Class 1	1,2,3,7
2	10
4	4,5
5	6,9
6	8
7	11,12,13
8	14,16,17

Management Control in
Nonprofit Organizations

The Irwin Series in Graduate Accounting

Fifth Edition

Management Control in Nonprofit Organizations

ROBERT N. ANTHONY, D.B.A.

Professor Emeritus
Graduate School of Business Administration
Harvard University

DAVID W. YOUNG, D.B.A.

Professor of Accounting and Control
Health Care Management and Public Management Programs
School of Management
Boston University

IRWIN

Burr Ridge, Illinois
Boston, Massachusetts
Sydney, Australia

Senior developmental editor: Diane M. Van Bakel
Marketing manager: John E. Biernat
Project editor: Karen M. Smith
Production manager: Diane Palmer
Art coordinator: Heather Burbridge
Compositor: Bi-Comp, Inc.
Typeface: 10/12 Times Roman
Printer: R.R. Donnelley & Sons Company

Library of Congress Cataloging-in-Publication Data

Anthony, Robert Newton, 1916–
   Management control in nonprofit organizations / Robert N. Anthony, David W. Young.—5th ed.
     p.   cm.
   Includes indexes.
   ISBN 0-256-08642-7
   1. Nonprofit organizations—Accounting. 2. Managerial accounting.
I. Young, David W.   II. Title.
HF5686.N56 1994
658.15′11—dc20   93–18016

Printed in the United States of America
1 2 3 4 5 6 7 8 9 0 DOC 0 9 8 7 6 5 4 3

Preface

Courses for which this text is designed have existed for about 20 years in many universities. As the field of management control in nonprofit organizations has developed, so have our own ideas about the material in this book. In addition, in the six years that have passed since the Fourth Edition, a great deal of literature has been published relating to both the management of nonprofit organizations in general, and *management control* in those organizations in particular. Finally, changes have taken place in the environments of most nonprofit organizations, forcing many of them to rethink the way they conduct their operations.

As a result of these developments, several substantive changes have been made in the content of the book. Organizationally, the book continues to be structured into four parts—introduction, management control principles, management control systems, and implementation of management control systems. However, many chapters have been completely rewritten, and some new appendixes have been included. In several of the chapters, we have introduced some new concepts being developed in both the management field in general, and management accounting in particular. We also look at how these emerging concepts relate to the management control effect in nonprofit organizations.

We also have introduced 13 new cases into this edition and have revised 4 cases from the Fourth Edition. The Fourth Edition had 64 cases; this edition has 68. This large number of cases permits instructors to use the book in courses for either beginning or advanced students. It also encourages instructors to explore a particular subject in some depth, beginning on a relatively elementary level and moving to a more advanced one. Moreover, the large number of cases allows instructors to focus attention on certain types of nonprofit organizations (e.g., health or education).

Use of the Book

This is not primarily a book on accounting. Rather, it is intended for a course on management control problems in nonprofit organizations in general. Such a course is often offered by an accounting department, but the book has also been used in courses offered by economics and finance departments, and by management departments in schools of education, medicine, public health, social work, theology, and public administration.

Although written to apply to all types on nonprofit organizations, including governmental entities, the book can easily be adapted for a course that focuses on a single type, such as education or health care, by the selection of cases appropriate to that type. The book also may be used in short programs designed for managers of nonprofit organizations. The selection of chapters and cases for such programs depends on the nature of the short program. In one type of program the principal topics of the whole book may be discussed; in another type, the focus might be on a specific area of management control, such as programming, budgeting, or the evaluation of performance. Finally, the book may also be used by individual managers in nonprofit organizations as background reading, or for reference purposes.

Case Reproduction

The 68 cases included in this book are listed in the index in alphabetical order. The first page of each case indicates its authors' names and affiliations, the copyright holder(s), and the source from which copies of the case may be obtained. For Harvard Business School cases, the first page also indicates the case number. Cases with no copyright designation are in the public domain.

Individuals wishing to obtain additional copies of cases should contact the source shown on the first page of the case. Harvard Business School cases are available from HBS Case Services, Harvard Business School, Boston, MA 02163. Addresses for other sources are as follows: Pew Curriculum Center, Department of Health Policy and Management, Harvard School of Public Health, 677 Huntington Avenue, Boston, MA 02115. Case Program, Kennedy School of Government, 79 JFK Street, Cambridge, MA 02138. Osceola Institute, c/o Professor Anthony, Apt. 332, 80 Lyme Road, Hanover, NH 03755. Accounting Curriculum Center, Department of Accounting, School of Management, Boston University, 685 Commonwealth Avenue, Boston, MA 02215. Massachusetts Health Data Consortium, 400-1 Totten Pond Road, Waltham, MA 02154. Colgate Darden Graduate Business School Sponsors, Box 6550, Charlottesville, VA 22906. Instituto Centroamericano de Administración de Empresas, Apartado 960, 4050 Alajuela, Costa Rica. Permission to reproduce other cases should be sought from the copyright holder.

Comments on the text or cases, or new ideas for teaching the cases, are welcomed, and should be sent to Professor Young at the Accounting Curriculum Center, Boston University School of Management.

Acknowledgments

We are grateful to many individuals for assistance in the preparation of both the text and the cases that we authored. These include Charles A. Anderson; C. Stewart Anthony; Professor Neil Charity, New York University; Charles Bowsher and Eleanor Chelimsky, U.S., General Accounting Office; Professors Charles Christenson and David Hawkins, Harvard Business School; William E. Cotter and Douglas Reinhardt, Colby College; Richard Depp, M.D., Thomas Jefferson Medical School, Philadelphia; Gregory Dorf, George Pereira-Ogan, and George Winn (all former MBA students at Boston University School of Management); Professor Patricia Douglas, University of Montana; James Farnum, Henry Harbury, and Richard Showalter, Dartmouth-Hitchcock Medical Center; Neil E. Harlan; Martin Ives, Governmental Accounting Standards Board; John Lordan, Johns Hopkins University; Leslie Pearlman, Boston University; Professor William Rotch, University of Virginia; Russy D. Sumariwalla, United Way of America; Stan Trecker, Art Institute of Boston; Eoin Trevelyan, Harvard School of Public Health; George Wilbanks, M.D., Rush-Presbyterian-St. Luke's Medical Center; and Susumu Uyeda.

We are also appreciative of the support we received from Boston University and Harvard University, and from the following sources for the preparation of certain cases:

Wyeth-Ayerst Laboratories [a grant to the Medical Education Foundation of the Association of Professors of Gynecology and Obstetrics] (Croswell University Hospital; Brookstone Ob-Gyn Associates (A) and (B); and Rush-Presbyterian-St. Luke's Medical Center)

The Boston Foundation (Boston Public Schools; Jefferson High School; Moray Junior High School; and Timilty Middle School)

The Edwin Gould Foundation for Children (Bureau of Child Welfare)

The Ford Foundation (Morazan and Izaltenango)

Line Publications (Centerville Home Health Agency)

The Pew Memorial Trust (Arnica Mission and Yoland Research Institute)

The U.S. Department of Health and Human Services, Public Health Service (Rural Health Associates (A) and (B))

Massachusetts Health Data Consortium (South Brookfield Hospital; Union Medical Center)

Two reviewers—Mark A. Covaleski of the University of Wisconsin at Madison and Ray Dillon of Georgia State University—provided us with formal reviews of the Fourth Edition, which were extremely useful in the preparation of this edition. We are most thankful for their ideas, many of which were incorporated into the text.

Finally, we greatly appreciate the editorial and secretarial assistance provided by Nancy Anthony, Elizabeth Baril, Audrey Barrett, Jane Barrett, Tracy O'Connor, Kelly Dwyer, Judith Grady, Eileen Hankins, Emily C. Hood, and Ann Whitehouse.

We, of course, accept full responsibility for the final product.

Robert N. Anthony
David W. Young

Contents

Chapter 4
Full-Cost Accounting

Chapter 5
Measurement and Use of Differential Costs   *235*

Chapter 10
Operations Budgeting

Chapter 11
Control of Operations

PART I

Introduction

Management control in nonprofit organizations—as an academic subject—is relatively new. Historically, many nonprofit organizations survived on the strength of their mission and their ability to attract increasing amounts of public and private support for their activities. Over the past 10 to 15 years, there has been a gradual change in the prevailing attitude toward nonprofit management on the part of both professionals (physicians, educators, artists, and so on) and managers (who generally are professionals themselves). It was not until recently, however, that these individuals recognized their need for stronger management skills. One of these skills is management control.

In this introductory section we discuss the scope of the material covered in this book and the nature of the organizations to which we intend to apply it. Chapter 1 outlines the territory of the field of management control, indicating both what it includes and, equally important, what it does not include. Chapter 2 discusses the nature and size of nonprofit organizations, as well as the types of services they offer.

Chapter 1

The Management Control Function

Any organization, even the tiniest, has a management control function. In large organizations management control tends to be formal; in smaller ones it is often quite informal. Management control has existed as long as organizations have been in existence, but it has not been the subject of much systematic study and analysis until quite recently. One of the early works on the subject was Chester Barnard's *The Functions of the Executive*.[1] Originally published in 1938, this landmark book dealt with management control as well as other management functions. Since then, managers and academics have contributed to the evolution and definition of principles for designing management control systems and carrying out the management control function.

As with most principles of management, the tenets of management control are incomplete, inconclusive, tentative, vague, contradictory, and inadequately supported by experimental or other evidence. Some initial *truths* have been proven wrong. Other principles, however, have shown sufficient validity in terms of managerial and organizational performance that managers increasingly are taking them into account.

Most studies of management control have been conducted in for-profit businesses, where most management control techniques originally were developed. Consequently, descriptions of management control tend to assume that the primary objective of the enterprise is earning a profit. This book, by contrast, looks at management control in nonprofit organizations. Our thesis is that the basic concepts of management control are the same in both for-profit and nonprofit organizations, but, because of the special characteristics of nonprofit organizations, the way managers apply these concepts will differ in some important respects.

---

[1] Chester I. Barnard, *The Functions of the Executive*, 30th anniversary ed. (Cambridge, Mass.: Harvard University Press, 1968).

3

PLANNING AND CONTROL ACTIVITIES

Managers engage in a wide variety of activities. They lead, teach, organize, influence, plan, and control. We focus on the latter two activities. In the planning activity, managers decide what should be done and how it should be done. In the control activity, managers attempt to assure that the desired results are obtained.

There are three different types of planning and control activities: (1) strategic planning, (2) task control, and (3) management control. Since our focus is on management control, we will describe the other two types of activities briefly. Our purpose in doing so is to clarify the boundaries of management control.[2]

Strategic Planning

An organization exists for the purpose of accomplishing something; that is, it has one or more goals. Senior management generally determines both the organization's goals and the general nature of the activities it will undertake to achieve them—the organization's strategies. *Strategic planning* is the process of deciding on the goals of the organization and on the strategies that are to be followed in attaining them.

At any given time, an organization has a set of goals and strategies. Strategies can be changed when senior management perceives *(a)* a threat to the organization, *(b)* new opportunities for the organization, or *(c)* a better way to achieve the goals. Since threats and opportunities do not arise in orderly, predictable ways, strategic planning decisions are not made according to a prescribed timetable. The strategic planning process therefore is essentially irregular and in many respects unsystematic.[3]

Task Control

At the other extreme are control processes used in carrying out the day-to-day operations of the organization, in particular the performance of specific tasks. *Task control* is the process of assuring that these operations are carried out effectively and efficiently.

Task control activities vary with the nature of the organization's operations. In a hospital, for example, maintaining an adequate inventory in the pharmacy is task

---

[2] For a more thorough description of these activities, see Robert N. Anthony, *The Management Control Function* (Boston: Harvard Business School Press, 1988).

[3] For additional details on the strategic planning process, see Kenneth R. Andrews, *The Concept of Corporate Strategy* (Homewood, Ill.: Dow Jones-Irwin, 1980), and Michael Porter, *Competitive Strategy* (New York: Free Press, 1980). For an application of strategic planning to health care, see Alan Sheldon and Susan Windham, *Competitive Strategy for Health Care Organizations* (Homewood, Ill.: Dow Jones-Irwin, 1984).

control. So is assuring adequate patient care procedures on the wards. Many task control activities do not involve managers. If they are automated, they do not even involve human beings, except to assure that the task control system is functioning properly and to deal with matters not included in the automated process. For example, in many organizations with sizable inventories (such as hospitals), when the quantity of an item on hand decreases to a preset limit, a computer places a replacement order directly with the appropriate vendor.

Management Control

Management control sits between strategic planning and task control. Management control accepts the goals and strategies determined in the strategic planning process as given. It focuses on the implementation of the strategies and the attainment of the goals. As such, management control attempts to assure that the organization designs effective programs and implements them efficiently. An effective program is one that moves the organization toward its goals. An efficient program is one that accomplishes its purposes at the lowest possible cost.

Unlike strategic planning, management control is a regular, systematic process with steps repeated in a predictable way. And, unlike task control, which may not even involve human beings, management control is fundamentally behavioral. It requires managers to interact with other people in the organization, particularly other managers. In many organizations, it also depends on managers interacting with the organization's professional staff.

In part, the management control function assists managers to decide on the optimum allocation of resources. In this respect, it is governed by the principles of *economics*. Management control also looks at the influence of accounting and reporting systems on the behavior of people in organizations. In this respect, it is governed by the principles of *social psychology*. Managers who experience initial difficulty in understanding the subject of management control should take comfort in the recognition that the principles found in these two disciplines are quite different, and that their relative importance to the management control function varies greatly in different situations. Throughout this book, we hope to help managers cultivate the critical eye (or at least the ability to ask the critical questions) that will enable them to incorporate the optimal mix of economic and behavioral factors in their management control efforts.

THE MANAGEMENT CONTROL ENVIRONMENT

The way the management control function is carried out in an organization is influenced by that organization's external and internal environments. The external environment is important because management control must be concerned with matters such as the actions of customers or clients, the constraints imposed by funding providers and legislative bodies, and the customs and norms of the society in which the organization exists. The internal environment is important because management control affects and is affected by the organization's structure, its members' behavior, its information systems, and its cultural norms. We discuss some of these aspects briefly here.

Organizational Structure

Organizations can be structured in a variety of ways, generally determined by the tasks that managers and employees need to perform. Some organizations have a *functional* structure, in which employees and managers are grouped according to common tasks such as production, marketing, or finance. Other organizations have a *program* structure, in which employees and managers who perform different functions (or tasks) are grouped according to common programs or services. Still others have a *matrix* structure in which programs and functional responsibilities have equal or reasonably equal weight.[4]

The management control function takes the existing organizational structure as given, and overlays it with a network of *responsibility centers*. A responsibility center is a group of people working toward some organizational objective. It is headed by a manager who is responsible for the actions of its members. The network of responsibility centers is called the *management control structure*. We will discuss the management control structure later in the chapter.

Organizational Relationships and Members' Behavior

Line and Staff.   Organization units can be classified as either line or staff units. Line units are directly responsible for carrying out the work of the organization. Staff units provide advice and assistance to the line units. Line managers are the focal points in management control. Their judgment is incorporated in the approved plans, they must work with others to accomplish their objectives, and their performance is measured via their responsibility center's performance.

Staff people collect, summarize, and present information that is useful in the management control function, and they make calculations that translate management judgments into the format of the management control system. Such a staff may be large in numbers; indeed, the control department is often the largest staff department in an organization. However, the significant program and control decisions are made by line managers, not by staff people.

---

[4] For a thorough discussion of these matters and other organizational issues in a health care context, see Martin P. Charns and Marguerite J. Schaefer, *Health Care Organizations* (Englewood Cliffs, N.J.: Prentice Hall, 1983).

Controller.   The person responsible for the design and operation of the management control system is the controller.[5] In practice, the controller may have other titles such as chief financial officer or chief accountant.

The idea that the controller has a broader responsibility than merely keeping the books is a fairly recent one in for-profit organizations, and it is not yet well accepted in many nonprofit organizations. Not too long ago, controllers were invariably called *chief accountants* and expected to confine their activities to collecting and reporting historical data. With the development of formal management control systems, and the increased emphasis on information needed for planning and decision making, the controller's function has broadened.

The controller is still a staff person, however, and thus does not make management control decisions. The job of the staff is to provide information that will facilitate good decision making by line managers. Sometimes an operating manager with a problem of inadequate resources is told, "Go see the controller." In making such a statement, senior management effectively has shifted line responsibility, and the controller has been put into a line capacity. The controller then becomes a de facto manager, with a corresponding diminution in the responsibility of the organization's other line managers. This usually leads to less than optimal management of the whole organization.[6]

Information

An important part of the management control environment is information. Information is a resource. As with any resource, its use involves both costs and benefits. Responsibility center managers must attempt to assure that the value of the information exceeds the cost of collecting and disseminating it.

Information may be either quantitative or qualitative; a report that "Ms. X is doing a good job" is qualitative information. A report that "Ms. X delivered 25 hours of client service" is quantitative information. Quantitative information may be either monetary or nonmonetary. A report that "Ms. X earned $200" is monetary information; a report that "Ms. X worked 15 hours" is nonmonetary information. Much of the information used in management control is monetary information. The system that collects, summarizes, analyzes, and reports such information is the *accounting system*.

Nature of Accounting Information.   An accounting system provides historical information; that is, what has happened, and what the organization's revenues

---

[5] The preferred term is *controller*. However, in some organizations, the word is spelled *comptroller*. In any event, the term is always pronounced as if it were spelled controller. Pronouncing it *"compt roller"* is archaic.

[6] Senior management may decide to assign responsibility for certain detailed decisions, such as approval of travel vouchers, to the controller. This is different from assigning line responsibility to the controller.

and costs actually were. This system collects information for three purposes: management control, reporting to outside parties, and special analyses.

Management Control.   Information for management control purposes usually is classified in two ways: by responsibility centers and by programs. As we discuss later, the management control system must have an ability to integrate these two sets of information.

Reporting to Outside Parties.   Some accounting information is contained in general-purpose financial reports. Principles governing the preparation of these reports are described in Chapter 3. Other information is prepared for outside agencies according to reporting requirements that they specify. State and local government agencies that accept funds from the federal government, for example, must prepare reports on their use of these funds. The content of these reports is specified by the agency that grants the funds. Ideally, the information contained in these special-purpose reports simply summarizes information in the management control system. This is because the information needs of outside agencies presumably do not exceed or vary greatly from those of management. The ideal is not always the case, however. The appropriation structure specified by the Congress for federal agencies, for example, rarely results in reporting configurations that are useful for the information and control needs of managers in those organizations.

Special Analyses.   Special analyses include information used in connection with litigation or one-time studies. In many organizations, for example, the accounting system collects information that is useful in strategic planning. Strategic decisions are made only occasionally, however, and each decision requires tailor-made information. This information cannot ordinarily be collected in any routine, recurring fashion. Rather, it must be assembled when the need arises and in the form required for the specific issue.

Although the management control system includes information found in the accounting system, it also provides two types of information not found in the accounting system: (1) estimates of what will happen in the future and (2) estimates of what should happen. The former are called *forecasts*, and the latter are called *standards* or *budgets*. We will discuss budgets in more detail later in this chapter, and in Chapter 10.

Cost Information.   The accounting system collects information on the resources used in an organization. This is information on inputs. Inputs can be expressed as physical quantities, such as hours of labor, quarts of oil, reams of paper, or kilowatt-hours of electricity. If these physical quantities are converted to monetary units, they are called *costs*. Money provides a common denominator that permits the quantities of individual resources to be combined.

Cost is a measure of the amount of resources used for a purpose. In accounting terms, this purpose is called a *cost object*. The education of a student, the care of a patient, the completion of a research project, and the development of a museum exhibit are all examples of cost objects. Ordinarily, responsibility centers work on cost objects.

Inputs are resources *used* by a responsibility center in working on a cost object. Thus, the patients in a hospital or the students in a school are not the inputs of a responsibility center. Rather, a responsibility center's inputs are the resources it uses in accomplishing its objectives of treating patients or educating students.

Input information consists of three basic types of cost construction: full, differential, and responsibility. Each is used for a different purpose, and considerable misunderstanding can arise if the cost construction for one purpose is used inappropriately for another. Full costs and responsibility costs ordinarily are collected in the accounts. For reasons discussed below, differential costs are not collected in the accounts.

Full Cost. Full cost is the total amount of resources used for a cost object. Since cost objects often are programs, full costs often are called *program costs*. The full cost of a cost object is the sum of its direct costs plus a fair share of the organization's indirect costs.

Direct costs are costs that can be traced to a single cost object. For example, the salaries and fringe benefits of persons who work exclusively on a single program (cost object) are direct costs of that program. *Indirect costs* are costs incurred jointly for two or more cost objects, and a fair share of these indirect costs must be allocated to each cost object to obtain its full cost. These matters are discussed in greater detail in Chapter 4.

Differential Costs. Costs that are different under one set of conditions from what they would be under another are differential costs. These costs are useful in many problems involving a choice among alternative courses of action. The analysis of such problems involves estimates of how costs would be different if different proposed alternatives were adopted. Since the costs that are relevant to a given problem depend on the nature of that problem, there is no general way of labeling a given item of cost as differential or nondifferential, and therefore no way of recording differential costs as such in the formal accounts. The analyst uses information from the program structure or the responsibility structure as raw material for estimating the differential costs of a particular proposed alternative.

In many alternative choice problems, an important classification of costs is whether they are variable or fixed. *Variable costs* are those that change proportionally with changes in volume; that is, in the level of activity. Since twice as many workbooks are required in teaching two fifth-grade students than in teaching one, the cost of books used in education is a variable cost. By contrast, the amount of depreciation expense for the school building does not change with the number of students, so depreciation is a fixed cost. Other costs, such as teachers' salaries share features of both, changing as volume increases or decreases but not in direct proportion. Differential costs are the subject of Chapter 5.

Responsibility Costs. Costs incurred by or on behalf of a responsibility center are responsibility costs. They provide managers information on the cost of the responsibility center as an organizational unit, rather than on the program or programs with which the responsibility center is involved. When measured in monetary terms, the total resources consumed by a responsibility center for a specific period of time are the costs of that responsibility center. Managers are cautioned, however, that total recorded costs are at best an approximation of total inputs. Some inputs are not included as costs, either because the effort required to translate them into monetary terms is not worthwhile (e.g., minor supplies and services or small amounts of borrowed labor) or because measurement is not possible (e.g., certain types of executive or staff assistance, or training).

Responsibility costs are classified as either controllable or noncontrollable. An item of cost is *controllable* if it is significantly influenced by the actions of the manager of the responsibility center in which it was incurred. Note that *controllable* always refers to a specific responsibility center; all items of cost are ultimately controllable by someone in the organization. Note also that the definition refers to a significant amount of influence, rather than complete influence. Few managers have complete influence over any item of cost.

Output Information.   Although inputs almost always can be measured in terms of cost, outputs are much more difficult to measure. In many responsibility centers, outputs cannot be measured at all. In a for-profit organization, revenue is often an important measure of output. But such a measure is rarely a complete expression of output, since it does not encompass everything that the organization does. For example, it excludes such activities as pollution control and environmental cleanup, which may be important outputs from a societal perspective.

Many nonprofit organizations do not have a good quantitative measure of output. A school can easily measure the number of students graduated, but it is much more difficult (usually impossible) to measure how much education each of them acquired. Although outputs may not be measurable, it is a fact that every organization unit *has* outputs; that is, it does something.

The degree to which outputs can be measured quantitatively varies greatly with circumstances. If the quantity of output is relatively homogeneous (e.g., membership certificates in an association), it often can be measured precisely. If the goods or services are heterogeneous (e.g., different types of health care services), however, problems arise in summarizing the separate outputs into a meaningful measure of total output. Converting dissimilar physical goods to monetary equivalents is one way of solving this problem. Such a monetary measure is called *revenue*. If fees are structured properly, the total quantity of output of a client-serving organization is reliably measured by the fees charged to clients; that is, by revenues. This is true even though the services rendered consist of dissimilar activities (e.g., the use of beds, nursing care, operating rooms, and various laboratory, X-ray, and other technical procedures in a hospital).

At best, revenue measures the *quantity* of output. Measurement of the *quality* of output is much more difficult, and often cannot be made at all. In many situations, quality is determined strictly on a judgmental basis. In some, there is a go-no-go measurement—either the output is of satisfactory quality or it is not. Moreover, it is always difficult, and often unfeasible, to measure, or even estimate, the outputs of such staff units as the legal or research departments of a company, or the outputs of schools, government agencies, or churches.

In addition to goods and services thought of as outputs, responsibility centers produce intangible effects—sometimes intentionally and sometimes unintentionally. They may prepare employees for advancement, for example, or instill attitudes of loyalty and pride of accomplishment (or, alternatively, attitudes of disloyalty and indolence). They may also affect the image of the organization as perceived by the outside world. Some of these outputs, such as better trained employees, are created in order to benefit operations in future periods; that is, they will become inputs at some future time. Such outputs are therefore *investments,* since an investment is a commitment of current resources in the expectation of deriving future benefits. Because of inherent obstacles to measurement, however, investments in intangibles are rarely recorded in the formal accounting system. We discuss output measures more fully in Chapter 12.

Efficiency and Effectiveness

Efficiency and effectiveness are the two criteria for judging the performance of a responsibility center. These criteria are almost always used in a relative, rather than absolute, sense. We do not ordinarily say that Organization Unit A is 80 percent efficient, for example. Rather, we say that Unit A is more (or less) efficient than Unit B, or that it is more (or less) efficient now than it was in the past, or that it was more (or less) efficient than planned or budgeted.

Efficiency. Efficiency is the ratio of a responsibility center's outputs to its inputs; that is, its output per unit of input. Unit A is more efficient than Unit B if it uses either (1) fewer resources than Unit B but has the same output, or (2) the same resources as Unit B but has more output. Note that the first measure of efficiency does not require us to quantify output; it only requires a reasonable judgment that the outputs of the two units are approximately equal. If management is satisfied that Units A and B are both doing a satisfactory job, and if their jobs are of comparable magnitude, then the unit with fewer inputs (i.e., lower costs) is more efficient. For example, if two elementary schools are judged to be furnishing adequate education, the one with lower per student costs is more efficient.

The second type of efficiency measure, which contrasts different levels of output given approximately equal levels of input, requires some quantitative indication of output. It is therefore more difficult to use in many situations. If two elementary schools have the same costs, for example, one can be said to be more efficient than the other only if it provides more education, but this is inherently difficult to measure.

In many responsibility centers, measures of efficiency can be developed that relate actual costs to some standard. The standard expresses the costs that should be incurred for a given level of output. Managers often find such measures useful as indicators of efficiency.

Effectiveness. The relationship between a responsibility center's output and its objectives is an indication of its effectiveness. The more its outputs contribute to its objectives, the more effective a responsibility center is. Since both outputs and success in meeting objectives may be difficult to quantify, measures of effectiveness are often difficult to obtain. Effectiveness, therefore, is usually expressed in qualitative, judgmental terms, such as "College A is doing a first-rate job" or "College B has slipped somewhat in recent years."

An organization unit should attempt to be both efficient and effective; it is not a matter of being one or the other. A manager who meets a responsibility center's objectives with the least resources may be efficient; but if the center's output is inadequate in its contribution to the unit's objectives, the manager is ineffective. If, for example, the employees in a welfare office are invariably busy, processing claims and applications with little wasted motion, the office is efficient. If the personnel have the attitude that their function is to ensure that every form is made out perfectly, however—rather than to help clients obtain welfare services—the office is ineffective.

The Role of Profit.   One important goal in a for-profit organization is to earn a satisfactory profit, and the amount of profit is therefore an important measure of effectiveness. Since profit is the difference between revenue, which is a measure of output, and expense, which is a measure of input, profit is also a measure of efficiency. Thus, in a for-profit organization, profit measures both effectiveness and efficiency. Since, by definition, a nonprofit organization does not have a goal to earn a profit, the difference between revenue and expense says nothing about effectiveness.

THE MANAGEMENT CONTROL STRUCTURE

As we discussed previously, the management control structure is an organization's network of responsibility centers. Large organizations usually have complicated hierarchies of responsibility centers: units, sections, departments, branches, and divisions. Within the exception of those at the bottom of the organization, each responsibility center consists of aggregations of smaller responsibility centers, and the entire organization is itself a responsibility center. One function of senior management is to plan and control the work of all these responsibility centers.

> *Example.* A university consists of a number of responsibility centers, such as its Schools of Law and Medicine and its College of Arts and Sciences. Each school or college is in turn composed of separate responsibility centers, such as the language department or the physics department. These departments may in turn be divided into separate responsibility centers; the language department may, for example, be composed of sections for each language. The management control function is to plan and coordinate the work of all these responsibility centers.

As discussed above, a responsibility center exists to accomplish one or more purposes; these are its objectives. These objectives should help the organization achieve its overall goals, which were decided in the strategic planning process. A responsibility center also has inputs of labor, material, and services. The language department in the above example has inputs of faculty, staff, educational materials, and maintenance services. The department uses these inputs to produce its

EXHIBIT 1–1 Nature of a Responsibility Center

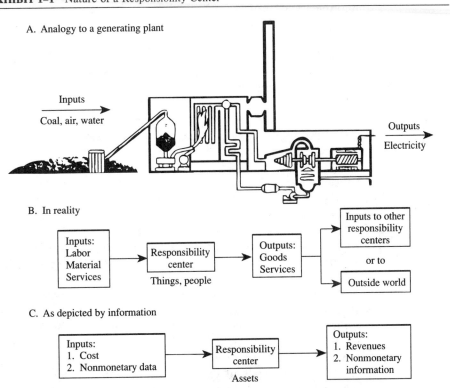

A. Analogy to a generating plant

Inputs
Coal, air, water

Outputs
Electricity

B. In reality

Inputs:
Labor
Material
Services

Responsibility
center

Things, people

Outputs:
Goods
Services

Inputs to other
responsibility
centers

or to

Outside world

C. As depicted by information

Inputs:
1. Cost
2. Nonmonetary data

Responsibility
center

Assets

Outputs:
1. Revenues
2. Nonmonetary
   information

outputs. If the responsibility center is effective, its outputs will be closely related to its objectives. One output of the language department is the knowledge and skill in language acquired by the students; another might be instructional recordings or tapes for use outside the university. These outputs are related to the language department's objectives and presumably help satisfy one or more of the university's goals.

Exhibit 1–1 shows the essence of what a responsibility center does, using a steam-generating plant as an analogy. The plant exists for a purpose, namely, to generate electrical energy. To accomplish this objective, it employs furnaces, turbines, smokestacks, and other physical resources which, in operating, use fuel. These are its inputs. The energy the plant generates is its output.

Types of Responsibility Centers

There are four principal types of responsibility centers: (1) revenue, (2) expense, (3) profit, and (4) investment. The principal factor in the selection of one type over another is control. That is, senior management's objective in choosing a given type of responsibility center is to hold the center's manager accountable for only those inputs and outputs over which he or she can exercise a reasonable amount of control (not necessarily total control, however).

Revenue Centers.   A revenue center is a responsibility center in which the manager is charged primarily with attaining some predetermined amount of revenue. Of course, a revenue center incurs expenses, and these are agreed upon between the manager and his or her superiors. However, the manager's *performance* is measured in terms of the amount of revenue earned by the responsibility center. Many marketing departments are revenue centers. A university's development office frequently is a revenue center.

Expense Centers.   In an expense center, the manager is held responsible for the expenses incurred during a specified time period.[7] This means that the management control system is concerned with the center's outputs. Although every responsibility center has outputs (i.e., it does something), in many cases it is neither feasible nor necessary to measure these outputs in monetary terms. It would be extremely difficult to measure the monetary value that the accounting department contributes to the whole organization, for example. And, although it would be relatively easy to measure the monetary value of the outputs of an individual production department (such as the department of radiology in a hospital), there may be no good reason for doing so. This would be the case, for example, if the department manager's responsibility was simply to produce a stated quantity of output at the lowest feasible cost.

There are two types of expense centers: discretionary expense centers and standard expense centers. A *discretionary expense center* ordinarily is used when there is no easy way to measure the center's outputs, such as in the accounting department example above. If this is the case, the manager is held responsible for a fixed amount of expenses for the month (or other reporting period) and is not expected to exceed this amount unless there are compelling reasons to do so.

A *standard expense center* is used when the units of output can be rather easily identified and measured, such as in the radiology department above. With a standard expense center, the manager is not responsible for a fixed amount of expenses, but for a predetermined expense for each unit of output. A standard expense center ordinarily is used when the manager cannot control the amount of output that his or her department is required to produce. Instead, the amount of output is determined by requests from other responsibility centers. When this happens, the manager's budget for each reporting period is determined by multiplying the actual output produced by the standard expense per unit. His or her performance is measured against this figure.

---

[7] The term *expense* is not synonymous with *cost*. Cost is a measure of resources consumed for any specified purpose, whereas expense always refers to resources that are consumed in operations of a specified time period. Outlays to manufacture a product are costs in the period in which the product is manufactured, but they become expenses only in the period in which the product is sold and the related revenue is earned. This distinction is discussed more fully in Chapter 3.

Example. During a particular month, a department of radiology received requests from the department of pediatrics for 500 chest X rays and 200 skull X rays. The agreed-upon expenses were $25 per chest X ray and $50 per skull X ray. The expense budget against which the radiology manager's performance is measured is $12,500 (500 × $25) for chest X rays and $10,000 (200 × $50) for skull X rays, for a total of $22,500.[8]

In a business enterprise most individual production departments are standard expense centers, and most staff units are discretionary expense centers. In many nonprofit organizations, both types of departments are discretionary expense centers. For these, the accounting system records expenses incurred, but not revenue earned or output produced.

Profit Centers. In a profit center, the manager is responsible for both revenue (a monetary measure of output) and expense (a monetary measure of input, or resources consumed). Profit is the difference between revenue and expense. Thus, a profit center manager's performance is measured in terms of both the revenue his or her center earns and the expenses it incurs.

Many nonprofit organizations have responsibility centers that charge fees for their services and incur expenses in delivering those services. This is the case with many hospital departments; with the housing, dining, and other auxiliary services of a university; and with utilities, refuse collection, and similar enterprises of a municipality. In these instances, the responsibility center can be thought of as a profit center, even though use of the term profit center in a nonprofit organization may seem contradictory. In order to avoid this connotation, some nonprofit organizations now refer to these units as *financial centers*.

Investment Centers. In an investment center, a manager is responsible for both profit and the assets used in generating the profit. This responsibility frequently is measured in terms of a return on assets (ROA), which is a ratio of profit to assets employed. The former usually is expressed as a percentage of the latter. Thus, an investment center adds more to a manager's scope of responsibility than does a profit center, just as a profit center involves more than an expense center. Although investment centers are rarely used in nonprofit organizations, they are nevertheless quite appropriate for those situations in which a manager is responsible for a clearly identified set of assets. This can happen in nonprofit organizations as well as in for-profit ones.

Mission Centers and Service Centers

Regardless of type, responsibility centers can be classified as either mission centers or service centers. The output of a *mission center* contributes directly to the objectives of the organization. The output of a *service center* contributes to the

---

[8] The computations are somewhat more complicated than this. We will return to this issue in Part III.

work of other responsibility centers, which may be either mission centers or service centers; its output is thus one of the inputs of these responsibility centers. A service center is often called a *support center*.

> ***Example.*** In a museum, the curatorial and education departments ordinarily are designated as mission centers—they contribute directly to the objectives of the museum. Finance and personnel departments usually are designated as service centers—they contribute to the work of other responsibility centers but do not contribute *directly* to the objectives of the museum.

Many mission centers are also profit centers, although some are designated as revenue or expense centers. A service center may be a discretionary expense center, a standard expense center, or a profit center. If the latter, it *sells* its services to other units, and its output is measured by the revenue generated from its sales. Its objective usually is not to make a profit (i.e., an excess of revenue over expenses) but rather to break even. The extension of the profit center concept to service centers is relatively new in nonprofit organizations. When properly designed, however, service centers functioning as profit centers can provide a powerful instrument for management control.

Responsibility Centers and Programs

Many organizations distinguish between responsibility centers and programs. These organizations have both program structures and responsibility center structures in their management control systems. The responsibility center structure contains information classified by responsibility center. This information is used for: (1) planning the activities of individual responsibility centers, (2) coordinating the work of several responsibility centers in the organization, and (3) measuring the performance of the responsibility center managers. Information about the programs that the organization undertakes or plans to undertake is contained in the program structure. Managers use the program structure for three principal purposes:

1. To make decisions about the programs to be undertaken and the amount and kind of resources that should be devoted to each.
2. To provide a basis for setting fees charged to clients or for reimbursement of costs incurred.
3. To permit comparisons with similar programs in other organizations. For example, managers in a hospital with an open-heart surgery program might wish to compare its costs with those of similar programs in other hospitals.

When there is both a responsibility center structure and a program structure, the management control system must identify their interactions. In some instances, a responsibility center may work solely on one program, and it may be the only responsibility center working on that program. If so, the program structure corresponds to the responsibility center structure. For example, this is the case in most municipal governments. One organization unit is responsible for providing police protection, another for education, another for solid waste disposal, and so on.

One-to-one correspondence between programs and responsibility centers does not always exist, however. For example, a regional office of the U.S. Department of Health and Human Services (DHHS), which is a responsibility center, works on several DHHS programs. When this happens, the management control system must identify the relationships between the organization's responsibility centers and its programs.

Exhibit 1–2 uses a hospital to depict the relationship between responsibility centers and programs. In this organization, responsibility centers are divided between mission centers and service centers. A given mission center, such as the outpatient department, can work for several programs. Here, it provides 12,500 visits for the sports medicine program, 10,000 visits for the alcohol detoxification program, and 8,500 visits for the drug rehabilitation program. At the same time, a given program, such as the drug rehabilitation program, can receive services from several mission and service centers. Here, it receives 300 days of care from the routine care mission center, 300 tests from the laboratory, and 8,500 visits from the outpatient department. It also receives housekeeping, dietary, laundry, administrative, and social services from the hospital's service centers. If these departments were established as profit centers, they might sell their services to both mission centers and programs; otherwise, their costs would be allocated to mission centers and programs.

EXHIBIT 1–2   Relationship between Responsibility Centers and Programs

Responsibility Centers	Programs			
	Sports Medicine	*Alcohol Detoxification*	*Drug Rehabilitation*	*Open-Heart Surgery*
Mission centers:				
Routine care	3,800 days	1,200 days	300 days	8,000 days
Surgery	1,000 operations	—	—	500 operations
Laboratory	2,000 tests	500 tests	300 tests	2,000 tests
Radiology	8,000 procedures	—	—	1,500 procedures
Outpatient care ...	12,500 visits	10,000 visits	8,500 visits	—
Service centers:				
Housekeeping		Costs allocated to mission centers		
Dietary		for purposes of measuring the full		
Laundry		cost of mission centers and the pro-		
Administration		grams using the resources of these		
Social service		mission centers.		

THE MANAGEMENT CONTROL PROCESS

The management control process takes place in the context of an organization's goals and the broad strategies senior management has chosen for achieving them. As discussed previously, decisions on goals and strategies are made in the strategic planning process, which is largely unsystematic and informal.

Much of the management control process also is informal. It occurs by memoranda, meetings, conversations, and even such signals as facial expressions—control devices not amenable to systematic description. Most organizations also have a formal system, in which the information consists of planned and actual data on both outputs and inputs. Prior to a given operating period, decisions and estimates (budgets) are made, which specify desired levels of outputs and inputs. During the operating period, records of actual levels of outputs and inputs are collected. Subsequent to the operating period, reports are prepared that compare actual outputs and inputs to their planned levels. If necessary, corrective action is taken on the basis of these reports.

The formal management control process has four principal phases:

1. Programming.
2. Budget preparation.
3. Operating and measurement.
4. Reporting and evaluation.

These phases occur in a regular cycle, and together they constitute a closed loop, as indicated in Exhibit 1–3.

Programming

In the programming phase, senior management determines the major programs the organization will undertake during the coming period and the approximate expenses that each will incur. These decisions are made within the context of the goals and strategies that emerged from the strategic planning activity. If a new program represents a change in strategy, the decision to initiate it effectively is part of the strategic planning activity, rather than the management control process. Strategic planning and management control merge in the programming phase.

Some organizations state their programs in the form of a *long-range plan* that projects outputs and inputs for several years ahead—usually five years, but possibly as few as three, or (in the case of public utilities) as many as 20. Other organizations do not have a formal mechanism for describing their overall future programs. They rely instead on reports or understandings as to specific, important facets of their programs, especially the amounts to be invested in capital assets and the means of financing these assets.

Programs in industrial companies are usually products or product lines, plus activities (such as research) that cannot be related to specific products. The plans state the amount and character of resources (inputs) that are to be devoted to each

EXHIBIT 1–3   Phases of Management Control

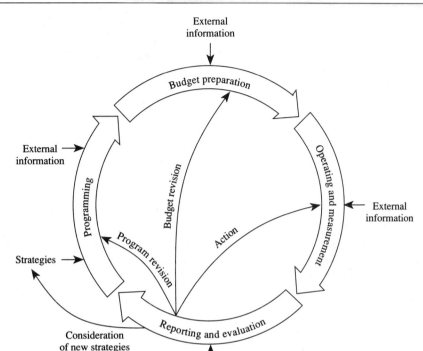

program and the planned uses of these resources. In a nonprofit organization, programs define the types of services the organization has decided to provide.

To the extent feasible, program decisions are based on economic analyses, which compare estimated revenues or other benefits from a proposed program with the program's estimated costs. In many for-profit companies, as well as in most nonprofit organizations, reliable estimates of a program's benefits cannot be made. Decisions on these programs tend to rest on senior management's ability to exercise sound judgment and evaluative capacity in the face of sometimes persuasive program advocates, political considerations, and the frequently parochial interests of external constituencies.

Budget Preparation

A budget is a plan, expressed in quantitative, usually monetary, terms. It covers a specified period, usually a year. In the budget preparation phase of the management control process, each program's objectives are translated into terms that correspond to the spheres of responsibility of the managers charged with implementing them. Thus, during the budget preparation phase, plans made in program terms are converted into responsibility terms.

> *Example.* In a university, an art program will have several interrelated goals: train a certain number of students, provide some cross-cultural experiences, raise a designated amount of support from alumni, and so forth. During the budget preparation process, the university determines the faculty and staff resources that are to be committed to the program, the budgeted operating expenses (e.g., travel) for the program, and, perhaps, some program objectives (e.g., admit a certain number of international students to the program). The manager of the program assumes responsibility for accomplishing these objectives within some specified amount of resources (the budget), department chairs assume responsibility for providing the requisite faculty to teach in the program, and the program manager may obtain commitments from his or her subordinates to achieve certain objectives (e.g., send three newsletters to 90 percent of alumni, develop a fund raising campaign).

The process of arriving at the budget is essentially one of negotiation between responsibility center managers and their superiors. The end product of these negotiations is a statement of the outputs expected during the budget year and the resources (inputs) to be used to achieve these outputs. As such, the agreed-upon budget is a *bilateral commitment*. Responsibility center managers commit to producing the planned output with the agreed amount of resources, and their superiors commit to agreeing that such performance is satisfactory. Both commitments are subject to the qualification "unless circumstances change significantly."

Operating and Measurement

During the period of actual operations, managers supervise what is going on and help the accounting staff keep records of actual resources consumed and actual output achieved. In many organizations, the records of resources consumed (i.e., costs) are maintained in such a way to reflect the costs incurred by both programs and responsibility centers. Program cost records are used as a basis for future programming; responsibility cost records are used to measure the performance of responsibility center managers.

Reporting and Evaluation

Accounting information, along with a variety of other information, is summarized, analyzed, and reported to those responsible for knowing what is happening in the organization as well as those charged with attaining agreed-upon levels of performance. The reports enable managers to compare planned outputs and inputs with actual results. The information in these reports is used for three purposes.

Operations. First, the reports help senior managers coordinate and control current operations of the organization. Using this information, together with information obtained from conversations or other informal sources, managers can identify situations that may be "out of control," investigate these situations, and initiate corrective action where necessary and feasible.

Performance Evaluation.   Second, the reports are used as a basis for evaluating operating performance. Such evaluations lead to actions related to responsibility center managers: praise for a job well done; constructive criticism if warranted; or promotion, reassignment, or, in extreme cases, termination. Such information is also used to guide managers of responsibility centers in the development of improved methods of operating.

Program Evaluation.   Third, the reports are used as a basis for program evaluation. For any of a number of reasons, the plan for a program may be suboptimal. If so, individual budgets or entire programs may need to be revised.

The reporting and evaluation phase thus closes the loop of the management control process. Evaluation of actual performance can lead back to the first phase, a revision of the program, or to the second phase, a revision of the budget, or to the third phase, a modification in operations. It can also lead to senior management reconsidering the organization's strategies for achieving its goals, or even to a revision of the organization's goals.

Characteristics of a Good Management Control System

Management control systems differ considerably from one organization to the next. In some organizations they work well; in others they are in need of considerable redesign if they are to play a significant role in helping the organization to achieve its goals and strategies. In assessing the quality of a management control system, analysts tend to focus on several criteria. The absence of one or more of these criteria is an indication that the system is in need of redesign.

A Total System.   Properly designed, a management control system is a *total* system; that is, it embraces all aspects of an organization's operations. It needs to be a total system because an important management function is to assure that all parts of the operation are in balance with one another. To monitor and maintain this balance, senior management must have information about all parts of the organization's operations. By contrast, information collected for the strategic planning process is usually specific to the plans under consideration, which rarely embrace the whole organization. Similarly, information used in task control is usually tailor-made for the requirements of each activity, and, therefore, limited in its scope.

Goal Congruence.   A basic principle of social psychology is that persons act according to their perceived best interests. Because of this, one characteristic of a good management control system is that it encourages managers to act in accordance with *both* their own best interests *and* the best interests of the organization as a whole. In the language of social psychology, the system should encourage *goal congruence*. It should be structured so that the goals of individual managers are consistent with the goals of the organization as a whole.

Perfect congruence between individual goals and organizational goals rarely exists. As a minimum, however, the system should not include evaluation and reward criteria that make the individual's best interests inconsistent with the best interests of the organization. For example, a lack of goal congruence exists if the management control system emphasizes reduced costs and, in doing so, encourages managers to sacrifice quality, provide inadequate service, or engage in activities that reduce costs in one department but cause more than an offsetting increase in another.

Financial Framework. With rare exceptions a management control system should be built around a financial structure; that is, estimates and measures are stated in monetary amounts. This does not mean that accounting information is the sole, or even the most important, part of the control system; it means only that the accounting system provides a unifying core to which managers can relate other types of information. Although the financial structure is usually the central focus, nonmonetary measures, such as minutes per operation, number of persons served, percent of applicants admitted, and reject and spoilage rates are also important parts of the system.

Rhythm. The management control process tends to be rhythmic; it follows a definite pattern and timetable, month after month, year after year. In budget preparation, certain steps are taken in a prescribed sequence and at certain dates each year: dissemination of guidelines, preparation of original estimates, transmission of these estimates up through the several echelons of the organization, review of these estimates, final approval by senior management, and dissemination back through the organization.

Integration. A management control system should be a coordinated, integrated system. Although data collected for one purpose may differ from those collected for another, these data should be reconcilable. The management control system is a single system, but it is perhaps more useful to think of it as two interlocking subsystems—one focused on programs and the other on responsibility centers. Furthermore, much of the data used in the management control system are also used in preparing a variety of other reports and analyses used by both line managers and professional staff.

BOUNDARIES OF MANAGEMENT CONTROL

Management control is an important function, but it is by no means the whole of management. Managers also must make judgments about people: their integrity, their ability, their potential, their fitness for a given job, or their compatibility with colleagues. Senior management is responsible for building an effective organization and for motivating the people who comprise that organization to work toward its goals.

Managers also have functions that are not "management" as such. Kotter illustrates the external activities of a manager by describing the external agencies and persons on which the head of a large municipal, urban teaching hospital must depend:

- The mayor's office, which must approve the hospital's budget, support the hospital publicly, and avoid employing everyone to whom the mayor owes a favor.
- Other parts of the city bureaucracy, which provide services such as construction.
- A dozen unions or employee associations that could call a strike or work stoppage.
- The civil service, which could make it easy or impossible to get adequate employees.
- The city council, which could call hearings that could take up a hospital manager's time and be a source of embarrassment.
- Accreditation agencies, which could put the hospital out of business.
- The state government, which could constrain hospital activities in a number of ways.
- Its medical school affiliate, which supplies the hospital with physicians.
- The local press, which could embarrass the hospital and upset the mayor.
- The federal government, which supplies the hospital with funds and regulates certain activities.
- Other hospitals in the city, whose major actions could have a positive or negative impact on this hospital.
- The local community, which, if organized, could constrain the hospital's actions through the press, the mayor, or the city council.[9]

BOUNDARIES OF THIS BOOK

The management control function helps an organization to reach its goals. Management control does not have anything to do directly with the existence of the organization or the formulation of its goals. This book therefore is not concerned with whether there should be an organization, or whether it should have its existing goals—be they good or bad. The management control function occurs both in UNICEF and the Mafia. Our focus thus precludes criticism of the goals themselves, on moral, public policy, or other grounds. We do not, for example, debate

---

[9] John P. Kotter, "Power, Success and Organizational Effectiveness," *Organizational Dynamics*, Winter 1978.

the question of the extent to which the government should be responsible for health care. We accept the fact that the Congress has assigned certain health care responsibilities to the Department of Health and Human Services, and start our analysis with this as a given.

Exclusion of Systems Approach

The focus on management control in an existing organization means that some exciting topics are not given the attention that their importance might otherwise warrant. Of these, perhaps the most important is the systems approach. Health care, for example, should be viewed as a system, comprising all the individuals, organizations, and policies that are intended to provide an optimal level of health care. When viewed in this way, it is apparent that the health care system in the United States is deficient. Our morbidity rates, infant mortality rates, and other indicators of health status rank nowhere near the top of the list of developed countries, despite the fact that we spend more on health care per capita than do most other nations. Health care facilities are poorly distributed. Many ill people who could be treated inexpensively in a clinic are sent unnecessarily to expensive hospitals. Many people cannot afford adequate health care. All these facts are indications that the health care *system* needs a drastic overhaul. It should be possible to provide better health care at substantially lower cost by emphasizing new organizational arrangements, such as more ambulatory care facilities; a new mix of personnel, such as more nurse practitioners and physician extenders; and more emphasis on preventive medicine. In short, a focus on health care as a system is fascinating, and an analysis of this system can lead to major improvements in its functioning. Similarly, governmental organizations, higher educational facilities, and volunteer organizations are all best understood when viewed in a systemic perspective.

This book takes a narrower focus, however, concerning itself with the activities of individual organizations. Within the health care system, our focus will be limited to a hospital, clinic, or nursing home, for example. Within the educational system, we will focus on individual schools, colleges, or universities. The book accepts the role of an organization and its goals essentially as given, and concentrates on how improvements in the management control function might help the organization to perform more efficiently and effectively.

Such a focus tends to be less than satisfying to many people because it rules out discussion of certain current, sometimes glamorous, high-payoff topics. These topics should of course be discussed, but in another context. Thus, in the chapters that follow, we put a relatively low emphasis on the systems in which nonprofit organizations exist, focusing instead on the individual organizations that comprise those systems. It is tempting, of course, to focus on global systems' problems and to neglect the problems of individual organizations, but we try to resist that temptation.

SUGGESTED ADDITIONAL READINGS

Bower, Joseph L. *The Two Faces of Management.* Boston: Houghton Mifflin, 1983.

Bryce, Herrington J. *Financial and Strategic Management for Nonprofit Organizations,* 2nd ed. Englewood Cliffs, N.J.: Prentice Hall, 1992.

Committee on Nonprofit Entities' Performance Measures. *Measuring Performance of Nonprofit Organizations: The State of the Art.* Sarasota, Fla.: American Accounting Association, August 1989.

Hay, Robert D. *Strategic Management in Non-Profit Organizations.* New York: Quorum Books, 1990.

Hopwood, Anthony, and Cyril Tomkins, eds. *Issues in Public Sector Accounting.* New Delhi, India: Heritage Publishers, 1985.

Marquette, R. Penny. *An Annotated Bibliography of Articles: Government, Accounting, Auditing, and Municipal Finance, 1971–85.* Sarasota, Fla.: American Accounting Association, Government and Nonprofit Section, August 1986.

Unterman, Israel, and Richard H. Davis. "The Strategy Gap in Not-for-Profits," *Harvard Business Review,* May–June 1982.

CASE 1–1   Hoagland Hospital(A)*

In September 1986, Dr. Richard Wells, Chief of Surgery at Hoagland Hospital in Chicago, Illinois, announced that all full-time doctors in the Department of Surgery were required to join the Surgical Group Practice or leave the hospital premises. In his eight years as chief, Dr. Wells had initiated numerous changes in the department, but never one as controversial as the Group Practice. Looking back on it in 1988, he said:

> This has been one of the ugliest things I've ever done—all the personal abuse, just for following the damn rules the university sent down. It is the closest I've come to quitting my job . . .

Dr. Wells had established the Group Practice or "trust" in 1984 to serve two purposes. First, it was intended to regulate each surgeon's professional income to comply with the Kent Medical School Salary Regulation, and secondly, it would augment the department's income with funds not otherwise attainable. Additionally, Dr. Wells was convinced that as an academic department of Kent Medical School, the Department of Surgery needed guidelines to ensure a standard of excellence:

> I think this has to be done in any academic institution. Doctors here are supposed to provide ongoing patient care, carry on research, and teach. Now if you're at all good as a surgeon, your private practice will skyrocket, and your research and teaching will lose out. It's fun and lucrative to practice medicine, but in a teaching hospital you have other responsibilities, too.

Background

The Department of Surgery was a clinical department of the 85-year-old Hoagland Hospital in Chicago. A private, 450-bed hospital, Hoagland had been a teaching affiliate of Kent Medical School since 1925. In its more than 60 years as a teaching hospital, Hoagland has demonstrated a firm commitment to teaching and research as well as patient care. Insisting that the three were interdependent units which together enhanced the quality of medical care, Hoagland's medical staff had distinguished itself among hospital teaching staffs. In 1980, Hoagland was the most popular hospital among Kent medical students and attracted graduates of the top medical schools for its 175 intern and resident positions.

As part of the teaching hospital, Hoagland's clinical departments were subject to the guidelines of Kent Medical School. Prior to 1980, Kent's guidelines, which

* This case was prepared by Patricia O'Brien under the direction of Professor David W. Young. Copyright © by the President and Fellows of Harvard College. Distributed by the Pew Curriculum Center, Harvard School of Public Health.

primarily stressed Kent's commitment to scholastic achievement, had had little effect on the school's clinical departments. Dr. Wells explained:

> For years, we'd had what you'd call a "Gentleman's Agreement" with the medical school. They gave the department a modest budget and paid doctors something for their teaching and research. Other than that, doctors could work for the hospital and carry on a private practice making about as much money as they wanted. There was some innocuous stipulation in our agreement allowing doctors to make as much money as "didn't interfere with their scholarly activities."

By 1980, Kent Medical School was feeling the financial constraints besetting most academic institutions. Unable to continue supporting their clinical departments, they altered the agreement, asking that patient fees support hospital clinical departments. The school issued a Salary Statement Regulation, from which the following is excerpted.

> Total Compensation paid to full-time members of the Faculty of Medicine as of December 1, 1981, may not exceed the level set for each individual in the *Appointments and Compensation Requirements for the Faculty of Medicine at Kent University*. The member's total income is equal to the sum of his/her Academic Salary plus Additional Compensation plus Other Personal Professional Income and may not at any level exceed twice the member's Academic Salary.
>
> Each Clinical Department head shall be responsible for maintaining the records and reporting the income of all full-time members of the Department. . . . Fees earned that are in excess of an individual's compensation level must be reported and disposed of as directed by the institution responsible for setting the level of compensation in consultation with the Dean of the Medical School.
>
> Inasmuch as the System was adopted by the faculty and approved by the Kent Corporation, it is understood that no Faculty member may continue in the full-time system unless he/she is in full conformity with the system and the procedures designed to implement it.

According to Dr. Wells, this was a difficult confirmation for the chiefs to give:

> The new guidelines caused quite a commotion, as you can imagine. Doctors were critical of the policy because they now had to report their salaries—something they'd never had to do before.
>
> When I asked people in my department for income disclosures, some of them tried everything to get around the rules. They were giving me their salaries after taxes and expenses—and it was *unreal* what they were calling "expenses." They were, of course, making just what they had been before. And it was becoming clear to me that I couldn't enforce the regulation.

Meanwhile, the Department of Surgery's income, now derived from the hospital and grants, was not meeting the department's needs. Some surgeons joined Dr. Wells in his concern about their financial problems. Dr. Eleanor Robinson, Associate Director of the Department of Surgery, explained:

> We were finding the department had needs, mostly of an academic nature, that we didn't have the money to support. Occasionally, we'd want to send residents to meetings or

postgraduate educational programs but couldn't afford to. Or someone would need financial assistance for a small research project that wasn't covered by long-term NIH grants and the money just wasn't there.

The Group Practice

Responding to these administrative and financial problems, in 1983, Dr. Wells decided to establish a group practice. He intended to structure the practice as a department fund that could pool surgeons' professional fees and pay them salaries, according to Kent's regulation. Any surplus of fees would be retained by the department for its use.

The Group Practice was organized as an educational and charitable trust fund with nonprofit, tax-exempt status. Although the hospital and medical school became the trust's beneficiaries, the trust maintained total responsibility for its policies and budget. Dr. Wells commented:

> I watched the Department of Anesthesia at Memorial Hospital form a group through their hospital about eight years ago. Everything goes into the hospital, and they give the group a yearly budget. The chief there is now having difficulty getting a run-down from the hospital on the department's contribution margin when he knows the department is making money. If he wants another anesthetist, he has to justify it to the hospital.
>
> I don't want to crawl to the hospital for what I need if I've got the space. Because of their problems, I chose not to do that.

Dr. Robinson, who aided in administering the trust, added:

> We generally agreed that patient income for the department's use should be administered outside of the hospital budget. Surgeons sometimes view themselves as more hardworking than the rest of the hospital and we didn't want our money used to subsidize other departments. We hadn't had problems with the hospital but it was a preventive measure.

The Surgical Trust offered members a salary in accordance with the medical school guidelines plus benefits and a conditional overage expense account. As an incentive, salaries were graded down from the guideline ceiling with increases based on yearly evaluation meetings between Dr. Wells and the doctor concerned. Dr. Wells explained:

> A doctor's salary is a function of his or her overall contribution to the department plus academic rank. What the medical school gave us is a maximum for each position. At the evaluation conferences, I decide, with the doctor, where he or she falls on that scale. In reality, we're all pretty close to our maximums but it's an incentive to get the work done.
>
> It is important to realize though, that salaries don't reflect the amount of patient fees generated by the doctor. If a surgeon has a steady practice and generates an average income in patient fees but is an invaluable teacher or researcher, he or she might be promoted academically and hence be paid more than another surgeon whose best skills are in seeing patients.

Dr. Wells acknowledged that this could also be a disadvantage:

> There's a practical problem with tying salaries to academic rank. It isn't always possible for people to do all three things equally well. If they don't do the academics, their salaries suffer. For example, we have some super neurosurgeons—absolutely super— but they don't have time to write academic papers. Their salaries are stuck at their academic rank, whatever happens.
>
> But the fact is, this is an academic hospital and if doctors are interested in making money, they shouldn't be here. They can move up the street and make as much money as they want.

The trust's benefits were health, life, and malpractice insurance, long-term disability insurance, and a tax-deferred annuity program. The plan was designed to provide members with benefits that had previously been purchased with members' after-tax dollars. Thus, it sought both to maximize members' income potentials within the Kent ceiling and to offer tax advantages.

If doctors generated more income than their salaries reflected, they received an overage account for professional expenses. That is, 50 percent of a doctor's surplus income would be credited to the doctor to cover expenses such as subscriptions, books, and conference travel. According to the by-laws of the trust, however, overage money could not be converted into salary. The remaining surplus income was to be used for department expenses.

The department would collect supplemental income from "chief-service patients." Prior to the trust, those patients who did not have private physicians were the responsibility of the chief resident and received free professional services. Because chief-service patients were admitted to the hospital without private physicians, the surgical services they received did not qualify for Blue Shield reimbursement.

When the department established the trust, they employed the senior chief resident as the Group's "junior-staff surgeon" and admitted all junior-staff patients as patients of the professional group practice. The trust could then bill junior-staff patients through its provider status. As a result, the trust collected fees that were not available when each doctor maintained an independent practice.

The trust was to be governed by a board of trustees. The five-member board would be responsible for trust policies and approving loans and budgets. Board members were to be Dr. Wells, who held a permanent position, two trustees appointed by him, and two trustees elected by the department. In addition, Dr. Wells would hold periodic meetings for all trust members.

Membership

By the winter of 1985, there were four members of the Surgical Group Practice: the junior-staff surgeon, Dr. Wells, and two other young surgeons. Critical of the trust's organization and planning methods, four or five doctors opposed joining.

Dr. Melvin Jefferson, a general surgeon at Hoagland for 10 years, was the most vocal about his position:

> I was not going to join the trust until I knew exactly what was being proposed. A number of the important issues were left extremely vague. The reasons for establishing the trust were even vague, in my mind at least, and our meetings did little to clarify the specifics. Some of the important issues, especially reconciling salaries, faculty rank, and academic and financial contributions to the department, were unresolved. I don't think these things had been thoroughly thought out, yet we were being asked to join. So a few other doctors and I refused to join until we knew more about the details.

In the spring of 1986, Dr. Wells asked all surgeons to join the trust. A few doctors who had verbally committed themselves to the trust but had postponed joining became members. But because attitudes in the department continued to differ, Dr. Wells decided membership had to be mandatory for all full-time academic surgeons. He explained:

> Membership had to be a prerequisite for remaining in the department because I knew what was going to happen. I had a few nice guys, resigned to the idea of the trust, carrying the department. And there were these other fellows, you know, friends of everyone; they'd been here a long time and didn't want to join the group. Some of them were taking home $200,000 a year. Others, their friends, were towing the line.
>
> I knew that some people wouldn't go along with it, and maybe for good reasons. You have to be realistic about the specialty you're talking about; if cardiologists can make $300,000 a year, how can you keep them down on the farm? In another one of our subdepartments, everyone is leaving. They're moving down the street to private offices. They're good specialists and it's too bad we're losing them, but if they're interested in making money, that's where they should be.

At the announcement of mandatory participation, every surgeon was forced to make a decision. Dr. Ben Lewis, head of the urology subdepartment, explained his decision to join the trust:

> We were TOLD by Dr. Wells that the department was not in compliance with the medical school's financial guidelines. He TOLD us that we had to change our system to comply and that if we didn't want to, we'd have to leave.
>
> I said fine. I trusted Dr. Wells totally, I admired him greatly, and I liked my work. I was willing to change even though I knew the financial and emotional costs. I knew the financial cost because I subtracted their guideline figure from my salary and . . . that was my loss. The emotional cost, loss of independence, is harder to evaluate and still troubles me.
>
> It makes you wonder why people stay here. Why do they? I guess it's because they like Wells—I think that's the main reason everyone stays. He's created a good faculty and a relatively favorable environment.

Other surgeons, however, were still opposed to the Group Practice. Dr. Jefferson, the most reluctant to join, explained that his reticence stemmed from his impression of the trust's operational structure:

> In thinking about the Group Practice earlier, I'd had exalted goals in mind. I thought we could use the trust to make a more unified and cohesive Department of Surgery. We

could spread the operative experience to the younger surgeons and improve the department academically by removing some of the economic motivations. Somehow the trust got sidetracked into an instrument whose *sole* purpose was to collect chief-service fees for the department, which resulted in a lot of devisiveness in the department.

For example, look at the method of remuneration as initially spelled out: a salary based on faculty rank and an admittedly extremely modest fringe benefit package. That left the question of overages and benefits essentially unresolved. We were being asked to sign a document involving a significant financial decision that could theoretically and legally involve making considerably less money than before, without having the specifics spelled out. We were just told that "no one would be hurt."

I also thought it was absurd to erect a gigantic administrative superstructure on what is essentially a small department. If the purpose was simply to conform to the medical school guideline and earn a little extra money for the department, we didn't need this whole organization with a billing office and everything else. I think we should have started small and built up—the fact is, we just don't have any big earners who can support a trust of this size.

From Dr. Wells' perspective, the trust had by then become

a tremendous can of worms. I had doctors philosophizing about everything, you should have heard them. All upset because of their "loss of control." It wasn't loss of control at all, it was loss of money. The absurd part of it was that a lot of those people weren't losing money. Believe me, surgeons can be a difficult bunch to work with.

Unfortunately, there's no uniformity in the way clinical departments interpreted the guidelines so doctors could point to other departments and claim that they weren't complying the way we were. They were right, particularly in this school, because the dean is afraid to interfere too much in the autonomy of the hospitals.

Billing System

At the outset of the trust, Dr. Wells intended to have all members' billing managed by a central billing office. In the spring of 1983, he hired a business manager to administer billings, collections, and reports for members. He planned that each doctor would submit a daily "activity sheet" to the business office, detailing services rendered, patient names, and fees.

However, so many present and future trust members opposed the centralized billing plan that Dr. Wells postponed implementing it. Instead, upon joining the trust, each doctor had the choice of centralized billing through the business office or their previous system wherein secretaries billed for doctors' private practices. Given the choice, half the surgeons chose central billing and half chose to remain with the old system. Ann Miller, the business manager explained:

Doctors really hold a spectrum of opinions on billing; some don't care at all about their bills while others want to see and discuss every one. I think some doctors don't like the business aspect of medicine—they prefer not having to handle it. The others don't like not having control of it. They feel removed from their practice if they don't see the bills go out.

The doctors who remained with private billing were to submit duplicate bills and their monthly collections to the business office. But most doctors never forwarded their duplicate bills, leaving the office with incomplete billing information. Ms. Miller was forced to establish a bill-receipt record system, posting bills and receipts simultaneously and setting them equal to each other.

> It was a crazy system and we knew it, but what could we do? Surgeons set their own fees, and we had no idea what they were. At the end of the month they would send us money with a record of patients' names and amounts paid. So we'd record that amount as billed and paid.
>
> But it was no way to run a business office. For example, one day a doctor brought in $15,000 in checks, just like that. We hadn't expected it at all. We never had any idea of our accounts receivable or collection rates.

However, Ms. Miller added that centralized billing had developed its own complications:

> Our main problem was that the information we received from doctors varied immensely from doctor to doctor. We didn't provide them with a formal activity sheet, so the doctors used their own systems of recording. As you can imagine, we were receiving dissimilar information from all of them.
>
> From what they gave us, my three assistants would compile standard data sheets which was unbelievably time-consuming. On top of that, we were billing for 5 doctors, collecting and recording for 11 doctors, and attempting individual monthly reports for 11. It was taking us three weeks to do just the monthly reports.

It was also becoming obvious to Dr. Wells that the trust billing had to be uniform and managed by a central computer system:

> Finally, I'd had it. The only efficient way to collect money for so many people was through one system. It had to be cheaper and more accurate plus it would keep everyone honest. I figured that if collections changed at all, they should increase because one office was handling all the data.

Many surgeons, however, disagreed with Dr. Wells on this issue. Among them was Dr. Lewis:

> I felt all along that it was crucial that we do our billing independently. Very simply, no one is more interested in his collections than the person who worked for it: I can do it better because *I care*.
>
> Secondly, there are complications in people's billings, which can only be settled by the doctor. A patient is on welfare and can't pay. After one bill, I'd know enough to drop it. A professional courtesy charge—I'm never sure what the billing office charged or if they understand my intention.
>
> Sometimes people come in and say, "doctor, I've been in here three times and I haven't received a bill yet, why?" I have to say, "I don't know," which makes me feel foolish. When my secretary did billing, I'd just step out, ask her and get the answer. Now with the business office all the way over in Talbot, geographically remote from the department, it is very difficult to know what the current situation is.

In January of 1987, the trust hired a computer company to manage all billings. The company was to receive billing and payment information from the business office and would process it by batches into claims and collections. They would apply claims and collections to physicians' balances and maintain a continual record of the trust's financial status. The computer company agreed to produce monthly printouts, by provider, so that doctors would have accurate records of their accounts.

Despite this contract, the computer company never produced the information. Ms. Miller explained:

> We had a terrible time with that company. The first problem was they never produced any reports according to doctor. We kept asking and they kept agreeing, but they never gave us anything useful.
>
> By the time we realized that we weren't going to get that out of them, we had a more serious problem: they had dropped $15,000 in payments from the records. They just hadn't applied it to any accounts, so although we had the money, we didn't know which accounts, i.e., doctors, it belonged to. That meant that the rates we had manually calculated were also meaningless. Well, we got rid of the company then, but I'm afraid it was too late.

Some doctors, affected by these errors, were already furious. With minimal billing information and startling fluctuations in collection rates, doctors blamed the centralized billing procedure. In an attempt to trace the problems, Dr. Robinson studied the collection data. After analyzing patient mix, payor class, and service mix, she reached no conclusion:

> I felt that centralized billing should, if anything, improve collections, but that wasn't our experience. Of course, with our other computer problems the issue became more complicated because our information was incomplete.
>
> Nevertheless, I think we have to separate questions of administrative efficiency from problems with the system itself. This is difficult to do, but we can't treat them as all one big problem with the billing system. Of course, we also have to consider that when surgeons turn their bills over to a collection office, they feel like they're losing control. That's the motive for doing the billing ourselves.

Dr. Wells considered the billing problem to be one of administrative oversights:

> Obviously, there were problems with that computer company but I don't see why this would be inherent to centralized billing systems. I've discussed the problem with other groups and our experience is atypical. It happened though, and we can't explain it.
>
> There's also the issue of overhead; doctors are seeing it now like never before. They can see costs that the hospital and department formerly picked up, like secretaries, coming directly out of the trust, and they're not pleased.

Other surgeons, including Dr. Lewis who had become an elected member of the board of trustees, maintained their opposition to the system. He commented:

> I've been against centralized billing from the start, and I think time has borne me out. For one year I've worked with no idea of what my collections have been. As a result, I don't know my overage, or if I even have one. If I submit receipts, I don't know if they'll be covered.
>
> I got some information for a few months last year and according to that, my collections had fallen by 33 percent. Yet, Dr. Wells calls this a more efficient system . . .

This method must be costing us more. My secretary still prepares the background information on bills and sends that to the billing office to finish. She might as well do the whole thing. It's unnecessary and inefficient to involve that whole office.

Dr. Jefferson thought that, for himself, the system was less efficient than his previous one:

Last year I tried to get some information about my collections and was appalled at how little they'd collected and how little they knew. They couldn't even give me records on patient payments. I did find out though that overhead was about 19 percent of my salary. We all agreed that this was excessive.

Dr. Lewis added that, in his opinion, the controversy over billing methods and other administrative matters was indicative of the trust's overall administrative policies:

What happened with billing is typical of the way the trust is run. I like and respect Dr. Wells, but our finances are in shambles because he isn't interested in and doesn't have financial skills. For example, look at what happened with the computer company he and Ms. Miller engaged.

What it comes down to is that the trust is really Dr. Wells's. It reflects his personality, plus he controls the majority of votes. Of the five board members, three are Dr. Wells and his two appointments, giving him 3/5 of any vote—it would be impossible to beat him. Not that there has been a showdown but the fact is, he's playing with a loaded deck. It's OK as long as you like and trust him, but it makes for an uncertain future.

Evaluation

By the winter of 1988, all 14 full-time surgeons at Hoagland had joined the trust. Five doctors had left the department in the previous two years for reasons both related and unrelated to the trust. Some joined the staffs at other hospitals, others left to establish independent private practices. Dr. Wells gradually filled their positions with surgeons who joined the trust upon joining the department.

Although reactions in the department still differed on some aspects of the trust, there were also points of general agreement among members. One such area concerned the trust's effect on the department's economic condition. Dr. Robinson commented on it:

One of the most important results of the trust has been the increased revenue generated for the department. It remains to be seen whether any of this is from the changes in the billing system, but collecting chief-service patient fees has certainly helped us financially.

Before the trust, the department was stretching to take care of the usual expenses. In the past few years we've not only covered our usual costs but we've been able to pay for postgraduate education and extend interest-free loans to residents. We even lent travel money to a resident so that his family could go to England with him when he was studying there.

The problems in the trust were really administrative and business problems. People here are devoted to academic pursuits so they're not concerned about who is generating the most income—that's not the point of medicine. I think these problems are getting smoothed out and the trust will run much better in the future. I also think it will improve as more people join the department.

Although Dr. Jefferson agreed with Dr. Robinson that the trust had helped the department, he remained critical of the trust's operations:

It's still difficult to get a handle on precisely what's going on. The process of forming the trust was not salutary on communication problems within the department, and these problems remain.

In a way, the trust has had no real effect on me. I do exactly what I did before and am not significantly better or worse off because of it. The available funds have allowed the department to survive, which was important, but when the trust was formed, Dr. Wells was never as frank as he should have been about the economic problems of the department. He said "we'd make a little extra money" but we never knew that there was a significant economic problem. If we had, we might have all discussed it and come up with an agreeable solution. The emphasis was always on the Medical School guidelines.

I think Dr. Wells is a much better chief of surgery than a businessman. There are many business issues and it was preposterous to go about them in an unbusinesslike way. I think Wells had the attitude that it isn't nice to talk about money. So because he can't talk about it we have a major communication problem. We still need frankness about this because we're getting new people into the trust and they have to know the details.

Dr. Lewis gave his opinion of the trust's shortcomings:

It's a nice feature of the department to have supplemental funds. I've set up a library in my office for medical students and residents in urology. I've also used money for honoraria and visual aids, and residents have been reimbursed for expenses from urological meetings.

I'd eventually like to see more money spent on teaching and conference equipment. We have considered a closed-circuit TV in the operating room.

As for the other side, I would say that reduced personal income and loss of independence are disadvantages of the trust. And there have been mistakes. The whole concept of centralized billing was a big mistake. I've voted against it every time it's come up, but it exists. Of course, the mistake was exacerbated by Wells's choice of computer companies.

I believe the real problem in organizing the trust was asking people to change. People were asked to go from a liberal, laissez-faire system to a structured one, and resisted. That's not unusual and could have been predicted.

Commenting on the trust four years after he'd organized it, Dr. Wells noted that some questions remained unanswered:

It's a difficult situation because there still is no uniformity in the medical school. I did what I thought had to be done to keep a Department of Surgery functioning academically, but some departments haven't done anything. And realistically, I know academic rank doesn't always reflect someone's contribution. But what could I do?

Then there's always been the budget problem. We never really know where we stand with any of our four budgets. We have budgets for the hospital, the medical school, the grants, and the trust; research funds for this department alone are $1 million. That's big business, and we're not trained for that.

You know, I sometimes wonder if the hospital could help us more than they have. I don't want them to run the trust, but I'd like to use them better than I have.

Questions

1. Classify the activities of Dr. Wells into the categories of strategic planning, management control, and task control. How, if at all, does this assist you in understanding the problems faced by the trust?
2. How would you characterize the management control structure of the trust? The management control process?

CASE 1–2   Boston Public Schools*

Edward Caton, a teacher in a midsize elementary school in Boston, Massachusetts, hoped someday to rise through the administrative ranks to serve as a principal of his own school, but he felt that in order to do so, he should understand more about the position to which he aspired. This was especially important to him in terms of the control he might have over the budget, which he knew was central to real power in many organizations.

In an effort to learn more about the operations of the Boston Public Schools, he set up some informational interviews with the principal/headmaster of an elementary school, a middle school, and a high school. Before making those rounds, however, he visited the headquarters of the Boston School Committee to obtain background information for his interviews.

Background

Mr. Caton learned that the department of implementation (DI) was responsible for carrying out the 1974 desegregation rulings issued by the federal government, and reported directly to the new superintendent of schools, who had been appointed in September 1985.

In addition to its responsibilities under the desegregation rulings, the DI also was responsible for making school enrollment projections each December for the coming fiscal year (which ran from July to June). These projections were important since annual staffing needs for each school were determined by a rather

---

* This case was prepared by Dena Rakoff under the direction of Professor David W. Young. Copyright © by David W. Young.

complex formula that used the DI's projections as the starting point. Moreover, since personnel formed the bulk of the budget, these projections effectively determined a school's budget. Each school had a few weeks to challenge the DI projections, and, if a convincing argument could be made, the projections would be modified. Final enrollment projections were established by mid-January of each year.

Mr. Caton learned that Boston, along with many other large cities, had seen declining enrollments during the 1970s and early 1980s. The decline was caused by a slowing of the birthrate, but also, in Boston's case, by flight from the city in the face of the desegregation orders which created busing and some violence within the schools. The result was not only a drop in enrollments, but also a change in the composition of the school system population. Specifically, the proportion of white students had dropped from 64 percent in 1970 to only 27 percent in 1985. Black students, by contrast, had increased during those same years from 30 to 48 percent, and Hispanics from 4 to 17 percent. Moreover, the proportion of students termed *very poor* had increased, by one estimate, to two-thirds of the total; 60 percent of the families of Boston public school students were classified as being at the poverty level of income as defined in federal guidelines.

Retrenchment had been necessary in the face of these shrinking enrollments, and pink slips to staff and closing of school buildings had become almost commonplace during this era. As of 1985, the BPS operated 77 elementary schools grades K-5, and 1 grades K-8; 22 middle schools grades 6-8, and 1 grades 7-8; and 17 high schools. Nearly 4,000 teachers worked in these schools.

The Fiscal Year 1987 Budget

Recently, the city had witnessed the beginnings of a rise in enrollments, and the DI was forecasting an increase to 58,625 students in fiscal year (FY)1987. The budget for FY1987 had been set at $293 million, divided between two funds: Fund Number 017 (General School Purposes [GSP]/City Funds), which comprised $285 million of the total, and Fund Number 027 (Facilities Management/Alterations and Repairs [A&R]), which accounted for the remaining $8 million.

Chapter 766 (Special Education) and Chapter 71A (Bilingual Education) of the Massachusetts State Laws mandated certain levels of spending for their constituents; in FY1987, the portion of the Boston School Committee budget assigned to those laws was 28 percent. Despite some state financial support for these mandates, much of the funding had to be provided by the School Committee, thereby limiting the funds available for regular education programs.

The State constitution prescribed a formula which determined the amount that the City of Boston was required to provide to Boston Public Schools; the school system received this automatically, without being required to make a justification. For the 1987 fiscal year, this "constitutional base" figure was $224.5 million. For additional revenue, the school system had to convince the city of its needs. For FY1987, this "supplemental appropriation" from the city was $57.9 million. In addition, the school system expected revenues from miscellaneous sources, mostly federal government entitlement programs, of $10.6 million. These amounts equaled the $293 million budgeted expenditures.

Control of the Budget Formulation Process

Much of the control of the budget process appeared to Mr. Caton to derive from the Central Office. Under the leadership of the new superintendent, there had been an emphasis given to centralizing much of the decision making. He advocated a tripartite objective—quality education, equal access, and accountability—and he wanted to reduce what he called *operational inefficiencies*. In his short tenure with the Boston schools he had developed the Boston Education Plan, a document outlining a mission and long-range goals for the system. Indeed, in December 1985, a few months after assuming office, he had launched a new budget system with new procedures and committees. This new budgeting system was explained in an April 1986 document of about 100 pages entitled *Superintendent's Budget Perspective for the Boston Public Schools, 1986–87,* and was supplemented with two budget manuals, each about 30–50 pages long. The FY1987 budget document itself was some 75 pages long.

In January 1986, in accordance with the new budgeting system, the principals and headmasters of each school had been given budget packets to assist them in preparing the FY1987 budget. These packets included forms such as a school profile, requesting formulation of goals and program directions; a program summary on which to detail plans for using allotted staff; and a programmatic reductions form, which allowed the principals and headmasters to make an argument for restoring previously withdrawn funds by documenting the impact of the cut. The principals and headmasters had about 20 days to complete these documents and to submit them to district superintendents; about a month after that, the district superintendents had been required to submit the packets to the Central Office. Reviews and hearings had taken place on several community and committee levels, as well as on the Central level, prior to arriving at a final budget.

Mr. Caton had read that the new superintendent's longer term objective for the budget formulation process was to rely on a zero-based budgeting model, where all spending would begin with an empty line and build on a program-by-program basis, in accordance with the rationale for each program. However, that plan had not been in place for the FY1987 budget, which had been simply a maintenance budget, keeping stable spending levels from the previous year, combined with a few initiatives and a few cuts. The result was an increase of about 8 percent over the fiscal 1986 budget of $270 million.

Mr. Caton noticed that of the $293 million, $190 million consisted of personnel expenditures, including $121 million for teachers and substitutes. He assumed that this money, and much but not all of the administrative support costs, were quite difficult to reduce, given enrollment levels and union contracts for salary levels and teacher-pupil ratios. Moreover, budget maneuverability appeared to him to be quite restricted by a variety of "givens" within the system: curriculum requirements, accompanied by citywide tests; promotion and graduation requirements; and even length-of-class-period dictates. All of these requirements were handed down by the school committee. He even had heard of rumors of an initiative being developed by the Massachusetts Department of Education to require schools to report on matters such as truant days, suspension days, dropouts, and high school seniors' postgraduation plans. He wondered what this would imply for the availability of state funds for individual schools within the system.

Mr. Caton also had observed what he thought to be a troublesome dichotomy within the system. On the one hand, he had seen an October 1985 memorandum from the deputy superintendent for finance and administration, describing some options that gave principals and headmasters greater budget flexibility (Exhibit 1). But on the other hand, Mr. Caton noted that the new Superintendent was in some ways decreasing the autonomy of schools. He continually heard, for instance, about the slowing of progress toward what the previous superintendent had called *School-Based Management*, a program that had made great strides in placing the locus for much decision making in the hands of each school and local community.

Perspective of the Principals and Headmasters

Armed with some sense of the school system at large, and toting a set of documents gathered from the Central Office, Mr. Caton next ventured out into the field to interview some school principals. He decided to first visit a senior high school, followed by an elementary school and a middle school.

The Senior High School.   The senior high school Mr. Caton visited was a relatively new one, with an enrollment of some 900 students. He began by attempting to learn more about the matter of budgetary discretion:

Caton: What I'd like to know is where you feel that you have any budgetary discretion. Is the entire procedure out of your hands?

Headmaster: Well, no, not entirely. Look, for instance, at my 620 account. That's the budgetary line that covers Instructional Materials. It's fairly broad, including mainly supplies—books, paper, that sort of thing. The total amount assigned to me in September—or actually in late spring—is determined by my projected student enrollment. A fixed part is removed from my allocation before I ever get the opportunity to assign it; that part covers equipment rental and that sort of thing. Let's say I get about an $85,000 allotment; $8,000–$9,000 of that might be assigned before I see the funds.

Then I have the rest to spend as I see fit. No, let me modify that. I have control over the items purchased with the rest and over the timing of that spending—but within certain guidelines. I must order books that appear on the list of School Committee-approved publications. I must use the vendors identified by them as approved. If there is something I want under $2,000, I can arrange my own vendor. However, I still have

---

EXHIBIT 1 Memorandum to Principals and Headmasters from the Deputy Superintendent, Finance and Administration

---

Subject: Budget Flexibility
Date: October 1, 1985

One major outgrowth of surveys and interviews done in connection with the Finance and Administration Task Force in the spring of 1985 is that desire for budget flexibility continues to be one of the highest priorities of principals and headmasters.

The School-Based Management Project had already given considerable impetus to this concept, and piloted it in certain schools. The Office of School Site Management has emphasized it as a priority for this school year.

Fiscal year 1986 promises to be a very tight budget period throughout. While the schools and programs appear to be adequately staffed, lack of appropriate initial funding and unanticipated large-scale costs in transportation and other areas will put a yearlong squeeze on the total school budget. However, since we will more than likely be in tight budget situations for years to come, we should not use that as a reason for totally avoiding the issue of budget flexibility. Therefore with the new superintendent's approval, we will undertake initial moves on a systemwide basis this year.

The budget flexibility options open to all principals and headmasters for 1985–1986 will include:

a. *Ability to move positions* within the individual school budget throughout the school year as long as there is compliance with state and federal mandates. This can be done by submission of a budget transfer (FA-01) and accompanying explanation to the Budget Office through the respective community superintendent.

b. *Use of lag funds* within the 312 account at all levels, and within the lunch monitor account at the elementary school level. This can be done beginning immediately by written request to the Budget Office through the community superintendent.

c. *Return to schools* of one-third of what is saved in substitute monies once we have factored out the use of district substitutes or building substitutes. This will be done early enough in the spring of 1986 to enable principals and headmasters to use any funds saved in late spring of 1986.

d. *Flexible use of 620 funds* to buy equipment, to pay part-time stipends to teachers for special programs for contracted services, for consultants, for tutors, or for hiring temporary help during peak periods. Use of 620 funds in this manner will be by submission of the appropriate FA-01 and explanation to the Budget Office through the community superintendent. (It should be noted that 620 funds cannot be used for creating extra permanent positions, whether full- or part-time.)

e. *Pooling of resources between schools.* Savings that accrue to an individual school may prove small but pooling resources among several facilities might offer opportunities that might not otherwise prove possible. For example, two or three small schools might find it possible to purchase jointly audio/visual equipment that neither could buy individually. In fact, smaller schools are most likely to obtain maximum benefits from these proposals only if they do cooperate and dovetail their efforts with each other.

It is my belief that this initial movement toward providing flexibility while small at first, will enable school principals and headmasters to purchase some important materials and to try some innovative approaches. It will also allow us as a system to test out ways to provide budget flexibility in a more comprehensive manner in the future.

I will be discussing this topic with principals and headmasters as I meet with you by level, and, along with the Budget Director, I will be available for any inquiries or recommendations.

Thank you for your continued cooperation.

cc: Superintendent
    Community Superintendents
    Budget Director

---

to go through the central purchasing format. And, to order books not on the list, I have to get approval from the Department of Curriculum and Instruction, which is quite time-consuming.

In terms of when I spend my funds, there is some pressure to use up the money quickly. You never know when the Central Office might issue a spending freeze, and those monies you were saving for a particular midyear purchase vanish. What's more, sometimes, your money is needed elsewhere—and it's wiped out of your account. So, spend quickly is my motto.

I very much wish I could use the money in a more measured way. Rolling over funds from year to year is a good example of a power that would enable me to save for items greatly needed, or to not spend when the need wasn't strong. But, we cannot keep any surplus till the following year, so I spend now!

If I could choose my vendors, I'm sure I could make more informed choices than the Central people can. I'm sure I could get better prices. But, as I said before, as soon as I make a purchase of over $2,000, I must use the approved sellers, or if no appropriate ones are listed, put the proposed purchase out to bid, which makes for a very lengthy procedure.

Caton: Tell me, I think I heard about money held for payment of substitutes, which reverts to you during the year if you do not call upon your full allotment of subs. Is that useful to you?

Headmaster: Sometimes, a portion of the unspent balance does come to the school for us to use as we see fit. We've gotten as much as $7,000 in a year that way. I leave the spending decision to the faculty senate. But, again, we bump up against the issue of inability to choose vendors by ourselves. And, you should consider the pressure felt by the faculty in knowing that their absences determine just how much of these funds all of us will have to use. Sometimes there are legitimate reasons to be out—personal sickness, ill children, etc. And, the teachers' union rises in agitation when they worry about too much pressure being put on people not to take advantage of their legitimate benefits. To tell you the truth, I'd rather spend my time solving real problems than focus too much on this "boon."

Caton: Is there any opportunity to handle your own money more directly when you are awarded grant money?

Headmaster: Yes and no. I recently got an outside grant, funded by the Bank of Boston and administered by the Central Office. In that case, I had to comply with the usual spending procedures. However, I also had a Carnegie grant of $30,000, and since that was not administered by Central, I could dispense the money as I saw fit.

Caton: I understand that your budget's size is determined by the projected student enrollment. What happens if you take in more students than either you or the Department of Implementation foresaw?

Headmaster: An addendum to the budget is possible. I do feel very strongly, though, that needs and program offerings, rather than numbers, should drive the budget. I'd like to be able to fund a program to train teachers to focus on problem-solving skills here, for instance.

Caton: Is there any way that you, here in your school, can control the numbers reported to Central?

Headmaster: Yes. I try to clean up my DNRs quickly. That stands for "Did Not Report"—in other words, students who were supposed to come to our school but either moved or are attending another school. I don't want them on my rolls any longer than necessary. I send out an attendance officer early to investigate those who do not report, and to drop them early.

Caton: But, doesn't that penalize you when it comes to determining your enrollment?

Headmaster: I run into union trouble if I don't drop them: they make the classes look unrealistically large. My truancy rate looks too large, also. I like clean books.

Caton: What control do you have over changes in budget procedure? How would you go about getting some of these revisions made?

Headmaster: I have a policy of always keeping parent groups informed. It's most important to know how to utilize your constituencies.

The Elementary School.   Next, Mr. Caton visited an elementary school, built in the 1970s, with an enrollment of about 700.

Principal: So, you want to know where I have any discretionary spending power. The 620 account, that's key. Maybe 12% of that is preassigned; the rest is mine to do with as I see fit.

Look, here's a copy of the latest expenditure report for this school from Central (Exhibit 2). As you can see, here's my 620 line. It shows me budgeted for about $59,000. Supposedly, according to this, $20,000 has already been spent by me—not by Central on its predetermined purchases. But I know that I've spent more than $20,000. It's very important for you to keep records in-house. That's the only way you can answer them downtown when they say you've overspent, or when they try to assign your funds elsewhere, or when you don't know how much you have left because the expenditure reports don't arrive in a very timely manner.

Caton: Don't you get funds from unfilled vacancies to use within your school?

Principal: They don't come here.

Caton: What about unspent substitute money?

Principal: I think that gets reassigned. I don't spend it. But, maybe the reason is that my per diem line gets charged for the long-term substitutes I seem to need each year.

I don't suffer, though. I manage to make things happen. I came into this school when it was a shambles. I've managed to create a very good faculty. Some of the people who contributed very little left.

Caton: How did you bring that about?

Principal: I simply let my expectations be known; if people wanted to work with me, they stayed; if they didn't, most of them left. Of course there are exceptions.

It took me a few years to get the support of the community. But look, now I can get parents in to help with the video workshop or with field trips any time I need them. I'm about to launch a program for parents to train them in carrying on at home the teaching that we begin here during the day.

Caton: Do you have any other sources of funds?

Principal: Grants. Grant application-writing, that's something my teachers spend a lot of time on. One of my teachers is presenting a workshop on that during the upcoming Teacher Professional Workshop Day. They really produce.

Grants give us some discretionary money. We sometimes get them for schoolwide use, and sometimes individual teachers get them for use with specific classes.

We really must look to external sources. Sales of candy or the like are another place where we turn up money we can use for whatever ends we choose. Parents and children help, last year we raised almost $7,500 through sales. That allows us to buy new blackboards, bulletin boards, to take field trips, and to do some repair of the facilities, which happen to be in fairly poor shape. Fortunately, neither this money, nor our 188 money from the State carry any vendor requirements.

As a matter of fact, look at the 730 account, repairs and maintenance of buildings and grounds. You can see I have an empty line there. The School Committee isn't paying for nonemergencies.

EXHIBIT 2 School Expenditure Report

012 GSP/CITY FUNDS

SELECTED ACCOUNT 87-87-012-***-***

EXP OBJ	ACCOUNT DESCRIPTION	CURRENT BUDGET	RE-SERVED	ENCUM-BERED	EXPEN-DED	ADJUST-MENTS	PCT YTD	AVLBLE BUDGET
131	REG. EDUCATION TCHR	690,289			58,151		8	632,137
133	PER DIEM SUBS	32,340						32,340
141	KDG TEACHER	121,752			9,214		7	112,537
161	BILINGUAL KDG TCHR	22,180			2,272		10	19,907
171	SPED RESOURCE TCHR	94,146			6,225		6	87,920
181	SPED SUB/SEP. TCHR	245,174			19,721		8	225,452
191	BILINGUAL TEACHER	202,642			17,893		8	184,748
312	SCH/DIST. ADMINIS.	123,714			30,629		24	93,804
341	PROGRAM SUPPORT	32,777			3,300		10	29,476
381	ATHLETIC INSTRUC.	24,976			2,272		9	22,703
391	P. T. PROF/STIPEND	588						588
521	CUSTODIAN	157,341			35,919		22	121,421
576	LUNCH MONITOR	24,486			858		3	23,627
577	BUS MONITOR	4,236						4,236
578	INSTRUCTIONAL AIDE	8,482						8,482
586	SPED RESOURCE AIDE	9,282						9,282
587	SPED SUB/SEP. AIDE	64,972			2,037		3	62,934
588	BILINGUAL ED. AIDE	30,809			564		1	30,244
620	INSTRUC. SUPPLIES	58,850	1,432	21,909	20,507		74	14,999
730	RPRS/MAINT. B&G							
810	INSTR. EQUIPMENT	1,750	985	753			99	11
820	NON-INSTR. EQUIP.							
	-DISTRICT C/E	1,950,786	2,417	22,663	209,570		12	1,716,134

As I say, though, I'm able to get what I need. And, if a teacher needs something, and makes a good case to me for that need, I can provide it. There's always a way.

But, I do have somewhere in my head a list of changes I feel are necessary. One item on that list is the method of determining the budget in the first place. What we need is a program-based budget. We should be able to designate the needs we must meet from the level of the school, and then be given the means and the responsibility to meet them. We shouldn't have to work on what Central says to work on. They claim they understand our programs, but then they do something like what they did this morning—send me a seventh "Behavior Lab" student when six is the limit.

As you know enrollment predictions are very important in determining the budget. Central sends me their estimate every year, and I'm allowed to counter it with my own predictions. In fact, my predictions for the past few years have been right on target. I've worked hard to prove to Central that my predictions are the accurate ones.

Once the budget is set, I can move teachers and use aides to cover if I need to. And, I've been able to distribute enrichment subjects among the student body in a fair way by creating a seven-day roster week; with that, each student gets music or art not once a week in the traditional way, but once every seven-day rotation. Thereby I keep my classes down to a manageable size.

The Middle School. Finally, Mr. Caton went to a middle school of about 600 pupils, constructed in the late 1960s. Some people had told him that middle schools were particularly difficult to manage because of their unstable demographics. He also had learned that high schools received more resources than middle schools due, in part, to the fact that high schools operated with departmentalized systems and differentiated staffing. But he also had been informed that, in the past few years, the middle schools had received funding for some additional positions, such as Directors of Instruction, Instructional Support teachers, and Targeted Reading teachers. He was anxious therefore to learn more about the perspective of a principal of a middle school.

Principal: You have to understand, Boston has a system of priorities in its school department. Most important is the high school. They get more personnel, more budget, and more discretionary funding; that's probably because the media features them, and media attention must be respected.

Next come the elementary schools, and finally the middle schools. Historically, our size and importance have been determined by the surges and retractions in the elementary school populations. As you probably know, the junior high schools, which middle schools supplanted, ran from grades 7 through 9. Because of this dependency on elementary school enrollment, we, at times, have been as inclusive as grades 4 through 8; sometimes we're 6 through 8. That variation has made it difficult to focus on an age group, and the abrupt changes have been disruptive to teachers as well.

Middle school years, especially 7th and 8th grades, are important years; those are when the decision to drop out is made. We're beginning to get some funds and programs now to combat middle-school-specific problems like overage students, dropouts, and teenage pregnancy.

Caton: Speaking of money, have you been able to take advantage of the "lag funds," that is, the unspent money from unfilled vacancies in your school that I understand reverts to you for your own use?

Principal: That's tricky. I have a vacancy right now for an assistant principal. I do get some of the salary money now, about three months' worth to cover August through this month of October, if I take a new person. But if I take a recall, I lose whatever funds are necessary to pay that person retroactively for the difference between his or her previous salary and this one. So, it's likely not to be as much money as you might expect.

But if I do get some money, I can file a Form FA-01, asking for the money to be transferred to my 620 account, and from there I have some discretion as to what it will buy.

You might think that leaving a position vacant could buy you the money you need for programs or whatever. Not really. The union has come in when positions remain unfilled if there are any unassigned teachers within that certificate area. They worry about their members not being utilized—and paid. And, what's more, if you leave a position unfilled for too long, Central might deem your need for the position reduced, and eliminate the funding for it in the coming budget year.

Numbers, in particular enrollments, are all-important. Special Education and Bilingual Education, both of which are programs mandated by the state, but only partially reimbursed by state or federal funds, put a drain on our resources. When it comes to regular education programs, we have trouble making a case for them.

The Department of Implementation each winter projects our enrollment for next year. My projected and actual enrollment figures are never the same. If you think the figures generated for your school are too small when the March budget figures are announced, you can petition to have the projections altered by making a good statistical argument. If your argument is considered valid, your teacher allotment will be raised, but your 620 account will not—it will be calculated on the basis of the original enrollment projections. Teacher allotments are contractual according to class size; instructional materials are not. The result is that if I get enough students to push a special education class over its limit, for example, I'm given an extra teacher, but I do not necessarily get enough extra 620 money to provide the students with books.

Caton: Do you find the 620 account something you can use to increase expenditures where you feel they're needed?

Principal: Yes, to some extent. But some of those expenditures are fixed: paper, Xerox supplies, art supplies, membership in various organizations; all those things are taken from your 620 account before the line is open to you. Prediction of costs is a bit difficult here also. Some years, for instance, maintenance of the Xerox is done by Central; some years, you have to absorb the costs yourself. It's important to stay in touch with Central each year to learn the current procedures.

After this final interview Mr. Caton looked forward to the evening, when he would sit back in his favorite armchair, notes in hand. From that vantage point, he would attempt to make a coherent whole from the various parts.

Questions

1. Define the key features of the current management control system in the Boston Public Schools.

2. As the manager (principal or headmaster) of a Boston public school, what changes would you like to see made in the management control system? (Your proposals should, of course, be limited to those that you think might be acceptable to headquarters.)
3. As the Deputy School Superintendent, what would be your reaction to these proposals?

Chapter 2

Characteristics of Nonprofit Organizations

Although the precise line between a for-profit and a nonprofit organization is fuzzy, the following definition is adequate for this book: A nonprofit organization is an organization whose goal is something other than earning a profit for its owners. Usually its goal is to provide services. This definition corresponds approximately to that found in most state statutes.[1]

The definition also emphasizes a basic distinction between the two types of organizations—a distinction that is the cause of many management control problems in nonprofit organizations. In a for-profit company, decisions made by management are intended to increase (or at least maintain) profits. Success is measured, to a significant degree, by the amount of profit the organization earns. By contrast, in a nonprofit organization, decisions made by management ordinarily are intended to produce the best possible service with the available resources. Success in a nonprofit organization is measured primarily by how much service the organization provides and by how well these services are rendered. More basically, the success of a nonprofit organization is measured by how much it contributes to the public well-being.

Since service is a more vague, less measurable concept than profit, it is more difficult to measure performance in a nonprofit organization. It is also more difficult to make clear-cut choices among alternative courses of action in such an organization; relationships between service costs and benefits, and even the amount of benefits, usually are hard to measure. Despite these complications,

---

[1] Some people prefer the term *not-for-profit* on the grounds that a business enterprise with a net loss is literally a nonprofit organization. *Black's Law Dictionary, Kohler's Dictionary for Accountants, Webster's Third New International Dictionary, Funk and Wagnalls Dictionary,* and *American Heritage Dictionary* do not list "not-for-profit," however. Practice varies widely among states and is not uniform for the statutes of a given state. In federal statutes, the usual term is *nonprofit.* In income tax regulations, *not-for-profit* refers to a corporation that is operated as a hobby of the owners.

EXHIBIT 2–1 Distribution of Short-Term General Hospitals and Beds, 1990

	Entities		Beds	
	Number	*Percent*	*Number*	*Percent*
Government...............................	1,444	26.8	169,228	18.2
Nongovernment, nonprofit.....................	3,191	59.3	656,755	70.8
Proprietary.................................	749	13.9	101,377	11.0
Total	5,384	100.0	927,360	100.0

Source: American Hospital Association, *AHA Guide to the Health Care Field,* (Chicago, Ill.: American Hospital Association, 1991).

management must do what it can to assure that resources are used efficiently and effectively. Thus, the central problem is to find out what management control policies and practices are useful for nonprofit organizations.

The distinction between for-profit and nonprofit organizations is not black and white. A for-profit company must render services that its customers find adequate if it is to earn a profit. A nonprofit organization must receive funds from operating revenues or other sources that are at least equal to its expenses if it is to continue to render services. Thus, the distinction is not based on the *need* for funds, per se, but on the predominant attitude toward the *uses* of funds.

Nor does the distinction relate solely to the types of services provided. Some hospitals, medical clinics, schools, even religious organizations operate as for-profit organizations, even though the services they provide often are thought of as being provided by nonprofit organizations. For example, Exhibit 2–1 shows the distribution among three classes of short-term general hospital entities and beds in 1990. In addition to the proprietary (i.e., for-profit) hospitals, an increasing number of nonprofit hospitals are being managed by for-profit companies.

NATURE OF THE NONPROFIT SECTOR

Any categorization of nonprofit organizations is certain to have gray areas.[2] Nevertheless, the categories shown in Exhibit 2–2 will serve as a useful frame of reference for this book. As this exhibit indicates, an important distinction exists between public (governmental) and private nonprofit organizations. Within the public category, the division among federal, state, and local government entities provides a useful organizing scheme; any of these entities can have agencies, commissions, or authorities.

---

[2] Work is under way to develop a common language to define, describe, and classify nonprofit organizations by major function and type. See Virginia A. Hodgkinson and Christopher Toppe, "A New Research and Planning Tool for Managers: The National Taxonomy of Exempt Entities," *Nonprofit Management & Leadership,* 1, 4 (Summer 1991).

EXHIBIT 2–2 Categories of Nonprofit Organizations

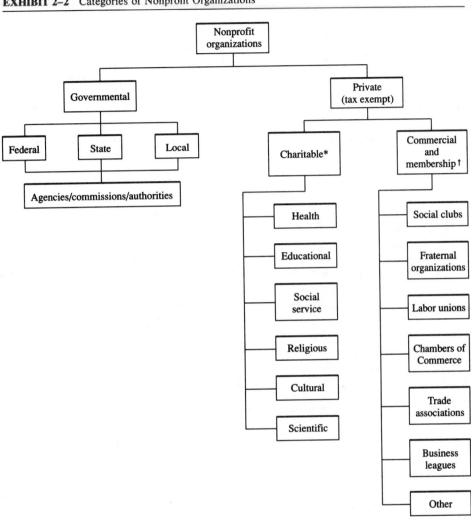

* Donor contributions are tax deductible.
† Donor contributions are not tax deductible.

Within the private category, an important distinction is between charitable organizations, for which donor contributions are tax deductible, and commercial and membership organizations, for which donor contributions ordinarily are not tax deductible. The former category includes health, educational, and social service organizations; in the latter are social clubs, fraternal organizations, labor unions, and similar entities.

Diversity of Demands on Managers

As Exhibit 2–2 suggests, the nonprofit sector comprises many different types of entities, with diverse activities, clientele, technological resources, and funding sources. Because of these and many other differences, any discussion of management control in nonprofit organizations must be viewed as a highly contingent one. That is, a management control system that works for one nonprofit organization quite likely will not work for another. Nevertheless, there are certain management control principles that are applicable to almost all nonprofit organizations, and certain issues that all nonprofit managers invariably confront as they attempt to improve the effectiveness and efficiency of their organizations. These are the focus of this book.

Size and Composition of the Nonprofit Sector

Exhibit 2–3 gives some idea of the magnitude of the class of organizations on which we focus our attention in this book. The figures are not exact because the census categories do not quite conform to the definition of nonprofit that is used here. They are, however, satisfactory as a basis for some general impressions. As can be seen, nonprofit organizations employ about a quarter of the nation's nonagricultural work force. As this exhibit indicates, local governments are by far the largest employers, with hospitals the largest nongovernmental employers (al-

EXHIBIT 2–3 Number of Nonagricultural Employees in Nonprofit Organizations

	Number of Employees (millions)			Average Annual Percent Change	
	1975	*1985*	*1989*	*1975–85*	*1985–89*
Federal government.........................	2.7	2.9	3.0	7.4	3.4
State government...........................	3.2	3.8	4.1	18.8	7.9
Local government	8.8	9.7	10.6	10.2	9.3
Health services:					
Nursing, personal care facilities	0.8	1.2	1.4	50.0	16.7
Hospitals	2.3	3.0	3.5	30.4	16.7
Education.................................	1.0	1.3	1.7	30.0	30.8
Social services	0.7	1.3	1.7	85.7	30.8
Membership organizations	1.5	1.5	1.8	0.0	20.0
Total nonprofit	21.0	24.7	27.8	17.6	12.6
Total nonagricultural work force..............	76.9	97.6	108.4	26.9	11.1
Nonprofit as percent of total	27.3	25.3	25.6		

Source: U.S. Department of Commerce, *Statistical Abstract of the United States* (Washington, D.C.: Government Printing Office, 1991).

though the numbers for this category are somewhat overstated since they include for-profit organizations).

The Internal Revenue Service (IRS) estimated that there were 1.1 million nonprofit organizations in 1991. The federal government is by far the largest single nonprofit organization. Its immensity is difficult to comprehend. In 1988 it owned 688 million acres of land and 442,000 buildings (occupying 2.8 billion square feet). The 1990 federal budget was $1.2 trillion. The Department of Health and Human Services (DHHS) had the largest share, $436 billion, followed by the Department of Defense with $312 billion. The largest department in terms of employees is the Department of Defense, which in 1989 had 1.1 million civilian employees. The Department of Health and Human Services had 122,000 employees in 1989.

Spending for nongovernmental nonprofit organizations is shown in Exhibit 2–4. As this exhibit indicates, when operating expenditures for the 1980–85 period are converted into constant (1982) dollars, they increased by an average of 12.5 percent per year, and by 7.2 percent on a per capita basis. Between 1985 and 1987, the average annual increases in constant (1982) dollars were 7.0 percent and 4.9 percent, respectively.

Many nonprofits make extensive use of volunteer labor. Because of this, Exhibit 2–3, which looks only at paid employees, understates the amount of effort expended on behalf of these organizations' clientele. Exhibit 2–5 corrects for this bias. As it shows, in 1987 (the most recent year for which data are available), the percentage of volunteers ranged from 0 percent in legal services to over 80 percent in foundations. The average was 45.3 percent.[3]

In general, it is quite difficult to find good information on the magnitude and activities of nonprofit organizations. In an effort to improve the quality of this information, the Ford Foundation made several grants during the 1980s. A number of publications emerged from these activities, some of which are listed in the references at the end of this chapter.

EXHIBIT 2–4 Operating Expenditures of Nonprofit Organizations (excluding government)

	1980	1985	1987	Percent Change 1980–85	Percent Change 1985–87
Current expenditures (billions)	$150.4	$242.4	$290.5	61.2%	19.8%
Constant (1982) dollars (billions)	181.6	204.3	218.5	12.5	7.0
Per capita (in 1982 dollars)	797.00	854.00	896.00	7.2	4.9

Source: Virginia A. Hodgkinson and M. S. Weitzman, *Dimensions of the Independent Sector: A Statistical Profile,* 3rd ed. (Washington, D.C.: Independent Sector Staff, 1989).

---

[3] These figures are volunteers as a percentage of the total paid and volunteer individuals; they are not measures of the percentage of work done by volunteers.

EXHIBIT 2–5 Paid Employees and Volunteers in Nonprofit Organizations, 1987

	Number of Paid Employees (000s)	Number of Volunteers (000s)	Total Employees	Volunteers as Percent of Total
Health services	3,367	1,049	4,416	23.8%
Education/research.	1,666	1.105	2,771	39.9
Religious	650	2,092	2,742	76.3
Social service.	1,182	645	1,827	35.3
Civic, social, fraternal	366	753	1,119	67.3
Arts and culture	122	390	512	76.2
Foundations	22	90	112	80.4
Legal services	15		15	0.0
Total	7,390	6,124	13,514	45.3

Source: Virginia A. Hodgkinson and M. S. Weitzman, *Dimensions of the Independent Sector: A Statistical Profile*, 3rd ed. (Washington, D.C.: Independent Sector Staff, 1989).

CHARACTERISTICS OF NONPROFIT ORGANIZATIONS

In the remainder of this chapter we discuss characteristics of nonprofit organizations that affect the management control process. These characteristics are arranged under the following headings:

1. The absence of a *profit* measure.
2. Different *tax and legal* considerations.
3. A tendency to be *service* organizations.
4. Greater *constraints* on goals and strategies.
5. Less dependence on clients for *financial support*.
6. The dominance of *professionals*.
7. Differences in *governance*.
8. Importance of *political influences*.
9. A *tradition* of inadequate management controls.

The absence of a profit measure is the most important characteristic. Since it affects all nonprofit organizations, we will discuss it at length. The other characteristics affect many, but not all, nonprofit organizations. They do so to varying degrees and are not unique to nonprofit organizations; they therefore are tendencies rather than pervasive characteristics.

THE PROFIT MEASURE

All organizations use resources to produce goods and services; that is, they use inputs to produce outputs. As we discussed in Chapter 1, an organization's effectiveness is measured by the extent to which its outputs accomplish its goals, and its efficiency is measured by the relationship between inputs and outputs. In a for-profit organization, profit provides an overall measure of both effectiveness and efficiency. The absence of a single, satisfactory, overall measure of performance comparable to the profit measure is the most serious problem nonprofit managers face in developing effective management control systems for their organizations. In order to appreciate the significance of this statement, we need to consider the usefulness and the limitations of the profit measure in for-profit organizations.

Usefulness of the Profit Measure

The profit measure has the following advantages: (1) it provides a single criterion that can be used in evaluating proposed courses of action; (2) it permits a quantitative analysis of those proposals in which benefits can be directly compared with costs; (3) it provides a single, broad measure of performance; (4) it facilitates decentralization; and (5) it permits comparisons of performance among entities that are performing dissimilar functions. We discuss each of these points below, and contrast them with the situation in a nonprofit organization.

1. Single Criterion.   In a for-profit business, profit provides a way of focusing the considerations involved in choosing among alternative courses of action. The analyst and the decision maker can address such questions as: Is the proposal likely to produce a satisfactory level of profits? Is Alternative A likely to add more to profits than Alternative B?

The decision maker's analysis is rarely as simple and straightforward as the profit criterion might imply. Even in a for-profit organization, most proposals cannot be analyzed in terms of their effect on profits—almost all proposals involve considerations that cannot be measured in monetary terms. Nevertheless, these qualifications do not invalidate the general point: profit provides a focus for decision making.

In a nonprofit organization, there often is no clear-cut objective criterion that can be used in analyzing proposed alternative courses of action. Members of the management team of a nonprofit organization often will not agree on the relative importance of various objectives. Thus, in a municipality, all members of the management team may agree that the addition of a new pumper will add to the effectiveness of the fire department. Nevertheless, some may disagree on the importance of an expenditure to increase the effectiveness of the fire department as compared to a comparable expenditure on parks, streets, or welfare.

2. Quantitative Analysis.   The easiest type of proposal to analyze is one in which estimated costs can be compared directly with estimated benefits. Such an analysis is possible when the objective is profitability: profit is the difference between expense and revenue, and revenue is equated to benefits.

For most important decisions in a nonprofit organization, managers have no accurate way of estimating the relationship between costs and benefits; that is, they have difficulty judging what effect the expenditure of X dollars will have on achieving the goals of the organization. Would the addition of another professor increase the value of the education that a college provides by an amount that exceeds the cost of that individual? How much should be spent on a program to retrain unemployed persons? Issues of this type are difficult to analyze in quantitative terms because there is no good way of estimating the benefits of a given increment in spending.

3. Performance Measurement.   Profit provides a measure that incorporates a great many separate aspects of performance. The best manager is not the one who generates the most sales volume, considered by itself; nor the one who uses labor, material, or capital most efficiently; or who has the best control of overhead. Rather, the best manager is the one who, on balance, does best on the combination of all these separate activities. Profit incorporates these separate elements. The key consideration is not the details of the operating statement, but the *bottom line*. This measure provides managers with a current, frequent, easily understood signal as to how well they are doing, and it provides others with an objective basis for judging a given manager's performance.

The principal goal of a nonprofit organization is to render service. Since the amount and quality of service rendered cannot be quantified, however, performance with respect to goals is difficult and sometimes impossible to measure. The success of an educational institution depends more on the ability and diligence of its faculty than on such measurable characteristics as the number of courses offered or the ratio of faculty to students, for example.

Although financial performance should be at most a secondary goal, managers sometimes overemphasize its importance. This can happen when managers with experience in for-profit companies become involved in nonprofit organizations. Accustomed to the primacy of profits, they frequently find it difficult to adjust to their new environment.

4. Decentralization.   For-profit organizations have a well-understood goal. The performance of many individual managers can be measured in terms of their contribution toward that goal. Because of this, senior management can safely decentralize, thereby delegating many decisions to lower levels in the organization.

If an organization has multiple goals and no good way of measuring performance in attaining them, it cannot delegate as many important decisions to lower level managers. For this reason, many problems in government organizations must be resolved in Washington or in state capitals rather than in local offices. The paperwork and related procedures involved in sending problems to senior management, and in transmitting the resulting decisions back to the field can be quite elaborate, giving rise to part of the criticism that is levied against bureaucracy. Frequently, such criticism is often unwarranted because, in the absence of something corresponding to the profit measure, there is no feasible way for governmental organizations to decentralize.

5. Comparison of Unlike Units. The profit measure permits a comparison of the performance of heterogeneous operations that is not possible with any other measure. The performance of a department store can be compared with the performance of a paper mill in terms of a single criterion: Which was more profitable? This usually is measured in terms of return on equity or return on assets.

Profitability therefore provides a way of combining heterogeneous elements of performance within a company, and a way of making valid comparisons among organizations. Organizations that have a goal of profitability can be compared, at least roughly, even though the size, technology, products, and markets of these companies are quite different from one another.

Nonprofit organizations can be compared with one another only if they have similar functions. One fire department can be compared with other fire departments, and one general hospital with other general hospitals. There is no way of comparing the effectiveness of a fire department with the effectiveness of a hospital, however.

TAX AND LEGAL CONSIDERATIONS

Most nonprofit organizations benefit from certain provisions of tax legislation. In this section, we summarize the general nature of these benefits. We also discuss briefly some of the legal implications of nonprofit status, particularly with regard to the generation and distribution of a financial surplus and the development of for-profit subsidiaries. The reader should use this information as a broadbrush approach only; it is not a substitute for a legal or tax opinion.

Tax Considerations

Nonprofit organizations ordinarily are exempt from income, property, and sales taxes. Individuals who lend money to these organizations may be exempt from paying taxes on the interest income they earn from their loans. Contributions and gifts to nonprofit organizations also may be tax deductible. We will discuss each item separately.

Income Taxes. Most nonprofit organizations are exempt from paying federal, state, and municipal taxes on income related to their nonprofit activity. (They do report their revenues and expenses to the Internal Revenue Service on Form 990.) They do, however, pay taxes on income generated from activities that fall outside their nonprofit charters. Such activities are known as unrelated business activities.

A nonprofit organization can lose its tax-exempt status if it engages in activities that are not considered "appropriate." These include substantial lobbying or participation in political campaigns. A nonprofit organization also can lose its tax-exempt status if a "substantial part" of its income results from activities that are unrelated to its charter.

The line between unrelated activities and tax-exempt activities frequently is not clear. For example, most YMCAs do not pay taxes on the income from their gymnasiums and swimming pools, even though these facilities compete directly with for-profit physical fitness centers that offer similar services. If, on the other hand, a YMCA shifts its service and program mix too radically, its tax-exempt status may be called into question.

There are essentially two ways a nonprofit organization can conduct for-profit activities and maintain its tax-exempt status: it can pursue a venture that is either (1) related to its tax-exempt purpose or (2) unrelated, but insubstantial. If the organization's for-profit activity falls into the first class, it will preserve its tax-exempt status and pay no federal income taxes. If the activity falls into the second class, the organization will pay "unrelated business" income taxes on the portion of its activity that is unrelated, but will maintain its general tax-exempt status. Many nonprofit organizations that engage in for-profit activities organize in such a way that these activities are carried out in separate, wholly owned subsidiaries. The key advantage of a separate corporate entity is that, for income tax purposes, it minimizes the risk to the parent organization's tax-exempt status.[4] It does not necessarily eliminate the risk that the organization's nonprofit status will be challenged by its state or municipality for property or sales taxes, however.

> ***Example.*** In 1990, the city of Erie, Pennsylvania, successfully challenged the tax-exempt status of Hamot Medical Center. Hamot owned several enterprises, including a boat marina on the shores of Lake Erie. The medical center appealed the decision to the Pennsylvania supreme court.[5]

Property Taxes and Sales Taxes. Government, charitable, religious, scientific, and educational organizations are exempt from local property taxes. In many states and municipalities, they are also exempt from sales taxes on the goods and services they sell. In addition, some are exempt from social security contributions and enjoy reduced postal rates. In comparing the costs of a nonprofit organization with those of a for-profit one in the same industry, the nonprofit's costs are inherently lower for these reasons. However, some nonprofit organizations make "contributions in lieu of taxes" to their local municipalities. The purpose of such a contribution is to pay for the services provided to a nonprofit organization by its municipality.

---

[4] The IRS now requires that nonprofits report their unrelated business activities. In 1989, IRS Form 990 was changed to make it easier for the IRS to identify potential unrelated business income and to impose additional penalties. For additional information see Laura Kalick and John Gardner, "Revised Form 990: Roadmap for the IRS," *Philanthropy Monthly,* December 1989.

[5] Dolores Kong, *The Boston Globe,* May 4, 1992.

Tax-Exempt Bonds. Individuals who purchase bonds issued by states and municipalities do not pay federal or state taxes on the bond interest income they receive. Some states issue bonds whose proceeds are used by nonprofit hospitals and educational institutions, and the income on these bonds usually is tax exempt also. Because holders of these bonds do not pay taxes on the interest income they receive, they are willing to accept a lower interest rate than they would on a bond of similar grade whose interest was taxable.

Contributions. Individuals and corporations that make contributions to charitable organizations can itemize and deduct these contributions in calculating their taxable income. The organizations that qualify for these deductions are spelled out in detail in Sections 170 and 501(c)(3) of the Internal Revenue Code. (For this reason, these organizations frequently are termed *501(c)(3) organizations*.) As Exhibit 2–2 indicates, they include entities established for religious, charitable, health, scientific, literary, or educational purposes. Nonprofit veterans' groups, cemeteries, and day-care centers also are included. States, municipalities, and fraternal organizations are included in this group if the contributions they receive are designated for the above purposes.

Legal Considerations

Three legal issues are of great concern to nonprofit managers: (1) ownership of the entity, (2) generation and distribution of a profit or surplus, and (3) legal obligations under a nonprofit charter.

Ownership of the Entity. A for-profit organization is owned by its shareholders, who expect to receive dividends and stock price appreciation as a return on the equity capital they furnish. By contrast, nonprofits cannot obtain equity capital from outside investors. Instead, the equity capital they obtain from outside sources must be from donations. Moreover, a nonprofit organization cannot distribute assets or income to, or otherwise operate for the benefit of, any individual. (Indeed, trustees usually serve without monetary compensation.) There is nothing comparable to stock options, for example, which constitute an important employee incentive in many for-profit organizations. However, under the current tax code, neither high salaries nor large cash reserves are necessarily a violation of these requirements. Considerable judgment is required, of course, in determining what is a high salary or a large cash reserve.

When a nonprofit organization is dissolved, the entity's value is transferred to another nonprofit organization or to the state or municipality where the organization operates, never to private individuals. In the case of a conversion from nonprofit to for-profit status, the determination of the amount of value is a central concern of the state agency charged with regulating nonprofit organizations. This is because the entity's market value may be greater than the difference between its recorded assets and liabilities, and, when this is the case, the determination of the appropriate amount becomes a matter of judgment.[6]

Surplus Generation and Distribution. Legally, a nonprofit organization is allowed to earn an excess of revenues over expenses, sometimes called a *surplus*. This is its principal means of accumulating the equity capital that may be needed for *(a)* expansion, *(b)* the replacement of fixed assets, or *(c)* a buffer in the case of hard times. A nonprofit organization is prohibited from paying out any of its surplus as cash dividends.

Under certain circumstances, nonprofit organizations can create for-profit subsidiaries, which are permitted to pay dividends. For example, a nonprofit research laboratory may have a subsidiary that holds patents developed by its employees. It gives these employees ownership shares in the subsidiary, and thereby rewards them with a share of license fees for patented products they develop.

Since 1983, the Internal Revenue Service has allowed nonprofit organizations to establish profit-sharing plans under certain conditions. In making this determination, the IRS decided that profit-sharing plans could have a favorable effect on employees' performance, and thus could further a nonprofit organization's charitable purposes.[7] The IRS prohibits a nonprofit organization from distributing a portion of its surplus to its managers after the fact, however. There must be a profit-sharing plan in place prior to any sort of distribution.[8]

Legal Obligations under a Nonprofit Charter. In exchange for their tax-exempt status, nonprofit organizations are required to provide benefits to their communities. A subject of some considerable debate among nonprofits concerns the nature and extent of these benefits. During the early 1990s, some states and municipalities, facing fiscal difficulties, began to look to the possibility of revoking the tax-exempt status of certain nonprofits. The argument they used was that these nonprofits were not providing sufficient benefits to their communities.

---

[6] For a discussion of this point, see David W. Young, "Ownership Conversions in Health Care Organizations: Who Should Benefit?" *Journal of Health Politics, Policy, and Law* 10, no. 4 (Winter 1986). See also Kenneth C. Dunn, Geoffrey B. Shields, and Joanne B. Stern, "The Dynamics of Leveraged Buy-Outs, Conversions, and Corporate Reorganizations of Not-for-Profit Health Care Institutions," *Topics in Health Care Financing*, Spring 1986.

[7] *IRS Revenue Procedure 83-36*. For a discussion of some of the issues involved in establishing such a plan see Charlotte P. Armstrong and Rylee Routh, "Profit-Sharing Choice for Non-Profit Organizations," *Pension World*, April 1984. For a broader discussion of compensation in nonprofit organizations (principally trade and professional associations, however), see Towers, Perrin, Forster & Crosby, "Not-for-Profit Compensation," *Public Relations Journal*, May 1984. For a more general discussion of employee job satisfaction and rewards in nonprofit organizations, see Philip H. Mirvis and Edward J. Hackett, "Work and Work Force Characteristics in the Nonprofit Sector," *Monthly Labor Review*, April 1983.

[8] For an expanded discussion of this point see Mark V. Pauly, "Nonprofit Firms in Medical Markets," *AEA [American Economic Association] Papers and Proceedings*, May 1987.

Example. Some cities require hospitals to meet "community care standards" before being exempted from property taxes. Hospitals wishing to retain their tax-exempt status are required to contribute to their communities in a variety of ways, such as by accepting medicaid patients or running a 24-hour emergency room.

SERVICE ORGANIZATIONS

Most nonprofit organizations are service organizations and thus do not have the same management control advantages as companies that manufacture and sell tangible goods. There are several important differences between the two types of organizations:

- Services cannot be stored. Goods can be stored in inventory, awaiting a customer's order. If facilities and personnel available to provide a service today are not used today, the potential revenue from them is lost forever.
- Service organizations tend to be labor intensive. Although such organizations require relatively little capital per unit of output, controlling this output is more difficult than controlling that of an operation whose work flow is paced or dominated by machines. People have a principle of motion of their own; machines do not.
- It is not always easy to measure the quantity of services. Keeping track of a quantity of tangible goods, both during the production process or when goods are sold, is usually easy. By contrast, a medical group practice can measure the number of patients a physician treats in a day, for example, and even classify patient visits by type of complaint. However, this is by no means equivalent to measuring the amount of service the physician provides to each of these patients.
- The quality of a service cannot be inspected in advance. The quality of tangible goods can be inspected in most cases before the goods are released to customers, and any defects are usually physically evident. At best, the quality of a service can be inspected during the time it is rendered to the client. Judgments as to the quality of most services are subjective, however, since for the most part, objective measurement instruments and unambiguous quality standards do not exist.

CONSTRAINTS ON GOALS AND STRATEGIES

Within wide limits, a for-profit organization can select the industry or industries in which it will do business. It can choose any of a number of different ways of competing in its industry, and it can change these strategies fairly easily should its management choose to do so. Most nonprofit managers have much less freedom of choice, and tend to change strategies slowly, if at all. A university adds or closes a professional school less frequently than a large corporation adds or divests an operating division. A municipality is expected to provide certain services for its residents, such as education, public safety, or welfare. It usually can make decisions about the amounts of these services it will provide, but it cannot as easily decide to discontinue them.

Furthermore, many nonprofit organizations must provide services as directed by an outside agency, rather than as decided by their own management or governing board. Private social service organizations must conform to state or municipal guidelines. Many hospitals must obtain a certificate of need to undertake a large-scale capital project. Organizations receiving support from the government must conform to the terms of the contract or grant. Moreover, the charters of many nonprofit organizations specify in fairly explicit terms the types of services that they can provide.

Finally, federal and state legislatures may limit total spending for an organization or certain programs. They also may dictate spending limits for certain cost objects, such as travel. Similarly, donors to nonprofit organizations may restrict management's options on the uses to which their contributions may be put.

Diversification through New Ventures

Despite the various constraints they face, many nonprofit organizations have grown and diversified considerably during the past decade. Many have done so through the formation of for-profit subsidiaries. The process a nonprofit follows in its decision to undertake a new venture is invariably complex, involving legal, strategic, and managerial concerns. We introduce some of these issues here and discuss them further in Chapter 8, under the topic of programming.[9]

In many instances, new ventures have helped nonprofit organizations subsidize activities that otherwise would not have been financially feasible. Indeed, during the 1980s and into the 1990s, faced with substantial reductions in federal assistance, many nonprofits saw diversification strategies as crucial to their survival.

For some nonprofits, the production of new types of goods and services has put them in direct competition with for-profit organizations, particularly small ones. One survey placed unfair competition from nonprofit organizations as third among the top concerns of small business people. The argument was that, since nonprofit organizations pay no taxes, they can compete unfairly with many small businesses.[10]

---

[9] For a good description of the issues associated with for-profit ventures, see Edward Skloot, "Should Not-for-Profits Go into Business?" *Harvard Business Review,* January–February 1983. See also Herrington J. Bryce, *Financial and Strategic Management for Nonprofit Organizations* (Englewood Cliffs, N.J.: Prentice Hall, 1986).

[10] The survey was of individuals attending the White House Conference on Small Business in summer, 1986. See also *Unfair Competition by NonProfit Organizations with Small Business: An Issue for the "80's,"* a booklet published by the Small Business Administration, Washington, D.C.

Example. In July 1983 Planned Parenthood began offering its own trademarked brand of condoms, and by May 1984 had sold over 1 million. It then began to develop its own line of over-the-counter contraceptives.[11]

Example. The nonprofit MacNeal Hospital, near Chicago, entered into a joint venture with Damon Corp., a diversified biotechnology company in Massachusetts, to conduct blood and urine tests, as well as cell and tissue studies. Damon splits its profits from commercial medical testing with MacNeal, and MacNeal saved an estimated $750,000 in purchasing costs because of the greater scale of operations at its testing lab.[12]

Example. The nonprofit Metro Washington Park Zoo in Oregon sells cans of "Zoo Doo," elephant manure that is used as fertilizer. Washington's National Zoo hosts champagne breakfasts in its reptile house. And the Minnesota Zoo charges crosscountry skiers $4 to traverse its grounds.[13]

The issue of competition between nonprofit and for-profit organizations is complicated by the presence of for-profit companies in activities traditionally conducted by nonprofit organizations. This is particularly true in health care, where considerable debate has raged over the merits of such a shift and its impact on the cost and quality of care.[14]

Competition of nonprofits with small businesses is further muddied because analysts attempting to address its financial consequences have paid little attention to distinguishing among three types of growth by nonprofits: (1) expanded sales of goods and services that do not compete with small businesses (e.g., hospital care), (2) expanded sales of goods and services that already were competing with small businesses (e.g., Girl Scout cookies), and (3) sales of goods and services that are relatively new to the nonprofit arena (e.g., tanning salons at a YMCA). Until a distinction of this sort is made, interested parties will not be able to address the issue fully.

SOURCE OF FINANCIAL SUPPORT

A for-profit company obtains financial resources from the sales of goods and services. If the flow of this revenue is inadequate, the company does not survive. A company cannot survive for very long if it makes a product that the market does not want. Moreover, it cannot sell products unless their quality is acceptable, and

---

[11] "New Profits for Nonprofits," *INC,* May 1984.

[12] Udayan Gupta, "Hospitals Enlist Profit-Minded Partners for Ventures to Generate New Business," *The Wall Street Journal,* January 23, 1987.

[13] Michael Allen, "Let's Hope Pythons Don't Enjoy a Sip of Veuve Clicquot," *The Wall Street Journal,* February 12, 1990.

[14] See A. S. Relman, "The New Medical-Industrial Complex," *New England Journal of Medicine,* 303 (1980), pp. 963–70; Carson W. Bays, "Why Most Hospitals Are Nonprofit," *Journal of Policy Analysis and Management* 2, no. 3 (1983); and Steven C. Renn et al., "The Effects of Ownership and System Affiliation on the Economic Performance of Hospitals," *Inquiry* 22 (Fall 1985).

their selling prices are in line with what the market is willing to pay. Thus, the market dictates the limits within which the management of a for-profit company can operate.

Some nonprofit organizations also obtain all, or substantially all, of their financial resources from sales revenue. This is the case with most community hospitals (as contrasted with teaching hospitals), private schools and colleges that depend entirely on tuition from students, and research organizations whose resources come from contracts for specific projects. These client-supported nonprofit organizations are subject to much the same forces as are their for-profit counterparts, such as proprietary hospitals and for-profit research organizations.

Other nonprofit organizations receive significant financial support from sources other than revenue for services rendered. In these public-supported organizations, there is no direct connection between the amount of services received by clients and the amounts of resources provided to the organization. Individuals receive essentially the same services from a government unit whether they pay high taxes or no taxes. Unrestricted grants by a foundation are not made because of services provided to the grantor. Appropriations made by a state legislature to a university or hospital are not related directly to the services received by the taxpayers from these organizations.

Contrast between Client-Supported and Public-Supported Organizations

In almost all instances, client-supported organizations want more customers. More customers imply more revenues, and more revenues imply greater success. In public-supported organizations there is no such relationship between the number of clients and the success of the organization. Indeed, additional clients may place a strain on resources. This is especially true when a nonprofit's available resources are fixed by appropriations (as in the case of government agencies) or by income from endowment or annual giving (as in the case of many educational, religious, and charitable organizations). Thus, in a public-supported organization, a new client may be only a burden—to be accepted with misgivings. In most for-profit, or client-supported nonprofit organizations, by contrast, a new client is an opportunity to be pursued vigorously.

This negative attitude toward clients gives rise to complaints about the poor service and surly attitude of bureaucrats. Clients of client-supported organizations tend to hear "please" and "thank you" more often than clients of public-supported organizations.

> ***Example.*** An investigation by the Comptroller of New York disclosed that 63.9 percent of the time, individuals calling food stamp dispensing centers could not get through to a staff person because of busy signals or a failure to answer within 15 rings. Moreover, 84.4 percent of the callers who reached a staff person were given incorrect and incomplete information.[15]

---

[15] *Comptroller's Report,* The City of New York, vol. 12, no. 6 (February 1988).

In some public-supported organizations, the contrast with the motivations associated with market forces is even stronger. A welfare organization should be motivated to decrease its clientele, rather than increase it; that is, it should seek ways of rehabilitating clients, and removing them from the welfare rolls. The Small Business Administration (SBA) should work to change high-risk businesses into low-risk businesses that will no longer need the special services of the SBA. The idea that an organization should deliberately set out to reduce its clientele is foreign to the thinking of for-profit managers.

Competition provides a powerful incentive to use resources wisely. Profits will decline if a firm in a competitive industry permits its costs to get out of control, its product line to become obsolete, or its quality to decrease. A public-supported organization has no such automatic danger signal.

As a substitute for the market mechanism for allocating resources, managers of public-supported organizations compete with one another for available resources. The sanitation, the parks, and the road maintenance departments all try to get as large a slice as possible of a city's budget pie. In responding to their requests, senior management tries to judge what services clients should have, or what is best in the public interest, rather than what the market wants. In the public interest, Amtrak provides railroad service to areas where it is not economically warranted. Similarly, the U.S. Postal Service maintains rural post offices even though they are not profitable.

Just as the success of a client-supported organization depends upon its ability to satisfy clients, the success of a public-supported organization depends on its ability to satisfy those who provide resources. Thus, a state university may maintain close contact with the state legislature, and a private university may place somewhat more emphasis on athletics than the faculty thinks is warranted so as to satisfy contributors to the alumni fund. Similarly, a sanitation department may place considerable emphasis on removing the mayor's garbage in a timely way. Furthermore, acceptance of support from the public frequently carries with it a responsibility for accounting to the public. In many instances, this accounting must be done to a greater degree than exists in a client-supported organization.

PROFESSIONALS

In many nonprofit organizations, the important people are professionals (e.g., physicians, scientists, combat commanders, teachers, pilots, artists, ministers). Professionals often have motivations that are inconsistent with good resource utilization. This creates a dilemma that has important implications for senior managers in nonprofit organizations.

Professionals are motivated by two sets of standards: those of their organizations and those of their colleagues. The former are related to organizational objectives; the latter may be inconsistent with organizational objectives. In fact, the rewards for achieving organizational objectives may be much less potent than those for achieving professional objectives. The reluctance of university faculty to serve on school or department committees is a direct reflection of this reward structure.

Many professionals, by nature, prefer to work independently. Examples are academicians, researchers, and physicians. Because the essence of management is getting things done through people, professionals with such a temperament are not naturally suited to the role of manager. This is one reason managers in professional organizations are less likely to have come up through the ranks than are those in for-profit organizations.

Although leadership in a nonprofit organization may require more management skills than professional skills, custom often requires that the manager be a professional. A military support unit is usually managed by a military officer, even though a civilian might be a better qualified manager. Traditionally, the head of a research organization is a scientist; the president of a university, a professor; the head of a hospital, a physician. This tradition seems to be diminishing, however.

In a professional organization, the professional quality of the people is of primary importance and other considerations are secondary. Promotion is often geared to the criteria established by the profession rather than those of the organization, per se. To the extent that these criteria reflect an individual's worth to the profession but not to the organization, they may run counter to the efficiency and effectiveness of the organization as a whole. Moreover, professionals tend to need a longer time to prove their worth to the profession than managers need to prove their worth to the organization.[16]

Traditionally, a professional's education has not included a management component. Most educators believe that training in the skills of the profession is far more important than training in the skills needed to manage organizations employing members of the profession. Consequently, sheer ignorance has often left professionals to underestimate the importance of the management function. While education and external pressures for better organizational performance are working to change this perception, the culture of many organizations has reinforced the tendency to look down on managers. The following quotation from Lewis Thomas, a physician, illustrates the typical attitude:

> A university, as has been said so many times that there is risk of losing the meaning, is a community of scholars. When its affairs are going well, when its students are acquiring some comprehension of the culture and its faculty are contributing new knowledge to their special fields, and when visiting scholars are streaming in and out of its gates, it runs itself, rather like a large organism. The function of the administration is solely to see that the funds are adequate for its purposes and not overspent, that the air is right, that the grounds are tidy—and then to stay out of its way.[17]

---

[16] See Joseph A. Raelin, "An Anatomy of Autonomy," *Executive,* The Academy of Management, vol. III, no. 3 (1989), pp. 216–28. Raelin describes the role of professionals at three levels, which correspond closely to strategic planning, management control, and task control, discussed in Chapter 1.

[17] Lewis Thomas, *The Youngest Science: Notes of a Medicine-Watcher* (New York: Bantam Books, 1983).

Financial incentives tend to be less effective with professional people. This is both because professionals usually consider their current compensation to be adequate and because their primary satisfaction ordinarily comes from their work. Professionals also tend to give inadequate weight to the financial implication of their decisions. Many physicians, for example, feel that no limit should be placed on the amount spent to save a human life. Unfortunately, in a world of limited resources, such an attitude is unrealistic. Nevertheless, in Thoreau's words, the professional "marches to the beat of a different drummer."

GOVERNANCE

Although the statement that shareholders control a corporation is an oversimplification, shareholders do have the ultimate authority. They may exercise this authority only in times of crisis, but it nevertheless is there. The movement of stock prices is an immediate and influential indication of what shareholders think of management. In for-profit organizations, policy and management responsibilities are vested in the board of directors, which derives its power from the shareholders. In turn, the board delegates power to the chief executive officer (CEO), who serves at the board's pleasure, acts as the board's agent in the management of the organization, and is replaced if there are serious differences of interest or opinion.

Governing Boards in Nonprofit Organizations

In many nonprofit organizations the corresponding line of responsibility is often not clear. There are no shareholders, members of the governing body are seldom paid for their services, and they may be chosen for political or financial reasons rather than for their ability to exercise sound judgment about the organization's management.[18] The governing body frequently is insufficiently informed about major issues facing the organization, and its decisions therefore are not always optimal. Thus, governing boards tend to be less influential in nonprofit organizations than in for-profit ones.

At an absolute minimum, the governing board of a nonprofit organization has the responsibility to act when the organization is in trouble. Since there is no profit measure to provide an obvious warning, the personal appraisal by board members of the health of the organization is much more important in a nonprofit organization than in a for-profit one. In order to have a sound basis for such an appraisal, board members need to spend a considerable amount of time learning what is

---

[18] The Council of Better Business Bureaus recommends that not more than 20 percent of the voting members of a nonprofit organization should be directly or indirectly compensated by the organization. See The Council of Better Business Bureaus, *Standards for Charitable Contributions* (Arlington, Va., 1982).

going on in the organization, and they need to have enough expertise to understand the significance of what they learn.

The juxtaposition of the previous two paragraphs points to one of the most serious governance problems faced by many nonprofit organizations. For reasons indicated in the first paragraph, many governing boards do an inadequate job of fulfilling the responsibilities outlined in the second. Frequently, there is not even a general recognition of the board's responsibility. In universities, for example, a widely quoted maxim is that "The function of a Board is to hire a president and then back him, period."[19] In hospitals, boards frequently are dominated by physicians who are qualified to oversee the quality of care but who have neither the expertise nor the willingness to assess the effectiveness and efficiency of hospital management. In government organizations at all levels, auditors verify compliance with statutory rules on spending, but few oversight agencies pay attention to how well management performs its functions. Although legislative committees look for headline-making sins, many committees do not have the staff or the inclination to arrive at an informed judgment on management performance.

Government Organizations

In government organizations, external influences tend to come from a number of sources, leading to a diffusion of power. In state and federal governments, for example, there is a division of authority among executive, legislative, and judicial branches. Consequently, there are often conflicting judgments about objectives and the means of attaining them. In a for-profit company the board of directors and the chief executive officer usually have similar objectives.

There may also be a vertical division of authority among levels of government (federal, state, and local), each responsible for facets of the same problem. For example, the federal government finances major and many minor highways, whereas local governments construct and maintain other highways.

Agencies, or units within agencies, may have their own special-interest clienteles (e.g., Maritime Administration and shipping interests) with political power that is stronger than that of the chief executive of the agency. Similarly, senior-management authority may be divided, particularly in states where expenditure authority is vested in committees of independently elected officials. The same problem occurs in localities governed by commissions whose members each administer a particular segment of the organization (e.g., streets or health). By

---

[19] Perhaps because the academic environment encourages writing, more has been written about college and university trustees than about other types of governing boards. Publications of the Association of Governing Boards of Colleges and Universities, One Dupont Circle, Washington, D.C., contain much material about the governance of colleges and universities. The classic book is still Beardsley Ruml and Donald M. Morrison, *Memo to a College Trustee* (New York: McGraw-Hill, 1959).

contrast, elected officials, such as the attorney general, the treasurer, the secretary of state, or the director of education, each may manage their organizations fairly independently.

A manager's latitude also may be determined by political boundaries that are structural in nature. For example, the mayor of Los Angeles has much narrower responsibility than does the mayor of New York because county government in California is responsible for many services that in New York fall under the city organization.

Often, too, government bureaucracy is insulated from senior management by virtue of job security and rules. Career civil servants may know that they will outlast the term of office of the elected or appointed chief executive. If a particular project cannot be sold to the current boss, the project's sponsors may bide their time and hope to sell it to the next one. Conversely, if they dislike a new policy, they may drag their heels long enough to allow new management to take over and possibly rescind the policy.

This fragmentation of authority complicates management control. A particularly significant consequence is that the public administrator comes to depend upon political power to influence those who cannot be controlled directly. Consequently, managers must focus on their political credit as well as their financial credit; they must measure the political costs and benefits of alternatives, as well as their financial costs and benefits. On the other hand, as the U.S. Constitution states, there are strong advantages to divided authority, with each branch serving as a check on the activities of the others.

POLITICAL INFLUENCES

Many nonprofit organizations are political—they are responsible to the electorate or to a legislative body that presumably represents the electorate. Some of the consequences of this status are discussed below.

Necessity for Reelection

In government organizations, decisions result from multiple, often conflicting, pressures. In part, these political pressures are inevitable, and up to a point desirable. In effect, since elected officials are accountable to voters, these pressures presumably represent the forces of the marketplace. Elected officials cannot function if they are not reelected. In order to be reelected, they must advocate the perceived needs of their constituents. In order to gain support for programs important to their constituents, however, elected officials must often support certain of their colleagues' programs, even though they personally do not favor them. This "logrolling" phenomenon is also present in for-profit organizations, but to a lesser extent.

Public Visibility

In a democratic society, the press and the public feel they have a right to know everything there is to know about a government organization. In the federal government and some state governments, this feeling is recognized by "freedom of information" statutes, but the channels for distributing this information are not always unbiased. Although some media stories describing mismanagement are fully justified, others tend to be exaggerated or to give inadequate recognition to the inevitability of mistakes in any organization. To reduce the potential for unfavorable media stories, government managers may take steps to reduce the amount of sensitive information that flows through the formal management control system. Unfortunately, this also lessens the usefulness of the system.

Multiple External Pressures

The electoral process, with institutionalized public review through the media and opposing political parties, results in a wider variety of pressures on managers of public organizations than on managers of private ones, whether nonprofit or for-profit. In general, elected public officials generate more controversy about their decisions than do business managers. In the absence of profit as a clear-cut measure of performance, these pressures may be erratic, illogical, or even influenced by momentary fads. Frequently, these pressures tend to induce an emphasis on short-term goals and on program decisions devoid of careful analysis. Shareholders demand satisfactory earnings, whereas the public and governing bodies of nonprofit organizations do not always channel their pressures toward good resource utilization.

Legislative Restrictions

Government organizations must operate within statutes enacted by the legislative branch, which are much more restrictive than the charter and bylaws of corporations, and which often prescribe detailed practices. In many instances it is relatively difficult to change these statutes.

Management Turnover

In some public organizations senior management tends to turn over rapidly because of administration changes, political shifts, military orders, and managers who only dabble in government jobs. Each change requires learning lead time and frequently a change in priorities. This rapid turnover results in short-run plans and programs that quickly produce visible results, rather than substantive long-range programs.

Civil Service

There is widespread belief that Civil Service regulations operate to inhibit good management control. It is by no means clear, though, that Civil Service regulations are different in any important respect from personnel regulations in some large companies. One important difference in many state and municipal governments is that Civil Service laws effectively inhibit the use of both the carrot and the stick. As a result, a Civil Service Syndrome may develop: "You need not produce success; you need merely to avoid making major mistakes." This attitude is a major barrier to employees and managers who wish to improve organizational effectiveness.

Nevertheless, Civil Service regulations in many government organizations may be no more dysfunctional than union regulations and norms in for-profit organizations. Examples are the restrictive and inefficient union rules regarding work assignments, such as the number of engineers and other personnel aboard trains, or the division between electricians and plumbers on a joint repair job. An important difference is that union rules generally affect individuals near the bottom of the organization, whereas Civil Service rules affect individuals throughout the organization, including most managers.

TRADITION

In the 19th century, accounting was primarily fiduciary in nature; that is, its purpose was to keep track of funds entrusted to an organization to ensure that they were spent honestly. In the 20th century, accounting in business organizations has assumed much broader functions. It furnishes useful information to interested outside parties as well as to management. Nonprofit organizations have been slow to adopt 20th-century accounting and management control concepts and practices, particularly the accrual concept.[20]

Barriers to Progress

Since nonprofit organizations lack the semiautomatic control provided by the profit mechanism, they need good management control systems even more than businesses. Why, then, have many such organizations, particularly government organizations, lagged behind? For government, there seem to be three principal explanations.

First, for many years, there was a prevalent attitude that the differences between government and business were so great that government could not use management control techniques developed by business. This attitude continues to be implicit in some texts on government accounting.

---

[20] For a brief history of the accounting function and its development in the last century, see William Steinberg, "Cooked Books," *The Atlantic Monthly,* January 1992.

Second, at the federal level, the Congress, particularly the House Committee on Appropriations, is reluctant to shift to a new budget format. Because of the importance of the budget, this reluctance affects the whole management control system. A similar problem exists in many states. In part the reluctance is based on simple inertia, but it also reflects a suspicion—generally unwarranted—that the change is an attempt by the executive branch to conceal something from the legislative branch.

Third, many career officials recognize that a good management control system is double-edged: it provides new information for management, but it also provides new information for outside agencies such as the Office of Management and Budget (OMB), the Congress, special interest groups, and the media. Sometimes, these officials are not anxious for outside agencies to have access to new and better information.

It is important to note that the first reason is based on the premise that good management control systems cannot be developed in the public sector. The second reason is based on the premise that the proposed formats provide poorer information. The third reason is based on the premise that a revised management control system will provide better information. All three reasons cannot be correct.

SUMMARY

The characteristics of nonprofit organizations described in this chapter can be grouped into two classes—technical and behavioral. Both are important to the material in this book.

Technical characteristics relate to the difficulty of measuring outputs and assessing the relationship between inputs and outputs. This difficulty is unique to a nonprofit organization. Great improvements in output measurement are possible, however, and managers need to spend considerable efforts to make such improvements. Nevertheless, it must be recognized at the outset that the resulting system will never provide as good a basis for planning or measuring performance as does the profit measure in for-profit organizations.

Behavioral characteristics encompass all the other topics in the book. The significance of these characteristics is twofold. First, most behavioral factors that impede good management control can be overcome by improved understanding and education. Second, unless these problems are overcome, any improvement in the technical area is likely to have little real impact on the management control function.

APPENDIX
Differences among Nonprofit Organizations

The description of nonprofit organizations in this chapter is intended to apply to nonprofit organizations in general. Clearly, the characteristics we discussed do not fit all such organizations equally well. In this appendix, we attempt to relate the broad description of nonprofit organizations contained in the text to each of the principal nonprofit sectors. Of course, these too are broadbrush generalizations to which many exceptions can be found in individual organizations.

Health Care Organizations

Nonprofit hospitals, nursing homes, health maintenance organizations, clinics, and similar health care organizations closely resemble their for-profit counterparts. Indeed, were it not for the difference in objectives—service rather than profit—their management control problems would be identical to those of their for-profit counterparts. There are few differences between a voluntary hospital and a proprietary hospital.

The health care environment is changing dramatically, and competition among health care organizations of all kinds has become much more intense in the past few years than ever before. Nevertheless, most health care organizations still have fewer competitive pressures than the typical for-profit business. Much of their revenue is still received from third parties (e.g., Blue Cross, commercial insurance companies, and the government) rather than directly from clients. Additionally, they are dominated by professionals, and they have no clear-cut line of responsibility to a defined group of owners. Spurred on by public concern about the rising cost of health care and by the necessity of justifying their fees on the basis of a plausible measurement of cost, many hospitals have made dramatic improvements in their cost accounting systems in recent years.[21]

Educational Organizations

Private colleges and universities whose tuition approximates the cost of education also resemble for-profit educational entities. To the extent that colleges and universities are supported by contributions and endowment earnings, however, the relationship between tuition revenues and the cost of services is less direct. Like hospitals, they are dominated by professionals, and their governing boards tend to be relatively uninfluential. They are also subject to increasing competitive pressures—in their case because of the decline in student population. In recent years, under the leadership of the National Association of College and University Business Officers (NACUBO), many have made substantial improvements in their management control systems.

State colleges and universities are supported primarily by appropriations from state legislatures. Although these appropriations may be based on a formula that takes into account the number of students or the number of credit hours, they are not the same as fees charged to clients because the individual student (or parent) ordinarily does not make the decision that the education received is worth the

---

[21] For a discussion of these improvements, see David W. Young and Leslie K. Pearlman, "Managing the Stages of Hospital Cost Accounting," *Healthcare Financial Management*, forthcoming, 1993.

amount charged. In other respects, state institutions are similar to private colleges and universities. In recent years, the legislative oversight bodies of some states have paid much attention to the financial management of their colleges and universities, and this has led to great improvements in their management control systems.

Public elementary and secondary schools generally use an accounting system developed under the auspices of the U.S. Office of Education, which is urged as a condition of federal support. Although revised in the late 1970s, it continues to be an inadequate system, and management control is hampered by its inadequacies. A few communities have developed excellent systems on their own initiative.

Membership Organizations

Membership organizations are those whose purpose is to render services to their members. They include religious organizations, labor unions, trade associations, professional associations, fraternal organizations, social and country clubs, cemetery societies, and political organizations. To the extent that they are supported by membership dues, fluctuations in the amount of such dues is an indication of the perceived value of services rendered by the organization. This is true even though there is rarely a direct connection between an individual's dues and the services he or she receives.

Many membership organizations are dominated by professionals and have weak governing boards. Certain membership organizations, such as religious organizations and some labor organizations, face strong competitive pressures. Others, such as professional associations, have no effective competition.

Historically, religious organizations have had notoriously weak management control systems. In recent years, however, several denominations have developed good systems and encouraged their use at local levels. Religious organizations have a particularly difficult problem in deciding on the programs to be undertaken and in measuring the value of services rendered. ("Souls saved per pew hour preached" is not a feasible measurement!)

Human Service and Arts Organizations

Human service organizations include family and child service agencies, the Red Cross, scouting and similar youth organizations, and various other charitable organizations. Arts organizations include museums, public broadcasting stations, symphony orchestras, theaters, and ballet companies.

Although they have quite different missions, human service and arts organizations share a characteristic that unites them from a management control perspective. With some notable exceptions, these organizations rely heavily on public support, either from the government or from contributions by individuals, companies, and foundations. Their revenues therefore do not directly measure the value of services provided to clients. Those who provide support tend to exercise an increasing amount of influence over the financial affairs of these organizations.

Considerable improvements have been made over the past several years in the management control systems of these organizations. These improvements are primarily a result of the influence of such organizations as the United Way of America and professional associations of museums and broadcasting stations. Significant opportunities for further improvement remain, however.

The Federal Government

Except for certain businesslike activities, such as the U.S. Postal Service, the federal government does not receive fees from clients. Its goals are multiple and fuzzy, and the value of its services is especially difficult to measure.

The federal government is subject to more external power and political influence than other nonprofit organizations. These forces make management control especially difficult. Furthermore, many federal agencies are unique (there is only one State Department), so there is no basis for comparing their performance with that of other units. Some improvements have occurred in recent years, but much remains to be done.

State and Local Governments

Collectively, state and local governments are by far the largest category of nonprofit organizations. Like the federal government, they are subject to a variety of external powers and political influences, and therefore have difficult management control problems.

Generally, their revenue is not directly related to services provided to clients. Although the person whose house is on fire is a client in one sense, the main function of the fire department is to protect the whole community. Proposals for specific programs are often political in nature, and frequently are not subject to economic analysis. The objectives of these organizations are difficult to define in ways that permit measurements of attainment. (What is adequate fire or police protection?)

Because management control in state and local government is inherently difficult, good systems are especially necessary. With a few notable exceptions, such systems currently do not now exist in most government units. Tradition has greatly hampered development of adequate systems. Many government units keep their accounts solely on a cash receipts and disbursements basis, a practice that has been obsolete since the 19th century. Only recently has pressure for change—public dissatisfaction with rising taxes and revelations of poor management—begun to emerge. There also are pressures from the federal government to implement revenue-sharing programs. Moreover, the Governmental Accounting Standards Board (GASB) is in the process of making substantial improvements in its accounting systems. These pressures seem likely to lead to improvements in the relatively near future.

SUGGESTED ADDITIONAL READINGS

Anthony, Robert N. *Financial Accounting in Nonbusiness Organizations.* Norwalk, Conn.: Financial Accounting Standards Board, 1978.

Clark, Robert C. "Does the Nonprofit Form Fit the Hospital Industry?" *Harvard Law Review,* May 1980, pp. 1417–89.

Drucker, Peter F. *Managing the Non-Profit Organization: Practices and Principles.* New York: Harper Collins, 1990.

Oleck, Howar L. *Nonprofit Corporations, Organizations and Associations,* Englewood Cliffs, N.J.: Prentice Hall, 1988.

Powell, Walter W., ed. *The Nonprofit Sector: A Research Handbook.* New Haven, Conn.: Yale University Press, 1989.

Rudney, Gabriel. *A Quantitative Profile of the Nonprofit Sector.* PONPO Working Paper No. 40, Yale University Program on Non-Profit Organizations, November 1981.

_____, and Murray Weitzman. *Significance of Employment and Earnings in the Philanthropic Sector, 1972–1982.* PONPO Working Paper No. 77 and ISPS Working Paper No. 2077, Yale University Program on Non-Profit Organizations, November 1983.

CASE 2–1   Boston Symphony Orchestra, Inc.*

For several years prior to 1982, Boston Symphony Orchestra, Inc. (BSO), operated at a deficit. For the four years 1978–81, the deficit totaled $4.5 million, an amount that had to be withdrawn from capital funds. Were it not for one special circumstance—a fund drive conducted in connection with BSO's 100th Anniversary in 1982—capital funds would have been exhausted within a decade if the deficit continued at the 1978–81 rate.

Background

BSO owned two properties. One was Symphony Hall in Boston. The orchestra performed there, except in the summer and when it performed in other cities. When Symphony Hall was not needed for performances, rehearsals, or recording sessions, it often was rented to other organizations.

The other property was Tanglewood, a large complex in the Berkshire Hills, about 130 miles from Boston. The orchestra performed there for nine weeks in the summer. Several hundred students participated in training programs at Tanglewood each summer. (The principal buildings at Tanglewood were not winterized and could be used only in the summer.) In the summer of 1982, attendance at Tanglewood totaled 308,000.

In 1981–82, in addition to Tanglewood, the orchestra gave 107 concerts, of which 13 were in foreign countries and 14 in other American cities. The Boston Pops Orchestra, formed from symphony orchestra players, gave 63 concerts in Symphony Hall and 7 free concerts at an outdoor concert shell in Boston, known as the Esplanade. At the July 4 Esplanade concert, a Boston institution, attendance was estimated at 200,000. Nearly all orchestra and pops performances were sold out.

Management estimated that Symphony Hall was used on 165 evenings a year, of which 130 were for BSO concerts and rehearsals, and 35 were for rentals to outside groups. In the afternoons there were 22 symphony orchestra concerts and approximately 25 rentals to outside groups. The orchestra used the hall on 125 to 150 afternoons annually for rehearsals, recording, or television sessions.

Proposed Plan

The "BSO/100" fund drive raised about $20 million of capital funds (primarily endowment) over a five-year period. Management recognized, however, that the special stimulus of the 100th Anniversary could not be counted on to provide the

---

* This case was prepared by Professor Robert N. Anthony. Copyright © by Osceola Institute.

EXHIBIT 1

BOSTON SYMPHONY ORCHESTRA, INC.
Analysis of Revenue Contribution to Fixed Costs
For the Year Ended August 31,
($000)

	Actual					Projections							
	1978	1979	1980	1981	1982	1983	1984	1985	1986	1987	1988	1989	1990
Fixed costs:													
Artistic	3,902	4,243	4,514	5,176	5,608								
Facilities	920	1,005	1,160	1,318	1,348								
Administration	1,377	1,472	1,768	1,940	2,204								
Total fixed costs	6,199	6,720	7,442	8,434	9,160	10,140	10,850	11,800	12,425	13,300	14,225	15,225	16,300
Results from operations:													
Operations:													
Concerts	2,666	2,986	3,161	3,827	4,006								
Radio (BSTT)	125	145	160	185	185								
Recording	320	384	510	543	827								
Television	139	225	289	223	246								
Occupancies	101	91	186	252	244								
Education	(100)	(60)	(87)	(34)	(77)								
Other Income	—	12	32	35	278								
Marginal contribution	3,251	3,783	4,251	5,031	5,709	6,160	6,675	7,325	7,775	8,375	9,025	9,750	10,500
Percent fixed costs	52.4	56.3	57.1	59.7	62.3	60.8	61.5	62.0	62.5	63.0	63.5	64.0	64.5
Operating (deficit):	(2,948)	(2,937)	(3,191)	(3,403)	(3,451)	(3,980)	(4,175)	(4,475)	(4,650)	(4,925)	(5,200)	(5,475)	(5,800)
Percent fixed costs	47.6	43.7	42.9	40.3	37.7	39.2	38.5	38.0	37.5	37.0	36.5	36.0	35.5
Endowment Income:	981	1,221	1,358	1,691	1,893								
Percent fixed costs	15.8	18.2	18.3	20.0	20.7								

Annual fund-raising:													
Total annual gifts	1,133	1,121	1,211	1,334	1,786								
Special-purpose gifts transferred to operations	(162)	(302)	(268)	(299)	(355)								
General-purpose gifts	971	819	943	1,035	1,431								
Net project revenues	176	209	229	264	723								
	1,147	1,028	1,172	1,299	2,154								
Fund-raising expenses	(549)	(441)	(414)	(553)	(442)								
Total	598	587	758	746	1,712	—	—	—	—	—	—	—	—
Percent fixed costs	9.7	8.7	10.2	8.8	18.7								
Total endowment													
Income and annual fund-raising	1,579	1,808	2,116	2,437	3,605	3,865	4,175	4,475	4,650	4,925	5,200	5,475	5,800
Percent fixed costs	25.5	26.9	28.5	28.8	39.4	38.1	38.5	38.0	37.5	37.0	36.5	36.0	35.5
Surplus (deficit)	(1,369)	(1,129)	(1,075)	(966)	154	(115)	-0-	-0-	-0-	-0-	-0-	-0-	-0-
Percent fixed costs	22.1	16.8	14.4	11.5	1.7	1.1							
Funding from (to)	1,369	1,129	1,075	966	(154)	115							
Unrestricted capital	-0-	-0-	-0-	-0-	-0-	-0-	-0-	-0-	-0-	-0-	-0-	-0-	-0-
Capital analysis:													
Added to endowment funds	442	1,750	1,433	1,308	3,540	3,500	3,500	3,500	3,500	3,500	3,500	3,500	3,500
Added (charged) to special reserve					150	(115)							
Funding of plant additions	433	980	493	1,641	326	1,021	500	500	500	500	500	500	500
Added to unexpended property fund balance					241	(241)							
Funding of deficit	1,369	1,129	1,075	966									
	2,244	3,859	3,001	3,915	4,257	4,165	4,000	4,000	4,000	4,000	4,000	4,000	4,000
Pooled investments:													
Cost	10,343	12,018	13,850	15,822	19,465	23,000	26,500	30,000	33,500	37,000	40,500	44,000	47,500
Market	11,645	14,015	15,817	16,356	20,536								
Endowment share unit value	12.54	13.20	13.67	13.78	14.19								

funds needed to balance the budget in the future. Alternative ways of financing operations were discussed, and the trustees eventually agreed on the plan given in Exhibit 1. In the BSO annual report for 1982 (i.e., for the fiscal year ended August 31, 1982), this plan was described as follows:

> As the orchestra embarks on the first decade of its second century, Trustees, Overseers, and Friends must make plans based upon the experience of the past and their best estimate of the economic climate in the years ahead. The single most important assumption in making such a projection is the rate at which "fixed costs" of maintaining the present organization and properties will increase due to inflation. Included in the Analysis of Revenue Contribution to Fixed Costs are projections based upon several assumptions:

1. That "fixed costs" will increase at a compound annual rate of approximately 7 percent through fiscal 1989–90.
2. That management will be able to increase the percentage of "fixed costs" financed by concert activities by ½ of 1 percent per year.
3. That the Investment Committee and the Resources Committee working together will be able to increase the percentage of "fixed costs" covered by endowment income by ½ of 1 percent per year.
4. That the Resources Committee will be able to raise on average about $6,000,000 per year, of which $2,000,000 per year will be available to balance the budget.
5. That the Buildings and Grounds Committee will be able to limit capital expenditures for depreciation, for necessary improvements, and for new facilities to $500,000 per year.

Perhaps the most significant conclusions to draw from the projections (Exhibit 1) are:

1. That, in the absence of some new source of revenue, ticket prices will have to continue to increase so that the marginal contribution from concert activities can increase from $5,709,000 in 1981–82 to $10,500,000, or 64.5 percent of "fixed costs," in 1989–90.
2. That Endowment Income available for unrestricted use must increase from $1,893,000 in 1981–82 to $4,000,000, or 24.5 percent of "fixed costs," in 1989–90.
3. That the book value of Pooled Investments must be increased from $19,465,000 at August 31, 1982, to $47,500,000 in 1990 if the yield on endowment funds averages slightly over 8 percent over the period.

During the past five years the orchestra raised a total of $20,000,000 for BSO/100 and $7,000,000 from Annual Fund Drives for a grand total of $27,000,000.

The goal of $6,000,000 per year, or $30,000,000 over the next five years, is challenging, but the task is not much greater than the task already accomplished during the period of the BSO/100 campaign, and the organization is in place to do the job.

The financial projections in the Analysis of Revenue Contribution to Fixed Costs and the above assumptions and conclusions will have to be reexamined annually in the light of economic conditions and the financial results of each year's operations, but the nature of the task facing management and volunteer fundraisers will probably not be materially changed by modest differences from the assumptions.

Contribution to Fixed Costs

The concept of "contributions to fixed costs" referred to in the above description was explained in the Annual Report as follows:

Each year the Trustees are faced with certain relatively fixed costs which are scheduled in the Analysis of Revenue Contribution to Fixed Costs report. These are primarily for the annual compensation of orchestra members, the general administration of the orchestra, and the basic costs of maintaining Symphony Hall and Tanglewood. Management earns a percentage of these "fixed costs" by presenting concert programs, through radio, television, and recordings, and through other projects which involve both direct expenses and related income from ticket sales, fees, and royalties.

Each program or activity, of which there are over 40, is expected to make a "marginal contribution" to "fixed costs." The "marginal contribution" is the difference between direct income and direct costs of the particular program or activity. The orchestra continued to make progress toward its goal of increasing the percentage of "fixed costs" contributed from operation activities.

The "marginal contribution" from all operations in 1981–82 covered 62.3 percent of "fixed costs" as compared to 59.7 percent last year and 43.0 percent in 1971–72.

In fiscal 1981–82, the "fixed costs" amounted to $9,160,000, compared to $8,434,000 in 1980–81, an increase of 8.6 percent. Operations earned $5,709,000, compared to $5,031,000 last year, a 13.1 percent increase. This left an "operating deficit" to be funded from other sources, e.g., endowment income and unrestricted contributions, of $3,451,000 in 1981–82, compared to $3,403,000 last year.

Other Information

The 1982 Annual Report contained the following explanation of endowment income:

Investment Income reached an all-time high of $2,134,000 as compared to $1,838,000 in the prior year. Of this amount, $219,000 was used for restricted purposes, e.g., supporting the winter season programs ($35,000), providing fellowships for the Berkshire Music Center and other BMC activities ($101,000), supporting the Esplanade concerts ($47,000), underwriting the Prelude Series ($29,000), and other miscellaneous activities. An additional $22,000 went to nonoperational uses, leaving $1,893,000 for unrestricted use in support of operations. This compares to $1,690,000 in 1980–81, a 12 percent increase.

EXHIBIT 2

BOSTON SYMPHONY ORCHESTRA, INC.
Balance Sheets
August 31, 1982 and 1981

Current Funds

Assets	1982	1981
Cash (including savings accounts of $49,835 in 1982 and $463,320 in 1981)	$ 119,888	$ 501,962
Short-term cash investments	2,600,000	1,666,222
Participation in pooled investments, at market	1,979,960	1,681,781
Accounts receivable—less allowance for doubtful accounts of $10,000 in 1982 and $32,000 in 1981	709,069	937,016
Grants and other receivables	285,900	291,071
Prepaid salaries and wages	343,962	345,195
Deferred charges	163,893	40,111
Prepayments and other assets	491,605	506,858
	$ 6,694,277	$ 5,970,216

Liabilities and Fund Balances	1982	1981
Accounts payable	$ 564,677	$ 591,559
Accrued pension liability	221,116	187,775
Accrued expenses and other liabilities	619,008	189,972
Advance ticket sales and other receipts	2,781,005	2,516,114
Advance receipts—special events	137,983	803,015
Due to other funds	240,528	—
	4,564,317	4,288,435
Fund balances:		
Unrestricted	150,000	—
Internally designated	1,979,960	1,681,781
	2,129,960	1,681,781
	$ 6,694,277	$ 5,970,216

Property Funds

Assets	1982	1981
Due from other funds	$ 240,528	—
Properties and equipment at cost, less accumulated depreciation of $2,209,622 in 1982 and $1,956,005 in 1981	4,766,216	4,693,885
	$ 5,006,744	$ 4,693,885

Liabilities and Fund Balances	1982	1981
Fund balance:		
Unexpended balances	$ 240,528	—
Investment in plant	4,766,216	4,693,885
	$ 5,006,744	$ 4,693,885

Endowment and Similar Funds

Assets	1982	1981
Cash management fund-annuities	$ 120,409	$ 179,390
Real estate and other property held for sale	712,223	862,233
Pooled investments at market	20,536,010	16,356,225
Less participation in pooled investments by other funds	(1,979,960)	(1,681,791)
	$19,388,682	$15,716,057

Liabilities and Fund Balances	1982	1981
Annuity payable	$ 67,778	$ 103,662
Fund balances:		
Endowment principal and income restricted	2,533,903	2,142,179
Funds functioning as endowment—trustee designated	16,787,001	13,470,216
	19,320,904	15,612,395
	$19,388,682	$15,716,057

The Annual Report also explained how the budget for 1982 was balanced, as follows:

The percentage of "fixed costs" that had to be provided by unrestricted gifts was reduced from 20.3 percent in 1980–81 to 17.0 percent in 1981–82, amounting to $1,558,000.

The sources of the $1,558,000 required to balance revenues and expenses in 1981–82 were:

1. Annual Fund (net): $989,000, up $250,000 or 34 percent over the previous year.
2. Projects (net): $723,000, up $459,000 or 174 percent over the previous year.

Since funds available from these two sources totaled $1,712,000, it was possible to transfer the excess gifts of $154,000 for other needs.

Exhibit 2 gives the balance sheet, taken from the Annual Report.

Questions

1. Do the plans for 1983–90 seem reasonably attainable?
2. Speculate as to other possible ways that BSO should seek to balance its budget this period.

CASE 2–2   Metropolitan Institute of Art

In January 1991, Simon E. Roberts, interim administrator of the Metropolitan Institute of Art (MIA), was in the process of attempting to obtain a loan. Despite a 20 percent increase in operating revenues between 1989 and 1990, the MIA was experiencing significant financial difficulties. According to Mr. Roberts, the Institute had a month left before it ran out of cash. He knew that if he could not obtain a loan soon, the organization's future was in jeopardy.

Background

The MIA was located in a major metropolitan area. Its building, which it owned, had five floors and 37,000 square feet of space. The facilities included a MacIntosh computing lab for graphic design, a production room with stat cameras and other production facilities, a photography lab with both black and white and color printing capabilities, a printmaking lab with a press, a clay lab with kilns, painting

---

* This case was prepared by George A. Pereira-Ogan under the direction of Professor David W. Young. It was prepared with the cooperation of an organization that wishes to remain anonymous. Copyright © by David W. Young.

and drawing studios, design and illustration classrooms, academic lecture rooms, offices, and a library containing 7,000 books, 30,000 slides, and 36 periodicals. The building was appraised in December 1990 at a value of $4,500,000.

The MIA offered bachelor of fine arts, diploma, and continuing education programs in design, fine arts, illustration, and photography. The mission of the Institute was "to provide students with the esthetic awareness, formal expertise, and humanistic perspective necessary to become professional artists in today's world." The Institute offered a full range of day and evening classes in both its degree and diploma programs, making it attractive to both full and part-time students. The Institute's student body was diverse with representatives from nine foreign countries and 23 states. The faculty was an equally diverse group drawn from the artistic, educational, and business communities. The Institute's students benefited from a low student to faculty ratio of 14 : 1.

Data

After experiencing a steady decline in enrollment during the early 1980s, the MIA's full-time equivalent (FTE) students began increasing steadily in 1988. This was despite an equally steady trend toward rising tuition costs for students. In 1990, MIA had 305 FTEs compared to 293 in 1989. Tuition was $7,150 and $6,500 in 1990 and 1989, respectively.

The MIA anticipated further tuition increases in the future, but it expected its tuition to be competitive with those of similar institutions. Indeed, its tuition in 1990 was approximately the same as a number of small art schools in the region, and was lower than the national average for comparable art schools. Despite these steady tuition increases, the Institute was projecting a steady increase in the number of FTEs in future years. It maintained an aggressive recruitment campaign in an effort to increase its applicant pool. In 1990, the Institute sent representatives to visit 200 schools, career fairs, and portfolio days. It also advertised nationally and it held two open houses a year.

Cash Flow

The MIA, like many educational institutions, had a very seasonal cash flow. It had plenty of cash on hand in the fall and spring when it collected tuition fees, but had significant cash flow problems in the summer when student enrollment was greatly reduced. Mr. Roberts felt the organization needed a loan to help alleviate these seasonal cash flow problems. Financial statements are shown in Exhibit 1.

The Banking Environment

The banking industry at this time had some significant problems of its own. The failure of Western Commerce Bank in late 1990 and the recent seizure by the Federal Deposit Insurance Corporation (FDIC) of the Bank of the Southwest, one of the region's largest financial institutions, had the industry in turmoil. That, coupled with the downturn in the economy, had caused most banks to adopt extraordinarily cautious lending policies. To complicate matters even further, the MIA had three primary obligations outstanding: two loans with the Western Health and Educational Facilities Authority (WHEFA) totaling $2,042,475 and one with the Western Commerce Bank totaling $446,103. However, since the Western Commerce Bank had been seized by the FDIC, this amount was due to the FDIC. Although the Western Commerce Bank loan had been a long-term one, secured by the building, the FDIC was requesting immediate payment of the full balance. As a result, Mr. Roberts was seeking another bank to assume the Western Commerce Bank loan on a long-term basis.

Despite all of this, Mr. Roberts felt that the Institute's financial outlook was improving. Although unrestricted cash had fallen by about $80,000 from 1989 to 1990, the organization's operating results had improved dramatically. The current unrestricted fund balance had increased by $10,537 in 1990, compared to a decrease of $325,454 in 1989. However, he suspected that the Institute's financial statements did not clearly communicate the organization's financial position to banks and other potential lenders. Indeed, one bank had told him they did not understand the statements, and another had said it would not grant a loan since the MIA had a negative fund balance.

Because of this, Mr. Roberts felt he needed to more clearly depict the MIA's financial status. He thought that if he could somehow present the information in a fashion more like he had seen in some for-profit organizations, he would have a better case with the banks. He also wondered if there was a way to clearly show how the organization's cash had been used during the year so that he could explain the large decrease to both banks and his board of directors.

Questions

1. Prepare an analysis that responds to Mr. Roberts' needs as described in the last paragraph of the case.
2. Over the longer term, what should the MIA do about its financial reporting problems?

EXHIBIT 1   Financial Statements

INDEPENDENT AUDITORS' REPORT

Board of Trustees
The Metropolitan Institute of Art, Incorporated

We have audited the accompanying balance sheet of The Metropolitan Institute of Art, Incorporated as of June 30, 1990, and the related statements of changes in fund balances (deficit), and current funds revenues, expenditures, and other changes for the year then ended. These financial statements are the responsibility of the Institute's management. Our responsibility is to express an opinion on these financial statements based on our audit. The 1989 financial statements were audited by other auditors whose report, dated September 7, 1989, expressed an unqualified opinion on those statements.

(continued)

EXHIBIT 1 *(continued)*

INDEPENDENT AUDITORS' REPORT *(concluded)*

We conducted our audit in accordance with generally accepted auditing standards. Those standards require that we plan and perform the audit to obtain reasonable assurance about whether the financial statements are free of material misstatement. An audit includes examining, on a test basis, evidence supporting the amounts and disclosures in the financial statements. An audit also includes assessing the accounting principles used and significant estimates made by management, as well as evaluating the overall financial statement presentation. We believe that our audit provides a reasonable basis for our opinion.

In our opinion, the financial statements referred to above present fairly, in all material respects, the financial position of The Metropolitan Institute of Art, Incorporated as of June 30, 1990 and the changes in fund balances (deficit), and the current funds revenues, expenditures and other changes for the year then ended, in conformity with generally accepted accounting principles.

Whitters, Prescott and McKernan, P.C.
August 29, 1990
(Except for Note 6 for which the date is September 7, 1990)

THE METROPOLITAN INSTITUTE OF ART, INCORPORATED
Balance Sheets
June 30, 1990 and 1989

Assets

	1990	1989
Unrestricted current funds:		
Cash	$ 3,666	$ 83,437
Marketable securities, at cost (market value of $19,672 in 1990 and $17,139 in 1989)	13,366	6,247
Accounts receivable, net of allowance for doubtful accounts of $55,000 in 1990 and 1989	103,377	58,232
Inventories (Note 2)	—	5,444
Due from restricted current funds	23,049	16,027
Due from loan funds	7,790	—
Prepaid expenses and other assets	9,359	28,225
Total	$ 160,607	$ 197,612
Restricted current funds:		
Cash	$ 1,416	$ 202
Investments	14,371	14,371
Due from federal and state governmental agencies	23,049	17,427
Total	$ 38,836	$ 32,000
Loan funds (Perkins Loan Program):		
Cash	$ 3,936	$ 12,548
Loans receivable students	116,735	134,473
Total	$ 120,671	$ 147,021
Plant funds: (Notes 3 and 4)		
Land	$ 136,000	$ 136,000
Building and improvements	2,666,752	2,666,752
Equipment and fixtures	257,849	247,049
Leasehold improvements	—	—
Deferred financing charges	31,909	31,909
Total	$3,092,510	$3,081,710

EXHIBIT 1 *(continued)*

Liabilities and Fund Balances (Deficit)

	1990	*1989*
Unrestricted current funds:		
Notes payable, bank (Note 3)	$ 446,103	$ 471,103
Accounts payable	67,237	90,617
Accrued expenses and other current liabilities	30,119	61,599
Deferred revenues	70,477	74,159
Estimated litigation settlement (Note 6)	36,000	—
Fund balance (deficit)	(489,329)	(499,866)
Total	$ 160,607	$ 197,612
Restricted current funds:		
Due to unrestricted current funds	$ 23,049	$ 16,027
Fund balance	15,787	15,973
Total	$ 38,836	$ 32,000
Loan Funds:		
Due to unrestricted current funds	$ 7,790	—
National direct student loan fund	112,881	$ 147,021
Total	$ 120,671	$ 147,021
Plant funds:		
Note payable, bank (Note 3)	$ 209,930	$ 209,930
Long-term debt (Note 4)	2,042,475	2,129,841
Fund balance	840,105	741,939
Total	$3,092,510	$3,081,710

See Notes to Financial Statements.

EXHIBIT 1 *(continued)*

THE METROPOLITAN INSTITUTE OF ART, INCORPORATED
Statement of Current Funds Revenues, Expenditures, and Other Changes
Years Ended June 30, 1990 and 1989

	Unrestricted	Restricted	Total 1990	Unrestricted	Restricted	Total 1989
Revenues:						
Tuition	$1,987,059		$1,987,059	$1,574,266		$1,574,266
Application, registration, laboratory, and class fees	166,480		166,480	145,802		145,802
Miscellaneous	41,933		41,933	72,322		72,322
Gifts and grants	29,496	$375,905	405,401	4,510	$376,310	380,820
Student activities fees	5,451	5,451	5,451		2,800	2,800
Investment income	14,403	1,480	15,883	16,069	396	16,465
Total current revenues	2,239,371	382,836	2,622,207	1,812,969	379,506	2,192,475
Expenditures and other transfers:						
Educational and general:						
Instruction	727,849		727,849	620,680		620,680
Academic support	24,877		24,877	21,457		21,457
Student services	5,451	7,117	12,568	2,800	3,005	5,805
Operation and maintenance of plant	171,972		171,972	117,230		117,230
Institutional support	1,010,549		1,010,549	985,944		985,944
Scholarships and fellowships	42,171	375,905	418,076	41,048	363,858	404,906
Bookstore, net loss				69,422		69,422
Total educational and general expenditures	1,982,869	383,022	2,365,891	1,858,581	366,863	2,225,444
Other transfers:						
Transfer to plant funds for:						
Plant expenditures	(10,800)		(10,800)	(45,758)		(45,758)
Principal and interest	(235,165)		(235,165)	(241,014)		(241,014)
Accounts payable				(28,000)		(28,000)
Notes payable, bank				34,930		34,930
Total other transfers	(245,965)	0	(245,965)	(279,842)	0	(279,842)
Net increase (decrease) in fund balances	$ 10,537	($ 186)	$ 10,351	($ 325,454)	$12,643	($ 312,811)

See Notes to Financial Statements.

EXHIBIT 1 *(continued)*

THE METROPOLITAN INSTITUTE OF ART, INCORPORATED
Statement of Changes in Fund Balances (Deficit)
Year Ended June 30, 1990

	Current Funds		Loan Funds	Plant Funds		
	Unrestricted	*Restricted*	*Loan Funds*	*Renewals and Replacements*	*Retirement of Indebtedness*	*Investment in Plant*
Revenues and other additions:						
Unrestricted current fund revenues..........	$2,195,472					
Gifts.......................	29,496	$ 1,480				$ 10,800
Investment income	14,403					
Expended for plant facilities........						87,366
Retirement of indebtedness........						
Grants, restricted..............		375,905				
Interest on loans receivable..........		5,451	$ 1,997			
Total revenues and other additions..........	2,239,371	382,836	1,997	0	0	98,166
Expenditures and other deductions:						
Educational and general expenditures........	1,982,869					
Expenditures for stated purposes..........		383,022				
Administrative and collection costs........			9,079			
Expended for plant facilities............				10,800		
Retirement of indebtedness............					87,366	
Interest on indebtedness					147,799	
Retirement of plant facilities............						
Student loans assigned to federal government.....			27,058			
Total expenditures and other deductions	1,982,869	383,022	36,137	10,800	235,165	0
Transfers among funds:						
Unrestricted funds transferred for:						
Plant expenditures............	(10,800)			10,800		
Principal and interest	(235,165)				235,165	
Total transfers	(245,965)	0	0	10,800	235,165	
Net increase (decrease) for the year	10,537	(186)	(34,140)	0	0	98,166
Fund balance (deficit), beginning of year	(499,866)	15,973	147,021			741,939
Fund balance (deficit), end of year	($ 489,329)	$ 15,787	$112,881	$ 0	$ 0	$840,105

See Notes to Financial Statements.

EXHIBIT 1 *(continued)*

THE METROPOLITAN INSTITUTE OF ART, INCORPORATED
Statement of Changes in Fund Balances (Deficit)
Year Ended June 30, 1989

	Current Funds		Loan Funds	Plant Funds		
	Unrestricted	*Restricted*		*Renewals and Replacements*	*Retirement of Indebtedness*	*Investment in Plant*
Revenues and other additions:						
Unrestricted current fund revenues	$1,792,390					
Gifts	4,510	$ 12,452				
Investment income	16,069	396				
Expended for plant facilities						$ 45,758
Retirement of indebtedness						122,866
Grants, restricted		363,858				
Interest on loans receivable			$ 1,925			
Student activities fees		2,800				
Total revenues and other additions	1,812,969	379,506	1,925	0	0	168,624
Expenditures and other deductions:						
Educational and general expenditures	1,858,581					
Expenditures for stated purposes		366,863				
Administrative and collection costs			5,625			
Expended for plant facilities				45,758		34,930
Retirement of indebtedness					87,936	
Interest on indebtedness					146,148	
Retirement of plant facilities						201,613
Total expenditures and other deductions	1,858,581	366,863	5,625	45,758	234,084	236,543
Transfers among funds:						
Unrestricted funds transferred for:						
Plant expenditures	(45,758)			45,758		
Principal and interest	(241,014)				241,014	
Accounts payable	(28,000)				28,000	
	34,930				(34,930)	
Total transfers	(279,842)	0	0	45,758	234,084	0
Net increase (decrease) for the year	(325,454)	12,643	(3,700)	0	0	(67,919)
Fund balance (deficit), beginning of year	(174,412)	3,300	150,721	0	0	809,858
Fund balance (deficit), end of year	($ 499,866)	$ 15,943	$147,021	$ 0	$ 0	$741,939

See Notes to Financial Statements.

EXHIBIT 1   *(continued)*

Notes to Financial Statements—Years Ended June 30, 1990 and 1989

Note 1.   Summary of significant accounting and reporting policies
Organization
   The Institute is a nonprofit organization, formed in 1912 for the purpose of instructing students for the development of creative professions in the visual arts.
Accrual Basis
   The financial statements of the Institute have been prepared on the accrual basis. The statement of current funds revenues, expenditures and other changes is a statement of financial activities of current funds related to the current reporting period. It does not purport to present the results of operations or the net income or loss for the period as would a statement of income, or a statement of revenues and expenses.
   To the extent that current funds are used to acquire plant assets or to amortize long-term debt, the amounts so provided are accounted for as transfers to the plant fund.
Fund Accounting
   In order to ensure observance of limitations and restrictions placed on the use of the resources available to the Institute, the accounts are maintained in accordance with the principles of "fund accounting." This is the procedure by which resources for various purposes are classified for accounting and reporting purposes into funds that are in accordance with activities or objectives specified. Separate accounts are maintained for each fund; however, in the accompanying financial statements, funds that have similar characteristics have been combined into fund groups. Accordingly, all financial transactions have been recorded and reported by fund group.
   The assets, liabilities and fund balances of the Institute are reported in four self-balancing fund groups as follows:

- Unrestricted current funds represent the portion of expendable funds that is available for support of the Institute's operations.
- Restricted current funds represent funds available which are restricted in use to a specific purpose, designated by the donor, grantor or other outside party.
- Loan funds represent funds available which were generated from the Perkins Loan Program.
- Under this program, the Institute offers long-term, low-interest loans to qualified students in need of financial assistance.
- Plant funds represent resources restricted for plant acquisitions and funds expended for plant.

Reclassification
   Certain reclassifications have been made to the 1989 financial statements in order to conform with the presentation for 1990.
Plant Funds
   Plant fund additions are recorded at cost or, if acquired by gift, at fair market value as of the date of the gift. Interest costs incurred for qualifying assets during the assets' construction period have been capitalized as a component of the asset. In accordance with institutional accounting practices, depreciation of educational buildings and equipment is not provided for in the accounts.
Deferred Financing Charges
   Deferred financing charges represent costs incurred principally in connection with the placement of financing on the renovation of the Institute's building.
Gifts and Pledges
   The Institute does not follow the practice of accruing pledges and gifts for either operating or permanent funds. When payments on pledges and gifts are received, they are accounted for in the year of receipt in the appropriate funds.

Note 2.   Inventories
   During the year ended June 30, 1989, the operations of the bookstore were discontinued. All bookstore supplies and materials were sold and the resulting gain or loss has been reflected in the statement of current funds revenues, expenditures, and other changes for the year ended June 30, 1989. At June 30, 1989, inventories in the amount of $5,444 represented supplies and materials in the Institute's stat room.

EXHIBIT 1   *(continued)*

Note 3. Notes payable, bank

The Institute is indebted to a bank under a commercial real estate loan agreement. The agreement provides that any borrowings are due in full on demand, and bear interest at 2 percent above the bank's prevailing prime lending rate. The outstanding balance is collateralized by the Institute's real estate. At June 30, 1990 and 1989, total borrowings under the agreement amounted to $656,033 and $681,033, respectively. Of the total amount outstanding $209,930 has been reported in the plant fund each year since the funds were used to finance the renovation of the Institute's building.

Note 4. Long-term debt

Long-term debt at June 30, 1990 and 1989, consists of loan agreements with the Western Health and Educational Facilities Authority (the Authority) and the Security Bank of the Southwest, trustee for the Authority. The Institute borrowed funds as required in order to finance the renovation of its building. At June 30, 1990 and 1989, the outstanding principal loan balances amounted to $2,042,475 and $2,129,841, respectively.

The loan agreements are secured by Irrevocable Letters of Credit issued by Western Commerce Bank and Trust Company. The loan agreements are also subject to various covenants. At June 30, 1990, the Institute is of the opinion that there are no violations that would cause the loans to become callable.

Maturities of long-term debt for each of the five years succeeding June 30, 1990, assuming a final repayment date of May 2005 and an interest rate of 6.45% per annum, are as follows:

Years ending June 30	*Amount*
1991	$ 93,681
1992	100,453
1993	107,715
1994	115,502
1995	163,851

Note 5. Pension plan

Retirement provisions for the Institute include contracts between each participating employee and the Teachers Insurance and Annuity Association and the College Retirement Equities Fund. Contributions are applied to individual annuity contracts that are fully funded and provide for full and immediate vesting of all contributions to the participant. The accrued benefit at any time for a participant is the current value of the annuity accumulation, including all contributions, less expense charges, plus investment results. The Institute's portion of contributions to these funds amounted to $7,016 in 1990 and $9,142 in 1989.

Note 6. Commitments and contingencies

Letters of Credit

The loan agreements, referred to in Note 4, are secured by Irrevocable Letters of Credit issued by the Western Commerce Bank and Trust Company.

Litigation

The Institute is a defendant in a lawsuit filed by the general contractor in charge of the building renovations. The suit alleges the Institute owes the contractor approximately $130,000 for services rendered. The Institute has filed a counterclaim in the amount of $2.2 million contesting some or all of the services that were performed in an unworkmanlike manner. The Institute intends to pursue this matter vigorously through completion.

The Institute is also a defendant in a lawsuit filed by the lessor of a building it leased through May 1989. The suit alleges the Institute prematurely terminated its lease agreement with the lessor and seeks damages of approximately $50,000. In September 1990, an out of court agreement was reached under which the Institute would pay the lessor $36,000 in full settlement of the dispute. Therefore this amount has been reflected as a liability in the balance sheet at June 30, 1990.

EXHIBIT 1 *(continued)*

INDEPENDENT AUDITORS' REPORT

Board of Trustees
The Metropolitan Institute of Art, Incorporated

Our audit was made for the purpose of forming an opinion on the basic financial statements taken as a whole. The information contained on the next two pages is presented for purposes of additional analysis and is not a required part of the basic financial statements. Such information has been subjected to the auditing procedures applied in our audit on the basic financial statements and, in our opinion, is fairly stated in all material respects in relation to the basic financial statements taken as a whole.

Whitters, Prescott and McKernan, P.C.
August 29, 1990

METROPOLITAN INSTITUTE OF ART, INCORPORATED
Schedule of Current Funds Expenditures
Years Ended June 30, 1990 and 1989

	1990		1989	
	Unrestricted	*Restricted*	*Unrestricted*	*Restricted*
Institutional support:				
Teacher's salaries	$628,982	$ 0	$561,591	$ 0
Models.......................................	26,922		19,506	
Materials and other classroom expense	71,945		39,583	
	727,849	0	620,680	0
Academic support:				
Library salaries	17,097		17,462	
Miscellaneous library expense	7,780		3,995	
	24,877	0	21,457	0
Student services:				
Miscellaneous.................................	5,451	7,117	2,800	3,005
Operation and maintenance of plant:				
Maintenance salaries	36,167		20,962	
Maintenance...................................	59,910		35,394	
Heat, light, and telephone.....................	67,789		54,240	
Water...	8,106		6,634	
	$171,972	$ 0	$117,230	$ 0

See Independent Auditors' Report on Accompanying Information.

EXHIBIT 1   (*concluded*)

	1990		1989	
	Unrestricted	*Restricted*	*Unrestricted*	*Restricted*
Institutional support:				
Administrative salaries..........................	$ 362,833	$ 0	$354,391	$ 0
Payroll taxes....................................	83,056		74,626	
Advertising and promotion	82,017		79,942	
Catalogue expense	66,022		30,319	
Postage	29,129		25,336	
Printing expense	13,422		6,000	
Dues and subscriptions	9,272		8,512	
Travel and entertainment........................	15,264		10,209	
Bad debts	5,006		44,713	
Collection expense	15,461		8,047	
Rent..	36,000		95,808	
Pension plan contribution	7,016		9,142	
Exhibition expense	6,169		4,227	
Professional services	39,566		58,183	
Office expense..................................	75,862		33,519	
Insurance	36,765		19,259	
Interest	80,165		82,968	
Fund-raising....................................	10,541		15,978	
Data processing................................	3,106		1,720	
Miscellaneous expenses.........................	33,877		23,045	
	$1,010,549	$ 0	$985,944	$ 0
Scholarships and fellowships:				
Scholarships...................................	$ 22,390	$ 0	$ 20,585	$ 0
Working grants	6,658		6,127	
College work study.............................	13,123	39,300	14,336	44,809
Educational opportunity grants	0	336,605	0	319,049
	$ 42,171	$375,905	$ 41,048	$363,858

See Independent Auditors' Report on Accompanying Information.

PART II

Management Control Principles

Before discussing management control systems and their implementation, we first outline some of the principles on which these systems are based. In Chapter 3, we describe general-purpose financial statements—the vehicles by which nonprofit organizations report their financial activities and results to outside parties. An appendix to Chapter 3 contains a primer on financial accounting for readers with no prior exposure to the topic. In Chapter 4 we look at full-cost accounting in terms of the decisions managers must make to establish a full-cost system. Chapter 5 takes up the topic of differential costs, discussing the bases on which different types of costs are calculated. Finally, in Chapter 6, we examine one of the more important aspects of management control in nonprofit organizations: pricing decisions. We discuss some considerations for managers who make these decisions.

A common theme in the final three chapters of this part is cost (and expense) measurement. Cost information plays a central role in many management decisions in nonprofit organizations. These decisions include:

- Determining the financial viability of programs, which requires full-cost information.
- Choosing among alternative courses of action, which relies on differential costs.
- Pricing, which uses a combination of full costs and differential costs.

Cost information is also important in decisions about the management control system. In setting up the management control system, senior management structures costs in terms of the managers who are responsible for incurring them. Costs structured in this way are called responsibility costs. Responsibility costs are discussed in Part III.

Full costs and responsibility costs are incorporated into an organization's accounts so that they can be collected on a regular basis. By contrast, a differential cost analysis is specific to the issue under consideration; therefore, differential costs, as such, are not included in the accounts.

Chapter 3

General-Purpose Financial Statements

All organizations, for-profit and nonprofit, periodically report their financial status as of a certain date and their financial performance for the accounting period (usually a year) ending on that date. Although the principles governing the preparation of these financial statements are largely the same for both types of organizations, this chapter focuses on principles applicable primarily to nonprofit organizations. We also describe variations in practice among different types of nonprofit organizations, particularly among local, state, and federal governments.

Our discussion assumes that the reader is familiar with the basic principles of accounting. Those who have not had a course in accounting or who want a refresher should review the appendix to this chapter for a discussion of these principles.

NATURE OF ACCOUNTING PRINCIPLES

Accounting information falls into two general categories: management accounting and financial accounting. The purpose of the former is to provide information to managers in an organization. The information provided by the management accounting system varies according to management's perception of the organization's needs. The purpose of financial accounting is to provide information to outside parties. In some cases, the outside party can prescribe the principles used to prepare the reports. These are called *special-purpose reports*. Nonprofit organizations, for example, must furnish information annually to the Internal Revenue Service in a specific format, using a report called *Form 990*. In other cases, the outside party does not prescribe the content or format of the report. These reports are called *general-purpose financial statements*. Reports to lending agencies and the general public are examples of general purpose financial statements. Because these reports must conform to a common set of principles, the information provided by various organizations is comparable. General-purpose financial statements are prepared according to generally accepted accounting principles (GAAP).

Source of Principles

Except for reports prepared by government units, generally accepted accounting principles are prescribed by the Financial Accounting Standards Board (FASB), a private-sector body comprised of seven full-time members supported by a large staff. The FASB has an annual budget of about $12 million, contributed by accounting organizations, accounting firms, and related businesses. Although many FASB principles (which it calls standards) apply to both for-profit and nonprofit organizations, it has published (as of 1992) only one standard relating specifically to nonprofit organizations. This standard deals with depreciation and continues to be highly controversial.

In general, instead of setting specific standards for nonprofit organizations, the FASB has designated four guides published by the American Institute of Certified Public Accountants (AICPA) as the source of preferred practices. These guides apply respectively to colleges and universities, voluntary health and welfare organizations, hospitals, and other nonprofit organizations.

Accounting standards for state and municipal organizations are set by the Governmental Accounting Standards Board (GASB), which is located in the same building as the FASB but has a much smaller staff. Its board has five members, three of whom are part-time. Although in operation only since 1983, the GASB has made considerable progress in writing a complete set of standards.

By law, standards for federal agencies are set by the Comptroller General of the United States. Implementation of these standards is the responsibility of the Department of the Treasury and the Office of Management and Budget (OMB). Despite the law, many agencies have accounting systems that are inconsistent with these standards. Partially because of this, in 1990 the Congress created a new advisory body to develop standards for federal government accounting.

Although generally accepted accounting principles are required only for the preparation of general-purpose financial accounting reports, they also influence many aspects of management accounting. If this were not the case, an organization would have to keep two sets of books, causing an additional bookkeeping cost and, more importantly, possibly causing confusion because of different ways of reporting the same event.

FINANCIAL STATEMENTS

An organization for which accounts are kept is called an *accounting entity*, and the time period for which reports are prepared is the accounting period. In all organizations the official reporting period, known as the *fiscal year*, is one year.

The fiscal year needn't end on December 31; in fact, many organizations end the fiscal year on June 30, September 30, or some other date. Usually the entity will prepare interim reports for shorter periods, such as monthly or quarterly. In this description we shall assume that the purpose is to prepare the annual financial statements.

Balance Sheet

Nonprofit organizations and for-profit companies report assets and liabilities in essentially the same way. The reporting of equity differs, however, because of differences in the nature of equity transactions in each type of organization.

In a for-profit entity, equity reflects the amount of capital obtained from two main sources: (1) investors and (2) the profitable operation of the entity. In a corporation, investors are known as *shareholders* or *stockholders*. They supply capital in exchange for the entity's stock, and the amount they supply is called *paid-in capital*. The entity generates additional equity by operating at a profit. The amount of profit in a period is the entity's net income or earnings. Some of this income may be paid to shareholders in the form of dividends, so the *net* amount of equity obtained from operations is the difference between earnings and dividends. The amount reported on the balance sheet is called *retained earnings*. It is the total earnings since the corporation first began to operate, less the total dividends paid during that time. This is sometimes called *operating capital*.

A nonprofit entity has no investors; therefore its balance sheet has no item for paid-in capital. It does, however, generate earnings from its operations. Since it is legally prohibited from paying dividends, the full amount of earnings it has generated is its equity. Nonprofit organizations do not use the term *retained earnings*. Instead they label this amount as *net assets* or *fund balance*. Whatever the label, the amount is conceptually the same as retained earnings or operating capital in a for-profit corporation.

Some nonprofit entities obtain capital from contributions. Capital contributed as money or its equivalent is called *endowment*, and the contribution of other assets is known as *contributed plant*. For reasons we discuss later, contributed capital must be kept separate from operating capital. This is done by preparing separate financial statements for capital contributions. (We will describe these statements later in this chapter.)

Operating Statement

Like for-profit organizations, nonprofit organizations prepare an operating statement (or income statement) that explains the change in operating equity between two balance sheets. The operating statement reports the revenues and expenses of the period.

A primary goal of a for-profit entity is to earn income on its invested capital, and its net income (often referred to as *the bottom line*) is an indication of how the entity has performed in attaining this goal. As a general rule, the larger an entity's net income in relation to its invested capital, the better it has performed.

The Statement of Cash Flows

Revenues and expenses are measured by what is called the *accrual concept*. According to this concept, revenue is recorded when earned, and expenses when incurred. This is not necessarily the same as the amount of cash received or paid out. Entities prepare a third statement—the statement of cash flows—that explains the reasons for a change in cash. This statement shows the changes in cash in three categories: operations, financing, and investing.

FEATURES OF NONPROFIT ACCOUNTING

In many respects, the principles of accounting in nonprofit organizations are the same as those in for-profit organizations. The Financial Accounting Standards Board has stated that, unless another treatment is specifically required, nonprofit entities should account for transactions according to standards that apply to all organizations. Some special aspects of nonprofit accounting are discussed in this section. All but one of them pertain to transactions that do not occur in for-profit entities, rather than to differences in treatment for the same types of transactions. The exception is depreciation.

Revenues

Revenues in nonprofit organizations are recognized in accordance with the same principles used in for-profit organizations.[1] Matters relating to the application of these principles are described below.

Sales Revenues.   Amounts generated through the sale of goods and services in a period are revenues of that period. Patient charges in a hospital are revenues of the period in which the patient received hospital services, for example, even though this is not necessarily the same period in which the patient (or a third-party payer) was billed or in which payment was actually received. The amount of revenue recognized is the amount that is most likely to be received. If some

---

[1] The term *income* is sometimes used instead of revenue, as in tuition income, interest income, and so on. This usage is incorrect and potentially confusing. Income always refers to a difference. *Income* is the difference between revenues and expenses—not the revenues, themselves.

patients are not apt to pay their bills, the recognized revenues are the amounts billed less an allowance for possible bad debts. Similarly, if third-party payers disallow certain items on a bill, the amount of revenue recognized is limited to the amount billed less these "contractual allowances."

Membership Dues.   Members of an organization pay dues in order to receive services for a specified period of time. These dues are revenues of that period, whether they are collected prior to the period (as is often the case), during the period, or after the period. If dues are not collected until after the period, the asset, *dues receivable*, must be adjusted downward at the end of the period to allow for the amount that probably never will be received. If the collection of dues is fairly uncertain (as is the case in an organization with a high membership turnover), an exception to the general principle may be made, and dues may be recorded as revenues only when cash is received.

Life membership dues present a special problem. Conceptually, a part of the total should be recorded as revenue in each year of the member's expected life. As a practical matter, this calculation is complicated and requires considerable recordkeeping. Many membership organizations therefore take the simple solution of recording life memberships as revenues in the year received.

Pledges.   In accordance with the basic revenue concept, pledges of future financial support of operating activities are revenues in the year to which the pledged contributions apply, even if the cash is not received in that year. Unpaid pledges are adjusted downward to allow for estimated uncollectible amounts, just as is done with other accounts receivable. Some people argue that the basic revenue concept should not apply to pledges because, unlike accounts receivable, they are not legally enforceable claims. Others maintain that the difficulty of estimating the amount of uncollectible pledges is so great that a revenue amount incorporating such an estimate is unreliable. Neither of these groups would count unpaid pledges as revenues.

Tax Revenues.   Property taxes are revenues of the period for which they are levied, whether or not the cash is collected during that period. Amounts to be collected from income taxes, sales taxes, gross receipts taxes, parking meter revenues, fines, and similar sources often cannot be estimated reliably in advance of receipt. Such taxes are therefore usually counted as revenue when the cash is received. The Governmental Accounting Standards Board describes this practice as a *modified revenue concept.*[2]

Operating Contributions.   A fundamental concept in accounting is the matching concept. According to the matching concept, when a given event has both a

---

[2] Actually, a for-profit company faced with similar uncertainties would also record revenues on a cash basis, so this is not really a modification of accounting practice.

revenue aspect and an expense aspect, the revenue and the expense should be reported in the same accounting period, that is, they should be *matched*. If, for example, a store purchases an item of merchandise for $60 in July and sells it for $100 in August, both the $100 revenue and the $60 cost are reported on the operating statement for August. The $60 is held in the asset account, *Inventory*, at the end of July.

In both for-profit and nonprofit organizations, a problem with matching arises with respect to advance payments. These are payments that are received in one period for a purpose that will cause expenses to be incurred in some other period. Suppose, for example, a foundation made a $30,000 contribution to a university in 19x1 on the condition that the university hold a conference in 19x2. The conference is held in 19x2, and $30,000 is spent on it. Clearly, there was an expense of $30,000 in 19x2. The matching concept requires that the $30,000 contribution be reported as revenue in 19x2, not in 19x1 when it was received. The $30,000 cash received in 19x1 is a liability as of the end of 19x1, representing the university's obligation to incur expenses for the conference in 19x2. It is reported on the balance sheet, with a title such as *precollected* (or *unearned*) *revenue*.

If the expenses of the conference were less than $30,000, and if the foundation did not require that the difference be returned, the university had income in 19x2. If the difference had to be returned, the revenue would be reduced by this amount, in which case the revenue would equal the expense. If the expense were more than $30,000, there would be a loss in 19x2.

Some nonprofit organizations do not apply the matching concept to such transactions. They report operating grants and contributions as revenues in the period in which they were received. This practice can lead to misleading operating statements during both the year when the grant was received and the year when the associated expenses were incurred.

Endowment Earnings. Some nonprofit organizations have endowment funds. The donors who provide these funds usually intend that the principal of the fund be held intact permanently, or at least for a long time, and that the earnings on the investment of this principal be used for current operating purposes.

Earnings on invested endowment principal are called *endowment revenues*. Traditionally, endowment revenues for a year were the sum of dividends, interest, rents, and other earnings of the endowment fund during that year. Although this is still the practice in some organizations, many organizations now calculate the amount of endowment revenues on a *spending-rate* basis. To do this, they apply a percentage, in most cases about 5 percent, to the average market value of the endowment fund. The 5 percent is the amount of endowment earnings recognized as revenue for operating purposes. The remaining earnings from the investment of the endowment fund are retained in the endowment fund.

There are three related reasons for using the spending-rate method. First, dividends on common stock typically do not reflect the real earnings on that stock. In most instances, the investor expects the stock to increase in value, and this increase is not reflected if the return is calculated on the basis of dividends alone. Second, if 100 percent of endowment earnings were used for operating purposes, the purchasing power of the endowment would decrease because of inflation. The use of a spending rate of 5 percent assumes that, if there were no inflation, invested funds would earn 5 percent. Earnings in excess of 5 percent are therefore expected to approximate the rate of inflation. They are retained in the principal of the endowment so as to maintain its purchasing power. Third, the 5 percent approach provides senior management with a more predictable flow of operating revenues than does the use of dividends and interest, which can vary widely from year to year, depending on the organization's investment policies. (This topic is discussed in more detail in Case 3–5, "Michael Morris University.")

Expenses

Nonprofit organizations report most expenses according to the principle that applies to all organizations. To understand this principle, we distinguish among the various possibilities for recognizing decreases in equity. As illustrated in Exhibit 3–1, these are the periods of obligation, expenditure, expense, and disbursement. Each is explained below.

An *obligation* or *encumbrance* occurs when the entity places an order for goods or services. If an entity places an order for $1,000 of fuel oil in September, this is an obligation of $1,000 in September. At one time, many entities reported obligations as decreases in equity, but this practice is now rare, except in the federal government. Instead of reporting obligations in the accounts, entities may keep separate records of them outside the formal accounting system.

An *expenditure* takes place when goods or services are received and either cash is paid or a liability (such as an account payable) for them is incurred. If the fuel oil is received in October, this is an expenditure of $1,000 in October.

An *expense* is incurred when resources are consumed; that is, used up. If $400 of the fuel oil is used up in November, this is an expense of $400 in November, and inventory is decreased by $400. If the remaining fuel oil is used up in December, this is an expense of $600 in December, and the fuel oil inventory is correspondingly reduced to zero.

EXHIBIT 3–1   Distinction among Certain Accounting Activities and Terms

Month	*September*	*October*	*November*	*Anytime*
Activity	Order is placed.	Resources are received.	Resources are consumed.	Cash is paid.
Accounting Term	**Obligation**	**Expenditure**	**Expense**	**Disbursement**
Affected Accounts	None	Inventory is increased. Accounts payable is increased.	Inventory is decreased. Equity is decreased.	Cash is decreased. Accounts payable is decreased.

For personnel costs, the expenditure and the expense usually happen at the same time—when the employee works or when the services are performed. If an automobile is repaired in October, this is an expenditure and an expense in October, whether or not the bill is paid in that month. Some entities report expenditures as decreases in net income (and hence in equity). Technically, this is incorrect. Ordinarily, for items added to inventory and for long-lived assets such as equipment, the expenditure occurs prior to the expense.

A *disbursement* occurs when cash is paid out. This can be at the same time as the expenditure, as in the case of a cash purchase, or it can be in a later period such as when a purchase is made on credit or when personnel are paid after the period in which they work. Disbursements can also take place earlier than the expenditure; this happens with advance payments, such as insurance premiums. Similarly, a disbursement can occur in the same period, an earlier period, or a later period than an expense.

Some small entities have cash-based accounting systems; they decrease net income (and equity) when disbursements are made. This is not in accordance with GAAP, but in organizations that have mostly cash transactions, the difference may not be great.

Inventory.   Some entities record inventory items as expenses in the period in which the item is received, rather than when it is consumed. Most entities do this for minor supplies on the grounds that the extra recordkeeping required to trace consumption is not worthwhile. Some do it for all items; they argue that if additions to inventory in a period are approximately equal to consumption from inventory, the results would be the same, and that in any event this practice records expenses earlier than the alternative of waiting until the item has been consumed, which is a more conservative reporting practice.

Long-Lived Assets and Depreciation.   Long-lived assets, by definition, provide service for several periods after the entity has made the expenditure to acquire them. If in 19x1 a truck is acquired at a cost of $30,000, there was an expenditure of $30,000 in 19x1. If the truck was estimated to provide transportation services for the next five years, $6,000 of depreciation expense is incurred in each of these years (assuming the usual straight-line method of depreciation and a zero salvage value). GAAP requires that this depreciation expense be recognized in each of the five years.

If an entity does not use the depreciation mechanism, and instead records a decrease in net income when the asset is purchased, it will not measure net income correctly. In the year of purchase, net income will be understated and in the succeeding years, net income will be overstated. Nevertheless, some non-profit entities do not depreciate their long-lived assets. As is the case with inventory, some people argue that this practice is conservative. Others use the principal repayments on loans made to acquire long-lived assets as a substitute for depreciation, arguing that the effect on equity will be approximately the same. This possibility is discussed next.

Debt Service.   Many entities acquire major long-lived assets, such as buildings, trucks, and other "big ticket" equipment items, by borrowing an amount approximately equal to the purchase price. Often, the terms of a bond issue or other form of borrowing require that annual payments be made to retire the issue over the useful life of the assets acquired. The annual payments are called *debt service*. A debt service payment has two components: (1) interest on the amount of the loan outstanding, and (2) repayment of a portion of the principal. Interest is properly an expense of the period. Under GAAP, a principal repayment is not an expense.

If, however, the term of the loan and the economic life of the asset are about equal, the principal payment will approximate the annual amount of depreciation that otherwise would have been charged as an expense. In these circumstances, treating debt service as if it were an expense, may have approximately the same effect on net income as recording depreciation and the related interest amount separately. The validity of such treatment depends, of course, on how closely the principal component of debt service comes to the amount that would have been charged as depreciation.

For many state and local governments this process works well, since all their large fixed assets are acquired with debt. Such a process would not work well for any organization that uses retained earnings as a source of fixed asset financing. With these sources, there is no debt service and hence no substitute for depreciation.

Contributed Services.   In many nonprofit organizations volunteers donate their services to the organization. Although these services are valuable, they are not ordinarily counted as either revenues or expenses. If management can control the activities of the volunteers in the same way that they control the work of paid employees, the services are measured at the going wage rate and are counted as expenses.[3] If these services are counted as expenses, an equal amount is reported as revenue, so there is no effect on net income.

In organizations operated by religious orders, the teachers, nurses, physicians, clergy, and other members of the order may be paid less than the going rate for their services. When this happens, the difference between the actual compensation and the going rate for similar services is considered to be a contribution. Although this was customary practice some years ago, most religious orders now bill the organization in which these persons work at the going rate, and this amount is clearly an expense. In this case, however, there is no revenue.

Fringe Benefits.   An entity's cost for its employees' services includes not only salaries but also the pension, health care, leave and holiday pay, and various benefits to which the employees become entitled by virtue of having worked. The total cost of these services is an expense of the period in which the work was

---

[3] This is sometimes referred to as the rule of reprimand: if volunteers can be reprimanded in the same fashion as paid employees, the value of their services is recognized.

done. The same amount is an expenditure of the period in which the work was done. This is because the organization has incurred a liability to pay for the total cost, including benefits, at the time the services were acquired. This is true even in the case of pensions and other postemployment benefits, where the actual cash disbursement may not be made until many years in the future.

Failure to record pension costs in the year in which they are incurred is one of the most serious weaknesses in some state and municipal government accounting systems. Not only does this omission understate the costs of current operations, but it also puts the burden of providing for the pensions on future generations, rather than on the current one, even though the current generation received the benefit of the labor services. In New York City, for example, the present value of the amount that had been earned by employees but not yet charged as an expense was approximately $6.1 billion in 1990.

The principles for measuring the current cost of payments that will be paid to employees when they retire are complicated, but well worked out for all organizations except government. They are set forth in FASB *Statement No. 87* for pensions and *Statement No. 106* for other postemployment benefits, such as health care, that is provided after the employee retires.

Significance of Net Income

As noted in Chapter 2, net income is an extremely important measure of the performance of a for-profit entity; it measures both the effectiveness and efficiency of an organization's operations.

Since the goal of a nonprofit organization is to provide service, rather than to earn income, the importance of its operating statement may be less obvious. Nevertheless, the operating statement does convey important information about financial performance. If revenues do not at least equal expenses (i.e., if the organization does not at least break even), there is a danger signal. If this situation persists, the organization eventually will go bankrupt. Conversely, if revenues exceed expenses by too wide a margin, the organization probably is not providing as much service as it should with the funds available to it.

Operating Capital Maintenance.   If, in a given year, an entity's revenues at least equal its expenses, it is said to have maintained its operating capital. Some entities try to maintain their operating capital each year; others do not. Fiscal policy in many governmental units specifies that spending should equal revenue. Many states require such a policy, and rates of taxation are set so that this relationship will occur. If a governmental unit operates at a loss, those responsible for its management have, in effect, drawn on either past resources or future resources (supplied by future taxes or grants) to finance current operations.

In many other nonprofit organizations, the amount of revenue available in a given year is essentially fixed, and the policy is to limit expenses to the amount of this revenue or, in other words, to break even. This is the case in many membership organizations, foundations, and health maintenance organizations. For example, in many membership organizations (e.g., clubs, professional associations, trade associations), the members expect the governing board (whose composition changes annually) to conduct the affairs of the organization in the year for which it is responsible so that it uses almost all, but not more than, the revenue of that year. If the board does not use almost all the revenue, then it may not be providing the amount of services that the members have a right to expect. If the board spends more than the year's revenue, then there is a loss that must be made up by future governing boards.

Other nonprofit organizations may decide to have some net income in a given year in order to recoup the loss of a prior year, provide funds for expansion, provide a reserve for contingencies, or for a variety of other reasons. An organization may also decide to operate at a deficit in a given year in order to use accumulated equity, to meet an unusual need, or for other reasons. If the organization is financially well managed, net income reflects the results of these policies.

Many nonprofit organizations have a policy of doing somewhat better than breaking even. They attempt to generate a net income (sometimes called a *surplus*) every year. Their reasoning is that they need additional equity for three purposes: (1) to acquire additional fixed assets, (2) to replace worn-out fixed assets in periods of inflation, and (3) to finance the working capital needs associated with a growth in services. Many nonprofits are unable or unwilling to issue bonds or incur other forms of debt for 100 percent of these requirements. Since they cannot obtain equity capital from investors, the only sources of equity are contributions and their own operating activities. When contributions are insufficient, a surplus is the only other possibility.

Generational Equity.   The capital maintenance idea is often described as *generational equity* or *interperiod equity*. The principle is that each generation affected by an entity should provide enough revenue to meet the expenses of the services it uses from that entity. If a municipality, college, or hospital operates at a loss in a given year, this indicates that taxpayers, students, patients, or donors have not provided enough revenues to meet the expenses incurred that year. Thus, future generations will have to make up the loss or the entity will go bankrupt. The idea, then, is that each generation, or more specifically each year, should pay its own way.[4]

Reporting Expenses and Revenues

On the operating statement, expenses may be classified either by *elements* (e.g., salaries, fringe benefits, supplies, depreciation) or by *programs*. A program is a set of activities that the entity undertakes in order to achieve its objectives. In a

---

[4] For a discussion of inter-period equity and its relation to operating and capital budgets in government, see Robert N. Anthony, "Observations on Government Financial Accounting Research," *Government Accountants Journal*, 38, no. 4 (Winter 1989–90).

college or university, for example, the National Association of College and University Business Officers (NACUBO) recommends that expenses be reported in two main program categories: (1) educational and general and (2) auxiliary enterprises. In the educational and general category, the programs include instruction, research, academic support, student services, institutional support, and student aid. Auxiliary enterprises included housing, food service, the bookstore, the student union, and similar activities. Usually it is desirable to report the entity's administration costs as a separate program item. Also, if the entity incurs significant expenses for fund-raising, it should report them separately.

Classification of expenses by programs is generally more informative than classification by elements. Some organizations report a main classification by programs and report expenses by elements under each principal program. They may report only two elements: employee compensation and all other; this is because employee compensation is a large fraction of total expenses. If expenses are incurred jointly for two or more programs, the accountant attempts to allocate an equitable share of such joint or common expenses to each program. Techniques for doing this are described in Chapter 4.

If revenues can readily be identified with programs, they too may be classified by program. Another common basis for classifying revenue is by its source. Examples of revenue sources in a university include tuition, contributions from private parties, government grants, and endowment earnings.

CONTRIBUTED CAPITAL AND FUND ACCOUNTING

Financial accounting focuses mainly on the *operating* performance of the entity. Many nonprofit entities have financial transactions that are not associated with operating performance, per se. These transactions are not reported among the assets, liabilities, and equity associated with operations. Instead they are reported in separate funds. The result is a need for a separate accounting and financial reporting process called *fund accounting.*

The principal class of nonoperating activity in nonprofit organizations is *contributed capital.* In this section we describe the nature of contributed capital transactions and how to account for them. We also describe fund accounting briefly. More thorough treatments are available in "Suggested Additional Readings" at the end of the chapter.

Capital Contributions

Contributions for operating purposes are revenues; they add to the resources available for use in operations and hence to the organization's operating equity. Capital contributions are not revenues; they are direct additions to an organization's equity. There are two general types of capital contributions: contributions for endowment and contributions for plant. When a donor contributes to an entity's endowment, the entity invests the amount received, and only the earnings on that amount are available for operating purposes.[5] Similarly, when a donor contributes money to acquire a building or other item of plant, this contribution must be used for the specified purpose; it is not available to finance operating activities. Both types of contributions add to equity—they make the entity better off—but neither is associated with operating activities.

Because it is not associated with operating activities, the receipt of a capital contribution does not affect the measurement of net income as reported on the operating statement. Nor do capital contributions affect the balance sheet items associated with operating activities because the cash or other assets received are not available to pay operating bills. To insulate operating activities from the effect of these capital contributions, the accounting system has separate funds for endowment and plant. Each of these funds is a separate accounting entity, with its own balance sheet, and its own way of reporting increases and decreases in equity. Each is governed by the fundamental accounting equation:

$$\text{Assets} = \text{Liabilities} + \text{Equity}$$

Financial Statement Presentation

The balance sheet for each fund reports the fund's assets, liabilities, and equity. For reporting purposes, each fund usually is contained in a separate column on a page that shows the balance sheet items for all of the entity's funds. Some entities also report the total amounts for all funds on the balance sheet, but these totals have little meaning. The total of the entity's cash, for example, might imply that the cash in any fund can be used to pay any bill, but this is not the case. Only cash in the operating fund can be used to pay operating bills. Sometimes an entity will borrow from a nonoperating fund to support cash needs in its operating fund, but this is only a temporary source of cash. Like any other loan, it must be repaid.

The most informative presentation is to report the balance sheet for each fund separately, as shown in Exhibit 3–2. Transactions related to operating activities are reported in an operating fund section (often called *general fund* or *current fund*). Note that each section of Exhibit 3–2 is a self-balancing set of accounts, with total assets equal to total liabilities plus equity. Note also that each section has a cash item. The cash in one fund should not be mingled with the cash in the others. The equity in each fund often is labeled in such a way as to clearly identify it with its fund. Sometimes it simply is called *fund balance.*

By definition, the terms *revenues, expenses,* and *net income* are associated with operating activities, so there is no operating statement as such for the endowment or plant funds. In order to summarize the transactions that occurred in the year, however, a flow statement of some sort is prepared for each fund. It shows the amounts that flowed into the fund during the period and the uses made of the fund's resources. It is often titled *statement of changes in equity* or *statement of changes in fund balance.* Such a statement for the endowment fund would report

---

[5] This restriction is a matter of law. The entity has a fiduciary duty not to use the principal of donor-restricted endowment funds for operations.

EXHIBIT 3–2

EXAMPLE ORGANIZATION
Balance Sheet
As of December 31, 19x1
($000)

Assets		Liabilities and Equity	
Operating Fund			
Cash..........................	$ 200	Accounts payable	$ 400
Accounts receivable..............	300	Precollected revenue	600
Inventory	400	Bonds payable..................	1,200
Investments	800	Total liabilities.................	2,200
Buildings and equipment.........	1,400	Operating equity	900
Total assets	$ 3,100	Total liabilities and equity........	$ 3,100
Endowment Fund			
Cash..........................	$ 10	Legal endowment	$ 7,000
Bonds	9,100	Board-designated endowment......	13,010
Stock..........................	10,900		
Total assets	$20,010	Total liabilities and equity........	$20,010
Plant Fund			
Cash..........................	$ 20	Accounts payable	$ 30
Investments	400	Plant equity	11,590
Buildings and equipment.........	11,200		
Total assets	$11,620	Total liabilities and equity........	$11,620

---

additional contributions to endowment and earnings from dividends, interest, and rent as additions. It would report the amount of earnings recognized as revenue and transferred to the operating fund as reductions.

Endowment Fund

Donors may specify that their contributions are for the organization's endowment; that is, only the earnings are to be used for operating purposes. Alternatively, even if a donor does not make a legally binding restriction, the circumstances may clearly indicate that the contribution is for endowment purposes. If, for example, a university receives $1 million from a bequest, the size of the gift makes it obvious that it was not intended for use in the year in which the university received the money.

Such contributions are called *board-designated endowment.* By contrast, a legally binding contribution to endowment is called *legal endowment.* The difference is that the principal amount of legal endowment can never be used for operating purposes, whereas the governing board could vote to use a portion of board-designated endowment for operating purposes. It normally would do so only in the event of a financial emergency, however.

Assets of the endowment fund consist principally of investments in stocks, bonds, and real estate. The assets are for the endowment fund as a whole. They are not separated according to individual donors, or even between those assets that relate to legal endowment and those that represent board-designated endowment.

A donor may specify that the income from his or her endowment may be spent only for a designated purpose, such as scholarship aid, or even a scholarship to a student from the donor's hometown. For internal management purposes, records of these restrictions must be maintained. These individual records do not appear in the general-purpose financial statements, however.

Plant Fund

Contributions for buildings, equipment, art and other museum objects, or similar purposes are often reported in a separate plant fund. These assets are recorded at their fair market value at the time they were received, even if their cost to the entity was zero. Because accounting usually does not recognize increases in market value, a subsequent increase in market value is not reflected in the accounts.

Since art and museum objects presumably have an indefinitely long life, they are not depreciated; they remain on the books at cost until they are sold or otherwise disposed of. FASB *Statement No. 93* requires that contributed buildings, equipment, and other depreciable assets be depreciated. Some organizations object to this requirement. They argue that because the buildings were contributed, they did not—and never will—require the use of revenues to finance them. Therefore, the inclusion of a depreciation component as an expense item on the operating statement would understate the amount of income earned through operating activities. FASB *Statement No. 93* is based on the premise that the buildings are used for operating purposes and that omission of depreciation would understate the real expenses of operating the organization.

A recently adopted solution to this dilemma is to report depreciation on contributed plant as an expense, and to report an equal amount as revenue of the period. The revenue component represents the donor's contribution to the operations of the period, while the expense component reports the cost of using the facilities. Since the two amounts are equal, there is no effect on income. Although recommended by an international accounting standards group, so far this practice is not yet widely used in the United States.

Other Fund Types

Although operating, endowment, and plant funds usually are the largest funds in nonprofit entities, many organizations have other types of funds. Some of these also exist in for-profit organizations, although texts on accounting in such organizations may not describe them.

Restricted Operating Funds.   Some entities set up a separate fund to account for operating contributions whose use is restricted to a specified purpose or to a specified period. This happens, for example, in the case of a grant or contract. Since these contributions are associated with operations, there is no strong reason for doing this. As noted earlier, such contributions are essentially advance payments, and they can be accounted for in the same way as advance payments in any organization: by recording a liability when the contribution is received. The liability is eliminated and revenue is recognized when the organization incurs the expenses for the specified purpose or in the specified time period.

Other Nonoperating Funds.   An entity may have a loan fund that makes loans to employees or students, a pension fund whose resources are used to pay pensions, a sinking fund used to guarantee payments due on bond issues, or other resources that must not be mixed with operating resources or included in reports on operating activities. Some nonprofit entities create separate funds for these purposes and report them as part of their general-purpose financial statements. Others follow the practice of for-profit organizations and treat them as entirely separate entities, excluded from the organization's annual financial report. For pension funds, such a separation is required by law.

Transfers

When an entity has several funds, it usually has transactions that involve transferring amounts from one fund to another. The transfer of endowment earnings from the endowment fund to the operating fund is an example. Such a transfer results, quite properly, in an item of revenue on the operating statement. Other types of transfers may or may not represent legitimate items of revenues or expense. For example, an entity that has earned a large income in a given year may transfer funds to its plant account to be used for the construction of new assets. If the transfer is reported as a deduction from revenue on the operating statement, the amount of surplus reported would be lower than the actual amount earned.

Transfers from the operating fund to the plant fund actually reflect decisions as to how the surplus earned in the period should be used. The transfer of an amount of cash equivalent to the depreciation expense is an example. This is called *funding of depreciation*, and entails making a transfer of cash from the operating fund to the plant fund. Organizations that fund depreciation claim that the transfers provide a pool of cash that can be used to pay for the replacement of assets. Because of this, many managers believe that funding depreciation enforces a degree of fiscal discipline on their organizations. (Since such a pool could be maintained in the operating fund just as easily, however, the funding of depreciation is purely a disciplinary matter. It serves no other purpose.)

Some transfers are mandatory, that is, they are required by contract. An example is the conditions imposed by bondholders to pay a specified amount to a debt service fund. Depending on their nature, these transfers may or may not represent expenses. As pointed out above, the amount of debt service may be an approximation of interest and depreciation expense on long-lived assets. In some health care organizations, the funding of depreciation is required by third-party payers. In these cases, the transfer is mandatory.

VARIATIONS IN PRACTICE

In due time the Financial Accounting Standards Board will issue standards for accounting in nonprofit organizations. Until then, the accounting practices of these organizations are influenced by *Audit Guides* and other pronouncements for several types of organizations.[6]

The *Audit Guides* for health care organizations, voluntary health and welfare organizations, and other nonprofit organizations recommend practices that generally are similar to the preceding descriptions. However, the *Audit Guide* for colleges and universities is different in several respects. Indeed, this *Audit Guide* states that the report that is closest to an operating statement "does not purport to present the results of operations or the net income or loss for the period," whereas we have emphasized that such information is the central focus of financial accounting.

State and Local Governments

The accounting details for state and local government are described in some of the texts listed in the "Suggested Additional Readings." "The City of Douglas" (Case 3–6) contains a description of municipal accounting.[7] A few of the more important points follow.

General Fund.   The general operating activities of a government unit are accounted for in a *general fund*. However, this fund reports expenditures rather than expenses, and the treatment of debt service, pension expense, and certain other items is different from the above descriptions.

Enterprise Funds.   If a governmental unit operates a utility (e.g., electric, gas, water, sewer), a subway, a toll bridge, a lottery, a hospital, or other activity that generates substantial amounts of revenue, these activities are accounted for in what are called *enterprise funds*. Accounting for enterprise funds is basically the same as accounting in for-profit entities. Because this accounting is inconsistent

---

[6] These *Audit Guides* are of a lower level of importance than FASB standards. Nevertheless, entities are expected to adhere to them.

[7] For a discussion of one state's decision to adopt GAAP, see Vivian L. Carpenter and Ehsan H. Feroz, "The Decision to Adopt GAAP: A Case Study of the Commonwealth of Kentucky," *Accounting Horizons* 4, no. 2 (June 1990), pp. 67–78.

with that used for other government activities, there is no way of presenting a single set of financial statements for the government unit as a whole.

Deviations from GASB Principles.   States are sovereign bodies; they can decide the principles that are to be followed in their accounting systems and in the systems of municipalities and other government units within their borders. These principles may be inconsistent with those of the Governmental Accounting Standards Board (GASB).

> *Example.* In a 1986 study with 567 respondents from cities, counties, and school districts, 75 percent of the respondents whose accounting practices are regulated by other governments reported that these regulations required them to conform to GASB standards, but 25 percent reported they were required to use different standards.[8]

Federal Government

The General Accounting Office (GAO) publishes a *prototype* (i.e., unofficial) balance sheet and operating statement for the government as a whole.[9] It is of less use than a set of conventional financial statements, however. The financial viability of the federal government depends basically on its authority to print money, rather than on its assets as listed on a balance sheet, or on activities that could be reported on an operating statement. Investors in government bonds know that because of this authority, the bonds will be repaid (short of a catastrophe that would destroy the whole fabric of government). These investors need not look to financial statements for an analysis of debt-paying ability; they know that the federal government will not declare bankruptcy.

The federal government has essentially three types of accounting systems: (1) appropriation accounting, (2) accounting systems required by the General Accounting Office, and (3) systems developed by individual agencies.

Appropriation Accounting.   Government managers and members of Congress are interested primarily in financial reports that show how much an agency actually spent compared with what it was authorized to spend. Because of this, the appropriation accounting system—which reflects the power of the purse—is the most important accounting system in the federal government. Its appropriations are of several types, each requiring somewhat different accounting procedures.

Annual Appropriations.   The operating activity of most agencies, including their authority to make certain types of grants and contracts, is financed by annual

---

[8] Robert Ingraham, *Financial Reporting Practices of Local Government* (Norwalk, Conn.: Governmental Accounting Standards Board, 1987).

[9] Copies of the GAO document may be obtained from the U.S. General Accounting Office, 441 "G" Street NW, Washington, D.C. 20548.

appropriations. An annual appropriation, sometimes called *budget authority,* is the authority to obligate funds during the year ending September 30. Funds are obligated when contracts are let or when employees work. Although rarely the case, an individual who is responsible for overobligating an appropriation is subject to a fine or other penalty under the Antideficiency Act (31 U.S.C. 665).

Annual appropriations that are not fully obligated by September 30 are lost. This is why many contracts may be written or grants made shortly before this date. As mentioned earlier, obligations are not recognized in the accounts of business accounting systems.

No-Year Appropriations.   Appropriations for the acquisition of major items of buildings and equipment and other types of grants are *continuing* or *no-year* appropriations. They grant authority to spend a specified amount of money on the particular project, rather than in a particular year. If a project turns out to be more costly than originally anticipated, either an additional appropriation is made or the project stops. Stories about cost overruns do not mean that more than the appropriated amount was actually spent on the project; they usually mean that the amount originally appropriated was too low, and that additional appropriations subsequently were made.

Entitlement Programs.   Amounts spent for entitlement programs are governed by formulas set by the Congress. These include social security, medicare and medicaid, and most subsidies. Agencies have the authority to spend whatever the formula permits, and the amounts set forth in the approved budget are estimates rather than ceilings that cannot be exceeded.

Control of Obligations.   With all three types of appropriations, the accounting focus is the control of obligations. There is no need to control expenditures or disbursements, often called *outlays,* since checks can be issued only for legal obligations.

Beyond this, government grants and contracts prescribe the type of costs that the government will reimburse for a given program. The recipients of these grants and contracts must keep records of costs incurred according to principles established by the granting agency or, in some cases, by the Office of Management and Budget in the executive office of the president. All cost-type defense contracts and many contracts in other agencies are governed by detailed rules established by the Cost Accounting Standards Board in the Office of Federal Procurement Policy, and published as Federal Acquisition Regulations.

General Accounting Office Systems.   Under the Budget and Procedures Act of 1950, the comptroller general of the United States prescribes principles and standards for accounting in government agencies. The General Accounting Office (which is the organization headed by the comptroller general) has done so on several occasions. Because they focus on expenses, these requirements generally provide more useful information for management purposes than do those in the appropriation accounting system with its focus on obligations. Since GAO standards do not have the power of the purse behind them, however, not much attention is paid to them.

Individual Agency Systems. Individual departments and agencies develop accounting systems to meet their own information needs. In general, these give heavy emphasis to accounting for obligations, but they also provide information on expenses, or at least on expenditures. Businesslike agencies, such as the U.S. Postal Service and the Tennessee Valley Authority, have businesslike accounting systems.

Problems with Inconsistent Practices

Some users are interested only in the financial statements of a specific type of organization, such as a museum. Those individuals learn the peculiarities of the accounting practices in that type of organization. Users who are interested in several types of organizations must understand the differences among practices in various types. The problem is especially complicated when a single entity operates several types of organizations. A medical center may have a hospital subject to the *Health Care Audit Guide*, a medical school subject to the *College and University Guide*, and a physician's clinic subject to business-type accounting principles. Such a medical center has difficulty in developing a meaningful set of financial statements for the whole entity.

Terminology presents still another problem. This is because, even if they use the same basic principles, entities tend to differ in the names they use for various items. Because of this, a reader frequently must look behind labels and headings and use the context to determine a report's meaning.

SUMMARY

Most revenues and expenses should be measured the same way in all organizations, both for-profit and nonprofit. Revenues increase operating equity, and expenses decrease it. Both should be reported in the accounting period to which they relate, in accordance with the realization and matching concepts.

Contributed capital, such as contributions of plant or endowment, is added directly to equity, and accounted for separately from operating transactions. Such a separation leads to individual funds for nonoperating items and the related practice of fund accounting, which has no counterpart in a business.

Despite the similarity of most transactions in all organizations, actual accounting practices vary greatly among various types of nonprofit organizations. These variations reflect primarily the different treatments suggested in the audit guides that apply to these organizations. The Financial Accounting Standards Board and the Governmental Accounting Standards Board are now responsible for developing accounting standards for nonprofit organizations. In due time, they will eliminate, or at least greatly reduce, these variations.

SUGGESTED ADDITIONAL READINGS

General

Douglas, Patricia P. *Governmental and Nonprofit Accounting: Theory and Practice.* Orlando, Fla.: Harcourt Brace Jovanovich, 1991.

Financial Accounting Standards Board, *Statement of Financial Accounting Concept No. 4. Objectives of Financial Reporting by Nonbusiness Organizations.* Norwalk, Conn., 1980.

————, *Statement of Financial Accounting Concept No. 6. Elements of Financial Statements.* Norwalk, Conn., 1985.

Gross, Malvern J., Jr., William Warshauer, Jr., and Richard F. Larkin. *Financial and Accounting Guide for Not-for-Profit Organizations,* 4th ed. New York: John Wiley & Sons, 1991.

Hay, Leon E., and Earl R. Wilson. *Accounting for Governmental and Nonprofit Entities.* Homewood, Ill.: Richard D. Irwin, 1992.

Henke, Emerson O. *Introduction to Nonprofit Organization Accounting,* 4th ed. Cincinnati, Ohio: South-Western Publishing Co., 1992.

Herbert, Leo, et al. *Accounting and Control for Governmental and Other Nonbusiness Organizations.* New York: John Wiley & Sons, 1987.

Lynn, Edward S., and Robert J. Freeman. *Governmental and Nonprofit Accounting: Theory and Practice,* 3rd ed. Englewood Cliffs, N.J.: Prentice Hall, 1988.

Pahler, Arnold J., and Joseph E. Mori. *Advanced Accounting: Concepts and Practice,* 3rd ed. New York: Harcourt Brace Jovanovich, 1988.

Razek, Joseph R., and G. A. Hosch. *Introduction to Government and Nonprofit Accounting,* 2nd ed. Englewood Cliffs, N.J.: Prentice Hall, 1992.

Education

American Institute of Certified Public Accountants. *Audits of Colleges and Universities.* New York, 1973.

National Association of Independent Schools. *Accounting for Independent Schools,* 2nd ed. Boston, 1974.

Ryan, L. V. *An Accounting Manual for Catholic Elementary and Secondary Schools.* Washington, D.C.: National Catholic Education Association, 1969.

Welzenbach, Lanore F. *College and University Business Administration,* 4th ed. Washington, D.C.: National Association of College and University Business Officers, 1982.

Federal Government

Comptroller General of the United States (General Accounting Office). *Accounting Principles and Standards for Federal Agencies.* Washington, D.C.: Government Printing Office.

U.S. Department of Transportation. *U.S. Government Standard General Ledger*. Washington, D.C.: Government Printing Office.

U.S. General Accounting Office. *GAO Policies and Procedures Manual, Title 2*. Washington, D.C.: Government Printing Office.

Health Care

American Hospital Association. *Chart of Accounts for Hospitals*. Chicago, 1976.

American Institute of Certified Public Accountants. *Health Care Accounting and Audit Guide*. New York, 1990.

Seawell, L. Vann. *Introduction to Hospital Accounting*. Dubuque, Ia.: Kendall/Hunt Publishing, 1992.

U.S. Department of Health, Education, and Welfare. *A Guide for Non-Profit Institutions. Cost Principles and Procedures for Establishing Indirect Cost Rates for Grants and Contracts with the Department of Health, Education, and Welfare*. DHEW Publication No. (OS)72-28. Washington, D.C.: Government Printing Office, 1970.

State and Local Government

Governmental Accounting Standards Board. *Codification of Governmental Accounting and Financial Reporting Standards*. Norwalk, Conn., Annual.

Other Sources

American Institute of Certified Public Accountants. *Audits of Voluntary Health and Welfare Organizations*. New York, 1974.

Association of Science—Technology Centers. *Museum Accounting Guidelines*. Washington, D.C., 1976.

Club Managers Association of America. *Uniform System of Accounts for Clubs*. 2nd rev. ed. Washington, D.C., 1967.

National Conference of Catholic Bishops. *Diocesan Accounting and Financial Reporting*. New York, 1971.

Sumarialla, Russy D. *Accounting and Financial Reporting, A Guide for United Ways and Not-for-Profit Human Service Organizations*. Alexandria, Va.: United Way of America, Systems, Planning, and Allocations Division, 1974.

Vargo, Richard J. *Effective Church Accounting,* San Francisco: Harper & Row, 1989.

CASE 3–1   Brookstone Ob-Gyn Associates (B)*

In mid-July 1991, Dr. Mark Amsted, chair of the department of obstetrics and gynecology at Brookstone Medical School, chief of Ob-Gyn at Brookstone Medical Center, and president of Brookstone Ob-Gyn Associates (BOGA), was concerned about his upcoming meeting with the Harris National Bank. He planned to present a request for an increase in BOGA's line of credit. As had happened in the past, the bank's approval of his request was critical to BOGA's continued operations. Although the dean of the medical school had approved his request to approach the bank again, Dr. Amsted was uncertain about the bank's reaction. The Brookstone Ob-Gyn Associates (A) case (Case 3A–1) contains background information on BOGA, and discusses the details of Dr. Amsted's first request to the bank (in January 1991).

In conjunction with Dr. Amsted's January request for a $300,000 line of credit (discussed in the (A) case), the bank had asked him to prepare some projections for the 1991 operating year. He had done this, indicating that he expected 1991 revenue to be 30 percent greater than 1990 revenue. After switching to an accrual system of accounting, Dr. Amsted had been pleased to learn that 1990 had been a profitable year for the group. His projections indicated that 1991 also would be profitable.

Problems

Despite the growth in revenues and the group's profitability, BOGA's cash flow was once again becoming an issue. Indeed, as he began to prepare for the meeting with the bank, Dr. Amsted realized that he faced two problems related to BOGA's cash flows. He commented:

> In January, I established a $300,000 line of credit with the Harris Bank. We expected to have some cash flow difficulties, and I thought this would help us cope with them until our cash caught up with our profitability. Now I'm not sure $300,000 is enough!
>
> There's a related problem, too. Until 1990, we kept our financial records on what the accountants called a modified cash basis. That was pretty simple. Revenues were recorded when we received a cash payment from a patient or third-party payer. Expenses were recorded when the cash was paid out. The only exception was plant and equipment purchases, where the accountants said we needed to use depreciation instead of cash as the expense.
>
> When I applied to the Harris Bank for the line of credit, Ms. Tanshel [the bank's loan officer] told me that a modified cash basis was not an acceptable way to present our financial statements. The bank required us to submit our statements on an accrual basis.

---

* This case was prepared by Professor David W. Young. Copyright © by David W. Young.

According to our accountants, the most significant change needed to satisfy the bank's requirement was to record revenue when a patient received services, rather than when we actually received the related cash payment.

1991 Expectations

Exhibit 1 contains a projected operating statement for calendar year 1991 (prepared by Mr. Weber [BOGA's business manager] and Dr. Amsted in January 1991), and actual operating statements for each of the first six months of 1991. The projected operating statement confirmed Dr. Amsted's expectation that 1991 revenue would grow by 30 percent over the 1990 level. Exhibit 2 contains actual balance sheets as of the end of each month for the first six months of 1991.

As the exhibits show, Dr. Amsted expected that 1991 would add $268,500 to retained surpluses. These retained surpluses, plus the medical center's start-up contribution of $1 million, would give BOGA equity (or a fund balance) of some $3 million as of the end of 1991.

EXHIBIT 1

BROOKSTONE OB/GYN ASSOCIATES (B)
Operating Statements (Accrual Basis)
($000)

	1991 Projected	1991 Actual January	February	March	April	May	June
Revenue:							
Professional services	$8,252.3	$678.2	$693.1	$704.9	$719.0	$732.7	$748.8
Less: allowances and bad							
debts	1,650.5	135.6	138.6	141.0	143.8	146.5	149.8
Net revenue	$6,601.8	$542.6	$554.5	$563.9	$575.2	$586.1	$599.0
Expenses:							
Physician payments	$1,573.6	$110.2	$113.3	$118.0	$122.7	$125.9	$130.6
Administrative salaries	820.8	57.5	61.6	61.6	65.7	65.7	73.9
Benefits....................	396.8	27.8	28.8	29.8	31.1	31.7	33.5
Medical supplies	123.8	10.2	10.4	10.6	10.8	11.0	11.2
Rent and utilities............	523.2	43.6	43.6	43.6	43.6	43.6	43.6
Billing/collection fees.........	660.2	54.3	55.5	56.4	57.5	58.6	59.9
Equipment depreciation.......	29.7	2.0	2.0	2.0	2.4	2.4	2.4
Office expense...............	60.0	5.0	5.0	5.0	5.0	5.0	5.0
Liability insurance	1,237.8	101.7	104.0	105.7	107.9	109.9	112.3
Contracted services	127.2	10.6	10.6	10.6	10.6	10.6	10.6
Other......................	54.0	4.5	4.5	4.5	4.5	4.5	4.5
Contribution to Dean.........	726.2	59.7	61.0	62.0	63.3	64.5	65.9
Total expenses..............	$6,333.3	$486.9	$500.2	$509.8	$525.1	$533.4	$553.5
Surplus (Deficit)	268.5	$ 55.6	$ 54.3	$ 54.2	$ 50.2	$ 52.8	$ 45.6

EXHIBIT 2

BROOKSTONE OB/GYN ASSOCIATES (B)
Balance Sheets (Accrual Basis)
($000)

	1991 Actual					
	As of Jan. 31	*As of Feb. 28*	*As of Mar. 31*	*As of Apr. 30*	*As of May 31*	*As of June 30*
Assets						
Cash	$ 44.3	$ 0.0	$ 0.0	$ 0.0	$ 0.0	$ 0.0
Accounts receivable (net)	1,932.2	2,025.0	2,105.3	2,171.5	2,223.0	2,279.5
Medical supply inventory	135.0	145.0	155.0	165.0	167.0	170.0
Prepaid insurance	275.0	300.0	320.0	320.0	330.0	340.0
Total current assets	$2,386.5	$2,470.0	$2,580.3	$2,656.5	$2,720.0	$2,789.5
Equipment (net)	1,248.0	1,246.0	1,294.0	1,291.6	1,289.2	1,306.8
Total assets	$3,634.5	$3,716.0	$3,874.3	$3,948.1	$4,009.2	$4,096.3
Liabilities and Equity						
Bank loan (line of credit)	$ 0.0	$ 15.5	$ 139.2	$ 153.9	$ 155.2	$ 218.8
Accounts payable	76.5	78.0	79.6	81.2	82.7	84.4
Payable to Dean	141.2	151.4	160.3	167.5	173.2	179.4
Total current liabilities	$ 222.8	$ 272.4	$ 420.6	$ 458.6	$ 481.6	$ 568.1
Note payable	630.0	630.0	600.0	600.0	600.0	570.0
Fund balance						
Start-up contribution	1,000.0	1,000.0	1,000.0	1,000.0	1,000.0	1,000.0
Retained surpluses	1,786.7	1,841.1	1,895.2	1,945.4	1,998.2	2,043.8
Total liabilities + Fund balance	$3,634.5	$3,716.0	$3,874.3	$3,948.1	$4,009.2	$4,096.3

1991 Results

The first six months of 1991 had gone much better than expectations. In fact, Dr. Amsted had expected that the annual surplus in 1991 would be about 4 percent of net revenue, and the monthly surpluses had been averaging between 8 and 10 percent. Although the surpluses had fallen off slightly in April, May, and June, Dr. Amsted expected them to grow, along with revenue increases, during the second half of the year.

Surpluses were not the problem, however. In January, shortly after Dr. Amsted had arranged for the line of credit, BOGA's cash balance declined from $110,000 as of the end of 1990 to just over $44,000. In February, BOGA used up all of its cash, and drew down $15,500 of its line of credit. The trend had continued, and by the end of June the line of credit had reached some $219,000. These figures are shown in Exhibit 2. Dr. Amsted commented on them:

> If we had continued with the modified cash basis of accounting this wouldn't have happened. How can it be that we earn a surplus in each month of the year and run out of cash? It just doesn't compute. When we used the cash basis, my life was much simpler. If we had a surplus, we had cash in the bank. No surplus, no cash.

It was BOGA's problem with cash that had led Dr. Amsted to arrange for the meeting with Ms. Tanshel. Ms. Tanshel had readily agreed to meet, but she also had insisted that Dr. Amsted think about BOGA's future plans. In particular, she wanted to know if BOGA would need more than $300,000 in its line of credit and, if so, how much more it would need. She also asked Dr. Amsted to think about a repayment plan, since the bank usually required its customers to fully repay a line of credit at least once a year.

Review of the Financial Statements

To respond to Ms. Tanshel's request, Dr. Amsted met with Mr. Weber to review the current situation and project figures for the remainder of 1991. Despite the problems with cash, Dr. Amsted was optimistic. One reason was salaries. The number of physicians and administrative staff in the group had grown slightly during the first six months of 1991, and some physician compensation arrangements had changed slightly. These changes had caused some increases in salary expenses. Salaries had more or less stabilized as of June 30, however, and Dr. Amsted expected they would remain constant for the rest of the year despite the expected increases in revenue.

In reviewing the financial statements, Mr. Weber and Dr. Amsted saw nothing surprising. In March and June, they had made the quarterly payments of $30,000 on the long-term note payable. They also had made some planned equipment purchases of $50,000 in March and $20,000 in June; both of these were cash purchases. The payments on the note and the equipment purchases were reflected on the balance sheet. Dr. Amsted's plans called for a cash purchase of another $30,000 of equipment in September. Mr. Weber expected that all equipment items would have a 10-year economic life with no salvage value.

Dr. Amsted also knew that the group's medical supply inventory and prepaid insurance payments needed to grow with the increase in the number of patients and physicians. For example, with the greater volume of patients being seen, the group needed to have a larger supply of inventory on hand. Similarly, as new physicians joined the group, BOGA needed to make some advance premium payments to the insurance companies for malpractice coverage.

Dr. Amsted realized that the growth in BOGA's accounts receivable was a result of both the accrual system and patients' paying patterns. The average collection period for a bill was five months, which meant that as volume grew (as it had been doing), accounts receivable would need to grow also. In fact, he was pleased that the entire $1,831,200 in net accounts receivable owed as of December 31, 1990, had been collected by the end of May. (*Net* accounts receivable is the portion of billings that BOGA actually expected to collect from patients and third parties.)

A Lack of Cash

Despite all of this, the decline in cash was perplexing. One problem was that, although the average time necessary to collect an account receivable was approximately five months, almost all of BOGA's expenses had to be paid immediately. Dr. Amsted had asked some of his medical supply vendors to wait a bit longer for their payments, but most were insistent on 30-day terms. Since billings were growing, however, so were the expenses related to billings. Because of this, accounts payable had been growing by about 2 percent a month for the first six months of 1991. Similarly, since BOGA's payment to the dean was based on cash collections, the account called *Payable to Dean* also was growing. Nevertheless, according to Mr. Weber, because this growth in the two payables accounts was so slow, there still was a strain on cash.

EXHIBIT 3 Projected Revenue, Expense, Asset, and Liability Behavior for July–December 1991

Revenue:

Professional services	Will grow at 2 percent a month for the rest of the year.
Allowances and bad debts	Will be 20 percent of revenue from professional services.

Expenses:

Physician payments	$141,600 per month for the rest of the year.
Administrative wages	$73,900 per month for the rest of the year.
Benefits	$0.20 per MD salary dollar; $0.10 per administrative salary dollar.
Medical supplies	1.5 percent of professional services revenue.
Rent and utilities	$43,600 per month for the rest of the year.
Billing and collection fees	8 percent of gross billings (i.e., the professional services line)
Equipment depreciation	$2,600 per month for July–September; $2,900 per month for October–December.
Office expenses	$5,000 per month for the rest of the year.
Liability insurance	15 percent of gross billings.*
Contracted services	$10,600 per month for the rest of the year.
Other	$4,500 per month for the rest of the year (includes interest on the long-term note and the line of credit).
Contribution to Dean	11 percent of net revenue.

Assets:

Accounts receivable	The five-month collection lag will continue for the rest of the year.
Medical supply inventory	Will grow by $3,000 per month for the rest of the year.
Prepaid insurance	Will remain constant at $340,000 for the rest of the year.
Equipment	Will increase with additional purchases in a given month, and decrease by the amount of the monthly depreciation expense.

Liabilities:

Accounts payable	Will grow by 2 percent a month for the rest of the year.
Payable to Dean	Will increase by 11 percent of net revenues and decrease by 11 percent of cash collections.
Note payable	Payment of $30,000 is scheduled for September.

* This item actually is related to the number of physicians, but 15 percent of gross billings provides a satisfactory approximation.

EXHIBIT 4

BROOKSTONE OB/GYN ASSOCIATES (B)
Worksheets
($000s)

Operating Statements

	1991 Forecast						Total for 1991
	July	*August*	*September*	*October*	*November*	*December*	

Revenue:
  Professional services
  Less: allowances and
    bad debts							

Net revenue							
Expenses:							
Physician payments Administrative wages Benefits Medical supplies							
Rent and utilities Billing/collection fees Equipment depreciation Office expense							
Liability insurance Contracted services Other Contribution to Dean							
Total expenses							
Surplus (Deficit)							

Balance Sheets

	1991 Forecast					
	As of July 31	*As of Aug. 31*	*As of Sept. 30*	*As of Oct. 31*	*As of Nov. 30*	*As of Dec. 31*

Assets:
  Cash
  Accounts receivable
  Medical supply inventory
  Prepaid insurance						

Total current assets Equipment (net)						
Total assets						

Liabilities and Equity Liabilities:
  Bank loan (line of credit)
  Accounts payable
  Payable to Dean						

Total current liabilities
Note payable
Equity:
  Start-up contribution
  Retained surpluses						

Total liabilities + fund balance						

Dr. Amsted did not know how much larger the line of credit needed to be to cover BOGA's cash shortfalls in the next six months. Ms. Tanshel, had indicated a reluctance to increase the ceiling above the current $300,000 level, but Dr. Amsted felt he could convince her to raise it if he presented her with a solid financial analysis. This meant he would need to give careful consideration to projecting the next six months of activity. As a first step in this effort, he asked Mr. Weber to address the behavior of each item on the financial statements. Mr. Weber reached the conclusions shown in Exhibit 3.

As they began to prepare for the meeting, Dr. Amsted and Mr. Weber realized that their request would need to incorporate more than just the cash needs associated with the timing differences of revenue and expenses. It also would need to include the changes they had forecasted in all of the current accounts on the balance sheet, as well as BOGA's cash needs for paying off the note and purchasing the equipment. Unless they included all this information, their analysis would not reflect BOGA's true cash needs.

Questions

1. Using the data in Exhibit 3 and the worksheets in Exhibit 4, project the changes in the line of credit during July–December 1991. Note that the line of credit effectively is negative cash. It will increase in any given month by the same amount that cash otherwise would decrease for that month.
2. What is causing the decline in cash? How big does the line of credit need to be to accommodate the cash shortfalls? When will BOGA be able to repay the line of credit to the bank? Would a return to a modified cash system eliminate the problem?
3. What should Dr. Amsted do?

CASE 3–2   Menotomy Home Health Services*

In November 1987, Ms. Carolyn Ringer, treasurer of the Menotomy Home Health Services (MHHS), was preparing a loan request to go to the Norten Municipal Bank. Less than eight months earlier, MHHS had expanded their staff by 30 percent. At that time, the home health service had been in a secure financial position and Ms. Ringer, anticipating no financial problems, had spoken to the agency's board of directors in favor of the increase in services. However, in July, Ms. Ringer realized that although MHHS had begun training and paying their new staff in June, the agency would not receive the additional revenue generated by the new staff until later in the year. With the staff totaling about 30 employees (full- and part-time), Ms. Ringer realized that MHHS could not always have on hand the cash they would require.

---

* This case was prepared by Patricia O'Brien under the direction of Professor David W. Young. It subsequently was modified and updated by David W. Young. Copyright © by David W. Young.

EXHIBIT 1

MENOTOMY HOME HEALTH SERVICES
Balance Sheet
As of September 30, 1985–1987

	1985	*1986*	*1987*
Assets			
Cash..	$143,460	$ 32,805	$ 22,860
Accounts receivable.........................	52,650	58,140	68,100
Inventory	26,622	30,780	39,960
Prepaid expenses............................	32,118	34,303	41,585
Total current assets	$254,850	$156,028	$172,505
Property and equipment (net).................	315,345	411,735	468,946
Other assets	13,590	15,975	16,650
Total assets	$583,785	$583,738	$658,101
Liabilities and Fund Balances			
Line of credit.............................	$ 0	$ 0	$ 65,400
Accounts payable	2,745	3,542	2,925
Salaries and benefits payable	31,050	32,400	35,100
Due to third-party payer	12,060	13,153	14,086
Note payable, current	21,240	26,235	29,070
Mortgage, current...........................	11,250	11,250	11,250
Total current liabilities.....................	$ 78,345	$ 86,580	$157,831
Mortgage payable	168,750	157,500	146,250
Other long-term debt	270,000	270,000	270,000
Total liabilities..........................	$517,095	$514,080	$574,081
Fund balances	66,690	69,658	84,020
Total liabilities and fund balances	$583,785	$583,738	$658,101

Faced with these unexpected expenses, Ms. Ringer had gone to the Norten Municipal Bank to apply for a short-term line of credit to cover the additional costs. Mr. Jansen, the bank officer, had granted MHHS a line of credit which had reached almost $66,000 by September 1987. Although he had allowed the agency to continue using its line of credit into its next fiscal year,[1] he had raised some important considerations.

He explained that the bank was willing to continue a line of credit for the agency but he was concerned that Ms. Ringer had not adequately anticipated the agency's cash needs. He asked Ms. Ringer to present the bank at the outset with a detailed monthly statement of MHHS's projected cash needs for fiscal year 1988. Consequently, Ms. Ringer began to review the agency's financial statements (contained in Exhibits 1 and 2) and collect data that would help her plan for MHHS's future cash requirements.

---

[1] MHHS's fiscal year ran from October 1 to September 30. Fiscal year 1987 ran from October 1, 1986, to September 30, 1987.

EXHIBIT 2

MENOTOMY HOME HEALTH SERVICES
Income Statements
Fiscal Years 1985–87

	1985	1986	1987
Gross patient revenue	$649,462	$722,493	$838,524
Less: Contractual allowances and uncollectable accounts	114,892	130,278	140,034
Net patient revenue	$534,570	$592,215	$698,490
Operating expenses:			
Salary and benefits	$372,600	$388,800	$421,200
Overhead and administration	63,129	89,807	136,310
Cost of medical supplies	24,477	27,967	34,471
Contract services	8,123	8,640	10,230
Equipment rental	17,250	18,750	19,650
Depreciation	22,500	28,500	33,000
Interest	–0–	15,947	14,935
Other expenses	3,058	10,836	14,332
Total operating expenses	$511,137	$589,247	$684,128
Excess of revenue over expenses	$ 23,433	$ 2,968	$ 14,362
Fund balance, September 30	$ 66,690	$ 69,658	$ 84,020

Background

Menotomy Home Health Services was a private, nonprofit home health agency founded in 1965 by four retired nurses. Each founder had between 10 and 35 years of experience working with elderly and disabled patients in Norten's hospitals. Realizing that a majority of their patients would not have needed hospitalization if Norten or the near vicinity had had a home health service, the nurses started their own agency. At first, MHHS was small and operated out of one person's home. The agency then employed the four founders, a part-time social worker, and six home health aides, three of whom were volunteers.

By 1974, the organization had outgrown its "office space" as well as its organizational structure and objectives. Although two visiting nurse associations had sprung up in Norten in the early 1970s, there was still a greater demand for MHHS's services than the agency could provide. Demand had risen at an average rate of 10 percent per year, and forecasts at that time indicated a steady increase at the 10 percent level.

During the mid-70s, MHHS underwent a gradual expansion. They purchased a small building in downtown Norten for management offices, employee training programs, and headquarters. They also bought some of the vehicles and equipment they had previously rented. In the subsequent 10 years, the staff grew from 10 to 20 people.

In the mid-1980s, in conjunction with increased pressures on hospitals to discharge their patients earlier because of medicare's diagnosis-based group (DRG) form of reimbursement, MHHS was again faced with an increasing demand for home health services. A poll taken at Norten's three hospitals in March 1987 indicated that there would be a 20 percent increase for them in home health care patients. MHHS management estimated that net patient revenue would reach $810,000 in FY 1988, an increase of 16 percent over the 1987 level. Further growth of between $75,000 and $100,000 a year was expected during the 1989–90 period.

Consequently, MHHS was forced to decide whether to hold staff and services steady and hope that other health service organizations would fill in the gaps or to launch an expansion program aimed at providing more services to a greater number of patients in the Norten area. After examining MHHS's financial position and talking to Norten's health care providers about the agency's services, the board voted overwhelmingly to expand.

Data

Demand for MHHS's services, like that for many other home health agencies, was seasonal. Over two-thirds of the agency's annual home visits were made during the late fall and winter months. Exhibit 3 contains the forecasted monthly revenue for FY 1988 based on the number of visits during FY 1987. In making these projections, Ms. Ringer took into account the contractual adjustments and bad debts from MHHS's third-party payers and indigent patients.

Although demand for the agency's services tended to be seasonal, MHHS's employee salaries and benefits were expected to be relatively steady throughout

---

EXHIBIT 3   Estimated Monthly Revenue and Month-End Accounts Receivable for FY 1987–88

	Gross Patient Revenue	Net Revenue*	Accounts Receivable End-of-Month
October	$ 67,500	$ 55,800	$117,450
November	96,000	78,750	148,050
December..........	135,600	111,150	212,850
January............	139,950	114,750	257,400
February	156,450	128,250	278,100
March.............	88,350	72,450	235,800
April	73,500	60,300	143,100
May...............	61,350	50,400	117,450
June	53,400	43,800	76,500
July...............	32,850	27,000	59,550
August	34,500	28,350	60,000
September	47,550	39,000	89,700
	$987,000	$810,000	

* After adjustments for contractual allowances and bad debts.

the year. The agency had a firm policy of regular employment for both full and part-time employees which, according to management, enabled MHHS to maintain a highly skilled and committed staff. MHHS's management also believed that its employment policy contributed significantly to the agency's reputation for quality home health care. Employees were paid on the first of each month for earnings from the previous month. Starting in October, employee salary and benefit earnings were expected to be $41,250 a month except for June when many employees would be on vacation and some part-time wages would be eliminated; payments in July would thus decrease to about $30,000.

Disbursements related to overhead and administration were scheduled at $15,000 a month throughout FY 1988. Included in that $15,000-a-month was Ms. Ringer's estimate of the monthly interest on the Norten Municipal Bank loan. The initial depreciation expense was forecasted to be $33,000. Medical and office supply purchases were projected at $3,420 per month. The agency's policy was to charge these items and pay for each month's purchases in the following month. Contract service expenses were forecast at $900 a month. Other miscellaneous expenses were projected to total about $1,500 per month.

The new van, ordered for the meals-on-wheels program, was due for delivery in December. The van cost $18,000 and would be paid for in four equal monthly installments, beginning on delivery. The vehicle had an economic life of four years, at the end of which its salvage value would be zero. Depreciation would begin in the month of delivery.

In FY 1988, MHHS would owe Dr. Wilson, one of the board members, $29,070 for a short-term, interest-free loan she had made to the agency. This amount was payable in equal installments in December and March. The agency was also the lessee on long-term leases of furniture, equipment, and automobiles, with terms ranging from three to five years, beginning at various dates. The payments owed on these operating leases totaled $22,500, payable in equal installments in December and June.

In October 1985, MHHS had borrowed $180,000 from a life insurance company under a 16-year mortgage loan secured by the property and equipment. The current portion of the loan was repayable in equal installments in March and September of each year. Interest of 9 percent per annum on the unpaid balance was payable at the same time. In preparing her financial forecasts, Ms. Ringer planned to show separately the two principal payments, totaling $11,250, and the two interest payments, totaling $13,922, due in FY 1988.

The only other expenditure Ms. Ringer anticipated was $14,086 due to medicare for payments received exceeding reimbursable costs for the period ending September 30, 1987. The sum payable was noninterest-bearing and due in equal installments in June and September. She did not expect to incur a liability of this sort during FY 1988. Inventory, prepaid expenses, other assets, and other long-term debt were expected to remain essentially unchanged during FY 1988.

Although Mr. Jansen had not hesitated to grant MHHS a line of credit, he had stressed the importance of the bank's credit regulations. The bank required that

EXHIBIT 4

MENOTOMY HOME HEALTH SERVICES
Cash Flow Worksheet

	Oct.	Nov.	Dec.	Jan.	Feb.	Mar.	Apr.	May	June	July	Aug.	Sept.
CASH IN												
CASH OUT: Salaries and benefits												
Overhead and administration												
Payment of A/P												
Contract services												
Miscellaneous expense												
Vehicle expenditure												
Payment of note/P												
Equipment leases												
Payment of mortgage/P												
Mortgage interest												
Payment of third-party/P												
TOTAL OUT												
Net inflow (+) or outflow (−)												
Financing: (1) cash drawn down (+) or increase (−)												
(2) Line of credit change												
Beginning balance, line of credit												
Ending balance, line of credit												

for a line of credit of $200,000 or less, the agency maintain a compensating cash balance of $20,000 at all times. Second, the entire line of credit, including the $65,400 currently owed by MHHS, was to be completely liquidated for at least one month during the year.

Using the worksheet in Exhibit 4, Ms. Ringer began to prepare a monthly cash flow forecast for FY 1988 that, she hoped, would show how much money the agency would need on a monthly basis.

Questions

1. Prepare the cash flow worksheet contained in Exhibit 4. What does this tell you about the operations of MHHS?
2. Prepare pro forma financial statements for FY 1988. What do these tell you about the operations of MHHS? How can you reconcile the information in the cash flow worksheet with that in the financial statements?
3. How do the cash flow problems being experienced by Menotomy Home Health Services compare with those of Gotham Meals on Wheels or Brookstone OB/GYN Associates? Please be as specific as you can: What is causing the problems in each organization? Is the solution the same for each?
4. What recommendations would you make to Ms. Ringer?

CASE 3–3   Transitional Employment Enterprises, Inc.*

In early August 1988, the chairman of the board of Transitional Employment Enterprises, Inc. (TEE) signed an Assurance of Compliance Agreement with the attorney general of the Commonwealth of Massachusetts. The agreement referred to a Massachusetts law requiring that public charities receiving more than $100,000 in gross support and revenue during a fiscal year must submit to the Division of Public Charities, Office of the Attorney General, a complete audited financial statement for that year, prepared in accordance with generally accepted accounting principles. According to the agreement:

> . . . TEE submitted to the Division of Public Charities an audited financial statement, examined by an independent certified public accountant. . . . However, the certified public accountant reported that because of an absence of certain accounting records and because of uncertainties about whether certain past cost allocations will be approved by regulatory agencies and whether TEE will be able to recover from its cumulative deficit position, he is unable to state that the financial statement in question presents fairly the financial position of TEE as of June 30, 1987, in conformity with generally accepted accounting principles applied on a consistent basis.

---

* This case was prepared by Professor David W. Young, using publicly available information obtained from the Division of Public Charities, Massachusetts Office of the Attorney General.

Under the terms of the agreement, TEE obligated itself:

> . . . to keep financial records sufficient to permit application of adequate audit procedures and, in maintaining such records, employ standard accounting methods so as to produce auditable financial results.

Failure to maintain adequate financial records created some potential financial problems for TEE. According to the Management Statement accompanying its 1987 financial statements:

> After providing supported work employment opportunities to disadvantaged populations for 14 years, TEE, as an organization, has recently suffered severe financial setbacks. These problems stem primarily from inadequate accounting and record keeping resulting in potentially large deficits in prior audited operating years.

Background

TEE had been organized as a Massachusetts Corporation in 1974. Since that time, it had developed and operated a variety of supported work programs in Massachusetts and New Hampshire. The goal of each program was to develop employment skills of difficult-to-employ individuals selected from target populations such as recipients of Aid to Families with Dependent Children (AFDC), mentally retarded individuals, people over 55, special needs high school students, and people with histories of mental illness. TEE provided work preparation services for these individuals by placing them on site at a private company or public agency. At the end of approximately six months, unsubsidized employment was sought for the participants.

A substantial proportion of TEE's funding came from state and federal agencies: the Massachusetts Department of Public Welfare (DPW), the Massachusetts Rehabilitation Commission, the Massachusetts Department of Social Services, the New Hampshire Division of Vocational Rehabilitation, and the U.S. Department of Education (Projects with Industry and Special Education for the Handicapped). Additional funds came from the City of Boston/Jobs and Community Services and from private companies and foundations.

Data

Exhibit 1 contains the opinion letter prepared by the auditors of TEE's financial statements. TEE's financial statements are contained in Exhibits 2 through 5.

EXHIBIT 1   Auditors' Opinion Letter

To the Board of Directors of
Transitional Employment Enterprises, Inc.:

1. We have examined the balance sheet of Transitional Employment Enterprises, Inc. ("TEE") as of June 30, 1987. Except as explained in paragraph 5 below, our examination was made in accordance with generally accepted auditing standards, and accordingly, included such tests of the accounting records and such other auditing procedures as we considered necessary under the circumstances.

2. As discussed in Note C to the balance sheet, there are pending administrative adjudications involving the results of a prior audit of the financial activities of TEE for the period from July 1, 1983 to June 30, 1984. These proceedings have resulted in the determination by the Department of Public Welfare (DPW) that TEE's methodology for allocating certain costs to various programs and funding sources may not be adequate, and approximately $450,000 in costs for that year have been questioned. Of that amount, $28,324 has been claimed by DPW as a disallowance. The disallowance amount has been accrued in the accompanying balance sheet. In addition, costs allocated to program and funding sources for fiscal years 1985 through 1987 are subject to future audits by DPW which may result in additional questioned costs or claims for cost disallowance.

3. As discussed in Note C to the balance sheet, the Massachusetts Office of the Inspector General is conducting an investigation of TEE's costs charged to the DPW Career Counseling Contract, and certain transactions between TEE and another organization named America Works. The ultimate outcome of this investigation cannot be presently determined.

4. As shown in the accompanying balance sheet, TEE's accumulated deficit as of June 30, 1987 and other factors discussed in Notes C, E, and I indicate that TEE may be unable to continue in existence. TEE's ability to continue as a going concern is contingent upon its ability to obtain adequate financing and funding, and to recover from its cumulative deficit position by achieving and sustaining revenues in excess of expenditures. The balance sheet does not include any adjustments relating to the recoverability and classification of recorded asset amounts or the amounts and classification of liabilities that might be necessary should TEE be unable to continue in existence.

5. As discussed in Note C to the balance sheet, evidence supporting the activity in advances under grants and contracts, and evidence supporting cost allocations made in 1987 to publicly funded grants and programs is not available. TEE's records do not permit application of adequate alternative procedures regarding these cost allocations.

6. Because of the significance of the uncertainties noted in paragraphs 2, 3, and 4 above, and because we were unable to apply adequate alternative audit procedures noted in paragraph 5, we are unable to express, and we do not express, an opinion on the balance sheet referred to above.

Boston, Massachusetts
April 22, 1988

EXHIBIT 2

TRANSITIONAL EMPLOYMENT ENTERPRISES, INC.
Balance Sheet
June 30, 1987

Assets		
Current fund:		
Current assets:		
Cash......................		$104,964
Accounts receivable (Notes D and E):		
Employment contracts and research grants..........	425,100	
Service Projects...........	232,482	
Other	50,599	
Allowance for doubtful accounts	(108,223)	
Total accounts receivable ..		599,918
Prepaid expenses............		11,209
Security deposits............		3,812
Total currents assets.......		$719,903
Total assets.....................		$719,903
Fixed asset fund:		
Furniture and office equipment		$112,564
Less: accumulated depreciation		(63,076)
Total fixed assets..........		$ 49,488

Liabilities and Fund Balances	
Current fund:	
Current liabilities:	
Accounts payable	$ 230,651
Accrued liabilities	38,305
Notes payable-current portion (Note E)	520,818
Accrued payroll and related taxes....................	107,510
Accrued vacation and sick pay	98,702
Total current liabilities.....	$ 995,986
Note payable-long-term portion (Note E)	300,000
Total liabilities	$1,295,986
Commitments and contingencies (Notes C and G)	
Fund balance	(576,083)
Total liabilities and fund balance ..	$ 719,903
Fixed asset fund:	
Fund balance	$ 49,488
Total fixed asset fund balance	$ 49,488

The accompanying notes are an integral part of the balance sheet.

EXHIBIT 3

TRANSITIONAL EMPLOYMENT ENTERPRISES, INC.
Statement of Support, Revenue and Expenses and Changes in Fund Balances
For the 12 Months Ended June 30, 1987

Support and Revenue	*Current Unrestricted Fund*	*Current Restricted Fund*	*Fixed Asset Fund*	*Total*
Public support:				
Massachusetts Department of Public Welfare	—	$1,286,981	—	$1,286,981
Massachusetts Rehab Commission..................	—	150,700	—	150,700
New Hampshire Dept. of Mental Health	—	142,175	—	142,175
Employment contracts	—	901,283	—	901,283
Welfare diversion................................	—	191,523	—	191,523
Grants and contributions	—	11,359	—	11,359
Total public support	—	$2,684,021	—	$2,684,021

EXHIBIT 3 *(concluded)*

Support and Revenue	Current Unrestricted Fund	Current Restricted Fund	Fixed Asset Fund	Total
Revenue:				
Service projects		$1,915,259		$1,915,259
Interest income	$ 222			222
Other	53,908			53,908
Total support and revenue	$ 54,130	$4,599,280		$4,653,410
Expenses:				
Program management	—	$1,759,359	$19,427	$1,778,786
Support work project	—	3,311,404		3,311,404
Total expenses	—	$5,070,763	$19,427	$5,090,190
Excess (deficiency) of support and revenue over expenses	$ 54,130	(471,483)	(19,427)	(436,780)
Transfer of restricted funds	(471,483)	471,483	—	—
Total changes in fund balance	(417,353)		(19,427)	(436,780)
Fund balance June 30, 1986	(216,046)		63,588	(152,458)
Prior year adjustments:				
Contract advances and receivables adjustments	57,316		5,327	62,643
Adjusted fund balance June 30, 1986	(158,730)		68,915	(89,815)
Fund balance June 30, 1987	(576,083)		49,488	(526,595)

EXHIBIT 4

TRANSITIONAL EMPLOYMENT ENTERPRISES, INC.
Statement of Functional Expenses
For the 12 Months Ended June 30, 1987

	Program Management	Supported Work Project	Totals
Current operating fund:			
Supported worker wages and expenses		$1,721,793	$1,721,793
Salaries and benefits	$ 842,973	1,139,329	1,982,302
Travel	10,215	50,398	60,613
Occupancy	252,060		252,060
Office operations	195,242		195,242
Project materials and supplies		4,235	4,235
Equipment rental and maintenance	17,841		17,841
Technical support consultants		259,910	259,910
Professional fees	47,565		47,565
Others	393,464	135,738	529,202
Total expenses excluding depreciation	$1,759,360	$3,311,403	$5,070,763
Fixed asset fund:			
Depreciation	19,427	0	19,427
Total expenses	$1,778,787	$3,311,403	$5,090,190

EXHIBIT 5 Notes to Balance Sheet

A. Nature of business
[All relevant information from this section is contained in the text of the case.]

B. Summary of significant accounting policies

Revenue recognition
  TEE recognizes revenue from contributions when received; from cost reimbursement contracts and grants when expenditures are incurred; and from performance contracts as services are performed. All contributions are considered to be available for unrestricted use, unless specifically restricted by the donor.

Welfare diversion funds
  TEE is permitted, through an agreement with the DPW and approved by the U.S. Department of Health and Human Services, to receive the portion of participants' AFDC grant which the DPW would normally retain when a recipient obtained employment.

Furniture and office equipment
  Furniture and office equipment are stated at cost. Depreciation is provided on the straight-line basis over the estimated useful lives of the assets. Expenditures for repairs and maintenance which do not improve or extend the life of assets are charged to operations as incurred. All equipment acquired with grant funds is expensed in the year of purchase in accordance with the grant agreements.

Income taxes
  TEE is exempt from Federal income taxes under Section 501(c) (3) of the Internal Revenue Code, and from Massachusetts income taxes.

C. Contingencies, uncertainties, and scope limitations
In 1986, the DPW contracted with an independent public accounting firm for an audit of the financial activities of TEE for the period from July 1, 1983 to June 30, 1984. The audit has resulted in the determination and claim by the DPW that TEE's methodology for allocating certain costs to various programs and funding sources may not be adequate and approximately $450,000 in costs for that year have been questioned. Of that amount, $28,324 has been claimed by DPW as a disallowance. The disallowance amount has been accrued on the accompanying balance sheet. TEE and DPW are in the process of resolving the findings from that audit. TEE's cost allocation methodology for fiscal years through June 30, 1987 has not been accepted by the DPW. The ultimate outcome of the 1984 audit and potential cost disallowances for fiscal years subsequent to June 30, 1984 cannot be determined at this time. Accordingly, no provision for any liability that may result has been accrued on the accompanying balance sheet.
  TEE is also being investigated by the Massachusetts Office of the Inspector General regarding the DPW Career Counseling contract and TEE's relationship with America Works. The ultimate outcome of this investigation cannot be determined. Accordingly, no provision for any liability that may result has been accrued on the accompanying balance sheet.
  At June 30, 1987, TEE's current liabilities exceeded its current assets by $276,083 and its total assets by $576,083. TEE continued to sustain an operating deficit in fiscal year 1987 and as shown on the balance sheet, the cumulative fund deficit is $576,083. These factors, among others discussed above and Notes E and I, indicate that TEE may be unable to continue in existence. TEE's ability to continue as a going concern is contingent upon its ability to obtain adequate financing and funding, and to recover from its cumulative deficit position by achieving and sustaining revenues in excess of expenditures.
  TEE's accounting records to support the following areas have not been located:

- TEE had recorded $77,995 as advances under grants and contracts as of June 30, 1986. Advances under grants and contracts represent amounts received in excess of the related program expenses incurred under cost reimbursement grants and contracts. TEE closed these advances to revenue as of June 30, 1987.
- Documentation of cost allocation made in fiscal year 1987 to publicly funded grants and program.

  In addition, TEE has not reconciled various grant/contract confirmation exceptions to its accounting records. The absence of the above described accounting records and reconciliations do not permit the application of adequate alternative audit procedures to related accounts.

EXHIBIT 5 *(continued)*

D. Accounts receivable

At June 30, 1987, accounts receivable consisted of amounts due from private companies for supportive work services (service projects), and grant contract billings to city, state, and federal agencies and other nonprofit organizations. The accounts receivable balances are used to collateralize notes payable to Bank of New England (see Note E).

Other accounts receivable balances consist of the following:

Due from America Works (Note H)	$46,827
Miscellaneous	3,732
Total	$50,559

E. Debt

On November 21, 1986, TEE entered into a $450,000 five-year term loan agreement with the Bank of New England (the Bank). The interest rate charged on outstanding loan balance is at prime rate plus 2.5 percent. The loan outstanding at June 30, 1987 was $390,000 of which $90,000 is payable in fiscal year 1988. TEE also has a $250,000 revolving line of credit arrangement with the Bank. On March 21, 1987, the Bank increased the line of credit by an additional $180,818. TEE is charged interest at prime rate plus 2 percent on the $250,000 portion, and prime rate plus 2.5 percent on the $180,818 portion of the outstanding line of credit balance. The outstanding borrowing at June 30, 1987 was $430,818.

All of the above borrowings are collateralized by TEE's accounts receivable.

The terms *loan and revolving credit facilities* contain various restrictions and covenants. Under the most restrictive of these covenants, the ratio of total liabilities to fund balance cannot exceed 2.9 : 1, and total borrowing outstanding is limited to 50 percent of qualified accounts receivable, as defined. As shown on the balance sheet, TEE has a cumulative deficit fund balance and total borrowing outstanding which exceeds gross accounts receivable at June 30, 1987. TEE is in violation of these covenants, therefore, the loans are in default, as defined. TEE has obtained from the Bank a waiver of the certain loan restrictions and covenants effective through April 22, 1988. In the event of a nonwaiver of those restrictions and covenants after April 22, 1988, the Bank has the right to demand payment on the loans, including the long-term portion of the term loan.

F. Pension plan

TEE has a defined contribution pension plan, covering all full-time employees after completion of one year of service, as defined. Program enrollees are not eligible to participate in the plan. TEE's policy is to fund pension costs accrued, contributing an amount equal to 8 percent of the participants' gross wages to the plan. For the year ended June 30, 1987, pension expense under the plan was $69,975.

G. Commitments

TEE has various lease agreements for office space and equipment. Since all leases are operating lease arrangements, the lease payments are charged to earnings as incurred.

On February 29, 1988, TEE terminated its certain office space lease and agreed to pay a total of $60,000 as termination fee, payable in equal monthly installments of $1,667 until February 1, 1991.

The following is a schedule of future minimum lease and lease termination fee payments required under such commitments:

Year Ending June 30	
1988	$209,735
1989	124,863
1990	125,284
1991	85,585
	$545,467

EXHIBIT 5   *(concluded)*

H.   Related party transactions

During fiscal year 1987, TEE provided technical consulting services to America Works, an employment and training company, and reflected billings of approximately $71,000. The president of America Works is married to a person who was the president of TEE during fiscal year 1987. At June 30, 1987, amounts due from America Works was $46,827 (see Notes C and D).

I.   Subsequent events

In December 1987, the DPW terminated two fiscal year 1988 contracts for supported work services and the contract for career assessment services was not renewed for the period beginning January 1988. One of the supported work service contracts (Access program for the psychologically disabled) was subsequently reinstated. The termination of the AFDC Supported Work Services Contract is effective as of February 29, 1988. The terminated contract provided a significant portion of the revenues of TEE for fiscal year 1987.

Question

1. Should the Bank of New England (see Notes D and E) demand payment on their outstanding loans? In preparing your response, please:

   a.   Identify the most significant *accounting* issues that you think TEE must concern itself with.

   b.   Identify the most significant *financial management* issues that you think TEE must concern itself with.

CASE 3–4   Michael Morris University*

For about 15 years, the board of trustees of Michael Morris University had wrestled with the policy governing the amount of endowment earnings that should be recognized as operating revenue. Throughout the period 1980–82, the topic had been discussed at several meetings of the Finance Committee, and the committee hoped that the matter could be resolved once and for all at its May 1982 meeting.

Arriving at a sound policy was important because the university adhered faithfully to a balanced budget each year. The amount of endowment revenue recognized had a significant effect on total revenue, and hence on the total amount of expenses that could be budgeted.

Michael Morris University was an old, relatively small, New England university. As shown in Exhibit 1, in June 1960 the market value of its endowment was

---

* This case was prepared by Professor Robert N. Anthony. Copyright © by the President and Fellows of Harvard College. Harvard Business School case 9-1183-115.

EXHIBIT 1   Basic Financial Data ($000)

Years Ending June 30	Market	Income	Additions	Cost	Book	Realized Gains
1953	$ 4,885	$234	$ 48	$ 3,942	$ 4,779	$ 88
1954	5,430	248	174	4,118	5,092	137
1955	6,608	263	131	4,249	5,478	255
1956	7,469	306	533	4,782	6,270	259
1957	7,881	341	442	5,224	6,844	132
1958	7,845	366	31	5,255	7,053	179
1959	8,739	363	169	5,424	7,600	378
1960	8,748	356	172	5,596	7,814	42
1961	10,520	384	585	6,181	8,453	53
1962	9,628	418	146	6,327	8,704	105
1963	11,815	418	593	6,920	9,303	6
1964	12,823	445	344	7,264	9,830	183
1965	14,679	468	1,868	9,132	11,770	72
1966	14,554	574	263	9,395	12,250	217
1967	16,712	565	503	9,898	12,908	155
1968	20,209	617	931	10,829	14,623	784
1969	21,006	652	505	11,334	15,589	462
1970	19,421	731	980	12,314	17,141	571

$8.7 million, and its book value was $7.8 million. In June 1969 the market value reached a peak of $21.0 million, and the book value was $15.6 million. At that time, the policy was to recognize as endowment revenue interest income on bonds and dividends on stocks (plus some income from faculty mortgages and miscellaneous sources not relevant to the case). In the 1960s, the university invested fairly heavily, and successfully, in growth stocks. The investment objective was capital appreciation, and the dividends on these stocks were typically zero or low.

Adoption of Total Return

In 1973 Michael Morris adopted a "total return" policy.[1] It recognized as endowment revenue 5 percent of the three-year average market value of the portfolio. Several other institutions shifted to a similar concept at about the same time, and

---

[1] *Total return* means dividends, interest, and appreciation in market value, whether or not realized. Although the policy is usually referred to as a *total return* policy, actually it is a revenue recognition policy. As used here the term does *not* mean that the total return is recognized as revenue. Rather, it means that endowment revenue is based, not on interest and dividends, but on a "prudent portion" of the total return.

the typical rate was approximately 5 percent. In his report to the board recommending the adoption of this policy, Mr. Clark, chairman of the Finance Committee, made the following comments:

The Finance Committee has been trying to define endowment earnings for a considerable length of time. This sounds simple, but it is not. Heretofore, we have not included any increase in market values in endowment earnings. By not including increases in market value, we have been robbing the present generation to benefit future generations. Much of the endowment is made up of common stocks that pay very low or no dividends but have tremendous potential for appreciation. Today's investors give as much weight in their investment decisions to appreciation as they do to dividends. We are all aware of the "glamour" stocks such as Eastman Kodak, IBM, J&J, and Xerox that sell at fantastically high price/earnings multiples but return 1.0 percent or less in cash dividends. Obviously, they are selling at such high P/Es because the investor is paying for future growth. Therefore, when we talk about a total return, we mean the total of both dividends and appreciation during any set period of time.

However, we cannot just take dividends plus appreciation because if this were done, inflation would reduce the purchasing power of the endowment. We also should use some sort of a multiyear moving average to even out peaks and valleys.

After more than 20 computer printouts covering the effect of various formulas on the results of past years, we finally have come to the realization (along with a number of other people!) that a figure of 5 percent of the endowment market value fits our purpose. This means that if we have a 9 percent "total return" (dividends and interest plus appreciation) and allow 4 percent for inflation, our endowment earnings are 5 percent. That is basically it. We have built in a number of safeguards, such as using average market values of the endowment over the past three years and taking into account unused restricted income.

The AICPA Audit Guide

In 1974, the American Institute of Certified Public Accountants issued an *Audit Guide* for colleges and universities. This contained a lengthy discussion of the total return concept, from which the following is excerpted:

The law and the legal profession, while by no means in accord on the subject, appear to be heading in the direction of elimination of limitations on the governing board's right to appropriate gains for expenditure. The total return concept continues, however, to cause accountants difficulty in that the concept thus far has produced few, if any, practical applications which appear to be *objectively determinable*. No clear *redefinition* of traditional income yield has evolved. The exercise of prudence is subjective and not susceptible to measurement in an accounting sense. The practical applications of the total return concept utilized to date amounts substantively to the selection of a "spending rate," usually relating the rate to the market value of the portfolio. They appear in some cases to involve an intolerable element of arbitrariness.

Consequently, until a general practice evolves which is *objectively determinable*, the guide would do a disservice to higher education and the accounting profession to sanction as a permissible accounting treatment the inclusion in revenue of gains utilized under a total return approach.

EXHIBIT 2 Basic Financial Data ($000)

	Beginning Market Value	Gifts and Other Additions	Appre-ciation	Interest and Dividends	Revenue Recognized	Ending Market Value
1972	$24,610	$ 837	$ 3,535	$ 831	$ (709)*	$29,104
1973	29,104	609	(4,997)	918	(778)	24,856
1974	24,856	532	(3,209)	1,047	(942)	22,284
1975	22,284	736	1,169	914	(852)	24,251
1976	24,251	(647)	(962)	1,003	(937)	22,708
1977	22,708	192	(1,091)	965	(930)	21,844
1978	21,844	506	214	955	(916)	22,603
1979	22,603	258	579	1,141	(1,116)	23,465
1980	23,465	1,314	1,523	1,322	(1,262)	26,362
1981	26,362	706	2,128	1,529	(1,358)	29,367
		$5,043	$(1,111)	$10,625	$(9,800)	

Summary:

Market value, June 30, 1971	$24,610
Gifts and other additions	5,043
Interest and dividends	10,625
Appreciation	(1,111)
Revenue recognized	(9,800)
Market value, June 30, 1981	$29,367

* Revenue Recognized excludes income on some restricted funds that could not be used during the year. Revenue actually recognized was therefore roughly 5–10 percent less than it would have been if these funds could have been used.

Some members of the Finance Committee had been uneasy about the new policy, and this statement led to a reopening of the question. Moreover, as indicated in Exhibit 2, the market value of the portfolio had been declining during this period. After considerable discussion, the committee recommended a return to the former policy, and the board approved this in May 1975. Because the portfolio at that time consisted of a smaller proportion of low-dividend stocks than in 1973, this change did not make a substantial difference in the amount of income recognized.

Return to Total Return

In 1980, the issue was reopened. One new factor was the high rate of inflation in recent years and the opinion of some committee members that the board had an obligation to protect the purchasing power of the endowment. In 1981, another factor arose in conjunction with the peculiar effect of a decision by the Investment Committee. The Investment Committee decided that too large a fraction of the endowment portfolio was invested in common stock, so it shifted several million dollars into bonds. Since the dividend yield on stocks was about 5 percent and the interest yield on bonds was about 14 percent, this change resulted in a reported increase in endowment income of about $300,000 a year. Some Finance Committee members doubted that the university's revenue actually was increased by this move.

A memorandum circulated to the Finance Committee at that time from Mr. Clark, its chairman, contained the following (references to other colleges and universities relate to a survey of their practices that the financial vice president had prepared for the committee):

> Our revenue recognition policy should not influence our investment policy. Investment decisions should not be influenced by a need to produce a specified amount of cash. If dividends and interest do not produce enough cash, securities can easily be sold to provide the balance.
>
> Our revenue recognition policy should be consistent with accounting standards. The bottom line on the published financial statements should be the same as the number we use for internal decision making. At present, the *College and University Audit Guide* recommends that endowment revenues consist only of dividends and interest; however, this is likely to be changed in the near future to accommodate the total return approach.
>
> Our revenue recognition policy should be rarely changed. It should not be subject to the board's judgment each year. Such a policy leads to the practice of recognizing whatever amount of endowment revenue is needed to balance the budget. This results in a meaningless bottom line. The bottom line should show whether we actually operated at a surplus or a deficit. Yale tried this approach in the 1960s, with disastrous results. In the early 1970s Wesleyan used up a substantial fraction of its endowment with such a policy.
>
> Our policy should not be to increase the previous year's revenue by a stated percentage. Such a policy bears no relationship to the actual performance of the portfolio, and would not, I believe, be acceptable under the new accounting standards. (This seems to be the policy at Harvard, MIT, and Bowdoin.)
>
> Our policy should be to maintain the purchasing power of the endowment. Because universities have relatively low productivity increases, such a policy will not permit existing programs to be financed with the existing endowment, even when the purchasing power of the endowment is held constant. Endowment revenue finances only a fraction of existing programs. We must count on new contributions to endowment to finance the balance.
>
> A policy of recognizing dividends and interest as revenue will maintain the purchasing power of the endowment only by coincidence, that is, if the proportion of low-yield, high-growth stocks to high-yield stocks and bonds happens to work out so that purchasing power is maintained. (This is the traditional policy, and is apparently still used by Amherst, Colby, Columbia, Johns Hopkins, Notre Dame, and several others.)
>
> Our revenue recognition policy need not be influenced by, nor govern, the rate of return used in calculating payments to annuitants.
>
> Our policy should be to recognize as revenue approximately 5 percent of the average market value of the endowment over three to five years, adjusted for additions to endowment during that period. (This is the policy of Brown, Cal Tech, Chicago, Dartmouth, Smith, and a number of institutions not listed in the material furnished us.)
>
> Such a policy does not necessarily result in a more volatile revenue stream than a policy of recognizing dividends and interest as revenue. Although dividends, or interest for a given security, change less rapidly than does the market value of that security, a percentage of the market value of the whole portfolio is not necessarily more volatile

than the total dividend and interest stream. In 1981 we saw how volatile this stream can be; a shift in the mix of debt and equity resulted in a great increase in interest income, even though this increase did not have much economic significance.

In meetings held to discuss the issue, some members supported the point of view of this memorandum. Others, however, pointed out that the college had been burned once by using the total return policy, and that the prudent course of action was to continue with the policy of recognizing only dividends and interest. Furthermore, they said, any departure from this policy probably would result in a qualified opinion by the university's auditors, and this might have an adverse effect on the attitude of creditors.

Mr. Henderson, the financial vice president, recommended a policy of recognizing 5 percent of the average market value of the endowment. He thought that the average should be lagged two years; that is, the amount recognized in 1983 should be the average for the five years ended in 1981. In preparing the 1983 budget (in April 1982), the latest available information was that for fiscal year 1981.

Questions

1. Assuming a revenue recognition policy based on average market value, how should the amount of revenue recognized in a given year be calculated?
2. What policy would you recommend? (Be prepared to discuss each of the alternative policies mentioned in the chairman's memorandum.)

CASE 3–5   City of Douglas*

Claire Dexter was appointed by the mayor of Douglas to a three-year term on the city's finance committee. The finance committee acted as an adviser to city officials and as a "watchdog" on behalf of the city's citizens. Under certain circumstances it could propose city budgets, and it had to approve large proposed capital expenditures. Its views were given considerable weight by city officials.

Ms. Dexter was senior vice president of the region's largest bank. She had extensive experience in analyzing corporate financial statements. As preparation for her committee work, she asked the city controller for financial statements. The controller promptly furnished a 102-page book, titled "Comprehensive Annual Financial Report, City of Douglas, Fiscal Year Ended June 30, 1987." The financial statements had been examined by a national public accounting firm, and in its opinion letter the firm stated that they "present fairly the financial position and results of operations . . . in conformity with generally accepted accounting principles."

---

* This case was prepared by Professor Robert N. Anthony. Copyright © by Osceola Institute.

Ms. Dexter searched through the book looking for an operating statement or income statement, which was in her opinion the most important financial statement for any organization. She did not find one. The closest to it appeared to be an exhibit with the title, "Combined Statement of Revenues, Expenditures, and Changes in Fund Balances: All Governmental Fund Types." She decided to recast this statement, as closely as possible, to the form and content of a business operating statement.

She particularly wanted to determine whether Douglas operated at a surplus or a deficit. Specifically, she believed that the financial goal of a municipality should be that the revenues applicable to a given year are approximately equal to the expenses of that year. She also wanted numbers for the various city programs so that spending on these programs could be compared with amounts for previous years and with amounts spent by other municipalities.

Exhibit 1 is adapted from the statement referred to above. Ms. Dexter had her secretary modify the actual statement in two ways. First, the numbers on the report were carried out to the last dollar, which she modified by rounding them to thousands of dollars. Second, there was a column on the statement headed "Totals (Memorandum only)," which contained the totals of the amounts in each row. It seemed to her that these totals were "adding apples and oranges," and she eliminated them.

Funds

Next, she read the notes accompanying the financial statements to determine whether the fund types listed in the report did in fact relate to operations. A summary of the description of these funds and Ms. Dexter's conclusions about them follows:

General Fund.   "The General Fund is the general operating fund of the City. It is used to account for all financial resources except those required to be accounted for in another fund. The General Fund accounts for the normal recurring activities of the city." Ms. Dexter concluded that the amounts in this column clearly related to operations.

Special Revenue Funds.   "Special Revenue Funds are used to account for the proceeds of specific revenue sources (other than special assessments or major capital projects) that are legally restricted to expenditures for specified purposes." An exhibit in the financial report showed that the amount reported in Exhibit 1 was the total of 13 separate funds, the largest of which were revenue sharing (amounts received from the federal government), special education grants (grants from the state), and school lunch program (grants from both state and federal sources). Ms. Dexter concluded that the amounts in the special revenue column were substantially related to operating activities.

EXHIBIT 1

CITY OF DOUGLAS
Combined Statement of Revenues, Expenditures, and Changes in Fund Balances
All Governmental Fund Types
Year Ended June 30, 1987
($000)

	General	Special Revenue	Debt Service	Capital Project	Special Assessments
Revenues:					
Taxes and assessments	$32,015	$ —	$ —	$ —	$ 82
Penalties	377	—	—	—	31
Licenses and permits	164	—	—	—	—
Intergovernmental	11,637	2,712	23	1,071	—
Charges for services	332	582	—	—	—
Investment earnings	960	128	—	166	154
Contributions	—	30	—	—	—
Miscellaneous	551	4	—	—	1
Total revenues	46,036	3,456	23	1,237	268
Expenditures:					
General government	1,435	415	—	—	—
Public safety	5,400	112	—	—	—
Public works	4,579	667	—	—	—
Health and welfare	1,461	634	—	—	—
Libraries	435	49	—	—	—
Parks and recreation	726	188	—	—	—
Education	23,028	1,958	—	—	—
Citywide:					
Employee benefits and pensions	3,793	—	—	—	—
General insurance	542	—	—	—	—
Capital outlay	—	—	—	1,937	8
Debt service:					
Principal retirement	—	—	1,872	—	—
Interest and fiscal charges	—	—	1,034	—	108
Miscellaneous	619	—	—	—	—
Total expenditures	42,018	4,023	2,906	1,937	116
Excess of revenues over (under) expenditures	4,018	(567)	(2,883)	(700)	152
Other financing sources (uses):					
Operating transfers in	160	952	2,693	142	—
Operating transfers out	(3,434)	(134)	—	(379)	—
Total	(3,274)	818	2,693	(237)	—
Net excess (under)*	744	251	(190)	(937)	152
Fund balance, July 1, 1987	2,955	1,984	1,259	2,115	(60)
Fund balance, June 30, 1988	$ 3,699	$2,235	$1,069	$1,178	$ 92

* The label for this line was "Excess of revenues and other sources over (under) expenditures and other uses."

Debt Service Fund. "The Debt Service Fund is used to account for the accumulation of resources for, and the payment of, general long-term debt principal, interest, and related costs." Ms. Dexter learned from the report used to construct Exhibit 1 that $2,693,000 was transferred to the Debt Service Fund from the General Fund. She concluded that this amount was probably related to operations and that to include the Debt Service Fund column would be double counting; she therefore eliminated it.

Capital Project Fund. "The Capital Project Fund is used to account for financial resources to be used for the acquisition or construction of major capital facilities." Ms. Dexter concluded that the expenditures recorded for this fund were similar to those for the account "construction in progress" in a business balance sheet, and that they related to fixed asset acquisitions, which are not operating activities.

Special Assessments Fund. "The Special Assessment Fund has been established to account for the financing and construction of various sewer extension projects deemed to benefit the properties against which special assessments are levied." Ms. Dexter concluded that this fund also related to the acquisition of fixed assets rather than to operating activities.

Ms. Dexter therefore combined the amounts in the general fund and special revenue fund columns of Exhibit 1 to obtain a first approximation to an operating statement.

Revenues

General Property Taxes. The report stated: "In accordance with GAAP, general property taxes are recorded as revenues in the period in which they become measurable and available. Taxes for the year that are not received within 60 days of year-end are assumed not to be 'available'." These unpaid taxes, reduced by an allowance for bad debts, were recorded as assets on the balance sheet, with an offsetting credit to a liability, deferred revenue.

Ms. Dexter concluded that the tax revenue for the year 1987 should be the amount assessed for 1987 (reduced by an allowance for bad debts). A table in the report gave information about tax assessments for the past 10 years. From it she learned that the assessment for 1987 was $32,343,000, and that the bad debt experience over the period was about 1.5 percent of the amount assessed. She therefore took $31,858,000 (98.5 percent of $32,343,000) as the amount of 1987 tax revenue, a decrease of $157,000 from the amount reported.

Other Revenues. The report stated that certain special revenue items were grants from government agencies that were recognized as revenues in the same period as that in which the expenditure was incurred, because this was required by the terms of the grant. Ms. Dexter viewed this treatment as appropriate.

Expenditures

The Douglas statement had the heading "expenditures," whereas the term *expenses* was used for similar items in business operating statements. In general, expenditures were recognized in the period in which the liability was incurred. Ms. Dexter concluded that regardless of the label, expenditures were the same as expenses, with the exceptions noted below.

Inventories. Inventories were recognized when the inventory items were received by the city. A business would recognize an expense in the period in which the items were consumed, which often would be a later period. However, the Douglas accounting system did not track the consumption of inventory items, so there was no way of making an adjustment for this.

Accumulated Unpaid Vacation and Sick Pay. In accordance with GAAP, Douglas recorded these amounts as a "long-term obligation," a memorandum account that did not affect the operating statement. In a business, the amounts earned by employees because of work done in the year would be recorded as an expense of the year. The amount of the obligation as of June 30, 1987, was $3,272,000. However, this was only $100,000 more than the amount reported a year earlier. Ms. Dexter decided that an adjustment for this amount was not worth the effort.

Pensions. Under business GAAP, the pension expense recognized for a given year an amount equal to the present value of that part of the benefits that employees would receive after they retired that was earned because of the work they did in that year. If the pension benefits were increased, the employee would be entitled to an additional amount for the earnings of prior years, and a fraction of this "past service liability" also would be included as pension expense of the current year. Douglas used a quite different approach to its calculation of pension expenditures. It contributed to its pension fund an amount "reasonably necessary to meet expenditures and benefits payable."

In 1987, the city paid $2,668,000 to its pension fund under this provision and recognized this amount as an expenditure. The pension fund at year-end had assets of $36,216,000, and the estimated present value of the pension benefits to which employees would become entitled by virtue of their earnings through 1987 was $46,739,000. Ms. dexter therefore concluded that the amount that had been contributed to the fund in this and prior years was about $10,500,000 too low. However, this deficiency related to several prior years, and she did not have data that would permit a calculation of the amount attributable to 1987. Pending further study, she decided to add $1,000,000 to the 1987 pension expenditure.

Program Expenditures. Exhibit 1 contained an item under "Citywide" for employee benefits and pensions, amounting to $3,793,000. Ms. Dexter decided that this amount, plus the $1,000,000 of inadequate pension expense, properly were part of the compensation earned by employees and therefore should be recorded as expenses in the programs to which their salaries were charged. (Programs were the items listed on Exhibit 1, from "general government" through "education.") She hoped to obtain information on the salary expense for each program, but lacking this information, she decided to allocate the $4,793,000 in proportion to the amount reported as expenditures for each program.

Depreciation

GAAP does not permit depreciation accounting in government activities. The city did have a record of the cost of depreciable assets, which totaled $85,737,000 as of June 30, 1985. However, a note to the financial statement listed some $48,000,000 of new projects that currently were in various stages of completion, which indicated to Ms. Dexter that the $85,737,000 cost of all assets in use was too low; these assets had been acquired over the past 50 years or more.

As another clue, a note to the statement indicated that $2,693,000 had been transferred from the General Fund to the Debt Service Fund, and that the Debt Service Fund had retired $1,872,000 principal amount of bonds during the year. If all the fixed assets had been acquired with borrowed funds, and if the repayment schedule corresponded to the life of the asset, the $1,872,000 would correspond to a depreciation charge. Since some assets were acquired with government grants and others with operating funds, and since the bond issues typically were for a shorter period than the life of the assets acquired with the proceeds of the bonds, this amount clearly was too low. Nevertheless, Ms. Dexter decided to use $1,872,000 as an indication of depreciation expense. Because of the uncertainty involved in this amount, she decided to show it as a separate item, rather than spreading it among the several programs.

Operating Transfers

The items labeled *transfers* apparently were something different from revenues and expenditures because they were shown separately. Of the transfers "in" and "out" of the General and Special Revenue Funds, $2,693,000 was the transfer to the Debt Service Fund already mentioned. Most of the other transfers were between the General and Special Revenue funds, which largely offset one another. Other transfers were to or from Capital Project and Special Assessment Funds, and Ms. Dexter believed that they were related to fixed assets rather than to operating expenditures. In constructing her statement, she therefore disregarded transfers other than the debt service item described above.

Proprietary Fund Type

In a separate section of the Douglas annual financial report, Ms. Dexter discovered a "Combined Statement of Revenues, Expenses, and Changes in Retained Earnings/Fund Balances—Proprietary Fund types," with a column headed "Enterprise Fund.'' A note stated: ''The Enterprise Fund is used to account for the operations of the Douglas Water Department. These operations are financed and operated in a manner similar to that of a private business enterprise where the intent is that all costs, including depreciation, related to the provision of goods and services to the general public on a continuing basis be financed or recovered primarily through user charges.''

As the title implied, this statement was a conventional business-type operating statement, recognizing revenues when earned and expenses as the amounts of resources applicable to the year, including depreciation. The bottom line reported a net loss of $420,000. Ms. Dexter concluded that the water department was a part of the City of Douglas, so she incorporated this loss in her operating statement.

EXHIBIT 2

CITY OF DOUGLAS
Operating Statement
Year Ended June 30, 1987
(with adjustments made by Claire Dexter)
($000)

	General +	Special Revenue =	Sub-total +	Other =	Total
Revenues:					
Property taxes	$32,015	$ —	$32,015	$ (157)	$31,858
Penalties	377	—	377	—	377
Licenses and permits	164	—	164	—	164
Intergovernmental	11,637	2,712	14,349	—	14,349
Charges for services	332	582	914	—	914
Investment earnings	960	128	1,088	—	1,088
Contributions	—	30	30	—	30
Miscellaneous	551	4	555	—	555
Total revenues	$46,036	$3,456	$49,492	$ (157)	$49,335
Expenses:					
General government	1,435	415	1,850	$ (157)	2,089
Public safety	5,400	112	5,512	624	6,136
Public works	4,579	667	5,246	623	5,869
Health and welfare	1,461	634	2,095	239	2,334
Libraries	435	49	484	48	532
Parks and recreation	726	188	914	96	1,010
Education	23,028	1,958	24,986	2,924	27,910
Benefits and pensions	3,793	—	3,793	(3,793)*	—
General insurance	542	—	542	—	542
Depreciation	—	—	—	1,872	1,872
Interest	—	—	—	1,034	1,034
Miscellaneous	619	—	619	—	619
Total expenses	$42,018	$4,023	$46,041	$ 3,906	$49,947
Operating income, government	$ 4,018	$ (567)	$ 3,451	$(4,063)	(612)
Loss, Water Department				(420)	(420)
Net loss					$(1,032)

* 3,793 + 1,000 = 4,793 assigned to programs.

Revised Operating Statement

Exhibit 2 summarizes the changes she made to Exhibit 1 to arrive at an operating statement. (If this type of statement were adopted, the reconciliation to Exhibit 1 would not be shown.) Her operating statement showed a net loss of $1,012,000, compared with the "Excess of revenues over expenditures" of $3,451,000, or the "Excess of revenues and other sources over expenditures and other uses" of $995,000, both numbers being the sum of the amounts in the General and Special Revenue Fund columns in Exhibit 1.

Discussions with Controller

Ms. Dexter explained to the controller what she had done and asked for his comment. He took issue principally with two items, pension expense and depreciation (although Ms. Dexter got the impression that he did not agree with any of the adjustments and refrained from saying so out of politeness).

With respect to pension expense, the controller said that taxpayers should not be asked to finance pension payments that might be made many years in the future. Proper provision should be made for the payments to retirees that were made in the current year, and that was enough.

With respect to depreciation, he said that the retirement of the current year's debt service principal is the amount for which this year's taxpayers should be responsible. Depreciation in excess of this amount would be misleading, especially for assets that have been paid for from other funds such as grants from the federal government. No present or future taxpayer would have to pay for these amounts.

The controller also pointed out that if Douglas did not prepare its reports in accordance with municipal GAAP, it would not receive a Certificate of Compliance from the Municipal Finance Officers Association. He thought that credit rating agencies gave favorable treatment to cities that had this certificate.

Questions

1. Do you agree with Ms. Dexter's decision to eliminate the Debt Service Fund, the Capital Project Fund, and the Special Assessments Fund from the operating statement?
2. Should the amounts for the General and Special Revenue Funds be combined?
3. Should the amount reported as pensions in Exhibit 1 be increased? If so, how should the revised amount be calculated?
4. Should depreciation be recognized, or is the "principal retirement" of Debt Service an adequate substitute? If you favor depreciation, how would you respond to the controller's remark about the unfairness of charging depreciation on assets that were acquired with grants?

5. In your opinion, did the revenues properly associated with the operating activities of 1987 exceed the expenses properly attributable to 1987? That is, did Douglas operate "in the black" or "in the red"?
6. In general, would you prefer an operating statement along the lines of Exhibit 2 to the corresponding report in Exhibit 1, or would you prefer some other alternative?
7. As a member of the finance committee, would you recommend that the City of Douglas prepare an operating statement similar to that in Exhibit 2, even though such a statement would not be in accordance with generally accepted accounting principles for municipalities?

APPENDIX
Basics of Financial Accounting

Every organization needs good records that show what resources it has, where it obtained the funds to acquire these resources, and how it has performed financially. An accounting system collects, summarizes, and reports this information. Its end products are financial statements, which are obtained by summarizing the detailed data that are recorded when an event that has an effect on the organization's financial status occurs or is recognized.

Amounts are recorded in an accounting system according to well-established conventions, which are called *generally accepted accounting principles* (GAAP). This appendix describes the main ideas contained in these principles.[1]

BASIC CONCEPTS

Financial accounting is based on several fundamental concepts. Three of the most important are (1) the accounting entity, (2) money measurement, and (3) double entry.

The Accounting Entity

A set of accounts applies to a single organization, which is called the *accounting entity*. These accounts are for the entity itself; they do not relate to individuals who may control or be employed by the entity. Throughout this description, we shall use as an example the Hollis Day Care Center, a nonprofit entity that has been created by the Hollis Church. The accounting system must record events that affect this entity: not the church, and not the individuals who manage or work in the day-care center.

---

[1] This material is adapted from Robert N. Anthony, *Essentials of Accounting.* Reading, Mass.: Addison Wesley, 1993.

Money Measurement

Accounts are kept in terms of money. The only arithmetic used in accounting is addition and subtraction. You can add one amount to another, or subtract one amount from another, only if the amounts have a common denominator. This denominator is money. You can't add 6 apples and 8 oranges and get a meaningful total, but you can add $2 of apples and $5 of oranges; the $7 total is the dollar amount of fruit. If things are not stated in terms of money, accounting can't record them.

Double Entry

The third concept, double entry, is more complicated. In order to explain it, we introduce the balance sheet, which is one of the reports that is the end product of an accounting system. (It is less important than another report, the operating statement, but the idea of double entry is easier to grasp if we start with the balance sheet.)

THE BALANCE SHEET

A balance sheet shows the financial position of the accounting entity at one moment in time. A balance sheet is therefore always dated "as of" a certain date. A balance sheet as of December 31, 1992 shows the entity's financial position as of the end of 1992. A balance sheet is prepared at least annually, and it can be prepared more frequently. For the purpose of this illustration, we shall prepare a balance sheet daily. The form of the balance sheet is as follows:

**HOLLIS DAY CARE
CENTER**
Balance Sheet
As of December 1

Assets   Liabilities and Equity

Note that the balance sheet has two sides. The left-hand side is called the *asset* side. Amounts listed on that side show the resources owned by the entity. The right-hand side is called the *liabilities and equity* side. Liabilities are amounts provided by outside parties. Equity represents the amount provided by the entity's owners plus the net amount of the entity's earnings since its inception. It also is equal to the difference between assets and liabilities. Its meaning will become clearer as we proceed. An essential feature of a balance sheet is that the totals of the amounts on the two sides are equal; that is, Assets = Liabilities + Equity.

Transactions

Each event that is recorded in the accounting records is called a *transaction*. We shall describe how certain transactions affect the balance sheet.

Borrowing. On December 2, Hollis Day Care Center had its first transaction. It borrowed $10,000 from a bank, signing a promissory note, that is, a legal document in which it promised to repay the $10,000 to the bank at some future date. The entity now has an asset, a valuable resource, of $10,000. The bank has a claim against the assets for $10,000, usually called a *Note Payable*. An outside party that has a claim against the assets is called a *creditor*. The amount of a creditor's claim is a liability. The balance sheet therefore shows the asset, Cash, $10,000 and the liability, Note Payable, also $10,000, and it looks like this:

HOLLIS DAY CARE CENTER
Balance Sheet
As of December 2

Assets		Liabilities and Equity	
Cash	$10,000	Note payable	$10,000
Total assets	$10,000	Total liabilities and equity	$10,000

Using Cash to Purchase Other Assets. On December 3, the entity used $3,000 of its cash to buy supplies. The accounting name for the asset that shows the amount of supplies owned by the entity is *Supplies Inventory*. Its cash therefore decreased by $3,000 and another asset, Supplies Inventory, increased by $3,000. The balance sheet for December 3 is as follows:

HOLLIS DAY CARE CENTER
Balance Sheet
As of December 3

Assets		Liabilities and Equity	
Cash	$ 7,000	Note payable	$10,000
Supplies inventory	3,000		
Total assets	$10,000	Total liabilities and equity	$10,000

Using Cash and Credit to Purchase Assets. On December 4, the entity purchased equipment at a cost of $12,000. It paid $1,000 cash and agreed to pay the supplier $3,000 before the end of December and the remaining $8,000 within three months. An asset, Equipment, increased by $12,000, Cash decreased by $1,000, and the entity now has an additional liability, $11,000, the amount it owes the supplier; this is called *Accounts Payable*. The balance sheet for December 4 is as follows:

HOLLIS DAY CARE CENTER
Balance Sheet
As of December 4

Assets		Liabilities and Equity	
Cash	$ 6,000	Accounts payable	$11,000
Supplies inventory......	3,000	Note payable	10,000
Equipment............	12,000		
Total assets	$21,000	Total liabilities and equity......	$21,000

Revenues. On December 5, parents of students enrolled in the day-care center paid December fees of $5,000. Cash increased by $5,000, but no other asset decreased and no liability increased. The $5,000 therefore must represent an increase in the entity's equity. The entity was better off as a result of this transaction. This transaction contrasts with the one on December 2 in which the entity obtained $10,000 cash but incurred a liability of an equal amount. Increases in equity that are associated with operating activities are called *Revenues*. The balance sheet after this transaction is as follows:

HOLLIS DAY CARE CENTER
Balance Sheet
As of December 5

Assets		Liabilities and Equity	
Cash	$11,000	Accounts payable	$11,000
Supplies inventory......	3,000	Note payable	10,000
Equipment............	12,000	Total liabilities	21,000
		Equity	5,000
Total assets	$26,000	Total liabilities and equity......	26,000

Payment of a Liability. On December 30, the entity paid $3,000 cash to the supplier who furnished the equipment. This resulted in a $3,000 decrease in Cash and an equal decrease in Accounts Payable. The balance sheet after this transaction is as follows:

HOLLIS DAY CARE CENTER
Balance Sheet
As of December 30

Assets		Liabilities and Equity	
Cash	$ 8,000	Accounts payable	$ 8,000
Supplies inventory......	3,000	Note payable	10,000
Equipment............	12,000	Total liabilities	18,000
		Equity	5,000
Total assets	$23,000	Total liabilities and equity......	$23,000

Expenses. During December the entity made the following payments, totaling $3,700: wages ($1,300), rent ($600), utilities ($300), other items ($1,500). This $3,700 was a decrease in cash, but no other asset increased nor did a liability decrease. These transactions therefore must have resulted in a decrease of $3,700 in equity. Decreases in equity that are associated with operating activities are called *Expenses*. The $3,700 of expenses represent a decrease in Cash of $3,700 and a decrease in Equity of $3,700. Assuming that no other transactions occurred in December, the balance sheet as of December 31 is as shown below. (It is labeled before adjustment because we still must make some changes to arrive at the final balance sheet for December 31.)

HOLLIS DAY CARE CENTER
Balance Sheet
As of December 31
(before adjustment)

Assets		Liabilities and Equity	
Cash	$ 4,300	Accounts payable	$ 8,000
Supplies inventory	3,000	Note payable	10,000
Equipment	12,000	Total liabilities	18,000
		Equity	1,300
Total assets	$19,300	Total liabilities and equity	$19,300

Double-Entry Concept

The transactions recorded above illustrate the six types of transactions that affect the balance sheet:

- The December 2 borrowing increased assets and increased liabilities by the same amount.
- The December 3 purchase of assets for cash increased one asset and decreased another asset by the same amount, leaving the total of assets unchanged.
- The December 4 purchase of assets on credit increased one asset, decreased another asset, and increased a liability by the amount of the net change in assets.
- The December 30 payment of a liability decreased an asset and decreased a liability by the same amount.
- Revenues received in cash increased an asset and increased equity by the same amount.
- Expenses paid in cash decreased an asset and decreased equity by the same amount.

Observe the following:

1. Each transaction affected at least two items on the balance sheet. The December 4 transaction affected more than two items.

2. After a transaction was recorded, the total of the assets side of the balance sheet always equaled or balanced the total of the liabilities and equity side. This is why the statement is called a *balance sheet.*

The double-entry concept is that each accounting transaction affects at least two items. After it has been recorded, the total of the left-hand side of the balance sheet continues to equal the total of the right-hand side. There is no exception to this rule; that is, there is no such thing as "single-entry accounting." This principle is stated as the fundamental accounting equation:

$$\text{Assets} = \text{Liabilities} + \text{Equity}$$

BALANCE SHEET CONCEPTS

The balance sheet reports the entity's financial status as of the end of an accounting period. The principal items on the balance sheet are described below.

Assets

Assets are resources that are owned or controlled by an entity. There are two main types of assets: monetary and nonmonetary. The amounts reported for each type are measured in quite different ways.

Monetary Assets. Monetary assets consist of cash and the entity's claims to specified amounts of cash. The amounts that hospitals have billed patients, tuition due from students in a university, or taxes levied on property owners by a municipality are monetary assets. They are called *receivables*. In each case, the entity is entitled to receive a specified amount of money. Cash is reported on the balance sheet as the actual amount on hand and in various bank accounts. Other monetary assets are reported as the amount of cash that is likely to be received. This may be less than the amount owed the entity because some patients (or payers on their behalf) may not pay their hospital bills, some students (or their parents) may not pay their tuition, and some property owners may not pay their taxes. If management decides that not all debtors will pay what they owe, the amount reported on the balance sheet is adjusted downward by an estimate of the amount that will not be collected. This adjustment is called an *Allowance for Bad Debts.*

Nonmonetary Assets. Nonmonetary assets include principally inventory and fixed assets (i.e., long-lived assets such as buildings and equipment). Nonmonetary assets are recorded at the cost of acquiring them. This *cost concept* is the cause of much misunderstanding about accounting numbers; many people think that the amounts reported on the balance sheet represent the value of these assets, but this is not the case. The value of the goods that a drugstore has on its shelves is the amount that the goods can be sold for, but this inventory is not reported at its selling price. Inventory, like other nonmonetary assets, is reported at its cost to the entity; that is, at the amounts paid to acquire the item. Subsequently, as these assets are sold or used by the entity, accounting traces this cost in a way that will be described later on.

Failure to appreciate this point is probably the most common source of misunderstanding about accounting. Accounting does not, except for monetary items, report values; it reports costs. Land acquired many years ago at a cost of $10,000 is reported on this year's balance sheet at $10,000, even though it currently could be sold for, say, $100,000. Thus, the asset side of the balance sheet does not show the entity's worth; it shows the amounts invested in various assets, measured at their cost. Except for contributed assets, a resource that did not cost the entity anything is not an asset. The most valuable resource of a university, for example, is its faculty, but no amount for this resource is reported on the balance sheet because, since the abolition of slavery, no one can legally buy another person. (The university buys the *services* of its faculty, but these are used up as soon as they are acquired, so there is no asset amount remaining to be listed on the balance sheet.)

Readers of a balance sheet would, of course, like to know what the assets are worth; that is, their value. Accounting does not attempt to measure the value of nonmonetary assets since to do so would involve a great deal of estimating and judgment. If the estimates were made by management, they probably would be biased. A system based on costs is much more objective.

Liabilities

The nature of liabilities can be described in either of two ways, both of which are correct. In the *source of resources view*, liabilities report the outside sources from which the entity has obtained the funds used to acquire its assets. The balance sheet shows the amount obtained from each source. When Hollis Day Care Center purchased inventory on credit, the vendor supplied the funds by its willingness not to require cash payment at the time of purchase. By contrast, with the *claims view*, liabilities report the claims of outside parties (i.e., creditors) against the entity's assets. Until paid, the vendor who supplied the inventory has a claim against Hollis Day Care Center's assets.

The amount of the liability is the amount that is owed the creditor as of the balance sheet date. If a bank loans $1,000 to the entity on December 31 to be repaid with interest three months later, the entity eventually must pay the bank $1,000 plus interest; however, as of December 31 the entity's obligation is only the $1,000 because the bank has not earned any interest as of that date. If the $1,000 is still owed on January 31, and if no interest payments have been made, the entity's obligation now is $1,000 *plus* one month of interest. That is, as of January 31, the bank has earned one month's worth of interest.

Equity

The claims view does not apply to the equity section of the balance sheet. The way to think of items in this section is as sources of funds from parties other than creditors. A for-profit corporation obtains funds from two principal sources: contributed capital and net income or earnings. A nonprofit does also, but with some important variations.

Contributed Capital. In a for-profit organization, contributed capital comes from shareholders or stockholders, who hope to receive a return on this investment, either in the form of dividends or by selling the stock at a price higher than the amount they paid. The amount reported as shareholder investment is the amount of funds that they furnished.

Net Income. Net income comes from an entity's own operations. As illustrated by the Hollis Day Care transactions, if an entity has revenues of $5,000 and expenses of $3,700 during an accounting period, it has earned $1,300 from operations. This is its net income, which increases its equity. When a for-profit company pays dividends to its shareholders, its equity is reduced by the amount of these dividends; only the difference between net income and dividends is retained in the entity; this is called *retained earnings*. Retained earnings is the total of the earnings (or net income) for all periods to date less the total of the dividends paid. In a profitable company that does not pay out all earnings as dividends (as is the case with most profitable companies), the amount of retained earnings increases with the passage of time.

Nonprofit Entities. A nonprofit entity does not receive funds from equity investors, nor does it pay dividends. Thus, its operating equity comes entirely from operating activities and is equal to the total net income since its inception. (If the entity has operated at a net loss, it has negative equity.) In a nonprofit entity, net income is often called *surplus* and equity often is called *fund balance*.

Some nonprofit entities receive contributions intended for capital purposes. These contributions are a source of equity capital. However, they are not associated with operating activities, and the funds received ordinarily are not mingled with operating assets. They are therefore excluded from the balance sheet for operating activities and are reported in separate financial statements, which are described in the text. The equity arising from operating activities is often titled with a term such as *operating equity* so as to distinguish it from contributed capital.

ACCRUALS

The transactions for Hollis Day Care Center described above come to the accountant's attention by means of a document of some sort: a bank deposit, a check drawn against the bank account, an invoice from a supplier, and the like. Other transactions that affect the accounts during the period are not represented by documents. In order to find the entity's actual financial position at the end of the accounting period, these transactions must be identified and their effect on balance sheet items must be recognized. These transactions are called *accruals*, and the entries made to recognize their impact on the financial statements are known as *adjusting entries*.

Most adjusting entries are expenses; that is, they represent decreases in equity arising from events that occurred during a particular accounting period. The accountant's job is to determine these events and compute the associated expenses.

Examples of Adjusting Entries

All the December accruals for Hollis Day Care Center are expenses. That is, they are accounting-related events that took place during the month that reduced equity, but for which there is no document. There are four such events:

Consumption of Supplies. Of the $3,000 supplies purchased, records show that only $2,400 was on hand on December 31. Therefore, the supplies inventory decreased by $600. This means that there was an expense of $600 for supplies consumed.

Accrued Wages. Employees earned $300 for work they did in December, but they had not been paid. This is because the pay period did not end on December 31, but in early January instead. Therefore, as of December 31, the entity owed them $300. This is a liability, called *Accrued Wages* or *Wages Payable*. The $300 is an expense and is subtracted from equity.

Recall from the earlier discussion of Hollis Day Care Center that the expense transaction of $3,700 included $1,300 of wages. The presence of $300 of accrued wages means that the total wage expense for the month was $1,600 ($1,300 + $300). Of this, $1,300 had been paid in cash and $300 was owed as of December 31.

Accrued Interest. The bank charged interest for the use of the $10,000 it loaned to the entity, but no interest was paid. Interest is a charge made for the use of money, and it is an expense of the period in which the money was used. If the interest rate is 12 percent, the entity's Interest Expense for December is $100 [($10,000 × 0.12) ÷ 12 months]. This is subtracted from equity. The $100 of unpaid interest is a liability, called *Accrued Interest* or *Interest Payable*. It is owed as of December 31.

Depreciation. Long-lived assets are called *fixed assets*. Except for land, which usually can be used indefinitely, long-lived assets have a limited useful life. A portion of the cost of these assets is an expense in each of the periods in which the asset is used. This portion is called the *depreciation expense* of the period. Most organizations calculate depreciation on the straight-line basis; that is, they calculate the expense in each month as an equal fraction of the asset's life. To calculate depreciation, we must make two estimates: (1) how long we will use the asset (called its *economic life*), and (2) the asset's market value at the end of this period (called its *residual value*).

If we estimate that the economic life of the Hollis Day Care Center equipment is 5 years (60 months), and that its residual value is zero, the depreciation expense for December is 1/60 of its $12,000 cost, or $200. The result is that the asset amount is reduced by $200 and there is a $200 decrease in equity. The depreciation expense for each accounting period accumulates on the asset side of the balance sheet, resulting in an accumulated depreciation figure. At any given time, the book value of the asset (as contrasted with its market value) is its original cost less whatever depreciation has accumulated.

BALANCE SHEET FORMAT

The effect of these adjusting entries is shown on the following balance sheet:

HOLLIS DAY CARE CENTER
Balance Sheet
As of December 31

Assets			Liabilities and Equity	
Cash..................		$ 4,300	Accounts payable	$ 8,000
Supplies inventory		2,400	Wages payable................	300
Equipment: Cost........	$12,000		Interest payable..............	100
Less: Accumulated				
depreciation	200	11,800	Note payable	10,000
			Total liabilities	18,400
			Operating equity	100
Total assets............		$18,500	Total liabilities and equity......	$18,500

Note that the new operating equity amount is the result of a beginning amount of $1,300 on the balance sheet before adjustment, less supply expenses ($600), accrued wage expense ($300), interest expense ($100), and depreciation expense ($200). Of these $1,200 in additional expenses, none has affected cash. Each has resulted in either (a) a decrease in an asset or (b) an increase in a liability.

This balance sheet shows assets on the left side and liabilities and equity on the right side. Alternatively, the same information can be given by listing the liabilities and equity items beneath the assets. This format is often easier to fit on a page.

Assets.   Assets are listed according to their nearness to cash; that is, the likelihood that they will be used up. Cash itself is always the first item. Supplies Inventory will probably be used up in a few months, so it is listed next.

For most items, only a single amount is shown. However, for equipment and other depreciable items, it is customary to list the cost of the item and subtract from it the amount of depreciation accumulated to date. The net amount, $11,800 in this case, is the *net book value* of the item. At the end of January, an additional $200 of depreciation would be added, making the accumulated depreciation $400; the net book value would then be $11,600. At the end of February the net book value would be $11,400, and so forth. Each time accumulated depreciation increases, the net book value of the asset decreases. Operating equity also decreases by this depreciation expense, which is what keeps the two sides of the balance sheet equal.

Liabilities. On the right-hand side, the liability items are also listed in approximate order of their nearness to cash; that is, those that will require cash payments in the near future (here, the first three items) are listed ahead of those that will not be paid until later. The liability for interest payable is listed separately from the liability for the $10,000 owed to the bank, which will presumably not be paid until later in the future.

Working Capital. Although not shown on the above statement, most balance sheets show current assets separately from other assets, and current liabilities separately from other liabilities. Current assets are cash and items that are expected to be used up or turned into cash within one year. Current liabilities are those items that will be paid in cash within one year. In the preceding balance sheet, Cash and Supplies Inventory are current assets, and all liabilities except the Note Payable are current liabilities. The difference between current assets and current liabilities is called *working capital*.

MEASUREMENT OF INCOME AND THE OPERATING STATEMENT

The Hollis Day Care Center's equity was zero at the beginning of December, and it was $100 at the end of December. It therefore increased by $100 during December. This was the net financial effect of its activities during December. Users of financial statements are interested in the causes of this increase. A second financial statement, called the *income statement* or *operating statement*, lists these causes. Since revenues are increases in equity and expenses are decreases, the operating statement lists all revenues and expenses.

In our simple illustration, we entered revenues and expenses directly to the equity item on the balance sheet. In actual practice an account would be set up for each item. The December operating statement would be prepared from these revenue and expense accounts. It would look as follows:

HOLLIS DAY CARE CENTER
Operating Statement for December

Revenues:		
Fees from parents......		$5,000
Expenses:		
Wages	$1,600	
Rent	600	
Utilities	300	
Supplies..............	600	
Interest	100	
Depreciation...........	200	
Other expenses	1,500	
Total expenses.........		4,900
Net income............		$ 100

The difference between revenues and expenses, or net income, is the net income for the period. It is literally the *bottom line* that is so often referred to. The operating statement describes the reasons for the $100 change in equity during the period.

In December, the first month, net income equals the equity as of December 31. This would not be true in subsequent months. In January, for example, the operating statement would report only the changes in equity that occurred in January. Thus, if net income for January were, say, $150, operating equity as of January 31 would be $250 ($100 from December plus $150 from January).

Note that the operating statement reports activities for a period of time, such as the month of December, whereas the balance sheet reports financial condition as of a moment in time, the close of business on December 31. Note also that the amount of net income is not related to changes in Cash. During December, cash decreased from $10,000 (as shown on the initial balance sheet prepared December 2) to $4,300 on December 31, a decrease of $5,700, but equity increased by $100.

There are two general reasons for the difference: (1) cash was used for purposes that were unrelated to changes in equity, such as the purchase of supplies, only part of which were consumed in the month; and (2) the adjusting entries affected equity but did not affect cash. Although some entities use an accounting system that records only cash receipts and cash disbursements, such a system will not tell what has happened to equity unless cash receipts in a period were approximately the same as revenues, and cash payments were approximately the same as expenses. A third statement, called the *statement of cash flows*, describes the reasons for the change in cash during an accounting period. This will be discussed later.

Income Measurement Concepts

The measurement of net income for a period is governed by certain concepts that are described briefly below. These are the matching concept, the realization concept, the conservatism concept, the consistency concept, and the materiality concept.

Matching Concept. The matching concept requires that if a given event affects both expenses and revenues, both the revenue transaction and the expense transaction are recorded in the same period. If, for example, Hollis bought some vitamin supplements in January at a cost of $60, and sold them to parents in February for $100, both the $100 revenue and the $60 expense would be reported on the February operating statement. As of January 31, the $60 paid for the vitamins would be an asset, Inventory. The expense occurs at the same time the vitamins are sold (i.e., it is matched with the related revenue).

The matching concept also requires that assets become expenses in the period in which they provide service. If fuel oil was purchased in January for $800, and if $200 of this oil was burned in January, $500 in February, and $100 in March, then the January expense would be $200 (not $800), the February expense would be $500, and the March expense would be $100. The asset, Fuel Oil Inventory, would be $600 as of January 31 and $100 as of February 28. The related computations are shown below:

Month	Event	Change in Asset	Change in Expense	Change in Cash
January	Purchase fuel oil	+800	0	−800
	Use fuel oil	−200	+200	0
February...	Use fuel oil	−500	+500	0
March	Use fuel oil	−100	+600	0

The same concept applies to equipment and other long-lived assets: a fraction of their cost becomes an expense in each period in which they provide service. As indicated above, the mechanism for doing this is called *depreciation*. The Hollis equipment was expected to provide service for 60 months, so 1/60 of its cost was depreciation expense in each of those months. Note especially that depreciation has nothing whatsoever to do with changes in the *value* of the asset; it is the accountant's way of writing off the asset's cost.

Finally, the matching concept requires that if the entity learns that an asset will not provide service in a future period, it is recorded as an expense of the current period. If in April, the management at Hollis discovers that some of the inventory has been damaged or lost, the amount is an April expense. Similarly, if equipment is destroyed by fire, its net book value is an expense in the period in which this happened, even though its remaining life may have been many months.

Realization Concept.   The realization concept has two aspects, one relating to when revenues are recognized, and the other to how much is to be recorded as revenues. With regard to the first, revenues are recognized in the period in which goods are delivered to the buyer or in which services are rendered. Thus, the fees that Hollis Day Care Center received from parents for taking care of their children in December are December revenues. If a parent paid ahead of time, such as paying for January's day care in December, the amount would not be considered revenue. Instead, it would be a liability, Precollected Revenue (or Unearned Revenue), in December; it would become revenue in January, the month to which it applied. Conversely, if a child attended the center in December, but the parent didn't pay until January, the revenue would still be recorded in December, with a corresponding entry to an asset, Accounts Receivable. When the parent paid in January, the increase in cash would be accompanied by a decrease in Accounts Receivable. January revenue would not be affected by this payment.

The amount recognized as revenue is the amount that is reasonably certain to be realized. If after building up its experience, Hollis decides that 5 percent of the money due from parents each month is never going to be collected, it reduces its revenue by 5 percent of the amount due. It does this by creating an expense called *Bad Debt Expense*. Gross Revenue, reduced by the Bad Debt Expense, becomes Net Revenue. Net Revenue is the amount the entity expects to actually collect.

Conservatism Concept.   Revenues are recognized only to the extent that they are reasonably certain, but expenses (including losses) are recognized as soon as their existence is reasonably possible. At one time this conservatism concept was stated as: "Anticipate no revenues, but provide for all losses." As a practical matter, such a rule is unrealistic. One never knows for sure that accounts receivable will be paid, but to ignore fees until the period in which the cash is received would understate the entity's performance in earlier periods. In fact, most clients will pay their bills. Similarly, to try to anticipate all possible losses would overstate expenses because many of the things that could happen are in fact not going to happen.

Consistency Concept.   The same accounting practices are used from one period to another, unless there is strong reason to change them. Without this consistency concept, comparisons of the current operating statement with those of past periods would be unreliable.

Materiality Concept.   Trivial matters are disregarded, but all important matters are disclosed. In the illustration given above, supplies were held in inventory until they were consumed. Many entities would record them as expenses when they were purchased on the grounds that the bookkeeping effort required to keep track of them would not be worthwhile. Utility bills are usually recorded as expenses of the month in which they are paid, even though they are bills for services rendered in the previous month. Conversely, the accountant is obligated to account for all events that have a significant effect on items on the operating statement and/or the balance sheet. Decisions about materiality frequently are a matter of judgment.

STATEMENT OF CASH FLOWS

In addition to the balance sheet and operating statement, general-purpose financial reports include a third statement called the *statement of cash flows (SCF)*. The SCF is prepared by rearranging information taken from the balance sheet and operating statement. It does not involve the collection of material in the accounts as is the case with the other two statements.

The SCF reports on the sources of cash that flowed into the entity during the period and the uses to which this cash was put. Prior to 1987, entities were permitted considerable latitude in determining the format of this statement. In 1987, the Financial Accounting Standards Board issued a standard that reduced this latitude considerably. As of 1987, entities are required to separate their sources and uses of cash into three categories: operating activities, investing activities, and financing activities. A SCF for Hollis Day Care Center for the month of December is shown below.

HOLLIS DAY CARE CENTER
Statement of Cash Flows for December

Cash generated from (for) operations:		
Cash received from clients		$ 5,000
Cash paid to vendors	$(5,400)	
Cash paid to employees	(1,300)	(6,700)
Net cash from operations....................		$(1,700)
Cash generated from (used by) investing activities:		
Purchase of equipment......................		(12,000)
Cash generated from (used by) financing activities:		
Loan from equipment supplier	$11,000	
Payment on loan to equipment...............	(3,000)	
Loan from bank ....:.......................	10,000	
Net cash from financing.....................		18,000
Net change in cash		$ 4,300
Plus: Beginning cash balance		0
Equals: Ending cash balance..................		$ 4,300

The $5,400 paid to vendors includes the $600 for rent, the $300 for utilities, the $1,500 for other expenses, and the $3,000 used to acquire the inventory. Thus, while the operating statement shows the supply expense associated with *consuming* $600 of inventory, the SCF shows the cash paid to *acquire* the inventory, regardless of how much was consumed. Also, the SCF shows only the cash paid to employees, not the accrued wages. The SCF excludes depreciation (a noncash item), showing instead the amount spent to acquire the equipment. It also distinguishes between the acquisition cost of the equipment and the amount financed by the loan from the supplier. Finally, it includes the cash received from the bank, but excludes the interest (since it has been accrued but not paid).

SUMMARY

Two of the concepts described in this appendix that give beginning students the most trouble are the cost concept and the matching concept. We therefore review them as part of our concluding comments.

Cost Concept

Accounting records an asset at its cost to the entity at the time of acquisition, and ordinarily holds the asset at its acquisition cost (also called its *historical cost*) until it becomes an expense. (In the case of long-lived assets, the transformation of an asset to an expense occurs via depreciation and may take place over many future periods.) There is a natural tendency to believe that assets should be reported on the balance sheet at their market values but this is not the case. Accounting uses costs rather than market value because changes in asset values are subjective; two people might have quite different opinions as to the market value.

Matching Concept

The other concept that frequently is difficult to understand is the matching concept, particularly the matching of expenses to the proper accounting period. When an entity acquires an asset, it makes an expenditure, either by paying cash or incurring a liability. Unless the transaction is carefully analyzed, there is a tendency to think that the acquisition has reduced equity; when in fact it was associated either with a decrease in cash or an increase in a liability. As the illustrations given earlier show, if the asset was not *consumed* in the current period, there was no expense in that period.

All expenditures result in assets at the moment they are made. If the asset is labor or other services that become an expense immediately, or if it is a supply that is consumed in the current period, the expenditure becomes an expense in the current period. If the asset is not consumed in the current period, it remains as an asset at the end of the period, and becomes an expense in one or more future periods. In short, all expenditures are assets initially, even if only for a moment. If they are on hand at the end of the period, they continue to be assets. When they are consumed, they become expenses.

Finally, accounting deals with events that can be expressed in monetary amounts. Every such event changes two or more items on the balance sheet. If the event affects equity, it is also reported on the operating statement. Although the brief description given above provides a way of accounting for such events, there are many complications. These complications include: *(a)* detailed rules for certain types of transactions, *(b)* generally accepted terms for many items in addition to those given here, and *(c)* practices for applying the general principles that differ across industries and among entities within a given industry. Moreover, accounting cannot report all important things about an entity. It cannot report the quality of the education that a college provides or the quality of the music furnished by an orchestra, for example, because quality cannot be measured in monetary terms.

CASE 3A–1   Brookstone Ob-Gyn Associates (A)*

In January 1991, Dr. Mark Amsted, chair of the Department of Obstetrics and Gynecology at Brookstone Medical School, chief of Ob-Gyn at Brookstone Medical Center, and president of Brookstone Ob-Gyn Associates (BOGA), was preparing for a meeting with the Harris National Bank. He planned to present a request for a $300,000 line of credit, the approval of which was critical to the BOGA's continued operations. He had discussed the need for the line of credit with the dean of the medical school, and had obtained the dean's approval to make the request to the bank, but he was by no means certain that the bank would agree to the loan. A great deal depended upon the bank's reaction to the financial information that he and his business manager, Randy Weber, planned to present.

Background

BOGA was a faculty practice plan comprised of university faculty physicians in obstetrics and gynecology (Ob-Gyn). All BOGA physicians were on the staff of Brookstone Medical Center (BMC), one of the city's major teaching hospitals. The hospital was affiliated with the Brookstone Medical School, and all of BOGA's physicians also held faculty appointments in the medical school.

BOGA had been organized several years earlier as a nonprofit educational trust. Initially, its offices had been located in the hospital, and it had grown slowly. During its first few years of existence, BOGA's physicians saw mainly medicaid, medicare, and self-pay (or uninsured) patients in the hospital's outpatient department.

In the mid- to late-1980s, many local Ob-Gyn specialists discontinued their obstetrics practices because of high malpractice insurance premiums. At about that time, Brookstone Medical Center began to experience declining Ob-Gyn admissions due to competition from some nearby community hospitals. As a result of these forces, BMC offered to contribute $1 million to BOGA if it would open a new suite of offices in a nearby office building. The idea was to make

---

* This case was prepared by Professor David W. Young. Copyright © by David W. Young.

BOGA's facilities more attractive to patients with private insurance. The medical center hoped these patients would use its services. If the idea worked, BMC would reverse the declining trend in its Ob-Gyn admissions, and would do so with fully insured patients. After discussing BMC's proposal with his colleagues, Dr. Amsted agreed to accept the offer.

Dr. Amsted supplemented the $1 million contribution from the medical center with a $630,000 long-term note from the Harris National Bank. The funds were used to purchase new medical and office equipment, renovate the space, and furnish the offices in the new facility.

The surrounding community responded positively to BOGA's move. The reputation of BOGA's physicians and the attractiveness of the new facilities led to increases in the number of private insurance patients treated. In both 1989 and 1990, revenue increased by some 20 percent over the previous year.

Problems

Despite the growth in revenues, BOGA's profitability was becoming an issue. Indeed, as he began to prepare for his meeting with the bank, Dr. Amsted was quite perplexed. He commented:

> It's crazy. Despite our rapid rate of growth, we're losing money. I don't understand why. Our salaries are competitive, and our physicians see as many patients per hour as Ob-Gyn physicians in other places. Our scheduling is good, so we don't have a lot of downtime. All our other costs seem quite reasonable. Yet, the figures speak for themselves. In 1990, we lost $850,000!
>
> According to Mr. Weber, if we don't get the line of credit from the bank, we won't be able to meet some of our payroll and other expenses next month. Even if the bank gives us the loan, I'm sure they'll ask me to either cut expenses or increase our charges so we'll be profitable. The problem is that the charges are restricted by our third parties, and I can see no place to cut expenses other than by laying people off. I'm reluctant to do that, though, since everyone seems somewhat overworked.

Modified Cash Accounting

BOGA used what was called a *modified cash form of accounting*. Under this system, with only one exception, revenue is recorded when cash is received, and expenses are reported when cash is paid out. The exception is equipment and other fixed assets, where the cash payment associated with a purchase is not treated as an expense. Rather, because each asset has a relatively long service life (usually 5 to 10 years for equipment), an annual depreciation figure is computed by dividing the cost of the equipment by its estimated service life. This depreciation figure is shown as an expense on the operating statement even though it is not represented by an actual cash payment (the cash payment is made when the equipment is purchased).

Exhibit 1 contains financial information for BOGA's 1990 operations. As it

EXHIBIT 1

BROOKSTONE OB–GYN ASSOCIATES (A)
1990 Financial Information
($000)

TABLE A   1990 Operating Statement
Modified Cash Basis

Revenue:	
Receipts from patients and third parties	$3,895.4
Expenses:	
Physician payments	$1,124.0
Administrative salaries.	684.0
Benefits	293.2
Medical supplies	95.2
Rent and utilities	436.0
Billing/collection fees (*a*) . . .	507.8
Equipment depreciation. . . .	24.0
Office expense	50.0
Liability insurance (*b*)	952.2
Contracted services	106.0
Other	45.0
Contribution to Dean (*c*) . . .	428.5
Total expenses.	$4,745.9
Surplus (deficit)	$ (850.5)

TABLE B   Account balances
As of 31 December 1990

Cash.	$ 110.0
Medical supply inventory	125.0
Prepaid insurance	250.0
Equipment (net).	1,250.0
Accounts payable	75.0
Payable to Dean	130.1
Long-term note payable.	630.0

TABLE C   1990 Accounts Receivable Activity

	Billings	Receipts
January	$ 423.2	199.9
February.	437.8	222.1
March	453.4	246.8
April	470.2	274.2
May	488.3	304.7
June	507.8	338.6
July	529.0	350.2
August.	552.0	362.7
September	577.1	376.2
October.	604.6	390.6
November	636.3	406.2
December.	668.2	423.2
Total	$6,347.9	$3,895.4

TABLE D   Accounts Receivable Activity for 1990

Beginning balance.		$ 648.4
Billings	$6,347.9	
Less: expected allowances and bad debts (*d*)	1,269.6	
Equals: net revenue		5,078.3
Subtotal		5,726.7
Less: actual collections (*e*).		3,895.4
Equals ending balance		$1,831.3

Notes:
a. 8 percent of billings.
b. Computed on a per-physician basis. 15 percent of billings is used here as an approximation.
c. 11 percent of collections.
d. Allowances and bad debts are expected to be 20 percent of billings.
e. Collections come with a five-month time lag from when the patient was billed.
Example: January billings = $423.2. Expected collections are 423.2 − (.2 × 423.2) = $338.6. In June (five months later) $338.6 is received.

shows (Table C), although BOGA billed patients for $6.3 million, it received only $3.9 million in cash during the year. The difference, less Mr. Weber's estimate of $1.3 million of contractual allowances and bad debts on the $6.3 million, went into its accounts receivable. Accounts receivable grew from $648,400 at the beginning of 1990 to $1.8 million as of the end of 1990 (Table D).

Exhibit 1 also shows BOGA's operating statement for 1990 (Table A). With revenue of $3.9 million and expenses of $4.7 million, BOGA's operating deficit slightly exceeded $850,000 for the year.

Accrual Accounting

Alice Tanshel, the Harris Bank's lending officer, had asked Dr. Amsted to come to the meeting with a set of financial statements prepared on both a modified cash *and* an accrual basis. In accrual accounting, revenue is recognized when it is earned (usually when the bill is sent out) rather than when the cash is collected, and expenses are recorded when they are incurred, rather than when the associated cash is paid out.

The main difference between the two approaches for BOGA was in the amount of revenue. The switch to an accrual basis would require Mr. Weber and BOGA's accountants to record revenue when services were delivered to a patient, rather than when cash was received. Because of this, Mr. Weber needed to estimate the portion of revenue that would not be collected. Contractual allowances and adjustments by third-party payers, as well as the fact that some patients would never pay their bills, meant that not all revenue that was billed actually would be received in cash. This was not a problem with the modified cash basis, since cash payments and revenue were the same. However, the switch to full accrual required Mr. Weber to make estimates of the allowances and bad debts. "Net revenue" was the difference between billings and these estimates.

Mr. Weber commented on the task that lay before him:

I remember learning about accrual accounting in school. Even then, it wasn't clear to me why it's advantageous to use it. With the modified cash system, life is quite simple. When we get a check, we've earned revenue. We don't have to worry about estimating bad debts formally, we just need to know about how much of our receivables we can expect to collect. When we pay out cash, except for equipment, we have an expense. What could be easier to understand?

Preparing a set of accrual statements is going to be a nightmare. I've spoken with our accountants, and they tell me that to prepare the statements for the bank, I'm going to have to estimate more than just revenues. Inventory, for example. Under the modified cash system, when we buy some medical supplies, we have an immediate expense. With the accrual system, we need to create an inventory, and we only incur an expense when we use an item, rather than when we buy it. Insurance is just like inventory. With an accrual system, we record the expense when we use the insurance, not when we pay the premium to the insurance company. That's a bit of a complication since we pay our premiums for several months in advance; it leads to what the accountants call a Prepaid Insurance account.

Accounts payable is just the opposite. Our vendors let us charge our supply purchases. Under the modified cash system we incur an expense when we pay a vendor. Not with the accrual system. But this is really tricky. When we buy some medical supplies, the goods go into inventory, and, as I said, we incur an expense when we use the inventory. But this means we can incur an expense even if we haven't paid the vendor yet. This is not just complex; it's *layers* of complexity!

Finally, the accountants tell me that after we've deducted our estimates of allowances and bad debts from billings, we owe the Dean 11 percent of this *net revenue,* as they call it. Although the Dean doesn't ask us to pay him until we receive the cash, the accountants tell me that we need to keep track of the difference. Let me give you an example. During 1990, our net revenue was $5,078,300 [see Table D of Exhibit 1]. At the 11 percent rate, we owed the Dean $558,600. By contrast, on a modified cash basis, we owed (and paid) the Dean $428,500, or 11 percent of our $3,895,400 in cash receipts [see Table A in Exhibit 1]. That's a difference of $130,100. The accountants tell me that this amount is a liability — we owe it to the Dean. Even though we don't have to pay him until we collect the cash, we still have to show the liability on our balance sheet.

PREPARING FOR THE MEETING

To prepare for the meeting with the bank, Dr. Amsted asked Mr. Weber to construct both an operating statement and a balance sheet using the accrual method. The operating statement would be for the entire 1990 calendar year, and the balance sheet would be as of December 31, 1990.

The accountants had provided Mr. Weber with a worksheet (Exhibit 2) to use in preparing the two statements. They also had given him their assessment of some of the account balances as of December 31. These are shown in Table B of Exhibit 1. With this information in hand, Mr. Weber began to prepare a set of financial statements on an accrual basis.

Questions

1. Using the accrual system, prepare an operating statement for 1990 and a balance sheet as of December 31, 1990 for BOGA. What do these statements tell you about BOGA's profitability?
2. In the absence of the bank's stipulation that accrual be used, which type of system — modified cash or accrual — would you recommend that Dr. Amsted use for BOGA? Why?

EXHIBIT 2

BROOKSTONE OB/GYN ASSOCIATES (A)
Worksheet (Accrual Basis)
($000)

Operating Statement	For Calendar Year 1990	Notes
Revenue:		
Professional services		Same as billings
Less: allowances and bad		
debts. . . . ./. . .		20 percent of billings
Net revenue		
Expenses:		
Physician payments		Same as on modified cash
Administrative wages		Same as on modified cash
Benefits		Same as on modified cash
Medical supplies		Same as on modified cash (assumes purchases = uses)
Rent and utilities		Same as on modified cash
Billing/collection fees		Same as on modified cash
Equipment depreciation . . .		Same as on modified cash
Office expense		Same as on modified cash
Liability insurance.		Same as on modified cash (assumes purchases = uses)
Contracted services		Same as on modified cash
Other		Same as on modified cash
Contribution to Dean		11 percent of net revenue
Total expenses		
Surplus (Deficit)		

Balance Sheet	As of December 31, 1990	Notes
Assets:		
Cash.		Given
Accounts receivable		Given
Medical supply inventory .		Given
Prepaid insurance		Given
Total current assets		
Equipment (net).		Given
Total assets.		
Liabilities and Equity:		
Liabilities:		
Bank loan (line of		
credit)		Not needed as of end of 1990
Accounts payable		Given
Payable to Dean.		Given
Total current liabilities		
Note payable		Given
Equity:		
Start-up contribution. . . .		Given
Retained surpluses		To be calculated
Total liability + fund balance		

CASE 3A–2   Early Years Day Care Center*

After six months of operations, Frances Nissen wanted to analyze the performance of Early Years Day Care Center, a nonprofit corporation. She wanted to know where the company stood as of December 31, 1986, and what its future prospects were.

Early Years Day Care Center was organized by Ms. Nissen early in 1986 to provide supervised care, preschool education, a snack, and a noonday meal, primarily for children of working mothers. For its initial capital, Ms. Nissen took out a $24,000 mortgage on her own house. She loaned $21,000 of this to the center. Friends of hers loaned $11,000 in cash. A government agency made a one-year loan of $6,500 to the center.

With these funds, the center purchased property for $40,000 of which $8,000 was for land and $32,000 was for a building on the land. The purchase was financed in part with a $27,000 mortgage, the remainder being paid in cash. Interest on the mortgage was to be paid quarterly, but no principal repayment was required until the company had become established. The center also purchased $13,200 of furniture and equipment for cash.

During the first six months of operations, which ended December 31, 1986, the center paid out the following additional amounts in cash:

Salary* to Ms. Nissen	$ 8,000
Salaries* of part-time employees......	5,120
Insurance	1,340
Utilities	1,019
Food and supplies..................	4,370
Interest and miscellaneous	3,642
Total paid out................	$23,491

* Includes payroll taxes

The center received $16,880 of fees in cash. In addition, it was owed $600 of fees from parents. As of December 31, 1986, Ms. Nissen estimated that $320 of supplies were still on hand. The center owed food suppliers $520.

In thinking about the future, Ms. Nissen estimated that for the next six months, ending June 30, student fees received (in addition to the $600 of fees that applied to the first six months) would be $25,600. This was higher than the amount for the first six months because enrollments were higher.

She estimated that the center would pay $13,120 of salaries; $1,280 cash for utilities (which was higher than the first six months because of expected colder

---

* This case was prepared by Professor James S. Reece, Graduate School of Business Administration, University of Michigan. Copyright © by Osceola Institute.

weather); $5,600 for additional food and supplies (higher because of the higher enrollment); and $2,720 for interest and miscellaneous (lower than the first six months because certain start-up costs were paid for during the first six months). She also expected to pay back the government loan.

She estimated that food and supplies on hand as of June 30 would be $320, and that nothing would be owed suppliers. She did not include any additional amounts for insurance because the amounts paid in the first six months covered these costs for the whole year.

She knew that many companies recorded depreciation on buildings, furniture, and equipment; however, she had a firm offer of $56,000 cash for these assets from someone who wanted to buy the center, so she thought that under these circumstances depreciation was inappropriate.

Questions

1. Prepare a balance sheet for Early Years Day Care Center as of December 31, 1986. (In order to minimize errors, it is suggested that you treat each event separately; show the items that are affected and the amount of increase or decrease in each item. For events that affect equity, increase or decrease the item "Equity." This item will have a minus amount, which should be indicated by enclosing it in parentheses. Show noncurrent assets at their original cost.)
2. Prepare another balance sheet as of June 30, 1987.
3. Prepare an operating statement for the periods June 1986–December 31, 1986, and January 1, 1987–June 30, 1987. How do these relate to the two balance sheets you have prepared?
4. Should the noncurrent assets be reported on the June 30, 1987, balance sheet at their cost, at $56,000, or at some other amount (the amount need not be calculated)? If at some amount other than cost, how would the balance sheet prepared in Question 1 be changed?
5. Does it appear likely that Early Years Day Care Center will become a viable entity? That is, is it likely to be financially solvent if Ms. Nissen's estimates are correct?

CASE 3A–3   National Helontological Association*

Each December the incoming members of the board of directors of the National Helontological Association (NHA) met in joint session with the outgoing board as a means of smoothing the transition from one administration to another. At the meeting in December 1987, questions were raised about whether the 1987 board had adhered to the general policy of the association. The ensuing discussion became quite heated.

---

* This case was prepared by Professor Robert N. Anthony. Copyright © by Osceola Institute.

EXHIBIT 1

NATIONAL HELONTOLOGICAL ASSOCIATION
Estimated Income Statement
1987

Revenues:

Membership dues	$198,500
Journal subscriptions	22,000
Publication sales	8,000
Foundation grant	30,000
Profit, 1986 annual meeting	4,261
Total revenues	$262,761

Expenses:

Printing and mailing publications	$ 64,200
Committee meeting expenses	28,200
Annual meeting advance	8,000
Purchase of computer..................	18,000
Administrative salaries and expense	116,840
Miscellaneous........................	21,000
Total expenses......................	$256,240
Excess of revenues over expenses	$ 6,521

NHA was a nonprofit professional association whose 3,000 members were experts in helontology,[1] a specialized branch of engineering. The association represented the interests of its members before congressional committees and various scientific bodies, published two professional journals, arranged an annual meeting and several regional meetings, and appointed committees that developed positions on various topics of interest to the membership.

The operating activities of the association were managed by George Tremble, its executive secretary. Mr. Tremble reported to the board of directors. The board consisted of four officers and seven other members. Six members of the 1988 board (i.e., the board that assumed responsibility on January 1, 1988) were also on the 1987 board; the other five members were newly elected. The president served a one-year term.

The financial policy of the association was that each year should "stand on its own feet"; that is, expenses of the year should approximately equal the revenues of the year. At the meeting in December 1987, Mr. Tremble presented an estimated income statement for 1987 (Exhibit 1). Although some of the December transactions were necessarily estimated, Mr. Tremble assured the board that the actual totals for the year would closely approximate the numbers shown.

Wilma Fosdick, one of the newly elected board members, raised a question about the foundation grant of $30,000. She questioned whether this item should be counted as revenue. If it were excluded, there was a deficit, and this showed that

---

[1] Disguised name.

the 1987 board had, in effect, eaten into reserves and thus made it more difficult to provide the level of service that the members had a right to expect in 1988. This led to detailed questions about items on the income statement, which brought forth the following information from Mr. Tremble:

1. In 1987, NHA received a $30,000 cash grant from the Workwood Foundation for the purpose of financing a symposium to be held in June 1988. During 1987 approximately $1,000 was spent in preliminary planning for this symposium and was included in the item, "Committee meeting expenses." When asked why the $30,000 had been recorded as revenue in 1987 rather than in 1988, Mr. Tremble said that the grant was obtained entirely by the initiative and persuasiveness of the 1987 president, so 1987 should be given credit for it. Further, although the grant was intended to finance the symposium, there was no legal requirement that the symposium be held; if for any reason it was not held, the money would be used for the general operations of the association.

2. In early December 1987 the association took delivery of, and paid for, a new computer costing $18,000. It would be put into operation early in 1988. Except for this new machine, the typewriters, desks, and other equipment in the association office were quite old.

3. Ordinarily, members paid their dues during the first few months of the year. Because of the need to raise cash to finance the purchase of the new computer, in September 1987 the association announced that members who paid their 1988 dues before December 15, 1987, would receive a free copy of the book which contained papers presented at the special symposium to be held in June 1988. The approximate per-copy cost of publishing this book was expected to be $6, and it was expected to be sold for $10. Consequently, $21,000 of 1988 dues were received by December 15, 1987.

4. In July 1987 the association sent to members a membership directory. Its long-standing practice was to publish such a directory every two years. The cost of preparing and printing this directory was $8,000. Of the 4,000 copies printed, 3,000 were mailed to members in 1987. The remaining 1,000 were held to meet the needs of new members who would join before the next directory came out; they would receive a free copy of the directory when they joined.

5. Members received the association's journals at no extra cost, as a part of their membership privileges. Some libraries and other nonmembers also subscribed to the journals. The $22,000 reported as subscription revenue was the cash received in 1987. Of this amount about $6,000 was for journals that would be delivered in 1988. Offsetting this was $2,000 of subscription revenue received in 1986 for journals delivered in 1987; this $2,000 had been reported as 1986 revenue.

6. The association had advanced $5,000 to the committee responsible for planning the 1987 annual meeting held in late November. This amount was used for preliminary expenses. Registration fees at the annual meeting were set so as to cover all convention costs, and it was expected that the $5,000, plus any profit, would be returned to the association after the committee had finished paying

the convention bills. The 1986 convention had resulted in a $4,261 profit, but the results of the 1987 convention were not known, although the attendance was about as anticipated.

Question

Did the association have a surplus or a deficit in 1987?

CASE 3A–4   Gotham Meals on Wheels*

"We're a success!" exclaimed Ethan McCall, executive director of Gotham Meals on Wheels, upon seeing that his March surplus had reached $2,000. "And if our projections for the next six months are accurate, we'll have earned enough to rent facilities in Newburytown and double our service area. My only concern is whether we'll have the cash on hand to do so."

With that, Mr. McCall set about predicting how his cash would change in accordance with his projected growth in volume of activity. Although March had been a good month, cash had been falling since December, and he was concerned about making sure he had enough on hand to purchase supplies and meet payroll for the remainder of the year.

Background

Gotham Meals on Wheels was a nonprofit agency that specialized in preparing and delivering nutritious yet appetizing meals to home-bound people. Its clientele included many elderly individuals plus victims of AIDS who, because of the debilitating nature of their disease, were unable to leave their homes, and did not have enough strength to prepare their own meals. Convinced that there was a large market for a specialized meal service, and supported by a $25,000 grant from a local foundation, the agency had begun operations in early October.

In order to assure that it wouldn't run short during any given month, the agency prepared its meals one month in advance and froze them. By basing production on the following month's anticipated sales, the agency had found that it could assure its clients of uninterrupted service. All the costs associated with these meals were paid in the month in which production took place.

Another advantage of freezing the meals was that they could be delivered in bulk to each client. The meals were easily stored in the freezing compartments of clients' refrigerators. From the agency's perspective, freezing the meals and de-

---

* This case was prepared by Professor David W. Young. Copyright © by David W. Young.

livering several of them at a time had allowed it to keep its transportation costs at a minimum. Clients seemed to have no complaints about the food being frozen, and many, in fact, had written Mr. McCall to tell him how much they enjoyed the meals.

Sales Results

November sales had been 325 meals, and December sales had been 450 meals. Mr. McCall had expected that 500 meals would be sold in January, and that sales would increase by 250 meals per month after that through the end of the year. Thus, by May, sales would be 1,500 meals, and by September they would reach 2,500 meals. His exuberance expressed in the first paragraph was because sales for January through March had been on target, and 1,250 meals had been produced and frozen for delivery in April.

Because of the relatively low volume of sales, the first two months had been somewhat difficult, and the agency had run small deficits in both October and November. But in December it had earned a surplus that was enough to erase the October and November deficits. The balance sheet as of December 31 is shown in Exhibit 1.

Financial Data

The ingredients and labor needed to produce each meal cost the agency $7.00. In addition, the agency incurred some monthly administrative costs, such as rent, that were not directly associated with the meals. These costs had grown from only $300 in October, when Mr. McCall had used his own home to produce and freeze the November meals, to $1,400 in November and December, and $1,600 in January. In February and March, they had reached $2,000, and were expected to remain at that level for the rest of the year. These monthly costs were incurred whether the agency sold any meals at all, whereas the $7.00 per meal was incurred only when meals actually were sold. The meals were sold at a price of $11.00 each.

EXHIBIT 1

GOTHAM MEALS ON WHEELS
Balance Sheet
As of December 31

Assets		Liabilities and Equity	
Cash....................	$12,975	Contributed capital	$25,000
Accounts receivable......	8,525	Retained surpluses.............	0
Inventory	3,500		
Total assets	$25,000	Total liabilities and equity	$25,000

Because many of the agency's clients were on limited incomes, Mr. McCall did not insist upon immediate payment. Instead, he billed the clients monthly. Because of some office inefficiencies the bills usually were not sent out until a month after the meals had been delivered, and most clients took a full month to pay their bills. So, for example, bills for January meals actually were sent in February, and payment was not received until March. All clients were extremely conscientious about paying on time, however, and none exceeded the 30-day time limit for payment.

Questions

1. What problems, if any, does Gotham Meals on Wheels have? Please be as specific as you can, clearly identifying the *cause(s)* of any problems you identify. To do so, you should do the following:*
   a. Reconcile Equity, Accounts Receivable, and Inventory for each month, beginning in November, and, for each account, using the basic formula:

$$
\begin{array}{rl}
 & BB \\
+ & \text{Additions} \\
- & \text{Reductions} \\
= & EB
\end{array}
$$

   b. Prepare actual balance sheets and operating statements for November through March, and pro forma balance sheets and operating statements for April through September. Remember that, because of the matching principle, cost of goods sold is recognized as an expense only when the meals actually are sold, not when they are produced.
   c. Prepare actual statements of cash flows (SCF) for January through March, and pro forma SCFs for April through September.
2. What advice would you give Mr. McCall?

---

* In doing so, try to set up a spreadsheet containing the balance sheet, the operating statement, and the statement of cash flows in such a way that they are all interconnected. That is, try to make the spreadsheet as "formula driven" as possible.

Chapter 4

Full-Cost Accounting

"What did it cost?" is one of the most slippery questions for managers in both for-profit and nonprofit organizations. Measures of the cost of *acquiring* resources such as supplies and labor usually can be obtained readily from invoices and other documents. Measuring the cost of *using* these resources for various purposes is another matter, however. Calculating a total cost per unit produced—be it a widget or 50 minutes of psychotherapy—is relatively easy as long as the organization produces a single type of product or a single service.[1] Complications arise when an organization produces different types of products because each type uses *different* amounts of resources, and each therefore has *different* costs.

This chapter discusses some of these complications. We begin with an overview of the uses to which full-cost information can be put. Next, we look at several decisions that managers make in developing full-cost accounting systems. We conclude the chapter with a discussion of several factors that complicate a full-cost analysis, an assessment of some of the problems that arise in using full cost information, and an examination of some of the issues that organizations must consider when attempting to comply with published cost principles.

USES OF FULL-COST INFORMATION

Information on the full cost of carrying out a particular endeavor has three basic uses: pricing, profitability assessments, and comparative analyses.

Pricing

One of the most basic functions of full-cost information is to assist management in setting prices. Clearly, full-cost information is not the only information that management uses for this purpose, but it is an important ingredient in the decision-

---

[1] As defined by the Institute of Management Accountants, the term *products* refers to both goods and services. Goods are tangible products; services are intangible products. Some people define *products* to include only tangible items, but this is incorrect.

making process. Many nonprofit organizations are *price takers*; that is, they must accept whatever price a third party or client can pay. In these instances, prices are not based on full costs, but on the market. For other organizations, full-cost information is much more important to the pricing decision. These include organizations whose reimbursement from clients or third parties is calculated on a cost-plus basis. We discuss pricing issues in greater detail in Chapter 6.

Profitability Assessments

Even nonprofit organizations that are price takers must calculate full costs if management is to know whether a particular program or product is losing money. In Chapter 5, we will examine what management might do if a product is losing money on a full-cost basis. For the moment, however, it is sufficient to say that if a product is not covering its full costs it is, by definition, a *loss leader*. Since even nonprofits cannot have all their products be loss leaders, full-cost accounting serves to highlight where the cross subsidization among programs and products is taking place. This allows management to assess whether that cross subsidization is consistent with the organization's overall strategy.

Comparative Analyses

Many organizations can benefit from comparing their costs with those of similar organizations delivering the same sorts of products. Full-cost information can assist in this effort.

In undertaking comparative analyses, we would need to be aware of potential comparability problems. For example, we would need to know whether the organizations with which we are comparing ourselves measure their costs in the same way we do. As the discussion in this chapter will indicate, there can be a variety of complexities in undertaking comparative analyses.[2]

Example. Northern College, a small private liberal arts college, is interested in comparing its cost per student with the cost per student in some other similar colleges. In making the comparisons, the college must consider issues such as average class size, the existence of specialized programs in athletics, art, music or other subjects, special services (such as career counseling), whether it wishes to include room and board costs in the comparison, the method used to calculate the cost of its library (e.g., whether it amortizes its collections, and if so, over what time period), whether it wishes to include the library cost in the comparison, and a wide variety of similar issues.

---

[2] For a discussion of the sorts of issues that an organization must consider, see David W. Young, "Cost Accounting and Cost Comparisons: Methodological Issues and Their Policy and Management Implications," *Accounting Horizons* 2, no. 1 (March 1988).

As this example suggests, even the definition of what is to be included in a full-cost calculation requires a managerial decision. Indeed, because there is such a wide range of choices embedded in an organization's full-cost accounting system, managers frequently find it difficult to compare costs between their organization and others where the choices may have been made differently.

COST ACCOUNTING SYSTEM DECISIONS

At a conceptual level, the problem of full-cost determination is quite basic: one attempts to measure the amount of resources consumed in the manufacture of a given product or the delivery of a particular service. Putting this concept into practice is more difficult, however, because of several decisions and determinations that must be made in designing a cost accounting system. These include: defining the final cost object, specifying intermediate cost objects, determining cost centers, distinguishing between direct and indirect costs, selecting the bases of allocation, deciding on an allocation method, and distributing costs to cost objects.

Cost accounting decisions frequently are made by an organization's accounting staff rather than its managers. This approach is not optimal. Senior management should take an active role in cost accounting decision making if it is to assure the design of a managerially useful system.

Final Cost Object

In designing any cost accounting system, a central question concerns the unit of activity being measured; that is, the unit for which we wish to know the cost. In health care, for example, a hospital's activity might be measured in terms of a day of care, an admission, an episode of illness, or any of a variety of other units.[3] The choices in an educational context might include the cost of a classroom hour, a course, or a department. If the system is to be useful, senior management should determine the most appropriate activity unit for the organization to use.

In cost accounting terminology this activity unit is called the *final cost object*.[4] In many instances, limitations in available data mean that compromises must be

---

[3] A day of care is a day spent in a hospital as an inpatient. An admission is usually several days, and includes all activities associated with the hospitalization, workup, treatment, and discharge of a patient. An episode of illness includes all activities that take place from the time a person gets sick (with an acute, i.e., non-chronic, illness) until he or she is cured. It can include both in-hospital (inpatient) and out-of-hospital (outpatient) activities (and costs).

[4] Cost accounting terminology is not completely uniform. Appendix A contains definitions of some key terms as we use them. For additional discussion of terminology and methodological considerations, see Charles Horngren and George Foster, *Cost Accounting: A Managerial Emphasis* (Englewood Cliffs, N.J.: Prentice Hall, 1991).

made. In health care, for example, some managers believe that the episode of illness is the most appropriate cost object in ambulatory care. Most health care organizations do not have data systems that permit easy retrieval of complete episode information, however. As a result, most comparisons tend to be made for a visit or an encounter, for which data can be obtained more easily.

Intermediate Cost Objects

A second question concerns the activities that take place in order to produce the cost object. A day of care in a hospital encompasses a wide range of activities, including differences in levels of nursing care provided, types of ancillary procedures used (including laboratory tests and radiological procedures), and amenities furnished. In a school system, the cost of educating a student in a given grade will depend on activities such as provision of remedial instruction, involvement in athletics, and use of counseling services. Each of these activities is an intermediate cost object, and part of its costs should be included in the final cost object.

In effect, differences in intermediate cost objects represent what might be called product differences. That is, for a given final cost object—such as the education of a first-grade student for one academic year—the product in reality is quite different from one individual to the next, depending on the aggregation of intermediate cost objects for each. Moreover, the cost may be different from one school to another, and the cost of delivering services to a particular type of client may differ from one social service agency to another. Similarly, the cost of caring for a patient with a particular diagnosis or diagnosis-related group (DRG)[5] may differ among hospitals. For example, the treatment of a patient with a given diagnosis might require five days in one hospital and six in another. Some physicians might order a surgical procedure, while others might not; some might order one combination of tests and procedures, while others might order a different combination. These different combinations of intermediate cost objects affect the cost of the final cost object, even though the end product—the discharge of a healthy patient, the education of a first grader, the treatment of a client and so on—is the same.

---

[5] A DRG-based reimbursement system for U.S. hospitals was introduced by medicare in 1983. Under this system, hospitals are reimbursed a fixed amount per patient admitted, and, with only a few exceptions, a hospital cannot receive more than this amount regardless of the cost it incurs in caring for a patient. Diagnoses are classified into several hundred groups—or DRGs—and the hospital is reimbursed according to the patient's group; that is, the reimbursement amount varies depending upon the patient's diagnosis.

For a discussion of the advantages and disadvantages of DRGs, see R. S. Stern and A. M. Epstein, "Institutional Responses to Prospective Payment Based on Diagnosis-Related Groups: Implications for Cost, Quality, and Access," *New England Journal of Medicine* 312 (1985), pp. 621–27. For a critique of DRGs as well as a discussion of some of their managerial implications, see D. W. Young and R. B. Saltman, "Medical Practice, Case Mix, and Cost Containment: A New Role for the Attending Physician," *Journal of the American Medical Association*, February 12, 1982, pp. 801–5.

Cost Centers

Before being assigned to intermediate cost objects, costs are first collected in cost centers.[6] A cost center might be thought of as a "bucket" into which an organization's costs are classified and accumulated for purposes of full-cost analysis. Frequently, an organization's departments are its cost centers. For example, in a hospital, the department of radiology might be one cost center, the social work department another, the housekeeping department a third, and so on. But this is not always the case. The department of radiology, for instance, might be divided into several separate cost centers: CT Scanning, angiography, and so on. Or, a language laboratory in a high school, while not a department, might be a cost center.

There are two broad types of cost centers: mission centers and service centers. *Mission centers* are directly related to the purposes of the organization. *Service centers* provide support to both mission centers and other service centers. In a hospital, the housekeeping, plant maintenance, and dietary departments are service centers, while the pediatrics, obstetrics, and medical/surgical departments are mission centers. A good rule of thumb for client-serving organizations is that mission centers charge clients for their services while service centers do not. For this reason, mission centers frequently are called *revenue-producing centers*.[7] In some instances, service centers may charge both mission centers and other service centers for their support activities, but they do not charge clients directly.[8]

The distinction between an intermediate cost object and a mission center is occasionally quite subtle since both may be viewed as purposes for which costs are collected. When this happens, mission centers are identical to intermediate cost objects.

> *Example.* The annual cost of caring for a child in the Western Home for Children (the final cost object) depends on the services (intermediate cost objects) the child receives. There are four basic types of services: foster home care, psychological testing, social work counseling, and psychotherapy. Each of these services also is a mission center, where a variety of costs are accumulated. The psychological testing center, for example, includes the costs of part-time psychologists, testing materials, and the fee the agency pays to an outside organization to have the tests processed and scored. The costs in the psychological testing mission center are accumulated for the year, and are divided by the number of children tested to give a cost per child tested. Each child who was tested has this cost added to his or her other costs to arrive at the total cost of caring for him or her for the year.

---

[6] Strictly speaking, as we discuss in Appendix A, a cost center is also a type of cost object.

[7] This rule of thumb works for all client-serving organizations, even those that do not charge clients directly. Where there are no charges, the accounting system nevertheless can calculate a cost that *could be used* as a basis for the charge.

[8] This internal charge is called a *transfer price*. It is discussed in greater detail in Chapter 6.

Direct and Indirect Costs

An appropriate analysis of costs should allow us to identify both the costs directly associated with (or that can be physically traced to) a particular cost center, as well as those that are associated with more than one. A full-cost accounting system should distinguish between these direct and indirect costs. That is, direct costs are unambiguously associated with a specific cost center. Indirect costs apply to more than one.

To carry out the full-cost accounting effort, the accounting system *assigns* all costs to cost centers. Direct costs, by definition, can be assigned quite easily. Indirect costs pose problems, however, because they are not clearly associated with a particular mission or service center. Ordinarily, their assignment is carried out by establishing formulas that distribute them as fairly as possible to the appropriate cost centers.[9] Also, by developing improved measurement techniques and appropriate records, an organization can convert some indirect costs into direct costs.[10]

> ***Example.*** A social worker in the foster home care department of Western Home for Children is supervised by a person who also supervises the psychologists in the testing department. Unless the time the supervisor spends in each department is traced, his or her salary is an indirect cost of the two departments—it applies to activities in both. In order to apportion the cost between the two, the accountants might develop a formula, using, say, relative hours of service or number of personnel in each cost center as the apportionment mechanism. Alternatively, the supervisor might be asked to maintain careful records of the time spent in each cost center, which the accountants then could use to distribute the salary. In this latter case, the cost (time) would be direct, since it is now traceable to each cost center.

Bases of Allocation

A full-cost analysis would be incomplete if it stopped with the assignment of direct and indirect costs to cost centers. We would then know the cost in each service and mission center, but not the full cost of the mission centers—which are the revenue-producing centers. Therefore, once the system has assigned all costs to

---

[9] This assignment process sometimes is called *allocation*. It contrasts with another type of allocation, discussed later in this chapter, of service center costs to mission centers.

[10] Government contracts normally permit the recovery of service center costs via an *indirect overhead rate*. When this happens, an organization receiving government funding for a particular project first calculates the direct costs of the project—usually personnel, supplies, transportation, equipment, and the like—and then adds its allowable (as determined by prior audits) indirect overhead rate to determine the full amount of funding to be received. In such a contract, the cost elements to be included in direct costs must be spelled out clearly.

either a mission center or a service center, the accounting staff must *allocate* the service center costs to the organization's mission centers.[11]

Allocation is the process of distributing service center costs to mission centers, in order to determine the full cost of each mission center. To allocate service center costs, the cost accounting system uses a separate *basis of allocation* for each. In general, the best basis for allocating the costs of a given service center is the one that most accurately measures its use by the cost centers that receive its services. In this regard, the main issue is *causality*. That is, to the extent possible the basis of allocation should reflect the receiving cost center's usage of a service center.

> *Example.* The basis for allocating the costs of the laundry service center in a hospital usually is pounds processed. Dietary uses the number of meals served as its allocation basis. In each instance, the hospital is seeking a basis of allocation that measures the *usage* of the laundry and dietary service centers by the cost centers receiving the allocations.

In selecting a service center's allocation basis, managers should carefully assess the need for precision. In general, greater precision increases the expense of operating the cost accounting system.

> *Example.* Housekeeping costs in a hospital frequently are allocated on the basis of the number of square feet occupied by the cost centers that use housekeeping services. Alternatively, and more accurately, housekeeping costs could be allocated on the basis of hours of service rendered to each cost center by the housekeeping department. Although hours of service is a more accurate measure of the cause of the cost, such a measure requires the housekeeping department and the accounting staff to maintain records of hours; this recordkeeping expense is not necessary in the simpler system.

In an effort to recognize that many service centers (such as housekeeping and laundry) are available regardless of whether they actually are used, some cost accounting systems isolate the fixed and variable costs of each service center.[12] Fixed costs are then allocated on the basis of anticipated use (e.g., the number of *budgeted* patients in the case of laundry), and variable costs are allocated according to actual use (e.g., the *actual* number of pounds of laundry processed).

---

[11] This is one area where terminology can be particularly confusing. The terms *assign*, *apportion*, and *allocate* sometimes are used interchangeably. Moreover, many managers consider all mission center costs to be direct and all service center costs to be indirect. Additionally, service center costs frequently are called *overhead costs,* although the definition of *overhead* varies considerably among organizations. In general, the context will make clear how the terms are being used.

[12] Fixed and variable costs will be discussed at length in Chapter 5. For the moment, it is sufficient to recognize that fixed costs are those costs that do not change with the volume of activity in a cost center, while variable costs fluctuate in direct proportion to the volume of activity. In the case of operating an automobile, insurance generally is a fixed cost, whereas gasoline is a variable cost. That is, insurance is the same regardless of the number of miles driven, while gasoline increases in direct proportion to the number of miles driven. On the other hand, insurance is a variable cost of *owning* *automobiles*; that is, it increases proportionately with the number owned.

The Allocation Method

Several methods are available for allocating service center costs. The easiest is known as *single-step* allocation. With this method, each service center's costs are allocated to the various mission centers that use its services, but not to any other service centers. For example, in a hospital, housekeeping would be allocated to pediatrics, surgery, and so forth based on, say, their share of the institution's square feet. However, this method fails to recognize that some service centers provide services to other service centers; for instance, housekeeping cleans the medical records department, another service center.

A *two-stage* or *stepdown* method corrects for this deficiency. With this method, the costs of the service centers are "trickled down" to other service centers and the mission centers using the chosen allocation bases. This method is illustrated in Exhibit 4–1. Typically, it begins with the service center that serves the greatest number of other service centers in the organization, and spreads its costs over the remaining cost centers. It continues in this fashion with all other service centers.

Clearly, Exhibit 4–1 is quite simple—it has only three service centers and two mission centers. The process used would be the same, however, in a system with many cost centers. That is, the allocation process begins with the first service cost

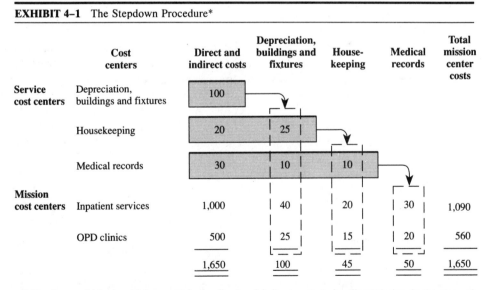

EXHIBIT 4–1 The Stepdown Procedure*

	Cost centers	Direct and indirect costs	Depreciation, buildings and fixtures	House-keeping	Medical records	Total mission center costs
Service cost centers	Depreciation, buildings and fixtures	100				
	Housekeeping	20	25			
	Medical records	30	10	10		
Mission cost centers	Inpatient services	1,000	40	20	30	1,090
	OPD clinics	500	25	15	20	560
		1,650	100	45	50	1,650

* The three solid horizontal bars contain the direct and indirect costs to be allocated plus, in the cases of housekeeping and medical records, those amounts allocated from the previous cost centers. The three dotted vertical bars contain the individual amounts allocated to each cost center from the three service cost centers. Note that, as the arrows indicate, the total amount in each horizontal bar has been redistributed within a vertical bar. This redistribution is done in accordance with the chosen allocation basis; for example, by square feet for housekeeping.

center, depreciation of buildings and fixtures in this case, and distributes its costs across all remaining cost centers. The column labeled "Depreciation, Buildings and Fixtures" shows this distribution. The amount to be distributed from the next service center (Housekeeping) now includes not only its own costs ($20) but also the amount allocated to it from the previous step ($25 of depreciation). The column "Housekeeping" allocates this total ($45) to the remaining cost centers. The third step, "Medical Records," includes its costs ($30), plus the amount of depreciation ($10) and housekeeping ($10) allocated to it, for a total of $50. The "Medical Records" column shows how this total was allocated to the two mission centers.

Exhibit 4–1 does not show the bases of allocation for the service centers. For example, the basis of allocation for depreciation might be square feet. The house-keeping department's share of depreciation then would be calculated based on its share of the hospital's total square footage.

Two important aspects of the stepdown method are (1) no reverse allocation takes place; that is, once a service center's costs have been allocated, that service center receives no additional allocations from other service centers; and (2) service center costs are allocated both to other service centers and to mission centers, but mission center costs are not allocated to other mission centers.

Because no reverse allocation takes place, the sequence of the steps in the stepdown is an important cost accounting decision. Although the effect of different stepdown sequences often is not great, in some circumstances the choice may have a significant influence on the costs allocated to the various mission centers.

The Reciprocal Method.   The need to select a stepdown sequence can be obviated by using the *reciprocal method*. With this method, service center costs are not stepped down. Rather, the accountant develops a set of simultaneous equations that measure and allocate each service center's costs based on the use of its services by *all* other cost centers, not just those below it in a stepdown sequence. This technique thus avoids the problem with the stepdown method that no reverse allocation can take place. The reciprocal method is illustrated in Appendix B at the end of this chapter.

In summary, accountants engage in three distinct activities in a cost accounting effort. First, they define cost centers. Second, they *assign* all costs to a cost center—either a mission or a service center. With direct costs, this is easy; with indirect costs it is more complicated. Third, they *allocate* service center costs to mission centers.

To carry out the allocation process, the accountants must take two steps. First, they must choose a *basis of allocation* (such as square feet) for each service cost center; this basis attempts to measure the use of the center's services by the other cost centers. Second, they must select a *method* of allocation (such as the step-down method) to distribute service center costs among mission centers. Some-times this process can become quite complex. For example, the CADMS model of the National Center for Higher Education that was developed for colleges and universities, provides 26 steps for allocating costs to mission centers.[13]

In many instances, service center costs are called *overhead costs*, although terminology is not consistent across all organizations. In some instances, for example, *overhead* is used to describe any cost element that is not directly associated with a final cost object. In this regard, the easiest approach usually is to determine the methodology being used rather than to attempt to discern the meaning of the terminology.

Distributing Mission Center Costs to Cost Objects

The last step in the cost accounting process is to determine the full cost of each final cost object. In some cases, mission centers also are final cost objects. If so, the preceding step completes the cost accounting process. In other cases, a mission center works on several cost objects, and its costs must be distributed to each.

Example. The research department of a university (a mission center) may work on several different research projects (final cost objects), and each project usually is costed-out individually.

Example. The counseling department of a social service agency (a mission center) comes into contact with many clients (final cost objects), and wishes to know the cost associated with each.

Example. The remedial education department of a junior high school (a mission center) provides services to many students (final cost objects) and wishes to know the cost for each student.

Example. The internal medicine department of a rural group practice (a mission center) sees many patients each day and wants to know the cost of each patient's visit (the final cost object).

Process Costing and Job Order Costing. In the above situations and other similar ones where mission center costs must be distributed to final cost objects, organizations are faced with two principal choices, each of which has several variations: the process method and the job order method. In manufacturing, the process method is used when all units of output are essentially identical, such as the production of chairs, phone directories, and fertilizer—activities that often are performed on a production line or in a chemical process. The job order method is used when the units of output are quite different, such as in an automobile repair garage or a specialty machine shop.

---

[13] For an example of the use of CADMS, see Michael E. Young and Ronald W. Geason, "Cost Analysis and Overhead Charges at a Major Research University," *Business Officer*, April 1983, pp. 17–20.

With the process costing method, all mission center costs for a given accounting period are calculated, totaled, and then divided by the total number of units produced to give an average cost per unit.[14] With the job order system, the labor, material, and other direct costs associated with each job are collected separately on a job cost record, and indirect costs are distributed to each job using an overhead rate.

Some nonprofit organizations use a process method and others use a job order one. In general, the choice between the two depends on the managerial significance of an average cost figure.

> *Example.* Most hospitals use a job order system. They sum the costs from several mission centers for each patient, based on the patient's actual use of those mission centers. Medications, special dietary services, operating room usage, ancillary procedures, special nursing care, and intensive care unit usage are accumulated on a patient's medical (job cost) record to obtain the cost of treatment for that individual. Each patient's cost will differ depending on the resources he or she used.

> *Example.* Third-party payers that reimburse a hospital on the basis of an all-inclusive per diem amount assume (perhaps implicitly) that the hospital is using a process method. The reimbursement system treats the entire hospital as a mission center, calculates all costs for the hospital, and determines the average cost per day by dividing the number of patient days delivered into total costs. The assumption underlying in this approach is that all patients served receive roughly similar services, and therefore an average cost per day is a meaningful figure.

> *Example.* A school with a remedial education program lies between a pure process system and a job order system. It recognizes that a student in a remedial education program will use resources that are different from those used by a student in a regular education program, but it assumes that all students using the remedial education program will use roughly the same services (i.e., that this average is a meaningful figure). The system does not attempt to find the cost of individual jobs (i.e., students).

In choosing between process and job order methods, managers must weigh the costs of the increased reporting and processing effort in the job order method against the benefits of greater management control (e.g., competitive pricing needs, management control potential) that the method usually provides. Differences among clients and services also are important, however. For example, most client- or patient-serving nonprofit organizations would benefit from a method that approximates job order, while most membership-type organizations or associations would find a process method acceptable.

---

[14] The accounting process actually is considerably more complicated than this, since *(a)* units frequently move through several production stages, each of which is a cost center, *(b)* at any given time there are partially completed units in each cost center, and *(c)* spoilage (both normal and abnormal) must be taken into account. For details, see Horngren and Foster, *Cost Accounting*.

Summary of Cost Accounting System Decisions

Exhibits 4–2 through 4–4 summarize the discussion thus far, using the example of a hospital. The hospital has selected an individual patient as its final cost object and has defined three mission centers and three service centers. The mission centers are inpatient care, the laboratory, and radiology. The service centers are housekeeping, laundry, and medical records. The mission centers provide intermediate cost objects, such as days of care, lab tests, and X rays. The hospital's accountants now must follow three separate steps.

Assignment of Indirect Costs. Step 1, shown in Exhibit 4–2, is the assignment of indirect costs to both mission and service centers. By definition, each indirect cost item applies to multiple cost centers; otherwise it would be a direct cost. The objective of step 1 is to use formulas or other techniques to assign the indirect costs to the cost centers to which they apply.

EXHIBIT 4–2   Full-Cost Accounting Process: Step 1—Assignment of Indirect Costs to Cost Centers*

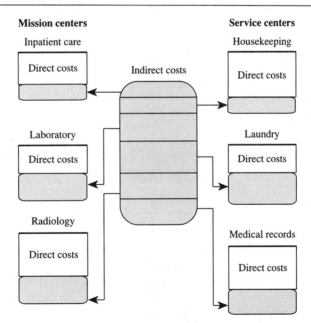

* Indirect costs (e.g., salaries and benefits of employees who work in more than one cost center) are assigned to both mission and service cost centers.

Allocation of Service Center Costs.   Step 2, shown in Exhibit 4–3, is the allocation of service center costs to mission centers. Note that each mission and service center can have both direct costs and assigned indirect costs (from step 1). The total of these costs in each service center is the amount that is allocated. As a result, each mission center's total costs will include its direct and indirect costs plus allocated service center costs. Ordinarily, the accountants also allocate a service center's costs to other service centers by using the stepdown or reciprocal method. Eventually, however, all service center costs end up in mission centers.

EXHIBIT 4–3   Full-Cost Accounting Process: Step 2—Allocation of Service Center Costs*

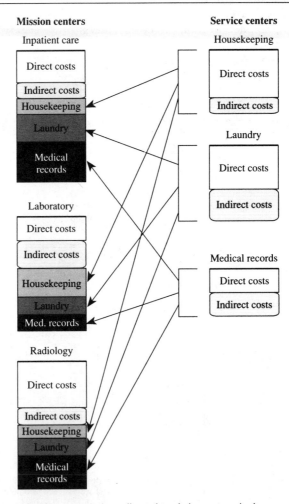

* Service center costs are allocated to mission centers via chosen bases of allocation (e.g., square feet for housekeeping, pounds processed for laundry, and so on).

Distribution of Mission Center Costs to Cost Objects.   Finally, in step 3 (Exhibit 4–4), the mission center costs are distributed to the final cost objects (a patient with a particular diagnosis). A final cost object receives some direct costs from each mission center plus some overhead costs. These overhead costs include both the mission center's indirect costs and the service center costs allocated to it.

EXHIBIT 4–4   Full-Cost Accounting Process: Step 3—Distribution of Mission Center Costs to Cost Objects*

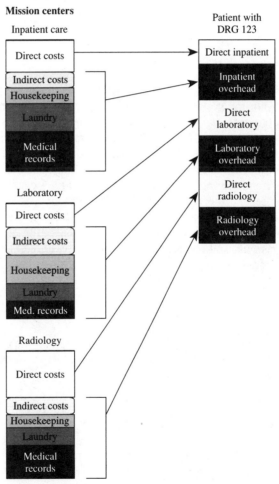

* Costs are assigned to final cost objects (e.g., a patient with DRG 123) by means of measuring the direct costs used in each mission center (e.g., hours of nursing time in inpatient care, films in radiology, and so on) and applying the overhead of each mission center by means of an overhead rate (e.g., $90 per inpatient day, $5 per lab test, and so forth).

In effect, each mission cost center delivers some intermediate cost objects, and each of these has a cost. The final cost object is the sum of all the intermediate cost objects. In this example, the final cost for a patient is the sum of the costs of all the services the patient received; for example, three chest X rays, two urinalyses, five days of inpatient care, and so on.

The calculation of the cost of an intermediate cost object sometimes becomes complicated. This happens when some costs that are direct for the mission center are indirect for the intermediate cost object. For example, the supervisor of a radiology department will be a direct cost of the mission center (radiology) but an indirect cost for any given X ray. A radiology film, by contrast, will be a direct cost for both the radiology mission center and the X ray.

Interactive Effects

As the above discussion indicates, the decisions involved in developing a full-cost accounting system may be quite difficult. Regardless of the difficulty, it is important to note that changes in the system that increase the cost of one cost object will always decrease the cost of one or more other cost objects. This is because the total costs of operating the organization are unaffected; the cost accounting system merely divides this total among the cost objects. Nevertheless, changes in cost accounting definitions and techniques can have a significant effect on the costs reported for a given cost center or cost object. In many organizations, managers' ability to analyze these effects is facilitated by computer software packages. The packages allow a manager or analyst to vary cost accounting decisions, and to examine the impact of such changes on individual cost centers and cost objects.

COMPLICATING FACTORS

The general framework described above contains many variations and complications. While most of them are appropriately dealt with in a cost accounting course, a few are discussed briefly below.

Defining Direct Costs

There are significant differences in the ways different organizations draw the line between direct and indirect costs. For example, in calculating the cost of university research projects, one university may count pension and other fringe benefits of researchers as direct costs, while another may count these items as indirect costs; one may charge secretarial assistance directly to projects, but another may charge all secretarial help to a common pool (a service center). Similarly, if heat, light and other utilities are metered, they are direct costs; if not, they are indirect costs.

These differences in accounting treatment may have no material effect on the *total cost* of a research project because approximately the same amount may wind up as a cost, whether charged directly or indirectly. They do, however, affect the *relationship* between direct and indirect costs. Because of this, comparisons of this relationship among organizations are of little use.

Example. A study of research costs in four universities showed that the reported percentages of indirect costs to direct salary and wages were as follows:

University	Overhead Percentage
A	85.77
B	79.95
C	57.00
D	54.23

Some people use data like these to infer that Universities A and B had much more overhead than C and D. Actually, the authors of the study concluded that the differences primarily reflected differences in the method of distinguishing between direct and indirect costs.[15]

Appropriateness of Indirect Costs

Frequently, the issue is not one of distinguishing between direct and indirect costs, but of the appropriateness of the indirect costs themselves. For example, in the case of universities, critics say indirect costs have been rising unchecked for years. These costs now total over 50 percent of direct costs for most major research universities, and have been reported to be as high as 74 percent in some cases. University officials contend that such costs are needed to run the university. At issue are several questions: (1) what costs should be allowable, (2) which projects should pay for them, and (3) the efficiency with which various university overhead units operate (such as how many librarians are needed to run the library).

In some instances, the debate has reached the faculty ranks, with faculty expressing concern that high indirect rates impede a university's ability to obtain research funding.

Example. In a flurry of letters and emotional meetings, [Stanford University faculty] deluged the administration with bitter complaints that a bloated bureaucracy and campuswide building fever was burdening them with costs that would strangle their research. The tinder for the explosion was the news that Stanford's overhead—already among the highest in the nation at 74 percent—would rise to 84 percent by 1993.[16]

---

[15] Peat, Marwick, Mitchell & Co., *Study of Indirect Cost Rates of Organizations Performing Federally Sponsored Research.* Prepared for Stanford University, November 1977.

[16] Marcia Barinaga, "Stanford Erupts over Indirect Costs," *Science,* 248 (April 20, 1990), p. 292.

On the other hand, some observers claim that government auditors tend to question those items that make headlines but that are of little importance to total costs. Clearly, there are merits to both arguments.

Standard Costs

Increasingly, nonprofit organizations are adopting cost accounting approaches that have proven to be successful in manufacturing settings. One such approach is the use of standard costs. In a standard cost system, each unit of product in a mission center is charged a predetermined (or standard) cost for direct labor, direct materials, and overhead. When this procedure is followed, the mission center's total standard cost for a given month (or other accounting period) is obtained by multiplying the standard unit cost by the number of units that flowed through the mission center for the month.

To implement a standard cost system, each mission center defines the products it provides and determines how much direct labor and direct material are necessary for each. The accountants then determine the mission center's costs that cannot specifically be identified with a particular product. They next calculate an overhead rate for each service unit by dividing the total indirect costs by the total units of all service, or by some other appropriate measure.[17] An example of how such a system might be structured for a mission center in a client-serving organization is given in Exhibit 4–5. As this exhibit shows, service providers who deliver services directly to clients (i.e., direct labor) have had standards developed for the number of minutes needed for each service. A service might be an office visit in a social service agency, an initial visit in a doctor's office, or a reading lesson in a remedial reading program.

Standards also are developed for supplies and any other material costs that can be directly associated with a service (i.e., direct materials). Indirect costs are listed and totaled separately and can be used to determine a standard overhead rate.

In Exhibit 4–5, the overhead rate of $46.56 has been calculated by dividing the total indirect costs ($74,500) by the standard (or anticipated) number of units of service (1,600). This amount then would be added to the direct cost per service unit to obtain the total cost per service unit. For example, in the case of Service 2, the total cost would be $60.94 ($14.38 + $46.56).

When a standard cost system is in place, management can use a technique called *variance analysis,* to identify whether deviations from the standard cost figure in a particular mission center are the result of volume changes (more or fewer units than anticipated), mix changes (a different combination of services

---

[17] In a manufacturing setting, this process can become quite detailed. For additional information, see Robert N. Anthony and James S. Reece, *Accounting: Text and Cases*, 9th ed. (Homewood, Ill.: Richard D. Irwin, 1992), chaps. 18 and 19.

EXHIBIT 4-5 Standard Cost Analysis for a Mission Center

							Mission Center A				
	Standards: Service 1			Standards: Service 2			Standards: Service n				
Direct Costs	Min.	$/Min.	Cost	Min.	$/Min.	Cost	Min.	$/Min.	Cost	Totals	
Personnel:											
Provider 1	15	.20	$3.00	10	0.20	$2.00	30	0.20	$6.00		
Provider 2	5	.30	1.50	3	0.30	.90	10	0.30	3.00		
...											
Provider n	10	.10	1.00	20	0.10	2.00	30	0.10	3.00		
Subtotal			$5.50			$4.90			$12.00		
Fringe benefits at .20			1.10			.98			2.40		
Personnel total			$6.60			$5.88			$14.40		
Supplies			1.50			3.50			9.00		
Purchased services			.50			5.00			1.50		
Total direct costs per unit			$8.60			$14.38			$24.90		
Number of units of service at standard			1,000			500			100.00	1,600	
Total direct costs at standard			$8,600			$7,190			$2,490	$18,280	
Indirect costs											
Personnel:											
Position 1										25,000	
Position 2										18,000	
...											
Position n										12,000	
Fringe benefits at .20										11,000	
Supplies										5,000	
Purchased services										3,500	
Total indirect costs										$74,500	
Overhead rate per unit ($74,500 ÷ 1,600 units of service)										$ 46.56	

195

than anticipated), efficiency changes (more or less time or materials needed per unit of service), or price changes (higher or lower wage rates and material prices). Additionally, by summarizing standard costs and variances for each mission center, and relating these figures to the standard and actual intermediate cost objects for each final cost object, management can determine why the total cost for a given cost object was higher or lower than anticipated.

As a consequence of using standard costs and variances, managers can gain much greater understanding of cost behavior in their organizations, as well as improved ability to control costs. Variance analysis is discussed in greater detail in Chapter 13.

Capital Employed

In a for-profit company, the full cost of using a fixed asset is greater than the asset's depreciation expense. The company's capital that is tied up in the asset also has a cost, even though a charge for the use of capital is not identified as a cost item in many accounting systems. If a nonprofit organization borrows money to finance the purchase of an asset, the interest on the loan is a cost. Similarly, all organizations need working capital to operate. Working capital has a cost, just as funds tied up in a fixed asset have a cost. There are other situations in which a cost of using capital exists but is not so obvious.

> *Example.* Suppose a university uses $1 million of its funds to finance the construction of a building. Some would argue that there is a capital cost associated with this transaction because, if the university had not used the $1 million to finance the building, it would have continued to invest it, earning perhaps $50,000 a year. Since it now forgoes these annual earnings, the $50,000 "opportunity cost" is appropriately part of the annual cost of using the building.

These cost elements are important in situations in which it is agreed that a client will reimburse the organization for the full cost of the service rendered as, for example, in a research contract. Unless the reimbursement includes an allowance for items such as the above, the organization's revenues will be insufficient to allow it to maintain its capital.

Opportunity Costs

As indicated above, one way to measure the cost of capital employed is with *opportunity costs*. That is, while costs in most systems are measured by monetary outlays, they also can be measured by opportunity losses.

> *Example.* The use of water is often controlled by public agencies, sometimes through investment in public works, and sometimes (at least under western states' water laws) because the agency is the legal holder of original water rights. As water becomes an increasingly scarce resource, the expense of some programs, such as waterfowl refuges,

may come to be measured as the opportunity cost of water consumption rather than solely in terms of monetary outlays. Similar instances can be cited for public lands and public controls of private land.

Imputed Costs

In certain situations, imputed costs, which are a form of opportunity costs, need to be incorporated into the cost accounting system. Both cost measurement and control are facilitated if imputed costs are converted to actual monetary outlays.

Example. In the United States the cost of polluting water is usually an imputed cost; that is, companies generally have not been charged for the social cost of the rivers that they pollute. In the Ruhr Valley in Germany, by contrast, polluters pay a charge based on the effect of the effluent on the river's need for dissolved oxygen, that is, its biochemical oxygen demand. The revenue derived from this charge is used to provide for water treatment. The effect is to convert an imputed cost into a monetary cost. In one study, conducted over 20 years ago, the amount involved was about $60 million per year.[18] That amount would be considerably higher in today's prices.

Example. The Dutch government is developing a system of national accounting to reflect the damage done to the air, water, soil, and animal and plant life, and to account for the cost of maintaining or restoring them. Sweden, France, and Norway also have begun similar efforts at what is now called *green accounting*. In the United States, the Congress has directed the Department of Commerce to work on a new system of calculating environmental costs and benefits.[19]

In some situations, the price charged by a tax-exempt organization is supposed to be a yardstick for for-profit organizations. This is the case with the Tennessee Valley Authority. In such a situation, the imputed cost of taxes also must be recognized. In other situations, the case is not so strong. If a tax-exempt hospital includes an allowance for property taxes in its full-cost calculation what does it do with the funds that this fee generates? Should it then pay some form of property tax?[20]

PROBLEMS WITH USING FULL-COST INFORMATION

Full costs are necessary if costs are to be used as a basis for pricing an organization's services, as in the TVA, the U.S. Postal Service, hospitals, and universities. They are also useful if judgments need to be made about the extent to which a

---

[18] From Barbara Ward and René Dubos, *Only One Earth*, an official report commissioned by the secretary general of the United Nations Conference on Human Environment (New York: W. W. Norton, 1972), chap. 7.

[19] Marlise Simons, "Europeans Begin to Calculate the Price of Pollution," *The New York Times*, December 9, 1990.

[20] For additional thinking on this latter point, see R. C. Clark, "Does the Nonprofit Form Fit the Hospital Industry?" *Harvard Law Review*, May 1980, pp. 1417–89.

program should "pay for itself," which is conceptually almost the same problem. Full-cost information may also facilitate the comparison of the cost of performing certain services in nonprofit organizations with the costs of comparable services in for-profit organizations.

The innate difficulties of making comparisons such as the above are considerable, however. Because of the complications discussed in the previous section, some people believe that the techniques of full-cost accounting do not actually provide a reasonable approximation of full cost. This is particularly important when, as will be discussed more fully in Chapter 6, full costs are a significant factor in setting prices.

> *Example.* In an otherwise excellent article on pricing blood services, the statement is made, "Since there can be no precise measurement of cost, there can be no sure correspondence between cost and price. Therefore, administrative decisions about prices must be made on the basis of criteria other than cost."[21] This statement is used as an argument for basing prices on public policy considerations, and specifically for setting the price of whole blood well above the prices of blood components—red cells, plasma, platelets, and factor VIII. A strong case can be made for such pricing differentials, but it is a case that should rest on its own merits, not on the premise that cost-based pricing is not feasible.

Problems with Statistical Systems

Some organizations base prices on cost, but they obtain cost data from a statistical system. Since a statistical system is not tied directly to the accounts, such cost data are likely to be of dubious validity. Furthermore, since prices are not related to the actual costs incurred in responsibility centers, managers of these centers are unlikely to accept them as reliable. Once designed and implemented, a cost system tied directly to the accounts requires little, if any, additional work to maintain than does a statistical cost system.

PUBLISHED COST PRINCIPLES

With the growth of full-cost pricing, many resource providers have published rules governing the way costs are to be measured for reimbursement purposes. The most broadly applicable set is that of the Cost Accounting Standards Board in the Office of Federal Procurement Policy, but there are many other rules for specific types of reimbursement. The Department of Health and Human Services prescribes rules for health care organizations. The Office of Revenue Sharing of the Treasury Department prescribes principles for state and local governmental units. The Office of Management and Budget (OMB) sets forth principles for educational institutions. These principles are not completely consistent with one

---

[21] D. M. Surgenor et al., "Blood Services: Prices and Public Policy," *Science*, April 27, 1973, p. 387.

another, and an organization must be thoroughly familiar with the specific rules that are applicable to its situation.

> ***Example.*** Much university research is supported by the federal government through contracts or grants. If the support comes in the form of a contract, the university is reimbursed in accordance with principles set forth in OMB *Circular A-21, Cost Principles for Educational Institutions*. These principles provide for direct costs plus an equitable share of indirect costs, including a use allowance for depreciation of buildings and equipment, operations and maintenance of plant, general administration and general expenses, departmental administration, student administration and services, and library.

Despite the presence of the OMB document, university overhead costs have presented an ongoing problem, and claims of overcharging for indirect costs are frequent. Similar claims have surfaced in other nonprofit organizations as well. In health care, for example, concerns have been voiced about the indirect costs that teaching hospitals charge medicare for medical education. Teaching hospital administrators claim that these costs are appropriate ones for medicare to pay in that, over the long term, they benefit medicare patients.[22]

In part, these claims reflect societal concerns about how tax dollars are spent. However, they are also partly reflective of a cost accounting effort that entails many managerial choices. To a great extent, those choices influence the amount of an organization's costs that wind up as overhead. This is one important reason why senior management must involve itself in the cost accounting choices discussed in this chapter.

APPENDIX A
Cost Accounting Terminology

As discussed in the text, cost accounting terminology can be confusing and occasionally contradictory. This appendix discusses several particularly tricky terms and concepts. It is not meant to be the final word, and readers usually must determine the precise meaning of a particular term from the context in which it is used.

A *cost object* is anything whose cost is collected. The Cost Accounting Standards Board (CASB) uses the term *cost objective* to mean the same thing. A *cost center,* therefore, is a cost object; *revenue* (or *mission*) *centers* and *service centers* are types of cost centers and, hence, also are cost objects. In many situations, a product is a *final cost object,* and cost centers are *intermediate cost objects*. Sometimes, there are several layers of cost objects, as when a final product consists of several intermediate products, each of which is produced in one or more cost centers.

---

[22] See United States General Accounting Office, *Medicare: Indirect Medical Education Payments Are Too High*. Washington, D.C.: GAO/HRD 89-33, January 1989.

A *cost item* is something that has been purchased: a pound of supplies, an hour of labor, a month of rent. It is expressed in units of currency (e.g., dollars) rather than some other measure. *Assign* is a verb referring to any recording of a cost item in a cost object. There are two ways a cost item can be assigned: (1) it can be assigned directly or (2) it can be allocated.

A cost item is *assigned directly* if it is traced to a single cost object. Such an item is a *direct cost* component of that cost object. If a cost item relates to two or more cost objects, it can still be assigned directly if appropriate measurement devices are used. For example, if a social worker carries out activities in two programs (cost objects) but keeps careful time records, his or her salary can be assigned directly to the two programs based on the percent of time spent in each. If a cost item cannot be assigned directly to a single cost object, it must be *allocated*. Therefore a cost item is allocated if it is assigned to two or more cost objects. When this happens, the cost item is an *indirect cost* of each cost object. Thus, all indirect costs are allocated costs and vice versa; but not all assigned costs are allocated costs—some assigned costs are direct.

These definitions are slightly different from those used by the CASB. The CASB says that costs are *assigned to accounting periods*. They then are allocated to cost objects within the accounting period. They may be either directly or indirectly allocated.

We believe our usage conforms to the ordinary usage of *allocated*. Few people would say (as the CASB does) that direct labor or direct material is *allocated* to a product. Moreover, almost everyone refers to the *basis of allocation,* which refers to indirect costs only. If the CASB were to be consistent, it would need to use the term *basis of **indirect** allocation,* which it does not.

APPENDIX B
The Reciprocal Method of Cost Allocation

To see how the reciprocal allocation method works, let us assume that we wish to allocate a museum's two service center costs of maintenance and administration to its two mission centers: curatorial and operations. Management has decided to allocate maintenance costs on the basis of the square footage in each department, and administration costs on the basis of the number of hours worked by the employees in each of their respective departments. Exhibit 4B–1 shows how the initial data for the museum might look.

Note that there are no square feet shown for maintenance and no labor-hours shown for administration. Since we are using square feet as the basis of allocation for maintenance, and labor hours as the basis of allocation for administration, we therefore exclude these measures from the two departments. In effect, we do not calculate the cost of maintaining the maintenance department or administering the administration department.

In order to perform the reciprocal allocation, we must set up two equations with two unknowns; the unknowns are the amount of administration to be allocated

---

EXHIBIT 4B–1   Example of Reciprocal Cost Allocation for a Museum

	Adminis-tration	Mainte-nance	Curato-rial	Opera-tions	Totals
Basic Information:					
Area occupied (square feet)	1,000	—	1,000	3,000	5,000
Labor-hours	—	100	100	400	600
Mission center costs ($000).........			$1,500	$4,000	$5,500
Service center costs ($000)	$1,200	$2,400			$3,600
Total costs ($000)					$9,100

(which is designated as *A*) and the amount of maintenance to be allocated (designated as *M*). Then, since maintenance costs are allocated on the basis of square footage, and administration occupies 1/5 (1,000/5,000) of the square footage,

$$A = \$1{,}200 + 1/5(M)$$

In effect, the amount of administration to be allocated is the sum of its direct costs plus its share of the maintenance costs.

Since administration costs are allocated on the basis of hours worked, and maintenance uses 1/6 (100/600) of the hours,

$$M = \$2{,}400 + 1/6(A)$$

That is, the amount of maintenance to be allocated is the sum of its direct costs plus its share of the administration costs.

We now can substitute terms, as follows:

$$A = \$1{,}200 + 1/5[\$2{,}400 + 1/6(A)]$$

or

$$A = \$1{,}200 + \$480 + 1/30(A)$$

Therefore,

$$A = \$1{,}738$$

And, since $M = \$2{,}400 + 1/6(A)$,

$$M = \$2{,}690$$

To complete the reciprocal allocation, we remove $1,738 from administration and allocate it to the remaining three cost centers on the basis of labor-hours, and we remove $2,690 from maintenance and allocate it to the three other cost centers on the basis of square footage. The result is that the service center costs are fully allocated to both the other service centers and the mission centers, and the full $9,100 in costs now resides only in the mission centers. These allocations are shown in Exhibit 4B–2.

As might be imagined, once the number of cost centers exceeds three or four, solving the set of simultaneous equations becomes quite complex for a person,

EXHIBIT 4B–2 Allocation of Service Center Costs to Mission Centers ($000):

	Adminis-tration	*Mainte-nance*	*Curato-rial*	*Opera-tions*	*Totals*
Initial costs	$1,200	$2,400	$1,500	$4,000	$9,100
Maintenance allocation*	538	(2,690)	538	1,614	—
Administration allocation†	(1,738)	290	290	1,158	—
Total costs			$2,328	$6,772	$9,100

* $2,690 from formula. Allocated ⅕ to Administration, ⅕ to Curatorial, ⅗ to Operations.
† $1,738 from formula. Allocated ⅙ to Maintenance, ⅙ to Curatorial, 4/6 to Operations.

although it can be done easily with a computer. Moreover, even the stepdown method can benefit from the use of a rather simple spreadsheet application that carries out the allocations automatically. Designed properly, the computer program will allow an analyst to determine how the costs of each mission center are affected by different cost center structures, different allocation bases, and different stepdown sequences

SUGGESTED ADDITIONAL READINGS

Anthony, R. N., and James S. Reece. *Accounting: Text and Cases,* 9th ed. Homewood, Ill.: Richard D. Irwin, 1992.

Cooper, Robin, and Robert S. Kaplan. *The Design of Cost Management Systems: Text, Cases, and Readings.* Englewood Cliffs, N.J.: Prentice Hall, 1991.

Hansen, Don R., and Maryanne M. Mowen. *Management Accounting,* 2nd ed. Cincinnati, Ohio: South-Western Publishing, 1992.

Heitger, Les, Ogan Pekin, and Serge Matulich. *Cost Accounting,* 2nd ed. Cincinnati, Ohio: South-Western Publishing, 1992.

Horngren, Charles, and George Foster. *Cost Accounting: A Managerial Emphasis.* Englewood Cliffs, N.J.: Prentice Hall, 1991.

Suver, James D., Bruce R. Neumann, and Keith E. Boles. *Management Accounting for Healthcare Organizations,* 3rd ed. Westchester, Ill.: Healthcare Financial Management Association; and Chicago, Ill.: Pluribus Press, Inc., 1992.

Young, David W. *Financial Control in Health Care: A Managerial Perspective.* Homewood, Ill.: Dow Jones-Irwin, 1984.

CASE 4–1   Croswell University Hospital*

Ann Julian, M.D., chief of the department of obstetrics and gynecology at Croswell University Hospital (CUH), was reviewing the hospital's most recent cost report. Disappointed with its contents, she was meeting with Jonathan Haskell, the director of fiscal affairs, whose department had generated the report. She was not pleased.

> This report doesn't describe where our costs are generated. We're applying one standard to all patients, regardless of their level of care. What incentive is there to identify and account for the costs of each type of procedure? Unless I have better cost information, all our attempts to control costs will focus on decreasing the number of days spent in the hospital. This limits our options. In fact, it's not even an appropriate response to the hospital's reimbursement constraints.

Background

With the advent of DRGs and other reimbursement limits in the early 1980s, CUH had felt the pinch of third parties' attempts to control hospital costs. The third parties effectively had placed hospitals at risk for their own costs. Croswell, like many other tertiary care institutions, had extended the cost control responsibility to its middle managers. It required each department head to become involved in the hospital's budgeting process, and to become accountable for the share of costs associated with his or her department's activities.

After considerable discussion with the board, the vice president for Medical Affairs had agreed that each clinical department chief should assume responsibility for the share of costs associated with the care of patients in his or her specialty. By enlisting the participation of chiefs in the cost control efforts, Croswell's senior management hoped to improve the hospital's overall financial performance.

The Present System

The hospital's present cost accounting system was based on an average standard costing unit applied to each department. For inpatient costs, the system used a cost-per-bed-per-day, known as a *bed/day*. For operating rooms (both inpatient and emergency), the standard unit was a cost-per-operation or procedure.

* This case was prepared by Emily Hayden, R.N., M.B.A., under the supervision of Professor David W. Young. It was prepared with assistance from Richard Depp, M.D. and with financial support from the Association of Professors of Gynecology and Obstetrics. Development of the case was made possible by a grant from Wyeth-Ayerst Laboratories to the APGO Medical Education Foundation. Copyright © by David W. Young.

To calculate the unit cost, the fiscal affairs department began with the direct costs of each department, as shown in Exhibit 1. It then allocated indirect costs, such as maintenance and depreciation, according to a predetermined method. It had developed this method in order to report costs to third parties such as medicare. The method used allocation bases such as size of plant, number of employees, salary dollars, and the total number of bed/days. For a given cost, the basis of allocation was designed to distribute indirect costs as fairly as possible across departments.

EXHIBIT 1   Cost Center Report for 1991

Cost Center: Inpatient Surgery-Gynecology

Number of available bed/days	16,425	
Number of occupied bed/days	14,602	
Occupancy rate	88.9%	
Direct costs:		
Wages:		
Nursing service	$3,182,330	
Clinical support staff	902,790	
Administrative staff	132,605	$ 4,217,725
Supplies:		
Pharmaceutical	$2,518,643	
Medical supplies	670,050	3,188,693
Diagnostic/Therapeutic:		
Diagnostic imaging	$ 687,361	
Laboratory tests	923,986	
Radiotherapy	279,486	1,890,833
Total direct costs		$ 9,297,251
Indirect costs:		
Patient Services:		
Dietary	$ 626,430	
Laundry	169,575	
Housekeeping	154,260	
Medical records	127,720	
Social service	120,897	$ 1,198,882
Capital equipment:		
Depreciation on major purchases	$ 174,000	
Minor purchases	34,000	208,000
General services:		
Operation of plant	$ 236,450	
Plant depreciation	382,680	
Employee benefits	469,950	
Administration	1,205,450	
Liability insurance	541,000	$ 2,835,530
Total indirect costs		$ 4,242,412
Total direct and indirect costs		$13,539,663
Average cost per day at full capacity		$824.33
Average cost per day at occupied capacity		$927.25

Once all direct costs had been assigned to departments, and indirect costs had been allocated, the fiscal staff would calculate the average cost per unit by dividing the department's total costs by the number of activity units for that department. Exhibit 2 shows the average cost per unit for several surgical specialty departments.

After reviewing the costs and activities of the department of Ob/Gyn, Dr. Julian felt that obstetrical procedures were fairly well defined in terms of their costs. By contrast, gynecological procedures were a problem. She commented:

> Gynecological procedures are less amenable to assignment into cost categories. This is mainly because of the age range and diversity of the patients, but it's also due to the distinctions among the surgical subspecialties in gynecology. Because of this, the present cost accounting system is of little use for gynecology cases. This is extremely frustrating, especially since the hospital is expecting me to utilize the average cost per day approach to manage costs in the department. The average figure simply does not account for the real use of clinical resources by gynecology patients.

Mr. Haskell disagreed.

> Dr. Julian just doesn't understand. This system is ideal for comparative purposes. It allows me to quickly compare the costs of services among different departments within the hospital. It also helps me to compare the cost of a particular department at Croswell with a similar department at another hospital. Additionally, I can use the information to estimate the cost of treating an entire illness at Croswell. For example, I can easily

EXHIBIT 2   Cost Summary for Surgical Specialties

Specialty	Costing Unit	Total Cost	Average Cost at Occupied Capacity	Average Cost at Full Capacity
General	Bed/day	$11,871,305	$ 797.36	$721.32
Orthopedic	Bed/day	12,274,636	938.24	794.56
Neurosurgery	Bed/day	15,837,594	1,105.80	808.80
Gynecology.......................	Bed/day	13,539,663	927.25	824.33
Obstetrics	Bed/day	9,483,625	819.12	733.80
Pediatrics.........................	Bed/day	11,847,364	882.28	802.68
Inpatient operating rooms		$13,789,475		
Major/general anesthesia	Procedure		$ 1,197	
Major/epidural or spinal..............	Procedure		1,163	
Major/local or regional	Procedure		760	
Minor/general anesthesia	Procedure		589	
Minor/epidural or spinal..............	Procedure		485	
Minor/local or regional	Procedure		274	
Emergency operating rooms		$ 4,842,631		
Minor/general anesthesia	Procedure		$ 486	
Minor/local or regional...............	Procedure		388	
Minor/no anesthesia	Procedure		178	
Total costs.........................		$93,486,293		

determine the approximate cost of treating a patient having a total abdominal hysterectomy [TAH].*

According to Mr. Haskell's figures, the cost of a nononcology TAH would be about $3,709 ($927.25 × 4), since an average procedure of this type required four days in the hospital. To this would be added the cost of a major operation with general anesthesia, or $1,197. This procedure might also be performed with epidural or spinal anesthesia at the discretion of the anesthesia staff, in which case the total cost of the procedure would be slightly less.

The inpatient operating room costs of specific operative procedures were based on a three-year study. These figures were updated regularly by the fiscal affairs department. Dr. Julian was not presently held accountable for these costs, nor for the costs of anesthesia management. She was held responsible only for the costs associated with the pre- and postoperative care of the patients in her department. These costs were the ones causing her difficulty. According to her:

> Some patients, especially those undergoing treatment for cancer, use more resources than others. This is mainly because the testing and therapeutic treatment of patients varies widely. Some require more or fewer diagnostic and therapeutic interventions, depending upon their admitting diagnoses. For example, radiation therapy is utilized almost exclusively by oncology patients.
>
> Somehow, a good cost accounting system must recognize these differences. I also don't want my department to appear overly costly simply because some patients don't conform to the norm. The current cost accounting system just does not account for the differences among patients, and it doesn't give me the data I need to manage costs.

The Use of Clinical Distinctions

After some discussion, Dr. Julian convinced Mr. Haskell that the average unit cost calculation could be revised to account for the differences among patients having different gynecology procedures. In an effort to address these clinical differences, Mr. Haskell suggested that the gynecology patients be divided into three categories according to clinical subspecialty:

1. General gynecology/urogynecology (Nononco Gyn).
2. Reproductive/in vitro fertilization (RE-IVF).
3. Oncology.

With the help of Dr. Julian, Mr. Haskell calculated time and material estimates for each type of patient stay. For example, he estimated that, in general, more medication was used on oncology patients than on general gynecology patients. Also, oncology patients were likely to need more of a variety of other resources, such as lab tests, drugs, and X rays.

---

* This is a procedure in which the uterus, fallopian tubes, and ovaries are removed. If the procedure is done for reasons other than cancer, then it is classified as a *nononcology procedure*.

Mr. Haskell conferred with his staff regarding the best method to apportion indirect costs among the three subspecialties. After much discussion, they decided to apportion most of these costs according to the number of patient days in each subspecialty. They made a few adjustments, however, to reflect unusual circumstances.

Although this new system maintained bed/days as the standard costing unit, Mr. Haskell pointed out that it was more accurate than the one currently in use because there were now three average costs per bed/day: one for general gynecology/urogynecology, another for RE-IVF, and a third for oncology. Exhibit 3 contains this information.

EXHIBIT 3   Department of Gynecology Cost Breakdown by Surgical Specialty

Costs	General Gynecology	Reproductive/ IVF	Oncology	Total
Direct:				
Wages:				
Nursing	$1,040,160	$ 903,080	$1,239,090	$ 3,182,330
Clinical support	302,900	247,210	352,680	902,790
Administration	41,825	37,475	53,305	132,605
Supplies:				
Pharmaceutical.	650,422	595,277	1,272,944	2,518,643
Medical supplies	119,470	238,940	311,640	670,050
Diagnostic/therapeutic:				
Diagnostic imaging	229,564	153,838	303,959	687,361
Laboratory tests	295,384	241,745	386,857	923,986
Radiotherapy	0	0	279,486	279,486
Total direct.	$2,679,725	$2,417,565	$4,199,961	$ 9,297,251
Indirect:				
Patient services:				
Dietary.	$ 180,480	$ 136,490	$ 309,460	$ 626,430
Laundry.	57,495	45,535	66,545	169,575
Housekeeping.	49,090	43,030	62,140	154,260
Medical records.	30,930	31,850	64,940	127,720
Social services	32,567	28,465	59,865	120,897
Capital equipment:				
Major equipment depreciation	36,692	82,540	54,768	174,000
Minor.	7,564	13,875	12,561	34,000
General services:				
Operation of plant.	79,160	59,155	98,135	236,450
Plant depreciation	102,230	113,370	167,080	382,680
Employee benefits.	141,550	153,280	175,120	469,950
Administration.	235,510	480,530	489,410	1,205,450
Liability insurance	195,771	187,243	157,986	541,000
Total indirect	$1,149,039	$1,375,363	$1,718,010	$ 4,242,412
Total direct and indirect	$3,828,764	$3,792,928	$5,917,971	$13,539,663
Number of bed/days.	4,002	5,023	5,577	
Cost per bed/day.	$ 956.71	$ 755.11	$ 1,061.14	

Dr. Julian and Mr. Haskell performed some calculations and compared the differences between the two systems. They computed the cost of an abdominal hysterectomy (nononcology) using each system. Dr. Julian estimated that an uncomplicated TAH generally required a four-day stay under general gynecology. They also compared the costs of patients undergoing two other procedures. One was a tuboplasty, a procedure in which the fallopian tube is opened or its lumen (passage) is reestablished. The other procedure was a total abdominal hysterectomy (TAH) with lymph node dissection. In this operation, the lymph nodes in the pelvic region are also excised. The tuboplasty would be categorized in the RE-IVF category, while, in this instance, the TAH with lymph node dissection would be classified in the oncology category.

From their findings, Dr. Julian and Mr. Haskell concluded that this specialty-based system could greatly increase Dr. Julian's ability to identify and control costs.

Intensities of Care

After Dr. Julian had compared a few more specialty-based costs of care, she continued to harbor some concerns about the system. Although it was an improvement over the average bed/day calculation, it still had problems. She was particularly disturbed about the intensities of medical and nursing attention given to patients within each subspecialty category. Dr. Julian explained to Mr. Haskell that, for example, a TAH patient with cancer required more nursing and medical care on the second postoperative day than did a laparoscopy patient, even if both patients were classified in the oncology category.

The new system did not address these differences. The system made it appear as if all oncology patients received the same amount of care on a given day in the hospital. From a clinical perspective, this clearly was not the case. Because of this, Dr. Julian felt that the subspecialty breakdown was still not a sufficiently accurate measure of the costs of care rendered to different patients. Working on her own, she developed a third cost accounting method based on levels of care delivered by the nursing and medical teams. In developing this new method, she divided the department's costs into three categories that were quite different from those used by Mr. Haskell:

1. Daily patient maintenance.
2. Medical treatment.
3. Nursing care.

Dr. Julian decided that medical treatment could be measured with an index of non-nursing clinical intensity. She worked with two other physicians in the department to determine the amount of laboratory, diagnostic radiology, therapeutic radiology, and pharmacy resources that would be used by a typical patient with a TAH (nononcology), a TAH (oncology), and a tuboplasty. She then translated these resources into units that could be counted and totaled easily. Dr. Julian knew that this type of information was not completely accurate. For example, a TAH (nononcology) patient in relatively good health would need fewer tests and drugs than a somewhat older patient, or a patient with complications. This could result in higher or lower medical intensity, even though the number of medical treatment units in the system would be the same for all patients with the same procedure. Despite these problems, she felt that she now had a way to measure medical resource use fairly accurately.

Levels of nursing care proved to be a similarly complicated issue. Dr. Julian consulted with nurses on the gynecology floors and, with them, developed a system to measure patient care needs. They defined three basic levels of nursing care, which are described in Exhibit 4. A patient could change levels during his or her stay. Within each level, a patient could be assigned a range of units, depending upon the intensity of nursing services being provided.

EXHIBIT 4   Levels of Nursing Care

Level 1. Basic Assistance (mainly for ambulatory patients)   **1–3 units**
   Feeds self without supervision or with family member.
   Toilets independently.
   Vital signs routine—daily temperature, pulse, and respiration.
   Bedside humidifier or blow bottle.
   Routine postoperation suction standby.
   Bathes self, bed straightened with minimal or no supervision.
   Exercises with assistance, once in eight hours.
   Treatments once or twice in eight hours.

Level 2. Periodic Assistance   **4–7 units**
   Feeds self with staff supervision; or tubal feeding by patient.
   Toilets with supervision or specimen collection, or uses bedpan. Hemovac output.
   Vital signs monitored; every 2 to 4 hours.
   Mist or humidified air when sleeping, or cough and deep breathe every 2 hours.
   Nasopharyngeal or oral suction prn.
   Bathed and dressed by personnel or partial bath given; daily change of linen.
   Up in chair with assistance twice in 8 hours or walking with assistance.
   Treatments 3 or 4 times in 8 hours.

Level 3. Continual Nursing Care   **8–10 units**
   Total feeding by personnel or continuous IV or blood transfusions or instructing
      the patient.
   Tube feeding by personnel every three hours or less.
   Up to toilet with standby supervision or output measurement every hour. Initial
      hemovac setup.
   Vital signs and observation every hour or vital signs monitored plus neuro check.
      Blood pressure, pulse, respiration, and neuro check every 30 minutes.
   Continuous oxygen, trach mist or cough and deep breathe every hour. IPPB with
      supervision every four hours.
   Tracheostomy suction every two hours or less.
   Bathed and dressed by personnel, special skin care, occupied bed.
   Bed rest with assistance in turning every two hours or less, or walking with assis-
      tance of two persons twice in eight hours.
   Treatments more than every two hours.

Source: Adapted from M. Poland et al., "PETO—A System for Assisting and Meeting Patient Care Needs," *American Journal of Nursing* 70 (July 1970), p. 1479.

In this third method, Dr. Julian expected to use not only bed/days as a costing unit, but also, the average number of medical treatment and nursing units per procedure. She enlisted the assistance of Mr. Haskell in devising a means to apportion costs to each of the categories in her new system. The resulting cost summary is shown in Exhibit 5.

EXHIBIT 5   Department of Gynecology Level of Care System

Costs	Daily Patient Maintenance	Medical Treatment	Nursing Care	Total
Direct:				
Wages:				
Nursing			$3,182,330	$3,182,330
Clinical support	$ 17,345	$ 429,756	455,689	902,790
Administration	132,605			132,605
Supplies:				
Pharmaceutical		$2,518,643		2,518,643
Medical supplies	229,310	328,140	112,600	670,050
Diagnostic/therapeutic:				
Diagnostic imaging		687,361		687,361
Laboratory tests		923,986		923,986
Radiotherapy		279,486		279,486
Total direct	$ 379,260	$5,167,372	$3,750,619	$9,297,251
Indirect:				
Patient services:				
Dietary	$ 626,430			626,430
Laundry	169,575			169,575
Housekeeping	154,260			154,260
Medical records	85,145	28,575	14,000	127,720
Social services	72,100	30,050	18,747	120,897
Capital equipment:				
Major equipment depreciation	35,276	138,724		174,000
Minor	6,748	17,928	9,324	34,000
General services:				
Operation of plant	236,450			236,450
Plant depreciation	382,680			382,680
Employee benefits		194,490	275,460	469,950
Administration	1,205,450			1,205,450
Liability insurance		502,000	39,000	541,000
Total indirect	$2,974,114	$ 911,767	$ 356,531	$ 4,242,412
Total direct and indirect costs	$3,353,374	$6,079,139	$4,107,150	$13,539,663
Total days care	14,602			
Cost per bed/day	$ 230			
Total medical treatment units		36,180		
Cost per medical treatment unit		$ 168		
Total nursing units			49,754	
Cost per nursing unit			$ 83	

Comparison of Costs

To compare her new system with the others, Dr. Julian again calculated costs for the same three procedures. According to her calculations, each required the following:

Procedure	Bed/days	Total Medical Treatment Units	Total Nursing Units
TAH-Nononcology......	4	12	10
Tuboplasty.............	3	10	5
TAH-Oncology.........	7	20	38

Dr. Julian was satisfied with the results of this cost accounting system. She believed that it accurately distinguished among the surgical procedures in the gynecologic subspecialties, and that the differences in costs reflected the actual differences in resources used by patients. She commented:

With this new information, I can identify cost problems easily since all costs are now categorized according to the nature as well as the intensity of the services. I plan to develop this system even further so that standard unit requirements for each type of procedure become well-known by the attendings and residents in my department. Then I'll be able to analyze gynecology costs according to the particular patient mix being treated, and in terms of the services being provided by different physicians in the department.

Mr. Haskell agreed with Dr. Julian that this third system might work well in gynecology, and in other departments having surgical subspecialties. However, he doubted that it could be transferred to all departments within the hospital. He felt that some departments would not be able to develop standard medical and nursing requirements since their patient diagnoses and procedures were less well-defined than in surgery. Furthermore, he was concerned about the complexity of the system, especially for department chiefs. Chiefs, in his view, might not have the inclination to use the system effectively or might not feel it worth the time to collect all of the necessary information.

Dr. Julian disagreed. She contacted the vice president of medical affairs and offered to present her system at the next meeting of chiefs of service. She was convinced that, unlike Mr. Haskell, the chiefs would see the value of the system.

Questions

1. What is the cost of a TAH (nononcology) under each of the cost accounting systems? A tuboplasty? A TAH (oncology)? What accounts for the changes from one system to the next?

2. Which of the three systems is the best? Why?
3. From a managerial perspective, of what use is the information in the second and third systems? That is, how, if at all, would this additional information improve Dr. Julian's ability to control costs? How might it help chiefs in nonsurgical specialties?
4. What should Dr. Julian do?

CASE 4–2   Jefferson High School*

"I'm sorry, but I'm having a very difficult time using the information on this cost report," said Mr. Adam King, principal of Jefferson High School. "I mean, salary totals and the average unit cost may be useful to you and the people in the central office, but I need to know more detail. We have so many different types of activities at Jefferson that I need to know the unit cost for each if I'm going to do anything about cost control."

Mr. King was discussing the Los Diablos school system's cost accounting system with Mr. Michael Abbott, director of the fiscal affairs department. Mr. King had requested the meeting because he felt he needed more information than that contained on his school's cost report, shown in Exhibit 1. Interested in improving cost control methods at Jefferson High, Mr. King argued that the average per-student cost calculation was not an accurate measure of Jefferson's costs because the type and content of a student's educational activities varied greatly depending on the student's grade, interests, and special needs. According to Mr. King, the school system's cost accounting system needed to be revised in order to identify the specific unit costs of various student-based activities. During the discussion, Mr. Abbott became interested in Mr. King's approach, and agreed to help him design a cost accounting system that made these distinctions.

Background

In 1986, in conjunction with the Los Diablos school system's move toward decentralizing its educational activities, a school-based cost accounting system had been developed. As one of the system's largest schools, Jefferson was among the first to implement such a system, which required the assistance of principals in monitoring their school's expenditures. By involving principals in the budgeting and expenditure review process, Ms. Nell Chamberlain, Los Diablos' school superintendent, hoped to gain more control over school-based costs and to improve the system's overall financial performance.

The School-Based Cost Accounting System (SBCAS) was based on a standard costing unit which each school could use to measure its overall costs. SBCAS

---

* This case was prepared by Professor David W. Young. Copyright © by David W. Young.

EXHIBIT 1   School-Based Cost Report, 1985–86

Statistics:

Number of registered students.....................	750	
Number of days in academic year..................	170	
Number of potential student days..................	127,500	
Actual number of student days	115,350	
Attendance rate................................	90.5%	

Direct costs—Instruction

Regular teacher salaries..........................	$1,175,000	
Special education teacher salaries..................	480,000	
Aide salaries....................................	58,500	
Substitute teacher salaries.......................	37,700	
Instructional supplies and library	85,200	
Other services*	327,500	
Total		$2,163,900

Direct costs—Administration

Administrative salaries...........................	$ 125,000	
Administrative supplies	15,500	
Operations and maintenance......................	270,000	
Other...	7,500	
Total		418,000

Total direct costs		$2,581,900

Indirect costs—Allocated from central office

School committee	$ 3,500	
Administration..................................	43,300	
Health/life insurance	135,200	
Operation and maintenance	7,400	
Rent and depreciation	3,500	
Contract services	2,200	
Travel	850	
Total		195,950

Total direct and indirect costs		$2,777,850
Average cost per registered student		$ 3,704

* Includes athletics, transportation, and counseling.

used a student as the basic cost calculation unit. To calculate an average cost per student for any given school, SBCAS first collected the direct costs on the School-Based Cost Report (SBCR), as shown in Exhibit 1. The fiscal affairs department then allocated the central office costs, such as depreciation, health and life insurance, and administration to each school according to a predetermined method. These allocation methods for indirect costs had been determined by Mr. Abbott, and included classroom space, number of student days, number of employees, and salary dollars. The basis of allocation for any given cost was designed to provide the fairest means possible for distributing it to the various schools in the system.

Once all costs had been allocated to schools, the fiscal staff would calculate the average cost per student by dividing the schools' total costs by the appropriate number of students. These calculations also are shown on Exhibit 1.

According to Mr. Abbott, the main advantage of this system was that it allowed him to quickly compare the cost of educating a child in different schools. He also thought the system could be used to calculate the cost of educating the students in a particular grade. For example, to determine the cost of educating students in the 12th grade, Mr. Abbott could multiply the number of students in that grade at Jefferson High by Jefferson's average cost per student, perform similar calculations for all other high schools in the system, and add the results together.

For Ms. Chamberlain, the SBCAS was to be the basis for greater fiscal accountability, and she had notified the principals in each school that she expected them to work with the SBCAS data in attempting to control costs. This was the main source of concern for Mr. King, since he thought that the average cost per student was not an accurate measure for most of the students at Jefferson High. According to him, the actual cost of a student varied because students at different grade levels required different types and levels of education. Mr. King argued that the average cost per student misrepresented the resource needs of most students, and, because of this, the SBCAS did not provide him with the data he needed for accurate budgeting and planning.

Grade-Based System

In an effort to address this problem, Mr. Abbott suggested that the SBCAS for Jefferson be based on grade distinctions. He therefore divided the school's students into three categories based on their grade levels—10th, 11th, and 12th—and, with Mr. King's help, calculated personnel and supply estimates for each grade level. For example, he estimated that although there were fewer students in the 12th grade than the 10th or 11th, many students in the 12th grade regularly used the school's career counselor, whereas most students in the 10th and 11th grades did not. From these estimates, Mr. Abbott assigned Jefferson's direct costs to each grade level.

Next, Mr. Abbott set about devising a method for allocating the indirect costs. After much discussion with Mr. King and his staff, he decided to allocate all these costs according to the number of students in each grade. His calculations are contained in Exhibit 2.

Although the new system maintained a student as the standard costing unit, Mr. Abbott argued that it was a more accurate approach than the system currently in use. Instead of an average cost per student, he now had three average cost figures: one for each grade level.

In evaluating the new cost accounting system, Mr. King and Mr. Abbott explored the differences in cost calculations resulting from the two systems. Some quick computations by the two pointed out the differences in the cost per student under different accounting procedures. From these findings, Mr. Abbott concluded that his "grade-based" system could greatly increase a principal's ability to budget and control costs.

EXHIBIT 2   Grade-Based Cost Report, 1985–86

	Grade 10	Grade 11	Grade 12	Total
Direct costs—Instruction				
Regular teacher salaries	$ 470,000	$411,250	$293,750	$1,175,000
Special education teacher salaries.........	240,000	144,000	96,000	480,000
Aide salaries	35,100	14,625	8,775	58,500
Substitute teacher salaries	15,080	13,195	9,425	37,700
Instructional supplies and library	34,080	29,820	21,300	85,200
Other services.........................	65,500	81,875	180,125	327,500
Total	$ 859,760	$694,765	$609,375	$2,163,900
Direct costs—Administration				
Administrative salaries	$ 50,000	$ 43,750	$ 31,250	$ 125,000
Administrative supplies..................	6,200	5,425	3,875	15,500
Operations and maintenance	67,500	108,000	94,500	270,000
Other................................	3,000	2,625	1,875	7,500
Total	$ 126,700	$159,800	$131,500	$ 418,000
Indirect costs—Allocated from central office				
School committee......................	$ 1,400	$ 1,223	$ 877	$ 3,500
Administration........................	17,320	15,126	10,854	43,300
Health/life insurance	54,080	47,230	33,890	135,200
Operation and maintenance	2,960	2,585	1,855	7,400
Rent and depreciation	1,400	1,223	877	3,500
Contract services	880	769	551	2,200
Travel	340	297	213	850
Total	$ 78,380	$ 68,453	$ 49,117	$ 195,950
Total direct and				
indirect costs......................	$1,064,840	$923,018	$789,992	$2,777,850
Number of registered students.............	300	262	188	
Average cost per registered student.........	$ 3,550	$ 3,523	$ 4,202	

As Mr. King reflected on the new system, a few problems continued to bother him. Although he agreed that the grade-based costs were more accurate than the school-based per-student calculations, he felt there were further distinctions in resource use that the system did not sufficiently address. He was particularly disturbed about the varying intensities of special education, athletics, and counseling received within each grade. Mr. King explained to Mr. Abbott that, according to the new accounting system, it appeared as though all students in the 12th grade received the same amount of educational resources, but from his perspective this clearly was not the case. He pointed out by way of example that a student in varsity athletics received far more athletic resources than one taking only regular physical education classes. Similarly, a student whose behavior resulted in a need to see the school counselor regularly used more counseling resources than one who was well-behaved. These sorts of distinctions could be made, he argued, for special education as well. As such, the grade-based breakdown was not a sufficiently accurate measure.

Service-Based System

Unable to convince Mr. Abbott of the importance of this additional refinement, Mr. King himself began experimenting with a third cost accounting method—based on levels of educational services received—that he thought might be more accurate. As the first step in his calculations, he divided the school's costs according to the type of service provided: regular education, special education, athletics, and counseling. He decided that a student's use of the regular education component could be measured most easily and accurately in terms of the number of days of school attendance during the academic year.

Examining Jefferson's student records, he decided that it was more complicated to measure special education. He consulted with some of the special education teachers and, with them, developed a system based on levels of special education needs. They decided to define special education intensity on three levels: one unit represented occasional assistance only; two units were for a student who received special education services for one or two days a week; three units represented three or more days a week.

Athletics and counseling were measured in a similar fashion. Students who participated in after-school athletic programs but did not play either junior varsity or varsity sports received one unit; two units were given for junior varsity; three units for varsity. Students who used counseling services on an infrequent basis received one unit; those who used them more regularly received two units; those who used them continually received three units.

Having developed these classifications, Mr. King solicited Mr. Abbott's assistance in allocating indirect costs; their cost summary is contained in Exhibit 3. In this analysis, Mr. King expected to use more than student days as the costing unit. For each student, he would need to calculate the number of days of school attendance, and estimate the number of units required for special education, athletics, and counseling.

To compare this system with the others, Mr. King chose three students at random in order to determine their costs. According to his calculations, each required the following:

Student	Grade	Regular Education	Special Education	Athletics	Counseling
Larry B	10	170 days	2 units	0 units	0 units
Michael R	11	150	0	3	2
Anna B	12	165	3	1	3

Mr. King was satisfied with the results of this cost accounting system. He thought that it accurately distinguished among the various types of services available, and that the differences in costs reflected actual differences in services received. He felt that because he could now isolate costs by both the nature and intensity of the service provided, he would be able to locate and manage cost

EXHIBIT 3   Service-Based Cost Report, 1985–86

	Regular Education	Special Education	Athletics	Counseling	Total
Direct costs—Instruction					
Regular teacher salaries	$1,112,300		$ 62,700		$1,175,000
Special education teacher salaries		$480,000			480,000
Aide salaries	15,300	43,200			58,500
Substitute teacher salaries	25,700	12,000			37,700
Instructional supplies and library	60,200	25,000			85,200
Other services.......................	18,200	50,300	204,000	$55,000	327,500
Total	$1,231,700	$610,500	$266,700	$55,000	$2,163,900
Direct costs—Administration					
Administrative salaries	$ 71,750	$ 35,266	$ 15,406	$ 3,178	$ 125,000
Administrative supplies	8,823	4,373	1,910	394	15,500
Operations and maintenance	153,685	76,175	33,277	6,863	270,000
Other	4,269	2,116	924	191	7,500
Total	$ 237,927	$117,930	$ 51,517	$10,626	$ 418,000
Indirect costs—Allocated from central office					
School committee	$ 1,992	$ 987	$ 431	$ 89	$ 3,500
Administration	24,648	12,216	5,337	1,101	43,300
Health/life insurance.................	76,956	38,144	16,663	3,436	135,200
Operation and maintenance	4,212	2,088	912	188	7,400
Rent and depreciation................	1,992	987	431	89	3,500
Contract services	1,252	621	271	56	2,200
Travel.............................	484	240	105	22	850
Total	$ 111,536	$ 55,283	$ 24,150	$ 4,981	$ 195,950
Total direct and indirect costs....................	$1,581,163	$783,713	$342,367	$70,607	$2,777,850
Total number of units	127,500	1,200	1,500	300	
Cost per unit........................	$ 12.40	$ 653.09	$ 280.13	$ 235.36	

problems in the school more easily, thereby complying more effectively with Ms. Chamberlain's expectations.

Mr. Abbott, however, remained skeptical. Although he thought Mr. King might be able to make effective use of the system at Jefferson, he doubted that it could be transferred to other schools since, in his view, other schools would not be able to develop resource utilization units for the various services. Furthermore, he was afraid that the system was too complicated to be implemented in all schools. Finally, he seriously questioned the ability of principals to use the system effectively.

Questions

1. What is the cost for each of the three students Mr. King chose at random? What explains the differences?
2. Which of the three systems is the best? Why?

3. What other systems, if any, would you propose?
4. What should Mr. King do?

CASE 4–3   Rosemont Hill Children's Center*

In March 1983, Mr. Frank Mitchell, Administrator of the Rosemont Hill Children's Center, expressed concern about the center's cost accounting system. The extensive funding Rosemont Hill had received during its early years was decreasing, and Mr. Mitchell wanted to prepare the center to be self-sufficient, yet he lacked critical cost information.

At a meeting with Mr. Robert Simi, Rosemont Hill's new accountant, Mr. Mitchell outlined the principal issues:

> Our deficit is increasing, and we obviously have to reverse this trend if we're going to become solvent. But, for that, we have to know where our costs are, in particular the cost of each of the services we offer.

Background

Rosemont Hill Children's Center was established in 1968 by a consortium of community groups. Situated in Roxbury, an inner-city residential neighborhood of Boston, Massachusetts, the center was intended to provide counseling and related services to residents of Roxbury and neighboring communities. Fifteen years after its inception, the center maintained strong ties with the community groups responsible for its development and subsequent acceptance in Roxbury.

Funding for Rosemont Hill was initially provided by the federal government as part of the Department of Health, Education and Welfare's attempt to provide social services to inner-city poverty areas in the United States. When these operating funds were depleted in 1981, the city of Boston supplemented Rosemont Hill's income with a small three-year grant. Because Mr. Mitchell realized that government support could not continue indefinitely, he intended to make the center self-sufficient as soon as possible. Rosemont Hill's income statement is contained in Exhibit 1.

The center was composed of eight client-service departments: Homemaker Service, Family Planning, Counseling, Parents' Advocacy, Mental Health, Alcohol Rehabilitation, Community Outreach, Referral and Placement. In addition, the center had a Training and Education Department, which saw no clients, and a

---

* This case was prepared by Patricia O'Brien under the direction of Professor David W. Young. Copyright © by the President and Fellows of Harvard College. Distributed by the Pew Curriculum Center, Harvard School of Public Health.

EXHIBIT 1

ROSEMONT HILL CHILDREN'S CENTER
Income Statement
For the Year Ended December 31, 1982

Revenue from patient fees............	$690,900
Other revenues.....................	10,000
Total revenue..................	$700,900
Expenses:	
Program services.................	$470,000
Recordkeeping....................	20,000
Training and education............	50,000
General and administrative........	184,000
Total expenses.................	$724,000
Surplus (deficit).....................	(23,100)

Client Records Department. The center had 22 paid employees and a volunteer staff of 6–10 students acquiring clinical and managerial experience.

Community Outreach, which had been designed by Rosemont Hill's consumers, was a multidisciplinary department providing a link between the health and social services at Rosemont Hill and the schools and city services of the community. The department was staffed by a part-time speech pathologist, a part-time learning specialist, and a full-time nutritionist.

The Referral and Placement Service was for clients whom Rosemont Hill felt, at the time it received a referral, it could not serve; the center attempted to locate another agency that could serve the client. Parents' Advocacy did not serve clients directly but rather worked on behalf of clients who were having difficulty with housing, schools, and so forth.

The Existing Information System

Rosemont Hill's previous accountant had established a system to determine the cost per client visit (or related activity such as advocacy). According to this method, shown in Exhibit 2, the cost was a yearly average for all client visits. The accountant would first determine the direct cost of each department. He would then add overhead costs, such as administration, rent, and utilities, to the total cost of all the departments to determine the center's total costs. Finally, he would divide that total by the number of visits. Increased by an anticipated inflation figure for the following year (approximately 8 to 10 percent), this number became the projected cost per client visit for the subsequent year.

In reviewing this method with Mr. Simi, Mr. Mitchell explained the problems he perceived. He said that although he realized this was not a precise method of determining costs for clients, the center's cost per visit had to be held at a reason-

---

EXHIBIT 2 Costs and Client Visits for 1982, by Department*

Department	Number Client Visits	Expenses Salaries†	Expenses Other‡	Expenses Total
Homemaker Service	5,000	$ 40,000	$ 16,000	$ 56,000
Family Planning	10,000	10,000	30,000	40,000
Counseling........................	2,100	60,000	32,000	92,000
Parents' Advocacy.................	4,000	54,000	12,000	66,000
Mental Health.....................	1,400	30,000	16,000	46,000
Alcohol Rehabilitation..............	1,500	64,000	16,000	80,000
Community Outreach	2,500	10,000	20,000	30,000
Referral and Placement.............	6,400	40,000	20,000	60,000
Subtotal	32,900	308,000	162,000	470,000
Administration		76,000	4,000	80,000
Rent			72,000	72,000
Utilities..........................			20,000	20,000
Training and Education.............		32,000	18,000	50,000
Cleaning.........................			12,000	12,000
Recordkeeping		14,000	6,000	20,000
Total		$430,000	$294,000	$724,000
Number of patient visits............				32,900
Average cost per visit..............				$ 22.00

* Client visits rounded to nearest 100; expenses rounded to nearest $1,000.
† Includes fringe benefits.
‡ Materials, supplies, contracted services, depreciation, and other nonpersonnel expenses.

---

able level to keep the services accessible to as many community residents as possible. Additionally, he anticipated complications in determining the cost per visit for each of Rosemont Hill's departments:

> You have to consider that our overhead costs, like administration and rent, have to be included in the cost per visit. That's easy to do when we have a single cost, but I'm not certain how to go about it when determining costs on a departmental basis. Furthermore, it's important to point out that some of our departments provide services to others. Parents' Advocacy, for example. There are three social workers in that department, all earning the same salary. But one works exclusively for Counseling, another divides her time evenly between Family Planning and Homemaker Service. Only the third spends his entire time in the Advocacy Department seeing clients who don't need other social services, although he occasionally refers clients to other social workers. In the Alcohol Rehabilitation Department, the situation is more complicated. We have two MSWs, each earning $24,000 a year, and one bachelor degree social worker earning $16,000. The two MSWs yearly see about 1,500 clients who need counseling, but they also spend about 50 percent of their time in other departments. The BA social worker cuts pretty evenly across all departments except Referral and Placement, of course.

Mr. Simi added further dimensions to the problems:

> I've spent most of my time so far trying to get a handle on allocating these overhead costs to the departments. It's not an easy job, you know. Administration, for example,

EXHIBIT 3 Rosemont Hill Children's Center Floor Space and T&E Usage, by Department

Department	Floor Space*	T&E Usage†
Homemaker Service	1,000	1,000
Family Planning	1,300	200
Counseling	1,800	2,400
Parents' Advocacy	300	100
Mental Health	1,000	—
Alcohol Rehabilitation	500	—
Community Outreach	1,100	100
Referral and Placement	1,000	200
Administration	500	—
Recordkeeping	300	—
Training and Education (T&E)	1,200	—
Total	10,000	4,000

* In square feet, rounded to nearest 100.
† In hours per year, rounded to nearest 100.

seems to help everyone about equally, yet I suppose we might say more administrative time is spent in the departments where we pay more salaries. Rent, on the other hand, is pretty easy: that can be done on a square-foot basis. We could classify utilities according to usage if we had meters to measure electricity, phone usage, and so forth, but because we don't we have to do that on a square-foot basis as well. This applies to cleaning too, I guess. It seems to me that record keeping can be allocated on the basis of the number of records, and each department generates one record per patient-visit.

Training and Education (T&E) is the most confusing. Some departments don't use it at all, while others use it regularly. I guess the fairest would be to charge for T&E on an hourly basis. Since there are two people in the department, each working about 2,000 hours a year, the charge per hour would be about $8.00. But this is a bit unfair since the T&E Department also uses supplies, space, and administrative time. So we should include those other costs in its hourly rate. Thus, the process is confusing and I haven't really decided how to sort it out. However, I have prepared totals for floor space and T&E usage (Exhibit 3).

The Future

As Mr. Mitchell looked toward the remainder of 1983, he decided to calculate a precise cost figure for each department. The center was growing, and he estimated that total client volume would increase by about 10 percent during 1983, spread evenly over each department. He anticipated that costs would also increase by about 10 percent. He asked Mr. Simi to prepare a stepdown analysis for 1982 so that they would know Rosemont Hill's costs for each department. He planned to use this information to assist him in projecting costs for 1983.

Questions

1. What is the cost per visit for each department?
2. How might this information be used by Mr. Mitchell?

CASE 4–4   Charles W. Morgan Museum*

In November 1978, Cabot M. Davis was appointed Managing Director of the Charles W. Morgan Museum, succeeding Daniel Sharkey who had retired earlier that year after twenty-three years as head of the museum. Soon after he took over, Davis discovered a nagging problem which his predecessor never thought important enough to confront directly but which now threatened to disrupt the smooth operation of the museum. The problem concerned the distribution of the cost of certain activities which served four adjacent institutions (three schools and a research center) as well as the museum. Though the legal entity of the museum owned the land and facilities of all five institutions, and technically could direct their operation, in practice each was governed by its own board of trustees and operated under its own budget. The problem with cost distribution arose because the heads and business managers of the neighboring institutions complained that they did not understand the distribution and no one had ever been able to explain it satisfactorily. Furthermore, the distribution seemed to them to be unfair in several respects.

Mr. Davis investigated and tried to understand the problem. However, the more he looked into it, the more complex and mixed up it seemed to become. He soon realized that it would not be wise to direct a solution, though he probably had the authority to do so. A good solution would be one that was acceptable to all the governing boards of the museum and neighboring institutions as well as their heads or directors. Therefore, to provide a broad base of experience and representation, he appointed a committee to analyze the situation and to recommend a method of distribution. The committee was to meet in August 1979.

Background

The Charles W. Morgan Museum had been established in 1875 by a generous bequest of one of the city's wealthier merchants. The bequest included a 52 acre site on the city's outskirts, a large mansion, a well-selected collection of European paintings and sculpture and a modest endowment.

---

* This case was prepared by Professor William Rotch, Colgate Darden Graduate School of Business Administration, University of Virginia. Copyright © 1980 by Colgate Darden Graduate Business School Sponsors. All rights reserved.

During the century that followed, the museum grew, constructing new buildings and adding to its collections. Also during that time, four other institutions were established on the museum's land. In 1907, on the completion of a major new museum building, the mansion became the site of a new school of art which had grown over the years to the 1970s. In the middle of the 30s, an existing elementary school moved from its central city location to the museum's land. In 1951 a drama school was also established on the museum's land. Finally, in 1956, a Center for Research on the Preservation of Art was established in its own building adjacent to the museum.

All of these institutions were supported primarily from donations, tuitions and fees. The museum and art school had modest endowments. The elementary and drama schools had to rely primarily on tuition. The research center was supported by grants and fees. All five worked separately to raise money from whatever private sources they could tap. The drama school was probably in the shakiest financial position, and in 1979 was particularly conscious of being caught between rising costs and a student body which could not afford tuition increases.

Over the years the museum had taken a leading role in providing support services for all five institutions. In 1979 these services fell into the following areas: Accounting; Switchboard; Purchasing and printing; Grounds maintenance; Heating; Service building; Security; and Administration.

In 1979 the total cost of these services amounted to slightly over $1 million. Exhibit 1 shows the budgeted distribution for the most recent three years.

Services Provided

The following is a description of the services provided in the eight categories:

Accounting. The accounting department provided accounting services for all five institutions and consisted of eight people:

The financial officer who managed the department.

An assistant, with particular concern for reconciliation of bank statements, distribution of investment income, insurance, and depreciation schedules.

Office manager, who managed work flow and filled in for others as needed.

Two accounts receivable and payable clerks.

One payroll clerk.

Cashier, concerned with transfer and accounting for cash and deposits.

Ledger machine operator.

Switchboard. Though all five institutions had outside lines, there was a central switchboard which was manned during the day and which could connect a person calling a central number with any of the numbers in the institutions. Recently a

EXHIBIT 1 Distribution of Budgeted Support Service Costs (distributed dollars in thousands)

	Total Budgeted Dollars	Museum		Elementary School		Art School		Drama School		Research Center		Other	
		$	%	$	%	$	%	$	%	$	%	$	%
Administration:													
FY 1977-78	52,300	36.6	70.0	4.9	9.3	6.5	12.5	3.1	5.9	1.2	2.2		
1978-79	61,600	26.1	42.4	9.4	15.2	15.9	25.8	7.3	11.9	2.9	4.7		
1979-80	75,540	32.0	42.4	11.6	15.4	18.3	24.2	8.7	11.5	3.6	4.7	1.3	1.8
Accounting:													
FY 1977-78	140,700	51.2	39.2	22.5	17.2	33.9	26.0	15.9	12.2	7.1	5.4	10.0	7.1
1978-79	148,340	59.7	40.2	26.0	17.5	38.9	26.2	16.8	11.4	6.8	4.6		
1979-80	168,390	83.4	49.5	22.2	13.2	33.3	19.8	16.1	9.6	9.1	5.4	4.2	2.5
Switchboard:													
FY 1977-78	42,400	16.0	37.8	11.2	26.5	9.9	23.5	3.9	9.1	1.3	3.0		
1978-79	40,870	10.7	26.1	10.9	26.6	11.9	29.1	4.5	11.1	1.4	3.5	1.4	3.5
1979-80	35,930	8.7	24.2	7.7	21.3	10.3	28.7	3.1	8.6	1.5	4.1	4.7	13.1
Purchasing and printing:													
FY 1977-78	68,000	35.7	52.5	13.2	19.4	12.2	17.9	3.7	5.5	3.2	4.7		
1978-79	68,410	26.5	38.7	14.7	21.5	14.9	21.7	6.7	9.7	5.6	8.2		
1979-80	72,910	21.0	28.7	18.9	25.9	18.1	24.9	8.0	11.0	6.9	9.5		
Grounds maintenance:													
FY 1977-78	269,500	116.2	45.7	46.1	18.1	66.2	26.0	22.7	8.9	3.2	1.2	15.0	5.6
1978-79	227,330	82.3	38.7	28.5	13.4	66.8	31.4	27.7	13.0	7.1	3.4	15.0	6.6
1979-80	235,440	87.2	37.0	39.6	16.8	69.7	29.6	33.1	14.0	5.8	2.5		
Heating:													
FY 1977-78	229,310	112.0	52.0	20.2	9.4	45.0	20.9	24.2	11.2	13.9	6.4	14.0	6.1
1978-79	238,740	80.7	35.3	21.5	9.4	75.7	33.1	33.7	14.7	17.2	7.5	10.0	4.2
1979-80	273,820	112.4	41.0	25.2	9.2	69.3	25.3	38.4	14.0	19.8	7.2	8.8	3.2
Service building:													
FY 1977-78	26,500	12.7	45.7	4.6	18.1	6.2	26.0	2.3	8.9	.7	1.2		
1978-79	30,500	12.6	44.2	4.2	14.4	7.7	25.9	4.1	10.9	1.9	4.6		
1979-80	39,500	15.9	40.3	5.4	13.7	9.8	24.9	5.6	14.2	2.7	6.8		
Security:													
FY 1977-78	174,000	131.9	78.7	14.6	8.7	3.4	2.0	15.2	9.1	2.3	1.4	6.5	3.7
1978-79	147,480	97.6	68.0	26.6	18.5	8.9	6.2	9.6	6.7	.8	.6	4.0	2.7
1979-80	168,280	92.6	55.0	33.5	19.9	30.3	18.0	10.4	6.2	1.5	.9		
Total													
FY 1977-78	1,002,710	512	51.1	137	13.7	183	18.3	91	9.1	33	3.3	45	4.5
1978-79	963,270	396	41.1	142	14.7	241	25.0	111	11.5	44	4.6	30	3.1
1979-80	1,069,810	453	42.3	164	15.3	259	24.2	123	11.5	51	4.8	19	1.8

more efficient system and a reduction in the hours of attendance had reduced the switchboard cost.

Purchasing and Printing. The four people in this department provided centralized purchasing for some of the supplies used by the institutions and did printing jobs as requested. The department also provided an internal messenger mail service including distribution of some outside mail that did not go directly to the institutions.

Grounds Maintenance. About 12 people worked on the grounds crew, doing three kinds of work. One kind was response to special requests from the institutions, for which they were charged directly. Another kind was "routine institutional" maintenance which clearly pertained to a single institution (mowing or raking that institution's grounds, for example). The third kind was "general" maintenance which served all five institutions. Daily trash pick-up, leaf removal, snow plowing the common driveways, street repair, and equipment maintenance were examples of the third kind of maintenance.

Heating Plant. All five institutions were served by one heating plant. The cost of running the plant was about 45% fuel expense and about 55% for the engineers running it and necessary repairs. The heat was distributed through steam lines which had meters to measure institutional consumption.

Service Building. The service building contained the heating plant (about 30% of the area) and shop areas used by the grounds crew. Included in the shop areas were an electrical shop and a carpentry shop. The carpenters and electricians were paid by the museum which charged other institutions for labor hours spent on jobs they requested. The building had been built in 1974 by the museum which, through a "depreciation" charge based on a 50-year life, was slowly recovering its cost. The annual cost of the building, therefore, was the depreciation charge plus building maintenance.

Security. There was a security force which patrolled the area and buildings 24 hours a day.

Administration. There were three people who were involved in administering the support services. Two of those people had other responsibilities which pertained only to the museum. Thus the cost of administration was the full salary of one person and part of the salary of two others, together with some secretarial expenses.

Budget

The budgets of the five institutions were on a fiscal year ending August 31. Hence in the early spring of each year a budget for the various support services was prepared as well as a set of allocation percentages. By March the amounts in the next year's budget which were attributed to each institution were made known to them so that they in turn could include these amounts in their own budgets which were usually prepared in late spring.

The support services were actually funded by the museum. As the year progressed each institution was billed monthly for its share (based on the budget percentages) of the previous month's actual expenses. Thus if the budget showed that the drama school was to pay 14% of heating costs, the drama school would be billed in November for 14% of the total heating costs incurred in October. Though the August bill was rendered in September, the institutions would include it as part of their actual expenses for the year ending August 31.

Distribution of Support Expenses

In 1979 the eight categories of support services were being distributed on the following bases:

Accounting. About 16% of total.

Basis. Computer line entries were counted and the number pertaining to each user was noted. Allocation of cost was based on the user's line entries as a percent of total line entries. Some 30,000–40,000 line entries were generated each year.

Timing. Counting was done once a year in January for the year ending the previous August 31.

Switchboard. About 4% of total.

Basis. The number of telephone numbers (or extensions) each user had listed, as a percent of total numbers listed.

Timing. Counted in March when the next year's budget was being prepared. The dollars charged covered labor and equipment.

Purchasing, Supply, and Printing. About 7% of total.

Basis. About 85% of this category was salaries. Bob Rust (the manager) estimated the percentage of time each of the four people spent on activities devoted to each user. The four percentages applying to each user were added and divided by four.

Timing. This was done once a year in March when the budget for the next year was being prepared.

Grounds Maintenance. About 23% of the total.

Basis. Total cost to be allocated was first reduced by the amount of labor cost for special work orders chargeable to those who made specific requests for work to be done. The time spent on special work orders represented from 2% to 20% of the total but averaged around 5%. The remainder was allocatable cost and included the cost of routine maintenance for specific institutions and the cost of general or common maintenance activities, plus the cost of equipment and supplies. The basis for allocation was the record kept of where the grounds people spent their time when working on routine maintenance at a specific institution.

Timing. When the budget was prepared in March, the previous twelve months' record of hours spent was used to develop allocation percentages.

Heating Plant. About 27% of total.

Basis. The basis was the amount of steam metered into the various buildings. In this case there were some users who were not among the five. These other users paid their share.

Timing. Steam usage was measured to as near the end of the heating season as the budget process would allow, usually March. Thus the 1978–79 heating season was the basis for the 1979–80 budget allocation.

Service Building. About 4% of total.

Basis. The operating costs of the building were combined with depreciation charges. Depreciation on the building was set at 2% of its cost (50 year life) and the total cost allocated according to a formula determined shortly after the building was completed, the basis of which no one could quite remember.

Security. About 16% of total.

Basis. About 60% of the total patrol hours were directly related to a user. In the past, the total cost of security had been allocated on the basis of proportional usage of that 60% of the total time.

Timing. Once a year Captain Mark estimated the time spent providing security services to each of the users, on both regular patrols and on special occasions.

Administration. About 7% of total.

Basis. The last category allocated, the amount charged each user was based on each user's total as a percent of total support services cost before administration was allocated.

The First Committee Meeting

Mr. Davis appointed eight people to the committee whose charge was to recommend a procedure for distributing the support costs. Five members, including the chairman, were treasurers of the boards of the five institutions. The other three were paid staff; one was Jill Gray, the financial officer in charge of accounting; another was Bill Calder who was the full-time operations manager for the support services; and the third was Tilford Burke who was recently hired as special assistant to the museum director and whose time would be partly devoted to administration of the support services.

Prior to the committee's first meeting on August 16, 1979, Mr. Davis asked Mr. Burke to review the situation, by talking with the five institute business managers and to present to the committee what he discovered to be their complaints about the present system.

At the meeting Mr. Burke reported the following comments:

- Derivation of the distribution percentages was hard to understand. The Research Center business manager, for example, had seen his total charges go from $33,000 to $51,000, an increase of 60% while the total costs of support services had risen only about 6%. The previous summer, in an effort to reduce costs, the center had undertaken to mow its own grass but had seen no reduction in the amount it was charged.
- One business manager had complained that another business manager had managed to get large amounts of grounds work charged on special work orders rather than as routine work. Mr. Burke was not quite sure why that was a complaint but he reported it anyway.
- Three business managers thought the allocation of purchasing and printing costs seemed a bit arbitrary, though two said they had no reason to believe it was not fair. The third, the drama school manager, said they rarely used the printing services because they had bought their own duplicating machine and thought they were charged too much.
- The elementary school business manager said that $30,000 for security was far more than they needed. They had their own janitorial service (as did all the institutions) and beyond that a night watchman, if needed at all, would cost less than half that amount.
- The drama school business manager said they didn't need the switchboard service.
- The elementary school business manager said they had installed storm windows and turned down thermostats in the winter of 1977–78 but saw no effect on heating costs.
- Several business managers complained that they were being charged for the space used by the electrical and carpentry shops in the service building, but used those services only in emergencies.
- One business manager noted that since most of the service costs seemed pretty well fixed, a reduction in usage by one user meant higher costs for the others even though they did not increase their usage.

The committee discussed these complaints at length. There was some agreement that they should investigate the separation of fixed costs, or "capacity costs" as one member called them, from variable costs. It was not entirely clear, however, how the two types of costs should be defined and identified. Furthermore, such a separation would not solve the problem of cost allocation, though if variable costs could be attributable to users, the amount to be allocated would be reduced.

Several members of the committee expressed concern that, while the proportions might or might not be equitable, there was no clear rationale, no basis on which the percentages could be defended. After some discussion of the need to have a defensible basis for allocating the capacity costs, the committee returned to a discussion of individual items.

At this first meeting of the committee there was no agreement on the most appropriate method of distribution. However, committee members did agree that they had gained a better understanding of the nature and extent of the problem.

At the end of the meeting the chairman asked Mr. Burke and Ms. Gray to prepare a summary of what seemed to be the most appropriate bases for the allocation percentages and to prepare a breakdown between fixed and variable costs.

Background for the Second Committee Meeting

Mr. Burke and Ms. Gray prepared a number of tables for use by the committee at its next meeting. They were as follows:

Accounting. Exhibit 2 shows a summary of accounting costs and three bases for allocation: the present method of line postings, by payroll population, and by checks issued. Ms. Gray favored one of the latter two over the present method because, she said, the present method was affected too much by the structure of accounts. The museum's fund accounting system had many interfund transfers, she said, which involved no actual transfer of cash. The museum's treasurer had even thought of combining funds to avoid the transfers and perhaps save $15,000.

Switchboard. Since the switchboard had caused some controversy, a count was made of the volume of calls handled by the operators during a four-week period

EXHIBIT 2 Measures of Accounting Activity

Function	Museum	Elementary School	Art School	Drama School	Research Center	Total
Accounts payable:						
June 1–Nov. 30:						
Checks issued	1,556	1,285	1,906	611	282	5,640
Monthly average	259	214	318	102	47	940
Percentage	17.55	22.77	33.83	10.85	5.00	100%
Payroll:						
Nov. 30:						
Population	124	101	137	60	14	436
Percentage	28.44	23.17	31.42	13.76	3.21	100%
Variables not included:						
Schools closing for summer						
Schools' summer programs						
Christmas card seasonal staff						
Machine postings:						
(Based on FY 1978 data, support services only)	50.05	13.70	20.27	10.06	5.92	100%
Posting percentages used in 1978–80 budget, recognizing 2.5% other	49.5	13.2	19.8	9.6	5.4	97.5%

from August 20 to September 14. It revealed the following distribution, shown alongside the allocation made during the past two years:

	Percent Calls	*Budget Allocation*	
		1978–79	*1979–80*
Museum	38.8%	26.1%	24.2%
Elementary school	27.0	26.6	21.3
Art school............	24.6	29.1	28.7
Drama school.........	8.4	11.1	8.6
Research center.......	1.3	3.5	4.1

An analysis of FY 1979 showed that switchboard costs totaled $45,732, a bit higher than the amount budgeted; that $31,430 represented personnel and basic equipment costs; and that $14,302 represented the telephone company's charge based on the number of line numbers provided.

Purchasing and Printing. The purchasing and printing department employees spent about 75% of their time on printing work, about 15% on purchasing, and about 10% on mail distribution. The materials used in printing work done for the several institutions were charged to them at cost, just as with other purchased supplies. The cost of running the department was allocated on the basis of the department manager's estimate of time spent in behalf of each institution.

Grounds Maintenance. Exhibit 3 is a report comparing previous allocations with the average distribution with and without inclusion of special work-order hours.

An alternative to the present system of allocation would be to eliminate separate charges for special work orders and charge a flat rate for all institution work, allocating the general maintenance costs according to the average institutional usage.

Another alternative would be to add the cost of the general maintenance to the hourly charge.

The general maintenance costs could also be divided according to population, area, or some other reasonable measure.

Bill Calder said the recording and distribution of grounds work hours to the three categories and five institutions consumed a good deal of time on his part as well as that of his groundsmen. The data were not useful to him in managing the grounds crew—there was too much delay—and he would be delighted if the data were found to be unnecessary.

Heating. The following table shows the percentage of actual steam consumption during the last three years, 1977 and 1978 for the full year, and 1979 through February:

	FY 1977	FY 1978	FY 1979
Museum	47.2%	39.2%	41.1%
Elementary school ...	9.5	8.3	9.2
Art school	19.0	28.0	25.3
Drama school	14.2	13.8	14.0
Research center	7.1	7.3	7.2
Other..............	3.0	3.3	3.2

The total pounds of steam used was much the same (within 5%) in all three years. Consumption at the art school was unusually high in FY 1978 because a broken steam line went undetected for over a month. Also in that year the museum's use of steam decreased significantly as a result of changed thermostats, reduced hours of opening, and energy saving weatherproofing. In FY 1979 the art school had mended the steam pipe but also added a new building. The elementary school also added a building in 1979.

EXHIBIT 3

Fiscal Year	Museum	Elementary School	Art School	Drama School	Research Center
Grounds:					
Previous allocations:					
1978	45.7	18.1	26.0	8.9	1.2
1979	38.7	13.4	31.4	13.0	3.4
1980	37.0	16.8	29.6	14.0	2.5
2-year average, including work orders					
General:					
42.3	23.5	9.1	15.6	8.2	1.3
2-year average, routine hours plus work orders					
	40.9	14.9	27.3	14.7	2.3
2-year average, routine hours only (present method)					
	36.4	17.3	28.8	15.2	2.4

1979 cost $222,982 (not including service building)

General maintenance hours includes the following:

Daily trash pick-up and disposal
Leaf pick-up and disposal
Snow and ice removal
Pick-up and delivery for purchasing
Maintenance of equipment
Gas service
Maintenance building custodial, grounds
Street cleaning and repair
Street sign maintenance
Street drain cleaning and maintenance
Special truck runs for support services

Of the $283,304 total costs of heating, $125,159 or 44.2% was for fuel costs; the rest was for labor and equipment maintenance costs.

Service Building. The cost of the service building, other than that part which housed the heating plant, was $26,719 in FY 1979. Of this space 3.5% was used by the art school and .7% by the drama school for storage areas; 35.7% was used by the carpentry and electrical shops and 60.1% was used for storage and repair of equipment used in grounds maintenance. The following table summarizes this.

	Space	Dollars
Grounds	60.1%	$16,058
Carpentry and electrical	35.7	9,539
Art school......................	3.5	935
Drama school...................	.7	187
Total	100.0%	$26,719

Security. There were about a dozen security officers who provided various kinds of services, including patrols 24 hours a day, museum duty, and traffic control. The grounds of the five institutions were surrounded by a fence and access was limited to four gates. Over the years the city had grown around and beyond the grounds and for many of the students and employees at the five institutions the fence and security force were a distinct benefit.

The costs represented in the security category were about 94% personnel, 3% vehicles, and 3% for other equipment and supplies.

The Business Manager's Proposal

Before the second meeting of Mr. Davis's committee on October 16, the business managers of the four non-museum institutions met and prepared a proposal. This was that fixed or capacity charges be separated from variable or direct charges and that each institution's share of the total of capacity charges be determined by dividing its total operating expenses (less interest and transfers to reserves) by the sum of these expenses for all institutions. Thus they said, "capacity costs would be divided among users according to their economic size. Each institution would have an equal stake in the management of capacity and these costs would be the same proportion of each institution's budget." The business managers figured that capacity costs would amount to about 60% of the total service costs and that this would be about 7.5% of total expenses. Each institution would therefore budget 7.5% of its total expenses for the capacity cost of support services.

The Second Committee Meeting

After reviewing the data that had been made available for the meeting, a number of alternative distribution methods were proposed and discussed.

EXHIBIT 4 Measures of Relative Demand

	Total	Museum	Per cent	Elementary School	Per cent	Art School	Per cent	Drama School	Per cent	Research Center	Per cent
Population served (hours of attendance):	2,786,732	495,844	18.8	652,800	23.4	831,000	29	705,320	25.3	101,468	3.6
Payroll—people	412	119	28.9	97	23.5	127	30	56	13.6	13	3.2
Payroll—$	331,129	88,072	23.1	100,977	26.5	121,547	31	58,268	15.3	12,265	3.2
Building area	431,037	116,037	26.9	95,000	22.0	146,600	34	40,900	9.5	32,500	7.5
Expenses	8,210,987	1,801,877	22.0	1,867,474	22.7	2,906,549	35	1,356,534	16.5	278,553	3.4
Assets	13,676,459	5,939,519	43.4	2,450,295	17.9	3,109,810	22	401,795	2.9	1,775,040	13.0
Fund balance	13,291,897	6,031,526	45.4	2,793,320	21.0	2,413,525	18	357,349	2.7	1,696,177	12.8

1. Population Served: Schools—No. of students, parents, other clients times hours. Museum—Visitors times hours average of 2 hours per visit.
2. Payroll: A typical monthly payroll, Fall 1979. Seasonal variation: Museum up in Fall, Schools down in summer, etc. Source: SS Accounts.
3. Building Area: From Business Managers and Insurance Records.
4. Expenses: 1978 Statement of Revenues; Total General Expenses.
5. Assets: 1978 Balance Sheet; Total Assets less Land and Buildings.
6. Fund Balances: Total Fund Balances less net investment in Land and Buildings.

One committee member thought the easiest way to proceed would be to use the present method and refine the percentages so that they did a better job in reflecting actual usage.

Two others argued in favor of the separation of fixed capacity costs from variable costs. There was some question whether "variable" should mean ultimately variable or costs which were traceable to the user.

Handling of the capacity costs proved to be another bone of contention. One person said he thought the simplest way would be not to try to use a confusing multiplicity of percentages but to find one basis for distributing all capacity costs, more or less as proposed by the business managers. This idea stimulated extensive discussion of what that base should be. At this point Ms. Gray produced a chart showing several possible bases that might be considered. (Exhibit 4)

After the committee had studied this chart for several minutes, one senior member who had said rather little up to this point said he thought the whole confusing process could be greatly simplified because there wasn't very much difference between the various bases. He proposed that the committee approve a division as follows: Museum 30%, elementary school 20%, art school 30%, drama school 16%, and research center 4%.

Spirited discussion followed with no sign of agreement as the time for adjournment approached. Recognizing that another meeting would be required, the chairman asked Mr. Burke to draw up a specific proposal, consulting whomever he wished, and using the actual FY 1979 figures noted in the following table.

	Actual FY 1979
Accounting	$ 174,051
Switchboard	45,732
Purchasing and printing	56,044
Grounds maintenance	236,491
Heating (including its share of the service building)	283,304
Service building	26,719
Security	162,435
Administration	56,607
	$1,041,383

Questions

1. Several ways of dealing with support costs were suggested in the second committee meeting. Comment on the advantages and disadvantages of each. Which approach would you recommend?
2. Assuming that support costs are to be allocated so that each institution is charged with a "fair share," is the approach of Mr. Burke and Ms. Gray the best way of doing this?

Chapter 5

Measurement and Use of Differential Costs

One of the most significant principles of cost accounting is the notion that "different costs are used for different purposes." The full-cost accounting principles discussed in Chapter 4 are valuable for activities such as pricing, profitability analysis, and reimbursement. They are inappropriate, however, for a variety of decisions—called *alternative choice decisions*—made regularly in both for-profit and nonprofit organizations. Examples of alternative choice decisions include:

1. Keep or drop a service.
2. Expand or reduce the amount of a service provided.
3. Perform work in-house or contract out for it.
4. Accept or reject a special request (such as that by a health maintenance organization to use a certain service provided by a hospital).
5. Sell or scrap obsolete supplies and equipment.

While alternative choice decisions frequently have strategic, organizational, and political dimensions, they also have a financial dimension. As we discuss in this chapter, the appropriate information to use for analyzing the financial dimension is differential costs, rather than full costs.

We begin the chapter with an assessment of the kinds of cost analyses that must be undertaken in an alternative choice decision. We then move to a discussion of cost behavior, addressing the distinction between the costs used for a full cost analysis and those used for a differential cost analysis. Next, we take up the topic of breakeven analysis, a special application of differential cost analysis. Following this, we review four important assumptions that underlie cost behavior in a breakeven analysis. We then discuss some of the techniques that analysts use to estimate the relationship between volume of activity and costs.

With the discussion of cost behavior complete, we are ready to examine the factors that can complicate a differential cost analysis. We conclude the chapter by examining some of the issues that can surface in a contract-out decision—a type of alternative choice decision that most organizations make quite frequently. We include a discussion of a special form of contracting out: privatization. The increasing use of privatization by government agencies at all levels suggests that it is worthy of careful examination as a management tool. This section highlights some recent developments in the nonprofit field that call for managers to be especially attuned to the need for sophisticated and thoughtful analyses of differential costs.

THE NATURE OF COST ANALYSES FOR ALTERNATIVE CHOICE DECISIONS

From a cost accounting perspective, the key question in an alternative choice analysis is: "How will costs (and revenues) change under the proposed set of circumstances?" That is, what costs and revenues will be *different*? In the keep/drop, expand/reduce, and in-house/contract-out decisions, for example, certain costs and revenues will be eliminated. Other costs may be incurred, however, and additional revenues may be realized if the alternative is adopted. In the special-request or obsolete-asset situations, certain items of revenue will be received, but costs will change only minimally or not at all.

Because of the presence of allocated or indirect costs in full-cost calculations, the use of full-cost information as a basis for deciding which costs will change or how certain costs will vary under alternative sets of circumstances can be misleading. Indeed, full-cost information can lead to decisions that will be more, rather than less, costly to the organization.

> *Example.* The full cost of educating a child in a certain public school system is $5,700 a year. This figure includes teachers' salaries, curriculum supplies and materials, a fair share of individual school overhead expenses (e.g., a principal's or headmaster's salary), and a fair share of the school system's overhead expenses (e.g., the school system superintendent's salary). The decision to reduce enrollment by 10 students clearly would not save $57,000 (= $5,700 × 10), since it is unlikely that teachers' salaries, individual school overhead expenses, and the school system's overhead expenses would be changed at all with a reduction of 10 students.
>
> Even the decision to close an entire school would not save $5,700 per student, since it is unlikely that the school system's overhead expenses would be reduced. Moreover, if closing a given school resulted in shifting tax revenues that had been assigned to the school system to some other use, and these revenues amounted to $5,700 per student, the school system would be worse off as a result of the closing. That is, its revenues would have declined by more than its costs. It is for reasons such as this that an understanding of cost behavior is essential to a differential cost analysis.

COST BEHAVIOR

Fundamental to the analysis of any alternative choice decision is the question of how costs behave with changes in volume. Chapter 4 described the distinction between direct and indirect costs; this chapter uses a different view, dividing costs among fixed, variable, and a variety of intermediate possibilities. This latter view gives us a better perspective on how an organization's costs actually will behave under various scenarios. It therefore will assist us to identify as clearly as possible the differential or nondifferential nature of those costs.

Fixed Costs

Fixed costs are those costs that do not vary with changes in the number of units of service delivered, at least in the short run. They can be graphed as shown in Exhibit 5–1.

An example of a fixed cost in most organizations is rent. Regardless of the volume of activity, the amount of rent that an organization pays in a given year will remain the same.

Step-Function Costs

Step-function costs are similar to fixed costs, except that each step has a much narrower relevant range. As such, they increase in relatively small "lumps" as volume increases. Graphically, step-function costs behave as shown in Exhibit 5–2.

EXHIBIT 5–1   Fixed Costs

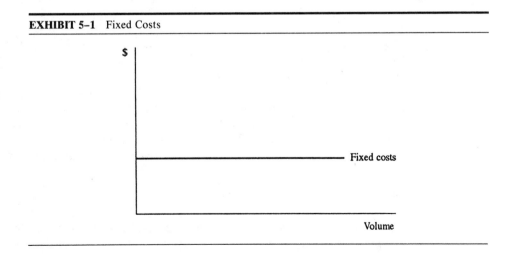

EXHIBIT 5–2   Step-Function Costs

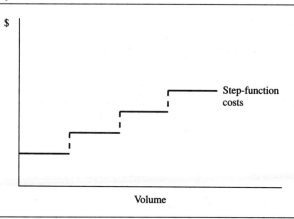

An example of a step-function cost is supervision. In a hospital or social service agency, for instance, as the number of nurses, social workers, and the like increases, supervisory personnel must be added, but not on a one-to-one basis. Since it is difficult for most organizations to add part-time supervisory help, the cost function for supervisors usually will behave in a steplike fashion. Similarly, in a school system or university, faculty costs tend to behave as step functions. New faculty members are added in steplike increments when either the total number of students in the school or a given course enrollment figure reaches a certain level.

Variable Costs

Variable costs behave in a roughly linear fashion with changes in volume. That is, as volume increases, total variable costs will increase in the same proportion. The result is a straight line, whose slope is determined by the amount of variable costs associated with each unit of activity, as shown in Exhibit 5–3.

An example of variable costs is supplies, such as textbooks for students in a public school system. Some organizations have relatively high-variable costs per unit, resulting in a line that slopes upward quite steeply. Other organizations have variable costs that are relatively low for each unit of output, with a variable cost line that slopes upward more slowly. An example of each is shown in Exhibit 5–4.

Semivariable Costs

Semivariable costs have a fixed component that is unrelated to the level of volume, plus a variable component. Consequently, they intersect the cost axis of a graph at some point above zero, and then slope upward in a linear fashion, as is shown in Exhibit 5–5.

EXHIBIT 5–3   Variable Costs

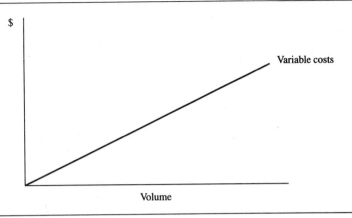

EXHIBIT 5–4   High- and Low-Unit Variable Costs

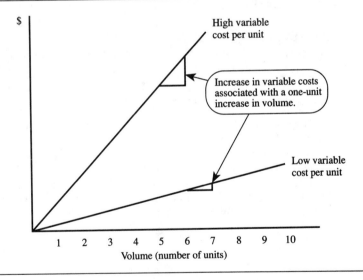

For many organizations, utilities are semivariable costs, since the organization typically pays a basic monthly service charge, followed by increments in cost according to use of the utility. Electricity, for example, typically has both a demand component (fixed) and a use component (variable).

EXHIBIT 5–5   Semivariable Costs

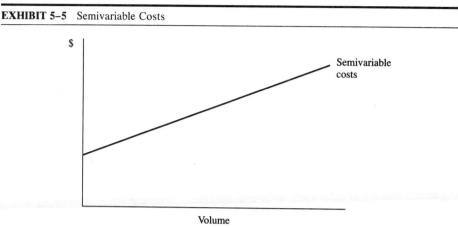

Total Costs

Total costs are the sum of the fixed, step-function, variable, and semivariable components. Because cost analyses combining all four types of costs are quite complex and difficult to work with, most analysts generally classify all costs as either fixed or variable. For semivariable costs, this can be accomplished by incorporating the fixed element into total fixed costs and adding the variable element to the variable costs. For step-function costs, the width of the relevant range typically dictates whether the cost is added to fixed costs or incorporated into the variable cost amount.

> *Example.* The Abbington Youth Center has rent and other fixed costs of $50,000 per year, and variable supply and material costs of $100 per student per year. Its meal costs have a fixed element (a part-time dietitian) of $7,000 per year, and a variable component (food and beverages) of $500 per student per year.
>
> In constructing a graphical representation of Abbington's costs, we can incorporate the fixed and variable components of the semivariable cost function for meals into the separate fixed and variable components, as follows:

Cost Element	Fixed Amount	Variable Amount (per student)
Rent, etc.	$50,000	$ 0
Supplies and materials	0	100
Meals....................	7,000	500
Total	$57,000	$600

Abbington also has student-teacher ratios of 3:1 for its infants and toddlers program and a 15:1 for its adolescent after-school program. Faculty salaries are $15,000 per year. The step-function relationships for these two programs are shown in Exhibits 5–6 and 5–7.

EXHIBIT 5–6   Step-Function Costs in the Infant and Toddlers Program

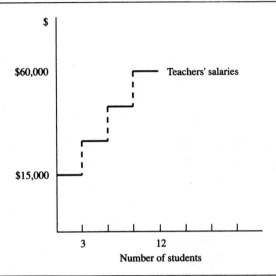

The narrow steps in the infant and toddlers program suggest that the relationship is close enough to a linear one that the costs can be treated as variable, whereas the wider steps in the adolescent after-school program would appear to call for these costs being treated as fixed, even though they have a shorter relevant range than, say, rent. Once

EXHIBIT 5–7   Step-Function Costs in the Adolescent After-School Program

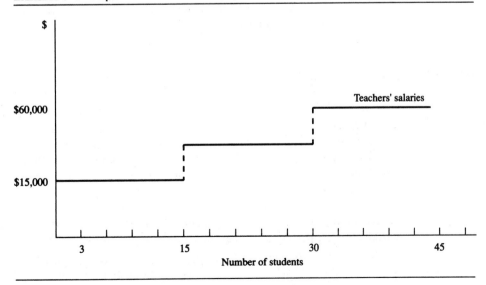

teacher salaries are simplified in this manner, they can be added to either the variable cost per student totals or the fixed cost totals as follows:

Program	Fixed Amount	Variable Amount per Year
Infant and toddlers	0	$5,000 per student
Adolescent after-school (30–45 students)	$45,000	0

With these simplifications, total costs are as follows:

Cost Element	Fixed Amount	Variable Amount per Student
Rent, etc.	$ 50,000	$ 0
Supplies and materials	0	100
Meals.	7,000	500
Teachers		
Infant and toddlers	0	5,000
Adolescent after-school (30–45 students)	45,000	
	$102,000	$5,600

Note that the fixed costs are only valid within a range of 30 to 45 students in the adolescent after-school program. Above 45 students, they jump to a higher step; below 30 students, they fall to a lower step. Also, the variable cost of $5,600 for each additional student is not quite accurate, since $5,000 of the increment is actually a portion of a step-function change. Nevertheless, because the steps in the infants and toddlers program are so small, the amount is a reasonable representation of the pattern of cost changes that are associated with volume.

BREAKEVEN ANALYSIS

One important technique used in differential cost situations is breakeven analysis. The purpose of breakeven analysis is to determine the volume of activity at which total revenue equals total costs. This usually is done for a program or other activity within an organization. A breakeven analysis begins with the fundamental equation:

$$\text{Total revenue} = \text{Total costs}$$

Since, as indicated above, total costs can be expressed as the sum of fixed and variable costs, the equation can be expanded as follows:

$$\text{Total revenue} = \text{Fixed costs} + \text{Variable costs}$$

Total revenue for most activities is quite easy to calculate. If we assume that an organization's charge or price per unit is represented by p and its volume by x, then total revenue is unit price times volume, or

$$\text{Total revenue} = px$$

Algebraically, fixed costs generally are represented by a and variable costs per unit by b. Thus, total variable costs can be represented by the term bx where, as before, x represents volume. The resulting breakeven formula can be shown as follows:

$$px = a + bx$$

Graphically, we can represent the formula as follows: First, revenue is an upwardly sloping straight line, whose slope is determined by price. Variable costs are similar, but with a less steep slope. Fixed costs are represented by a horizontal line. Total costs are shown by adding the variable cost line to the fixed cost line. Exhibit 5–8 is the result. Point x_1 where $px = a + bx$ is the breakeven volume; that is, it is the point at which total revenue (px) equals total costs ($a + bx$). Thus, if we know unit price, fixed costs, and variable costs per unit, we can solve the formula algebraically for x, which would be our breakeven volume.

Example. The Valley Wine Association has fixed costs of $10,000, variable costs per member of $18, and charges a $38 annual membership fee. What is its breakeven volume (number of members)?

EXHIBIT 5–8   Breakeven Analysis

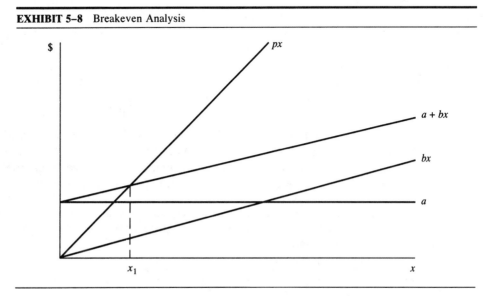

Analysis

$$px = a + bx$$

$$\$38x = \$10,000 + \$18x$$

$$\$20x = \$10,000$$

$$x = 500$$

Breakeven thus would be 500 members. To confirm:

Revenue	$38(500) =		$19,000
Less: costs:			
Variable...........	$18(500) =	9,000	
Fixed		10,000	
Total			$19,000
Surplus (deficit)			$ 0

Unit Contribution

An alternative way to think of a breakeven analysis is in terms of the contribution that each unit sold makes to the recovery of fixed costs. Returning to the basic breakeven formula, we can see that unit contribution is the difference between price and unit variable cost, or $p - b$. Thus, by rearranging some of the terms, we can see that breakeven is simply fixed costs divided by unit contribution, as follows:

$$px = a + bx$$

$$px - bx = a$$

$$x(p - b) = a$$

$$x = \frac{a}{(p - b)}$$

In effect, price less unit variable cost tells us how much each additional unit of service contributes to the coverage of our fixed costs. Since breakeven volume is the level where all our fixed costs are being covered, we simply need to divide fixed costs by the unit contribution margin to determine the figure.

Example. The Federated Milk Producers Association has fixed costs of $900,000 and variable costs of $200 per member. Its annual membership dues are $500. Therefore its breakeven volume is

$$\$900,000 \div (\$500 - \$200) = 3,000 \text{ members}$$

Fundamental Assumptions of Breakeven Analysis

Four important assumptions are fundamental to the behavior of costs in a breakeven analysis: relevant range, linearity, homogeneity of volume, and underlying conditions. The first two of these already have been mentioned briefly. Before proceeding with a more analytical discussion of cost behavior, we need to examine all four in some detail.

Relevant Range. As mentioned in the discussion of fixed costs, an implicit assumption made for analytical purposes is that cost behavior does not change within a given range of volume, called the *relevant range*. With fixed costs, the graphs in Exhibits 5–1 and 5–8 give the impression that costs are fixed from a level of zero volume to whatever number is shown at the far right of the graph.

Clearly, this impression is not realistic, since at near-zero volume, some so-called *fixed costs* probably could be eliminated. Basic clerical staff, cleaning staff, and so forth, while generally considered fixed, most likely could be reduced if a very low level of services were being delivered. By contrast, once volume exceeds a certain level, an organization will find it necessary to incur additional fixed costs. For example, once its activities grow beyond a certain level of volume, an organization will need additional space. At that point, rent—the prototypical fixed cost—will increase. Consequently, it is necessary in a differential cost analysis to stipulate the assumptions about the range within which fixed costs truly are considered to be fixed.

Identifying the relevant range, while important for fixed costs, is even more important for step-function costs. These costs, by definition, have a rather narrow relevant range, and hence must be considered carefully in the analytical effort. As suggested previously, if the range is narrow enough, the step-function costs can be treated as variable; indeed the narrower the width of the steps, the more the line looks like a variable cost line. On the other hand, if the steps are relatively wide, step-function costs must be considered as fixed costs and added to the other fixed costs for analytical purposes.

The distinction between fixed and variable costs is also greatly influenced by the length of the time period that is used in the analysis. If the time period is short, such as a week, relatively few costs are variable. If the time period is a year, many more costs are variable. This point is sometimes overlooked in an analysis because cost accounting systems treat costs as being variable that actually are fixed in the short run. For example, direct labor costs often are classified as variable, but if volume falls within a given week, it is unlikely that employees will be laid off. Even if there are layoffs, they probably will not be proportionate to the change in volume.

Linearity. In most differential cost analyses, the assumption is made that the relationship between volume and cost is a linear one. That is, each cost, even if fixed, can be depicted by a straight line. Clearly this is not true for step-function costs. Moreover, there can be situations in which the relationship between volume and cost is curvilinear; that is, the cost line is curved.

Calculating costs when the cost line is curvilinear is complicated, and unless the curvilinear force is strong, an assumption usually is made that a linear relationship is close enough for analytical purposes. On the other hand, a linear assumption may not be adequate with step-function costs. Moreover, if a step-function cost is assumed to be fixed, the analyst must then check the resulting breakeven figure to determine if it is within the relevant range. If not, it will be necessary to move up or down the step function and recalculate the breakeven volume until a figure is reached that satisfies the relevant range of the step-function relationship.

Example. The Valley Wine Association charges its members $38 per year. It has fixed costs of $10,000, variable costs per member of $18, and supervisory costs that behave as follows:

Members	Costs
0–500........	$ 5,000
501–1,000......	10,000
1,001–1,500......	15,000
1,501–2,000......	20,000

To calculate a breakeven membership volume, we must determine the appropriate level of supervisory (i.e., step-function) costs to use. This means that we must assume some level of membership. If we begin with the first level, we add the $5,000 in supervisory costs to our fixed costs of $10,000 and undertake the breakeven analysis, which looks as follows:

$$px = a + bx$$

$$\$38x = \$10,000 + \$5,000 + \$18x$$

$$\$20x = \$15,000$$

$$x = 750$$

The problem is that, although the breakeven volume is 750 members, the relevant range for the step-function costs was only 0 to 500 members. Thus, the solution is invalid, and we must move to the next step on the step function, which gives us the following equation:

$$\$38x = \$10,000 + \$10,000 + \$18x$$

$$\$20x = \$20,000$$

$$x = 1,000$$

This solution is within the relevant range for step 2 and, therefore, is valid.

The conclusion we can draw from this example is that the incorporation of step-function costs in the breakeven formula requires a trial-and-error process to reach the breakeven volume; that is, each time a breakeven volume is determined, it must be checked against the step used in the calculation to be certain it is valid. If it is not, another step must be used for the calculation until a breakeven volume is found that is within the range of the step used in the calculation.

Homogeneity of Volume. In conducting breakeven analyses, an assumption is made that the units of volume being considered are all essentially identical. In the above analysis, for example, we assumed that all members were treated equally and, thus, that the $18 per member variable costs and the step-function supervisory costs would be affected in an identical manner any time a new member was added to the organization.

Clearly this is not always the case. In many instances the differences average out so that the assumption of volume homogeneity is adequate. In others, however, separate analyses may be necessary for different types of service units.

> *Example.* In the analysis of the Abbington Youth Center described earlier in this chapter, the presence of different step-function relationships for the Infant and Toddler Program and the Adolescent After-School Program means that there is an absence of volume homogeneity. Thus, although the fixed, variable, and semivariable cost relationships may be analyzed with this assumption, the step-function relationship may not. That is, under the step-function relationships described above, the addition of one child to the Infant and Toddler Program is assumed to add $5,000 to costs, while the addition of an adolescent to the Adolescent After-School Program will not add anything to costs unless the relevant range is exceeded. Therefore, each program should be considered separately. This creates another complication, namely the need to determine how much of the $57,000 in fixed costs is applicable to each program.

When there is an absence of volume homogeneity, the breakeven analysis becomes considerably more complex. Techniques for dealing with this complexity are discussed in most cost accounting textbooks.[1]

Underlying Conditions. A *ceteris paribus* (other things being equal) set of assumptions underlies a breakeven analysis. If any underlying conditions should change, the analysis becomes obsolete and must be recalculated using the new set of conditions. For example, if the variable cost per unit of $18 above is derived from certain supply prices for stationery, photocopying, and so forth, and if those prices increase, a new breakeven analysis must be undertaken using the new prices.

ESTIMATING THE COST-VOLUME RELATIONSHIP

To construct a cost-volume graph, an analyst estimates the costs that will be incurred at various levels of volume. These estimates often are made as part of the operations budgeting process, described in Chapter 10. Frequently, the analyst

---

[1] See, for example, Charles Horngren and George Foster, *Cost Accounting: A Managerial Emphasis,* 6th ed. (Englewood Cliffs, N.J.: Prentice Hall, 1987).

relies on historical data, modified as appropriate for the changing circumstances the organization expects to face in the future. Any of five methods can be used to construct a cost line.

High-Low Method

Under the high-low method, total costs are determined for each of two volume levels. This establishes two points on the total cost line. Next, the costs at the lower volume are subtracted from the costs at the higher volume, and the difference in units between the two levels is determined. The difference in costs is then divided by the difference in units to obtain the variable cost per unit; that is, the slope of the variable cost line, or *b* in the breakeven formula. Finally, for either of the two volumes, the variable cost per unit is multiplied by the volume, and the result is subtracted from the total cost figure initially determined. The difference between the two is the fixed component.

Example. The Federated Producers Association had total costs of $1,500,000 with a membership of 3,000, and $2,300,000 with a membership of 7,000. To determine its cost line, it can take the following steps:

1. Difference in total costs:

$$\$2,300,000 - \$1,500,000 = \$800,000$$

2. Difference in volume:

$$7,000 - 3,000 = 4,000$$

3. Variable cost per unit:

$$\$800,000 \div 4,000 = \$200$$

4. Total variable costs with 3,000 members:

$$\$200 \times 3,000 = \$600,000$$

5. Total fixed costs with 3,000 members:

$$\$1,500,000 - \$600,000 = \$900,000$$

Therefore fixed costs are $900,000 and variable costs per unit are $200. The formula for its cost line is:

$$\text{Total costs} = \$900,000 + \$200x$$

Scatter Diagram Method

Instead of using the high-low method with just two points, it is possible to plot several historical cost points on a graph, with total costs on the vertical axis and volume on the horizontal axis. The number of data points varies depending on the information available. Outliers—or unusual circumstances (e.g., the presence of a

EXHIBIT 5-9   Example of a Scatter Diagram

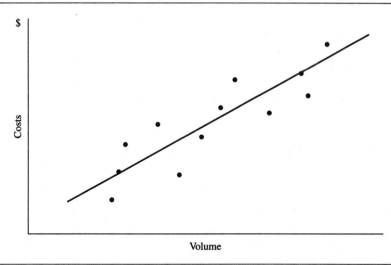

strike during a particular year that required using outside contractors to perform work normally done by employees)—usually are omitted. Using visual inspection, the analyst then fits a line to the points. Two points then can be chosen from this line to use for the high-low method. An example of a scatter diagram is shown in Exhibit 5-9.

Least Squares or Linear Regression Method

This is a modification of the scatter diagram method in which the line is fitted by a statistical technique rather than by visual inspection. This method is more mathematically correct than visual inspection and, if outliers are omitted, is probably more accurate. However, because much of the process is necessarily judgmental, many analysts prefer the visual inspection approach over a mathematical one.[2]

Incremental Method

This method is used when there is only one data point; that is, one total cost figure and its associated volume. When this is the case, the analyst must estimate how an assumed increment in volume would affect total costs. Once this has been done, two data points are available, and the high-low method can be used.

---

[2] A more detailed discussion of the least squares and linear regression methods can be found in Robert N. Anthony and James S. Reece, *Accounting Principles,* 9th ed. (Homewood, Ill.: Richard D. Irwin, 1992), chap. 16.

Element Analysis

This method is used when there are no historical data points available. The analyst therefore must estimate each cost category separately (e.g., salaries and wages) and dissect it into its various cost elements: fixed, step-function, variable, semivariable. Once this is done, simplifying assumptions can be made concerning step-function and semivariable costs, and the totals for each cost element can be summed to produce a total cost equation.

COMPLICATING FACTORS

In addition to the difficulties associated with estimating costs and breaking them into their various elements, several other complications may be encountered in a differential cost analysis. Some of these are associated with the need on occasion to use full-cost reports as the source of cost information; others are associated with the relationship between the fixed/variable distinction and the differential-cost concept.

Use of Information from Full-Cost Reports

Two potential problems arise from the frequent need to obtain information for differential-cost analyses from full-cost reports: cost distinctions and the behavior of allocated costs. Each of these potential problems calls for the analyst to exercise caution in obtaining and working with full-cost data.

Cost Distinctions. The analysis of differential costs would be simplified if, as occasionally is assumed, all indirect costs were fixed and all direct costs were variable. This is not always the case. Exhibit 5–10 contains an illustration of four different cost types and their fixed/variable, direct/indirect distinctions. Note that each of the four cells in the matrix contains a possible cost, leading to the conclusion that all direct and indirect costs in a full-cost accounting system must be analyzed individually in order to determine how they can be expected to behave as volume changes.[3]

Behavior of Allocated Costs. Three problems exist in differential cost analysis when allocated costs are associated with a particular effort for which the differen-

---

[3] A detailed analysis of this sort of cost classification can be found in Kenneth J. Smith, "Differential Cost Analysis Techniques in Occupational Health Promotion Evaluation," *Accounting Horizons*, June 1988.

EXHIBIT 5–10   Cost Examples: Fixed/Variable versus Direct/Indirect in a Social Service Agency

	Fixed	*Variable*
Direct	Supervisor's salary in the foster home care program	Payments to foster parents for room and board
Indirect	Portion of executive director's salary (which is a cost of administration that is allocated to the foster home program)	Electric bills (which are mainly variable, and costs of administration that are allocated to the foster home program)

tial analysis is to be made: misleading allocation bases, shared savings, and complexities of the stepdown methodology.

Misleading Allocation Bases.   The bases of allocation used in the full-cost accounting system do not necessarily reflect actual use by mission or service cost centers. Thus, if the costs of a particular mission center are reduced, the service center costs allocated to that center automatically will be reduced. However, these costs will not necessarily be reduced proportionately, and they may not be reduced at all.

> *Example.* A reduction of staff in a given mission center will lead to a reduction in total salaries in that center. If general and administration (G&A) costs are allocated to cost centers on the basis of salary dollars, there also will be a reduction in the amount of G&A costs allocated to the center. It is unlikely, however, that there will be a proportionate reduction in the staff or other costs associated with the G&A service cost center.

Shared Savings.   While some service center costs actually may be reduced as a result of reduced activity in a given mission center, the reduction may not accrue entirely to that mission center. Indeed, when the allocation basis does not change, the savings will be shared with other cost centers.

> *Example.* A reduction in volume in a given mission center may reduce that mission center's need for housekeeping services. If housekeeping costs are allocated on a square footage basis, however, and the space used by the mission center does not change, the housekeeping allocation will not change by the full amount of housekeeping's savings. Instead, the savings will be shared with other mission centers that receive housekeeping allocations. Thus, although costs allocated to the mission center will fall as a result of the lower amount of housekeeping costs overall, the reduction *indicated* on the full-cost report will be much less than the *real* reduction that took place.

Complexities of the Stepdown Methodology.   When the stepdown methodology is in use, it blurs the impact of cost changes. Specifically, since each service center is allocated to all remaining cost centers as one moves down the steps in the stepdown, the service centers farthest down in the report will have portions of the cost centers above them included in their totals. And, since the total to be allocated from each service center includes both its direct costs and the costs that have been allocated to it from previous "steps" in the stepdown, the allocation from a service center far down in the stepdown will include cost from several other cost centers.

> *Example.* If social service is far down on the list in a stepdown, the total social service cost allocated to a particular mission center will carry a significant allocated component with it (e.g., administration, housekeeping, laundry and linen, and so on). While it may be possible to reduce the use of social workers in a mission center by reducing the number of patients treated, the full impact of that reduction on the costs in the social service cost center will be overstated if one uses the fully allocated social services totals (including both direct and previously allocated costs). That is, the allocated component from social services contains costs from a variety of other cost centers that may not be affected at all by the reduction in patient volume.

Recognizing these problems and incorporating them into analytic efforts is one of the most challenging aspects of cost accounting in any organization. Determining which costs are indeed differential and the extent of their differential nature is extremely difficult, particularly when a full-cost report is the principal source of information.

Differential Costs versus Variable and Fixed Costs

Another erroneous assumption that frequently is made in the analysis of differential costs is that there is no change in *unit* variable costs. In some situations, for example, volume will not change at all, but alternative cost scenarios will be possible for the same volume of activity. In other situations, a reduction in volume may eliminate some unit cost savings in supplies because of a loss of volume discounts; alternatively, an increase in volume may result in a volume discount. Both of these scenarios will change unit variable costs.

Some analysts assume that fixed costs are not differential. That is, when they analyze the various alternatives under consideration, they assume that the only cost changes they need to consider are those associated with variable, semivariable costs, and step-function costs. Actually, many alternative choice problems faced by an organization involve movements outside the relevant range for fixed costs, and, hence, changes in fixed costs as well. The following example illustrates the nature of this problem as well as one of the problems associated with incorporating allocated costs into a differential cost analysis.

> *Example.* Clearwater Ambulance Service operates a fleet of two ambulances. It charges 95 cents per mile for each service mile driven. Ambulance 1 drives 60,000 service miles a year; Ambulance 2 drives 30,000 service miles a year. The variable cost per mile for each ambulance is 25 cents. The organization's revenues and costs are as follows:

Item	Ambulance 1	Ambulance 2	Total
Revenue..........................	.95 × 60,000 = $57,000	.95 × 30,000 = $28,500	$85,500
Costs:			
Variable costs.....................	.25 × 60,000 = $15,000	.25 × 30,000 = $ 7,500	22,500
Drivers.........................	15,000	15,000	30,000
Overhead costs (rent and administration)	20,000	10,000	30,000
Total costs....................	50,000	32,500	82,500
Surplus (Deficit).....................	$ 7,000	$(4,000)	$ 3,000

Question. Would the profitability of Clearwater Ambulance Service be improved if Ambulance 2, which is losing money, were discontinued?

Analysis. The question is not whether Ambulance 2 is losing money on a full-cost basis, but rather the nature of its differential costs and revenues. More specifically, if Ambulance 2 were discontinued, which revenues and costs would be eliminated and which would remain. It appears that if we eliminate Ambulance 2, we discontinue all of its revenue, all of its variable costs, and the fixed cost of the driver. From all indications, however, the rent and administrative costs will remain; that is, they are nondifferential. The result is a shift from an overall *surplus* of $3,000 to a *deficit* of $3,000, as the analysis below indicates.

Item		Ambulance 1
Revenue (.95 × 60,000).......................		$57,000
Costs:		
Variable costs (.25 × 60,000)................	$15,000	
Driver....................................	15,000	
Overhead costs (rent and administration)......	30,000	
Total costs..............................		60,000
Surplus (Deficit).............................		$ (3,000)

This example illustrates several important points. First, full-cost information can produce misleading results if used for differential cost decisions—in this instance a keep/drop decision. In the case of the Clearwater Ambulance Service, the full-cost data would seem to indicate that we could increase the surplus by dropping Ambulance 2, but this clearly was not the situation.

Second, differential costs can include both fixed and variable costs. In the above example, the driver generally would be considered a fixed cost, but the elimination of Ambulance 2 eliminates this fixed cost. The key point here is that as long as we operate the ambulance, we have the fixed cost of the driver's salary; it does not fluctuate in accordance with the number of miles driven within the relevant range. But when we eliminate the ambulance, we also eliminate this cost in its entirety; it is thus differential in terms of the decision we are analyzing. In effect, we have dropped below the relevant range for this cost.

A third point is that differential cost analysis invariably requires assumptions. Since we do not have perfect knowledge of the future, we must make some guesses about how costs will behave. In this example, there are three important assumptions: (1) the number of miles driven by Ambulance 1 will not increase with the elimination of Ambulance 2; (2) we will not be able to reduce or eliminate any overhead costs with the elimination of Ambulance 2; and (3) the unit costs and revenues will be the same in the future as in the example. Changes in these assumptions clearly would have an impact on the new surplus (deficit) figure, and might in fact actually make it financially feasible to eliminate Ambulance 2. It is therefore important in undertaking any form of differential cost analysis both to clarify the assumptions one is making, and to explore how changes in these assumptions would affect the conclusions of the analysis. This latter activity is called *sensitivity analysis.*

Contribution to Overhead Costs

In discussing breakeven analysis earlier in this chapter, we introduced the notion of unit contribution, defining it as the amount that each unit sold contributes to the recovery of fixed costs. The concept of contribution also can be used in differential cost analyses.

As the above example indicated, a key question in many differential cost analyses is the behavior of overhead costs. In the Clearwater Ambulance illustration, a key assumption was that overhead costs (rent and administration) for the ambulance service would not be reduced if the second ambulance were eliminated. As indicated above, and as will be discussed in greater detail later, an assumption of this sort is not necessarily valid. Nevertheless, in most instances an analysis of differential costs is most easily performed when the direct fixed and variable costs of the particular activity itself are analyzed separately from the overhead costs of the organization. Such an analysis can be structured in terms of the contribution of the particular service or program to the organization's overhead costs.

More specifically, a program (an ambulance in this instance) provides some revenues and incurs some direct costs. The difference between the revenue provided and the direct costs (both fixed and variable) is the contribution of that program to the organization's overhead costs.

Returning to the example above, the cost data for the ambulance service could be structured in the following way:

Item	Ambulance 1	Ambulance 2	Total
Revenue.....................................	$57,000	$28,500	$85,500
Less: Variable costs	15,000	7,500	22,500
Margin (for fixed and overhead costs)...........	$42,000	$21,000	$63,000
Less: Fixed costs (drivers)	15,000	15,000	30,000
Contribution (to overhead costs)	$27,000	$ 6,000	$33,000
Less: Overhead costs	20,000	10,000	30,000
Surplus (Deficit).............................	$ 7,000	$(4,000)	$ 3,000

As this example indicates, both Ambulance 1 and Ambulance 2 are contributing to the coverage of overhead costs. Consequently, elimination of either ambulance will reduce the total contribution to overhead, thereby either reducing the organization's surplus or increase its deficit. In fact, it is the $6,000 contribution from Ambulance 2 that led to the change from a $3,000 surplus to a $3,000 deficit when we considered the impact of eliminating it.

THE CONTRACT-OUT DECISION

Up to this point, we have discussed the use of differential costs in situations where an alternative choice decision involved a change in volume. This is the characteristic of most keep/drop and special-request decisions. Many other types of alternative choice decisions do not involve a change in volume. Perhaps the most common of these is what is called the *contract-out* (or *make-or-buy* or *outsource*) decision. We discuss the general nature of this decision below, and provide some illustrations of a special form of contract-out decision making—called *privatization*—that has become increasingly popular in government organizations.

Nature of the Contract-Out Decision

An organization provides some services by using its own resources, and it obtains other services by buying them from other organizations. Almost all of the things it does internally conceivably could be done for it by an outside organization. At the extreme, the total operation could be contracted out, as the federal government does in the operation of certain nuclear generating plants that it owns. Conversely, a large organization could rely on its own resources for most of its needs, even building a power plant to generate electricity, rather than buying electricity from a public utility. At any given time, there is a balance between what an organization makes and what it buys. Management frequently must reexamine whether this balance is the most appropriate one.

A wide variety of strategic considerations generally enters into the contract-out decision. Nevertheless, in considering a proposal to buy a service that it is now making or to make a service that it is now buying, an organization ordinarily also looks at the applicable costs and revenues. In particular, management wishes to identify the alternative that has the lower costs and/or higher revenues. The relevant revenues and costs are the differential ones associated with each alternative.

Example. A trade association cleans its headquarters with employees who are hired for this purpose. Someone has proposed that an outside cleaning crew be engaged. The differential cost of contracting with an outside organization is relatively easy to determine; it is the amount specified in the proposed contract. Finding the differential cost of continuing to use the association's own employees is more complicated, however. The salaries and benefits of the cleaning crew and the supplies they use obviously are differential costs; they would disappear if the cleaning were contracted out. The other differential costs associated with this activity are more difficult to estimate. Would there be a reduction of costs in the payroll accounting department? The personnel department? In other overhead costs? In estimating the amount of differential overhead costs, management must be aware of the cautions made in earlier sections of this chapter about possible misinterpretations of the effects of overhead allocations.

Absence of General Principles

There are few general principles for deciding what items of cost are differential in a contract-out problem. Each problem is unique, and each must be analyzed separately to decide what costs would be different under the particular circumstances. One generalization can be made, however: the longer the time period involved, the more costs are differential. If the alternative being considered is to contract out a single printing job rather than use in-house facilities, for instance, the only reduction in costs might be the savings in paper and ink; the printing presses remain, payment to employees probably would not be reduced, and no overhead costs would be affected. If, however, the proposal is to discontinue the in-house print shop permanently, all the costs associated with operating that shop, both direct and overhead, would be saved.

Role of Depreciation

A common error in calculating differential costs for contract-out problems is to include depreciation on existing plant and equipment as a cost that would be saved if the organization bought the service from an outside contractor. Depreciation is not a differential cost, however. Once assets have been acquired, the costs incurred to purchase them are *sunk costs*. Depreciation is simply an accounting mechanism to charge the expense of using up an asset to each year of its useful life. The expenditure itself took place at the time the asset was acquired. Unfortunately, the past cannot be undone, and money spent cannot be recovered. Therefore, deciding not to use an asset does not result in a saving of its depreciation. Of course, if an asset is sold, the amount realized can be a differential gain associated with the contract-out decision, but this amount rarely corresponds to the asset's book value.

If the contract-out time frame is a sufficiently long one, such that the acquisition of additional assets would be required under the *make* option but not under the *buy* option, then depreciation might be used as a surrogate for the cost associated with replacing existing assets as they wear out. If this is done, the analyst must be certain that the existing depreciation figure is adjusted for changes in prices, technology, and other factors that would cause replacement assets to cost more or less than existing ones. Again, the replacement amount rarely corresponds to the existing depreciation expense. Moreover, if asset acquisition is a significant aspect of the decision—if, that is, assets must be acquired in order for the *make* option to be pursued—then depreciation alone will not suffice. Rather, a technique known as net present value is required. This is discussed in Chapter 9.

The Move toward Privatization

In government—federal, state, and local—the strategy of contracting out has become extremely popular during the past 10 to 15 years. Called *privatization*, this activity has touched on a wide variety of services that only a few years ago were seen as the exclusive domain of a federal, state, or local government agency. In almost all instances, the principal driving force behind the decision to contract out has been cost savings. Unfortunately, it has not always been evident that the decision makers knew the relevant costs.

> *Example.* The British National Health Service (NHS) purchases much of its long-term geriatric care from private vendors, but it purchases little surgery. The surgery it does purchase appears to come from situations that require little in the way of careful cost analysis, such as from suppliers with excess capacity that are willing to sell at marginal cost. One reason for this situation seems to be that the NHS does not know its own costs with sufficient precision to undertake useful differential cost analyses.[4]

The privatization movement has been characterized by two quite different activities: (1) the divestment of assets or programs, such as national land, railroads, and the post office, and (2) actual contracting out for services, such as prison operations, health care delivery, garbage collection, and dog catching. The former has a one-time effect only, whereas the latter has the potential for ongoing savings over many years.

> *Example.* Butte, Montana, is saving $600,000 a year by contracting a private firm to run its municipal hospital. Newark, New Jersey, uses a private firm to collect about one-third of its refuse, at a [reported] annual savings of over $200,000, and hires private contractors to provide services such as tree trimming, garbage collection, building demolition, snow plowing, and street sweeping. The Southern California coastal community of Rancho Palos Verdes pays a private law firm to act as town prosecutor. Farmington, New Mexico, contracts with an independent firm to run its airport control tower at a cost of $99,000 per year, compared with the $287,000 the Federal Aviation Administration had been paying out. A private paramedic/ambulance service saves Newton, Massachusetts, some $500,000 a year. New York, Philadelphia, Washington, D.C., and 70 other cities use private *meter persons* to enforce parking regulations. And, Scottsdale, adjoining Phoenix, Arizona,—the first U.S. city to use a private company for fire protection—boasts of better-than-average fire response times, at less than half the cost to cities of comparable size.[5]

---

[4] Alain Enthoven, *Reflections on Improving Efficiency in the National Health Service*, A Nuffield Occasional Paper, the Nuffield Provincial Hospitals Trust, 1985.

[5] Neil A. Martin, "When Public Services Go Private," *World*, May–June 1986, pp. 26–28.

Privatization Concerns.   One of the main questions that emerges when a government agency decides to privatize is which services to contract out. A related concern is the difficulty of making comparisons between the contractor's charge and the cost of maintaining services inhouse. A third is the private contractor's possible lack of commitment to and involvement with the organization and its goals.[6]

With regard to costs, the federal government Office of Management and Budget *Circular A-76* directs departments and agencies to study privatization possibilities, and gives detailed rules for estimating the differential costs appropriate for such a study. In general, *Circular A-76* focuses on the differential costs associated with personnel, although it emphasizes the need to consider all significant costs, including overhead items.[7]

Problems with a shared commitment are particularly apparent when a government agency contracts with the private sector. In particular, some concerns have been raised about quality and other delivery-related issues associated with converting what is essentially a public-sector responsibility into a private enterprise. According to one analyst,

> In theory, contracting out government services brings to the public realm all the virtues of the private market—flexibility, innovation, and competition. In practice, however, contracting-out government begs the ancient political question: *Quis custodiet ipsos custodes*? (Who will watch the watchers?).[8]

Although both for-profit and nonprofit contractors have been employed to carry out privatization, many nonprofit professionals are especially concerned when the contract is with a for-profit organization. Indeed, this concern extends outside of government into nonprofit organizations that contract out for services with for-profit vendors.

> ***Example.***   A few years ago, the trustees of Massachusetts General Hospital (MGH) announced that the Hospital Corporation of America had indicated an interest in purchasing McLean Hospital, an inpatient psychiatric facility affiliated with both MGH and the Harvard Medical School (HMS). MGH trustees saw the potential purchase as an opportunity to raise some needed capital financing and to introduce greater efficiency into the operations of McLean.
>
> The proposal evoked a strong negative reaction from both the staff at McLean and physicians at HMS. Opponents of the sale were concerned with such matters as staffing patterns, quality of care, research focus and quality, and the general purpose and values of McLean. In the end, the proposal was not accepted.

---

[6] For a discussion of these points, see Mary Kelaher, "Commercializing the Public Sector," *Australian Accountant* 61, no. 2 (March 1991).

[7] For a summary of *Circular A-76* and its intent, see "Enhancing Government Productivity through Competition: Targeting for Annual Savings of One Billion Dollars by 1988," Office of Management and Budget, March 1984. For an example of an analysis carried out under *Circular A-76*, see David R. Solenberger, "The Cost of a Federal Employee: An Input to Economic Analysis," *GAO Review,* Spring 1985.

[8] Robert Kuttner, "Viewpoint: The Private Market Can't Always Solve Public Problems," *The Privatization Review* 2, no. 2 (Spring 1987), p. 7.

While privatization issues frequently evoke more passion than substance,[9] the phenomenon nevertheless is an important aspect of nonprofit management—particularly for city, state, and federal agencies. From the perspective of this chapter, the critical question is that of cost analysis. Later chapters will introduce issues related to designing and utilizing appropriate and effective management control systems to manage private contractors. Indeed, according to one author, difficulties with privatization seem more often than not to rest with inadequate monitoring by the contracting public agency.[10] In this regard, *inadequate* monitoring also can include *inappropriate* monitoring.

> *Example.* The growth of the contracting system [in Massachusetts] over the past decade has caused a corresponding growth of paperwork, ostensibly to ensure accountability for the taxpayer's dollar, but in reality merely documenting, in excruciating detail, the smallest of expenditures. In this way, the state *micromanages* provider agencies. This *micromanagement* is also carried through to state audit operations. Potentially nine audit agencies can descend on the provider to audit the same year, the same program, and the same line items. At best, providers are subject to onerous reporting requirements demanded by multiple state agencies, all asking for the same basic information. None of this annual paper blizzard addresses the question of the outcome of service delivery. The system, in focusing on the paper chase, has lost focus on the client.[11]

SUMMARY

Differential costs provide the proper analytical focus for keep/drop, contract-out, special request, or obsolete asset decisions. However, they do not make either the decisions themselves or the analytical efforts that underlie them easy. Indeed, as suggested in the discussion above, a variety of strategic and other nonquantifiable factors usually enter into these decisions which go beyond financial analysis, and which create highly complex situations. An adequate differential analysis must incorporate all of these factors.

SUGGESTED ADDITIONAL READINGS

Anthony, Robert N., and James S. Reece. *Accounting: Text and Cases.* Homewood, Ill.: Richard D. Irwin, 1992.

Demone, Harold W., Jr., and Margaret Gibelman, eds. *Services for Sale: Purchasing Health and Human Services.* New Brunswick, N.J.: Rutgers University Press, 1989.

---

[9] For examples of the substantive arguments, see E. S. Savas, "Tax Plan's Boost to Privatizing Services," *The Wall Street Journal,* July 10, 1985; and John R. Miller, "Privatization Shifts Government Responsibility," *American City & County* (Communication Channels Inc., Atlanta, GA), June 1986. For an example of the passionate argument, see Arnold S. Relman, "The New Medical Industrial Complex," *The New England Journal of Medicine* 303 (1980), pp. 963–70.

[10] Miller, "Privatization Shifts Government Responsibility."

[11] Peter Nessen, "The Business of Human Services," *Industry,* Associated Industries of Massachusetts, April 1990.

Donahue, John D. *The Privatization Decision.* New York, Basic Books, 1989.

Hay, Robert D. *Strategic Management in Non-Profit Organizations.* New York: Quorum Books, 1990.

Henke, Emerson O. *Introduction to Nonprofit Organization Accounting.* Cincinnati, Ohio: South-Western Publishing, 1992.

McKinney, Jerome B. *Effective Financial Management in Public and Nonprofit Agencies.* New York: Quorum Books, 1986.

Suver, James D., Bruce R. Newman, and Keith E. Boles. *Management Accounting in Healthcare Organizations,* 3rd ed. Westchester, Ill: Healthcare Financial Management Association, and Chicago, Ill.: Pluribus Press, Inc., 1992.

U.S. Department of Education. *Tough Choices: A Guide to Administrative Cost Management in Colleges and Universities.* Washington, D.C.: Government Printing Office, 1991.

Young, David W. *Financial Control in Health Care.* Homewood, Ill.: Dow Jones-Irwin, 1984.

CASE 5–1   Centerville Home Health Agency*

In December, Mr. Joseph Blanchard became the controller of the Centerville Home Health Agency (CHHA). After 10 years in the accounting department of a consumer products firm, Mr. Blanchard decided to move into the nonprofit field where he felt his expertise would be needed. CHHA, a small social service agency in East Hampshire, Kentucky, offered him that opportunity.

Before Mr. Blanchard accepted the position of controller, Ms. Louise Tucker, the director of the agency, briefed him on the agency's financial position. Like other home health agencies, CHHA was reimbursed for all its patient visits by Medicare on an average-cost-per-visit basis. At the end of each fiscal year, the agency would total their operating costs, adjusting them according to Medicare regulations. They then divided the total costs by the number of visits to derive an average cost per visit which became the Medicare reimbursement rate. CHHA's average cost per visit calculation for 1987 is contained in Exhibit 1.

In September of 1987, CHHA was notified by Medicare that the agency's average cost per visit exceeded the "reasonable cost guideline" established by the Division of Direct Reimbursement for that Standard Metropolitan Statistical Area (SMSA). The letter read as follows:

> We have reviewed your current interim rate of Medicare reimbursement in accordance with applicable Medicare regulations, and have found in accordance with Regulation No. 5, Subpart D, 405.451(C)(2), that your agency is being reimbursed at a rate which is substantially out of line with other home health agencies.
>
> The program recognizes that the cost of provider services may vary from one institution to another and the variations generally reflect differences in the scope of services, intensity of care, geographical location, and utilization. Regulation No. 5, Subpart D, 405.451(C)(2) states:
>
> > "The provision in title XVIII of the Act for payment of reasonable cost of services is intended to meet the actual costs, however widely they may vary from one institution to another. This is subject to a limitation where a particular institution's costs are found to be substantially out of line with other institutions in the same area which are similar in size, scope of services, utilization and other relevant factors."
>
> Our records indicate that your agency is currently being reimbursed at an average cost per visit of $57.89 for Part A billings. In order to adjust your interim rate of reimbursement to a level of reimbursement that will not exceed the reasonable cost of services incurred by similar institutions, it will be necessary to reduce your interim rate to $55 per visit.
>
> We will institute the revised rate of interim reimbursement 90 days from the date of this letter, unless you are able to provide acceptable written documentation which would

---

* This case was prepared by Patricia O'Brien under the direction of Professor David W. Young. Copyright © by the President and Fellows of Harvard College. Distributed by the Pew Curriculum Center, Harvard School of Public Health.

EXHIBIT 1 Expense Record—1987

	Detail	Total
1. Salaries		$283,997
Director, assistant director, controller	$82,570	
Nurses (2).................................	52,960	
Psychologist (1)..........................	28,000	
Social workers (2).........................	38,500	
Physical therapists (2)	45,167	
Support staff (3)...........................	36,800	
2. Transportation costs.........................		28,000
Automobile operation and insurance..........	8,000	
Automobile allowance for staff	20,000	
3. Services purchases		2,350
4. Medical and nursing supplies		7,400
5. Space occupancy costs		17,330
Rent.....................................	16,500	
Maintenance and repairs	600	
Taxes....................................	230	
6. Office costs.................................		12,656
Stationery and printing.....................	6,042	
Telephone................................	5,440	
Postage and express	1,174	
7. Other general costs...........................		17,860
Depreciation on furniture and equipment.......	1,300	
Legal and accounting fees....................	5,300	
Insurance (other than auto)..................	5,510	
Other	3,600	
Interest	2,150	
Total cost		$369,593
Number of visits..............................		6,384
Average cost per visit		$57.89

clearly provide evidence that the high costs incurred by your agency are unavoidable. The rate will be applied against services rendered as of December 1, 1987.

If you have any questions, or if we can be of any further assistance, please feel free to contact us.

Ms. Tucker was concerned because the 1987 charge had been $57.89 per visit and, according to her, at $55 per visit the agency could not meet its expenses. Ms. Tucker hired Mr. Blanchard with the hope that he could resolve this problem.

Background

The Centerville Home Health Agency opened in 1970 to provide nursing visits to elderly and disabled residents of East Hampshire and neighboring towns. In 1973 the agency expanded to offer physical therapy and medical social service visits.

Because another organization in town, The Hampshire Home Service, provided home health aide care, CHHA did not offer aide services.

In 1987, CHHA had a staff of 13. Two registered nurses, two physical therapists, two social workers, and one psychologist were responsible for the home health visits. The administration consisted of a director, an assistant director, the newly appointed controller, and a support staff of three. The skilled nursing care visits were handled by the two registered nurses. The two physical therapists worked exclusively on patient visits, and the social workers, with the help of the psychologist, provided all the social service visits.

The two registered nurses who handled all nursing visits could provide as many as seven visits a day each. However, because the case visits varied significantly in time, effort, and location for 1987, the nurses averaged only 5.54 visits per day. The physical therapists averaged 3.3 visits per day, although Ms. Tucker thought their capacity could be increased by at least 33 percent if they had the demand. CHHA's medical and social service visits were the most complicated. With the help of the psychologist, the social workers averaged 4.46 visits a day for 1987. Ms. Tucker thought these visits could be increased to about 5.5 a day, however. The CHHA staff worked an average of 240 days a year.

Data

In his first few weeks, Mr. Blanchard reviewed CHHA's financial statements, employee service sheets, and other working papers to become familiar with the agency's financial status and planning needs. He realized the agency had been operating without any cost objectives before Medicare imposed a guideline. After a cursory review of past records, Mr. Blanchard decided his first priority was to ensure that their current revenue met their costs. According to him, the agency needed to know the capacity at which their revenue would balance their costs.

Examining CHHA's Expense Record, shown in Exhibit 1, Mr. Blanchard determined that the agency had two types of costs: those that changed according to the number of visits provided and those that were unchanged, regardless of volume. Mr. Blanchard reasoned that at their breakeven point, CHHA's revenue of $55 per visit would equal the total cost of the expenses generated by each visit plus the fixed expenses.

Mr. Blanchard reviewed each item on the Expense Record to determine which type of cost it was. He thought the medically related salaries and the medical and nursing supplies were items that varied directly with the number of visits. When he discussed his analysis with Ms. Tucker, she suggested that staff automobile allowance varied with the number of visits because it referred to mileage incurred by the medical staff in making home visits.

"Terrific," thought Mr. Blanchard. "Now I can calculate a variable cost per visit and in no time I'll know the breakeven point. I can show them their costs and revenues, and where we'll have to operate to keep this agency in business."

Questions

1. Identify the fixed and variable costs.
2. What is the breakeven point?
3. What assumptions were necessary in answering questions 1 and 2?

CASE 5–2   Springfield Handyman Program*

In January 1990, Donald Hoover, program coordinator of the Springfield Handyman Program, was in the process of deciding whether to employ full-time handymen or to subcontract services from a local general contractor on a daily basis. Inasmuch as the program was experiencing some financial difficulties, he knew that this decision could have some important consequences for its financial viability.

Background

The Springfield Handyman Program was a division of the Springfield, Oregon, Community Visiting Nurse Association (VNA). The program had been initiated as part of an effort to develop services that were needed by the elderly in the community, but that historically had been provided by for-profit organizations. The hope was that the handyman program could eventually subsidize other, less-financially viable, programs in the VNA. Unfortunately, because of the program's financial difficulties, just the opposite had been taking place. Mr. Hoover had been hired with the explicit mandate to put the program on a sound financial footing.

Revenue and Expenses

The fixed costs of the handyman program were estimated to be $900 a month for rent and other expenses. The variable costs of supplies (measured on a per-day-of-service basis) were expected to be $80. Mr. Hoover believed that the program could collect revenue of $200 per day of service.

In terms of personnel, Mr. Hoover saw two options. The first was to hire full-time handymen to meet expected demand each month. Each person would work a maximum of 20 days per month. His or her monthly salary would be $1,500, regardless of the number of days actually worked during the month.

---

* This case was prepared by Wendy Raber, Research Assistant, under the supervision of Professor David W. Young. Copyright © by David W. Young. Distributed by the Accounting Curriculum Center, Boston University School of Management.

The second option was to contract services as needed from the general contractor. The rate, which Mr. Hoover found to be competitive with other general contractors in the area, was $100 per day of service. As was customary in the industry, partial days would be billed at the full rate.

With this information on revenue and expenses, Mr. Hoover felt he could calculate a breakeven for each option, and use this as a basis for making his decision.

Questions

1. Calculate the breakeven for each option. Why do these breakeven volumes differ?
2. Which option is preferable? Why?
3. What other factors or options should Mr. Hoover consider?
4. What should Mr. Hoover do?

CASE 5–3   Abbington Youth Center*

Mark Thomas, a recently graduated M.B.A., had been hired three months ago as assistant director of the Abbington Youth Center. Prior to earning his M.B.A., he had worked in several manufacturing firms, but he had never worked in a non-profit organization. He knew little about Abbington's programs or the educational and social theories in use by the professional staff, but had decided to take the job since he had been impressed with the center's attempts to provide high-quality programs for the children in his community.

Despite his lack of experience in organizations like Abbington, Mr. Thomas had brought some much-needed management skills to the center's operations. In his short tenure with the center he not only had introduced some new management techniques, but had regularly made attempts to educate the professional staff in the use of those techniques.

This afternoon's staff meeting was no exception. In attendance would be the center's director, Helen Fineberg, and the coordinators of the center's three programs: Fiona Mosteller (Infants and Toddlers Program), Joanne Olivo (Pre-school Program), and Don Harris (After-School Program). As the names suggested, each program was aimed toward a different age-group: the first accepted children up to the age of three; the second from three to five years of age; and the third from five to seven years.

Mr. Thomas planned to instruct the program directors in the concept of breakeven analysis; in order to do so, he had gathered some data on the revenues

* This case was prepared by Professor David W. Young. It is based in part on the case "Bill French" by R. C. Hill and N. E. Harlan, Harvard Business School. Copyright © by David W. Young. Distributed by the Accounting Curriculum Center, Boston University School of Management.

EXHIBIT 1 Program Cost Analysis, Normal Year[1]

	Infants and Toddlers	Preschool	After-School	Aggregate
Students at full capacity.............				150
Actual number of students	50	40	25	115
Fee per student	$ 4,520	$ 5,320	$ 5,970	$ 5,113
Total revenue......................	226,000	212,800	149,250	588,050
Variable cost per student.............	480	1,040	896	765
Total variable cost..................	24,000	41,600	22,400	88,000
Contribution to program fixed costs	$202,000	$171,200	$126,850	$500,050
Less: Program fixed costs	130,000	118,000	80,000	328,000
Contribution to allocated fixed costs....	$ 72,000	$ 53,200	$ 46,850	$172,050
Less: Allocated fixed costs[2]	42,675	51,210	76,815	170,700
Surplus (deficit)	$ 29,325	$ 1,990	$(29,965)	$ 1,350

1. All figures rounded to the nearest dollar.
2. Allocated on the basis of square feet

and costs of the three programs (see Exhibit 1). Using this information, he determined that each student contributed $4,348 to fixed costs after covering his or her variable costs. Given total fixed costs of $498,700 ($328,000 in the programs and $170,700 for the center overall), he had calculated that 115 students were needed to break even.

He had prepared the breakeven chart, shown in Exhibit 2, which he planned to distribute to everyone at the meeting prior to giving a short lecture on the concept of breakeven analysis. His intent was to make clear to everyone that enrollment was exactly breakeven, which did not allow any margin of safety, and to encourage the program directors to expand the size of their programs by a few students each so as to provide a more comfortable margin and, if all went well, a substantial surplus for the center.

The Meeting

At the meeting, several issues arose that Thomas had not anticipated, and a rather hostile atmosphere developed. Ms. Mosteller pointed out that 50 students was the maximum her program could accommodate, given current classroom space, and wondered exactly how Mr. Thomas expected her to increase the program's size. Ms. Olivo said she would be happy to expand her program by another 10 students, but in order to do so, she would need to hire another teacher, at a cost of $22,000. She wondered how Mr. Thomas might include this fact in his analysis, and, under the circumstances, whether the teacher should be considered a fixed or a variable cost. Mr. Harris told Mr. Thomas that he had been planning all along to add another 15 students to his program, and wondered why Mr. Thomas had not

EXHIBIT 2 Breakeven Chart—All Programs

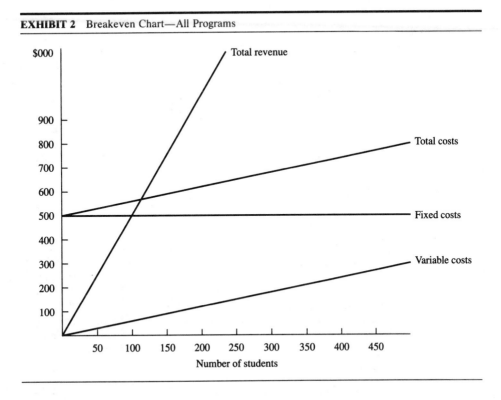

checked with him about this prior to preparing the figures and the chart. He too would need to hire another teacher, however, at a cost of $25,000, and also wondered whether this was a fixed or variable cost.

Ms. Fineberg seemed quite perplexed by the discussion, and began her comments by asking Mr. Thomas why he was using averages when the center had three separate programs. She also indicated that $1,350 was far too low a surplus, since she was hoping to have some extra money available during the year for painting and some minor renovations, which would cost about $10,000. She asked Mr. Thomas how he might incorporate this need into his analysis. She also expressed some concern about Mr. Thomas's per-student fees, stating that in conversations with people in other centers she had learned that Abbington's fees were about 10 percent below what others were charging. She thought an across-the-board increase to make up the difference was called for.

Finally, all three program directors queried Mr. Thomas about his variable-cost-per-student figure. They asked him how he had derived these figures and whether they included some recent price increases of about 5 percent in educational supplies. Mr. Thomas stated that they included both supplies and food, divided about 75 percent/25 percent between the two, but he confessed that he had not included any price increase in his calculations.

Next Steps

The meeting ended on a less-than-happy note. Mr. Thomas had not had an opportunity to give his lecture, the program managers felt frustrated that their concerns and plans had not been included in his analysis, and Ms. Fineberg was quite upset because it appeared as though the center would not have the funds necessary to pay for the much-needed painting and renovations.

Mr. Thomas returned to his office and wondered whether his decision to work at the center had been a wise one. Perhaps, he thought, life would be simpler in a manufacturing firm.

Questions

1. What assumptions are implicit in Mr. Thomas's determination of a breakeven point?
2. Using the data in Exhibit 1, calculate a breakeven point for *each* of the three programs. Why is the sum of these three volumes not equal to the aggregate breakeven volume?
3. On the basis of the suggestions and comments made at the meeting, and making assumptions where necessary, prepare revisions to Exhibit 1. What is the new breakeven volume for the center? What is it for each of the three programs?
4. Based on the information in Exhibit 1, Ms. Fineberg is considering eliminating the After-School Program. What advice would you give her?

CASE 5–4   Lakeside Hospital*

"A hospital just can't afford to operate a department at 50 percent capacity," said Dr. Peter Lawrence, Director of Specialty Services at Lakeside Hospital. "If we average 20 dialysis patients, it costs us $257 per treatment, and we are only reimbursed for $138. If a department like this can't cover its costs, including a fair share of overhead, it isn't self-sufficient and I don't think we should carry it."

Dr. Lawrence was meeting with Dr. James Newell, chief nephrologist of Lakeside Hospital's Renal Division, about the recent change in the medicare reimbursement policy regarding hemodialysis treatments. A few years ago, medicare had begun reimbursing independent dialysis clinics for standard dialysis treatments; the policy change had caused the dialysis unit's volume to decrease to 50 percent of capacity this year, producing a corresponding increase in per treatment costs. By February of the current fiscal year,[1] Dr. Lawrence and Lakeside's

* This case was prepared by Patricia O'Brien under the direction of Professor David W. Young. Copyright © by the President and Fellows of Harvard College. Distributed by the Pew Curriculum Center, Harvard School of Public Health.
[1] Lakeside's fiscal year (FY) ran from October 1 to September 30.

medical director were considering phasing down or closing the dialysis unit. At the end of February, Dr. Lawrence met with Dr. Newell to discuss the future of the dialysis unit.

Dr. Newell, who had been chief nephrologist since he'd helped establish the unit, was opposed to cutting down renal disease services and even more opposed to closing the unit. Although he was impressed by the quality of care that independent centers offered, he was convinced that Lakeside's unit was necessary for providing back-up and emergency services for the outpatient centers. Furthermore, although the unit could not operate at the low costs of the independent centers, Dr. Newell disagreed with Dr. Lawrence's cost figure of $257 per treatment. He resolved to prepare his own cost analysis for their next meeting.

Background

At Dr. Newell's initiative, Lakeside had opened the dialysis unit in 1972 in response to the growing number of patients with chronic kidney disease. The hospital's renal division had long provided acute renal failure care and kidney transplants, but by the 1970s, the most common treatment for end-stage renal disease was hemodialysis. During dialysis, a portion of a patient's blood circulates through an artificial kidney machine and is cleansed of waste products. Used three times a week for four to five hours, the kidney machine allows people with chronic kidney disease to lead almost normal lives.

Lakeside's dialysis unit had 14 artificial kidney machines, but they were limited by their certificate of need to using 10 stations at any one time; thus 4 machines were reserved for breakdowns and emergencies. Open six days a week with two shifts of patients daily, the unit could provide 120 treatments a week or accommodate 40 regular patients. From 1973, the year that medicare began reimbursing for dialysis, all of Lakeside's dialysis patients were covered by medicare. By 1975, the unit was operating close to or above 100 percent capacity, extending its hours and staff to accept emergency cases and to avoid turning away patients.

Beginning in October of 1977, most patients spent their first three months of dialysis in a hospital facility; if there were no complications when this "start-up" period had passed, patients were then required to transfer to independent centers. Currently, medicare paid Lakeside $138 per dialysis treatment.

The independent dialysis centers were developed in the mid-1970s throughout the United States. Many were centrally owned and operated, and were organized into satellite groups of 8 or 10 spread throughout metropolitan and suburban areas. The centers' facilities were modern and attractively designed and, because they were separate from hospitals' institutional environments, they offered psychological advantages to patients dependent on dialysis. Centrally managed with low overhead, the independent centers could achieve economies unobtainable by similar hospital units. Supplies and equipment were purchased in bulk, and administrators watched staff scheduling and cost efficiency closely. As a result, the cost per treatment in outpatient centers was significantly lower than comparable treatments in a hospital facility. For example, treatments in a center operating at 100 percent capacity with 40 patients could cost the center as little as $80. Center charges varied from $113 to $150, depending on the volume and location.

Lakeside Data

Lakeside's direct and allocated costs for the Renal Dialysis Unit in the previous fiscal year are detailed in Exhibit 1. Dr. Newell also obtained the unit's cost center report for the same fiscal year (Exhibit 2), which provided a breakdown of the unit's direct costs.

EXHIBIT 1

LAKESIDE HOSPITAL
Cost Allocation
For Prior Fiscal Year

Cost Center	Direct Expenses	Appor-tioned Expenses	Total for Appor-tionment	Depre-ciation	Adminis-tration and General	Employee Health and Welfare	Opera-tion of Plant	Laun-dry and Linen
				Square Footage	Payroll ($)	Payroll ($)	Square Footage	Pounds Processed
1 *General Services*								
2 Depreciation	3,185,102		3,185,102					
3 Admin. and general	7,416,669	85,998	7,502,667	85,998				
4 Employee health and welfare	4,774,196	956	4,775,152	956				
5 Operation of plant	2,379,838	295,941	2,675,779	177,092	72,626	46,223		
6 Laundry and linen	530,249	106,312	636,561	35,036	23,934	15,233	32,109	
7 Housekeeping	1,364,177	642,554	2,006,731	38,221	344,372	219,179	35,053	5,729
8 Dietary	98,735	989,973	1,088,708	153,203	349,174	222,236	140,211	17,187
9 Maintenance of personnel	204,327	838,166	1,042,493	306,725	17,106	10,887	280,957	6,366
10 *Professional Care—General*								
11 Nursing service	604,183	84,327	688,510	27,392			25,152	1,591
12 Physician salaries	1,237,980	485,096	1,723,076		251,790	160,254		
13 Medical supplies	352,954	1,041,454	1,394,408	181,869	306,859	195,304	166,701	14,641
14 Pharmacy (general)	932,181	285,848	1,218,029	36,310	105,037	66,852	33,180	891
15 Medical records	276,355	345,465	621,820	53,510	114,791	73,060	48,967	
16 Social services	221,804	286,975	508,779	23,888	125,144	79,650	21,941	
17 Intern–resident services	438,547	630,658	1,069,205	89,820	143,676	91,444	82,146	1,082
18								
19 *Professional Care—Special*								
20 Operating rooms	1,589,868	1,877,383		178,366	424,651	270,274	163,490	177,601
21 Electrocardiology	174,776	101,372		18,155	27,760	17,668	16,590	159
22 Anesthesiology	616,494	807,737		37,583	327,866	208,674	28,898	1,082
23 Radiology	1,454,540	1,622,683		188,876	579,206	368,642	173,123	14,577
24 Laboratory	2,086,649	1,878,882		245,890	656,483	417,826	225,301	7,639
25 Blood bank	444,595	414,876		65,932	131,297	83,565	60,473	1,719
26 Physical therapy	387,735	183,484		22,296	61,822	39,347	20,336	6,175
27 Pharmacy (special)	254,426	673,570						
28 Renal dialysis	525,142	277,267		4,778	69,550	44,266	4,281	1,782
29 Oxygen therapy	532,757	30,086		5,733	7,728	4,918	5,352	318
30								
31 *Professional Care—Ambulatory*								
32 Emergency	223,082	921,647		16,881	118,542	75,447	15,252	12,094
33 Other (OPD)	796,023	1,854,084		168,492	316,613	201,511	155,195	2,419
34								
35 *Routine Services—Inpatients*								
36 Adults and children	4,810,077	8,902,811		438,589	1,546,300	984,159	401,367	327,861
37 Intensive care	388,417	1,456,321		102,879	492,925	313,727	94,187	35,011
38 Nonpatient		3,015,094		480,632	887,415	564,806	445,517	637
39								
40 Total	38,301,878			3,185,102	7,502,667	4,775,152	2,675,779	636,561

He intended to use the prior year's costs to calculate the per treatment cost at various volume levels for the current year. More importantly, he wanted to find the point at which the unit's revenue would meet its costs. He planned, however, to use only those costs that could be traced directly to dialysis treatments, omitting all overhead expenses. According to Dr. Newell, if the unit's revenue met those costs, the unit was self-sufficient. Dr. Newell considered Dr. Lawrence's treatment cost of $257 misleading because it included substantial overhead. He argued that this year's overhead would differ from last year's because of the dialysis unit's changes in volume. However, Dr. Newell knew that this year's overhead could not be calculated until the end of the fiscal year. He felt that an accurate cost analysis would first calculate

House-keeping	Dietary	Mainte-nance of Personnel	Nursing Service	Physician Salaries	Medical Supplies	Phar-macy	Medical Records	Social Services	Intern Resident Services	Total Expense	
Square Footage	Number of Meals	Payroll ($)	Hours of Service	Hours of Service	Direct Supplies ($)	Phrm. Revenue ($)	Number of Records	Hours of Service	Hours of Service		
											1
											2
											3
											4
											5
											6
											7
107,962											8
216,125											9
											10
19,305	10,887								*		11
	33,750	39,302									12
128,230		47,850									13
25,566		16,367			1,645						14
37,727		17,410									15
16,857		19,495									16
63,292	136,089	23,039			70						17
											18
											19
100,337		66,615		143,015	78,645	114,008			160,381	3,467,251	20
12,843		4,378		1,723	418	609			1,069	276,148	21
26,489		54,210		12,062	2,468	108,405				1,424,231	22
134,451	15,242	90,384		5,169	7,251	45,067			695	3,077,223	23
173,181		102,373			3,904	46,285				3,965,531	24
46,556		20,433			516	4,385				859,471	25
15,653		9,591		5,169	42			3,053		571,219	26
						673,570				927,996	27
3,411	9,471	10,842		65,477	279	1,827		50,878	10,425	802,409	28
4,013		1,251			42	731				562,843	29
											30
											31
11,839		18,452		177,477	28,864	20,706	52,233	7,123	366,737	1,144,729	32
118,397		49,414		286,031	10,319	13,520	171,000	132,791	228,382	2,650,107	33
											34
											35
321,077	883,269	241,233	688,510	937,353	1,191,424	138,977	310,910	285,425	206,357	13,712,888	36
72,242		76,415			68,186	48,721	27,360	29,509	95,159	1,844,738	37
351,178		133,439		89,600	335	1,218	60,317			3,015,094	38
											39
2,006,731	1,088,708	1,042,493	688,510	1,723,076	1,394,408	1,218,029	621,820	508,779	1,069,205	38,301,878	40

EXHIBIT 2   Cost Center Report—Dialysis Unit, Actual Expenses, Prior Fiscal Year

Expense	Oct.–Nov.	Dec.–Jan.	Feb.–Mar.	Apr.–May	June–July	Aug.–Sept.	Total
Medical supply:							
Dialyzers....................	1,792	1,750	1,728	1,720	1,750	1,759	
C-Dak coils.................	5,772	5,631	5,560	5,537	5,629	5,654	
Needles and syringes	6,370	6,290	6,136	6,108	6,213	6,250	
General supplies.............	12,446	12,070	11,981	11,938	12,142	12,190	
Concentrate.................	2,058	2,008	1,982	1,974	2,014	2,018	
Saline	4,390	4,283	4,229	4,211	4,283	4,301	
Blood tubing...............	5,743	5,602	5,532	5,468	5,564	5,633	
Miscellaneous...............	3,381	3,258	3,257	3,243	3,298	3,312	
Total..............	41,952	40,892	40,405	40,199	40,893	41,117	245,458
Purchased lab services..........	2,116	2,026	2,000	1,994	2,042	2,060	12,238
Salaries and wages:							
Nursing	17,500	17,500	17,500	17,500	17,500	17,500	
Technicians.................	15,340	15,340	15,340	15,340	15,340	15,340	
Administration	3,560	3,560	3,560	3,560	3,560	3,560	
Total..................	36,400	36,400	36,400	36,400	36,400	36,400	218,400
Employee expense..............	2,350	2,350	2,350	2,350	2,350	2,350	14,100
Water usage	1,764	1,740	1,728	1,720	1,748	1,748	10,448
Minor equipment	1,904	1,904	1,904	1,904	1,904	1,904	11,424
Major equipment depreciation ...	2,188	2,188	2,188	2,188	2,188	2,188	13,128
Number of treatments..........	980	956	944	940	956	960	5,736

the "real" cost of a treatment and, from there, define a "fair share of over-head."

In reviewing the cost center report, Dr. Newell realized that the nature of the costs varied. He defined three types of costs for his analysis: those that varied in proportion to volume, those that varied with significant changes in volume, and those that remained the same regardless of the unit's volume.

He first separated the costs of medical supplies, purchased laboratory services, and water usage because they changed according to the number of treatments provided. He then examined the salary and wages and employee expense costs; although these costs had not changed during the last year, the unit's number of treatments had also remained fairly steady during that year. Dr. Newell thought that the significant reduction in volume this year might cause a corresponding reduction in salary and employee expenses. In the prior year, the unit had employed eight hemodialysis technicians, seven nurses, and two administrative people (their eight consultant nephrologists were on the hospital's physicians' payroll). However, anticipating that the unit's volume would fall, Dr. Newell had not replaced the nurse and two technicians who'd left in January of the current year. Consequently, by February, the unit's monthly salaries and employee expenses had decreased by $3,000. Dr. Newell determined that the remaining costs on the cost center report would stay essentially the same regardless of the number of treatments.

As a final step in preparing for his meeting with Dr. Lawrence, Dr. Newell called a hospital equipment supply manufacturer to discuss the resale value of

Lakeside's 14 artificial kidney machines. The company informed him that machines used for four years or more could not be sold, even for scrap. Lakeside had purchased the 14 machines five years ago for $105,000.

Questions

1. What is the breakeven volume for the dialysis unit? What assumptions are necessary for calculating it?
2. What will happen to total costs and revenues at Lakeside if the dialysis unit is closed? What other options are available and what are their financial consequences?
3. What are the nonquantitative considerations?
4. What should Dr. Newell do?

CASE 5–5   Town of Belmont*

It was 10 A.M., January 4th. Mr. James Castanino, the newly promoted head of the Highway Department, sat at his desk looking out across the sloping park toward the town's busy main shopping district. Opposite him was a member of his staff who had recently begun a project to determine the appropriate mix of town-owned and subcontract snow removal equipment.

The study came at an opportune time. The town's aging six Walther Snow Fighters were rapidly reaching the point of replacement, and it was Mr. Castanino's intention to replace them at a rate of one per year. Belmont, like most town governments, was finding it ever more difficult to increase its revenues rapidly enough to maintain previous levels of service. All of the town's departments were undertaking sustained cost cutting measures. The Highway Department had been a leader in such cost savings, doing volume purchasing and repairing all its vehicles. However, further cost cutting was necessary. With snow removal being the largest component of the department's budget, a reexamination of its snow removal subcontracting policies might yield significant savings.

In simplified terms, the decision Mr. Castanino faced contained two options. The first option was to replace the six Walther Snow Fighters on a one-to-one basis. The second was to not replace the Walthers and subcontract six more vehicles. Before making his decision he felt a number of important variables needed to be considered.

Belmont (triple A bond rating) was a suburb of Boston. Its population was predominantly middle class, with a high proportion of professional people. The town had a well-deserved reputation for providing its citizens with high-quality services, and the maintenance of this reputation was important. Indeed, during the two large blizzards of 1978 the Highway Department had managed to keep all

* This case was prepared by Professor Roy D. Shapiro, Harvard Business School. Copyright © by the President and Fellows of Harvard College. Harvard Business School case 9-182-046.

roads passable and was one of the first in the state to have restored road conditions to normal.

The department heads reported to a part-time Board of Selectmen. This provided them with considerable autonomy in their day-to-day decision making. Capital expenditures greater than $5,000 required approval by the selectmen, the warrant committee, and the town meeting. As a result, Mr. Castanino was aware that any capital expenditure would face searching scrutiny before approval. The town also desired to maintain good relations with its employees. Thus, any cost-saving measure which improved working conditions would be highly attractive.

The town had 90 miles of roads, of which 40 were considered main thoroughfares. When salting or sanding was required, the main thoroughfares were covered each hour by four trucks equipped with spreaders.

The use of spreaders varied according to conditions. If only a trace of snow was expected, road conditions were watched closely. If road conditions seemed likely to worsen, one truck would be dispatched to cover the steeper gradients. If more than a trace but less than an inch was expected, four trucks with spreaders would be dispatched to cover the main thoroughfares. They would generally have to make two sweeps (at 10 miles an hour). If greater than an inch but less than three inches fell, seven trucks with spreaders would be dispatched to cover all roads. They would generally spend an hour per inch with an hour for mopping-up operations. If greater than three inches were expected, snowplowing procedures were initiated. Exhibit 1 contains relevant snowfall data, averaged for 30 years.

EXHIBIT 1   Snowfall Data, 1950–1979

November

11 percent of November days had snow, sleet, or hail; of these days, measured snowfall was as follows:

Snowfall (inches)	Proportion of Days Having that Amount
Trace	72%
Under 1	18
Over 1	10

December

34 percent of December days had snow, sleet, or hail; of these days, measured snowfall was as follows:

Snowfall (inches)	Proportion of Days Having that Amount
Trace	54%
Under 1	27
1–3	9
3–5	5
5–10	1
10–15	1
Over 15	0.5

EXHIBIT 1 *(concluded)*

January

41 percent of January days had snow, sleet, or hail; of these days, measured snowfall was as follows:

Snowfall (inches)	Proportion of Days Having that Amount
Trace	47%
Under 1	29
1–3	11
3–5	7
5–10	4
10–15	1
Over 15	0.2

February

39 percent of February days had snow, sleet, or hail; of these days, measured snowfall was as follows:

Snowfall (inches)	Proportion of Days Having that Amount
Trace	47%
Under 1	30
1–3	11
3–5	5
5–10	4
10–15	1
Over 15	1

March

28 percent of March days had snow, sleet, or hail; of these days, measured snowfall was as follows:

Snowfall (inches)	Proportion of Days Having that Amount
Trace	50%
Under 1	27
1–3	12
3–5	6
5–10	4
10–15	1
Over 15	0.4

Source: Local Climatological Data Monthly Survey (for Boston Logan International Airport) compiled by the National Oceanic and Atmospheric Administration Environmental Data Service.

The department's resources consisted of its own vehicles and subcontractors. Belmont had 15 vehicles which could be used for snowplowing. They consisted of the 6 Walther Snow Fighters and 9 other vehicles that were used for other purposes in addition to snowplowing. On the average, 13 were available during a storm. Also on call were 15 subcontracted vehicles. Typically, 90 percent of those

EXHIBIT 2   Cost of Operating a Town Vehicle, Salting and Sanding

Labor..........................	2 persons per vehicle*
Salt...........................	$27 per ton at 3 tons per hour†
or	
Sand..........................	$3 per ton at 3 tons per hour†
Fuel...........................	$6/hour
Repairs and maintenance...........	$10/hour

Snow Removal with New Vehicles

Labor..........................	1 person per vehicle*
Fuel...........................	$6/hour
Repairs and maintenance...........	$10/hour
Cost of new 18 GVW vehicle.......	$30,000

* Labor costs were $6 per hour, time-and-a-half for overtime.
† Normally half of the material spread was salt and half was sand.

called in any storm would turn out. To ensure good relations with the subcontractors, Castanino's policy was to divide them into two groups—one group of seven and one of eight. If the expected snowfall was greater than three inches but less than five inches, he would call in only one group. The two groups would be chosen on an alternating basis. If greater than five inches was expected, all 15 subcontractor vehicles would be called. Subcontractors only performed plowing services, not the salting and sanding of roads. Like town employees, subcontractors would work until the snow was cleared, but they did not receive overtime pay. While the size and rental cost of subcontracted vehicles varied, an appropriate average was $34 per hour. Cost data for a town vehicle is contained in Exhibit 2.

Normal procedures called for the employees and/or subcontractors to work until the storm was cleared up. For all storms, this took roughly an hour for each inch of snow. "Mop-up" for a three-inch storm required an additional three-hour shift of all vehicles. For an eight-inch snowfall, an additional four hours was required for mop-up, and for a snowfall greater than 16 inches, an additional eight hours was required. For any storm which dumped more than 12 inches, the usual policy required working 16-hour shifts. This meant that only two-thirds of the vehicles would be on the road at any time. For snowfall in excess of two feet, all crews would be sent home for eight hours rest before clean-up operations were resumed. It was not a surprising demonstration of the innate perversity of weather conditions that, historically, 70 percent of all town employees' time spent on snow removal had been at overtime rates.

It also had come to Mr. Castanino's attention that if the Walthers were retired but not replaced, it would be possible to redeploy their drivers as replacements for other drivers, reducing the expected time any individual driver would spend on the road in a 12-inch storm by 6.5 hours without increasing labor costs. The total labor cost per town vehicle would, however, remain the same.

Having discussed operating procedures, Mr. Castanino and his assistant began to discuss ways of determining the costs of these two options.

Question

What action would you recommend?

Chapter 6

Pricing Decisions

Management control in a for-profit company does not usually encompass decisions about the price to charge for the company's products.[1] By contrast, for reasons we discuss in this chapter, pricing decisions are an important aspect of management control in nonprofit organizations. Nevertheless, many nonprofit managers have given insufficient thought to pricing policies. In fact, many tend to regard all marketing activity as something to be ignored. Such an attitude can result in a nonprofit organization giving insufficient attention to the needs and decision-making behavior of its clients. It also can result in the organization pricing its services in a way that is unfair to some of its clients, or developing pricing policies that inhibit the achievement of its strategic goals.

In the first section of this chapter we explain why pricing decisions are important to management control in nonprofit organizations. We then describe the basis of normal pricing, which is a product's full cost plus a profit margin. Next, we describe two variations from normal pricing: services provided at subsidized prices and services provided at no charge. Finally, we discuss transfer pricing, a technique used by many organizations to charge for services provided by one responsibility center to another.

RELEVANCE OF PRICING TO MANAGEMENT CONTROL

In for-profit companies, pricing is usually the responsibility of the marketing department. Apart from the provision of relevant cost information from company accounts, the topic rarely is mentioned in a description of management control

---

[1] Recall that, by definition, the word *product* includes services as well as goods.

278

practices. In most nonprofit organizations, however, prices are an important consideration in management control. There are three reasons for this:

- Prices influence the behavior of clients.
- Prices provide a measure of output.
- Prices influence the behavior of managers.

Client Behavior

The amount that a client (or third party on behalf of a client) pays for a service indicates that the service is worth at least that much to the client. Indeed, the better a pricing scheme fits with client decision-making options, the more powerful its impact on client behavior.

> *Example.* Residents of a city or town can be charged for use of water in any of at least three different ways: (1) everyone can be charged the same amount (or, at the extreme, nothing); (2) everyone can be charged a monthly or quarterly flat rate, based on the number of bathrooms and kitchens in their residences; or (3) everyone can be charged individually for the water they actually consume, as measured by a meter. In the first case, residents are not motivated to conserve water, and consumers who use little water subsidize those who use more. In the second case, the charge is somewhat more equitable because water usage tends to vary with the number of outlets. However, such a system does not motivate consumers to conserve water (although it may influence their decisions to add or delete bathrooms). If meters are installed, consumers are more likely to give thought to conserving water. This occurred in New York City some decades ago when, after meters were installed, water consumption fell by nearly 50 percent.

Strength of Motivation. Prices that affect clients directly tend to have the greatest influence on consumption. Normally, as the price for a unit of service increases, clients consume fewer units. The influence may not be as strong if charges are paid by third parties, however. Some observers claim, for example, that third-party insurance for health care services, by insulating patients from the full cost of those services, has contributed to escalating health care costs.[2]

In other situations, price is a mere bookkeeping charge with no direct effect on client behavior. Some universities, for example, allocate computer resources by providing students and faculty with monetary allowances that entitle them to a certain amount of computer time. These allowances may be set so high or may be so easily supplemented, however, that they do not motivate at all, and do little more than track computer usage. The motivating force of such systems would be much stronger if clients were allowed to trade *dollars* of computer time for other resources, or receive a refund for time not used.

---

[2] See Joseph Newhouse et al., "Some Interim Results from a Controlled Trial of Cost Sharing in Health Insurance," *New England Journal of Medicine* 17 (December 1981), pp. 1501–07.

Price can sometimes provide an automatic means of rationing a service. For example, if motorists who renew their automobile registrations in person are charged more than those who complete their renewal by mail, fewer are likely to use the window services of the registry.

Measure of Output

Measurements of output in nonmonetary terms, such as the number of visitors to a community health center or the number of hours faculty spend in contact with students, are likely to be cruder than monetary measurements. If, for example, each service furnished by an organization is priced at its cost, the total revenue for a period approximates the total amount of service provided during that period. Even if reported revenue does not measure the real value of an organization's services to individual clients or society, the revenue-based approximation may provide useful information to managers. For example, if revenue one year is lower than that of the previous year (after adjustments for inflation), managers have a good indication that the organization's real output has decreased.

If the quantity of service provided varies among an organization's clients, a single price will not accurately measure the variations. At one time, for example, hospital patients were charged a flat rate per day, even though the services they received varied greatly based on their illnesses. Today hospital charges vary more directly with the quantity of services provided. If the unit price of a service reflects the relative magnitude of that service, then total revenue, which is the aggregate of these prices, is in effect a weighted measure of output. That is, total revenue incorporates differences in the types of services rendered.[3]

Behavior of Managers

If services are sold, the responsibility center that sells them frequently becomes a "profit center."[4] In general, profit center managers are motivated to think of ways to: (a) render additional services so as to increase revenue, (b) cut costs, or (c) change prices. Under these circumstances, the manager of a profit center in a nonprofit organization behaves much like a manager in a for-profit company.

---

[3] While most health care managers and policymakers consider this evolution an improvement, we caution against pursuing such precision in all pricing and control situations. For reasons we will describe later, linking prices directly to the types of services provided may not be optimal in all circumstances.

[4] Recall that a profit center is an organizational unit in which both outputs and inputs are measured in monetary terms. The manager of a profit center is responsible for operating the unit in such a way that it achieves the budgeted difference between revenues and expenses.

Example. In an organization with a computer center, if computer services are furnished without charge, assignment of computer time is the responsibility of the manager of the center, and time assignments are made according to his or her perception of users' needs (or sometimes, friendship with users). In any case, the manager has little financial incentive to provide quality computer services in a cost effective manner.

If the computer center were set up as a profit center, however, and dissatisfied users were free to go elsewhere, the manager would be motivated to offer quality services at competitive prices—or risk underutilized facilities, unmet revenue goals, and poor performance. In addition, when internal clients must pay for their use of computer resources (which reduces the profit in their profit centers), they tend to think much more carefully about their use of those resources.

In this and other pricing situations, if customers do not buy a product in the quantity that managers think is reasonable, there is an indication that something is wrong. Perhaps not enough people believe the product is worthwhile at the stated price. Perhaps they can obtain a similar or better product at a lower price elsewhere. Whatever the reason, management will want to reexamine the product and its price. Can its costs be reduced? Is there a need for better marketing? Can the product be made more attractive? If not, should it be discontinued?

NORMAL PRICING

In general, the price of a product or service provided by a nonprofit organization should be its full cost (i.e., the sum of its direct costs and a fair share of its indirect costs) plus a modest margin. This is the same approach that is used in normal pricing in for-profit companies, except that in for-profit companies the margin ordinarily is higher, for reasons discussed below.

Rationale for Normal Pricing

An important goal of a for-profit company is to earn a satisfactory level of profit. Its success is measured, at least in part, by the amount of profit that it earns; in general, the higher its profit, the more favorably investors view its performance. If a company sets prices that cover full cost plus a satisfactory profit margin for each product, or for its average product, it will attain its goal of earning a satisfactory total profit.

A nonprofit organization does not have earning a satisfactory *profit* as a goal. Its basic goal is to provide services. To survive, however, it must generate revenues that at least equal its expenses. Otherwise, it will go bankrupt. In this regard, the *profit* figures in accounting reports of a for-profit company overstate real profit in the sense that economists use the term. Accounting profits include a return for the use of equity capital, which economists, quite properly, count as an element of expense. That is, accounting principles allow a company to include the interest incurred for the use of debt capital as an expense but do not treat dividends as an expense. Together, dividends plus the appreciation in stock prices that shareholders expect when they invest in a corporation's stock constitute the cost of using equity capital.

Need for a Satisfactory Margin.   For-profit companies must earn a profit for more than just satisfying investors' need for a return. One of the principal uses of profit is to generate some of the funds needed to grow, acquire new assets, and replace existing assets as they wear out. In this respect, there is no difference between for-profit and nonprofit organizations. Like their for-profit counterparts, nonprofit organizations need an excess of revenue over expenses to finance needed working capital (such as for inventories and receivables) and fixed assets (such as new buildings and equipment). Moreover, because inflation usually increases replacement costs, depreciation on the historical costs of existing assets does not provide sufficient financing for their replacement.

The following example shows why there is a need for additional working capital in a growing organization.

Example. An organization with revenues growing at the rate of 2 percent per month, with revenues equal to expenses, might have an income statement for a six-month period that appears as follows:

	Month					
	1	*2*	*3*	*4*	*5*	*6*
Revenue.......	100	102	104	106	108	110
Expenses......	100	102	104	106	108	110
Profit.........	0	0	0	0	0	0

If, however, the organization does not collect its accounts receivable until two months after the revenue is recognized, yet must pay its expenses immediately (a common situation), its cash account will appear as follows:

	Month					
	1	*2*	*3*	*4*	*5*	*6*
Cash in*...........	96	98	100	102	104	106
Cash out...........	100	102	104	106	108	110
Change in cash......	(4)	(4)	(4)	(4)	(4)	(4)
Cumulative change ..	(4)	(8)	(12)	(16)	(20)	(24)

* From two months ago.

Under these circumstances, if the organization does not wish to slow its growth and cannot accelerate the collection of its accounts receivable or delay payment of its expenses, it will need to earn a profit that equals the amount of change in its cash. A loan would not be an acceptable alternative since the cash needed to repay it would not be available until growth were slowed, receivable collections accelerated, or expense payments delayed.[5]

Nonprofit organizations could finance some of their working capital and fixed asset needs by borrowing, just as for-profit companies do. However, there is a limit to the amount that any organization can borrow. Consequently, nonprofits need equity capital for basically the same reason that for-profit companies do, because lenders are unwilling to provide amounts that equal an organization's total capital needs. Indeed, many nonprofits believe that financing entirely with borrowed funds is too risky.

The same principle holds for an individual family. Mortgage lenders will not lend an amount equal to 100 percent of the cost of a house.

If, for example, a nonprofit organization can finance only 80 percent of its fixed asset replacements through borrowing or contributions, it needs to generate equity funds from either contributions or operations for the balance. In the absence of a constant and predictable source of capital contributions from donors or other sources, the organization will need to generate additional equity capital in the form of a profit from its own operations.

Furthermore, in addition to financing capital needs that cannot or should not be met through borrowing, a nonprofit organization needs a reserve against *rainy days,* or periods in which revenues do not equal expenses. Earning a profit during good times will assist the organization to weather bad times.

In summary, as we discussed in Chapters 2 and 3, accounting measures profit essentially the same way in both for-profit and nonprofit organizations. In nonprofit organizations, profit is often called *surplus.* Regardless of the terminology, the purpose of an excess of revenue over expenses is to increase the retained earnings portion of the organization's equity. The need for equity capital is smaller in nonprofit organizations because they do not have stockholders who expect cash dividends. In other respects, however, the need for generating equity capital from operations is the same in both types of organization—as a source of financing and as protection against bad times.

Full Cost

As we discussed in Chapter 4, the full cost of a product is the sum of its direct costs and its allocated share of the indirect costs incurred jointly for it and any other products. In arriving at prices, the relevant costs are estimates of *future* costs, not historical costs.

---

[5] For details on the underlying theory of this example, see David W. Young, "Nonprofits Need Surplus Too," *Harvard Business Review,* January–February, 1982.

Recall from Chapter 4 that direct costs are those that can be traced directly to a single cost object. In nonprofit organizations, the typical cost object is a program. Indirect costs of a cost object include items of cost that, although incurred in part for that cost object, are not traced directly to it. Indirect costs are allocated to cost objects by means of overhead rates. These rates are set so that at the expected volume, 100 percent of indirect costs are allocated to the cost objects whose prices are being calculated. The pricing principles discussed above, therefore, assume that a specified volume of output will be attained.

Depreciation.   In nonprofit organizations, there is a difference of opinion as to whether depreciation on buildings and equipment that were financed with contributions should be included as an element of cost. Some argue that such buildings and equipment were acquired at zero cost and that, because the purpose of depreciation is to recover an organization's cost, there is nothing to depreciate. Others maintain that depreciation is necessary in order to provide for replacement of these assets. Also, some people argue that the services a nonprofit organization provides are just as valuable as the services provided by a for-profit company, and that clients should pay a comparable amount for them. Thus, by including depreciation as an element of cost, nonprofits are in keeping with the pricing practices of for-profit companies. Indeed, many clients of nonprofit organizations, including government agencies, are willing to include depreciation on contributed assets (or its equivalent as a *use charge*) as an element of cost. The government does not permit inclusion of depreciation on equipment it has already paid for in the prices it is charged, however; to do so would be double counting.

Many organizations do not depreciate fixed assets. Instead they arrive at an approximation of depreciation by summing the principal repayment on borrowed funds, plus an annual allowance for renewal and replacement. They supplement this approach with a policy of expensing all except major equipment purchases. They argue that this adds up to approximately the same amount as depreciation in an average year.

Revenue Offsets.   Some services are partially financed by revenue from endowment or other contributed sources. Opinions differ as to whether these *revenue offsets* should be deducted from costs in order to arrive at the price a client should pay.

If revenue is directly related to a service—as is the case with endowment that is specifically designated for financial aid to students—a good case can be made for taking this revenue into account in arriving at the price. Even if this is done, however, it may be desirable to report this amount as a component of the service's revenue on the operating statement, rather than as an offset to costs. Then the operating statement will show the total resources earned by and for the service.

If the contributed revenue is for general operating purposes rather than for a specific service, many organizations do not treat some fraction of it as an offset to full cost in calculating the price for a specific service. Rather, they prefer to reduce the required margin included in the price of all services by the amount of this revenue.

Estimating the Margin

The best conceptual way for managers to estimate the margin to include in a price is to calculate the cost of using the equity capital that the organization needs, and to include this cost in the total cost of a service. Most managers do not make such calculations, however. Instead, they rely on rules of thumb. For example, there is a widespread belief among managers of hospital and research organizations that their organizations' margin should be 3 or 4 percent of revenue.

Some organizations base their prices on a conservative estimate of volume, and plan for no surplus. When actual volume exceeds the estimate, the incremental amount (i.e., revenues minus variable expenses) provides the necessary margin. For example, a college may base its tuition on an enrollment that is 5 percent lower than what it actually expects. If its actual enrollment reaches the expected level, the difference is its surplus for the year. Similarly, an organization may make a conservative estimate of its revenue from annual giving, with the expectation that the anticipated excess will be its surplus.

This approach works when the estimate of volume is truly conservative. Difficulties arise when volume falls below the anticipated level. When this happens, an organization's revenues do not cover its expenses. In such circumstances continued existence is precarious and often rests on the hope that, in times of crisis, special appeals to donors will bail the organization out.

> *Example.* It is said that for many years the Metropolitan Museum of Art presented its annual deficit to its board of trustees, and the trustees then wrote personal checks that totaled the needed amount. Today, few nonprofit organizations (including the Metropolitan Museum) are able to do this.

The Pricing Unit

In general, the smaller and more specific the unit of service that is priced, the better. Senior management's decisions about the allocation of resources are improved, and its measures of output for control purposes are more accurate. A price that includes several discrete services with different costs is not a good measure of output because it masks the actual mix of services rendered. The practice of isolating progressively smaller units of service for pricing purposes is called *unbundling*.

There is considerable disagreement about this practice. Those who reject it argue that price should reflect an average mix of services, and that detailed information needed for management control can be obtained in other ways.

Managers who decide to unbundle services should be mindful of two qualifications: First, and an obvious problem, beyond a certain point, the paperwork and other costs associated with pricing tiny units of service outweigh the benefits. Some hospitals charge for individual aspirin tablets, a practice that is difficult to defend. The precise location of this point is, of course, uncertain.

The second qualification for managers considering unbundled prices is that the consequences of such pricing should be consistent with the organization's overall policy and goals. This qualification extends beyond the size of the unit to matters that are much more strategic in nature.

Example. Undergraduate English instruction costs less than undergraduate physics instruction, and these differences could be reflected by charging different prices for these courses. However, a separate price for each course might cause students to select courses in a way that university management considers to be educationally unsound. By contrast, in most universities there are significant differences in the overall costs of graduate and undergraduate programs. Thus, there may be good reasons for charging different tuition rates to graduate students than to undergraduate ones. University administrators who unbundle in this way do not feel these differences motivate individual students to make unwise choices.

Example. The Port Authority of New York and New Jersey charges the same amount for a tunnel crossing of the Hudson River as for a crossing using the George Washington Bridge, despite a lower full cost per vehicle for bridge traffic. The pricing decision is based on transportation policy, rather than on the cost of the separate services.

Hospital Pricing as an Example of Unbundling. Exhibit 6–1 shows several approaches that could be used in pricing the services provided by a hospital. Moving from Column A to Column D, one can see pricing practices that involve (1) an increase in recordkeeping, (2) a corresponding increase in the amount of output

---

EXHIBIT 6–1 Pricing Alternatives in a Hospital

(A) All-Inclusive Rate	*(B)* Daily Charge plus Special Services		*(C)* Type of Service		*(D)* Detailed	
$820/day	Patient care	$500/day	Medical/surgical:		Admittance	$500
	Operating room	$300/hour	1st day	$550	Work-up, per hour	50
	Pharmacy	$ 7/dosage	Other days	475	Medical/surgical bed, per	
	Radiology	$ 35/film	Maternity:		day	400
	Special nurses	$ 75/day	1st day	$350	Maternity bed, per day	150
	Etc.		Other days	300	Bassinet, per day	125
			(Plus special services as in *B*)		Nursery care, per hour	30
					Meals, per day	40
					Discharge	50
					(Plus special services as in B)	

information for use in management control, and (3) a basis for charging to clients that more accurately reflects the services they received.

At one extreme, the hospital could charge an all-inclusive rate, say $820 per day. This practice is advocated by some people on the grounds that patients then know in advance what their bills will be (assuming their lengths of stay can be estimated), and because recordkeeping, at least for billing purposes, is simplified. They point out that detailed information required for administration can be collected in the management control system, even though such information would not be reflected in the prices charged. The weakness of the latter argument is that if detailed information is going to be collected for management anyway, an all-inclusive price will not result in significant savings in recordkeeping (unless short-cuts and estimates are substituted for sound data collection methods). The only savings would be in the billing process, which is a small part of a hospital's total accounting function.

A common variation on the all-inclusive price is shown in Column B. Here the hospital charges separately for the cost of each easily identifiable special service, and makes a blanket daily charge for everything else. Radiology prices, for example, are frequently calculated according to a rather detailed point system that takes into account the size of the radiology plate and the complexity of the procedure; each point is worth a few cents. There is some incongruity in calculating prices for certain services in terms of points worth a few cents each, while lumping other service costs into an overall rate of, say, $500 per day.

Column C unbundles the daily charge. Different charges are made for each department, and more is charged for the first day than for subsequent days. This pricing policy accounts for the admitting and work-up costs associated only with the first day of a patient's stay.

Column D is the job-cost approach that managers in many for-profit companies use. Managers of automobile repair shops, for example, cost each repair job separately. Each repair is charged for the services of mechanics according to the number of hours they work on the job, as well as for each part and significant item of supply required for the job's completion. The sum of these separate charges is the basis for the price the customer pays. Customers of a repair garage would not tolerate any other approach. They would not, for example, tolerate paying a flat daily rate for repairs, regardless of the service provided.

Prices Influenced by Outside Forces

Some prices are set by outside agencies. Examples are the diagnosis related group (DRG) prices that are used by medicare to reimburse hospitals, and the price ceilings sometimes specified by government agencies as a condition for providing services funded by government grants. In these instances, managers still need to make cost calculations even though their selling price is given. If, for example, a hospital's full cost of treating a patient with a particular diagnosis is greater than the associated DRG price, the hospital will need to determine whether it wishes to avoid accepting patients with that diagnosis.[6] Of course, this decision is subject to the hospital's legal obligation to treat the ill.

DRG prices also affect the way physicians behave. Consciously or unconsciously, they may treat the patient in a way that generates the most income, rather than in an alternative way.

> *Example.* A General Accounting Office study of 264 oncologists found that 64 percent of them administered chemotherapy in a hospital rather than in their private office, although the treatment in many cases could have been conducted equally well in their private office. Reimbursement for office treatment was low, but costs were higher in the hospital.[7]

Price may also be indirectly influenced by outside forces. For example, no college could charge much more than its competitors; to do so would indicate that it was inefficient. Nor would a college charge less than its competitors because it could make good use of any additional amount to strengthen its curriculum. Furthermore, most colleges are convinced that small differences in tuition do not influence a student's decision as to which college to attend.

> *Example.* In 1990 the Department of Justice considered investigating the possible incidence of illegal price fixing by a group of colleges whose tuition charges were within 5 percent of one another. Its decision not to pursue this matter was probably influenced by the recognition that such a situation is likely among competing organizations.

Similarly, if a ceiling price required by a government grant is lower than the full cost of the service to be provided, the organization has to decide whether to accept the grant. It may decide to do so if the price exceeds the variable costs of providing the service; that is, if the grant makes a contribution to overhead.

VARIATIONS FROM NORMAL PRICES

There are many situations in nonprofit organizations where circumstances call for variations from the normal approach to setting prices. In some instances, these situations arise because of the presence of third-party payers. In others, they arise because the organization wishes to distinguish between services provided as part of its main mission and those that are more peripheral.

Cost Reimbursement

Revenue for many services consist of reimbursement for costs actually incurred, rather than a preset selling price. Although the intent of the buyer usually is to pay the full cost of the service, often the definition of full cost varies considerably from

---

[6] Such diagnoses have come to be called *DRG orphans*. For a discussion of this problem, see Michael Shwartz, Melanie Lenard, and Joseph Restuccia, "Pricing DRGs to Improve Patient Access," Paper presented at the American Public Health Association annual meeting, September 1986.

[7] U.S. General Accounting Office, "Medicare Reimbursement Policies Can Influence the Setting and Cost of Chemotherapy" (GAO/PEMD-92-28), July 1992.

one buyer to another. In particular, a new component called *unallowable costs* enters the calculation. These are costs that, although incurred by the organization, cannot be included in the cost pool that is used to arrive at the overhead rate. Contracting agencies may also specify ceilings for certain items, such as the compensation of executives or the daily amount that can be spent for travel.[8]

Some of these requirements are extremely detailed. Moreover, they change frequently. As a result, managers of nonprofit organizations receiving cost-based reimbursement must be sure to be both thoroughly familiar and current with the regulations that govern their organization's reimbursement.

> *Example.* According to OMB *Circular A–21*, travel and subsistence costs of college and university trustees are unallowable. The reasonable cost of meals served in connection with a trustee meeting is allowable, except that the cost of alcoholic beverages served at such meals is unallowable.

Market-Based Prices

Managers ordinarily apply a normal pricing policy to services that are directly (or closely) related to their organization's principal objectives. In dealing with peripheral activities, however, they usually make sure their prices correspond to market prices for similar services.

> *Example.* Many universities believe that room and board charges should be based on full cost because students live in dormitories and eat in dining rooms as a necessary part of the educational process. For similar reasons, they believe that textbooks, laboratory supplies, and the like, should be priced at full cost. By contrast, they believe that the rental of space to outside groups, the provision of special programs requested by outside groups, or the sale of items at campus soda fountains is not closely related to the main objective of the university. Accordingly, the prices of these services are set at market levels. Similarly, many universities base tuition for graduate and undergraduate programs on full cost, whereas they use market rates for executive development programs.

In making pricing decisions, managers often have difficulty drawing the line between programs that are closely related to the organization's objectives and those that are more peripheral. For example, market rates seem appropriate for the executive development programs mentioned in the example above, but the use of market rates for university extension courses or adult education programs in municipal school systems is much less clear. Moreover, as we indicated in Chapter 2, these decisions involve not only pricing issues, but legal issues as well.

---

[8] See the following U.S. Office of Management and Budget (OMB) publications: *Circular A–21*, "Cost Principles for Educational Institutions"; *Circular A–87*, "Cost Principles for State and Local Governments"; *Circular A–122*, "Cost Principles for Nonprofit Organizations"; and *Circular 133*, "Audits of Institutions of Higher Education and Other Non-Profit Organizations." (Dates are not given because these circulars are revised from time to time.) United Way organizations also publish guidance on allowable costs. In most of these guidelines, even if an item is not specifically described, it must meet the general test that it be "reasonable."

Prospective Prices

As a general rule, management control is facilitated when the price is set prior to the performance of a service. When this happens, prices provide an incentive for managers to keep costs within prescribed amounts. No such incentive exists for managers who know that costs will be recouped no matter how high they are.

This principle can be applied, of course, only when it is feasible to estimate the cost of a service. With many research and development projects, for example, there is no reliable basis for estimating how much money should be spent to achieve the desired result. Even so, it is usually possible to establish overhead rates based on budgeted overhead costs and to require adherence to these rates.

Opponents of prospective pricing assert that it leads to an overemphasis on cost control, with a consequent lowering of the quality of service. Advocates counter that a well-designed management control system should help managers and service providers overcome any tendency to emphasize reduced cost at the expense of quality.

Danger of Normal Pricing

If a nonprofit organization provides a worthwhile service, clients are usually willing to pay the normal price. In this case, the organization usually will earn its desired margin. This is so even if the organization has competitors with lower priced services, because clients often do not select a service provider on the basis of price alone.

The danger of this situation is that the normal price may conceal cost inefficiencies. For-profit companies must face the test of the marketplace; an inadequate profit is a danger signal that may not exist in a nonprofit organization. Because of the absence of such a danger signal, the nonprofit governing board has the responsibility of ensuring operating efficiency in other ways. It does this by careful analysis of proposed budgets, as explained in later chapters, by comparing the costs with the costs of comparable organizations if this is feasible, and by other devices that lead management to "get the message" that efficiency is important.

PRICING SUBSIDIZED SERVICES

Services are being subsidized when the price charged for a service to one client is lower than the price charged to another, or when the price to all clients is lower than the full cost of the services they receive. We shall discuss three types of subsidy: (1) the subsidy of certain services, (2) the subsidy for some clients, and (3) the subsidy of all clients.

Subsidy of Certain Services

A nonprofit organization may decide to price a certain service at less than the normal price. Such a price is called a *subsidy price*. It may want to encourage the use of the service by clients who are unable or unwilling to pay the normal price. Or, as a matter of policy, the organization may want clients to select services on some basis other than their ability to pay. Examples are public education and low-cost housing. Economists tend to argue that, in most circumstances, providing a service at a subsidy price is preferable to providing it for free. This is because a price, even if low, motivates clients to give thought to the value of the service they receive. However, an organization should be careful to determine whether the price deters clients from requesting *needed* services.

> *Example.* Milton Roemer reported that when medicaid patients in California were charged $1 per visit for primary care, there was a sharp decline in the number of patient visits. Some months later, however, there was an increase in these patients' rates of hospitalization—hospitalization that could have been avoided had the individuals received timely primary care. Overall, the cost to medicaid was higher as a result of this pricing policy.[9]

An organization may decide that its price will be the same for all services even though some services cost more than others. In this case, the higher cost services are said to be *cross-subsidized* by lower cost services. More broadly, any difference in price that does not reflect a difference in cost results in cross-subsidization. Although cross-subsidization is frowned on in public utility rate regulation, there may be sound reasons for using it in other circumstances. As mentioned in the discussion of unbundling, one reason is that the work of establishing equitable prices for narrow units of service may not be worth the cost. A more important reason is that the organization may not want clients to choose one service over another on the basis of price.

> *Example.* Courses in Latin and Greek, and seminars in a college typically have small enrollments, with the resulting faculty cost per student for these courses two or three times that for more popular courses. Because the college does not want to discourage enrollment in these courses, it charges the same tuition to all students. Thus, its low-enrollment courses are subsidized by high-enrollment courses.

Even if managers do not use cost as the basis for pricing, they may find it helpful to calculate the actual costs of subsidized services. Knowing the difference between price and full cost can help flag areas for managerial decision making. For example, if a particular service does not cover its full costs, managers have several possible courses of action:

- Accept the loss, recognizing that the service is either a *loss leader* or sufficiently important to the organization's strategy to warrant subsidization.

---

[9] M. Roemer et al., "Copayments for Ambulatory Care: Penny-Wise and Pound-Foolish," *Medical Care,* June 1975, pp. 457–66.

- Reduce the variable costs or fixed costs directly associated with the service.
- Increase volume (if the service makes a contribution, there is some breakeven volume at which full costs will be covered).
- Raise the price of the service.
- Phase out the service.

Example. A university discovered that the cost of operating its nuclear reactor was $50,000 per student using the reactor. The reactor probably should be shut down unless: (1) it is important to the university's strategy, (2) its operating costs can be reduced, or (3) the number of users can be increased.

Example. The U.S. Postal Service subsidizes rural post offices because it is public policy to provide convenient mail service to everyone; this principle is rarely challenged. However, the Postal Service also subsidizes its money order service, even though commercial banks provide adequate facilities for transferring money. Some observers question whether this latter subsidy is warranted.

Subsidies as a Motivating Device.   Most subsidies are intended to encourage the use of a service by clients who would not otherwise do so.

Example. Many public bathing beaches and other recreation facilities charge a lower price on weekdays to encourage off-peak use. By contrast, the Mexican government had a policy of eliminating recreational charges on Sundays. This had the effect of further crowding recreation facilities on their busiest day, which would appear to be counterproductive. The policy was judged to be sound, however, because it encouraged use of the facilities by working-class families on the only day they could do so—a purpose judged more important than reducing crowding.

Subsidies for Some Clients

A client who is not charged the same amount as other clients who receive the same or comparable services is being subsidized. The reason for this subsidy is that the organization's objective is to provide the service to all qualified clients, some of whom are unable to pay the normal price. The subsidy may be in the form of a lower price (or no charge), or the client may be charged the normal price and the subsidy treated as a deduction. The latter is often preferable because the gross revenue resulting from this method provides a better measure of the amount of service rendered by the organization than does net revenue (gross minus the subsidies).

Example. Colleges and universities provide subsidies to certain students in the form of scholarships and other financial aid. The amount of financial aid is reported as an expense item, so tuition revenue measures the gross amount that the college has earned in its educational programs. Tuition revenue thus provides a sound measure of actual output.

Example. Nonprofit hospitals are usually charitable organizations and, as such, are obligated to provide certain levels of care to indigent patients. Until recently, hospitals deducted revenue lost from charitable care from the gross revenue that measured charges for all services rendered. A 1990 pronouncement by the American Institute of Certified Public Accountants (AICPA) changed this practice for external reporting purposes.[10] Managers of hospitals that follow this recommendation will not have as sound a measure of actual output as they had under the previous practice. This will reduce the value of this information for management control purposes.

Estimating Subsidies.   In situations such as those described above, managers must take care to incorporate subsidies into their analyses when they are considering price increases. For example, when subsidies are present, a 10 percent increase in university tuition rates or hospital charges will not necessarily result in a 10 percent increase in *net revenue*.

> *Example.*   Assume a college has 1,000 students who are charged $15,000 each for tuition. Gross tuition revenue is $15,000,000. Students receive financial aid in the amount of $1,000,000. An increase of 10 percent in tuition will result in an increase of $1,500,000 in gross revenue. However, if the criteria for deciding what students receive financial aid are unchanged, financial aid will also increase by 10 percent, or $100,000. Therefore, the college's net case inflow will increase by only $1,400,000 (= $1,500,000 − $100,000). (This is a simplified calculation because the inflation that caused the increase in tuition may also reduce parents' ability to pay, thus requiring more than a 10 percent increase in financial aid.)

Relating Subsidies to Need.   Some clients are subsidized because they need the service but do not have the resources to obtain it. In some cases, this general idea is applied to a class of clients even though some members of the class have ample resources. Examples are subsidies for handicapped and elderly persons by both nonprofit organizations and for-profit companies—for transportation, movies, restaurants, drugs, and a variety of other services. Conceptually, the subsidy should be limited to those in need, but finding a practical way of applying this concept is difficult. A *means test* usually is not feasible because it is expensive and time consuming, and, more importantly, because many people resent being classified as being needy. Moreover, such a subsidy is politically popular, and attempts to eliminate or modify it would encounter considerable resistance from lobbying groups such as the American Association of Retired Persons (the largest and one of the most effective lobbying groups in the country).

Subsidies for All Clients

Some organizations receive contributions or appropriations intended to subsidize their services for all clients. When this happens, no client pays the normal price for services. Museums, symphony orchestras, and state universities are exam-

---

[10] American Institute of CPAs, *Audits of Providers of Health Care Services* (New York: AICPA, 1990), para. 7.2.

ples. The question then arises: Should the gross revenue resulting from the normal price of these services be reported with an offset from the contributed amount, or should only the actual amount of service revenue charged should be reported? For museums and symphony orchestras, there is little reason to report the gross amount; the operating statement will show how much revenue came from clients and how much from contributions.

The case of public universities is more controversial, and relates to the reason for the existence of a subsidy in the first place. Tuition in a public university is never as high as the full cost of education (except, in some cases, for out-of-state students). The principal argument against full-cost tuition is that it would deprive some students of the opportunity for education, and educated people are valuable assets to society. The counterargument is that all students could obtain the education if they received adequate financial aid. If tuition were set at full cost, those who could afford to pay would do so, and the cost to the taxpayers would be only the amount of financial aid. Moreover, in times of financial stringency, many state governments tend to reduce appropriations to higher education, and this makes for unsettling conditions in public universities. If tuition were set at full cost, the reduced appropriation would affect only those students receiving financial aid. The university could then determine how it wished to award this aid consistent with its overall goals and objectives.

Traditions are difficult to change, and many state legislatures perceive that voters would not approve of a move to full cost tuition. Nevertheless, there has been a recent tendency to move tuition rates upward to incorporate a higher percentage of total costs. By reporting gross revenue as the full cost of tuition, and using the state subsidy as an offset, public universities could identify more clearly the extent to which the state subsidy is serving as financial aid for needy students rather than as a benefit to all students. Few public universities do this, however.

FREE SERVICES

Some services are provided free to clients. This usually happens when public policy officials determine that it would be discriminatory to charge for a particular service, or when managers determine that attempting to collect for a service would be impossible or infeasible.

Public Goods

The most important class of services furnished without charge is that of public goods. Public goods are services provided for the benefit of the public in general, rather than for specific users. Examples are police protection (as contrasted with a police officer who is hired by the manager of a sporting event), and foreign policy and its implementation (as contrasted with services rendered to an individual firm doing business overseas). Public goods are well described in the following passage:

> These are goods and services that simply cannot be provided through the market. They have two related qualities. First, they inevitably have to be supplied to a group of people rather than on an individual basis. Second, they cannot be withheld from individuals who refuse to pay for them.
>
> Take national defense, for example. The national security provided by our military forces is extended to all persons in the country. They all receive the same protection, whether they are willing to pay for it or not. There is no way of withholding the service, of creating a market which separates those who pay from the freeloaders. In fact, in this type of situation, rational consumers who are interested only in economics will never pay since they will get the benefit in any event.
>
> In the case of ordinary private goods, this difficulty does not occur. If one person likes some item of food or clothing or a service, and another does not, one will pay for it and receive it, and the other will not. If someone should refuse to pay yet wishes to obtain the product, the sellers would simply refuse to give the item or service.[11]

Quasi-Public Goods

Many services that superficially seem to meet the definition of public goods turn out upon analysis to be services for which prices could be charged.

> *Example.* A classic instance of a public good is a lighthouse. It is said that one ship's "consumption" of the warning light does not leave less warning light for other ships to "consume," and there is no practical way that the lighthouse keeper can prohibit ships from consuming. On the other hand, a ship cannot refuse to consume the light. However, it can be argued that shipowners, as a class, should pay for lighthouses. Then, if lighthouse costs become too high, the objections of shipowners may help bring them back in line.[12]

The lighthouse example is similar to the practice of charging users of highways for their cost via tolls or taxes on gasoline and diesel fuel, or of charging airlines and owners of private aircraft for the cost of operating the air traffic control system. In many countries, users of air waves are charged through a tax on television sets; in the United States, the air waves are regarded as a public good.

Tuition Vouchers. A useful way to think about whether a given service should be sold or given away is to separate the question of whether a price should be charged from the question of who ultimately should pay this price. For example, it is generally agreed that all children are entitled to an education and that the

---

[11] Otto Eckstein, *Public Finance*, 2nd ed. (Englewood Cliffs, N.J.: Prentice Hall, 1967), p. 8.

[12] In a fascinating article, Coase describes the history of British lighthouses, showing that they in fact successfully charged fees from the 17th century until the present. R. E. Coase, "The Lighthouse in Economics," *Journal of Law and Economics* 17 (October 1974), pp. 357–76.

community as a whole is responsible for providing this education. Education is therefore a public good—in this case, not because it is impossible to withhold the service but because it is against public policy to do so. Nevertheless, it may be possible to accept this principle and still gain the advantages of "selling the service."

This is the idea behind the *tuition voucher* plan. Parents are given vouchers that can be used to *pay* for their children's education. On the voucher is a dollar amount, which generally is the average cost per pupil in the public school system. Within certain limits, the voucher can be used at any school that the parent elects, including private schools (but perhaps not parochial schools because of constitutional prohibitions). The purpose of such a pricing mechanism is not to affect client's decisions as to whether to obtain the services, but rather to permit a consumer choice as to what school will provide the service. By using the tuition vouchers at the school of their choice, parents can express their pleasure or displeasure with individual schools and thus introduce an element of competition among schools.

There is much controversy about whether the tuition voucher idea is sound public policy. It has been used experimentally in a few locales, and yet there remains much disagreement among researchers as to whether it has improved education in those places.[13]

Housing Vouchers.   Vouchers also have been used in the housing field. This was done through the Experimental Housing Allowance Program (EHAP), established by the U.S. Department of Housing and Urban Development (HUD). An evaluation of that program concluded that, because of relatively low-income elasticities of demand for housing, the vouchers did not increase housing purchases. They did increase recipient well-being, however, presumably because they freed up rent funds for other purposes.[14]

Charges for Peripheral Services

Even when the principal service of an organization is a public good provided at no charge, managers may discover opportunities to charge for certain peripheral services rendered by the organization. For example, the Congress charges a fee for copying certain documents in its files,[15] federal agencies charge fees for copy-

---

[13] Much of the literature discusses the first experiment, which was started in Alum Rock, California, in 1972. For an analysis and a bibliography, see Paul M. Wortman and Robert G. St. Pierre, "The Educational Voucher Demonstration: A Secondary Analysis," *Education and Urban Society*, August 1977, p. 471.

[14] Joseph Friedman and Daniel H. Weinberg, *The Economics of Housing Vouchers,* Studies in Urban Economics Series (New York: Harcourt Brace Jovanovich, 1982).

[15] In this case the price was deliberately set quite high in order to discourage copying of these documents. Many people regard this as an abridgment of the public's right of access to information.

ing documents made available under the Freedom of Information Act, municipal governments charge for dog licenses, and some public school systems charge for after-school athletics.

Other Free Services

In addition to the general class of public goods, there are other situations in which prices should not normally be charged for services. These include the following situations:

- Services are provided as a public policy, but clients cannot afford to pay for them. Examples include welfare investigations and legal aid services.
- It is public policy not to ration the services on the basis of ability to pay. Examples include legislators, who do not charge fees for assisting constituents, even though a legislator's time is a valuable resource.
- A charge is politically untenable. Examples include public tours of the White House and Capitol. The public clamor over such charges could be harmful to overall organizational objectives, even though a charge would be equitable and would promote good management control.
- Client motivation is unimportant. A nominal charge to a public park or bathing beach will not measure actual output, nor will it influence a client's decision to use the facilities. A charge equal to full cost, by motivating less wealthy individuals to avoid using these facilities, may be inconsistent with public policy.

TRANSFER PRICES

When one responsibility center receives goods or services from another responsibility center and is charged for them, the charge is called a *transfer price*. A transfer price is used exclusively for transactions *within* an organization, as contrasted with an external price, which is used for transactions between an organization and its clients. The example given earlier concerning charges for services of a central computer center was an illustration of the use of a transfer price.

Motivational Considerations

In all organizations—for-profit and nonprofit—transfer pricing provides a mechanism for encouraging the optimal use of an organization's resources. This is because the behavior of profit center managers (and to a lesser extent standard expense center managers) frequently is influenced considerably by the way transfer prices are structured (or by the requirement that products be furnished without charge under certain circumstances).

If a service is free, users are not motivated to consider its value. They tend to request as much of the service as they can get without considering how much it is worth to them. Resources available to most users are limited by their budgets. If a service can be obtained free, the user need not even think about how its value compares with alternative services that require resources. For example, if a motor pool provides automobiles without charge, a user who is about to take a trip need not consider whether use of a taxi, public transportation, or private automobile would be more efficient. Other things being equal, the choice is the motor pool.

> *Example.* One organization had a motor pool that delivered freight by trucks without charging users. It found that managers were requesting trucks to deliver small quantities of freight that could be delivered less expensively by private trucking companies. The trucking company price was a charge against their budget, whereas the use of the motor pool truck was free. When the organization started to charge for motor pool deliveries, managers gave thought to the cost of alternative methods of transportation. They were also motivated to combine shipments to a given destination to further reduce costs.

The use of transfer prices also fosters an equitable distribution of services. If a motor pool provides automobiles without charge, for example, the motor pool manager's decisions about who gets an automobile may be made on the basis of favoritism or a user's persuasive talent. With a transfer pricing system, however, the user who is willing to pay gets an automobile, just as with a car rental agency. (Of course, in periods of heavy demand, when the motor pool is operating at full capacity, favoritism or pleading capability may still be influential.)

Setting Transfer Prices

In general, the transfer price should be the market price used for sales to an outside customer. It therefore might appear that if a responsibility center did not sell its products to outside customers, there would be no reliable way of establishing its transfer prices. But this is not so. Almost all service centers have counterparts in for-profit organizations. Motor pools are like car rental agencies; maintenance, housekeeping, laundry, and similar departments are like private contractors; computer departments are like computer service bureaus. The principles used to set prices in these organizations usually can be adapted rather easily to nonprofit organizations.

In cases where there is no for-profit counterpart, the time-and-material basis of pricing usually is adequate. In these instances, the transfer price normally should be based on the standard full cost of the responsibility center that provides the product (i.e., the product's direct cost plus its fair share of the organization's overhead costs, as described in Chapter 4). In some situations the transfer price is based on the standard direct cost only. In others, the transfer price is set higher than full cost to discourage undesirable practices, such as excessive use of facilities or services subject to transfer.

Because of these variations, there is no single "best" approach to establishing transfer prices. There are, however, four basic principles that organizations have found to be helpful:

Principle 1. If a valid market price exists for the product, it ordinarily should be the basis for the transfer price. This price may be adjusted downward to reduce the profit component in prices charged by for-profit companies. It also may be adjusted downward to eliminate bad debts or selling expenses that do not exist with internal transactions. If, however, the market price is a distress price—that is, a price well below the one at which market transactions usually take place—it normally does not provide a valid basis for the transfer price.

Principle 2. If no valid market price exists, the transfer price ordinarily should be the product's full cost. This rule corresponds to the normal practice for arriving at normal selling prices to outside customers, except that it has at most only a small margin above costs. As with market prices, some organizations also exclude bad debts and selling expenses.

Principle 3. The transfer price should be based on standard costs, rather than on actual costs. If based on actual costs, the selling unit could pass its inefficiencies to the units receiving its services.

Principle 4. In special circumstances, the buying and selling units may be permitted to negotiate the transfer price. If the selling unit is operating below capacity, for example, it may be willing to accept a lower price that will make some contribution to its overhead. Conversely, if the selling unit provides an especially high-quality product or certain special services or guarantees, the manager of the buying unit may be willing to pay a somewhat higher transfer price.

Measure of Efficiency

A market price above the selling unit's full cost indicates that the unit is operating efficiently, whereas a market price below the selling unit's full cost suggests inefficiency. That is, if users can obtain needed services from either an internal responsibility center or an outside source, total revenue of the responsibility center providing the service is a good measure of its efficiency. This assumes, of course, that purchasers are motivated to seek the supplier who can furnish a service of an acceptable quality at the lowest price.

If a responsibility center cannot furnish services at competitive prices, or if the revenue it earns is not equal to its costs, its operating statement will report a loss. This is an indication that something is wrong. If the responsibility center's charges are similar to those of alternative providers of the service, but its revenue is low, the center may be providing service of poor quality. If this is the case, the manager presumably will be motivated to seek quality improvements. If, by contrast, the responsibility center has comparable quality to alternative providers, but charges more than the market price, its low revenue is a sign that costs are too high. In this case, the manager will be motivated to reduce costs. If volume large enough to cover fixed costs is unattainable, senior management may decide to discontinue the service. Thus, charging for services provides senior management with information about the efficiency and quality of the service, and whether the service should be offered at all.

Need for Caution.   In making decisions about efficiency and quality, managers must be cautious. Quality, service, and other considerations may mean that a responsibility center is providing a different product from the one for which a market price is available. If this is the case, the comparison between full cost and market price is invalid and potentially dysfunctional. Moreover, if the organization's full-cost accounting system is not well designed, it may be providing misleading information.[16]

> *Example.*   Within a few years after designing a transfer pricing system based on full cost for word processing, graphics, technical publications, and secretarial services, one organization noticed some unintended consequences: researchers and engineers were spending time typing documents and making overhead slides because their departments could not afford the transfer prices. Upon investigation, the organization found that the existing cost allocation mechanisms did not measure usage of service center resources appropriately, and the people-intensive service centers were getting an unfair share of administrative overhead. When better measures were used to allocate overhead costs, the full cost of the people-intensive service centers fell. The transfer prices for these service centers then fell to a level that research and engineering departments were willing to pay.[17]

SUMMARY

The prices that a nonprofit organization charges (or decides not to charge) for its services influence the behavior of clients, provide a measure of output, and influence the behavior of managers and service providers. The price that is usually charged is called the *normal price*. It is the sum of the full cost of a service plus a modest margin.

Prices charged for subsidized services are less than normal prices. Subsidized prices may be charged only for certain services, only to certain clients, or to all clients. In some instances, for sound public policy purposes, a service may be provided free of charge.

Pricing decisions exist not only between an organization and its clients, but between two responsibility centers as well. The latter price is called a *transfer price*. The principles of transfer pricing are similar to those for external pricing. Properly designed, transfer prices can have important and beneficial motivational effects on managerial behavior. They also can be used to measure the efficiency of an organization's responsibility centers.

---

[16] For additional details on transfer pricing, see Robert N. Anthony, John Dearden, and Vijay Govindarajan, *Management Control Systems* (Homewood, Ill.: Richard D. Irwin, 1992).
[17] Edward J. Kovac and Henry P. Troy, "Getting Transfer Prices Right: What Bellcore Did," *Harvard Business Review,* September–October 1989.

SUGGESTED ADDITIONAL READINGS

Anthony, Robert N., and James S. Reece. *Accounting: Text and Cases*. Homewood, Ill.: Richard D. Irwin, 1993.

Arrow, Kenneth J. *Social Choice and Individual Values*, 2nd ed. New York: John Wiley & Sons, 1973.

Bryce, Herrington J. *Financial and Strategic Management for Nonprofit Organizations*, 2nd ed. Englewood Cliffs, N.J.: Prentice Hall, 1992.

Kotler, Philip, and Roberta N. Clarke. *Marketing for Health Care Organizations*. Englewood Cliffs, N.J.: Prentice Hall, 1986.

McKinney, Jerome B. *Effective Financial Management in Public and Nonprofit Agencies*, New York: Quorum Books, 1986.

Musgrave, R. A. *The Theory of Public Finance*. New York: R. E. Krieger Publishing, 1982.

Schultze, Charles L. *The Politics and Economics of Public Spending*. Washington, D.C.: The Brookings Institution, 1968.

Shapiro, Benson P. "Marketing for Nonprofit Organizations." *Harvard Business Review*, September–October 1973, pp. 123–32.

CASE 6–1   Harlan Foundation*

Harlan Foundation was created in 1951, under the terms of the will of Martin Harlan, a wealthy Minneapolis benefactor. His bequest was approximately $3,000,000, and its purpose was broadly stated: income from the funds was to be used for the benefit of the people of Minneapolis and nearby communities.

In the next 35 years, the trustees developed a wide variety of services. They included three infant clinics, a center for the education of special needs children, three family counselling centers, a drug abuse program, a visiting nurses program, and a large rehabilitation facility. These services were provided from nine facilities, located in Minneapolis and surrounding cities. Harlan Foundation was affiliated with several national associations whose members provided similar services.

The Foundation operated essentially on a breakeven basis. A relatively small fraction of its revenue came from income earned on the principal of the Harlan bequest. Major sources of revenue were fees from clients, contributions, and grants from city, state, and federal governments.

Exhibit 1 is the most recent operating statement. Program expenses included all the expenses associated with individual programs. Administration expenses included the costs of the central office, except for fund-raising expenses. Seventy percent of administration costs were for personnel costs. The staff members (excluding two senior officers) earned an average of $18,000 per year in salaries and fringe benefits.

In 1987, the Foundation decided to undertake two additional activities. One was a summer camp, whose clients would be children with physical disabilities. The other was a seminar intended for managers in social service organizations. For both of these ventures, it was necessary to establish the fee that should be charged.

Camp Harlan

The camp, which was renamed Camp Harlan, was donated to the Foundation in 1986 by the person who had owned it for many years and who decided to retire. The property consisted of 30 acres, with considerable frontage on a lake, and buildings that would house and feed some 60 campers at a time. The plan was to operate the camp for eight weeks in the summer, and to enroll campers for either one or two weeks. The policy was to charge each camper a fee sufficient to cover the cost of operating the camp. Many campers would be unable to pay this fee, and financial aid would be provided for them. The financial aid would cover a part, or in some cases all, of the fee and would come from the general funds of the Foundation or, it was hoped, from a government grant.

---

* This case was prepared by Professor Robert N. Anthony. Copyright © by Osceola Institute.

EXHIBIT 1

Operating Statement
For the Year Ended June 30, 1986

Revenues:
Fees from clients.....................	$ 917,862
Grants from government agencies	1,792,968
Contributions	683,702
Investment income	426,300
Other	24,553
Total revenues	3,845,385

Expenses:
Program expenses:
Rehabilitation......................	1,556,242
Counselling.........................	157,621
Infant clinics.......................	312,007
Education	426,234
Drug abuse	345,821
Visiting nurses	267,910
Other	23,280
Total program expenses...........	3,089,115

Support:
Administration	480,326
Dues to national associations	24,603
Fund-raising	182,523
Other	47,862
Total support	735,314
Total expenses.................	3,824,429
Net income...........................	$ 20,956

As a basis for arriving at the fee, Henry Coolidge, financial vice president of the Foundation, obtained information on costs from the American Camping Association and from two camps in the vicinity. Although the camp could accommodate at least 60 children, he decided to plan on only 50 at a time in the first year, a total of 400 camper-weeks for the season. With assured financial aid, he believed there would be no difficulty in enrolling this number. His budget prepared on this basis is shown in Exhibit 2.

Coolidge discussed this budget with Sally Harris, president of the Foundation. Harris agreed that it was appropriate to plan for 400 camper-weeks, and also agreed that the budget estimates were reasonable. During this discussion, questions were raised about several items that were not in the budget.

The central office of the Foundation would continue to plan the camp, do the necessary publicity, screen applications and make decisions on financial aid, pay bills, and do other bookkeeping and accounting work. There was no good way of estimating how many resources this work would require. Ten staff members

---

EXHIBIT 2   Budget for Camp Harlan

Staff salaries and benefits	$ 90,000
Food	19,000
Operating supplies	4,000
Telephone and utilities....................	9,000
Insurance	15,100
Rental of equipment.......................	7,000
Contingency and miscellaneous (5%)	7,200
Total	$151,300

---

worked in administration, and as a rough guess about half a person-year might be involved in these activities. There were no plans to hire an additional employee in the central office. The workload associated with other activities usually tapered off somewhat during the summer, and it was believed that the staff could absorb the extra work.

At the camp itself, approximately four volunteers per week would help the paid staff. They would receive meals and lodging, but no pay. No allowance for the value of their services was included in the budget.

The budget did not include an amount for depreciation of the plant facilities. Lakefront property was valuable, and if the camp and its buildings were sold to a developer, perhaps as much as $500,000 could be realized.

The Seminar

The Foundation planned to hold a one-day seminar in the fall of 1987 to discuss the effect on social service organizations of the Income Tax Act passed in 1986 and other recent regulatory developments. (Although these organizations were exempt from income taxes, except on unrelated business income, recent legislation and regulations were expected to have an impact on contributions, investment policy, and personnel policies, among other things.) The purposes of the seminar were partly to generate income and partly to provide a service for smaller welfare organizations.

In the spring of 1987, Harris approved the plans for this seminar. The following information is extracted from a memorandum prepared by Coolidge at that time:

It is estimated that there will be 30 participants in the seminar.

The seminar will be held at a local hotel, and the hotel will charge $200 for rental of the room and $20 per person for meals and refreshments.

Audiovisual equipment will be rented at a cost of $100.

There will be two instructors, and each will be paid a fee of $500.

Printing and mailing of promotional material will cost $900.

Each participant will be given a notebook containing relevant material. Each notebook will cost $10 to prepare, and 60 copies of the notebook will be printed.

Coolidge will preside, and one Harlan staff member will be present at the seminar. The hotel will charge for their meals and for the meals of the two instructors.

Other incidental out-of-pocket expenses are estimated to be $200.

Fees charged for one-day seminars in the area range from $50 to $495. The $50 fee excluded meals and was charged by a brokerage firm that probably viewed the seminar as generating customer goodwill. The $495 fee was charged by several national organizations that run hundreds of seminars annually throughout the United States. A number of one-day seminars are offered in the Minneapolis area at a fee in the range of $150 to $250, including a meal.

Except for the number of participants, the above estimates were based on reliable information and were accepted by Harris.

Questions

1. What weekly fee should be charged for campers?
2. Assuming a fee of $100, what is the breakeven point of the seminar?
3. What fee should be charged for the seminar?

CASE 6–2   Grindel College*

At its meeting in January 1981 the board of trustees of Grindel College adopted a new policy governing charges made to off-campus students. This policy resulted in student dissatisfaction, culminating in a boycott of the annual drawing for dormitory rooms. At its meeting in April 1981 the board discussed whether this policy should be changed.

Background

Grindel College was a private, four-year, coeducational college with 1,800 students. It had dormitory accommodations for 1,650 students, including fraternity houses owned by the fraternities but located on college property. Fraternity houses had no dining facilities. The other 150 students lived in the community.

---

* This case was prepared by Professor Robert N. Anthony. Copyright © by the President and Fellows of Harvard College. Harvard Business School case 9-183-088.

All residential students paid the same amount for room rent and meal charges, regardless of the age or location of the dormitory in which they lived. The amount of room rent collected from each resident in a fraternity house (200 students) was held by the college and used for fraternity house upkeep. All freshmen were required to live in dormitories.

The policy was to fill dormitories to their design capacity. (In practice, withdrawals, unexpectedly large enrollments, and other considerations resulted in minor variations between actual occupancy and design capacity.) Since more than 150 students wanted to live off campus, a lottery was held each April to determine those who would be permitted to do so. Preference was given to students living with their parents (usually about 12), married students, and students age 24 or older. The remaining off-campus permissions were decided by lot.

Financial Policies

Each January the board adopted a schedule of tuition, fees, room rent, and meal charges for the following academic year. The budget was prepared according to the principal financial policies summarized below (certain policies not relevant to this case have been omitted):

1. Tuition and fees are to be competitive with other colleges.
2. Tuition and fees, plus estimated revenue from annual gifts, endowment, and miscellaneous sources gives the total amount available for academic and general operations. Academic and general expenses are budgeted to equal this amount, approximately.
3. Auxiliary enterprises are to operate on a breakeven basis.
4. Budgeted student resident expenses are divided by the number of dormitory residents (excluding fraternity residents) to give the room rent.
5. Budgeted food service costs (reduced by the estimated amount of revenue from casual meals and miscellaneous sources) are divided by 1,650 to give the meal charge.

Student resident and food service expenses included both direct cost and an equitable portion of common maintenance and operating costs (but not college-wide administration expenses). Student resident costs also included debt service, in lieu of depreciation, on funds borrowed to construct dormitories. For several years prior to 1979–80, the amount of debt service had been nominal.

In 1980–81, (i.e., the year ended August 31, 1981) tuition and fees were $6,120, room rent was $1,070, and board was $1,310. As shown in Exhibit 1, these charges were not quite consistent with the financial policies, in that the student residences were budgeted to operate at a loss. The reason for this was that a new dormitory was completed in 1979, and in accordance with long-standing practice its cost was financed by a 25-year bond issue. Inclusion of the full amount of its debt service in the calculation of room rents would have increased room rents by an amount that

EXHIBIT 1

GRINDEL COLLEGE
Condensed Financial Data on Operations
($000 except per-student charges)

	Budget 1980–81	Current Estimate 1980–81	Proposed Budget 1981–82
Education and general:			
Tuition and fees......................	$11,010	$11,375	$12,870
Other revenue........................	3,145	3,495	3,606
Total revenue	14,155	14,870	16,476
Educational and general expenses	13,782	13,964	16,245
Educational and general income.........	$ 373	$ 906	$ 231
Auxiliary enterprises			
Student residences:*			
Revenue...........................	$ 1,547	$ 1,555	$1,842†
Expenses	1,811	1,865	2,020
Net	(264)	(310)	(178)
Food service:			
Revenue...........................	2,177	2,244	2,352
Expenses	2,175	2,167	2,337
Net	2	77	15
All other:‡			
Revenue...........................	1,215	1,208	1,346
Expenses	1,301	1,248	1,404
Net	(86)	(40)	(58)
Auxiliary net....................	$ (348)	$ (273)	$ (221)
Net income	$ 25	$ 633	$ 10
Charges per student:			
Tuition and fees (1,800 students)	$ 6,120		$ 7,150
Room (1,450 students)	1,070		1,250
Board (1,650 students)	1,310		1,410

* "Student residences" excludes fraternity expenses.
† Includes revenue from off-campus students.
‡ Includes student union, bookstore, conferences using campus facilities, and a few minor items.

was believed to be too great for one year. Thus, it was decided to increase room rents in 1979–80, and in the next three or four years also, by a smaller amount than the increase in estimated costs.

Meeting of January 1981

In January 1981, the administration recommended charges for 1981–82 to the Budget and Finance Committee of the board. Exhibit 1 is a condensed version of material used at that meeting (details of revenues and expenses have been omitted). It showed that although the budget for 1980–81 was essentially a breakeven budget, the current estimate of revenues and expenses for 1980–81 indicated a surplus of $633,000. This was primarily because more students than budgeted were enrolled and because endowment earnings were higher than anticipated.

At this meeting John Bard, the president, and Russell Strong, financial vice president, recommended tuition and fees of $7,150, room rent of $1,250, and board charges of $1,410. These were consistent with the financial policies except that, as was the case in 1979–80, student residences were budgeted at a loss because of the decision not to recover the full amount of debt service.

The administration also proposed a change in the charges made to off-campus students. Until that time, they had not paid room or board charges. (They could eat meals on the campus at rates set on a per-meal basis.) The administration proposed that in 1981–82 and thereafter off-campus students be given a credit of 85 percent of the room rent and board charges. Students living with their parents would be given a credit of 100 percent of these charges.

Reasons given for, in effect, charging off-campus students 15 percent of the room rent and board charges were as follows:

1. Grindel was a residential college, and its facilities are available to all students whether they choose to use them or not. Off-campus students could, and did, visit friends in the dormitories and attend functions held in the dormitories. If some students choose not to live and eat on campus, this does not free them of an obligation to pay at least a portion of the residential costs.

2. Most dormitory costs were fixed. If a student moved off campus, dormitory costs were reduced only by an insignificant amount. Therefore, off-campus students were in effect being subsidized by dormitory residents because they did not pay anything toward the fixed costs of the dormitories. This was unfair to dormitory residents.

3. Off-campus students used a "commuter room" in the student union, and they often traveled to the campus in a college bus; they should bear the cost of these special facilities. (No student paid a separate charge for use of the student union.)

Mr. Strong reported that the Financial Priorities Committee, an advisory body of students and faculty, had voted approval of the new policy in principle, but had not felt competent to judge whether the 85 percent credit was the appropriate amount. After considerable discussion, the Budget and Finance Committee voted unanimously to recommend the policy to the board. At its meeting the following day, the board unanimously approved the proposed tuition, room, and board charges and the new policy for off-campus students.

Developments after the January Meeting

Shortly after the January meeting, Mr. Bard, the president, notified parents of the charges for 1981–82. (Through an oversight, the letter went only to parents, and some students did not hear of the charges until some weeks thereafter.)

A number of students thought that the new policy for off-campus students was unfair. These included most students who wanted to live off campus, and some on-campus students. About 75 students met for more than two hours with the financial vice president, Mr. Strong. The points made at that meeting are summarized below, as excerpted from a lengthy, well-written letter sent subsequently to each member of the board of trustees:

> Grindel cannot house all its students, so off-campus living is an integral part of its activities . . . occasional use of the dormitories by off-campus students does not incur costs that come close to the claimed 15 percent surcharge . . . off-campus students promote closer town/gown relations . . . the surcharge would discriminate in favor of well-to-do students . . . the 15 percent surcharge should be applied to all students benefiting from the residential aspects but who also are not housed in dormitories, namely fraternity members . . . under the proposed policy, women have no opportunity to seek alternatives to dormitory life without paying extra, while men do (because only men can live in fraternity houses) . . . immediate implementation of an extra charge is grossly unfair to students who are currently enrolled and who planned to live off campus before knowing of the surcharge . . . students have not been told the rationale for the surcharge, and in particular for the amount of 15 percent.

Students requested that in 1981–82 the new charge be applied only to students not now enrolled, and that during that time the merits of the policy be restudied. This would in effect be a two-year delay because all freshmen were required to live in dormitories.

A number of letters expressing similar views were printed in the Grindel student newspaper. No letters supported the administration position.

As it happened, the deadline for signing up for the off-campus lottery was the day after the April board meeting. As an indication of the depth of their feeling, only one student had signed up as of the day before the meeting.

Meetings of April 1981

At the Budget and Finance Committee meeting held on the day before the board meeting in April 1981, the president summarized the discussions, and reported that the financial vice president had proposed a compromise solution in his meeting with students: for the year 1981–82 off-campus students would be credited for $2,380, the amount of board and room charges for 1980–81, that is, this amount would be subtracted from the proposed board and room charges. The new policy would go into full effect in 1982–83. The president recommended adoption of this policy by the committee.

Mr. Bard also pointed out that if few students signed up for off-campus housing, all of them could be housed in the dormitories by putting in additional beds. In some prior years, the number of beds had been increased temporarily by similar measures, when enrollments had turned out to be higher than expected.

Most committee members continued to believe that the new policy was sound. Some, however, sought to defuse the issue by postponing implementation of the policy entirely until 1982–83. The president indicated that this was agreeable with him. Others pointed out that the financial vice president had already gone on record with a compromise solution and that to postpone implementation entirely would both undercut the administration and give the signal that students were free to question financial charges; this might open the door to controversy on other financial questions in future years.

Because a large "kick-off" dinner for a major capital funds drive took place that evening, the committee meeting had to adjourn before all views had been aired. By a small majority, the Budget and Finance Committee voted to recommend the compromise position to the full board, and this was done.

Questions

1. As a member of the Budget and Finance Committee, what position would you have taken at the January meeting?
2. As a member of the board, not on the Budget and Finance Committee, what position will you take at the meeting in April 1981?

CASE 6–3   Town of Waterville Valley*

At the 1980 town meeting, residents of Waterville Valley, New Hampshire, would be asked to authorize a major expansion of the town's water system. Some residents believed that the supply was adequate for the foreseeable future. Others, including the area's developer, thought that the supply was inadequate and would inhibit growth in the town.

The method of paying for an expanded water system was also at issue. The capital expenditure would be financed by a municipal bond issue. Alternatives for payment of the principal and interest on this issue were: (1) a lump sum to be charged to each new housing unit, to be paid by the developer and included in the price of the unit, (2) higher water rates for all users, or (3) an annual charge made to all new water users, that is, those whose service began after the expanded system went into operation.

Finally, there was the question of how water was to be charged to users. At present, residential users were charged a flat monthly amount, and some people thought that the charge should be based on usage.

Background

The Town of Waterville Valley is in a valley surrounded on all sides by the White Mountain National Forest. The area of the town is about 700 acres, and it is unlikely that its area can grow because the U.S. Forest Service probably would not sell additional land to private parties. One well-paved road, 11 miles long, provides access to the valley from an interstate highway. Waterville Valley is 130

---

* This case was prepared by Professor Robert N. Anthony. Copyright © by the President and Fellows of Harvard College. Harvard Business School case 9-179-203.

miles from Boston and 60 miles from the state capital, Concord, which is the nearest city.

The town was incorporated in 1829. In 1965 the permanent structures consisted of an inn, accommodating 60 guests, 16 homes of residents, most of whom lived in the valley year round, and a small town hall.

In 1965 the inn and 506 acres of land were purchased by the Waterville Company, a privately owned corporation. Thomas Corcoran, president, moved to Waterville Valley. He planned to develop the area as a year-round resort and to sell land to developers and individuals.

By 1979 the area had become a major ski facility, with 10 lifts, 35 miles of downhill trails, many with snowmaking facilities, and many miles of cross-country trails. About 4,000 skiers used the facilities on peak days. The ski area was leased from the Forest Service by the Waterville Company. In addition, there was a nine-hole golf course, a pond for bathing and sailing, and 15 tennis courts. There were five inns with a capacity of about 200, a bunk house, 65 single-family houses, 6 condominium developments totaling approximately 300 units, a conference center with a capacity of 500, and a number of restaurants and stores. There were sleeping accommodations for about 2,000 persons. The ultimate capacity was estimated to be 7,000 persons. The official population, however, was 199.

Water Supply

Until 1967, property owners provided their own water. The original inn was served by a spring, and individual homeowners used artesian wells. One consequence was that whenever a fire started, the property burned to the ground, as had happened to the inn twice before, and again in 1967.

In 1967, the Waterville Company, at its expense, drilled new wells and constructed a pumping station, a reservoir, a distribution system with an 8-inch main, and fire hydrants. In the 1968 town meeting, the voters unanimously agreed to buy this system from the Waterville Company, and voted a bond issue of $135,000 for this purpose and to finance further exploration for water.

In 1970, a bond issue of $105,000 was authorized to expand the water system, and in 1972 a third bond issue of $235,000 was authorized for this purpose. After this construction, the town had a half-million gallon storage capacity and water distribution lines throughout the town. However, by 1979, according to the town manager, existing wells were being used to 85 percent of capacity, and "a new source is necessary." Two pumps were used, and if one of them broke, water pressure would be seriously affected.

Sewer System

The initial sewer system consisted of collection mains and a series of lagoons for filtering wastes. These were built, owned, and maintained by the Waterville Company. By 1972 these facilities had become inadequate. The Waterville Company, however, wanted to get out of the sewer business, and it proposed the following:

1. The company would give the existing system, preliminary engineering for an expanded system, and land for a sewage treatment facility to the town, without consideration.

2. The town would set up a municipal services department to operate the water and sewer systems.

3. If in any year the operations of this system resulted in a cash loss, the town's maximum obligation from the general tax levy would be $2 per $1,000 of assessed valuation, assuming that the town would continue to assess property at full fair market value. Any additional loss would be made up by the Waterville Company. Payments made by the Waterville Company would be repaid in future years if operations (including the $2 tax levy) produced a profit in those years.

4. Water and sewerage fees would be at an agreed-upon schedule and would increase at stated percentages thereafter (details of these fees are described subsequently).

5. The town would build a municipal sewer system, with the most modern sewage treatment facilities, to be financed with a bond issue of $1.8 million. This system would be adequate for the ultimate development of Waterville Valley to a 7,000-bed capacity.

6. The agreement would last until January 1, 1983, or until three years beyond the date of an additional bond issue to expand the water system, whichever was longer.

This proposal was approved at the 1973 town meeting, the bonds were issued, and the facilities were built. As shown in Exhibit 1, losses were experienced in 1975, 1976, and 1977; the Waterville Company reimbursed the town for these losses. In 1978, a profit was earned.

Water and Sewer Rates

Users were charged a one-time, fixed, "tap" fee which entitled them to tap into the town water and sewer system. The fee was determined by a point and unit system. Points were determined by the number of bedrooms, bathrooms, and other water use outlets, such as kitchens, outdoor spigots, and sinks, that were part of a unit.

Ten points comprised one water or sewer unit. For example, a half-bath was assessed at ¼ point, a sauna at ¼ point, and a full bath at 3 points. Kitchens were assessed at 2½ points; bedrooms, living rooms, hallways, and lofts at 1 point. Water coolers, ice machines, and extra sinks were assessed at ¼ point each. There was a minimum of one sewer unit and one water unit per dwelling unit. The point system was also used to establish usage rates. See Exhibit 2 for recent rates.

Meters were used only for commercial establishments. The fee for installing a meter was $10, paid by the building's owner. It had been suggested that meters be installed in residential units as well as commercial ones. The town treasurer favored this plan because it would probably provide more revenue for the system. In addition, he felt that it would be a more equitable way of determining charges

EXHIBIT 1

TOWN OF WATERVILLE VALLEY
Water and Sewer Calculations
($000)

	1974	1975	1976	1977	1978
Revenues:					
Operations:					
Usage charges	$ 59.6	$ 85.3	$ 106.1	$ 121.9	$ 139.0
Tap fees.............................	45.2	30.7	9.3	19.5	46.7
Other	5.6	3.7	1.3	2.1	2.3
Subtotal...........................	110.4	119.7	116.7	143.5	188.0
State contribution (40% of debt service)......	—	59.0	57.7	56.5	55.3
Town tax revenues ($2/$1,000)...............	32.5	36.3	36.5	45.5	50.6
Other revenues..........................	40.4	55.6	—	—	—
Total revenues	183.3	270.6	210.9	245.5	293.9
Expenditures:					
Operating expenses......................	44.8	68.3	54.4	58.4	67.9
Debt service:					
Principal	27.6	100.8	100.9	100.9	102.1
Interest	89.0	110.5	106.1	100.6	95.5
Total expenditures..................	161.4	279.6	261.4	259.9	265.5
Excess of revenues over expenditures	$ 21.9	$ (9.0)	$ (50.5)	$ (14.4)	$ 28.4
Tax base: Assessed valuations...............	$16,243.0	$18,165.0	$18,261.0	$22,763.0	$25,321.0
Tax rate/$1,000	12.7	13.0	16.8	13.4	14.0
Water consumption (millions of gallons)		19.4	22.9	25.2	27.0
Sewage treated (millions of gallons)		10.5	16.3	21.0	22.0

Source: Town records.

and thus sharing expenses, and it would encourage conservation of water. This would become more important as it became more and more difficult to find new sources of water.

He noted that the only conservation measures now being applied were mandatory installation of water-saver toilets and showers in new condominium and residential units. He felt that in the near future, there could conceivably be an

EXHIBIT 2 Water and Sewer Department Rate Schedule

	1977	1978	1979
Tap fee—per water unit.............................	$315.00	$330.00	$345.00
Tap fee—per sewer unit	525.00	550.00	575.00
Water usage—per water unit per month	9.45	10.00	10.50
Water usage—commercial metered per 1,000 gallons	1.90	2.00	2.10
Sewer usage—per sewer unit per month	12.39	13.00	13.65
Sewer usage—commercial rate		(130% of water bill)	
Turn on–turn off charge—water	20.00		

Source: Town records.

outright ban on saunas and pools because of their prodigious consumption of water. He cited expense as the main reason the town had not seriously considered requiring installation of meters on residential units. Residential water meters cost $60 installed.

A large consumer of water was the snowmaking operations of the Waterville Company. The equipment, when operating, consumed 1,000 gallons per minute. The company had its own water supply for this purpose, which came partially from the Mad River and partially from one of the town's original wells. The company considered this "free" water and charged only the capital cost of the equipment, and the electricity and manpower to operate it, as expenses.

Many experts believe that the era of an inexpensive potable water supply is over.[1] As demands mount, nearby sources become inadequate. In addition, capital costs of developing new and large surface supplies of water are increasing. The possibility of using the pricing mechanism to control demand has become a widely considered alternative to increasing supplies.

In the past, consumption/pricing decisions made by public utility managers have caused inefficient supply and demand relationships. Peak users of water who create high short-term demands requiring expensive investment in equipment are not required to pay for the added capacity. Block prices are offered to major users, thus encouraging the inefficient use of water. States and communities have subsidized local utilities by developing reservoirs at public expense and by charging less than the cost of the water.

In a recent study for the National Water Commission undertaken by Resources for the Future, it was found that little incentive exists for homeowners to install water-saving devices. Currently available technologies could reduce residential water use (frequently considered to be inelastic) by more than 30 percent. Even greater reductions could be achieved for swimming pools and lawn sprinklers, with a more effective pricing mechanism.

This same study indicated that a change in price from 40 cents per 1,000 gallons (an average price) to $1 per 1,000 gallons would reduce the projected increase in residential demand for the Northeast, in this decade, by almost 20 percent.

Present Operations

The new sewer treatment plant was completed and operational in 1974. At that time water and sewer were combined into a Municipal Services Department with a separate budget and financial statement. All receivables and payables for the department were handled by the town bookkeeper. She estimated that she spent about five days per quarter billing and paying bills for this department. No part of

---

[1] Based on Michael Greenberg and Robert W. Hordon, *Water Supply Planning: A Case Study and Systems Analysis* (New Brunswick, N.J.: Rutgers State University Press, 1976).

her $9,095 annual salary was allocated to the department, nor were other town costs.

Similarly, the Public Safety Department was not charged for its use of water in firefighting. Although hydrants used in firefighting belonged to the town, they were paid for by the developer. The town manager estimated that each new hydrant cost $800.

The municipal services budget did not include an allowance for depreciation. The town treasurer said that the town budgets were based on a system of direct costs and that it would be confusing and arbitrary to try to allocate indirect costs.

EXHIBIT 3

TOWN OF WATERVILLE VALLEY
Municipal Services Department
1978 Summary

	Sewer	*Water*	*Solid Waste*	*Total Department*
Revenues:				
Tap fees...................	$ 29,029.01	$17,622.31		$ 46,651.32
Usage.....................	73,903.78	65,069.33	$ 11,556.00	150,529.11
Other	638.32	1,651.36		2,289.68
Revenues from operations	103,571.11	84,343.00	11,556.00	199,470.11
Additional revenues:				
State grant.................	55,274.00			55,274.00
Total revenues	158,845.11	84,343.00	11,556.00	254,744.11
Operating expenses:				
Wages	15,961.30	9,442.40	6,820.76	32,224.46
Vehicle operations..........	1,128.02	1,390.81	3,896.97	6,415.80
Telephone	618.05	126.00		744.05
Electricity	8,912.11	2,805.71	113.60	11,831.42
Heating fuel	6,743.88	501.51		7,245.39
System/plant maintenance	3,919.91	12,494.91	310.76	16,725.58
Chemicals	3,394.41			3,394.41
Disposal costs			7,991.09	7,991.09
Training and seminars	90.83			90.83
Retirement		336.04	336.02	672.06
Total operating expenses	40,768.51	27,097.38	19,469.20	87,335.09
Income (loss) before debt service	118,076.60	57,245.62	(7,913.20)	167,409.02
Debt service:				
Principal	66,080.00	35,999.45	5,101.97	107,181.42
Interest	82,040.00	13,503.11	1,054.50	96,597.61
Total debt service	148,120.00	49,502.56	6,156.47	203,779.03
Net profit (loss) of departments	$(30,043.40)	$ 7,743.06	$(14,069.67)	$(36,370.01)

Source: Annual Report.

He also felt that since the town did not pay taxes, depreciation wasn't a necessary component of the budget.

Many water districts do not depreciate their capital plant and equipment for the following reasons: plants usually take a number of years to reach their full income potential although, from year one, their facilities must be adequate to serve the entire district; if depreciation were charged, the accumulating losses would have a disastrous effect on the sale of bonds; if rates were set high enough to allow for depreciation, they might not be affordable by users.

Details of the Municipal Services Department revenues and expenditures for 1978 are given in Exhibit 3. (The collection of solid waste was also a function of that department.) By comparison, total expenditures in 1970 were $22,500, of which $18,500 was for debt service.

Total revenues and expenditures for the town, as presented to the 1979 town meeting, are given in Exhibit 4.

EXHIBIT 4

TOWN OF WATERVILLE VALLEY
Income and Expenditures—1978

	1978 Estimated	1978 Actual	1979 Projected
Revenues:			
State sources:			
Interest and dividends tax	$ 27,000.00	$ 25,489.40	$ 25,500.00
Savings bank tax	600.00	558.36	600.00
Meals and rooms tax	900.00	998.96	1,000.00
Highway subsidy	1,284.54	1,270.51	1,552.37
Town road aid	1,676.48		2,111.49
Forest Service lands reimbursement	21,500.00	13,851.90	14,000.00
Business profits tax	350.00	372.52	400.00
Sewage treatment grant	55,274.00	55,274.00	54,062.00
Antirecession funds	–0–	224.00	–0–
Local sources:			
Dog licenses	60.00	90.30	100.00
Motor vehicle permits	6,500.00	7,250.50	7,250.00
Permits and filing fees	300.00	297.00	300.00
Interest on taxes and deposits	2,250.00	2,207.47	1,500.00
Cemetery	1,000.00	500.00	–0–
Public Safety Department	13,700.00	16,412.25	14,300.00
Municipal Services Department	180,000.00	199,470.11	215,000.00
Highway Department	–0–	1,010.62	–0–
Recreation Department	–0–	–0–	7,000.00
Resident taxes	1,200.00	1,540.00	1,500.00
Timber yield taxes	1,500.00	2,686.75	2,800.00
Town Office	25.00	24.92	25.00
Revenue sharing	3,000.00	3,811.00	4,500.00
Short-term loans	39,250.00	31,200.00	46,575.00
Fire truck	72,000.00	72,000.00	–0–
Police cruiser sale	800.00	–0–	–0–
Proceeds—insurance claim		2,400.00	
Total revenues	$430,170.02	$438,940.57	$400,075.86

EXHIBIT 4 *(concluded)*

	1978 Appro- priation	1978 Expenses	1979 Requests
Expenditures:			
Town officers salaries...................	$ 4,075.00	$ 4,147.52	$ 3,400.00
Town Office expense	31,725.00	30,908.43	33,473.40
Town Office—Public Safety			
Building maintenance	5,900.00	6,543.34	6,650.00
Property appraisal.....................	1,000.00	1,411.63	1,500.00
Surveying and drafting.................	4,500.00	3,720.00	2,000.00
Osceola Library.......................	800.00	1,246.73	1,100.00
Employees benefits....................	11,241.97	9,680.09	15,226.64
Public Safety Department	97,516.30	103,161.36	114,006.12
Municipal Services Department	97,894.25	87,335.09	113,360.47
Highway Department	20,850.00	22,266.39	24,315.25
Legal services	5,944.65	4,303.61	5,000.00
Planning and zoning	500.00	4.00	1,200.00
Advertising and regional	4,275.00	4,275.00	2,025.00
Hospitals and health...................	887.25	877.25	873.25
Conservation Commission...............	800.00	800.00	1,000.00
Municipal recreation...................	2,000.00	3,691.86	20,250.00
Post Office	3,000.00	3,000.00	4,000.00
Street lights..........................	1,200.00	1,230.94	1,570.00
Cemetery.............................	600.00	–0–	250.00
Insect control........................	4,200.00	3,170.00	1,000.00
Insurance.............................	19,000.00	20,998.00	25,000.00
Capital equipment	88,200.00	89,060.95	24,575.00
Capital construction	23,050.00	27,808.38	22,000.00
Debt service	228,072.61	232,488.07	246,136.07
Contingency	5,200.00		6,000.00
Total expenditures..................	$662,432.03	$662,128.64	$675,911.20
Insurance proceeds—applied to			
principal............................		2,400.00	
		$664,528.64	

The total estimated revenues from all sources except property taxes deducted from total appropriations in the ensuing fiscal year gives estimated amount to be raised by property taxes.

Current Issues

At the 1980 town meeting, the selectmen planned to present a proposal for additional water capacity. They would hire engineers to bore holes in a search for additional water. (A $17,000 survey in 1977 had found one additional well with an estimated flow of 80 to 100 gallons per minute. This well had not yet been developed.) The capacity of the system at that time was 400 gallons per minute.

Based on the findings of engineers, a plan for expansion of the water system would be submitted at a subsequent meeting. The cost of this plan would depend on the engineers' findings and on several alternatives for expansion. Each new well would cost from $30,000 to $40,000; and an additional storage facility would cost from $200,000 to $300,000. Engineers already had recommended some expansion of the 8-inch main distribution system, at a cost of roughly $200,000. In total, expansion of the system to accommodate the town's ultimate capacity might cost from $400,000 to $600,000, but this was a rough estimate because of the uncertainty of the exploration efforts and debate as to when ultimate capacity should be installed.

There was concern over the additional debt burden. Exhibit 5 shows the payments required by the bonds issued to date. It was customary to issue bonds with a 30-year maturity, with an equal amount of principal payments each year and interest on the outstanding balance. The life of the bonds could be shorter than 30 years. The principal payment was not necessarily the same each year, although changing this practice might make the bonds less attractive.

The state of New Hampshire agreed to pay 40 percent of the debt service on the sewer bond issue of 1973. It was hoped that the state would similarly pay part of the cost of water expansion, but this was not certain.

Because of recent improvements in the water system, the town experienced a 12 percent reduction in insurance on private homes and a 10 percent reduction on commercial establishments. The State Insurance Commission indicated that additional water would likely result in another rate reduction.

One long-time resident of Waterville Valley, who considered himself a spokesman for the group who opposed further expansion of the system, expressed the concern that more water and another bond issue could not help but increase the tax rate beyond the promised $2 per thousand. He felt that the future residents, if there were to be any, should bear the entire cost of any improvements that they required. He stated the concerns of a number of retired residents, living on fixed incomes, who were alarmed at the present 5 percent yearly increase in their taxes. He felt that the past 12 years of development were already taking their toll on the community in terms of the impact on ecology, increased traffic, and the need for additional municipal services.

EXHIBIT 5 Debt Payments (shown at five-year intervals)

| Year | Water | | Sewer | | Total |
	Principal	Interest	Principal	Interest	Payments
1970	$10,000	$ 8,504			$ 18,504
1975	26,520	16,780	$65,000	$91,000	199,300
1980	26,520	9,433	65,000	75,010	175,963
1985	10,000	4,420	65,000	58,110	137,530
1990	10,000	1,820	60,000	42,120	113,940
1995			60,000	26,520	86,520
2000			60,000	10,920	70,920

Note: Approximate amounts for the years not shown can be found by interpolation, except that in 1974 the total payments were $44,878. The final bond issue matures in 2003.

The president of the Waterville Company, who was also a selectman and a resident of the town, was convinced that the town was committed to expansion of its facilities to the limits imposed by its geography and should also be committed to expansion of its water supply. He felt that past records showed that municipal services could pay their own way from the revenues they generated. He believed that his company could work compatibly with the town. He acknowledged that his company benefited from the town's ability to borrow at favorable rates, but he also believed that the town had benefited from the company's expenditures for early water and sewer development and its help in underwriting the initial losses of the sewer system. He agreed that current residents should not have to shoulder all expenses for future improvements, and felt that through municipal borrowing, future residents would be sharing in the cost of improvements by helping to repay the debt.

Questions

1. As a matter of general policy (but without attempting to arrive at specific numbers), how should the cost of an additional water system be divided between those who are now on the system, those who may subsequently become customers, and the general taxpayers (i.e., included in the tax rate)?
2. As a matter of general policy, how should the "tap charge" (i.e., the amount to amortize capital costs) and the "usage charge" be determined?
3. What is your estimate of the cost of the Municipal Services Department in 1978?
4. In calculating the cost that should be used in arriving at charges, should the capital cost be the amount of debt service (i.e., principal and interest) actually paid in the year, or is some other approach better?
5. Can you suggest tentative rates for each item on Exhibit 2 for a year in which expenditures are like those in 1978, with an additional capital charge of $500,000 financed by a 30-year bond issue?
6. Should meters be used to record usage by residential customers so that charges can be based on usage?

CASE 6–4 White Hills Children's Museum*

Jan Sweeney, director of the Urban Life Program of White Hills Children's Museum, was outraged. A few weeks ago, she had asked the design and engineering (D&E) department of the museum for a bid to build the Central Artery Exhibit of her Cities and Streets project. The D&E bid was some $7,000 more than a bid she had received from a local construction firm, yet it seemed that the museum's director was encouraging her to use the D&E department anyway.

---

* This case was prepared by Professor David W. Young. Copyright © by David W. Young.

Background

White Hills Children's Museum was a medium-sized nonprofit museum located in northern California, just outside San Francisco. Its charter stipulated that it was to orient its activities and exhibits toward the environment, and it had been enormously successful in attracting a wide following of regular visitors. The museum also enjoyed a national reputation, and attracted a sizable number of visitors who were vacationing in northern California.

Recently, under the leadership of a new director, the museum had been organized into profit centers, and Ms. Sweeney's program had been designated as one of the programmatic profit centers. As such, she was encouraged, but not required, to "purchase" all design and construction services for her program from the museum's design and engineering department, a service profit center. Both managers—as well as all other profit center managers—had the possibility of earning annual bonuses based upon the profits of their profit centers.

The services of the D&E department ranged from the construction of relatively simple display cases to the design and manufacture of rather complex exhibits. Some of the recent exhibits the D&E department had developed included a miniature waterfall and an artificial windstorm.

Because of the complexity of the demands made upon it, and the resulting need for a wide variety of technical skills, the D&E department needed a rather large staff. Since the museum was too small to fully utilize its staff, however, the department also sold its services to other organizations, including several smaller museums located within a radius of about a hundred miles from White Hills. At the moment, because it was a slow period for most museums, the department's staff was not fully utilized. This was not an unusual situation.

The Central Artery Exhibit

In planning her Cities and Streets project, Ms. Sweeney knew that she would need to have several exhibits designed and built to rather exacting specifications. One of these was the Central Artery exhibit, a large-scale illustration of the environmental impact of placing an expressway underground. Her plans called for four phases of construction, showing how the environment would be affected by each phase. The exhibits would need to be large enough to allow children to explore them from the inside, thereby allowing them to experience as well as learn about the impact of a project of this sort.

Data

Because the exhibit was a large one, Ms. Sweeney had asked John Harp, the director of the D&E department to assist her in putting together the design and engineering specifications. The two had spent several days discussing the ex-

---

EXHIBIT 1   Budget Information Prepared by the Design and Engineering Department

Central Artery Project:

Materials	$ 7,000
Direct labor (1).	10,000
Variable overhead (2)	2,000
Fixed overhead (3)	5,000
Total costs	$24,000
Markup	3,000
Total bid	$27,000

Notes:

1. Carpenters, plumbers, electricians, painters, and gofers. All currently are on staff; that is no one would be hired especially for this project.

2. Miscellaneous cleaning solvents, sandpaper, and other minor materials that will not be purchased specifically for this project but that would not be used without the project. Also includes the cost of supervision.

3. Allocated portion of the cost of the department head, administrative assistant, and secretary, as well as several other administrative costs, such as the rent charged the department by the museum's central administration.

---

hibit's objectives and constraints, and Mr. Harp had prepared some architectural and engineering drawings. At that point, Ms. Sweeney had asked him for an estimate of the cost, and, after a few days of gathering the necessary information, he had provided her with the $27,000 figure. His calculations are shown in Exhibit 1.

Shocked at the amount, Ms. Sweeney had called Mr. Harp to complain. At his suggestion, she had taken the drawings to a local construction firm and asked them for a bid. Using the drawings plus the design and engineering specifications prepared by Mr. Harp, the local firm had given Ms. Sweeney a figure of $20,000. The firm had indicated that this figure was all-inclusive and was firm; that is, it included all supplies, materials, labor, and profit, and Ms. Sweeney would be charged a flat $20,000 regardless of the actual costs the firm incurred in constructing the exhibit.

The Decision

When he heard of the situation, Mike Sampson, the museum's new director immediately had called the two managers into his office, and asked for an explanation. Mr. Harp was the first to speak:

I simply can't do the job for less. I've been working for several months now to establish a fair pricing structure, not only for people inside the museum but for my external customers. This is the price I would use for our neighboring museums, and it's the one I feel I must use for Jan as well. Besides, I spent all that time helping her design the project and preparing the drawings—that must be worth something.

Ms. Sweeney responded:

When I was in school, we were taught that the transfer price should be the market price. I think I've pretty well established what the market price is, and I should not be asked to pay any more than that. If I did, my profits would fall, and you've been asking us to worry about our bottom lines. This $7,000 difference would make a big difference at the end of the year, particularly in terms of my bonus.

Mr. Sampson's main concern at this point was with the overall surplus of the museum. It was clear that if Ms. Sweeney used the local construction firm to build her exhibit, the cost to her department would be less; but he felt quite certain that the impact on the museum's surplus would be worse than if she used Mr. Harp's department. He was not sure if he should intervene in the decision or not, and if he did, what his intervention should be.

Questions

1. What is the impact on the museum's surplus of each of the two possibilities?
2. Should Mr. Sampson intervene in this decision? Why or why not?
3. If Mr. Sampson intervenes, what should he do? Please be specific: For example, should he tell Ms. Sweeney to purchase the work for the exhibit from Mr. Harp? If so, at what price?
4. If Mr. Sampson does not intervene, what do you think will happen? Is this good or bad for the museum in the short term? In the long term?
5. What other advice would you give Mr. Sampson? Ms. Sweeney? Mr. Harp?

CASE 6–5   National Youth Association*

"If I were to price this conference any lower than $480 a participant," said James Brunner, manager of National Youth Association's Housing Division, "I'd be countermanding my order of last month for our marketing organization to stop shaving their bids and to bid full-cost quotations. I've been trying for weeks to improve the quality of our business, and, if I turn around now and accept this at $430 or $450 or something less than $480, I'll be tearing down this program I've been working so hard to build up. The division can't very well accomplish its objective by putting in bids that don't even cover a fair share of overhead costs, let alone give us a safety margin."

---

* This case was adapted with permission from case 158–001 prepared by William Rotch under the supervision of Neil Harlan, Harvard Business School. Copyright © by the President and Fellows of Harvard College.

National Youth Association (NYA) was an organization with several hundred local chapters. It provided support for these chapters, published a magazine and books, held a national convention, and arranged a number of conferences. At the national headquarters were several divisions. Among them was the Conference Division, which developed and managed a number of professional development conferences for members. Another was the Housing Division, headed by Mr. Brunner, which operated a conference center in the headquarters city; its facilities were used both by NYA and by other organizations. A third was the Produce Division, which operated a cattle, poultry, and produce farm, located outside the headquarters city. This property had been willed to NYA many years ago.

For several years, each division had been judged independently. The financial objective of each was to provide a margin above its costs; this margin was intended to help finance headquarters activities and to provide a cushion against unforeseen contingencies. Senior management had been working to gain effective results from a policy of decentralizing responsibility and authority for all decisions except those relating to overall association policy. The association's senior officials believed that in the past few years the concept of decentralization had been successfully applied and that the association's financial position had definitely improved.

The Conference Division had developed a three-day conference that it planned to offer several times a year. Mr. Brunner had spent many hours with the Conference Division in working on these plans.

When all the plans were completed, the Conference Division asked for bids from the Housing Division and from two outside companies. Each division manager was normally free to buy from whatever supplier he wished; and, even on sales within the company, divisions were expected to meet the going market price if they wanted the business.

During this period, the profit margins of hotels and other conference facilities were being squeezed. Because NYA did not run conferences steadily throughout the year, many of Housing's sales were made to outside customers. If Housing got the order from the Conference Division, it probably would buy much of its raw food from the NYA Produce Division. About 70 percent of Housing's out-of-pocket cost of $400 for the conference represented the cost of raw food purchased from the Produce Division. Though the Produce Division had excess capacity, it quoted the market price, which had not noticeably weakened as a result of the oversupply. Its out-of-pocket costs were about 60 percent of the selling price.

The Conference Division received bids of $480 a participant from the Housing Division, $430 a participant from Magnolia Hotel, and $432 a participant from Golden Eagle Hotel. Golden Eagle offered to buy from the Produce Division raw food at a price equivalent to $90 a participant.

Since this situation appeared to be a little unusual, William Kenton, manager of the Conference Division, discussed the wide discrepancy of bids with NYA's executive director. He told the executive director: "We sell in a very competitive market, where higher costs cannot be passed on. How can we be expected to show a decent margin if we have to buy our accommodations at more than 10 percent over the going market?"

Knowing that Mr. Brunner had on occasion in the past few months been unable to operate the Housing Division at capacity, it seemed odd to the vice president that Mr. Brunner would add the full 20 percent overhead and margin to his out-of-pocket costs. When asked about this, Mr. Brunner's answer was the statement that appears at the beginning of the case. He went on to say that having helped in the planning for the conference, and having received no reimbursement for his time spent on that, he felt entitled to a good markup on the use of his facilities.

The executive director explored further the cost structures of the various divisions. He remembered a comment that the controller had made at a meeting the week before to the effect that costs which were variable for one division could be largely fixed for the company as a whole. He knew that in the absence of specific orders from senior management Mr. Kenton would accept the lowest bid, which was that of Magnolia Hotel for $430. However, it would be possible for senior management to order the acceptance of another bid if the situation warranted such action. And though the volume represented by the transactions in question was less than 5 percent of the volume of any of the divisions involved, other transactions could conceivably raise similar problems later.

Questions

1. Which bid should the Conference Division accept that is in the best interests of National Youth Organization?
2. Should Mr. Kenton accept this bid? Why or why not?
3. Should the NYA executive director take any action?
4. In the controversy described, how, if at all, is the transfer price system dysfunctional? Does this problem call for some change, or changes, in NYA's transfer pricing policy? If so, what specific changes do you suggest?

PART III

Management Control Systems

As we indicated in Chapter 1, management control systems consist of both a structure and a process. Structure describes what the system is, and process describes what it does—in much the same way that anatomy and physiology describe the human body.

In this part of the book, we discuss the important aspects of management control systems. Chapter 7 focuses on structure, placing it in the broader context of a management control environment. Understanding the management control environment is critical to understanding the management control structure, which is highly situational and governed in large measure by the organization's external and internal environments.

Chapters 8–15 describe the management control process—a set of activities encompassing a wide variety of interactions among individuals in an organization. Each phase in the management control process—programming, budgeting, operating and measuring output, and reporting and evaluating performance—is the subject of at least one chapter, sometimes two. Some chapters consider specific aspects of a phase in detail. For example, Chapter 11 looks in depth at the control of operations, a part of the operations and measurement phase of the cycle. Similarly, Chapter 15 is devoted to an aspect of the management control process that is particularly important for nonprofit organizations: evaluation of program and organizational performance. In most for-profit organizations, profit is the primary means of evaluation. Most nonprofit organizations, however, do not have a corresponding means of evaluation that is as uniform or accessible. We discuss some aspects of evaluation that are useful when there is no profit measure.

Chapter 7

The Management Control Environment

The management control function is affected by many forces outside the organization. Together, these forces constitute the organization's *external environment*. In Chapter 2, we discussed the external forces that affect nonprofit organizations. These include tax and legal considerations, constraints on goals and strategies, professional norms, unsophisticated governance, and political influences.

External environments vary greatly from one organization to the next, and these differences affect the design of the management control system. For example, management control in an entity with relatively certain revenues, almost no competition, and programs that are essentially unchanged from one year to the next, is considerably different from management control in an entity whose sources of funding are relatively uncertain, whose competitors are numerous, and whose program emphases shift rapidly.

Government organizations, as well as organizations that receive substantial funds from government sources, are subject to a variety of pressures and scrutiny from legislative bodies and the general public. In these cases, the desires of the press and the public for information constitute an important design consideration for the management control system.

Organizations also have *internal environments*, and in designing an organization's management control system, senior management must give careful consideration to the fit among a variety of elements that constitute this internal environment. These elements include the organizational structure, the program structure, the information structure, and a variety of administrative, behavioral, and cultural factors. Not only must these elements fit with each other, but they must fit with the external environment as well. As we will discuss in this chapter, the management control system is an important tool for senior management to use in helping the organization attain these fits.

THE ORGANIZATIONAL STRUCTURE

Organizational structure refers to the *formal* reporting relationships among managers and other individuals in an entity. An entity also has an *informal* structure that is unwritten and perhaps unintended. The informal structure encompasses a network of interpersonal relationships that has important implications for management. Because it is unwritten, however, the informal structure of the organization is difficult to identify and describe. For this reason, we concentrate here on the formal structure.

Senior management weighs many considerations in determining the best formal structure. These considerations involve questions such as the most appropriate division of tasks, the activities that should be carried out by specialized staff units, the activities that should be the responsibility of line managers, the decisions that should be made at or near the top of the organization, and the decisions that should be delegated to lower levels. Some of these considerations are related to individuals; that is, in part, the entity is organized to take into account the skills and personality traits of individual managers.

An organization's formal structure can take one of several forms. In a functional structure, tasks are classified according to function, and all personnel who work in the same functional area are under the direction of a manager. In a social service agency, for example, all social workers might report to a director of social work, or in a hospital all nurses might report to a director of nursing.

As organizations grow and become more diverse, many shift from a functional structure to a divisional one. In a divisional structure, functional tasks are grouped into a logical cluster according to clients served, regions, or programs. For example, if a large home health care agency had a divisional structure, its personnel might be grouped into teams according to geographic region. If so, its home care workers would report to a team manager or regional manager, rather than to a director of home care. In a hospital, nurses would report to a department head, such as the chief of surgery or chief of medicine, rather than to a director of nursing.

The most complex organizational structure is the matrix form. In this form, individuals have two supervisors—a divisional or program supervisor and a functional supervisor. Social workers might report to a team manager for their day-to-day activities, for example, and to a director of social work for their professional development and training. In a hospital, nurses might have similar dual reporting responsibilities.[1] In some universities, faculty have dual reporting responsibilities: to both a department chair and a program director.

---

[1] For additional details on these organizational types in a health care context, see Martin Charns and Marguerite J. Schaefer, *Health Care Organizations* (Englewood Cliffs, N.J.: Prentice Hall, 1983).

Responsibility Centers

As we discussed in Chapter 1, the formal organizational structure for management control purposes is defined in terms of responsibility centers, with line control exercised by the managers of these responsibility centers. Although the type and degree of control exercised by a manager may be difficult to pinpoint, at some level someone in an organization has control over each resource-related decision. In some cases control is infrequent and has long-term implications, such as in the acquisition of a fixed asset or the commitment to a long-term lease. In other cases, it is of shorter duration, such as in the decision to sign a one-year supply contract. In still other cases, control is very short run, such as in the decision to ask employees to work overtime.

The key question senior management asks in defining the organization's responsibility center structure is "Who controls what resources?" Each manager's responsibility then should be aligned with the resources over which he or she exerts reasonable, although not necessarily total, control.

Types of Responsibility Centers

As the above discussion suggests, a responsibility center is an organizational unit headed by a manager who is responsible for its activities. In any organization, except the smallest, there is a hierarchy of responsibility centers. At the lowest level in the organization there are responsibility centers for sections or other small organization units. At higher levels there are departments or divisions that consist of several smaller units plus overall departmental or divisional staff and management people; these larger units are also responsibility centers. From the viewpoint of senior management, trustees, or legislative oversight bodies, the whole entity is a responsibility center. In general, however, even though such large units fit the definition of a responsibility center, the term usually is used to refer to smaller, lower level units within the organization.

In Chapter 1 we described four types of responsibility centers: revenue centers, expense centers (standard and discretionary), profit centers, and investment centers. Exhibit 7–1 lists these four types and the management control implications of each.

All types of these responsibility centers can be found in some nonprofit organizations, but the most common are: discretionary expense centers, standard expense centers, and profit centers. In a discretionary expense center the focus is on total expenses regardless of the volume and/or mix of activity. In a standard expense center the focus shifts to expenses per unit of output rather than total expenses. The budget each period (called a *flexible budget*) is adjusted based on the actual volume and mix of units of output. In a profit center, the focus is on both revenues and expenses.

Recall from discussions in earlier chapters that revenues are monetary mea-

---

EXHIBIT 7–1   Types of Responsibility Centers

Type of Responsibility Center	*Responsible for*
Revenue center..........	Revenue earned by the center.
Expense center:	
Standard..............	Expenses per unit of output, but not total expenses, incurred by the center.
Discretionary..........	Total expenses incurred by the center.
Profit center.............	Total revenues and expenses of the center.
Investment center........	Total revenues and expenses of the center, computed as a percentage of the assets used by the center, that is, the center's return on assets.

---

sures of a responsibility center's output. They may be generated by sales of services both to other responsibility centers and to outside clients. To some people, the idea that profit centers exist in a nonprofit organization seems peculiar, but the profit center idea can be an important way of facilitating management control. As such, it is not at all inconsistent to have a profit center in a nonprofit organization—the term simply refers to a manager's scope of financial responsibility.

Criteria for Profit Centers

An important set of considerations for understanding a management control system relates to the criteria that senior management uses to decide which responsibility centers should be profit centers and which should be expense centers. Because a profit center encompasses more elements of managerial performance than an expense center, it also requires more recordkeeping. Indeed, in some circumstances the creation of a profit center may have dysfunctional consequences. For example, it may encourage managers to place too much attention on the revenue side of the equation, or to cut expenses in a given accounting period without concern for the longer term consequences of these cuts.

Despite these potential dysfunctional consequences, a profit center generally is desirable if a manager has a reasonable amount of influence over both the outputs and the inputs of his or her responsibility center. In effect, a profit center manager behaves almost as if he or she were running a separate organization. In most organizations, managers who carry out identifiable programs, especially ones that are geographically separate, usually have their units designated as profit centers. In determining whether a responsibility center should be a profit center, senior management should consider five key criteria:

Degree of Influence.   The manager of a responsibility center should be able to exert *reasonable* influence over both revenues and expenses of the center. This does not imply that the manager must have *complete* control over outputs and inputs, for few, if any, profit center managers have such authority. However, a profit center manager usually should be able to exercise some control over the volume of activity of the responsibility center, the quality of the work done, the center's variable unit costs, and its direct fixed costs. Sometimes he or she also can influence the prices charged.

Perception of Fairness.   The manager should perceive that the profit reported for the unit is fair as a measure of its financial performance. This does not mean that the amount of reported profit is completely accurate or that it encompasses all aspects of performance, for no profit measure does this. If a service center is designated as a profit center, for example, its usual financial objective is to break even; that is, to provide services whose revenues approximate the costs of the center. If this is the case, both the manager and his or her superior need to agree that breakeven performance is good financial performance.

Absence of Dysfunctional Incentives.   The competitive spirit that the profit center concept fosters should not have dysfunctional consequences to the organization. For instance, in some cases when a unit is organized as a profit center, the desirable degree of cooperation with other responsibility centers does not occur. The manager of a profit center may make decisions that add to the profit of his or her own unit to the detriment of other units in the organization. For example, he or she may be reluctant to incur overtime costs even though the services may be badly needed by other responsibility centers. Senior management should attempt to avoid or minimize such dysfunctional consequences by designing the management control system so that cooperative actions have a positive impact on the profit center's reported performance (or at least do not adversely affect it).

Existence of Transfer Prices.   Internal users of a responsibility center's services should be expected to pay for those services via transfer prices. If there are internal users and no transfer prices, senior management ordinarily should not designate the unit as a profit center. An internal audit organization, for example, usually provides services without charge and therefore should not be a profit center. Similarly, if senior management encourages operating units to use the services of certain staff units, these staff units probably should not be profit centers, at least not until operating units come to accept the value of the staff services and are willing to pay for them.

As discussed in Chapter 6, transfer prices constitute a monetary way of measuring the amount of a responsibility center's internally furnished services. As such, they measure the unit's output. The problem of arriving at satisfactory transfer prices is complicated, however. Some of the more important considerations were discussed in Chapter 6.

Some people believe that if a responsibility center does not sell a substantial percentage of its products to external customers, it cannot be a true profit center; it is, at most, a *pseudo profit center*. If the profit center concept is properly understood and applied, however, sales to other responsibility centers are just as real to a profit center manager as sales to outside clients.

Low Recordkeeping Costs. The benefits of having a profit center should be greater than the extra cost of recordkeeping and other administrative activities that are required. The cost of measuring the output of most accounting departments, for example, is large enough that establishing the accounting department as a profit center probably would not be worthwhile. If, however, an accounting department does recordkeeping for several outside organizations, as is the case in some municipalities, it may be worthwhile to incur the additional recordkeeping costs needed to make the department a profit center.

Profit Centers and Managerial Autonomy

Profit centers vary considerably as to the degree of autonomy they give to their managers. While a profit center may operate almost as if it were an independent company, its manager does not have all the autonomy of a chief executive officer of an independent company. This is because profit centers are part of a larger organization, and their managers are subject to the policies of that organization. Profit center managers rarely have the authority to initiate new programs or commit to major capital expenditures, for example. Those decisions, like others that significantly influence the organization's overall strategy, usually are made by senior management.

Restrictions on autonomy imposed by senior management may be communicated by formal rules described later in this chapter, by programming systems, and by budgeting activities. No matter how carefully these formal devices are constructed, however, informal mechanisms constitute powerful indicators of a manager's autonomy. These mechanisms include unwritten rules concerning, for example, what decisions *(a)* are appropriately made by a profit center manager, *(b)* require approval of higher authority, or *(c)* require consultation with (but not necessarily approval of) staff offices or higher line managers. In general, chief executives tend to give more autonomy to subordinates whom they know well and whose judgment they trust. As a result, despite the presence of a variety of formal devices in an organization, some profit center managers may have considerably more decision-making latitude than others.

THE PROGRAM STRUCTURE

Every organization exists to carry out programs. Fixing responsibility for control over programs would be relatively easy if each program were a responsibility center and each program's resources were controllable in the same way. For example, the design of the control structure would be quite easy if: (1) each program sold its services, (2) each program were staffed by personnel who worked in no other program, and (3) each program manager had reasonable control over hiring and other personnel decisions, as well as decisions on program supply purchases. Under these circumstances, each program would be a profit center.

Most entities are not organized in a fashion that permits such tidy and well-defined control structures. Many organizations operate over large geographic areas and must consider this fact when designing their structure. For example, does a multihospital system have one director of alcoholic rehabilitation services with broad geographic responsibilities, or several area directors, each of whom has responsibility for all programs in his or her area, including the alcoholic rehabilitation program?

In other organizational settings, the program and functional lines become similarly blurred. Does the director of the summer festival program for a symphony orchestra have control over the number of personnel taking part in the festival, or their salaries? Does the director of a master's degree program in a large university control the number of applications received, the tuition charged, or the salaries of the faculty who work in the program? Moreover, while performers in the orchestra or faculty in the university may take part in a particular program, their reporting relationships within the organization generally are not to the director of one program only.

In summary, a separate program structure is needed when responsibility for the execution of programs involves more than one responsibility center. A municipality organized so that each responsibility center performs a defined type of service (e.g., public safety, highway maintenance, education, and so on) does not need a separate program structure. By contrast, a federal government agency that executes many separate programs through several regional offices does. So does a research organization that draws on the resources of several departments to carry out its research projects.

> **Example.** In the Department of Defense (DoD) in the 1960s, the lines of organizational responsibility ran to the Secretary of the Army, the Secretary of the Navy, and the Secretary of the Air Force, whereas defense programs cut across these lines. For example, the DoD had a strategic mission (or program) that was related to a possible nuclear exchange with the Soviets. Different parts of this program were the responsibility of the army (antiballistic missiles), the navy (Polaris submarines), and the air force (strategic missiles and bombers). A mechanism that facilitated decision making about the program as a whole was necessary. The defense program structure (in which Program 1 was Strategic Forces) provided such a mechanism.
>
> In recent years, some authors have argued that the DoD's success in accommodating the cutbacks it faces in the post-cold-war era will depend to a great extent on the existence of a structure such as this with transfer prices linking mission and support centers' interactions.[2]

---

[2] See Fred Thompson, "Management Control and the Pentagon: The Organizational Strategy-Structure Mismatch," *Public Administration Review* 51, 1 (January–February 1991).

Many organizations have found that selecting a good program structure is a difficult task. In fact, several efforts to establish programming systems in the federal government failed because the program structure was not arranged in a way that facilitated management decision making. Consequently, managers did not find the information they received useful, and paid no attention to it.

In short, the process of aligning responsibility with control and developing a responsibility center structure within an organization's broader organizational structure is by no means a simple endeavor. For this reason, the selection of a program structure is one of the most critical tasks facing senior management in nonprofit organizations.

Components of a Program Structure

In a large organization, the program structure usually consists of several layers. At the top are a few major programs; at the bottom are a great many program elements—the smallest units in which information is collected in program terms. A program element represents some definable activity or related group of activities that the organization carries on either directly, to accomplish an organizational objective, or indirectly, in support of other program elements.

Between programs and program elements are summaries of related program elements, which we call *program categories,* and, depending on how many layers are needed, *program subcategories.* In a relatively flat organization, there may be no need for program categories (or subcategories); program elements can be aggregated directly into programs. In a more hierarchical organization, by contrast, there may be several levels of program categories.

Exhibit 7–2 contains a simple example of programs, program categories, and program elements. A more complex example is contained in Appendix A at the end of this chapter.

EXHIBIT 7–2   Hierarchy of Programs, Program Categories, and Program Elements

Program	100. Formal Education
Program categories	101. Pre-elementary school service
	102. Elementary and secondary school service
	103. Post-secondary school education service
	104. Special education service for exceptional persons
Program subcategories (for Program Category 102)	1. Kindergarten
	2. Primary or elementary school education
	3. Secondary or high school education
	4. Vocational and/or trade high school
Program elements (for Program Subcategory 2)	.1 Language instruction
	.2 Music instruction
	.3 Art instruction
	.4 Social sciences instruction

Types of Programs. In designing the program structure, senior management focuses its attention on several different types of programs.

Direct and Support Programs. Programs can be classified as either *direct* or *support* (sometimes called *mission* and *service* programs). Direct programs relate to the organization's objectives and usually are focused on clients. Support programs provide services to more than one other program but usually don't work directly with clients. In making decisions about the allocation of resources, management usually focuses its attention on direct programs. Within limits, the amount of resources required for support programs is roughly dependent on the size and character of the direct programs.[3]

> *Example.* In a college or university, the direct programs would be those related to instruction and research. The support programs would include buildings and grounds maintenance, publications, and financial aid.

Administration. Ordinarily, there should be a separate program for administration. This support program typically includes certain miscellaneous program categories or elements that, although not strictly administrative in character, do not belong logically in other programs and are not important enough to be set up as separate program categories or elements. Alternatively, these miscellaneous program elements might be grouped in a separate program category.

The rationale for a separate program for administration is that it permits senior management to focus special attention on administrative activities. Senior management usually wishes to devote as much of the organization's total resources as possible to direct programs, and as little as possible to administration. In the absence of special attention, however, administrative activities tend to grow. A program for administration encourages senior management to direct attention to these activities.

Development. In organizations that obtain financial resources from contributors, there should be a separate program for the costs associated with development (or fund-raising). Contributors and others usually are interested in how much of the donated amounts was used for the direct programs of the organization and how much was spent on development activities. Occasionally there are practical difficulties in drawing the line between development costs and direct program costs, but this should not deter senior management from attempting to keep track of development costs as accurately as possible. A separate program facilitates this effort.

---

[3] Some organizations, primarily governments and philanthropic foundations, carry out some or all of their programs by making grants to other organizations. These other organizations actually perform the programmed activities. Although grants and other transfer payments should be reported separately from the expenses actually incurred in operating the organization, they nevertheless are a part of the direct program costs.

Example.   Major contributors to a symphony orchestra or other arts organization may be given special preferences, such as use of a patrons' lounge. Although conceptually these are fund-raising costs, the amounts are rarely segregated as such. As a result, the organization's reported development costs are understated.

Program Elements.   If feasible, a program element should be the responsibility of a single manager. If this is not feasible, senior management should attempt to relate program elements to the responsibility of a relatively small number of persons. Items for which responsibility is widely diffused, such as long-distance telephone calls, are not satisfactory program elements. Such items should appear not as program elements but as functional categories or expense elements in the responsibility structure.

Management decisions regarding program elements cannot be enforced unless these elements are related to personal responsibility. An alignment of individual responsibility with specific program elements also leads to an increased sense of personal identification with programs, and thus helps foster a greater degree of commitment among responsibility center managers.

Example.   A museum of natural history might have a program for exhibit halls. This program might have a program element for each exhibit hall. Each of these is the responsibility of a manager. One job of the program manager is to coordinate the work of these program-element managers.

As is the case with programs, program elements can be classified as either direct or support. Many programs also have a separate program element for administration. This element includes administrative activities associated with the program (as contrasted with the administration of the organization as a whole), and may also include miscellaneous catchall activities.

Criteria for Selecting a Program Structure

Since the primary purpose of the classification of programs is to facilitate senior management's judgment on the allocation of resources, the program structure should correspond to the principal objectives of the organization. It should be arranged so as to facilitate decisions having to do with the relative importance of these objectives. Stated another way, it should focus on the organization's outputs (i.e., what it achieves or intends to achieve) rather than on its inputs (the types of resources it uses) or on the sources of its support. A structure that is arranged by types of resources (e.g., personnel, material, or services) or by sources of support (e.g., tuition, legislative appropriations, and gifts in a university) is not a program structure.

The optimal number of programs in an organization is approximately 10. The rationale for this limit is that senior management cannot weigh the relative importance of a large number of disparate items. There are many exceptions to this generalization, however.

The designation of major programs helps clarify the objectives of the organization. The development of the program structure may also clarify organizational purpose and, thus, suggest improvements in the overall structure of the organization. Therefore, the program structure should correspond to those areas of activity that senior management expects to use for decision-making purposes.

The idea that programs should be related to decision making is, of course, a general one. The following questions can be used to make the idea more specific:

1. Is the program structure output oriented? Specifically, does it focus on what the organization does and the target groups it serves or plans to serve?
2. Does the program structure assist senior management in deciding whether to expand or reduce a program?
3. Within a program, are there opportunities for trade-offs; that is, for different ways of achieving the objectives? Benefit/cost analysis, for example, is often feasible within a program but rarely between programs. Can senior management actually influence the scope and nature of the activities that are conducted for a designated program?
4. Is there an identifiable outside pressure group interested in a part of the organization's activities? If so, is there a program that corresponds to the interests of this group?
5. When a criticism arises that not enough (or too much) effort is being devoted to a certain activity, can the program structure provide information to address this criticism?
6. Does the structure identify all important activities so that none is hidden from management's view? For example, if a research organization has no separate program for basic research, the pressure to devote resources to more attractive development projects will be strong, and basic research may be slighted. Alternatively, basic research may be conducted clandestinely within a supposed applied project.
7. Does the structure require a relatively small amount of cost allocation? (If a large fraction of the program cost is an allocated cost, the structure is suspect.)
8. Is the structure of some help to operating managers? At a minimum, it should never impede the work of operating managers.
9. Can program elements be associated with a quantitative measure of performance? At the broad level of programs no single reliable measure of performance ordinarily can be found. But as one moves down the hierarchy in the program structure, it should be possible to identify rather specific quantitative measures of performance. More will be said about performance measures in Chapter 12.

Matrix Organizations

Although the program structure need not match the organization structure, there should be some person who has identifiable responsibility for each program (as well as each program category and each program element in large organizations).

This need for a fit between the organizational structure and the program structure often results in a matrix organization. The matrix consists of program managers along one dimension and managers of functionally organized responsibility centers along the other. Program managers may have other responsibilities, and they may call on other parts of the organization for much of the work that is to be done on their programs, but they nevertheless are advocates for their programs, and they are held accountable for their program's performance.

> *Example.* Faculty members of a business school typically have a home base in a subject-area department (such as organizational behavior, accounting, or marketing). They also may be assigned to one or more programs, such as undergraduate education, graduate education, or executive education. Program managers call on departments for work to be done on their programs. In these circumstances, responsibility is divided between the department head and the program head.

An example of a matrix structure is contained in Exhibit 7–3. This is for a large agency—the Department of Mental Health in a state government. As this exhibit shows, the complexity in this agency exists along several dimensions, which affect both its management control structure and its budget preparation process. Some of those dimensions are as follows:

- The agency does not generate revenues. Therefore it is an expense center. Since its budget probably cannot be changed with changes in volume during the year, the agency quite likely is a discretionary expense center.
- Resource allocation is along two dimensions. One is based on field operations and facilities, which corresponds to the agency's organizational structure (the left side of the matrix). The other is based on the agency's major programs, such as community mental health (the right side of the matrix). The major programs correspond to appropriation accounts in the state's budget, and are the responsibility of *account executives*.
- Both field operations and the major programs have several layers of responsibility. The field operations activity is comprised of regions at the highest level, followed by facilities, areas, and units within the facilities. The major programs are comprised of program categories (or subprograms as they are called here).
- Overall program control is the responsibility of the account executives, who presumably cannot spend more than the amount allotted to their appropriation accounts. The programs cut across all regions, although not all regions or all facilities have all programs or all subprograms. As a result, one of the jobs of an account executive is to determine the regions and facilities that can best meet the needs of each major program and its various subprograms.
- Control over the activities in regions and facilities is the responsibility of the field operations and facility managers. They receive budgets from the account executives and must adhere to them while striving to meet the objectives of the programs and subprograms that the budgets fund.
- Although the agency is a discretionary expense center, some units within it may be standard expense centers. This is because the managers of these units have no control over the number or mix of individuals who need their services. For

EXHIBIT 7-3   Matrix Structure in a Large State Agency

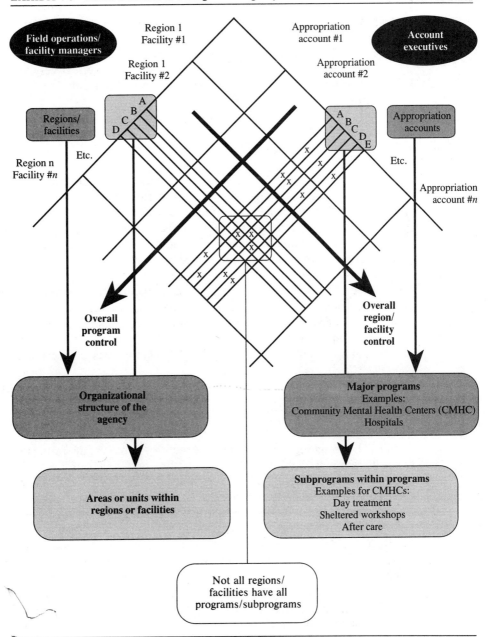

these units, the account executives should assure that increases in one region or facility are matched by decreases in other regions or facilities, since the appropriation account budgets are fixed. Nevertheless, with an appropriate flow of information to both account executives and field operations and facility managers, such a structure might provide greater motivation to the field operations and facility managers to run their operations more effectively and efficiently—each would be competing for scarce resources from the appropriations accounts.

THE INFORMATION STRUCTURE

Information is needed by both program planners and analysts as well as responsibility center (or operating) managers. Program planners and analysts need information for two purposes: (1) to facilitate decision making about programs and (2) to provide a basis of comparison of the cost and output of similar programs. Responsibility center managers need information on the outputs and inputs of their organizational units; this is used to facilitate their control of revenues and expenses.

These information needs relate to the distinction between the program structure and the organizational structure. The program structure is designed principally to meet the needs of planners and analysts, and emphasizes the full costs of carrying out programs. The responsibility structure is designed to meet the needs of operating managers, and emphasizes the controllable costs of operating responsibility centers.

In designing a program structure, the needs of planners and analysts should be given more weight than the needs of operating managers. For example, a program structure may cut across lines of responsibility, even though such a structure is not as useful to operating managers as one that is consistent with lines of responsibility. In designing a responsibility structure, however, operating managers' needs are paramount. Such a structure must be consistent with lines of responsibility, and this principle cannot be compromised to meet the needs of the planners.

To ensure that these conflicts are resolved in the most equitable way, senior management must be certain that the team designing (or modifying) the management control system not be dominated by people who represent the viewpoint of either the planners or the operating managers. Ideally, systems designers should be independent of both types of users, and should weigh equally the arguments of each.

The information structure should be able to reconcile most needs. This is especially important since senior management usually is interested in summaries of information provided to all other groups. An information structure to serve these multiple purposes is complicated since the information needed for one purpose may differ from that needed for another. In some cases, compromise in designing the structure may be necessary, but in most situations, the information structure can be designed to serve both sets of needs.

Example. The director of a Latin-American studies program in a university needs information on courses, enrollment, student satisfaction, and job placement. For the most part, this information is used for operating the program and not for comparisons with other similar programs. On the other hand, the dean of the school may wish to compare the Latin-American studies program with similar programs in other universities. To do this, he or she will need information on applications, standardized test scores, admission yields, and so forth. A well-designed program structure will provide information for both the program director and the dean.

Information for Comparative Purposes

Using information for comparative purposes can be particularly tricky, even with a well-designed program structure. If, for example, a number of similar organizations (e.g., schools, colleges, and hospitals) use the same program structure, then great care needs to be taken to assure not only that the structure is well designed, but that the participating organizations agree on the kinds of data that they will provide, and the meaning of these data. By having comparable data, managers can compile averages and other measures, and they can compare data from their own programs with these averages.

Example. There are several structures that provide data for interprogram comparison. Good structures exist for health care organizations, colleges and universities, social service organizations, and certain municipal services. In some states there are good structures for primary and secondary education, higher education, municipal activities, and certain other functions. Some religious organizations have systems for their local units, as do other membership organizations such as college fraternities, professional associations, chambers of commerce, and civic organizations.[4]

Compromises frequently are necessary in designing a structure for comparisons. This is because the participating organizations rarely view their programs in the same way. Because of this, the program structure that is used for comparisons should be quite broad, specifying only the data that actually will be used for comparative purposes. Each participating organization can then modify this structure (usually by subdividing the program into program categories and elements) to collect the more detailed information that is needed by its own management.

The Account Structure

To provide information needed by all relevant parties, the management control system should contain an account structure that is responsive to multiple demands. In addition to providing information to program planners and analysts,

---

[4] An abridged version of the program structure used by the United Way is contained in Appendix A at the end of this chapter. References of publications that describe structures for various nonprofit organizations are given in the list of "Suggested Additional Readings" for Chapter 3.

and to operating managers, the account structure must provide information to two other categories of users:

- *Senior managers and governing bodies.* These groups make policy decisions regarding the balance among programs and the relation of programs to objectives. Both groups need information on how the organization is performing.
- *Resource providers*, including contributors, legislative bodies, grantors, members, taxpayers, third-party payers, oversight bodies, and regulatory agencies acting in their behalf. These groups need information about what the organization did with the resources they provided. The needs of some resource providers can be met by general-purpose financial reports, which were discussed in Chapter 3. Other resource providers, particularly legislatures and grantors, require reports prepared according to their specifications.

Conflicts among Information Needs.   Since the needs of these parties frequently conflict with one another, the management control system must strike a balance. A well-designed account structure should be able to reconcile most needs, however. This is especially important since senior management usually is interested in summaries of information provided to all other groups. The system also must represent a balance between users' needs for information and the cost of collecting and processing that information. Appendix B at the end of this chapter discusses the types of accounts that typically are included in the account structure.

The Need for Articulation.   Ideally, all the accounts in the account structure make up a single, coordinated system. Technically, such a system is called an *articulated system*; each account is related to all other accounts. Serious management control problems can arise if program accounts are not tied with responsibility accounts, and if the historical costs in each set of accounts are not related to the budgeted costs.

Problems with Systems that Don't Articulate.   In some systems, a good program structure is used for planning and budgeting purposes, but after the program has been planned and the budget approved, this structure is not rearranged according to the responsibility centers that must execute the program. Instead, a separate budget is prepared for responsibility centers, often without any relationship to the program budget. As a result, both budgets and actual spending are recorded by responsibility centers but not by programs. Indeed, some systems do not even collect actual spending according to the same account structure used for the responsibility center budgets. When this happens, actual results cannot be compared to budgets in any meaningful way.

Example. Please refer to Exhibit 1–2 in Chapter 1. For this arrangement to be useful, plans for each program must be translated into the resources required from each responsibility center. The result is requested outputs (e.g., visits, days, tests) for each responsibility center. The responsibility center managers then must submit a budget for the inputs (e.g., salaries, supplies) they need to deliver the requested outputs. Finally, actual results—both outputs, inputs, and outputs per unit of input—must be calculated and compared to the budget.

There are two problems with systems that don't articulate. First, since the system cannot ascertain costs by program, program planners do not have the information they need to estimate future program costs. Second, without program-based costs, senior management has no adequate way of determining whether its program decisions are actually being implemented. If senior management decides that $1 million should be spent on a certain program, it needs to know whether the organization is in fact carrying out this program at the level of effort that $1 million represents. It cannot find this out unless the records classify actual spending in terms of programs.

One may ask why a system with defects such as these is permitted to exist. A possible explanation is that the idea of a program structure is relatively new in many nonprofit organizations. Some nonprofits that have adopted a program structure have not yet had the time to design accounting systems that permit the recording of costs by program elements as well as responsibility centers. Such changes are complicated and time-consuming, and involve training many people, both accountants and managers.

> *Example.* In the Department of Defense, a formal program structure for planning purposes was begun in 1962, but the conversion of the accounting system to one that collected costs by program elements did not take place until 1968, six years later.

ADMINISTRATIVE FACTORS

Another aspect of the internal management control environment is the set of rules, practices, guidelines, customs, standard operating procedures, and codes of ethics that exists in any organization. For brevity, we lump these together as administrative factors, or rules. Unlike the management control system, which involves continual change, administrative factors typically change infrequently. Some rules, such as those set forth in manuals, are formal; others, such as understandings about acceptable behavior, are informal. They relate to matters that range from the most trivial (e.g., paper clips will be issued only on the basis of a signed requisition) to the most important (e.g., capital expenditures of over $200,000 must be approved by the board of trustees).

Types of Rules

Some rules are guides. An organization's members are permitted (and expected) to depart from them, either under specified circumstances or if the manager judges that departure is in the best interests of the organization. For example, a guideline may state that overtime is not ordinarily paid, but managers may approve overtime payments under certain circumstances, either on their own authority or after obtaining approval from their superior. Other rules are literally rules—they should never be broken. Rules that prohibit paying bribes or taking illegal drugs are examples.

Some specific types of rules, procedures, and similar actions are listed below:[5]

1. *Physical control procedures.* Security guards, locked storerooms, vaults, computer passwords, television surveillance, and other physical controls are part of the internal control environment. Most of them are associated with task control, rather than with management control.
2. *Administrative control procedures.* There also are actions specifically designed to enhance task control, such as requiring that checks for more than a specified amount be countersigned. Their enforcement frequently is the responsibility of the controller's office.
3. *Administrative rules.* These are prescribed ways of performing certain functions, such as how to use time cards or how to complete expense reports.

Role of Manuals.   Much judgment is required in deciding which rules and procedures should be made formal (i.e., put in a manual), which should be guidelines rather than fixed rules, and which should be subject to managerial discretion. There are no clear-cut prescriptions for these judgments, although there are some fairly obvious patterns. Bureaucratic organizations have more detailed manuals than other organizations, large organizations have more than small ones, and centralized organizations have more than decentralized ones. Additionally, with the passage of time, some formal rules become obsolete. Manuals and other sets of rules therefore need to be reexamined periodically to ensure that they are consistent with current needs.

The Reward Structure

An important administrative factor is the reward structure. Ideally, managers should be rewarded on the basis of actual performance compared with expected performance under the prevailing circumstances. This ideal cannot be achieved, however, for two basic reasons. First, the performance of a responsibility center is influenced by many factors other than the actions of its manager, and the performance of the manager usually cannot be cleanly separated from the effects of these other factors. Second, managers are supposed to achieve both long- and short-run objectives, but the management control system usually focuses primarily on the short run. This is because the system can only report what has happened; it cannot report what will happen in the future as a consequence of the manager's current actions. As a consequence, responsibility centers and program managers are motivated to focus on achieving short-run goals. Indeed, our lack of knowledge about how best to measure and reward a manager's performance on a

---

[5] This list is derived from the work of Kenneth A. Merchant, who calls them specific action controls. See Kenneth A. Merchant, *Control in Business Organizations* (Aulander, N.C.: Pittman Publishing, 1985), chap. 3.

long-term basis is probably the most serious weakness in management control systems in both for-profit and nonprofit organizations.[6]

BEHAVIORAL FACTORS

Management control involves interactions among human beings. The behavior of people in organizations is therefore an important environmental factor. The major issue that senior management must address here is the congruence between the *personal* goals and needs of managers and professionals, and the goals and needs of the *organization* itself.

Personal Goals and Needs

People join an organization because they believe that by doing so they can achieve their personal goals. Once they have joined, their decision to contribute to the work of the organization is based on their perception that this will help them achieve their personal goals.

An individual's personal goals can be expressed as needs. Some of these needs are material and can be satisfied by the money earned on the job. Other needs are psychological. People need to have their abilities and achievements recognized; they need social acceptance as members of a group; they need to feel a sense of personal worth; they need to feel secure; they need to be able to exercise discretion; they need to feel good about themselves.

These personal needs can be classified as either extrinsic or intrinsic. Extrinsic needs are satisfied by the actions of others. Examples are money received from the organization and praise received from a superior. Intrinsic needs are satisfied by the opinions people have about themselves. Examples are feelings of achievement or competence, or a clear conscience.

The relative importance of these needs varies with different persons, and their relative importance to a given individual varies at different times. Moreover, the relative importance that people attach to their own needs is heavily influenced by the attitudes of their colleagues and superiors. For some people, earning a great deal of money is a dominant need; for others, monetary considerations are less important than serving society. Only a relatively few individuals attach much importance to the need to exercise discretion or the need for achievement, but these persons tend to be the leaders of the organization.[7]

---

[6] For-profit organizations sometimes use stock options as a way to motivate managers to think about the long-term consequences of their decisions. Some nonprofit organizations have used sabbatical leaves as a form of long-term incentive, but it is difficult to link leave time to long-run performance.

[7] McClelland argues that there is a relationship between the strength of the achievement need of the leaders of an organization and the success of that organization. See David McClelland, *The Achieving Society* (New York: Irvington Publishers, 1976).

How do people behave to satisfy their needs? One answer to this question is based on the expectancy theory model of motivation. This theory states that the motivation to engage in a given behavior is determined by (1) a person's beliefs or expectancies about what outcomes are likely to result from that behavior, and (2) the attractiveness of these outcomes; that is, their ability to satisfy needs.[8]

Individuals are influenced by both positive and negative incentives. A positive incentive, or reward, is an outcome that is expected to result in increased need satisfaction. A negative incentive, or punishment, is the reverse. Incentives need not be monetary. Praise for a job well done can be a powerful reward. Nevertheless, many people regard monetary rewards as extremely important. Such rewards may include a bonus based on a comparison between planned and actual results. As we discussed in Chapter 2, this incentive is being used increasingly by nonprofit organizations.

> *Example.* A survey of 587 hospitals conducted by William M. Mercer-Meidinger-Hansen, Inc., found that 18 percent of those surveyed had incentive compensation programs for executives. Another 21 percent were designing programs, and 29 percent were considering them. The survey found that the average target level for hospital CEOs (chief executive officer) was 24 percent of salary, and 17 percent for executives reporting directly to CEOs. While 85 percent of the plans were based on annual goals, 12 percent included longer term goals, and 21 percent included either a mandatory or optional deferral feature.[9]

Goal Congruence

Since an organization does not have a mind of its own, it literally cannot have goals. Organization goals are actually the goals of the board of trustees and senior management. Senior management wants the organization to attain these goals, but the organization's goals are not always congruent with the personal goals of operating managers and professionals. Because participants tend to act in their own self-interest, the achievement of organizational goals may be frustrated.

This distinction between organizational goals and personal goals suggests a central purpose of a management control system. Wherever possible, the system should be designed so that the actions it induces participants to take in accordance with their perceived self-interest are actions that also are in the best interests of the organization. That is, the incentives inherent in the management control sys-

---

[8] Texts on industrial psychology expand on these points at length. See Paul R. Lawrence and Jay W. Lorsch, *Organization and Environment* (Homewood, Ill.: Richard D. Irwin, 1969); and B. F. Skinner, *Beyond Freedom and Dignity* (New York: Appleton-Century-Crofts, 1971).

[9] Reported in "Hospitals Adopt New Strategy to Keep Top Executives," *Journal of Accountancy,* March 1988, pp. 14–17.

tem should encourage *goal congruence*.[10] If this condition exists, a decision that a manager regards as sound from a personal viewpoint also will be a sound decision for the organization as a whole.[11]

Perfect congruence between individual and organizational goals does not, and cannot, exist. For example, many individuals want as much compensation as they can get, whereas from the organization's viewpoint there is an upper limit to salaries. As a minimum, however, the management control system should not encourage individuals to act against the best interests of the organization.

> ***Example.*** An organization has a goal of low-cost, high-quality services, but its management control system rewards managers exclusively for reducing costs. If some managers decrease costs by reducing the quality of service, there is an absence of goal congruence.

Given these sorts of difficulties, senior management must ask two separate questions when evaluating its management control system:

1. What action does it motivate people to take in their own perceived self-interest?
2. Is this action in the best interest of the organization?

Cooperation and Conflict

Generally, the lines connecting the boxes on an organization chart imply that organizational decisions are made in a hierarchical fashion. Senior management makes a decision, this decision is communicated down through the organizational hierarchy, and operating managers at lower levels proceed to implement it. Clearly, this military model is not the way most organizations actually function.

Operating managers react to an instruction from senior management in accordance with their perception of how it affects their personal needs. Additionally, interactions between managers affect what actually happens. For example, the manager of the maintenance department may be responsible for maintenance work done in other departments. Maintenance work in one operating department may be slighted, however, if there is friction between the maintenance manager and the operating manager. Also, actions that a manager takes to achieve personal

---

[10] There actually are two levels of analysis here: (1) between *organizational goals* and *personal goals* and (2) between *organizational goals* and *incentives*. The determination of organizational goals and incentives is part of the management control system. However, senior management also can *influence* the personal goals of the organization's managers and professionals. It does so by using its hiring, promotion, and termination policies to select and retain individuals who have personal goals that are closely aligned with the organization's goals.

[11] For an elaboration of this idea, see Douglas McGregor, *The Human Side of Enterprise* (New York: McGraw-Hill, 1960). This book is considered a classic in management literature.

goals may adversely affect other managers. Managers may argue about which departments should get the use of limited computer capacity or other scarce resources. For these and many other reasons, conflict exists within organizations.

Clearly, an organization will not achieve its objectives unless managers work together with some degree of harmony. Thus, there also must be cooperation in an organization. Participants realize that without cooperation the organization will founder or even dissolve, and they will then be unable to satisfy the needs that motivated them to join it in the first place.

Senior management must maintain an appropriate balance between the forces that create conflict and those that create cooperation. Some conflict is both inevitable and even desirable. It results from the competition between participants for promotion or other forms of need satisfaction; within limits, such competition is usually healthy. Conflict also arises because different members of an organization see the world differently, and believe that different actions are in the organization's best interests. One need look no farther than the federal budget formulation process to see this.

Similarly, conflict also arises in museums over the most suitable exhibits, in school systems over the most desirable courses, and in hospitals over the most appropriate treatment patterns for patients. To a certain extent, this sort of conflict is beneficial in that it frequently brings out the best in an organization's members. Thus, if undue emphasis is placed on fostering a cooperative attitude, the most able managers and professionals may be denied the opportunity to use their talents fully. Somehow, senior management must seek to foster the right balance.[12]

The Bureaucracy

There are many comments to the effect that in government organizations and in certain other large nonprofit organizations effective management control is inhibited by the existence of the *bureaucracy*. Bureaucracy is often used as a label for any organization that operates by complicated rules and routines, or that is characterized by delays and buck-passing, or that treats its clients impolitely. In particular, government organizations are labeled as bureaucracies with the implication that nongovernmental organizations are not bureaucracies.

In fact, any large and complex organization is necessarily a bureaucracy. The classic analysis of bureaucracy is that of Max Weber.[13] Weber described a bureaucratic organization as one in which the chief executive's authority was derived by

---

[12] For further discussion on conflict and its benefits, see Lawrence and Lorsch, *Organization and Environment.*

[13] Max Weber, *The Theory of Social and Economic Organization* (1922). See the English translation by A. M. Henderson and Talcott Parsons (New York: Oxford University Press, 1947).

law or through election by an authorized body, rather than by tradition or charisma. Subordinates are responsible to the chief executive through a clearly defined hierarchy and are selected on the basis of their technical competence, rather than by election; they are promoted according to seniority or achievement, or both; and they are subject to systematic discipline and control.

In the Weberian bureaucracy, complex problems are solved by segmenting them into a series of simpler ones, and delegating authority for solving each of the segments to specialized subunits. The subunits consist of experts who are equipped to solve problems in their area of expertise. Such technical superiority, based on increased specialization, is supposed to lead to objective and impersonal decision making at the subunit level. Weber noted that an individual who applied personal subjective values to policy or decision making could seriously lessen the effectiveness of the organization. A bureaucracy avoids this possibility by replacing the subjective judgment of individuals with routinized work tasks and by a set of rules, values and attitudes, or goals, which are approved by the individual's superior.[14]

Bureaucracy is essential in an organization where several different units perform the same function. Each office of the Internal Revenue Service (IRS) is supposed to give the same advice to a taxpayer. There would be no way of coming close to that goal without a comprehensive set of rules and regulations used by all offices.

Researchers have paid considerable attention to the bureaucratic form of organization in recent years. Some have suggested that senior management can achieve the consistency needed in an organization such as the IRS without the complex hierarchy and red tape that generally characterize these organizations, and that give the word bureaucracy such a pejorative flavor. In part, this combination of consistency and flexibility can be achieved through the design of a good management control system.[15]

Role of the Controller

In most organizations, the controller is the person responsible for the operation of the management control system. The controller department is a staff unit, in contrast with the management control function itself, which is a line function. The responsibility of this staff unit is similar to that of a telephone company: it assures

---

[14] For an argument that just the opposite takes place in a bureaucracy, see Michel Crozier, *The Bureaucratic Phenomenon* (Chicago: The University of Chicago Press, 1964).

[15] For a discussion of this idea, see David W. Young, "Management Control in the Public Sector: Overcoming the Barriers to Progress," in A. P. Kakabadse, P. R. Borvetto, and R. Holzer (eds.), *Management Development and the Public Sector: A European Perspective* (Aldershot, England: Gower Publishing Company, 1988).

that messages flow through the system clearly, accurately, and promptly. It is not responsible for the content of these messages, however, or for the way managers act on them.

The controller ordinarily works with senior management to design the management control system in such a way that goal congruence is maximized. Most of this effort is associated with designing the responsibility center structure and the transfer pricing arrangements along the lines discussed earlier in the chapter. The controller also works with senior management to design the phases of the management control process, which are discussed in Chapters 8 through 15. Because of the major impact that design choices can have on managers' and professionals' behavior, senior management should be heavily involved in these choices. In many organizations, senior management completely delegates these choices to the controller, which is a mistake since the controller typically does not have a sufficiently broad perspective of the organization and its goals.

CULTURAL FACTORS

Every organization has its own culture—a climate, an atmosphere, a feeling for which attitudes are encouraged and which are discouraged. Cultural norms are derived in part from tradition, in part from external influences, such as its unions and the norms of society, and in part from the attitude of the organization's senior management and directors. The 1980s' best-seller, *In Search of Excellence*, was primarily an attempt to describe the culture in several companies that were judged at the time to be well managed. The failure of that book to provide an accurate assessment (as evidenced by the fact that several of these companies ran into serious trouble shortly after the book was published) illustrates the difficulty of explaining the influence of culture in a given situation. Nevertheless, cultural norms are extremely important. They explain why each of two entities may have an adequate management control system but why one has much better actual control than the other.

Cultural norms are almost never written down, and attempts to do so almost always result in platitudes. Instead, norms are transmitted partly by hiring practices and training programs. They also are conveyed by managers, professionals, and other organization members using words, deeds, and body language to indicate that some types of actions are acceptable and others are not.

Management Attitude

Perhaps the aspect of culture that has the most important impact on management control is the attitude of a manager's superior toward control. In a well-managed organization, the chief executive officer sets the tone. He or she may express this attitude in a number of ways. If performance reports typically disappear into the executive suite and no response is forthcoming, managers soon perceive that these reports are not important. Conversely, if a report is discussed at length with a manager, the signal is that the report is important. Conversations of this sort convey senior management's expectations about performance as powerfully as the formal budget does.

Other Aspects of Culture

The control climate also is affected by the attitudes of a manager's peers and by staff units. The culture within a responsibility center is also important. The organization may have ways of reacting to stimuli which in some cases reflect long tradition.

> *Example.* Despite the prestige and power of the office, a cabinet officer in the federal government may find it impossible to create the desired control climate no matter how hard he or she tries. Usually, the bureaucracy has firmly accepted certain behavioral norms and has found ways to perpetuate them. There is little that a political appointee can do in the short tenure he or she has with the organization.

Finally, the culture in the *external* environment affects the control climate within the organization. Some attitudes appear to be industrywide. For example, when times are tough, people tend to take the control process more seriously than when the economy is booming. In many nonprofit settings, the cultural norms of a professional group (e.g., physicians, nurses, social workers, artists, musicians) will have a major influence on the culture of the organization itself.

SUMMARY

One of the most difficult aspects of designing a management control system is defining the system's structure—its network of responsibility centers. In determining what sort of responsibility center given a manager's unit will be, senior management needs to pay careful attention to the resources the manager can control. This is the driving force behind responsibility center design. Beyond this, senior management needs to consider ways to attain goal congruence between the personal goals of each responsibility center manager and its goals for the organization as a whole. In part, a responsibility center manager's goals are determined by the incentives that senior management creates to reward certain forms of behavior. One of the major aspects of this incentive system is the organization's transfer prices, and senior management must be careful to establish the transfer pricing structure in such a way that it promotes behavior on the part of individual managers that is supportive of the organization's overall goals.

Beyond these considerations, senior management also must pay close attention to the fit between programs and responsibility centers. Programs represent the operational definition of an organization's strategy, and can be broken into program categories, subcategories, and elements. Each aspect of a program must be assigned to a responsibility center, and the management control system must be designed in such a way that it can provide information on both program and responsibility center activities. This calls for a careful design of the account structure, a task that ordinarily is carried out by the accounting staff but needs considerable guidance from senior management. Otherwise there is a danger that the accounts will not articulate.

Senior management must constantly bear in mind that management control is fundamentally behavioral. The various control tools are effective only to the extent they influence behavior, and they will influence behavior only to the extent that the culture of the organization is conducive to their doing so. A delicate balance must be struck between cooperation and conflict so that individuals—both managers and professionals—work together toward the attainment of organizational goals and yet are able to have legitimate and healthy conflicts over the best ways to attain them.

SUGGESTED ADDITIONAL READINGS

Anthony, Robert N., John Dearden, and Vijay Govindarajan. *Management Control Systems*. Homewood, Ill.: Richard D. Irwin, 1992.

Barnard, Chester I. *The Function of the Executive*. Cambridge, Mass.: Harvard University Press, 1938.

Charns, Martin, and Marguerite J. Schaefer. *Health Care Organizations*. Englewood Cliffs, N.J.: Prentice Hall, 1983.

Cyert, R. M., and J. G. March. *A Behavioral Theory of the Firm*. Englewood Cliffs, N.J.: Prentice Hall, 1963.

Lawrence, Paul R., and Jay W. Lorsch. *Organization and Environment*. Homewood, Ill.: Richard D. Irwin, 1969.

McGregor, Douglas. *The Human Side of Enterprise*. New York: McGraw-Hill, 1960.

Merchant, Kenneth A. *Control in Business Organizations*. Aulander, N.C.: Pittman Publishing, 1985.

Sathe, Vijay. *Controller Involvement in Management*. Englewood Cliffs, N.J.: Prentice Hall, 1982.

Simon, Herbert A. *The New Science of Management Decision*. Englewood Cliffs, N.J.: Prentice Hall, 1960.

APPENDIX A
A Program and Expense Element Structure

United Way of America has published a 319-page manual for use by the organizations whose activities it supports.[16] This appendix gives an abridged version of the program structure and the expense elements in this manual.

---

[16] United Way of America, *UWASIS II: A Taxonomy of Social Goals & Human Service Programs* (Alexandria, Va.: United Way of America, 1976). Used by permission.

Program Structure

Goals. The structure has eight goals (corresponding to programs as the term is used in the text):

1. Optimal income security and economic opportunity.
2. Optimal health.
3. Optimal provision of basic material needs.
4. Optimal opportunity for the acquisition of knowledge and skills.
5. Optimal environmental quality.
6. Optimal individual and collective safety.
7. Optimal social functioning.
8. Optimal assurance of the support and effectiveness of services through organized action.

Programs and Program Categories. The manual lists and carefully defines 587 programs, corresponding to program elements used in the text. These are grouped into 231 services, which in turn are grouped into 33 service systems; these correspond to program categories (and subcategories) as used in the text. In addition, the numbering system provides for additional programs, as desired by the individual agency.

The programs are classified as either (1) substantive (or direct), or (2) supportive (or indirect). The supportive programs are:

Comprehensive Planning and Development

Policy Planning

Research and Information Dissemination

Program Development

Programs Evaluation

Programs Coordination

Consultation and Technical Assistance

Standards Setting, Accreditation, and Monitoring

Public Education and Awareness

Personal Development and Training

Equal Access and Opportunity

Material Resources Provision

Ombudsman

Advocacy

As an example, a partial list of service systems, services, and programs for Goal 4, "Optimal opportunity for the acquisition of knowledge and skills," is given below:

100. Formal Educational Services System
    101. Pre-Elementary School Service
    102. Elementary and Secondary School Service
        01. Kindergarten
        02. Primary or Elementary School Education
        03. Secondary or High School Education
        04. Vocational and/or Trade High School
    103. Post-Secondary School Education Service
    104. Special Education Service for Exceptional Persons
200. Informal and Supplementary Educational Services System
300. Supportive Services System for the Acquisition of Knowledge and Skills
    301. Comprehensive Planning and Development Service
    302. Education Policy Determination Service
    303. Education Research and Information Service
    304. Educational Programs and Curriculum Development Service
    305. Educational Program Evaluation Service
    306. Education Program Coordination Service
    307. Education Program Consultation and Technical Assistance Service.

Expense Elements

Following is a partial list of the expense elements recommended by the United Way:

Employee compensation and related expenses:

Salaries

Employee health and retirement benefits

Payroll taxes, etc.

Other expenses:

Professional fees

Supplies

Telephone

Postage and shipping

Occupancy

Rental and maintenance of equipment

Printing and publications

Travel

Conferences, conventions, meetings

Specific assistance to individuals

Membership dues

Awards and grants

Depreciation or amortization

Miscellaneous

APPENDIX B
Types of Accounts in the Account Structure

To meet the wide variety of information needs of most organizations, the management control system usually includes several different types of accounts. They are included in the control system's account structure, and are the subject of this appendix.

Functional Accounts

To facilitate the collection of data on the cost of performing functions that are common to several responsibility centers, the accounting staff may prescribe a set of functional accounts within the responsibility centers. Ordinarily, one of these accounts should be designated as a mission account, in which the costs of performing the mission are collected.

> *Example.* In the various regional and local offices of a job training program, there may be one functional account for the job training mission itself. Other accounts are established for public relations, training of agency personnel, building operation and maintenance, and administration.

Expense Accounts

To facilitate analysis and, under certain circumstances, to control spending for discretionary elements of expense, the accounting staff usually sets up several expense accounts for each responsibility center (e.g., salaries, rent, utilities, travel). These accounts are called *object* (or *natural*) *accounts*. An example is given in Appendix A, above.

Cost Center Accounts

Every organization needs information about the cost of performing various functions or carrying on various activities. To the extent program elements are set up as cost centers, or to the extent program elements are represented by functional categories in the responsibility structure, cost information can be obtained either directly, from the accounts described above, or indirectly, from the cost accounting system. In some situations, however, such information is too detailed to be of interest to management (other than the manager of the responsibility center directly involved) and, hence, it is not worthwhile to clutter the program and responsibility accounts with this detail. In these situations, the information can be collected exclusively through the cost accounting system.

> *Example.* The highway departments of municipal governments use a great deal of detailed information on the cost of constructing, repairing, resurfacing, and maintaining roads of various types. They collect this information in a cost system.

Accounts for Outside Agencies

The accounts described above are those that management needs to plan and control the activities of the organization. Many organizations also must provide information to outside parties. Agencies of the federal government, for example, must report to the Congress and to the public. The U.S. Department of Education, which makes grants to public schools, is naturally interested in knowing what the schools do with those funds, and it consequently requires schools to submit reports on how the funds were used. State agencies are interested in information about the entities (e.g., hospitals, mental health clinics) that they regulate.

As a general proposition, it seems clear that no outside agency would need more information than the organization's internal management needs for its own purposes; indeed, one would think that an outside agency should need much less information than internal management. Furthermore, the nature of the information that interests an outside agency should correspond to the information that management finds useful. Rationally, therefore, information furnished to outside agencies should be a summary of the information collected for internal use.

Unfortunately, the real world is not this rational. A great many organizations must collect and report information which they consider useless, simply because an outside party requires it. When the outside party can enforce its request—because it provides funds, licenses the organization, and so on—the organization has no choice but to furnish the information. It can do so in one of two ways.

The safe, but expensive, way is to create a special account structure to collect the required information. Federal agencies furnish information to the Congress according to an appropriation structure that the agencies do not need for management purposes. In addition to being expensive, such a solution has the disadvantage of requiring the maintenance of two sets of accounts to collect information about essentially the same phenomena. At a minimum, this can cause confusion within the organization since managers may be uncertain as to which type of information should be used for decision making. A more serious possibility is that operating managers may pay too much attention to the outsider's structure and give inadequate attention to the structure that actually best fits management's needs.

An alternative used by some organizations is to prepare reports for outside agencies based on estimates rather than actual accounting information. A skilled accountant can construct a plausible list of costs, classified in any way that an outside agency specifies. Such a report does not, of course, reveal what *actual* spending has been, except by coincidence, but it often is a reasonable approximation. This method frequently is used when the requests from the outside agency seem obviously worthless, particularly when they require an undue amount of detail.

Fund Accounts

If an organization receives funds whose use is restricted to a specified purpose, then the accounting system must be set up in such a way that the amounts spent for this purpose are separately identified. Such a separation is made in the program structure. Mechanically, many nonprofit organizations control the use of these resources through fund accounting.

Fund accounting is not used in a for-profit organization. In business accounting, all available resources are, in effect, in one "pot." In a nonprofit organization, by contrast, resources may be accounted for in several separate pots, each of which is called a *fund*. As described in Chapter 3, each fund has its own self-balancing set of accounts, and each fund is therefore a separate entity, almost as if it were a separate business. The purpose of this device is to ensure that the organization uses the resources made available to each fund only for the purposes designated for that fund.

In recent years, many managers have recognized that control over spending can be obtained without an elaborate fund-accounting mechanism, and some have greatly reduced the number of separate funds. In general, those funds that remain serve a useful purpose, although in many cases it is quite possible that the same objective could be accomplished without the fund mechanism at all. In some other organizations, by contrast, the segregation by funds has been carried to extremes.

Example. Some years ago, the U.S. Post Office had one fund for first-class postage, another for third-class postage, another for money orders, and so on. Each post office maintained a separate bank account for each fund.

Relation between Funds and Programs. When accounts are set up for restricted funds, management should take care to ensure that the separate funds do not obscure the total amount spent for programs.

Example. All states collect a gasoline tax, which is used for maintenance of highways. In some states the amount of this tax is adequate to provide for all maintenance expenses; in other states, part of the amount needed comes from general tax revenues. In the latter states, highway maintenance costs should be recorded in two separate funds, with the system designed so that these separate amounts can be aggregated to show the total cost of the highway maintenance program.

CASE 7–1   Rural Health Associates (A)*

In July 1981, Paul Judkins, executive director of Rural Health Associates (RHA), was evaluating his organization's management structure and systems. Located in Farmington, Maine, RHA had been undergoing a period of rapid growth, and Mr. Judkins wondered whether the existing structure and systems were appropriate to meet the organization's needs in the future. During an interview, he commented on some of the important aspects of RHA's current situation. The remainder of this case consists of his comments and those of Jack Bourbeau, his business manager.

Background

RHA was conceived in 1971 in the midst of a hospital war between two groups in West Central Maine. After each applied separately for Hill-Burton money and was rejected, the two groups were compelled to cooperate and compromise on the hospital's present site here in Farmington. At the time, I worked for the Ford Foundation, and was also a member of the hospital's Board of Trustees. Meanwhile, four physicians practicing out of the nurses' home of the old hospital got together with the Community Action Program, funded by the Federal Office of Economic Opportunity. They documented the need for improvement in the geographical and financial access to health care for the 30,000 residents who lived in the 27 rural townships in the mountainous and heavily forested areas around here. RHA was set up to help fill this need, and was awarded a two-year federal grant.

I became executive director of RHA one year ago, in June of 1980. At that time, the organization had undergone rapid growth, but with no logical or deliberate planning. The separation of the organization into the three divisions of Rural Group Practice (RGP), Franklin Area Health Plan (FAHP, our HMO), and Research and Development (R&D), occurred as a reactive stance. The corporation had grown unwieldy and there was intraorganizational fighting over the budget and public image. My activities this year have been focused on remedial and corrective efforts. We've worked through a lot of problems and I've made some changes in the organization. The organization is at a juncture now, and we need to think ahead. I am concerned about whether our management structure and systems can facilitate a more progressive and less reactive posture.

---

* This case was prepared by Margaret B. Reber under the direction of Professor David W. Young. Copyright © by the President and Fellows of Harvard College. Distributed by the Pew Curriculum Center, Harvard School of Public Health.

Organizational Goals and Structure

RHA was chartered to develop a group practice, a prepaid health plan and minibus transportation system for the poor, and a research program in the rural health application of broadband microwave television. RHA's goals included:

1. The areawide delivery of comprehensive primary medical care with continuity and a strong preventive emphasis.
2. The recruitment of only board-certified or board-eligible physicians.
3. Peer review and audit, especially in the outpatient setting.
4. The necessity for and support of continuing education of its providers.
5. The teaching of predoctoral and postdoctoral health professions students.
6. Research and demonstration projects in clinical areas, health services delivery, health education, and nutrition.

I serve as executive director of RHA; Ron McAllister is our controller, and Dave Dixon is our medical director. I also serve as director of FAHP and R&D. The Rural Group Practice has a business manager, Jack Bourbeau, and an executive committee composed of three elected providers. I've considered designating divisional heads, but if we did that, what would I do? The job isn't big enough yet.

We have a 15-member board of directors, with 8 consumers and 7 providers. The board has a standing Committee on Goals and Objectives which I reactivated when I became executive director. We had a few meetings this year but then it fell by the wayside. I have another meeting with this committee next week. We need to start thinking ahead and plot where the need is going to be. For example, at the time we started RHA, there were 13 physicians in the region. Six of them are still here, but now the total is 24, 12 of whom practice at RHA. They are all young and about the same age. In fact, at age 51, I'm the oldest member of this organization. If we don't phase the M.D.s, they'll all be retiring at about the same time and we'll have a shortage all over again.

Very few of the M.D.s are native "Maineiacs." There are lots of people who want to get the hell out of Boston and other big cities. Last week we had a husband and wife team from Cleveland who were interested in moving up here. Physicians get tired of the routine office work and the isolation and overload of solo practice. Some want to get away from being the 24 hour per day country doctor. They want to share records and coverage, and get professional stimulation. They also seek challenge. Our R&D activities and FAHP alternative delivery project attract physicians. I encouraged one of our physicians, who was bored with day-to-day activities, to submit a grant. Now he has funding to examine early intervention with emotionally disturbed kids. Motivation for some physicians is money; for others it's free time. In terms of quality, we don't take a back seat. In no rural setting will you find more talent. The M.D.s have been very well trained and are all board certified.

Franklin Area Health Plan

FAHP is an individual practice association type of health maintenance organization. We call it a foundation. It provides comprehensive, prepaid health care to 2,700 poverty-income level and 500 commercial residents in the area. Ninety percent of each low-income enrollee's premium is paid by the federal government through a grant from the Bureau of Community Health Services (BCHS). Subscribers are required to make a copayment on emergency room care and prescription services. Unfortunately this year, the Feds told us they wouldn't pay for inpatient care due to Reagan's budget cuts. So I'm looking for other means of coverage.

I have a financial director, Debbie Belcher, and a marketing director for the plan. Debbie uses a COSTAR computer linkup with Massachusetts General Hospital to provide us with patient information and accounting for the plan. We submit reports to BCHS on financial and quality of care measures on a semiannual and quarterly basis.

The plan has been in operation for five years now and has done well, so we decided to market it to employers in the area. Initially, all 24 physicians in the area were members of FAHP, 10 of whom were also practicing in RGP, but when we decided to market FAHP to companies on a prepayment basis, all but 2 of the physicians outside of RGP got out of it. They weren't willing to accept a change in philosophy from fee-for-service to prepayment. Before this, the plan was a means of getting paid for services rendered to the poor; people who couldn't otherwise pay. But the physicians weren't willing to be at risk for people who would pay anyway through the fee-for-service system.

FAHP also has four full-time, internally-trained social workers who report to a social worker with a Bachelor of Social Work degree. These people work with three social workers from the Community Action Program. They run a house insulation program, dole out food stamps, run a parenting program, etc. In general they do a lot of outreach for RHA. People don't understand how to use the system. They won't use the facilities until they're at death's door. Attitudes are slowly changing as new people move into the area who are used to sophisticated medical systems. It takes time for patients to adjust to the less personal setup we have after being treated by an M.D. in a boarded-up back porch in the boondocks. To some patients we are considered the "General Electric" of health care.

Rural Group Practice

RGP is a group practice that provides medical, optometry, and dental services to about 60 percent of the people living in the service area. We have been able to reach many patients through the use of satellite centers located in secluded sections of our service area. Twenty percent of the physician encounters are with prepaid patients from FAHP. Eventually, I'd like to see 40 to 50 percent of the patients enrolled on a prepaid basis. This would help out on our seasonality problem. In the winter we have heavy usage of the facilities, whereas, in the summer, usage is the lightest. Our costs are fixed, but our fee-for-service revenues fluctuate. If more of our patients were prepaid, we could reduce our cash flow problems.

I don't think there is a conflict of interest between FAHP incentives to encourage physicians to underutilize services and the RGP fee-for-service incentives to increase utilization. The physicians see the same patients over and over again so there is continuity of care. They wouldn't treat the FAHP patients differently from the fee-for-service patients just because of the patients' payment mechanism. The patients receive equal quality of care. I want FAHP and RGP to operate side by side to provide patients with a prepaid alternative to more expensive health care and a traditional fee-for-service mode where it is more appropriate.

The services offered could be categorized into five departments: Family Practice/Pediatrics, Internal Medicine, Surgery, Dentistry, and Optometry. There are no formal or informal department heads because we are trying to maintain an overall group identity.

We have 10 physicians, two dentists and one optometrist in the group. There are three internal medicine specialists, three family practitioners, one pediatrician, one otolaryngologist, a general surgeon, and an orthopedic surgeon. In addition, we have two physician assistants, one nurse practitioner, one dental hygienist, and one optometric assistant on the provider team. Ideally, I'd like to see the group practice expanded to 15 physician providers. We need two more family practitioners. Two additional physicians would help spread our costs over a broader base and also provide more personal care. In addition, we could have more flexible scheduling and provide better weekend coverage.

Every time a new physician joins the group we have a publicity release. We take the opportunity to reiterate the hours and types of services offered. In general, we have real problems with our marketing. We can't use an objective form of marketing; we have to have a more personal form. An advertisement in the newspaper would have an impact like a sledge hammer on the head. So we try to use indirect means, like cooperation with area agencies. For example, we have a blood pressure program for the Bass Shoe Company employees, and this week I'm speaking at the Rotary Club. The physicians also contribute to the marketing of the group practice through their professional relations with various individuals and organizations.

We also have an active medical staff. The executive committee meets for lunch on Mondays and Thursdays to discuss problems that affect quality of care and physician well-being. The administration meets with them at their beck and call.

Unfortunately, the committee often turns out to be a discussion group, and won't arrive at decisions unless an administrator is present to provide input information and to act as facilitator. Even so, the physicians must have a voice in the running of the organization and a sense of control over their destiny. Recently we hired Jack Bourbeau as business manager of the group practice. He has an undergraduate degree in History with a Masters in Human Relations and 21 years in the Navy Medical Administration. Up until we hired Jack, I spent 75 percent of my time in the day-to-day operation of the group practice; now it's more like 25 percent. In a setting like this, Jack doesn't have line authority. He doesn't run things; he sees that things are run.

Satellite Centers. We used to have three satellite clinics located in isolated sections of Maine's western mountains. These centers have never been able to break even financially. In two cases, physicians have practiced at the satellite clinic just long enough to build up a practice and then they left. It's difficult to keep the clinics staffed. The providers always have a feeling of being odd-man-out or stepchildren of the Farmington Clinic. They develop a persecution complex. Rangeley is the only satellite we have left.

Research and Development

I can't conceptualize the group without the R&D component. It is a must for serving the needs of the community, for providing expanded services, and for developing alternative delivery systems. R&D has many different projects which fall into three main categories of educational services, community services, and the Early Periodic Screening and Diagnostic Treatment (EPSDT) Program. We also do some pure research such as testing blood pressure medicine for drug companies. The projects operate independently with each project director reporting to me.

R&D supports patient education projects in areas such as blood pressure, diabetes, nutrition, and obesity. I hope it will provide the financial support for these preventative health activities through grant money until such time as they are reimbursable by third-party payors. FAHP needs more patient education, and eventually we'd like to build some patient education services into the prepaid premium. We also have a pediatrician in RGP who is active in a school health program sponsored by R&D.

EPSDT is a federally funded program for Medicaid youngsters. Unlike most of our other R&D programs, the grant pays for some overhead costs, so it eases up the financial load for R&D. The community services program provides services to employees of local industries. We have tried to keep the full-time coordinator, a half-time secretary, and several part-time nurses. It has become known as the West Central Maine Health Services, and it is financially self-sufficient. I'm considering making it a fourth division. You see, we use R&D as a means to develop programs. If they fail to develop beyond the dependency stage, we disband the program. When they become self-sufficient we try to incorporate them into another division or perhaps set them up as a separate division.

Reporting Relationships

We adhere to the "each tub on its own bottom" philosophy for each division. So far the triadic structure has worked well. The organizational skeleton is just right. The major weakness in the system is working with the physicians. It's like a college president working with the faculty. Professionals have to have a voice in running the organization.

As executive director, I try to maintain a team with which I have rapport. I need to be kept informed. I do a lot of internal management, but about 50 percent of my job involves politics. For example, I'm beginning to develop a program with the elderly, which means negotiating a contract with Medicaid.

Budgetary Process

The budgetary process differs for each division. In R&D each project director submits to me a proposed budget with the expected revenues and expenses for the coming year. I read the budget and then meet individually with the project directors to firm up the figures. In FAHP, the financial director, the controller of RHA, and I develop a budget jointly and we talk about it. In RGP, Jack Bourbeau and the controller develop the budget and then they discuss it with me. In all cases the final figures are examined and approved by a committee of five board members, Jack Bourbeau, the controller and myself.

RGP is our main problem area; this is where we've had such a large discrepancy between budgeted and actual, and we've incurred considerable deficits in the last few years in growing proportions. Jack Bourbeau can fill you in on some of the details.

Interview with Jack Bourbeau, Business Manager

Our fiscal year runs from July to June, and we start the budgetary process in May. Ron McAllister, the RHA controller, provides me with revenue totals for the year to date. Unfortunately, the time lag for our computer information is from 30 to 45 days, so March is the most up-to-date revenue report available. The report provides us with a summary of actual revenues generated by each practitioner, including the three RN/PAs (Underwood, Hennesey, and Nurse).

Using the March report, we extrapolate the revenue for the three remaining months of the fiscal year. This then provides us with a baseline figure for each physician. We then make modifications to this expected revenue according to anticipated changes in physician productivity, patient volume increases, and price changes in various categories. We consider each physician separately. For example, one of our family practitioners recently came down with Hodgkins disease, and an internist had a nervous breakdown. Obviously, the expected productivity of these providers must be modified for the new fiscal year.

Last year, we factored in a 10 percent increase in volume. But what we've actually experienced was a 2 percent decrease in volume. I'd really like to examine the trends for the area. Everybody tells me the population is going up, but some demographic information would be helpful in determining expected volume increases.

If we are planning on a 5 percent charge increase for office visits, then we must adjust the expected revenue for each physician separately. For example, a charge increase in office visits will affect a family practitioner more drastically than it will a general surgeon. We use a detailed Revenue Analysis Report, which indicates the revenue generated by each physician in various charge categories.

We show these figures to each individual physician and he or she tells us whether or not we're on target. For example, an M.D. might say, "I think that's a little high." Then I might remind the physician that he's supposed to be available for office calls, a minimum of 20 hours per week. So, we compromise and adjust the revenue accordingly.

Then we aggregate the revenue for the providers and subtract 10 percent of the total to account for uncollectibles which include bad debts and third-party disallowances. This amount is divided by 12 to get the monthly expected revenue.

Physician Compensation

Up until this year, 45 percent of the projected revenue was allocated to cover the salaries of the 13 providers. This means that a predetermined amount was set aside for physician payment regardless of revenue actually generated.

We have recently changed that practice. Now the reimbursement allotment is 48 percent of the *previous year's* revenue. Out of this amount 40 percent is equally allocated to each physician for a base salary. Fifteen percent is distributed on the basis of the physician's contribution to the total number of encounters, 40 percent on the basis of their contribution to the total dollars generated, and 5 percent is allocated on the basis of the number of years the physician has been a member of RGP.

Changing the payment mechanism was an unpopular move. It took us four months to resolve the issue. There is a difference between managing professionals versus nonprofessionals. For every hour that I spend with a physician, I spend 12 to 15 hours in hard work documenting the case. When I showed them the figures for expenses and revenues they were more willing to accept it.

At first all of the providers wanted to take a $2,000 pay cut. However, Paul and I just wouldn't accept this, as it wouldn't have provided a long-lasting solution, and then we would have been on the defensive. So, we provided several different formula options to the physicians to consider.

Fortunately, there was an economically minded M.D. with a high regard for the dollar who realized what was happening. He pointed out that the higher generators were bringing in a higher percentage of what was put on the books. Essentially, the high generators were subsidizing the low generators. Under his influence, the physicians adopted the present payment mechanism.

It was rough, though, because for some of them it meant a salary cut. Some were so overpaid that it was a shock. There was a lot of turmoil. One of the physicians decided to leave, as she thought she could do better by herself.

The PA/NP salaries, as well as coverage of administrative and overhead costs, must come out of the 52 percent remaining after physician compensation, which is a big problem. The PA/NPs are each assigned to a preceptor, but we keep track of each one's encounters and generations separately, just as we do for the physicians. Bob Underwood works fairly independently in Family Practice and sees many of his own patients. Maria Hennesey works in Internal Medicine and is primarily a physician extender. She helps the M.D. with new patients, does initial screenings, does preoperative and postoperative visits, and also visits the nursing home patients. Pat Nurse is a nurse practitioner who works with the general surgeon. She does preop and postop work. In addition, she works with cancer patients and gives lectures to females on breast cancer. She is popular with teenage girls for physicals and family planning services. I guess she is straightforward, but she charges lower rates than expected. I don't know if it is right or wrong, but it causes problems for me. If the PA/NPs don't generate as much as their salary, we lose money. I spoke to a physician who worked with one of the PA/NPs about the low generation and he said, "She's worth her weight in gold. If you get rid of my PA/NP, you'll get rid of me." But, he isn't willing to pay the PA/NP out of his salary, or even out of the physician's pot. So, I compromised in this area for now.

The remainder of the expenses are budgeted by using the previous year's actual amounts and giving each section of Medical, Dental, Optometry, Pharmacy, Laboratory, X-ray, Medical Records, Facilities, and Administration some target amounts to strive for. Up until now the core was small enough to do this. When the nursing supervisor wanted to know if she could buy a piece of equipment, she would just call up Ron and he'd tell her if there was enough money available to make the purchase. Now, we're at the point where we need a more efficient system. Here are our budget reports for May (Exhibit 1).

Overhead costs of RHA are allocated to each division somewhat arbitrarily. For example, up until now RGP was arbitrarily assigned 50 percent of all facility and administrative costs. Recently, I've gone through the Medical Arts Building floor plan and I've come up with some figures of exclusive use areas for RGP, FAHP, R&D, and EPSDT. I figured out the exclusive and common use areas for the Surgical, Internal Medicine, Family Practice, Dental, and Optometry sections as well as for individual physicians. Now I should be better able to allocate costs on a square-foot basis.

Performance Review

I developed a monthly report on revenue generation, which I give to each provider. It shows total office charges for each physician for the month, the average price charged per patient, the actual number of hours spent, and the average number of patients seen per hour. I compare these figures with what was possible, and show the physician the difference between what he could earn and what he did earn in that month.

This has really helped out. When I first started giving the physicians this report in November, I would sit down and discuss the figures with them individually. Now they know how to use them, and I just send out the reports.

In general, the physicians have responded well. In fact, a few have come to my office for suggestions on ways to improve generation. One physician in particular has been very receptive to my suggestions. He was taking several unnecessary

EXHIBIT 1

RURAL GROUP HEALTH ASSOCIATES (A)
RURAL GROUP PRACTICE
Statement of Operations and Comparisons

	1980 Month May	1981 Month May	1980 Year to Date 5/31/80	1981 Year to Date 5/31/81	1980–1981 Budget
Generation:					
Medical	109,941	100,794	1,057,539	1,157,234	
Dental	14,511	18,685	140,431	163,694	
Optometry........................	10,185	14,984	122,943	142,061	
Pharmacy	3,218	2,778	33,007	35,949	
Laboratory	11,431	12,042	102,508	117,396	
X-ray	8,332	7,044	85,109	80,646	
Total..........................	157,618	156,327	1,541,537	1,696,980	2,097,980
Grants	2,823	2,039	34,299	24,931	30,000
Other income	(29)	(8)	13,603	1,064	
Total operating support	160,412	158,358	1,589,439	1,722,975	2,127,980
Less uncollectibles					
Provision for bad debts	4,431	4,402	43,663	47,964	
Cash discount.....................	1,473	1,367	13,133	15,502	
Courtesy and employee discount......	195	214	13,001	2,546	
Disallowed charges.................	9,885	12,878	104,125	131,486	
Total uncollectibles.............	15,984	18,861	173,922	197,498	212,798
Total operating revenue...............	144,428	139,497	1,415,517	1,525,477	1,915,182
Operating expenses:					
Medical	75,224	66,966	758,746	837,488	1,022,252
Dental	8,751	9,686	101,844	117,134	133,759
Optometry........................	11,853	15,341	105,491	124,971	121,761
Pharmacy	2,734	3,055	30,706	36,858	38,000
Laboratory	4,510	4,297	49,916	56,504	60,600
X-ray	3,874	5,353	53,993	56,082	64,800
Medical records...................	1,556	1,735	18,892	19,049	21,700
Facilities	11,887	11,350	132,823	131,512	156,560
Administration....................	17,900	21,584	198,905	235,251	290,250
Total operating expenses..............	138,289	139,367	1,451,316	1,614,849	1,909,682
Interest	1,000	746	7,593	5,573	4,000
Total operating expenses including interest..................	139,289	140,113	1,458,909	1,620,422	1,913,682
Excess of revenue over expenses (expenses over revenue)	5,139	(616)	(43,392)	(94,945)	1,500

breaks during his daily schedule. When the breaks were cut out, his productivity increased drastically.

The physicians also have their own quality of care report in which I'm not involved. At the end of each month, a patient's name is randomly picked from each of the doctor's schedules and the chart is pulled. Each doctor is assigned a chart (other than his own) to review. Upon completion of review, the audit is sent to the provider for his perusal. If there are any discrepancies, the auditor and the provider may get together and discuss them. Eventually all of the audit forms are analyzed by one person (a doctor) and any problems or trends are brought up at the monthly medical staff meeting.

Questions

1. What is the strategy of RHA? Please be as explicit as possible, focusing on markets, personnel policies, and financing mechanisms in particular.
2. Sketch out the organizational structure of RHA, making assumptions where necessary.
3. What kinds of responsibility centers are there at RHA? Are they appropriate according to the criteria for the design of responsibility centers? Why or why not?
4. What recommendations would you make to Mr. Judkins? To the physicians?

CASE 7–2   Piedmont University*

When Hugh Scott was inaugurated as the 12th president of Piedmont University in 1984, the university was experiencing a financial crisis. For several years enrollments had been declining and costs had been increasing. The resulting deficit had been made up by using the principal of quasi-endowment funds. (For true endowment funds, only the income could be used for operating purposes; the principal legally could not be used. Quasi-endowment funds had been accumulated out of earlier years' surpluses with the intention that only the income on these funds would be used for operating purposes; however, there was no legal prohibition on the use of the principal.) The quasi-endowment funds were nearly exhausted.

Scott immediately instituted measures to turn the financial situation around. He raised tuition, froze faculty and staff hirings, and curtailed operating costs. Although he had come from another university and was therefore viewed with some skepticism by the Piedmont faculty, Scott was a persuasive person, and the faculty and trustees generally agreed with his actions. In the year ended June 30, 1986, there was a small operating surplus.

In 1986, Scott was approached by Neil Malcolm, a Piedmont alumnus and partner of a local management consulting firm, who volunteered to examine the situation and make recommendations for permanent measures to maintain the university's financial health. Scott accepted this offer.

Malcolm worked about half time at Piedmont for the next several months and had many conversations with Scott, other administrative officers, and trustees. Early in 1987 he submitted his report. It recommended increased recruiting and fund-raising activities, but its most important and controversial recommendation was that the university be reorganized into a set of profit centers.

---

* This case was prepared by Professor Robert N. Anthony. Copyright © by Osceola Institute.

EXHIBIT 1   Rough Estimates of 1986 Impact of the Proposals ($ millions)

Profit Center	Revenue	Expenditures
Undergraduate liberal arts school	$30.0	$29.2
Graduate liberal arts school..........	5.6	11.5
Business school	15.3	12.3
Engineering school	17.0	17.3
Law school	6.7	6.5
Theological school..................	1.2	3.4
Unallocated revenue*	5.0	
Total, academic	80.8	80.2
Other		
Central administration	10.1	10.1
Athletic	2.6	2.6
Computer........................	3.4	3.4
Central maintenance	5.7	5.7
Library.........................	3.4	3.4

* Unrestricted gifts and endowment revenue, to be allocated by the president.

At that time the principal means of financial control was an annual expenditure budget submitted by the deans of each of the schools and the administrative heads of support departments. After discussion with the president and financial vice president, and usually with minor modifications, these budgets were approved. There was a general understanding that each school would live within the faculty size and salary numbers in its approved budget, but not much stress was placed on adhering to the other items.

Malcolm proposed that in the future the deans and other administrators would submit budgets covering both the revenues and the expenditures for their activities. The proposal also involved some shift in responsibilities and new procedures for crediting revenues to the profit centers that earned them and charging expenditures to the profit centers responsible for them. He made rough estimates of the resulting revenues and expenditures of each profit center using 1986 numbers; these are given in Exhibit 1.

A series of discussions about the proposal were held in the University Council, which consisted of the president, academic deans, provost, and financial vice president. Although there was support for the general idea, there was disagreement on some of the specifics, as described below.

Central Administrative Costs

Currently, no universitywide administrative costs were charged to individual schools. The proposal was that these costs would be allocated to profit centers in proportion to the relative costs of each. The graduate school deans regarded this as unfair. Many costs incurred by the administration were in fact closely related to the undergraduate school. Furthermore, they did not like the idea of being held responsible for an allocated cost that they could not control.

Gifts and Endowment

The revenue from annual gifts would be reduced by the cost of fund-raising activities. The net amount of annual gifts plus endowment income (except gifts and income from endowment designated for a specified school) would be allocated by the president, according to his decision as to the needs of each school, subject to the approval of the Board of Trustees. The deans thought this was giving the president too much authority. They did not have a specific alternative, but thought that some way of reducing the president's discretionary powers should be developed.

Athletics

Piedmont's athletic teams did not generate enough revenue to cover the cost of operating the athletic department. The proposal was to make this department self-sufficient by charging fees to students who participated in intramural sports or who used the swimming pool, tennis courts, gymnasium, and other facilities as individuals. Although there was no strong opposition, some felt that this would involve student dissatisfaction, as well as much new paperwork.

Maintenance

Each school had a maintenance department that was responsible for housekeeping in its section of the campus and for minor maintenance jobs. Sizable jobs were performed at the school's request by a central maintenance department. The proposal was that in future the central maintenance department would charge schools and other profit centers for the work they did at the actual cost of this work, including both direct and overhead costs. The dean of the business school said that this would be acceptable provided that profit centers were authorized to have maintenance work done by an outside contractor if its price was lower than that charged by the maintenance department. Malcolm explained that he had discussed this possibility with the head of maintenance, who opposed it on the grounds that outside contractors could not be held accountable for the high-quality standards that Piedmont required.

Computer

Currently, the principal mainframe computers and related equipment were located in and supervised by the engineering school. Students and faculty members could use them as they wished, subject to an informal check by people in the computer rooms on overuse. About one-quarter of the capacity of these computers was used for administrative work. A few departmental mainframe computers and hundreds of microcomputers and word processors were located throughout the university, but there was no central record of how many there were.

The proposal was that each user of the engineering school computers would be charged a fee based on usage. The fee would recover the full cost of the equipment, including overhead. Each school would be responsible for regulating the amount of cost that could be incurred by its faculty and students so that the total cost did not exceed the approved item in the school's budget. (The computers had software that easily attributed the cost to each user.) Several deans objected to this plan. They pointed out that neither students nor faculty understood the potential value of computers and that they wanted to encourage computer usage as a significant part of the educational and research experience. A charge would have the opposite effect, they maintained.

Library

The university library was the main repository of books and other material, and there were small libraries in each of the schools. The proposal was that each student and faculty member who used the university library would be charged a fee, either on an annual basis, or on some basis related to the time spent in the library or the number of books withdrawn. (The library had a secure entrance at which a guard was stationed, so a record of who used it could be obtained without too much difficulty.) There was some dissatisfaction with the amount of paperwork that such a plan would require, but it was not regarded as being as important as some of the other items.

Cross Registration

Currently, students enrolled at one school could take courses at another school without charge. The proposal was that the school at which a course was taken would be reimbursed by the school in which the student was enrolled. The amount charged would be the total semester tuition of the school at which the course was taken, divided by the number of courses that a student normally would take in a semester, with adjustments for variations in credit hours.

Questions

1. How should each of the issues described above be resolved?
2. Do you see other problems with the introduction of profit centers? If so, how would you deal with them?
3. What are the alternatives to a profit center approach?
4. Assuming that most of the issues could be resolved to your satisfaction, would you recommend that the profit center idea be adopted, rather than an alternative?

CASE 7–3   New York City Sanitation Department*

The Bureau of Motor Equipment of the New York City Sanitation Department had about 1,200 employees and an operating budget of about $38 million. It was responsible for maintaining the department's 5,000 vehicles. It operated 75 repair garages located throughout the city and one major central repair facility.

According to a report of the New York State Financial Control Board, conditions in the Bureau of Motor Equipment in 1978 were chaotic. Over half the vehicles it was responsible for servicing were out of service on the average day, resulting in huge amounts of overtime pay for the personnel assigned to the remaining vehicles. Mr. Ronald Contino was placed in charge of the bureau in late 1978. Within two years, the bureau was supplying 100 percent of the primary vehicles needed every day. Mr. Contino estimated that $16.5 million of costs had been avoided during that period.

Mr. Contino attributed the change to two main factors: (1) a change in labor/management relations, and (2) the creation of "profit centers" as a substitute for work standards in the central repair facility.

Mr. Contino set up labor/management committees, each consisting of shop supervisors, trade people, and a shop steward. Their mandate was to investigate ways to solve problems, to improve the quality of work life, and to increase productivity. A committee was formed in each of the eight principal departments, called shops, in the central repair facility. (This case focuses only on the central repair facility.) The committees met monthly with the manager of the central repair facility.

In 1978 the central repair facility operated under negotiated work standards that covered practically every job, from rebuilding an engine to fixing a generator. Committee members were concerned that if suggestions for improving productivity were made and implemented, management would subsequently adjust the work standards upward.

After a number of discussions, the following plan was adopted: Management would no longer be interested in work standards as applied to specific jobs and

---

* This case was prepared by Professor Robert N. Anthony. Copyright © by the President and Fellows of Harvard College. Harvard Business School case 9-184-039.

individuals; individual records of time spent on jobs would no longer be required. Instead, management would be interested only in whether the shop as a whole was producing at an acceptable level. The "value" of output would be measured by what it would cost to purchase the same items or services from outside vendors, and the total value of output for a period would be compared with the total cost of operating the shop.

The output values were determined by checking outside price lists or by obtaining price quotes for specific jobs. If the electric shop repaired an alternator, for example, the shop would receive a credit equal to what it would cost to buy a rebuilt alternator from a private supplier. The input costs included labor costs (salary, fringe benefits, sick pay, vacations, and jury duty), material costs, depreciation of machinery, and other overhead costs. The difference between output values and cost was called "profit," and the eight shops were therefore called profit centers.

According to Mr. Contino, the "profit center" work measurement system had a significant impact on production:

> This system provides a mechanism which measures productivity without threatening the individual worker . . . and labor has responded enthusiastically to this concept. . . . In addition, employees in individual shops can now see how well they are doing compared to the private sector (each shop has a large chart in a visible location) and a degree of competitiveness has developed, further spurring their desire to increase efficiency. The combination of the "profit motive" and the elimination of threats has worked like magic.

As evidence of progress, Mr. Contino referred to the table in Exhibit 1. He also had data showing that productivity and profits had improved with the passage of time.

As shown in Exhibit 1, all profit centers except the motor room reported a profit in 1981. The situation in the motor room illustrated the difficulty of measuring

EXHIBIT 1   Profit Center Status for 1981

Profit Center	Number of Weeks Operation from Inception to End of 1981	Annualized ($000)			
		Input	Output	Profit	Productivity Factor*
Transmission	37	$ 350	$ 716	$ 366	2.05
Unit repair	40	1,280	2,146	866	1.68
Upholstery	35	126	183	57	1.45
Radiator	36	263	438	175	1.67
Machine	23	643	1,562	919	2.43
Passenger cars	30	494	534	40	1.08
Electric	37	603	717	114	1.19
Motor room	43	1,272	822	(451)	.65
Total		$5,031	$7,117	$2,086	1.41

* Output ÷ Input

output. Initially, the shop's credit for rebuilt engines was the same as the cost to buy new motors because reliable data on the price of rebuilt motors was not available. The first reports showed that productivity was less than 1.0, meaning that the city could have purchased new engines for less than it spent rebuilding engines. As a result of decisions made by the shop's labor/management committee, the motor room subsequently doubled its productivity and appeared to be producing at a substantial "profit." However, once a data base of the outside price of rebuilt engines had been developed, all the shop's past reports were converted to the rebuilt values, the reports then showed that the shop was operating at a "loss." This led the labor/management committee to take further steps to increase productivity, including the discontinuation of unprofitable products and the transfer of personnel from support functions to line functions. By March 1982, the motor room's productivity factor hit 1.19.

The relatively low productivity in the passenger car shop had a different cause. The problem was that shop employees were required to list the actual time it took to do each job on a "job sheet," and they feared that if they consistently beat readily available industry-wide standards, sooner or later management would either require more work from individuals or would track each individual's daily performance. Thus, they tended to omit certain jobs done from their daily work sheet.

After the low productivity became apparent, meetings between the labor/management committee and the entire shop's work force were held, and it was agreed that it would no longer be necessary for employees to list the actual time it took to do a job. The February 1982 report for the shop showed the results: productivity moved from 1.05 to 1.30.

Mr. Contino summarized his impressions of the results of the program as follows:

> I have found that the process of getting labor involved in the running of an operation is not only exciting and rewarding, but also extremely worthwhile in terms of improving productivity and service quality. BME's experience belies the common notions that the government worker cannot be productive or that the output of a government operation cannot be measured. There is no simple formula for succeeding in the change from a traditional approach to the labor/management approach, and there should be no doubt that management's commitment to the process is a critical factor. But given the effort and the true desire to see it succeed, it does work. The simple proof is what has been achieved by BME in operating in this fashion.

Questions

1. What are the strengths and weaknesses of the profit measure developed for the central repair facility? Should its use be continued? Can you suggest possibilities for improving it?
2. Records on performance by individuals or on costs for individual jobs were discontinued. Do you agree with this policy?

3. Under what circumstances, if any, should work be contracted out to the vendors whose price lists were used in measuring output?
4. The 75 garages operated by the bureau did minor repairs and maintenance. Because of the specialized nature of the department's vehicles (e.g., street cleaning trucks, solid waste collection trucks), it was estimated that output values were available for only 20 to 30 percent of their work. Could some variation of the profit center idea nevertheless be applied to these garages?
5. Assume that adequate measures of value eventually can be developed for the 75 garages. Thereafter, should the work they do be charged to the responsibility centers that own the vehicles? If so, should the charge be the output value of this work, or should it be the cost?

CASE 7–4   Office of Economic Opportunity*

In September, Mr. Robert Oliver became chief of the Programs and Evaluation Division of the Office of Research, Plans, Programs and Evaluation (RPP&E) within the Office of Economic Opportunity (OEO). At that time, OEO was considering a proposal to transfer its Budget Branch from the Office of Management to Mr. Oliver's new bailiwick, P&E. A meeting was scheduled for mid-November for all involved to reach a decision.

In addition, it had been suggested that the program and evaluation functions currently joined under P&E be split into separate divisions. That proposal, however, would not be studied carefully until the Budget Branch question was resolved.

Between September and November, Mr. Oliver hoped to formulate his own recommendations concerning the transfer and to draft a suggested reorganization for P&E to accommodate the Budget Branch should the transfer be approved.

OEO

Although Mr. Oliver had just joined OEO, he had been well briefed on the special circumstances that led to the proposed transfer. He explained: "Since the early planning days, OEO has been described as a 'high-visibility' agency. It was created to eliminate the paradox of poverty in the midst of plenty. The personal interest of the president and the energy of its director helped the new agency achieve a rapid beginning. There was a sense of urgency in planning, an impatience with bureaucratic delays, and a driving desire to achieve results. A new agency had to be rapidly created, organized and staffed, and new programs launched, under intense public scrutiny.

"Since there was no fund of accumulated wisdom at the bottom, as in an established agency, OEO inevitably developed 'top-down' organizational proce-

---

* This case was prepared by Graeme Taylor, Management Analysis Center.

dures, particularly in the area of planning. To a much greater degree than in an established agency, in which ongoing programs comprise the bulk of operations and consume most of the budget, the top planners in OEO had considerable freedom in determining the magnitude and direction of OEO's effort. It was natural, therefore, that the director of RPP&E at that time, Dr. Kendall, had a major role in shaping the form and substance of OEO.

"RPP&E quickly became the principal point of contact between OEO and such external organizations as the Bureau of the Budget (BoB), other federal agencies, congressional staff, and the White House, particularly on substantive budgetary matters. Because of the newness of OEO programs, RPP&E was frequently the most logical source of ready information on OEO's developing programs and budgets. Particularly during the congressional hearings, Dr. Kendall and his staff developed an excellent rapport with the external groups most closely connected with OEO's activities. In a well-established agency, these external groups would most probably have dealt with the agency's budget office.

"Due to the background of many OEO officials, including Dr. Kendall, program planning at OEO tended to develop along PPB lines, even before the advent of PPBS. The process of defining a 'universe of need' against which goals could be set and programs evaluated appeared ideally suited to the nature of OEO programs, besides appealing to the inclination and training of Dr. Kendall and others.

"But the budget not only had to be conceived and formulated as the 'financial expression of the underlying program plan,' its format had to conform to statutory requirements monitored by BoB and Congress, and be supported by technically sound accounting and financial reporting systems. On these more technical aspects of the budget, the natural source of information was the Budget and Finance (B&F) Division within the Office of Management, where we had the accumulated expertise of an experienced budget officer and his staff. Thus, almost inevitably, outside groups had two principal sources of information on OEO's budget. Substantive questions were most often addressed to RPP&E; technical questions went to B&F. But many issues and questions could not clearly be labeled 'substantive' or 'technical'; on matters concerning such 'grey areas,' a degree of confusion tended to exist.

"This, then," Mr. Oliver concluded, "is the primary reason for the proposal to transfer the Budget Branch from B&F to RPP&E. RPP&E would become the sole source of information on all budgetary matters for external groups. In addition, some people believe that the change would also greatly simplify internal coordination during the preparation, execution, and review of the budget."

Existing Organization

Exhibit 1 is the organizational structure for the pertinent divisions within OEO at the time of Mr. Oliver's appointment, as well as changes under consideration.

As of September, RPP&E consisted of two divisions: Research and Plans, and Programs and Evaluation. The chief of each division reported to Dr. Roger Latimer, the assistant director of OEO for RRP&E, a post held until August by Dr.

EXHIBIT 1   Organizational Structure

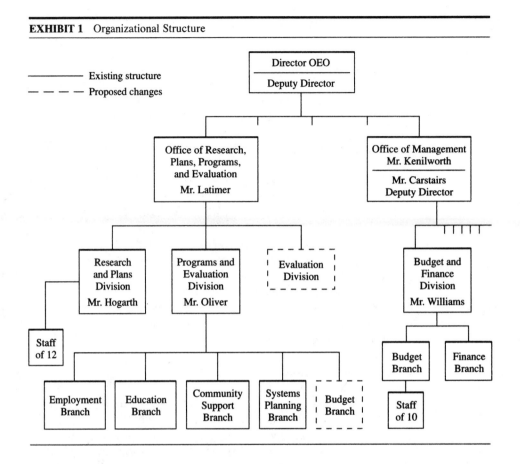

Kendall. "Dr. Latimer," Mr. Oliver explained, "is an economist whose interests lie primarily in the planning and programming of the War on Poverty, and in the necessary support functions of research and evaluation."

Mr. Hogarth, the chief of Research and Plans, supervised 12 professionals, all of whom reported directly to him with no intermediate organization—an arrangement that permitted the flexible assignments of workload Mr. Hogarth believed necessary in a dynamic organization like OEO.

When Mr. Oliver took over P&E, his division was similarly organized. However, despite the flexibility of assignments and the absence of any formal suborganization, his 11 staff members had tended to specialize in various areas. Mr. Oliver believed that he needed an intervening organizational level to reflect this division of labor, so he created four subordinate centers of responsibility, each with a branch chief reporting directly to him: Employment, Education, Community Support, and Systems Planning. Staff members were assigned to each according to their areas of specialization.

Each of the three "program" branches was concerned with a different set of OEO programs. For example, the Employment Branch was primarily interested in Manpower Programs, including the Neighborhood Youth Corps, Work Experience, and the Job Corps. Education Branch personnel were mainly involved with Head Start and Upward Bound, and the Community Support Branch was principally concerned with VISTA and the Community Action Program. Personnel in each of the branches worked closely with their counterparts in the "line" offices managing the programs.

The currently designated budget officer for the agency was Mr. Wilson Williams, the chief of the Budget and Finance Division (B&F) who reported to Mr. Wilfred Kenilworth, OEO's assistant director for Management. Both Mr. Williams and Mr. Kenilworth, and also Mr. Kenilworth's deputy, Mr. Ralph Carstairs, were experienced administrators who had been associated with OEO since its inception, and had participated in establishing and organizing the new agency.

The Budget Branch of B&F, the candidate for the proposed transfer, had 10 positions for professionals assigned to it as of September, although not all positions had been filled. The organizational entity remaining after the transfer of the Budget Branch from B&F would be redesignated the "Finance Division."

In the event that the transfer was approved, Mr. Oliver was considering assigning four of the old Budget Branch's ten professional positions to the new Budget Branch under his jurisdiction, and two of the remaining six positions to each of the three "program" branches—Employment, Education, and Community Support. Explaining this proposal, Mr. Oliver said, "This is a rather novel organizational scheme, but I am hoping that it will permit a complete integration of all the functions of program analysis and budget preparation, thus strengthening the role of my program analysts and promoting the fullest possible coordination. The more technical aspects of the budget function would be handled by my Budget Branch."

"However," Mr. Oliver concluded, "the internal reorganization of RPP&E is largely a matter for Dr. Latimer, Mr. Hogarth, and me to resolve. The main question to be discussed at the meeting is whether or not the Budget Branch should be transferred to RPP&E in the first place."

To help answer that question, a consultant had been hired to evaluate the pros and cons of the proposed transfer. The Appendix contains extracts from his report; below is his conclusion:

> In OEO, as elsewhere, the budget function is involved in so many widely different areas of work that both advantages and disadvantages can be found in its assignment to any one of several different organizational locations.
>
> However, it has been my observation over the years in government that the budget function properly belongs and can operate more effectively in the finance organization than in a general administrative or planning organization. I am quite familiar with recent developments establishing Program-Planning-Budgeting systems throughout government. I do not believe that the net advantage of locating budgeting in the finance organization is at all changed by the concepts and techniques of PPBS. Bureau of the Budget *Bulletin 66-3* establishing PPBS says on this point, "Planning-Programming-Budgeting

activities are functionally linked but it is not essential that they be located in the same office, so long as they are well-coordinated'' (par. 10c).

Budgeting is still basically grounded in finance and accounting. Its removal from the Budget and Finance Division will, in the long run, in my opinion create more problems than it will resolve. What appears to be needed in OEO is a strengthening of the Budget Branch staff where it is so that it may provide better service in meeting the budgetary needs of RPP&E and others.

In anticipating his colleagues' reactions at the November meeting, Mr. Oliver concluded:

The present director of RPP&E, Dr. Latimer, is oriented toward research and planning, but I think that he is relatively neutral on the question of the move. As for the Office of Management, my estimate is that Mr. Kenilworth and Mr. Williams are opposed to the move, while Mr. Carstairs is neutral. And, of course, some groups outside OEO would also be affected by the move. I think that certain BOB examiners would probably favor the move, and that White House and congressional staffs would likewise concur because the pattern of contacts established under Dr. Kendall's tenure at RPP&E could continue unchanged.

Questions

1. Should the Budget Branch be transferred from the Office of Management to RPP&E?
2. If so, what internal reorganization for RPP&E would you recommend?

APPENDIX
Extracts from Consultant's Report on Organizational Location of the Budget Function

Description of the Budget Function

The work of the Budget Branch staff must be closely coordinated with the work of several widely different administrative activities located in different parts of the OEO organization: long-range planning, programming and evaluation, program administration, general management control, contracting, auditing, personnel, and finance and accounting. The budget function also involves the exercise of a variety of technical skills. The staff must be thoroughly familiar with government budget and fiscal regulations, among them the OMB's Call for Estimates, which is one of the most technically complicated procedures in the federal government. The Budget Branch staff should also be thoroughly familiar with OEO accounting and financial procedures in order to structure budget estimates, allowances, and procedures in conformity with the accounting system and to comprehend the significance of monthly financial data.

Advantages of Transfer

1. *Closer integration of budgeting and programming.* Budget estimates and operating plans are essential steps in the implementation of the approved Multiyear Program and Financial Plan in the current budget year. By being part of the office responsible for the development of the plan, the Budget Branch staff should be more knowledgeable about its content and philosophy, and of contemplated revisions thereto. In addition, having the Budget and Planning/Programming staffs under the same administrative head would enable differing interpretations of long- and short-range plans to be resolved without reference to the director, his deputy, or to more than one assistant director.

   In the present PPBS cycle the annual transition from programming to budgeting involves a difficult shift of responsibilities and work from one major organizational unit in OEO to another (RPP&E or B&F). In addition, staff in the Bureau of the Budget and OEO program divisions often do not know whether to contact RPP&E or B&F staff on matters relating to both fields of responsibility. The inclusion of the budget function in RPP&E would minimize both these problems.

   Furthermore, having the budget function in the RPP&E organization would expand the working relations of that organization with OEO program staff. The programming, evaluation, and budget functions would all be enriched by the cross-fertilization thus made possible.

2. *Staff resources available to the budget function would be increased.* It has been stated that RPP&E would have more positions and possibly higher grade positions available for the budget function than are presently available to B&F for this purpose. If this statement is true and the availability of positions cannot otherwise be changed, this is an argument for the transfer since the function is presently not adequately staffed.

Disadvantages of Transfer

1. *Diffuses management control responsibilities.* The development and administration of the annual budget, including manpower ceilings, are powerful tools of management control. As such, they are more oriented to management than to the staff functions of programming and evaluation. Transfer of the budget function out of the Office of Management would weaken management control by diffusion of some control responsibilities into nonmanagement areas.

2. *Would increase problems of coordinating budgeting with finance and accounting.* Budget estimates are really "forward accounting" and, to be effective, must follow the same format as the accounting system that records the actual financial transactions. Some budget schedules must be developed jointly by the Budget Branch and accounting staff. In analyzing current performance to determine budget status the Budget Branch also must thoroughly understand and be able to interpret financial statements in order to identify significant trends at

variance with approved plans. All of these activities require not only close working relations with the accounting section but frequently also direct reference to supporting accounting documents such as trial balances and other machine runs and original vouchers. If the budget function is transferred to RPP&E, close daily working relations between Budget Branch and accounting would be made more difficult and technical differences now resolved by the chief of B&F might require the attention of the director, his deputy, or two assistant directors for resolution.

3. *Places a technical area in an organization where the head would not ordinarily be qualified to administer it.* By its very nature the RPP&E organization should always be primarily oriented toward research, long-range planning, and evaluation. There would be no assurance that a person qualified to direct such an organization also had the experience necessary to direct the budget function, aspects of which are highly technical and specialized.

4. *Probability of program and evaluation work suffering under the more immediately pressing demands of Budget Branch activities.* At least five times a year, Budget Branch staffs must do extensive preparation for hearings. During these periods, the program analysts would inevitably be overwhelmed with a mass of technical, detailed work, likely to the detriment of their primary missions.

5. *Weakening of accounting function.* In most organizations, budgeting, accounting, and related financial functions are under the common direction of a controller or other high-level finance officer. Removing the budget function from the financial area of responsibility would make it more difficult to attract a broad-gauge finance officer, as a result of which the remaining finance functions—particularly accounting—would suffer.

CASE 7–5   Lomita Hospital*

Dr. Charles Russell, Chief of Pathology at Lomita Hospital, was in the process of formulating his budget for fiscal year 1987. He had just received statistics from the Fiscal Affairs Department detailing the number of patient days and ancillary services used in the past two years and estimating the figures for FY 1987 (see Exhibit 1). One of Dr. Russell's responsibilities was to review the FY 1987 estimates and make whatever revisions he deemed appropriate. Once he and the other department heads had completed this process, the Fiscal Affairs Department could aggregate the totals and make overall hospital volume projections. The volume projections then were used to estimate hospital revenue which, in turn, determined the costs that the Fiscal Affairs Department allowed each department within the hospital. Since the beginning of intensified cost control measures by

---

* This case was prepared originally by Pamela A. Sytkowski, Ph.D., under the direction of Professor David W. Young. It subsequently was modified and updated by David W. Young. Copyright © by the President and Fellows of Harvard College. Distributed by the Pew Curriculum Center, Harvard School of Public Health.

EXHIBIT 1 Ancillary Service Statistics—Pathology and Laboratories

| Patient days | 110,579 | 111,000 | 110,500 |
| Patient visits | 134,119 | 130,000 | 126,000 |

Expense Code	Department/ Laboratory	Inpatient				Outpatient (OPD)				Totals			
		Fiscal 1985	Projected 1986	Estimated 1987	Percent +(−)	Fiscal 1985	Projected 1986	Estimated 1987	Percent +(−)	Fiscal 1985	Projected 1986	Estimated 1987	Percent +(−)
212	Cystoscopy lab.	602	612	600	(2.0)	800	726	725	—	1,402	1,338	1,325	(1.0)
213	Blood gas lab.	20,465	23,296	25,000	7.3	998	1,378	1,600	16.1	21,463	24,674	26,600	7.8
220	Chemistry lab.	214,824	205,888	206,000	0.1	104,593	70,327	70,000	(0.5)	319,417	276,215	276,000	—
221	Bacteriology lab.	69,769	70,250	72,000	2.5	31,893	32,987	33,000	0.2	101,662	103,187	105,000	1.8
222	Hematology lab.	154,312	162,234	162,000	(0.1)	86,655	84,049	85,000	1.1	240,967	246,283	247,000	0.3
228	Coagulation lab.	433	894	900	0.7	899	857	970	13.2	1,332	1,751	1,870	6.8
229	Outside lab.	14,673	16,028	17,000	6.1	10,239	9,323	9,300	(0.2)	24,912	25,351	26,000	3.7
230	Blood tests.	93,004	98,894	108,600	9.3	21,875	22,305	24,200	8.5	114,879	121,199	132,800	9.6
233	Tissue typing.	100	76	90	18.4	975	720	990	37.5	1,075	796	1,080	35.7
235	EKG lab.	18,552	18,472	18,400	(0.4)	7,493	7,376	7,575	2.7	26,045	25,848	25,975	0.5
236	Cardiac cath lab.	2,187	2,974	3,900	31.1	952	1,278	2,190	71.4	3,139	4,252	6,090	43.2
240	EEG lab.	2,140	1,292	1,450	12.2	2,585	1,096	1,200	9.5	4,725	2,388	2,650	10.8
242	Tissue typing–IHOB	110	94	90	(5.3)	1,339	826	1,340	62.2	1,499	920	1,430	55.4
245	Pathology.	4,618	4,524	4,700	3.9	3,705	3,513	3,820	8.7	8,323	8,037	8,520	6.0
246	Cytology lab.	1,907	1,830	1,860	1.6	7,752	6,290	6,506	3.4	9,659	8,120	8,366	3.0
247	Frozen sections	638	654	770	17.7	337	511	605	18.4	975	1,165	1,375	18.0
257	Vascular lab.	—	130	750	576.9	—	35	500	1,428.6	—	165	1,250	757.6
264	Blood preservation lab.	50	44	50	13.6	22	10	10	—	72	54	60	11.1

EXHIBIT 2 Review of Test Statistics

| | 1986–1979 Differences | | Est. | | | | | | | |
	Percent	Total over (under)	1986	1985	1984	1983	1982	1981	1980	1979
Surgicals	68.5	3,820	9,396	8,546	8,490	7,791	7,461	6,810	6,109	5,576
Autopsies	13.77	46	380	327	324	363	358	340	339	334
Cytology	(20.29)	(1,935)	7,600	9,358	10,579	10,457	13,676	12,426	12,097	9,535
		(1986–1980)								
Specials:										
Electron microscopy	94.33	77	130	117	119	110	82	85	53	—
Fluorescence microscopy	594.44	107	125	118	97	84	31	62	18	—

Comparison of Fiscal Years, by Quarters

	Q1	Q2	Q3	Subtotal	Q4	Total
Surgical pathology 1984–85	2,141	2,126	2,173	6,440	2,025	8,465
1985–86	2,156	2,188	2,385	6,729	2,085	8,814
Difference/% increase	15	62	212	289	60	349
Autopsies 1984–85	87	89	67	243	79	322
1985–86	92	95	98	285	101 (est.)	386
Difference/% increase	5	6	31	42	22	64
Cytology 1984–85	2,501	2,401	2,361	7,263	2,361	9,624
1985–86	2,239	1,910	2,014	6,163	2,201 (est.)	8,364
Difference/% increase	(262)	(491)	(347)	(1,100)	(160)	(1,260)
Electron microscopy 1984–85	30	37	33	100	21	121
1985–86	27	21	25	73	25 (est.)	98
Difference/% increase	(3)	(16)	(8)	(27)	4	(23)
Fluorescence microscopy 1984–85	17	26	23	66	15	81
1985–86	15	20	24	59	22 (est.)	81
Difference/% increase	(2)	(6)	1	(7)	7	—

medicare and other third parties in 1983, a tight rein had been put on departmental costs. Therefore, these statistics became highly meaningful to the Chief of Pathology as well as other service chiefs in the hospital. Each service chief had his or her own set of statistics which had to be analyzed in light of the hospital as a whole.

Dr. Russell's primary objection to the accounting statistics was that they were aggregated figures and, therefore, did not show the distribution of procedures undertaken by the various sections within his department. As a result, fluctuations within these sections were concealed. Since he felt that realistic projections of future volume could only be made on the basis of statistics for each section, he kept his own record of numbers of procedures, broken down according to section and specific laboratory process (Exhibit 2).

Dr. Russell was especially concerned with the projections of expenses insofar as they related to the cytology section of his department. There was a quite reliable rumor that the staff of the Gynecology Department would be leaving Lomita to set up their own clinic. If this should happen, it was by no means clear that the new, perhaps lesser known, staff would have the same volume of patients so as to generate the cytology work which the present staff gave to the Pathology Department.

Besides contemplating these issues and their effects on his budget proposal for the coming year, Dr. Russell was concerned about the request of one of his section heads, Dr. Pamela Gordon. She and Dr. Cornell Johnson were responsible for the major portion of the surgical service pathology done in the department, and Dr. Gordon was directly responsible for the administration of the histology lab (see Exhibit 3). Over the past few years Dr. Gordon had indicated that her lab was

EXHIBIT 3 Pathology Organization Chart

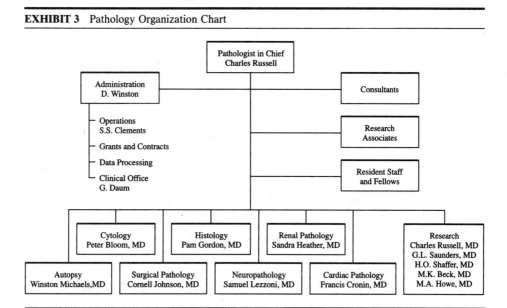

understaffed, and once again this year she had requested that a new technician be hired. She felt that the pressure put on the technicians as well as that put on herself was creating an unbearable situation in which both the quantity and quality of work in her lab were suffering. A new technician had not entered into Dr. Russell's initial calculation of expenses, and although the projected volume seemed to warrant the addition, these projections had not been available to him in January when he had made an emergency appeal for extra help. At that time, his request for an additional technician had been approved by Mr. Malcolm Gunderson, the Laboratory Administrator of the hospital, only after a detailed analysis of the pathology logs had been prepared. Dr. Russell knew that the histology lab technicians were still overworked—he *personally* was taking their overtime pay directly out of his Pathologist-in-Chief funds—yet administration had not been convinced in the past by overall hospital statistics, and it was now necessary to attempt again to justify this need. Dr. Russell, therefore, had asked Dr. Gordon and Dr. Johnson to prepare a detailed quantitative justification. Dr. Russell explained his problems in this regard:

> I ask my people to prepare a justification for all requests since I do not feel a hospital is any different from industry in this respect. In industry, expenses and budgets must routinely be justified either to the board of trustees or to the stockholders. A service chief must learn to do the same thing within the hospital setting. The problem is that my staff most often gives me emotionally charged justifications. There is never a justification in terms of numbers. Professionals must become aware of the necessity of using quantitative data in budgetary justifications. Very often I will get four or five justifications before one is finally written in terms of numbers which I can then relate to the administration. If the request cannot be put in terms of generating income or increasing productivity, the justification must be even more convincing. These statements can be in terms of loss of time, ease in handling, or better service. *But* none of these justifications can be emotional.

Background

Lomita Hospital was a 325-bed teaching hospital located in the heart of a large metropolitan area and affiliated with a local medical school. It employed some 2,000 persons and delivered well over 100,000 patient days of service a year. It admitted over 10,000 patients a year, had an average daily census of approximately 300, and an average occupancy rate of 92 percent. Its outpatient department handled over 100,000 patient visits a year. Exhibit 4 contains an organizational chart for Lomita Hospital.

The Budgetary Process

Budgeting at Lomita depended on the justification procedure which took place at various levels in the line of management. Projected expenses for the Pathology Department and other ancillary service departments were based on the projected

EXHIBIT 4 Administrative Organization Chart

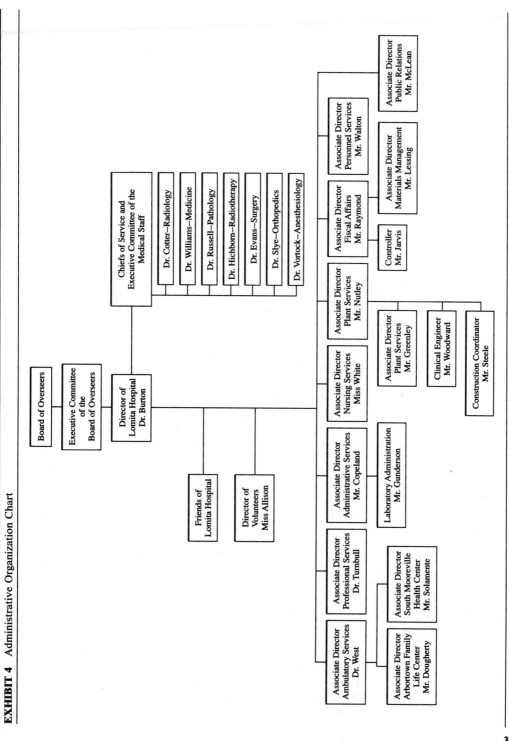

number of patient days and the related service units (e.g., number of tests) as determined by the accounting unit, using historical data as well as trend analysis and simulation modeling. These projections were open to revision by the service departments if they were able to show that their numbers were more realistic. Each department chief, his or her administrator, and, if appropriate, the Laboratory Administrator weighed the accounting unit projections against the department's own projections. When the department and the accounting unit agreed upon a projected volume, the accounting unit calculated a projected expense figure. Following this, the department and the Laboratory Administrator could contest the numbers on the basis of previous years' experience. In this respect, both past experience and the distribution of specific procedure projections were relevant since the accounting unit based its projected expense figure on a "weighted average cost" which was not always consistent with the department's evaluation of the distribution of procedures. These projections were extremely important since the department was held responsible for both projected expenses and projected volume.

Dr. Russell indicated that the projected expense figures for FY 1987 were more than simply a matter of estimating volume:

> The problem of cost accounting becomes especially acute when an increase in cost is seen as not merely due to an increase in volume but rather due to differences in efficiencies. The only increase the hospital will accept as a justifiable increase is one in terms of workload. For example, because of the advances in science, it has become easier but more time-consuming to classify lymphomas according to their types. There are many tests that can be performed before the exact classification of the lymphoma is agreed upon. To the administration or to Malcolm Gunderson, a lymph node is a lymph node. We must try to explain the difficulty in classification in terms of the number of slides which are necessary to thoroughly classify it. But when the number of slides hasn't changed, the argument becomes more and more difficult. Another problem in budgeting new expenses results when a situation has existed for such a long time that the administration feels that there is no reason to change it.

Dr. Cornell Johnson, Chief of Surgical Pathology, amplified on this:

> Arguments based on cost can cut both ways. For example, if the pressure to cut costs becomes too strong, one may undersample specimens in order to lower the cost of processing the specimens. This may result in extra hospital days for the patient because of the need to return and take another sample of the specimen, or even because of an error in diagnosis. Although I do not see this as a problem now, I believe one must bear in mind the potential hazards of undersampling as efforts are made to cut costs.

Dr. Russell also realized that any modifications he made to the budget for FY 1987 or any additional staff he wished to hire had to be justified not only through the Fiscal Affairs Department but to Mr. Gunderson as well. Mr. Gunderson reported directly to the Associate Director for Administrative Services of the hospital, and as such was required to approve every change in status and every requisition for each clinical laboratory in the hospital.

Mr. Gunderson's main concern in the budgetary process was that each department head had the resources necessary to run his or her department efficiently.

However, he also had an obligation to see that any increase in resources was justified appropriately. He commented:

> I feel that I am working with the departments, helping them to obtain budgetary approval for all of the personnel, supplies, services, and capital equipment demonstrably necessary to operate the clinical laboratory. The interest and ability in, or time available for, budget preparation varies from department to department. My role is to make sure that no major need or expense has been omitted from the budget. The budget workpapers are based on seven months actual expense extrapolated to twelve months. It is, therefore, imperative to identify any continuing expense commitments made part way through the fiscal year or to be made subsequent to the preparation of the budget projection. I also work with the departments to identify anticipated new needs for the coming fiscal year and to develop justifications for the requests. For proposed new clinical tests I assist in the development of need analysis, a revenue and expense projection, and a cost/price analysis.
>
> I try to remain unbiased and truly evaluate the necessity of new projects and equipment requested in the budget. Then I call it as I see it. If the analysis supports the request, I will recommend approval; if not, I will recommend disapproval.
>
> With respect to personnel, the Budget Worksheet provided by the Fiscal Affairs Department is not always complete (due to the time interval between the data processing run and actual budget preparation). Any positions vacant on the date the worksheet is run are automatically deleted and justification for continuing the availability of any such position, along with an indication of the length of time the position has been vacant, must be provided. The rationale for this is that if a department has been able to get along for a number of weeks without a position being filled it may be that the position is not essential and should be carefully scrutinized.
>
> One of the functions of the Laboratory Administrator in the budgetary process is to carefully review each department's personnel worksheet to be sure that: (1) all of the hours for which they have received prior authorization, and which are demonstrably necessary, are reentered on the worksheet and the required justification submitted; and (2) that all anticipated position upgradings and new position requests have been included, also along with the required justification. Assistance is provided in developing the justifications.
>
> If, by reviewing the laboratory test volume statistics, annual trends, and technical staff productivity—when possible employing the College of American Pathologists' (CAP) "Laboratory Workload Recording Method"—I conclude that a position should not be filled, I will so advise the laboratory director and the Associate Director for Administrative Services. He will either act on the recommendation or, in some circumstances, review it with the Director of the Hospital. In some instances a recommendation will be made for a complete study by the Management Engineering Department.
>
> I did not approve a request for a new technician in the Pathology Department when it was initially requested in January of 1986. This was between budgetary periods. Our fiscal year runs from October 1 to September 30. Since the position had been vacant for a long time, there was a question as to whether it was necessary. Moreover, an examination of the Fiscal Affairs Department's Expense Distribution Report revealed that the overall test volume in Pathology had declined 6 percent between calendar year 1984 and calendar year 1985. Excluding Cytology, chargeable test volume was nearly stable over the two years, having only a 1 percent increase. Useful as these data were as a very broad measure or indicator, I felt that a detailed count of the historical workload taken from the laboratory logs for at least the period covering the preceding two years (per-

haps on a sampling basis) was needed to make a valid evaluation. The logs indicate the number of blocks, slides, routine and special stains prepared for each accession number. CAP workload units could then have been applied so as to approximate total workload. I asked the Pathology Administrator to provide this summary, offering to supply clerical assistance if it was necessary.

Although this detailed summary from the logs, necessary for a workload computation, was not compiled, summary data were provided by Pathology comparing the total number of surgicals and autopsy slides prepared in 1985 with 1975 and providing a calculation of the average number of slides per "surgical" and per autopsy case. However, lacking the detailed summary, the position was disapproved again when it was requested in the budget in May. Later, in the summer of 1986, Pathology again requested approval for this position. Data taken from lab records were submitted indicating that the number of surgicals and autopsies in total had increased about 9 percent over the two-year period despite the fact that accounting data revealed almost no increase. A small part of this increase was represented by autopsies. However, a surgical represents a workload of 5.27 slides while an autopsy represents a workload of 28.6 slides. Therefore, to produce a meaningful basis of comparison, I converted both surgical and autopsies to "slides prepared" and compared the total slides prepared for fiscal 84 with fiscal 85. This showed an increase of only 3 percent which did not appear to represent a significant increase in workload.

This analysis was presented to the Pathologist-in-Chief, who then directed his senior staff physician in charge of histology to carry out a tally of the pathology logs, summarizing the total number of slides stained, categorized by the type of stain. This showed an actual annual increase of 10,032 H&E[1] stained slides over the most recent two-year period, while the number of special stains rose by 2,614 slides. Since the CAP workload allocation for these two staining procedures is six and 23 man-minutes per slide, respectively, there apparently had been an increase in histology workload of 120,314 man-minutes which represents an increase in workload in excess of one full-time equivalent. On the basis of this analysis, approval of the position was granted and a budget addendum obtained.

I also try to distinguish the uses for which money is budgeted. If I determine that the operating budget is being inflated with research-related supplies or services, research employees, or other expenses, they will be deleted from the lab budget. I look at every increase and expenditure which is above the allowable inflationary increase and make sure there is a justification, in quantitative terms whenever possible, which Fiscal Affairs and the Director will require. If an additional employee is requested in the budget, I will assist the department, to the extent necessary, in preparing a justification which should include an explanation of the medical or other necessity of the work to be performed—including quantification of demand by diagnosis for proposed new tests, a workload analysis, a revenue and expense analysis showing (when possible) that the expense will be recovered through additional revenue generated, and also, for proposed new tests, a cost-price analysis. Similar justification is often required for capital requests. However, there may be other justifications for a capital purchase; for example, the age of an instrument, poor instrument repair record and high repair expense, equipment obsolescence, unsafe equipment, improved method, all of which cannot or need not be justified with a revenue and expense analysis. Here documentation of the problem

---

[1] Hematoxylin and Eosin.

with records and other factual material greatly facilitates obtaining approval. Although quality of care is an important argument in any justification, it must be factually supported. Frequently a cost-benefit analysis is required to properly evaluate such a request. A request based on "quality of care" need without supporting justification will not hold.

Dr. Johnson, who was also an adviser to Dr. Russell on capital budget items for the Pathology Department, indicated that responding to the administration's needs was no simple matter:

> The hospital doesn't increase costs without justification, and the review process is necessary. Administration will always ask the question whether the needed item will generate revenue or increase quality of care. Therefore, a cost-benefit analysis always colors our perception of needs. This analysis takes into consideration the requirements of quality service, efficiency, and quality of care. For example, the department wished to purchase an ultraviolet microscope; it knew that it would need a highly-trained technician. The estimated cost of the technician was $20,000/year plus the cost of training. Before going to administration and requesting the microscope, the department estimated the amount of revenue that would be generated through its use. It was decided that this use justified the purchase of such a large item. It could be seen that the microscope would be used by many people both within and outside the department.

Others in the hospital pointed out the difficulties inherent in the interrelationship among the three activities of patient care, teaching, and research. Frequently, equipment as well as personnel cut across all three areas and the costs incurred for various items could not easily be separated. Third-party payors had indicated they would not reimburse hospitals for the research and teaching portions of a particular item, thereby posing a difficult dilemma for a chief attempting to cost-justify a request.

An additional concern of Dr. Russell's was the need to defend his budget not only to the Laboratory Administrator, but to several other levels in the hospital's hierarchy. He commented:

> At each level, attempts will be made to cut the budget. Whether the cut is successful or not depends on the strength of your justification and the availability of funds. The checks and balances within the Lomita system are very good. Everyone operates under the impression that people under them inflate their needs—I know I do. Sometimes needs *are* inflated; sometimes not. The problem is that at times administration can be very capricious about matters.

The Fiscal Affairs Department

The Fiscal Affairs Department of Lomita had the role of coordinating the budget preparation process. Once the data on volume and expenses had been submitted by each department, the Fiscal Affairs Department prepared a pro forma budget. This budget had both revenue and expenses which were determined in accordance with third-party reimbursement requirements and limitations. Mr. Kenneth Javits, the hospital controller, pointed out the value of the pro forma:

This is termed our "Expense Budget before Adjustment." From this, we are able to deduce what the net income will be before the need for an expense reduction. The next problem is where to look when a cut is necessary. We usually do this in terms of measuring increases in productivity. We generally can judge where the budget looks spongy and where it looks quite hard. We look for excessive increases to be tied to the volume of business. We then look at new programs and determine whether a commitment has been made, whether the program appears necessary for the standing of the hospital, or if an impact is questionable in terms of any goal or policy of the hospital. This part of the budget is somewhat subjective and is the initial stage of the budget reduction process.

If Fiscal Affairs determined that the budget contained any "soft areas," it would request the Chief of Service to cut expenses. After as many cuts as possible had been negotiated, the budget was turned over to the hospital's Director, Dr. Henry Burton. According to Mr. Javits, the Fiscal Affairs Department played a coordinating role in this process but did not impose decisions on the various departments:

Fiscal Affairs "proposes" expenses and "requests" cuts. We do not "cut." The Chiefs and Dr. Burton do that. After the budget has been negotiated as far as possible, we provide data and recommendations for the budget *we* propose to Dr. Burton. He must decide which items among the departments should be pushed and which should not. He must make an indirect evaluation of the contribution of each item on the budget to the hospital's final goal. At times, there is need for clinical judgment. In these instances, the Associate Directors, or "Administrative Physicians," as they are termed, will be called in to give judgment of clinical value. Dr. Burton will notify the Chief of Service that he has received specific budget recommendations from the budget unit which are contrary to the Chief's. The Chief is then allowed to decide whether he will push or not push for his decision over that of Fiscal Affairs. Ultimately, Henry Burton is able to negotiate through this process very well. If the Chief of Service does not feel that he is heard, he may request that the Board of Overseers intervene and make a judgment, but normally this does not occur.

The budget, as recommended by the budgeting unit and revised by Dr. Burton, then went to the Budget Finance Committee (a Board of Overseers Committee) which was composed of Dr. Burton, Mr. Colin Raymond (the Associate Director for Fiscal Affairs), and various board members. The chief of each service could address this group also if he specifically felt that his program needs were not being met.

According to one observer:

Uppermost in the minds of both Mr. Raymond and Dr. Burton is the hospital "Statement of Changes in Fund Balances" which reflects last year's costs and is the basis for the projection of the expected costs for the following year. This statement governs the budget from the beginning to the end, since administration is very concerned with the impact of the budget on the image of Lomita Hospital. Therefore, they are interested in working from the *bottom line* and fitting their costs and income in order to meet *this* objective.

The question now facing Dr. Russell was whether it would be possible for him to build an additional technician into his new budget. He did not feel, however, that this decision could be considered independently of the other decisions confronting him, namely the department's projected volume and expenses, and the volume projections for the cytology section, considering the change in the staffing of the Gynecology group. He knew that whatever changes and projections he made would have to be justified in a highly convincing manner.

Questions

1. Trace through the steps in the budgetary process at Lomita. Who are the key actors in this process and how can/do they influence the final budget?
2. What is your assessment of the way in which the request for an additional technician was handled? How, if at all, would you have changed the role that Mr. Gunderson played?
3. What are the key aspects of the management control environment at Lomita? (In answering this question, please analyze the kinds of the responsibility centers that have been established.) How does the management control environment influence the budgetary process?
4. What changes, if any, would you make to the budgetary process at Lomita? The management control environment?

Chapter 8

Programming

In Chapter 7 we described the management control environment. We turn now to a description of the management control process. The first step in this process, called *programming*, is described in this chapter and the next. In Chapters 10 through 15 we describe the other steps: budgeting, operating, measuring output, reporting, and evaluating performance.

In the first section of this chapter, we distinguish the programming process from the strategic planning and budgeting processes. We also distinguish among goals, objectives, and programs.

We then discuss the two types of programming activities. The first is the development and analysis of proposed new programs. It occurs whenever someone has a possibly worthwhile idea for doing something new, and it focuses on that idea. The second type is the formal programming process. It occurs annually, according to a prescribed timetable, and it focuses on all the organization's programs collectively.

NATURE OF PROGRAMMING

A program is a planned course of action intended to help an organization achieve its goals. It involves the commitment of a significant amount of resources, large enough to warrant the attention of senior management. Presumably, the adoption of a program will have a significant effect on the activities of the organization. Also, implementation of a new program usually requires several years, and the program's impact often is not apparent until some time after it has been initiated.

Programming and Budgeting

Many organizations do not make an explicit, formal distinction between programming and budgeting. Some organizations combine the two. Since the two activities are conceptually different, however, it is useful to think about these differences even if no formal distinction is made.

Both programming and budgeting involve planning, but the types of planning activities are quite different. Budgeting typically focuses on a single year, whereas programming focuses on activities that extend over a period of several years. A budget is, in a sense, a one-year slice of the organization's programs, although, for reasons we will discuss in Chapter 10, this is not a complete description of a budget. Also, a budget is structured in terms of responsibility centers, while many programs cut across the responsibility center structure.

The budget represents a commitment by responsibility center managers to attain some specific financial and programmatic results. A program is not such a firm commitment; rather, it is an estimate or best guess as to what will happen financially over a period of several years. The numbers for the first year of the program should be close to those of the budget. In the later years, the numbers state what is likely to happen if current policies are unchanged.

Programming and Strategic Planning

In Chapter 1, we drew a line between two management activities: strategic planning and management control. Programming, although part of management control, is close to the line dividing these two activities. While some authors use the term *long-range planning* to encompass both strategic planning and programming, we believe that it is important to distinguish between them.

In the strategic planning process, management decides on the goals of the organization and the main strategies for achieving them. Conceptually, the programming process takes these goals and strategies as givens, and seeks to identify programs that will facilitate their implementation. In practice, there is a considerable amount of overlap. For example, studies made during the programming process may indicate the desirability of changing goals or strategies. Conversely, strategic planning often includes some consideration of the programs that will be adopted to help achieve organizational goals and strategies.

An important reason for making a separation in practice between programming and strategic planning is that the programming process frequently becomes institutionalized, and this tends to put a damper on purely creative activities. Since strategic planning requires creative, innovative thinking, a separation between strategic planning and programming can help to foster this creativity.

The following comment emphasizes the importance of strategic planning. It provides a good rationale for giving adequate management attention to the process of selecting goals, which is a prerequisite to programming.

> Nonprofit institutions need strategy far more than profit-making organizations. Their goals are more complex, their sources of support are more complex, and the interaction between their support and performance is more complex. Consequently, the problem of identifying optimal policies and potential strategies must be inherently more complex. In fact, most institutions would find their planning and policy formulation much easier if they were profit-making organizations. Then at least they would have a common denominator for their objectives and strategies.

Strategy has many definitions but all definitions imply a goal, a set of constraints, and a firm plan for allocating resources. All of these factors interact and affect each other. Therefore, they must be considered simultaneously. Change one, and you may change them all.

The goal of most nonprofit institutions is clear enough. Be it a hospital, a school or a government unit, the intuitive goal is this: "Get as much as possible in the way of resources; do as much as possible with these resources."

But if the resources available are not enough to do everything, the definition of goals becomes more complicated. Which objective should be given priority? Should a school or hospital provide service to those who are willing to pay for its full cost; or should it be provided to those who can benefit most?

Any strategy requires a compromise between the choice of goals and the resources available. To this extent, every institution or organization is profit-making. It must attract resources at least equal to the requirements of its goals. . . .[1]

Goals, Objectives, and Programs

The nature of programs becomes clearer if they are distinguished from goals and objectives.

Goals. A goal is a statement of intended output in the broadest terms. It normally is not related to a specific time period. Goals ordinarily are not quantified, and hence cannot be used directly as a basis for a measurement system. A statement of goals has essentially two purposes: (1) to communicate senior management's decisions about the aims and relative priorities of the organization, and (2) to draw rough boundaries around the areas where senior management has decided the organization will operate.

Goals as Communicators of Aims and Priorities. In most organizations, senior management devotes significant effort to thinking about what the organization's goals should be and to expressing them as concretely as possible. Such an exercise greatly facilitates later steps in the management control process.

Example. The dietary goals of the United States, as recommended by the McGovern Committee, are as follows:

To avoid overweight, consume only as much energy (calories) as is expended; if overweight, decrease energy intake and increase energy expenditure.

To increase the consumption of complex carbohydrates and "naturally occurring" sugars from about 28 percent of energy intake to about 48 percent of energy intake.

To reduce the consumption of refined and processed sugars by about 45 percent to account for about 10 percent of total energy intake.

---

[1] The Boston Consulting Group, *Strategy for Institutions* (Boston, Mass., 1970). Used with permission.

To reduce overall fat consumption from approximately 40 percent to about 30 percent of energy intake.

To reduce saturated fat consumption to account for about 10 percent of total energy intake; and balance that with polyunsaturated and mono-unsaturated fats, which should account for about 10 percent of energy intake each.

To reduce cholesterol consumption to about 300 mg a day. To limit the intake of sodium by reducing the intake of salt to about 5 g a day.[2]

This is not to say that management should try to state *all* the goals of the organization. Every organization carries on some activities that are not directly or obviously related to its stated goals. Rather, management should focus on the principal goals of the organization.

Although thinking about goals and attempting to express them in words is often a useful exercise, it can become frustrating beyond a certain point, and not worth additional effort. For example, if a hospital has decided that it wants to be a general hospital, there may be no need to reduce to words an exact statement of the goals of a general hospital. Similarly, although many faculty committees have spent long hours attempting to find words that state the goals of a liberal arts college, the results sometimes are so vague that they have little operational impact. Nevertheless, particularly in large organizations, a clearly articulated set of goals is a prerequisite to effective program planning by middle-level managers.

Goals as Constraints. Goals alternatively, but less desirably, may be expressed as constraints, as indicated in the following comment:

The operational goals of a [government] organization are seldom revealed by formal mandates. Rather, each organization's operational goals emerge as a set of constraints defining acceptable performance. Central among these constraints is organizational health, defined usually in terms of bodies assigned and dollars appropriated. The set of constraints emerges from a mix of the expectations and demands of other organizations in the government, statutory authority, demands of citizens and special interest groups, and bargaining within the organization. These constraints represent a quasi-resolution of conflict—the constraints are relatively stable, so there is some degree of resolution; but the constraints are not compatible, hence it is only a quasi-resolution. Typically, the constraints are formulated as imperatives to avoid roughly specified discomforts and disasters.

For example, the behavior of each of the U.S. military services (Army, Navy, and Air Force) seems to be characterized by effective imperatives to avoid: (1) a decrease in dollars budgeted, (2) a decrease in personnel, (3) a decrease in the number of key specialists (e.g., for the Air Force, pilots), (4) reduction in the percentage of the military budget allocated to that service, (5) encroachment of other services on that service's roles and missions, and (6) inferiority to an enemy weapon of any class.[3]

---

[2] Select Committee on Nutrition and Human Needs, *Dietary Goals for the United States* (Washington, D.C.: Government Printing Office, 1977).

[3] Graham T. Allison, *Essence of Decision: Explaining the Cuban Missile Crisis* (Boston: Little, Brown, 1971), p. 82.

Objectives.   An objective is a specific result that is to be achieved within a specific time, usually one year or a few years.[4] A statement of objectives is a key element in the management control system in a nonprofit organization because an organization's effectiveness can be measured only if actual output is related to objectives.

Objectives are derived from goals, and provide the link between strategic planning and programming. In general, goals relate to strategic planning, while objectives relate to programming. Where feasible, an objective should be stated in measurable terms. Otherwise, performance toward achieving it cannot be evaluated with any precision; performance can only be judged subjectively. If a particular objective cannot be stated in measurable terms, management should consider modifying the objective so that it can be. Otherwise, senior management will have difficulty judging whether it has been achieved.

> ***Example.***   With some effort, it is often feasible to state objectives in a measurable way. The following quotation is a vague objective for third-grade instruction in geography:
>
> > To learn to use the vocabulary, tools, skills, and insights of the geographer in interpreting and understanding the earth and our relation to it.[5]
>
> This objective becomes more useful if it is recast as follows:
>
> > That 90 percent of the third-grade students attending the Booth Elementary School, by next June 30 will score between 90 and 100 percent, and the remaining 10 percent will score between 80 and 90 percent on a wide evaluative instrument and/ or process which measures their ability:
> >
> > a. To understand why we have maps and why they are important.
> > b. To understand the importance of the globe being marked with horizontal and vertical lines which represent degrees of longitude and latitude, and that the earth consists of hemispheres, continents, and oceans.[6]

Exhibit 8–1 shows a set of goals and objectives for a church. Note that although the objectives are not stated in quantitative terms, some quantitative measures are implied. Also, the statement shows the date by which each objective is to be attained.

Objectives versus Routine Activities.   Ordinary, ongoing activities that require little management judgment usually are not included in a statement of objectives. Objectives are nonroutine, and they provide a focus for program and other line managers, efforts. As such, they warrant the careful attention of senior management. Without this level of judgment, they may be simply platitudes with little managerial significance.

---

[4] Some writers use *goal* for the idea that is here described as *objective,* and vice versa. Care must be taken to determine the intended meaning from the context.

[5] From Larry Pauline, Education Systems Consultants.

[6] Ibid.

EXHIBIT 8–1 Programs and Objectives, Fairfield Baptist Church, Chicago, Illinois (excerpts)

Programs

1. To Proclaim the Gospel to All People
   Objectives:
   a. To establish a church evangelism committee by April 15.
   b. To contact every person within the city limits (for whom we can find record) who ever attended a church function, but no longer does, with a personal visit from this church by May 1.
   c. To contact every home in our immediate census tracts by May 1.
   d. To adopt a comprehensive churchwide missionary education program by September 1.

2. To Promote Worship
   Objectives:
   a. To establish a church worship committee by April 15.
   b. To implement systemic membership participation in the church worship services by May 8.
   c. To involve all institutionalized (elderly and otherwise) members in regular church worship by June 1.

* * * * *

6. Community Service
   Objectives:
   a. To establish a church community service by April 15.
   b. To define the meaning of "service" and the extent of "community" by May 8.
   c. To establish communication with all community service agencies by May 1.

Source: Contributed by Dennis W. Bakke (private correspondence).

Example. A statement of objectives from the City of Long Beach Department of Community Development reads as follows:

- Completion of the City's Community Analysis Program and development of a schedule of programs to prevent and correct blighted areas as well as predisposing and precipitating factors.
- Expansion of the federally approved low-income housing program for additional housing units.

These objectives are not stated in measurable terms, nor are the dates given by which they are supposed to be accomplished. They thus are of little help in the management control process.

Linking Goals, Objectives, and Programs

If program proposals are to be analyzed properly, they need to be considered in light of the objectives and goals they are designed to support. Exhibit 8–2 contains an example of these relationships. While the objectives are not specified as clearly as they might be, senior management nevertheless can see the relationship between each objective and its supporting programs. Having information of this sort, along with the approximate level of resources required to carry out each program's activities, allows senior management to make trade-offs among various

---

EXHIBIT 8–2   Excerpts from a Typical Narcotics Program

Program goals:
1.0 Reduce the abuse of narcotics and dangerous drugs in the United States.
1.1 Reduce the supply of illicit drugs.
    1.1.1 Reduce the amount of legally manufactured drugs available for abuse.
    1.1.2 Reduce domestic supply of illicit drugs.
    1.1.3 Reduce foreign supply of illicit drugs introduced into the United States.
1.2 Reduce demand for illegal use of drugs.
1.3 Expand understanding of the problem.
1.4 Improve program management and administrative support.
Operating program objectives (for Goal 1.1.3):
    1.1.3.1 Reduce smuggling into United States at ports and borders.
    1.1.3.2 Reduce foreign cultivation, production, and trafficking.
Operating program activities (for Objective 1.1.3.1):
    1.1.3.1.1 Conduct investigations of smuggling.
    1.1.3.1.2 Arrest smugglers and conspirators and seize smuggled drugs.
    1.1.3.1.3 Support prosecutions.
    1.1.3.1.4 Identify international border points vulnerable to smuggling and
         strengthen them.
    1.1.3.1.5 Inspect carriers, cargo, persons, baggage, and mail.
    1.1.3.1.6 Develop and operate a program of mutual exchange of intelligence.

---

program proposals. Also, program proposals related to a particular objective can be assessed in light of the existing programs designed to accomplish that objective.

PARTICIPANTS IN THE PROGRAMMING PROCESS

Five principal participants are involved in the programming process: (1) the advocate, the person who wants a proposed program (or change) adopted; (2) the analyst, the person who analyzes the merits of the proposal; (3) senior management, who decides on the adoption of the proposal; (4) resource providers, who must be sold on the merits of the proposal before they will provide funds for its execution; and (5) the controller, who operates the programming system. We shall focus primarily on the program analyst, who usually is a member of the planning staff.

Planning Staff

An organization that must make many decisions about programs usually has a staff of program analysts to facilitate this process. We refer to the unit housing the program analysts as the planning staff, but other common names are programming staff, program office, or systems analysis office. The planning staff should be close to the top of the organizational hierarchy; that is, it should report directly to either the chief executive officer (CEO) or the controller.

If the planning staff reports to the controller, there is a danger that it will become too heavily involved in the budget preparation process, which is also the controller's responsibility. The budget preparation process necessarily has a short-range focus and is often carried out under considerable time pressure. Involving the planning staff too heavily in budgeting, or allowing the ''budgeteers'' in the controller organization too much influence over the programming process, can stifle the long-range view that is essential to good programming. Thus, if the planning staff is housed in the controller organization, it should be kept separate from the part of that organization that is involved in budget preparation.

If an appropriate separation between programming and budgeting can be achieved, there may be good reasons for having the planning staff in the controller organization. This arrangement can reduce the number of staff units reporting to senior management, increase the likelihood that planners will have easy access to financial data, and possibly even out the workload in the controller organization (since the planning staff tends to be most heavily involved in programming for only a few months of the year, and can assist with other controller activities during the rest of the year).

In organizations where the idea of formal programming is relatively new, there may be friction between the planning staff and the operating organization, especially program advocates. The planning staff may consist of young, technically oriented, bright, but inexperienced persons who tend to be unaware of, or to minimize the importance of, the rules of the bureaucratic game. Such a staff may underestimate the value of experience and the importance of the pressures of day-to-day operations. Analysts also tend to use jargon that is unfamiliar to operating managers. To the operating organization, the planning staff may represent a challenge or even a threat to the established way of doing things.

To minimize the dysfunctional effect of such conflicts, senior management may build the planning staff gradually, starting with a small group and increasing it only as it develops credibility, and as resistance from operating managers subsides. Where feasible, senior management may also try to draw some members of the initial planning staff from the existing organization.

The planning staff must never forget that it is a staff, not a line, unit; that is, it does not make decisions itself. Because of its importance in linking strategic planning to programming, however, it needs to spend considerable time—much more than it usually prefers to spend—communicating with line managers. It must explain its approaches to analysis and attempt to establish good working relationships. The planning staff also must gain and maintain the firm support of senior management. Line managers must perceive that the programming effort is a permanent part of the management process, not a trial or a fad. This message can only be communicated by senior management.

Role of the Controller

Whether or not the planning staff is part of the controller organization, the controller's office, as the office responsible for all information flows, should be responsible for the flow of programming information. If there is a formal programming system, the controller's office should oversee the operation of this system; that is, it should set up procedures governing the flow of information through the system, and it should assure that these procedures are adhered to. In some agencies, the planning staff operates the programming system, but this often leads to an unnecessary duplication of data and to a lack of coordination and consistency between programming data and other data.

PROCESS FOR CONSIDERING A PROPOSED NEW PROGRAM

In some organizations, the process for considering a proposed new program is quite informal; in others, there are formal procedures. In either case, essentially six steps take place: (1) initiation, (2) screening, (3) technical analysis, (4) political analysis, (5) decision, and (6) selling.

Initiation

The idea for a new program may come from anywhere—from any level—within the organization, or it may come from people outside the organization. To encourage the internal generation of ideas, senior management needs to emphasize that new ideas are welcome, and it must provide a clear mechanism for bringing them to the attention of the planning staff.

Generally, wherever an idea originates, it becomes part of the programming process only after it has attracted the favorable attention of an influential person within the organization. In many instances this is the manager of a mission or service center, who then becomes the program advocate. The program advocate may do considerable work personally in developing the idea, or he or she may submit it in rough form to the planning staff for development. Planning staffs and members of senior management also may be program advocates.

Screening

From the many ideas that come to its attention, the planning staff selects the few that seem to be worth detailed analysis. Ideas proposed by senior management are obviously in this category, unless the planning staff can demonstrate clearly that they are unsound. Ideas proposed by resource providers generally are also worth detailed analysis since funding for the endeavor is probable.

An important criterion in the screening process is whether the proposal is consistent with the goals of the organization. In their natural desire to grow or to obtain funding for their overhead costs, some organizations pursue ideas that are unrelated to their goals.

> *Example.* Although the goal of the Port Authority of New York and New Jersey is to facilitate the movement of people and goods in metropolitan New York, it sponsored the construction of two huge office buildings in the most crowded section of Manhattan. The

purpose of the buildings was to generate additional revenue for the Port Authority. Unfortunately, movement of people to and from these buildings exacerbated the city's transportation problem.

Similarly, a university that attempts to cover its overhead costs by developing research proposals for projects outside its area of competence, or by undertaking new programmatic efforts that are only marginally related to its goals, is making a screening mistake. Such projects are quite likely to be unsuccessful and thereby not only waste scarce resources but also potentially damage the institution's credibility and its ability to raise funds in the future.

The goals of the organization need to be specific if the screening process is to be effective. Without specific goals, program advocates may spend a considerable amount of time promoting new programmatic endeavors that subsequently are rejected.

> *Example.* The stated goal of the United Nation's International Children's Emergency Fund (UNICEF) is to help children in developing nations. However, there are at least 100 such nations and well over a billion children in them, with a wide variety of needs. A narrower focus is essential if program advocates are to promote programmatic ideas designed to move the organization ahead in a consistent way.

The Program Proposal. At some time in the early stages of the process, a formal program proposal is prepared. This happens after the program advocate has "tested the water" sufficiently to be assured that reducing the proposal to writing is worthwhile.

The proposal describes *what* is to be done, but ordinarily it does not contain details on *how* it is to be done. These details are the responsibility of operating management, and typically are worked out after the proposal has been approved. The program proposal should include:

1. A description of the proposed program, and evidence that it will accomplish the organization's objectives.
2. An estimate of the resources to be devoted to the program over the next several years, divided between investment costs and operating costs. Since the principal purpose of this estimate is to show the approximate magnitude of the effort, the costs usually are "ballpark" amounts. Detailed cost analysis ordinarily is deferred until after the program has been approved in principle.
3. The benefits expected from the program over the same time period, expressed quantitatively if possible. One purpose of quantifying the benefits is to permit subsequent comparison of actual results with planned results.
4. A discussion of the risks and uncertainties associated with the program.

The purpose of a program proposal is to aid the decision maker. Because of this, the analysis it contains should be as thorough and objective as possible. A program proposal is quite different from a proposal designed to sell a project. This latter proposal is prepared after the programming decision has been made. Examples of selling proposals include most environmental and economic impact statements.

Taking Account of Inflation. The monetary amounts in a program proposal can be based either on the assumption that prices will not change or on the assumption of a specified amount of inflation. Either basis will work as long as all parties understand it and act consistently. If the program proposal assumes no inflation, changes in monetary amounts reflect purely physical magnitudes; this means that calculations are easier to make, and the program proposal is easier for readers to understand and evaluate. If estimates of inflation are incorporated, readers may have difficulty separating physical changes from changes in purchasing power.

On the other hand, inflation is a fact, and it may be unrealistic to disregard it. A program proposal that incorporates expected rates of inflation is particularly useful if there is good reason to believe that the several revenue and cost elements have different rates of inflation. An inflation assumption is especially important if high rates of inflation are likely to persist, or if there is a high rate of inflation in a particular sector of the economy related to the proposed program (e.g., health care technology).

Technical Analysis

Proposals that survive the initial screening process are analyzed by the planning staff. A technical analysis involves estimating the costs of a proposed program, attempting to quantify its benefits, and, if feasible, assessing alternative ways of carrying it out. The results of the technical analysis ordinarily are included in the program proposal. Techniques for carrying out technical analyses are discussed in Chapter 9.

Political Analysis

The final decision on a proposed program involves political considerations (such as the predisposition of a member of Congress toward a certain policy, or the desirability of favoring a certain congressional district), as well as economic, social, and organizational considerations. Usually, the decision maker takes political considerations into account separately and subsequent to his analysis of technical considerations. The analysis of the technical considerations is likely to be less lucid if it includes political considerations.

Political considerations properly are a part of some analyses, however. If, for example, several political solutions are proposed to a problem, an analysis might be able to show the lowest cost solution and the incremental cost of other solutions. The decision maker can use such an analysis as an aid in deciding whether the incremental political benefits of a higher cost solution outweigh the incremental cost.

Example. The Agricultural Stabilization and Conservation Service Peanut Program accomplishes important economic objectives with respect to the supply and price of peanuts. The economic effects of various program proposals can be estimated with a fair degree of reliability. At the same time, the particular program selected must take into account the desires of peanut growers and of legislators in peanut growing states. For political reasons, the program proposal finally selected may not be optimal in an economic sense. Therefore senior management may ask for estimates of the economic consequences of proposals that are favored for political reasons, so as to judge whether the economic sacrifice is worth the political gain.

Regardless of a proposal's technical merits, senior management may not be able to sell it to those who must provide the funds. Among the important considerations are political interference, postelection administration changes, the priorities of control agencies, and the demands of special interests.[7] Senior management frequently must make an extremely difficult judgment call as to the salability of a program before developing the proposal and formally putting it forth. Much of the relationship between the president and the Congress reflects such judgment.

> ***Example.*** The Family Assistance Plan was a proposal to guarantee each low-income family of four a minimum annual income, and consequently to do away with many separate welfare programs. It was originally proposed in 1969. Under various names, such as the negative income tax, it is still advocated by some. It has never been acceptable to the Congress, however.

Decision and Selling

Following analysis, the proposal is submitted to senior management for decision; or, more frequently, tentative proposals are discussed with senior management and then sent back for further work. This process may be repeated several times and usually involves the program advocate as well as the planning staff. The staff analysis may emphasize the technical aspects of the proposal, but the decision maker places considerable emphasis on the political aspects as well.

Most proposals are not submitted as "take-it-or-leave-it" propositions. Rather, they describe several alternative ways of accomplishing an objective, along with the merits and costs of each. Although the planning staff may not state formally a preference for one alternative, its views usually become clear in the discussion. At the same time, the program advocate ordinarily has a strong preference for one of the alternatives.

Since programs are important to the achievement of an organization's strategy, and since they normally involve substantial amounts of resources, they usually must be sold to resource providers before they can be implemented. In government organizations, resource providers are the Congress or corresponding legislative bodies at state and local levels. In other nonprofit organizations, resource providers are the governing boards of the organization, clients, third-party payers,

---

[7] See Peter W. Colby and Eileen Bonner, "Managing for Productivity Improvement: Successes and Failures," *New York Case Studies in Public Management*, no. 12 (Binghamton, N.Y.: State University of New York at Binghamton, November 1984).

or outside organizations and individuals who provide contributions and grants. This sales effort usually is carried out by senior management and the program advocate, often assisted by the planning staff.

Advocacy Proposals.   The decision maker should consider the extent to which a proposal has been prepared by, or greatly influenced by, the program advocate. An advocacy proposal is essentially a document that is designed to sell the proposal to the decision maker, and may not contain a thorough, objective analysis. Most proposals initiated by operating managers are advocacy proposals; indeed, if the manager is not an enthusiastic supporter of the proposal, there is probably something wrong with it. Proposals initiated by a top-level planning staff presumably are more neutral, but even staff-generated proposals can incorporate an element of advocacy under certain circumstances.

Ideally, the natural tension between a program advocate and the planning staff should lead to an objective presentation of the program, but this is not always the case. In general, therefore, it is safe to assume that most proposals reflect someone's advocacy.

Biases.   A proposal may be biased in one of four ways:

1. Consequences are asserted without adequate substantiation. (In a benefit/cost analysis, the proposal may first estimate the program's cost and then plug in a *benefit* number, such that the resulting benefit-cost ratio looks good.)
2. Technical matters beyond the comprehension of the decision maker are discussed at length. (This is one of several possible varieties of "snow jobs" that are attempted in proposals.)
3. Opposing views are omitted or not fully and accurately reported.
4. Costs and the time required to implement the proposal are underestimated.

Countering Biases.   Decision makers attempt to allow for these biases and to minimize them by discouraging deliberate omissions or distortions, but they usually do not have either the knowledge or the time to detect all elements of bias embedded in a proposal. In reviewing proposals, therefore, they need ways of compensating for biases. As indicated above, the planning staff provides one important resource for this purpose. Subject to the qualification that a planning staff can develop its own biases, the staff exists to help the decision maker. In many circumstances, the staff works with the initiator of the proposal to remove unwarranted assumptions, errors in estimations or calculations, and other weaknesses before the proposal is submitted to the decision maker. The staff also may list questions for the decision maker to raise with the advocate that will shed light on the real merits of the proposal.

An outside consultant may be hired to make the same type of review. If the consultant has special expertise in the topic, his or her appraisal can be useful, but it may also be unnecessary. In many situations, the internal planning staff has built up a background that permits it to do the same job more effectively. A consulting firm may be useful for another purpose: to associate its prestige either for or against a proposal, and thus either aid or hurt the proposal's chances for approval.

Adversarial Relationships.   Another approach to the advocacy proposal is to establish an adversarial relationship. For every important proposal, there is some group that opposes it, if only because it diverts resources the group would like to have for its own programs. If arrangements are made to identify an adversarial party and to provide for debate between it and the program advocate, the merits and weaknesses of the proposal often can be illuminated. The danger exists, however, that the adversaries will develop a "back-scratching" relationship. The presumed adversary may not argue forcefully against the proposal with the understanding, or at least the hope, that when the roles are reversed in connection with some other proposal, the other party will act with similar charity.

In short, for a variety of reasons, there is no such thing as a decision on an important proposal that is based entirely on rational, economic analysis. Instead, there is a continuum, with purely economic proposals at one extreme and purely social or political proposals at the other. Nevertheless, a decision must be made. Because resources are limited, not all worthwhile proposals can be accepted. The decision maker must determine which of the worthwhile projects are in the best interests of the organization. Only in the rarest of occasions does a decision maker have the luxury to proceed with all desirable projects.

Example.   In 1942, Dr. James Conant, the decision maker for the atomic bomb, was presented with five possible methods of producing fissionable material, each of which required enormous expenditures. He decided to proceed with all five. Two were abandoned a few months later, but the remaining three were actively pursued. There are few situations in which this luxury of adopting several competing alternatives is possible.[8]

FORMAL PROGRAMMING SYSTEMS

Most organizations, at some time, consider individual program proposals, but many do not have a formal programming system. In a formal system, *all* of the organization's programs are examined according to a prescribed timetable and procedure. The total of all programs is called by a variety of names. One of the most common is the *long-range plan*. We will use this term in the discussion that follows.[9]

Formal programming systems are needed primarily in large organizations, such as most government organizations whose programs are subject to considerable

---

[8] See Stephane Groveff, *Manhattan Project* (Boston: Little, Brown, 1967).

[9] The term *strategic plan* has come to be generally accepted in most business organizations instead of *long-range plan* or *program summary*. It is probably less widely used in nonprofit organizations. Regardless of the name it is given, a long-range plan is a plan for *implementing* strategies; it is not part of the process of deciding what the strategies should be.

change. Organizations with stable programs, such as hospitals, colleges, and membership organizations, normally do not need formal systems, although from time to time their managements may find it useful to construct long-range plans.

In general, a formal programming system is worthwhile if one or more of the following conditions exists:

- Several program decisions need to be made each year.
- Relationships among different parts of the organization are complicated.
- Implementation of program decisions requires a fairly long lead time.
- Complex scheduling of programs is required to bring activities and capital investments into a particular sequence.
- The number of desirable programs is quite large.

When a formal programming system exists, senior management usually is better equipped to make judgments about the overall balance and relative priorities among different programs. Furthermore, if the system is well understood by operating managers, it can help them to think in a creative and disciplined way about their problems. They tend to take a longer run point of view, relate activities more closely to objectives, and consider the impact of their activities on other responsibility centers.

The Planning, Programming, and Budgeting System

The most widely known type of formal programming system in nonprofit organizations is the Planning, Programming, and Budgeting System (PPBS). PPBS has three central ideas. First, it is a formal programming system. Second, it uses a program budget, as contrasted with a line-item budget.[10] Third, it emphasizes benefit/cost analysis.

PPBS, first discussed in the 1950s, was applied in the Department of Defense in 1962. By 1966 it had spread to other government agencies. In 1971 it was officially abandoned by the federal government. Because of its short life in the federal government, PPBS has become a pejorative term. Its basic ideas, however, live on under other labels in many federal agencies, state and municipal governments, and other nonprofit organizations. We will discuss the concepts of PPBS in greater detail in Chapter 9.

The Programming Period

The period customarily covered by a long-range plan is five years, although in organizations with large programs for capital spending, such as for highways, dams, or reclamation projects, the programming period may be as long as 20

---

[10] The difference between these will be discussed in Chapter 10.

years. In all cases, the first year is called the *budget year*, and the other years are *out years*. Rather than prepare separate numerical estimates for each year, many organizations require numerical estimates for the budget year, and for a few out years, such as Year 3 and Year 5.

> ***Example.*** The Forest Service in the Department of Agriculture has a multibillion dollar annual budget. By law, the Service is required to develop a 50-year plan. Every 10 years, an assessment is made of outputs produced (e.g., board feet of timber) and expected demand based on population projections and demand data. During the assessment process, a supply/demand model is developed for the next 50 years. From this, a plan is developed for producing the output needed to meet projected demand. This assessment plan is updated every five years, and a management program is developed based on the plan.

Steps in a Formal Programming System

The programming process starts shortly after the beginning of the organization's fiscal year and is completed just prior to the beginning of the budget preparation process. Thus, in an organization whose fiscal year starts on July 1, programming begins in July and ends in the following spring. The process typically involves the following steps:

1. Updating last year's long-range plan.
2. Deciding on assumptions and guidelines.
3. First iteration of this year's long-range plan.
4. Analysis.
5. Second iteration of the long-range plan.
6. Review and approval.

Updating Last Year's Long-Range Plan.   Usually, during the past year, decisions were made that changed the nature of an organization's programs. Management makes these sorts of decisions whenever there is a need to do so, not in response to a set timetable. These decisions might involve undertaking new programs, as described in the preceding section, or modifying certain ongoing programs. Conceptually, the implications of each of these decisions should be incorporated into the long-range plan as soon as the decision is made; otherwise, the long-range plan no longer represents the path the organization expects to follow. In particular, the long-range plan may no longer be a valid base for testing proposed new programs, which is one of its principal values. As a practical matter, however, very few organizations continuously update their long-range plan. Such updating would involve more paperwork and computer time than management judges to be worthwhile.

Since an organization begins its formal programming process early in its fiscal year, the planning staff uses the budget that has just been adopted as the starting point in updating the long-range plan. This budget may be based on assumptions that differed from those in the previous long-range plan. For example, during the year, new equipment, or even new facilities, may have become operational. The update incorporates the effect of these changes on expenses. In addition, the current budget assumptions may be used to update the out years of each program in the plan.

Deciding on Assumptions and Guidelines.   With the updated long-range plan as a starting point, senior management can examine the plan's most important assumptions. This is not done in great detail. A rough approximation is adequate as a basis for management decisions about the guidelines for the new long-range plan. The principal guidelines are assumptions on wage and salary increases (including new benefits programs that may affect expenses) and changes in the prices of other inputs.

An important guideline is the relationship of the new long-range plan to programs that were approved during the most recent year. Some organizations require the planning staff to assume that only these programs will be initiated; other organizations permit proposed, but not yet approved, programs to be incorporated in the plan, provided that they are separately identified.

It is essential for senior management to state resource and other constraints clearly, and to communicate them to line managers. Otherwise, initial updates to the plan are likely to be "wish lists" rather than realistic statements on what is feasible. In particular, managers will be reluctant to come to grips with the difficult problem of priorities; they will tend to recommend the continuation of all worthwhile programs rather than focus on those that are most important.

In some organizations, resource constraints are stated as a range; that is, managers are asked to prepare program updates for three funding levels: *(a)* the most probable level, *(b)* 5 percent (or 10 percent) above this level, and *(c)* 5 percent (or 10 percent) below this level. The purpose of this practice is to identify additional program opportunities and low-priority programs. Most organizations, that have used this practice have found it unsatisfactory, however. Busy managers tend to devote their time to preparing the most probable program; they usually give little thought to the other alternatives.

Management Meetings.   Some organizations hold a meeting where senior management and operating managers discuss the proposed guidelines and assumptions. Such a meeting (sometimes called a *summit conference* or a *retreat*) is usually held at a site distant from headquarters and lasts for several days. In addition to the formal agenda, such a meeting provides an opportunity for managers throughout the organization to get to know one another better.

First Iteration of the Long-Range Plan.   Based on the assumptions and guidelines, operating managers prepare their *first cut* of their part of the long-range plan. Much of the analytical work in this effort is done by their staffs, but the important decisions are those of the managers. Depending on their personal relationships, staffs in operating units may seek the advice of their counterparts at headquarters, and headquarters staff members may visit the operating units to make suggestions and answer questions. Among other advantages, these interactions help the operating units decide what amounts are likely to be salable at headquarters.

The proposed plan is prepared in some detail, but in much less detail than that involved in the preparation of the budget. Each operating unit sends its plan to headquarters.

Analysis.   When the individual plans are received at headquarters, they are aggregated into an overall plan, which is analyzed in depth. The planning staff asks questions such as: Are the guidelines adhered to? Are staff increases proposed by Division A really necessary? Do central service units provide adequate resources to meet the needs of mission units whose plan assumes that additional services will be provided?

This first cut at the long-range plan probably will reveal either or both of the following problems: (1) the total of individual programs exceeds the resources available, or (2) there is a lack of balance among the proposals; that is, mission units are planning to use more resources from service units than the service units can provide, or two managers are planning overlapping programs for the same objective.

Second Iteration of the Long-Range Plan.   Analysis of the first submission may lead to a revision of the programs of certain responsibility centers, or it may lead to changes in certain assumptions. The planning staff discusses these inconsistencies with program managers, attempting to resolve as many of them as a staff unit can, but remembering that senior management must make the actual decisions.

In many organizations, the second iteration focuses on the projected gap between revenues and expenditures. The City of New York, for example, must balance its budget each year (as is the case with many municipalities). The first iteration of its five-year plan always results in a gap, and the second iteration is based on a document that identifies the amount of the gap and describes possible gap-closing measures; that is, actions currently being considered to increase revenues or decrease expenditures.

Technically, the revision in the second iteration is much simpler to prepare than the original submission because it requires changes in only a few numbers. Organizationally, however, since it involves final decisions about cuts in programs, it usually is the most painful part of the process.

Final Review and Approval.   The end product of the programming process is a plan that shows revenues, expenses, capital expenditures, and, if feasible, outputs of each part of the organization for the next five years. Although the planning staff can provide clarification, data, and other assistance, and can undertake or revise the technical analysis, the decisions on these matters are made by operating managers. Discussions may take place at each level in the organization. When they have completed at one level, they are repeated at the next higher level, with the process concluding at the level of the person or group that makes final decisions on the allocation of funds. Final decisions can only be made by senior management.

SUMMARY

As the first step in the management control process, programming provides the link between strategic planning and management control. Programming accepts the goals and strategies of the organization as givens, and develops individual programs that are consistent with the strategies and are intended to help attain the goals.

There are two distinct activities that take place in programming. The first is the identification, development, and analysis of proposed new programs. Every organization has a process for doing this, although in many organizations it is implicit and unstructured: when a new idea comes along, it is evaluated, and a decision is made. If there is an explicit way of dealing with proposed new programs, it should be loosely enough structured that it fosters the flow of creative ideas.

The second process is the formal programming system. Large organizations that make several program decisions a year, and that consist of units that must work together need a formal system. In other organizations it generally is not worthwhile. The formal programming system typically focuses on updating the organization's long-range plan. Thus, the long-range plan becomes a "living" document that is revised annually, based on decisions to add, continue, or eliminate programs.

ADDITIONAL SUGGESTED READINGS

Anthony, Robert N., John Dearden, and Vijay Govindarajan, *Management Control Systems,* 7th ed. Homewood, Ill.: Richard D. Irwin, 1992.

Bryce, Herrington J. *Financial and Strategic Management for Nonprofit Organizations,* 2nd ed. (Englewood Cliffs, N.J.: Prentice Hall, 1992.

Hay, Robert D. *Strategic Management in Non-Profit Organizations.* New York: Quorum Books, 1990.

Koteen, Jack. *Strategic Management in Public and Nonprofit Organizations.* New York: Praeger Publishers, 1989.

Kotter, John P., and Paul R. Lawrence. *Mayors in Action.* New York: John Wiley & Sons, 1974.

Young, David W. *The Managerial Process in Human Service Agencies.* New York: Praeger Publishers, 1979.

CASE 8–1   Suard College*

In October 1988, the management and the Trustee Budget Committee of Suard College would meet to discuss the question of whether the college should prepare a five-year program. There was disagreement as to whether such an effort was desirable, and if so, whether the results would be worth the cost.

Background

Suard College was a coeducational, residential, four-year liberal arts college of 1,800 students, of whom 1,700 lived in dormitories on the campus. Established in 1836, the original campus was small and located near the commercial center of a city. As the city grew, the environment became increasingly unattractive. Accordingly, in 1950 a new campus was started on 120 acres of land, a mile outside the city.

By 1982, the new campus was essentially completed. There were classrooms, laboratories, a library, a chapel, a museum, dormitories and cafeterias, a student center, indoor and outdoor athletic facilities, and administrative and faculty offices. The newest dormitory, accommodating 100 students, was completed in 1981; it was financed by a 30-year $4 million bond issue. A renovation of the library was completed in 1985, at a cost of $8 million. Most of the new plant had been financed from capital fund campaigns. The college had an endowment of $60 million.

Suard was invariably included in lists of "selective" liberal arts colleges, usually defined as the top 100 or so of the 3,000 colleges and universities in the United States. As was the case with other selective colleges, its tuition was relatively high.

Generally, Suard operated with a balanced budget. Revenues had equaled or exceeded expenses in most of the past 25 years. Faculty salaries were in the top quartile of all four-year colleges, according to the survey made annually by the American Association of University Professors. The student/faculty ratio was similar to the average of competing colleges. Approximately 55 percent of the faculty had tenure, a percentage that had been fairly stable for some years. Operating statements are given in Exhibit 1.

---

* This case was prepared by Professor Robert N. Anthony. Copyright © by the President and Fellows of Harvard College. Harvard Business School case 9-184-010.

EXHIBIT 1

SUARD COLLEGE
Operating Statements
(000s)

	1985–86 Actual	1986–87 Actual	1987–88 Budget
Educational and general:			
Revenues:			
Student charges................	$16,697	$18,394	$20,473
Endowment	1,730	1,960	2,100
Gifts........................	1,089	1,230	1,450
Government grants............	737	1,041	1,023
Other (principally interest)	1,006	991	959
Total	$21,259	$23,616	$26,005
Expenditures:			
Instruction	$ 7,375	$ 7,754	$ 8,917
Research.....................	218	219	175
Academic support.............	2,024	2,144	2,292
Student services	2,984	3,268	3,427
Institutional support...........	2,923	3,123	3,625
Educational plant	2,464	2,832	3,069
Financial aid	3,388	3,712	4,402
Major renovation	—	763	537
Transfer to endowment			162
Total	$21,376	$23,815	$26,606
Net educational and general........	$ (117)	$ (199)	$ (601)
Auxiliary enterprises:			
Revenue	$ 7,320	$ 8,407	$ 9,497
Expenditures	7,146	8,158	8,846
Auxiliary, net.................	$ 174	$ 249	$ 651
Net income.....................	$ 57	$ 50	$ 50

Outlook

In the 1960s and 1970s, the total college population expanded dramatically, in part because a higher percentage of the college-age population attended college, but primarily because the baby boom after World War II resulted in a higher college age population. By 1979, total college population reached a plateau, and forecasts were that by 1983 or 1984 it would start to decrease, reaching a low in 1995 at about 75 percent of the 1983 level. In Suard's region of the United States, the percentage decline was forecast to be even greater because of the shift in population from this region to the Sun Belt of the Southwest. Although Suard's total applications had declined slightly in the past few years, the admissions office currently had no difficulty in admitting a class that was equal to those of recent years in all measurable aspects of quality.

The majority of board members and members of the administration believed that with its reputation and its new campus, Suard could maintain its enrollment at 1,800 high-quality students despite the decrease in the total population. These people believed that less selective colleges would suffer, that some of them would be forced to close (some already had closed), and that the selective colleges could maintain their enrollment by drawing students that otherwise would have gone to these colleges. Suard had increased the size and activities of its admissions and public relations offices in recent years so as to provide greater assurance of enrolling the necessary number of high-quality students. A minority thought the view of the majority was too optimistic.

Discussion of a Five-Year Plan

From time to time, most recently in 1979, committees had made studies of long-range strategy. These long-range planning committees usually had members from the faculty, administration, trustees, and the student body. Their reports had led to some changes in the curriculum, but these were generally considered to have been minor. In particular, every study concluded that the emphasis on the liberal arts should continue, and that graduate programs or vocationally oriented programs (e.g., nursing) should not be instituted. Long-range financial projections had been made from time to time, in some cases in connection with the long-range studies and in other cases as a separate exercise.

In the May 1988 meeting of the Budget Committee, a trustee suggested that the time had come to make a five-year program and financial plan, to consider its implications thoroughly, and to revise it annually thereafter. Time did not permit discussion of this proposal then, but it was decided to discuss it at the next meeting, in October 1988. In informal discussions subsequent to the May meeting, it became clear that the idea was controversial.

A programming effort obviously would be concerned with the decline in student-age population, and might develop strategies for dealing with a possible decline in Suard enrollment. Some committee members thought that the fact that such strategies were being considered would alarm the faculty unnecessarily and therefore would hurt morale. If the plan assumed faculty reductions in specified departments, the members of those departments would be upset; if it did not specifically describe departmental manning, everyone would wonder how a reduction would affect them.

Others pointed out that previous five-year financial plans had not amounted to much. These plans were primarily mechanical extrapolations of current revenues and expenditures, with assumptions as to tuition, salary, and other cost increases as a consequence of inflation. It was pointed out that tuition and other charges for a given year could not be estimated much in advance because Suard's tuition had to remain competitive with other colleges, and the decisions of these colleges were not typically made until January. Although the rate of inflation in 1988 was relatively low, no one knew what future inflation rates would be. Thus, although the annual budget was discussed thoroughly, little attention had been given to longer projections.

As an alternative to long-range planning, some believed that the college should adopt the policy of meeting a financial stringency when the need arose. Specifically, if opening enrollment in a given year was below the budgeted amount, the college would reduce discretionary expenses by about $400,000 and absorb the remaining deficit in that year from the operating surplus of some $800,000 that had been accumulated in prior years. It would immediately plan the expenditure reductions necessary to balance the budget in the following year. An enrollment decline would affect initially only the first-year class; thus, if the entering class was, say, 8 percent below budget, total revenues should decrease by only one-fourth of this, or 2 percent below budget.

Those favoring a formal programming effort pointed out that the library renovation and other factors might have long-range expenditure implications that needed to be explicitly considered. Suard now had a software program that quickly, and at relatively low cost, would provide five-year financial projections under any specified set of assumptions.

Questions

1. Assuming that the college decided to prepare a five-year program and financial plan, how should the assumptions incorporated in it be arrived at? Should the plan be a single "best estimate," or should several alternatives be studied?
2. Should the college prepare a formal five-year program and financial plan?

CASE 8–2   Wright State University*

Dr. Michael J. Cusack, director of athletics at Wright State University, described a way of evaluating certain athletics programs in a paper presented at a conference on college sports sponsored by Skidmore College. Dr. Cusack's men's basketball team won the national championship in Division II of the National College Athletic Association in 1982–83. He stated that his method would be useful as Wright State debated whether or not to move to N.C.A.A.'s Division I.

The paper is summarized in the following paragraphs. Dr. Cusack used as an illustration both Wright State University and Mercyhurst College (where Dr. Cusack was formerly athletic director), but in the interest of brevity, only the data for Wright State University are given here.

---

* This case was prepared by Professor Robert N. Anthony. Copyright © by the President and Fellows of Harvard College. Harvard Business School case 9-184-040.

The current state of the economy is causing most institutions to scrutinize their budgets very closely. The demographics for the remainder of the 80s and into the 90s are very disturbing. They are especially disturbing, however, within education. As federal aid reductions are coupled with a diminishing student pool, budgetary cuts in the form of retrenchment and program elimination will become more and more likely at various institutions.

In many colleges, and universities, cost effective programs could be the difference between the existence and extinction of the institution. In situations where programs and expenditures are examined and cuts are indicated, the first place that often comes to mind is the athletic program. Cuts made within the athletic program are often made in the form of elimination of one or more sports. The activities eliminated typically fall in the category of "nonrevenue" or so-called minor sports. Those making the decisions point to the savings generated by the elimination of the operating budget and the scholarship allotment for those particular sports. They will often combine these budgetary savings with the position that the programs serve a limited number of students and generate little or no fan support or public interest.

If the examination of athletic programs is limited to that level, it might be a logical conclusion to eliminate particular programs. It should be noted, however, that there are several factors which might be worthy of consideration before such a conclusion is drawn.

Among these factors are a determination as to whether the nonrevenue sports are, in fact, generating no revenue. In addition, consideration should be given to the benefits the Athletic Department provides to the Admissions Office through the recruiting efforts of the athletic staff.

Furthermore, the retention rates of student athletes should be examined to determine the difference between their rates and those of students who do not participate in intercollegiate athletics.

Finally, the publicity value of each program should be computed and considered in determining its financial impact on the institution.

Each of these areas is discussed below. The figures presented are those of Wright State University, which is a state-supported institution of 12,000 students in Dayton, Ohio. The data are derived from a study of the sports of baseball, soccer, softball, men's and women's swimming, men's tennis, volleyball, and wrestling. These sports are used because they are considered nonrevenue generating, receive limited scholarship aid, and have been eliminated at several institutions.

Revenue Generation

Intercollegiate athletic programs conducted on a partial or nonscholarship basis will provide revenue to the institution through the amount paid by each student-athlete above the athletic or other institutional aid provided. This amount will vary according to the cost of attendance, the amount of athletic and other institutional aid provided, and the amount of federal and state aid received by the student-athletes.

With the help of the Financial Aid Office, the maximum amount of aid to which each student is entitled can be generated. Coaches should be instructed that every student-athlete recruited must complete the financial aid forms before they will receive any institutional aid.

EXHIBIT 1 Total Revenue Generated by Nonrevenue Sports

Sport	Revenue Generated	Retention Benefits	Publicity Value	Total Financial Benefits
Baseball....................	+$12,341	$ 775	$ 6,685	+$19,801
Soccer.....................	+ 6,607	− 100	4,315	+ 10,822
Softball	+ 23,105	+ 300	585	+ 23,990
Swimming (men)	− 7,488	− 200	454	− 7,234
Swimming (women)	− 21,684	+ 150	370	− 21,164
Tennis	+ 11,815	+ 100	370	+ 12,285
Volleyball	− 16,526	+ 175	745	− 15,606
Wrestling..................	+ 1,500	+ 300	396	+ 2,196
	$ 9,670	$1,500	$13,920	$25,090

Regardless of the amount of athletically related aid a coach anticipates providing a particular individual, the completion of the appropriate forms should be required, since every dollar received from outside sources is that much more available to the institution.

We found that the tuition generated in the sports under discussion totaled an amount substantially greater than the costs involved in conducting the programs. In baseball, for example, the average revenue received per student-athlete was $1,415, there were 37 athletes, and the total revenue generated was $52,361. The total budget for baseball was $40,020, so the net revenue generated was $12,341. The results of similar calculations for the other sports are shown on the first column of Exhibit 1.

Admissions Benefits

Coaches are, by virtue of their recruiting efforts, an arm of the admissions office. The recruitment of student-athletes, who will be a positive factor on the campus, is as essential to their programs as it is for the admissions department. Furthermore, the contacts usually enjoyed by coaches and the specificity of their needs provide them with an excellent position in generating students for an institution.

In some cases it is possible to determine the unit cost incurred by the Admissions Office in the recruitment of students. When this is possible, the actual savings generated by the coaches who recruit student-athletes and add to the institutional population without the Admissions Office's involvement can be computed.

Due to the nature of the student body and the various populations the Admissions Office works with, the development of a recruiting figure was not possible at Wright State University. At Mercyhurst College we found that the average cost of recruiting a student by the Admissions Office was $500. In a survey conducted during the 1980–81 academic year we found that 10 student-athletes were recruited by the athletic staff in the nonrevenue sports. At $500 per student, this would represent a savings to the institution of $5,000.

Retention Benefits

It is generally accepted that students who are involved in an activity at an institution are more likely to remain at that institution. Furthermore, Admissions Offices are constantly attempting to find a match between what their institution has to offer, and the needs and interests of the prospective students.

An athletic program provides the opportunity for students to become involved in an activity, and the recruitment efforts of the coaching staff are predicated upon matching the needs of the athletic program with the abilities of the prospective student-athletes.

It would seem, therefore, that members of the athletic teams are more likely to remain at the institution than the nonathletic students. If there are, in fact, a greater proportion of student-athletes remaining at the institution than other students, then the athletic program is generating revenue to that institution. The retention rate in 1980–81 for the whole freshman class was 65 percent; for the student-athlete population, it was 75 percent.

An indication of the financial benefit generated by these retention rates can be determined by multiplying the cost of attendance for the fall term by the number of student-athletes who would have attrited if their rates were at the same level as the general student population. The cost of enrollment for the fall term was $500, the average cost of tuition and fees. The number of student-athletes who would have had to attrit in order to reach the general student level was 3, and the financial impact of the higher retention rates was, therefore, $1,500.

Publicity Value

The sports pages of every newspaper in the country provide college results in almost every sport each day. Institutions have long pointed to the publicity value of an athletic program, and have generally pointed to the high visibility sports as an example.

All sports, however, generate some publicity for which an institution would otherwise have to pay. By simply measuring the amount of space generated in the sports pages for each activity, and multiplying the figure by the cost of advertising space, the value of each sport can be computed. For example, baseball generated 538 inches of space during the year, with a value of $6,685.

It should be noted that no attempt was made to evaluate the space generated in the student-athletes' home newspapers, releases which are generated by other institutions, or any other form of media.

Utilizing the figures generated in each of the categories discussed, it is possible to objectively assess the financial impact of "nonrevenue" sports. The formula which can be utilized to compute the collective impact of the program or of each individual sport is as follows: Tuition generated + Admissions savings + Retention benefits + Publicity value. The benefits that Wright State derived from nonrevenue sports during the 1980–81 academic year totaled $25,090, not counting the value of admissions savings. (The benefits for Mercyhurst College, calculated in the same manner, were $85,714 for revenue generated, $5,000 for admissions savings, $13,200 for retention benefits, and $1,742.06 for publicity value, a total of $105,656.06.)

Reduced Use of Retention and Counseling Services

Counseling services will typically attempt to help the student connect with some part of the institution, with the expectation that it will help the student attain a more positive feeling about his or her role at that institution. The student-athlete already has a connection with the institution through his or her team. He or she also has a relationship with a coach which often transcends the field of competition. Often this relationship approaches that of a parent figure and/or counselor.

We have found that student-athletes utilize the college's counseling and retention service significantly less than the general student population. We feel that this reduced usage is due to the relationship within the teams and with the coaches. We have not attempted to quantify this position, but the reduced usage of the services certainly frees the counselors to spend more time with other students.

Unit of Delivery Cost

It is essential that an institution provide activities for their students throughout the school year. The Student Services area of an institution is budgeted to provide entertainment and activities which will help enhance the quality of life of the student body. Most of those activities require a financial outlay by the institution. Dances, concerts, lectures, and the like cost the Student Services something to stage, and are cost efficient in terms of the number of students who attend those activities. The unit of delivery cost can be determined by dividing the cost of the activity by the number of students who attend that activity. For example, a dance which cost $500 to run, and is attended by 500 students would have a unit of delivery cost of $1.

Athletic events are generally paid for through the athletic budget, and typically are free to the students. There would, therefore, be no unit of delivery cost to the Student Services budget, or any budget of the institution with the exception of the Athletic Department. Since we have already shown that the programs examined more than offset the budgets provided, there would also be no unit of delivery cost in this area.

While the actual financial value of these programs in unit of delivery costs is not easily computed, the value to the Admissions Office in recruiting and to the institution's student body in entertainment and spirit is obviously substantial.

In examining an individual activity or an entire program, the number of students attending those events, and the cost to the institution of staging them should be considered. It is generally accepted that events usually cost the institution something to stage, and that those costs are well spent if they improve the atmosphere on the campus. If, however, those activities are free of cost to the institution, and are in fact proving to be financially rewarding, then those programs would appear to be very valuable assets to the institution.

Other Uses

Beyond justifying a program's existence, the use of the formula presented, and an examination of the additional categories discussed has several potential values to an institution.

It can serve to identify areas within a program which are in need of improvement or which show particular strength. Coaches could be given a printout which would show

how they have performed in each area, and where they might consider working toward improvement.

It could serve as a major component of a planning procedure. Activities can be evaluated on their revenue-generating potential, admissions benefits, and the other areas discussed. The results of such studies could be used in making decisions as to initiating new programs, as well as eliminating or curtailing existing ones.

An analysis of full scholarship programs can also be conducted using the formula to determine the true cost of those programs. Traditionally, full scholarship programs have been justified by their revenue production through gate receipts and media contracts. It might turn out that scholarship programs that do not generate this type of revenue actually do offset much of their cost in other areas.

Finally, the method of study outlined and the formula developed can serve as a basis for studying other areas within an institution. As financial accountability becomes more necessary, all programs will come under close scrutiny. Every program has variables which are important to their existence, and many of them can be quantified and their total value to the institution established. Conversely, where programs show weakness in various areas, administrators would have a basis for determining means of improving them or deciding to eliminate them.

At the Skidmore conference Mr. Robert Atwell, vice president of the American Council on Education, disagreed with this approach. As reported in the *Chronicle of Higher Education* (April 20, 1983), he said:

> I don't buy this at all. First of all, the formula assumes that it doesn't cost anything to educate these athletes once you bring them to the institution. It costs money to do that. That's not profit.
>
> Also, the formula assumes that athletes are irreplaceable as students. The assumption is that an institution couldn't drop the football program, for example, and begin to attract non-athletes instead of football players. The non-athletes would pay full tuition, room, board, and other costs, but wouldn't have to be supplied with an expensive football program.

Questions

1. What is your assessment of the general approach advocated by Dr. Cusack?
2. Is there a feasible alternative approach?

CASE 8–3   South Brookfield Hospital*

Megan Charles looked across her desk at the pile of reports lying on the table. As Director of Systems Support at South Brookfield Hospital (SBH), she had overseen the task of merging patient diagnostic information with corresponding billing

---

* This case was prepared by Susan Koch under the direction of Professor Nancy M. Kane, Harvard School of Public Health. Copyright © 1983 by the Massachusetts Health Data Consortium. Distributed by the Pew Curriculum Center, Harvard School of Public Health.

data. This information had then been classified into Diagnosis-Related Groups (DRGs), allowing the hospital to see for the first time the charges associated with each type of case it treated.

The original impetus for this effort had been a 1981 State Rate Setting Commission (RSC) regulation requiring every hospital to provide case mix information merged with billing information by 1983. The project had been given additional impetus by the Tax Equity and Fiscal Responsibility Act of 1982, which mandated certain changes in the way in which hospitals were reimbursed for their medicare patients. The most significant of these changes was the use by medicare of 467 DRGs as the bases of payments to hospitals. Within the hospital, managers hoped that the reports generated by the project would provide a wealth of information useful for internal planning and management purposes.

Ms. Charles was not so sure now of the planning and management utility of the data. In spite of her best efforts to publicize the reports, which included teaching other administrators what type of information was contained in them and how it might be used, the reports were still sitting in her office, untouched and gathering dust. The stack of reports was seven inches thick and weighed about 15 pounds.

She had two sets of reports at this point. One set, from a statewide data consortium, was based on case mix information only and provided 1980 information on the number, distribution, and average lengths of stay (ALOS) for each DRG; these figures were provided for SBH as well as its "group,"[1] and included statewide averages. The second set, from another software vendor, included both case mix and financial information from 1980 in a detailed series of reports on SBH only.

As Ms. Charles wondered again how she could get people interested in using the thick stack of reports, an idea occurred to her. The Pediatrics Department had recently been pinpointed as an area of general management concern to the hospital. Pediatric admissions had declined over the past few years, reflecting a decline in the pediatric population of the community. Lengths of stay (LOS), on the other hand, had increased over the same period. Unless the types of cases treated in the hospital had changed in some way to account for the longer LOS, it might be that pediatric cases were being overtreated, a situation with potentially negative financial implications to the hospital.

The likelihood of financial penalties was increased with the recent passage of reimbursement legislation by the state. Under the new reimbursement system, by FY 1985 all payors—medicare, medicaid, Blue Cross and charge payors—would pay for hospital services based on each payor's percentage of total charges, applied to a universally recognized cost base. While the hospital would be allowed to keep all "savings" generated if actual costs were less than the cost base allowed, they also were not allowed to pass on to third parties any shortfall in revenues occurring if actual costs were above the cost base allowed. Furthermore, the formula which determined increments to the 1981 cost base year was expected to

---

[1] Based on hospitals that are similar with respect to bed size, location, teaching status, and other measurable characteristics believed to influence costs.

penalize hospitals with lengthening LOS as well as hospitals with rapidly growing use of inpatient ancillary services. Finally, certain payors—especially medicaid—were permitted large discounts off their share of the cost base, discounts which would not be recoverable from other payors.

Perhaps these case mix reports could be used to provide supporting data on the nature and underlying causes of the long pediatric lengths of stay. In using these reports to provide such an analysis, Ms. Charles also hoped to publicize their worth to the other administrators.

Background—RSC Regulation

In January 1981 the State Rate Setting Commission had required each hospital to submit patient demographic, diagnostic, and billing data in a specified format with unique physician identifiers. The data were to be sent to the RSC starting on March 31, 1982, and quarterly thereafter.

For the year preceding this submission, 12 hospitals volunteered to participate in a pilot program known as the Integrated Data Demonstration (IDD) project. The IDD project was sponsored jointly by the RSC, Blue Cross, and the statewide health data consortium; it was funded by a demonstration grant from the Health Care Financing Administration (HCFA). The project sponsors hoped that the experiences of the 12 pilot hospitals would be useful to the remaining 100 or more hospitals in the state as they set about merging their patient discharge and billing information.

South Brookfield, a 260-bed acute care general community hospital in a small suburban town, was one of the 12 pilot hospitals. It chose to participate in the pilot project in order to gain a better understanding of the RSC regulations, and to learn more about itself. Specifically, it hoped that the data would give it the capability to: (1) define its product mix and associated costs, (2) maximize reimbursement, (3) improve its competitive position, and (4) assist it in planning and marketing of new services and equipment.

Overview of IDD Project

Within the hospital, the IDD project was overseen by a committee made up of representatives from a cross-section of hospital departments. Included on the committee were the controller, the manager of patient accounts, the data processing manager, the medical records director, and the vice president of Ancillary Services. An outside consultant was hired to work with the committee on the more technical, data processing aspects of the project.

In March 1982, Ms. Charles was hired to direct the committee. With a background in both health care information systems and data processing, Ms. Charles had the skills and expertise which had become necessary to the hospital with this and related "case mix" projects. The committee met once every two weeks to discuss problems as they arose and to decide upon specific solutions.

The major difficulty encountered in merging patient discharge information with the corresponding billing information was organizational in nature. Traditionally, the billing and medical records departments in a hospital had little to do with one another. This led to the development of two completely separate flows of information: the medical record with its assigned number, and the billing record with a different assigned number. In order to merge these two data flows, a file had to be created to match each patient's medical record number and billing number. As Ms. Charles explained, this was not an easy task:

> There are basically two ways in which patient diagnostic information can be merged with billing information. You can maintain the two separate information systems (i.e., medical records and billing) and put them together at the end after each has been completed (i.e., after the patient has been discharged). Or you can use a shared system in which patient diagnostic and billing information is collected together in an integrated system while the patient is still in the hospital. For the IDD project we used the first approach, but the hospital now has an integrated system in place. The advantage of the integrated system is that it enables you to monitor what is going on in the hospital as it happens.
>
> In developing this merged file, we encountered a variety of problems with data definitions, consistency, and precision. But the committee put a great deal of time and effort into solving these problems, and when the first merged tape was run it was more than 99% successful, there being only 80 mismatched records out of approximately 9,000. I therefore felt confident about the internal consistency of the data across the billing and medical record information.

The committee identified the following 11 different reports that it thought would be helpful in the planning and management effort:

1. Case Mix Profile.
2. Outlier Control Report.
3. DRG Cost Distribution by Cost Center.
4. LOS Analysis by Admission Status.
5. Average and Total LOS by DRG and Payor Source.
6. Detailed Chart List of Cases Exceeding High Value.
7. Analysis of Cases by Physicians.
8. Analysis of Change in Case Mix Over Time.
9. Year to Year Comparison Report.
10. Payor Per Diem Analysis by DRG.
11. Analysis of Average and Total Costs by DRG and Payor.

Pediatric Service

As Ms. Charles thought about the ways in which the reports could be useful for investigating the questions raised in the pediatric service, she considered that a first step might be to break down the information in some systematic way. One option would be to define categories corresponding to areas of administrative responsibility. She thought she would start by considering the informational needs of the vice presidents in charge of Planning, Ancillary Services, and Finance.

After preliminary discussions with each of these administrators, she felt that the needs of each illustrated distinctive ways in which the data could be used. The planning department needed information on the present and future need for services provided at SBH, as well as for services provided at competing hospitals. For the VP of Ancillary Services, information describing variations in physician practice patterns seemed very important. The VP of Finance was concerned with his ability to compare the relative costs, revenues, payor mix, and lengths of stay across diagnostic categories. Each of these areas is discussed in greater detail below.

Planning Department Needs

The Planning Director, Mr. Harold James, explained that he wanted to know whether or not he could expect the need for pediatric beds to fall over the next three to five years. He had recently met with the Strategic Planning Committee of the Board where he was asked to develop a service-by-service bed need projec-

EXHIBIT 1 South Brookfield Pediatrics (Ages 0–17), 1978–1980

ICDA-8 DRGs	Description	1978		1980	
		Cases	ALOS	Cases	ALOS
112	Inflam. of middle ear..................	8	3.1	10	3.30
114	Disease of ear with surgery............	10	1.2	17	1.20
146	Circ. system	41	3.6	21	3.80
159	T & A..............................	150	1.4	110	1.50
160	URI/influenza	42	3.4	37	3.30
165	Simple pneumonia	110	5.4	107	5.60
169	Bronchitis	108	4.1	111	4.20
172	Asthma............................	33	4.1	53	4.20
197	Hernia	26	1.7	33	1.80
206	Intestine w/o surgery	75	4.0	101	4.40
322	Nerv. resp. circ. no surg.............. no 2nd dx indications	104	3.1	68	3.50
327	Indications-gast. intest................ Urinary w/o Surg. w/o major dx	78	2.2	52	3.20
341	Fx forearm, hand, lower foot,.......... closed reduction	25	3.0	35	2.80
354	Int. Inj. skull w/o surg. .... w/o Dx 2	65	1.5	37	1.70
355	Int. Inj. skull w/o surg. .... w/Major Dx 2	50	2.5	33	2.60
		925	2.91*	825	3.35*

* Not weighted averages.

tion. Specifically, the Committee hoped to find some beds "freed up" in the plans so that they might be converted into new services for the community. Mr. James asked Ms. Charles if any of her reports could help him.

Ms. Charles went back to her office and pulled figures from her stacks of reports for a few hours. By the end of the afternoon she had prepared Exhibits 1 and 2 which she hoped might help Mr. James. Exhibit 1 showed the change in distribution and LOS of the top 15 DRGs treated on the pediatric service which represented almost 90% of the total pediatric caseload in 1980.

Exhibit 2 showed the distribution of pediatric cases in 1980 using the new (ICD-9-CM) DRGs which specifically break out the pediatric age group (Ages 0–17) for a number of diagnoses. Although some pediatric cases fell into other general categories (such as fractures and circulatory diseases) which were not broken down by these age groups, the bulk of the hospital's cases were covered. The new DRGs were particularly useful because comparable frequency and LOS statistics for the state and for SBH's "group" of similar hospitals were available based on this system.

Ms. Charles thought Mr. James might find a way to incorporate this information into his pediatric bed need projections. She knew that the service was currently

EXHIBIT 2 Pediatric Service*—Comparative LOS and Frequency†—SBH, Rate Setting Group, and State, 1980

| | | | SBH | | RSC Group | | State | |
| | ICD-9-CM (All Ages 0–17) | | % of Total | | | | | |
DRG	Description	Cases	Cases	ALOS	%	ALOS	%	ALOS
026	Seizure, headache...............	19	.2	3.5	.2	3.1	.3	3.3
033	Concussion....................	45	.6	1.8	.3	1.6	.3	1.5
060	T & A........................	92	1.2	1.4	.8	1.6	.6	1.7
070	Otitis Media, URI..............	32	.4	4.3	.4	3.5	.4	3.5
074	Other NET....................	7	.1	2.1	<.1	1.9	.1	2.2
081	Resp. infections...............	1	<.1	1	<.1	2.8	<.1	8.4
091	Simple pneumonia	99	1.2	5.6	.5	4.7	.5	4.7
098	Bronchitis asthma..............	141	1.7	4.2	.8	3.9	.8	3.7
163	Hernia procedures	33	.4	1.9	.4	1.8	.3	2.0
184	Esoph, gastro, misc. diges.	100	1.2	3.7	1.1	3.2	.9	3.3
190	Other digestive	19	.2	2.8	.1	2.2	.1	2.2
298	Nutritional/metabolic...........	1	<.1	10.0	.1	5.6	.1	6.7
322	Kidney, urinary inf.	7	.1	7.0	.1	4.1	.1	4.2
327	Kidney/urin. signs & symptoms	2	<.1	3.0	<.1	3.3	<.1	2.7
343	Circumcision	2	<.1	1.0	<.1	1.5	<.1	1.5
448	Allergic Rx...................	1	<.1	4.0	<.1	3.2	<.1	2.5
451	Toxic effect-drugs‡	7	.1	1.9	.2	2.4	.2	2.6
		608§						
	ALOS			4.13				3.83

* Based on Puter Associates' definition (all DRGs with 0-17 criteria).
† Frequency % is % of all hospital discharges, not just pediatrics.
‡ Five outliers omitted; ALOS = 49 days
§ Total 1980 Ped. Disch. = 883 (difference due to cases falling into DRGs without the 0–17 age classification).

operating at about 80% capacity with 10 licensed beds. She planned to talk with him about what she found, as well as to discover what other data he would like to have for making his projections.

Ancillary Services Department Needs

"My major concern is with how physician practice patterns affect operating costs," stated Alice Ward, the VP of Ancillary Services and one of the most enthusiastic supporters of the DRG system at the hospital. "The important parameters here are LOS and ancillary usage. Eventually we would like to develop standards of expected resource consumption per DRG so that when a physician admits a patient with a certain diagnosis, we know the expected LOS for that patient and the types and numbers of ancillary services that should be ordered. These standards could be developed with help and input from the physicians. Any time the practice varied from the expected, a red flag would be raised and the variance investigated. This type of immediate feedback system gives us some hope of controlling costs. Right now we can only question a physician's practice after the fact and it is almost impossible to affect behavior retrospectively like that."

She continued, "My problem is that I don't have time to pore through all the data we have here. I need to be able to glance at exception reports and know who

---

EXHIBIT 3 Average Ancillary Costs per DRG

Ancillary Cost Centers	DRG 165 (Pneumonia) Average Cost	DRG 169 (Bronchitis) Average Cost	DRG 159 (T & A) Average Cost
ORR/RR			410
Delivery			
X Ray—diagnosis	45	31	16
X Ray—therapy			
Lab	70	53	66
EEG			
Physical therapy			
Inhalation therapy	207	122	1
Blood			
Pharmacy	75	41	5
Medical supplies	5	5	17
Dialysis			
Cardiac	1		
Kidney			
Skin			
Ancillary—other	9	10	
Total ancillary	412	262	515
ALOS	5.6	4.2	1.5

is keeping patients too long, or using too many ancillaries. The important thing here is exceptions. However, the fact there is an exception is not the final answer and should not be used in a prescriptive sense. It simply allows a manager to look further into what might be causing the difference, and ideally, to assess the financial implications."

Ms. Charles compiled a set of reports based on data from the software vendor that she thought might provide the sort of information in which Ms. Ward was interested. One report that was several pages in length, showed for three DRGs the distribution of charges incurred by each patient in 1980 as well as the patient's age, sex, and length of stay. Another (Exhibit 3) offered some supplemental ancillary "cost" data on those DRGs, and a third (Exhibit 4) provided some LOS data, by physician, for the same DRGs. She hoped Ms. Ward could be more specific about what she might consider an "exception." She was also interested in hearing what Ms. Ward would actually do with "exception" information once she had it.

EXHIBIT 4 Frequency and LOS Variations by Physician

| | MD# | Number of Cases | % Total | Average Length of Stay | | |
				Mean	Median	Mode
DRG 165:	001	26	24.3	5.73	5	4
Pneumonia.....	020	49	45.8	5.59	5	5
	Other*	32	29.9			
	Total	107		5.62		
	State			4.7		
	RSC Group			4.7		
DRG 159:	101	52	46.4	1.54	1	1
T & A.........	201	38	33.9	1.55	1	1
	301	8	7.1	1.50	1	1,2
	401	4	3.6	1.75	1	1
	501	10	8.9	1.50	1	1
	Total	112		1.53		
	State			1.70		
	RSC Group			1.60		
DRG 169:	001	53	45.7	4.55	4	4
Bronchitis	020	33	28.4	4.85	4	4
	605	15	12.9	3.87	4	4
	705	6	5.2	3.33	3	3
	Other†	9	7.8			
	Total	116		4.20		
	State			3.70		
	RSC Group			3.90		

* A total of 15 MDs admit patients under DRG 165.
† A total of 9 MDs admit patients under DRG 169.

Finance Department Needs

"At the hospital in which I worked previously, we were losing money on our neonatal intensive care unit. When we tried to figure out why, we discovered that a disproportionately high number of those cases were medicaid patients whose reimbursement rates did not cover the costs of the unit. So payor mix by DRG could help to pinpoint the cases that attract a 'losing' payor mix,'' explained Sam Goode, VP of Finance. Ms. Charles had in hand two reports which showed the number of cases in each payor class within a DRG as well as differences in LOS among the classes. "Although I am not as familiar as I would like to be with the merged data reports, I think they could provide me with good information about shifts in the types of cases we are seeing, in the intensity of resource usage, and in payor class. One important thing for me is the measure of relative costs provided in these reports; that is, which types of cases are more expensive relative to our average case cost. This is particularly useful in the new financial environment where we get rewarded for reducing our costs especially if we maintain our volume. Although it won't be the sole criteria for determining which services to emphasize and which to cut back, it certainly is an important one. I wonder if your data can help me identify potential 'winners and losers'."

EXHIBIT 5 Pediatric DRGs. Average and Relative Cost and LOS

DRG No.	Description	Number of Cases	ALOS	Total Average Cost	Cost SIW*	LOS SIW†
112	Inflam. of middle ear..............	10	3.3	$ 688	.83	1.01
114	Disease of ear with surgery........	17	1.2	787	.95	.38
146	Circ. system	21	3.8	885	1.07	1.18
159	T & A..........................	110	1.5	736	.89	.47
160	URI/influenza....................	37	3.3	803	.97	1.03
165	Simple pneumonia................	107	1.6	1,270	1.53	1.91
169	Bronchitis	111	4.2	918	1.11	1.30
172	Asthma.........................	53	4.2	1,037	1.25	1.25
197	Hernia	33	1.8	55	.91	.55
206	Intestine without surgery..........	101	4.4	871	1.05	1.35
322	Nerv. resp. circ.	68	3.5	1,147	1.38	1.08
327	No surg. no 2nd dx indications Indications—gast. intest. urinary w/o surg. w/o major dx	52	3.2	744	.89	.98
341	Fx forearm, hand, lower foot, closed reduction...............	35	2.8	783	.94	.85
354	Int. inj. skull w/o surg. w/o Dx 2...	37	1.7	448	.54	.54
355	Int. inj. skull w/o surg. w/major Dx 2	33	2.6	654	.79	.79

* Cost SIW = {Average Cost/Case for DRB sub i} over {sum Average Cost/Case for all DRGs}
† LOS SIW = {Average LOS for DRG sub i} over {sum Average for all DRGs}

Mr. Goode went on to say that what he really needed was some better information for pricing purposes. He and the hospital's administrator, Mr. Breen, were contemplating bidding on a preferred provider contract with one of the largest employers in the area. He wondered whether the data on cost per DRG that Ms. Charles had in her reports could be useful in that respect. Ms. Charles added that question to her growing agenda.

Ms. Charles returned to her office and started anew. First, she considered the best way to look at the "winners and losers." Exhibit 5 showed average costs per DRG of the pediatric DRGs. The exhibit included two index numbers related to service intensity weights (SIW). These numbers indicated the average amount of resources used for each DRG relative to the average resources used by all other

EXHIBIT 6   Top 15 Pediatric DRGs (includes all ages) Payor Mix

(Old) DRG No.		Medicare	Medicaid	Blue Cross	Commercial	Other	Total
114	Cases (%)	1 (5%)	3 (18%)	7 (41%)	5 (29%)	1 (5%)	17
	ALOS	4	1	1.14	1	1	1.24
146	Cases	4 (19%)	0	11 (52%)	3 (14%)	3 (14%)	21
	ALOS	7.25	0	3.55	2.33	2	3.86
159	Cases	0	9 (8%)	58 (53%)	39 (35%)	4 (4%)	110
	ALOS		1.56	1.50	1.56	1.50	1.53
160	Cases	0	6 (16%)	15 (41%)	14 (38%)	2 (5%)	37
	ALOS		3.33	3.13	3.57	4.0	3.38
165	Cases	0	19 (18%)	60 (56%)	20 (19%)	8 (7%)	107
	ALOS		6.58	5.28	5.70	5.63	5.62
169	Cases	0	12 (11%)	52 (47%)	40 (36%)	7 (6%)	111
	ALOS		4.83	4.10	4.4	3.71	4.26
172	Cases	0	4	29	15	5	53
	ALOS		4.25	4.07	4.47	4.4	4.23
197	Cases	0	2 (6%)	23 (70%)	5 (15%)	3 (9%)	33
	ALOS		2	1.87	1.6	1.67	1.82
206	Cases	16 (16%)	10 (10%)	46 (46%)	19 (19%)	10 (10%)	101
	ALOS	6.56	4	3.93	4.42	3.7	4.43
322	Cases	10 (15%)	3 (4%)	40 (59%)	9 (13%)	6 (9%)	68
	ALOS	3.5	4	3.68	3.78	2.17	3.54
327	Cases	5 (10%)	1 (2%)	25 (48%)	12 (23%)	9 (17%)	52
	ALOS	3.8	1	3.16	3.5	2.89	3.21
341	Cases	1 (3%)	2 (6%)	24 (69%)	5 (14%)	3 (9%)	35
	ALOS	5	6	2.42	2.8	3.	2.8
354	Cases	0	3 (8%)	21 (57%)	9 (24%)	4 (11%)	37
	ALOS		1.67	1.62	1.78	2.50	1.76
355	Cases	0	3 (9%)	16 (48%)	6 (18%)	8 (24%)	33
	ALOS		3	2.5	2.67	2.63	2.61
112	Cases	0	3 (30%)	3 (30%)	3 (30%)	1 (10%)	10
	ALOS		3.67	1.67	4.67	3	3.3
Overall 15 DRGs Payor Mix	Cases	55	77	405	189	69	795
	% Cases	7%	10%	50%	24%	9%	100%

EXHIBIT 7   Brief Description of Method by Which DRGs Are Costed

---

Step 1.   All hospital costs (direct, indirect, and overhead) are allocated to final cost centers.* (Financial information is taken largely from Medicare cost reports.) The total patient service charges associated with each cost center are also calculated. These two figures are then used in determining the ratio of costs-to-charges (RCC) for each cost center.

Step 2.   The billing data (i.e., charges) for each case are assigned to the proper final cost centers, and the RCC developed in Step 1 is applied to give an estimated cost for the case in each cost center.

Step 3.   The cases (with the costs calculated in Step 2) are then grouped into DRGs. Within each DRG, the costs in each cost center are totaled and then divided by the number of cases in that DRG in order to get an average cost for each cost center for each DRG.

* There are 15 ancillary final cost centers, and 6 routine. They are:

Ancillary Cost Center	*Routine Cost Center*
Pharmacy	I.C.U.
IV therapy	Medical-surgical unit
Medical-surgical supplies	Obstetrical unit
Laboratory	Psychiatric unit
X-ray diagnostic	Newborn unit
Operating room	Pediatric unit
Anesthesiology	
Physical therapy	
Pulmonary function	
Labor and delivery	
E.K.G.	
E.E.G.	
Renal dialysis	
Psychiatry	
Other ancillary	

---

cases in all other DRGs in the hospital. With this information, one could quickly identify both the more expensive cases and those requiring longer lengths of stay relative to the hospital average. Ms. Charles wondered what to make of this analysis of "winners and losers." She also had payor mix information by DRG shown in Exhibit 6. She hoped this might clarify the winners-losers concept a bit. Her understanding of the incentives of the new reimbursement system was still a bit fuzzy. The pricing question was really difficult; she wrote up a quick description of how the DRGs were costed (see Exhibit 7) and thought that might provide a useful starting ground for getting Mr. Goode to clarify what he really needed to make a pricing decision.

Conclusion

Ms. Charles looked over the reports she had assembled one last time in preparation for the special meeting she had called with the three vice presidents. She hoped that by having organized the DRG reports around the specific information needs of these managers, and focusing only upon the Pediatrics Department, she might finally be able to engage their interest and prove to them that the reports were both usable and useful.

Questions

1. Which pediatric DRGs are financial "winners" for the hospital? Which are financial losers? Why? How might this information assist the hospital in making programming decisions?
2. How might information on physician practice patterns affect the hospital's programming decisions?
3. Mr. James, the planner, has just discovered that the ENT specialist on the medical staff has applied for privileges at another hospital. How might the potential loss of business affect occupancy in the Pediatric Ward? Is this good or bad?
4. What is your assessment of the way in which costs have been calculated? What would happen to costs if there were a change in South Brookfield's case mix?

Chapter 9

Program Analysis

As we discussed in Chapter 8, technical analysis is a key step in the programming process. In this chapter we discuss topics related to this step. Technical analysis has essentially two dimensions: (1) making estimates of those costs or benefits of proposed programs that can be stated in monetary terms, and comparing the costs with the benefits, and (2) making an overall judgment about the proposed programs, based on the idea that not all relevant costs and benefits can be expressed monetarily.

BENEFIT/COST ANALYSIS

The underlying concept of *benefit/cost analysis* is the obvious one—that a program should not be undertaken unless its benefits exceed its costs. The term *cost-effectiveness analysis* sometimes is used, incorrectly, as a synonym for benefit/cost analysis. One way to clarify the distinction between the two terms is to compare two proposals that offer approximately the same benefits. If one has lower costs, it is considered to be more cost effective than the other.

> *Example.* An economic analysis of education programs usually addresses two questions: (1) Does the monetary value of benefits produced by expenditures on education equal or exceed the cost of those expenditures? (2) Given their current budgets, are schools and other educational efforts producing as much learning as possible? The first question requires a benefit/cost analysis; the second a cost-effective analysis.[1]

---

[1] David Stern, "Efficiency in Human Services: The Case of Education," *Administration in Social Work* 15, no. 2 (1991), pp. 83–104.

Status of Benefit/Cost Analysis

The idea of comparing the benefits of a proposed course of action with its costs is not new. Certain government agencies, such as the Bureau of Reclamation, have made such analyses for decades; proposals to build new dams, for example, frequently were justified on the grounds that the benefits exceeded the costs. Nor are such comparisons unique to nonprofit organizations. Techniques for analyzing the profitability of proposed business investments involve essentially the same approach.

Interest in benefit/cost analysis at the federal government level grew rapidly in the 1960s when the Department of Defense applied it to problems for which no formal analysis previously had been attempted. During this time, a variety of promotional brochures, journal articles, and proposals implied that benefit/cost analysis did everything, including taking ". . . the guesswork out of management." Suddenly, nonprofit organizations began to apply benefit/cost analysis to all sorts of proposed programs. When these efforts produced mixed results, public policy experts began to question the merits of the approach.

> *Example.* A proposal for a $275,000 research project submitted to the National Institute of Education promised to "address the Cost-Effectiveness Benefit questions by making a Macro Management and Policy analysis of alternate Cost opportunities in Elementary-Secondary and Post-Secondary Education," and to provide the results in nine months. Translated, this means that the proposer promised to use benefit/cost analysis to find the optimum amount and character of educational programs from kindergarten through college, in nine months, and all for $275,000!

Role of Benefit/Cost Analysis

Although overexuberant advocates of benefit/cost analysis (and outright charlatans) do exist, and their works are properly criticized, there is no doubt that many benefit/cost analyses have produced valuable information. To assure useful results, however, decision makers should consider two essential points:

1. Benefit/cost analysis focuses on those consequences of a proposal that can be estimated in quantitative terms. Because there is no important problem where all relevant factors can be reduced to numbers, benefit/cost analysis will never provide the complete answer. Not everything can be quantified, and no one should expect a benefit/cost analysis to do so. Analyses that claim to have quantified everything are of dubious merit.
2. To the extent that managers, decision makers, or analysts can express some important factors in quantitative terms, they are better off doing so. This narrows the area where the decision maker must operate in the more judgment-based dimension of technical analysis. Thus, while the need for judgment is not eliminated, it can be reduced.

Charles Schultze, former director of the U.S. Bureau of the Budget, summarized this middle ground in a statement that has become a classic:[2]

Much has been published on PPB.[3] Learned articles have treated it sometimes as the greatest thing since the invention of the wheel. Other articles attack it, either as a naïve attempt to quantify and computerize the imponderable, or as an arrogant effort on the part of latter-day technocrats to usurp the decision-making function in a political democracy.

PPB is neither. It is a means of helping responsible officials make decisions. It is not a mechanical substitute for the good judgment, political wisdom, and leadership of those officials. . .

PPB does call for systematic analysis of program proposals and decisions, concentrating upon those decisions which have budgetary consequences. But systematic analysis does not have to be and is not coextensive with quantitative analysis. The word "analyze" does not, in any man's dictionary, have the same meaning as the words "quantify" or "measure," although analysis often includes measurement.

Systematic analysis is an aid to policy debate. Too often these debates revolve around a simple list of pros and cons. There are no means of making progress in the debate, since participants simply repeat, in different words, their original positions. . . .

Now such analysis often does, and must, involve quantitative estimates. Most of our decisions—in fact, all of our budgetary decisions—willy-nilly involve quantitative consideration. For example, take the question of how many doctors to train and how much aid to give to medical schools. We can debate this simply in terms of arguing more or fewer budget dollars for the program. Alternatively, we can calculate the current and projected ratio of doctors to population, examine the relationship between the doctor/population ratio and various indices of health, review the distribution of doctors throughout various areas in the nation, estimate the costs of training doctors, and a host of similar factors. We cannot, of course, measure precisely, or even close to precisely, the national advantages to be gained from a program of aid to medical schools, nor can we account for all of the costs. But we can isolate, in a quantitative form, a number of the key elements involved in the program. The debate then can proceed in terms of weighing fairly specifically the advantages the nation gains from alternative increases in the supply of doctors against the costs of achieving each alternative.

In short, the issue is not whether benefit/cost analysis is a panacea or a fraud, for in general it is neither. Rather, the issue is to define the circumstances under which it is likely to be useful. There are many.

Example. The City of Edmonton, Alberta, decided to extend its light rail transit (LRT) system without undertaking a formal benefit/cost analysis. However, an analysis of the benefits and costs of LRT, incorporating data on population densities and air pollution, suggested that alternative transportation systems, such as express buses, were likely to achieve the city's public transit objectives at a lower cost. The authors of the benefit/cost analysis contended that the city had not produced any economic evidence that LRT was,

---

[2] From his Statement to the Subcommittee on National Security and International Operations of the Committee on Government Operations, U.S. Senate, 90th Cong., 1st sess., August 23, 1967.

[3] PPB stands for planning, programming, budgeting, which was the name given to the overall approach of which benefit/cost analysis was one part.

in fact, the low-cost transit alternative. They recommended that the city's transportation program require detailed benefit/cost analyses of major transportation project proposals.[4]

In the remainder of this section, we discuss some of the factors to consider in the decision to employ benefit/cost analysis.

Clarifying Goals

The benefit in a benefit/cost analysis must be related to an organization's goals; there is no point in making a benefit/cost analysis unless all concerned agree on these goals. That is, the purpose of benefit/cost analysis is to suggest the best alternative for reaching a goal. The formulation of goals is largely a judgmental process. Various members of management and various staff people may have different ideas of an organization's goals. Unless these groups reconcile their views, middle managers will find it difficult to formulate and implement programs to reach the goals.

Example. Several years ago, the federal government started to support local transportation for handicapped people. Since the U.S. Department of Transportation then subsidized local bus and subway lines, its natural inclination was to finance the modification of buses to provide lifts that would permit easy access for wheelchairs. The extra capital and maintenance costs of such equipment turned out to be huge, and usage was not high because handicapped people had no way of getting from their homes to the buses. Consequently, the cost per passenger was high—$1,283 per trip in Detroit in 1980, for example.

Subsequently, transportation was provided by vans that picked up handicapped people at their doors and took them directly to their destinations. This was both more convenient and less expensive—between $5 and $14 per passenger trip in most cities that tried it.

A focus on the goal of transporting handicapped people, rather than one of modifying existing modes of transportation, might have avoided the costly installation of passenger lifts in buses. Moreover, speculating on alternative ways of reaching the goal could also have produced a more effective solution.[5]

Just as it is important to agree on goals, it also is important to make sure that the goals are reasonable and achievable, or, stated somewhat differently, that the problem being presented is real, and that the program being proposed will help to alleviate it.

Example. In the late 1980s, locusts threatened the crops of many African nations. The U.S. Agency for International Development and other international aid agencies re-

---

[4] John Kim and Douglas S. West, "The Edmonton LRT: An Appropriate Choice?" *Canadian Public Policy* 17, no. 2 (June 1991), pp. 173–82.

[5] Based on Alice L. London, "Transportation Services for the Disabled," *The GAO Review,* Spring 1986, pp. 21–27.

sponded with $275 million and a fleet of aircraft that helped bomb crops with millions of liters of pesticides. A few years later, a report by the Office of Technology Assessment (OTA) said the campaign may have been a wasted effort. The OTA concluded that "Massive insecticide spraying . . . tends to be inefficient in the short-term, ineffective in the medium term, and misses the roots of the problem in the longer term." Moreover, the study suggests that the justification for the entire operation may have been flawed because locusts aren't as big a threat as had been thought.[6]

Proposals Susceptible to Benefit/Cost Analysis

Benefit/cost analysis has two general principles: (1) management should not adopt a program unless its benefits exceed its costs; and (2) when there are two competing proposals, the one with the greater excess of benefits over costs is preferable. In order to apply these principles, we must be able to relate benefits to costs.

Economic Proposals. For many proposals in nonprofit organizations, an analyst can estimate both benefits and costs in monetary terms. These economic proposals are similar to capital budgeting proposals in for-profit companies. A proposal to convert the heating plant of a high school from oil to coal involves the same type of analysis in either a for-profit or a nonprofit organization. Problems of this type are common in all organizations, and while important administratively, they frequently have little programmatic impact. Conversely, for problems that do have programmatic effects, analysts have difficulty making monetary estimates of benefits. Frequently, because benefits are so elusive, analysts cannot make a reliable estimate at all.

Alternative Ways of Reaching the Same Objective. Even if benefits cannot be quantified, a benefit/cost analysis is useful in situations where there is more than one way of achieving a given objective. If each alternative would achieve the objective, then management ordinarily will prefer the one with the lowest cost.

This approach has many applications because it does not require that the objective be stated in monetary terms, or even that it be quantified. We need not measure the degree to which each alternative meets the objective; we need only make the go-no-go judgment that any of the proposed alternatives will achieve it. Of these, we then seek the least costly.

> *Example.* The output of an educational program is difficult to measure. It is especially difficult to find a causal relationship between a certain teaching technique and the resulting quality of education. Nevertheless, educators can compare the costs of alternative teaching techniques, such as team teaching, computer-assisted instruction, and conventional tests and workbooks. In the absence of a judgment that one method provides better education than another, an educational manager presumably would prefer the technique with the lowest cost.

---

[6] Ann Gibbons, "Overkilling the Insect Enemy," *Science,* August 10, 1990.

Example. The objective of a benefit/cost analysis was to provide the optimal ground transportation and airport facilities for passengers arriving and departing Washington, D.C., by air. Analysts estimated the costs of various airport locations and associated ground transport services. Senior management chose the proposal that provided adequate service with the lowest cost. There was no need to measure the benefits of "adequate service" in monetary terms.

Equal Cost Programs. If two competing proposals have the same cost but one produces more benefits than the other, it ordinarily is the preferred alternative. This conclusion can be reached without measuring the absolute levels of benefits. Analysts often use such an approach to determine the best mix of resources in a program.

Example. Will $1 million spent to hire more teachers produce more educational benefits than $1 million spent on a combination of teachers and teaching machines, or $1 million spent on team teaching rather than individual teaching? The analysis involves an estimate of the amount of resources that $1 million will buy, and a judgment of the results that will be achieved by using this amount and mix of resources. It requires only that benefits be expressed comparatively, however, not numerically.

Different Objectives. A benefit/cost comparison of proposals intended to accomplish different objectives is likely to be worthless. For example, an analysis that attempted to compare funds to be spent for primary school education with funds to be spent for retraining unemployed adults is not worthwhile. Such an analysis would require assigning monetary values to the benefits of these two programs, which is an impossible task.

On the other hand, since funds are limited, policymakers must recognize that there is an opportunity cost associated with any given program. While experienced managers may have an intuitive feel for these opportunity costs *within* their organizations, relatively few managers have sufficient experience or skill to make such trade-offs *across* organizations, particularly when those organizations have disparate goals and clientele. Nor are there many managers with the *authority* to make such trade-offs. Funds used for pollution-control programs, for example, are not available for social welfare programs.[7]

Causal Connection between Cost and Benefits. Many benefit/cost analyses implicitly assume that there is a causal relationship between benefits and costs. That is, spending X produces Y amount of benefit. Unless a causal connection such as this actually exists, a benefit/cost analysis is fallacious.

---

[7] Some insightful analyses of opportunity costs can be found in Steven E. Rhoads, *The Economist's View of the World: Government, Markets, and Public Policy* (Cambridge, England: Cambridge University Press, 1985).

Example. An agency defended its personnel training program with an analysis indicating that the program would lead participants to get new jobs. The new jobs would increase their lifetime earnings by $25,000 per person. Thus, the $5,000 average cost per person trained seemed well justified. However, the assertion that the proposed program would indeed generate these benefits was completely unsupported; it was strictly a guess. There was no plausible link between the amount requested and the projected results.

Benefit/Cost as a Way of Thinking

Because of the difficulty of quantifying benefits, benefit/cost *analysis* is feasible for only a small portion of the problems that arise in nonprofit organizations. These tend to be well-structured administrative-type problems. Nevertheless, a benefit/cost *way of thinking* is useful for a great many problems. One of the characteristics of competent managers is their ability to evaluate program proposals, at least in a general way, by comparing the expected benefits with the proposed costs. They may not be able to quantify the relationship, nor do they need to do so in many cases. Nevertheless, this way of looking at problems tends to distinguish factors that are relevant from those that are not.

Example. The president of a liberal arts college was considering a proposal to join a consortium of three other colleges in the general area. Advocates of the proposal argued that the consortium movement originated in Oxford in the 15th century, and that the idea therefore was good because it had a long and noble history. They also pointed out that there were 67 American consortia at the time, compared with only 7 three years earlier, and that the idea therefore was good because it was growing rapidly. They said that it was advantageous for college faculties to cooperate with one another, that central purchasing is more efficient than having each college do its own purchasing, and so on.

The president said that, although these statements were interesting, none of them directly addressed the questions that were on his mind: How many students were likely to benefit from the activities of the consortium? Was the benefit likely to be worth the cost per student (the annual fee was $15,000)? What would a central purchasing office cost? Would it be likely to reduce costs sufficiently to pay for itself plus the cost of the consortium? Could a central purchasing office be created without having a formal consortium? In effect, the president was engaging in a benefit/cost analysis, even though he had no quantified measures of benefits available to him.

Overreliance on the Benefit/Cost Approach.   Benefit/cost thinking can be carried to extremes. If a manager rejects all proposals in which no causal connection between costs and benefits has been demonstrated, middle managers will be reluctant to submit innovative program proposals. A primary characteristic of many new, experimental—and promising—schemes is that there is no way of estimating their benefit/cost relationships in advance. Undue insistence on benefit/cost analyses can therefore result in overly conservative programs. The risk of failure of an innovative proposal may be high, but it frequently is worth taking if an organization wishes to serve its clients in the best way possible.

SOME ANALYTICAL TECHNIQUES

The literature on benefit/cost analysis is voluminous. In the remainder of the chapter, we summarize some of the principal techniques used to conduct them, along with particularly difficult problems that arise in the application of these techniques to nonprofit organizations. More details and techniques can be found in the "Suggested Additional Readings" at the end of this chapter.

CAPITAL INVESTMENT ANALYSIS

A typical capital investment proposal is one that involves an outlay of money at the present time so as to realize a stream of benefits sometime in the future. For example, a proposal might be to install storm windows at a cost of $10,000, with an estimated savings in heating bills of $3,000 per year. In evaluating this proposal one asks: Is it worth spending $10,000 now to obtain benefits of $3,000 per year in the future? There are several approaches to answering this question.

Payback Period Analysis

One approach determines the number of years that the benefits will have to be obtained to recover the investment. This is the payback period, calculated as follows for the storm window example:

$$\text{Payback period} = \frac{\text{Initial Investment}}{\text{Annual benefits}} = \frac{\$10,000}{\$3,000} = 3.3 \text{ years}$$

If the storm windows are expected to last fewer than 3.3 years, the investment is not worthwhile. If more than 3.3 years, the storm windows will have "paid for themselves," and the benefits thereafter will contribute to the organization's surplus.

Present Value Analysis

The payback period analysis assumes that savings in the second and third years are as valuable as savings in the first year, but this is not realistic. No rational person would give up the right to receive $3,000 now for the promise to receive $3,000 two years from now. That is, if a person loans $3,000 to someone now, he or she expects to get back more than $3,000 at some time in the future. The promise of an amount to be received in the future therefore has a lower *present value* than the same amount received today.[8]

---

[8] The concept of present value is discussed in the appendix at the end of this chapter.

Use of the present value technique is important in the capital budgeting process. By incorporating the time value of money into the analysis, the technique recognizes that money received in the future does not have as much value as money received today.

Net Present Value Analysis

The present value technique, or *discounting* technique, as it sometimes is called, is used in what is called the *net present value approach* to capital budgeting analysis. Net present value is the difference between the present value of a project's estimated benefits, and the amount to be invested in the project. The benefits often are called the project's *cash flows*. The approach involves the following steps:

1. Determine the estimated annual cash flows associated with the project. These may be either increased revenues or decreased costs to the organization, but they must result exclusively from the project itself and not from any activities that would have taken place without the project.
2. Determine the estimated economic life of the investment. This is not necessarily the physical life of the investment. Rather, it is the time period over which the cash flows will be received. The economic life may be shorter than the physical life because of obsolescence, change in demand, or other reasons.
3. Determine the net amount of the investment. This is be the actual purchase price of the new asset, plus any installation costs, plus any disposal costs for the asset it is replacing, and less the salvage value received for the asset being replaced.
4. Determine the required discount rate, or rate of return. This topic will be discussed in greater detail later in the chapter.
5. Compute the proposed project's net present value according to this formula:

$$\text{Net present value} = \left(\text{Cash flow} \times \text{Present value factor} \right) - \text{Investment amount}$$

$$\text{NPV} = (CF \times pvf) - I$$

The $(CF \times pvf)$ portion of this equation is known as *Gross Present Value,* and becomes *Net Present Value* when the investment amount is deducted from it.

6. If the NPV is greater than zero, the investment is financially feasible. That is, once we have determined the desired rate of return, a project that yields a net present value of zero or greater is earning the desired rate, and therefore is acceptable from a pure financial perspective.

As discussed in the appendix at the end of this chapter, when the cash flow is the same every year, the present value factor can be obtained from Table 9A–2 (p. 457) by looking at the intersection of the year row and the percent column selected in steps 2 and 4 above. Present value factors for one-time cash flows can be found in Table 9A–1 (p. 456).

Example. Assume we estimate that the storm windows in the above example will last five years, and that our required rate of return is 8 percent. The analysis would be performed as follows:

Step 1. Annual cash flow = $3,000
Step 2. Economic life = 5 years
Step 3. Net investment amount = $10,000
Step 4. Rate of return = 8 percent
Step 5. NPV = $(CF \times pvf) - I$
$$= (\$3,000 \times 3.993) - \$10,000$$
$$= \$11,979 - \$10,000$$
$$= \$1,979$$
Step 6. The investment has a NPV that is greater than zero, and therefore is financially feasible.

Points to Consider.   Several important points should be made about an analysis of net present value. First, the above example assumed identical cash flows in each of the years, which permits us to use Table 9A–2. If the cash flows were not the same in each year, we would need to calculate the term $(CF \times pvf)$ for each year separately, using Table 9A–1, and add the results together.

Second, although an analysis of this sort appears to be quite precise, we should recognize that its significant elements are estimates or guesses, and may be quite imprecise. Specifically, cash flows projected beyond a period of two to three years ordinarily are not precise, nor are estimates of the economic life of most investments. Thus, we should be careful about attributing too much credibility to the precision that the formula seems to give us. Because of this, many managers look for the NPV to be a *comfortable margin* above zero. Of course, what is comfortable for one manager may not be so for another.

Third, inflation is a factor. It is quite likely, for instance, that potential increases in wage rates, will cause labor savings from an investment to be greater five years from now than they are today. If, however, we are to adjust our cash flow factor for the effects of inflation, we also need to adjust the required rate of return to reflect our need for a return somewhat greater than the rate of inflation. By excluding an inflation effect from both the cash flow calculations and the required rate of return, we neutralize the effect of inflation. We thus do not need to undertake the rather complex calculations that otherwise might be necessary.

Finally, the financial analysis is only one aspect of the decision-making process. As we discussed in Chapter 8, there are many more considerations, including political analyses. Managers must be careful not to let the financial analysis dominate a decision that has political or strategic consequences that cannot be quantified. In these instances, a manager's judgment and "feel" for the situation may be as important as the quantitative factors. Indeed, if a project is *required* for nonquantitative reasons (e.g., for accreditation), its net present value is irrelevant. In short, almost all capital budgeting proposals involve a wide variety of nonquantitative considerations that will influence the final decision. The use of present value or any related techniques serves mainly to formalize the quantitative part of the analysis.

Benefit/Cost Ratio

Since most organizations do not have sufficient capital investment funds to engage in all financially feasible projects, managers must devise some method to rank projects in order of their financial desirability. One such method is to calculate their *benefit/cost ratio,* as follows:

$$\text{Benefit/cost ratio} = \frac{\text{Gross present value}}{\text{Investment}}$$

To illustrate this approach, suppose we have two proposals, one requiring an investment of $2,000 that yields a cash inflow of $2,400 one year from now, and the other requiring an investment of $3,000 that yields a cash inflow of $900 a year for five years. If the required rate of return is 10 percent, the benefit/cost ratio indicates that the second proposal is preferable, as indicated below:

Proposal	Investment	Cash Inflow	Present Value Factors at 10 percent	Gross Present Value	Benefit/ Cost Ratio
A	$2,000	$2,400, Year 1	0.909	$2,182	1.09
B........	$3,000	$900, Years 1–5	3.791	$3,412	1.14

In this instance, Proposal B is more valuable on a benefit/cost basis than Proposal A.

Internal Rate of Return

Another way of ranking projects is by their *internal rate of return (IRR).* The IRR method is similar to the net present value method, but instead of determining a required rate of return in advance, we set net present value equal to zero and calculate the *effective rate of return* on the investment. Proposed projects can then be ranked in terms of their rates of return.

To use this method, we usually assume identical cash flows in each year of a project's life.[9] Given this assumption, the IRR method begins with the net present value formula

---

[9] Computer programs can solve for unequal cash flows, but they are time consuming, and ordinarily are not readily available.

$$NPV = (CF \times pvf) - I$$

but sets NPV equal to zero, so that

$$CF \times pvf = I$$

or

$$pvf = \frac{I}{CF}$$

Once we have determined the present value factor, we can use it in conjunction with the project's economic life to determine the effective—or *internal*—rate of return. We do this with Table 9A–2. For instance, in our storm window example, if we divide the $10,000 investment amount by the $3,000 annual cash flows, we get 3.33. We now find the figure 3.33 in Table 9A–2 in the row for five years, and can see that it lies somewhere between 15 and 16 percent. This is the internal rate of return for the storm window project.[10]

Choice of a Discount Rate

In any capital investment analysis, the choice of a discount rate is an important consideration. The approach used by many organizations, both for-profit and nonprofit, involves the calculation of an entity's weighted cost of capital, which is then adjusted as necessary to account for the riskiness of the particular proposal under consideration.

Weighted Cost of Capital.   As we discussed in Chapter 3, an organization's assets are financed by a combination of liabilities and equity. Some liabilities, such as accounts payable, are usually interest free, but both short- and long-term debt carry a rate of interest that the organization must pay for the use of the lender's money. Equity generally comes in two forms: (1) contributions and grants, which are called *contributed equity* (*contributed capital* in a for-profit organization), and (2) *retained surpluses* or *operating equity* (*retained earnings* in a for-profit organization).

In choosing a discount rate, we begin with the cost of each of these sources of capital and weight them by their relative amounts. For example, assume that the right side of an organization's balance sheet appears as follows, with interest rates as shown:

---

[10] See James F. Gaertner and Ken Milani, "The TRR Yardstick for Hospital Capital Expenditure Decisions," *Management Accounting,* December 1980, for a discussion of another approach, called the *true rate of return method.*

Item	Amount	Interest Rate
Accounts payable.....................	$ 3,000	0.0%
Accrued salaries.....................	2,000	0.0
Short-term note payable	10,000	12.0
Total current liabilities	15,000	
Long-term note payable	75,000	10.0
Mortgage payable....................	150,000	8.0
Total liabilities.................	240,000	
Contributed equity	150,000	0.0
Operating equity.....................	50,000	0.0
Total liabilities and equity	$440,000	

In calculating a weighted cost of capital, we (1) determine the percentage of the total liabilities and equity that each source represents, (2) multiply this by the appropriate interest rate, and (3) add the resulting totals together. The calculations for the above situation would look as follows:

Item	Amount	Percent of Total	Interest Rate	Weighted Rate
Accounts payable.....................	$ 3,000	0.6	0.0	0.0 %
Accrued salaries.....................	2,000	0.5	0.0	0.0
Short-term note payable	10,000	2.3	12.0	0.28
Total current liabilities	15,000			
Long-term note payable	75,000	17.0	10.0	1.70
Mortgage payable....................	150,000	34.1	8.0	2.73
Total liabilities	240,000			
Contributed equity....................	150,000	34.1	0.0	0.0
Operating equity.....................	50,000	11.4	0.0	0.0
Total liabilities and equity	$440,000			
Totals		100.00		4.71

Cost of Equity. This weighted cost of capital in the above example is low because both sources of equity—contributed and operating—have been assigned a zero interest rate. An ongoing debate in many nonprofit organizations concerns the appropriate interest rates for these sources. Although some nonprofit organization managers argue that these funds are essentially free, and therefore should be assigned a zero interest rate, most managers believe there is a real cost for using their organizations' equity capital.

While managers may agree on the relevance of a cost of equity, there is considerably less agreement among them on how to determine the appropriate rate of interest. Some argue that contributed equity tends to be invested either in property and plant or in the entity's endowment fund. Funds tied up in property and plant obviously are not available for other investments. Endowment funds on the other hand, usually are invested in securities, real property, or other earning assets. If some of these funds are used for a particular project, the amount available for investment elsewhere is reduced by that much. The cost of using these funds on the proposed project, therefore, can be thought of as the rate they would have earned if invested in securities or other similar assets (i.e., their opportunity cost). Like all future estimates, this rate is uncertain, but most managers have a fairly good idea of what their investments can earn.

If an organization expects that it can invest its equity funds to earn a rate of 12 percent, the weighted cost of capital calculated above would change considerably, as is shown below:

Item	*Amount*	*Percent of Total*	*Interest Rate*	*Weighted Rate*
Accounts payable......................	$ 3,000	0.6	0.0%	0.0 %
Accrued salaries......................	2,000	0.5	0.0	0.0
Short-term note payable................	10,000	2.3	12.0	0.28
Total current liabilities	15,000			
Long-term note payable	75,000	17.0	10.0	1.70
Mortgage payable......................	150,000	34.1	8.0	2.73
Total liabilities	240,000			
Contributed equity....................	150,000	34.1	12.0	4.09
Operating equity......................	50,000	11.4	12.0	1.37
Total liabilities and equity	$440,000			
Totals...............................		100.0		10.17

Most managers would argue that this approach yields a realistic average for a nonprofit organization to use as a discount rate in its capital investment decision-making analyses. Of course, the actual amount of the weighted cost of capital will differ from one organization to the next depending on capital structure and interest rates.

Problems Associated with Low Discount Rates

There are many instances in which nonprofit organizations have analyzed a capital investment decision using a discount rate that is too low. This problem is particularly important with respect to government proposals for public works and other capital expenditures whose benefits accrue over a long period. Until fairly recently, most government agencies either did not discount the streams of costs and benefits at all, or they used the interest rate on government bonds as the discount rate. Most government officials now agree that a government bond rate is too low. Indeed, as we will show below, its use can result in the approval of projects that actually should not be undertaken.

In the 1960s there was considerable discussion about the appropriate discount rate to use for the federal government. The eventual consensus was that the rate should approximate the average rate of return on private sector investments. In March 1972 the U.S. Office of Management and Budget (OMB) effectively ended the controversy with *Circular A-94*, which specified that in most circumstances a rate of 10 percent should be used. (*Circular A-94* also gives concise, useful guidance on applying the discounting principle.)

Exhibit 9–1 illustrates the nature of the errors that can result from the failure to discount at all or from the use of a discount rate that is too low. The exhibit lists the essential characteristics of three projects, together with the present value of the benefits under three discount rates: 0 percent, 5 percent, and 10 percent. It leads to several generalizations:

1. If benefits are not discounted, projects may be undertaken that are financially unfeasible. Project C is an example. At a 10 percent discount rate, the present value of Project C's benefits is only $8,500, which is less than its cost, so the project should not be undertaken. Prior to 1940, the Soviet Union did not use discount rates and consequently invested large amounts in projects similar to Project C. These were typically capital-intensive, long-lived projects such as hydroelectric power facilities.
2. With a low discount rate, projects that are capital-intensive and long-lived appear more attractive than they actually are. For example, if a government agency is deciding how best to spend a fixed sum of money and therefore must rank projects in order of desirability, it will favor Project B over Project A if it uses a 5 percent discount rate. At this rate, Project B's benefits of $13,900 exceed Project A's of $12,900. If the agency uses a 10 percent rate, however, Project A is better than Project B ($11,400 compared with $11,000). In India, the mistake of using low-discount rates led to the construction of large cement plants built at infrequent intervals, rather than to smaller plants built more frequently.
3. If agencies are permitted to use different rates, an agency that uses a low rate can justify a larger capital budget than an agency that uses a high rate. For

---

EXHIBIT 9–1 Effect of Discount Rates

	Project		
	A	*B*	*C*
Investment	$10,000	$10,000	$10,000
Annual benefits	3,000	1,800	1,000
Life (years)	5	10	20
Present value of benefits:			
At 0%	15,000	18,000	20,000
At 5%	12,900	13,900	12,500
At 10% (proper rate)	11,400	11,000	8,500

example, an agency that uses 5 percent can justify Projects A, B, and C, since in each case the benefits exceed the cost. An agency that uses 10 percent can justify only Projects A and B.

The desirability of long-lived projects is extremely sensitive to the discount rate used in the feasibility analysis. For example, some years ago, the Water Resources Council surveyed 245 authorized Corps of Engineers projects. The survey showed that for about one-third of them, costs would exceed benefits if the discount rate were raised from the 5-3/8 percent actually used in the analyses to 7 percent.[11]

Incorporating Risk into the Analysis

Capital investment proposals are not risk free. Since all capital investment projects involve future cash flows, there is always the possibility that the future will not be as anticipated. This risk element should be incorporated into the analysis. If risk is not considered explicitly, then a very risky proposal might be evaluated in the same way as one that has a high probability of success.

There are a number of ways to incorporate risk into an analysis. With all of them, an increase in risk reduces the net present value of a proposal. Many organizations adjust their weighted cost of capital either upward or downward to account for perceived risk. The problem with this approach is that there is no easy way to establish a meaningful risk scale or otherwise make adjustments to the required rate of return. Statistical techniques are available for incorporating the relative riskiness of a project, but they require analysts to estimate the probabilities of possible outcomes. This is quite difficult to do.

Another approach, taken by many organizations, is to heavily discount any projected cash flows beyond some predetermined time period, such as 5 or 10 years. They use the weighted cost of capital as the discount rate for all cash flows in, say, the first five years of an investment. They then use a much higher rate for all subsequent years. Some even exclude all cash flows beyond a certain number of years. In all instances, the reasoning is that the future is highly uncertain, and the farther out the projections the greater the uncertainty. While this approach tends to bias decisions in favor of projects with short payback periods, many organizations in industries experiencing rapid technological change believe that short payback periods are justified.

Finally, in considering risk, some organizations give greater weight to projections of cost savings than to projections of additional revenues. When a particular technological improvement, say a new piece of equipment, has demonstrated its ability to produce certain cost savings in other organizations, managers reason that projections of cost savings are quite reliable. By contrast, a projection that a

---

[11] Luther J. Carter, "Water Projects: How to Erase the 'Pork Barrel' Image?" *Science* 19, October 1973, p. 268.

certain investment will result in new business and hence additional revenue is far more uncertain. Factors such as clients' willingness to use the new service, competition, third-party reimbursement changes, and so forth will also affect a new investment's return. Some organizations incorporate this risk into the analysis by using lower discount rates for projects with cost savings and higher ones for projects that are expected to yield additional revenues.

In summary, when we consider the formula

$$\text{NPV} = (CF \times pvf) - I$$

the only element that is reasonably certain is the amount of the investment. Both cash flow estimates and economic life can be highly speculative. Organizations can include adjustments for uncertainty either by shortening economic life or by raising the required rate of return. Either approach requires managers and analysts to exercise considerable judgment.

USE OF MODELS

All benefit/cost analyses rely on an underlying model that describes both the essential variables in the situation being studied and the relationships among them. Many studies explicitly attempt to construct such a model as an aid to estimating the benefits and costs of each alternative. The model need not be complicated; indeed, the use of models has been greatly facilitated over the past 5 to 10 years by the development of spreadsheet software for microcomputers.

Example. Exhibit 9–2 shows a simple financial model that focuses on the relationships of important variables for the instructional program of a college. All the "initial values" are entered except one: tuition and fees per student. The *baseline equations* are established in accordance with the college's policies concerning section sizes, faculty workloads, faculty salaries, the number of nonteaching faculty, and other expenses.

With this information, the college can "solve" for the amount of tuition and fees per student necessary to put the model into "equilibrium." It is in equilibrium in the sense that the revenues available for instruction equal the costs of instruction. The first *management decision equation* does this, indicating that the tuition and fee figure would need to be $8,767.

Alternatively, tuition could be entered into the model at the level set by senior management and the trustees, and the model could be used to solve for the number of students needed to reach equilibrium (that is, to break even). The second management-decision equation does this, using a tuition and fee figure of $8,000. The number of students needed for equilibrium is 1,723.

By changing the unknown in a management-decision equation, or by changing the college's policy concerning section sizes, faculty workloads, or salaries, this model could be used to answer many questions: By how much, for example, could we increase average faculty compensation if we reduced *(a)* the number of sections by *X*, *(b)* the number of nonteaching faculty by *Y*, or *(c)* nonfaculty instruction costs by *Z*? If we increased the course offerings, by how much would tuition have to be increased? What would happen if we increased the number of students by 10 percent?

EXHIBIT 9–2   College Financial Model

Variables

Abbreviation	Name	Initial Value
TUITN	Tuition and fees, per student.............................	To be determined
STUDS	Number of students......................................	1,572
OTREV	Other revenue available for instruction (e.g., endowment) (000)......................................	$ 400
OTCOS	Instruction cost other than faculty compensation (000)........	$ 7,993
COURSE	Number of courses per student, per semester................	5.0
SECSI	Average number of students per section....................	24.3
SECTS	Number of sections offered	323
TEFAC	Number of FTE teaching faculty	107.7
NOFAC	Number of FTE nonteaching faculty (sabbaticals, department head, slippage)	12.3
SALRY	Average compensation per faculty	$ 51,525
LOAD	Number of sections per teaching faculty....................	3.0

Baseline Equations		*Results*
SECTS	= (STUDS × COURSE) ÷ SECSI	
	= (1,572 × 5.0) ÷ 24.3	323
TEFAC	= SECTS ÷ LOAD	
	= 323 ÷ 3.0	107.8
EXPENSES	= SALRY(TEFAC + NOFAC) + OTCOS	
	= $51,525 (107.8 + 12.3) + $7,993,000	$14,182,128

Management Decision Equations		*Results*
TUITN	= (EXPENSES − OTREV) ÷ STUDS	
	= ($14,182,128 − $400,000) ÷ 1572	$ 8,767
STUDS	= (EXPENSES − OTREV) ÷ TUITN	
	= ($14,182,128 − $400,000) ÷ $8,000	1,723

Moreover, beginning with this simple model, we can refine the analysis by substituting a frequency distribution of section sizes for the average section size, by substituting a distribution of faculty compensation by rank for the overall average, by bringing in noninstruction costs, or by being more specific about any of several other variables.

Computer models such as this are available for many types of nonprofit organizations, and spreadsheet packages can be adapted to meet managers' needs in a wide variety of circumstances. Frequently these models serve to quantify an organization's policy decisions, and require analysts, senior management, and governing bodies to determine which variables are policy driven and which can be formula driven. In so doing, the models help to bring considerable discipline to an organization's financial analyses, and add a great deal of power to the decision-making processes undertaken by senior management and the board.

Example. Some hospitals use a model called *HOFPLAN*. HOFPLAN can compute: *(a)* fees by class of patient, *(b)* direct costs and charges by cost center, *(c)* reimbursement by financial class, and *(d)* financial statements. The model relies on assumptions entered by the user. These assumptions include the type of patient, the length of stay, unit variable costs, total fixed costs, units of service for each cost center, allocation method preferred, growth rates, seasonal patterns, endowment revenue, depreciation, bad debts, and similar financial data. The user can quickly see the "bottom line effect" of varying any of these assumptions. Equally important, the model allows senior management to identify the individuals in the hospital setting who control the variables entered into the equation, thereby adding an important dimension to the analytical effort.

Limitations of Models

In many situations, attempts to construct models have turned out to be fruitless. Persons contemplating model building for public-sector problems should read Brewer's *Politicians, Bureaucrats, and the Consultant* to be forewarned about what can go wrong.[12] Brewer describes several attempts to build models of the demand for housing in San Francisco and Pittsburgh. Over $1 million was spent on each of these models, but no useful results emerged. There were several reasons for the failure:

1. The goals were not clearly set forth at the beginning of the study (essentially, they consisted of the vague statement: "Provide the best housing at the lowest cost for all our citizens").
2. The consultants did not understand the housing problem.
3. The historical data used in the model were so voluminous and detailed that a single run of the model required many hours of computer time.
4. By contrast, the assumptions about population growth patterns were naive and simplistic.
5. The output of each computer run was several inches thick, and decision makers could not comprehend it.

In short, to develop useful models, an analyst needs reliable data, and such data often are not available.

QUANTIFYING THE VALUE OF A HUMAN BEING

In their analyses of proposed programs, nonprofit organization managers frequently encounter a factor that rarely is relevant in proposals originating in for-profit companies: the value of a human being. This dilemma arises because some programs are designed to save or prolong human lives. Such programs include automobile safety, accident prevention, drug control, and medical research. In these programs, the value of a human life, or of a workday lost to accident or illness, is a relevant consideration in measuring benefits.

---

[12] Gary D. Brewer, *Politicians, Bureaucrats, and the Consultant: A Critique of Urban Problem Solving* (New York: Basic Books, 1973).

Analysts are often squeamish about attaching a monetary value to a human life since there is a general belief in our culture that life is priceless. Nevertheless, such a monetary amount often facilitates the analysis of certain proposals. In a world of scarce resources, it is not possible to spend unlimited amounts to save lives in general.

There are, of course, circumstances in which society is willing to devote significant resources to saving a specific life, as when hundreds of people, supported by helicopters and various high technology devices, are brought together to hunt for a child who is lost in the woods. In most situations, however, the focus is not on saving a single life, but rather on saving the lives of a class of people (such as motorcyclists or cancer victims) or on valuing a life that already has been lost (such as in cases of litigation for medical malpractice).

Analytical Approaches to Valuation. Analysts have advocated several approaches to estimating the value of a human life. All of them present difficulties. One approach is to discount the expected future earnings of the person or persons affected by the program; this discounted present value presumably represents the person's economic value to his or her family or to society. A related approach subtracts the person's food, clothing, and other costs from the earnings to find the *net* value of his or her life.

These two approaches frequently are used in litigation involving "wrongful deaths." They are relevant to cases involving deceased persons, automobile accidents, industrial pollution, or the release of toxic chemicals.

Example. In a study of the costs of firearm injuries, the U.S. General Accounting Office (GAO) reported on an outside study to determine the average lifetime cost of a firearm injury. The costs used in the study included actual dollar expenditures related to illness or injury, including amounts spent for hospital and nursing home care, physician and other medical professional services, drugs and appliances, and rehabilitation. The cost estimates also included life years lost and the indirect cost associated with loss of earnings from short- and long-term disability and premature death from injury. The study's conclusion was that injuries not requiring hospitalization cost $458 per person, while those requiring hospitalization were $33,159 per person. The average lifetime cost of a firearm *fatality* was $373,520, which the GAO characterized as ". . . the highest of any cause of injury." Using annual figures for injuries and deaths attributable to firearms, the GAO went on to conclude that the estimated lifetime costs for accidental shootings was close to $1 billion every year.[13]

Among the problems encountered in applying these approaches is the difficulty of: *(a)* estimating the amount of future earnings and related costs, *(b)* choosing an

---

[13] U.S. General Accounting Office, *Accidental Shootings: Many Deaths and Injuries Caused by Firearms Could Be Prevented,* Report to the Chairman, Subcommittee on Antitrust, Monopolies, and Business Rights, Committee of the Judiciary, U.S. Senate, Washington, D.C., March 1991. The study cited by the GAO was Dorothy P. Rice, et al., *Cost of Injury in the United States: A Report to Congress* (San Francisco, Institute for Health and Aging, University of California, and Injury Prevention Center, The Johns Hopkins University, 1989).

appropriate time period, and *(c)* selecting the correct discount rate. Perhaps more important, these approaches tend to discriminate against persons with relatively low-expected lifetime earnings, such as elderly people, homemakers, members of minority groups, ministers, college professors, and artists.[14]

A third analytical approach computes the value of a life in terms of society's willingness to spend money to prevent deaths. One might imagine, for example, that the development and enforcement of occupational safety regulations and building codes are based on benefit/cost comparisons. This is rarely the case, however. Spending on many of these programs frequently is based on emotional arguments or political posturing, as happens, for example, when members of Congress suggest that economic costs are irrelevant for questions related to human lives.

> *Example.* In the early 1990s, the state of Oregon planned to change its medicaid program by covering more poor residents but offering fewer services. The state computer-ranked 1,600 medical procedures according to costs, benefits, and patients' "quality of well-being." Under the scheme, immunizations ranked higher than treatment for gallstones and depression; cosmetic surgery and sex-change operations fell in the lowest rank. Ultimately, the state drew a line through the list, with funding to be provided for procedures above the line and denied for those falling below it.[15]
>
> The state needed a federal waiver to implement the plan since medicaid rules required that states fund "all medically necessary" services. In 1992 (a presidential election year), the waiver was denied based, in part, on the argument that the plan valued some human lives higher than others, and that such a valuation was unfair.

A fourth approach seeks to measure the value people place on their own lives as indicated by, say, the amount they are willing to spend on life or disability insurance, or by risk premiums they earn in hazardous occupations. This implies that these individuals' decisions are based on economic considerations, but many other considerations may be involved.

> *Example.* At one time the exposure standard for benzene was 10 parts per million averaged over an eight-hour working day. At this rate, one benzene worker would die of benzene-related cancer every third year. According to the Occupational Safety and Health Administration (OSHA), a standard of one part per million would have eliminated the risk, but would have cost $100 million annually for the 30,000 workers who were exposed to benzene.
>
> One analyst asked the following questions: Would each of the 30,000 benzene workers be willing to pay $3,333 a year (his or her share of the $100 million) to eliminate the risk?

---

[14] Ralph Estes makes an attempt to adjust for some of these factors in *Estes® Economic Loss Tables* (Wichita, Kans., A.U. Publishing, 1987). He provides separate data for different educational levels, different genders, whites and nonwhites, persons with and without established earnings histories, and for persons who earn the minimum wage. In cases of wrongful death, he also provides data that adjust for terminated personal consumption.

[15] Health One® and Deloitte & Touche, *Managing Care and Costs: Strategic Choices and Issues: An Environmental Assessment of U.S. Health Care, 1991–1996* (Minneapolis, Health One Corporation, 1991).

If not, would the $100 million be better spent in a highway-improvement or cancer-screening program that could save more than one life every third year?[16]

Example. Merril Eisenbud, a member of the Three Mile Island Advisory Board, and former chairman, North Carolina Low-Level Radioactive Waste Management Authority, criticized some states' regulations concerning the design of low-level radioactive waste disposal sites. He argued that, in response to public pressure, some states require more protection be provided than is specified by the Nuclear Regulatory Commission. According to Mr. Eisenbud: "The additional protection involves expenditures of more than $100 million over the life of a facility, which is the equivalent to many *trillions* of dollars per premature death averted!"[17]

Despite its limitations, a benefit/cost approach may be better than any alternative. It may show that a proposal is outside a reasonable boundary in either direction—that it is obviously worthwhile or obviously not worth its cost from an economic standpoint. Unfortunately, this does not guarantee either its acceptance or rejection.

Example. Studies of the effect of a 55-miles-per-hour speed limit show that the benefits may not be worth the costs. Benefits are lives saved. Costs can be measured in terms of the additional time taken to reach a destination. Even when time is valued at low amounts per hour, and lives are given a high value, the cost exceeds the benefits in most of these studies. Nevertheless, the 55-mile-per-hour speed limit persists in many states.

Alternatives to Valuation.   The cost of saving lives may be a useful way of choosing among alternative proposals even when it is not possible or feasible to measure the value of a life. Specifically, the alternative that saves the most lives per dollar spent generally is considered preferable from an economic viewpoint. The Federal Highway Administration uses this approach in ranking the attractiveness of various highway safety alternatives. Such an analysis is limited to judging whether a particular program saves more lives per dollar spent than other lifesaving or life-prolonging programs. It does not compare costs with monetary benefits.

SUMMARY

Managers of most nonprofit organizations frequently must choose between two or more competing programs. When this is the case, some attempt to quantify both benefits and costs usually can assist in the decision-making effort.

When two or more proposals have roughly the same benefits, the comparison is relatively easy since only costs need to be calculated. Similarly, when competing proposals have the same costs but one clearly produces more benefits than the

---

[16] From Steven E. Rhoads, "Kind Hearts and Opportunity Costs," *Across the Board,* December 1985.

[17] Merril Eisenbud, "Disparate Costs of Risk Avoidance," *Science* 9, September 1988, pp. 1277–78.

other, the decision usually is quite easy. The decision becomes complicated, however, when benefits and costs extend over several years (as is the case with almost all proposed new programs), and when competing proposals have both different benefits and different costs.

When both benefits and costs can be expressed easily in monetary terms, calculating either present values or internal rates of return can facilitate a decision. When these analyses are being used, the choice of a discount rate is a key decision; many relatively undesirable projects have been undertaken because analysts used a discount rate that was too low. Models also can assist in the decision-making effort in that they allow managers and analysts to measure the implications of changing certain key variables.

Frequently, benefits and costs cannot be expressed easily in monetary terms. This happens, for example, when managers attempt to incorporate risk into the analysis, since risk is inherently difficult to measure. It also happens when managers attempt to quantify the value of a human being, and include that in the analysis. Additionally, there are a variety of nonquantitative considerations that are part of almost every proposed program. In all these instances, although some quantitative analysis usually can be carried out, managers must be careful not to allow the quantitative factors to dominate the decision. In most program decisions, managers will need to exercise their judgment, which may override the results of the quantitative analysis.

APPENDIX
The Concept of Present Value

The concept of present value rests on the basic principle that money has a *time value*. That is, that $1 received one year from today is worth less than $1 received today. To illustrate the concept, consider the following situations:

> ***Question.*** A colleague offers to pay you $1,000 one year from today. How much would you lend her today?

Presumably, unless you were a good friend or somewhat altruistic, you would not lend her $1,000 today. You could invest your $1,000, earn something on it over the course of the year, and have more than $1,000 a year from now. If, for example, you could earn 10 percent on your money, you could invest your $1,000 and have $1,100 in a year. Alternatively, if you had $909, and invested it at 10 percent, you would have $1,000 a year from today.

Thus, if your colleague offers to pay you $1,000 a year from today, and you are an investor expecting a 10 percent return, you would most likely lend her only $909 today. With a 10 percent interest rate, $909 is the present value of $1,000 received one year hence.

> ***Question.*** Under the same circumstances as the previous question, how much would you lend your colleague if she offered to pay you $1,000 two years from today?

Here we must incorporate the concept of compound interest; that is, the fact that interest is earned on the interest itself. For example, at a 10 percent rate, $826 loaned today would accumulate to roughly $1,000 in two years, as shown by the following:

Year 1 $826 × .10	= $ 82.60
Year 2 ($826 + $82.60) × .10	= $ 90.86
Total at end of Year 2 = $826 + $82.60 + $90.86	= $999.46

Thus, you would be willing to lend her $826.

> *Question.* The previous question consisted of a promise to pay a given amount two years from today, with no intermediate payments. Another possibility to consider is the situation in which your colleague offers to pay you $1,000 a year from today, and another $1,000 two years from today. How much would you lend her now?

The answer requires combining the analyses in each of the above two examples. Specifically, for the $1,000 received two years from now, you would lend her $826, and for the $1,000 received one year from now you would lend her $909. Thus, the total you would lend would be $1,735.

Our ability to make these determinations is simplified by present value tables. Two such tables follow the suggested additional readings in this chapter. Table 9A–1, "Present Value of $1," is used to determine the present value of a single payment received at some specified time in the future. For instance, in the first example above, we could find the answer to the problem by looking in the column for 10 percent and the row for one year; this gives us 0.909. Multiplying 0.909 by $1,000 gives us the $909 we would lend our colleague. Similarly, if we look in the row for two years and multiply the entry of 0.826 by $1,000, we arrive at the answer to the second example: $826.

Table 9A–2, "Present Value of $1 Received Annually for *N* Years," is used for even payments received over a given period. Looking at Table 9A–2, we can see that the present value of 1.736 (for a payment of $1 received each year for two years at 10 percent) multiplied by $1,000 is $1,736. With a minor rounding error, this is the amount we calculated in the third example above. We also can see that the 1.736 is the sum of the two amounts shown on Table 9A–1 (0.909 for one year hence, and 0.826 for two years hence). Thus, Table 9A–2 simply sums the various elements in Table 9A–1 to facilitate calculations.

SUGGESTED ADDITIONAL READINGS

Anthony, Robert N., and James S. Reece. *Accounting: Text and Cases,* 9th ed. Homewood, Ill.: Richard D. Irwin, 1993.

Clayton, P. Gillette, and Thomas D. Hopkins. *Federal Agency Valuations of Human Life.* Washington, D.C.: Administrative Conference of the United States, 1988.

Eisenberg, J. M. "New Drugs and Clinical Economics: Analysis of Cost Effectiveness in the Assessment of Pharmaceutical Innovations." *Review of Infectious Diseases,* November–December, 1984.

Gramlich, E. M. *Benefit-Cost Analysis of Governmental Programs,* 2nd ed. Englewood Cliffs, N.J.: Prentice Hall, 1989.

Karam, J. A.; S. M. Sundre; and G. L. Smith. "A Cost/Benefit Analysis of Patient Education." *Hospital and Health Services Administration* 31, no. 4 (July–August, 1986).

Mowitz, Robert J. *The Design of Public Decision Systems.* Baltimore, Md.: University Park Press, 1980.

Portney, P. R., ed. *Public Policies for Environmental Protection.* Washington, D.C.: Resources for the Future, 1990.

Rhoads, Steven E. *The Economist's View of the World: Government Markets, and Public Policy.* Cambridge, England: Cambridge University Press, 1985.

Schultze, Charles L. *The Politics and Economics of Public Spending.* Washington, D.C.: The Brookings Institution, 1968.

Stevenson Smith, G., and M. S. Tseng. "Benefit-Cost Analysis as a Performance Indicator." *Management Accounting,* June 1986.

Zeckhauser, R. J. "Procedures for Valuing Lives." *Public Policy,* Fall 1975, pp. 419–64.

Table 9A–1 Present Value of $1

Years Hence	1%	2%	4%	6%	8%	10%	12%	14%	15%	16%	18%	20%	22%	24%	25%	26%	28%	30%	35%	40%	45%	50%
1	0.990	0.980	0.962	0.943	0.926	0.909	0.893	0.877	0.870	0.862	0.847	0.833	0.820	0.806	0.800	0.794	0.781	0.769	0.741	0.714	0.690	0.667
2	0.980	0.961	0.925	0.890	0.857	0.826	0.797	0.769	0.756	0.743	0.718	0.694	0.672	0.650	0.640	0.630	0.610	0.592	0.549	0.510	0.476	0.444
3	0.971	0.942	0.889	0.840	0.794	0.751	0.712	0.675	0.658	0.641	0.609	0.579	0.551	0.524	0.512	0.500	0.477	0.455	0.406	0.364	0.328	0.296
4	0.961	0.924	0.855	0.792	0.735	0.683	0.636	0.592	0.572	0.552	0.516	0.482	0.451	0.423	0.410	0.397	0.373	0.350	0.301	0.260	0.226	0.198
5	0.951	0.906	0.822	0.747	0.681	0.621	0.567	0.519	0.497	0.476	0.437	0.402	0.370	0.341	0.328	0.315	0.291	0.269	0.223	0.186	0.156	0.132
6	0.942	0.888	0.790	0.705	0.630	0.564	0.507	0.456	0.432	0.410	0.370	0.335	0.303	0.275	0.262	0.250	0.227	0.207	0.165	0.133	0.108	0.088
7	0.933	0.871	0.760	0.665	0.583	0.513	0.452	0.400	0.376	0.354	0.314	0.279	0.249	0.222	0.210	0.198	0.178	0.159	0.122	0.095	0.074	0.059
8	0.923	0.853	0.731	0.627	0.540	0.467	0.404	0.351	0.327	0.305	0.266	0.233	0.204	0.179	0.168	0.157	0.139	0.123	0.091	0.068	0.051	0.039
9	0.914	0.837	0.703	0.592	0.500	0.424	0.361	0.308	0.284	0.263	0.225	0.194	0.167	0.144	0.134	0.125	0.108	0.094	0.067	0.048	0.035	0.026
10	0.905	0.820	0.676	0.558	0.463	0.386	0.322	0.270	0.247	0.227	0.191	0.162	0.137	0.116	0.107	0.099	0.085	0.073	0.050	0.035	0.024	0.017
11	0.896	0.804	0.650	0.527	0.429	0.350	0.287	0.237	0.215	0.195	0.162	0.135	0.112	0.094	0.086	0.079	0.066	0.056	0.037	0.025	0.017	0.012
12	0.887	0.788	0.625	0.497	0.397	0.319	0.257	0.208	0.187	0.168	0.137	0.112	0.092	0.076	0.069	0.062	0.052	0.043	0.027	0.018	0.012	0.008
13	0.879	0.773	0.601	0.469	0.368	0.290	0.229	0.182	0.163	0.145	0.116	0.093	0.075	0.061	0.055	0.050	0.040	0.033	0.020	0.013	0.008	0.005
14	0.870	0.758	0.577	0.442	0.340	0.263	0.205	0.160	0.141	0.125	0.099	0.078	0.062	0.049	0.044	0.039	0.032	0.025	0.015	0.009	0.006	0.003
15	0.861	0.743	0.555	0.417	0.315	0.239	0.183	0.140	0.123	0.108	0.084	0.065	0.051	0.040	0.035	0.031	0.025	0.020	0.011	0.006	0.004	0.002
16	0.853	0.728	0.534	0.394	0.292	0.218	0.163	0.123	0.107	0.093	0.071	0.054	0.042	0.032	0.028	0.025	0.019	0.015	0.008	0.005	0.003	0.002
17	0.844	0.714	0.513	0.371	0.270	0.198	0.146	0.108	0.093	0.080	0.060	0.045	0.034	0.026	0.023	0.020	0.015	0.012	0.006	0.003	0.002	0.001
18	0.836	0.700	0.494	0.350	0.250	0.180	0.130	0.095	0.081	0.069	0.051	0.038	0.028	0.021	0.018	0.016	0.012	0.009	0.005	0.002	0.001	0.001
19	0.828	0.686	0.475	0.331	0.232	0.164	0.116	0.083	0.070	0.060	0.043	0.031	0.023	0.017	0.014	0.012	0.009	0.007	0.003	0.002	0.001	
20	0.820	0.673	0.456	0.312	0.215	0.149	0.104	0.073	0.061	0.051	0.037	0.026	0.019	0.014	0.012	0.010	0.007	0.005	0.002	0.001	0.001	
21	0.811	0.660	0.439	0.294	0.199	0.135	0.093	0.064	0.053	0.044	0.031	0.022	0.015	0.011	0.009	0.008	0.006	0.004	0.002	0.001	0.001	
22	0.803	0.647	0.422	0.278	0.184	0.123	0.083	0.056	0.046	0.038	0.026	0.018	0.013	0.009	0.007	0.006	0.004	0.003	0.001	0.001		
23	0.795	0.634	0.406	0.262	0.170	0.112	0.074	0.049	0.040	0.033	0.022	0.015	0.010	0.007	0.006	0.005	0.003	0.002	0.001			
24	0.788	0.622	0.390	0.247	0.158	0.102	0.066	0.043	0.035	0.028	0.019	0.013	0.008	0.006	0.005	0.004	0.003	0.002	0.001			
25	0.780	0.610	0.375	0.233	0.146	0.092	0.059	0.038	0.030	0.024	0.016	0.010	0.007	0.005	0.004	0.003	0.002	0.001	0.001			
26	0.772	0.598	0.361	0.220	0.135	0.084	0.053	0.033	0.026	0.021	0.014	0.009	0.006	0.004	0.003	0.002	0.002	0.001				
27	0.764	0.586	0.347	0.207	0.125	0.076	0.047	0.029	0.023	0.018	0.011	0.007	0.005	0.003	0.002	0.002	0.001	0.001				
28	0.757	0.574	0.333	0.196	0.116	0.069	0.042	0.026	0.020	0.016	0.010	0.006	0.004	0.002	0.002	0.001	0.001	0.001				
29	0.749	0.563	0.321	0.185	0.107	0.063	0.037	0.022	0.017	0.014	0.008	0.005	0.003	0.002	0.002	0.001	0.001	0.001				
30	0.742	0.552	0.308	0.174	0.099	0.057	0.033	0.020	0.015	0.012	0.007	0.004	0.003	0.002	0.001	0.001	0.001					
40	0.672	0.453	0.208	0.097	0.046	0.022	0.011	0.005	0.004	0.003	0.001											
50	0.608	0.372	0.141	0.054	0.021	0.009	0.003	0.001	0.001	0.001												

TABLE 9A–2   Present Value of $1 Received Annually for N Years

Years N	1%	2%	4%	6%	8%	10%	12%	14%	15%	16%	18%	20%	22%	24%	25%	26%	28%	30%	35%	40%	45%	50%
1	0.990	0.980	0.962	0.943	0.926	0.909	0.893	0.877	0.870	0.862	0.847	0.833	0.820	0.806	0.800	0.794	0.781	0.769	0.741	0.714	0.690	0.667
2	1.970	1.942	1.886	1.833	1.783	1.736	1.690	1.647	1.626	1.605	1.566	1.528	1.492	1.457	1.440	1.424	1.392	1.361	1.289	1.224	1.165	1.111
3	2.941	2.884	2.775	2.673	2.577	2.487	2.402	2.322	2.283	2.246	2.174	2.106	2.042	1.981	1.952	1.923	1.868	1.816	1.696	1.589	1.493	1.407
4	3.902	3.808	3.630	3.465	3.312	3.170	3.037	2.914	2.855	2.798	2.690	2.589	2.494	2.404	2.362	2.320	2.241	2.166	1.997	1.849	1.720	1.605
5	4.853	4.713	4.452	4.212	3.993	3.791	3.605	3.433	3.352	3.274	3.127	2.991	2.864	2.745	2.689	2.635	2.532	2.436	2.220	2.035	1.876	1.737
6	5.795	5.601	5.242	4.917	4.623	4.355	4.111	3.889	3.784	3.685	3.498	3.326	3.167	3.020	2.951	2.885	2.759	2.643	2.385	2.168	1.983	1.824
7	6.728	6.472	6.002	5.582	5.206	4.868	4.564	4.288	4.160	4.039	3.812	3.605	3.416	3.242	3.161	3.083	2.937	2.802	2.508	2.263	2.057	1.883
8	7.652	7.325	6.733	6.210	5.747	5.335	4.968	4.639	4.487	4.344	4.078	3.837	3.619	3.421	3.329	3.241	3.076	2.925	2.598	2.331	2.108	1.922
9	8.566	8.162	7.435	6.802	6.247	5.759	5.328	4.946	4.772	4.607	4.303	4.031	3.786	3.566	3.463	3.366	3.184	3.019	2.665	2.379	2.144	1.948
10	9.471	8.983	8.111	7.360	6.710	6.145	5.650	5.216	5.019	4.833	4.494	4.192	3.923	3.682	3.571	3.465	3.269	3.092	2.715	2.414	2.168	1.965
11	10.368	9.787	8.760	7.887	7.139	6.495	5.937	5.453	5.234	5.029	4.656	4.327	4.035	3.776	3.656	3.544	3.335	3.147	2.752	2.438	2.185	1.977
12	11.255	10.575	9.385	8.384	7.536	6.814	6.194	5.660	5.421	5.197	4.793	4.439	4.127	3.851	3.725	3.606	3.387	3.190	2.779	2.456	2.196	1.985
13	12.134	11.343	9.986	8.853	7.904	7.103	6.424	5.842	5.583	5.342	4.910	4.533	4.203	3.912	3.780	3.656	3.427	3.223	2.799	2.468	2.204	1.990
14	13.004	12.106	10.563	9.295	8.244	7.367	6.628	6.002	5.724	5.468	5.008	4.611	4.265	3.962	3.824	3.695	3.459	3.249	2.814	2.477	2.210	1.993
15	13.865	12.849	11.118	9.712	8.559	7.606	6.811	6.142	5.847	5.575	5.092	4.675	4.315	4.001	3.859	3.726	3.483	3.268	2.825	2.484	2.214	1.995
16	14.718	13.578	11.652	10.106	8.851	7.824	6.974	6.265	5.954	5.669	5.162	4.730	4.357	4.033	3.887	3.751	3.503	3.283	2.834	2.489	2.216	1.997
17	15.562	14.292	12.166	10.477	9.122	8.022	7.120	6.373	6.047	5.749	5.222	4.775	4.391	4.059	3.910	3.771	3.518	3.295	2.840	2.492	2.218	1.998
18	16.398	14.992	12.659	10.828	9.372	8.201	7.250	6.467	6.128	5.818	5.273	4.812	4.419	4.080	3.928	3.786	3.529	3.304	2.844	2.494	2.219	1.999
19	17.226	15.678	13.134	11.158	9.604	8.365	7.366	6.550	6.198	5.877	5.316	4.844	4.442	4.097	3.942	3.799	3.539	3.311	2.848	2.496	2.220	1.999
20	18.046	16.351	13.590	11.470	9.818	8.514	7.469	6.623	6.259	5.929	5.353	4.870	4.460	4.110	3.954	3.808	3.546	3.316	2.850	2.497	2.221	1.999
21	18.857	17.011	14.029	11.764	10.017	8.649	7.562	6.687	6.312	5.973	5.384	4.891	4.476	4.121	3.963	3.816	3.551	3.320	2.852	2.498	2.221	1.997
22	19.660	17.658	14.451	12.042	10.201	8.772	7.645	6.743	6.359	6.011	5.410	4.909	4.488	4.130	3.970	3.822	3.556	3.323	2.853	2.498	2.222	1.998
23	20.456	18.292	14.857	12.303	10.371	8.883	7.718	6.792	6.399	6.044	5.432	4.925	4.499	4.137	3.976	3.827	3.559	3.325	2.854	2.499	2.222	1.999
24	21.243	18.914	15.247	12.550	10.529	8.985	7.784	6.835	6.434	6.073	5.451	4.937	4.507	4.143	3.981	3.831	3.562	3.327	2.855	2.499	2.222	1.999
25	22.023	19.523	15.622	12.783	10.675	9.077	7.843	6.873	6.464	6.097	5.467	4.948	4.514	4.147	3.985	3.834	3.564	3.329	2.856	2.499	2.222	1.999
26	22.795	20.121	15.983	13.003	10.810	9.161	7.896	6.906	6.491	6.118	5.480	4.956	4.520	4.151	3.988	3.837	3.566	3.330	2.856	2.500	2.222	2.000
27	23.560	20.707	16.330	13.211	10.935	9.237	7.943	6.935	6.514	6.136	5.492	4.964	4.524	4.154	3.990	3.839	3.567	3.331	2.856	2.500	2.222	2.000
28	24.316	21.281	16.663	13.406	11.051	9.307	7.984	6.961	6.534	6.152	5.502	4.970	4.528	4.157	3.992	3.840	3.568	3.331	2.857	2.500	2.222	2.000
29	25.066	21.844	16.984	13.591	11.158	9.370	8.022	6.983	6.551	6.166	5.510	4.975	4.531	4.159	3.994	3.841	3.569	3.332	2.857	2.500	2.222	2.000
30	25.808	22.396	17.292	13.765	11.258	9.427	8.055	7.003	6.566	6.177	5.517	4.979	4.534	4.160	3.995	3.842	3.569	3.332	2.857	2.500	2.222	2.000
40	32.835	27.355	19.793	15.046	11.925	9.779	8.244	7.105	6.642	6.234	5.548	4.997	4.544	4.166	3.999	3.846	3.571	3.333	2.857	2.500	2.222	2.000
50	39.196	31.424	21.482	15.762	12.234	9.915	8.304	7.133	6.661	6.246	5.554	4.999	4.545	4.167	4.000	3.846	3.571	3.333	2.857	2.500	2.222	2.000

CASE 9–1   Yoland Research Institute*

Ms. Brooke Russell, executive director of Yoland Research Institute, was contemplating a proposal recently submitted to her by Dr. Russ Roberts, the head of the nutrition studies department. Dr. Roberts' request was for the purchase of new equipment to perform operations currently being performed on different, less efficient equipment. The purchase price was $150,000 delivered and installed.

Background

Yoland Research Institute was a nonprofit, university-affiliated organization, specializing in research in a wide variety of fields. In large part, its activities were determined by a combination of the faculty affiliated with it and their research interests, although most of its projects tended to be of a basic, rather than applied, nature. As such, it was constantly involved in projects that were attempting to advance the state of the art in the particular field of investigation. One such area was nutrition, where much of the work required sophisticated equipment. Sometimes the purchase of this equipment was funded by a particular research grant or contract.

Dr. Roberts' Request

Dr. Roberts had worked closely with the equipment manufacturer to determine the potential benefits of the new equipment, and estimated that it would result in annual savings to the Institute of $30,000 in labor and other direct costs, as compared with the present equipment. He also estimated that the proposed equipment's economic life was 10 years, with zero salvage value.

In the case of this request, no grant or contract funds were available, and, hence, Yoland would need to finance the cost of the new equipment itself. The Institute had recently borrowed long-term to finance some other projects, and Ms. Russell was certain that it could obtain additional funds at 12 percent, although she would not plan to negotiate a loan specifically for the purchase of this equipment. She did feel, however, that an investment of this type should have a return of at least 20 percent, even though the Institute paid no taxes.

---

* This case was prepared by Professor David W. Young. Copyright © by David W. Young. Distributed by the Accounting Curriculum Center, Boston University School of Management.

Complicating Factors

There were several complications associated with Dr. Roberts' request. The first was that, although the present equipment was in good working order and would probably last, physically, for at least 20 more years, it was being depreciated at a straight-line rate of 10 percent per year. As such, it had a book value of $72,000 (cost $120,000; accumulated depreciation, $48,000). It had no resale value, however. Dr. Roberts thought the Institute would be able to find someone to remove it at no charge, but that was about all.

The second complication was that Dr. Roberts' proposal had arrived on the same day as a proposal from Dr. Sharon Kim in the sanitary engineering department. Two years ago, the Institute had approved a proposal from Dr. Kim involving the same economic life and dollar amounts as Dr. Roberts' proposal. Dr. Kim's new proposal was for what she termed even better equipment that, in her view, rendered her other equipment completely obsolete with no resale value. The new equipment would cost $300,000 delivered and installed, but was expected to result in annual savings of $75,000 above the cost of operating the two-year-old equipment. Dr. Kim estimated that the economic life of this new equipment was 10 years.

The third complication was that a board member had pointed out that the Institute had a debt/equity structure as follows:

	Percent of Total	Average Interest Rate	Weighted Interest Rate
Debt	40%	12.0%	4.8%
Equity......	60	0.0	—
Total	100%		4.8%

According to the board member, this situation arose because the Institute's equity consisted of donations and other gifts that are essentially free; that is, there is no interest charge. Thus, the proper discount rate to use is not 20 percent, as suggested by Ms. Russell, but only about 5 percent.

The Decision

Although funds could be obtained to finance the purchase of both Dr. Roberts' and Dr. Kim's proposed new equipment, Ms. Russell was concerned about the apparent mistake that had been made two years ago with Dr. Kim's request. She wanted to be sure that a similar mistake not be made this year with Dr. Roberts' request. She also was not certain that Dr. Kim's request was justifiable.

Questions

1. What is your response to the argument made by the board member concerning the appropriate discount rate to use? If not 5 percent, what figure would you use?
2. Should the Institute buy the proposed equipment for Dr. Roberts? For Dr. Kim?
3. If the Institute decides to purchase the new equipment for Dr. Kim, a mistake apparently has been made somewhere, because good equipment, bought only two years previously, is being scrapped. How did this mistake come about? What might be done to avoid similar mistakes in the future?

CASE 9–2   Downtown Parking Authority*

In January a meeting was held in the office of the mayor of Oakmont to discuss a proposed municipal parking facility. The participants included the mayor, the traffic commissioner, the administrator of Oakmont's Downtown Parking Authority, the city planner, and the finance director. The purpose of the meeting was to consider a report by Richard Stockton, executive assistant to the Parking Authority's administrator, concerning estimated costs and revenues for the proposed facility.

Mr. Stockton's opening statement was as follows:

As you know, the mayor proposed two months ago that we construct a multilevel parking garage on the Elm Street site. At that time, he asked the Parking Authority to assemble all pertinent information for consideration at our meeting today. I would like to summarize our findings briefly for you.

The Elm Street site is owned by the city. All that stands on it now are the remains of the old Embassy Cinema, which we estimate would cost approximately $80,000 to demolish. A building contractor has estimated that a multilevel structure, with space for 800 cars, could be built on the site at a cost of about $4 million. The useful life of the garage would be around 40 years.

The city could finance construction of the garage through the sale of bonds. The finance director has informed me that we could probably float an issue of 20-year tax-exempts at 5 percent interest. Redemption would commence after three years, with one-seventeenth of the original number of bonds being recalled in each succeeding year.

A parking management firm has already contacted us with a proposal to operate the garage for the city. They estimate that their costs, exclusive of the fee, would amount to $480,000 per year. Of this amount, $350,000 would be personnel costs; the remainder would include utilities, mechanical maintenance, insurance, and so forth. In addition, they would require a management fee of $60,000 per year. Any gross revenues in excess of $540,000 per year would be shared 90 percent by the city and 10 percent by the management firm. If total annual revenues are *less* than $540,000, the city would have to pay the difference.

---

* This case was prepared by Graeme Taylor, Management Analysis Center, and Professor Richard F. Vancil, Harvard Business School.

I suggest we offer a management contract for bid, with renegotiations every three years.

The city would derive additional income of around $100,000 per year by renting the ground floor of the structure as retail space.

We conducted a survey at a private parking garage only three blocks from the Elm Street site to help estimate revenues from the prospective garage.

The garage, which is open every day from 7:00 A.M., until midnight, charges: $1.50 for the first hour; $1.00 for the second hour; and 50 cents for each subsequent hour, with a maximum rate of $4. Their capacity is 400 spaces. Our survey indicated that during business hours, 75 percent of their spaces were occupied by "all-day parkers"—cars whose drivers and passengers work downtown. In addition, roughly 400 cars use the garage each weekday with an average stay of three hours. We did not take a survey on Saturday or Sunday, but the proprietor indicated that the garage is usually about 75 percent utilized by short-term parkers on Saturdays until 6:00 P.M., when the department stores close; the average stay is about two hours. There's a lull until about 7:00 P.M., when the moviegoers start coming in; he says the garage is almost full from 8:00 P.M., until closing time at midnight. Sundays are usually very quiet until the evening, when he estimates that his garage is 60 percent utilized from 6:00 P.M. until midnight.

In addition, we studied a report issued by the City College Economics Department last year, which estimated that we now have approximately 50,000 cars entering the central business district (CBD) every day from Monday through Saturday. Based on correlations with other cities of comparable size, the economists calculated that we need 30,000 parking spaces in the CBD. This agrees quite well with a block-by-block estimate made by the traffic commissioner's office last year, which indicated a total parking need in the CBD of 29,000 spaces. Right now we have 22,000 spaces in the CBD. Of these, 5 percent are curb spaces (half of which are metered, with a two-hour maximum limit for 40 cents), and all the rest are in privately owned garages and open lots.

Another study indicated that 60 percent of all auto passengers entering the CBD on a weekday were on their way to work, 20 percent were shoppers, and 20 percent were business executives making calls. The average number of people per car was 1.75.

Unfortunately, we have not yet had time to use the data mentioned thus far to work up estimates of the revenues to be expected from the proposed garage.

The Elm Street site is strategically located in the heart of the CBD, near the major department stores and office buildings. It is five blocks from one of the access ramps to the new crosstown freeway, which we expect will be open to traffic next year, and only three blocks from the Music Center, which the mayor dedicated last week.

As we all know, the parking situation in that section of town has steadily worsened over the last few years, with no immediate prospect of improvement. The demand for parking is clearly there, and the Parking Authority therefore recommends that we build the garage.

The mayor thanked Mr. Stockton for his report and asked for comments. The following discussion took place:

Finance Director: I'm all in favor of relieving parking congestion downtown, but I think we have to consider alternative uses of the Elm Street site. For example, the city could sell that site to a private developer for at least $2 million. The site could support an office building from which the city would derive property taxes of around $400,000 per year at present rates. The office building would almost certainly incorporate an underground parking garage for the use of the tenants, and therefore we would not only improve our tax base and increase revenues but also increase the availability of parking at no cost to the city. Besides, an office building on that site would improve the amenity of downtown; a multilevel garage built above ground, on the other hand, would not.

Planning Director: I'm not sure I agree completely with the finance director. Within a certain range we can increase the value of downtown land by judicious provision of parking. Adequate, efficient parking facilities will encourage more intensive use of downtown traffic generators such as shops, offices, and places of entertainment, thus enhancing land values. A garage contained within an office building might, as the finance director suggests, provide more spaces, but I suspect these would be occupied almost exclusively by workers in the building and thus would not increase the total available supply.

    I think long-term parking downtown should be discouraged by the city. We should attempt to encourage short-term parking—particularly among shoppers—in an effort to counteract the growth of business in the suburbs and the consequent stagnation of retail outlets downtown. The rate structure in effect at the privately operated garage quoted by Mr. Stockton clearly favors the long-term parker. I believe that if the city constructs a garage on the Elm Street site, we should devise a rate structure that favors the short-term parker. People who work downtown should be encouraged to use our mass transit system.

Finance Director: I'm glad you mentioned mass transit because this raises another issue. As you know, our subways are not now used to capacity and are running at a substantial annual deficit borne by the city. We have just spent millions of dollars on the new subway station under the Music Center. Why build a city garage only three blocks away that will still further increase the subway system's deficit? Each person who drives downtown instead of taking the subway represents a loss of $1.00 (the average round trip fare) to the subway system. I have read a report stating that approximately two-thirds of all persons entering the CBD by car would still have made the trip by *subway* if they had *not* been able to use their cars.

Mayor: On the other hand, I think shoppers prefer to drive rather than take the subway, particularly if they intend to make substantial purchases. No one likes to take the subway burdened down by packages and shopping bags. You know, the Downtown Merchants Association has informed me that they estimate that each new parking space in the CBD generates on average an additional $20,000 in annual retail sales. That represents substantial extra profit to retailers; I think retailing aftertax profits average about 3 percent of gross sales. Besides, the city treasury benefits directly from our 3 percent sales tax.

Traffic Commissioner: But what about some of the other costs of increasing parking downtown and therefore, presumably, the number of cars entering the CBD? I'm thinking of such costs as the increased wear and tear on city streets, the additional congestion produced with consequent delays and frustration for the drivers, the impeding of the movement of city vehicles, noise, air pollution, and so on. How do we weigh these costs in coming to a decision?

Parking Administrator: I don't think we can make a decision at this meeting. I suggest that Dick Stockton be asked to prepare an analysis of the proposed garage that will answer the following questions:

Questions

1. Using the information presented at this discussion, should the city of Oakmont construct the proposed garage?
2. What rates should be charged?
3. What additional information, if any, should be obtained before making a final decision?

CASE 9–3   New York City Asphalt Plant (A)*

Prior to 1963, four of the five boroughs of the City of New York owned and operated their own asphalt plants. As the demand for asphalt grew and the condition of the plants deteriorated, the city increased its purchases from the private sector. By the early 1970s it appeared inevitable that the city would soon be out of the asphalt-producing business altogether. Some officials viewed this prospect with alarm. For example, a February 1973 memo from Peter Stangl, an assistant administrator in the Transportation Department, to the Office of Management and Budget argued:

> The city of New York should maintain its own capacity for producing asphalt even if it can be purchased more cheaply from private vendors. The reason is that a benchmark against which to measure vendor performance must be provided.

At that time, there were eight private plants: one in the Bronx, one small one in Brooklyn, two on Staten Island and four in Queens, on so-called "asphalt row."

Paving asphalt is a mixture of sand and gravel stuck together with a petroleum product called asphalt cement. The asphalt cement is analogous to the portland cement in concrete, but hardens at room temperature rather than by chemical reaction. Asphalt making consists of mixing appropriate proportions of aggregates and cement at 325° F., to produce a product that is soft enough to apply and roll smooth as long as it stays hot. The asphalt is unusable if allowed to cool below 250° F., as occurs if a truck is delayed or if paving is attempted in winter weather.

At the time of Stangl's memo the price of asphalt to the city was rising and there were allegations of collusion between the contractors in the bidding process. (According to the memo, prices rose almost 80% from 1968 to 1972, from $7.53 per ton to $13.50 per ton.) Nevertheless, no last-ditch action was taken to forestall the loss of in-house production capacity—at least in part because such a step would have required a capital expenditure of several million dollars on a new plant, and at the time New York City was extremely hard pressed for funds. (In 1975, the city's financial crisis triggered an emergency bailout from the federal and state

---

* This case was prepared by Paul Starobin under the direction of Associate Dean Peter Zimmerman, John F. Kennedy School of Government. Copyright © by the President and Fellows of Harvard College. Distributed by the Case Program, Kennedy School of Government.

governments.) To meet its asphalt needs, the city adopted a competitive bidding process. Under this system, the Transportation Department divided the city's streets into four geographic zones, and let annual contracts to serve each of the zones. (The zones were Queens; Staten Island; the Bronx and Manhattan north of 59th Street; and Brooklyn and Manhattan south of 59th Street.)

The Stangl memo had accurately reflected widespread concern among city officials about the prices being charged by vendors located in the city; and in 1975 the city decided to increase competition by making vendors from New Jersey eligible to bid on the city contracts. According to one official:

> What happened was that the [bids] came in significantly cheaper than the ones from the vendors in New York City. And I don't mean by a dollar, I'm talking five or six dollars a ton. So right away people started saying "What's going on here? What's the price of asphalt? What should we be paying?
>
> . . . I don't know the full story. A lot of people thought that it was chicanery, but perhaps it wasn't. I did know that the New Jersey vendors had cheaper labor and energy costs.

While the New Jersey "option" proved advantageous in terms of price, it left much to be desired: the chief shortcoming was that the trucks bearing loads of freshly made asphalt tended to get delayed, and therefore cold, in the traffic flowing into the city each morning from across the Hudson River. Also, given a fixed number of trucks, the closer the plant was to the work site, the less time the crew had to wait for trucks to arrive with fresh loads of asphalt.

The experiment revived arguments in favor of in-house capacity for producing asphalt. The city official who was perhaps the most dissatisfied with the loss of this capacity—and the best positioned to do something about it—was Henry Fulton, chief of the Transportation Department's Bureau of Highway Operations. The bureau was responsible for the asphalt hauling and road resurfacing functions, and the asphalt contracting system. Also, the responsibility for the operation of an asphalt plant, should the city decide to build one, would fall in its bailiwick.

Fulton saw advantages to building a plant in addition to the "benchmark" argument cited by Stangl. For one, as an aide of his commented: "We knew it would be cheaper: It had to be. The City of New York would be buying the [raw materials] aggregate at least for the same price as the vendors. We would be paying the people working at the plant approximately the same salary. But there's no profit. If you eliminate the profit margin the city can produce it for less."

Various analyses undertaken at Fulton's initiative supported the cost-savings argument. One such analysis, completed in July 1975, estimated that the city could produce asphalt for $14.72 per ton. This price included a per ton operating cost of $12.36 (made up mainly of labor, energy, and materials[1]) and a finance and

---

[1] The most expensive item was the asphalt cement, a petroleum derivative, which accounted for nearly 60% of the materials cost. The price of the cement was rising sharply over this period, due to rising oil prices.

capital cost of $2.36 (this assumed borrowing to pay for the plant at an interest rate of 9%). The price per ton charged by vendors was put at $19.00; the savings in production costs of $4.28 per ton could amortize the finance and capital costs in seven years, according to the analysis. (The analysis also indicated that the amortization would increase to 7.93 years, and decrease to 6.6 years, under the assumption of a 10% and 8% interest rate, respectively.)

City officials claimed also that a city asphalt plant could operate for 12 months of the year. This would enable the city to get out of premium-priced winter asphalt contracts. (The "peak season" for producing and laying asphalt was April 1– December 15; during the "winter season" road work was limited to filling potholes. Low production volume meant high production costs—and prices.) One official commented in a memo that a city-owned asphalt supply would not be affected, "by strikes or other disruptions in the private sector"; the city could experiment with new, and possibly better types of asphalt; and city trucks would spend less time queuing at private plants. Proponents also argued that a city plant could come equipped with an asphalt recycling capability otherwise unavailable. This capability, they argued, could both produce environmental benefits and reduce raw material and waste disposal costs. (The vendors claimed that recycling was an untried and costly technology.)

Finally, there were some officials, chief among them Henry Fulton, who believed that city workers, in general, did better quality work than those from the private sector, and that a city plant would enable the bureau to improve its roadway program, thus raising the "public image" of city workers. As Fulton said: "I see a bad street, and a city team comes in, leaves two days later, and we've got a brand new street. That's good PR—the best you can get." Fulton also relished the prospect of a "little friendly competition" with the "big guys" in the private sector. As he put it:

> I pictured the city as another business entity. The Bureau of Highway Operations was in the business of repairing and maintaining roads, and I was firmly convinced that the bureau personnel did the best asphalt work that was being done in New York City . . . Sure the profit motive means something, but we had personal satisfaction, personal drive we get from hearing we did a good job, and hearing criticism from the contractors that we're putting them out of business. We liked to compete, that kind of criticism felt all right.

These arguments were apparently persuasive to many in the city government, but because of continuing financial problems, and the political opposition of private vendors to a city-operated plant, Fulton's project remained on the back burner for some time. In May 1978, sensing the timing was right to clear the political and financial obstacles, Fulton wrote a memo recommending the project to Acting Transportation Commissioner Dave Love. The memo, which included the 1975 analysis, referred to an updated analysis indicating that:

> The price of asphalt paid to private vendors has been rising steadily and is now estimated at $20/ton or approximately $4.0/ton more than the projected cost of City produced asphalt. Based upon an annual production level of 250,000 tons per year, savings of $1,000,000 could be anticipated in future expense budget appropriations.

The total Highways Department yearly asphalt needs are estimated at 500,000 tons. The balance of the asphalt would be purchased, as is the current practice, from private vendors. The city plant would therefore create a competitive situation possibly providing an additional benefit by becoming a barometer and, hopefully, regulator of the private asphalt market.

The details of Fulton's calculations are contained in Exhibit 1.

EXHIBIT 1   Analysis of Costs and Benefits of In-House Asphalt Production

---

1. Production cost:
   Costs have been evaluated from 1974 data. The following breakdown is for a production of 250,000 tons/year.

		Per Ton
Labor = 11 personnel + 100%......................	$ 336,000	$ 1.34
Grease and oil.......................................	5,000	0.02
Electricity...	82,500	0.33
Fuel...	50,000	0.20
Materials: (1) Asphalt cement @ $62/ton................	930,000	3.72
(2) Sand, stone and dust.....................	1,062,500	4.25
Waste	12,500	0.05
Repair and maintenance	50,000	0.20
		$10.11

Considering 22% cost increase over 1974, the cost for 1975 is projected to be $12.36/ton.

2. Capital cost and amortization:

1. Plant...............	$3,660,000
2. Bulkhead	870,000*
3. Dredging	75,000
4. Electrical...........	475,000*
5. Mechanical	300,000
Total.................	$5,380,000

   * This cost has been reduced by charges applied to shop area.

   It must be pointed out that the life expectancy as well as the cost of items 3 and 5 is much less than that for the remainder. Therefore the life expectancy for the whole system can be taken to be that of the plant—20 years.

   Considering the cost of financing to be 9% we have the following:

   20-year recovery factor at 9% = .1095466

   Finance and amortization cost per year = $5,380,000 × .1095466 = $589,361

   For a production of 250,000 tons/year the F & A cost is $2.36/ton

3. Total cost:
   For a production of 250,000 tons/year it follows:

Per Ton	
Operating cost...........	$12.36
F & A cost..............	2.36
Total	$14.72

   The finance and capital cost is 16% of the total cost for 250,000 tons of production and decreases to 11.9% for 350,000 tons.

4. The plant is designed for a maximum production of 300 tons/hour. Demand is affected by construction cycle and the geographical location of field operation. This may change the demand for *efficient*

EXHIBIT 1 *(concluded)*

production from one year to another between 150,000 tons and 350,000 tons per year. It is estimated however that over the long run production will stand at the 250,000-ton mark.

5. Cost benefit:
Material currently being purchased from vendors strategically located for maximum efficiency of field operation costs $19/ton.

The savings which the City can incur by building the plant are illustrated by the difference between the vendor cost and the City cost. It follows that 147,500 tons/day is the break-even production quantity below which the City will incur losses. At a production level of 250,000 tons/year the saving is as follows:

$$\text{Saving} = (\text{Cost by vendor} - \text{Cost by City})\ 250,000.$$
$$\text{Saving} = (19. - 14.72)\ 250,000$$
$$\text{Saving} = (4.23)\ 250,000$$
$$\text{Saving} = \$1,070,000 \text{ per year}$$

The saving increases as production increases. For a production of 350,000 tons/year the savings can be increased to $2,117,500 per year.

It must also be noted that the effective savings are even larger than those illustrated herewith when considering the investment gains on such savings.

If the net savings are assumed to remain the same over a period of years regardless of what the absolute costs may be then these prorated savings can be utilized toward the subsequent amortizations of the finance and capital cost. Then:

$$\left(\begin{array}{c} \text{Yearly} \\ \text{charges} \end{array} + \begin{array}{c} \text{Yearly} \\ \text{savings} \end{array} \right) \times \left(\begin{array}{c} \text{Number} \\ \text{of years} \end{array} \right) = \begin{array}{c} \text{Total finance and capital cost} \\ \text{paid over 20 years} \end{array}$$

For 250,000 tons/year of production we obtain:

$(589,361 + 1,070,000)$ years $= (589,361)(20)$; years $= 7.09$. This means that the savings incurred can reduce the payment for finance and capital cost from 20 years to 7.09 years. However, note that the effective years are even less when considering the investment gains from such savings.

6. Interest rate:
The effect of an interest rate other than 9% retained in the previous sections is considered for the long-range production of 250,000 tons/year.

	Interest Rate		
	8%	*9%*	*10%*
Operating cost per ton............	$12.36	$12.36	$12.36
F & A cost per ton..............	2.19	2.36	2.53
Total cost per ton................	$14.55	$14.72	$14.89
Cost from vender per ton	$19.00	$19.00	$19.00
Savings per ton...................	4.55	4.28	4.11
Yearly savings...................	1,387,500.00	1,070,000.00	1,027,500.00
Yearly charges	547,760.00	589,361.00	631,935.00
Total charges....................	$10,955,200.00	$11,787,220.00	$12,638,696.00
No. of years for payment of the plant	6.6	7.09	7.93

Obviously a large interest rate for financing the capital investment, reduces the savings and consequently increases the effective time period for paying off the plant. The analysis indicates that the effect is not drastically adverse with respect to the savings incurred. The 10% interest rate extends the effective time for paying off the plant by 1.27 years (19%) over the time required for an 8% interest rate.

At the time this memo was written, Fulton was intending to locate the plant in Queens, at a site of one of the city's old asphalt plants. Due to political opposition to this site, however, and shortly after the memo to Love, he made a new proposal to locate the plant at a city-owned site in Brooklyn. The plant would serve all of the Brooklyn-Manhattan south zone and—if necessary—other areas as well. (The plans for the facility and the analysis of the operating and financing costs remained the same.) Fulton and other bureau officials argued that a Brooklyn site was even better than a Queens location: as things stood, the contractor for the Brooklyn-Manhattan south zone was located on "asphalt row" in Queens; a Brooklyn plant would increase the productivity of the road resurfacing work performed in this zone by shortening the amount of time it took asphalt haulers to get from the production point to the work site.

It was up to Love to decide whether to submit to the Mayor's Office of Management and Budget a request for a capital appropriation to finance the construction of a plant.

Questions

1. Assuming a discount factor of 10 percent, what was the net present value of the proposed asphalt plant?
2. Was the analysis described in Exhibit 1 an acceptable basis for arriving at a decision on the proposed asphalt plant?
3. Considering only the economics, should New York City build the proposed asphalt plant?
4. Would consideration of factors in addition to the economics change your conclusion?

CASE 9–4   New York City Asphalt Plant (B)*

In April 1981, the City of New York constructed a 300 ton-per-hour asphalt plant at 448 Hamilton Avenue in Brooklyn. Operated by the Transportation Department's Bureau of Highway Operations, the facility supplied all the asphalt needs of the Brooklyn-Manhattan South zone. Private vendors continued to service the other three zones—Queens, Staten Island, and the Bronx-Manhattan North. In a March 1982 memo to Anthony Ameruso, commissioner of the Transportation Department, Henry Fulton, chief of the Bureau of Highway Operations, quoted the price of asphalt produced by the Brooklyn plant at $23.46 per ton for the period April 1, 1981, to December 1981. To get the same grade material from the contractor for Queens would cost $27.55/ton; from the Bronx-Manhattan North vendor $27.27; and from the Staten Island vendor, $26.50.

---

* This case was prepared by Paul Starobin under the direction of Associate Dean Peter Zimmerman, John F. Kennedy School of Government. Copyright © by the President and Fellows of Harvard College. Distributed by the Case Program, Kennedy School of Government.

The memo also cited "productivity" gains resulting from the favorable siting of the plant; in the first half of FY 1982, as compared to the first half of the previous fiscal year, 46% more asphalt was laid down over the area served by the Brooklyn plant. The recycling equipment, on the other hand, was not being put to much use; plant workers discovered assorted problems with the technology that prevented its use more than "15% of the time." Still, Fulton and others in the Highways Bureau declared the venture a success.

In fact, Fulton was so pleased with the performance of the first plant, and so enamoured of the idea of the city "making" a product it needed, that he considered proposing to Commissioner Ameruso the construction of a second plant, to serve the Queens zone. (Queens required 900–1,000 tons of asphalt per day.) The site for the facility would be at the mouth of the Flushing River in Queens—a site originally proposed, and rejected, for the first plant. The long-time contractor for the Queens zone, Jet Asphalt Company, was located just across the river from the site Fulton had in mind, and the company's president, Frank Castiglione, was understandably not very enthusiastic about Fulton's proposal. Some 60%–65% of his plant's total annual asphalt production of 250,000 tons was purchased by the city.

EXHIBIT 1   1982 Asphalt Costs (Information Collected by Joan Kaden)

Fixed costs:		
Capital (finance charges, 20-year amortization at 11.44%)		$365,000
Personal services	$293,178	
Overhead (35% of Personal services)	102,612	
		$395,790
Parts		30,000
		$790,790
Fixed cost per ton:		
100,000 tons		$ 7.91
175,000 tons		4.52
250,000 tons		3.16
Variable costs per ton:		
Materials:		
Sand (38%)	$ 2.25	
Gravel (53%)	5.22	
Asphalt cement (6%)	9.54	
Mineral dust (3%)	.54	
	$ 17.55	
Energy (10%)	2.00	
Total variable costs per ton		$ 19.55
Total costs per ton:		
100,000 tons		$ 27.46
175,000 tons		24.07
250,000 tons		22.71

EXHIBIT 2   Recent Bids from Private Contractors

	Per Ton
Queens	$27.42
Staten Island	24.45
Bronx-Manhattan	27.94

Getting Analysis

Meanwhile, Commissioner Ameruso decided to probe more deeply into the cost-effectiveness of in-house asphalt production. The official asked a former colleague, Joan Kaden, an analyst with the mayor's Office of Operations, to compare "in-house" and vendor costs of production at different production levels (Exhibit 1), recent bids for asphalt from private operators (Exhibit 2), and the daily in-season asphalt needs of the city (Exhibit 3).

EXHIBIT 3   Daily Asphalt Needs

Laying asphalt is a seasonal activity. The manufacture is likewise seasonal. The production goals for the Hamilton Avenue plant are 150,000 tons during the season, and 25,000 tons off season. The season is April to December 15. Activity tends to peak in May and June, level down in July and August due to hot weather and vacations, peak again in September and October, and decline in November and December due to holidays and bad weather. From December 15 to March 30, roadwork typically is limited to pothole repair. During the first thirteen months of operations (April 1981–May 1982), output was approximately 189,000 tons, and in line with production goals.

The Hamilton Avenue plant supplies Brooklyn and Manhattan, and the three City road crews assigned to those boroughs. Daily asphalt requirements for these boroughs range between 725 and 900 tons during the season. The borough assignment and approximate daily asphalt requirements of each of the City's eight road crews are as follows:

Road Crews	Borough Assignment	Daily Asphalt Needs (tons)		Source of Asphalt
1	Manhattan	225	(low due to traffic)	City/vendor
2	Brooklyn	500–725	(assumes use of 1 drag spreader and 1 automatic paving machine)	City
1	Staten Island	600	(assumes asphalt produced in Staten Island)	Vendor
1	Bronx	400		Vendor
3	Queens	900–1,000		Vendor
6		2,525–2,950 tons per day		

To meet production goals, the Hamilton Avenue plant must produce 900 tons per day for 166 days of the season, which has a maximum of 170 working days (8½ months × 20 working days per month). Alternatively, they could supply night emergency crews or double shifts and produce on fewer days. Bad weather or plant breakdowns will preclude production four to six days per season.

Questions

1. With the benefit of hindsight, was the decision to build the asphalt plant a sound one?
2. Assuming that the cost estimates in Exhibit 1 were the best that could be made, would you recommend the construction of a second asphalt plant? If so, what should be its size?

CASE 9–5   Disease Control Programs*

In February 1967, Mr. Harley Davidson, an analyst in the office of the Injury Control Program, Public Health Service (Department of Health, Education and Welfare) was reviewing DHEW's recently published Program Analysis 1966–1 titled *Disease Control Programs–Motor Vehicle Injury Prevention Program.* Included therein were nine program units. Mr. Davidson was a member of a task force established within DHEW to evaluate a series of benefit/cost analyses of various proposed disease control programs. In addition to motor vehicle injury prevention, benefit/cost studies had been made of programs dealing with control of arthritis, cancer, tuberculosis, and syphilis. Mr. Davidson's specific responsibility was to review Program Unit No. 8 of the Motor Vehicle Injury Prevention Program (Increase Use of Improved Safety Devices by Motorcyclists) in order to (*a*) evaluate the methodology and results of the benefit/cost analysis of Program Unit No. 8, and (*b*) recommend whether or not the analysis justified the level of funding contemplated in the program unit.

The Motorcycle Program

The following is the description of Program Unit No. 8, which appeared in Program Analysis 1966–1:

Increase Use of Improved Safety Devices by Motorcyclists.   To prevent accidental deaths due to head injuries of motorcycle riders through appropriate health activity at the national, state, and local levels.

Approach.   The Public Health Service approach to solving the motorcycle injury problem will involve four phases. Although each of the four phases of activity is identified separately, all will be closely coordinated and carried out simultaneously. The four phases of activity are:

1. A national education program on use of protective head gear aimed primarily at motorcycle users. It will also include efforts to prepare operators of other motor vehicles to share the road with motorcycles.

---

* This case was prepared by Professor Charles J. Christenson, Harvard Business School.

2. A cooperative program with other national organizations and the motorcycle industry to improve protective and safety devices.
3. Involvement of state and local health departments and medical organizations in programs and activities designed to minimize accidental injury in motorcycle accidents.
4. Conduct surveillance activity on appropriate aspects of the motorcycle accident and injury problem.

The program unit was estimated to require the following level of new funding during the five-year planning period 1968–72:

	Estimated Program Level (millions of dollars)
1968	$1.679
1969	1.609
1970	1.574
1971	1.569
1972	1.569

Exhibit 1 gives a summary of the way in which the proposed funds would be spent.

The benefit/cost study estimated that the above program would result in the saving of 4,006 lives over the five-year period 1968–72 (no reduction in injuries was considered). The cost of the program discounted at 4 percent was $7,419,000;

EXHIBIT 1 Proposed Budget for Program to Increase Use of Protective Devices by Motorcyclists (1968–1972; $000)

	1968	1969	1970	1971	1972
Total number of persons	42	42	42	42	42
Total costs	$1,679	$1,609	$1,574	$1,569	$1,569
Personnel	504	504	504	504	504
Program	1,175	1,105	1,070	1,065	1,065
Staff:					
Central office	13	13	13	13	13
Regional office	9	9	9	9	9
State assignees	20	20	20	20	20
Personnel	$ 504	$ 504	$ 504	$ 504	$ 504
Evaluation and surveillance	300	300	300	300	300
State projects*	500*	500	500	500	500
National TV spots	60	60	60	60	60
Educational TV series	100	100	100	100	100
Safety films	40	40	20	20	20
Publications	100	30	30	30	30
Exhibits	30	30	15	15	15
Community projects	25	25	25	25	25
Campus projects	20	20	20	15	15

* Ten projects at $50,000 per project.

EXHIBIT 2 Costs per Death Averted and Benefit/Cost Ratios for All Program Units Studied

Program Unit	Program Cost per Death Averted	Benefit/Cost Ratio
Motor vehicle injury prevention programs:		
Increase seat belt use........................	$ 87	1,351.4 : 1
Use of improved restraint devices............	100	1,117.1 : 1
Reduce pedestrian injury....................	600	144.3 : 1
Increase use of protective devices		
by motorcyclists	1,852	55.6 : 1
Improve driving environment	2,330	49.4 : 1
Reduce driver drinking.....................	5,330	21.5 : 1
Improve driver licensing	13,800	3.8 : 1
Improve emergency medical services	45,000	2.4 : 1
Improve driver training	88,000	1.7 : 1
Other disease control programs studied:		
Arthritis..................................	n.a.	42.5 : 1
Syphilis	22,252	16.7 : 1
Uterine cervix cancer.......................	3,470	9.0 : 1
Lung cancer	6,400	5.7 : 1
Breast cancer	7,663	4.5 : 1
Tuberculosis..............................	22,807	4.4 : 1
Head and neck cancer	29,100	1.1 : 1
Colon-rectum cancer........................	42,944	0.5 : 1

n.a. = Not available.

the benefits of the program, based on the lifetime earnings discounted at 3 percent of those whose deaths would be averted, were estimated at $412,754,000. Hence, the benefit/cost ratio equaled 55.6 : 1. Another measure of program effectiveness was the cost per death averted, $1,852. Exhibit 2 summarizes the benefit/cost ratios and the costs per death averted for all nine motor vehicle injury prevention program units and for the arthritis, cancer, tuberculosis, and syphilis programs. Exhibit 3 presents, for all programs, the estimated five-year reduction in numbers of injuries and deaths and the estimated discounted five-year program dollar costs and benefits.

Overall Methodology

In this effort to apply benefit/cost analysis to the domain of vehicular accidents, three major constraints were laid down:

1. The problem of motor vehicle accidents is examined exclusively in terms of public health concerns. This mandate focused on the role of human factors in vehicular accidents and the amelioration of injury caused by vehicular accidents. In adopting this posture, three major factors in vehicular accident complex—law enforcement, road design, and traffic engineering—were, for the most part, excluded. This constraint had the effect of limiting the problem to

EXHIBIT 3 Reduction in Injuries and Deaths and Total Discounted Program Costs and Savings for All Program Units Studied (1968–1972)

Program Unit	Discounted Program Costs ($000)	Discounted Program Savings ($000)	Reduction in Injuries	Reduction in Deaths
Motor vehicle injury prevention programs:				
Seat belts	2,019	2,728,374	1,904,000	22,930
Restraint devices	610	681,452	471,600	5,811
Pedestrian injury................	1,061	153,110	142,700	1,650
Motorcyclists...................	7,419	412,754	—	4,006
Driving environment	28,545	1,409,891	1,015,500	12,250
Driver drinking	28,545	612,970	440,630	5,340
Driver licensing.................	6,113	22,938	23,200	442
Emergency medical services.....................	721,478*	1,726,000	†	16,000
Driver training..................	750,550	1,287,022	665,300	8,515
Other disease control programs studied:				
Arthritis	35,000	1,489,000	n.a.	n.a.
Syphilis.......................	179,300‡	2,993,000	n.a.	11,590
Uterine cervix cancer	118,100‡	1,071,000	n.a.	34,200
Lung cancer....................	47,000‡	268,000	n.a.	7,000
Breast cancer...................	22,400	101,000	n.a.	2,396
Tuberculosis...................	130,000	573,000	n.a.	5,700
Head and neck cancer...........	7,800	9,000	n.a.	268
Colon-rectum cancer	7,300	4,000	n.a.	170

n.a. = Not available.
* Includes $300 million state matching funds.
† This program does not reduce injury; however, it is estimated to reduce hospital bed/days by 2,401,000 and work loss days by 8,180,000.
‡ Funding shown used as basis for analysis—includes funds estimated to come from sources other than DHEW.

considerations traditionally within the purview of DHEW, while excluding those elements which are traditionally handled by the Department of Commerce and other government agencies.

2. The problem of motor vehicle accidents is handled by nine programs which, in the opinion of committee members, were feasible and realistic. Criteria for determining "feasible and realistic" were not made explicit. However, program proposals which were rejected, such as no person under 21 being allowed to drive, reduction of maximum speeds on all roads by 20 percent, the federal government paying for the installation of $100 worth of safety devices on all automobiles, indicate the cultural values and assumed cost factors which were two issues involved in judging "feasible and realistic."

3. The problem of motor vehicle accidents is handled by programs based on what is known today. This constraint ruled out dependence on new findings based on future research. Unlike the other constraints, this ruling, in the minds of the committee members, constituted a basic condition for undertaking a benefit/

cost analysis of alternative program strategies. Unless the analysis was re-stricted to "what is known," the "need for more research" would allow one partner in the dialogue to withdraw from the struggle without even having been engaged.

The report then went on to describe the rationale behind benefit/cost analysis:

The reasoning behind the benefit/cost analysis is quite straightforward. The idea is to allow for a meaningful comparison of the change which results in a given situation as a result of applying alternative programs. In order to bring about this state of affairs, a measurable common denominator is useful for rating program outcome and program costs. This common denominator is dollars. Granting the existence of the common denominator, there must, in addition, be a point on which to take a "fix" in order to support the contention that change has, in fact, taken place. This point for fixing position and shifts in relation to change wrought by program is the baseline.

In this exercise the baseline was created by assessing past rates for motor vehicle and pedestrian deaths and injuries. The assumption was made that the current level of program effort in DHEW would remain constant through 1972 with the exception of increases for obligated administrative costs. The observed trend was then projected and applied to the anticipated population distribution for the years 1967–72. Program costs and savings due to the introduction of the program were limited to the five-year period 1968–72, although certain programs were just gathering momentum by the end of this period. . . . The required common denominator was incorporated into the baseline by converting fatalities into lost earnings and by translating lost work days, bed disability days, length of hospitalization, physician visits, and other medical services resulting from injuries into the direct and indirect costs represented by these statistical measures. . . . Throughout this analysis, the total dollar costs and benefit for the five-year period are discounted to 1968, the base year, to convert the stream of costs and benefits into its worth in the base year. . . .

With the baseline and common denominator established, the Committee was able to examine the potential payoff for a variety of program units even though these units differed with respect to such factors as cost of implementation, target group to be reached, method to be employed, and facet of the total program addressed by the proposed program.

With the establishment of the baseline and the development of techniques to convert all elements of the equation to a common denominator, the energies of the Committee were given over to the creation of program units. There are a number of variables which may contribute to the occurrence of a vehicular accident and its resultant injury or death. The skill of the driver, the condition of the road, the speed of the vehicle, the condition of the car, the failure to have or to use safety devices incorporated in the car are just a few of many that are mentioned in the literature. What we know about vehicular accidents is expressed in terms of these variables and, as a consequence, program formulations are generally placed in the context of managing these variables, either singly or in combination. A program unit, as developed by the Committee, usually addressed a single variable.

There are two links needed to effect the benefit/cost analysis in vehicular accidents. The first link is associated with the estimate of reduction that could be realized if a given variable were addressed by a program of some sort. This link is supplied in vehicular accidents by the expertise of the Committee members and recourse to studies on the particular variable in question. The second link is associated with the effectiveness of the program proposed to bring about the estimated reduction. In vehicular accidents this is supplied by the experience with programs of the Committee members and the success in the past of programs, similar in content, devoted to public health problems.

Estimate of Benefits

The benefit/cost studies of the motor vehicle injury prevention programs began with a stipulation of a "base line," or the number of deaths and injuries to be expected if the level of DHEW effort remained constant. Next, an estimate was made of the number of deaths and injuries which would be avoided if the proposed program unit were adopted. Finally, the reduction in deaths and injuries was translated into dollar terms. These three steps will now be described as they applied to Program Unit No. 8.

The Baseline.   The team working on the motorcycle unit had available the information given in Table 1.

The team estimated that (1) the number of registered motorcycles would continue to increase at an increasing rate, and (2) the death rate would decline, in the absence of new safety programs, to a level of 110 deaths per 100,000 registered motorcycles. Accordingly, the number of motorcycle accident deaths to be expected without the safety program was projected as shown in Table 2.

Effectiveness of the Program Unit.   Calculation of the anticipated reduction in the number of deaths resulting from the proposed program unit involved two separate estimates: (1) the effectiveness of the program in persuading motorcyclists to wear helmets and protective eyeshields; and (2) the effectiveness of these devices in reducing deaths (injuries were not considered in the analysis of this program unit). The team's judgment was that the program would result in use of helmets and eyeshields to the degree shown in Table 3.

TABLE 1   Historical Data on Motorcycle Registrations and Fatalities

Year	Total Number of Registered Motorcycles in the U.S.	Number of Deaths from Motorcycle Accidents	Rate of Deaths per 100,000 Motorcycles
1959	565,352	752	133.0
1960	569,691	730	128.1
1961	595,669	697	117.0
1962	660,400	759	114.9
1963	786,318	882	112.2
1964	984,760	1,118	113.5

TABLE 2 Projected Baseline Case

Year	Projected Total Number of Registered Motorcycles in the U.S.	Projected Number of Deaths from Motorcycle Accidents without Program (based on 110 deaths per 100,000 registered motorcycles)
1968	2,900,000	3,190
1969	3,500,000	3,850
1970	4,200,000	4,620
1971	5,000,000	5,500
1972	6,000,000	6,600

TABLE 3 Estimated Effectiveness of Program in Encouraging Protective Devices

Year	Estimated Percentage of Motorcyclists Using Helmets and Eyeshields
1968	20
1969	30
1970	40
1971	50
1972	55

Regarding the second factor, the effectiveness of protective devices in reducing deaths, the team relied on a study entitled "Effect of Compulsory Safety Helmets on Motorcycle Accident Fatalities" which appeared in *Australian Road Research,* vol. 2, no. 1, September 1964. This study reported that the number of motorcycle fatalities occurring in the Australian state of Victoria in the two years following the effective date of a law requiring the wearing of helmets was only 31 while the number of fatalities projected on the basis of the experience of the two preceding years was 62.5, for a reduction of about 50 percent. Other states, which did not have such a law, had shown a reduction of about 12 percent in the same period, a difference of 38 percent. The committee concluded that 100 percent usage of helmets and eyeshields by American motorcyclists would reduce the number of deaths by about 40 percent.

Multiplication of the figures for projected usage of protective devices given in Table 3 by 40 percent gave the estimated percentage reduction in deaths, and application of these percentages to the baseline data of Table 2 gave the estimated reduction in number of deaths. The results are summarized in Table 4.

Conversion to Economic Benefits. For the purpose of calculating the lifetime earnings lost in the event of a motorcycle fatality, it was necessary to estimate the

TABLE 4 Estimated Reduction in Deaths from Proposed Program

Year	Projected Number of Deaths from Motorcycle Accidents without Program	Estimated Percentage Reduction in Deaths with Program	Estimated Reduction in Number of Deaths with Program
1968	3,190	8	255
1969	3,850	12	462
1970	4,620	16	739
1971	5,500	20	1,100
1972	6,600	22	1,450
5-year total	23,760	—	4,006

TABLE 5 Estimated Reduction in Deaths by Age and Sex

Year	Age 15–24 Males	Age 15–24 Females	Age 25–34 Males	Age 25–34 Females	Total
1968	207	23	22	3	255
1969	374	42	41	5	462
1970	598	67	67	7	739
1971	891	99	99	11	1,100
1972	1,174	131	130	15	1,450
Total	3,244	362	359	41	4,006

distribution of fatalities by age and sex. In 1964, approximately 90 percent of the victims of motorcycle accidents had been male and 10 percent female; similarly, about 90 percent had been in the age group 15–24 and 10 percent in the age group 25–34. The data were not cross-classified, so it was considered necessary to assume that the sex distribution of fatalities in each age group was the same as the overall distribution, i.e., 90:10. Projecting these percentages into the future, it was calculated that, of the 255 fatalities which the proposed program was expected to avoid in 1968, 207 would be males between 15 and 24 inclusive (i.e., .9 × .9 × 255). Combining this procedure for all categories and years resulted in the estimates of the distribution of death reductions over the five-year period shown in Table 5.

The final step in calculating the expected benefits of the proposed program was to assign the appropriate dollar benefits to the above estimates of decreases in deaths by age group and sex. This was done by multiplying the decrease in deaths in each sex-age group "cell" in the above table by the applicable discounted lifetime earnings figure for that particular cell.

Table 6 shows lifetime earnings by age and sex, discounted at 3 percent used in computing the dollar benefits of reducing motorcycle accident fatalities. (The

TABLE 6 Discounted Lifetime Earnings by Age and Sex

Age	Males	Females
Under 1	$ 84,371	$50,842
1–4	98,986	54,636
5–9	105,836	63,494
10–14	122,933	73,719
15–19	139,729	81,929
20–24	150,536	84,152
25–29	150,512	81,702
30–34	141,356	77,888

TABLE 7 Discounted Savings Resulting from Program to Promote Use of Protective Devices by Motorcyclists (000s)

Year	Total	Age 15–24		Age 25–34	
		Males	Females	Males	Females
Total.	$412,754	$334,002	$27,164	$48,714	$2,874
1968	36,140	30,347	1,976	3,578	239
1969	61,972	52,423	3,282	5,895	372
1970	97,152	82,363	5,059	9,248	482
1971	39,547	17,928	7,408	13,393	818
1972	177,943	150,941	9,439	16,600	963

report contained a detailed description of the methodology used in deriving these amounts.)

The number of deaths saved in each cell of Table 5 was multiplied by the appropriate earnings figure from Table 6, and discounted at 3 percent to the base year, 1968. For example, Table 5 indicates that it was estimated that, in 1968, the lives of three females between the ages of 25 and 34 would be saved. The discounted lifetime earnings of females in this age group was found from Table 6 by averaging the discounted lifetime earnings for females 25–29 and 30–34, the average of $81,702 and $77,888 being $79,795. This was multiplied by 3 to give $239,385; using a present value factor of 1 (since 1968 was the base year), the figure derived was $239,385. Similarly, discounted figures were obtained for each year by age group and sex; the results are shown below in Table 7.

Thus, over the five-year program period, 1968–72, it was estimated that 4,006 deaths could be averted (Table 5), at a present-value cost of $7,419,000. The present value of the lifetime earnings of the 4,006 persons whose lives would be saved during this period was shown in Table 7 to be $412,754,000.

These data were summarized in the form of two measures of program effectiveness:

$$\text{Program cost per death averted} = \frac{\$7,419,000}{4,006} = \underline{\underline{\$1,852}}$$

$$\text{Benefit/cost ratio} = \frac{\$412,754,000}{\$7,419,000} = \underline{\underline{55.6}}$$

Questions

1. As Mr. Davidson, prepare a critique of the methodology and findings of the benefit/cost analysis of Program Unit No. 8.
2. Based on your evaluation of the analysis, would you recommend the level of funding proposed?

Operations Budgeting

A budget is a plan expressed in monetary terms. There are essentially three types of budgets: (1) the *capital budget,* which lists and describes planned capital acquisitions, (2) the *cash budget,* which summarizes planned cash receipts and disbursements, and (3) the *operating budget,* which describes planned operating activities. In this chapter, we put most of our emphasis on the operating budget. The capital budget is derived more or less automatically from decisions made during the programming process, as described in Chapters 8 and 9; we discuss it briefly to show its link to both programming and the operating budget. The cash budget is derived from the operating budget, and forecasts planned cash flows on a monthly (or sometimes more frequent) basis during the operating year. We do not discuss the cash budget in this chapter.[1]

THE CAPITAL BUDGET

The capital budget contains a list of capital projects that are proposed for financing during the coming year. In effect, the capital budget includes all acquisitions of long-lived assets planned for the year.

In most organizations, items to be included in the capital budget emerge from decisions made during the programming process. If the total approved capital expenditures are larger than can be financed, senior management must reduce the capital budget. Since capital projects affect program execution for years to come, such reductions require careful consideration.

Capital expenditures ordinarily have an impact on operating costs. For this reason, there is an important link between the capital budget and the operating budget. For example, if a capital expenditure was approved because it would lead

---

[1] "Menotomy Home Health Services," Case 3–2 in Chapter 3, required the preparation of a cash budget.

to some labor savings, senior management must be certain that line managers include those labor savings in their operating budgets. Similarly, if the capital budget includes some expenditures for new equipment as part of a new program, there no doubt will be new operating costs and new revenues associated with the new program. Senior management should expect these to be included in the operating budget.

GENERAL NATURE OF THE OPERATING BUDGET

The operating budget is always for a specified period, usually one year, although some organizations use a different time frame.[2] For example, some states prepare a biennial (once every two years) budget. The Old Globe Theater in San Diego, by contrast, has a semiannual budget: one for the winter season and one for the summer season.[3]

The general character of the budgeting process in a nonprofit organization is similar to that in a for-profit one. There are significant differences in emphasis, however. This chapter focuses on both the similarities and the differences.

Relationship between Programming and Budgeting

In concept, budgeting follows, but is separate from, programming. The budget is supposed to be a "fine tuning" of an organization's programs for a given year. It incorporates the final decisions on the amounts to be spent for each program, and specifies the organizational unit that is responsible for carrying out each program. In some organizations, these decisions take place within the context of basic decisions made during the programming process. In most organizations, however, no such clean separation between programming and budgeting exists. Even organizations that have a well-developed programming system frequently discover circumstances during budgeting that require revisions of program decisions. In organizations that have no recognizable or separate programming activity, program decisions are made as part of budgeting.

Despite this overlap, it is useful to think about the two activities separately because they have different characteristics. As discussed in Chapter 8, programming decisions typically have multiyear consequences. The purpose of budgeting, by contrast, is to decide on the details of the actual operating plan for a year. Budgeting requires careful estimates of expenses and revenues, using the most

---

[2] Budget (or fiscal) years end in different months of the calendar year. In colleges and universities, for example, the fiscal year usually ends June 30, July 31, or August 31. In nongovernment organizations, the budget year is usually the calendar year. In the federal government, the fiscal year ends September 30. In many state and local governments the fiscal year ends June 30.

[3] See Donald V. Tartre and Derek H. Hurd, "One for the Money, Two for the Show," *Management Focus*, September–October 1983.

current information on prices of both outputs and inputs. Moreover, a budget usually is formulated within a ceiling of estimated available resources.

Since a budget is a plan against which actual performance is compared, senior management must be certain that it corresponds to individual responsibility centers. As such, the budget provides a basis for measuring the performance of responsibility center managers. If a program is to be used as a basis for performance measurement, senior management generally must designate it as a responsibility center. Otherwise, responsibility for many of a program's elements may be too diffused throughout the organization to permit the measurement of the performance of any given manager.

Two-Stage Budgets

This chapter refers to the operating budget as if there were only one. In government organizations and some other nonprofit organizations, there actually are two budgets.

1. The *legislative budget* is essentially a request for funds. It does not correspond to the budget that is prepared in a for-profit company. Its closest counterpart is the prospectus that a company prepares when it seeks to raise money. Most media reports about government budgets relate to the legislative budget, and many textbook descriptions of government budgeting focus on this budget.

2. The *management budget* is prepared after the legislature has decided on the amount of funds that is to be provided (or, if the legislature is dilatory, it is prepared as soon as the executive branch can make a good estimate of what the legislature eventually will approve). This budget corresponds to the budget prepared in a for-profit company; that is, it is a plan showing the amount of authorized spending for each responsibility center. If the amount of revenue is known within reasonable limits, the management budget can be an accurate reflection of the organization's plans for the year. Our discussion concerning the operating budget focuses almost exclusively on this management budget.

Contrast with For-Profit Companies

Budgeting is an important part of the management control process in any organization. It is even more important in a nonprofit organization than in a for-profit company, however, for two reasons—cost structure and spending flexibility.

Cost Structure. In a for-profit company, particularly a manufacturing company, many costs are engineered. The amount of labor and the quantity of material required to manufacture products are determined within close limits by design and engineering specifications. Consequently, little can be done to affect these costs during the budgeting process. By contrast, in most nonprofit organizations many costs are discretionary; that is, the amount to be spent can vary widely depending on management's decisions. Many of these decisions are made during the budget formulation process.

Spending Flexibility.   In a for-profit company, a budget is a fairly tentative statement of plans. It is subject to change as conditions change, and such changes, particularly in the volume and mix of sales, can occur frequently during the year. Furthermore, there is general agreement on the way managers should react to such changes; they should make revised plans that are consistent with the overall objective of profitability.

In many nonprofit organizations, conditions are more stable and predictable. In a university, the number of students enrolled in September governs the pattern of spending for the whole year. A hospital gears up for a certain number of beds, and, although there may be temporary fluctuations in demand, these ordinarily do not cause major changes in spending patterns. A federal agency or a public school system has a certain authorized program or set of programs for the year that it must carry out. Under these circumstances, the budget is a fairly accurate statement of both its activities and the resources to be used. It is therefore important to prepare the budget carefully. Much time, including much senior-management time, should be devoted to it.

COMPONENTS OF THE OPERATING BUDGET

The numerical part of the operating budget (which is often supplemented by explanatory text) consists of three components: (1) revenues, (2) expenses and expenditures, and (3) output measures.

Revenues

As we discussed in Chapter 2, the general purpose of a nonprofit organization is to provide as much service as it can with available resources. In many nonprofit organizations, the total amount of resources (revenue) in any given budget year is, for all practical purposes, confined within quite narrow limits. The approach to budgeting, therefore, is to decide how best to spend it. This suggests that the basic approach to budgeting should be, first, to estimate the available resources—that is, revenues—and, second, to plan spending to match those resources.

Most managers would agree that the policy of anticipating revenues first, and then budgeting expenses below or equal to them, is fiscally sound. The policy also provides a bulwark against arguments, often made by highly articulate and persuasive people, that an organization should undertake a program even though it cannot afford to do so.

In federal or state governments, application of this principle requires that public managers make careful estimates of the level of funds that the legislature is likely to appropriate. In state and municipal governments, it requires judgment as to feasible taxation and other revenues. In other organizations, it requires estimating the revenues to be derived from fees charged to clients, gifts and grants, endowment earnings, and other sources.

Discipline Required for a Revenue-First Policy. Carrying out a revenue-first policy requires considerable discipline in two respects. First, it requires a careful and prudent estimate of total revenues from all sources, including clients, grants, contracts, third-party payers, and endowment earnings. Once this figure has been established, it is "locked in."

Second, it requires a commitment to engage in cost cutting if necessary. That is, if the first approximation to the budget indicates a deficit, the least painful course of action is to anticipate additional sources of revenue that will eliminate it. This is a highly dangerous course of action. If the original revenue estimates have been made carefully, all feasible sources of revenue were included. New ideas that arise subsequently may produce additional revenue, but the evidence that they will do so usually is not strong. If they do not produce the additional revenue, operations may proceed without taking the steps needed to balance revenues and expenses. The safer course of action is to take whatever steps are necessary to bring expenses into balance with revenues.

> *Example.* Some churches and religious organizations adopt a "God will provide" approach to budgeting. Many have discovered, much to their dismay, that the Lord has *not* provided.

> *Example.* During one fiscal year, the Baltimore Ballet budgeted its expenses first, and then compared them with estimates of earned revenue. The excess of expenses over earned revenue was deemed "to be raised" through contributors. This sum was overly optimistic as were estimates of earned revenue. Although monthly statements indicated unfavorable revenue and expense variances, no corrective action was taken by the board for eight months. The result was a deficit of several hundred thousand dollars.[4]

Preliminary versus Final Budgets. Some colleges prepare a preliminary budget in early summer, prior to the beginning of their fiscal year on July 1. This gives department heads the spending authority needed to prepare for fall classes. In September, once actual enrollments are known with almost total certainty, they prepare a final budget. This final budget uses total revenue as the ceiling for total expenses. Such a process works if the total revenue is known with considerable certainty early in the fiscal year, and if line managers have enough discretionary items in their budgets (such as part-time faculty) so they can make cuts if necessary.

Hard and Soft Money. A college with a reasonable expectation of meeting its enrollment quota can count on a certain amount of tuition revenue; this is *hard money*. Income from endowment is also hard money. It is prudent to make long-

---

[4] From a report by Rosemary Dougherty (personal correspondence).

term commitments, such as tenured faculty appointments, when they will be financed by hard money. By contrast, revenue from annual gifts or short-lived grants for research projects is *soft money*. In a recession, gifts may drop drastically and grantors may decide not to renew their grants. Managers must be careful about making long-term commitments that are financed with soft money.

Exceptions to the Revenue-First Policy.   The policy that budgeted revenue sets the limit on expenses is not applicable under certain conditions. Some of these are discussed below.

The Federal Budget.   The considerations mentioned above do not apply to the federal budget. This budget may be either a surplus or a deficit. The amount of either is determined by the administration's conclusion (with the concurrence of the Congress) as to the proper fiscal policy in a given year. The federal government rarely plans for a balanced budget.

Discretionary Revenue.   In some organizations management has an ability to increase revenues. For example, it may be able to increase revenues from current gifts by an intensified fund-raising effort. This idea of "spending money to make money" is the nonprofit counterpart of a for-profit company's marketing budget. To the extent that this argument is valid, it is appropriate to speak of discretionary revenue as well as discretionary expenses. Ordinarily such opportunities are not of major significance, however. In most situations, the organization has already used all the fund-raising devices that it can think of, and managers must take the probable revenues from such efforts as a given, not subject to major upward revision.

Anticipated Revenue.   Some organizations such as universities, research institutes, and social service agencies include anticipated grant revenues in their budgets. This is because they frequently apply for grants, but do not learn whether the funds will be approved until well into the fiscal year. If the budget were prepared only on the basis of *known* revenues, key professional staff might be laid off, obtain employment elsewhere, and not be available if the grant is awarded. Thus, some organizations decide to incur deficits in anticipation of receiving grant awards. Such a strategy is risky and clearly can be sustained only if grants of sufficient magnitude are received.

Example.   Some years ago, New York University embarked on a major expansion program. Substantial amounts of additional revenue were obtained from additional enrollments, fund-raising campaigns, and government grants. Several years later, funds from all these sources began to shrink. Instead of cutting costs to meet the lower level of revenues, however, deficits were permitted, which reached a peak of $14 million. Drastic steps were finally taken to bring costs in line with revenue, but by then a considerable portion of the university's capital had been dissipated.[5]

-----

[5] Condensed from a report in *Science* December 8, 1972, pp. 1072–75.

Short-Run Fluctuations. When managers expect short-term revenue fluctuations around an average, it is appropriate to budget for the average revenue, rather than for the specific level of revenue in a given year; that is, in some years expenses may exceed revenue if in other years revenues exceed expenses by a corresponding amount. Indeed, some nonprofit organizations consciously adopt a "countercyclical" fiscal policy as a strategy. They reason that when the economy is in a downswing, more clients who cannot pay will need their services, with the opposite effect taking place during economic expansion. They thus plan to incur deficits in bad times and surpluses during good times. This strategy must be carefully managed. If, for example, the policy is overly conservative, it deprives current clients of services. Conversely, as is the case with uncertain revenue, if management assumes that next year will be better, and when this doesn't happen, that the following year surely will be better, the institution may be headed for disaster.

The Promoter. Occasionally, the amount of resources available can be increased by a dynamic individual. The governing board thereupon authorizes an operating budget in excess of current revenues in anticipation of the new resources that the promoter will provide. Such a decision is obviously a gamble. If it works, the institution may be elevated to a permanently higher plateau. If it doesn't work, painful cutbacks may be necessary to bring expenses back in line with revenues.

Deliberate Capital Erosion. There are situations where the current revenue is deliberately not regarded as a ceiling, and part of the organization's permanent capital is used for current operations. This may represent a gamble in anticipation of new resources as described above, or it may reflect a conscious policy to go out of existence after the capital has been consumed.

In effect, any budget with a deficit is consuming permanent capital. Thus, decisions to use permanent capital for current operations should be made with great care. No organization can live beyond its means indefinitely.

> *Example.* One university had its schools organized as profit centers. Each school was responsible for achieving a balanced budget every year. One year, when a school was facing its third substantial deficit in three years, the university's central administration informed the school's dean that the deficit would be financed with the principal from the school's endowment fund. Faced with the prospect of capital erosion, the dean balanced the budget.

Expenses and Expenditures

There are two general formats for the spending portion of the budget. The traditional format is called the *line-item budget*, although this term is not descriptive because every budget has items arranged in lines. A line-item budget focuses on expense elements; that is, wages, fringe benefits, supplies, and other types of resources. The other format is called a *program budget*. It focuses on programs and program elements that represent the activities for which the funds are to be spent. Examples of each type for the public safety department of a municipality are shown in Exhibit 10–1. Although the focus of a program budget is on programs, condensed element information—such as the amount of personnel costs, supplies, and other operating costs—is usually shown for each program as well.

The program budget permits a decision maker to judge the appropriate amount of resources for each activity, and hence the emphasis to be given to that activity.

EXHIBIT 10–1   Examples of Types of Budgets—Municipal Public Safety Activities ($000)

A. Line-Item Budget

	Estimated Actual 19x1	*Budget 19x2*
Wages and salaries	$4,232	$4,655
Overtime	217	72
Fringe benefits	783	861
Retirement plan	720	792
Operating supplies	216	220
Fuel	338	410
Uniforms	68	70
Repairs and maintenance	340	392
Professional services	71	0
Communications	226	236
Vehicles	482	450
Printing and publications	61	65
Building rental	447	450
Other	396	478
Total	$8,597	$9,151

B. Program Budget

	Estimated Actual 19x1	*Budget 19x2*
Crime control and investigation	$2,677	$2,845
Traffic control	1,610	1,771
Correctional institutions	470	482
Inspections and licenses	320	347
Police training	182	180
Police administration	680	704
Fire fighting	1,427	1,530
Fire prevention	86	92
Fire training	64	70
Fire administration	236	260
Other protection	563	560
General administration	282	310
Total	$8,597	$9,151

It also permits senior management to match spending with measures of each activity's planned outputs. These are important advantages of the program budget format.

Link to the Capital Budget. If the operating budget is prepared on an expenditure (rather than expense) basis, it may include amounts for equipment and other long-lived assets. When this is the case, only buildings and major capital acquisitions will be included in the capital budget.

When the operating budget is prepared on an expenditure basis, senior management should make a clear distinction between the types of items included in these two budgets. Otherwise, there is a temptation to balance the operating budget by moving some items from it into the capital budget.

Example. Officials in New York City made many maneuvers in the early 1970s to hide the true operating deficit. One was to shift operating items to the capital budget where they presumably would be financed by bonds rather than by current revenues. An extreme example was vocational education expenses, which were shifted to the capital budget on the grounds that students would enjoy the benefits for many years to come and that vocational education was therefore a long-lived asset!

Output Measures

The third component of a budget is information about planned outputs. As we describe in Chapter 12, output information usually consists of either process measures or results measures. The former is usually called a *workload measure* and the latter a *measure of objectives*. Some organizations commit themselves to specific results measures as part of the budgetary process.

Example. In one public school system, principals' budgets were determined in part by a combination of expected enrollments and centrally mandated student-teacher ratios; these ratios are process or workload measures. The principals also committed themselves to achieving certain levels of reading scores for students completing different grades. Senior management believed that these scores helped to measure how well teachers achieved the school system's objectives.

Example. An article on university budgeting lists several output criteria that can be used to determine merit salary increments for faculty: dollar amounts of research grants generated, number of Ph.D.s graduated, number of journal publications, and teaching quality.[6] These criteria help to link the budget to a university's objectives.

Management by Objectives. The use of quantified measures of planned objectives during the budget period is often called a *management by objectives* (MBO)

---

[6] Allen G. Schick, "University Budgeting: Administrative Perspective, Budget Structure, and Budget Process," *Academy of Management Review* 10, no. 4 (1985), pp. 794–802.

EXHIBIT 10–2   Statement of Objectives for a Motor Vehicle Registry

---

Objectives to Maintain Operations

The direct salary cost per letter produced by the Correspondence Unit will be maintained at the current level of $— (year to date).

Objectives to Strengthen Operations

By June 30, the process time from mail receipt at the work processing center to receipt by Data Processing, will be decreased from current level of — days to — days.

By June 30, the processing time, from Data Processing release to internal files, will be decreased from current level of — weeks to — weeks.

By June 30, the methods of handling current categories of "Go-back" letters will be altered, resulting in a 10 percent reduction in mailed correspondence—a reduction of 2,000 letters per month from the current level of 20,000 at an estimated cost savings of — per month (i.e., — per letter).

By June 30, the distribution of forms to the public will be tightened in such a way that the total purchase quantity for the year will be reduced from — million to — million (a reduction of approximately 5 percent).

Objectives to Improve Operations

By June 30, the time taken for release of an I.D. card from the work processing center to issuance of a plate to the public will be reduced from — days to — days.

By June 30, the time for release of the application from the work processing center to the issuance of a title will be reduced from — days to — days.

By June 30, the average processing time for routine title applications will be reduced from the current — week average to — working days.

Source: Michael J. Howlett, "Strategic Planning in State Government," *Managerial Planning,* November/December 1975.

---

system. An example is given in Exhibit 10–2. In some nonprofit organizations, budgetees commit themselves to objectives such as these as part of the budgetary process.

Note that the objectives in Exhibit 10–2 are quantified so that actual performance can be compared with them. These statements of objectives take the place of the profitability objective which is a key part of the budgeting process in a for-profit company.

Some organizations use a management by objectives (MBO) procedure that is quite separate from the budgeting process. Generally, this separation comes about because the MBO procedure is sponsored by persons outside the controller organization. Such a separation is undesirable. In discussing plans for next year, both the expenses and the results expected from incurring these expenses should be considered together.

STEPS IN THE OPERATIONS BUDGETING PROCESS

The principal steps involved in the operations budgeting process are: (1) dissemination of guidelines, (2) preparation of the budget estimates, (3) review of these estimates, and (4) approval of the budget. The review process may lead to revision of the original estimates, so the proposed budget may be recycled several times before being approved. In this regard, timing is an important consideration. If the budget is prepared too far in advance, it will not be based on the most current information. If, on the other hand, not enough time is allowed, the process may be rushed and incomplete. In the federal government, for example, the budgeting process starts about six months before the budget is submitted to the Congress, and well over a year before the budget year begins. In less complex organizations, the period is considerably shorter.

Dissemination of Guidelines

Senior management usually begins the budgetary process by formulating the budget guidelines and disseminating them to operating managers. Considerable attention by senior management to the guidelines is warranted; if the budget is formulated on the basis of unrealistic assumptions, it may have to be redone with consequent wasted effort.

If approved programs exist, one guideline is that the budget should be consistent with them. This does not necessarily mean that the budget should consist only of approved programs, since this can be frustrating for operating managers. Moreover, desirable innovations may come to light, if managers are permitted to propose activities that are not part of approved programs. These unapproved activities should be clearly distinguished from those in the approved programs, however, and operating managers should understand that the chances for approval of new programs during budget formulation are slight. Any other impression downgrades the importance of programming.

Even if there are no formal programs, operating managers should be made aware of the constraints within which the budget is prepared. These constraints can be expressed in an overall statement such as "budget for not more than 105 percent of the amount spent this year," or they can be stated in much more detail. These details might include:

- Planned changes in the activities of the organization.
- Assumptions about wage rates and other prices.
- Conditions under which additional personnel can be requested.
- Number of personnel who may be promoted.
- Services to be provided by support responsibility centers.
- Planned productivity gains.

In the absence of guidance to the contrary, the usual assumption is that next year's activities will be similar to this year's.

In addition to the substantive guidelines, there are also guidelines about the format and content of the proposed budget. These are intended to ensure that the budget estimates are submitted in a fashion that both facilitates analysis and permits their subsequent use in comparing actual performance with planned performance.

Preparation of Budget Estimates

In many organizations, managers at the lowest levels are responsible for preparing a budget for their activities. This "participatory" budgeting approach contrasts with the practice of "imposed" budgeting in which budgets are prepared by top-level staffs and then imposed on operating managers. Under participatory budgeting staff assistants may help managers by making calculations and filling out the forms, but the basic decisions that are reflected in the proposed budget are made by operating managers, not by staff.

Relation to Programs.   If an approval program exists, the expense budget usually is constructed by fine tuning the estimated program costs. For new programs, this involves assigning program responsibility to responsibility centers and constructing careful cost estimates in each responsibility center. For example, a research and development program may be budgeted at $400,000 simply by estimating that it will require four professional work years at $100,000 a work year. In constructing the budget, the salaries of professionals and the other support costs that make up the overall estimate of $100,000 per work year will be stated. The resulting total will approximate $400,000 but will vary somewhat from this estimate as the costs are examined in more detail.

Arriving at Budget Amounts.   Assuming the current level of spending is used as a starting point, the budget can be constructed by adjusting for:

- Changes in wage rates and prices.
- Elimination of unusual factors that may have affected current spending.
- Changes in programs.
- Possible adjustments in certain discretionary items (such as expenses for attendance at conventions) that may have been mandated in the guidelines.

In the 1970s considerable publicity was given to a system called *zero-base budgeting* (ZBB), and many organizations experimented with this type of system. Essentially, a ZBB approach required managers to justify their entire budgets each year; no base level of spending was assumed.[7] Experience demonstrated that not enough time was available to permit the use of this technique, and ZBB during the budget preparation process has pretty much disappeared.[8]

Variable Budgets.   If the workload for the budget year can be estimated and if unit costs are available, the budget can be constructed so as to take changes in

---

[7] A process called *zero-base review*, used frequently as part of the evaluation process, is described in Chapter 15.

[8] For a contrasting view, see Stanley B. Botner, "Utilization of Decision Units and Ranking Process in Budgetary Decision-Making by Federal Departments and Agencies," *The Government Accountants' Journal*, Winter 1985–86. Botner speculates that, as resources become more and more scarce at the federal level, ZBB procedures may reappear.

workload into account. In a welfare office, for example, if the number of cases can be predicted, the number of budgeted social workers can be found by using a standard number of cases per social worker. Other elements of cost can be estimated as a function of the number of social workers.

If revenues and expenses vary with volume, as happens with, say, food service costs, the expense budget may be stated in terms of a fixed amount plus a variable rate per unit of volume (e.g., $300,000 + $9 per patient day). It is appropriate to budget, say, food service in a hospital or a private school in this fashion because the revenue from patient care or student board varies with volume. (The amount reported in the budget would be the total cost of food service at the estimated number of meals served.)

In circumstances, where revenue does not vary with volume, a variable budget allowance can be potentially misleading.

Example. The snow removal budget in a municipality may be computed by estimating costs at $10,000 per inch of snow, that is, $300,000 if 30 inches of snow falls. Since the actual snowfall will not be exactly 30 inches, actual snow removal costs are likely to be more or less than $300,000. Nevertheless, it usually is desirable to set the snow removal budget at the fixed amount of $300,000 and to require the appropriate manager to seek a budget revision when the actual snowfall exceeds the budget amount. If the budget were permitted to vary automatically with the amount of snowfall, there would be no way of assuring that the total appropriation was not exceeded. When a budget revision is required, an offsetting change can be made in some other item or, if necessary, supplemental funds can be sought.

Despite the logic of developing the budget from workload estimates and unit costs, the budget guidelines may prohibit increases above a certain amount, regardless of the workload. This requirement overrides the workload calculations. The manager may point out, however, that the budgeted amounts are inadequate to carry out the planned workload so that trade-off decisions must be made.

Advanced Techniques. Various analytical techniques, such as the use of subjective probabilities, preference theory, multiple regression analysis, and models, have been advocated as an aid to budget formulation. For a variety of reasons, few of these are used in practice.

Example. The operating budget for a hospital or a health care system (such as a state, region, or country) could be determined by a model that incorporates morbidity estimates (types and number of cases expected), physician treatment protocols for each diagnosis, expected efficiency measures and factor prices for physician-ordered services, and fixed facility costs. Such a model would permit policymakers to determine where and how expenditures might be reduced by focusing on specific cost-related elements. Policymakers could stipulate, for example, whether reductions should take place by refusing to treat certain types of cases, by changing physician treatment protocols, by seeking improved administrative efficiency, or by guaranteeing certain factor prices. The model could permit policy analysts to test the impact of each of these options, as well as combinations of options, on total health care costs. Although such an approach is being used with some success in individual hospitals, it clearly would en-counter a great deal of political resistance at the health system level.[9]

Budget Detail.   Many dollar amounts in the budget are the product of a physical quantity times a cost per unit. For example, personnel costs are a product of the number of staff times average compensation. These amounts should be shown separately because a breakdown of quantities and unit costs both facilitates re-view of the budget and also is useful in subsequently analyzing differences be-tween budgeted and actual expenses.

In addition to the numbers, the proposed budget usually includes explanatory material. In particular, if additional personnel are requested, a justification may be required.

Review of Budget Estimates

The budget review and approval process has both a technical and a behavioral dimension. Although the two are closely related, we discuss them separately to illustrate the important distinctions.

Technical Aspects.   The technical aspects of the process usually are carried out by budget analysts, who are quite different in makeup from the program analysts discussed in Chapters 8 and 9. A program analyst usually does not work under tight time constraints, and is less interested in accuracy than a budget analyst. He or she is more interested in judging, even in a rough way, the relation between costs and benefits of a proposed program. A budget analyst, by contrast, must be concerned with accuracy, but also must work under great time constraints, pos-sess a feel for what is the right amount of cost, and be able and willing to get to the essence of the calculations quickly.

Time Constraints.   An important, but sometimes overlooked, fact about the review process is that not much time is available for it. The proposed budgets for every responsibility center must be examined in the space of, at most, a few weeks. This is in contrast with the programming process in which one program, covering only a small fraction of the organization's activities, can be examined in depth. Because there is not enough time to do otherwise, the level of current spending is typically taken as the starting point in examining the proposed budget. Although the burden of proof to justify amounts above that level is on the budge-tee, there is an implication that budgetees are "entitled" to the current level. This practice is widely criticized (it sometimes is called the *blight of incrementalism*), but there is little that can be done about it as a practical matter, simply because of

---

[9] David W. Young and Richard B. Saltman, "Resource Planning and Control in Health Care," *Australian Health Review* 9, no. 4 (1986).

time pressure. The place for a more thorough analysis of spending needs is the programming process. As discussed earlier, zero-base budgeting attempted to correct this problem, but it encountered the difficulty of being too time consuming.

Methods of Analysis. Frequently, proposed budgets are first reviewed by the budget staff, which then makes recommendations to line managers. This review has two aspects, one relating to direct programs, and another to support programs.

If a direct program is new, little can be done to change the revenue and expense estimates during the budget review process. Not only has a rough budget ordinarily been agreed to during the programming phase, but there is no experience with actual operations of the program that can be used as a basis for assessing the adequacy of the budget.

If a direct program is ongoing, the appropriateness of actual and proposed expenses can be analyzed. Many budget analysts develop unit cost guidelines that assist them in judging proposed increases in items such as staffing and supplies for a program. For example, a budget analyst, whose programs include restaurant inspections for a state department of public health, knows that each inspector should cover a certain number of restaurants in a year. By obtaining information on the number of new and closed restaurants, the analyst can judge the adequacy of proposed staffing levels.

The budget analyst also focuses on support programs. If the entity's size will change because of direct program decisions, corresponding adjustments must be made in the current level of spending for support activities. After making adjustments for changes in size, a budget analyst also can make a careful review of the details of support activities, using the adjusted current levels of spending as a starting point.

There is a tendency for support costs to creep upward, especially in affluent organizations.[10] Because of this, analysts make special efforts to detect and eliminate unnecessary increase in these costs. If unit costs or ratios can be calculated, a comparison of these with similar numbers in other responsibility centers, or with published data for other organizations, may be helpful. In the absence of such a basis for comparison, reviewers frequently rely on their feel for the appropriateness of the requested amounts.

Finally, the analyst makes comparisons among the unit costs of similar activities within the organization. The budget is checked for consistency with the guidelines; wage rates and costs of significant materials are checked for reasonableness; and other checks—including the simple but essential check of arithmetic accuracy—are made.

---

[10] In a survey of 91 public high school districts, it was found that budgets of schools in affluent communities had a significantly higher proportion of administrative costs than did budgets of schools in poorer communities. Richard L. Daft, "System Influence on Organizational Decision-Making: The Case of Resource Allocation," *Academy of Management Journal*, March 1978, p. 6.

Behavioral Aspects.   In estimating the labor cost of making shoes, there is little ground for disagreement on the part of well-informed people: the cost of each operation can be estimated within close limits, and the total labor cost can be found by adding the costs of each operation and multiplying by the number of pairs of shoes. As noted above, such engineered costs constitute a relatively large fraction of the costs of an industrial company. By contrast, discretionary costs—costs for which the optimal amount is not known, and often is unknowable—constitute a relatively large percent of the budget of a nonprofit organization. Since there is no scientific way to estimate the amount of discretionary costs, these costs do not lend themselves to analysis by the budget staff. Rather, the budget amounts must be determined through negotiation. Negotiation is also required because there is no objective way to decide which requests for funds have the highest priority.

On one level, this negotiation process can be thought of as a *zero-sum game*. Specifically, in many organizations, each budgetee negotiating with a particular supervisor is competing with all other budgetees who report to that supervisor for a share of the resources the supervisor controls. In instances where resources are not abundant, such an arrangement generally produces a great deal of conflict and game-playing by budgetees in order to obtain as large a share of resources as possible.

Senior management can eliminate the zero-sum aspect of this process, and potentially lessen conflict, by decentralizing the budgetary process and increasing the number of budgetary decisions to be made. Doing so tends to reduce the stakes in such a way that each budgetee can gain something.[11]

On another level, the process of negotiation in a decentralized budgetary process has been described as a two-person, nonzero-sum game.[12] The players are the budgetee, who is advocating a proposed budget, and the supervisor, who must approve, modify, or deny the request. Except for the lowest echelon, all managers are supervisors at one stage in the budget process, and they become budgetees in the next stage. Even senior management becomes a budgetee in presenting the budget to the outside agency or board that is responsible for providing the funds. Although in one sense a new game is played each year, there are important carryover consequences from one year to the next. The judgment that each party develops in one year about the ability, integrity, and forthrightness of the other party affects attitudes in subsequent years.

As in any negotiation, the two parties have a common interest in reaching a satisfactory outcome, but they usually have conflicting interests in what that outcome should be. The essence of this conflict is that budgetees generally want as large a budget as possible, and supervisors usually want to cut the proposed budget as much as they safely can.

---

[11] Schick, "University Budgeting," pp. 794–802.
[12] See G. H. Hofstede, *The Game of Budget Control* (Assen, Neth.: Van Gorcum & Co., N.V., 1967).

A budgetee's desire for resources is particularly troublesome in responsibility centers whose output cannot be reliably measured. Under these circumstances, not only are budgetees motivated to acquire as many resources as they can, but it is extremely difficult for supervisors to measure the effectiveness of their use of the resources. This phenomenon has been analyzed by economists in socialist countries where it is crucial to understanding the budget preparation process.

> *Example.* Kornai lists the following factors as particularly significant in the budget preparation process in Hungary: (1) a good manager wants to do the job properly and therefore wants all the resources that may be needed to accomplish it; (2) the manager wants the operation to run smoothly and for this purpose needs slack in order to meet peaks in demand; (3) the manager wants the unit to be viewed favorably in comparison with other units and therefore wants the resources to be up to date; (4) the manager's power and prestige is perceived as being related to the size of the responsibility center, and, in contrast with profit centers, there is no penalty in having too many resources in a discretionary expense center.
>
> For these reasons, the manager's desire for resources is insatiable. Moreover, if supervisors grant all the budget requests this year, it is likely that the requests next year will be even larger.[13]

Role of Professionals. The attitude of professionals is also an important factor. For example, in a hospital, the budgetee may be a physician and the supervisor a hospital administrator. Physicians are primarily interested in improving the quality of patient care, improving the status of the hospital as perceived by their peers, and increasing their own prestige. Their interest in the amount of costs involved generally is secondary. By contrast, hospital administrators are primarily interested in costs, although they realize that costs must not be so low that the quality of care or the status of the hospital is impaired. Thus, the two parties weigh the relevant factors considerably differently.

Role of Norms. The budget process is most effective when the two parties conform to certain norms. In general, effective behavior by supervisors includes:

- Trusting their subordinates.
- Assuming their subordinates are competent and have goodwill and honesty.
- Allowing subordinates to develop their own solutions to budget-related problems.
- Not feeling threatened if a subordinate does not agree with them.
- Sharing information with subordinates.
- Not forcing their personal goals onto subordinates.

Similarly, budgetees need to be able to also trust their superiors. A budget ordinarily is based on certain assumptions about the external world; these assumptions often prove to be wrong. If budgetees do not trust their supervisors to recognize this fact, they will be reluctant to make realistic estimates. Indeed, they

---

[13] For a development of this analysis in Hungary, see Janos Kornai, *Economics of Shortage* (Amsterdam, Neth.: North-Holland Publishing, 1980), especially pp. 62–64 and 191–95.

may be so afraid of their supervisors that they cannot negotiate; that is, enter into a give-and-take collaboration with them.

Role of the Analyst. In general, both senior management and lower level line managers must trust the budget analysts' recommendations as to the details of the budget. If the analysts' calculations indicate that four, not five, new employees are needed for a new function, these calculations ordinarily must be accepted. If each of these detailed decisions is challenged, the whole process will bog down. Moreover, as the budget goes up the chain of command, decision makers may have difficulty identifying and concentrating on key issues. In short, the budget process will work smoothly only if line management has confidence in the judgment of the budget analysts. The solution, if such confidence is lacking, is to reeducate, or in the extreme, replace the analysts.

Rules of the Game and Budget Ploys. As in any game, rules exist for the budget process; many of these rules are unwritten. Moreover, they vary considerably from organization to organization. They also depend in large part upon the size of the organization and the relationships between supervisors and budgetees.

> ***Example.*** One study of budget games that managers play in manufacturing organizations identified five major activities: (1) understating volume estimates, (2) undeclared (or understated) prices increases, (3) undeclared (or understated) cost reduction programs, (4) overstated expenses (such as for research), and (5) undeclared extensions of a product line. A principal reason given by one manager was "senior management just doesn't have the time for checking every number you put into your plans . . . so one strategy is to 'pad' everything. If you're lucky, you'll still have 50% of your cushions after the plan reviews."[14] Similar, sometimes identical, games are played in many nonprofit organizations.

Even when the formal rules are clear, the budget game frequently is characterized by certain ploys. To play the budget game well, each party should be familiar with these ploys and the appropriate responses to them.

Ploys can be divided into two main categories: (1) *internal*—those used primarily within an organization, and (2) *external*—those used between the head of the organization and the legislative body or governing board that authorizes funds for the organization. External ploys are well described in Wildavsky's *The Politics of the Budgeting Process.*[15] Some internal ploys are given in the appendix at the end of this chapter.

The Commitment. The end product of the negotiation process is an agreed-upon budget that represents a commitment by both the budgetee and the supervisor. Some organizations go so far as to state this commitment in the form of a formal contract, in which the budgetee agrees to deliver specified services for a specified sum of money. This becomes the amount in the approved budget.

---

[14] Christopher K. Bart, "Budgeting Gamesmanship." *The Academy of Management Executive* II, no. 4 (1988), pp. 285–94.

[15] Aaron Wildavsky, *The Politics of the Budgetary Process,* 2nd ed. (New York: Harper Collins, 1992).

By agreeing to the budget estimates, the budgetee says, in effect: "I can and will operate my responsibility center in accordance with the plan described in this budget." By approving the budget estimates, the superior in effect says, "If you operate your responsibility center in accordance with this plan, you will be doing what we consider to be a good job." Both statements contain the implicit qualification, "subject to adjustment for unanticipated changes in circumstances."

> ***Example.*** In the one and one-half months that elapsed following its submission on May 10, 1985, the fiscal year 1986–87 budget for New York City became obsolete because of changes in circumstances. Among the changes were: (1) a tentative union agreement covering the city's uniformed employees, which necessitated wage increases of 6 percent; (2) receipt of notice from the state of New York that the city's estimates of state aid were unrealistic; (3) a refinancing of the city's general obligation bonds; (4) an agreement between the state and the city to jointly finance a housing program; (5) a budget resolution passed by the U.S. Congress, which, among other things, made it clear that the Federal General Revenue Sharing Program would likely be terminated; and (6) the city received two additional months of revenue collection information as well as indications of final real property assessments, that resulted in changes in its local revenue estimates for the budget year. As a result, the city submitted a revised financial plan on June 26, 1985.

Budget Approval

The final set of discussions is held between senior management and whatever body has ultimate authority for approving the organization's plans—trustees or similar groups for private nonprofit organizations, or legislatures for public ones. After approval, the budget is disseminated throughout the organization and becomes the authorized plan to which managers are expected to adhere unless compelling circumstances warrant a change.[16]

SUMMARY

Many aspects of operations budgeting in nonprofit organizations are similar to those in for-profit companies. Perhaps the most important difference is on the revenue side of the budget. Many nonprofit organizations are not "self-financing." Because of this, they must be careful to forecast their revenues accurately, and to assure themselves that expenses will not exceed revenues. Although there are some exceptions to this rule, and most organizations can have a year or two

---

[16] Some people refer to actual operations as "executing the budget." This is an unfortunate term because it implies that the operating manager's job is to spend whatever the budget says can be spent. A better term is *executing the program.* This implies that the manager's primary job is to accomplish program objectives. The budget simply shows the resources available for this purpose.

where expenses exceed revenues, the effective result of such a policy is to erode the organization's capital.

Some other differences between nonprofit and for-profit organizations are (1) the presence of two-stage budgets in some nonprofit organizations, (2) the existence of soft money and the uncertainty about grant revenue in some nonprofits, (3) the need for output measures as well as measures of revenue and expenses, and (4) the role of professionals.

In all organizations, the budget frequently has a "gamelike" quality to it. Because of this, the players have developed many ploys to assure their success in the game. These ploys are described in some detail in the following appendix.

APPENDIX
Some Budget Ploys

Internal ploys used in the budget game can be divided into roughly four categories:

1. Ploys for new programs.
2. Ploys for maintaining or increasing ongoing programs.
3. Ploys to resist cuts.
4. Ploys primarily for supervisors.

There is some overlap among the categories, with some relating to programming as well as to budgeting. Each ploy is described briefly, and an appropriate response is given.

Ploys for New Programs

1. Foot in the Door
Description.   Sell a modest program initially, with the idea of concealing its real magnitude until after it has gotten under way and has built a constituency.

> *Example.* In a certain state, the legislature was sold on a program to educate handicapped children in regular schools rather than in the special schools then used. The costs were said to be transportation costs and a few additional teachers. Within five years, the definition of handicapped had been greatly broadened, and the resources devoted to the program were four times the amount originally estimated.

> *Response.* This ploy can elicit either of two responses: (a) detect the ploy when it is proposed, consider that it is merely a foot in the door and that actual costs eventually will exceed estimates by a wide margin, and therefore disapprove the project (difficult to do); or (b) hold to the original decision, limiting spending to the original cost estimate despite pleas for more funds (effective only if the ploy is detected in time).

Variations.   One variation on this ploy is *buying in*; that is, underestimating the real cost of a program. An example is the B-1 bomber program. In the early 1980s, this program was estimated to cost $11.9 billion. The Air Force submission for the B-1 bomber for FY 1983 "certified" that the cost of the program was $20.5 billion. However, two independent audit groups within the Pentagon estimated its cost as $23.6 billion and $26.7 billion, respectively. The Congressional Budget Office estimated the cost at $40 billion.

Another variation is bait and switch; that is, initially requesting an inexpensive program but increasing its scope (and cost) after initial approval has been obtained. This differs from the "foot in the door" ploy in that the changes in the program take place before the program begins rather than after it has been operating for a while.

2. Hidden Ball

Description.   Conceal the nature of a politically unattractive program by hiding it within an attractive program.

> *Example.*   Some years ago the Air Force had difficulty in obtaining funds for general-purpose buildings but found it easy to get funds for intercontinental ballistic missiles, so there was included in the budget for the missile program an amount to provide for construction of a new office building. Initially this building was used by a contractor in the missile program, but eventually it became a general-purpose Air Force office building.

Response.   Break down programs so that such items become visible.

3. Divide and Conquer

Description.   Seek approval of a budget request from more than one supervisor.

> *Example.*   The City Planning Commission in New York City was organized so that each member was supposed to be responsible for certain specified areas. The distinctions were not clear, however, so budgetees would deal with more than one supervisor, hoping that one of them would react favorably.

Response.   Responsibilities should be clearly defined (easier said than done).

Caution.   In some situations, especially in research, it is dangerous to have a single decision point. It is often desirable to have two places in which a person with a new idea for research may obtain a hearing. New ideas are extremely difficult to evaluate, and a divided authority, even though superficially inefficient, lessens the chance that a good idea will be rejected.

4. Distraction

Description.   Base a specific request on the premise that an overall program has been approved when this is not in fact the case (difficult, but not impossible, to use successfully).

Example. At a legislative committee, a university presented arguments to replace buildings prior to implementing an approved plan for doubling the capacity of a certain professional school. The argument was that newer buildings would be more useful and efficient than the existing buildings. The merits were discussed in terms of the return on investment arising from the greater efficiency of the new buildings. This discussion went on for some time until a committee member asked who had approved the plan for expansion of the school in the first place. It turned out that the expansion had never been approved; approval of the new buildings would have de facto approved the expansion.

Response. Expose the hidden aims, but this is sometimes very difficult.

5. Shell Game

Description. Use statistics to mislead supervisors as to the true state of affairs.

Example. The budgetee was head of the Model Cities program for a certain city. He wanted available funds to be used primarily for health and education programs but knew that his superiors were more interested in "economic" programs (new businesses and housing). He drew up the following table:

	Source		
Purpose	*Federal*	*Other*	*Total*
Health and education	$2,000,000	$ 15,000	$2,015,000
Economic	50,000	2,300,000	2,350,000

The budgetee emphasized to the mayor and interested groups that over half the funds were intended for economic purposes. The catch was that the source of "other" funds was not known, and there were no firm plans for obtaining such funds. This was not discovered by the supervisor until just prior to the deadline for submitting the request for federal Model Cities funding, at which time the budgetee successfully used the delayed buck ploy (No. 17).

Response. Careful analysis.

6. It's Free

Description. Argue that someone else will pay for the project so the organization might as well approve it.

Example. States often decide to build highways, reckoning the cost is low since the federal government reimburses 95 percent of the cost. These states overlook the fact that maintenance of the highway is 100 percent a state cost.

Response. Require analysis of the long-run costs, not merely the costs for next year. This technique, called *life-cycle costing*, is becoming increasingly popular.

7. Implied Top-Level Support

Description. The budgetee says that, although the request is not something that he personally is enthusiastic about, it is for a program that someone higher up in the organization asked to be included in the budget (preferably this person is not well known to, and more prestigious than, the budgetee's superior). The budgetee hopes that the supervisor will not take the time to bring this third party into the discussion.

Response. Examine the documentation. If it is vague, not well justified, or nonexistent, check with the alleged sponsor.

Note. In a related ploy, the end run, the budgetee actually goes to the supervisor's boss without discussing the matter with the supervisor first. This tactic should not be tolerated.

8. You're to Blame

Description. Imply that the supervisor is at fault, and that defects in the budget submission therefore should be overlooked.

> *Example.* It is alleged that the supervisor was late in transmitting budget instructions or that the instructions were not clear, and that this accounts for inadequacies in the justifications furnished.

Response. If the assertion is valid, this is a difficult ploy to counter. It may be necessary to be contrite, but arbitrary, in order to hold the budget within the guidelines. (It also may be necessary to reexamine one's management style.)

9. Nothing Too Good for Our People

Description. Used, whether warranted or not, to justify items for the personal comfort and safety of military personnel, for new cemeteries, for new hospital equipment, for research laboratory equipment (especially computers), and for various facilities in public schools and colleges.

Response. Attempt to shift the discussion from emotional grounds to logical grounds by analyzing the request to see if the benefits are even remotely related to their cost. Emphasize that in a world of scarce resources, not everyone can get all that is deserved.

10. Keeping Up with the Joneses

> *Example.* Minneapolis must have new street lights because St. Paul has them.

Response. Analyze the proposal on its own merits.

11. We Must Be Up to Date

Description. This differs from Ploy No. 10 in that it does not require that a "Jones" be found and cited. The argument is that the organization must be a leader and must therefore adopt the newest technology. Currently, this is a fashionable ploy for computers and related equipment, for hospital equipment, and for laboratory equipment.

Response.   Require that a benefit be shown that exceeds the cost of adopting the new technology.

Caution.   Sometimes the state of the art is such that benefits cannot be conclusively demonstrated. If this leads to a deferral of proposals year after year, opportunities may be missed.

12. If We Don't, Someone Else Will

Description.   Appeal to people's innate desire to be at least as good as the competition.

> *Example.*   A university budgetee argued that a proposed new program was breaking new ground, and was important to the national interest. She stated that if her university didn't initiate the program, some other university would. Moreover, the other university would obtain funds from the appropriate government agency, and thus make it more difficult for her university to start the program later on.

Response.   Point out that a long list of possible programs have this characteristic, and the university must select those few that are within its capabilities.

13. Call It a Rose

Description.   Use misleading, but appealing, labels.

> *Example.*   The National Institutes of Health were unable to obtain approval for the construction of new buildings but were able to build annexes. It is said that Building 12A (the annex) is at least double the size of Building 12.

Response.   Look behind the euphemism to the real function. If the disguise is intentional, deny the request and discourage recurrence.

14. Outside Experts

Description.   The agency hires outside experts to support its request, either formally in hearings, or informally in the press.

Response.   Determine whether these experts are biased, either because they have connections with the agency or because they are likely to benefit if the request is approved. Seek other experts with contrasting views.

Ploys for Maintaining or Increasing Ongoing Programs

15. Show of Strength

Description.   Arrange demonstrations in support of a request; occasionally, threaten violence, work stoppages, or other unpleasant consequences if the request is not approved.

Response. Have fair criteria for selecting programs, and have the conviction to stand by your decision.

16. Razzle-Dazzle

Description. Support the request with voluminous data, arranged in such a way that their significance is not clear. The data need not be valid.

Example. A public works department submitted a 20-page list of repairs to municipal buildings that were said to be vitally needed, couched in highly technical language. This was actually a "wish list," prepared without a detailed analysis.

Response. (a) Ask why the repair budget should be greater next year than in the current year. (b) Find a single soft spot in the original request and use it to discredit the whole analysis.

17. Delayed Buck

Description. Submit the data late, arguing that the budget guidelines required so much detailed calculation that the job could not be done on time.

Example. The budget guidelines requested a "complete justification" of requested additions to inventory. The motor vehicle repair shop of a state did not submit its budget on time. At the last minute, it submitted an itemized list of parts to be ordered, based on a newly installed system of calculating economic order quantities. It argued that its tardiness was a consequence of getting the bugs out of the new system (which was installed at the controller's instigation), but that it was generally agreed that the economic order quantity formula was the best way of justifying the amount of parts to be purchased.

Response. This is a difficult ploy to counter. Complaining about the delay may make the supervisor feel better but will not produce the data. One possible response, designed to prevent recurrence, is to penalize the delay by making an entirely arbitrary cut in the amount requested, although this runs the risk that needed funds will be denied.

18. Reverence for the Past

Description. Whatever was spent last year must have been necessary to carry out last year's program; therefore, the only matters to be negotiated are the proposed increments above this sacred base.

Response. As a practical matter, this attitude must be accepted for a great many programs because there is not time to challenge this statement. For selected programs, there can be a zero-base review (see Chapter 15).

19. Sprinkling

Description. "Watering" was a device used in the early 20th century to make assets and profits in prospectuses for new stock offerings look substantially higher than they really were. "Sprinkling" is a more subtle ploy, which increases budget estimates by only a few percent, either across-the-board or in hard-to-detect areas. Often it is done in anticipation that the supervisor will make arbitrary reductions, so that the final budget will be what it would have been if neither the sprinkling nor the arbitrary cuts had been made.

Response. Since this ploy, when done by an expert, is extremely difficult to detect, the best response is to remove the need for doing it; that is, create an atmosphere in which the budgetees trust the supervisor not to make arbitrary cuts.

Ploys to Resist Cuts

20. Make a Study

Description. The budget guidelines contain a statement that a certain program is to be curtailed or discontinued. The budgetee responds that the proposed action should not be taken until its consequences have been studied thoroughly.

Response. Make the study; be persistent; supplement with other ploys.

21. Gold Watch

Description. When asked in general terms to cut the budget, propose specific actions that do more harm than good.

Example. This well-known ploy derives its name from an incident that occurred when Robert McNamara was with the Ford Motor Company. In a period of stringency, all division heads were asked to make a special effort to cut costs. Most responded with genuine belt tightening. However, one division manager, with $100 million sales, reported that the only cost reduction opportunity he had found was to eliminate the gold watches that were customarily given to employees retiring with 30 or more years of satisfactory service.

Response. Reject the proposal. (In the example, disciplinary action was also taken with respect to the division manager.)

22. Arouse Client Antagonism

Description. When a budget cut is ordered, cut a popular program, hoping to provoke complaints from clients that will pressure the supervisor to restore the program. A classic case is known as the "Washington Monument elevator ploy," where the manager of the Washington Monument proposes to cut the monument's budget by eliminating its elevator service, knowing that doing so will arouse considerable antagonism from hundreds of thousands of visitors each year.

Example. When Mayor Abraham Beame was asked in 1975 by the federal government to reduce spending in New York City to avoid bankruptcy, he responded by dismissing 7,000 police officers and firefighters and closing 26 fire houses. Many people believe he did this to inflame public opinion against budget cuts. It did have this effect, and the order was reversed.

Response. Try to redirect client attention by publicizing areas where cuts are feasible.

23. Witches and Goblins

Description. The budgetee asserts that if the request is not approved, dire consequences will occur. It is used often by the House Armed Services Committee in its reports to Congress. For example, an antiballistic missile system was recommended as a counterdefense to the "Talinin System" that the Soviets were alleged to be building. In fact, the Soviets were not building such a system.

Response. Analysis based on evidence rather than on emotion.

24. We Are the Experts

Description. The budgetee asserts that the proposal must be accepted because he or she has expert knowledge that the supervisor cannot possibly match. This ploy is used by professionals of all types: military officers, scientists, professors, physicians, and clergy.

Response. If the basic premise is accepted, the budget process cannot proceed rationally, for the supervisor tends to be a generalist and the budgetee a specialist. The supervisor should insist that the expert express the basis for his or her judgment in terms that are comprehensible to the generalist.

25. End Run

Description. Go outside normal channels to obtain reversal of a decision.

Example. In Massachusetts in the early 1980s, many hospitals that had been denied a certificate of need (CON) to engage in capital building projects asked their state legislators to introduce a bill overriding the decision by the public health council (an executive branch agency) and permitting the project to proceed. Other legislators, knowing that the next CON denial might be in their district, supported their colleagues, and the entire CON process was weakened.

Response. If the end run is made to the legislature or an equivalent powerful body, the executive probably has no choice except to grin and bear it (pressures for a veto frequently are hard to muster). In other cases, anyone who attempts an end run should be reprimanded and the request denied, because attempts to go outside proper channels upset the authority of the whole budgetary process.

Ploys Primarily for Supervisors

26. Keep Them Lean and Hungry

Description. The supervisor tells the budgetee that the latter's organization will work harder and possibly more effectively if it doesn't carry so much fat.

Response. Show that the analogy with human biology is false, or go along with the analogy and show that the cuts represent muscle rather than fat.

27. Productivity Cuts

Description. It is assumed that many capital expenditures are made with the intention of cutting operating costs. Although few systems permit individual cost reductions to be identified, it is reasonable to assume that they, together with continuing management improvements, should lead to lower operating costs in the aggregate. Some organizations therefore reduce personnel-related costs by about 1.5 percent from the previous year's level. In the entire economy, productivity increases by about 3 percent annually. The lower percentage assumes that non-profit organizations are only half as susceptible to productivity gains as the economy as a whole.

In some organizations the cost reductions can be specifically traced. When an organization makes a large capital expenditure to convert its recordkeeping to computers, this presumably results in lower operating costs, and the planned savings should be specifically identified. If an approved program for, say, 1991 contains an item for the installation of a new computer system that is designed, in part, to reduce clerical expenses beginning in 1993, the budgeted clerical expenses in 1993 should reflect the promised reduction.

Response. Point out that dismissals are politically inexpedient, and retirements and resignations may not be rapid enough to permit costs to be reduced to the desired level.

28. Arbitrary Cuts

> *Example.* The supervisor, who was director of research of a large company, followed the practice of reducing the budget for certain discretionary items (travel, publications, professional dues) in certain departments by approximately 10 percent. Although the supervisor did this on a purely random basis, he achieved a reputation for astute analysis.

Response. Challenge the reason for the cuts (but the items tend to be so unimportant and difficult to defend that such challenges may consume more time than they are worth).

29. I Only Work Here

Description. The supervisor says she cannot grant the budgetee's request because it is not within the scope of ground rules that her superiors have laid down.

Response. Ask that the issue be brought to the appropriate decision-making authority. This, of course, relies on a good relationship (trust) between the budgetee and the supervisor.

30. Closing Gambits

Description. The supervisor uses various tactics to bring the negotiation to a close. A simple one is simply to glance at his or her watch, indicating that time is valuable. Another is to "split the difference" between the amount requested and the amount the supervisor initially wanted to approve. Still another is the proposal to settle on a small amount now, with an indication that a larger amount will be considered later on.

Response. Suggest that another meeting be scheduled to complete the negotiation. If this is not possible, be sure to clarify in writing those decisions that have been made.

SUGGESTED ADDITIONAL READINGS

Anthony, Robert N. "Zero-Base Budgeting: A Useful Fraud?" *The Government Accountant*, Summer 1977, p. 7.

Harmer, W. Gary. "Bridging the GAAP between Budgeting and Accounting." *Governmental Finance*, March 1981, pp. 19–24.

Hofstede, G. H. *The Game of Budget Control*. Assen, Neth.: Van Gorcum & Co., NV., 1967.

Lynn, Laurence E., Jr., and John M. Seidel. "Bottom Line Management for Public Agencies." *Harvard Business Review*, January 1977, pp. 13–23.

McLeod, R. K. "Program Budgeting Works in Nonprofit Organizations." *Harvard Business Review*, September–October, 1971.

Wildavsky, Aaron. *The Politics of the Budgetary Process*, 2nd ed. New York: Harper Collins, 1992.

CASE 10–1   Orion College*

Orion College was a small, private, liberal arts college located in Fleming, Ohio. It granted a bachelor of arts degree. Originally founded as a men's college, it had remained as such until four years ago when, after several heated trustee meetings, it had opened its doors to women.

The admissions office felt that the decision to go coed had significantly offset the negative reaction to the small, rural Ohio town in which the college was located. Over the past four years, its applications from both men and women had increased, and projected enrollment for next year was 1,600 students (all residents). Despite the strong enrollment figures and a large endowment, a deficit of $530,000 was projected (see Exhibit 1).

In its recent meeting, the trustee finance committee had not approved the proposed budget. Instead, it asked President Haas to review the budget with the business officer, academic department heads, and other department heads in order to reduce costs. The finance committee was unwilling to consider even an increase in tuition and fees until it was convinced that adequate measures had been taken to control expenses. In addition, they felt that the budget, as submitted, gave them no indication of where the college's resources were being consumed. Any cost reductions, they felt, should be considered in the light of explicit educational objectives. They requested that President Haas and his business officer prepare a budget format that would be more informative in this regard.

Data

In trying to understand how the college's resources were being consumed, President Haas studied the data presented below. To this he added some notes to expedite the business office's first cut at a new budget format, using a worksheet they had designed (Exhibit 2).

1. Revenue from auxiliary enterprises represents the surplus of income over expenses for the bookstore, faculty club, and college printing office. It does not include any revenue from the college infirmary (health services). A health service fee of $225 is included in the total tuition charge of $7,800 per student.
2. The health services expenses includes expenses for medicine and drugs dispensed in the infirmary but not special prescriptions which students pay for themselves. The health services expense also includes salaries for nurses and doctors but does not include any costs for plant, housekeeping, food, or utilities.
3. For next year, there are 10 full-time equivalent (FTE) faculty assigned to research. Average faculty salaries are budgeted for $38,000 per year. Salaries

---

* This case was prepared by Professor Claudine B. Malone, Harvard Business School. Copyright © by the President and Fellows of Harvard College. Harvard Business School case 9-178-025.

EXHIBIT 1 Operating Budget

	Preliminary Budget Next Year ($000)	*Actual Last Year ($000)*
Revenues:		
Student tuition and fees	$12,480	$11,747
Dining	4,394	4,001
Housing	5,371	4,912
Auxiliary enterprises	2,494	1,966
Gifts for current use	1,139	1,025
Endowment income	1,546	1,092
Reimbursement of direct and indirect expenses related to research grants	130	117
Total revenue	$27,554	$24,860
Expenses:		
Salaries:		
Faculty (teaching and research)	$11,020	$ 9,583
Administration	1,945	1,691
Staff	4,500	3,914
	$17,465	$15,188
Student support:		
Library and audiovisual	$ 696	$ 583
Equipment and supplies	170	146
Food	3,353	2,913
Student activities and athletics	546	476
Scholarships	563	514
	$ 5,328	$ 4,632
Plant:		
Maintenance (salaries, supplies, and minor parts)	$ 569	$ 493
Utilities	644	514
Equipment	482	608
Interest	74	61
	$ 1,769	$ 1,676
General and administration:		
Employee benefits	$ 1,393	$ 1,212
Insurance	100	87
Professional fees	64	56
Communications and data processing	691	640
Travel	135	117
Services purchases	72	63
Security	109	51
Health services	439	381
Miscellaneous	19	23
	$ 3,022	$ 2,630
Research costs (excluding faculty salaries)	500	435
Total expenses	$28,084	$24,561
Surplus (deficit)	$ (530)	$ 299

EXHIBIT 2 Orion College Worksheet ($000)

Programs

Line Items		Admin- istration	Instruc- tion	Re- search	Plant	Housing
Salaries:						
Faculty	(1)					
Administrative	(2)					
Staff	(3)					
Student support:						
Library and audiovisual	(4)					
Equipment and supplies	(5)					
Food	(6)					
Student activities and athletics	(7)					
Scholarships	(8)					
Plant:						
Maintenance	(9)					
Utilities	(10)					
Equipment	(11)					
Interest	(12)					
General and administrative:						
Employee benefits	(13)					
Insurance	(14)					
Professional fees	(15)					
Communication and data process	(16)					
Travel	(17)					
Services purchases	(18)					
Security	(19)					
Health services	(20)					
Miscellaneous	(21)					
Research	(22)					
Subtotal	(23)					
Allocation in (out)	(24)					
	(25)					
	(26)					
Total	(27)					

Programs

Dining Center	Health Services	Student Activities and Athletics	Development	Total	Adjustments	Adjusted Total
				11,020		
				1,945		
				4,500		
				696		
				170		
				3,353		
				546		
				563		
				569		
				644		
				482		
				74		
				1,393		
				100		
				64		
				691		
				135		
				72		
				109		
				439		
				19		
				500		
				28,084		

for faculty secretaries are included in the budget line for staff salaries. For budgeting purposes, each member of the faculty (whether a department head, teaching faculty, or assigned to research) is considered to have 0.3 FTE secretaries at an average salary of $16,800 for an FTE. The budget line for salaries does not include fringes. Next year's teaching faculty (including department heads) number 290 FTEs.

4. For budgeting purposes, administrators are assumed to have 0.2 FTE secretaries. The one exception is the development office. The director of development (salary $39,000) has a full-time secretary, and the office staff comprises an additional six FTE secretary/clerks as well as three administrators (average administrative salaries are $29,500).

5. Salaries for librarians, library clericals, and the audiovisual staff are included in the budget line for library and audiovisual. However, the chief librarian's salary of $29,600 is included in the budget line for administrative salaries.

6. The budget line for student activities and athletics includes all the expenses for the varsity sports program, as well as intramural athletic activities, the student association, required physical education classes, athletic equipment, travel for athletic activities, and other student organization expenses. Revenues from athletic fees and game receipts have been credited to these expenses. Salaries totaling $99,000 for the athletic director, assistant athletic director, and the director of student services have been included in the budget line for administrative salaries.

7. There is very little information readily available on the breakdown of plant expenses. The business office records indicate that utilities for the dormitories have been budgeted for $200,000. The utility budget for all the athletic buildings is $120,000. The dining center utility budget is $80,000. And the infirmary utility expense is planned for $36,000. It was not possible to separate administrative and classroom building utilities since administrators and student activities personnel share space in the classroom complex of buildings. Nor was it possible to isolate housekeeping salaries and expenses from other maintenance salaries and expenses. The salary for the director of the physical plant ($36,900) is in the budget line for administrative salaries.

It was possible to allocate building space among the different users, as indicated in the following table:

Program	Percent of Building Square Feet Used
Administration	5
Instruction	40
Research	10
Plant	1
Housing	40
Dining center	1
Health services	1
Student activities	1
Development	1

8. Professional fees cannot be immediately identified by program. Nor have travel expenses ever been broken down by department. Travel requests have to be approved in advance by the business office except for the $4,000 in travel expenses included in the development office budget and the $9,000 in travel expenses designated for the recruiting office.

9. The $691,000 budgeted for communications and data processing includes $206,000 for the college switchboard, telephones, and operators' salaries. The remainder covers computer rental and data processing personnel salaries except for the $38,000 salary for the director of computer services included in the budget line for administrative salaries.

10. Professional services purchased include legal fees, consulting fees, and auditing fees. Historically, legal fees have been very low because of the long-standing relationship between the college and the firm. Likewise, the fee for the annual audit was well below market.

11. Maintenance of the athletic fields costs about $30,000 a year.

Questions

1. Restructure the preliminary budget in "program format" using the worksheet in Exhibit 2, and making assumptions where necessary. All administrative expenses and plant expenses should be allocated to one of the programs.
2. What action should President Haas take?

Note: For this first budget review, no attempt will be made to examine the individual faculty department salaries and expenses.

CASE 10–2   Moray Junior High School*

Ms. Hilda Cook, principal of Moray Junior High School, stared at her 1986–87 budget. She had just returned from the March 1986 meeting of the Moray Public School System's School Committee, where she had agreed to attempt to cut her school's budget by almost 12 percent. Although Ms. Cook did not consider her projected costs to be excessive, neither did several of the other principals, who also had agreed to attempt to reduce their budgets. According to Ms. Cook:

> This budget cut is a serious problem for us. I don't know quite how to reduce our costs because there really wasn't much flexibility in the budget to begin with. However, we're all in the same situation; we expect to have only $2.2 million to spend on Moray and we have to find some way to live with that.

---

* This case was prepared by Professor David W. Young. Copyright © by David W. Young. Distributed by the Accounting Curriculum Center, Boston University School of Management.

Background

Moray Junior High School was one of three junior high schools in the town of San Pedro, Arizona. Built in the late 1970s, the school was in excellent physical condition, and had an enrollment of approximately 700 students a year. The quality of education was considered extremely high, and a student-teacher ratio of no more than 15:1 had always been maintained. Among the school's special programs were a highly-regarded Drug and Alcohol Awareness Program, and an Understanding Handicaps Program, in which trained parents and handicapped speakers provided a course of instruction to both students and teachers to acquaint them with the various handicapping conditions, such as epilepsy, blindness, physical handicaps, retardation, and deafness.

Moray was best known, however, for its Spanish Language Program, which used native speakers of Spanish to teach courses that began in the 7th grade and continued through the 9th grade. A special language laboratory with 30 student "stations" and three instructor stations was equipped with the latest in audio technology, including an "interrupt" feature that allowed an instructor to listen in on a student practicing with a cassette tape and to intervene electronically, when necessary, to correct the student's pronunciation or grammar. Students successfully completing the program were considered to be extremely proficient in the Spanish language, and a special field trip to a "sister" junior high school in Anguila, Mexico, was organized each year for the 9th graders. The students lived with local families for an entire week while actively participating in the Anguila school system's activities.

As principal of Moray since 1980, Ms. Cook had witnessed numerous changes in the school. For over 40 years, Moray had been the only junior high school in San Pedro; however, in the late 1970s, when migration from the northern United States had led to a large influx of new residents, additional demands had been placed on the school system. As a result, Moray had been expanded and two new junior high schools had been built.

With such a dramatic increase in services, the School Committee had become increasingly concerned with budgeting, cost control, and accountability. Accordingly, in the past few years, Ms. Cook had become more actively involved in the financial management of Moray. By 1986, she, along with other principals in the San Pedro system, had assumed responsibility for constructing her school's annual budget. Moray's proposed budget for 1986–87 is contained in Exhibit 1.

Budget Data

San Pedro's budget process began in January. At that time, the Central Office made enrollment projections, and, using these figures, all school principals held conferences with their teachers and program heads to determine their school's requirements for staffing, supplies, and other cost items. In 1986, all budget needs for Moray were calculated on the basis of a projected enrollment of 690 students, although not all programs served all 690 students. In particular, as Exhibit 1

EXHIBIT 1 Budgeted Statistics and Expenses 1986–87

	Regular Instruction Program	Special Education Program	Spanish Language Program	Other Programs	Total*
Statistics:					
Number of registered students	615	75	180	450	690
Number of days in academic year					170
Number of potential student days					117,300
Expected number of student days					110,497
Attendance rate					94.20%
Direct costs—instruction:					
Regular teacher salaries	$1,119,300	$376,875	$ 85,000	$15,000	$1,596,175
Substitute teacher salaries	37,200	12,500	0	0	49,700
Aide salaries	20,300	9,100	6,500	3,000	38,900
Instructional supplies and library	84,870	37,275	8,280	1,100	131,525
Travel and lodging........................	0	0	3,000	0	3,000
Depreciation	12,300	8,000	40,000	0	60,300
Total.............................	$1,273,970	$443,750	$142,780	$19,100	$1,879,600
Direct costs—administration:†					
Administrative salaries (regular teacher salaries)	$ 87,655	$ 29,514	$ 6,657	$ 1,175	$ 125,001
Administrative supplies (regular teacher salaries)	10,869	3,660	825	146	15,500
Operations and maintenance (square feet)	175,500	40,500	27,000	27,000	270,000
Other (regular teacher salaries).............	5,259	1,771	399	70	7,499
Total.............................	$ 279,283	$ 75,445	$ 34,881	$28,391	$ 418,000
Total direct costs	$1,553,253	$519,195	$177,661	$47,491	$2,297,600
Indirect costs—allocated from Central Office:					
School Committee	$ 2,419	$ 815	$ 184	$ 32	$ 3,450
Administration	30,362	10,223	2,306	407	43,298
Health/life insurance......................	94,514	31,824	7,177	1,267	134,782
Operations and maintenance	4,739	1,093	729	729	7,290
Rent and depreciation.....................	2,243	518	345	345	3,450
Contract services	1,048	128	307	767	2,250
Travel...................................	581	195	44	8	828
Total.............................	$ 135,905	$ 44,796	$ 11,092	$ 3,555	$ 195,348
Total direct and indirect costs................	$1,689,158	$563,991	$188,753	$51,046	$2,492,948
Average cost per registered student...........					$3,613

* Registered students do not crossfoot, since students are enrolled in more than one program.
† Basis for allocations to programs shown in parentheses ( )

shows, Regular Instruction was scheduled to serve 615 students, Special Education 75 students, and the Spanish Language Program 180 students. (As Exhibit 1 indicates, some students were enrolled in more than one program.) The student-teacher ratio in Regular Instruction was scheduled to be 15 : 1, while in the Special Education Program it was only 6 : 1.

Shortly before the budget was completed, Ms. Cook and other principals met with the Director of Finance and Administration to discuss the Central Office

---

EXHIBIT 2   Allocation Bases 1986–87

Indirect Cost	*Basis for Allocation to Moray*
School committee	$5.00 per registered student
Administration	$62.75 per registered student
Health/life insurance.	$0.08 per teacher salary dollar (regular teachers, substitute teachers, and aides)
Operations and maintenance.	$0.027 per Operations and Maintenance dollar in the school
Rent and depreciation.	$5.00 per registered student
Contract services.	$0.018 per administrative salary dollar
Travel.	$1.20 per registered student

Indirect Cost	*Basis for Allocation to Programs within Moray*
School committee	Proportion of regular teacher salaries
Administration	Proportion of regular teacher salaries
Health/life insurance.	Proportion of regular teacher salaries
Operations and maintenance.	Proportion of floor space: 65% to Regular Instruction; 15% to Special Education; 10% to Spanish Language Program; 10% to Other Programs
Rent and depreciation.	Same as Operations and Maintenance
Contract services.	Proportion of registered students
Travel.	Proportion of regular teacher salaries

Examples of Calculations for Allocation to Programs within Moray

School committee	Regular teacher salaries = $1,119,300; Total salaries = $1,596,175. Proportion = .7012. Therefore Regular Instruction share = .7012 × $3,450 = $2,419.
Administration	Regular Instruction share = .7012 × $43,298 = $30,362
Health/life insurance.	Regular Instruction share = .7012 × $134,782 = $94,514
Operations and maintenance.	Regular Instruction share = .65 × $7,290 = $4,739
Rent and depreciation.	Regular Instruction share = .65 × $3,450 = $2,243
Contract services.	Regular Instruction share = $[615/(615 + 75 + 180 + 450)] \times \$2,250 = \$1,048$
Travel.	Regular Instruction share = .7012 × $828 = $581

---

costs. These indirect costs were allocated to individual schools based on measures such as salary expenses and student enrollments. The specific allocation bases for 1986–87 are shown in Exhibit 2.

In reviewing her budget for Fiscal Year 1986–87 (which ran from July 1, 1986, to June 30, 1987), Ms. Cook realized that the nature of the costs varied. She quickly ascertained that the budget contained no superfluous costs that simply could be cut; indeed, the instructional and administrative supply costs reflected only higher supply prices, and the teacher and administrative salaries were based on a very small increase in the wage rate. It appeared that if Ms. Cook wanted to reduce the budget by 20 percent, she would have to analyze the behavior of each cost, and adjust those that were flexible. If necessary, she also was prepared to alter Moray's operations to comply with the School Committee's budget ceiling.

In order to prepare a modified budget for the School Committee, Ms. Cook decided to meet with some of Moray's teachers and program heads, who she thought could provide information concerning some of the budgeted expenses. Her first meeting was with Mr. Steven Hartman, the teacher with the greatest seniority in the school, and the designated representative of the teachers' union, to discuss the teachers' salary expense. Ms. Cook hoped to make substantial cuts in the teacher salary expense item by increasing the average class size from 15 to 20 students. Mr. Hartman's response was not particularly encouraging:

> We can't possibly cut teachers' salaries in the way you envision because the teachers are already overworked. We have to cover lunch and recess periods, and most of us substitute regularly during our break periods for teachers who are out sick. So we need a minimum of 1 teacher for every 15 students. Unless we cut down on students, we can't possibly reduce the number of teachers.

Next, Ms. Cook met with Dr. Mariana Olivera, the lead teacher for the Special Education Program, and Ms. Lillian Higgins, the librarian. Ms. Higgins, the most senior of the two, discussed the use of books and other instructional supplies, and her ideas for reducing costs:

> The instructional supplies and library item does appear to be a large amount, but there is really nothing included in it that's excessive. I think we're already quite frugal in our supply use, and we can't just stop ordering pencils, paper, books, or anything else we need for instructional purposes.
>
> I do see one problem with the budget, however; we're budgeting for a full 690 students when, in fact, due to absences, we probably have only about 650 students in school at any one time. If we adjust the budget to reflect our actual attendance, we can cut costs by at least 5 percent.

Dr. Olivera also had an idea for cutting costs. She suggested that the school reduce or eliminate the Spanish Language Program, thereby reducing the budget by almost $189,000. In considering Dr. Olivera's suggestion, Ms. Cook called the audio equipment manufacturer to discuss the resale value of some of the school's equipment. The company informed her that machines used for four years or more could not be sold, even for scrap. All of the equipment in Moray's language laboratory had been purchased prior to 1982.

Ms. Cook also reviewed the salaries for the Spanish Language Program and found that $35,000 was for a lead teacher, with the remaining $50,000 designated for two regular teachers, at $25,000 each. No substitutes were budgeted since, in the case of a teacher absence, the aide could cover. She also noted that the program's size was limited by the number of teachers. That is, since a strict 10 : 1 student-teacher ratio was maintained, and the students attended the lab daily, the maximum number of students the program could accept was 180 (30 per class period with six class periods in a day). This did not mean that the lab equipment was fully utilized, however, since the nature of the instructional process was such that some days the students would not use the lab at all.

As she reflected on the nature of the task before her, Ms. Cook realized that she had to consider the interactive effects of several factors. First, there was the question of the nature of the direct costs in her budget. Although Mr. Hartman had given her a good indication of how teachers' costs might change with changes in enrollment, the behavior of the other costs was less clear. Administrative salaries and supplies, she reasoned, would remain about the same regardless of the number of students. This would probably be true for operations and maintenance expenses as well. Instructional supplies and library expenses, on the other hand, would probably change in direct proportion to the number of students.

A second consideration of Ms. Cook's was the level of indirect costs. When she called the Central Office to learn more about the allocation process, she was told that the distribution of indirect costs among programs within Moray used a different set of allocation bases from those used to allocate the costs to the school; these are shown in Exhibit 2. She also realized that at least some of the indirect costs allocated to Moray from the Central Office would change as both student enrollment and the level of Moray's direct costs changed. Nevertheless, she felt quite certain that the School Committee would hold her responsible for whatever amount was allocated. But then, if she was responsible for these costs, she wondered about the extent to which she could control or reduce them.

Finally, Ms. Cook mused about Dr. Olivera's suggestion. Reducing or eliminating services did not seem appropriate, yet it might be the only way to meet the targeted budget reduction. If she were to cut the Spanish Language Program in half, she thought she might be able to reduce some of the Program's costs, but she was not at all sure. She also noted that approximately two-thirds of the depreciation in her budget was for language laboratory equipment.

As she began to prepare her budgetary modifications, Ms. Cook realized that Dr. Olivera's suggestion posed some very difficult issues. She decided to revise her budget first by making the appropriate changes in costs associated with an average attendance of 650 students. Only if this failed to produce the requisite reduction, would she consider cutting back the Spanish Language Program. However, in order to demonstrate to the School Committee the true impact of its request, she also decided to calculate what her average attendance in the Regular Instruction Program would have to be in order to meet the Committee's requested cut without curtailing the Spanish Language Program. Since several teachers were expected to retire at the end of the current fiscal year (FY1985–86), she realized that if attendance levels were cut on a permanent basis, she might be able to get by without hiring replacements.

Since Ms. Cook would soon be required to make employment offers for any new or replacement teachers, she realized that preparing revised budgetary projections and gaining School Committee approval for them was of the utmost priority.

Questions

1. What is the average teacher salary for the Regular Instruction and Special Education Programs?
2. Please analyze the costs in the category "Direct Costs-Instruction," and classify each line item as either fixed, variable, semivariable, or step-function. If variable, semivaria-

ble, or step-function, please indicate specifically how the cost behaves. How, if at all, is this analysis useful to Ms. Cook?

3. What are the budgetary options open to Ms. Cook? What are the cost savings associated with each?

4. What should Ms. Cook do?

CASE 10–3   Urban Arts Institute*

In May 1992, Tim Stanley, president of the Urban Arts Institute (UAI), had just received some good news and some bad news. The good news was that the Institute's bank had approved the conversion of a portion of a long-term note (secured by a second mortgage on the Institute's property and building) to an increase in its short-term line of credit. The increase had allowed the Institute to close its budget gap for the fiscal year ending June 30, 1992. The bad news was that the bank also had informed Mr. Stanley that the additional drawings on the line of credit needed to close the budget gap had taken the line of credit up to its maximum. Since the Institute had virtually no endowments or other reserves, there was no margin for error left for the upcoming fiscal year.

Mr. Stanley realized that unless he took some immediate steps to improve UAI's budgeting system, the Institute was headed toward financial disaster. With the budget formulation process for fiscal year 1993 (July 1992 to June 1993) almost complete, he turned his attention to UAI's fiscal operations with the following questions:

1. With no reserves to fall back on, the Institute needed a balanced budget in FY 1993. What measures should he put in place to assure himself that this would happen?

2. How could the overall budget formulation process be changed to reflect his management style and support some of his other strategic goals, such as improved communications among faculty, administration, and the board?

Background

UAI was founded in 1911 as a private for-profit enterprise with a mission to provide training for business and commercial applications of art skills. In 1965, to permit it to tap into additional revenue sources (e.g., government grants, scholarships, and so on), the UAI changed its legal status to private nonprofit. Despite this change, the management of the Institute retained its for-profit flavor, operating as a family-owned business. Until 1990, it was run by the same family that had

---

* This case was prepared by William Wubbenhorst, under the supervision of Professor David W. Young. Copyright © by David W. Young.

founded it, with decision-making authority vested in a small circle, and board members comprised of friends of the family.

Historically, the school always had been highly tuition-dependent, with almost no endowment to contribute toward operating expenses. In 1985, the UAI financed about $2 million in building renovations entirely through bonds issued by the Massachusetts Health and Education Financing Authority (HEFA). In 1989, the UAI became accredited as a four-year institution, having previously offered only a three-year diploma to its students. To receive accreditation, the UAI needed to increase its curriculum to include the requisite number of liberal arts credits for its students.

In mid-1990, the Institute's president of 11 years resigned. In the ensuing weeks, several board members also resigned, marking an end to the founding family's control over the Institute. Steven Roberts, Dean of Academic and Faculty Affairs, stepped in as interim president until a new president could be recruited. Mr. Stanley assumed the position in August 1991.

Organizational Structure

The Institute's president reported to the Board of Trustees. The current chairperson of the board, Henry Hunter, was elected in May 1990, while the Institute was still under the leadership of the previous president. The turnover of trustees following in the wake of the president's resignation marked a period of awakening for the board. Mr. Hunter took the opportunity to recruit new board members who were committed to playing a much more active role in the Institute's affairs than had been expected previously.

Three administrative deans (for Academic/Faculty Affairs, Student Affairs, and Admissions) reported directly to the president. Also reporting to the president were the directors for public relations, financial aid, development, and the business manager. The bulk of the Institute's professional staff, mainly faculty, reported to Dean Roberts.

The instructional side of UAI consisted of six academic departments, each with its own chair. The six chairs also reported to Dean Roberts. The Fine Arts, Liberal Arts, and Foundation departments comprised the institute's "core" curriculum through which students received a common grounding in art skills. In the case of Liberal Arts, this curriculum was also required as part of the school's authority in granting bachelor's degrees. As described by Mr. Hunter:

> All of our students, regardless of concentration, receive a grounding in Fine Arts and Foundation. This integrated approach to our curriculum is one aspect of the school that makes us different and unique from other art schools.

The other three departments (Design, Illustration, and Photography) were the principal areas of concentration students pursued after completing the core curriculum. Each year, a small number (some four to five) chose a concentration in Fine Arts.

Tim Stanley

Prior to assuming his role as president, Mr. Stanley had served as director of a nearby university-affiliated arts center, a position he held for 11 years. Previously, he had earned Master's degrees in both Business Administration (with concentration in international banking) and Fine Arts (concentrating in arts management).

Mr. Stanley's first few months at UAI were spent acclimating himself to the school through both informal conversations as well as a formal survey of staff, faculty, and trustees. He also conducted some informal research into current issues around the external environment of higher education in general and art schools in particular. He reflected on his key findings:

> One of the first things I discovered at the UAI was the lack of a common vision or goal for the institute among staff, faculty and board members. However, I knew from my previous experiences that these types of creative differences around issues like traditional versus contemporary teaching techniques, are common in an arts education environment.
>
> Another thing that leapt out at me was the impact that UAI's previous management style had had on staff and faculty. Previously, the school's affairs were managed by a very tight circle of decision-makers, especially as it applied to fiscal and budget matters. As a result, I found many of the staff and faculty surprisingly ill-informed about the fiscal condition we were in. The previous leadership clearly had left a management legacy characterized by extremely poor communication and coordination with the instructional and programmatic side of the school.
>
> There was also an atmosphere of annual crisis management, with severe cash flow problems arising from unanticipated budgetary shortfalls on a regular basis. Furthermore, the MIS in place was unable to give critical and timely answers to questions concerning enrollment and the budget.
>
> Lastly, there really hadn't been any kind of market research or analysis around the school's "fit" with its external environment, specifically the market of prospective art students. There were no data on current demographic and historical enrollment trends, both for the school in particular and for higher education in general.

In response to these findings, Mr. Stanley and Mr. Hunter (who shared many of Mr. Stanley's concerns and observations about the school's condition) assembled a two-day retreat with staff, faculty, and trustees. The primary purpose of the retreat was to communicate their findings and to begin to forge a common understanding of the problems and challenges facing the school in the future.

The retreat, according to Mr. Stanley:

> . . . was a great success. People had been left in the dark for so long, they were very receptive and attentive to what Henry and I had to say. The retreat got people enthusiastic and they welcomed the opportunity to share more responsibility in the change process. Our message to all of them was: "You are an active partner," and they heard that.
>
> The retreat was also successful in developing some common agreement and discussion around such critical issues as student enrollment, recruitment and retention, as well as ideas for new program delivery systems.

As he reflected on the retreat and looked toward the future, Mr. Stanley saw a number of challenges:

In a sense, everything I had done to date, in terms of the interviews and the retreat, was the easy part. Now, I had to figure out how to change the fiscal, and especially the budgetary, decision-making and communication processes in a way that would support my participatory management style. Now that I had gotten everybody excited about being a part of the school, I needed to figure out how to channel the energy and efforts of the staff, faculty, and trustees toward solving the school's critical financial problems.

The Budgetary System

The Institute's budgeting system had gone largely unchanged in recent years. As described by one of the school's administrators, the system was a reflection of the school's history of management:

> It was a very closed process, with almost all of the decisions being made by the president, the Dean of Student Affairs [who had since left the school], and a couple of the trustees, including the chairman [who also had left]. The budget process itself wasn't really very rigorous, and we were constantly having to make mid-fiscal year reductions because of unanticipated cash flow problems.

Budget Structure.   Revenues were recorded in 14 different accounts. Expenses were tracked through approximately 140 different accounts. These accounts and the relevant amounts for fiscal years 1992 (as of 4/30/92) and 1993 (budget) are shown in Exhibit 1 (Revenues) and Exhibit 2 (Expenses). (Exhibit 2 has been abbreviated somewhat due to length considerations.) The original FY 1992 budget, which was approved by the board in October 1991, contained a surplus of $2,062, up from a loss in FY 1991 of $28,350.

The largest expense, accounting for over half of the Institute's expenses in FY 1992, was personnel costs. For budget planning purposes, these costs were determined centrally, based on department heads' estimates of the number of classes they would be providing. The academic heads generally used historical information, along with their own projections of enrollments, to estimate their staffing needs for the coming semester. These projections then were collected and added to the administrative staffing costs to determine the total projected personnel budget. Exhibit 3 provides a breakout of full- and part-time faculty by academic department, along with actual enrollment figures (credit hours).

Most department heads controlled only a very small discretionary budget to pay for models, speakers, supplies, and equipment. The exceptions to this were the heads of the Design and Photography departments, who controlled considerably larger budgets for operating two labs each. The Design Department operated the production room and the computer lab; the Photography Department operated the photo lab and the video lab.

The Budget Formulation Process.   UAI's budget formulation process typically began in early March and was completed in mid-October, when the board of trustees formally adopted the budget. Exhibit 4 contains a memo prepared by the

EXHIBIT 1

URBAN ARTS INSTITUTE
Revenues

FY 1993 Budget	FY 1993 Proposed	% Revenue	FY 1992 (revised 2/13)	% Revenue
1. Federal work study............	$ 45,000	1.5%	$ 45,000	1.62%
2. Tuition—day students	2,514,700	83.6	2,370,990	85.30
3. Registration—day students.....	9,600	0.3	8,000	0.29
4. General fees—day students	160,400	5.3	133,530	4.80
Day students (subtotal)	2,729,700	90.7	2,557,520	92.01
5. Continuing education	107,300	3.6	101,500	3.65
6. Registration—continuing education.........................	6,900	0.2	5,750	0.21
7. Summer.....................	65,075	2.2	64,575	2.32
8. Application fee	9,000	0.3	9,000	0.32
9. Pre-college	37,125	1.2		0.00
Other tuitions/fees (subtotal) .	225,400	7.5	180,825	6.5
10. Miscellaneous	2,500	0.1	6,100	0.22
11. Interest	0	0.0	12,000	0.43
Earned income (subtotal)	2,500	0.1	18,100	0.7
12. Gifts—unrestricted...........	25,000	0.8	15,000	0.54
13. Gifts–restricted	25,000	0.8	5,000	0.18
14. HGCC/bazaar................	0	0.0	3,000	0.11
Contributed income (subtotal)..	50,000	1.6	23,000	0.8
Total revenue	$3,007,600		$2,779,445	

EXHIBIT 2

URBAN ARTS INSTITUTE
Expense Accounts
FY 1993 Proposed Budget

Expenses	Account Number	FY 1993 Proposed	% Expense	FY 1992 (Revised 2/13)	% Expense
Personnel:					
Instruction........................	4001	$ 700,000	23.0%	$ 698,134	25.2%
Department heads	4002	81,120	2.7	81,120	2.9
Department staff....................	4003	3,000	0.1	2,000	0.1
Administration heads...............	4004	215,280	7.1	215,280	7.8
Administration staff................	4005	400,000	13.1	384,344	13.9
Nonpersonnel:					
Foundation:					
Materials	5030	600	0.0	650	0.0
Models	5050	7,000	0.2	8,200	0.3
Equipment......................	5070	600	0.0	0	0.0
Fine Arts:					
Materials—General	5130	200	0.0	2,220	0.1
Print materials...................	5131	2,000	0.1	0	0.0
Sculpture	5132	2,000	0.1	0	0.0
Speaker	5140	1,000	0.0	500	0.0
Models	5150	14,000	0.5	13,280	0.5
Equipment......................	5170	1,800	0.1	1,720	0.1

EXHIBIT 2   *(continued)*

Expenses	Account Number	FY 1993 Proposed	% Expense	FY 1992 (Revised 2/13)	% Expense
Design (+2 labs):					
Materials	5230	$ 1,500	0.0	$ 1,500	0.1
Speaker	5240	500	0.0	300	0.0
Models	5250	0	0.0	900	0.0
Equipment	5270	0	0.0	0	0.0
Illustration:					
Materials	5330	500	0.0	200	0.0
Speaker	5340	1,000	0.0	500	0.0
Models	5350	2,800	0.1	3,800	0.1
Equipment	5370	240	0.0		
Photo (+2 labs):					
Materials	5430	4,000	0.1	2,050	0.1
Speakers	5440	1,500	0.0	1,200	0.0
Models	5450	900	0.0	600	0.0
Video	5455	0	0.0	0	0.0
Equipment	5470	2,000	0.1	1,020	0.0
Liberal Arts:					
Materials	5530	500	0.0	600	0.0
Speaker	5540	1,100	0.0	900	0.0
Equipment	5570	600	0.0	200	0.0
Continuing education:					
Materials	5630	850	0.0	200	0.0
Models	5650	1,500	0.0	1,000	0.0
Summer:					
Materials	5730	250	0.0	150	0.0
Models	5750	1,500	0.0	1,500	0.1
High school					
Materials	5830	2,500	0.1	500	0.0
Models	5850	600	0.0	600	0.0
Production room (design lab):					
Materials	5911	5,000	0.2	9,800	0.4
Equipment	5912	2,000	0.1	700	0.0
Photo lab:					
Materials	5921	20,500	0.7	23,950	0.9
Equipment	5922	9,000	0.3	7,280	0.3
Repair	5923	3,000	0.1	1,000	0.0
Computer lab (design):					
Materials	5931	2,500	0.1	2,000	0.1
Equipment	5932	11,816	0.4	16,900	0.6
Video lab (photo):					
Materials	5940	75	0.0	0	0.0
Equipment	5941	2,500	0.1	3,700	0.1
Repair	5942	1,500	0.0	0	0.0
Student affairs (8 accounts)		26,500	0.9	19,380	0.7
Admissions (6 accounts)		34,800	1.1	29,335	1.1
Gallery (4 accounts)		11,100	0.4	9,400	0.3
Library (7 accounts)		21,100	0.7	16,200	0.6
Dean of faculty (1 account)		0	0.0	0	0.0
Front desk (1 account)		33,408	1.1	40,240	1.5
Institutional:					
Bank fees	8110	2,700	0.1	2,700	0.1
Bad debts	8115	4,000	0.1	4,000	0.1

EXHIBIT 2 *(concluded)*

Expenses	Account Number	FY 1993 Proposed	% Expense	FY 1992 (Revised 2/13)	% Expense
Collection expense...............	8120	$ 7,000	0.2	$ 6,000	0.2
Professional fees..................	8125	52,500	1.7	43,000	1.6
Insurance........................	8130	20,000	0.7	20,000	0.7
Workmens compensation..........	8135	9,500	0.3	8,000	0.3
Dues............................	8140	12,500	0.4	9,000	0.3
Interest.........................	8145	7,500	0.2	600	0.0
Miscellaneous....................	8150	2,500	0.1	2,000	0.1
Supplies........................	8155	9,500	0.3	7,800	0.3
Postage/delivery.................	8160	32,000	1.0	27,000	1.0
Reserve	8165	100,000	3.3	25,000	0.9
Printing.........................	8170	12,950	0.4	16,000	0.6
Phone..........................	8180	30,800	1.0	7,500	0.3
Unemployment...................	8185	10,000	0.3	20,000	0.7
Pension.........................	8190	10,000	0.3	8,500	0.3
Travel..........................	8195	1,500	0.0	10,000	0.4
Data processing	8210	10,500	0.3	1,500	0.1
Equipment rental	8215	8,215	0.3	9,000	0.3
IBM............................	8216	18,000	0.6	10,040	0.4
Equipment purchase	8220	2,500	0.1	17,400	0.6
Equipment maintenance	8225	12,800	0.4	4,325	0.2
Health..........................	8230	44,084	1.4	10,900	0.4
State health	8235	1,400	0.0	36,400	1.3
Social security	8240	114,582	3.8	1,500	0.1
Tuition reimbursement	8250	3,000	0.1	108,716	3.9
President (4 accounts)..............		7,500	0.2	12,500	0.5
Publicity:					
Day catalogs	8630	70,000	2.3	68,000	2.5
Continuing education catalogs......	8645	19,000	0.6	20,000	0.7
High school catalogs	8650	5,000	0.2	4,200	0.2
Advertising	8730	65,000	2.1	60,000	2.2
Public transit campaign...........	8731	4,000	0.1	0	0.0
Special event....................	8745	0	0.0	0	0.0
Miscellaneous	8780	500	0.0	200	0.0
New ad campaign.................	8760	0	0.0	4,000	0.1
Production costs.................	8755	2,500	0.1	2,000	0.1
Development (4 accounts)		29,000	1.0	10,300	0.4
Building maintenance (4 accounts)....		35,075	1.2	35,350	1.3
Utilities (4 accounts)		59,000	1.9	56,200	2.0
Building renovation (2 accounts)		0	0.0	0	0.0
Finance:					
HEFA interest	9700	118,000	3.9	118,000	4.3
HEFA principal	9750	87,000	2.9	87,000	3.1
Bank interest....................	9762	60,000	2.0	83,000	3.0
Bank principal...................	9763	20,000	0.7	13,000	0.5
Scholarship:					
CWS federal	9800	45,000	1.5	45,000	1.6
Work grant	9900	12,000	0.4	10,000	0.4
UAI............................	9905	206,000	6.8	96,500	3.5
DWA UAI.......................	9915	20,000	0.7	15,000	0.5
Special	9920	5,800	0.2	3,204	0.1
Total Expenses......................		$3,048,145		$2,765,388	

EXHIBIT 3 Faculty and Enrollments by Department (faculty figures are from the 1992–93 Budget)

	No. of Full-Time Teaching Faculty*	Average Salary†	No. of Part-Time Teaching Faculty	Average Salary	Enrollment (Number of Credit Hours)		
					Fall 1991	Winter 1992	Fall 1992
Fine Arts	4	$26,250	5	$10,215	608.0	484.5	642.0
Foundation	4	28,593	2	12,913	593.5	595.0	721.0
Liberal Arts	3	30,000	5	6,025	1,155.0	1,317.0	1,236.0
Design‡	1 ½	25,000	12	4,898	756.0	475.5	715.0
Illustration‡	¾	26,667	6	4,583	541.0	632.5	426.5
Photography	4	28,750	7	3,571	514.0	602.0	603.0
	17 ¼		37				

 * Some faculty have part-time administrative responsibilities. Their time in administrative activities is not counted here. Also, some faculty who reside in one department actually spend some of their time teaching in another department. These shifts are not shown here.
 † Includes chair's salary.
 ‡ Chair is part-time.

EXHIBIT 4 The Budget Preparation Schedule

February 21, 1992

To: Department Heads
From: Edward Carlton
Re: FY 93 budget process

This year's budget process will be essentially the same as it has been in prior years. We will use the following schedule:

March 9	Proposals for new programs, courses, building projects, and major purchases due to Carlton (use attached form).
During March	Academic Dept. heads meet with Frank Angelo for proposals for classes and programs and with Steven Roberts for all other proposals. Dept. heads responsible for setting appointments.
	All Dept. heads meet with Tim Stanley, Roberts, Carlton, and Angelo regarding general plans for the depts. for FY 93.
April 1	Carlton announces decisions on proposals if the decision has not been given before.
During April	Dept. heads prepare detailed budgets on the basis of FY 92 and the approved proposals. Carlton will supply basic information for FY 92.
April 24	Detailed budgets due to Carlton, including faculty hours.*
May	Dept. heads individually meet with Stanley, Carlton, and Angelo.
June 1	Carlton announces proposed budget.
June 15	Dept. heads submit revised budgets to Carlton if desired.
June 30	Stanley and Carlton announce Preliminary Budget for FY 93.
During Sept.	Stanley and Carlton review Preliminary Budget in light of enrollments.
Sept. 30	Carlton announces proposed changes in Preliminary Budget.
Oct. 7	Dept. heads submit revised budgets to Carlton if desired.
Oct. 15	Board of Trustees adopts budget.

 * This projection was based on the department head's estimate of students and classes to be taught for the fall semester.

EXHIBIT 4 *(concluded)*

New Proposals for FY 1993

Use for proposals for new programs, courses, building changes, and major new purchases or expansions to be undertaken in FY 93. Complete one form for each proposal and deliver it to Edwards by March 9.

Brief Description

Person making proposal

Approval by appropriate department head

Detailed description of proposal

Anticipated benefits

Anticipated costs (financial and other)

Impact on other departments

Effective date

school's business manager, Edward Carlton, outlining the timetable for the FY 1993 budget.

Dean Roberts described one of his main frustrations surrounding the budget formulation development process:

> Because the school is so highly dependent on tuition revenues, the information around the number of enrolled students is a critical element in preparing the budget. However, due to the school's "open" admissions policy, which permits students to register for courses up to one week before fall semester classes are scheduled to begin, both revenue projections and course planning are subject to last minute revisions. These revisions sometimes take place as late as two months into the fiscal year.

Budget Monitoring. Once the preliminary budget was finalized at the beginning of the fiscal year, Mr. Carlton began monitoring budget-to-actual expenditures on a monthly basis, beginning with the end of August. Exhibit 5 shows a portion of this report for April 1992. Mr. Carlton commented:

> Since Tim arrived, I have continued to do essentially the same things that I did before. I look at the budgeted versus actual year-to-date spending for each account and send the information out to each academic head and administrative dean and director. If there is a small variance, I'll usually just have a quick informal chat with the person responsible for that account. If it's a big variance, I generally communicate those accounts directly to the president.

Perspectives on the Budget Process

Not surprisingly, different members of the organization had different perspectives on the budget process. For example, most academic department heads considered themselves outside of the budget decision-making process. As Sally Ames, the chair of the Fine Arts Department explained:

> At UAI, the budget is run kind of like a shopping mall. All of us operate in our own little world without much knowledge about how each department or the school as a whole is doing. The budget process here has always been shrouded in mystery to me. I don't really know if and when budget decisions are made. In the past few years, we've been sent back mid-semester on several occasions to reassess our budget, and to make more cuts. It becomes very difficult to do any kind of long-term planning or to try to administer new ideas or course expansion because of the uncertainty over whether you'll actually get to spend what you think you're budgeted for.

John Christopher, chair of the Photography Department, also cited the poor communication associated with department budgets:

> After I sat down and negotiated my budget with the business manager and Steve [Dean Roberts] back last May, I assumed that the result of that conversation led to my final budget, since I didn't hear anything back from either of them. So, when the new fiscal year started, I began making needed equipment and supply purchases based on that budget. Then, at the end of August, I received the first end-of-month summary report, only to find out that my final budget was less than I thought. If I knew then what I did at the end of August, I would have spent my budget differently during the first two months, but it's too late now.

Walter Robertson, chair of the Liberal Arts Department added:

> The uncertainty on what my budget really is causes me to make purchases in a more cautious, and expensive, piece-meal fashion. Furthermore, I feel the budget categories are not really relevant for me. I know what my total budget is, and I'll stay within that bottom line, but I might overspend and underspend in certain accounts.

Others, such as Mary Susans (the chair of the Design Department) and Scott Davidson (the chair of the Illustration Department) were frustrated with the lack of full-time faculty in their departments. Mr. Christopher also noted how the poor communication with management had made staff indifferent in responding to administrative tasks:

EXHIBIT 5

URBAN ARTS INSTITUTE
Monthly Financial Report
Sample Pages from Report Dated May 21, 1992

CODES:

A	12-month expense	83%	
B	12-month salary	85%	22
C	9-month expense	89%	
D	9-month salary	94%	17

FY 92 Revised per 2/13

Account Name	Account Number	Year to Date April 30	FY92 Revised	FY92 Original	Year to Date FY92 Revised (percent)	CODE
Net total		$ 90,054	$ 14,057	$ 2,062		
Revenue:						
Federal work study	1910	$ 28,731	$ 45,000	$ 45,000	63.85%	
Tuition day	3105	2,312,345	2,370,990	2,370,990	97.53	
Registration day	3110	5,240	8,000	8,000	65.50	
Day general fee	3150	132,255	133,530	133,530	99.05	
Student health						
Continuing education (Coned)		93,776	101,500	101,500	92.39	
Registration, Coned...	3210	4,350	5,750	5,750	75.65	
Summer		3,127	64,575	64,575	4.84	
Application fee	3015	8,176	9,000	9,000	90.84	
Miscellaneous	3440	15,030	6,100	6,100	246.39	
Interest	3410	1,453	12,000	12,000	12.11	
Art kits	3610					
Gifts, unrestricted	3800	7,446	15,000	15,000	49.64	
Gifts, restricted	3830	0	5,000	5,000	0.00	
HGCC/Bazaar	3920	2,377	3,000	3,000	79.23	
Total revenue		$2,614,306	$2,779,445	$2,779,445	94.06	
Expenses:						
Instruction	4001	$ 693,263	$ 698,134	$ 698,134	99.30	
Department heads	4002	70,027	81,120	81,120	86.33	
Department staff	4003	0	2,000	2,000	0.00	B
Administration heads	4004	194,764	215,280	215,280	90.47	B
Administration staff	4005	314,498	384,344	384,344	81.83	
Payroll adjustment				(20,713)		C
Foundation:						C
Materials	5030	175	650	650	26.92	C
Models	5050	7,750	8,200	8,200	94.51	
Equipment	5070		0	500		
Fine arts:						C
Materials	5130	3,427	2,220	2,220	154.37	C
Speaker	5140	400	500	500	80.00	C
Models	5150	14,396	13,280	13,280	108.40	C
Equipment	5170	596	1,720	1,720	34.65	
Design:						C
Materials	5230	488	1,500	1,500	32.53	C
Speakers	5240	374	300	300	124.67	C
Models	5250	0	900	900	0.00	
Equipment	5270	0				
Illustration:						C
Materials	5330	220	200	200	110.00	
Speaker	5340	460	500	500	92.00	C

EXHIBIT 5   *(concluded)*

Account Name	Account Number	Year to Date April 30	FY92 Revised	FY92 Original	Year to Date FY92 Revised (percent)	CODE
Models	5350	$ 2,335	$ 3,800	$ 3,800	61.45%	C
Equipment	5370					
Photo:						
Materials	5430	2,345	2,050	2,050	114.39	C
Speakers	5440	570	1,200	1,200	47.50	C
Models	5450	495	600	600	82.50	C
Video	5455	0				
Equipment	5470	104	1,020	1,020	10.20	C
Liberal Arts:						
Materials	5530	618	600	600	103.00	C
Speaker	5540	1,130	900	900	125.56	C
Equipment	5570		200	200		
Continuing education:						
Materials	5630	757	200	200	378.50	C
Models	5650	1,511	1,000	800	151.10	C
Summer:						
Materials	5730	175	150	150	116.67	
Models	5750	1,510	1,500	1,500	100.67	
High school:						
Materials	5830	189	500	500	37.80	C
Models	5850	270	600	600	45.00	C
Production room:						
Materials	5911	5,681	9,800	9,800	57.97	A
Equipment	5912	256	700	700	36.57	A
Photo lab:						
Materials	5921	15,632	23,950	23,950	65.27	A
Equipment	5922	10,986	7,280	7,280	150.91	A
Repair	5923	2,385	1,000	1,000	238.50	A
Computer lab:						
Materials	5931	2,038	2,000		101.90	A
Equipment	5932	15,373	16,900	21,438	90.96	A
Video lab:						
Materials	5940	41				
Equipment	5941	3,081	3,700	3,700	83.27	

Also included were expenses for:
Student affairs (8 accounts)
Admissions (6 accounts)
Gallery (4 accounts)
Library (7 accounts)
Dean of faculty (1 account)
Front desk (1 account)
Institutional (26 accounts)
President (4 accounts)
Publicity (12 accounts)
Development (4 accounts)
Building maintenance
  (4 accounts)
Utilities (4 accounts)
Building renovation
  (2 accounts)
Finance (4 accounts)
Scholarship (4 accounts)

Total expenses		$2,524,252	$2,765,388	$2,777,383	91.28%	

In past years, we've received various directives from the administration around certain planned purchases for the school. One year, they told us they were going to make a major purchase of new books for the library, so a bunch of us, including faculty, spent a number of months researching and compiling a list of books. By the time we were about done, we found out there was no money to buy the books after all. After a few of these wasted exercises, we and the involved faculty have become somewhat wary and indifferent to these types of requests from the administration.

These problems around budget uncertainty and communication also made it difficult for the department heads to manage their faculty, especially the part-time teachers. Because of the open admissions policy, teachers often did not know if they were going to teach a particular section until a week before the first class. The school also had a policy whereby full-time faculty were guaranteed a certain number of classes before determining whether classes were available to be taught by part-time faculty.

According to Ms. Ames, this class scheduling and faculty selection process was seen by many teachers as having political dimensions:

The whole process by which the administrative deans plan classes and sections is seen by many faculty as a process driven by political considerations, in which teachers had a "favored" or "unfavored" status in the eyes of UAI administrators.

In contrast to the department heads, the administrative staff faced the difficult task of managing a budget process with high tuition-dependency. The Institute's open admissions policy meant that enrollments, and therefore tuition revenues, were not certain until the fall, but the summer was often the best time for discretionary spending projects like restocking supplies and fixing the building. As Mr. Carlton explained:

In past years, we have gotten ourselves into a jam because we spent our discretionary funds during the summer, only to find enrollments, and thus revenues, coming in lower than expected. By that time, we have essentially lost any flexibility in terms of our spending, and are forced to lay people off and cancel classes at the 11th hour, which is very disruptive to the school's instructional operations.

Amy Danielson, the Dean of Admissions, had a similar concern:

For my office, the summer is a critical time for outreach, both through printing and mass mailings of UAI course catalogs as well as travel and attendance at portfolio days [recruitment conventions for prospective art students to learn more about various art school programs and offerings] and other recruitment efforts.

She also had some concerns over how the school set enrollment goals for budgetary purposes:

Over the past few years I've been here, I've detected a distinct and recurring sense of eternal optimism around the numbers of students, and subsequently the revenues, that will be coming through the door on a given year. The question around setting admissions goals seems to be framed around the question: "How many students do we need in order to cover the school's expenses?" I think, perhaps, that we've been putting the cart before the horse on this matter.

The board of directors also had some concerns not only about the budget process, but about the kind of information it was receiving on the Institute's financial situation. The critical need from Mr. Hunter's perspective was related to the quality of cost information and reporting:

> For many years, the UAI had been run more like a family-owned business than a nonprofit corporation. As the UAI's fiscal condition worsened in recent years, this small circle of decision-makers, consisting primarily of a handful of trustees and the president, became more and more defensive and secretive of the school's fiscal operations. During that time, the remainder of the board served effectively a rubber-stamp function, approving decision with little or no inquiry or involvement.
>
> Consequently, there is no MIS in place to answer critical questions, such as: "How much are the instructional costs related to this department?" or "What does it cost us to operate the public art gallery?"

One reason why Mr. Hunter wanted to have more detailed information about the Institute's expenses was reflected in his broad definition of what he saw as the Institute's mission:

> I feel that a part of our mission is not just to teach art, but also to serve a role of supporting the local artist community through our part-time teaching positions. Many of these teacher/artists are in great need of the steady income that teaching provides to support them while they pursue their creative aspirations.

When Mr. Hunter took the helm, he recruited new members onto the board who wanted to know more about the school's finances and operations. Both he and the new board members felt it necessary for the school to take a "leave no stone unturned" approach to revamping the school's fiscal operations, with special attention to the budgeting and information systems. From his perspective, there were three key ingredients needed in an improved MIS:

> We need to develop specific guidelines on reporting. For example, I think we need to know how much each academic department generates in revenue, and how much it costs to operate. In addition, we should know the administrative overhead costs on a per student basis. Secondly, reports should be generated on at least a weekly basis. These reports should pay close attention to the bottom line and anticipate any cash flow problems. Finally, we need to establish specific conditions under which a particular department or administrative office should be permitted to exceed its budget.
>
> I also want the information in these reports to focus on two key policy objectives for the school: (1) To increase the school's "standard of living" through a more efficient allocation of the existing revenue base; and (2) To provide detailed cost information on each of the school's academic departments to help ascertain "what we do best" and, presumably, concentrate resources in those areas.

In considering these and other issues relating to the budget process, Mr. Stanley categorized the problems into three main areas: information/reporting, timeliness, and communication. He commented on the first area:

> My initial frustration in the area of MIS was with the lack of comparable historical data for multi-year trend analyses of the school's finances. I was also frustrated, as was Henry, with our inability to retrieve needed current budget information in a timely manner. For example, there was no ability to even provide a projected cash flow report

to anticipate possible short-term borrowing needs during the course of the year. In addition, data on enrollment, both past and current, were difficult to retrieve and analyze.

The second area, timeliness, appeared to be somewhat less complicated. Under the current fiscal year, although the preliminary budget was put into place in July, final enrollment figures were not available until the last week in August. Furthermore, the board didn't officially adopt the budget until mid-October, more than one quarter into the fiscal year. If changes needed to be made at that time, they would likely have to occur in the middle of the fall semester, often causing disruptions in academic scheduling.

Mr. Stanley was considering whether changing to a federal fiscal year (October 1st to September 30th), a calendar year, or some other fiscal year might mitigate these mid-year adjustment problems.

The last, and probably most important, area for Mr. Stanley was communication. He commented:

> Years of being excluded from the school's financial decision-making has left most staff, faculty, and department heads largely ignorant of budget issues and concerns. In fact, prior to the retreat, most of the staff, faculty, and trustees were largely unaware of the extent of the school's financial difficulties.
>
> Furthermore, because the budget had been subjected to so many revisions during the course of the year, there was widespread confusion over what the actual budget was. In FY 1992, this confusion led the director of the Financial Aid office to significantly overspend her budget. This meant we had to approach the bank to increase our long-term debt.

To avoid these and other problems, Mr. Stanley knew that improved communication of budgetary information would be essential if the school were to successfully navigate itself through the coming years. With the mixed news from the bank, Mr. Stanley came to understand that UAI had perhaps escaped the frying pan only to face falling into the fire. With no financing options to fall back on, the school would now survive based solely upon its ability to live within its tuition revenue base. With this in mind, he set out to change the budgeting process. He had four objectives:

> First, I want to involve faculty and staff in UAI operations through the budget decision-making process. Second, I want to be able to provide budget information by department. Everyone should know how much they're spending, including salaries. Third, I think Trustees should have cost and budget information, but on a programmatic basis, not on a line-item basis. Finally, all of this must help us to keep the school within the bottom line. We simply cannot have any more deficits.

Questions

1. What measures should Mr. Stanley put in place to assure himself of a balanced budget in FY 1993?
2. How, if at all, should the budget formulation process be changed to reflect Mr. Stanley's management style and his goals for the organization?

CASE 10–4   Fernwood College*

The nose of the United 727 aircraft sliced through the crisp, cool October morning sky. Jason Bourne liked to fly, especially in the morning. Even airline coffee tasted good.

But the coffee was only a diversion. Bourne's mind shifted to his purpose. The D.C. to Columbus flight would take 45 minutes, and he needed the time to think. As his left hand mechanically pressed the plastic coffee cup to his lips, Bourne's right hand dug through the deep, Italian-leather attaché case. There he found the president's letter. With his forefinger and thumb, Bourne pinched the six frayed white pages, and his eyes, like waterbugs on a pond, raced through the letter for the umpteenth time.

The letter contained a recommendation from Thomas Hartman, president of Fernwood College, to the finance committee of the Board of Trustees, suggesting a $550,000 supplemental allocation to the 1979–80 budget. Late that same Friday afternoon, the finance committee, of which Bourne was the youngest member, was to discuss the subject. Jason was unsure whether he could go along with the president's recommendations. He was especially concerned with the president's proposal that $207,000 of the allocation be used for an increase in compensation for faculty and administration.

Bourne knew that the nine members of the finance committee were split into two camps: four who sided with the president on all compensation issues and four who, for various reasons, did not always follow the president's recommendations. Bourne wasn't sure which camp he fell into, but he was sure of one thing: the meeting that afternoon would be long and heated.

Background

Fernwood College was located in Fernwood, Ohio, a city of about 5,000 people located 20 miles south of Columbus. It was founded in 1866 as an academy under the patronage of the Episcopal Church. Fernwood had an average enrollment of 2,200 students, a faculty of about 160 full-time persons (175 Full-Time Equivalents) and a roster of more than 15,000 living alumni. It was coeducational, undergraduate, and primarily a liberal arts college. In recent years, several types of vocational programs had been added that emphasized the importance of preparation for a career.

---

* This case was prepared by Richard J. Parsons and Robert E. Harvey, under the direction of Professor John L. Snook, Jr., Colgate Darden Graduate School of Business Administration, University of Virginia. Copyright © by Colgate Darden Graduate Business School Sponsors. All rights reserved.

Fernwood's financial affairs were regarded by the administration as "excellent." Revenues regularly exceeded expectations, private donors contributed record amounts, and the value of endowment assets increased significantly. Exhibit 1 shows sources and uses of college funds for 1977–79.

EXHIBIT 1

FERNWOOD COLLEGE
Comparison of Educational and General
Expenditures and Mandatory Transfers
For the Years Ended June 30, 1979, 1978, and 1977

	Dollar Amounts			*Percent*		
	1979	*1978*	*1977*	*1979*	*1978*	*1977*
Unrestricted sources:						
Tuition	$ 8,926,283	$ 8,293,989	$ 7,574,181	72.3	72.7	72.7
Summer term fees	134,197	56,021	65,627	1.1	.5	.6
English language program fees	391,789	283,993	314,104	3.2	2.5	3.0
Other student fees	183,463	180,618	170,788	1.5	1.6	1.6
Total student fees	9,635,732	8,814,621	8,124,700	78.1	77.3	77.9
Gifts	715,293	655,778	632,861	5.8	5.8	6.1
Endowment income distributed	453,212	412,631	349,918	3.7	3.6	3.4
Other general resources	160,889	100,426	86,275	1.3	.9	.8
Auxiliary enterprises contribution margin	97,834	164,124	93,626	.7	1.4	.9
Total unrestricted sources	11,062,960	10,147,580	9,287,380	89.6	89.0	89.1
Restricted current funds used	1,281,410	1,249,510	1,137,066	10.4	11.0	10.9
Total provided	12,344,370	11,397,090	10,424,446	100.0	100.0	100.0
Deduct amounts used for:						
Additions to current funds	118,070	121,866	34,814			
	$12,226,300	$11,275,224	$10,389,632			
Instruction and research:						
General	$ 4,546,648	$ 4,265,100	$ 3,945,946	37.2	37.8	38.0
Summer term	84,514	43,984	44,568	.7	.4	.4
English language program	338,999	188,568	217,338	2.8	1.7	2.1
Institutes	139,998	132,636	112,708	1.1	1.2	1.1
Academic development	11,060	20,562	68,845	.1	.2	.7
Research	75,187	69,054	37,170	.6	.6	.3
Total instruction and research	5,196,406	4,719,904	4,426,575	42.5	41.9	42.6
Library and audiovisual	412,808	385,284	356,893	3.4	3.4	3.4
Academic administration	278,671	153,957	145,269	2.3	1.4	1.4
Student services	884,480	814,091	705,611	7.2	7.2	6.8
Athletic equipment and game costs	243,975	211,790	169,792	2.0	1.9	1.6
Institutional support	1,481,787	1,450,996	1,366,446	12.1	12.9	13.1
Educational plant operation	1,549,236	1,489,781	1,335,817	12.7	13.2	12.9
Unfunded pension payments	300,912	297,691	286,722	2.5	2.6	2.9
Student financial aid grants	1,876,469	1,746,905	1,594,219	15.3	15.5	15.3
Mandatory transfers, net	1,556	4,825	2,288			
	$12,226,300	$11,275,224	$10,389,632	100.0	100.0	100.0

Governance

The college was governed by a Board of Trustees of 45 members (42 elected, 3 ex-officio). They were elected, respectively, by the Alumni Association (15), the Ohio East Area Conference of the Episcopal Church (6), and the Ohio West Area Conference of the Episcopal Church (6); the remainder were elected as trustees-at-large (15). Each trustee was elected for a three-year term; after three consecutive three-year terms, rotation was mandatory.

The trustees constituted a working board, were generally kept well informed by the president, and took an active and strong interest in policy determination for the institution. Much of the work of the board was conducted by the various committees (Executive, Organization, Finance, Endowments, Student Affairs, Academic Affairs, University Facilities, and University Relations). The Board of Trustees met three times during the school year (October, February, and May). Committee meetings took place on Fridays, with the full board meeting on the following Saturday.

The $550,000 Allocation

Fernwood College's annual budget for 1979–80 had been approved by the Board of Trustees at their February 1979 meeting. The February budget was based on an enrollment of 2,220 students. The actual enrollment for 1979–80 was considerably higher (2,290 actual in the Fall Quarter, 2,250 estimated in the Winter Quarter, and 2,210 estimated in the Spring Quarter). The higher enrollment made necessary a revision of the school's budget in order to accommodate the resulting increase in tuition income of approximately $550,000. The finance committee had been asked to consider the president's proposed use of the unallocated funds. He suggested the sum be divided among the following areas: (1) accumulated unrestricted reserve for operations; (2) salaries and compensation; (3) accumulated plant deficits; (4) deferred maintenance and special project needs; and (5) academic projects.

The Finance Committee Meeting

The October Finance Committee meeting began promptly at 2 P.M. In attendance were: James Matlock, chairman (attorney); Bernard Osterman (chairman of board, engineering firm); Peter Chancellor (vice president, IBM); Victor Fontine (investment banker); David Spaulding (professor, Ohio college); Gretchen Beaumont (publisher); Jason Bourne (graduate student); Noel Holcroft (bank president); Brandon Scofield (attorney); Munro St. Clair, chairman, Board of Trustees (attorney); Thomas Hartman, president, Fernwood; and Merle Smit, vice president for Business Affairs, Fernwood. The major item of business was the $550,000 allocation. Chairman Matlock opened the meeting by referring to the five recommendations made by President Hartman in the letter he had sent to the committee members 10 days earlier. The recommendations from the president's letter were as follows:

I. Accumulated, Unrestricted Reserve for Operations

Summary Statement

1. Neither the Board nor the Committee on Finance has established a target for the contingency reserve. The Committee has given the administration a guideline that the annual contingency in the February budget should be not less than 1 percent of the total budget ($165,000 for 1979–80 February budget). A reserve which allows for a 5 percent decrease in enrollment in one year should be more than adequate to deal with a random fluctuation. The reserve will need to increase in size at least as rapidly as tuition rises merely to provide the same enrollment coverage. The 1 percent guideline will provide sufficient reserve funds to increase the enrollment coverage by 20 students per year (see Exhibit 2).

Recommendation

We should continue to add to that reserve until we have a coverage of 100 students (Exhibit 2). When that is achieved, we can evaluate our position. We would need to set aside about *$157,000* of the expected current supplemental allocation for that purpose in 1979–80.

II. Salaries and Compensation

Summary Statements

1. Since 1971–72, the real salary for a representative faculty member has dropped almost 15 percent; total compensation has dropped about 6 percent. (See Exhibit 3 for a table showing Consumer Price Index changes and salaries and compensation for continuing faculty.)
2. We had made steady progress from 1975 through 1978; real salaries increased 4 percent and total compensation 6 percent during that three-year period.
3. Our budget and salary decisions for 1978–1979 were intended to continue that upward trend. Rapid inflation (10%), however, caused a decrease in real salaries of 3.1 percent and a decrease in total compensation of 2.1 percent last year.
4. Our budget and salary decisions for 1979–80 also were intended to increase real salaries and compensation. However, if the present 13 percent inflation rate

---

EXHIBIT 2 Accumulated Unrestricted Reserve for Operations

End of	*Total*	*Enrollment Coverage**
1973–74	$250,000	89
1974–75	28,000	9
1975–76	43,000	13
1976–77	78,000	22
1977–78	199,000	50
1978–79	318,000	74
1979–80 (projected)	475,000	100

* Accumulated reserve as related to tuition per student.

EXHIBIT 3   Consumer Price Index Change and Salaries and Compensation for Continuing Faculty

Year	Prices Percent Change Annual	Prices Percent Change Cumulative 1971–72	Tuition Percent Change Annual	Tuition Percent Change Cumulative 1971–72	Salaries Percent Change Annual	Salaries Percent Change Cumulative 1971–72	Compensation Percent Change Annual	Compensation Percent Change Cumulative 1971–72
1972–73......	4.6	4.6	3.1	3.1	4.0	4.0	6.6	6.6
1972–74......	9.8	14.9	5.0	8.2	3.9	8.0	5.2	12.1
1974–75......	10.6	27.1	5.7	14.3	7.6	16.3	6.5	19.4
1975–76......	6.5	35.3	9.8	25.5	7.7	25.2	7.6	28.5
1976–77......	6.0	43.4	9.8	37.8	7.1	34.1	8.3	39.2
1977–78......	6.9	53.3	7.4	48.0	7.5	44.2	8.2	50.6
1978–79......	10.0	68.6	9.0	61.2	6.9	54.1	7.9	62.5
Projected 1979–80....	12.5	89.7	10.2	76.1	10.0	69.5	10.5	79.4

continued for the entire academic year (through August 1980), real salaries would fall another 3 percent, total compensation another 2.5 percent.

5. The estimated salary and compensation for 1978–79 are as follows:

Wages and salaries......	$6,000,000
Fringe benefits..........	1,455,000
Total compensation	$7,455,000

Because not all fringe benefits are wage-related, we estimate that a 1 percent increase in wages and salaries would cost about $69,000 if discretionary fringe benefits are included as well.

Type of Adjustment	Costs ($000) 1979–80	Costs ($000) 1980–81
A. 3%–full year, eff. Sept. 1 ...	$207	$207
⅚ year, eff. Nov. 1	173	207
⅔ year, eff. Jan. 1	138	207
B. 2%–full year, eff. Sept. 1 ...	138	138
⅚ year, eff. Nov. 1	115	138
⅔ year, eff. Jan. 1	52	138
C. 1%–full year, eff. Sept. 1 ...	69	69
⅚ year, eff. Nov. 1	58	69
⅔ year, eff. Jan. 1	46	69

Recommendation

We recommend a *3 percent* adjustment including all fringe benefits effective retroactively to September 1, 1979. This move will cost approximately *$207,000* in both 1979–80 and 1980–81, which represents just over one half of the funds available from the supplemental allocation after setting aside $157,000 for the unrestricted contingency reserve.

III. Accumulated Plant Deficits

Summary Statements

1. Over the last decade we have accumulated substantial deficits in the plant accounts. These deficits are of two types:

   a. *Land*—a result of outlays for land acquisition in excess of inflow of funds from the sale of excess property.

   b. *Plant Projects*—the result of accumulated interest charges arising because available plant funds have not been sufficient to meet project costs. The balance has been borrowed against pledges. The interest deficit continues to grow as long as total plant fund balances are negative.

2. These deficits have been financed by borrowing from current funds. At the end of 1976–1977, our auditors, Ernst & Whinney, urged (but did not order) us to develop a mechanism to reduce and eventually to eliminate such deficits. Our response was to adopt a policy that designated annually $25,000 or 20 percent of the undesignated plant gifts, whichever is larger, to reduce these deficit balances. In 1977–78, $51,000 was allocated to these deficits; in 1978–79, $26,000, for a total of $77,000 over the two-year period. The table below shows the balances in these types of plant deficit amounts over the recent years:

		Plant Deficits End of Year ($000)			
		1975–76	1976–77	1977–78	1978–79
1.	Land	$129	$137	$159	$ 41
2.	Total plant projects	309	288	275	328
3.	Interest accumulated	56	117	177	189
4.	Total	494	558	611	558
5.	Less cumulative reduction	—	—	51	77
6.	Balances	$494	$542	$560	$481

Recommendation

Since these facilities are in use and no depreciation expense is charged against current operations, it is appropriate that the current interest being accumulated on these plant debts be carried as an expense in the budget. We recommend that *$40,000* of the projected contingency be applied to meet the interest costs on the plant deficit accounts for 1979–80.

IV. Deferred Maintenance and Special Project Needs

Summary Statements

1. In the 1979–80 budget we budgeted $165,000 to fund special projects and deferred maintenance. The particular projects to be undertaken in any year are determined by the administration.

2. Several such projects (see below) have a high priority with the administration but could not be funded in the present budget.

Recommendations

The following allocations should be made for maintenance and special projects.

1. Conversion of the Student Union area formerly occupied by the bowling alleys to an area to be used by students as a coffee house and pub (*$35,000*).

2. Conversion of the public safety and buildings and grounds communication system from VHF to UHF (*$25,000*).
3. Additional hookup of electrical power users (motors, lights) to the Buildings and Grounds mini-computer to control energy usage (*$25,000*).
4. Acceleration of the conversion and upgrading of administrative computer operations (*$36,000*).

V. Academic Projects

Recommendation

We would like to recommend that *$25,000* be designated for academic projects such as the following: books for the library, expansion of the Learning Resources Center, and modest funding for student research projects.

Discussion centered first on the compensation increases. Chairman Matlock first explained to new committee members the actions taken regarding compensation at the February meeting. The committee had then approved an average 10 percent increase which was intended to cover inflation plus some real economic increase. Projected inflation at that time was 9 percent. The rate at the time of the October meeting was 13 percent.

Mr. Spaulding moved adoption of all of President Hartman's proposals. Extensive discussion, particularly of the compensation increase, followed:

Mr. Osterman: I second. We all know that the faculty is the life-blood of Fernwood. Despite the Board's sincere efforts in the past to improve the faculty's real purchasing power, the faculty has fallen behind. [Osterman referred to the figures shown in Exhibit 3.] If President Hartman says that faculty morale is hurting due to inadequate compensation levels, I believe him. We pay him to understand the day-to-day operations of the school. If the President says a salary adjustment is needed, then I back him on it.

Mr. Holcroft: I'm opposed to any increases in compensation *at this time*. This committee sets a dangerous precedent in reopening the issue of salaries. Last February we adopted, after much discussion, a budget which we honestly believed would provide adequate measures for keeping faculty and staff compensation ahead in real terms. At some point in time, and I think this is that time, this Board must stand firm. We've done the best we can, and we'll continue to try, but not mid-year in the budget!

Mr. Scofield: I really wonder if we have any choice but to approve the 3 percent compensation package recommended by President Hartman. Hasn't the Faculty Governance Committee already learned that there is a "windfall" $550,000? I understand from what I read in the student newspaper that a representative for the faculty stated that he expected that the lion's share of the $550,000 would be used to improve compensation for faculty and staff.

Mr. Holcroft: Since the $550,000 "windfall" resulted from an unexpected increase in enrollment, does that mean that, if we approved a compensation increase now, we could cut back compensation in the future if enrollment unexpectedly fell? Something tells me that the faculty will not view this issue as a two-way street.

Mr. Spaulding: As Mr. Osterman said, the faculty of Fernwood is the school's greatest asset. Fernwood's salaries must remain competitive.

Mr. Fontine: [interrupting] First, who says that we need to be "competitive"—the market is glutted with talented Ph.D.s. President Hartman has told us himself that every time the school has an open faculty position, nearly 100 applicants vie for the position. Maybe our faculty is paid too much? Which brings me to my second point: My understanding is that our faculty is well paid relative to their colleagues throughout the country. I recently read in the August 1979 issue of the *Chronical of Higher Education* that the average compensation for Fernwood faculty in all three categories (i.e., professor, associate, and assistant) is in the highest quintile distribution among four-year colleges.

Mr. Osterman: I have a question for President Hartman: the survey referred to by Mr. Fontine includes all four-year colleges throughout the country. I'm particularly interested in how Fernwood compares with colleges like itself in the Midwest. Have you any data on this?

President Hartman: According to a recent survey among 24 colleges in the Associated Colleges of the Midwest, Fernwood's average compensation ranks fourth. [President Hartman distributed the list of colleges. The top four colleges were Kalamazoo with average compensation of $27,096; Carleton, $26,913; Oberlin, $26,230; and Fernwood $25,517. The median was $24,300, the lower quartile was $23,500, and the lowest was $20,674.]

Ms. Beaumont: We must remember that this committee and the full Board made a commitment four years ago to maintain and improve the real income level of staff and faculty. During the past eight months, inflation heated up and ate into what we thought last February was an improvement in real income. We must not forget our commitment.

Chairman Matlock: I agree with Ms. Beaumont, our Board cannot forget our commitment made four years ago. I am concerned, however, that the comparative measuring stick that we have used in the past to gauge real income against inflation is adequate. I am referring to the Consumer Price Index. Although I'm not an economist, I understand that the CPI can overstate real inflation. My understanding is that the CPI includes the effect of rising mortgage rates, which is a factor that does not affect people who already own a house. In addition, we all know that the cost of living in Fernwood, Ohio, is lower than most places in the country.

Mr. Fontine: I want the committee members to remember that last February I voted in favor of the 10 percent compensation increase for 1979–80. At that time, the committee agreed to my proposal that future compensation for faculty and administration would be contingent on improvements in efficiency. The Faculty Governance Committee was told this back in February. Why haven't I heard during this meeting anything about improvements in efficiency? I ask you, President Hartman, what improvements have taken place?

President Hartman: I think this group will recall that in February there was considerable debate as to what exactly "efficiency" meant for an academic institution. I don't believe we adequately defined efficiency. I will report that the Faculty Governance Committee and my staff are committed to increasing the student/faculty ratio from the present 14.5/1 ratio to 15/1. Also, many faculty members have become involved in special tutorial programs for students of exceptional ability.

Mr. Chancellor: I, too, am concerned with the efficiency issue. Perhaps we should set aside some time later to adequately define the term. The point I wish to make at this time has to do with the accumulated plant deficits. I believe that President Hartman's figure of $40,000 is horrendously too low. There should be more attention given to this. Our auditors have strongly recommended that we develop definitive plans for funding these deficits. I don't believe that our current plan will accomplish this. We must be more fiscally responsible here. I recommend we use President Hartman's original $40,000 together with the $207,000 originally earmarked for compensation increases to extinguish part of the accumulated plant deficit.

Chairman Matlock: Before our committee considers another recommendation, we first must vote on Mr. Spaulding's motion that we accept all of President Hartman's proposals. Are there any last questions or comments relevant to Mr. Spaulding's motion?

Mr. Bourne: I have a question for President Hartman. In your table showing a comparison of the CPI to salaries and compensation (Exhibit 3), you used 1971–72 as your base year. Why?

President Hartman: It was in 1971–72 that faculty compensation was considered to be at its peak level of real purchasing power.

Chairman Matlock: Any other questions or comments? If not, let's vote.

Question

How should Mr. Bourne vote?

CASE 10–5   Rush-Presbyterian-St. Luke's Medical Center*

George D. Wilbanks, M.D., Chair of Obstetrics/Gynecology at Chicago's Rush-Presbyterian-St. Luke's Medical Center, and Chair of the Department of Obstetrics/Gynecology at Rush Medical College, sat in his office pondering his new managerial responsibilities. He was especially concerned about the additional level of accountability he would have under a new budgeting approach that he and his colleagues in Women's and Children's Services had proposed recently to the medical center's budget committee.

The medical center had undergone significant organizational and structural changes during the last year, one of which was to consolidate obstetrics/gynecology, pediatrics, and maternal-child nursing into a strategic business unit, called Women's and Children's Services, with accountability for its bottom line. The implementation of a flexible budgeting system, in which departments' budgets were adjusted according to changes in the volume of patients served, was a key ingredient in the consolidation. Dr. Wilbanks knew his role in the budgeting process would be significant under the new system, and he wanted to identify the processes he would have to manage to assure its success.

* This case was prepared by George A. Pereira-Ogan under the direction of Professor David W. Young. Financial support for its preparation was provided by the Association of Professors of Gynecology and Obstetrics. Development of the case was made possible by a grant from Wyeth-Ayerst Laboratories to the APGO Medical Education Foundation. Copyright © by David W. Young.

Background

Rush-Presbyterian-St. Luke's Medical Center had a long history. Rush Medical College was over 150 years old, and was actually incorporated several days before the city of Chicago. Presbyterian and St. Luke's were two very old and established hospitals in Chicago that merged with Rush Medical College in the 1960s to form Rush-Presbyterian-St. Luke's Medical Center, or "Rush," as it frequently was called.

In 1992, Rush was the largest academic medical center in Chicago. Its downtown campus housed a 912-bed tertiary care hospital, a 176-bed rehabilitation facility, and a health university that comprised four colleges: Rush Medical College, the College of Nursing, the College of Health Sciences, and the Graduate College. In 1991, these four colleges enrolled 1,228 students in several health fields, ranging from medicine to health care administration. In addition, in the fall of 1991, there were 447 residents and 97 fellows enrolled in graduate medical education tracks.

Rush also was a vertically and horizontally integrated health care system. In addition to its downtown campus, the Rush system contained two community hospitals, a staff model HMO with 150,000 members, an IPA-model HMO, a PPO, and a for-profit subsidiary that was involved in a variety of different ventures including home health care, home pharmacy, and the operation of eight occupational health centers. Total operating revenues for 1991 were over $733 million, and total assets as of the end of 1991 were approximately $900 million.

Mission. Like most teaching hospitals, Rush's mission had four themes: patient care, teaching, research, and community service. Rush saw itself as different from most other teaching hospitals, however, in that its primary mission was patient care. Michael A. Maffetone, D.A., associate vice president and administrator of Women's and Children's Services, explained:

> Usually, when a hospital is associated with a medical school, the hospital essentially exists for the medical school; it is a laboratory in which medical students practice. The typical teaching hospital might not exist if it did not have the medical school. Even though we focus on patient care, teaching, research, and community service, everyone at Rush understands the *primary* mission, without a doubt, is patient care. Patient care is the driver, so if we didn't have the medical college, we wouldn't have as good a hospital, but we would still have a hospital. However, it's not as though the medical college is just stuck on the side. We try to fully integrate it, similar to other medical schools, but the major driver is patient care. To a degree, because of that, the organization is very structured around classical hospital operations lines.

Organization. For the past 20 years, Rush had been managed in terms of what Dr. Maffetone called a "matrix." An organizational chart depicting this arrangement is contained in Exhibit 1. A senior management committee, composed of senior level representatives from nursing, administration, and medicine, oversaw the operations of the medical center.

EXHIBIT 1 Organizational Chart

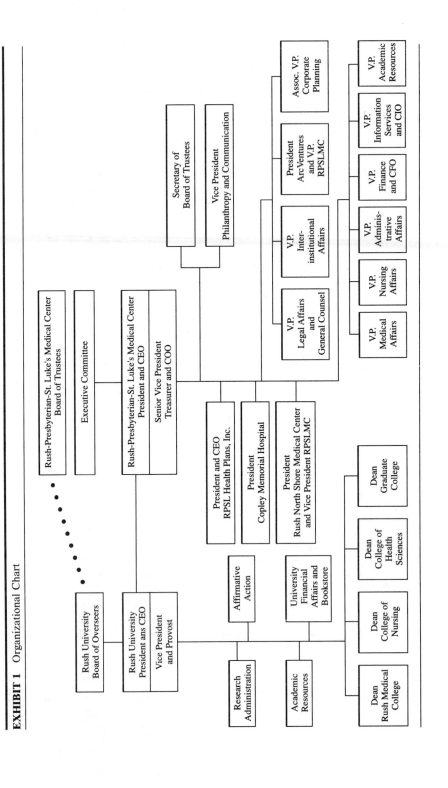

The structure was a "consolidated governance model," meaning that Leo Henikoff, M.D., the CEO of the medical center, was also the president of the university. That management theme was carried all the way down the hierarchy to the department chair level. For example, the vice president for medical affairs in the medical center, Roger Bone, M.D., was also the dean of the medical college. The vice president for nursing, Kay Andreoli, D.S.N., was also the dean of the nursing college. And Peter Butler, vice president for administration, was the chair of the graduate program in health systems management. As Dr. Maffetone characterized it:

> There is no duality. In most medical school settings, you have the Dean and all of the faculty on one side, and the hospital guys on the other side. At times, there is duplication. For example, even in the clinical labs, you'll have a lab in the university doing hematology and then you'll have one in the hospital. There is duality of function all the way down the line and a lot of competition for resources. Here, it doesn't exist. All of the medical staff functions come through the Dean when he wears his vice-president-of-medical-affairs hat. He negotiates with himself. George Wilbanks is the head of Ob/Gyn Services and he is also the chairman of Ob/Gyn in the university. This is a key point that drives the way we approach our mission and is one reason that we are unique as a medical center.

Dr. Henikoff described the vision of Rush as being a true vertically integrated regional health care system. He likened the structure of this system to a pyramid with primary care forming the base, the corporately-integrated community hospitals comprising the center, and Rush-Presbyterian-St. Luke's Medical Center at the top. In 1992, there were two corporately-integrated community hospitals in the Rush system. Rush also was negotiating with several others. Its eventual goal was to have eight community hospitals, forming a significant referral base for the tertiary care provided at the downtown campus.

The 1991 Strategic Reorientation

In 1991, Rush embarked upon an ambitious new strategy and structure. There were several underlying reasons for this strategic reorientation. First, according to Dr. Henikoff, Rush was probably the first hospital in the country to institutionalize total quality management (TQM) in a serious way. They had been using TQM tools to solve operational problems for about five years. At the same time, when the senior managers were developing the long-range strategic plan for the medical center, they decided to form institutes of excellence in six areas, including a Heart Institute and a Cancer Institute.

Hospitals within a Hospital. To facilitate the development of these institutes, Rush planned, within five years, to build a new patient care building on the campus. The new building was to be designed to house "hospitals within a hospital." Specifically, each floor of the new building was to be a 148-bed, self-contained hospital within the larger hospital. Each would represent one of the institutes of excellence. Dr. Henikoff spoke about the transition:

> Eventually, we want to have six or eight of these hospital-within-a-hospital institutes of excellence. These institutes will operate with a multidisciplinary approach—each will have its own basic research, its own patient care, and its own clinical research. Teaching will be incorporated throughout. The Heart Institute, for example, will house cardiology, cardiac surgery, cardiac rehabilitation, and preventive care all together. This will reduce the huge amount of wasted time elapsed in the process of seeing a doctor for chest pain until being ready for cardiac surgery.
>
> Additionally, each hospital will have its own support services in-house, i.e., radiology, laboratory, dietary, housekeeping, transport, etc. And all of these service employees will be cross-trained, with the expectation that they will be able to perform several tasks. Historically, we suffered a loss of productivity on the basis of logistics. There are typically over 300 job descriptions in a hospital, so there are people sitting on their hands, "pigeonholed" because of narrow job descriptions. Just getting a wheelchair somewhere is a logistical nightmare. Because of restrictive job descriptions, people are forced to sit around and say "that's not my job." So, we're cross-training these service employees with the ultimate goal being the concept of patient-focused hospital care.

Just prior to the strategic planning session in 1991, Peter Butler, Vice President for Administrative Affairs, had returned from the position of CEO of one of Rush's community hospitals. Butler's experience there was a key factor in the strategic changes that were to follow. He reflected on the experience:

> I came to Rush originally as the Budget Director. Then I went out to one of our community hospitals as the CEO. When I came back as Vice President for Administration, I realized that decisions had been made more easily at that 250-bed hospital. Administration was able to work with physicians and nurses, and I asked myself why we couldn't be more efficient decision-makers here. I wanted to move decision-making down while maintaining the benefits of matrix input at the operating unit level.

The senior management of the medical center decided that this would be an excellent opportunity to test the concept of hospitals within a hospital before officially making the move with the construction of the new patient care building and the implementation of the institutes of excellence. They divided the hospital into four smaller hospitals: Psychiatric Services, Medical/Surgical, Rehabilitation, and Women's and Children's. The stated goal was to decentralize decision-making to test the theory that, with local governance, the smaller hospitals could actually maximize revenue, while simultaneously improving operational efficiency and the quality of patient care. At that time, Rush's senior management approached Dr. Maffetone about directing one of the hospitals. He chose Women's and Children's.

Women's and Children's Hospital

The mission of the Women's and Children's Hospital (W&C) was to provide the highest level of patient care with the advantages of both a large, tertiary medical center and a smaller, less encumbered facility. The hospital planned to employ a strong and cohesive multidisciplinary approach to patient care, teaching, research, and operational management so as to maximize the resources devoted to achieving the corporate mission. W&C also wanted to develop the necessary synergy for sustained growth, a quality work environment, and an ability to maintain services to the community.

Rush's vision was that W&C would be the hospital of first choice for women's and children's services in the Chicago metropolitan area, and a regional referral center for specialty and subspecialty care. Systematic, planned growth was a goal, as was the development of a comprehensive, consumer-oriented service unit that would remain fiscally sound. A continuous improvement philosophy was a critical component, designed to enhance the clinical expertise, unique services, state-of-the-art technology, and recognized research that distinguished W&C's programs. Moreover, W&C was to serve as a model within the Rush system, and in the health care industry, for quality of care, operating efficiency, level of service, and work environment.

Organization. W&C's senior management decided not to use Rush's traditional matrix management structure, where each individual reported to a person in the same discipline at the next highest level. Instead, they decided that the W&C hospital would be managed by a team, consisting of medicine, nursing, and administration. This team would be responsible for everything in the W&C hospital. As the organizational chart in Exhibit 2 shows, the team consisted of four individuals: Samuel Gotoff, M.D. (the Chair of Pediatrics), Barbara Durand, Ed.D., R.N. (the Chair of Maternal/Child Nursing), Dr. Maffetone, and Dr. Wilbanks.

Need for a New Budgeting Process. The management team recognized that if W&C was to be a pilot project for the new organizational structure and strategic thrust at Rush, they would need to run their own hospital relatively independently. To do so, they would need to make changes in the way the hospital's operations were managed, including the budgeting process. Dr. Maffetone spoke about the changes:

> The first thing we did was assemble the management team—George, Sam, Barbara, and me—to see what budgetary information we had. What we had was a bunch of financial spreadsheets that the medical center had broken up on a cost center basis. They aggregated certain cost centers, assigned them to W&C, and said, "OK, now you're a hospital, so manage the bottom line." Of course, that was very difficult because we had not previously been structured to understand the overhead allocation, let alone determine what real net income was.
>
> So, I told the management team that we shouldn't look at this as if these are our cost centers and this is our budget. The budget had already been put to bed for FY92 when the organizational changes at Rush took place, so there was no opportunity to actually form a new budget for W&C in that year. That meant, we could do one of two things. We could spend our whole next year looking at the current structure justifying our budgets based on what we've done in the past. Or, we could sit back and say that we just built a brand new hospital out in the middle of nowhere—what is the executive information system that we need to run it? What is the costing information we need to manage? Let's

EXHIBIT 2 Organizational Chart—Women's and Children's Hospital and Services

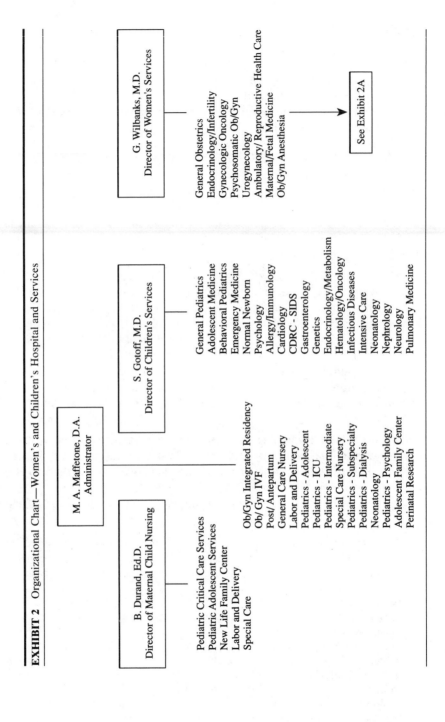

EXHIBIT 2A   Organizational Chart—Department of Obstetrics and Gynecology

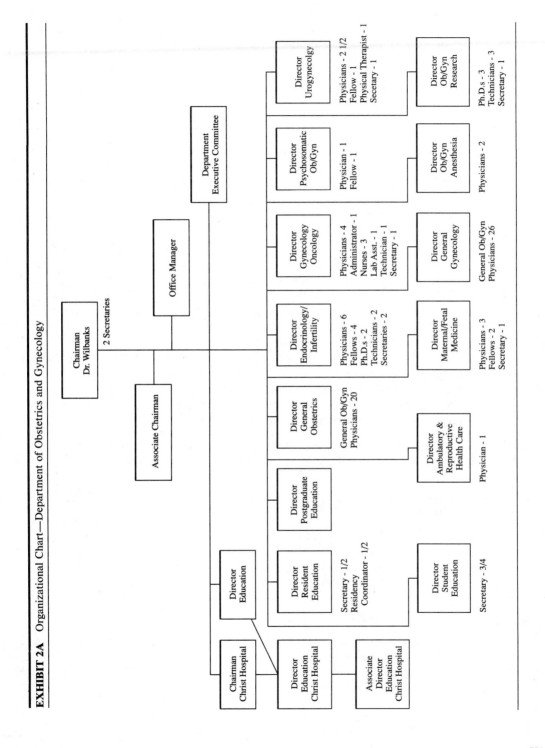

get our information straight so that we can be creative in approaching the medical center on what we wanted to do with budgeting at W&C for FY93.

Budgetary History.   The budgeting process at Rush had undergone some changes over the last three years. Prior to fiscal year 1991, the process was somewhat disjointed because of Rush's reporting structure. Dr. Wilbanks would meet with the associate vice president of surgical services for about a half-hour to discuss the number of bed-days that would be provided by the Obstetrics/Gynecology (Ob/Gyn) department. At the end of the meeting, the two would agree on the number of bed-days. The associate v.p. of surgical services would have similar conversations with all of the other department chairs. The numbers from all of the departments would be aggregated to arrive at the total patient day and revenue figures for the medical center.

At the same time as total revenues were being determined, the associate v.p. of surgical services would send budget papers to all of the departments, requesting them to submit budgeted expenses. To keep expenses in check, the departments often would be asked to budget flat (at the same level as the year before).

Once the budget was in place, the administrative and nursing managers would be held accountable for living within their budgeted expense limits, and the clinical chairs were expected to deliver the budgeted number of patient days. The department's budget would not decrease during the year if fewer patient days occurred. If, however, its surplus of revenue over expenses was not sufficient, the medical center often would impose across-the-board cuts in several areas, especially nursing. Susan Kilburg, assistant administrator for W&C and former Ob/Gyn administrative manager, described the process:

> The typical budgeting process that occurred at Rush is that the budget would be just about put to bed, and as the completion got close, an inadequate difference between

EXHIBIT 3   Departmental Volume Forecast Worksheet

	Patient Days						Admissions		
Obstetrics/ gynecology	*Actual FY 1987*	*Actual FY 1988*	*Actual FY 1989*	*3 Months Annualized FY 1990*	*Budget FY 1990*	*Submitted* Budget FY 1991*	*Actual FY 1987*	*Actual FY 1988*	*Actual FY 1989*
Gynecologic endocrinology/ infertility	751	753	607	670		650	183	195	160
Maternal/fetal medicine	2,267	3,193	4,544	5,483		5,550	500	639	1,116
Oncology	2,782	3,215	2,626	2,317		2,400	439	485	449
Other	14,285	12,654	10,468	10,970		10,300	3,602	3,198	2,890
Total obstetrics/ gynecology . . .	20,085	19,815	18,245	19,440	17,500	18,900	4,724	4,517	4,615

* Please list major assumptions in projecting FY 1991 volume.

expenses and revenues would become apparent. So, administrative management would go back to the department chairs and say, "can you do a few more days?" The chairs would say "sure," and they would boost up the days in order to justify the expenses, but without the appropriate increase in expenses to support the increased volume. Then half-way through the year, they would realize that the days hadn't materialized, but they're still spending their budget. So, expenses were reduced, often resulting in across the board cuts.

Responding to what she perceived to be a need for more concrete numbers for the Ob/Gyn budget, Ms. Kilburg set out to improve the budgeting process. In FY91, she and Dr. Wilbanks started interviewing all of the physicians in the department to obtain more accurate projections of their actual patient day volumes. They categorized the department's physicians into four clinical sections: Gynecologic Endocrinology/Infertility, Maternal/Fetal Medicine, Gynecologic Oncology, and Other. The "other" was a "catch-all" category that largely represented normal obstetric and gynecologic care. Exhibit 3 shows the Departmental Volume Forecast Worksheet that Ms. Kilburg used for FY91. (During FY91, a fifth section, Urogynecology, was added.)

At that time, the medical center's budget was built by hospital cost center (or operating unit), rather than by clinical section. Therefore, when building the Ob/Gyn department budget, Ms. Kilburg needed to classify the patient volume in each clinical section into the various operating units from which the revenue and expense sides of the hospital budget would be built. After determining what she believed to be adequate expenses to deliver the projected number of patient days, she would submit the expense side of the budget to administration. Following any budget reductions requested in the budget reconciliation process, this amount would then become the Ob/Gyn department's budget. The department would need to live within this budget, and there would be no adjustments according to changes in the volume of patient days actually delivered.

						Length of Stay			
3 Months Annualized FY 1990	*Budget FY 1990*	*Submitted* Budget FY 1991*	*Actual FY 1987*	*Actual FY 1988*	*Actual FY 1989*	*3 Months Annualized FY 1990*	*Budget FY 1990*	*Submitted* Budget FY 1991*
143		160	4.1	3.9	3.8	4.7		4.1
1,424		1,350	4.5	5.0	4.1	3.8		4.1
452		414	6.3	6.6	5.8	5.1		5.8
3,063	___	2,776	4.0	4.0	3.6	3.6	___	3.7
5,082	4,100	4,700	4.3	4.4	4.0	3.8	4.3	4.0

The FY 1992 Budget.   The above process continued into the FY92 budget development effort. Although there were improvements in the methodology used to predict patient day volume, Dr. Wilbanks once again had a fixed expense budget for the Ob/Gyn department. By the beginning of FY92, however, the Ob/Gyn department had been consolidated with the Pediatrics department and Maternal/Child Nursing department to form Women's and Children's Services. The W&C budget consolidated all of the relevant departmental budgets, and consisted of six operating units and 19 cost centers.

At the end of FY 92, W&C had lived within its consolidated budget. However, it had done so by having fewer patient days than budgeted. When the medical center's budget committee looked at the number of patient days W&C had provided, they cut the budget for FY93. The budget committee's rationale was that even though Dr. Wilbanks had not overspent his budget, his department had not delivered as many patient days as expected. Because the hospital's revenue had fallen, the committee reduced his budget for the following year.

The FY 1993 Budget.   In preparing the patient day projections for the FY93 budget, Ms. Kilburg and Dr. Wilbanks decided to engage in a somewhat more sophisticated process than in previous years. Dr. Wilbanks sent projection sheets to each section head (section heads are shown on Exhibit 2A). He asked his section heads to think about whether physicians would be joining or leaving their groups, and about which physicians would be expanding or contracting their practices. He also asked the section heads to project the impact of these changes on the kinds of DRGs that would be provided by each section. A similar process was used in pediatrics.

Ms. Kilburg translated the section heads' DRG projections into patient day projections. The results are contained in Exhibits 4 and 5. She then classified each section's patient days into one of the six W&C operating units, or "nursing units," as they sometimes were called: Pediatric Adolescent Services, Pediatric Intensive Care Unit (PICU), Intermediate Pediatrics, Special Care Nursery (SCN), Obstetrics and Gynecology, and General Care Nursery. These operating units and Ms. Kilburg's projections are shown in Exhibit 6.[1]

As Exhibit 6 shows, W&C expected to deliver 3,398 more patient days in FY93 than in FY92. Of this total, 1,232 days were to come from the General Care Nursery, and 2,166 days from the remaining units.[2]

Introduction of the Flexible Budget.   At the same time as the FY93 W&C budget was under preparation, Rush's Board of Trustees was applying significant pressures on Dr. Henikoff because the medical center had just embarked upon a

---

[1] Exhibit 6 shows both the name and account number of each nursing unit, such as 4670 for Pediatric Adolescent Services. For internal resource allocation purposes, two of the units were subdivided. SCN (Unit 4673) was broken into an Intermediate Unit (INT) and an Intensive Care Unit (ICU); Ob/Gyn (Unit 4630) was broken into Ob and Gyn. (The term "6KEL/6PAV" refers to the location of the nursing unit.)

[2] Total Gynecology days in the entire medical center were expected to be approximately 7,560 for FY93. As Exhibit 6 indicates, only 730 of those days are included in the W&C operating units.

EXHIBIT 4 Changes in Patient Days by Section

	FY 1993 Budget	FY 1992 Actual (annualized)	Day Increase or (Decrease)	
Pediatrics:				
Anchor	675	668	7	
General—full time	2,000	2,721	−721	Correction—Volume at status quo
General—voluntary	735	728	7	
Neonatology...............	10,200	10,875	−675	Boarder babies to General Care Nursery due to staffing
Other pediatrics—				
Subspecialties	1,700	1,283	417	Peds G.I. +350 days
Pediatrics cardiology	658	917	−259	Less Guerrero-Tiro; +372 new program
Pediatrics hematology/ oncology	1,230	1,100	130	
Pediatrics intensive care	1,850	223	1,627	948 Hayden/711 Barnes/474 Boyer/Heiliczer—Clardy 711
Pediatrics nephrology........	1,375	1,120	255	
Pediatrics neurology.........	275	151	124	Volume unreasonably low in FY 1992
Pediatrics pulmonary	200	0	200	
Net change—pediatrics			1,112	
Obstetrics/gynecology				
Endocrinology/infertility	432	300	132	Fellow to join section
Oncology..................	2,700	2,657	43	Recruiting additional Oncologist
Urogynecology	1,035	644	391	Fenner/Retzky/Benson
Maternal/fetal..............	4,750	4,830	−80	Shorter COS/declining medicaid
Other—obstetrics	6,634	6,340	294	Additional volume Nye/Gorens/ Roth/Dreyer HMO
Other—gynecology.........	3,399	2,621	778	Additional volume Nye/Gorens/ Maclin
Net change—obstetrics/ gynecology			1,558	
Total			2,670	

$350 million philanthropy and borrowing campaign to build the new patient care building. The board made the medical center promise that, over the next five years, $60 million of the total would come from the corporate bottom line. Consequently, Dr. Henikoff announced that he would no longer accept additional days as justification for balancing the budget. He wanted the expense base to be cut and the days to be budgeted flat (at the same level as the year before).

As Ms. Kilburg pointed out, this decision had severe repercussions for the W&C budget:

> The budget committee told us they didn't think we could deliver the patient days that we had predicted in our original budget. They gave us some revised projections [Exhibit 7] that were over 4,000 days *below* ours. In fact, they were projecting that we would have fewer patient days this year than last. Yet, we were confident that we could do the days in our original budget.

EXHIBIT 5   Departmental Volume Forecast FY1993

Obstetrics/ Gynecology	Patient Days						Admissions		
	Actual FY 1989	*Actual FY 1990*	*Actual FY 1991*	*6 months Annualized FY 1992*	*Budget FY 1992*	*Submitted* Budget FY 1993*	*Actual FY 1989*	*Actual FY 1990*	*Actual FY 1991*
Gynecologic endocrinology/ infertility	607	578	466	300		432	160	153	109
Maternal/fetal medicine	4,544	5,410	5,133	4,830		4,750	1,116	1,354	1,391
Oncology	2,626	2,598	2,415	2,657		2,700	449	444	397
Other	10,468	10,722	8,845	9,361		10,033	2,890	2,868	2,641
Urogynecology..	0	0	555	644		1,035	0	0	114
Total obstetrics/ gynecology ...	18,245	19,308	17,414	17,792	18,767	18,950	4,615	4,819	4,652

* Please list major assumptions in projecting FY 1991 volume.

EXHIBIT 6   FY1993 Changes in Patient Days by Nursing Unit (original projections by Women's and Children's Hospital)

Nursing Unit	*FY 1993 Budget*	*6 Month FY 1992 Actual Annualized*	*Day Increase (Decrease)*
PEDS/ADOL SVS—4670	8,760	7,462	1,298
PICU—4671..	1,825	1,322	503
PEDS INT—4672.....................................	1,825	1,456	369
SCN-INT—4673.......................................	3,742	4,596	(854)
SCN-ICU—4673.......................................	6,296	6,358	(62)
Net changes—PEDS			1,254
6 KEL/6 PAV OB—4630	11,384	11,202	182
6 KEL/6 PAV GYN—4630	730	0	730
Total	34,562	32,396	2,166
Average daily census.................................	94.7	88.8	5.9
GCN—4631	7,200	5,968	1,232
Total (including GCN)................................	41,762	38,364	3,398
Average daily census.................................	114.4	105.1	9.3

Key:
   PEDS/ADOL. SVS—Pediatrics/Adolescent Services.
   PICU—Pediatrics Intensive Care Unit.
   PEDS—INT—Pediatrics Intermediate.
   SCN—INT—Special Care Nursery—Intermediate.
   SCN—ICU—Special Care Nursery—Intensive Care Unit.
   6KEL/6PAV OB—Refers to the location of the nursing unit.
   6KEL/6PAV GYN—Refers to the location of the nursing unit.
   GCN—General Care Nursery.

6 months Annualized FY 1992	Budget FY 1992	Submitted* Budget FY 1993	Length of Stay					
			Actual FY 1989	Actual FY 1990	Actual FY 1991	6 months Annualized FY 1992	Budget FY 1992	Submitted* Budget FY 1993
84		120	3.8	3.8	4.3	3.6		3.6
1,072		1,289	4.1	4.0	3.7	4.5		3.8
444		450	5.8	5.9	6.1	6.0		6.0
2,823		2,947	3.6	3.7	3.3	3.3		3.4
141	—	225	0.0	0.0	4.9	4.6	—	4.6
4,564	4,912	5,031	4.0	4.0	3.7	3.9	3.8	3.8

EXHIBIT 7 FY1993 Changes in Patient Days by Nursing Unit (with proposed days by Medical Center Budget Committee)

Nursing Unit	FY 1993 Budget	6 Month FY 1992 Actual Annualized	Day Increase (Decrease)	Proposed FY 1993 Days*	Proposed Day Increase (Decrease) from Sub 93†
PEDS/ADOL SVS—4670.............	8,760	7,462	1,298	7,197	1,563
PICU—4671.........................	1,825	1,322	503	1,460	365
PEDS INT—4672....................	1,825	1,456	369	1,460	365
SCN-INT—4673.....................	3,742	4,596	(854)	3,742	0
SCN-ICU—4673.....................	6,296	6,358	(62)	6,296	0
Net changes—PEDS			1,254		2,293
6 KEL/6 PAV OB—4630	11,384	11,202	182	10,912	472
6 KEL/6 PAV GYN—4630	730	0	730	0	730
Total	34,562	32,396	2,166	31,067	3,495
Average daily census.................	94.7	88.8	5.9	85.1	9.6
GCN—4631........................	7,200	5,968	1,232	6,648	552
Total (including GCN)................	41,762	38,364	3,398	37,715	4,047
Average daily census.................	114.4	105.1	9.3	103.3	11.1

Key:
PEDS/ADOL. SVS—Pediatrics/Adolescent Services.
PICU—Pediatrics Intensive Care Unit.
PEDS—INT—Pediatrics Intermediate.
SCN—INT—Special Care Nursery—Intermediate.
SCN—ICU—Special Care Nursery—Intensive Care Unit.
6KEL/6PAV OB—Refers to the location of the nursing unit.
6KEL/6PAV GYN—Refers to the location of the nursing unit.
GCN—General Care Nursery.

* Proposed by the medical center's budget committee.
† Difference between Women's and Children's FY1993 budget and budget committee's proposal.

According to Dr. Maffetone, this new budgeting methodology would have dev-astated W&C. W&C needed the additional 3,400 non-general care nursery days that the section heads had projected to secure enough funds to both operate W&C's existing programs, and to support several new program initiatives that the management team planned to implement. Consequently, the team had to come up with a strategy to retain the incremental days in the budget, the result of which was their proposal for a flexible budget. Dr. Maffetone spoke about proposing the flexible budget to the Budget Committee:

As FY92 progressed, it became evident that we were overspending the expenses as related to the days that had been promised, but we were probably spending about the right amount of expenses for the amount of days that we were actually doing. So, along comes the new budget process. You get to the budget committee and the first thing they say is that you're spending too much for the amount of days. This is typical of what has happened in the past, and the whole idea of a hospital within a hospital may not work because nothing has changed. So, we asked them if we could do some decent costing, and break out the cost of our services into nursing costs, administrative costs, and physician costs. Then we wanted to distinguish between our average costs and marginal costs at the operating unit level [pediatric intensive care, special care nursery, etc.] for each of the additional days of care we provide next year. We proposed a flexible budget so that they would have the option to either give us the money up front and flex down, or not give us the money and flex up. They agreed to give us the money up front.

Ms. Kilburg added:

We agreed that the *budget committee's* proposed days would form the base. Everything above that [column 5 in Exhibit 7] would be part of the flexible budget.

Preparing the Flexible Budget. Based on this decision, the W&C management team began to prepare for the next meeting with the Budget Committee. They used the Baxter Consulting Group's methodology to do some baseline costing for each of their DRGs and operating units. The final result of this analysis was a flexible budget proposal.

Exhibit 8 contains an example of the analysis for three of Ob/Gyn's most fre-quent case types: a C-Section with Complications (DRG 370), a C-Section without Complications (DRG 371), and a Vaginal Delivery with Complications (DRG 372).[3] As it shows, both the variable and fixed expenses differed considerably for each case type. This fact, combined with the varying number of actual cases, led to significantly different net income amounts for each.

Exhibit 9 contains the flexible budget. Columns 1 through 5 of the exhibit contain the same information as Exhibit 7. The remaining columns show the unit and total marginal costs of both administration and nursing for each W&C operat-ing unit. Overall, W&C (not including the general care nursery) had an average marginal cost of $286 for nursing and $55 for administration.

---

[3] A Vaginal Delivery without Complications (DRG 373) was not included. This DRG comprised approximately 75 percent of the department's cases.

EXHIBIT 8 1993 Budget by Diagnosis Related Group (DRG) Obstetrics and Gynecology

Overall Budget	DRG 370	DRG 371	DRG 372
Number of cases (actual 1990)....................	183	573	267
Net revenue/case	$ 7,157	$ 5,519	$ 4,334
Total revenue	1,309,731	3,162,387	1,157,178
Variable expense per case	2,854	1,967	1,727
Total variable expenses............................	522,352	1,127,062	461,106
Contribution......................................	787,379	2,035,325	696,072
Total fixed expenses	473,985	1,484,116	691,551
Net income	313,394	551,209	4,521
Variable expense detail			
Labor:			
Number of days per case	6.78	4.65	3.73
Expense per day.................................	$ 187	$ 215	$ 196
Total expense per case	1,268	1,000	731
Supplies:			
Number of income test cost occurrence	6.78	4.65	3.73
Expense—including test code	$ 82	$ 48	$ 128
Total expense per case	556	223	477
Laboratory:			
Number of tests per case	6.78	4.65	3.73
Expense test	$ 26	$ 18	$ 18
Total expense per case	176	84	67
Pharmacy:			
Number of units per case	6.78	4.65	3.73
Expense per unit.................................	$ 85	$ 86	$ 48
Total expense per case	576	400	179
Other:			
Number of units per case	6.78	4.65	3.73
Expense per unit.................................	$ 5	$ 4	$ 8
Total expense per case	34	19	30
Overhead:			
Number of units per case	6.78	4.65	3.73
Expense per unit.................................	$ 36	$ 52	$ 65
Total expense per case	244	242	242
Total variable expense per case	$ 2,854	$ 1.967	$ 1,727

Source: Baxter Cost Analysis.

The $286 and $55 were averages for all of W&C. As Exhibit 9 shows, each operating unit had a different marginal cost per day. For example, in the Pediatric Intensive Care Unit (PICU), the marginal daily cost was $400 for nursing and $149 for administration. Consequently, an extra patient day in the PICU would be much more costly than an extra day in, say, general gynecology.

The differences in nursing cost per day were due largely to the intensity of nursing required in each of the units, with some variation caused by different skill levels of nurses that were needed to staff the units. Administrative cost per day, also varied in terms of both the intensity and type of services used by the unit.

EXHIBIT 9   FY 1993 Flexible Budget Marginal Cost/Day by Nursing Unit

Nursing Unit	*(1)* FY 1993 Budget	*(2)* 6 Month FY 1992 Actual Annualized	*(3)* Day Increase or (Decrease)	*(4)* Proposed FY 1993 Days	*(5)* Proposed Day Increase or (Decrease) from Sub 93 (Flexible Amount)
PEDS/ADOL SVS—4670	8,760	7,462	1,298	7,197	1,563
PICU—4671	1,825	1,322	503	1,460	365
PEDS INT—4672	1,825	1,456	369	1,460	365
SCN-INT—4673	3,742	4,596	(854)	3,742	0
SCN-ICU—4673	6,296	6,358	(62)	6,296	0
Net changes—Peds			1,254		2,293
6 KEL/6 PAV OB—4630	11,384	11,202	182	10,912	472
6 KEL/6 PAV GYN—4630	730	0	730	0	730
Total	34,562	32,396	2,166	31,067	3,495
Average daily census	94.7	88.8	5.9	85.1	9.6
GCN—4631	7,200	5,968	1,232	6,648	552
Total (including GCN)	41,762	38,364	3,398	37,715	4,047
Average daily census	114.4	105.1	9.3	103.3	11.1

PROPOSED ADDITIONAL PROCEDURES

	Proposed Increase in Procedures (Flexible Amt)	Total Marginal Cost per Procedure
Pediatric Day Hospital (Cardiology)	37	$137
Pediatric Echo	1,718	36
Pediatric Dialysis Program	380	120
CDRC Program	282	189
Lactation Consulting*	224	78
Antepartum/Ultrasound Program*	426	21
	3,067	$ 63

Key:
   PEDS/ADOL. SVS—Pediatrics/Adolescent Services.
   PICU—Pediatrics Intensive Care Unit.
   PEDS—INT—Pediatrics Intermediate.
   SCN—INT—Special Care Nursery—Intermediate.
   SCN—ICU—Special Care Nursery—Intensive Care Unit.
   6KEL/6PAV OB—Refers to the location of the nursing unit.
   6KEL/6PAV GYN—Refers to the location of the nursing unit.
   GCN—General Care Nursery.

   * See Exhibit 9A for details.

(6) Marginal Administrative Cost per Day	(7) Marginal Nursing Cost per Day	(8 = 6+7) Total Marginal Cost per Day	(9 = 5×6) Marginal Administrative Costs	(10 = 5×7) Marginal Nursing Costs	(11 = 9+10) Total Marginal Cost for Flexible Amount
$ 37	$235	$272	$ 57,831	$367,305	$ 425,136
149	400	549	54,385	146,000	200,385
46	375	421	16,790	136,875	153,665
59	396	455	0	0	0
59	396	455	0	0	0
103	406	509	48,616	191,632	240,248
19	215	234	13,870	156,950	170,820
			191,492	998,762	1,190,254
Average Daily Marginal Cost			55	286	341
17	0	17	9,384	0	9,384
			200,876	998,762	1,199,638
Average Daily Marginal Cost			50	247	296

Total Marginal Cost for Flexible Amount

$ 5,069
62,463
45,669
53,402
17,406
9,069

$193,078

EXHIBIT 9A Women's & Children's FY 1993 Submitted Incremental Revenue/Cost Analysis

Payor	Payor Mix	Reimbursement	Incremental			Gross Revenue	Incremental Net Revenue	Net Revenue per Case	Incremental	
			Cases	Days	ALOS				Average Cost	Net Income
Lactation Consulting Program										
BC/BS	8%	55%	18	n/a	n/a	$ 2,747	$ 1,511	$ 84	$ 1,392	$ 119
COMM	25	87	56	n/a	n/a	8,585	7,469	133	4,352	3,117
SELF	5	45	11	n/a	n/a	1,717	773	70	870	(97)
HMO/PPO	16	70	36	n/a	n/a	5,494	3,846	107	2,785	1,061
ANCHOR	19	43	43	n/a	n/a	6,524	2,806	65	3,307	(501)
MEDICAID	26	35	58	n/a	n/a	8,928	3,125	54	4,526	(1,401)
MEDICARE	1	50	2	n/a	n/a	343	172	86	174	(2)
	100%		224	n/a	n/a	$ 34,338	$19,702	$ 88	$17,406	$ 2,296

Average Charge = $153.30/case
Note: Total program cost = $17,406
Cost/Case = $78
Cost Center 4630: 6 Kellogg/pavilion

Payor	Payor Mix	Reimbursement	Cases	Days	ALOS	Gross Revenue	Net Revenue	Net Revenue per Case	Average Cost	Net Income
Antepartum/Ultrasound Program										
BC/BS	8%	55%	34	n/a	n/a	$ 8,203	$ 4,512	$133	$ 726	$ 3,786
COMM	25	87	107	n/a	n/a	25,635	22,302	208	2,267	20,035
SELF	5	45	21	n/a	n/a	5,127	2,307	110	453	1,854
HMO/PPO	16	70	68	n/a	n/a	16,406	11,484	169	1,451	10,033
ANCHOR	19	43	81	n/a	n/a	19,482	8,377	103	1,723	6,654
MEDICAID	26	35	111	n/a	n/a	26,660	9,331	84	2,358	6,973
MEDICARE	1	50	4	n/a	n/a	1,025	513	128	91	422
			426	0	0	$102,538	$58,826	$138	$ 9,069	$49,757

Total Program cost = $1,569 + .25 FTE $7,500 = $9,069
Cost/Case = $9,069/426 FY 92 Cases = $21.29/case.
Charge/case = Weighted avg chrg/case of $240.70.
Cost Center 4630: 6 Kellogg/pavilion

Key:
BC/BS—Blue Cross/Blue Shield.
COMM—Commercial.
SELF—Self pay (i.e., patient pays his/her medical coverage).
HMO/PPO—Health Maintenance Organization/Preferred Provider Organization.
ANCHOR—Anchor health care plan.

SOURCE: MSS DETAIL PAY CATEGORY ANALYSIS 8 MO. FY 92

Exhibit 10 shows these variations. In cost center 4630, (Obstetrics and Gynecology) for example, medical/surgical supplies were $6.92 per day, compared to $95.35 in cost center 4671 (Pediatric Intensive Care). But cost center 4671 also contained some administrative cost elements, such as office supplies, medicare/ambulance services, and medical/surgical instruments, that were not required in cost center 4630.

EXHIBIT 10 Administrative Cost per Day—Obstetrics and Gynecology Based on Actual FY92 Expense

Cost Center Variable	Per Patient Day	
4630	Patient supply	$ 0.74
	Lab supply	0.13
	Medical/surgical supply	6.92
	Paper supply	2.02
	Housekeeping supplies	0.32
	Bedding	0.05
	Minor equipment	0.17
	Office supplies	0.17
	Electrical supplies	0.03
	Dry cleaning/laundry	0.50
	Rent/lease equipment	0.82
	Subtotal	$ 11.87
	Recharge drugs	$ 1.49
	Recharge linen	4.54
	Recharge office supplies	0.83
	Subtotal	$ 6.86
	Total	$ 18.73
4671	Patient supply	$ 2.44
	Office supplies	0.64
	Patient supply items	4.00
	Lab supply	2.27
	Medical/surgical supplies	95.35
	Housekeeping supplies	0.20
	Medicare/ambulance service	21.92
	Electrical supplies (50%)	0.39
	Books and publications	0.16
	Electronic supplies	0.44
	Electrical supplies (50%)	0.39
	Equipment repair outside control	0.27
	Dry cleaning/laundry	0.23
	Medical/surgical instruments equipment	0.99
	Minor equipment purchase	0.47
	Subtotal	$130.16
	Recharge drugs	$ 8.92
	Recharge central service	0.97
	Recharge linen	6.47
	Recharge print shop	2.90
	Subtotal	$ 19.26
	Total	$149.42

Relation to Net Income. The overall impact of the incremental 4,047 days included in the flexible budget is shown in Exhibit 11. As this exhibit shows, these days were expected to increase W&C's contribution margin by almost $3 million.

Current Issues

Despite having convinced the Budget Committee of the merits of the flexible budget, the W&C management team still had several concerns about the actual management of the hospital. Everyone was worried about delivering the incremental volume of patient days that they had promised when asking for the flexible budget, and each manager had several issues to deal with.

Dr. Maffetone was concerned about both organizational and accounting matters:

What could make it difficult as an administrator is that, even though I'm the "CEO" of W&C, there is no formal reporting line from nursing or medicine to me. At this time, everyone on the organizational chart reports up their own lines to their vice presidents, so leadership is very important. I think the common goal that's driving the management team together is a desire to make it work.

Another worry I have is that the flexible budget is based on the average marginal costs for W&C as a whole. So, if there's a disproportionate increase in one of the more marginally expensive operating units, our actual spending will be higher than our flexible budget. Initially, we had to pull out all of the growth in what was considered discretionary spending (i.e., money for resident projects, a marketing budget, travel, publications, etc.) as a budget reduction. The flexible budget idea provides some opportunities for effecting operating efficiencies, which would allow us to purchase the discretionary items if our actual spending comes in under the flexible budget.

If the budget could be managed on a bottom line basis, we could make all of these things work out. This is important, because marketing would bring me in extra revenue and so forth. I'm asking the budget committee to consider not only days, but admissions and payer mix as well. What if LOS goes down, but revenues actually increase because of getting a better payer mix and getting the patients out more quickly? How will we be recognized for that?

Ms. Kilburg was acutely aware of Dr. Maffetone's concerns about having actual spending come in under the flexible budget amount:

What about the things we can't control that get into our budget? How can we be responsible for them? For example, sometimes the ancillaries like pharmacy jack up their prices to make their own budgets work. That has a direct impact on our budget. We can control the volume of drugs we order, but we have no control over the prices the pharmacy charges. Housekeeping is another problem. We can't control either their efficiency or the rate of pay to their personnel. Unless we can control these things, this hospital within a hospital thing is not going to work.

Dr. Durand had some concerns related to nursing:

This is a big experiment for us. The greatest proportion of the budget is dependent on nursing costs, which sometimes makes me nervous. In the past, our costs have gone up

EXHIBIT 11 Women's & Children's FY 1993 Budget Balance Sheet for New Volume

	Net Revenue	Expenses	Net Income Impact	Target Net Income Impact	Base	Net Days	ADC Base	EW	Total
Pediatric cardiology (inpatient and outpatient)	$1,015,721	$ 441,155	$ 574,566			372			
Gynecology expansion	1,249,395	162,060	1,087,335			730			
New OB recruits	589,764	227,504	362,260			472			
PICU growth	239,805	129,015	110,790			235			
PICU intermediate growth	206,517	84,315	122,202			365			
Additional pediatrics days	653,646	325,104	328,542			1,321			
Subtotal	$3,954,848	$1,369,153	$2,585,695		31,067	3,495	85.1	9.6	94.7
General care nursery boarder babies	$ 229,190	$ 9,384	$ 219,806		0	552	0.0	1.5	1.5
					85.1	4,047	85.1	11.1	96.2
Other outpatient revenue									
Pediatric dialysis growth	$ 44,996	$ 45,669	$ (673)						
CDRC program	133,399	53,402	79,997						
Lactation consulting	19,702	17,406	2,296						
Antepartum diagnostic program	58,826	9,069	49,757						
Total	$4,440,961	$1,504,083	2,936,878						

Note: Medical affairs salaries (neonatology, pediatrics cardiology, pediatrics psychiatry, and miscellaneous) of $480,000 not included in total.

because we had to use a lot of agency nurses. My average hourly staff rate is $17.62. Agency nurses can cost up to $45–$55 per hour. Historically, we have staffed at the average daily census (the mean), but the Obstetric and Pediatric floors have very volatile censuses—there can be 14 patients one day and 40 the next. So, now, we're trying something new. We're staffing at the mode. But, that presents problems because some units are bimodal. We need to consider the level of risk that we're willing to accept if staffed at the mode, but at least it lessens some of the unpredictability associated with staffing at the mean. And we also have the pressures of a general shortage of nurses to deal with.

Finally, Dr. Wilbanks expressed his concerns about the future of W&C:

Right now, it seems like I'm worried about everything. Before, all I had to worry about was whether or not we had our number of bed days filled. Now, I have to worry about how much toilet paper we use, what medicines my doctors are prescribing, whether they're using 10 sutures when they could be using five, a name brand antibiotic rather than a generic one, etc.

Eventually, I'll also be expected to worry about our payer mix. I would never do this because of my ethics, but sometimes I think we should tag all of the patients and say, Mrs. Jones has a red tag so we can keep her longer, but Mrs. Smith has a white tag so we have to get her out quickly.

I'm not sure how to respond to the changes that have taken place at W&C. On the one hand, we want our actual daily expenses to come in under our flexible budget amount. One way to do that would be to stretch out the length of stay since the last days are usually less expensive. But, on the other hand, I know that W&C is a pilot for the eventual implementation of the hospital-within-a-hospital concept. And these hospitals are going to be treated as totally separate entities, responsible for everything from the quality of patient care to the financial bottom line.

Questions

1. What are the key changes that have been made in the budgetary process at Rush? What is your assessment of these changes?
2. How have responsibility centers been designed at Rush? Specifically, what kind of responsibility center is the Women's and Children's Hospital? What kind of responsibility center is a section in the W&C hospital? An operating (nursing) unit? Are there other responsibility centers? Are the responsibility centers well designed?
3. What factors can cause W&C to come in under or over budget? Please be as specific as you can in identifying these. What role can each of the participants on the team play in managing those factors? Are any factors left unmanaged?
4. What should Dr. Wilbanks do?

Control of Operations

The third phase in the management control cycle is that of operations and measurement. Although described as a single phase, it actually consists of two separate but related activities: control of operations and measurement of output. This chapter describes tools and techniques that are useful in the control of operations. Chapter 12 looks at the measurement of output.

Control of operations encompasses two quite distinct activities: financial control, and performance control. The former, as the name implies, is related to spending activities. Financial control systems are designed to assure that proper steps are taken, and appropriate records are maintained, to preserve the financial integrity of the organization's activities.

Performance control focuses on the activities of line managers, professional staff, technical support staff, clerical employees, and other members of the organization. Its goal is to assure that performance is in accordance with the organization's objectives. It concentrates on matters of productivity, and on managers' motivations to operate their programs and projects effectively and efficiently.

Since many of their programs are not subject to market forces, nonprofit organizations must be especially concerned with performance control activities. Performance control can help to assure clients and other constituents that the organization's resources are being used as efficiently as possible in carrying out ongoing operations.

The first half of this chapter is devoted to financial control, where we focus on matters such as accounting systems and auditing. In the second half we discuss performance control, including both technical and behavioral matters.

FINANCIAL CONTROL IN GENERAL

The approved operating budget, consisting of both planned expenses and expected outputs, is the principal financial guideline for operations. Presumably, management wants the organization to operate in a way that is consistent with this plan unless there is good reason to depart from it. This qualification is important, for it means that the control process is more complicated than simply insisting that the organization do what the budget prescribes. One of the principal purposes of management control is to assure that objectives are accomplished as efficiently as possible. If changed conditions suggest that a different course of action than that specified in the budget will do a better job of attaining the objectives, that course of action should be followed. Thus, the financial control activity should have two aspects: (1) to assure that, in the absence of reasons to do otherwise, the plan set forth in the budget is adhered to, and (2) to provide a way to change the plan if conditions warrant.

Types of Financial Control

The total amount in the approved budget ordinarily is a ceiling that should not be exceeded. Indeed, as discussed below, if funds are received from a legislative appropriation, it is a ceiling that legally *cannot* be exceeded. Within this ceiling, there are more detailed controls. These usually take the form of ceilings for specific activities or programs, but in some cases they may be floors.

> *Example.* In a social work agency, each program manager has a budget ceiling. However, senior management also requires that a minimum amount of resources (a floor) be spent on each family.

Although the budget may contain a detailed listing of amounts for expense elements (e.g., wages, supplies, travel, utilities), these amounts are normally guides rather than ceilings. The primary focus should be on programs and responsibility centers, not on expense elements. Some years ago, financial control focused on individual line items of expense. Although some nonprofit organizations persist in using line-item controls, most have shifted their focus to programs and responsibility centers.

Need for Some Line-Item Restrictions. Despite the shift to a focus on programs and responsibility centers, most organizations also require line managers to obtain approval for shifts among line items above a certain amount or percentage. Although this policy may seem inconsistent with the shift to program control, there are several reasons that justify its existence.

Lack of Experience. Many line managers are professionals (such as artists, teachers, or social workers), and have not had much experience with budgets. Overspending one line item by a large amount early in the fiscal year (such as for travel to professional meetings) may use up funds that are needed later in the year for ongoing program operations.

> *Example.* In a college of arts, one department head gave out considerably more financial aid early in the fiscal year than he had in his budget. Later in the fiscal year, he informed management that there were no funds left in his budget to pay for models for art classes.

Potential Changes in Objectives.   When the budget was agreed upon, it represented a commitment between the line manager and senior management that it was the most appropriate way to use the organization's resources to accomplish certain objectives. A large change in the use of resources suggests a change in the activities of a program or responsibility center and, hence, may inhibit the attainment of certain objectives. Senior management needs to be a party to this sort of decision.

Long-Run Implications.   Some expenses represent long-term commitments. If personnel are added to the organization, for example, the corresponding increase in costs tends to be relatively permanent. This is especially true if the newly hired person occupies a union or civil service position, or otherwise assumes a position with some sort of tenure commitment. Therefore, the number of personnel (i.e., a "head count"), frequently constitutes a ceiling that cannot be exceeded without senior-management approval.

Potential for Duplication.   Since line managers do not have a complete view of the organization, senior management needs a way to avoid duplication in the use of resources. This was an important aspect of the budget preparation process. If line managers are permitted to make large changes in their operating budgets without the review and approval of senior management, they may be undertaking activities that overlap or conflict with activities of other programs or responsibility centers.

For these reasons, most organizations require program and responsibility center managers to obtain approval from higher levels of authority for major deviations from their budgets. Depending on the size of the organization and the dollar amounts involved, this approval may be required from several higher levels of authority. Despite this approval process, line managers usually have sufficient flexibility to carry out their programs as planned if two conditions are in place: (1) they are allowed to make minor shifts among line items in their budgets without higher level approval, and (2) there is an efficient and noncapricious approval process in place that will allow them to make larger shifts if necessary to attain programmatic objectives more efficiently.

Flow of Spending Authority

The flow of spending authority within an organization generally should follow the lines of operating management responsibility; that is, spending should be authorized from higher levels to lower levels according to the formal organizational hierarchy. Difficulties arise when funds are received directly by organizational units, rather than through the organizational hierarchy. If it does not control the distribution of spending authority, senior management often cannot exercise appropriate control over subordinate elements because it does not have "the power of the purse."

Example.   In New York City, mental health services are provided to the public on a contractual basis by private institutions. These institutions are supposed to be accountable to the city's Department of Mental Health; however, operating funds for these institutions are provided directly by the state, and the institutions therefore tend to disregard the city agency.

There are two types of difficulties that senior management encounters in attempting to control the flow of spending authority: compartmentalized funds and funds from several sources. Each constrains senior management's ability to exercise spending authority.

Compartmentalized Funds. If a legislature or other source of funds specifies in great detail the way the funds can be spent, managers can be inhibited from making sound decisions on the best use of operating resources. This is because some activities may turn out to be overfunded while others are underfunded. Without the ability to shift funds from one "compartment" to another, senior management's ability to coordinate the various activities of the organization is impeded.

Example. In the Navy, ships have been known to steam on unneeded missions, even though they lacked vital parts for radar, because they had ample funds for fuel, but no funds for radar parts. The overall effectiveness of the ship would have been enhanced if some of the money budgeted for steaming had been shifted to radar repair, but there was no mechanism that permitted the easy shifting of funds among line items.

Funds from Several Sources. If program managers have funding from several sources, they can play off one funding source against another. Thus, while senior management may desire that the overall level of spending be reduced, a program manager can sometimes defeat this desire by finding one source, among the several available, to provide the additional funds.

Example. The manager of a program in a university wanted to purchase an expensive computer with funds from her operating budget, but was denied permission by the dean, who was attempting to control overall spending. The manager then used grant funds to purchase the computer, and operating funds to pay for a research assistant who otherwise would have been paid with funds from the grant.

Example. The University of Minnesota spent $1.7 million for the renovation of the campus office and official residence of the president. The money came from a $55 million reserve fund of "unrestricted private donations, interest on university investments, and surpluses from the campus food and housing services and bookstores." Neither the Board of Regents nor legislators were fully aware of the existence of this fund. Further, although the Board of Regents was required to approve all capital expenditures in excess of $100,000, this project was carried out "through a series of smaller projects costing less than $100,000 each."[1]

---

[1] *Chronicle of Higher Education*, March 21, 1988, p. 1.

In addition, if funds are received from several sources, performance measurement may be difficult. This is because each funding source tends to focus on a different aspect of operations, rather than evaluating the organization's activities as a whole.

Budget Adjustments

In many nonprofit organizations, the total annual budget constitutes an absolute ceiling that cannot be exceeded except under highly unusual circumstances. Nevertheless, changed circumstances may call for modifications in detailed spending requirements. This raises the problem of accommodating these modifications within the prescribed ceiling. There are two general techniques for solving this problem: contingency allowances and revisions. The choice between the two is largely a matter of management preference.

Contingency Allowances. In this approach, amounts are set aside at various levels in the organization for unforeseen circumstances. Thus, the budgeted expenses for each responsibility center and program are targets that can be exceeded, if necessary, with the excess being absorbed by the contingency allowance. Ordinarily, a contingency allowance is not more than 5 percent of the budget for each organizational level.

An advantage of contingency allowances is that increases in spending can be accommodated without the sometimes painful task of finding an offsetting decrease. A risk is that if there is a 5 percent contingency allowance, there may be a tendency to regard the actual ceiling as 105 percent of the target in all responsibility centers. This defeats the purpose of the contingency allowances.

A variation of the contingency allowance is the practice of releasing somewhat less than the proportionate amount of funds in the early part of the year. For example, in an agency whose spending is expected to be spread evenly throughout the year, only 22 percent of the funds, rather than 25 percent, might be released in the first quarter. As the year progresses and spending needs become clearer, subsequent releases of the contingency allowance are allocated to those responsibility centers that need them the most.

Revisions. In this approach, 100 percent of the authorized amount is divided among responsibility centers. Changed circumstances are accommodated by increasing the budget of one responsibility center and making a corresponding reduction in the budget of one or more other responsibility centers. Under this plan the budget for each responsibility center cannot be exceeded without specific approval. Moreover, some responsibility centers will be asked to spend less than their budget to accommodate the needs of other responsibility centers.

When the revision approach is used, operating managers frequently will create an informal contingency allowance to avoid having to seek formal approval for changed spending needs. Thus, allowances exist in both approaches, even though they are not visible in the second type.

Whichever approach is used, senior management should recognize the likelihood that changes will be necessary. It therefore should be certain that the mechanism for making these changes is well understood. Otherwise, the budget may not conform to the demands managers face, and thus will not serve as a reliable instrument for measuring their performance.

> *Example.* Some states have three budgets: the originally approved one, a supplemental budget, and a deficiency budget. The supplemental and deficiency budgets are submitted to the legislature by the governor during the course of the fiscal year. The supplemental budget is a request for a budget increase. The deficiency budget, by contrast, is submitted after the state incurs obligations that exceed the funds provided in either the original or the supplemental budget. This process calls the legislature's attention to the situation, and permits it to: *(a)* approve the proposal as warranted, *(b)* disapprove it, or *(c)* approve it but criticize the governor's performance.

FINANCIAL CONTROL VIA THE ACCOUNTING SYSTEM

The central device for reporting internal operating information is the accounting system. It is central because accounting deals with monetary amounts, and money provides the best way to aggregate and summarize information about a wide variety of inputs, including labor, supplies, and purchased services.

General Characteristics

In Chapter 3, we described the nature of accounting systems in nonprofit organizations. Several important aspects of these systems are relevant for financial control purposes: donor restrictions, double entry, consistency with the budget, and the need for integrated systems.

Donor Restrictions. The accounting system must assure that restrictions placed on contributions are observed. If a donor specifies that a scholarship may be used only for residents of a particular state or community, for example, this restriction must be honored. Many organizations set up a separate account for each type of restriction as a device for exercising this control, even though there is no need to report the details of the restrictions in the financial statements. The result often is considerably more detail in the accounting system than one typically would find in a for-profit setting.[2] The principal purpose of this detail is to assure donors that

---

[2] Some colleges and universities, where the number of separate funds typically is quite large, will not accept restricted contributions unless they exceed a given amount. They reason that the extra cost of controlling for the restrictions is only warranted for large contributions.

their funds were used only for the specified purposes. Since the auditor can provide this assurance (or, identify the rare instance where restrictions were not observed), there is no need to report the detail.

Double Entry. The accounting system should be a double-entry system; that is, a system in which debits equal credits. A sentence like the preceding would never appear in a description of the accounting system of a for-profit company because double-entry accounting is taken for granted in these companies. Some nonprofit organizations, however, including some very large government organizations, collect important types of information in single-entry systems.

Information collected in a single-entry system is not likely to be reliable since there is no way to assure that all items have been recorded. For example, in a double-entry system, every cash expenditure gives rise to a credit to cash and a debit to some asset or expense account; otherwise, the accounts will not balance. In a single-entry system, the debit may be omitted, and there is therefore no way of knowing whether all expenditures have been recorded. Technically, it is a simple matter to convert such a system to double entry.

Consistency with the Budget. The accounting system should be consistent with the budget. The budget states the approved plan for spending, and the accounting system reports actual spending. Unless the two are consistent, there is no reliable way of determining if actual spending occurred according to plan. This does not mean that the accounting system should contain *only* the accounts that appear in the budget, however. Management usually needs more accounting detail than is suggested by the budget items, and it needs rearrangements of the basic data for various purposes. Nevertheless, as a minimum, the accounting system should contain accounts that match each item on the budget.[3]

Need for Integrated Systems. Not only should budget and accounting data be consistent with one another, but the accounting system should be an integral part of a total information system for reporting on both inputs and outputs. Achievement of such integration is a difficult task, but some organizations are succeeding.

> ***Example.*** The federal government, through its Federal Urban Information Systems Interagency Committee Program, has encouraged municipalities to develop integrated systems, and has provided substantial funding for this purpose. Such systems include budget and accounting information along with information on demographics, physical and economic development programs, and public safety. Accounting data on costs (inputs) are integrated with output data throughout the system.

---

[3] If accounts do not match the budget, it generally is possible to develop a mechanism for reconciling the two. This mechanism, called a *crosswalk*, is a rearrangement of the accounts to match the budget categories. A crosswalk is not as reliable as recording amounts in the proper accounts in the first place.

Encumbrance Accounting

An *encumbrance* occurs when an organization becomes obligated to pay for goods or services. This happens when a contract is entered into or when personnel work (At the time they work, they become entitled to salaries and related benefits.) An appropriation by a state or local government usually is an authority to encumber (a federal appropriation is an authority to *obligate,* which means the same thing).

In federal government organizations, amounts appropriated in accordance with the budget cannot legally be exceeded, and violators are subject to criminal penalties under the federal Anti-Deficiency Act (R.S. Sec. 3679). Most states have similar legislation.[4]

Appropriations for operating purposes usually cannot be encumbered after the end of the fiscal year; that is, they lapse. There is therefore a natural tendency to fully encumber all appropriated funds. Thus, while an encumbrance accounting system is designed to avoid spending more than the amount appropriated, it also discourages spending less than the amount appropriated. The accounting process for encumbrances is described in the appendix at the end of this chapter.

FINANCIAL CONTROL VIA AUDITING

No matter how well an accounting system has been designed, there is always the possibility of error or fraud. To detect such irregularities, many nonprofit organizations have an internal audit function called *compliance auditing*. Most nonprofits have their financial statements and financial control systems audited by an external body, usually an independent public accountant. This latter function is called an *external audit*.

Compliance Auditing

A well-designed management control system contains its own financial controls. When there is an internal audit staff, its responsibility is to ensure that these controls are effective. Internal financial controls have three general purposes: (1) to minimize the possibility of financial loss by theft, fraud, or embezzlement; (2) to ensure adherence to senior management's rules governing the receipt and spending of money, and the use of other resources; and (3) to ensure that information flowing through the system is accurate.

---

[4] As a practical matter, punishment under these acts is rare. In the Department of Defense there are only a few dozen violations per year, most of them for trivial amounts. Some years ago, because of a breakdown in its control system, the Army spent $225 million more than was appropriated, but no one went to jail, much less paid back the $225 million. Nevertheless, the possibility of legal action is a deterrent.

Some organizations, including many state and municipal governments, do not have even minimal controls. This problem is revealed by frequent newspaper exposés of contracts let in an unauthorized manner, persons on the public payroll who do not actually work, or welfare payments made to persons not entitled to receive them.

> *Example.* For 11 years, John T. Glennon was purchasing agent at the University of California, San Francisco. He was considered to be an "extremely valuable employee" until three months after he left the university in 1987, when it was discovered that during the preceding four years he had embezzled $310,000 by billing fake purchases to a dummy corporation. He was in complete charge of placing orders, receiving the goods, and paying for them.[5]

Internal controls are never perfect. Their limitations are well described in the AICPA's *Statement of Auditing Standards No. 30*, a document that describes the objectives and difficulties of compliance auditing.

> The objective of internal accounting control is to provide reasonable, but not absolute, assurance as to the safeguarding of assets against loss from unauthorized use or disposition, and the reliability of financial records for preparing financial statements and maintaining accountability for assets. The concept of reasonable assurance recognizes that the cost of a system of internal control should not exceed the benefits derived and also recognizes that the evaluation of these factors necessarily requires estimates and judgments by management.
>
> There are inherent limitations that should be recognized in considering the potential effectiveness of any system of internal control. In the performance of most control procedures, errors can result from misunderstanding of instructions, mistakes of judgment, carelessness, or other personal factors. Control procedures whose effectiveness depends upon segregation of duties can be circumvented by collusion. Similarly, control procedures can be circumvented intentionally or with respect to the estimates and judgments required in the preparation of financial statements. Further, projection of any evaluation of internal control to future periods is subject to the risk that the procedures may become inadequate because of changes in conditions, and that the degree of compliance with the procedures may deteriorate.[6]

Resources devoted to internal auditing in government agencies have increased greatly in recent years. In most agencies, this additional effort has resulted in the detection of fraud and waste many times larger than the additional cost, but there is still a long way to go.

> *Example.* In one study of 77,000 cases, only 2.5 percent of fraud exposed was uncovered through audit effort. Much of the rest was uncovered by chance or by scheduled

---

[5] *Chronicle of Higher Education*, April 10, 1991.

[6] American Institute of Certified Public Accountants, *Statement of Auditing Standards (SAS) No. 30.* Subsequent *SAS*s have expanded upon this basic definition. See, for example, *SAS* numbers 53, 54, and 55.

compliance and eligibility reviews by program units. Additionally, reports by alleged victims and gratuitous reports by private individuals helped uncover some of the fraud.[7]

Since both chance discoveries and discoveries associated with scheduled reviews revealed deficiencies in the internal control systems in use, one conclusion is that more attention needs to be devoted to designing good control systems.

> *Example.* As a result of publicized scandals, the National Religious Broadcasters (NRB) agreed to regulate themselves and monitor one another's business practices. The new code requires full annual audits disclosing every expenditure and source of income; fund-raising records submitted upon request; and governing boards controlled by outsiders rather than family members and employees. Compliance with the code is now a requirement for NRB membership.[8]

Incorrect Charges.   One possible reason for the relative ineffectiveness of internal auditing is its focus. Many nonprofit organizations spend considerable effort assuring that certain rules are obeyed precisely (for instance, checking every travel voucher to ensure that per diem calculations are accurate and that mileage between points is stated correctly). They also have voucher systems, locked petty cash boxes, and other devices that inhibit obvious possibilities for theft or losses by individuals. By contrast, the same organizations may pay little attention to procedures for assuring that expenditures are charged to the proper accounts; that is, to projects or other items that correspond to those for which the costs actually were incurred. If the amounts charged to accounts are used as a basis for reimbursement by a client, as is often the case, deliberate mischarging amounts to stealing. The situation is even more flagrant when the persons responsible sign their names to a certificate that states that costs are recorded correctly, knowing full well that they are not.

In addition to the illegality of this practice, one obvious consequence is that recorded data are inaccurate. Reports prepared from such data give management an incorrect impression about current performance, and a misleading basis for future plans. In general, internal auditors do not pay enough attention to the prevention and detection of incorrect charges.

> *Example.* Some years ago, auditors at one university found that 7 percent of faculty members charged more of their time to research projects than they actually spent. Over a 2½-year period, this amounted to $100,000 of excess charges. Recent disclosures are much larger.

An interesting ethical question arises when the rules under which an agency is forced to operate are such that efficient operations are inhibited. Should managers get the job done and cover up the fact that, to do so, they had to break rules, or should they use the existence of the rules as an excuse for not getting the job

---

[7] Mortimer A. Dittenhofer, "Internal Control and Auditing for Fraud," *The Government Accountants' Journal*, Winter 1983–84.

[8] *Nonprofit World* 6, no. 3 (May–June 1988), p. 6.

done? Managers with different temperaments answer this question in different ways.

Example. A certain state legislature set maximum payment rates for part-time psychiatrists employed by state mental health institutions. These rates were about half the going rate for psychiatrists. At these rates, few psychiatrists would work for the state. Consequently, administrators hired psychiatrists for half a day and paid them for a full day. They said that this was the only way they could hire a sufficient number of psychiatrists. On balance, have they done wrong? Whether or not they have done wrong, the records show that twice as many psychiatrist work-hours were provided as actually was the case.

External Auditing

In many states, the Office of the Attorney General requires most tax-exempt organizations to submit financial statements annually. For large organizations, they require that these statements be audited. Moreover, any state or local government unit receiving more than $25,000 annually in federal assistance is subject to audit at least once every two years, and organizations that receive grants from government agencies are also subject to audit.[9] Although government auditors conduct many of these audits, outside independent public accountants increasingly are engaged to perform them.[10]

Even where audits are not required by law or by grantors, there is a general recognition that, for purposes of reliability and continuity, such reports should be prepared by an outside auditor. These audits determine whether: *(a)* financial operations were conducted properly, *(b)* the financial reports of an audited entity were presented fairly, and *(c)* the entity complied with applicable laws and regulations.[11] When defects in an organization's financial control system prevent the auditors from undertaking a thorough analysis of compliance, the organization may have to spend a considerable sum upgrading its system.

Example. According to one study, auditors of the Department of Health and Human Services found it impossible to resolve salary and related charges claimed by large universities under research contracts when the universities did not maintain or properly supervise the after-the-fact (i.e., after the budget) time and effort reports required by

---

[9] Because the requirements for conducting a government audit generally are somewhat different from those for a nongovernment audit, special training is needed. See American Institute of Certified Public Accountants, *Report of the Task Force of the Quality of Audits of Governmental Units*, March 1987.

[10] For details on the various audit requirements, see Office of Management and Budget, *Circular A-102* (for state and local governments), OMB *Circular A-110* (for other nonprofit organizations), and U.S. Office of Revenue Sharing, *Audit Guide and Standards for Revenue Sharing and Antirecession Fiscal Assistance Receipts*.

[11] Comptroller General of the United States, *Standards for Audit of Governmental Organizations, Programs, Activities, and Functions* (Washington, D.C.: Government Printing Office), p. 2.

governmentwide standards. Ultimately, the auditors identified a need for universities to upgrade their payroll distribution and support systems.[12] For many universities this was an expensive endeavor.

PERFORMANCE CONTROL

Apart from establishing financial control systems to assure that funds are spent as intended, nonprofit managers also must be concerned about assuring the effective and efficient performance of their organizations. Chapters 12, 13, and 14 discuss the process of measuring and reporting performance. In the remainder of this chapter we address several issues related to managers' need to exert control over the *day-to-day operations* of their organizations.

Relationship to Task Control

In many respects, performance control is concerned with the processes that we defined in Chapter 1 as task control: the rules, procedures, forms, and other devices that govern the performance of specific tasks to assure that they are carried out effectively and efficiently. For example, professionals in a research organization must report the time they spend on various projects; payroll checks must be issued in a timely way; inventories must be replenished before they are depleted, but must not be maintained at excessively high levels; and accounts receivable must be monitored and steps taken to collect delinquent accounts. The larger and more complex the organization, the larger the number of these rules. Also, a mature organization tends to have more formal rules and procedures than a young organization.

Although most managers dislike rules, they also recognize that many rules are necessary to assure that members of the organization handle similar situations in a similar manner. Some rules, however, may have been devised to deal with situations that no longer exist, or they may unduly restrict the ability of managers to use good judgment. Because of this, an organization needs to review its rules from time to time, and eliminate those that no longer serve a useful purpose. Otherwise, frustrations such as those implicit in the following apocryphal description of procurement procedures may impede the smooth functioning of the organization:

> . . . If you want to buy a short length of coaxial cable, please fill out a requisition sheet, university budget form 16-j. (Use the orange form if the money is to come from operating funds, and blue if the money is to come from capital funds.) Never indent on any line more than five spaces or the form will be returned. Submit in triplicate to the Office of Budget Approval, Administration Building, Room 1619, attention Mrs. Bagley. After

---

[12] Edward W. Stepnick, "Accountability for Government-Sponsored University Research: A Lesson from the Behavioral Sciences," *The Government Accountants' Journal,* Winter 1985–86.

Mrs. Bagley initials the form signifying that you have the $38 in your budget, the form is sent to the Technical Buyer, located in Room 1823. There Mr. Ted Rosler puts out a request for bids. If there is only one coaxial cable distributor in the region, it presents difficulties, but they can be surmounted with a special Sole Source form, which should be approved by the Comptroller's Council of Purchases and Services. The Council meets bimonthly. To get on their agenda, you must submit, in duplicate. . . .[13]

Relationship to Productivity

Many nonprofit organizations have instituted measures designed to improve employee productivity. These include attempts to classify costs into controllable and noncontrollable categories so managers can focus on costs that might be reduced without affecting the organization's programmatic outcomes. They also include investment in equipment that will reduce operating expenditures, principally labor.

In some instances these measures call for consolidation of activities across two or more organizational units. In others, they attempt to assure that the time of professionals is being used as much as possible in the activities for which they were hired.

Example. Many colleges and universities have undertaken a variety of measures to improve productivity. These include: renegotiating banking relationships to obtain less expensive transaction processing and credit services; consolidating purchasing for five science labs in one large university; and conducting on-site surveys of facilities maintenance to determine the average time for completion of certain activities so that standards can be established.[14]

Example. In one public school system, managers found that significant savings could be achieved by consolidating certain functions, such as that of a registrar. Since the optimum-size school was determined to be one with about 1,500 students, principals of schools with fewer than 800 students were encouraged to share registrars with similarly small nearby schools.

Example. A rural health clinic found that it could significantly improve the productivity of its physicians by using a nurse practitioner (NP). The NP was able to screen patients, treat those who did not require a physician, and conduct many tests and procedures that physicians formerly conducted. As a result, the clinic greatly increased the productivity of its physicians with consequent reductions in the cost of a patient visit and a higher volume of patients seen.

Selection of a Measure.   Efforts to improve productivity require measures that managers can use to judge their success. The major difficulty in selecting a mea-

---

[13] By Frederick Brietenfeld, Jr., executive director, the Maryland Center for Public Broadcasting (personal correspondence).

[14] See Clark L. Bernard and Douglas Beaven, "Containing the Costs of Higher Education," *Journal of Accountancy*, October 1985.

sure of productivity is choosing a unit that is sufficiently homogeneous to provide a reliable indicator of improved (or worsened) performance. In a membership organization, for example, clerical staff might be evaluated according to the number of applications processed per hour. Since each application is about the same as all others, this can be a reliable measure. In an ambulatory care clinic, on the other hand, there are many different types of visits and levels of severity associated with different patients. Therefore, a patient visit is at best only a rough measure of productivity.

Operational Auditing

Compliance auditing, as described above, is used to determine whether financial data are being recorded properly and whether financial rules (such as those concerning spending authorizations) are being followed. Another type of auditing, called *operational auditing*, has become increasingly important in recent years. Its development was fostered by the U.S. Comptroller General's 1973 publication *Standards for Audit of Governmental Organizations, Programs, Activities and Functions*. According to this booklet, operational auditing

> . . . determines whether the entity is managing or utilizing its resources (personnel, property, space, and so forth) in an economical and efficient manner and [attempts to identify] the causes of any inefficiencies or uneconomical practices, including inadequacies in management information systems, administrative procedures, or organizational structure.[15]

By showing where changes in policies or procedures are desirable, operational auditing can help an organization improve both its effectiveness and efficiency. If properly conducted, it can be a valuable tool in the management of a nonprofit organization. If not properly conducted, however, it can be a source of friction and frustration, with no constructive results.

> ***Example.*** James Watkins, head of the Department of Energy, created "tiger teams" in 1989 to serve as a special inspection force to enforce compliance with federal rules on environmental purity, worker safety, and public health. While some of the teams identified serious problems, others focused on the trivial. In one reported instance, a team member discovered a paint brush left under a fume hood in a laboratory. Someone in the lab had used it to apply ordinary paint to a piece of equipment, setting it down to dry so that it could be disposed of safely in the trash later. The tiger team threatened to cite the lab for a violation. As a result, the lab staffer was forced to wrap the brush in two layers of plastic, and dispose of it as costly hazardous waste.[16]

---

[15] Comptroller General of the United States, *Standards for Audit of Governmental Organizations, Programs, Activities, and Functions* (Washington, D.C.: Government Printing Office), pp. 1–2.

[16] Eliot Marshall, "Tiger Teams Draw Researchers' Snarls," *Science* 252 (April 19, 1991), pp. 366–69.

The operational auditor must recognize that all managers make mistakes, and that hindsight permits identification of decisions that should have been made differently. There is no point, however, in publicizing such decisions if they were made in good faith, given the information available at the time. Operational auditing serves a useful purpose if, and only if, it shows how future decisions can be made in a better way.

Skills Required. Because of the above needs, operational auditing requires a quite different approach and a quite different type of auditor than does compliance auditing. This is evidenced by the fact that the General Accounting Office hires approximately equal numbers of accountants and nonaccountants. Operations analysts, economists, and social psychologists are well represented among the nonaccountants.

Use of Flowcharts. One technique that has proven quite effective in operational auditing is the use of flowcharts. Flowcharts can map levels of decision making for a particular activity, thereby assisting managers to focus on potential problem areas or gaps in the way clients are handled by the organization's employees. While a flowchart can become highly complex, depending on the activity being analyzed, the technique itself is quite simple, relying essentially on the three symbols shown in Exhibit 11–1.

Using these three symbols, the flowchart lays out all tasks, decision points, and documents generated in conjunction with a particular activity. Managers can then determine if all possible tasks have been considered, and where, if at all, tasks should be monitored to compare their performance with expectations.

The flowchart shown in Exhibit 11–2 provides a simplified example of decisions that are made in some social service agencies when they receive a referral of a potential new client. Note that the flowchart shows not only the sequence of decisions that must be made, but also the reports that have been developed to monitor key decision points. For example, an analysis of the reasons for the inability to serve clients quite likely would be helpful to senior management and the board of directors in reviewing the work of the agency. An analysis of lengths of waiting time for a social worker might assist the director of social work in considering personnel reassignments or in preparing next year's budget. Senior

---

EXHIBIT 11–1 Flowchart Symbols

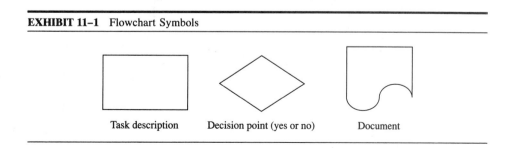

Task description   Decision point (yes or no)   Document

EXHIBIT 11–2 Simplified Flowchart for a Social Service Agency

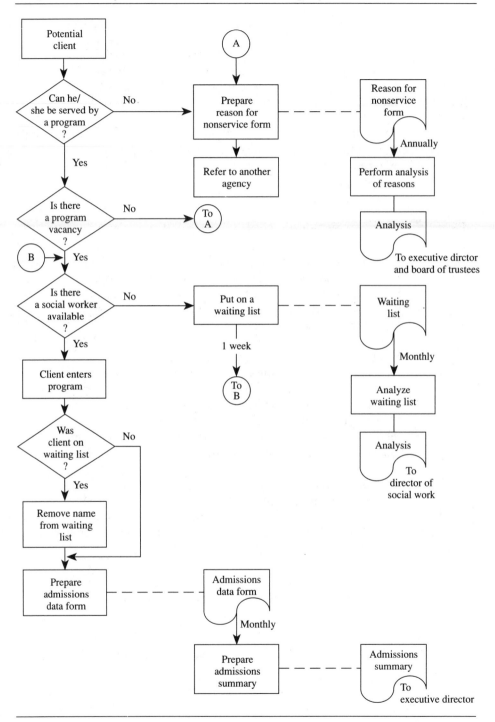

management also might be interested in an analysis of the characteristics of clients admitted to the agency.

The value of a flowchart is that it identifies in a very specific way the decisions that are made in conjunction with a particular activity. Since there can be no loose ends (i.e., paths that are left undefined), managers can view the decision-making process in its entirety and identify potential problem areas. Managers can monitor these areas, and take corrective action when necessary.

Flowcharts have become increasingly important in organizations implementing continuous quality improvement (CQI) and total quality management (TQM). These organizations effectively ask line managers to engage in operational auditing. If senior management fosters an organizational environment that supports such an effort, line managers will be able to undertake operational analyses on their own. They do not have to wait for, or rely on, operational auditors to conduct them.

Controls on Effectiveness. Some management control systems omit effectiveness considerations; that is, comparisons of actual versus planned outputs. Indeed, the absence of information on effectiveness frequently is used as a reason for not giving appropriate attention to information that *is* provided by the system. For example, in a hospital there may be no adequate formal mechanism for measuring the quality of care, and this fact leads some people to conclude that little attention should be given to the control of costs because of the danger that such attention might lead to a lowering of quality.

Notwithstanding the absence of good data, there actually are powerful forces at work in hospitals and other nonprofit organizations, where professionals deliver services, to ensure that the quality of service is adequate. If it becomes inadequate, this fact usually is brought to senior management's attention. Physicians, nurses, and other hospital professionals are vitally interested in patient welfare, and usually will not tolerate reductions in quality. Additionally, if there are problems with nonclinical quality, patients may complain. When these complaints are about poor food, dirty floors, or other matters within the patient's competence, they are relevant. They may even come to the attention of the general public or the trustees, which is an outcome senior management certainly wants to avoid.

The presence of competition also may affect quality, for if quality levels deteriorate in one hospital, physicians may threaten to use (or actually use) another. Accrediting and licensing agencies also make periodic inspections and check actual conditions against prescribed standards. Thus, physicians, patients, trustees, competition, and outside agencies are all of some help in assuring adequate quality levels, even in the absence of a formal method of measurement. Some hospitals use volunteers or paid patient care representatives to question patients about the quality of care they receive, and to bring patient complaints to the attention of management.

Example. In the Mid-Maine Medical Center, a volunteer interviews eight patients a month, following a printed interview guide. Serious problems, if any, are brought to the attention of management immediately. A summary report is discussed monthly at a meeting of management and the volunteer team.

Peer Review.   Several professions have devised methods to ensure a satisfactory quality of service. Although the movements have different labels, they share in common the concept that a professional's work should be subject to review by his or her peers.

Of these efforts, the most important—and the most controversial—were professional standards review organizations (PSROs) in the medical profession. PSROs began to function in 1976 to review the service provided by hospitals to medicare patients. Staffed by practicing physicians, PSROs looked at three questions: (1) Was the service medically necessary? (2) Was the treatment up to recognized standards? (3) Were the services delivered in the most economical fashion?

At the peak of the program's activity, there was at least one PSRO in each state, and many states had several. The PSRO program was all but eliminated in the early 1980s because of massive budget cuts at the federal level.

Although PSROs as such have been effectively dismantled, peer review continues to exist in most hospitals. Hospitals have medical records committees, tissue committees, and utilization review committees. These committees review the accuracy and completeness of records, the accuracy of surgical diagnoses, and the clinical treatments and lengths of patient stay.

Peer review also exists in other organizations in which professional decision making is a critical activity. Colleges and universities have mechanisms for reviewing the performance of faculty members, and the schools are themselves subject to review by accrediting agencies. In research organizations, work done by one group is reviewed by other groups.

In general, when the principal output of an organization is the work of professionals, the quality of that output is best judged by other professionals. Professionals tend to resist peer review activities, however, and there is a strong possibility of back scratching, so the mechanism needs senior management attention if it is to be effective.[17]

Results of Operational Auditing.   Despite 20 years of emphasis on operational auditing, little in the way of management reform has taken place in the federal government. For example, the President's Private Sector Survey on Cost Control (the Grace Commission) in 1984 identified programs that it claimed would reduce

---

[17] It should be noted that peer review focuses on the effectiveness of an organization's *professionals* and not on the broader question of the effectiveness of its *programs*. It may be, for example, that individual teachers in a bilingual education program are all extremely well qualified and carry out their responsibilities in a highly effective manner, but that the nature of the student population has changed such that the program no longer is needed. Questions such as these are part of an evaluation review, discussed in Chapter 15.

waste and improve management for total savings of $424.6 billion in five years.[18] Relatively few of its proposals were implemented.

Confusion with Compliance Auditing. Some organizations have not been successful at operational auditing because they do not appear to be aware of the differences between operational auditing and compliance auditing. As a result, they use persons with an accounting background for operational auditing, simply because the current auditing organization consists exclusively of accountants. When accountants imply that they know how to run a school, hospital, or any other organization better than the professionals who have spent their careers working in and managing such organizations, or when they attempt to recommend changes that are outside their areas of competence, their work is resented and frequently disregarded.

PROJECT CONTROL

The foregoing description has focused on the control of individual responsibility centers. Somewhat different techniques are appropriate for the control of projects, such as individual research projects or the building of a major capital asset. Specifically, in controlling a responsibility center, the focus is on work done in a specified period, such as a month or a quarter. In project control, by contrast, the focus is on the accomplishment of a project that, in many instances, may extend over a period of several years.

A project control system must consider three aspects of the project: cost, quality, and time requirements. The essentials of the system for controlling these are summarized below.

Specification of Work Packages

Senior management specifies the responsibility centers that will do the work. Responsibility center managers estimate the activities to be done and the resources and time required to complete them. These estimates should be made as near to the inception of the project as possible and in terms of *work packages*—relatively small, measurable increments of work that can be related to a physical product, milestone, or other measurable indicator of progress. These units should be of short duration, with discrete starting and completion points, and should be the responsibility of a single organizational unit.

---

[18] President's Private Sector Survey on Cost Control, *War on Waste,* 1984. For current efforts to improve performance in the federal government, see *Management of the United States Government,* a report prepared annually by the Office of Management and Budget.

Preparation of Schedules and a Budget

Based on the work packages, responsibility center managers prepare a work schedule and a budget. These should show:

- Physical products, milestones, technical performance goals, or other indicators that will be used to measure output.
- Budgets for costs expected to be incurred for each work package and for overhead costs.
- Starting and completion time for each work package.
- The organizational unit responsible for the work.
- Interdependencies among work packages.

Reporting of Outputs and Costs

The accounting staff maintains records of actual outputs and actual costs incurred. At frequent intervals, it prepares reports from these records showing, both for the interval and cumulatively, significant differences between:

- Incurred budgeted costs and direct work performed.
- Incurred and budgeted overhead costs.
- Budgeted costs for work actually performed and budgeted costs for work scheduled.
- Actual and planned schedule.
- Actual and planned performance.

Revisions to the Plan

Based on these reports, managers make revisions to the project plan and budget to reflect current estimates of the work schedule, the expected level of technical performance, and costs. Once they have revised plans and budgets, subsequent management reports should show comparisons both with the original (i.e., baseline) budget and with the current budget. The reasons for significant revisions should be readily identifiable in these reports.[19]

BEHAVIORAL CONSIDERATIONS

Thus far we have focused mainly on the technical aspects of performance control systems. While these matters are important, so too are the attitudes of those who use, and are affected by, the information from these systems. In this section, we discuss several matters related to the use of performance control information.

---

[19] For a more complete description of project control, see Robert N. Anthony, John Dearden, and Vijay Govindarajan, *Management Control Systems*, 6th ed. (Homewood, Ill.: Richard D. Irwin, 1992).

Senior Management Involvement

A management control system is likely to be ineffective unless operating managers and professionals perceive that it is considered important by their superiors. This requires that both senior management and line managers use information from the system in decision making, in appraising the results of performance, and as a basis for salary adjustments, promotions, and other personnel actions. It also requires that superiors at all levels discuss the results of operations with their subordinates.

Some managers convene regular meetings at which performance of the entire organization is discussed. Others prefer individual discussions with responsibility center heads. Still others prefer to make comments in writing, holding only infrequent meetings.

In discussions of performance, subordinates should be given an opportunity to explain circumstances not revealed in the reports. If corrective action seems called for, constructive suggestions for such action should be put forth and agreed upon. If the performance is good, managers should convey appropriate recognition of this.

Sometimes it is difficult for management to convey the correct impression about the importance of quantitative information, especially the comparison of budgeted and actual revenues and expenses. Inadequate attention leads to a common disregard of these numbers. On the other hand, if senior management places too much emphasis on numerical measures of performance, operating managers may act in such a way that their performance looks good according to the measures that are emphasized, but to the detriment of the real objectives of the organization. These actions are called *playing the numbers game*. They can be avoided only by convincing operating managers that they should concentrate on accomplishing the real objectives of the organization and that they will not be penalized if such efforts do not show up in numerical measures of performance.[20]

Importance of Adequate Staffs

Quantitative information for appraising performance cannot be used unless qualified people are available to make the calculations. Except in very small organizations, managers do not have time to make the calculations themselves. Unfortunately, a great many nonprofit organizations, including some very large ones, do not have staffs large enough to undertake such analyses in a thorough and systematic way. For example, one state government agency with a multibillion dollar budget has only six professionals who are engaged in the regular analysis of operating reports. Some states have none at all.

---

[20] For a good discussion of some of the important aspects of performance review, see Berkley Rice, "Performance Review: Examining the Eye of the Beholder," *Across the Board*, December 1985.

Balance between Freedom and Restraint

In any organization, for-profit or nonprofit, the right balance has to be struck between freedom and restraint. *Freedom* is needed to take advantage of the ability and knowledge of the person on the firing line. *Restraint* is needed to ensure that management policies are followed and to reduce the effect of poor judgments or counterproductive decisions by lower level managers.

In nonprofit organizations, there are two complications to attaining an appropriate balance between freedom and restraint. First, the absence of profit as an overall basis for measuring performance usually calls for somewhat less freedom and somewhat more restraint than in a for-profit organization. Second, the presence of professionals in many nonprofits introduces a level of knowledge about client needs that senior management must consider carefully.

This is a matter of degree. Many nonprofit organizations, particularly government organizations, impose far too many and too detailed restraints on first-line managers. Sometimes this is caused by the *goldfish bowl problem.* Errors are likely to be played up in the newspapers, and, as a protective device, managers prescribe rules, which they can point to when errors come to light: "I am not to blame; he (the sinner) broke my rule." The detailed restraints also result from encrustation: a sin is committed, and a rule is promulgated to avoid that sin in the future; but the rule continues even after the need for it has disappeared. No one considers whether the likelihood and seriousness of error is great enough to warrant continuation of the rule.

Motivation

A central purpose of any control system is to motivate operating managers to take actions that help accomplish the organization's objectives efficiently and effectively. As discussed in Chapter 7, the problem of inducing the desired degree and direction of motivation is a difficult one in any organization, but it is particularly difficult in a nonprofit organization. In a school system, for example, all groups are interested in better education, but teachers as individuals are concerned with salary, educational advancement, and professional status, as well.

The Problem of Budget Conformance.   The fact that performance in a nonprofit organization is measured in part by how well managers conform to their budgets can have dysfunctional consequences. Suppose a manager has a $1 million budget, and by careful, hard work performs the required job, but spends only $990,000. In many organizations, the budget for the following year, other things equal, will be $990,000. In effect, the manager is punished, rather than rewarded, for reducing costs—his or her department now has less money to work with than would have been the case if the entire $1 million had been spent.

The following cartoon illustrates a typical attitude toward budgets—that it is almost sinful not to spend the full amount that is available.

Beetle Bailey

It is a difficult matter to create the right attitude in these circumstances. On the one hand, if the program can be run more efficiently or if demand for it has fallen, its budget should be less than before. On the other hand, managers need incentives to be efficient this year that do not penalize them in future years. There are several possible ways to do this.

One possibility is to guarantee managers that their budgets will not be reduced for the current year or the succeeding year, even if the job can be done at less than the amount budgeted. To make this policy work, senior management may need to expand the definition of operating expenses to include minor capital expenditures, for it is on items of this type that managers tend to spend the extra money. (In government, however, the person who makes such a promise may not be in the same job long enough to make good on it.)

A second possibility is to convince operating managers that a budget reduction, per se, should not be viewed as a punishment, and that senior management recognizes and rewards cost reductions. An effective and efficient manager is rewarded with a combination of promotion, salary, and the respect of peers, superiors, and subordinates. If senior management successfully stresses the importance of cost reduction and rewards, it may be able to avoid negative reactions to reducing the budget.

The third possibility is to release substantially less (say, 20 percent less) than the funds managers need. They know that additional funds are available, but they can never be sure of getting them. This may make them more than ordinarily careful in spending available funds. There is a risk, of course, that this practice will stifle their initiative, resulting in a reluctance to both introduce new programs and maintain existing facilities.

A fourth possibility is to hold next year's budget constant, but expect managers to accomplish more work with the same amount of resources. This approach increases efficiency just as much as a policy of expecting a unit to do the same amount of work with fewer resources. It also assumes that the organizational unit can, in fact, accomplish more work with the same amount of resources.

Use of Monetary Incentives. For-profit organizations often pay cash bonuses or give stock options when savings are realized or profits are high. Increasingly, as we discussed in Chapters 2 and 7, nonprofit organizations are paying bonuses; frequently the bonuses are related to nonfinancial as well as financial performance.

Example. A survey of hospitals found that, in many instances, bonuses paid to executives were related to both net operating income and at least one measure relating to quality of care or improvement of services delivered.[21]

Example. The state of Tennessee permitted a college or university to earn a bonus of up to 2 percent of its budget based on its performance with regard to five variables:

- Number of academic programs accredited.
- Performance of graduates on outcomes related to general education, as measured by tests administered to alumni.
- Performance of graduates on tests in their major fields.
- Evaluation of programs by students, alumni, and community representatives, by questionnaires
- Evaluation by peers at other institutions.[22]

Some organizations also emphasize the importance of collaboration and teamwork in their incentive systems.

Example. One nonprofit organization has an incentive system in which a portion of each manager's salary is withheld monthly with the understanding that it may not be paid at all. Depending on the extent to which the organization as a whole achieves its financial and programmatic objectives for the year, all or a portion of this withheld salary is then paid out as a bonus. Since all managers receive the same proportion of the amount withheld, and since the proportion is based on the performance of the entire organization, managers have a major incentive to collaborate, which is essential activity for the success of the organization.

All of the above bonus arrangements relate to performance in the short term. In general, nonprofit organizations have not been successful in designing incentive compensation plans that motivate managers to consider the long-term consequences of their decisions. One important reason is that they cannot use stock options. Stock options frequently are used by for-profit companies to attempt to motivate managers to think in terms of the long run.

Some nonprofit organizations have attempted to design incentive plans that encourage managers to adopt a long-term perspective. The accumulation of extra vacation days is one such approach, with the possibility of an extended sabbatical leave at some point in the future. If the system is designed in such a way that these days are not paid if the employee leaves the organization voluntarily, there is an incentive for the employee to remain with the organization.

---

[21] "Hospitals Adopt New Strategy to Keep Top Executives," *Journal of Accountancy*, March 1988, pp. 14–17.

[22] E. Grady Bogue and Wayne Brown, "Performance Incentives for State Colleges," *Harvard Business Review*, November–December 1981, pp. 123–28.

Gainsharing. Increasingly, nonprofit organizations are incorporating financial rewards into productivity improvement programs. Sometimes called *gainsharing,* these programs allow the savings generated by increases in productivity to be shared between the employee and the organization. At the federal level, the major barriers to gainsharing programs are the lack of legislation authorizing such programs, the presence of existing regulations that limit managers' flexibility in designing and operating the programs, and the absence of specific policies and guidelines from the Office of Personnel Management. Nevertheless, several instances have been reported in the Department of Defense of successful efforts, including elimination of work backlogs, decreased equipment downtime, reduction in time lost from on-the-job injuries, and substantial reductions in overtime and sick leave.[23]

There are also gainsharing successes outside the federal government. For example, one hospital paid bonuses to employees of departments where productivity exceeded historical standards. The result was an increase of productivity of 8 percent, producing $2 million in savings; employee bonuses averaged 4.3 percent of base salaries.[24]

If properly designed, a gainsharing program takes advantage of the knowledge of possible improvements that usually exists in the lower levels of an organization. While there can be problems with gainsharing, such as a tendency to hold back some ideas for next year so that there will be constant evidence of effort, the program nevertheless provides managers with a financial incentive to reduce costs.

SUMMARY

Control of operations consists of both financial control and performance control. The former focuses on assuring that the spending limitations of the budget are adhered to. The latter is concerned with effective and efficient managerial performance. The distinction between the two types of control is highlighted by the kind of auditing that takes place in each. Financial control uses the compliance audit, an audit that is relatively narrow in scope, and is concerned with safeguarding the organization's assets against loss from unauthorized use or disposition. It also verifies the reliability of the records used for preparing financial statements. Its main focus is on the accounting system.

Performance control uses the operational audit, which is relatively broad in its scope, and focuses on how an organization is managing its resources. It attempts to identify the causes of any inefficiencies or uneconomical practices. The opera-

---

[23] U. S. General Accounting Office, *Gainsharing: DOD Efforts Highlight an Effective Tool for Enhancing Federal Productivity,* Briefing Report to the Chairman, Subcommittee on Defense, Committee on Appropriations, House of Representatives, GAO/GGD86-143BR, September 1986.

[24] Ibid.

tional audit's main units of analysis are the management information system, administrative procedures, and the organizational structure.

Behavioral considerations are important in the control of operations. In particular, senior management should seek an appropriate balance between freedom and restraint. That is, they should give program heads and responsibility center managers the freedom to exercise judgment in their operating activities, but they also must ensure that overall management policies are followed, and that the possibilities for poor judgment or counterproductive decisions by lower level managers are minimized. One tool to help attain this balance is a system of monetary incentives that is used to reward managers for attaining superior financial and programmatic operating results.

Rewarding managers for good performance is more difficult in a nonprofit organization than in a for-profit one, largely because the "bottom line" doesn't measure effectiveness or efficiency in the same way it does in a for-profit company. Thus, senior management must seek ways to reward managers for the programmatic results they attain. This requires measuring output, which is the subject of Chapter 12.

APPENDIX
The Encumbrance Accounting Process

Encumbrance accounting is used when an organization wishes to maintain accounting records of *obligations* to pay for goods or services. An encumbrance arises when such an obligation is made. Usually, encumbrance accounting takes place when a state or local authority is appropriated funds by its legislative body, thereby giving it the authority to encumber. Accordingly, the first step in an encumbrance accounting is to record the amount appropriated for each fund. The next step is to charge the appropriated amount for encumbrances.

> *Example.* If the legislature appropriates $10 million for a certain activity in 1992, this amount is set up in the accounts, and it is reduced as contracts are entered into, so the accounts show at all times how much of the $10 million has not yet been encumbered. The organization has complied with the law if, by the end of 1992, it has not encumbered more than $10 million, whether or not goods or services contracted for have been received, and whether or not cash disbursements to vendors or employees have been made.

A formal business accounting system starts when goods or services are received; it does not record purchase orders. From this point on, the accounting process is the same in many nonprofit organizations as in a business; that is, resources are held in asset accounts until they are used, at which time they are charged as expenses to responsibility centers and programs.

Some nonprofit organizations charge responsibility centers and programs as soon as the amounts are encumbered; others make these charges when the goods or services are acquired, rather than when they are consumed. (The latter is called the *expenditure basis* of accounting.) Alternatively, the charge may be made to the responsibility center that *incurs* the encumbrance or the expenditure, which is not necessarily the same as the responsibility center that *uses* the resources.

> **Example.** Consider $1,000 of supplies to be used by an operating agency but purchased by a central supply office. The supplies are purchased in March and consumed in April. Under encumbrance accounting, the $1,000 is recorded as a charge to the central supply office in the month of March; it may never be recorded as an expense of the operating agency. Under accrual accounting, it is recorded as an expense of the operating agency in the month of April.

As explained in Chapter 3, these differences can have a significant effect on the amount of resources reported as consumed by a given responsibility center.

Reconciling Encumbrance and Expense Accounting

It is feasible to design an accounting system that keeps track of encumbrances, expenditures, and expenses. This is accomplished by the use of working capital accounts that hold costs in suspense until the resources are consumed. The inventory account in a business accounting system serves this purpose, and inventory accounts can be used for the same purpose in organizations that record encumbrances. In addition, such organizations need an account called *Undelivered Orders* that holds items in suspense between the time a contract is placed and the time goods are received.

The procedure for doing this is illustrated in Exhibit 11–3. As it indicates, in the month of April, labor services of $100,000 were used, and orders were placed for $80,000 of material and $60,000 of other services (e.g., a contract was let for painting buildings). Total encumbrances for the agency in April (shown in Account A) were therefore $240,000.

Labor is accounted for essentially the same on an encumbrance basis as on an expense basis, so labor expense is here assumed to be equal to the encumbered $100,000. This is shown in Account C. To record material expense and services expense, however, two types of working capital accounts are necessary. One is Undelivered Orders (Account B); the other is Inventory (Account D). Inventory is of the same nature in a nonprofit organization as in a for-profit business; namely, it records the amount of material that is on hand at any time (which, by definition, is an asset). Thus, it holds the cost of material between the time of acquisition and the time of consumption.

As orders are placed, Account B is debited, and Account A is credited. As the services are rendered, Account B is credited and Account C is debited. Thus, for $70,000 of services performed in April (e.g., the buildings were painted and $10,000 of work was done under contracts let in earlier months), a credit is made to Undelivered Orders (Account B), with a corresponding debit to an expense account (Account C). The Undelivered Orders account has no counterpart in a for-profit company.

EXHIBIT 11–3 Reconciliation of Encumbrance and Expense Accounting Transactions for April ($000)

A. Encumbrance Accounts		B. Undelivered Orders			C. Expense Accounts	
Labor	100	Balance	200	Services 70	Labor	100
Material ordered	80 →	Material	80	Material 50	Services	70
Services ordered	60 →	Services	60		Material	40
Encumbrances	240	Balance	220		Total expenses	210

D. Inventory

Balance	90	Used	40
Received	50		
Balance	100		

To reconcile:
Change in working capital + Expenses = Encumbrance

Undelivered orders (220 − 200)	20
Inventory (100 − 90)	10
Total	30 + 210 = 240

As material is received, Undelivered Orders (Account B) is credited and Inventory (Account D) is debited. When the inventory is used, Account D is credited and an expense account (Account C) is debited. To illustrate, in the above example, $50,000 of material was received in April, reducing Undelivered Orders by $50,000 and increasing Inventory by the same amount. In April, $40,000 of material was issued from inventory for use in current operations, so Inventory was credited $40,000, with a corresponding debit to an expense account.

As Exhibit 11–3 shows, total expenses and total encumbrances for April can be reconciled by measuring the changes in the two working capital accounts. Undelivered orders increased by $20,000 (from $200,000 to $220,000) and Inventory increased by $10,000 (from $90,000 to $100,000). The sum of these two changes ($30,000), plus the expenses for the month of $210,000 is the same as total encumbrances.

If senior management wishes, a manager's budget can include these working capital accounts. The budget report can show the amount of expenses authorized for each program, and also the amounts authorized for changes in working capital (which may be either positive or negative). As a result, the total amount budgeted is the sum of these amounts.

The mechanism described above provides a way of holding charges in suspense between the time an asset is acquired and the time it is consumed. Working capital accounts also hold items in suspense so as to differentiate between the organizational unit acquiring the asset, and the unit consuming it. Again, this is a function that inventory accounts serve in a business. In a manufacturing company, all the costs of manufacturing goods are accumulated in Work-in-Process Inventory accounts until the manufacturing process is completed. At that time, the costs are moved from Work-in-Process Inventory to Finished Goods Inventory, effectively shifting *responsibility* for the goods from the manufacturing department to the marketing department. Similarly, the costs incurred by service centers in non-profit organizations can be held in suspense in working capital and inventory accounts until the goods or services are consumed. At that point, the expense account of the responsibility center that benefits from the goods or services can be debited, reflecting their consumption.

SUGGESTED ADDITIONAL READINGS

Azad, Ali N., and Ted D. Skekel. "Personal Attributes and Effective Operational Auditing: Perceptions of College and University Internal Auditors." *Governmental Accountants Journal* 39, no. 3 (Fall 1990).

Barzelay, Michael, and Babak J. Armajani. *Breaking through Bureaucracy: A New Vision for Managing in Government,* 1992.

Bordelon, Barbara, and Elizabeth Clemmer. "Customer Service, Partnership, Leadership: Three Strategies that Work." *The G.A.O. Journal,* Winter 1990/91.

Coate, L. Edwin. "TQM on Campus: Implementing Total Quality Management in a University Setting." *NACUBO Business Officer,* November 1990.

Epperly, Mary Lou. "Audits of Academic Programs." *Internal Auditing* 5, no. 4 (Spring 1990).

Forrester, Robert. "Are Your Not-for-Profit Clients Ready for Compliance Auditing?" *Journal of Accountancy* 170, no. 1 (July 1990).

Gabor, Andrea. *The Man Who Discovered Quality: How W. Edwards Deming Brought the Quality Revolution to America—The Stories of Ford, Xerox, and GM.* New York: Times Books (Division of Random House), 1990.

Ganguli, Gouranga, and Sue Winfrey. "Auditing Medical Records Helps Reduce Liability." *Healthcare Financial Management* 44, no. 10 (October 1990).

Holley, Charles, and Ross Mcdonald. "Operational Auditing of Health Care Ancillary Departments." *Internal Auditing* 6, no. 1 (Summer 1990).

Krallman, John, and Wayland Winstead. "Operational Audits in a University Environment." *Internal Auditing* 5, no. 2 (Fall 1989).

Levin, Henry M. "Raising Productivity in Higher Education." *Journal of Higher Education* 62, no. 3 (May/June 1991).

Miller, John R., and Frederick D. Wolf. "A Look at the New Yellow Book: Tomorrow's Government Audits." *Journal of Accountancy,* November 1988.

Smith, L. Murphy, and Jeffrey R. Miller. "An Internal Audit of a Church." *Internal Auditing* 5, no. 1 (Summer 1989).

Wilson, James Q. *Bureaucracy: What Government Agencies Do and Why They Do It.* New York: Basic Books, 1989.

CASE 11–1   Hospital San Pedro*

Sr. Julio Rivera, Director General of Health of the Social Security Administration of the country of Ilobasco, sat down at his desk one morning late in September, and began to open his mail. One of the first items he came to was a letter from Sr. Fidel Sanchez Hernandez. The letter read as follows:

Sonsonate
September 20

Sr. Director General of Health
San Miguel

Dear Sir,

In a routine examination which took place last April 3, Dr. Magaña, the primary care doctor for my community, discovered that my son, Gabriel, suffered from a visual defect. Since it was necessary for him to be treated by an eye specialist, Dr. Magaña gave me a referral to go to the ambulatory care center in our county capital, Santa Ana, where all the medical specialists are located.

The 8th of that month, at noon, the hour specified for ophthalmology consultations, my son and I were in the clinic waiting to be seen by Dr. Duarte, the center's ophthalmologist. You can't imagine my surprise when, after a MINIMAL examination, the doctor gave me a referral so that my son could be seen in Hospital San Pedro, in Santa Telca, since, as was patently clear, the center at Santa Ana DOESN'T HAVE THE MINIMUM REQUIRED FACILITIES NECESSARY TO CONDUCT AN EYE EXAMINATION.

That was the beginning of the Odyssey of a patient seeking to find and obtain a diagnosis.

On April 13, in the afternoon, I had to return to the center at Santa Ana so that the Inspector[1] could authorize the referral, so that I could go to the Hospital San Pedro, as we had been directed.

I was informed by his office that in San Pedro, specialist visits begin at 8:30 A.M. daily.

The following day, April 14, at 8:30 in the morning, accompanied by my son, I arrived at the facilities of Hospital San Pedro, and completed the administrative transactions related to my son's case. After ONE HOUR in line, they gave me a visit for the 4th of June (ALMOST TWO MONTHS!), telling us that we should arrive at 8:30 in the morning.

On the 4th, at 8:30 in the morning, my son and I were in front of the door of the ophthalmology clinic of San Pedro, awaiting our turn. After waiting TWO HOURS, my

---

* This case was prepared by Antoni Garcia Prat, Instituto de Estudios Superiores de la Empresa, Barcelona, Spain. It was translated and modified slightly by Professor David W. Young. Copyright © by Antoni Garcia Prat and David W. Young. Distributed by the Accounting Curriculum Center, Boston University School of Management.

[1] An Inspector is a Social Security Officer, always a physician, who, among other duties, is responsible for authorizing patients to be treated in contracted (i.e., non-Social Security) hospitals.

son was seen in one of the offices, where we were asked to go to another room for the next step . . . and to wait some more.

At last, we entered the clinic. After conducting various tests, the doctor indicated to us that it was necessary to dilate the pupils in order to complete the exam thoroughly, and that therefore we should return another day, telling us that we should put in some drops a few hours before the consultation. Returning to the reception desk, after waiting A HALF HOUR we were given a new visit time on the 5th of August (TWO MORE MONTHS). At the same time, the clerk requested from us a new referral form, P–10, from the Inspector in which he should ask the Hospital to conduct the test that the specialist at San Pedro already had told me they would give to my son.

The same day, the 4th, I had to make another trip to Santa Ana in order to obtain Form P–10 from the Inspector, and, in the afternoon I had to go to San Miguel, to the Chaparestique Clinic on Madrazo Street, so that the Inspector there could authorize the referral since the Inspector at Santa Ana was on vacation (ARE THERE NO SUBSTI-TUTES?).

The 5th of August. 8:30 in the morning. We arrive at San Pedro. My son with drops in his eyes. We enter the clinic at TEN O'CLOCK. After the visit, the doctor tells me that we have to return another day since the results of the exams conducted on June 4th have been lost (!!??!!) and it was impossible to repeat them now with the pupils dilated. Because of the expression on my face and because of what I had on the tip of my tongue to spit out at him, the doctor understood my justified indignation, and he himself gave us a new date, for the 12th of August, eight days later, without any type of referral.

On the 12th, at 8:30 in the morning, once again in the clinic of San Pedro. My son was not seen until ELEVEN O'CLOCK. The doctor diagnosed strabismus.

That's the story until now. Now, I request that you, as the person responsible for health in Ilobasco, answer the following questions for me.

1. Is it necessary to pass FOUR MONTHS, visit after visit, from clinic to clinic, in order to be seen and learn what type of illness a person suffers from, especially in the case of my son, in which the diagnosis of the specialist of San Pedro coincides exactly with that given to me on the 14th of April, free and in half an hour, by an optometrist?
2. Who will reimburse me for the costs that I have been obliged to incur for travel and lost working hours?
3. Of what use is an ophthalmology consultation at Santa Ana if they don't know how or can't diagnose a basic defect such as astigmatism?
4. Why is there the confusion such as exists at San Pedro, and why is it tolerated, where patients gather at 8:30 A.M., the physicians arrive at 9:00, and visits are conducted until 1:00 P.M.?
5. Why were we sent to San Pedro, when there is a Social Security Hospital in my own service area which has an ophthalmology service?

Awaiting your answer, I would like to take this opportunity to give you my best wishes.

Signed

Fidel Sanchez Hernandez

Background

Hospital San Pedro was a private general hospital with some 300 beds, reimbursed in part by the Social Security Administration (SSA) in order to alleviate the deficit of beds in the densely-populated area of Santa Tecla. The reimbursement system established a method with a monthly payment based on the services delivered to SSA patients. Units of payment for ambulatory consultation distinguished among first visits, subsequent visits, and emergency visits. Separate payment units existed for inpatient care. The rates for each one of these visit types were determined by the SSA, and, without exception, each hospital received rates which corresponded to the group and level in which it had been classified. Traditionally, Hospital San Pedro had been incurring significant losses owing to the fact that the SSA's rates were below its costs. Even so, the hospital had begun, in the last few years, some new services and programs.

The new investments, small in comparison with the requests of the medical staff, served to give the hospital a greater base of facilities and equipment. With these it had an opportunity to move to a higher reimbursement group and level, and therefore an ability to increase its rates by 10 percent.

Another concern of the hospital had been to widen its geographic service area and broaden its scope of services. This was due to the fact that management feared, because a Social Security Hospital existed in the same area, the SSA authorities would prefer to fill their own hospital, thereby saving reimbursement monies.

On the other hand, the hospital faced a serious problem of waiting lists in its clinics, owing to the traditional inadequacy of primary care in SSA facilities. This was quite serious since long waiting lists of SSA patients could threaten that portion of the utilization which was made up of patients affiliated with private insurance companies, or who were self-pay. Both of these groups not only paid more for a clinic visit, but also could decide to utilize the services of other clinics or private centers if they were dissatisfied with their care at Hospital San Pedro.

Next Steps

Sr. Rivera realized that a nicely written letter of apology probably would pacify Sr. Sanchez Hernandez, but he also knew that the case presented in the letter was not an unusual one. In part, it indicated some serious deficiencies in the patient referral system, but it also called into question the government's newly formulated policy of decentralization with an emphasis on primary care, and the role of private hospitals in that effort. It was because of these latter matters that he decided to convene a meeting of the Director of Hospital San Pedro, the SSA's Director of Reimbursement, and the Director of Primary Care Services for the Ministry of Health. He then set about preparing for the meeting.

Questions

1. Based on the information in Sr. Sanchez Hernandez's letter, prepare a flowchart for a patient in Ilobasco seeking a diagnosis for a medical problem. Make assumptions where necessary.
2. How, if at all, does this assist you in suggesting ways to improve the country's health care delivery system?
3. What should Sr. Rivera do?

CASE 11–2 Northeast Research Laboratory (A)*

In the fall of 1974, the problem of assuring that the time of professionals was recorded properly (which is a chronic problem in research and development organizations) seemed to Andrew Carter, president of Northeast Research Laboratory, to be becoming acute. Carter wondered what, if any, additional steps should be taken to mitigate this problem.

Northeast Research Laboratory (NRL) was a large, multidisciplinary research and development organization, employing approximately 1,000 professionals. Approximately half its revenue came from contracts for research projects that were undertaken for various government agencies, particularly agencies of the Department of Defense, and the other half came from industrial companies and from nonfederal government agencies.

The typical research contract specified that the client would reimburse NRL for direct costs involved in the project, plus an allowance for overhead, plus a small fee, with total reimbursement being limited to a specified ceiling. For this amount, NRL agreed to deliver reports or other completed work. The overhead allowance was determined on the basis of an overhead rate which was expressed as a percentage of direct labor costs. For defense contracts, the overhead rate was negotiated annually with the Department of Defense. Some nondefense agencies negotiated a separate rate because they did not allow the same overhead components as were allowed by the Department of Defense. For example, the Department of Defense permitted the cost of preparing bids and proposals for contracts to be included as an item of overhead cost, but the Atomic Energy Commission excluded this cost. Exhibit 1 shows the principal components of overhead and their magnitude. The type of work that was to be charged to the various overhead accounts was spelled out in a five-page section of the NRL procedures manual. Exhibit 2 summarizes this material.

---

* This case was prepared by Professor Robert N. Anthony. Copyright © by the President and Fellows of Harvard College. Harvard Business School case 9-175-183.

EXHIBIT 1   Overhead Costs

	First Ten Months ($000)	
	1974	*1973*
Administration and planning	6,490	6,644
Information dissemination	2,500	1,958
Division research and development	845	824
General research and development	189	165
Staff development	623	371
Staffing	673	465
Facility expense	6,506	5,298
Interim technical studies	389	278
Proposal liaison	243	238
Concept formulation	551	515
Proposal preparation	1,475	1,155
Total overhead	20,484	17,911

Employees were supposed to fill out weekly timecards on which they recorded how they spent their time to the nearest 0.1 hour. The time was charged either as a direct cost of a research project or to one of the overhead activity codes listed on Exhibit 2. The timecard was also signed by the employee's supervisor.

Problems with Time Reporting

As was the case with all defense contractors, NRL was subject to audit by representatives of the Defense Contract Audit Agency (DCAA). In 1964, DCAA had made a spot check of the timecards, had uncovered several errors, and consequently had disallowed $150,000 of overhead costs; that is, NRL's revenue from defense was $150,000 less than it would have been if this disallowance had not been made. This was about 25 percent of NRL's profit for 1964. As a consequence of this experience, NRL management had placed increased emphasis on accurate time recording, by means of talks at management meetings and memoranda to the staff.

In the period 1965–72, DCAA did not check on time recording, but beginning in 1973, DCAA auditors showed renewed interest in the topic. On three occasions in 1973, auditors made a *gate check;* that is, they stood at the NRL entrance, took the names of employees who arrived after the official starting time, and then checked to see whether these employees had recorded their correct starting time on their timecards. Although no action was taken as a result of these gate checks, they led to resentment on the part of employees who learned of them. It was felt that professionals should be trusted to do a good day's work and that if a person

---

EXHIBIT 2   NRL Activity Codes

Administration and planning:
  511   Administrative duties (such as handling personnel actions, timecards, requisitions, financial reports, etc.); costs of nonproject office supplies, stationery, etc. (see also 561).

Information dissemination:
  521   Formal NRL publications; work order required (see also 525).
  522   Technical articles and papers (writing, editing, and publishing charges); reprints.
  523   Symposia or seminars, nonproject; work order required.
  525   Client liaison and tours, nonproject (use 581 for proposal followup); preparation and publication of division/department brochures or program descriptions.

NRL research and development:
  532   Division IR&D task; subnumber required (use NRL form 4823).
  535   General IR&D task; subnumber required (use NRL form 4823).

Staff development:
  541   Formal education and training courses.
  542   Orientation and staff training.
  543   Professional society participation.
  544   Overseas travel, nonproject.

Staffing:
  551   Recruiting, review of applications, and interviews.
  552   Relocation and transfer, nonproject; new hire moving costs.

Facility expense:
  561   Support services by Central Staff, nonproject translations, periodicals, books, small hand tools, toolboxes, and small parts cabinets—division personnel time charges only for work on security and property.
  562   Nonproject laboratory equipment maintenance, calibration, and repair.
  563   Minor laboratory and office moving costs; work order required if cost is to exceed $250.
  564   Minor construction including leasehold or building improvements less than $250; work order required.

Interim technical study:
  571   Informal study and assigned reading of journals, technical articles, or other library materials.

Bid and proposal expense:
  581   Proposal liaison; work order required.
  582   Concept formulation; work order required.
  583   Proposal preparation; work order required.

---

started late, he usually quit late; on balance, most employees put in more than the 40 hours a week that their employment contract called for, it was felt.

The controller of NRL reported to Mr. Carter that in the spring of 1974 DCAA auditors had conducted at least three *floor checks* (a type of audit that is described in the following section). The auditors had made no comments to him, nor to anyone else so far as he knew, as to what the results of these floor checks were.

The controller suspected that the auditors were gathering ammunition that would be used in connection with the next overhead rate negotiation, which took place in November.

Internal Audits

In 1974 NRL's Internal Audit Department conducted a series of floor checks to validate time recording practices. The first of these, on March 6, involved 15 professionals assigned to one of the engineering departments. Of these 15 persons, 7 were away from the department premises for one reason or another, so only 8 were interviewed. These eight were asked to describe the nature of the work they were doing. Subsequently, their timecards were examined, and in each case the work was correctly reported on the timecard.

The next floor check was on June 12 in another engineering department. Eight employees were selected who in the preceding week had charged three or more hours to overhead accounts. Each of these persons was asked to describe the nature of the work for which an overhead account was charged. In all cases, the work described was clearly of an overhead nature, as contrasted with work on research projects, but in three of the cases, there was some question to whether the correct overhead account had been charged. There was room for difference of opinion as to this, however, so the auditors did not take a formal "Exception," which was the standard practice when an improper procedure was observed.

On June 25, 1974, a similar floor check of seven employees in still another department produced similar results for six of them; that is, although there were some differences of opinion as to the proper overhead account to be charged, there was no doubt that the work was of an overhead nature. For the seventh employee, 27.5 hours were erroneously charged to overhead. The report stated that the person "had been told to charge work on Project 8366 the previous week to Interim Technical Study, an overhead account. Project 8366 is in an overrun condition, and management felt that since it would eventually have to be charged to overhead the charge may as well go there now."

In a study of five employees on July 25, one person was found to have charged time to the wrong overhead account. For another employee, the report read:

> When we checked the timecard of one of the employees who was working at home, we noted he had charged five hours on that day to Interim Technical Study. We had discussed the matter of working at home with the director of his organization on the day of the test. The director stated it was sometimes necessary for employees who are trying to meet deadlines to stay home to prevent unimportant interruptions from personnel and telephones. He further stated that he practiced this policy himself occasionally.
>
> It does not seem necessary, however, to stay at home for the sake of privacy to study because of the lack of other work or to keep up with professional journals, technical articles, and so forth, either on an assigned or unassigned basis.
>
> We recommend using NRL facilities, rather than working in the home.

A floor check of six employees on August 12, 1974, revealed several errors in the proper overhead account to be charged, but no project work charged to overhead.

On September 19, a follow-up audit was made on eight of the employees who had made incorrect or questionable charges as reported in earlier audits. In this follow-up, two exceptions were noted:

a. A biologist had charged four hours to grounds maintenance and described his work to the auditor as "fertilizing and watering the plants landscaping our building." The auditor recommended that when the biologist noted the need for maintenance, he should notify the grounds maintenance department rather than doing the work himself.

b. The other employee said he could not remember the nature of the work for which he had charged time to overhead, in the preceding week. It turned out that the timecard had been made out by his supervisor, and the supervisor had made an erroneous entry.

On September 20, an incident was reported to the controller that was relevant to the floor check program. On September 10, an internal auditor telephoned the Chicago office, asked for K. Smithson, and was told that he was not available. In a subsequent conversation with Smithson, the auditor was told that he had been participating in a TV program on September 10. Smithson's timecard for the week showed that he worked 40 hours on Project 8122, however. Further investigation showed that Smithson participated in a TV program, unrelated to NRL work, approximately two days a month, but that all of his time, except vacation and illness, was charged to some project. It turned out that timecards in the Chicago office were made out by an administrative assistant, based on her general knowledge of the activities there, but without checking with the employees involved.

The foregoing is a summary of all internal audit floor checks for the first nine months of 1974. The internal audit staff consisted of two professionals and an assistant.

The persons involved and their supervisors were informed of the results of these audits, but no formal disciplinary action was taken.

The McCabe Memorandum

On May 3, 1974, partly motivated by the reports of DCAA and internal audit floor checks, Robert McCabe, vice president for research operations, circulated the following memorandum to all professionals in the organization:

> Many members of the staff may not be aware of the reasoning behind the structure of NRL overhead charge numbers. As a consequence, they are sometimes not as careful as they should be when filling out their weekly timecards, with resulting erroneous apportioning of time charges between accounts.
>
> Under our pricing system, we agree to charge each customer the direct costs of performing his project, plus an allocated share of the indirect costs necessary to the

general operations of NRL. Our federal government customers have the right (and obligation) to audit not only the direct charges but the pool of expenses upon which the indirect allocation is based. In order to furnish the detail upon which they can base an audit, our accounting system provides a series of descriptive activity codes. Errors in proper accounting result in a cost disallowance and the reduction of net earnings available for capital purchases.

As a part of their audit function the government auditors make periodic floor checks to determine the relationship between the time charges and the work actually performed. These checks take two forms. In one case, they ask selected personnel what accounts they are charging on a particular day, and later check the timecards to make sure that the time charges correspond. In the other case, they select a number of people who have charges against a particular charge number and ask them what they were doing on the day they charged that number. Recent floor checks have revealed a serious number of discrepancies between time charges and activities. It is absolutely essential that we charge time to the project account or to the overhead activity code directly related to the work being performed. Errors in this area raise questions concerning the validity of our entire system and could have serious consequences.

The attached abbreviated schedule of activity codes has been prepared for your use. [This is reproduced as Exhibit 2.] I suggest that you keep this in a handy place for ready reference when you are filling out your timecards. If there are any questions, consult your supervisor or business office; they can furnish a schedule with more complete activity code definitions if you need them.

I would expect most overhead charges for project professionals to be recorded against Codes 525, 532, 535, 581, 582, and 583. Code 511 will more frequently be used by directors, managers, and their administrative staff.

It is absolutely essential that each of you take the care necessary to assure that your time is accurately charged.

Views of the Financial Vice President

Carter discussed the time charging problem on several occasions with Spencer Bean, financial vice president. Bean said that professionals did not appear to realize that deliberate falsification of timecards was as much a crime as submitting a fraudulent invoice. In both cases, a client was billed for work that actually had not been done. The situation in NRL was probably no different from that in similar organizations. For example, Bean knew of a case in a large, highly regarded university in which the salary of a professor had been charged to a research project for a whole year, even though the professor did no work on the project. Instances of this type had been uncovered and publicized from time to time by the U.S. General Accounting Office, but the publicized examples were "only the tip of the iceberg."

Bean thought that in NRL, the principal reasons for erroneous charging were as follows:

1. On the one hand, an important measure of employee performance was the percentage of "billed time"; that is, the percentage of his total time that was

recorded as a direct charge to some research project. Staff members were motivated to keep this percentage high, since it was invariably taken into account in their semiannual performance review. They, therefore, were tempted to charge time to projects even when their activities were temporarily of an overhead nature.

2. On the other hand, professionals were also judged on the basis of whether they were able to complete projects within the stated ceiling. A project overrun was considered by some managers to be as bad a sin as a low billed time percentage, and by other managers it was considered to be a worse sin. This was particularly the case with the "old-timers" because some years ago the evils of overrunning a project had been much more strongly stressed than they were currently. An overrun could occur simply because the project turned out to be more time-consuming than originally anticipated. It could also occur because project leaders made overly optimistic estimates of time requirements when the project proposal was being prepared. In some cases there was a deliberate underestimate of requirements so that a low price could be quoted in order to help get the contract, with the hope that additional funds could be negotiated when the original amount was used up. In particular, in the 1970s, government research/development funds were "tight," and some agencies insisted on an unreasonably low contract ceiling because they did not have adequate available funds. Project leaders accepted these contracts because they wanted to continue on work for such agencies, particularly when they considered the work as being exciting, important to the national interest, and leading to scientific advances.

3. Some professionals didn't see any substantial difference between a direct project charge and overhead. Either way, the client pays—in the one case as a direct charge, in the other case via the overhead rate. Getting the work done somehow was more important than who paid for it.

4. Professionals tend to be idealists. They spend their time in ways that they judge to be best, and they sincerely believe that their work benefits society. They don't want a superior, and especially they don't want an auditor, to second-guess them. They regard timekeeping in general as unnecessary paperwork.

5. Some types of overhead activity were regarded as being less desirable than others, and this tended to affect how time was charged. For example, bid and proposal costs were regarded as being high. Within this general category, "concept formulation" was regarded as being less defensible than "proposal preparation," although the line between these two activities was not sharp.

Bean had the following suggestions as possible ways to mitigate the problem:

1. There should be more training of lower level supervisors so that they would learn to act as managers, rather than as researchers. It was their responsibility, in Bean's view, to see to it that the staff charged time correctly.

2. Top management should do more to get across the message that the government has rules and NRL personnel must abide by these rules no matter how

much it may hurt to do so, and also the message that without reliable data on project and overhead costs, management would be likely to make erroneous decisions.

3. In performance reviews, there should be less criticism of project overruns and less emphasis on the billed time percentage.

Bean cautioned against overreacting to the problem. Scientists and engineers, he said, had strong opinions. Their loyalty is primarily to their profession and only secondarily to the organization in which they happen to work. If they feel that their professional activities are being affected adversely by the organization's policies, they will as a minimum resent these policies, and they may well leave the organization.

Conclusion

Carter thought that there was a good chance that alleged erroneous charges would be an important factor in the next overhead negotiation with the Department of Defense, and he wanted to have a course of action in mind if this occurred. Even if NRL got through these negotiations unscathed, the danger of trouble at some future time was present so long as erroneous charges continued to be made.

Question

What course of action should Mr. Carter pursue?

CASE 11–3   Northeast Research Laboratory (B)*

On a Friday morning in late December 1973, Sam Lacy, head of the Physical Sciences Division of Northeast Research Laboratory (NRL) thought about two letters which lay on his desk. One, which he had received a few weeks before, was a progress report from Robert Kirk, recently assigned project leader of the Exco project, who reported that earlier frictions between the NRL team and the client had lessened considerably, that high-quality research was under way, and that the prospects for retaining the Exco project on a long-term basis appeared fairly good. The other letter, which had just arrived in the morning's mail, came from Gray Kenney, a vice president of Exco, and stated that the company wished to terminate the Exco contract effective immediately.

---

* This case was prepared by Professor Robert N. Anthony. Copyright © by the President and Fellows of Harvard College. Harvard Business School case 9-175-184.

Lacy was puzzled. He remembered how pleased Gray Kenney had been only a few months before when the Exco project produced its second patentable process. On the other hand, he also recalled some of the difficulties the project had encountered within NRL which had ultimately led to the replacement of project leader Alan North in order to avoid losing the contract. Lacy decided to call in the participants in an effort to piece together an understanding of what had happened. Some of what he learned is described below. But the problem remained for him to decide what he should report to senior management. What should he recommend to avoid the recurrence of such a situation in the future?

Company Background

Northeast Research Laboratory was a multidisciplinary research and development organization employing approximately 1,000 professionals. It was organized into two main sectors, one for economics and business administration and the other for the physical and natural sciences. Within the physical and natural sciences sector, the organization was essentially by branches of science. The main units were called divisions and the subunits were called laboratories. A partial organization chart is shown in Exhibit 1.

EXHIBIT 1 Organization Chart (simplified)

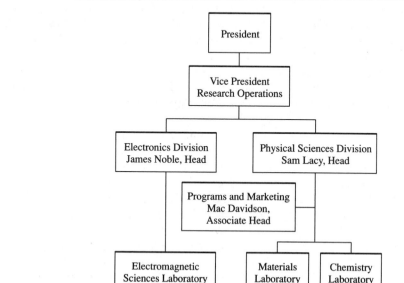

Most of the company's work was done on the basis of contracts with clients. Each contract was a project. Responsibility for the project was vested in a project leader, and through him up the organizational structure in which his laboratory was located. Typically, some members of the project team were drawn from laboratories other than that in which the project leader worked; it was the ability to put together a team with a variety of technical talents that was one of the principal strengths of a multidisciplinary laboratory. Team members worked under the direction of the project leader during the period in which they were assigned to the project. An individual might be working on more than one project concurrently. The project leader could also draw on the resources of central service organizations, such as model shops, computer services, editorial, and drafting. The project was billed for the services of these units at rates which were intended to cover their full costs.

Inception of the Exco Project

In October 1972, Gray Kenney, vice president of Exco, had telephoned Mac Davidson of NRL to outline a research project which would examine the effect of microwaves on various ores and minerals. Davidson was associate head of the Physical Sciences Division and had known Kenney for several years. During the conversation Kenney asserted that NRL ought to be particularly intrigued by the research aspects of the project, and Davidson readily agreed. Davidson was also pleased because the Physical Sciences Division was under pressure to generate more revenue, and this potentially long-term project from Exco would make good use of the available work force. In addition, senior management of NRL had recently circulated several memos indicating that more emphasis should be put on commercial rather than government work. Davidson was, however, a little concerned that the project did not fall neatly into one laboratory or even one division, but in fact required assistance from the Electronics Division to complement work that would be done in two different Physical Sciences Laboratories (the Chemistry Laboratory and the Materials Laboratory).

A few days later Davidson organized a joint client-NRL conference to determine what Exco wanted and to plan the proposal. Kenney sent his assistant, Tod Denby, who was to serve as the Exco liaison officer for the project. Representing NRL were Davidson; Sam Lacy; Dr. Robert Kirk, director of the Materials Laboratory (one of the two Physical Sciences laboratories involved in the project); Dr. Alan North, manager of Chemical Development and Engineering (and associate director of the Chemistry Laboratory); Dr. James Noble, executive director of the Electronics Division; and a few researchers chosen by Kirk and North. Davidson also would have liked to invite Dr. James Ross, director of the Chemistry Laboratory, but Ross was out of town and couldn't attend the pre-proposal meeting.

Denby described the project as a study of the use of microwaves for the conversion of basic ores and minerals to more valuable commercial products. The study was to consist of two parts:

Task A—An experimental program to examine the effect of microwaves on 50 ores and minerals, and to select those processes appearing to have the most promise.

Task B—A basic study to obtain an understanding of how and why microwaves interact with certain minerals.

It was agreed that the project would be a joint effort of three laboratories: (1) Materials, (2) Chemistry, and (3) Electromagnetic. The first two laboratories were in the Physical Sciences Division, and the last was in the Electronics Division.

Denby proposed that the contract be open-ended, with a level of effort of around $10,000–$12,000 per month. Agreement was quickly reached on the content of the proposal. Denby emphasized to the group that an early start was essential if Exco was to remain ahead of its competition.

After the meeting Lacy, who was to have overall responsibility for the project, discussed the choice of project leader with Davidson. Davidson proposed Alan North, a 37-year-old chemist who had had experience as a project leader on several projects. North had impressed Davidson at the pre-proposal meeting and seemed well suited to head the interdisciplinary team. Lacy agreed. Lacy regretted that Dr. Ross (head of the laboratory in which North worked) was unable to participate in the decision of who should head the joint project. In fact, because he was out of town, Ross was neither aware of the Exco project nor of his laboratory's involvement in it.

The following day, Alan North was told of his appointment as project leader. During the next few days, he conferred with Robert Kirk, head of the other Physical Sciences laboratory involved in the project. Toward the end of October Denby began to exert pressure on North to finalize the proposal, stating that the substance had been agreed upon at the pre-proposal conference. North thereupon drafted a five-page letter as a substitute for a formal proposal, describing the nature of the project and outlining the procedures and equipment necessary. At Denby's request, North included a paragraph which authorized members of the client's staff to visit NRL frequently and observe progress of the research program. The proposal's cover sheet contained approval signatures from the laboratories and divisions involved. North signed for his own area and for laboratory director Ross. He telephoned Dr. Noble of the Electronics Division, relayed the client's sense of urgency, and Noble authorized North to sign for him. Davidson signed for the Physical Sciences Division as a whole.

At this stage, North relied principally on the advice of colleagues within his own division. As he did not know personally the individuals in the Electronics Division, they were not called upon at this point. Since North understood informally that the director of the Electromagnetic Sciences Laboratory, Dr. Perkins, was quite busy and often out of town, North did not attempt to discuss the project with Perkins.

After the proposal had been signed and mailed, Dr. Perkins was sent a copy. It listed the engineering equipment which the client wanted purchased for the project and described how it was to be used. Perkins worried that performance characteristics of the power supply (necessary for quantitative measurement) specified in the proposal were inadequate for the task. He asked North about it and North said that the client had made up his mind as to the microwave equipment he wanted and how it was to be used. Denby had said he was paying for that equipment and intended to move it to Exco's laboratories after the completion of the NRL contract.

All these events had transpired rather quickly. By the time Dr. Ross, director of the Chemistry Laboratory, returned, the proposal for the Exco project had been signed and accepted. Ross went to see Lacy and said that he had dealt with Denby on a previous project and had serious misgivings about working with him. Lacy assuaged some of Ross's fears by observing that if anyone could succeed in working with Denby it would be North—a flexible man, professionally competent, who could move with the tide and get along with clients of all types.

Conduct of the Project

Thus the project began. Periodically, when decisions arose, North would seek opinions from division management. However, he was somewhat unclear about whom he should talk to. Davidson had been the person who had actually appointed him project leader. Normally, however, North worked for Ross. Although Kirk's laboratory was heavily involved in the project, Kirk was very busy with other Materials Laboratory work. Adding to his uncertainty, North periodically received telephone calls from Perkins of the Electronics Division, whom he didn't know well. Perkins expected to be heavily involved in the project.

Difficulties and delays began to plague the project. The microwave equipment specified by the client was not delivered by the manufacturer on schedule, and there were problems in filtering the power supply of the radio frequency source. Over the objection of NRL Electromagnetic Sciences engineers, but at the insistence of the client, one of the chemical engineers tried to improve the power supply filter. Eventually the equipment had to be sent back to the manufacturer for modification. This required several months.

In the spring of 1973, Denby, who had made his presence felt from the outset, began to apply strong pressure. "Listen," he said to North, "top management of Exco is starting to get on my back and we need results. Besides, I'm up for review in four months and I can't afford to let this project affect my promotion." Denby was constantly at NRL during the next few months. He was often in the labs conferring individually with members of the NRL teams. Denby also visited North's office frequently.

A number of related problems began to surface. North had agreed to do both experimental and theoretical work for this project, but Denby's constant pushing for experimental results began to tilt the emphasis. Theoretical studies began to lapse, and experimental work became the focus of the Exco project. From time to time North argued that the theoretical work should precede or at least accompany the experimental program, but Denby's insistence on concrete results led North to temporarily deemphasize the theoretical work. Symptoms of this shifting emphasis were evident. One day a senior researcher from Kirk's laboratory came to North to complain that people were being "stolen" from his team. "How can we do a balanced project if the theoretical studies are not given enough work force?" he asked. North explained the client's position and asked the researcher to bear with this temporary realignment of the project's resources.

As the six-month milestone approached, Denby expressed increasing dissatisfaction with the project's progress. In order to have concrete results to report to Exco management, he directed North a number of times to change the direction of the research. On several occasions various members of the project team had vigorous discussions with Denby about the risks of changing results without laying a careful foundation. North himself spent a good deal of time talking with Denby on this subject, but Denby seemed to discount its importance. Denby began to avoid North and to spend most of his time with the other team members. Eventually the experimental program, initially dedicated to a careful screening of some 50 materials, deteriorated to a somewhat frantic and erratic pursuit of what appeared to be "promising leads." Lacy and Noble played little or no role in this shift of emphasis.

On June 21, 1973, Denby visited North in his office and severely criticized him for proposing a process (hydrochloric acid pickling) that was economically infeasible. In defense, North asked an NRL economist to check his figures. The economist reported back that North's numbers were sound and that, in fact, a source at U.S. Steel indicated that hydrochloric acid pickling was "generally more economic than the traditional process and was increasingly being adopted." Through this and subsequent encounters, the relationship between Denby and North became increasingly strained.

Denby continued to express concern about the Exco project's payoff. In an effort to save time, he discouraged the NRL team from repeating experiments, a practice that was designed to ensure accuracy. Data received from initial experiments were frequently taken as sufficiently accurate, and after hasty analysis were adopted for the purposes of the moment. Not surprisingly, Denby periodically discovered errors in these data. He informed NRL of them.

Denby's visits to NRL became more frequent as the summer progressed. Some days he would visit all three laboratories, talking to the researchers involved and asking them about encouraging leads. North occasionally cautioned Denby against too much optimism. Nonetheless, North continued to oblige the client by restructuring the Exco project to allow for more "production line" scheduling of experiments and for less systematic research.

In August, North discovered that vertile could be obtained from iron ore. This discovery was a significant one, and the client applied for a patent. If the reaction could be proved commercially, its potential would be measured in millions of dollars. Soon thereafter, the NRL team discovered that the operation could, in fact, be handled commercially in a rotary kiln. The client was notified and soon began a pilot plant that would use the rotary kiln process.

Exco's engineering department, after reviewing the plans for the pilot plant, rejected them. It was argued that the rotary process was infeasible and that a fluid bed process would have to be used instead. Denby returned to NRL and insisted on an experiment to test the fluid bed process. North warned Denby that agglomeration (a sticking together of the material) would probably take place. It did. Denby was highly upset, reported to Gray Kenney that he had not received "timely" warning of the probability of agglomeration taking place, and indicated that he had been misled as to the feasibility of the rotary kiln process.[1]

Work continued, and two other "disclosures of invention" were turned over to the client by the end of September.

Personnel Changes

On September 30, Denby came to North's office to request that Charles Fenton be removed from the Exco project. Denby reported he had been watching Fenton in the Electromagnetic Laboratory, which he visited often, and had observed that Fenton spent relatively little time on the Exco project. North, who did not know Fenton well, agreed to look into it. But Denby insisted that Fenton be removed immediately and threatened to terminate the contract if he were allowed to remain.

North was unable to talk to Fenton before taking action because Fenton was on vacation. He did talk to Fenton as soon as he returned, and the researcher admitted that due to the pressure of other work he had not devoted as much time or effort to the Exco work as perhaps he should have.

Three weeks later, Denby called a meeting with Mac Davidson and Sam Lacy. It was their first meeting since the pre-proposal conference for the Exco project. Denby was brief and to the point:

Denby: I'm here because we have to replace North. He's become increasingly difficult to work with and is obstructing the progress of the project.

Lacy: but North is an awfully good man . . .

Davidson: Look, he's come up with some good solid work thus far. What about the process of extracting vertile from iron ore he came up with. And . . .

Denby: I'm sorry, but we have to have a new project leader. I don't mean to be abrupt, but it's either replace North or forget the contract.

---

[1] Ten months later the client was experimenting with the rotary kiln process for producing vertile from iron ore in his own laboratory.

Davidson reluctantly appointed Robert Kirk project leader and informed North of the decision. North went to see Davidson a few days later. Davidson told him that although management did not agree with the client, North had been replaced in order to save the contract. Later Dr. Lacy told North the same thing. Neither Lacy nor Davidson made an effort to contact Exco senior management on the matter.

Following the change of project leadership, the record became more difficult to reconstruct. It appeared that Kirk made many efforts to get the team together, but morale remained low. Denby continued to make periodic visits to NRL but found that the NRL researchers were not talking as freely with him as they had in the past. Denby became skeptical about the project's value. Weeks slipped by. No further breakthroughs emerged.

Lacy's Problem

Dr. Lacy had received weekly status reports on the project, the latest of which is shown in Exhibit 2. He had had a few informal conversations about the project, principally with North and Kirk. He had not read the reports submitted to Exco. If the project had been placed on NRL's "problem list," which comprised about 10 percent of the projects which seemed to be experiencing the most difficulty, Lacy would have received a written report on its status weekly, but the Exco project was not on that list.

With the background given above, Lacy reread Kenney's letter terminating the Exco contract. It seemed likely that Kenney, too, had not had full knowledge of what went on during the project's existence. In his letter, Kenney mentioned the "glowing reports" which reached his ears in the early stages of the work. These reports, which came to him only from Denby, were later significantly modified, and Denby apparently implied that NRL had been "leading him on." Kenney pointed to the complete lack of economic evaluation of alternative processes in the experimentation. He seemed unaware of the fact that at Denby's insistence all economic analysis was supposed to be done by the client. Kenney was most dissatisfied that NRL had not complied with all the provisions of the proposal, particularly those that required full screening of all materials and the completion of the theoretical work.

Lacy wondered why Denby's changes of the proposal had not been documented by the NRL team. Why hadn't he heard more of the problems of the Exco project before? Lacy requested a technical evaluation of the project from the economics process director, and asked Davidson for *his* evaluation of the project. These reports are given in Exhibits 3 and 4. When he reviewed these reports, Lacy wondered what, if any, additional information he should submit to NRL senior management.

EXHIBIT 2 Weekly Project Status Report

| PROJECT/ACCOUNT STATUS REPORT | ORG 325 | PROJ/ACCT 3273 | SUB 000 | W/O 000 | WEEK ENDING DATE 12-22-73 | TYPE PROJ | REV TYPE INDUS | PRICE SCA | CLIENT YD | INT/DOM DOMESTIC | NOTICES | PAGE 1 |

DIVISION	DEPARTMENT	SUPERVISOR	LEADER
PHYSICAL SCI	CHEMISTRY LAB	ROBERT KIRK	ROBERT KIRK

PROJECT TITLE: MICROWAVES IN CONVERSION OF BASIC ORES AND MINERALS

INST	READY DATE	STOP WORK DATE	TERM DATE	BURDEN %	OVERHEAD %	FEE %
EXCO	11-06-72	- -	11-06-74	28.00	105.00	15.00

COST CATEGORIES	OBJECT CODE	DOLLARS PTD13WK1	TO DATE	LABOR HOURS ESTIMATE	TO DATE	BALANCE
SUPERVISOR	(11, 12)		560			36
SENIOR	(13)	192	17986			1348
PROFESSIONAL	(14)	150	16787			1678
TECHNICAL	(15)	529	5299			1037
CLER/SUPP	(16, 17, 18)		301			84
OTHER	(19)	72	72			12
LABOR (S. T.)	(10, 19)	943	41005			1644
BURDEN	(41, 42)	248	11481			
OVERHEAD		1227	55110			
OVERTIME PREM	(21)	160	1540			
OVS./OTH. PREM	(22-29)	242	476			
TOTAL PERSONNEL COSTS		2820	109612			
TRAVEL	(56-59)		776			
SUBCONTRACT	(36)					
MATERIAL	(41, 42)		3726			
EQUIPMENT	(43)					
COMPUTER	(37, 45)					
COMMUN	(62, 63, 70, 71)	2	507			
CONSULTANT	(74, 75)					
REPORT COST	(44, 47)					
OTHER M&S		54	99			
TOTAL M&S COST		56	5098			
COMMITMENTS			26847			
TOTAL LESS FEE		2876	141557			
FEE (15.00)		158	24376			
TOTAL		3031	165933			

LAST BILLING: DATE 11-30-73, AMOUNT 11350

ACCOUNT STATUS TO DATE: BILLED 154583, PAID 154583

		ESTIMATED	BALANCE
TIME BALANCE %	39.4	250435	108878
COST BALANCE %	43.5	37565	13189
TIME BALANCE WKS.	41	288000	122067

TRANSACTIONS RECORDED 12-15-73 - 12-22-73

LABOR

ORG	ID	W/E DATE	T S NO	OBJ	NAME	WEEK	TO DATE
322	02345	12-22-73	363073	13	KIRK	6.0	150
322	02345	12-22-73	363073	22	KIRK	6.0	
322	03212	12-22-73	363082	13	DENSMORE	8.0	25
322	03260	12-22-73	236544	14	COOK	15.0	30
325	12110	12-08-73	C30093	15	COOK	15.0	82
325	12110	12-15-73	236548	15	HOWARD	36.0	
325	12110	12-22-73	376147	15	HOWARD	8.0	
325	12357	12-22-73	376149	15	SPELTZ	15.0	68
325	12369	12-22-73	376150	15	GYURE	15.0	17
325	12384	12-22-73	R08416	15	DILLON	40.0-	44
325	2397	12-22-73	336527	15	NAGY	31.0	31
325	12397	12-22-73	336527	21	NAGY	15.0	
652	12475	12-22-73	236548	15	KAIN	8.0	20
652	12475	12-22-73	236548	21	KAIN	15.0	

	HOURS	DOLLARS
LABOR (STRAIGHT TIME)	117.0	943
PAYROLL BURDEN		248
OVERHEAD RECOVERY		1227
OVERTIME PREMIUM LABOR	30.0	160
OTHER PREMIUM LABOR	6.0	242
TOTAL PERSONNEL COSTS		2820 S

MATERIALS & SERVICES

PO NO	REF NO	OBJ	DESCRIPTION	REQUESTOR	
61289	54065	48	438 REA EXPRESS	KIRK	42
17234	87413	48	456 GEO SUPPLY CO	COOK	10
	04461	71	448 P.T.&T. 326-6200	NAGY	2
			TOTAL M&S COSTS		56 S
			FEE		158
			TRANSACTION TOTAL		3034 T

COMMITMENT STATUS TO DATE

PO NO		OBJ	VENDOR/DESCRIPTION	TOTAL	CHARGES	BALANCE
A61289	11-21-73	41	MINNESOTA MINING	111	61	50
A61313	11-23-73	41	ALDRICH CHEMICAL	348		348
A95209	11-28-73	43	TENNECO CHEMICAL CO	5		5
A95093	11-15-73	41	UNION CARBIDE CORP	23194		23194
B95104	11-19-73	37	SCIENTIFIC PRODUCTS	600		600
B95232	11-25-73	41	VAN WATERS & ROGERS	2500		2500
018046	12-15-73	57	ROGER MD	300	150	150
				26847		26847 T

EXHIBIT 3 Technical Evaluation

BY RONALD M. BENTON

Director, Process Economics Program

Principal Conclusions

1. The original approach to the investigation as presented in the proposal is technically sound. The accomplishments could have been greater had this been followed throughout the course of the project, but the altered character of the investigation did not prevent accomplishment of fruitful research.
2. The technical conduct of this project on NRL's part was good despite the handicaps under which the work was carried out. Fundamental and theoretical considerations were employed in suggesting the course of research and in interpreting the data. There is no evidence to indicate that the experimental work itself was badly executed.
3. Significant accomplishments of this project were as follows:

    a. *Extraction of vertile from iron ore by several alternative processes.* Conception of these processes was based on fundamental considerations and demonstrated considerable imagination. As far as the work was carried out at NRL, one or more of these processes offers promise of commercial feasibility.
    b. *Nitrogen fixation.* This development resulted from a laboratory observation. The work was not carried far enough to ascertain whether or not the process offers any commercial significance. It was, however, shown that the yield of nitrogen oxides was substantially greater than has previously been achieved by either thermal or plasma processes.
    c. *Reduction of nickel oxide and probably also garnerite to nickel.* These findings were never carried beyond very preliminary stages and the ultimate commercial significance cannot be assessed at this time.
    d. *Discovery that microwave plasmas can be generated at atmospheric pressure.* Again the commercial significance of this finding cannot be appraised at present. However, it opens the possibility that many processes can be conducted economically that would be too costly at the reduced pressures previously thought to be necessary.

4. The proposal specifically stated that the selection of processes for scale-up and economic studies would be the responsibility of the client. I interpret this to mean that NRL was not excluded from making recommendations based on economic considerations. Throughout the course of the investigation, NRL did take economic factors into account in its recommendations.
5. Actual and effective decisions of significance were not documented by NRL and only to a limited extent by the client. There was no attempt on NRL's part to convey the nature or consequences of such decisions to the client's management.
6. The NRL reports were not well prepared even considering the circumstances under which they were written.
7. It is possible that maximum advantage was not taken of the technical capabilities of personnel in the Electromagnetic Sciences Laboratory. Furthermore, they appeared to have been incompletely informed as to the overall approach to the investigation.
8. There was excessive involvement of the client in the details of experimental work. Moreover, there were frequent changes of direction dictated by the client. Undoubtedly these conditions hampered progress and adequate consideration of major objectives and accomplishments.
9. In the later stages of the project, the client rejected a number of processes and equipment types proposed by NRL for investigation of their commercial feasibility. From the information available to me, I believe that these judgments were based on arbitrary opinions as to technical feasibility and superficial extrapolations from other experience as to economic feasibility that are probably not valid.

Evaluation of Client's Complaints

Following are the comments responding to the points raised by the client management during your conversation:

1. *Client anticipated a "full research capability." He had hoped for participation by engineers, chemists, economists and particularly counted on the provision of an "analytical capability." It*

EXHIBIT 3 *(continued)*

---

was this combination of talents that brought him to NRL rather than [a competitor]. He feels that the project was dominated almost exclusively by chemists.

This complaint is completely unfounded. All the disciplines appropriate to the investigation (as called for in the proposal) were engaged on the project to some degree. In addition, men of exceptional capabilities devoted an unusually large amount of time to the project. The client never officially altered the conditions of the proposal stating that no economic studies should be performed by NRL and there was no explicit expression of this desire on the part of the client until near the project termination.

2. *The analytical services were poor. They were sometimes erroneous and there were frequent "deviations." Data was given to the client too hastily, without further experiment and careful analysis, and as a result a significant amount of the data was not reproducible. NRL was inclined to be overly optimistic. "Glowing reports" would be made only to be cancelled or seriously modified later.*

There is no way of determining whether the analytical services were good or bad, but one can never expect all analytical work to be correct or accurate. Because the client insisted on obtaining raw data, they would certainly receive some analyses that were erroneous. With respect to the allegation that NRL was overly optimistic, there were no recommendations or opinions expressed in the NRL reports or included in the client's notes that can be placed in this category. Whether or not there were verbal statements of this kind cannot of course be ascertained.

3. *There were "errors in the equations and the client was not informed of the changes." This refers to the case of a computer program that had not been "de-bugged." It was the client who discovered the errors and informed NRL of the discrepancies. (The program was eventually straightened out by the Math Sciences Department.)*

The client's complaint that they were given a computer program which had not been "de-bugged" is valid, but it is not certain that the project leadership gave them the program without exercising normal precautions for its accuracy. The program was developed by a person not presently with NRL and for another project. He transmitted it without any warning that "de-bugging" had not been conducted. It is even possible that the existence and source of error could not have been determined in his usage and would only appear in a different application.

4. *NRL told the client that the "vertile from iron ore" process could be handled commercially in a rotary kiln process and then was informed by his Engineering Division that this was completely infeasible. Plans were then shifted to a fluid bed process and much time and money had been wasted. Client claims that he was not warned that in the fluid bed agglomeration would probably take place. Agglomeration did take place the first time the process was tried ("open boats") and the client was greatly upset.*

It is unclear whether the original suggestion that a rotary kiln be used in the vertile process came from the client or NRL. In any event, it is a logical choice of equipment and is used for the production of such low cost items as cement. Without the benefit of at least pilot plant experience that revealed highly abnormal and unfavorable conditions leading to excessive costs, no one would be in a position to state that such equipment would be uneconomic. It is true that a completely standard rotary kiln probably could not be employed, if for no other reason than to prevent the escape of toxic hydrogen sulfide gas from the equipment. At least special design would be needed and probably some mechanical development. However, it is rare that any new process can be installed without special design and development and it is naive to expect otherwise.

I do not know, of course, how much time was actually spent on the "elaborate plans" for the vertile process using a rotary kiln. I can, however, compare it with generally similar types of studies that we carry out in the Process Economics Program. For this kind of process we would expend about 45 engineering man-hours, and the design calculations would be more detailed than the client's engineer made (his cost estimates incidentally reflected inexperience in this field). I doubt, therefore, that this effort represented a serious expenditure of money and would not have been a complete waste even if the process had been based on a partially false premise. The contention that the client was not informed of the agglomeration properties of the vertile while the reaction was taking place seem unlikely. The client's representatives were too intimately

EXHIBIT 3 *(continued)*

concerned with the experimental work that it would be unusual if the subject had not been raised. Moreover, it is doubtful that the client would have been deterred by NRL's warning, in view of their subsequent insistence that considerable effort be devoted to finding means by which a fluid bed could be operated.

5. *The meetings were poorly planned by NRL.*

There is no way of evaluating this complaint, but certainly the extreme frequency of the meetings would not be conducive to a well-organized meeting.

6. *Experimental procedures were not well planned.*

Apparently this refers to the client's desire that experiments be planned in detail as much as three months in advance. Such an approach might conceivably be useful merely for purposes of gathering routine data. It is naive to think that research can or should be planned to this degree and certainly if NRL had acceded to the request it would have been a fruitless time-consuming exercise.

7. *Economic support was not given by NRL.*

As mentioned above, the proposed specifically excluded NRL from economic evaluations, but NRL did make use of economic considerations in its suggestions and recommendations.

8. *NRL promised to obtain some manganese nodules but never produced them.*

Manganese nodules were obtained by NRL but no experiments were ever run with them. Many other screening experiments originally planned were never carried out because of the changed direction of the project. It seems likely, therefore, that the failure to conduct an experiment with manganese nodules was not NRL's responsibility.

9. *The client claims that he does not criticize NRL for failing "to produce a process." He says that he never expected one, that he wanted a good screening of ores and reactions as called for in the proposal, and that he had hoped for results from the theoretical studies—Task B. This he feels he did not get. We did not do what the proposal called for.*

The statement that a process was not expected seems entirely contrary to the course of the project. There was universal agreement among NRL personnel involved that almost immediately after the project was initiated it was converted into a crash program to find a commercial process. In fact, the whole tenor of the project suggests a degree of urgency incompatible with a systematic research program. It is quite true that the theoretical studies as a part of Task B were never carried out. According to the project leader this part of the proposal was never formally abandoned, it was merely postponed. Unfortunately, this situation was never documented by NRL, as was the case with other significant effective decisions.

Additional Comments

1. It appears that the first indication that the client expected economic studies or evaluations of commercial feasibility occurred during the summer of 1973. At this time the project leader was severely criticized by the client's representatives for having proposed a process (hydrochloric acid pickling) that was economically infeasible. The basis for this criticism was that hydrochloric acid pickling of steel had not proved to be economically feasible. It is totally unreasonable to expect that NRL would have access to information of this kind, and such a reaction would certainly have the effect of discouraging any further contributions of an economic or commercial nature by NRL rather than encouraging them. Actually it is patently ridiculous to directly translate economic experience of the steel industry with steel pickling to leaching a sulfided titanium ore. Nevertheless, I directed an inquiry to a responsible person in U.S. Steel as to the status of hydrochloric acid pickling. His response (based on the consensus of their experts) was diametrically opposite to the client's information. While there are situations that are more favorable to sulfuric acid pickling, hydrochloric acid pickling is generally more economic and is becoming increasingly adopted.

2. The reports written by NRL were requested by the client, but on an urgent and "not fancy" basis. If such were the case, it is understandable that the project leader would be reluctant to expend enough time and money on the report to make it representative of NRL's normal reports. However, the nature of the report seems to indicate that they are directed toward the same individuals with whom NRL was in frequent contact, or persons with a strong interest in the purely scientific aspects. The actual accomplishments of the project were not brought out in a manner that would have been readily understandable to client's management.

EXHIBIT 3   *(concluded)*

Recommendations

It is recommended that consideration be given to the establishment of a simple formal procedure by which high risk projects could be identified at the proposal stage and brought to the attention of the division vice president. There should also be a formal procedure, operative after project acceptance, in which specific responsibilities are assigned for averting or correcting subsequent developments that would be adverse to NRL's and the client's interests.

Some of the factors that would contribute to a high risk condition are insufficient funding, insufficient time, low chance of successfully attaining objectives, an unsophisticated client, public or private political conditions, and so forth. The characteristics that made this a high risk project were certainly apparent at the time the proposal was prepared.

EXHIBIT 4

MEMORANDUM

January 8, 1974

To: Sam Lacy
From: Mac Davidson
Re: The Exco Project—Conclusions

The decision to undertake this project was made without sufficient consideration of the fact that this was a "high risk" project.

The proposal was technically sound and within the capabilities of the groups assigned to work on the project.

There was virtually no coordination between the working elements of Physical Sciences and Electronics in the preparation of the proposal.

The technical conduct of this project, with few exceptions, was, considering the handicaps under which the work was carried out, good and at times outstanding. The exceptions were primarily due to lack of attention to detail.

The NRL reports were not well prepared, even considering the circumstances under which they were written.

The client, acting under pressure from his own management, involved himself excessively in the details of experimental work and dictated frequent changes of direction and emphasis. The proposal opened the door to this kind of interference.

There was no documentation by NRL of the decisions made by the client which altered the character, direction, and emphasis of the work.

There was no serious attempt on the part of NRL to convey the nature or consequence of the above actions to the client.

Less than half of the major complaints made by the client concerning NRL's performance are valid.

The project team acquiesced too readily in the client's interference and management acquiesced too easily to the client's demands.

Management exercised insufficient supervision and gave inadequate support to the project leader in his relations with the client.

There were no "overruns" either in time or funds.

Questions

    1. What additional information should Dr. Lacy submit to NRL senior management?
    2. What should Dr. Lacy recommend be done to avoid similar problems with other contracts?

CASE 11–4   WIC Program*

In late 1986, Emily Foster, the Assistant Director for Food Delivery at the Women, Infants, and Children Program (WIC), was pressing National Bank for its monthly report, which provided essential information for monitoring most aspects of the supplemental food program. Bank officers were responding that it was impossible to produce a timely report when WIC was responsible for the delay. A tense situation threatened to impair an otherwise good relationship.

As part of its contract with the food program, the National Bank provided space for three WIC Voucher Monitors, whose job it was to screen WIC's food and infant formula vouchers deposited by store owners in their bank accounts, and to reject violative vouchers. WIC routinely rejected 3,500 to 4,500 vouchers a month for violations, at an average voucher price of $7.60.

Data on valid payments and *bounces* (as rejections were called) were keyed into the bank's computer system and became part of a comprehensive monthly report of food delivery activity in the WIC Program. The bank's contract called for it to file the report for each month at WIC on or before the 21st day of the following month.

Vouchers were similar to checks. Issued to participants in the WIC Program, they were redeemed at authorized food stores, which deposited them directly in their bank accounts. Like regular checks they were cleared through the Federal Reserve System and were subject to a state law requiring payment within 24 hours. In fact, since the WIC Program was liable for payment of any voucher that was not cleared within the required 24 hours, they were assumed to be paid unless rejected by the WIC Voucher Monitors within the 24-hour period.

At one point that fall, WIC screening activity was 21 workdays behind schedule; and, therefore, vouchers that were found to be in violation of WIC redemption regulations were being rejected by the monitors as much as a month after the vendors had deposited them.

---

* This case was prepared by Nancy E. Fiske under the direction of Professor David W. Young. Copyright © by David W. Young. Distributed by the Accounting Curriculum Center, Boston University School of Management.

Background

The Special Supplemental Food Program for Women, Infants, and Children was established in 1972 (with an amendment to the federal Child Nutrition Act of 1966) to provide supplemental foods to low-income, pregnant, postpartum, and nursing mothers, and to infants and children up to age 5 who were diagnosed to be at nutritional risk. (Standards for determining *nutritional risk* were defined by the United States Department of Agriculture and further refined by each state administering a program.) In addition to specially prescribed foods, WIC also provided nutrition counseling, education, and access to health care.

WIC enjoyed strong bipartisan support in Congress. In fact, when funding for other nutrition programs was being cut in the early years of the first Reagan administration, WIC received a substantial increase. In hearings before the Senate Subcommittee on Nutrition, the Assistant Secretary of Agriculture testified:

> [WIC] is amazingly cost-effective. Our 1982 budget contains a substantial increase for the program, primarily because several recent studies have demonstrated the value of the WIC Program. One study . . . found that the incidence of low birthweight among infants whose mothers participated in the WIC Program during the prenatal period was markedly less than among infants whose mothers, although eligible for the Program, did not participate.
>
> The reduction in incidence of low birthweight babies led to much lower hospitalization costs. The study estimated that each dollar spent in the prenatal components of the WIC Program resulted in a $3 reduction in hospitalization costs, since the number of low birthweight infants who had to be hospitalized was significantly reduced.[1]

Other national evaluations and studies linked WIC with increasing weight gain among low-income pregnant women, reduced late fetal deaths, improved cognitive development among children, and increased head circumference at birth.

The Local WIC

"I like WIC. It's a good, essential program," began Jack Mason, the National Bank calling officer assigned to manage the WIC account in the Governmental Services Division of the bank. As a former staff person in the state legislature and manager of a number of low-income advocacy and planning agencies, Mason understood the issues posed by publicly funded human services programs.

> I'm spending much more time with WIC now—and I like that. WIC represents to me where I come from—it's a movement type of organization. People there are absolutely dedicated to the reason WIC exists, and you can feel it when you go there. Working with WIC gives me a chance to do good things for people.

---

[1] Carol Tucker Foreman, in hearing before Senate Subcommittee on Nutrition, April 1980; as quoted in *Performance and Credibility,* Joseph S. Wholey, ed. (Lexington, Mass.: Lexington Books, 1986), p. 277.

There are two things that WIC needs to be concerned about. First, WIC should be primarily concerned with providing food to low-income women and children. Secondarily WIC needs to be concerned about the business aspects of the program—but not at the expense of the first goal.

My superiors here don't necessarily have a strong love for human service clients, but they'll work on the issue if the contract can earn a profit. And WIC is a good contract for this bank. We reconcile about three million vouchers annually, and the profit is considerable. It's good public policy and it's good business for the bank to support WIC.

The philosophy here is one of relationship banking. It's important not only to earn the client's faith and confidence, but also to give a high quality product. This is probably the only bank in town that the WIC director could call up if funding were in trouble, and our lobbyist would be down at the capital in a minute speaking to the Senate President.

Program Organization

Eighty percent of the WIC Program funding was through a cash grant from the Food and Nutrition Service of the United States Department of Agriculture. The remaining 20 percent was from supplemental funding by the state legislature. In Fiscal Year 1987, the WIC budget was $34.3 million, which was intended to service a projected monthly caseload of 68,500 participants. Eighty percent of that budget, or $27.4 million, was designated for food costs; the remaining 20 percent was budgeted for administration.

The WIC Program had experienced significant growth since its inception in 1975. During the three most recent fiscal years, the actual caseload had grown by 40 percent from a monthly average of 46,000 participants to 64,200, but a needs assessment done in the spring of 1986 put the eligible population at 145,000.

The WIC Program was administered by the State Department of Public Health. The WIC unit was located in the Maternal and Child Health Section of the Division of Family Health Services. It was a relatively small unit, with approximately 30 employees. The WIC unit administered the program through contracts awarded to local agencies—usually either a health agency or a Community Action Program—in 35 different catchment areas in the state. Local agencies in turn established local WIC programs, which then received programmatic direction from the state agency.

The local programs determined the nutritional needs of their participants, and prescribed packages of vouchers which could be redeemed for the foods designated on the face of each voucher. "Food messages" contained on each voucher stipulated the kinds of foods for which the voucher could be exchanged, and included infant formula, milk, cheese, cereal, juice, peanut butter, beans, and eggs, in specified amounts. Participants could purchase up to the entire amount of the food message within 30 days from the issuance date on the voucher; they were required to use a WIC-authorized food vendor or pharmacy, that is, a vendor who contracted with the local program.

A sample voucher is shown in Exhibit 1. There were 66 different voucher types, each with a different maximum redemption price determined by the shelf prices

EXHIBIT 1 Sample WIC Voucher

Front (voucher face):

WIC PROGRAM

WIC

005 LOCATION · 9907797 VOUCHER NO · 14 · 9907797 DATE OF ISSUE · 15

NAME OF PARTICIPANT

IRON-FORTIFIED INFANT FORMULA (MILK/SOY BASED)
8 (13 OZ.) CANS CONCENTRATE
OR
2 (1 LB.) CANS POWDERED

NOT VALID WITHOUT WIC VENDOR AUTHORIZATION STAMP

6-2/110 ACTUAL WIC PURCHASE PRICE $

UNAUTHORIZED VENDORS MAY NOT ACCEPT THIS VOUCHER

I CERTIFY RECEIPT OF VOUCHER FROM THE WIC PROGRAM

THE CORRECT PRICE WAS WRITTEN IN MY PRESENCE

PARTICIPANT ID NO

H

IMPROPER USE OF THIS VOUCHER IS SUBJECT TO STATE AND FEDERAL PROSECUTION

NOT VALID IN EXCESS OF $20.
PAY ONLY TO THE ORDER OF AN AUTHORIZED WIC VENDOR
VENDOR: VOID FOR PURCHASE 30 DAYS AFTER DATE OF ISSUE
VENDOR MUST DEPOSIT WITHIN 60 DAYS FROM DATE OF ISSUE

Back (voucher reverse):

I CERTIFY, UNDER PENALTY OF PERJURY, THAT THE PRICE SHOWN ON THE FACE OF THIS VOUCHER IS THE CORRECT AND TRUE PRICE OF THE AUTHORIZED WIC FOODS PURCHASED.

VENDOR ENDORSEMENT

WIC APPROVED FOODS

MILK No chocolate milk

Fluid - whole, lowfat skim/nonfat
(gallons, half gallons, or quarts)
Evaporated - whole, skim
Dry - whole, lowfat, nonfat

CHEESE Domestic only

(No cheese food, cheese food product or cheese spread allowed)
American
Brick
Colby
Cheddar
Monterey Jack
Mozzarella - whole, part-skim
Muenster
Provolone
Swiss

JUICE 100% fruit juice only

Orange - bottle, carton, frozen
Apple - DeMoulas, frozen
Seneca, frozen in red cans
Hood, carton
West Lynn Creamery - carton
Grapefruit - bottle, carton, frozen
(One 12-oz. can frozen may substitute for two 6-oz. cans frozen.

EGGS

Grade A large

PEANUT BUTTER

Any brand

DRIED PEAS or BEANS

Any type or brand, in bags only

CEREAL

Cream of Wheat
Regular
Quick
Instant
Mix 'n Eat Regular
Halfsies
Kellogg's Bran Flakes
Kix
Maypo
30-Second Oatmeal
Vermont Style Hot Oat Cereal
Maltex
Product 19
Quaker Instant Oatmeal
Regular
Total
Total Corn Flakes

INFANT FORMULA

Iron-fortified Liquid concentrate or powder milk- or soy-based (Ready-to-feed, low-iron, non-iron or prescription formulas only when specified on voucher face)*

INFANT CEREAL

Dry, iron-fortified, any brand
(No cereals with added fruit allowed)

INFANT JUICE

Any flavor or brand

Front   Back

submitted competitively by vendors, initially as part of their application, and quarterly thereafter.

At the time a participant picked up vouchers, he or she was required to sign both a register and the vouchers. At the time of purchase the participant was required to sign the voucher again as certification that the price written on the voucher by the vendor was correct. Signatures had to match. The vendor would later stamp the voucher with an authorizing vendor identification stamp, endorse the voucher, and submit it to his or her bank for deposit like any other check. This voucher system is shown schematically in Exhibit 2.

EXHIBIT 2 WIC Voucher System

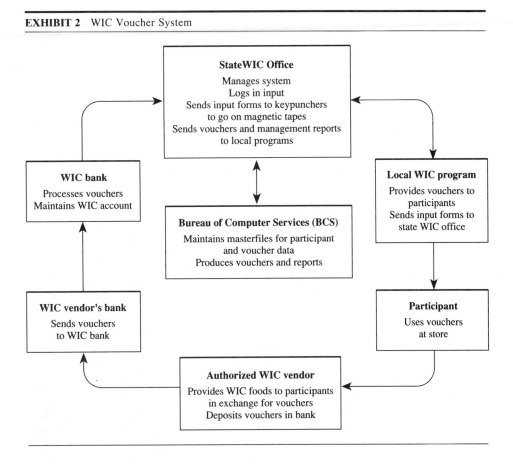

Vendor Controls

In order to become WIC-authorized, a vendor had to sign a five-page agreement containing a total of 58 requirements for the proper acceptance of vouchers. Incorporated into the agreement was a sanction policy which described the method of disqualifying vendors, and itemized sanction points applicable for each type of violation. Point values ranged from 0 to 10, and accumulation of 10 or more points was a basis for disqualification.

The state agency and local programs shared the responsibility for monitoring vendors for compliance with WIC regulations. Local programs were authorized to perform on-site reviews of the business as well as to respond to participant complaints about vendor abuse. The state agency monitored vendors through visual screening of vouchers and through investigative "compliance buys," which were often initiated because of a suspected violation.

An important component of vendor monitoring was the local programs' education of participants in the proper use of WIC vouchers: certification that the correct price had been entered *before* countersigning the voucher, selection of only WIC-authorized foods, not using the voucher before the issuance date noted on the front, etc. A typical complaint from a vendor was that many of the redemption violations were due to participant abuse and that the local program was not doing an adequate job of preparing participants to use the program properly.

Sanctioning of vendors involved warnings, application of sanction points, denial of payment, disqualification, and recoupment of payment. Much of the sanctioning activity depended on the availability of WIC Voucher Monitors stationed at the bank for locating and screening either current or previously-paid vouchers for abuse.

Voucher Processing

Vouchers were drawn on the WIC food account at the National Bank. Two part-time WIC Voucher Monitors worked in the space provided by the bank, and visually screened the vouchers for violations of the redemption procedure. Reasons for violations included missing or non-matching signatures, missing or invalid vendor identification stamp, missing or invalid local WIC program stamp, submission after the expiration date, missing or invalid vendor endorsement, the price written in pencil, overcharging, and charging a fixed price for a voucher with combinations of foods.

The WIC Voucher Monitors screened approximately 12,000 to 15,000 vouchers a day. When a violation was found, the monitor recorded the serial number, vendor code, reason for rejection, and voucher price on both a purge sheet and a credit slip. The data were then given to the bank's bookkeeping department so that the payment could be removed from the list of checks paid on that day.

When the payment activity for the month was completed, the bank had 10 days to submit three magnetic tapes to the state agency. These tapes reflected vouchers paid, vouchers bounced, and vouchers remaining undistributed to participants that month. The contents of each tape are shown in Exhibit 3.

Information on the tapes was then reconciled against master files of vouchers issued. From this reconciliation, the WIC Program could obtain information about average voucher prices, value and proportion of vouchers bounced, and the cost of errors due to mismatches of the MICR (Magnetic Ink Character Recognition) data with voucher masterfile data. Exhibit 4 contains an excerpt from the National Bank's September, 1986 monthly report.

Payment for some bounced vouchers could be arranged if the vouchers were submitted directly to the state agency. There were several reasons for exceptions of this sort, including instances where the price written on the voucher had been altered because of a cashier error or where the price of special infant formulas exceeded $20. In these cases, the WIC Unit's Vendor Compliance Assistant

EXHIBIT 3 Contents of Magnetic Tape Files

Paid Vouchers File

An itemized listing of all food vouchers paid from the Food Voucher Payment Accounting during the month's transactions. Voucher serial number, amount paid, and date paid are listed for each item. Items are sorted by sequential serial number in ascending order. Standard information for bank number, account number, and transaction type are also included for each item. A trailer record is included at the end of the file, identifying the total number of items and total dollar amounts.

Bounced Vouchers File

An itemized listing of all food vouchers presented for payment and rejected (returned to the depositor) during the month's transactions. Voucher serial number, dollar amount, and date rejected are listed for each item. Items are sorted by sequential serial number in ascending order. Standard information for bank number, account number, and transaction type are also included for each item. A trailer record is included at the end of the file, identifying the total number of items and total dollar amount.

Undistributed Vouchers File

An itemized listing of items identified and processed as undistributed vouchers. The voucher serial number is listed for each item, and dollar amounts are zero filled. Standard information for bank number, account number, transaction type, and date processed are also included for each item. A trailer record is included at the end of the file, identifying the total number of items.

manually authorized the National Bank's Office of Government Services to pay whatever amount of the voucher was *undisputed* out of a separate reimbursement account. Vendors who thought their vouchers might be bounced inappropriately, and who wished to avoid bounced check fees, submitted their vouchers directly to the state agency, thereby bypassing their checking account. Additionally, vendors who thought a voucher *had been* bounced inappropriately, could resubmit it directly to the state agency.

When the contract for services was originally signed with National Bank in 1984, these manual authorizations were projected to be approximately 10 to 15 per month. In recent months, the average monthly manual reimbursement activity had reached 300 authorizations, covering approximately 1,400 vouchers.

Copies of the authorization (or letter of denial) and the vouchers in question were filed by date of authorization. These payments and denials were not reconciled with the voucher masterfile, and data were neither tallied nor reported. The entire automated system is shown schematically in Exhibit 5.

Evaluation of the WIC Control System

In April 1986, an external evaluation of the WIC computer system focused almost entirely on the voucher distribution system. Among other things, the evaluators noted that the system was antiquated and expensive, and that, while it supported minimum operational requirements, it was deficient in its provision of information for management purposes. The current system, designed in 1977, had been opera-

EXHIBIT 4 Summary of Activity by Voucher Code, Report—1

VOUCHER STATUS	JUNE		JULY		AUGUST		SEPTEMBER	
	VOUCHERS	AMOUNT	VOUCHERS	AMOUNT	VOUCHERS	AMOUNT	VOUCHERS	AMOUNT
VALID..............	241413	$1,845,561.57	261259	$2,001,459.21	229168	$1,762,605.24	248106	$1,907,695.52
RESUBMITTED AND PAID....	000000	$ 0.00	000000	$ 0.00	000000	$ 0.00	000000	$ 0.00
VALID: 61–89 DAYS.......	000257	$ 2,009.69	000245	$ 1,852.24	000283	$ 2,159.61	000492	$ 3,699.49
EXPIRED.............	000024	$ 183.99	000047	$ 409.93	000046	$ 362.95	000092	$ 671.78
FUTURE DATED........	001932	$ 16,207.37	001448	$ 12,268.84	001657	$ 13,731.17	001509	$ 12,605.41
EXCESSIVE AMOUNT.......	000006	$ 90,807.48	000005	$ 3,778.37	000003	$ 609.11	000003	$ 64.59
SUBTOTAL...........	243632	$1,954,770.10	263004	$2,019,768.59	231157	$1,779,468.08	250002	$1,924,736.79
CASH ERROR..........	001227	$ 10,127.51	001422	$ 11,580.49	001598	$ 13,606.05	001439	$ 11,876.78
SUBTOTAL MAIN ACCT.....	244859	$1,964,897.61	264426	$2,031,349.08	232755	$1,793,074.13	251641	$1,936,613.57
REIMBURSEMENT ACCT.....	000000	$ 0.00	000000	$ 0.00	000000	$ 0.00	000000	$ 0.00
REIMBURSEMENT ERROR....								
TOTAL PAID..........	244859	$1,964,897.61	264426	$2,031,349.08	232755	$1,793,074.13	251641	$1,936,613.57
BOUNCED............	001727	$ 13,273.11	003508	$ 27,283.66	004240	$ 34,264.53	003317	$ 25,605.70
BOUNCED ERROR........	000967	$ 7,478.19	000892	$ 6,695.57	000332	$ 2,767.34	000192	$ 1,520.01
TOTAL USED—NOT PAID....	002694	$ 20,751.30	004400	$ 33,979.23	004572	$ 37,031.87	003509	$ 27,125.71

626

EXHIBIT 5 WIC Automated System for Food Delivery

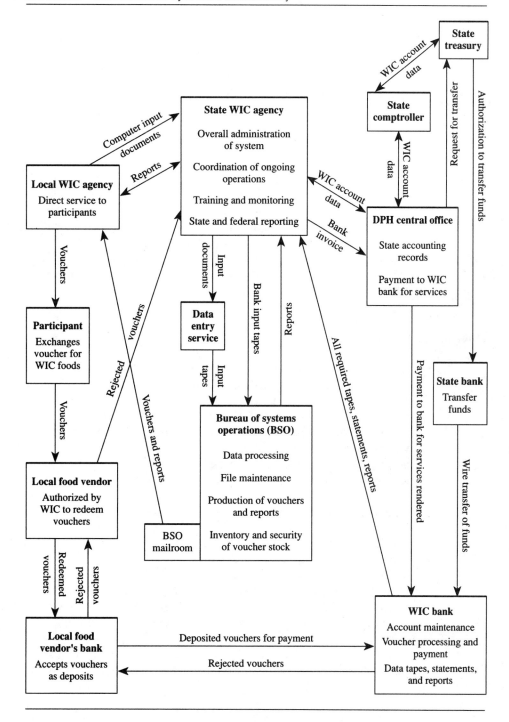

tional for nine years, whereas the expected life span of such systems was typically five years. Moreover, the inability of the bank to capture the vendor code for vouchers that were paid rendered impossible the timely gathering of vendor-specific payment data.

The result, according to the evaluators, was that vendor monitoring strategies were extraordinarily labor intensive. The evaluators noted the lack of reliable national data concerning retailer fraud, but cited case study estimates in other states of 5 to 15 percent of total food costs. A more conservative estimate by a National Bank official put the statewide loss from fraud at a minimum of $1 million.

The report mentioned the voucher reimbursement system, indicating that a major problem of that system was the failure to include manual reimbursements in the monthly reconciliation report as items paid, thus violating the agency's financial integrity. It criticized the method of estimating food cost obligations outstanding, the lack of vendor identification in redemption data, the high labor-intensiveness of monitoring strategies, and the lack of meaningful vendor reports. The evaluators noted that the present system was functional only to the degree that it was supported by manual intervention and data manipulations, and warned of the increasing potential for system breakdowns. None of the recommendations specifically addressed reimbursement controls.

Dilemma at the Bank

Prompted by staff turnover in the summer of 1986, Ms. Foster made several visits to the National Bank operations offices where the WIC vouchers were screened. While there, she discovered that, contrary to her instructions, the voucher monitors were using a less-than-100 percent method of review.

Asked by Foster to screen *all* vouchers for all possible violations, the monitors' workload doubled immediately. At the same time WIC management requested that monitors spot and pull vouchers submitted by certain suspect vendors. This job entailed identifying the payment date through the computer and microfiche, then retrieving the actual voucher from the storage area. Old vouchers were stored for up to three months in boxes labeled by the pay date, with approximately 3,500 in a box, filed sequentially by the last two digits of the serial number. Retrieval of one voucher could take up to an hour. The increased screening activity was adding to the workload.

Concurrent with additional work demands, the regular staff were taking vacations, uninspired temporary help was being trained, and supervision was changing. Over the course of the summer and fall months, the boxes of vouchers had piled up. One worker sympathized with the temps in admitting that the work was boring and difficult on the eyes. She noted that the slightest irregularity or required variation in the work was enough to slow them down to the point of getting further behind. One temp had complained of headaches and had joined the Army.

A bank official warned that the problem was exacerbated by an increase in the number of vouchers being processed, and that when the food budget was increased, the number of vouchers would increase still further, and WIC would fall even further behind in screening them.

Another bank official commented that WIC needed to figure out how it wanted to handle staffing, and speculated that perhaps it wouldn't be such a bad idea to make National Bank responsible for the screening and staffing. He suggested that with being responsible for screening, the bank would be better able to control its ability to deliver its monthly reports on time. Recognizing that a long-term plan was being shaped that would include the capture of vendor identification, he predicted that in the intervening two or more years, paralysis in problem solving might set in at WIC.

Ms. Foster summed up her view of the problem:

> There are ways to save money, but you have to spend money in order to save it. The resources are hard to get on a tight budget so that you can set up the systems to ultimately save the money, and also to draw the connections to be able to show that if we spend money here, we can save money there. I have to lobby for resources for such things, and it's difficult to show that there would be a savings. It takes time to get decisions made. And when it comes to hiring staff, the constraints of the state personnel system are enormous.

Questions

1. Prepare a flowchart for the voucher processing activity of the WIC Program. What problems, if any, does it reveal? What is the cost of these problems?
2. What other operational problems does the WIC Program have? What must it do well if it is to be successful?
3. What recommendations would you make to Ms. Foster?

Measurement of Output

No single overall measure of the performance of a nonprofit organization is analogous to the profit measure in a for-profit company. The goals of nonprofit organization's are usually complex and often intangible. The outputs of such organizations are difficult or impossible to measure.

In general, output information is needed for two purposes: (1) to measure efficiency, which is the ratio of outputs to inputs (i.e., expenses), and (2) to measure effectiveness, which is the extent to which actual output corresponds to the organization's goals and objectives. In a for-profit organization, gross margin or net income are useful measures for both these purposes. In a nonprofit organization, no such monetary measure exists because, as we discussed in Chapter 2, revenues do not approximate true output as they may in a for-profit company. This chapter looks at alternative ways of measuring output in nonprofit organizations.

In the absence of a profit measure, analyses of efficiency and effectiveness require adequate substitute measures of output. Despite the importance of devising such alternatives, current nonprofit management control systems tend to be deficient in this respect. For instance, a survey of 128 government and private nonprofit organizations in the Lehigh Valley area of Pennsylvania found that only 48 percent of government and 31 percent of private nonprofit agencies had specific, written criteria for measuring organizational effectiveness.[1]

> ***Example.*** Until 1970 the New York City Sanitation Department, with 15,000 employees, did not have a single person engaged in the analysis of output. A for-profit company of comparable size would probably have had a sizable group making such analyses.

The problem of measuring output in nonmonetary terms is not unique to nonprofit organizations. The same problem exists in responsibility centers in for-profit organizations in which discretionary costs predominate (e.g., research, law, per-

---

[1] Ralph E. Drtina, "Measurement Preconditions for Assessing Nonprofit Performance: An Exploratory Study," *Government Accountants' Journal*, Summer, 1984, pp. 13–19.

sonnel). Conversely, the output of many individual activities in nonprofit organizations can be measured as readily as can that of corresponding activities in for-profit ones (e.g., food service, vehicle maintenance, clerical work).

> ***Example.*** A library estimated that it should take two minutes to reshelve a book (including an allowance for personal time). One hundred books were replaced by a staff person who took four hours to complete the task.
>
> The output (100 books replaced) multiplied by the standard time per book (2 minutes) gave a total expected time of 200 minutes, or 3.3 hours (200 ÷ 60 minutes per hour). This can be compared with the actual total of four hours in order to measure productivity. This sort of analysis could be performed in a library of any sort, whether in a for-profit company or a city government.

BASIC MEASUREMENT CATEGORIES

Many different terms are used to classify output measures according to what they purport to measure. For our purposes, three will suffice: (1) social indicators , (2) results measures, and (3) process measures.

Social Indicators

A social indicator is a broad measure of output that reflects the impact of an organization's work on society at large. Unfortunately, few social indicators can be related to the work of a single organization because in almost all cases they are affected by external forces; that is, forces other than those of the organization being measured. The crime rate in a city may reflect the activities of the police department and the court system, but it is also affected by unemployment, housing conditions, and other factors unrelated to the effectiveness of these organizations. Similarly, life expectancy (or its converse, mortality) is partly influenced by the quality of health care, but it is also affected by nutrition, environment, and other factors.

> ***Example.*** The Peace Corps sponsored an attempt to measure the effectiveness of its program in Peru, using measures that purported to show the change in the well-being of Peruvians during a two-year period. Since there was no plausible way of relating the measures of well-being to the efforts of Peace Corps workers, the effort to measure output was probably a waste of time and money.

Valid social indicators are difficult to collect. Indeed, those that can be collected fairly easily are likely to be of dubious validity. Social indicators also are difficult to use properly because there ordinarily is no demonstrable cause-effect relationship between what an organization does and the change in a social indicator. Likewise, proxy indicators for intangible factors, such as percentage of registered citizens voting as an indicator of citizenship, or crime and disturbance statistics as an indicator of social unrest, may be collected fairly easily, but are of limited reliability.

Thus, social indicators are nebulous, difficult to obtain on a current basis, little affected by an organization's current programmatic efforts, and much affected by external forces. As a result, they are, at best, a rough indication of what an organization has accomplished, and therefore are of limited usefulness for management control purposes.

Social indicators can be useful in strategic planning, however, in that they can help guide senior management's decisions about the overall directions the organization should take. Because of this, social indicators are often stated in broad terms (e.g., "the expectation of healthy life free of serious disability and institutionalization"). For management control purposes, output objectives need to be expressed in more specific, preferably measurable, terms (e.g., infant mortality rates, life expectancy).

Results Measures

Results measures attempt to express output in terms that are related to an organization's objectives. As such, they tend to avoid many of the difficulties inherent in social indicators. Ideally, objectives are stated in measurable terms, and output measures are stated in these same terms. When it is not feasible to express objectives in measurable terms, as is often the case, the results measure represents the closest feasible way management has to both specify the objectives and measure the organization's progress toward them.

Properly designed, a results measure relates to an organization's success in attaining its goals. If the organization is client oriented, its results measures should relate to what it did for its clients. Organizations that render services to a class of clients, such as alcoholics or unemployed persons, may measure output in terms of results for the whole class or a target group.

Although results measures usually are easier to collect and use than social indicators, they still pose difficulties in both collection and use. Moreover, the closer a results measure comes to indicating an organization's impact on society, the more difficult it is to establish valid cause and effect relationships.

Example. A program to rehabilitate alcoholics might measure results in terms of either the percent of enrollees successfully completing the program or the rate of recidivism. While the latter is a more accurate results measure, it is complicated by three factors: (1) the choice of an appropriate time period, (2) the difficulty of identifying clients who resume drinking but do not notify the program of this fact, and (3) the influence of forces outside the organization's control on an individual's decision to resume drinking. The third complication is similar to a complication associated with social indicators.

Process Measures

A process measure (also called a *productivity* measure) relates to an activity carried on by the organization. Examples are the number of livestock inspected in a week, the number of lines typed in an hour, the number of requisitions filled in a month, or the number of purchase orders written in a day. The essential difference between a results measure and a process measure is that the former is *ends oriented,* while the latter is *means oriented* (the terms *performance oriented* and *work oriented* are other names for the same distinction).

A process measure relates to what a responsibility center or an individual does to help an organization achieve its objectives. Thus, process measures help managers gauge efficiency. Since they do not measure effectiveness, however, they ordinarily are only remotely related to the organization's goals and objectives. Because of this, senior management should be careful not to put too much emphasis on process measures, especially if they are unrelated or only tenuously related to results measures.

> *Example.* A U.S. Air Force Command measured performance of its squadrons by the number of hours flown, which is a process measure. As a consequence, squadrons sometimes would build up a record of performance simply by flying for many hours in large circles around a base, without any real accomplishments.

Need for Cause and Effect Relationships. In developing process measures, management must be careful to assure itself of a cause and effect relationship between the processes it wants employees to engage in, and the results it wants to accomplish. There frequently is an implicit assumption that a responsibility center's work helps the organization achieve its objectives, but this is not always the case.

> *Example.* In an air pollution program, the change in the amount of SO_2 in the atmosphere is a results measure, while the number of inspections made of possible violators is a process measure. The implication of a causal relationship between the number of inspections made and the amount of air pollution may or may not be valid.

Process measures are most useful in the measurement of current, short-run performance, and are particularly helpful in the control of lower level responsibility centers. They are the easiest type of output measure to interpret, presumably because there is a close causal relationship between them and inputs. Indeed, for those activities whose costs are related to inputs, process measures can be useful in constructing relevant parts of a budget.

> *Example.* In a department of public health, restaurant inspections are considered an important process measure. If each restaurant inspection (including travel time, office time, and other factors) should take approximately one hour and 15 minutes (a measure of efficiency), and there are 10,000 restaurant inspections to be made, there is a need for 12,500 inspector hours (10,000 restaurants x 1.25 hours per restaurant). This can be converted into the number of inspectors needed, which can be multiplied by the average inspector compensation to arrive at a budget.

Development of Standards. As the above example suggests, process measures require *(a)* identification of the activities of a person or a responsibility center, and *(b)* development of a *unit standard.* A unit standard is the amount of time needed to complete a single activity. For instance, in the above example, a unit standard is the amount of time needed to inspect a single restaurant. When the total activity count is multiplied by the unit standard, the resulting amount can be compared with the actual time spent, and can be used to evaluate performance.

Example. In the above example, if 3,000 restaurants were actually inspected during a given period of time, the 3,000 could be multiplied by the unit standard of 1.25 hours to give a total of 3,750 hours. This amount could be compared with the actual number of inspector hours used during the same period to obtain a measure of the efficiency of the inspectors. For example, if the inspectors did the job in 3,500 hours, they would be considered more efficient than anticipated.

In an office or clerical setting, there are three approaches to arriving at unit standards:

1. Using time standards for individual office operations developed by standard-setting organizations. One is called MODAPTS (Modular Arrangement of Predetermined Time Standards) developed by the Australian Association for Predetermined Time Standards and Research.
2. Having employees keep detailed records of the time taken to perform specific activities, and using averages of these records.
3. Having external observers record the time required to perform activities and the amount of idle time, according to a random plan of observations, and using averages of these records. (This procedure is called *work sampling*.)

Example. The National Institutes of Health established productivity measurement systems for many of its support activities. One is the Accounts Payable section, whose function was to examine about 30,000 vouchers monthly to determine whether they were a proper basis for payment.

Various types of vouchers required different amounts of examination time, and standard times were established by engineering studies. For convenience in calculating, these unit standards were expressed as *equivalent units*. The simplest voucher, a transportation request, had a standard time of 7.37 minutes, and this was designated as one equivalent unit. Equivalent units for the 14 other types of documents were determined based on the ratio of their standard time to 7.37. For example, a purchase order accompanied by a record of the call had a standard time of 16.68 minutes, which was 2.3 standard units (16.68 ÷ 7.37).

Exhibit 12–1 shows how these measures were used to calculate one person's productivity for a four-week period. Employee F worked 125 productive hours during this period and produced 2,163 equivalent units or 17.31 per productive hour. The standard per productive hour is 8.14 units (60 minutes ÷ 7.37). Employee F therefore performed at 213 percent of standard.[2]

Definitional Problems.   Productivity *should* mean output per unit of input. The inputs in the ratio should include labor, energy, equipment, and all the other resources used to achieve the output. In practice, however, productivity usually has a much narrower definition. Specifically, because labor is the critical resource in most nonprofits, the term usually means output per person-hour or person-year. However, an increase in output per person-hour is equivalent to an increase in efficiency *only if* all input factors other than personnel remain constant.

---

[2] From *Measuring Productivity in Accounting and Finance Offices,* Washington, D.C.: Joint Financial Management Improvement Program, September 1981, pp. 4–12.

EXHIBIT 12–1   Productivity Calculation

Name: Team <u>02</u>   Employee: <u>F</u>

Workstation: <u>15</u>

Period Reported: <u>June 2 to June 28</u>

Type of vouchers processed	*Equivalent Units*	*Invoices Quantity*	*Processed Equivalent Units*
Telephone charge order	1.20	170	204.00
Purchase order—No ROC	2.10	197	413.70
Purchase order—ROC	2.30	237	545.10
Research contract	2.80	2	5.60
Contract—ROC	2.30	341	784.30
Contract—No ROC	2.20	51	112.20
Library MOD	2.10	47	98.70
Total invoices processed		1,045	2,163.60

	Hours
Total available hours	160
Less annual leave	
Less sick leave	8
Less others	
Total regular hours	152
Plus overtime hours	40
Total hours worked	192
Less nonproductive hours	67
Total productive hours	125

Equivalent units produced
per productive hour (2,163.60 ÷ 125) 17.31

Performance rating (17.31 ÷ 8.14) 2ĺ3%

Total treasury rejections
charged to the individual   2

Terminology Problems.   Not all writers use the terms in the same way we have. In the work done by the Governmental Accounting Standards Board (GASB) to develop service effort and accomplishment (SEA) measures, a slightly different set of terms is used from what we have described above. The overall thrust is the same, however. The GASB distinguishes among inputs, outputs, and outcomes. Inputs are expenditures, outputs are what we call process measures (e.g., number of visits per month in a clinic, number of student-days in a school), and outcomes are what we call results measures (e.g., infant mortality rates in a clinic, academic test scores in a school). The GASB's work also measures efficiency as a cost per unit (e.g., cost per immunization in a clinic, average cost per student-day in a school). Efficiency measures are computed for both outputs and outcomes. Ex-

---

EXHIBIT 12–2 Recommended SEA Measures for Public Health Agencies

---

Indicator	*Rationale for Selecting Indicator*
Maternal and Child Health (MCH) Care	
Inputs:	
Expenditures (may be broken out by program or activity) in current and constant dollars...........	Measure of resources used to provide services.
Output:	
Number of clients admitted to MCH program	
Number of clinic visits per month.................	Widely reported measures that provide an indication of MCH program outputs.
Number of prenatal and postnatal mothers contacted.....................................	
Outcome:	
Infant mortality rate	
Low birth-weight rates..........................	
Teenage pregnancy rate.........................	Widely accepted measures used by public health officials to measure MCH program outcomes.
Rate of lead poisoning cases.....................	
Reported cases of preventable diseases in children ...	
Number of clients authorized to be served and actually served by WIC program.................	
Percentage of low birth-weight babies in target population...................................	Widely reported measures by MCH program to provide indicators of the accomplishment of short-term MCH program objectives.
Projected low birth-weight births prevented	
Projected infant deaths prevented	
Cases of measles prevented	
Efficiency:	
Cost per immunization...........................	Indication of the agency's efficiency in purchasing immunizations.
Cost of WIC supplements per unit	Indication of the agency's efficiency in purchasing WIC supplements.
Number of premature births/number of patients......	Indication of the agency's efficiency in reducing premature births.
Projected health care costs saved through routine checkups/costs of routine checkups	Indication of the agency's efficiency in reducing future health care costs.

Source: Governmental Accounting Standards Board.

hibit 12–2 shows these measures for public health agencies. Several of the readings at the end of this chapter refer to publications emerging from the GASB's efforts.[3]

Linkage among Measures

Some organizations have had success in linking process measures to results measures, and even in suggesting a link between results measures and social indicators. For reasons discussed earlier, the latter linkage is difficult to identify with

---

[3] For additional details, see Vivian L. Carpenter, "Improving Accountability: Evaluating the Performance of Public Health Agencies," *Association of Government Accountants Journal,* Fall Quarter 1990. Carpenter considers the usefulness of GASB's recommended performance indicators for assessing the performance of public health agencies.

any certainty, but the former is quite feasible. Specifically, for many activities, once an organization has determined its objectives, management can specify the corresponding results measures, and can link those measures to the process measures required to achieve them. The process measures also can be linked to the productivity of the organization's employees. Then, if objectives are not achieved, or if the cost of achieving certain objectives is higher than anticipated, the measurement system can help to pinpoint the reasons.

> *Example.* A social service agency undertook a special program to operate a group home for delinquent adolescent girls. In an effort to measure the program's success, the agency worked with each girl entering the program to determine: *(a)* vocational and living goals, *(b)* related objectives for each goal, and *(c)* service needs for each objective. For example, if a girl wished to become a beautician, this was established as a vocational goal. The related objectives might have been obtaining a high school diploma, completing beauticians' school, improving the girl's relationships with adults, and developing her ability to manage personal finances. The associated service needs might then be 10 hours per week of tutoring, tuition for beauticians' school, three hours a week of psychotherapy, structured summer employment in a job entailing interaction with adults, and so forth.
>
> The entire structure of goals, objectives, and service needs was then time phased, and the progress of each girl was assessed every three months. During the quarterly assessments, program managers asked the following questions:
>
> 1. Were service needs delivered as anticipated? If not, what changes were made and why?
> 2. Were the service needs delivered at the cost anticipated? If not, why not?
> 3. If an objective was scheduled to be accomplished, was it? If not, why not? Was it because designated service needs were not delivered, because needed services were not designated as such, or for some other reason?
> 4. If the objective was accomplished, did it have its anticipated effect? If not, why not?
> 5. Do any new objectives need to be established?
> 6. Is the goal still desired by the girl, and is it realistically attainable? If not, what new goal, objectives, and service needs are required?
>
> Over several years, the program was able to develop a results measure that focused on the target population: percent of girls who achieved their goal. In addition, managers developed a number of process measures, such as percent of objectives accomplished, percent of services delivered as anticipated, and actual expenditures per girl as compared to budget.

ISSUES IN SELECTING OUTPUT MEASURES

In selecting output measures, senior management makes several choices. Sometimes these choices are made consciously, and sometimes they are made by default. The choices have a major impact on the kind of output information that managers will see, however, and consequently on how they and others will view the effectiveness and efficiency of the organization. It therefore is important for senior management to think through these choices carefully.

Subjective versus Objective

An output measure may result from the subjective judgment of a person or a group of persons, or it may be derived from data that (unless consciously manipulated) are not dependent on human judgment. In many instances, a judgment made by a qualified person can be a better measure of the quality of performance than any objective measure. This is because humans incorporate the effects of circumstances and nuances of performance into their judgment. No set of objective measures can take all of these factors into account.

> *Example.* Hospitals are usually reluctant to measure the performance of physicians by any means other than peer review. Professors also prefer peer review judgments but will increasingly accept ratings made by students. Many will not accept the number of students electing a course or the number of articles published as valid measures of performance, however.

On the other hand, subjective judgments necessarily depend on the person making the judgment, and thus may be affected by the prejudices, attitudes, and even the person's emotional and physical state at the time the judgment is formed. Objective measures, if properly obtained, do not have these defects. Ideally, an organization's output measures should include both.

Quantitative versus Nonquantitative

Strictly speaking, any measure is, by definition, quantitative. Information in a measurement system is usually quantitative so that it can be summarized or compared. Some subjective information also is quantitative, and some kinds of output cannot be measured quantitatively.

> *Examples—Subjective Judgments Expressed in Quantitative Terms.* Grades in schools, even though numerical, are an expression of the instructor's judgment as to where the student's performance is located along some scale. Performance in figure skating contests, gymnastics, and certain other athletic events is measured by the subjective judgments of the judges; however, the performer is ranked along a numerical scale by each judge, and these ranks are then averaged to give a quantitative measure.

> *Example—Subjective Judgments Expressed in Nonquantitative Terms.* Most case files in a social service agency contain narrative statements of the social workers' assessments of clients. In many instances, these statements contain judgments about the kind of progress the client is making. While these statements frequently do a good job of measuring results of each case, they ordinarily cannot be summarized and reported to management in a quantitative way. Unless it reviews each case file, which is an impossible task, senior management has considerable difficulty measuring overall performance of the agency's social work professionals.

Discrete versus Scalar

A measure of performance may be either discrete; that is, a dichotomy ("satisfactory/ unsatisfactory" or "go-no-go"), or it may be measured along a scale. For example, to measure performance of a reading program in a school, a target could be established, such as "80 percent of students should read at or above grade level on a standardized test." If the measure were discrete, any performance of 80 percent or higher would be counted as success, and any performance below 80 percent would be counted as failure. If the measure were scalar, the percentage of students reading at each grade level on a standardized test would be used as the measure of output.

In general, scalar measures are preferable to discrete ones. However, there are many situations where discrete measures are appropriate. For example, most colleges do not measure how close their applicants came to being admitted; they simply use a discrete measure: x percent of all applicants met the admission criteria.

Actual versus Surrogate Measures

Whenever actual output can be measured, an organization should do so. If actual output cannot be measured, a surrogate measure may be used instead. In this case, the surrogate measure should be closely related to an objective. By definition, however, a surrogate does not correspond exactly to an objective, and managers should keep this limitation in mind. If this limitation is not recognized, the organization may focus too much attention on the surrogate, which may be dysfunctional. Achieving the surrogate should not be permitted to become more important than achieving the objective.

Example. A city used "number of complaints" as a surrogate measure for the performance of the agency that managed low-cost rental housing units. It was later discovered that after this measure was introduced, the agency put considerable pressure on tenants not to make complaints. This made performance, as measured by the surrogate, appear to improve, whereas service to tenants actually had deteriorated.

Example. When "effectiveness" of a Job Corps training program was being calculated by the contractor, "completions" were the mark of success; "dropouts" were the failures. When the latter appeared to be on the increase, "certificates of completion" were issued every other Saturday instead of the diploma originally given at the end of six months. Immediately, the number of completions rose, and the proportion of dropouts declined. As a result, the effectiveness of the enterprise was assured, and so was its continued funding.

Example. The success of other U.S. Department of Labor employment programs was measured by the proportion of people placed in jobs. This led to the practice known as *cream skimming*: accepting as job applicants the cream of the unemployed (persons temporarily unemployed and with a high probability of being placed).

Example. Performance of Veterans Administration hospitals was measured in part by the percentage of beds occupied. Because many hospital costs were fixed, a high occupancy rate resulted in a low cost per patient day. Studies showed that some veterans hospitals tended to keep patients, particularly mental patients, longer than their legitimate need for hospitalization.

The inappropriateness of a surrogate output measure may cause the discontinuance of a useful program, but more likely it will support the continuance of a marginally useful one, with a corresponding waste of resources. Inappropriate surrogate measures also may cause agencies to be complacent even though they are not reaching their objectives.

Quantity versus Quality

Although performance has both a quantity and a quality dimension, it usually is more feasible to measure quantity than quality. Despite this difficulty, the quality dimension should not be overlooked.

Frequently, the indicator that is chosen to measure quantity implies some standard of quality. "Number of lines typed per hour" usually carries with it the implication that the lines were typed satisfactorily; there may even be an explicit statement of what constitutes a satisfactory line of typing, such as the requirement that it be free of errors. Similarly, the measure "number of students graduated" implies that the students have met the standards of quality that are prescribed for graduation.

In some situations, judgments about quality are limited to discrete measures such as those given above: either a line of typing was error-free or it was not; either students met the requirements for graduation or they did not. In these situations, it is not feasible to measure quality along a scale, and this precludes a determination of, say, whether this year's graduates received a better education than last year's.

Importance of Quality.   In nonprofit organizations, measures of quality tend to be more important than in for-profit companies, where the market mechanism provides an automatic check on quality. If a pair of shoes is shoddy, people will not buy it. The company will then have to raise quality to stay in business. If the company does not raise quality, other companies will take its customers away.

Similar market mechanisms exist for some nonprofit organizations. For example, a university that gives poor quality education most likely will lose students to other universities. A museum that has poor quality exhibitions will not have as many visitors as otherwise. However, in some nonprofits, there is no such mechanism for consumer reaction to output. Hospital patients generally are not competent to judge the quality of their care, and, even if they are dissatisfied, there may be little they can do. Clients of welfare departments, courts, public safety departments, license bureaus, and other government offices cannot "vote with their feet" as customers of commercial businesses can; they have nowhere else to go. Because of the absence of market-oriented client checks on quality in nonprofit organizations, it is usually worthwhile for an organization to devote considerable effort to developing quality measures. If possible, these measures should be linked to the individuals responsible for attaining them.

> ***Example.*** U.S. Healthcare, Inc., a health maintenance organization (HMO), integrates quality indicators with a physician payment and recertification system. Twenty percent of each physician's payment is withheld. Return of the amount withheld is based on a 50/50 split—partly on corporate utilization goals and partly on four quality measures: (1) patient satisfaction, (2) chart audits, (3) transfer rates, and (4) a general assessment of the physician office's ability to operate as expected. Recertification of physicians takes place yearly, and high dissatisfaction rates lead to close scrutiny.[4]

Further, in some programs where a market mechanism might provide a measure of quality, an individual's personal motive for participating in the program may diverge from the social motive for sponsoring it, so that personal and social measures of quality differ. For example, even if a preschool program produces indifferent results or neurotic children, parents may still send their children to the program just to get them out of the home. Similarly, if a job training program neither trains nor places its clients well, unemployed people may still participate in it out of boredom, or out of hope it will assist them, or because they receive a stipend for participation. In such circumstances, unless there are adequate measures of quality, management may be misled about the value of the program's services.

Measuring Quality. During the past 5 to 10 years, many nonprofit organizations have begun programs in total quality management (TQM) or continuous quality improvement (CQI). One of the dilemmas faced by these organizations is measuring improvements in quality. As indicated above, the measurement of quality is inherently subjective. Yet, unless management can find some way to measure quality changes in a relatively objective fashion, the claim that quality has improved will have little credibility. There are three approaches that managers generally take to measure quality: crude measures, estimates, and surrogates.

Crude Measures of Quality. The absence of quality measures may lead to an emphasis on quantity. For example, people may be pushed rapidly through an education program, or inspectors may make a large number of quick and careless pollution inspections; or construction jobs may be done in a quick and shoddy manner. Thus, managers should make every effort to find acceptable quality measures, even if they are crude ones.

> ***Example.*** In preschool programs, one can measure a child's degree of literacy, social acclimation, and so forth before and after the program. In personnel training, one can ask employers to rate graduates. In construction, one can test fulfillment of construction standards.

---

[4] Maria R. Traska, "HMO Uses Quality Measures to Pay Its Physicians," *Hospitals* 62, Issue 13 (July 5, 1988).

Even though some measures are crude, and even though they may not even contain the "proper" attribute of quality, they may, if nothing else, serve as good motivators for the program's management and service delivery personnel. This assumes, of course, that there is a clear relationship between inputs and quality. If there is no demonstrable relationship between the two, senior management may not find it worthwhile to attempt to measure quality.

Estimates of Quality. In the absence of objective data, estimates of quality may be useful. For example, in a university, comparisons can be made between the standing of a college or department within its professional discipline, or its position currently with its position in the past. Similar judgments can be made about the kinds of positions graduates hold and the kinds of organizations that employ them.

Surrogates for Quality. In some nonprofit organizations, surrogates for the quality of services provided, such as accuracy and response time, are important indicators of quality. Often, objective measures of such surrogates are readily obtainable. Examples are the backlog of information requests, the number of checks returned because of error, average time taken to process an application, and the number of applications completed within seven days after their receipt. In using surrogates, managers must be cautious to avoid some of the problems discussed above, however.

IMPLEMENTING OUTPUT MEASURES: SOME GENERAL PROPOSITIONS

As the foregoing discussion has suggested, the selection and implementation of output measures for a management control system is an extremely complex task. It also is highly situational; that is, what works for one organization quite likely will not work for another. This is certainly true if two organizations have contrasting missions and clientele, but it also is likely to be the case even if the two have similar missions and clientele. What works for one community health center may not work for another.

Despite dissimilarities among organizations, we can state some general propositions that are relevant in selecting and implementing the output measures for an organization's management control system. These propositions are very general; there are no doubt exceptions to each rule. Nevertheless, they provide some useful guidance to managers concerned with measuring their organizations' output.

Proposition 1: Some Measure of Output Is Usually Better than None

Valid criticism can be made about almost every output measure, since few measures, if any, are perfect. There is a tendency on the part of some managers to magnify the imperfections and, thus, downgrade the attempt to collect and use any output information. In most situations a sounder approach is to take account of the imperfections and to qualify the results accordingly. In general, some output data, however crude, are of more use to a manager than none at all.

Although several caveats were expressed earlier concerning the use of inappropriate output measures, most organizations can develop reasonable, albeit imprecise, indicators of output. Rather than using such indicators as absolute bases for judgment, managers can use them as the means for asking questions to determine if a significant problem really exists. Moreover, the whole idea of benefit/cost analysis, which was discussed in Chapter 9, rests on the foundation of some measure of benefits, which means output. It follows that a considerable expenditure of effort in finding and developing output measures is worthwhile.

Example. The Income Maintenance Program of Canada administers many social programs. Its ultimate output is the well-being it provides to the families it serves. Its management believes that the following are satisfactory measures of this output:

- Number of accounts administered per employee-year.
- Units of service performed for clients per employee-year.
- Processing error rates.
- Average waiting time for client interviews.
- Percentage of checks returned.

Inputs as a Measure of Outputs. Although generally less desirable than a true output measure, inputs are often a better measure of output than no measure at all. For example, it may not be feasible to construct output measures for research projects. In the absence of such measures, the amount spent on a research project may provide a useful clue to output. In the extreme, if no money was spent, it is apparent that nothing was accomplished. (This assumes that the accounting records show what actually was spent, which sometimes is not the case.)

Example. The New Communities Program offered assistance to private and public developers of new communities. Although funds were available, no new projects were financed for 10 years. This was conclusive evidence that the program was not generating outputs.

As with other surrogates, when inputs are used as surrogate output measures, managers must be careful to avoid undue reliance on them. An organization should continually try to develop usable measures of output.

Proposition 2: If Feasible, Compare Output Measures to Measures Available from Outside Sources

Several professional associations, including those for hospitals, schools, colleges and universities, and welfare organizations, collect information from their members, and compile averages and other statistics. These statistics may provide a valuable starting point in analyzing the performance of an organization. Similar data are available from government sources, such as the Office of Productivity and Technology of the Bureau of Labor Statistics (although not much for non-profit organizations), the U.S. Department of Health and Human Services, and various state agencies. In some cases the measures reported are too detailed or not well suited to management needs, but some of the available statistics may nevertheless be useful.

Problems with Comparability.   When one organization's output information is being compared with averages of other organizations, it is important that the data be comparable. This requires that the detailed definitions used in compiling the averages be studied carefully; the user should not rely on the brief titles given in the tables themselves. Moreover, in using published statistics, an organization must be sure that its data are prepared according to the same definitions and ground rules as those used by the compiling organization.

> *Example.* The reporting system of the Department of Health of the state of New York defined hospital bed three different ways: certified beds, bed complement, and total beds. Unless users knew which of these definitions corresponded to the meaning of beds that they were accustomed to (e.g., which of them included bassinets), they could not make valid comparisons.

Comparability is especially important when data are reported for costs per unit of output. If the organization's definitions do not correspond to those used for both the numerator and the denominator of this ratio, the comparison is invalid. "Cost per FTE (full-time equivalent) student" can be a valuable statistic, but there are several different ways of defining the denominator of this ratio, and innumerable ways of defining the elements of cost that make up the numerator.

Problems with Reliability.   Managers also should ensure that the underlying data from which the statistics were derived are reliable. For example, many people believe that certain statistics on education published by the Department of Education were compiled from data of dubious validity. Obviously, one cannot expect to obtain valid comparative information from poor raw data.

Within an organization, if costs per unit of output are desired, output measures must be comparable with expense measures. In some organizations, the output measurement system is developed by one group and the expense reporting system by another; under such circumstances comparability is unlikely. Furthermore, if the cost-per-unit ratio is for responsibility centers, the responsibility center must be defined in the same way in measuring outputs as it is in measuring inputs (expenses); this is also the case for program elements or for other cost objects.

Proposition 3: Use Measures that Can Be Reported in a Timely Manner

There is no point in furnishing information after the need for it has passed. If managers need information quickly as a basis for action, the controller's staff must develop some way of compiling the information quickly. Timeliness requirements are different for different types of information, however.

Example. The Rand Corporation reported on an intensive evaluation of the educational voucher program at Alum Rock, California. The technique used was to measure the performance of pupils after the program. This measurement, at best, reflected the performance of the schools at least a year previously, and therefore was of no use in making decisions about the current performance in such schools. Nevertheless, it was undoubtedly useful to those responsible for making strategic decisions about continuing, dropping, or redirecting the educational voucher program.[5]

Importance of Timeliness.   For management control purposes a timely, but less accurate, output measure is usually preferable to an accurate, but less timely, one. Timeliness is not equivalent to speed in this context, but rather is related to the time span of the task.

Example. Mortality from emphysema, which can be measured only years after the occurrence of the cause of the disease, is less useful for control of air pollution programs than less accurate but more timely measures, such as the number of persons with eye/ear/nose/throat irritations, the number of persons who are advised by physicians to move to another locality, or the amount of effluent in the air.

Reasons for Timeliness Problems.   The problem of timeliness is different in nonprofit organizations (especially government) than it is in for-profit organizations for several reasons.

Lack of Prompt Feedback.   Output often cannot be measured immediately after a program's efforts have taken place. The results of funds invested in a school program in September may not be measurable until the following June, for example. The effect of interest rate subsidies on the supply of low-income housing may not be measurable for two or three years after the program is initiated because of the time necessary to design and construct buildings. The impact of reforestation programs may take a decade or two to measure.

Organizational Hierarchy.   Reports on a program may have to work their way through several organizational layers and thus become too old to be of use.

Example. Title I, an educational program, provides grants through a state educational agency, then through a local educational agency, and ultimately to the local Title I administrator. The data that work their way back through this chain could well be several months old by the time they reach program analysts in Washington.

Slowly Changing Circumstances.   Some data, although not timely, may describe a situation that is not likely to have changed since the time of measurement. Thus, old data are as accurate as if they were current. School desegregation programs are examples of programs for which data need not be collected frequently or processed quickly.

---

[5] Margaret A. Thomas, "Multiple Options in Education," *A Working Note* (Santa Monica, Calif.: Rand Corporation, 1976).

Proposition 4: Develop a Variety of Measures

There is no such thing as a general-purpose report on output that is analogous to a general-purpose financial statement. Just as management accounting information must be tailor-made to the needs of individual managers, so too must output measures.

For most responsibility centers, and for an organization as a whole, there are usually a few *key result measures* that are the important indicators of the quality and quantity of performance. In a given situation, opinions may differ as to what these are, but it is usually worthwhile to give careful thought to identifying them.[6] When there are several measures, each tends to be used for a different purpose. For example, with respect to health care in a community:

1. There can be a measure of the total cost of the health care system as a basis for comparison with the cost of other community services; this measures the relative emphasis given to each service. Expressed as a cost per person in the community, this can be compared with costs per person in other communities as another expression of relative emphasis.
2. There can be a measure of the overall cost per patient day in each hospital as a basis for detecting gross differences in the operating characteristics of each hospital. Per-patient costs for each service (medicine, surgery, pediatrics, psychiatry, and so forth) are useful for similar reasons.
3. At a lower level, information can be collected on the cost per episode of care, or cost per admission, perhaps classified by diagnosis.
4. At a still lower level, costs per unit of service rendered, such as cost per meal served, can be collected.

A Continuum of Output Measures.   When several types of output measures are used in a given organization, they tend to be arranged along a continuum. At one end are rough social indicators that are closely related to the goals of the organization, and at the other end are precisely stated process measures that are only remotely related to the goals of the organization.

> *Example.* At one extreme, the U.S. Information Agency measures the degree to which the agency influences international behavior through its activities. This might be called a *social indicator*. A second level measures the extent to which specific attitudes and opinions of the governing members of other nations have been changed by the agency's work. A third level represents a measurement of the increase of understanding of people overseas in regard to specific issues. A fourth level counts the number of times people have been reached by media of different kinds. A fifth and the lowest level counts the number of "media products" produced by the agency; this clearly is a process measure.

It is useful to think of output measures in terms of this continuum for two reasons. First, higher level output measures generally are better indicators of

---

[6] For an excellent discussion of this point, see David V. Mollenhoff, "How to Measure the Work of Professionals," *Management Review*, November 1977, p. 39.

program effectiveness than lower level measures, which often are not closely related to program goals. Second, lower level indicators are easier to specify and quantify than are higher level indicators. This fact explains the prevalence of measures of personnel efficiency in situations where personnel efficiency is only marginally related to overall program goals.

The continuum also corresponds to the relative usefulness of particular types of output indicators at various levels in the organization's hierarchy. Social indicators and results measures are most useful to senior management, governing bodies, and funding sources, whereas process measures are most useful to first-line supervisors.

> *Example.* A regional Air Pollution Control Administration headquarters has a wide variety of measures. It is concerned with its own efficient functioning; that is, it has its own process measures (how fast a request is considered, how quickly budget and project requests can be handled, and so on). At the other end of the spectrum, it has objectives for air quality in each region. The progress toward these objectives can be measured by the appropriate instrumentation.
>
> Between these process measures and results measures are several measures related to the functioning of the regional administrator and the state programs within a region. For example, the agency may establish as an objective the improvement of air quality in the New England region by more vigorous antipollution efforts on the part of the Commonwealth of Massachusetts.

Combined Output Measures.   Sometimes it is feasible to combine several output indicators into an aggregate that provides an indication of output quality and organizational performance. This sometimes is called a *combined output measure*.

The weights placed on each component of a combined output measure should reflect the values of the policymakers who govern the organization, not of the systems analysts or accountants who staff its programs. The output of many programs conceivably could be described by such a measure if enough work were devoted to constructing it. The question for management is whether the effort is worthwhile.

> *Example.* For many years, the Strategic Air Command evaluated its wings by a combined output measure that was computed by weighting scores for each of several dozen measures of performance. Some observers judged this system to be highly valuable; others doubted it was worth its cost.

In general, many managers decide that developing a combined output measure is more time consuming than the results justify, but simplified versions of this general approach may be eminently worthwhile.

Proposition 5: Don't Report More Information than Is Likely to Be Used

Although a variety of output measures may be necessary, managers should avoid receiving too much information. In part, this problem arises because there is a reluctance in many organizations to discontinue the use of certain output measures when they no longer serve an important managerial purpose. This reluctance must be overcome if the measurement system is to remain valuable and cost effective.

Example. In response to a request from a manager, the information services department in a social service agency developed a report that classified clients according to race and age. This was valuable output information to the manager at the time. Several years later, after that manager had left the agency, and the kinds of problems and issues the agency faced had changed, the Information Services Department continued to prepare the report, even though no one now used it.

A similar problem also arises when output measurement systems are being designed initially. In developing a new system, system designers have a tendency to collect a great mass of data so that somewhere within the mass are data that will meet everyone's desires. Too much data swamps the system, increases its "noise level," draws attention away from important information, and lessens the credibility of the system as a whole. This problem will be discussed in greater detail in Chapter 16.

Proposition 6: Don't Give More Credence to Surrogates than Is Warranted

As discussed previously, a surrogate can be a useful approximation of actual output, but it never should be interpreted as representing actual output. Its limitations must be kept in mind when developing a measurement system for output information.

COMPARISON OF OUTPUT MEASURES FOR STRATEGIC PLANNING AND MANAGEMENT CONTROL

The management control system should provide output information that is useful for both strategic planning and management control. Managers should recognize, however, that the criteria governing output measures useful for making strategic plans tend to differ from those that are useful for management control in the following ways:

Precision

For strategic planning, rough estimates of output generally are satisfactory. For management control, the measure must be more precise to be credible, although, as indicated above, timeliness considerations sometimes outweigh the desire for precision.

Example. One hospital's strategic planning activities included the purchase of a magnetic tape from the local telephone company; the tape contained information on new telephone installations. This information was used to analyze rough changes in the number of potential new patients in the hospital's service area. The fact that the tape contained data on people who had moved within the service area, and thus did not indicate precisely how many new residents there were, was not considered a serious limitation.

Causality

For management control, there should be a plausible link between the effort (i.e., inputs) of the organization and the output measure. For strategic planning, the connection can be more tenuous. If output measures are to be used in analyzing a proposal for a specific program, however, there should be some connection between inputs and outputs. To include correlating but noncausal output numbers in an analysis is not only a waste of time, but may do more harm than good if it leads people to believe erroneously that a causal connection exists.

> *Example.* In one rural community there was a high positive correlation between the number of storks observed in the spring and the number of babies born in the following winter. If health planners wish to determine the demand for maternity services, a model that used the number of storks as a predictive indicator probably would suffice. If, however, health planners wish to lower the birthrate, the systematic extermination of storks would not work, since the causal factor for both storks and babies was something entirely different: the richness of spring crops. Rich crops caused the storks to come in the spring because there was plenty of food for them; the rich crops also were a cause for optimism among the farmers and their wives, resulting in higher birthrates.[7]

The absence of a demonstrated causal connection is no reason to avoid analyzing *plausible* connections to assess the impact of a certain program. When there is no causal connection, decisions must be based on judgments unaided by quantitative information. For example, it seems obviously desirable to spend money on a judiciary system even though no good measurement of output is available.

Responsibility

For management control, the output measure must be related to the responsibility of a specific person or organization unit. For strategic planning, this is unnecessary. Thus, strategic considerations may require operating personnel to collect data for which they themselves have no use.

> *Example.* Title I education programs are intended to provide funds for improvement of education of low-income and disadvantaged children. In connection with these programs, planners in Washington require the collection of data (e.g., test scores) that will be of no use to operating managers. They are nevertheless necessary for reformulating program goals and strategies.

---

[7] Richard Normann, *A Personal Quest for Methodology*, SIAR Dokumentation AB (Stockholm, Sweden: Scandinavian Institutes for Administrative Research, 1975), pp. 7–9.

Timeliness

For management control, data on output must be available shortly after the event. For strategic planning, this is less important.

> ***Example.*** Measures of the high school and college performance of students who attended an elementary school are useful for strategic planning, but they cannot be part of a management control system.

Cost

For both strategic planning and management control, the benefits of obtaining information about inputs and outputs must exceed the costs of obtaining the information. For strategic planning, it may be possible to obtain certain data on an ad hoc or sampling basis, however, whereas the continuous collection of the same data for management control may be prohibitively expensive.

Relation to Program Elements

If output measures are to be useful for strategic planning, they must be related to overall goals and objectives. If it is not feasible to do this directly, it may be necessary to relate them to program categories or even to individual program elements. Ideally, they should be related to all three.

SUMMARY

Just as the economy has many indicators of prosperity that various people interpret differently, nonprofit organizations have numerous ways of looking at their complex outputs. The results in the social field are often indirect and unexpected. A variety of output measures, including a number of surrogates, often is necessary for a valid impression of the effectiveness of a program. Although a series of indirect output measures may make it difficult to measure the effectiveness of a responsibility center, it is unfair and depressing to morale to define output in terms that are too narrow.

In selecting a set of output measures, management must give consideration to three separate but related matters. First, it must look at measures that strike a balance between *(a)* subjective and objective, *(b)* quantitative and nonquantitative, *(c)* discrete and scalar, and *(d)* quantity and quality. Second, it must determine how it will respond to six propositions concerning the implementation of output measures: *(a)* the need for some measurement, *(b)* the ability to make comparisons, *(c)* the need for timely information, *(d)* the importance of having a variety of measures, *(e)* the avoidance of an excessive quantity of information reported, and *(f)* the avoidance of the use of surrogates. Finally, it must recognize that the demands for management control purposes are quite different from those for strategic planning. It therefore must be careful to choose output measures that are appropriate for the purposes to which they will be put.

SUGGESTED ADDITIONAL READINGS

Association of Government Accountants. *Executive Reporting on Internal Controls in Government*. Washington, D.C.: General Accounting Office, 1980.

Blickendorfer, Richard, and Jane Janey. "Measuring Performance in Nonprofit Organizations." *Nonprofit World* 6, no. 2 (March/April 1988).

Comptroller General of the United States. *Standards for Audit of Governmental Operations, Programs, Activities, and Functions*. Washington, D.C.: General Accounting Office, 1981.

Department of Health. *Comparing Health Authorities: Health Service Indicators, 1983–1986*. London, England: DHSS Publications, March 1988.

Epstein, Paul D. *Using Performance Measurement in Local Government*. New York: National Civic League Press, 1988.

Harr, David J., and James T. Godfrey. *Private Sector Financial Performance Measures and Their Applicability to Government Organizations*. Montvale, N.J.: National Association of Accountants, 1991.

Hatry, Harry P.; Marita Alexander; and James R. Fountain, Jr. *Service Efforts and Accomplishments Reporting: Its Time Has Come. Elementary and Secondary Education*. Norwalk, Conn.: Governmental Accounting Standards Board, 1989.

Hatry, Harry P., et al. *Service Efforts and Accomplishments Reporting: Its Time Has Come. An Overview*. Norwalk, Conn.: Governmental Accounting Standards Board, 1990.

U.S. General Accounting Office. *Evaluating a Performance Measurement System*. FGMSD 80-57, May 12, 1980.

————. *Pay for Performance: State and International Public Sector Pay-for-Performance Systems*. GAO/GGD-91-1, October 1990.

————. *Tax Administration: IRS Needs to Improve Certain Measures of Service Center Quality*. GAO/GGD-91-66, March 1991.

U.S. Joint Financial Management Improvement Program. *Implementing a Productivity Program: Points to Consider, 1977* (with minor updates in reprinted versions).

————. *Measuring Productivity in Accounting and Finance Offices*. September 1981.

U.S. Office of Personnel Management. *Increasing Federal Work Force Productivity*, January 1980.

Wallace, Wanda. *Service Efforts and Accomplishments Reporting: Mass Transit*. Norwalk, Conn.: Governmental Accounting Standards Board, 1991.

CASE 12–1   Morazan and Izaltenango*

In late 1982, the government of the Latin American republic of Soledad agreed to assign a share of the national budget for public health to family planning. Soon afterward, a Family Planning Office was established as a dependency of the Maternal-Child and Nutrition Division of the Ministry of Public Health. By the end of 1987, family planning services were being offered at over 80 health facilities throughout the republic.

Dr. Arturo Vivas, head of the Family Planning Office since late 1987, had just completed the annual evaluation of the performance of each clinic. The evaluation was based upon the percentage of "target population," or women of fertile age (generally considered to be 20 percent of the total population), that each clinic had been able to attract new users of family planning services. He believed that this was the most appropriate standard of evaluation, since national program goals were defined in terms of coverage, by percent, of Soledad's target population.

At a meeting of the Division's central office staff held on a warm afternoon in February 1988, Dr. Vivas circulated a list of the family planning clinics, ordered by percentage of target population covered. "As you can see from these statistics," he said, "performance among the clinics varied widely during 1987."

Dr. Luis Delgado, Director of the Division and Vivas' immediate superior, ran his finger down the list and said, "I notice that the Morazan clinic is near the top of the list, but that Izaltenango is down toward the bottom."

"That's right," Dr. Vivas responded. "Morazan did a tremendous job and attracted 5.4 percent of the target population in the area that it serves as new users during 1987. But Izaltenango turned in a poor performance, attracting only about 1.6 percent."

"Do you have the monthly statistics on those two clinics, Dr. Vivas?" he asked. Vivas nervously dug through the papers in his briefcase and produced the reports shown in Exhibits 1 and 2.

"Morazan may attract a lot of new users," Dr. Delgado continued, "but I think it is insufficient. In fact, I would bet that a consultation there costs double what it does at Izaltenango. When you evaluate your family planning clinics, don't you take cost efficiency into account?"

Dr. Vivas was momentarily silent. He knew why Dr. Delgado had chosen to comment on these particular clinics. Several months earlier Dr. Delgado had been asked by the Minister to serve on a special commission charged with analyzing costs within the health facilities. They had chosen four facilities—two urban clinics and two outlying health centers—for comparative analysis, including Morazan and Izaltenango. The final report was not yet complete, but now Dr.

---

* This case was prepared by Professor John C. Ickis. Instituto Centroamericano de Administración de Empresas (INCAE), Managua, Nicaragua. It is based on a real situation in which only the names have been changed to preserve the anonymity of the individuals involved. Copyright © by INCAE.

EXHIBIT 1 Morazan: Family Planning Statistics, 1987

Medical Consultations	Jan.	Feb.	Mar.	Apr.	May	June	July	Aug.	Sept.	Oct.	Nov.	Dec.	Total
IUD													
First visit	0	10	31	16	16	10	15	5	12	9	9	7	140
Subsequent	0	0	1	8	8	14	13	18	17	44	20	9	152
Oral contraceptive													
First visit	0	96	140	84	80	71	59	79	64	43	66	26	808
Subsequent	0	0	28	78	78	92	94	77	59	83	47	36	672
Other													
First visit	0	1	8	1	1	1	3	3	4	4	1	1	28
Subsequent	0	0	0	0	0	0	0	0	0	1	4	0	5
Total													
First visit	0	107	179	101	97	82	77	87	80	56	76	34	976
Subsequent	0	0	29	86	86	106	107	95	76	128	71	45	829
Total visits	0	107	208	187	183	188	184	182	156	184	147	79	1,805
Deserters	0	0	0	31	31	30	27	27	56	0†	36	21	259
Cycles of oral contraceptives distributed*	0	106	294	453	449	472	532	453	493	0†	459	396	4,107

* May be distributed without medical consultation.
† No data available.

EXHIBIT 2 Izaltenango: Family Planning Statistics, 1987

Medical Consultations	Jan.	Feb.	Mar.	Apr.	May	June	July	Aug.	Sept.	Oct.	Nov.	Dec.	Total
IUD													
First visit	0	2	2	0	0	4	0	0	6	9	3	3	29
Subsequent	3	1	0	5	1	3	6	3	9	10	3	7	51
Oral contraceptive													
First visit	11	2	5	9	12	8	11	7	7	7	5	10	94
Subsequent	12	17	25	19	20	24	25	8	22	22	20	10	224
Other													
First visit	0												0
Subsequent	0												0
Total													
First visit	11	4	7	9	12	12	11	7	13	16	8	13	123
Subsequent	15	18	25	24	21	27	31	11	31	32	23	17	275
Total visits	26	22	32	33	33	39	42	18	44	48	31	30	398
Deserters	3	1	2	2	3	2	2	1	3	2	1	0	22
Cycles of oral contraceptives distributed*	154	141	151	154	116	157	179	70†	176	155	140	122	1,715

* May be distributed without medical consultation.
† Stockout of oral contraceptives recorded during this month.

EXHIBIT 3 Selected Statistics from Results of an Analysis of Four Health Facilities, Ministry of Public Health, Soledad

	(A) Rural Health Center	(B) Izalte- nango	(C) Mora- zan	(D) Urban Clinic
1. Cost per outpatient medical consultation (does not include hospitalization)				
a. Direct costs (P/)*.............	5.80	5.48	8.54	9.10
b. Indirect costs†	3.66	2.36	4.86	2.76
c. Total......................	9.46	7.84	13.40	11.86
2. Cost of personnel per medical hour (outpatient only)				
a. Doctors	10.00	8.00	20.00	24.00
b. Nurses	7.00	6.00	10.00	6.50
c. Auxiliaries...................	4.00	6.00	6.00	6.00
d. Filing secretaries	1.50	1.50	5.00	1.50
e. Total......................	22.50	21.50	41.00	38.00
3. Cost of medicines and surgical articles per medical hour (outpatient only)	2.40	2.26	2.00	2.88
4. Number of consultations per medical hour (outpatient only)..........................	6.1	7.3	5.9	5.5
5. Number of laboratory examinations per outpatient consultation	0.37	0.40	1.47	0.95

* The currency of Soledad, the peso (P/), is equal to U.S. $0.20.

† Indirect costs include administration, laboratory costs, and pharmacy costs.

Delgado was passing Vivas a summary of the analysis (Exhibit 3). "Does this change your evaluation of those two clinics?" Delgado asked.

"But these costs are for the health services in general," Dr. Vivas protested. "Not just family planning."

"Maybe we can't attribute all the high costs to family planning," conceded Dr. Delgado. "Still, it is an important part of the health services at Morazan and it has to share the blame."

Dr. Roberto Fernandez, head of the National Nutrition Program, interrupted: "I know the family planning doctor out at Izaltenango personally. He is also the director of the health center. He is a dedicated man and I'm sure he's doing the best he can. But he has to face attitudes and beliefs that have been formed over centuries. It is not fair to compare his situation with Morazan, where the women eagerly line up at the doctor's door."

"It is true that there is a lot of activity in the Morazan clinic and they work very hard there," said Dr. de Reyes, head of the Division's Education Department. "But it is my impression that the rotation of users there is quite high. A lot of women drop out after only a short time in the program. Don't you take that into account?"

"This brings up another point," interjected Dr. Fernandez before Dr. Vivas could respond. "Just because a clinic looks active doesn't really mean that they are seeing a lot of people. I know of one clinic where the doctor just sees the same women over and over again. In order to do any kind of evaluation it seems to me that you need to know the total number of women being served by a clinic."

"It seems to me that we have to do a lot more thinking about the evaluation of our family planning clinics," said Dr. Delgado, directing his words at Dr. Vivas. "If we expect to increase the effectiveness of the program we have simply got to know which clinics are using their resources well or poorly in providing services to those who desire them. At next week's meeting I would like you to recommend a system that will give us this information."

The session came to a close and Dr. Vivas soon found himself sitting alone at the long conference table. He continued to puzzle over the many factors that would have to be taken into account in the design of an evaluation system. He decided to begin by reviewing his experiences during visits that he had made to the clinics back in November of 1987, when he was first getting acquainted with his new job. Among his recollections of these visits he hoped to find some clues as to which factors might or might not be important in evaluating clinic performance.

Visit to Morazan

Until the end of 1986, family planning services in the Morazan clinic had been provided by the Association for Family Orientation, a private organization of citizens concerned with problems arising from unwanted pregnancies. The Association had been assigned certain hours when their own staff offered family planning services in a designated area of the clinic. When it was announced that the Ministry of Public Health would offer family planning services, the Association's doctor resigned and family planning services were not offered until the Ministry program was begun in February 1987. The new doctor, Dr. de Mendoza, gave family planning consultations five days a week from 5 to 7 in the evening.

Morazan was a lower-middle-class neighborhood in the capital of Soledad, only a five-minute drive from the buildings that housed the Ministry. The neighborhood was composed of over 90,000 people. Many of them were employed as workers in industry, and many others had small shops and garages or were otherwise self-employed. Nearly half of Morazan's population was covered by the national social security system and used its health facilities. The remainder, most of whom could not afford private medical services, used the facilities of the Ministry of Public Health.

Finding doctors to staff the Morazan clinic had never been a problem, as it had been in some outlying health facilities. The clinic's convenience to the center of the capital made it much sought after by the most senior and best-paid doctors employed by the Ministry.

The Morazan clinic was located in a large, two-story wooden structure, built in Spanish style, with an interior courtyard. During the early 1900s it had been the fashionable residence of one of Soledad's wealthy families, but like the structures that surrounded it the house had been left to deteriorate over the years. The wood was warped with age and the paint was old and chipped.

There were 54 persons employed at the Morazan clinic. It had no hospitalization facilities and normal working hours were from 7 to 12 and 3 to 5. Those who worked beyond 5 P.M., including the family planning doctor and the nurse and auxiliary who assisted her, received additional pay for the extra hours.

Dr. Vivas arrived at the Morazan clinic on a late afternoon in November. It was his first visit to a clinic since he had been named head of the Family Planning Office, and he was still not completely familiar with all the standards and procedures. He decided that, rather than pretending that he "knew it all," he would momentarily forget what he had read in the documents his predecessor had left behind, assume he knew nothing at all about the operations of the family planning clinics, and ask some very basic questions in each location he visited.

Family planning medical consultations were given in a room on the first floor, to the left of the main entrance. The door of the room faced on a corridor along which 15 or 20 women were seated on a wooden bench. Several wore colorful dresses and high-heeled shoes. Just outside the door was a desk, cluttered with papers. From behind it, the auxiliary nurse, Mrs. Gonzalez, stood up to greet Dr. Vivas as he entered. He introduced himself and asked her to explain the operation of the clinic.

Auxiliary: Dr. de Mendoza should be here any minute. She will see up to 12 women between 5 and 7 P.M., after the rest of the clinic is closed. In that room over there the graduate nurse is just finishing up her interviews with women who have come for the first time. These women will have to return in another month to see the doctor again, but those without any side effects or problems will not have to return for a third time for another year. Of course, if a woman is using the oral contraceptive, she will have to make monthly return visits to pick up cycles of pills. But she does not have to see the doctor for that.

Dr. Vivas: What are your tasks?

Auxiliary: Taking care of the paperwork. Also, I have to prepare the women for the medical consultation. I arrive about 3 P.M., two hours before the doctor does. Women with medical appointments are expected to be here at that time. If there are more than 12 waiting I select the most important cases and make another appointment for the others. Then I take each woman's weight, temperature, and blood pressure, ask her the date of her last menstrual cycle, and record this information in the medical history forms. Then I send her to see the nurse.

Dr. Vivas: What problems do you have?

Auxiliary: Trying to keep up with my work is the biggest problem. You see, in addition to my other tasks I have to give out cycles of pills to women who return for them each month. That's what these women here are waiting for. But this is nothing . . . you should see this place on a *busy* afternoon!

Dr. Vivas: How long do you work in family planning?

Auxiliary: For four hours, from 3 P.M. to 7 P.M. Sometimes I have to stay longer to hand out pills. The nurse arrives a bit later, around 4 or 4:30 P.M.

Dr. Vivas: How long must the women wait for cycles of pills?

Auxiliary: That depends. If there are women waiting for pills when the clinic opens at 3, I try to see that they get them immediately. But I also have to make sure that all the women with medical appointments are ready for the nurse when she arrives. On some afternoons we may get 40 or 50 women in here wanting cycles of pills. So I have to tell them to wait until I have finished with the women who have medical appointments. Also, I must take the weight and blood pressure of each woman returning for pills and ask her whether she has experienced any side effects. Sometimes the doctor finishes before I do.

Dr. Vivas: Do these women sometimes get upset about having to wait?

Auxiliary: Do they! They get very angry sometimes . . . some women march out of here and we never see them again.

Dr. Vivas: How do you determine when a patient is inactive?

Auxiliary: Cards are kept on all patients in this file box. If an appointment is missed, a woman is put into a category known as *"faltista."* If in the case of IUD users three months pass or in the case of OC users two months pass, the woman is classified inactive. If, after that time, she chooses to re-enter the program, she is recorded as a new user.

Dr. Vivas: How many "actives" does the Morazan clinic have at the present time?

Auxiliary: It would be quite a job to go through these hundreds of cards and figure that out. Some of the cards may be in the wrong categories. I try to keep this card file up to date but with all my other tasks here there is just no time. Last month I got so far behind that I could not turn in a report on the number of women who left the program.

Dr. Vivas: Have you always worked in family planning?

Auxiliary: No, we rotate from one job to another. There are some problems, but we all enjoy working in family planning, and we are eager for our turn to come around. Especially the nurses. But I think their job is easier.

Dr. Vivas: Do you find much resistance to family planning here?

Auxiliary: Here? No. . . . Women here are experienced in family planning. They accept it.

Journey to Izaltenango

A week after his visit to Morazan, Dr. Vivas went on a trip with several other Ministry personnel to see the health facilities in the northern, mountainous provinces of Soledad. After an exhausting drive along winding and dusty roads, they arrived at the village of Izaltenango. Its rough cobbled streets, lined with white adobe walls and red-tiled roofs, were practically deserted in the mid-morning heat.

The health center at Izaltenango was a large, two-story concrete structure located on the extreme north end of town. The original structure had been built in the 1940s, but some additions had been made over the years to accommodate the growing medical demands of the area. Even the expansion of the hospital wing to 80 beds in 1985 had not been sufficient and it was sometimes necessary to place two patients in one bed.

The health center served a population of 38,000 including the 6,000 inhabitants of the village of Izaltenango. The remainder came from small settlements scattered widely among the mountains, some as far as 30 kilometers from the village. The only form of transportation from these settlements was by muleback or on foot, and they remained isolated by swollen rivers during the rainy season.

Family planning services were held for two hours per day, from 11 to 12 in the morning and from 2 to 3 in the afternoon. This schedule allowed most of the rural women ample time to travel to the clinic and to return to their communities before nightfall.

Izaltenango had been one of the first clinics in which the Ministry of Public Health had begun offering family planning services, and the director of the health center, Dr. Sandino, had served as its family planning doctor since the program's inception in 1983. Two additional doctors who were recent graduates from medical school and were serving their required one year of government social service, worked in the center. During this period they received a salary of about 8 pesos (5 pesos = U.S. $1) per medical hour or 1,600 pesos per month for an eight-hour day. Regular doctors were generally paid a minimum of twice that amount. These "social-service" doctors were assigned to facilities in remote parts of the country and seldom, if ever, worked in urban clinics like Morazan.

After they had introduced themselves, Dr. Sandino began to describe for Dr. Vivas the history of family planning in Izaltenango.

Dr. Sandino: When family planning was introduced here by the Ministry, we were sent educational materials and we were told to go out and motivate the members of the community. There was a strong reaction to our educational campaign by religious groups. This is a very conservative area and there are many religious societies and leagues. People were warned to stay away from the family planning clinic. There was also some opposition from the clinic personnel. The decision to introduce the program was taken very rapidly and it was done without consulting them. The social-service doctors, just out of the University, thought that it was part of a foreign-inspired plan to limit our population. Many of the nurses and auxiliaries had religious reservations.

Dr. Vivas: How do people feel about family planning now? Do these attitudes persist?

Dr. Sandino: There is now less vocal opposition by the community, but perhaps this is because we discontinued our publicity campaigns. The social-service doctors who are with us now do not object. They understand that it is a voluntary program which contributes to maternal health and to the improvement of living conditions.

Dr. Vivas: How about the nursing personnel?

Dr. Sandino: We have nine nurses here, and several of them are really motivated toward family planning. The problem is that they rotate jobs every couple of weeks, so that when you do get a nurse who is really interested she doesn't stay very long.

Dr. Vivas: If some nurses really want to work on family planning, why not let them do it full time?

Dr. Sandino: It's not that simple. Because of the hospital wing, this health center operates during 3 shifts, 24 hours a day. No nurse wants to be stuck with the night shift all the time. So we have to rotate.

Dr. Vivas: What are some of your other problems?

Dr. Sandino: Because we are located so far from the warehouse in the capital we sometimes have difficulty getting the supplies we need. But the real problem is with the laboratory results. This is true for all medical consultations, not just family planning. We have sent in many laboratory samples by public transportation and never heard about them again. We have decided it's just not worth the trouble, and we only take tests when it's absolutely necessary.

On his way out of Dr. Sandino's office, Dr. Vivas stopped to talk to the nurse in charge of family planning.

Dr. Vivas: What are your duties?

Nurse: I give the educational talks to women who come to the clinic for the first time and I hold an interview with each woman before she sees the doctor. After the medical appointment I make any necessary explanations. If she is using oral contraceptives, I give her one cycle.

Dr. Vivas: Do you ever give her more than just one?

Nurse: No, almost never. We like the women to return to the clinic once each month so that we can make sure that they are using the pills correctly and see whether they are having any reaction to them.

Dr. Vivas: How many family planning users see the doctor each day?

Nurse: Possibly three or four.

Dr. Vivas: Do you have any idea why more do not come?

Nurse: I think there are many reasons. Some of the women must walk for hours to get here. Many feel ashamed to sit in the waiting room among their neighbors who come in for health problems. These women do not want more children, but they do not want anyone to know that they are using family planning services. There are many religious and social taboos in this area.

Dr. Vivas: How many active patients does the clinic have?

Nurse: That is difficult to say . . . we would have to go through the card file. Over one hundred women joined the clinic last year, but many of them have not come back for cycles of pills. They are probably pregnant now.

As he left the Izaltenango health center, Dr. Vivas looked around the waiting room. Most of the people seated on the wooden benches were women, several of them breast-feeding babies. He noticed their calloused bare feet and the hard lines of hunger on their faces and thought to himself how sharply they contrasted in appearance to the well-dressed women he had seen in the Morazan clinic.

Questions

1. What issues does Dr. Vivas need to consider in measuring the performance of the clinics?
2. What changes, if any, should Dr. Vivas make to the management control system?

CASE 12-2 Davidson Community Health Center*

The Davidson Community Health Center was a family-centered, primary care facility offering services in health education, mental health, prevention of disease, and medical and dental care. The Center opened in September 1971 in what was formerly the outpatient department of Davidson Hospital in August, Georgia. August, a city of 59,000, was located in Richmond County, whose population was 162,000, many of whom were below poverty level. Prior to 1971 the county had no program for comprehensive primary health care.

About 70 percent of the Health Center's funding came from HEW, under its Public Health Service Act; the balance was from private grants, services donated by Davidson Hospital, and direct and third-party payments for patient care.

The Center's objectives were listed in a progress report issued in December 1972, at the end of its first year:

1. To make accessible to a large proportion of the poor of Richmond County a comprehensive scope of personal primary health services.
2. To improve access to the more specialized services not provided by the Center.
3. To decrease the need for and amount of hospitalization among the people served by the Center, by carrying out intensive early case-finding and prompt treatment of conditions that if left uncontrolled would subsequently require care in the hospital.
4. To contribute to improving the health of the community at large.
5. To contribute to the economic and social well-being of certain members of the community who have low levels of income and formal education, by training and employing such people in the Center and by providing built-in opportunities for career advancement.

The Center's services were open to any resident of Richmond County who met eligibility requirements. Priority went to families whose income fell within the OEO Poverty Index, which in 1972 was approximately $1,900 for one person plus $600 for each additional family member. Families with incomes somewhat above these limits were also eligible but were expected to pay part of the cost of the services provided. The eligible population totaled about 30,000. By July 1, 1972, 8,445 people had registered with the Center, about half of whom had been seen at least once (see Exhibit 1).

---

* This case was prepared by Martha Dula under the direction of Professor Robert N. Anthony. Copyright © by the President and Fellows of Harvard College. Harvard Business School case 1-175-254.

EXHIBIT 1 Summary Statistics and Summary Budget

Summary Statistics
January–December 1972

Total Registered Population, cumulative:

Quarter	January–March	April–June	July–September	October–December
Families	1,850	2,606	3,370	4,103
Individuals	6,255	8,445	10,631	12,693

Total encounters, registered and nonregistered:

Quarter	January–March	April–June	July–September	October–December	Total
Medical.......................	5,337	6,703	6,275	6,267	24,582
Mental health..................	19	27	24	91	161
Dental	1,192	1,397	1,222	1,595	5,406
Home health	627	528	522	820	2,497
Hearing screening..............	—	—	165	275	440
Social and community services.....................	375	327	292	316	1,310
Total	7,550	8,982	8,500	9,364	34,396

Note: Total registered patients seen at least once since registration as of July 1, 1972 = 4,175, which was 49 percent of the registered population at that time.

Summary Budget
July 1, 1972–June 30, 1973

	Total Amount Required	Source of Funds	
		Applicant and Other	Requested from HEW
Personal services......................	$1,052,974	$178,223	$ 874,751
Patient care..........................	163,130	29,000	134,130
Equipment...........................	105,145	34,940	70,205
Construction.........................	15,625	15,625	
Other	455,798	308,576	147,222
Trainee costs			
Total direct costs................	$1,792,672	$566,364	$1,226,308

Organization of the Center

The Center's board of directors operated under powers delegated to it by the grantee, Davidson Hospital Board of Trustees. Registered Davidson Center patients and several neighborhood councils together had two-thirds representation on the board. The other third was made up of representatives of county and state health agencies, the August Academy of Medicine, a nearby university medical school, and Davidson Hospital.

Care at the Center was delivered by teams composed of a physician, a family care nurse, a family health worker, and a dentist. Social work consultation was also available. The Center arranged backup services at the three hospitals in the area. In addition, prenatal and family planning services were available in cooperation with the Richmond County Health Department, and mental health services were available in cooperation with the Richmond County Mental Health Center. The Center also used the Home Health Service of the Richmond County Health Department.

Evaluating the Center's Performance

The administration of the Davidson Center kept conventional statistical and financial records to monitor the Center's performance (see Exhibits 1 and 2 for sample data). These reports were compiled every quarter. But its director, Dr. Rose Chadwick, felt that such records would provide only part of the information that she and other interested parties needed. Before the Center opened in the fall of 1971, she consulted Dr. Dennis Gillings, research associate with the Health Services Research Center of the University of North Carolina, who had recently developed a methodology for evaluating the effectiveness of social programs in meeting their own goals.[1] She asked Dr. Gillings to help apply his system to the Davidson Center.

The measurement system that Dr. Gillings devised is summarized in Exhibit 2.

Overall Approach

First, the Center's aims were broken down into eight goal areas:

1. Define and serve the target population.
2. Establish and maintain the Health Center as an operational unit.
3. Ensure that health care is accessible to the target population.
4. Improve the health of the target population.
5. Deliver high-quality health care.
6. Contribute economically and socially to the quality of life of the community.
7. Establish the role of the Center in relation to other programs.
8. Develop the Center as a catalyst for social reform.

Then, a list of activities that contributed to each goal was compiled. For each activity, a measurable target was set for the Center's first year of operation. The combination of an activity and a target made up an objective. A goal area was composed of a series of specific objectives, but an objective might appear under more than one goal area if it related to more than one.

---

[1] See "Evaluation: A Methodology for Determining the Effectiveness of a Social Program in Terms of Goal Fulfillment," Dennis Gillings, Ph.D., Department of Biostatistics, School of Public Health, University of North Carolina, Chapel Hill, N.C., October 1, 1974.

EXHIBIT 2 Direct Health Care and Supporting Activity Cost Center–Summary

NAME OF CENTER:
Davidson Community Health Center

CITY AND STATE:
August   Georgia

FOR THE QUARTER ENDING:
December 31, 1972

	(1) Personnel	(2) Outside Services In Center	(3) Outside Services Out of Center	(4) All Other	(5) Total Direct Costs	(6) Distributed Costs	(7) Total Functional Costs	(8) Percentage of Total	(9) Units of Service Provided	(10) Unit Cost
1. Medical	$ 79,280	$ 2,294	$ 371	$16,557	$ 98,502	$ 60,045	$158,547	45.2%	6,267	$25.30
2. Laboratory		16,279	4,993	116	21,388		21,388	6.1	3,512	6.09
3. X ray		12,114		9	12,123		12,123	3.4	820	14.78
4. Pharmacy		25,411		3,099	28,510		28,510	8.1	4,294	6.64
5. Mental health	4,198	840			5,038	2,126	7,164	2.0	91	78.73
6. Home health	6,038			1,246	7,284	7,030	14,314	4.0	820	17.46
7. Dental	23,817	14	6	5,100	28,937	15,577	44,514	13.0	1,595	27.91
8. Hospitalization										
9. Other direct (hearing/screening)	1,375			514	1,889	2,155	4,044	1.1	n.a.	n.a.
10. Total health care	114,708	56,952	5,370	26,641	203,671	86,933	290,604	82.9		
11. Social and community services	21,265			2,464	23,729	11,584	35,313	10.1		
12. Transportation	5,704			2,769	8,473	3,289	11,762	3.4		
13. Training										
14. Community organization										
15. Research and evaluation	6,340		3,750	237	10,327	2,153	12,480	3.6		
16. Environmental										
17. Other										
18. Total supporting activity costs	33,309		3,750	5,470	42,529	17,026	59,555	17.1		
19. Total health care and supporting activity costs	148,017	56,952	9,120	32,111	246,200	103,959	350,159	100.0%		
20. Medical records	23,124			6,008	29,132					
21. Other allocable (steno pool)	2,860			451	3,311					
22. Total allocable	25,984			6,459	32,443					
23. Administration	35,197	1,182		17,911	54,290					
24. Housekeeping and maintenance				16,028	16,028					
25. Other general services (security)				1,198	1,198					
26. Total general services	35,197	1,198		33,939	71,516					
27. Total allocable and general services	61,181	2,380		40,398	103,959					
28. Grand total	$209,198	$59,332	$9,120	$72,509	$350,159					

Note: n.a. = Not available.

Activities

A total of 55 activities (those listed under two goals were counted twice) were included for the eight goals, a number the data processing backup could comfortably manage. Personal details of each patient and family were collected at registration, and information about each encounter was routinely completed. All data were punched onto cards and tabulations produced by computer. The information collected corresponded to the standard reporting requirements developed by the Office of Economic Opportunity (OEO) for the neighborhood health centers that they had funded in recent years.

The activities listed were selected at the beginning of the year as representative of the tasks to be emphasized. Some had to be completed before others were started. For example, the Health Center building needed to be reconstructed before most of the staff were employed, and both of these were antecedent to delivering the health care. In future years, the evaluation would be more ambitious in the activities and outcome measures it included, but starting out with a fairly simple scheme allowed the staff to gain experience in applying the methodology.

Targets

Once the activities were listed, the targets were specified. Initially, this was a painful intellectual exercise, but after the first few activities had been allocated targets, it was surprisingly easy to work through the remainder of the list.

The targets were then assessed as a whole, to see if a realistic workload had been set, and to put them in perspective. For example, it was decided originally that 50 percent of adults registered with the Center should be given health assessments, but after other activities such as child assessments, sickle cell anemia screening, and treatment of walk-in patients were also given targets, the cumulative workload seemed unreasonable.

Most of the targets were set during September–December 1971, but occasionally it was necessary to gather preliminary information first, before deciding what expectations to set.

Outcome Measures

In order to evaluate the Center's overall performance, a standard numerical measure of achievement had to be developed. It was decided to let the real line [0, 1] represent a failure/success continuum, where 0 = complete failure and 1 = complete success. The point 0.6 was designated the minimum desirable level of achievement, that is, the target that the staff had chosen for a particular activity; any score in excess of 0.6 would show the degree to which a target had been surpassed. A score of 0.4 was taken to indicate that the Center had failed to achieve an objective; any score below 0.4 would show a proportionally greater degree of failure. The interval (0.4, 0.5) represented a "blurred region" suggestive of failure and (0.5, 0.6) a "blurred region" indicative of success.

Four different types of outcome measures were used to translate objectives to a [0, 1] continuum: (i) subjective, (ii) yes-no, (iii) linear, and (iv) distributional. The four types may be illustrated by considering the first activity in goal 3: "Register eligible persons with the Center." The target for this activity is to register 6,000 persons in the first year.

(i) Subjective. At the end of the first year, the program director, in consultation with the senior staff, considers how well registration has gone and makes an assessment on an 11-point scale 0.0, 0.1, 0.2, . . . , 0.9, 1.0. This assessment is taken to be the achievement for the registration activity. Alternatively, an external panel of judges may be used. This is likely to be less biased but difficult to arrange.

(ii) Yes-No. This is the simplest type of outcome measure and may always be used. Score 0.6 if the target is reached and 0.4 otherwise. It is appropriate to use the scores 0.6 and 0.4 since they correspond to the failure and success borderlines and such a crude measuring rod should not allow too high a level of relative success or failure.

(iii) Linear. A suitable linear scale should be set up. In this case a definite failure level must be specified—suppose this is 5,000 persons. Then an outcome of 5,000 will score 0.4 and 6,000 will score 0.6.

It is easy to see how this scale may be refined by using a quadratic scale or some higher degree of polynomial.

(iv) Distributional. An evaluator sets a target for an activity but initially is uncertain about the actual outcome. However, he/she may be willing to make probability statements about the chances of a given outcome. These probability statements may be used to determine an outcome measure. The evaluator must set up a distributional form that represents degrees of belief about the outcome, given that the staff work toward the target level. A target level and a failure level must be specified. As usual, the target level will correspond to an achievement of 0.6 and the failure level to 0.4. In this case 5,000 persons or less was felt to be a failure. Then a normal distribution is constructed with 6,000 as the 60 percentage point and 5,000 as the 40 percentage point. This corresponds to a normal distribution with mean 5,500 and standard deviation 2,000 (the 60 percentage point of a normal distribution is approximately one quarter of a standard deviation from the mean). The outcome measure is taken to be the percentage point at which the outcome falls. This may be found by calculating

$$\frac{|X - \text{Mean}|}{\text{Standard deviation}}$$

where X is the outcome and referring the result to percentage points of the standard normal distribution. The outcome in the example was 8,445 persons registered.

$$\frac{|X - \text{Mean}|}{\text{Standard deviation}} = \frac{8,445 - 5,500}{2,000} = 1.473$$

1.473 corresponds to the 93 percentage point. Hence, the achievement is given by 0.93.

The normal distribution is appropriate here, but other distributions may be relevant in some cases. For example, if it is felt that exceeding the target by a certain amount is not equivalent, in terms of achievement, to falling below the target by that same amount, then a skewed distribution such as a gamma may be more realistic than a symmetrical one like the normal.

Type (iv) was the outcome measure used for the registration activity. However, types (ii) and (iii) are the most common in the other tables. Usually, type (iii) was applied without specifying a failure level. Instead, the target level was transformed to 0.6 by using a suitable multiplying factor. For example, for the activity, "Encourage patients to keep appointments," the target was "65 percent of appointments should be kept." A naturally occurring outcome measure is the proportion (p) of kept appointments. This must be multiplied by 12/13 so that the target level of 0.65 corresponds to an achievement of 0.6, that is, $0.65 \times 12/13 = 0.60$. Another approach would have been to specify a failure level, for example, 50 percent, and use the points (50 percent, 0.4), (65 percent, 0.6) to determine the linear outcome measure. The second method is to be recommended, but the approach used here was easier to apply.

Weights

Weights were assigned to reflect the relative importance of activities to each goal, but they also depended on the outcome measures that were used. If a measure was felt to be imprecise (e.g., a subjective judgment), the weight assigned to the activity was less than it would have been if a more sophisticated measure were available. For example, the activity, "Make available suitable medical facilities to deliver primary care," was measured subjectively and so received a weight of 3 on a 5-point scale. If an objective measure had been developed, a weight of 4 or 5 would have been allocated.

Each goal was also weighted by its relative importance for the first year of the total program. Again the precision of the outcome measures used for the activities was taken into account when deciding on these weights. The last three goals were measured very imprecisely and so in the summary (Exhibit 4) were given a relatively lower weight.

Finally, those activities included (and hence measured) under more than one goal were weighted less, so that they did not receive disproportionate emphasis in the overall evaluation.

EXHIBIT 3 Evaluation of Effectiveness, Year 1—Goal II: Establish and Maintain the Health Center as an Operational Unit; Goal Weight = 5

		Assessment Regime				
Activity	Target	Outcome Measure	Weight	Outcome	Achievement	Effectiveness
Complete the reconstruction of the Health Center building.	Reconstruction complete by January 1972.	$\left[\begin{array}{c}\text{Estimated proportion of building completed by January 1972}\end{array}\right] \times \frac{6}{10} + \left[\begin{array}{c}\text{No. of days early completion}\end{array}\right] \times \frac{1}{60}$	5	Completed by January 1972	0.60	1.00
Employ a staff of qualified personnel.	90% of total staff requirement as of January 1972 will be employed and qualified.	$\left[\dfrac{\text{No. qualified staff at January 1972}}{\text{No. staff required}}\right] \times \frac{6}{9}$	5	100%	0.67	1.12
Make available suitable medical facilities to deliver primary care.	Adequate facilities available by January 1972.	Judgment by program director on scale [0, 1].	3	0.5	0.50	0.83
Deliver health care in a courteous manner.	85% of a sample of patients will answer positively to the question: "Are the people at the Center courteous when they deal with your problems?"	$\left[\begin{array}{c}\text{Proportion of a sample of registered patients who answer positively}\end{array}\right] \times \frac{12}{17}$	2	95%	0.67	1.12
Decorate the Center in a pleasant manner.	85% of a sample of patients will answer positively to the question: "Do you think the Center is decorated in a pleasant manner?"	$\left[\begin{array}{c}\text{Proportion of a sample of registered patients who answer positively}\end{array}\right] \times \frac{12}{17}$	2	89%	0.63	1.05

Objective	Criterion	Measurement			Achievement	Weight
Establish an appointment system.	60% encounters by appointment by March 1972.	Proportion of encounters by appointment during January–March 1972.	4	79%	0.79	1.32
Make arrangements to deal with walk-in patients.	Arrangements completed by December 1971.	$x = \begin{cases} 0.4 \text{ if no} \\ 0.6 \text{ if yes} \end{cases}$ Achievement $= x$	4	Yes	0.6	1.00
Encourage patients to make appointments.	From April 1972, 70% of encounters are by appointment.	$\left[\text{Proportion of center encounters by appointment during April–June 1972} \right] \times \frac{6}{7}$	3	56%	0.48	0.80
Establish mechanisms for reimbursement for services rendered.	Mechanisms established by June 1972.	$x = \begin{cases} 0.4 \text{ if no} \\ 0.6 \text{ if yes} \end{cases}$ Achievement $= x$	3	Yes	0.60	1.00
Design and test registration and encounter forms.	September 1971.	$x = \begin{cases} 0.4 \text{ if no} \\ 0.6 \text{ if yes} \end{cases}$ Achievement $= x$	4	Yes	0.60	1.00
Establish a reporting system to describe persons registered and details of encounters.	January 1972.	$x = \begin{cases} 0.4 \text{ if no} \\ 0.6 \text{ if yes} \end{cases}$ Achievement $= x$	4	Yes	0.60	1.00
Draw up an evaluation regime.	July 1972.	$x = \begin{cases} 0.4 \text{ if no} \\ 0.6 \text{ if yes} \end{cases}$ Achievement $= x$	4	Yes	0.60	1.00

Goal II Achievement = 0.62.

Goal II Effectiveness $= \dfrac{\text{Actual Achievement}}{\text{Target}} = \dfrac{0.62}{0.60} = 1.03.$

After weights had been assigned, a weighted mean achievement was computed for each goal, and the weighted mean goal achievement was computed as an indicator of overall program effectiveness. The achievement, measured on a [0, 1] scale, is divided by 0.6 to give the effectiveness scale. An effectiveness of 1.00 indicates that the objectives have been fulfilled. Degrees of under- or overfulfillment are then reflected by comparison with unity.

Reliability

Some attention should be paid to the question of reliability, that is, if the evaluation was repeated in a similar situation, would the same results be obtained? Many of the outcome measures used were objective and so can be taken to be fairly reliable. Of course, care must be taken to collect accurate information, and, ideally, quality control checks should be carried out. No such checks were made for the case example.

The reliability of the allocation of weights is more open to question. No studies were conducted to investigate this, although a fairly straightforward method of checking the weight allocation would be to paraphrase each activity, and three to six months later, ask the staff to weight the paraphrased version. The time lag would help eliminate the memory effect as far as possible. The correlation between the different weight assignments would be an indicator of reliability.

A more complex question is the original choice of activities. It is not realistic to think that another center, no matter how similar, would choose the same objectives. If one takes the objectives as given, the question is laid to rest. If not, it is likely to take more time to answer than is worthwhile.

Validity

It would be possible to go to absurd lengths to check the validity of the outcome measures and weights assigned to each objective. A more pragmatic approach is to consider the extent to which the system is used and the opinions of the program staff when they see the results. In this case, the findings corresponded with the general feelings of the staff, and so this is felt to be an important indicator of validity. More detailed aspects of validity are being investigated.

Discussion of the System

An example of the activities and calculations for one of the goals is given in Exhibit 3. Exhibit 4 is a summary of the achievement and effectiveness for all eight goals and indicates a very successful first year. The evaluation may be a little flattering, but it concurs with the staff's own perceptions.

EXHIBIT 4 Evaluation of Effectiveness, Year 1—Summary

	Goal I Target Population	Goal II Operation of Center	Goal III Accessibility of Health Care	Goal IV Improvement of Health	Goal V Quality of Care	Goal VI Contribution to Quality of Life	Goal VII Relation to Other Programs	Goal VIII Catalyst for Social Reform	Overall
Weight..........	4	5	5	5	5	4	3	2	
Achievement......	0.71	0.62	0.80	0.59	0.60	0.66	0.64	0.69	0.66
Effectiveness	1.18	1.03	1.33	0.98	1.00	1.10	1.06	1.15	1.11

In addition, the performance for each activity was summarized to allow the director to plan for the year ahead. It might, for instance, make sense to reduce resources given to activities that were overfulfilled and redistribute the excess to those that achieved less than 0.6.

A survey of the attitudes of registered patients was conducted during July 1972, and this information was used in the evaluation. It was appreciated that patients are often reluctant to give negative statements to questions like "Do you feel comfortable about expressing your health needs to the people that care for you at the Center?" High targets (85 percent) were set for these attitudinal objectives in order to compensate for the reluctance to criticize.

Evaluation of the System

According to Dr. Chadwick:

The major advantage of the system was that performance was measured in a way that administrators and staff can easily understand. In addition, it required little specialized professional input beyond the limited help of a statistician in formulating some of the outcome measures. Also, the system could easily be used to evaluate a program in midstream, since it was possible to start the process at any stage.

So far, it has only been used to aid internal planning and administration, but it need not be limited to this. If standard types of activities and associated targets are developed, then comparisons between different programs may be made. Also, an external evaluator could change the targets to investigate the performance by a different set of standards. If a program felt it could not conduct an evaluation on its own, an outside agency could be contracted to assist.

The total cost of data collection and processing in the first year was about $30,000. This included one dedicated biostatistician on the staff of the Center. An outside biostatistician devoted about 20 percent of his time during the year developing the methodology, applying it, and assisting with the organization of data processing. Numerous discussions with the staff were involved. It would be reasonable to estimate that in the future, up to 20 percent of a biostatistician's time may be necessary to undertake an evaluation on this scale. For a program funded with several hundred thousand dollars this would not be a prohibitive cost.

Questions

1. Should Dr. Chadwick continue to evaluate the Center by the statistical system described in this case?
2. Is the financial evaluation system one she should continue?
3. Should she suggest that HEW require that it be used by all community health centers?

CASE 12–3   Charlottesville Fire Department*

In December 1976, the Research Triangle Institute (RTI), in collaboration with the National Fire Protection Association (NFPA) and the International City Management Association (ICMA), issued preliminary findings of an 18-month evaluation of fire protection delivery arrangements in a nationwide sample of 1,400 fire departments. Charlottesville Fire Chief Julian Taliaferro immediately began using the RTI criteria to measure the effectiveness and productivity of the Charlottesville Fire Department, in relation to similarly constructed fire departments in cities of comparable size nationwide.

Background

The Charlottesville Fire Department protected both the City of Charlottesville and part of Albemarle County. The city itself included some 10.4 square miles, a population of approximately 56,000, and property valued at $766,143,984 (true market value).

Fire department resources included 5 engine companies, 1 aerial ladder, 68 paid personnel, and a volunteer force that functioned in an auxiliary capacity.

Albemarle County itself had no paid fire department. Protection was maintained through a network of 6 volunteer companies numbering 250 persons. The county also had, for a number of years, a verbal agreement with the city that the latter would automatically respond to fire alarms originating within a specified 30-square-mile area of the county, comprised mostly of that urbanized portion surrounding the city. This area had a population of approximately 19,800 and property valued at $202,365,670. While there were no county volunteers located within this area, those in close proximity would respond to fire alarms there.

The county contributed to the annual budget of the city fire department in proportion to the services it was rendered. In fiscal year 1977 this amounted to $163,303 of a total budget of $831,629. The county also maintained one engine company located at the main fire station, this being the engine the city normally used to respond to county fires. Therefore, it can be seen that the city fire department served two distinct regions: the city itself and a portion of Albemarle County. Chief Taliaferro's study attempts to evaluate and compare levels of fire protection provided by the city fire department to each area.

---

* This case was prepared by S. Y. Young and C. J. Tompkins; revised by C. J. Tompkins, College of Engineering, West Virginia University. Copyright © 1979 by C. J. Tompkins.

Measurement Criteria

RTI reduced all departments studied to 4 categories: fully volunteer, mostly volunteer (50 to 90 percent), mostly paid (50 to 90 percent), and fully paid departments. The departments were then further divided by size of population and type of community protected, whether center, ring, or fringe. A center city was described as an urban area with a population greater than 25,000 having considerable fire hazard and a paid fire department. A ring city was defined as a suburban community with a population of less than 100,000, and with a fire department composed of some volunteer personnel. A rural, low density community on the edge of an urbanized or suburban area was considered to be a fringe city.

The city of Charlottesville was classified as a center city of population between 25,000 and 100,000 with a fully paid fire department. It may be noted that RTI offered no category for a center city with a mostly paid force. This is ideally what Charlottesville would be considered, but since that classification did not exist, the next most accurate one was chosen. Chief Taliaferro felt the fully paid description to be closest to the true situation as over 90 percent of all fire alarms were handled with available paid personnel.

The 30 square miles of Albemarle County protected by the city was classified as a ring city of a population between 5,001 and 25,000 with a mostly volunteer force. The force was considered mostly volunteer because, while the city did respond to fire alarms in the area, its function was considered to be auxiliary to county volunteer companies that also responded to alarms in the area. Criticality of city response depended upon response time for county units and the seriousness of the fire. The city would normally respond to alarms with one engine company and three firefighters, but would usually be outnumbered by volunteer equipment and personnel.

RTI evaluated all departments as related to measures of effectiveness and productivity, using information gathered from years 1973, 1974, and 1975. Most of the figures used are averages for the three-year period and all are corrected for inflation.

Effectiveness was described as the extent to which the incidence of fire, loss of life, personal injury, and property loss was minimized. The seven measures used to operationalize the concept were:

1. Number of fires per 1,000 of population protected.
2. Dollars of property loss per capita.
3. Dollars of property loss per $1,000 of market value of property.
4. Dollars of property loss per fire.
5. Number of civilian injuries and deaths per 100,000 of population protected.
6. Number of civilian injuries and deaths per 100 fires.
7. Number of firefighter injuries and deaths per 100 fires.

Productivity was defined by RTI as the measure of the relationship between results obtained and resources utilized. Rather than rely strictly on levels of effort (expenditures) to measure fire department costs, RTI preferred to speak of *total cost*, defined as the sum of expenditures and dollar property losses.

Indicators used to reflect productivity were:

1. Expenditures per capita.
2. Expenditures per $1,000 of market value of property.
3. Total cost per capita.
4. Total cost per $1,000 of market value of property.
5. Total cost per fire.

After obtaining all measurement figures for each fire department, an average of each was computed for those departments considered to be in the lower quartile of service delivery (more effective), those at the median or average level of delivery, and those in the upper quartile or less effective level of service delivery. Those were the figures used for comparison in this study, target figures being those in the lower quartile.

Charlottesville's Performance

As shown in Exhibit 1, the number of fires per 1,000 of population protected in the city averaged 10.68 for the 1973–1975 period; this pushes the city above the lower quartile figure of 7.24. Chief Taliaferro believed the difference might be attributed to the fact that Charlottesville did not have a well-developed fire prevention program. In 1977 there was only one fire prevention officer, and, therefore, the program was conducted on a somewhat hit-and-miss basis. The Chief felt more time spent on public education and prevention programs would decrease the figure substantially.

The county figure of 2.98 compared favorably with the more effective target 6.63. This would be due to the low population density in the county which provided for less fire hazard than a high density area such as the city. The Chief expected this figure to rise as population and age of structures in the county increased.

Property loss per capita and per $1,000 of market value of property for the city are both higher than the median figures. This is in part due to the relatively low average manning of 2.6 firefighters per engine company. The number of firefighters immediately present at a fire would help determine the number and type of suppression activities that could be initiated. The longer certain activities must be delayed, the greater the chance of increased property loss.

In contrast, the property loss per fire for the city was below the median. This was in part due to the fact that Charlottesville had relatively little industry as compared to other cities of the same size. More industry would increase the risk of industrial fires, where property loss is normally greater than in dwelling fires (the type with the greatest frequency in Charlottesville).

EXHIBIT 1 Effectiveness Measures

Effectiveness Measures	Albemarle County Charlottesville	Target More Effective (Lower 25%)	Median	Less Effective (Upper 25%)
Prevention:				
Number of fires/1000 of	2.98	6.63	9.43	15.95
population protected	10.68	7.24	12.78	19.23
Suppression:				
Dollar property loss	27.47	5.10	7.69	11.98
per capita.................	10.90	5.39	10.40	14.96
Dollar property loss per	2.69	.34	.50	.75
$1,000 of market value	1.25	.31	.54	2.10
Dollar property loss	9,219.00	438.51	938.21	1,647.40
per fire	1,021.00	393.94	1,111.97	2,210.82
Civilian injuries and				
deaths per 100,000	5.05	0.00	7.93	21.73
population	35.71	13.84	19.09	28.48
Civilian injuries and				
deaths per 100 fires	1.70	0.00	.85	1.79
	3.34	.86	1.66	2.23
Firefighters injuries and	1.70	0.00	.58	2.65
deaths per 100 fires	.84	1.07	2.51	4.14
Levels of effort: .				
Expenditures per	5.28	8.08	15.02	21.02
capita...................	8.61	20.92	24.77	31.75
Expenditures per $1000				
market value of	.52	.51	.98	1.44
property	.62	.86	1.84	3.22
Productivity measures:				
Total cost per	32.76	18.36	28.75	30.77
capita...................	19.51	23.12	33.10	44.17
Total cost per $1,000				
market value of	3.20	.96	1.38	2.05
property	1.42	1.01	1.66	5.99
Total cost per	10,993.00	1,467.00	2,635.00	3,638.00
fire.....................	1,827.00	2,373.00	3,041.00	4,134.00

A comparison of property loss per capita and per $1,000 of market value of property would indicate the county to be high above the less effective range. But these figures are somewhat misleading. The property loss totals used here are averaged for the three-year period 1973–1975. In 1973 and 1974 there were two large industrial fires in the county, one where loss was estimated at $270,000, the other at $750,000. Without these two fires, property loss would have been substantially less for both years. For example, in 1973 loss was actually $97,000. Chief Taliaferro believed these two catastrophic fires inflated what property loss might routinely have been. Calculations with these two fires deleted showed property loss indicators to fall, although they still hovered in the less effective range (i.e., per capita, $9.38 and per fire $3,102).

Also, when using property loss figures in terms of per capita and per fire, Chief Taliaferro believed it was important to keep in mind the low population density of the county area (19,800 total) and also the low number of fires occurring in the county (i.e., 59 in 1975 as opposed to 598 for the city). Another contributing factor to higher property losses in the county was the longer response time experienced; meaning the fire was already somewhat advanced by the time the engine company arrived.

Civilian injuries and deaths per 100 fires were very high for Charlottesville as compared to other cities of its size. One reason may be the way in which injuries and deaths were reported in Charlottesville and other cities, a factor for which the RTI survey makes no allowance. Chief Taliaferro indicated that the Charlottesville Fire Department reported any civilian injury at the scene of a fire, however slight. Other cities may have reported the same way, or they may report only those injuries of a more serious nature. Those departments who follow the latter policy would compare more favorably in this measure than the former.

Grouping together injuries and deaths may also have distorted the meaning of the rating. Charlottesville averaged one death due to fire per year. The year 1975 saw 19 injuries and one death. Considering some injuries were probably slight, do those figures carry the same meaning as do 19 deaths and one injury?

Civilian injuries and deaths were also relatively high in the county. This again may be due to the reporting procedure. Also involved may be longer response time averaged for county alarms. Chief Taliaferro felt that possibly 25 percent of injuries could be related to this last factor.

The fighter injuries and deaths per 100 fires for the city were extremely low—well below the lower 25 percentile figure. This was due in part to mandatory protective clothing and required training for the firefighters. Also fewer injuries were reported in this fire department than may be the case in others.

Those explanations would also apply to firefighter injuries and deaths in the county as related to city firefighters. But the county figure was high as compared to the city figure probably due to the county volunteers that would respond to these fires. Volunteer firefighters normally wore less protective clothing and had fewer training hours, two factors that would increase chances of firefighter injuries.

Fire department expenditures per capita and per $1,000 of market value of property were low for both the city and county. But low expenditures do not automatically indicate efficiency. For a comparison with the target figures it must be kept in mind that while expenditures were lower than the 25 percentile, property loss figures were higher. This would indicate that the fire department was not as effective in the provision of fire protection as it might have been—whether this be due to resource misallocation or underfunding, a more likely factor in this case.

The extremely low expenditure per capita for the city might also relate to an additional factor. It must be kept in mind that the target figure for Charlottesville corresponds to that for a fully paid department and that Charlottesville was not strictly all paid, as there was an auxiliary force available. It seems probable that if Charlottesville had not had this auxiliary force, the city would have had to hire additional personnel at added cost.

Total Cost

The concept of total cost, while more informative than that of expenditures alone, may be somewhat misleading in its implications. As a combination of property losses and expenditures, it purports to be a productivity measure of effectiveness and efficiency where maximum productivity is achieved when total cost is minimized. RTI admitted that the calculation is indifferent to trade-offs between property loss and fire department expenditures.

For example, the same total cost could be achieved both by a department with low expenditures and high property losses and one with higher expenditures and lower property losses. Chief Taliaferro believed that a service-oriented agency such as a fire department cannot be indifferent to these trade-offs. The departmental goal of minimizing property loss due to fire must be part of any productivity measure. Chief Taliaferro was not certain that equal total costs reflect equal productivity when one department may spend more money, but have a good suppression record, and another may spend a minimal amount, but have a history of high property loss.

Chief Taliaferro thought the productivity concept would be more useful if property loss and expenditure could be weighted in a manner to reflect departmental goals and objectives.

For the city, total cost per capita was low, a commendable figure upon first inspection. But closer examination shows that this figure was a combination of extremely low expenditures per capita and higher than average property losses.

Total cost per $1,000 of market value of property for the city was below the median for comparable fire departments. This again was the result of low expenditures and high property loss in this category.

Total cost per fire for the city was below the target figure mostly as a result of low expenditures as property loss per fire was closer to the median level.

In contrast to the city, total cost per capita and per $1,000 of market value of property for the county was above the median level. This was due to extremely high property loss in the county as discussed earlier.

Questions

1. Assume that the information furnished by Research Triangle Institute was the only information available as a basis of comparison. What is your judgment as to the performance of the Charlottesville Fire Department?
2. What additional information, if any, would you like to have, if it could be obtained at a reasonable cost, in order to improve your judgment of performance?

Reporting on Performance: Technical Aspects

Management generally reviews an organization's performance in two somewhat different ways. First, it monitors the performance of current operations on a regular, recurring basis, using a set of reports designed for this purpose, together with other information. This type of review is discussed in this chapter and the next. Second, management conducts reviews of programs and activities at infrequent intervals, using information that is developed specifically for each program or activity. These reviews, called *program evaluations,* are discussed in Chapter 15.

Reports concerning the performance of current operations customarily are called *management control reports* since their purpose is to aid in the management control process. The dissemination of such reports, coupled with an analysis of the information they contain, is only one facet of this process, however. The whole process consists of several activities as well as a variety of formal and informal devices. Many of these activities and devices were discussed in Chapter 7.

This chapter discusses the technical aspects of the management control reports. We focus, in particular, on variance analysis, a technique that allows managers to determine in some considerable detail why actual revenues and expenses diverged from budgeted ones. In Chapter 14, we look at how the reports themselves can be structured, and how variance analysis can be combined with other information to facilitate managerial action to improve organizational performance.

TYPES OF INFORMATION

In monitoring performance, managers typically rely on both quantitative and nonquantitative information. Quantitative information can be either financial or nonfinancial. For example, as we will see in this chapter, variance analysis uses financial information. By contrast, as we discussed in Chapter 12, output information, while frequently quantitative, is not usually financial.

> *Example.* The New York City school system measures output at each school by a combination of: (1) attendance figures, (2) extracurricular activity participation, (3) number of diplomas, (4) number of scholarships, (5) percent of pupils with five or more major subjects, (6) percent of pupils with an 85 percent grade average or above, (7) standard test results, and (8) number of students discharged.

Quantitative information also can include nonmonetary information on inputs, such as the number of employees or the number of hours of service. This supplements the financial information on expenses. Output and input information frequently is shown on the same page as financial information, and the two types are related by reporting, say, cost per unit of output.

Quantitative information usually is included on reports that are prepared according to a regular schedule. The reports may arrive weekly, monthly, quarterly, or according to some other schedule that provides the information to managers in a timely way. As we discussed in Chapter 12, timely means that the information arrives soon enough to help managers make needed decisions.

In addition to receiving these routine reports, which tend to have the same format and content month after month, managers also can receive a variety of nonroutine, unsystematic, and generally nonquantitative performance information. Some of it comes from trade publications, newspapers, and other outside sources. Some of it comes from conversations within the organization, from memoranda, or from managers' personal observations as they visit responsibility centers and talk with people there.

Although the routine reports serve as a useful starting point in monitoring performance, additional information picked up from these other sources is essential to understanding how organizational units are performing and what factors are affecting them. Indeed, this nonquantitative information often is more important than that contained in the routine reports.

TYPES OF ORGANIZATIONS

Some nonprofit organizations, or parts of such organizations, have activities that are quite similar to those in for-profit businesses. Analysis of management performance in these *businesslike* organizations is essentially the same as it is in a for-profit company. Other nonprofit organizations are unlike a business in that they are not self-financing. Instead, the amount of resources they have available for operation in a given year is fixed in advance. We call these *fixed-resource* organizations. Still other nonprofit organizations are required to do a job that is relatively fixed, regardless of the amount of resources planned. We call these *fixed-job* organizations.

Businesslike Organizations

We use the term *businesslike organization* to describe an entity that obtains a substantial fraction of its revenues from fees charged to clients, either directly or through third parties (such as medicare for hospitals, state governments for some mental health agencies, or city governments for some foster care agencies). A businesslike organization ordinarily can exert a significant amount of influence over either the amount of revenues earned, the amount of expenses incurred, or both. Analysis of its operating performance, thus, is similar to analysis of the performance of a for-profit company.

> ***Example.*** A hospital cannot influence the number of individuals in its community who need hospital care, but it can—through a variety of techniques—influence the number of individuals who are admitted to its facility. Moreover, although management cannot directly influence physician-ordering patterns, it can have a direct effect on unit costs in terms of efficiency of personnel, wage rates, and unit prices for supplies and materials.

> ***Example.*** A museum or symphony orchestra can engage in a wide array of marketing activities in an attempt to increase the number of clients using its services. Choices about programming, prices, promotional activities, and the like are all comparable in nature to those of a for-profit company. Furthermore, cost analysis and control are of equally great significance.

Fixed-Resource Organizations

In many nonprofit organizations, the amount of resources available for operations in a given year is essentially fixed. This is the case with many religious organizations and other membership organizations whose resources are fixed by the amount of pledges or dues. Colleges with a fixed enrollment know their available resources, within narrow limits, as soon as the students enter. Health maintenance organizations (HMOs) know their resources based on annual enrollments.

Fixed-resource organizations must carefully monitor their spending to assure that they spend no more than the amount of available resources. Moreover, their success is measured by how much service they provide with these resources. In such organizations, spending more than the budget could portend financial disaster, and spending too far below the budget may be the first sign of impending client dissatisfaction.

In some fixed-resource organizations, the amount of service provided is a subjective judgment rather than a measured quantity. When this is the case, the reporting system cannot express the output for the whole organization in quantitative terms, and overall measures of efficiency therefore cannot be developed. Nevertheless, within such an organization there may well be service units whose output can be measured, and it may be possible to develop output and efficiency measures for these units. It also may be possible for managers to use quantitative information to help them determine when and where they need to take corrective action.

Fixed-Job Organizations

A fire department has a specific job to do; it must be ready to fight all fires that occur in its service area. Differences between the budget and actual amounts of spending may exist in either direction because of the nature of the job that had to be done. Similarly, if there are many snowstorms, the budget for snowplowing may need to be exceeded. Judgments about the performance of such organizations must therefore be in terms of how well they did whatever they were supposed to do, and whether a minimum amount of resources was used in doing whatever they did. It is more important, for example, to consider the cost of snow removal per snowstorm or per inch of snow than the total snow removal cost of the year.

In fixed-job organizations, there is a tendency to ascribe differences between actual and budgeted amounts in a general way to the requirements of the job, whereas a detailed analysis may reveal inefficiencies. It is not sufficient to explain away a budget overrun in the highway maintenance department on the grounds that the winter was severe. Analysis of the variable costs that are caused by snowstorms of varying depths may indicate that the overrun was greater than it should have been. Thus, in almost all of these situations, a quantitative analysis of the reasons why actual results diverged from the budget is an essential management tool.

Role of Responsibility Centers

All three types of organizations can use both quantitative and nonquantitative information. In all but the smallest, the information usually is identified with responsibility centers. This is because senior management usually acts by communicating with heads of responsibility centers. For ease of comparison, the same format usually is used for all responsibility centers. Most of the examples in our discussion of variance analysis assume that the computations are being made for a single responsibility center within a larger organization.

VARIANCE ANALYSIS

In most types of organizations, the difference, or *variance,* between planned (or budgeted) performance and actual performance can be explained by five factors:

1. Volume (number of units of service).
2. Mix of units of service.

3. Revenue per unit of service (or selling price).
4. Rates paid for inputs (such as labor wages and cost per unit of raw materials).
5. Usage and efficiency of inputs (usage of raw materials and efficiency of labor).

Ordinarily, these variances are considered separately. There are three reasons for the separation: (1) they have different causes, (2) they usually involve different responsibility center managers, and (3) they require different types of corrective action.

Basic techniques for calculating these variances are given in the appendix at the end of this chapter; more complex techniques are described in cost accounting textbooks. Computer programs are available to perform the actual calculations.

Volume Variances

If the actual quantity of services rendered differs from the quantity assumed in the budget, both revenue and certain expense items will be different from the budgeted amounts. For this reason, there are several different volume variances. The *revenue volume variance* shows the amount of change in revenue due exclusively to a change in volume (assuming that selling price remained constant). Similarly, the *expense volume variance* shows the change in expenses due exclusively to a change in volume (assuming that the expense per unit of volume remained constant). The sum of these two is the *contribution margin variance*.

Revenue Volume Variance. The revenue volume variance is the difference between the actual volume and the budgeted volume multiplied by the budgeted unit price:

$$RVV = (V_a - V_b) \times P_b$$

Example. If a museum budgets 10,000 visitors per month at $6 per visitor, its budgeted monthly revenue is $60,000. If in April it had 11,000 visitors, its revenue volume variance would be a favorable $6,000 [= (11,000 - 10,000) × $6].

Expense Volume Variance. The expense volume variance is the difference between the budgeted volume and the actual volume multiplied by the budgeted variable expense per unit:

$$EVV = (V_b - V_a) \times E_b$$

The calculation of the expense volume variance therefore requires classifying expense items as either fixed or variable. Recall from Chapter 5 that fixed expenses do not vary at all with volume, while variable items vary directly with volume.

Fixed versus Flexible Budgets. A budget that has no variable expense component is called a *fixed budget*. A fixed budget typically is used in a discretionary expense center. In a discretionary expense center, the manager is held responsible for spending no more than the budgeted, fixed amount each month (or other reporting period).

A budget developed from a classification of expenses into their fixed and variable elements is called a *flexible budget*. Rather than being a fixed amount, a flexible budget is expressed as a cost formula using agreed-upon fixed expenses and agreed-upon variable expenses per unit. An expected level of volume is specified to make sure that the fixed expenses are within their relevant range. This budget is then "flexed" each month (or other reporting period) by applying the actual volume of activity to the cost formula. The difference between the budget using the original estimate of volume and the budget using actual volume is the expense volume variance.

> *Example.* Assume that the budget for the kitchen of a shelter for the homeless consists of $12,000 per month of salaries and benefits, occupancy costs, and other costs that are unaffected by the number of meals served. The cost of ingredients, supplies, utilities, and other costs that vary with the number of meals served is expected to be $4 per meal. The cost formula for the kitchen therefore is $12,000 + $4x. The kitchen expects to serve 900 meals a month. Its monthly costs therefore are expected to be $15,600 [= $12,000 + ($4 × 900)].
>
> If, in April, the kitchen served 1,000 meals, the flexible budget would be $16,000 [= $12,000 + ($4 × 1,000)]. The expense volume variance would be an unfavorable $400 (= $15,600 − $16,000). It is unfavorable because the increase in meals, other things equal, would cause higher expenses and thus lower income. As indicated above, the expense volume variance also can be computed by multiplying the difference between actual and budgeted volume by the budgeted variable expense per unit; this results in the same unfavorable $400 [= (900 − 1,000) × $4].

A flexible budget typically is used in a standard expense center. In this sort of responsibility center, the manager is not expected to exert any control over volume, but he or she is expected to adhere to the amount determined by the flexible budget. Thus, for the manager of the kitchen in the above example, actual expenses for the month of April would be compared to a flexed budget of $16,000 to measure financial performance.

Contribution Margin Variance.   Differences in volume affect income by the difference between revenue per unit of volume and variable expenses per unit of volume. As we discussed in Chapter 5, this difference is called the *contribution margin*. The contribution margin variance is the sum of the revenue volume variance and the expense volume variance:

$$CMV = EVV + RVV$$

> *Example.* Assume that a food and wine association charges $50 per year for a membership, and expects that member service activities will cost $30 per year. The association has $380,000 in fixed costs. Assume that the management anticipated 20,000 members, but that only 15,000 joined. The revenue volume variance would be an unfavorable $250,000 [= (15,000 − 20,000) × $50]. The expense volume variance would be a favorable $150,000 [= (20,000 − 15,000) × $30]. The contribution margin variance would be an unfavorable $100,000 (= $150,000 − $250,000). Alternatively, the association thought

it would have \$400,000 [= (\$50 − \$30) × 20,000] of contribution to its fixed costs, but it had only \$300,000 [= (\$50 − \$30) × 15,000], a \$100,000 unfavorable variance.

Mix Variances

The volume variance computed above assumes that every unit of volume has the same selling price and unit variable expense associated with it. In many organizations, different types of services have different selling prices and different unit variable expense amounts. When this is the case, the volume variances are calculated using weighted averages of the selling price and variable expense amounts. If there is a change in the budgeted proportions of the different service types, a *mix variance* develops.

Many organizations do not calculate mix variances. In these organizations, the mix variance is automatically a part of the volume variance.[1] In a hospital, a mix variance can result either from a change in the hospital's case types (e.g., relatively more coronary artery bypass surgery cases than influenza cases), from a change in the mix of services used to treat a given case type (e.g., more or different radiological procedures ordered for each patient undergoing coronary artery bypass surgery), or from some combination of the two.[2]

Selling Price Variances

The selling price variance is the difference between the actual selling price and the budgeted selling price, multiplied by the actual level of volume:

$$SPV = (P_a - P_b) \times V_a$$

If, for example, a day-care center changed its fees during the year, there is a selling price variance. The computations for a selling price variance are shown in the revenue portion of the section, "Making the Computations," in the appendix at the end of this chapter.

Rate Variances

If the actual rates an organization pays for its material and labor inputs change from their budgeted levels, there is a rate variance. Rate variances usually are for either raw materials or labor. To compute them, we must know the unit amounts (raw material prices or wage rates) that were used in developing the budget. This

---

[1] For an explanation of the process of calculating mix variances, see Robert N. Anthony and James S. Reece, *Accounting Principles* (Homewood, Ill.: Richard D. Irwin, 1989).

[2] For additional discussion of this point, see David W. Young and Richard B. Saltman, "Preventive Medicine for Hospital Costs," *Harvard Business Review*, January–February, 1983.

is the reason we suggested in Chapter 10 that the budget show both quantity and unit price components.

Raw Material Rate Variances.   If the prices (rates) an organization pays for its raw materials change from what was budgeted, there is a raw material rate variance. The raw material rate variance is the difference between the budget rate and the actual rate, multiplied by the actual quantity of raw materials purchased:

$$MRV = (R_b - R_a) \times Q_a$$

Example. If an association planned to purchase paper for its newsletters for $10 a ream, and paid $8 instead, there is a material rate variance. If the association purchased 500 reams, the total material rate variance is a favorable $1,000 [= ($10 − $8) × 500].

Wage Rate Variances.   If the wages we pay our staff change from the budgeted levels, there is a wage rate variance. The wage rate variance is the difference between the budget rate and the actual rate, multiplied by the actual hours worked:

$$WRV = (R_b - R_a) \times H_a$$

The computations for wage rate variances are shown in the appendix.

Example. If a laboratory planned to pay its technicians $12 an hour, but paid them $14 instead, there is a wage rate variance. If the technicians worked 600 hours, the total wage rate variance is an unfavorable $1,200 [= ($12 − $14) × 600].

Usage/Efficiency Variances

Usage and efficiency variances measure, respectively, the actual productivity of raw materials and labor as compared to budgeted productivity levels. Typically, the term *material usage variance* is used for raw materials and the term *labor efficiency variance* is used for labor.

Material Usage Variance.   If the amount of raw materials used per unit of output differs from what was budgeted, there is a material usage variance. The material usage variance is the difference between the budget usage and the actual usage, multiplied by the budgeted rate, multiplied by actual volume of output:

$$MUV = (U_b - U_a) \times R_b \times V_a$$

The computation for a material usage variance is the same as the computation for a wage volume variance, as shown in the appendix.

Example. A free-standing radiology laboratory budgeted an average of 1.3 films per chest X ray, but actually used 1.6 films. The raw materials in each film had a budgeted cost of $12 each. The lab performed 2,000 chest X rays during the most recent month. The usage variance is an unfavorable $7,200 [= (1.3 − 1.6) × $12 × 2,000].

Labor Efficiency Variances.   If the actual amount of labor time needed to produce a unit of output differs from the budgeted amount of time, there is a labor efficiency variance. The labor efficiency variance is the difference between the budgeted time per unit and the actual time per unit, multiplied by the budgeted rate, multiplied by actual volume of output:

$$\text{LEV} = (T_b - T_a) \times R_b \times V_a$$

The appendix at the end of this chapter diagrams the computations for a labor efficiency variance. It is labeled there as a volume variance.

> *Example.* A welfare department's social workers were budgeted to spend an average of one-half hour per interview with potential clients, but actually spent an average of one-third hour. The social workers were paid $18 an hour. They interviewed a total of 300 clients during the most recent month. The efficiency variance is a favorable $900 [= (3/6 hours − 2/6 hours) × $18 × 300].

Use of Variance Analysis.   An important feature of variance analysis is the ability it gives senior management to link managerial responsibility to changes in revenues and expenses. By way of summary, Exhibit 13–1 lists each variance, and identifies in a general sense the department or responsibility center manager who controls it. Although Exhibit 13–1 is most applicable to a businesslike organization, it also has validity for fixed-resource and fixed-job organizations. The principal difference is that certain fixed-resource and fixed-job organizations will not be concerned with some of the variances. For example, a fixed-resource organization ordinarily will not be concerned with selling price variances.

In general, operating managers do not control the volume or mix of services supplied, nor do they usually set wage rates for employees, or control the rates paid for raw materials and other items of expense. Consequently, the principal reason for identifying the volume, mix, selling price, and rate variances is to

---

EXHIBIT 13–1   Types of Variances and Controlling Agents

Variance	*Controlling Agent*
Volume variance (revenue/expense)..........	Marketing department/senior management/the environment (depending on the organization).
Mix variances	Same as above.
Selling price variances.....................	Senior management/marketing department/ program managers (depending on the organization).
Raw material price variances................	Purchasing department/program managers.
Wage rate variances.......................	Senior management (who negotiate union contracts)/program managers (who make job offers).
Usage variances	Program managers/department heads.
Efficiency variances.......................	Program managers/department heads.

isolate them so management can focus attention on efficiency variances (and, therefore, the individual managers responsible for these variances). This is the principal reason for preparing a flexible budget.

In any event, senior management needs to have an adequate explanation of the reasons underlying large efficiency variances, and it especially needs to know whether unfavorable variances are likely to persist or whether steps are under way to correct them. By distinguishing between efficiency variances and all other variances, senior management is in a better position to discuss these steps with operating managers.

AN ILLUSTRATION OF VARIANCES IN A HOSPITAL SETTING

To illustrate how the above variances can be used, assume that Nucio Hospital has prepared the somewhat simplified budget shown in Exhibit 13–2. As this budget shows, the hospital anticipates four different kinds of cases: acute myocardial infarction (heart attack), influenza, pneumonia, and phlebitis. Its budgeted variable expenses per case are based on four different services: routine care (i.e., the hospital stay itself), radiology films, laboratory tests, and pharmacy units (such as prescriptions). (Obviously, there are many more services and many more case types in a hospital than this, so the overall totals may not be completely realistic. Nevertheless, the numbers are sufficient for illustrative purposes.)

Operating under a diagnosis-based form of reimbursement, the hospital is paid on a per case basis. For each case type, the anticipated "selling price" is shown, along with the anticipated utilization and variable expense per unit for each service. The total variable expense per case for each case type is then calculated, and the revenue and total variable expense per case are multiplied by the anticipated number of cases to give total revenue and total variable expenses by case type. The latter is deducted from total revenue to give the contribution to fixed expenses from each case type. The fixed expenses are then deducted from the total contribution to give a total budgeted income of $77,000 for the accounting period.

Exhibit 13–3 is a flexible budget based on the actual number of cases served. The flexible budget shows what the surplus *would have been* if everything remained the same as the original budget except volume and mix of cases. That is, the calculations use budgeted figures for both revenue per case and variable expense per case to calculate what the budget would have been if the actual number and mix of cases had been known in advance. Fixed expenses are shown as budgeted because the new volume amounts did not affect them. The result is that there would have been an income of $43,450 instead of the original $77,000.

The flexible budget is followed by revenue and expense volume variances, and a contribution margin variance. There are several items worth noting in these computations. First, as discussed in the appendix, in computing the revenue variance, budgeted cases are subtracted from actual cases, whereas in computing the expense variance the reverse is true. Second, when the unfavorable $33,550 contri-

EXHIBIT 13–2 Original Budget

	Acute MI	Influenza	Pneumonia	Phlebitis	Total
Overall budget:					
Number of cases..............	300	200	100	50	650
Revenue per case	$ 6,000	$ 1,000	$ 1,500	$ 3,000	
Total revenue	1,800,000	200,000	150,000	150,000	2,300,000
Variable expenses per case	3,590	910	1,031	1,218	
Total variable expenses.........	1,077,000	182,000	103,100	60,900	1,423,000
Contribution..................	$ 723,000	$ 18,000	$ 46,900	$ 89,100	$ 877,000
Total fixed expenses					800,000
Income					$ 77,000
Variable expense detail:					
Routine care:					
Number of days per case	21	5	6	7	
Expense per day.............	$ 150	$ 150	$ 150	$ 150	
Total expense per case	$ 3,150	$ 750	$ 900	$ 1,050	
Radiology:					
Number of films per case	5	1	2	0	
Expense per film.............	$ 25	$ 25	$ 25	$ 25	
Total expense per case	$ 125	$ 25	$ 50	$ 0	
Laboratory:					
Number of tests per case	10	5	3	7	
Expense per test.............	$ 15	$ 15	$ 15	$ 15	
Total expense per case	$ 150	$ 75	$ 45	$ 105	
Pharmacy:					
Number of units per case	55	20	12	21	
Expense per unit.............	$ 3	$ 3	$ 3	$ 3	
Total expense per case	$ 165	$ 60	$ 36	$ 63	
Total variable expense per case ...	$ 3,590	$ 910	$ 1,031	$ 1,218	

bution margin variance is added to the original budget of $77,000, the result is $43,450, the same amount as the flexible budget. Third, when we disaggregate the contribution margin variance, we see that the hospital lost $125,000 in revenue that it had anticipated receiving, but saved $91,450 in expenses that it had anticipated incurring.

Finally, note that the actual number of cases was 675, compared to 650 in the original budget. The fact that volume has increased but income under the flexible budget declined by $33,550 indicates that there was a fairly significant mix variance. Indeed, the reason for the decline is that the mix shifted away from high margin cases to low margin ones. Had the mix (the proportion of each case type) remained the same as budgeted, the flexible budget surplus would have increased with the increase in the volume of cases.

Exhibit 13–4 shows the actual results for the 675 cases that were served during the accounting period. Although revenue per case remained as budgeted, there were several changes in expenses between the original and flexible budgets: the average length of stay (i.e., number of patient days) was different for three of the

EXHIBIT 13–3   Flexible Budget and Variances

	Acute MI	Influenza	Pneumonia	Phlebitis	Total
Overall budget:					
Actual number of cases..........	250	150	200	75	675
Revenue per case	$ 6,000	$ 1,000	$ 1,500	$ 3,000	
Total revenue	1,500,000	150,000	300,000	225,000	2,175,000
Variable expenses per case	3,590	910	1,031	1,218	
Total variable expenses..........	897,500	136,500	206,200	91,350	1,331,550
Contribution....................	$ 602,500	$ 13,500	$ 93,800	$133,650	$ 843,450
Total fixed expenses					800,000
Income					$ 43,450
Revenue volume variance:					
Actual-budgeted cases...........	−50	50	100	25	
Budgeted unit revenue...........	$ 6,000	$ 1,000	$ 1,500	$ 3,000	
Variance......................	$ (300,000)	$ (50,000)	$ 150,000	$ 75,000	$ (125,000)
Expense volume variance:					
Budgeted—actual cases	50	50	−100	−25	
Budgeted expense per case	$ 3,590	$ 910	$ 1,031	$ 1,218	
Variance......................	$ 179,500	$ 45,500	$(103,100)	$ (30,450)	$ 91,450
Contribution margin variance:					
Revenue volume variance + Expense volume variance ...	$ (120,500)	$ (4,500)	$ 46,900	$ 44,550	$ (33,550)

four diagnoses and the average variable expense per day was $10 more than budgeted; the average number of radiological films was different for three of the four case types, and the average expense per film was $2 less than budgeted; the average number of laboratory tests differed, and the average expense per test was $5 more than budgeted; the average number of pharmacy units was different, although the average expense per unit remained as budgeted.

The result is a total average variable expense per case. Because of the above changes, it differs from the budgeted average variable expense per case. This total is multiplied by the actual number of cases served to give total variable expenses per case. As is shown in the totals at the top of Exhibit 13–4, the resulting actual income is $41,250, which is $2,200 below the $43,450 income in the flexible budget.

Exhibit 13–5 shows the calculation of the variances resulting from changes in the mix of services offered (e.g., length of stay, radiology, and so on). By multiplying the change in units of service per case by the budgeted unit expense figure, we isolate the impact on the budget of changes in utilization for each service. The total dollar effect for each case type (the product of the actual number of cases and the sum of the mix variance for each service) is shown at the bottom of the exhibit. Acute MI cases, with a total of $82,750, had the biggest reduction in service utilization, while influenza had somewhat higher service utilization (an unfavorable variance of $21,750). Overall, the hospital saved a total of $87,025 from reduced service utilization.

EXHIBIT 13–4 Actual Results

	Acute MI	Influenza	Pneumonia	Phlebitis	Total
Overall results:					
Actual number of cases..............	250	150	200	75	675
Revenue per case	$ 6,000	$ 1,000	$ 1,500	$ 3,000	
Total revenue	1,500,000	150,000	300,000	225,000	2,175,000
Variable expenses per case	3,491	1,126	991	1,252	
Total variable expenses..............	872,750	168,900	198,200	93,900	1,333,750
Contribution.......................	627,250	(18,900)	101,800	131,100	$ 841,250
Total fixed expenses					800,000
Income					$ 41,250
Variable expense detail:					
Routine care:					
Average number of days per case....	19	6	5	7	
Average expense per day	$ 160	$ 160	$ 160	$ 160	
Total average expense per case......	$ 3,040	$ 960	$ 800	$ 1,120	
Radiology:					
Average number of films per case....	4	2	2	0	
Average expense per film	$ 23	$ 23	$ 23	$ 23	
Total average expense per case......	$ 92	$ 46	$ 46	$ 0	
Laboratory:					
Average number of tests per case....	10	3	5	3	
Average expense per test	$ 20	$ 20	$ 20	$ 20	
Total average expense per case......	$ 200	$ 60	$ 100	$ 60	
Pharmacy:					
Average number of units per case ...	53	20	15	24	
Average expense per unit	$ 3	$ 3	$ 3	$ 3	
Total average expense per case.......	$ 159	$ 60	$ 45	$ 72	
Total average variable expense per case	$ 3,491	$ 1,126	$ 991	$ 1,252	

Exhibit 13–6 isolates the effect of the changes in expense per unit, or what can be called *rate/efficiency variances*. The reason this is both rate and efficiency is that the expense per service actually is the result of two separate elements: the rate paid for the input units in each service (e.g., the laboratory technician wage rate) and the efficiency of those units. For example, in the laboratory a change in expense per test could be the result of a change in the wage rate of the lab technicians performing tests, a change in their efficiency in conducting tests, or some combination of the two.

The average rate/efficiency variance per case can be multiplied by the number of cases served to give a total rate/efficiency variance for each service department. This figure, since it consists of variable expenses only, is independent of both the number and mix of cases served, and the utilization of the service. That is, given the *actual* number and mix of cases served, and the number of units of service *actually* ordered, the rate/efficiency variance shows how well the service department performed in meeting its budget. As can be seen, routine care, with an

EXHIBIT 13–5 Mix of Services Variances

Type of Service	Acute MI	Influenza	Pneumonia	Phlebitis	Total
Routine care:					
Budgeted—actual days per case	2	−1	1	0	
Budgeted expense per day.........	$ 150	$ 150	$ 150	$ 150	
Mix variance....................	$ 300	$ (150)	$ 150	$ 0	
Radiology:					
Budgeted—actual films per case	1	−1	0	0	
Budgeted expense per film	$ 25	$ 25	$ 25	$ 25	
Mix variance....................	$ 25	$ (25)	$ 0	$ 0	
Laboratory:					
Budgeted—actual tests per case	0	2	−2	4	
Budgeted expense per test.........	$ 15	$ 15	$ 15	$ 15	
Mix variance....................	$ 0	$ 30	$ (30)	$ 60	
Pharmacy:					
Budgeted—actual units per case	2	0	−3	−3	
Budgeted expense per unit	$ 3	$ 3	$ 3	$ 3	
Mix variance....................	$ 6	$ 0	$ (9)	$ (9)	
Total mix of services—Variances per case........................	$ 331	$ (145)	$ 111	$ 51	
Actual number of cases	250	150	200	75	
Total mix of services variances	$82,750	$(21,750)	$22,200	$3,825	$87,025

EXHIBIT 13–6 Rate/Efficiency Variances

Type of Service	Acute MI	Influenza	Pneumonia	Phlebitis	Total
Actual number of cases...............	250	150	200	75	
Routine care:					
Budgeted—actual expense per day....	$ (10)	$ (10)	$ (10)	$ (10)	
Actual number of days per case	19	6	5	7	
Rate/efficiency variance per case	$ (190)	$ (60)	$ (50)	$ (70)	
Total rate/efficiency variance.........	$(47,500)	$(9,000)	$(10,000)	$(5,250)	$(71,750)
Radiology:					
Budgeted—actual expense per film ...	$ 2	$ 2	$ 2	$ 2	
Actual number of films	4	2	2	0	
Rate/efficiency variance per case	$ 8	$ 4	$ 4	$ 0	
Total rate/efficiency variance.........	$ 2,000	$ 600	$ 800	$ 0	$ 3,400
Laboratory:					
Budgeted—actual expense per test....	$ (5)	$ (5)	$ (5)	$ (5)	
Actual number of tests	10	3	5	3	
Rate/efficiency variance per case	$ (50)	$ (15)	$ (25)	$ (15)	
Total rate/efficiency variance.........	$(12,500)	$(2,250)	$ (5,000)	$(1,125)	$(20,875)
Pharmacy:					
Budgeted—actual expense per unit ...	$ 0	$ 0	$ 0	$ 0	
Actual number of units	53	20	15	24	
Rate/efficiency variance per case	$ 0	$ 0	$ 0	$ 0	
Total rate/efficiency variance.........	$ 0	$ 0	$ 0	$ 0	$ 0
Total rate/efficiency variance..........					$(89,225)

unfavorable variance of $71,750, performed considerably worse than budget; the laboratory also had an unfavorable variance ($20,875). The radiology department performed slightly better than anticipated, and pharmacy was right on budget.

Since the rate effect is not isolated from the efficiency effect in this illustration, the term rate/efficiency variance is used. However, managers of routine care, the laboratory, and the other service units most likely would want to undertake a more detailed variance analysis to isolate the individual effects of rate and efficiency in their departments. The approach to doing this would be similar to that for calculating all other variances; that is, the effect of each item would be determined by holding everything else constant and calculating the impact of that item alone.

To illustrate, assume that the following data are available for the laboratory:

	Time per Test (minutes)	Wage Rate $ per minute	Total Expense per Text
Budget......	75	$0.20	$15.00
Actual	80	0.25	20.00

To perform the calculations, we look first at the change in wage rate:

(Budgeted rate − Actual rate) × Actual efficiency = Wage rate variance

or

$$(\$0.20 - \$0.25) \times 80 \text{ minutes} = (\$0.05) \times 80 \text{ minutes}$$
$$= \$4.00 \text{ unfavorable}$$

Next, we look at the change in efficiency:

(Budgeted time − Actual time) × Budgeted wage = Efficiency variance

or

$$(75 \text{ minutes} - 80 \text{ minutes}) \times \$0.20 = (5 \text{ minutes}) \times \$0.20$$
$$= \$1.00 \text{ unfavorable}$$

These per-test variances can be applied to the total number of tests to obtain the total variances. The computations are as follows:

Case Type	Number of Cases	Tests per Case	Total Tests	Wage Rate Variance $(4.00)/test	Efficiency Variance $(1.00)/test	Total
Acute MI	250	10	2,500	$(10,000)	$(2,500)	
Influenza........	150	3	450	(1,800)	(450)	
Pneumonia	200	5	1,000	(4,000)	(1,000)	
Phlebitis	75	3	225	(900)	(225)	
Total			4,175	$(16,700)	$(4,175)	$(20,875)

Note that the total variance for the laboratory shown here is the same as the total shown on Exhibit 13–6. With this additional information, however, the laboratory manager can now see that the total is divided between $16,700 that is due to a change in the average wage rate of technicians, and $4,175 that is the result of lower than expected technician efficiency (minutes per test).

VARIANCE ANALYSIS AND MANAGEMENT CONTROL

The principal purpose of variance analysis is to facilitate the management control process. In this regard, it is important to structure the variance calculations so that managers find them useful for taking corrective action. In the case of Nucio Hospital, for example, the $33,550 unfavorable contribution margin variance is due largely to factors outside the control of the hospital, namely a reduction in acute MI and influenza cases. (Some might argue that this variance is senior management's responsibility, since senior management is charged with improving the hospital's competitive position vis-à-vis other hospitals in the area.)

The $33,550 negative contribution margin variance reduces the originally budgeted income of $77,000 to a flexible budget income of $43,450. However, as discussed above, the actual income was $41,250, or $2,200 less. This rather small difference is somewhat misleading, since it is due to the combination of a favorable variance of $87,025 in the mix of services and an unfavorable variance of $89,225 in the rate/efficiency of the delivery of those services.

Since physicians tend to control the mix of services, they would appear to be responsible for the former variance. By contrast, cost center or department managers, who are responsible for the efficient delivery of physician-ordered services, would appear to be responsible for the latter variance. It is for this reason that department managers most likely would want to compute the separate rate and efficiency variances associated with their activities. Most no doubt would argue that they have greater control over efficiency than they have over wage rates.

Although there is a favorable variance in the mix of services, the medical director of the hospital might still have some concern, since, as Exhibit 13–5 indicates, the $87,025 favorable variance is the result of both favorable and unfavorable variances for individual case types. Specifically, the mix of services was $21,750 unfavorable for the influenza cases, and the large favorable variance for the acute MI cases might suggest potential problems with the quality of care.

From a management control perspective, discussions with the medical staff about these matters are greatly facilitated by variance analysis. For example, all of the variances in Exhibit 13–5 are due exclusively to changes in the mix of services; that is, they reflect only the cases actually treated (not those that were budgeted to be treated), and both rate and efficiency have been held constant by using the budgeted expense per unit (e.g., day, film, and so on).

With information on variances, senior management can discuss the reasons underlying the variances with the managers who are involved, and who can take corrective action, if appropriate. Managers should note, however, that a variance is not designed to be used as a "club"; rather, it is intended as a tool to assist in diagnosing the reasons why actual costs diverged from budget and for exploring these reasons with the appropriate managers so that, if possible, action can be taken to bring costs back in line.

OTHER MEASURES

As discussed in Chapter 12, in addition to a concern with inputs, many nonprofit organizations attempt to report on outputs. As Chapter 12 suggested, there are two broad types of output measures that are used by most nonprofits: results and process. Variance analysis is concerned principally with process measures. As such, it says little about results, and whether the organization is *effective,* that is, whether it is moving toward the attainment of its objectives.

By definition, effectiveness in a nonprofit organization cannot be measured by financial data alone. If reliable measures of the organization's accomplishments can be found, a comparison of planned and actual output provides a numerical measure of effectiveness. As discussed in Chapter 12, however, in many situations the most that quantitative measures can do is give clues to the organization's effectiveness. Nevertheless, in designing its reporting system, senior management should make an effort to provide quantitative reports on effectiveness as well as efficiency.

SUMMARY

In this chapter we have discussed some of the technical aspects of the management control reports, focusing on variance analysis. Variance analysis allows managers to determine in some considerable detail why actual revenues and expenses diverged from budgeted ones. In particular, it disaggregates differences between budget and actual data into five general categories:

1. Volume.
2. Mix of units of service.
3. Selling price.
4. Rates paid for inputs.
5. Usage and efficiency of inputs.

Variance analysis can be used in any of three types of organizations: businesslike, fixed-resource, or fixed-job. Although it is more limited in the latter two than the first, it nevertheless can help management focus on questions like why actual expenses exceeded the fixed resources, or why a particular job cost more than anticipated. In this regard, managers must bear in mind that variance analysis does not answer questions, as such; rather, it directs management's attention to areas where problems appear to exist. As such, it is not a substitute for, but rather an aid to, conversations with managers to decide what action, if any, is needed to change operations.

APPENDIX
Computing Variances

The concept of variance analysis can be illustrated graphically, using an example of labor costs. Total labor costs are the product of the number of hours worked and the wage rate per hour. Assume that the labor budget for a particular activity is 100 hours of work at $8 per hour, for a total of $800. Graphically, this can be represented by a rectangle, with the vertical axis indicating the wage rate and the horizontal axis the number of hours, as shown in Diagram 1.

Diagram 1

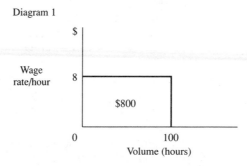

Now, assume that actual labor costs for the period are $1,200. A typical budget report indicates the variance as:

Item	Budget	Actual	Variance
Labor cost......	$800	$1,200	$(400)

The parentheses indicate an unfavorable variance; that is, one that reduces income. In this instance, the variance is negative because actual expenses were greater than budget.

While this information may be useful to managers, it does not indicate why the variance occurred. Specifically, in this instance, we cannot tell whether it was the result of a higher wage than anticipated, more hours than anticipated, or some combination of the two. If the variance were solely the result of a higher wage, it would be viewed graphically as shown in Diagram 2.

Diagram 2

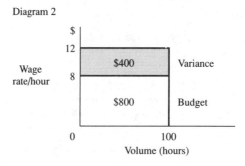

If, on the other hand, it were the result solely of more hours, it would be viewed as depicted in Diagram 3.

Diagram 3

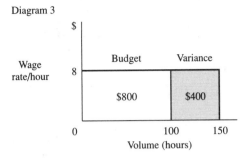

If the variances were a result of a combination of a higher wage *and* more hours, it could be depicted by a variety of wage/hour combinations; Diagram 4 is one example.

Diagram 4

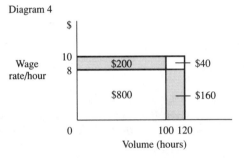

Note that, in this last instance, we have a problem because the $40 rectangle in the upper right portion of the graph is the result of a combination of *both* the wage variance *and* the hour (or volume) variance. The combination variance is referred to as the gray area, because it cannot reasonably be assigned to either the higher price or the higher volume; rather it is caused by the *combined effect* of the two. In this instance, $200 of the total variance can be attributed to the higher wage rate, $160 to the higher number of hours (volume), and $40 to the combination effect.

For ease of calculation, the gray area typically is assigned to the factor represented on the vertical axis, which usually is the factor that measures the rate. In this case, it would be assigned to the wage variance, such that, graphically, the analysis looks as shown in Diagram 5 (at the top of the next page).

This type of information makes the budget report much more useful to management. The resulting report might look something like the one shown on the next page. This report is useful because, in most organizations, different managers are responsible for different elements of a total variance, and, for management control purposes, it is important to designate the variance that is attributable to each individual manager.

Diagram 5

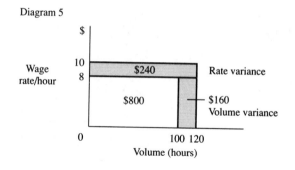

Item	Budget	Actual	Variance
Labor costs.............	$800	$1,200	$(400)
Wage-rate variance ...			(240)
Volume variance			(160)
Total variance			$(400)

Making the Computations

The technique used to calculate a variance isolates the change between budget and actual for each item and calculates its effect independent of other changes. The calculations are slightly different for expense variances than for revenue variances.

Expense Variances. An expense variance is calculated by subtracting the *actual* amount from the *budgeted* amount. For a rate variance, the result is multiplied by the actual volume amount. For a volume variance, the result is multiplied by the budgeted rate amount.

Let us return to the above example and perform the calculations:

$$\frac{\text{Wage rate}}{\text{variance}} = \left(\frac{\text{Budgeted}}{\text{wage rate}} - \frac{\text{Actual}}{\text{wage rate}}\right) \times \frac{\text{Actual}}{\text{hours}} = \text{Variance}$$

$$(\$8 \quad - \quad \$10) \quad \times \quad 120 \quad = \quad \$(240)$$

$$\frac{\text{Volume}}{\text{variance}} = \left(\frac{\text{Budgeted}}{\text{hours}} - \frac{\text{Actual}}{\text{hours}}\right) \times \frac{\text{Budgeted}}{\text{wage rate}} = \text{Variance}$$

$$(\$100 \quad - \quad \$120) \quad \times \quad \$8 \quad = \quad \$(160)$$

Revenue Variances. For a revenue variance, the process is the same with one exception: we subtract the *budgeted* amount from the *actual* amount. When this is done, a negative result of the computation will indicate an unfavorable variance; that is, a variance that, other things equal, reduces the organization's income.

To illustrate, if, in the above example, we had budgeted a selling price of $20 per hour, and actually had earned $25 per hour, our total variance would have been the difference between the budget of $2,000 [= $20/hour × 100 hours] and $3,000 [= $25/hour × 120 hours]. This has a $1,000 favorable effect on income. The computations would be as follows:

$$\begin{array}{c}\text{Selling price/} \\ \text{Hour variance}\end{array} = \left(\begin{array}{c}\text{Actual} \\ \text{rate}\end{array} - \begin{array}{c}\text{Budgeted} \\ \text{rate}\end{array}\right) \times \begin{array}{c}\text{Actual} \\ \text{hours}\end{array} = \text{Variance}$$

$$(\ \$25\ -\ \$20)\ \times\ 120\ =\ \$600$$

$$\begin{array}{c}\text{Volume} \\ \text{variance}\end{array} = \left(\begin{array}{c}\text{Actual} \\ \text{hours}\end{array} - \begin{array}{c}\text{Budgeted} \\ \text{hours}\end{array}\right) \times \begin{array}{c}\text{Budgeted} \\ \text{revenue/hour}\end{array} = \text{Variance}$$

$$(\$120\ -\ \$100)\ \times\ \$20\ =\ \$400$$

Note that, although this technique was performed in a situation involving only two variances (wage rate and volume), it could be performed equally well with several variances. The only difference is that the multiplication would involve more than just two factors. Indeed, a complete explanation of the divergence from budget in most organizations usually calls for an analysis of mix and efficiency variances as well as volume and prices (or wages). We discuss variances involving these four factors in the text.

SUGGESTED ADDITIONAL READINGS

Anthony, Robert N., and James S. Reece. *Accounting Principles*. Homewood, Ill.: Richard D. Irwin, 1989, chaps. 20 and 26.

Bennett, James P. "Standard Cost Systems Lead to Efficiency and Profitability." *Health Care Financial Management*, September 1985, pp. 46–54.

Finkler, Stephen A. "Flexible Budgets: The Next Step in Health Care Financial Controls." *Health Services Manager*, May 1981.

Heitger, Les; Pekin Ogan; and Serge Matulich. *Cost Accounting,* 2nd ed. Cincinnati, Ohio: South-Western Publishing, 1992.

Horngren, Charles T., and George Foster. *Cost Accounting*. Englewood Cliffs, N.J.: Prentice Hall, 1991.

Messmer, Victor C. "Standard Cost Accounting: Methods that Can Be Applied to DRG Classifications." *Health Care Financial Management*, January 1984, pp. 44–48.

CASE 13–1   Pacific Park School*

Ms. Audrey Hollingsworth, director of the Pacific Park School (PPS) was reviewing the results of the school's Summer Camp Program in preparation for the upcoming academic year. On her desk was a report (Exhibit 1) showing that instead of the $6,000 surplus she had budgeted, the Summer Camp Program had operated at a $50 loss. While the loss was not great, she had been planning to use the surplus to make some much needed improvements in the school's playground and classroom facilities. She now would need to either postpone these plans or find alternate sources of financing. Unhappy with this prospect, she resolved to determine exactly why the $6,000 surplus had evaporated.

Background

Pacific Park School was established in 1981 as an alternative to the many custodial day-care programs that operated in the city and its nearby suburbs. It accepted children as young as two years of age and worked with them until they reached the age of five, when they enrolled in a regular school.

Located in the annex of a church, the school had five classrooms and a playground. Enrollment during the academic year was limited to 50, and admission was extremely competitive. PPS enjoyed an excellent reputation in the community, and its graduates were virtually assured of admission to one of the city's prestigious private schools.

Parents could enroll their children on either a half-day or a full-day schedule. In either case, a wide variety of activities was available, and children could choose among them in a relatively unstructured way. Classrooms resembled those of a well-run elementary school, with amenities such as books, paints, blocks, toys, an aquarium, and small animals, such as turtles. Since most of the children could not read, each child had his or her own symbol (such as a triangle) that was used to indicate certain responsibilities (such as feeding the turtle). In all of their activities, the children were supervised by certified teachers and aides, who interacted with them constantly. Low child-teacher ratios were carefully maintained.

Summer Camp Program

The Summer Camp Program was almost identical to the program during the regular academic year. The only differences were that, with summer camp, children could enroll for as little as 1 week or as long as 10 weeks, outdoor activities

---

* This case was prepared by Professor David W. Young. Copyright © by David W. Young. Distributed by the Accounting Curriculum Center, Boston University School of Management.

EXHIBIT 1 Summer Camp Program: Budgeted and Actual Revenues and Expenses

	Budget	*Actual*	*Variance*
Revenue...............	$65,000	$60,750	$(4,250)
Expenses:			
Teachers and aides	40,000	40,250	(250)
Supplies..............	2,500	2,700	(200)
Administration........	12,000	13,500	(1,500)
Rent and utilities	4,500	4,350	150
Total................	$59,000	$60,800	$(1,800)
Surplus (deficit)	$ 6,000	$ (50)	$(6,050)

---

were somewhat more prevalent, and the term *camp* was used to make the program more appealing to children who might have grown tired of *school*.

Because the amount of time a child could spend in camp ranged from 1 to 10 weeks, and because parents did not need to commit themselves in advance to more than 1 week, budgeting was a little tricky. Instead of basing the budget on the number of children, Ms. Hollingsworth used *child-weeks* as the basic building block. As Exhibit 2 indicates, the budget had been based on 500 child-weeks, whereas only 450 actually materialized. In addition, qualified teachers and aides were in short supply, and instead of paying an average of $500 per week as she had anticipated, Ms. Hollingsworth had been obliged to pay an average of $575. She had, however, been able to operate with one fewer teacher than budgeted due to the reduced enrollment.

A similar salary problem had arisen on the administrative side, and in order to remain competitive, she had had to pay $1,350 a week in administrative salaries, rather than the $1,200 she had budgeted. At $6.00 per week per child instead of $5.00, curriculum supplies also had turned out to be more expensive than anticipated. Finally, she had managed to cut back a bit on telephone and electricity usage, thereby lowering her rent and utilities from the $1,500 per month budgeted to $1,450.

Because she had seen some of these problems coming, Ms. Hollingsworth had been able to send out a special notice to parents, informing them of a small

---

EXHIBIT 2 Summer Camp Program: Budget and Actual Statistics

	Budget	*Actual*
Number of child-weeks........................	500	450
Tuition (per week)............................	$ 130	$ 135
Teacher and aide average salary (per week)	500	575
Supplies (per child-week)......................	5	6
Administration and clerical total (per week)	1,200	1,350
Rent and utilities (per month)	1,500	1,450

increase in tuition of $5.00 per student week. At the time, she had thought this would defray the additional costs; obviously it had not.

With all of this in mind, Ms. Hollingsworth set about determining exactly why her budgeted surplus had not materialized. She also knew that she owed her board of directors an explanation, since it was at their insistence that she had planned to undertake the improvements to the school's facilities.

Questions

1. Calculate all relevant variances.
2. Prepare a nontechnical memorandum to the board of directors, explaining why the $6,000 budgeted surplus turned into a $50 loss.
3. What should Ms. Hollingsworth do to avoid similar problems in the future?

CASE 13–2   Arnica Mission*

Arnica Mission was located in the heart of a large metropolitan area in the north-central United States. Founded in the late 1800s, it had been serving the homeless ever since, providing hot meals, shelter, and companionship. Situated on a busy urban thoroughfare, it was a haven of last resort for many of the city's indigent, and "home" for many others. As might be expected, the demand for its services was especially high in the winter, when temperatures frequently dropped to below zero, and life "on the street" became unbearable.

The Mission provided three types of services. By far, its most significant activity was the Hot Meal Program, in which it served hundreds of meals a day. A meal of hot soup and a sandwich was available to anyone who arrived between the hours of 12:00 and 2:00 in the afternoon and 5:00 and 7:00 in the evening. Its second program was its Overnight Hostel, in which it made available 150 beds on a first-come, first-served basis. The linen was changed daily, so that its clients could look forward to "clean sheets and a hot shower." Finally, it had a counseling program, in which a staff of three full-time social workers assisted the Mission's clients in coping with the difficulties which had brought them to the Mission, and in establishing themselves in a more self-sufficient lifestyle.

In March 1983, Arnica Mission had hired a new administrator to improve its business activities. A business school graduate with prior experience in manufacturing and service companies in the private sector, one of his first steps had been to introduce responsibility accounting. The new budget reporting system had been

---

* This case was prepared by Professor David W. Young. Copyright © by the President and Fellows of Harvard College. Distributed by the Pew Curriculum Center, Harvard School of Public Health.

announced along with the provision of quarterly cost reports to the Mission's department heads. (Previously, cost data had been presented to department heads only infrequently.) The following is an excerpt from the memorandum and report received by the laundry supervisor in mid-January, 1984.

The Mission has adopted a responsibility accounting system. From now on you will receive quarterly reports comparing the costs of operating your department with budgeted costs. The reports will highlight the differences (variations) so you can zero in on the departure from budgeted costs. (This is called *management by exception.*) Responsibility accounting means you are accountable for keeping the costs in your department within the budget. The variations from the budget will help you identify what costs are out of line and the size of the variation will indicate which ones are the most important. Your first such report accompanies this announcement.

ARNICA MISSION
Performance Report—Laundry Department
October–December, 1983

	Budget	Actual	(Over) Under Budget	Percentage (Over) Under Budget
Bed days	9,500	11,900	(2,400)	(25)
Pounds of laundry processed	125,000	156,000	(31,000)	(25)
Costs:				
Laundry labor...................	$ 9,000	$ 12,500	$(3,500)	(39)
Supplies.......................	1,100	1,875	(775)	(70)
Water and water heating and softening	1,700	2,500	(800)	(47)
Maintenance	1,400	2,200	(800)	(57)
Supervisor's salary	3,150	3,750	(600)	(19)
Allocated administration costs	4,000	5,000	(1,000)	(25)
Equipment depreciation	1,200	1,250	(50)	(4)
	$ 21,550	$ 29,075	$(7,525)	(35)

Administrator's comments: Costs are significantly above budget for the quarter. Particular attention needs to be paid to labor, supplies, and maintenance.

The annual budget for fiscal year 1984 (July 1983–June 1984) had been constructed by the new administrator. Quarterly budgets were computed as one-fourth of the annual budget. The administrator compiled the budget from an analysis of the prior three years' costs. The analysis showed that all costs increased each year, with more rapid increases between the second and third year. He considered establishing the budget at an average of the prior three years' costs hoping that the installation of the system would reduce costs to this level. However, in view of the rapidly increasing prices, he finally chose FY 1983 costs less 3 percent for the FY 1984 budget. The activity level measured by bed days and pounds of laundry processed was set at FY 1983 volume, which was approximately equal to the volume of each of the past three years.

Questions

1. What is your assessment of the method used to construct the budget?
2. Recast the budget and performance report assuming the following:
   a. Laundry labor, supplies, water and water heating and softening, and maintenance are variable costs. The remaining costs are fixed.
   b. Actual prices are expected to be approximately 20 percent above the levels in the budget prepared by the administrator.
3. What does this new information tell you about the activities of the laundry department?
4. What should be done about the variations from the budget?

CASE 13–3   Nucio Hospital*

The chief financial officer of Nucio Hospital was concerned that the results of the year's operations were considerably worse than budgeted. One reason for this was that medicare had lowered the rates for three of the four case types served by the hospital, but there appeared to be some other explanations as well. Exhibit 13–2 in the text contains the original budget for Nucio Hospital. Actual results were as follows:

	Acute MI	Influenza	Pneumonia	Phlebitis	Total
Number of cases	275	250	100	75	700
Revenue per case...............	$5,500	$900	$1,400	$3,300	
Variable expense detail:					
Routine care:					
Average number of days per case	22	5	7	9	
Average expense per day	$ 140	$140	$ 140	$ 140	
Radiology:					
Average number of films per case	6	2	1	1	
Average expense per film....	$ 24	$ 24	$ 24	$ 24	
Laboratory:					
Average number of tests per case	8	5	6	7	
Average expense per test	$ 21	$ 21	$ 21	$ 21	
Pharmacy:					
Average number of units per case	60	22	12	20	
Average expense per unit....	$ 2	$ 2	$ 2	$ 2	

---

* This case was prepared by Professor David W. Young. Copyright © by David W. Young. Distributed by the Accounting Curriculum Center, Boston University School of Management.

He asked his staff assistant to give him a report on results for the year, as well as a complete breakdown of the reasons why the hospital's actual surplus diverged from budget. This report would be submitted to the hospital's chief executive officer and, quite likely, to the board of trustees.

Questions

1. Prepare a report showing actual results for the year.
2. Calculate all necessary variances and prepare a brief report for the hospital's board of trustees explaining in nontechnical terms what happened.

CASE 13–4   University Daycare Center*

Susan Brooks, Director of the University Daycare Center, was reviewing the year-to-date Budget Performance Report from the Finance Department of the university. As she tried to analyze the components of the report, she realized that something needed to be done about the Center's financial status. The variance analysis for the Daycare Center showed a shortfall of over $89,000 (Exhibit 1).

Background

The University Daycare Center (UDC) was affiliated with a large urban university and maintained a facility located two miles from the main campus. It had passed state inspection in April, and had opened in July, just in time for the beginning of the fiscal year. The building in which the UDC was located had formerly been an elementary school. The Center occupied one corridor, with four large classrooms on each side. Two other corridors in the same building were unoccupied and had not been renovated. At the end of the hallway was the director's office and a small reception area where parents arrived with their children, usually by eight o'clock in the morning.

The rooms had been carpeted and all of their doors had been removed to decrease the possibility of injuries. Additionally, the walls had been remodeled so that glass panels occupied the upper half of each wall on the corridor side. This made it possible for teachers and aides to observe children directly from the hallway. Each room was supplied with furniture, supplies, and toys appropriate to different age-groups of children. The infant room, for example, had cribs and

---

* This case was prepared by Emily Hayden, R.N., M.B.A., under the supervision of Professor David W. Young. Copyright © by David W. Young.

EXHIBIT 1 Variances from Budget Based on Actual Enrollment and Estimated Annualized Expenses

	FTES*		Budget	Actual Expenses	Variance
	Budget	Actual			
Revenues:					
Enrollee tuition..............................			$ 329,194	$ 141,926	$(187,268)
Expenses:					
Salaries:					
Director	1	1	$ 32,000	$ 31,990	$ 10
Instructors..............................	3	3	66,000	66,500	(500)
Teachers.................................	6	6	120,000	114,108	5,892
Aides....................................	5	1.5	83,200	27,140	56,060
Clerical.................................	0.5	0.5	9,000	9,000	0
Subtotals	15.5	12	$ 310,200	$ 248,738	$ 61,462
Fringe benefits			68,244	54,722	13,522
Supplies:					
Training			4,000	2,190	1,810
Conference			1,650	904	746
Food....................................			16,000	8,762	7,238
Disposables.............................			4,200	2,300	1,900
Classroom supplies			4,800	2,629	2,171
Field trips			1,100	602	498
Equipment..............................			1,000	548	452
Laundry.................................			500	274	226
Contingency			4,000	2,190	1,810
Maintenance			13,000	7,119	5,881
Telephone			500	274	226
Supplies subtotals			$ 50,750	$ 27,792	$ 22,958
Rent			60,000	60,000	0
Total expenses			$ 489,194	$ 391,252	$ 97,942
Total revenues less expenses			$(160,000)	$(249,326)	$(89,326)
Plus budgeted deficit			$ 160,000	$ 160,000	
Variance from budgeted deficit				$(89,326)	

* Full-time equivalents.

---

bassinets and was stocked with various sizes of disposable diapers. The facility was cleaned and maintained, respectively, by the housekeeping and maintenance departments of the university.

In December of the previous year, the university's Department of Human Resources had surveyed 300 of the 1,250 university employees, including professors, administrative personnel, laboratory workers, and office assistants, to determine whether they would utilize a day-care center. The survey included questions regarding fees, hours of operation, and coverage for emergencies. The response was overwhelmingly in favor of providing such a service. The Human Resources director, therefore, had drafted a proposal for the following year's budget and received approval for a one-year $160,000 subsidy for the operation of a day-care center. Funds for the remodeling and furnishing of the Center were to be obtained from the Capital Improvement Fund and the building was to be rented at a cost of $60,000 a year, with a one-year renewable lease.

The Department of Human Resources began promoting the Center two months prior to its opening. Flyers were posted throughout the university and were placed in the mailboxes of virtually every permanent employee. A Human Resources representative attended orientation sessions for new employees and answered questions regarding the Center's services. The promotion approach emphasized the presence of the Center as an employee benefit, despite the fact that employees would pay for most of the operating expenses in the form of tuition fees. No fees were printed on the promotional literature, and all tuition discussions between potential enrollees and the UDC director were to be held confidential.

The proposal stated that the Center intended to provide day care at reasonable rates (based on parental income) for any permanent university employee. A sliding fee scale would guarantee access for employees of all income levels. The Department of Human Resources hoped that the UDC would become a permanent service and envisioned that its implementation and operation would become a model for other university-affiliated day-care centers. Additionally, its presence could be an attractive incentive for employees to stay with the university or to choose employment there in the first place.

Fees and Enrollees

After considerable market research and consideration of various fee structures, a sliding fee scale had been developed. It incorporated not only income measures, but also intensity of care. Thus, the tuition charged for infants was generally higher, since they required closer supervision (Exhibit 2).

EXHIBIT 2   Sliding Fee Scale

Annual Family Income Range	Total Annual Tuition		
	Infant	Toddler	Preschool
$0–19,999	$ 5,980	$4,680	$3,900
20,000–24,999.	6,644	5,200	4,333
25,000–29,999.	7,309	5,720	4,767
30,000–34,999.	7,973	6,240	5,200
35,000–39,999.	8,638	6,760	5,633
40,000–44,999.	9,302	7,280	6,067
45,000–49,999.	9,967	7,800	6,500
50,000–59,999.	10,631	8,320	6,933
60,000–69,999.	11,296	8,840	7,367
70,000—Above	11,960	9,360	7,800

EXHIBIT 3   Annual Individual Tuition Contributions (revenues) Based on Present Enrollment

	Infants	Toddlers	Preschoolers	Totals
Number of full-time slots	7	18	17	42
Tuition payments	$11,296	$ 4,680	$ 3,900	
	11,960	8,320	3,900	
	3,588*	7,800	4,767	
	10,631	7,800	7,367	
		8,320	3,120	
		5,720	6,500	
		5,720	5,633	
		4,680	2,340*	
		3,744*	2,340*	
		7,800		
Revenue subtotals	$37,475	$ 64,584	$39,867	$ 141,926
Budgeted revenue.....................	$73,694	$156,048	$99,452	$ 329,194
Variance from budgeted revenue............................				$(187,268)
Average tuition per enrollee............	$ 9,369	$ 6,458	$ 4,430	
Budgeted average tuition per enrollee	$10,528	$ 8,669	$ 5,850	

* Part-time enrollees.

The UDC was licensed to have seven spaces for infants (2 to 18 months old), 18 spaces for toddlers (18 months to 2 years old), and 17 for preschoolers (2 to 5 years old). In October, the enrolled population consisted of 4 infants, 10 toddlers, and 9 preschoolers (Exhibit 3). Some of the children did not attend every day because their parents were part-time employees or had other child-care arrangements for the remaining days of the week. All parents were required to submit documentation of immunizations, as well as a physician statement attesting to the health of each child.

Staffing

The original budget allowed for staffing consisting of the director, three instructors, six teachers, five aides, and a half-time clerical worker. The Center was not fully staffed in some of these categories, but, since the staffing budget had assumed full enrollment, some positions were, in fact, overstaffed (Exhibit 4). In anticipation of high demand for the service, Ms. Brooks had hired all of the instructors and teachers one month before the Center's opening, both to accommodate an immediate full enrollment, as well as to comply with state requirements concerning child-to-teacher ratios. All instructors and teachers were certified in child care. Aides were trained and supervised by the instructors.

EXHIBIT 4 Salary Variances Based on Actual Enrollment

A:

Salary Category	Budgeted FTEs at Full Capacity	Budgeted FTEs Needed for Current Enrollment*	Budgeted Salaries at Full Capacity	Budgeted Salaries Adjusted for Current Enrollment	Variances
Director	1.0	1.0	$ 32,000	$ 32,000	0
Instructors	3.0	1.5	66,000	33,000	$ 33,000
Teachers	6.0	3.0	120,000	60,000	60,000
Aides	5.0	3.0	83,200	49,920	33,280
Clerical	0.5	0.5	9,000	9,000	0
Totals	15.5	9.0	$310,200	$183,920	$126,280

B:

Salary Category	Budgeted FTEs Needed for Current Enrollment*	Actual FTEs	Budgeted Salaries Adjusted for Current Enrollment	Actual Salaries	Variance
Director	1.0	1.0	$ 32,000	$ 31,990	$ 10
Instructors	1.5	3.0	33,000	66,500	(33,500)
Teachers	3.0	6.0	60,000	114,108	(54,108)
Aides	3.0	1.5	49,920	27,140	22,780
Clerical	0.5	0.5	9,000	9,000	0
Totals	9.0	12.0	$183,920	$248,738	$(64,818)

* Budgeted positions have been adjusted here to account for the current staffing needs of the Center. Amounts are budgeted to nearest half FTE (full-time equivalent) except director.

Budgeting Problems

The university's $160,000 subsidy was to be used to finance the deficit at full enrollment; that is, at full enrollment, tuition fees were expected to contribute a total of $329,194; and expenses were expected to total $489,194. Since expenses had not fallen proportionately to revenue, the university was facing a subsidy of $249,326 (Exhibit 1).

Ms. Brooks believed that the Center should remain an integral part of the university community; however, she also recognized the need to maintain financial viability. She knew that if she did not make the necessary adjustments in expenses, revenues, or both, that these decisions would simply be made by someone from the Department of Human Resources. This would reflect poorly on her ability to manage the budget and might also make the Center a target for elimination if budget cuts became necessary.

As she reviewed the set of reports generated by the Finance Department, a number of items remained unclear as to what impact they would have on the continuing operation of the Center. For example, adjustments made for the actual enrollment showed a variance of almost $65,000 for staff positions alone (Exhibit 4).

Supply expenses, by contrast, included many start-up items. Some of these were relatively long-lasting objects, such as toys and linens. Others, including disposable diapers and snack foods, were consumables. Many of the invoices for various classroom items had not yet been received. Additionally, charges for various services provided by the university, such as maintenance and laundry, were only generated every two to three months. Since this was the Center's first year of operation, however, the clerk had been instructed to carefully record the nature and the amount of each purchase, so that a better estimate could be submitted for the following year's budget. As a result, Ms. Brooks believed that the expenses shown in Exhibit 1 accurately reflected the results of the Center's activities.

As of November, the UDC had increased its enrollment to over 50 percent of capacity in each category. Still, total revenues from all contributions were far below what had been projected (Exhibit 3). Ms. Brooks knew that part of this was due to the empty slots as well as the partial attendance by some children; however, even if adjustments were made for full enrollment by the end of the year, there would still be a revenue shortfall of approximately $67,000, assuming that average tuition in each category remained unchanged (Exhibit 5). It was clear that revenue could probably be increased if enrollment were limited to those in the highest paying scales. One of the goals of the UDC, however, was to provide access to all employees, and charging the maximum tuition for the remaining slots would effectively limit the service to high-income applicants. Also, since the Center was not at full capacity upon opening, Ms. Brooks had seen no reason to exclude part-time attendance by some children. She had assumed that the revenue provided by part-time enrollees would offset at least some of the losses from the empty slots.

EXHIBIT 5   Annual Individual Tuition Contributions (revenues) Based on Full Enrollment

	Infants	*Toddlers*	*Preschoolers*	*Totals*
Number of full-time slots	7	18	17	42
Tuition payments	$11,296	$ 4,680	$ 3,900	
	11,960	8,320	3,900	
	3,588*	7,800	4,767	
	10,631	7,800	7,367	
	9,369†	8,320	3,120*	
	9,369†	5,720	6,500	
	9,369†	5,720	5,633	
		4,680	2,340*	
		3,744*	2,340*	
		7,800	4,430†	
		6,458†	4,430†	
		6,458†	4,430†	
		6,458†	4,430†	
		6,458†	4,430†	
		6,458†	4,430†	
		6,458†	4,430†	
		6,458†	4,430†	
Revenue subtotals	$65,582	$116,248	$79,737	$261,567
Budgeted revenue	$73,694	$156,048	$99,452	$329,194
Variance from budgeted revenue				$ (67,627)

* Part-time enrollees.
† Assume future enrollees pay the current average tuition and attend full-time.

Decisions

Complicating all of these considerations was the fact that even though future revenues and expenses were uncertain, both could be substantially manipulated. For example, decisions concerning the hiring or firing of staff could have a large impact on salary expenditures. Ms. Brooks was reluctant to make these decisions too quickly. If teachers were laid off and then enrollment suddenly increased, she would have to rehire them in order to maintain the required child-to-teacher ratios. By contrast, discretion in the use of supplies was limited, but she wondered if it might be worthwhile to investigate different vendors for expensive items like disposable diapers.

With only four months of operation as a basis for making predictions, Ms. Brooks was uncertain as to how soon, if ever, the Center would be at full capacity. She also did not know what type of enrollee mix would best fit the mission of the Center and, at the same time, generate enough revenue to ensure its survival. The sliding fee scale might be flawed, but the university's budget department was reluctant to do any more research on this item. They maintained that day-care centers throughout the city had comparable fee schedules. Ms. Brooks doubted that she could duplicate the efforts of the research by herself and, therefore, decided to accept the fee scale, and perhaps make minor adjustments for individual applicants.

Whether to encourage the presence of more part-time enrollees presented another dilemma. The child-to-teacher ratio on any given day could be compromised by the presence of too many part-time children attending on the same days. The Center might be overstaffed on other days due to such uneven attendance. This not only created problems in the scheduling and hiring of staff, but also meant that the partial slots occupied by part-time enrollees could no longer be used by potential full-time enrollees. Ms. Brooks had wanted to make the service available to all employees, but wondered if she should limit attendance to full-time children. On the other hand, if additional full-time applicants never materialized, the part-time attendees were needed, even if they did create staffing problems.

Although much of the promotional effort was ongoing, Ms. Brooks was unclear as to whether there were better ways of advertising the service to employees. The option of promoting to potential applicants outside the university community had occurred to her, although she doubted if the university's trustees would approve of funding for this. In addition to questions of how to increase enrollment, she wondered if the Center should instead opt to simply maintain the present enrollment or even to decrease it (by attrition). This would make the task of laying off teachers easier, since fewer children would provide a suitable justification for terminating the teachers' employment. If the Center could run at less than full capacity, but not run a deficit, then she might be in a better position to bargain for a larger subsidy in next year's budget proposal.

She also questioned the $160,000 subsidy amount. Was this just a token gesture to demonstrate to the community how progressive the university was, but one without real support from those who controlled the budget? The amount had seemed generous at first, but clearly there were problems in complying with the revenue and expenditure targets on which the subsidy was based.

Although Ms. Brooks did not expect the university to subsidize any shortfalls in enrollment completely, she realized that she would need to make a convincing argument for the continued operation of the Center. Unless she could do this by the time budget negotiations began in February, the closure of the UDC would no doubt become a subject for discussion at the annual trustees' meeting in March.

Questions

1. What is the source of the financial problems at the UDC? Please be as specific as you can, explaining all the reasons why actual results differ from budgeted ones.
2. What might Ms. Brooks do to correct the financial problems? Please be as specific as you can in outlining a course of action that you believe she should follow.
3. What action would you recommend the trustees take at their March meeting?

Chapter 14

Reporting on Performance: Management Control Reports

In all organizations—nonprofit and for-profit—managers need an ongoing flow of information to assist them in carrying out the management control process. As we discussed in Chapter 13, much of this information comes from talking with people and observing performance directly, but much also comes from formal reports. This chapter discusses the types of formal reports used by nonprofit organizations, the contents of the reports used for management control purposes, the technical criteria for control reports, and some of the issues managers face in using these reports.

TYPES OF REPORTS

There are essentially two types of formal reports: information reports and performance reports. Our primary interest in this chapter is performance reports, but first we shall briefly discuss information reports.

Information Reports

Information reports are designed to tell management "what is going on." Such reports do not always lead to action. Each reader studies these reports to detect whether or not something has happened that requires investigation. If nothing of significance is noted in an information report, which is often the case, the report is put aside without action. If something does strike the reader's attention, an inquiry or other action is initiated.

The information contained in such reports may come from the accounting system or from a variety of other sources. Information reports derived from accounting records include income statements, balance sheets, cash flow statements, and details on such items as cash balances, the status of accounts receivable and inventories, and lists of accounts payable that are coming due.

A list of nonaccounting information reports could easily be quite long. These reports might include internal information such as the number of new clients or patients, the number of discharges, the incidence of service delivery that did not meet quality standards, rates of absenteeism, admission applications, yield rates (the percentage of accepted applicants who decide to attend a college or university), number of failing grades, or the position titles of members of an association who did not renew. Information reports might also include external information, such as general news summaries, legislative updates, new regulations, information on the industry from trade associations, and general economic information published by the government.

Performance Reports

Performance reports look at two general types of output: economic performance and management performance. A conventional income statement can be prepared for a separate program, a profit center, or an entire organization. When this is done, the surplus shown at the bottom of the income statement is a basic measure of the unit's *economic performance*.

A *management performance report* focuses on the performance of a manager of a responsibility center. This report also is called a *control report*. A control report may show that a manager is doing an excellent job. If, however, an economic performance report shows that the responsibility center is operating at a loss, or is not producing a satisfactory surplus, action may be required despite the good performance of the manager.

> *Example.* An economic performance report showed that the nursing school in a private university was operating at a loss. This continuing loss was explained by the fact that a state university nearby had opened a nursing school and was charging much lower tuition rates. The dean of the nursing school was not responsible for this environmental trend, and, indeed, the control reports showed the dean's performance to be quite good. Nevertheless, a thorough analysis revealed no way to eliminate the ongoing loss in the nursing school; that is, to make it a sound economic entity. The decision therefore was made to close the nursing school and devote the university's resources to other activities.

In sum, there are two quite different ways to judge the performance of a responsibility center. First, there is the analysis of the responsibility center as an economic entity; in such an analysis, economic considerations are dominant. Second, there is the analysis of the performance of the responsibility center manager vis-à-vis the commitments made during the budget preparation process; the principal consideration in this analysis is behavioral. It is this latter analysis that is carried out in part by control reports.

Sources of Information

Information on economic performance typically is derived from conventional accounting information, including the full-cost accounting system. Control reports are prepared from responsibility accounting information, and attempt to distinguish between controllable and noncontrollable costs.

CONTENTS OF CONTROL REPORTS

Each responsibility center in an organization is expected to do its part in helping the organization achieve its objectives. To the extent that at least some of these expectations consist of achieving targeted revenues, controlling costs, or both, they are set forth in the budget for the responsibility center. The purpose of control reports is to communicate how well managers of responsibility centers performed in comparison with the budget as well as any other standard of performance.

If the budget is a valid statement of expected performance, the control report simply calculates the difference between budgeted and actual performance. Positive differences represent good performance and negative differences represent poor performance. However, such labels are valid only if there has been no change in the circumstances that were assumed when the budget was prepared. This is rarely, if ever, the case.

The purpose of a control report, then, is to compare actual performance with what performance should have been considering the actual circumstances. If inflation is greater than expected, if volume is down for uncontrollable reasons, or if any of a number of other circumstances has altered original assumptions, a negative variance does not necessarily represent poor performance.

Good control reports have three essential characteristics:

1. They are related to personal responsibility.
2. They compare actual performance to the best available standard.
3. They focus on significant information.

We will discuss each characteristic separately, using the sample set of control reports shown in Exhibit 14-1.

Relationship to Personal Responsibility

As described earlier, responsibility accounting classifies the costs assigned to each responsibility center according to whether they are controllable or noncontrollable. Many control reports show only controllable costs, but some control reports also show a separate category of noncontrollable costs for information purposes. In Exhibit 14–1 the majority of costs are controllable, but some noncon-

EXHIBIT 14–1   State Human Service Agency ($000)

A. Fourth-level report

Program Summary
(Agency Director)

	Actual		(Over) or under budget	
	June	Year to date	June	Year to date
Direct costs:				
Family planning	$ 2,110	$ 12,030	$ (315)	$ 35
Maternal/Infant Nutrition	**24,525**	**147,280**	**(710)**	**(2,590)**
Early childhood screening	1,235	7,570	(125)	(210)
Remedial reading	1,180	7,045	95	75
Adolescent drug counseling	3,590	18,960	(235)	245
Job training	4,120	25,175	160	(320)
Senior citizen drop in	2,245	13,680	180	(160)
Hospice.....................	3,630	22,965	(70)	(730)
Total direct	$42,635	$254,705	$(1,020)	$(3,655)
Controllable overhead	$27,120	$161,970	$ 3,020	$ 5,130
Total	$69,755	$416,675	$ 2,000	$ 1,475

B. Third-level report

Maternal/Infant Nutrition
Program Direct Cost Summary
(Program Director)

	Actual		(Over) or under budget	
	June	Year to date	June	Year to date
Direct labor:				
Counselors...................	$ 5,340	$ 35,845	$(625)	$(1,380)
Nutritionists	**3,310**	**19,605**	**(30)**	**(620)**
Physicians	3,115	18,085	90	(135)
Supplies and materials:				
Food and beverages...........	5,740	33,635	(65)	(640)
Stationery...................	1,865	9,795	(175)	825
Contract services:				
Computer expense	3,195	18,015	210	35
Housekeeping	1,960	12,300	(115)	(675)
Total direct	$24,525	$147,280	$(710)	$(2,590)

(from next page)

EXHIBIT 14–1 *(concluded)*

C. Second-level report

Nutritionists (Supervisor)	Actual		(Over) or under budget	
	June	Year to date	June	Year to date
Output:				
Standard direct labor-hours (000)....................	135	906	85	401
Direct-contact time cost:				
Amount...................	**$2,187**	**$12,524**	**$(265)**	**$ 90**
Efficiency variance............			(115)	515
Rate variance................			(150)	(425)
Noncontact time cost:				
Meetings.....................	420	1,916	180	91
Community/collateral work	284	1,748	(75)	(530)
Professional development......	115	808	(121)	(384)
Administrative activities	60	721	160	(82)
Sick and vacation time	244	1,888	91	195
Total noncontact time cost.....	$1,123	$ 7,081	$ 235	$(710)
Total direct labor cost...........	$3,310	$19,605	$ (30)	$(620)

D. First-level report

Regional Summary of Nutritionists Direct-Contact Time (Regional Supervisors)	Actual		(Over) or under budget	
	June	Year to date	June	Year to date
Output:				
Standard direct labor-hours (000)				
Region 1	50	342	20	120
Region 2	45	340	35	165
Region 3	40	224	30	116
Total	135	906	85	401
Direct contact time cost:				
Amount				
Region 1	$ 750	$ 4,140	$ (85)	$ 27
Region 2	795	3,890	(70)	30
Region 3	642	4,494	(110)	33
Total	$2,187	$12,524	$(265)	$ 90
Efficiency variance				
Region 1			$ (15)	$ 120
Region 2			(25)	155
Region 3			(75)	240
Total			$(115)	$ 515
Rate variance				
Region 1			$ (70)	$ (93)
Region 2			(65)	(120)
Region 3			(15)	(212)
Total			$(150)	$(425)

trollable costs, such as rate variances (on the first- and second-level reports) also are shown for completeness.

Levels of Reports.   To facilitate analysis and appropriate action, the total amount of controllable cost is classified by program, as shown in the fourth-level report. On this report, controllable overhead is reported separately from direct costs, but noncontrollable costs are excluded.

Direct costs for each program are broken down by item (also called *object, line item*, or *cost element*) in the third-level report. Direct costs in this organization include not only direct labor, but also supplies and materials and contract services, as well.

On the second-level report, the direct labor cost for each job category, such as nutritionists, is divided into direct-contact time and noncontact time for purposes of analyzing the activities of employees and the associated costs. Efficiency and rate variances are calculated for direct-contact time; noncontact time is divided into as many categories as are meaningful for the responsible supervisor.

Finally, on the first-level report, the costs and variances for direct-contact time are broken down by region. This allows responsibility to be decentralized to a very low level in the organization: in this instance, a regional supervisor of nutritionists.

Essentially, then, responsibility accounting requires that: (1) costs be classified by responsibility center (e.g., Maternal/Infant Nutrition Program); (2) costs within each responsibility center be classified according to whether they are controllable or noncontrollable; and (3) controllable costs are broken down into cost elements of sufficient detail to provide a useful basis for analysis and action. If it is not possible to give a positive answer to the question "Is there any conceivable action a manager could take on the basis of this report?" the report is a candidate for either revision or elimination.

Comparison with a Standard

A report that contains information on actual performance only is virtually useless for control purposes. To be useful, control reports must compare actual performance with a standard. There are three types of standards: budgeted, historical, and external.

Budgeted Standards.   If carefully prepared, a budget is the best standard. It takes into account the conditions that are expected to exist in the budget year, and the revenue and expense items show the expected monetary effect of these conditions. Although budgeted amounts per se are not shown in Exhibit 14–1, it is clear that budgeted standards exist, since the last two columns are labeled "(Over) or under Budget."

Historical Standards.   Some organizations compare current performance with past performance. Results for the second quarter of 1992, for example, could be compared with those of the first quarter of 1992 or the second quarter of 1991. Ordinarily, a historical standard is not as good as a well-prepared budget for at least two reasons: (1) conditions in the current period are probably different from those of the prior period, which lessens the validity of the comparison, and (2) performance in the prior period may not have represented good performance.

Despite these limitations, historical data are better than those in a sloppily prepared budget. Since they are drawn directly from the accounting records, they are not influenced by the judgments and persuasive arguments that sometimes affect the budget numbers. Furthermore, if the environment in which the organization operates is relatively stable from one year to the next, a historical standard may be practically as good as a budget.

External Standards.   The standard for analyzing performance in a given responsibility center may be the average performance in similar responsibility centers in the same organization or performance in similar outside organizations. The performance of one hospital in a multi-institutional chain can be compared with all other hospitals in the chain, for example. If the conditions in each hospital are reasonably similar, a comparison of this sort can provide a reasonable basis for judging the performance of hospital managers.

In practice, even reasonably similar conditions may not exist. A hospital's size, demographic and epidemiological environment, labor market, supply market, and other factors all affect its performance in some way. Senior management must decide if these conditions are sufficiently different to invalidate any sort of meaningful comparison.

Many industry associations compile and distribute useful information about changes in the general environment of their member institutions, and about current data on average costs and other statistics. Management can use such data for comparative analyses that may provide helpful indicators of whether the organization is drifting out of line with its peers.

> *Example.* The Healthcare Financial Management Association publishes detailed data on hospitals in its *Hospital Industry Analysis Report*. A typical report contains 29 financial ratios based on information supplied by 675 hospitals, with hospitals classified by type and bed size. Medians, upper quartiles, and lower quartiles are published.

As pointed out in Chapter 12, external data are of little use unless they are prepared in accordance with carefully worked out and well-understood definitions.

> *Example.* State governments publish data on cost per mile of highway maintained. Some states define this amount as "trunkline miles" (i.e., linear miles of main highways). Other states use miles adjusted for number of lanes; still others use "equivalent trunkline miles." In the absence of an agreed-upon definition of "mile of highway," these data are useless for comparison purposes.

Comparative measures are especially useful for control in situations involving a large number of moderately small, discrete, and independent entities with similar clientele, operations, and cost structures, such as day-care centers, urban schools, suburban schools, community hospitals, and inner-city job placement programs. In these cases the indicators measuring similar aspects of performance (such as pupil-teacher ratio, cost of instruction, cost of supervisory personnel, and cost of maintenance and construction) may be valid indicators of *relative performance* even in the absence of an absolute measure of performance.

Focus on Significant Information

The problem of designing reports is one of deciding on the right type of information to give to management. With the advent of computers, this task has become even more critical. Clearly, whenever feasible, managers should be given all the information they request. At the same time, a computer can spew out more data in a few minutes than a manager can assimilate in a day; to swamp managers with more information than they can assimilate (called *information overload*) is not helpful. Indeed, experiments have shown that if information overload exists—that is, if too much information flows through the reporting system—there is a tendency to disregard the whole reporting mechanism.

> *Example.* A high school in Sacramento, California, had a computerized attendance system installed at a cost of $100,000. It electronically transmitted to the accounting office the attendance of each pupil in each class period. One full-time person was required to operate the system. It provided instantaneous data, but data that no one needed instantaneously.[1]

> *Example.* A reporting system installed in naval shipyards some years ago produced 5,000 pages of computer printout per month in each shipyard. This was far more than managers could use.

Because of these sorts of problems, the controller should assure that line managers are receiving only the information they need. Periodic discussions with line managers to ascertain what information is being used for what sorts of purposes can facilitate this process. Clearly, a similar review process should take place for the information senior management itself receives.

Role of Personal Computers.   In the past, because control reports in most organizations were prepared centrally, it usually was difficult to tailor them to the needs of each individual manager. Increasingly, however, with the use of personal computers, managers are finding it possible to have information downloaded from a central computer to their personal computer, and then to structure and present the information in ways that best suit their individual needs.

Even when personal computers are used, there can be a tendency to report too much information, or to design reports in too complex a fashion. Senior managers

---

[1] Ida Hoos, *Systems Analysis in Public Policy* (Berkeley: University of California Press, 1972), p. 153.

generally need highly aggregated output data, while operating personnel or individuals responsible for program elements need more detailed data at more frequent intervals. Moreover, if their level of sophistication is low, operating personnel will require information that is neither too complex nor displayed in a format that is too difficult to understand.

Definition of Significant.   Finally, what is significant for one type of manager may not be significant for another. In general, significant items are those that can make a difference in the way a manager acts. There is no way of specifying exactly what such items are; they vary depending on the situation and on the wishes of individual managers. Nevertheless, some generalizations can be made:

- The significance of an item is not necessarily proportional to its size. In particular, certain discretionary cost items, such as travel, or dues and subscriptions, may be significant even though they are relatively small.
- Minor items should be aggregated. For example, costs for heating, air-conditioning, electric lighting, and perhaps telephone can be reported as utilities. Indeed, reporting a long list of cost items, many of which are relatively minor, can tend to obscure the few relatively significant items.
- The higher the management level using a report, the more aggregated it should be. Exhibit 14–1 illustrates this point. The report for each of the four successively higher levels contains less detail than the one below it. (Despite this aggregation, higher level managers may want access to reports prepared for lower levels so they can follow up on the details of items that appeared problematic on a summary report.)
- Managers do not care about the calculations. Note that Exhibit 14–1 does not show the budgeted amounts, but only the difference between actual and budget; the budget amount could be included to show how the difference was calculated, but it is omitted because the manager does not need to make this calculation. Similarly, calculations for the variances also are omitted.

Key Indicators.   In most organizations and the responsibility centers within them, there are a few factors that must be watched closely. We call these *key results measures;* they also can be called *key success factors* or, in some instances, *danger signals*. The quantitative measures that allow managers to focus on them are called *key indicators*. These indicators often can signal upcoming problems, particularly financial ones. For example, in many nonprofit organizations, the number of new clients or client inquiries is a key indicator; in a hospital average length of stay, classified by diagnosis, may play this role.

Example.   In a college, management needs to be alert to such danger signals as:

- A decrease in the number of inquiries.
- A decrease in the number of applications.
- A decrease in the quality of applicants.
- A decrease in yield (i.e., percentage of admitted applicants who enroll).
- A shift in enrollment among majors.

- An increase in student aid needs.
- An unplanned change in sections per faculty member.
- An increase in student attrition rates.
- An increase in administrative and support personnel.
- A decrease in gifts.

These danger signals are associated with several different responsibility centers within the college.

The number of key indicators typically is small, perhaps only numbering five or so for each responsibility center, but the reporting system must be designed so that managers can focus on them.

Example. The director of a mental health clinic states that in order to know how well the clinic is doing financially, she needs to focus on three items: (1) billed hours (i.e., the number of hours spent with clients), (2) accounts receivable as a percent of monthly billings (an indication of how promptly clients are paying their bills), and (3) the ratio of expenses to revenues.

TECHNICAL CRITERIA FOR CONTROL REPORTS

In addition to the basic characteristics listed above concerning their content, control reports also must satisfy certain technical criteria. While the satisfaction of these criteria is largely the controller's responsibility, senior management needs to be aware of the criteria so it can guide the controller in the design effort, and so that it can diagnose problems when they arise.

The Control Period

The period of time covered by one report should be the shortest period in which management can usefully take action, and in which significant changes in performance are likely. If a serious out-of-control condition develops, management needs to know immediately; otherwise substantial losses can occur. By contrast, reports on overall performance are usually made monthly or quarterly, because management does not need to act sooner.

Of particular importance is the fact that key indicators usually need to be reported separately from revenues, expenses, and variances. They also need to be distributed more frequently than financial information so as to facilitate timely intervention.

Example. The principal of a junior high school receives a daily report on absences. The report shows the cumulative number of days of absence in the school year for each pupil who is absent on a particular day. Since there is a strong correlation between attendance and performance, and since 10 days of absences mean that the pupil must repeat the school year, a growing number of absences for any given pupil is an important danger signal. Frequently, the only action necessary is for the principal to express concern to the pupil the next time they see one another; the fact that the principal knows—and the pupil knows that the principal knows—often provides the proper motivation.

Bases for Comparison

A control report should compare actual year-to-date amounts with budgeted amounts for the same time period. That is, unless revenues and expenses flow evenly during the fiscal year, budgeted amounts for, say, a quarterly report should not be obtained by taking one-quarter of the annual budget, but, rather, should be constructed by estimating the correct proportion of the annual budget that is applicable to the quarter. This is extremely important. Some organizations compare actual spending for a quarter with one-fourth of the annual budget. Others compare actual spending for the quarter with the total annual budget. Neither comparison is of much use to management.

Similarly, comparisons ordinarily should be made with the budget, not with the corresponding period from the prior year. Historical comparisons represent a holdover from the days when budgets were generally nonexistent or unreliable. A good budget provides a much better basis for comparison than last year's performance because the budget presumably incorporates the significant changes that have occurred since last year.

Timeliness

In all instances, it is important that reports be made available in a timely fashion; that is, soon enough to facilitate whatever action might be called for. A good rule of thumb is that an organization should make monthly reports available to its managers within a few days after the end of the month, certainly not more than a week. Indeed, one large multinational for-profit company invested several hundred thousand dollars in modifications to its computerized reporting system so that the waiting period for monthly financial statements could be shortened by *one day!*

Generally, obtaining a short reporting interval means that some accuracy is sacrificed in the interest of speed. However, approximately accurate reports available soon enough to provide a basis for action are far preferable to precisely accurate reports unavailable until so long after the event that nothing can be done about the problems they reveal.

Clarity

A control report is a communication device, and it is not doing its job unless it communicates its intended message clearly. This is much easier said than done. Those who design control reports, therefore, spend much time carefully choosing terminology that conveys the intended meaning and arranging the numbers in a way that emphasizes the intended relationships.

Clarity may also be enhanced if the variances are expressed as percentages of budget as well as in absolute dollars. The percentage gives a quick impression of how important the variance is relative to the budget. Particularly in reports for profit centers, clarity may be enhanced if ratios are used to call attention to important relationships.

Depending on the audience, clarity can be achieved by using graphs and narrative explanations. Computers and their associated software have made graphical presentations far easier to prepare than ever before, and many managers find them quite helpful in explaining trends or other changes to their superiors.

> *Example.* The reporting system for the finance operation of the Town of Concord, Massachusetts, includes: (1) a statement of results for the period, (2) a comparison of the results with an acceptable benchmark, (3) comparisons of the town's cash position to prior periods, (4) a comment on market conditions, (5) a summary of performance results, (6) a log of investments, and (7) a graphical depiction of the results. The report is useful not only to the town treasurer but also to the elected officials and the citizenry.[2]

Narrative explanations often are used to clarify the quantitative information in a report. A good narrative explanation needs to go beyond restating what a report already says. In general, such explanations are used to describe the reasons underlying a variance.

> *Example.* In Exhibit 14–1, a narrative explanation might say: "The unfavorable rate variance was the result of the use of three nutritionists in Pay Grade 14, whereas the job called for Grade 12. This condition has existed since April because no Grade 12 employees were available. We are actively working to recruit Grade 12 people, and hope to have the situation corrected by July."

Rounding.   To help focus managers' attention on significant information, the accounting staff should round the numbers in control reports, rather than calculate them to the last penny. Most managers care little about cents; some, depending on the magnitude of the budget, may not care about the last thousand dollars. An amount of $433,876 might just as easily be reported for control purposes as $434, with the report headed "Dollar Amounts in Thousands" or "$000."

As a rule of thumb, most control reports do not need dollar amounts reported with more than three digits, although decimal points might be used to make a column easier to understand or add. For example, the above amount might be reported as $433.9. In general, the amount of rounding depends on the size of the responsibility center and what makes most sense for the managers charged with controlling costs.

---

[2] Anthony T. Logalbo, "Spotlighting Small Governments: Performance Reporting—The Forgotten Element in Cash Management," *Government Finance Review* 3, Issue 4 (April 1987), pp. 41–43.

Integration

Ordinarily, control reports should consist of an integrated package. Specifically, reports for lower-level responsibility centers should be consistent with, and easily relatable to, summary reports prepared for higher-level responsibility centers.

Exhibit 14–1 illustrates this process of integration. The second-level report is for the supervisor of nutritionists, who is on the next higher level in the organization hierarchy above the regional supervisors (first-level report). Data for the regions for which the supervisor is responsible appear in summary form in Level 2. Note that the amounts reported on a single line in Level 2 for the nutritionists' direct-contact time are the same as the totals on the Level 1 control report.

The third-level report is for an even higher level of management, the Maternal/Infant Nutrition Program. It includes the nutritionists as reported in detail in Level 2, plus the other professionals who are affiliated with the program. It also includes the other direct expenses of the program (supplies and materials, contract services). Note that the total direct labor cost figures for nutritionists at the bottom of Level 2 appear as a single line on the Level 3 report.

Level 4 is the most highly summarized report and is used by the agency director or governing body to review financial results of all the agency's programs. Note that the total direct costs of the Maternal/Infant Nutrition Program at the bottom of Level 3 appear as a single line in Level 4.

Benefit/Cost

A reporting system, like anything else, should not cost more than it is worth. Unfortunately, there are great difficulties in applying this obvious statement to practical situations. For one thing, it is difficult to measure the cost of a given report. This is partly because most preparation costs are joint costs with other reports, and partly because the real cost includes not only the preparation cost, but also the opportunity cost of the hours that managers spend reading reports when they might be doing something else.

Because of the difficulty in assessing the benefit/cost ratio of reports, it is worthwhile to review an organization's management control reports periodically and eliminate those no longer needed. Useless reports are not uncommon. Frequently they exist because a new problem area created a need for a report at some earlier time, and the report continues to be prepared even though the problem no longer exists. A report structure, like a tree, is often better if it is pruned regularly.

An Illustration

Not all control reports follow the above criteria. Many organizations, for sound management reasons, diverge from these criteria. The control report shown in Exhibit 14–2 is an example of how a report might depart from some of the above

EXHIBIT 14–2

Illustrative College Budget Report
For the Period July 1, 1991, to December 31, 1991
($000)

	Fiscal 1992 Budget	Fiscal 1992 Estimate	Variance Total	Variance Previously Reported	Variance New This Quarter
Audited student enrollment.................	1,650	1,692	42	38	4
Educational and general:					
Revenues:					
Student charges:					
Tuition.............................	$19,866	$20,374	$ 508	$ 457	$ 51
Fees...............................	2,754	2,903	149	16	133
Endowment	2,867	2,867	—	—	—
Gifts:					
Unrestricted........................	1,198	1,250	52	52	—
Restricted..........................	660	1,062	402	285	117
Government grants.....................	965	1,034	69	45	24
Other revenues	888	1,064	176	30	146
Total revenues....................	$29,198	$30,554	$1,356	$ 885	$ 471
Expenditures:					
Instruction:					
On-campus programs...................	$ 9,380	$10,018	$ (638)	$ (410)	$(228)
Off-campus programs..................	1,283	1,377	(94)	—	(94)
Academic support.......................	2,680	3,091	(411)	(40)	(371)
Student services	3,926	4,025	(99)	(75)	(24)
Institutional support....................	3,955	4,109	(154)	(149)	(5)
Educational plant:					
Expenditures	2,870	2,909	(39)	16	(55)
Renovation.........................	220	278	(58)	—	(58)
Student aid............................	5,151	4,951	200	200	—
Contingency...........................	631	316	315	158	157
Total expenditures	$30,096	$31,074	$ (978)	$ (300)	$(678)
Educational and general net income (loss)	$ (898)	$ (520)	$ 378	$ 585	$(207)
Auxiliary enterprises:					
Revenues	$10,578	$10,736	$ 158	$ 185	$ (27)
Expenditures	9,642	9,975	(333)	(189)	(144)
Net income (loss)	$ 936	$ 761	$ (175)	$ (4)	$(171)
Summary:					
Gross revenues	$39,776	$41,290	$1,514	$1,070	$ 444
Gross expenditures......................	39,738	41,049	(1,311)	(489)	(822)
Net income.....................	$ 38	$ 241	$ 203	$ 581	$(378)

	Fall Term 1991	Fall Term 1990	Fall Term 1989
Admissions data:			
Average SAT scores	945	952	958
Percent requesting financial aid	25%	22%	21%
Percent minority applications	18%	16%	15%
Percent applicants below 20 years old..........	96%	97%	97%
Full-time students to part-time	17:1	15:1	14:1
Applicants admitted.........................	87%	82%	64%
Admits enrolled	54%	55%	59%

criteria, and yet serve management's purposes well. The report is the operating statement for a college.[3] It summarizes results for the fiscal year to date; that is, from July through December. It was prepared for a January meeting of the board of trustees. Some comments about it follow.

Numbers Are Rounded. The report is short, and the numbers are rounded so that a maximum of four digits is shown. It nevertheless conveys the significant information the board needs so that it can understand what has happened and what is likely to happen.

Management's Current Estimates Are Included. In a departure from the criteria discussed above, the report does not compare actual expenses for the year to date with the year-to-date budget; rather it compares the budget for the *entire year* with management's current *estimate* of revenues and expenses for the *entire year*. In the board's view, this is one of the most important parts of the report. Management must explain each significant difference, then seek board approval of controllable differences *before* the expenses actually are incurred.

Auxiliary Enterprises Are Shown Separately. The report is structured so that revenues and expenses of auxiliary enterprises are shown separately from educational revenues and expenses, and so that the net income of these activities is shown. (It may be desirable to show separately the revenues and expenses of each important auxiliary activity, such as dormitory, food service, bookstore, and varsity athletics.) In some reports all revenues are presented first, and then all expenses, so that important programmatic relationships are difficult to determine. This report is structured so that attention is focused on the revenues and expenses of the primary program, education, and then on the revenues and expenses of the auxiliary programs.

Approved Variances Are Separated. The variances that the board has considered and approved at earlier meetings are listed separately, so that attention is focused on variances that have developed since the last meeting. (A separate, two-page memorandum explains the important new variances.)

Unfavorable Variances Are Highlighted. "Unfavorable" variances, that is, those that reduce income, are enclosed in parentheses. These are revenue items for which the estimated actual is less than budget, and expense items for which the estimated actual is more than budget.

---

[3] Additional examples of operating statements can be found in Leon E. Hay, *Accounting for Governmental and Nonprofit Entities* (Homewood, Ill.: Richard D. Irwin, 1988); Malvern J. Gross, Jr., *Financial and Accounting Guide for Nonprofit Organizations* (New York: Ronald Press, 1991); and Edward S. Lynn and Robert J. Freeman, *Fund Accounting: Theory and Practice* (Englewood Cliffs, N.J.: Prentice Hall, 1991).

USE OF CONTROL REPORTS

If control reports are to have any value, they must be used; that is, managers must rely on them as an important resource. In this regard, an issue that frequently arises concerns the value of a comparison between expected and actual performance after the performance already has taken place. Since the work has been completed, and the past cannot be changed, of what value is such a report? There are two answers to this question.

First, if a manager understands that his or her performance is being measured, reported, and evaluated, there is at least some tendency to attempt to influence the results so as to obtain a good report. Assuming that the reporting system is fair—so that a "good" action (one that benefits the organization) on the part of a manager will be reflected accordingly on the control reports—a manager ordinarily will tend to act in ways that benefit the organization.

Second, although the past cannot be changed, analysis of the past can be extremely helpful. Among other things, such analysis may help identify ways in which performance can be improved in the future. Specifically, a good set of control reports can help managers to take whatever corrective action appears appropriate. Clearly, an important aspect of this process is the involvement of the manager's superior, who can praise, constructively criticize, or otherwise suggest ways to improve performance. At the extreme, a good reporting system can assist a manager to determine whether a subordinate should be promoted or terminated.

Feedback

Viewed in the above way, a good set of control reports functions as a *feedback mechanism*. In engineering, feedback refers to electrical circuits that are arranged so that information about a machine's performance is fed back to a control mechanism that can make adjustments. A thermostat is a feedback device. If the temperature in a room falls below a certain level, a thermostat will activate a furnace that will return the room to its prescribed temperature.

Control reports are feedback mechanisms, but they are only one part of the process. Unlike the mechanical cause-and-effect pattern of a thermostat, the feedback process associated with a set of control reports is not automatic. A control report by itself does not lead to a change in performance; this happens only when a manager gets involved and takes action. For a manager to take action, the three-step process shown schematically in Exhibit 14–3 must occur. Specifically,

- A *review* must take place, and one or more areas must be *identified* as candidates for action.
- Each area must be *investigated* to determine whether action is warranted.
- When necessary, some sort of *action* must take place.

We discuss each of these steps separately.

EXHIBIT 14–3   Flowchart for Use of Control Reports

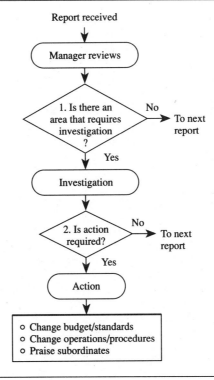

Review and Identification

A good control report will suggest areas that require investigation. An investigation sometimes, although not always, may come about because of a significant variance between budgeted and actual performance. Large unfavorable variances are not necessarily a reason for investigation, however, nor are large favorable variances a reason for complacency. Good managers will interpret the information on a control report in light of their own knowledge about conditions in the responsibility center and their "feel" for what is right.

Example. If a manager has learned from conversations and personal observations that, because of personnel shortages, there was need for considerable overtime (and therefore the payment of premium wage rates) in a particular responsibility center, there is little need to investigate a large wage rate variance. On the other hand, a large favorable price variance in the purchase of medical supplies in a hospital may indicate that low-quality supplies were purchased, perhaps implying problems later on when those supplies are used.

Some managers argue that an essential characteristic of a good management control system is that the reports contain no surprises. They expect their subordinates to inform them when significant events occur so that appropriate action can be taken immediately. When the control report subsequently appears, the manager will not be surprised by a particular variance, since the factors leading up to it were known and corrective action was taken.

The Exception Principle.   Problem identification is facilitated if the control system operates on the exception principle. According to this principle, a control report focuses a manager's attention on those limited number of items where performance differs significantly from the standard. Little or no attention is given to the rather large number of situations where performance was satisfactory.

Obviously, no control system can make this sort of distinction perfectly. Sometimes, as mentioned above, a large positive variance can be as much of a red flag as a large negative one. Sometimes a negligible variance masks underlying factors that a manager needs to address.

> *Example.* When the program director reads the Program Direct Cost Summary third-level report in Exhibit 14–1 (p. 716), his or her attention is not called to the performance of the nutritionists in June, because actual costs were only $30,000 in excess of standard, an insignificant amount. We can observe from the details of nutritionists' performance in Level 2, however, that costs for direct contact time, community collateral work, and professional development are considerably in excess of standard, and these excesses may indicate that problems exist.

The exception principle is tricky to apply in practice because it requires that significant items be identified, and significance is a matter of judgment. Nevertheless, a good set of control reports will at least attempt to highlight problem areas so as to save managers as much time as possible in the process of review and problem identification.

Engineered and Discretionary Costs.   In reviewing a set of control reports, a manager must distinguish between items of engineered cost and items of discretionary cost. In general, managers are looking for engineered costs to be as low as possible vis-à-vis the standard (consistent, of course, with quality and safety standards). Discretionary costs, on the other hand, are somewhat more complicated, since optimal performance frequently consists of spending the amount agreed upon in the budget; that is, spending too little may be as problematic as spending too much.

> *Example.* To reduce expenses, a manager in a research organization can easily skimp on maintenance or on training; the manager of the information services department can turn down desirable requests for special computer runs; senior management can cancel an unfunded research project. All of these actions result in lower costs during the current budget year, but none may be in the long-run best interest of the organization.

Limitations of the Standard.   No standard is perfect. Sometimes standards are derived in ways that are not methodologically sound. Even if a standard cost is carefully prepared, it may not be an accurate estimate of what costs should have been under the particular set of circumstances a manager faced during a reporting period.

>   ***Example.*** The standard direct labor cost for a particular procedure is $13.72. This may not be accurate if the engineering analysis that led to the standard was conducted improperly. Even if the engineering analysis was methodologically sound, the rate may not be an accurate estimate of current direct labor costs because of methods changes, changes in technology, changes in wage rates, or changes in the kind of personnel conducting the procedure.

In short, even with a valid budget, managers should exercise caution in using variances as indicators of performance. A variance may have a combination of causes, some of which were controllable, some not. At best, a good variance analysis provides the starting point for evaluating performance and discovering the underlying causes of performance that deviate from the budget. Therefore, in deciding what action to take, managers should utilize not only the control reports, but also whatever information they obtain through other channels, and their intuitive judgment regarding areas that need attention.

Investigation

Ordinarily, an investigation consists of a conversation between the manager of a responsibility center and his or her superiors and subordinates. In these conversations, the superior typically probes to determine whether corrective action of some sort is needed. Frequently, it turns out that special circumstances gave rise to the variance; that is, the assumptions that underlay the budget did not hold. If these changes were not controllable by the subordinate, there is little that can be done. Certainly there is no cause to criticize the subordinate. This does not mean that no corrective action can be taken, however; rather, it suggests that corrective action must be taken at some level other than the subordinate's.

It also is possible that the variance resulted from a random occurrence that probably will not repeat itself, such as an equipment breakdown or a strike. In this case, about all that can be done is to accept the variance and hope that it will not recur.

Finally, it is possible that the variance came about from performance that needs to be modified. In this case, the superior wants to determine the underlying causes of the deviation from budget, and assist the subordinate in taking corrective action to reverse the trend.

Action

Usually, a course of action comes about as a result of a meeting between a superior and a subordinate; the meeting generally revolves around a particular variance. If the variance is negative, the two individuals agree on the steps that must be taken to remedy the situation. If a favorable variance is the result of good performance, praise is appropriate.

In all respects, it is important for superiors to weigh the trade-offs between current performance and the long-run interests of the organization. An inherent weakness of management control systems is that they tend to focus on short-run rather than long-run performance. They measure current revenues and expenses, rather than the effect of current actions on the future financial health of the organization or the quality of services provided. Thus, if too much emphasis is placed on financial results as they are depicted in current control reports, long-run performance may be affected. We explore this dilemma more fully in the next chapter.

SUMMARY

Performance reports, as distinct from information reports, typically focus on two types of output: economic performance and management performance. Most of our attention in this chapter was directed toward management performance, which is the subject of the management control reports.

Good control reports have three essential characteristics: (1) they are related to personal responsibility, which typically calls for several levels of reports; (2) they compare actual performance to a standard, usually the budget; and (3) they focus on significant information, which frequently includes key indicators, many of which are nonfinancial in nature. By focusing on key indicators, managers frequently can see a problem developing and take action to avert it before it affects net income.

Good control reports also must satisfy certain technical criteria. They must (1) cover a period of time that facilitates management action; (2) be timely enough to allow management's actions to have an effect; (3) clarify important relationships, which frequently requires using graphs and narrative explanations, and rounding numbers to only three or four digits; (4) consist of an integrated package in which the reports for lower-level responsibility centers are consistent with and easily relatable to the reports for higher-level responsibility centers; and (5) be worth more than they cost.

A good set of control reports functions as a feedback mechanism that guides managers in identifying and investigating areas for possible action. To do this, the reports should function on the exception principle, which typically allows managers to focus their attention on a few areas where investigation is required. In so doing, managers need to bear in mind that a standard, no matter how carefully prepared, may not be an accurate estimate of what costs or revenues should have been under actual circumstances. Therefore, variances should be used with caution; they are a means to guide a manager's investigation and subsequent action, but not necessarily a reason for criticism of subordinates.

SUGGESTED ADDITIONAL READINGS

Anthony, Robert N., and James S. Reece. *Accounting Principles*. Homewood, Ill., Richard D. Irwin, 1989, chap. 26.

Nackel, John, Paul J. Fenaroli, and George M. J. Kis. "Product-Line Performance Reporting: A Key to Cost Management." *Healthcare Financial Management*, November 1987, pp. 54–62.

Usher, Charles L., and Gary C. Cornia. "Goal Setting and Performance Assessment in Municipal Budgeting." *Public Administration Review*, March–April 1981, pp. 229-35.

CASE 14–1   Rural Health Associates (B)*

In July 1981, Margaret Reber, Research Assistant at the Harvard School of Public Health, interviewed Jack Bourbeau, manager of Rural Group Practice (RGP), for the purpose of writing a case on the management control system at RGP. RGP was a division of Rural Health Associates, a large health care organization located in the rural community of Farmington, Maine (see Rural Health Associates (A) in Chapter 7 for a description). At the time of the interview Mr. Bourbeau had worked at RGP for eight months, and had already instituted some changes in the group practice, which he described in the following interview.

Bourbeau: When I first came here in November 1980, I looked at the physicians' generation of revenue and the corresponding expenses, and I knew something was wrong. Here, look at the Statement of Operations and Comparisons for that month (Exhibit 1). You can see how the generation figures in all categories were less than budgeted, but the expenses were not proportionally less, so we ended up with a big deficit.

Reber: Was meeting budgeted figures a matter of high priority to RGP providers when you came?

Bourbeau: No. At that time, the physicians didn't care whether or not they met budgeted amounts. They had no incentives to do so, as they were paid prospectively based on anticipated revenue for the budget year.

Reber: How did you interest the providers in the problem?

Bourbeau: The providers eventually became concerned when they realized the group practice would go under if we didn't reverse the deficit trend. Then I had their support.

Reber: How did you approach the problem?

Bourbeau: I decided to do an analysis to find out why our actual revenue was lower than budgeted. I focused on each individual provider. Although the year's budgeted values for physician generation were derived somewhat subjectively from discussions with individual physicians and examination of past trends, there were some standards I thought I could use to find the revenue we could expect from each physician. First, I identified each physician's specialty area and used the fee guidelines to determine the typical fee per visit for each provider (Exhibit 2). Next, I talked to the physicians to determine how many hours per week they were scheduled to be in the office (Exhibit 2). Although all of our providers are full time, some of them spend a greater percentage of their working time at RGP. For example, Dr. Sewall, one of our dentists, is available for office visits 40 hours/week, whereas Dr. Dixon, our general surgeon, spends a good deal of time at the hospital.

Reber: What happened next?

Bourbeau: Using some general guidelines, each provider determined how many patients she or he could see in an hour's time based on the length of an average office visit (Exhibit 2). Then I multiplied the expected number of hours worked per week by the expected number of patients in a week. In order to give the physician some leeway for

---

* This case was prepared by Margaret B. Reber under the direction of Professor David W. Young. Copyright © by the President and Fellows of Harvard College. Distributed by the Pew Curriculum Center, Harvard School of Public Health.

EXHIBIT 1

RURAL HEALTH ASSOCIATES (B)
Rural Group Practice
Statement of Operations and Comparisons*

	1979 Month November	1980 Month November	1979–80 YTD 11/30/79	1980–81 YTD 11/30/80	1980–81 Prorated Budget
Generation:					
Medical	$ 81,349	$ 81,073	$454,111	$486,622	$574,319
Dental	13,658	13,023	60,104	66,603	77,621
Optometry	10,788	11,030	56,587	55,955	69,807
Pharmacy	3,076	2,799	14,155	15,160	17,269
Laboratory	8,634	8,165	43,953	46,948	53,623
X-ray	7,253	5,296	34,338	32,187	41,892
Total	124,758	121,386	663,248	703,475	834,531
Grants	3,054	2,039	15,269	12,696	12,500
Other income	504	(9)	4,746	989	—
Total operating support	128,316	123,416	683,263	717,160	847,031
Less uncollectibles:					
Provision for bad debts	3,569	3,455	19,022	20,014	
Cash discount	1,173	1,066	5,685	6,791	
Courtesy and employee discount	1,635	189	9,936	1,152	
Disallowed charges	12,108	11,960	38,454	42,171	
Total uncollectibles	18,485	16,670	73,097	70,128	84,703
Total operating revenue	109,831	106,746	610,166	647,032	762,328
Operating expenses:					
Medical	62,933	65,453	326,936	386,170	398,383
Dental	7,844	8,701	45,501	51,170	55,277
Optometry	8,868	9,582	45,093	50,726	50,015
Pharmacy	3,738	2,933	14,024	15,475	15,834
Laboratory	4,785	4,518	20,819	21,996	25,252
X-ray	5,058	4,075	23,086	23,485	25,753
Medical records	1,606	3,056	8,706	9,948	9,042
Facilities	12,197	11,571	60,100	56,329	65,239
Administration	19,022	18,269	88,290	96,303	114,614
Total operating expense	126,051	128,158	632,555	711,602	759,409
Interest	300	244	3,749	2,215	1,667
Total operating expense including interest	126,351	128,402	636,304	713,817	761,076
Excess of revenue over expenses (expenses over revenue)	$(16,520)	$(21,656)	$(26,138)	$(66,785)	$ 1,252

* The fiscal year was from July–June. FY 1981 began on July 1, 1980.

---

telephone calls and paperwork, we use a 4.5 day workweek. This amount was multiplied by the expected number of provider days in the month, which I determined by subtracting all legitimate sick and vacation days for the particular month (Exhibit 2). This gave me the expected number of patients per month. Finally, I multiplied this number by 0.80 to get a more realistic number of patients the physician was expected to see for a month.

EXHIBIT 2   Expected Provider Charges, Office Hours, Visits, and Workdays

		(a)	(b)	(c)	(d)
			Expected	Expected	Expected
		Average	Number of	Number of	Number of
		Fee per	Office	Office	Workdays
Provider	Specialty	Visit	Hours/Week	Visits/Hour	in May
Bitterauf	Orthopedic surgery	$20	16	4	16
Condit	Family practice	$17	32	4	20
Dixon.	General surgery	$18	16	4	15
Fuson	Family practice	$17	32	4	15
Haeger.	Dentistry	$30	40	2	20
Hurst	Otorhinolaryngology (ENT)	$20	16	4	16
MacMahon	Pediatrics/family practice	$17	32	6	10
Prior.	Internal medicine	$17	23	4	18
Record.	Internal medicine	$17	23	4	16
Sewall	Dentistry	$30	40	2	20

Reber: Why did you provide the physicians with this additional leeway?

Bourbeau: The physicians engage in many nonincome generating activities and they thought some allowance should be incorporated to account for the time they spend in the reexamination of patients, delivery of medication and shots, and public relations activities for which there is a minimal charge or perhaps no charge at all.

Reber: I see. Anything else?

Bourbeau: Well, my final step was to take this adjusted figure and multiply it by the average fee per visit to get the revenue which I could expect each provider to generate.

Reber: Then you compared this expected revenue with actual?

Bourbeau: Yes. Using the physicians' schedule books, my secretary tallied up office visits, office surgery, and injection charges for the month for each physician to get the actual office visit generation. She also computed the number of patients seen, the total hours worked, the number of appointments rescheduled or canceled and the number of no shows. My secretary spent about six hours each month tabulating this information. She gave this information to me (Exhibit 3) and then I subtracted the actual from the expected and prepared a report for each physician contrasting expected and actual values. I have been doing this since November. Here is a sample of a recent report showing performance for Dr. Bitterauf for the month of May (Exhibit 4), as well as the totals for all departments for May (Exhibit 5).

Reber: What have you learned from the reports?

Bourbeau: Well, as might be expected, the revenue of some providers was way below expected. In certain cases, it was due to low productivity; in others, it was because the physicians weren't charging enough or they weren't spending enough time in the office. So I decided to talk to the providers.

Reber: How did the physicians respond?

Bourbeau: Pretty well. The first time I produced the report, I sat down with each physician individually and explained the figures. I had to convince them that I was right. I had to be able to back up my words with figures. For every hour I spent with a physician, I

EXHIBIT 3   Actual Provider Visits, Hours Worked, and Generation

Provider	Actual Number of Visits in May	Actual Number of Hours Worked in May	Actual Generation in May
Bitterauf	208	44	$ 3,816
Condit	413	107	6,890
Dixon.............	88	30	2,398
Fuson	242	87	4,271
Haeger............	218	130	7,493
Hurst.............	203	61	6,704
MacMahon	191	43	3,758
Prior..............	207	70	3,860
Record............	182	56	3,717
Sewall	211	133	10,100
Totals	2,163	761	$53,007

spent 12 to 15 hours in hard work documenting what I was talking about. When I showed them all the data, they accepted it. Let me give you an example of a conversation I had with one of our physicians who was undercharging patients. I said, "Roger, I've been studying the way you've been practicing, and I'd like to talk to you about it. Although you see a lot of patients, your total generation is under what we expected." Then Roger said, "How do you know?" After I showed him the numbers, we progressed to a discussion of his pattern of undercharging. Roger told me that some people didn't have much money, so he didn't charge as much. Then I told him, "You can't do that. You can't charge one patient less than another for the same service. That's discrimination." Now, we're gradually getting Roger's fees up to what they should be. But I couldn't do it without this report.

Reber: So you feel that the physician's report has been a useful tool for controlling revenue?

EXHIBIT 4   Sample Physician's Report

Dr. Bitterauf   May 1981

$$16 \text{ hrs/wk} \times 4 \text{ pts/hr} = 64 \text{ pts/wk}$$

No. of pts. (patients)	No. of hrs.	Generation
208	44	$3,816
$18.35	$86.73	4.7 pt/hr

$$64 \text{ pt/wk} \div 4.5 \text{ days/wk} = 14.2 \text{ pt/day}$$

$$14.2 \text{ pt/day} \times \#\text{provider days } (16) = 227 \text{ pt/mo (max)}$$

$$227 \text{ pt/mo} \times .80 = 182 \times \$20.00 = \$3,640$$

$$\$3,816 - \$3,640 = \$176$$

EXHIBIT 5

RURAL HEALTH ASSOCIATES (B)
Rural Group Practice
Statement of Operations and Comparisons

	1980 Month May	1981 Month May	1979–80 YTD 5/31/80	1980–81 YTD 5/31/81	1980–81 Budget
Generation:					
Medical..............................	$109,941	$100,794	$1,057,539	$1,157,234	$1,443,817
Dental...............................	14,511	18,685	140,431	163,694	195,136
Optometry...........................	10,185	14,984	122,943	142,061	175,492
Pharmacy...........................	3,218	2,778	33,007	35,949	43,414
Laboratory..........................	11,431	12,042	102,508	117,396	134,806
X-ray...............................	8,332	7,044	85,109	80,646	105,315
Total	157,618	156,327	1,541,537	1,696,980	$2,097,980
Grants...............................	2,823	2,039	34,299	24,931	30,000
Other income........................	(29)	(8)	13,603	1,064	
Total operating support............	160,412	158,358	1,589,439	1,722,975	2,127,980
Less uncollectibles:					
Provision for bad debts..............	4,431	4,402	43,663	47,964	
Cash discount	1,473	1,367	13,133	15,502	
Courtesy and employee discount	195	214	13,001	2,546	
Disallowed charges..................	9,885	12,878	104,125	131,486	
Total uncollectibles	15,984	18,861	173,922	197,498	212,798
Total operating revenue	144,428	139,497	1,415,517	1,525,477	1,915,182
Operating expenses:					
Medical..............................	75,224	66,966	758,746	837,488	1,022,252
Dental...............................	8,751	9,686	101,844	117,134	133,759
Optometry...........................	11,853	15,341	105,491	124,971	121,761
Pharmacy...........................	2,734	3,055	30,706	36,858	38,000
Laboratory..........................	4,510	4,297	49,916	56,504	60,600
X-ray...............................	3,874	5,353	53,993	56,082	64,800
Medical records	1,556	1,735	18,892	19,049	21,700
Facilities............................	11,887	11,350	132,823	131,512	156,560
Administration......................	17,900	21,584	198,905	235,251	290,250
Total operating expense	138,289	139,367	1,451,316	1,614,849	1,909,682
Interest..............................	1,000	746	7,593	5,573	4,000
Total operating expense including interest	139,289	140,113	1,458,909	1,620,422	1,913,682
Excess of revenue over expenses (expenses over revenue)..............	$ 5,139	$ (616)	$ (43,392)	$ (94,945)	$ 1,500

Bourbeau: Yes indeed. This report has enabled me to pinpoint the sources of our low revenue generation problem and it has provided me with the necessary back-up to discuss problems with the providers. We have seen some dramatic increases in certain physician's office visit revenue since we instituted the report. We have a ways to go, but this report is helping us to get our feet back on the ground.

Reber: What additional activities do you plan?

Bourbeau: The most important thing to do now is to be able to give the providers a breakdown of why they are not achieving their budgeted levels of performance. This is going to require designing a somewhat more sophisticated report than we have right now.

Questions

1. Prepare a variance analysis for Dr. Bitterauf.
2. How would you report this information to him/her?
3. Design a set of reports for RHA that more adequately addresses the needs of management and the physicians.

CASE 14–2   Cook County Hospital*

Mr. Lou Pinckney, Administrative Assistant in the Department of Radiology at Cook County Hospital, was assessing the new reporting system that he and the Chief of Radiology had developed to measure the department's performance. The system had been developed in response to some new directions being taken by the hospital, and Mr. Pinckney wondered if the reports being prepared were adequate in light of the new demands being placed on the department.

Background

In November 1970, Dr. James G. Haughton assumed the position of Executive Director of the Health and Hospital Governing Commission of Cook County. At the time he assumed the position, Cook County was one of the largest and most famous hospitals in the world. It had a bed capacity of 1,800 and a daily census of about 1,500. The hospital opened its doors to patients in 1876 in the heart of Chicago's west side, and had expanded to comprise 21 buildings. In addition to inpatient services, it operated a large clinic for outpatients. CCH provided a wide range of medical services and was particularly known for its Koch Burn Unit, trauma center, and pain clinic. The research wing of CCH was the Hektoen Institute, incorporated in 1943 as a nonprofit research organization.

CCH was the primary health care institution for the county's indigent sick.

---

* This case summarizes two cases that were prepared by C. K. Prahalad, under the direction of Professor J. B. Silvers, Case Western Reserve University. Copyright © by the President and Fellows of Harvard College. Harvard Business School cases 9-273-178 and 9-273-179.

Emergency cases were admitted without regard to any eligibility requirement. However, according to a 1976 article in *The Wall Street Journal,*

> by the late 1960s, the institution had become too old, too big, and too enmeshed in the county's political patronage system to care for the poor effectively. Large, overcrowded wards were dirty and lacked sufficient nurses, privacy, or supplies. Surgeons sometimes had to swat flies while operating. . . .
>
> Politicians and the press clamored to close the "medical snakepit," and in 1970 the hospital seemed about to lose its accreditation.

When Dr. Haughton came to Cook County, he refused an employment contract, but insisted that the Commission give him full operating authority and support. He then, according to *The Wall Street Journal:*

> . . . recruited a top caliber medical staff, streamlined the administrative structure, and collected $25 million in unpaid Medicare and Medicaid bills. In spending $12 million to clean up and modernize the facilities, he bought new beds rather than used ones, for the first time in memory. He ordered installation of patient call buttons and bed curtains and doubled the amount of nursing care. His improvements helped slash the hospital's death rate in half.

These changes did not come about without some difficulty, though; there was a threat of a walkout by hospital physicians in 1971, a nurses' strike in 1972, a strike by interns and residents in 1975, the firing of several key physicians, and a series of threats on Dr. Haughton's life. Many of these difficulties resulted from Dr. Haughton's controversial style and unilateral approach to decision making. According to *The Wall Street Journal,* Dr. Haughton

> thinks the broader issue is whether he or physicians should run the hospital. "The Commission hired me to make decisions," he says flatly. "If I can wait for consensus, fine. Otherwise, I will make decisions myself."

Organization

Until 1969, CCH was governed by the County Board. In 1969, the general assembly created the Health and Hospitals Governing Commission to remove the hospital from the political arena. The Commission had general responsibility for organizing, supervising, and managing Cook County Hospital, the Cook County School of Nursing, and Oak Forest Hospital.

According to Dr. Haughton, the Commission as constituted in July 1, 1969, was ineffective as an institution. "It was given all the responsibility for running the three institutions but none of the authority. It did not control its budget or its hiring practices, it could not set salaries, and it could not purchase. It was not until the spring of 1970 that amendments were passed giving the Commission all of these very necessary authorities."

Policies and Goals

One of Dr. Haughton's earliest moves was to work with the Health and Hospitals Governing Commission to clarify the hospital's policies and goals. At a meeting in late August 1971, the Commission adopted the statements shown in Exhibit 1. With these as a basis, Dr. Haughton then required all his chiefs of service and other department heads to develop a statement of objectives. The statement developed by the Department of Radiology is shown in Exhibit 2.

EXHIBIT 1   Policies and Goals for the Health and Hospitals Governing Commission of Cook County

---

POLICIES

1. To deliver patient care that is based on appropriateness and timeliness instead of mere cost effectiveness. For example, it might be impossible to justify the cost of the enormous expenditures involved in cancer therapy, but these expenditures are a necessary adjunct to delivering adequate health care to the community.
2. To encourage teaching and research in our health care system in order to create the environment to support excellence in patient care.
3. To foster community participation in identifying health care programs that will be truly responsive to the needs of the people of the community.
4. To create an atmosphere in which voluntary institutions, the Governing Commission and community groups working cooperatively at a local level will make acceptable health and medical care readily available to all people of the community.
5. To encourage programs for improvement of housing, education, welfare, and transportation insofar as these are necessary components of effective health care.
6. To encourage opportunities for the participation of members of minority groups in all of the Commission's programs and relationships; and, to associate or affiliate only with organizations which adhere to this philosophy. (As amended October 2, 1971.)

GOALS

1. To promote primary neighborhood family care in areas of greatest need throughout the county.
2. To establish a system of backup facilities for this primary care in order to provide specialty and inpatient care for patients.
3. To establish a decentralized system for chronic care and to coordinate it with backup facilities.
4. To develop outreach programs that place less reliance on physical facilities.
5. To develop educational programs that foster health maintenance within our communities.
6. To stress the benefits of ambulatory care over inpatient care to third-party payors and providers as well as to consumers.
7. To train paramedical personnel to such a level of competence that they may be relied upon for many basic medical procedures.
8. To examine and redefine the functions of Fantus Clinic and other services at Cook County Hospital as well as Oak Forest Hospital.
9. To promote the development of a countywide system of rapid registry and retrieval of medical records.
10. To examine and recommend participation in such regional programs as are appropriate for health care in the community.

In order to accomplish the above goals, it will be necessary for the Governing Commission to coordinate its role with the activities of voluntary and proprietary institutions as well as other governmental agencies.

Adopted: September 21   , 1971

EXHIBIT 2

Departmental Objective Statements

Department: Main Department, Radiology

Overall Objective Statement for Forthcoming Year

A. Reason for Existence of Budget Unit

1. *Specific Activities Performed:* Upgrading the Division of Diagnostic Radiology to give acceptable consultation by this specialty, and to improve qualitative and quantitative, the aspect of the overall department operations.

To improve the efficiency and effectiveness in performing various subfunctions within the department, such as patient scheduling, film filing, storage and retrieval, quality of X-ray procedures, diagnostic reporting and the Radiological Technical School.

To perform radiological services for the patients of Cook County Hospital and the citizens of the County of Cook.

2. *Problem Areas:* Severe space shortage. No employee lounge area, inadequate locker space and inadequate office space.

Need for additional radiographic rooms, especially in the Main Department and the Outpatient, Fantus Clinic Radiology Department.

Future plans must comprehend the radiologic growth problem and not be confined by thinking of architectural designs and equipment designs.

3. *Budget:* Monthly financial statements concerning expenditures and revenues of the department were to have been made available. To date, however, this information has not been received. Therefore, it is virtually impossible to make a completely accurate estimate of capital, operational and impersonal needs.

Medical "A"

1. *Problem Areas:* Severe space shortage. No employee lounge area, inadequate locker and office spaces. Future plans must comprehend the radiologic growth problem and not be confined by thinking of architectural designs and equipment designs.

2. *Budget:* Monthly statements concerning expenditures and revenues have not been made available to the department to this date. Therefore, it is virtually impossible to make a completely accurate estimate of capital, operational and impersonal needs.

Pediatrics

1. *Problem Areas:* New construction is presently being completed.

2. *Space:* Waiting area for patients is of utmost importance.

Fantus Clinic for Outpatients

1. *Problem Areas:* Severe space shortage. Additional space is urgently needed for additional radiographic rooms. This need is acute if we are to provide adequate radiological service for the Outpatient Department. Future plans must comprehend the radiologic growth problem and not be confined by thinking of architectural designs and equipment designs. A hospital this size must have complete radiological facilities for proper outpatient radiological services.

2. *Budget:* Monthly financial statements are not available, therefore making it impossible to accurately project our future estimate of operational cost.

B. New Objectives for Forthcoming Year

List of New Objectives Planned

1. *Quality of Personnel:* Needs vast improvement. More work-study programs, procedural check, formal and informal teaching programs.

EXHIBIT 2 *(concluded)*

---

2. *Scheduling System:* Each section has to be reassessed with new efficiency and effectiveness applied, especially as it relates to transportation of patients to and from the radiology department.

3. *Quality Level of Diagnostic Interpretation:* The present level is not high enough. This should include a senior staff member with an equivalent of five years' training to receive this kind of personnel.

4. *Quality Level of Diagnostic Procedures:* All technical personnel must attend quality control conferences and will be evaluated according to their technical abilities. This level of quality must also improve.

5. *Film Viewing Area:* To install alternators for each surgical and orthopedic chief for viewing of radiological films and reports with the staff radiologist.

6. *Time Span between Writing of the Requisition to the Delivery of the Final Report Back to the Unit:* The scheduling system has improved this procedure. However, the proper flow still remains a problem.

7. *Patient Master and Teaching Cards:* The Master Card is of utmost importance to any proper filing system and patient examination control. The Teaching Card System is a requirement of the American College of Radiology for accreditation.

8. *Projected Volume by Section:* Check daily average procedure and volume chart. Nationwide, the average increase is usually 10 percent. We expect at least a 12 percent increase over last year (1972).

9. *Film File Libraries:* The file areas need new equipment, personnel changes, as well as additions. They also need a filing program.

10. *Lounge and Locker Areas:* Must continue to push for additional space for an employee lounge and locker space.

Why Activity Should Be Pursued

To continue to improve radiological services for better patient care. It should also be realized that this division is presently functioning on an above average of what is expected of a Radiology Department in this Medical Center and Community.

How You Intend to Reach Goal

Hopefully by getting the cooperation and assistance from the Hospital Administration and the Health and Hospitals Governing Commission for additional space, equipment, and personnel.

When You Should Realize Objective

With the cooperation and assistance, hopefully within the next year.

C. Activity to Be Eliminated or Curtailed in Forthcoming Year

1. *Why Reduction:* Deletion of Radiology Medical Specialist "12"

2. Additional staff residents.

3. Utilization of registered X-ray technologists who have been trained by medical staff for injection of IVP. Approved by the AMA and ACR.

The Department of Radiology

Mr. Pinckney had extensive experience in the Department of Radiology. A fully trained technician, he had taken courses in business administration. He described his job as follows:

> I think we have come a long way. The concept of management of a department as extensive and complex as this [radiology] is being appreciated. People recognize it as a key function, not paper shuffling. We need managerial skills. I am called an Administrative Assistant but my job is that of a Business Manager.

Exhibit 3 is an illustration of Mr. Pinckney's conception of his job and the nature of the relationships that were involved.

EXHIBIT 3 Administrative Assistant—Radiology Division: A Conception of the Job

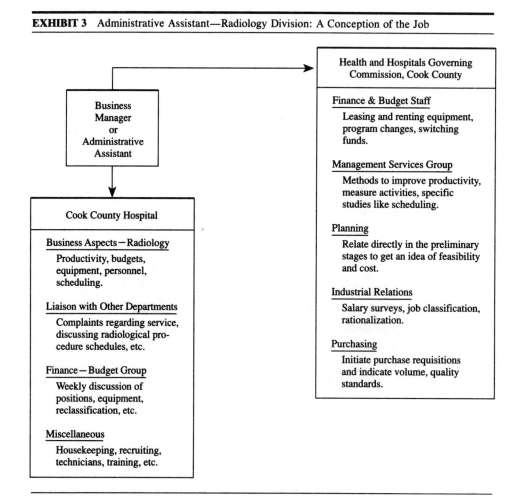

Q: How would you characterize the nature of changes that have taken place in the radiology department in the last three years?

Pinckney: I would say we have built up a whole new concept of patient care and have acquired the capability to deliver it, almost from scratch. It has been a very challenging and rewarding experience.

Q: What has been the role of the budgeting system?

Pinckney: Substantial. The budget has provided us the impetus. It is no more whom you know in downtown that matters but what is the merit of your programs. We have a better managed operation now.

Q: As an administrative assistant in the division, what sources of data do you use to develop your budget and evaluate your performance?

Pinckney: As you know we work on the basis of programs. Development of programs is based on our judgment and understanding of the demand for specific services or procedures. We make the equipment decisions as well as personnel decisions on that basis. We do not use management techniques like discounted cash flows or return on investment but I am confident that we can satisfy any accountant of the reasonableness of our decision.

   We do not have data on cost per procedure by the type of procedures, but we use extensive checks on technician productivity to measure efficiency. Basically, the controls that I exercise here are based on controlling output in physical terms, not in financial terms. Financial data can mask a lot of trends and shifts that are taking place. Moreover, we are at present concerned about increasing the quality of patient care and we do not want to get caught in a numbers game.

   Mr. Pinckney received a variety of reports from his supervisors and maintained a series of charts showing trends in a variety of performance indices. Some of the important reports were the following:

1. *Average waiting time per patient* (Exhibit 4). The total time for which a patient waited in the radiology unit was recorded on patient slips and this was used to compile the report. The "in" and "out" times of all patients divided by the number of patients provided an average waiting time. The waiting time for regular and special cases was separately computed. The segment of the total waiting time that was measured is shown below:

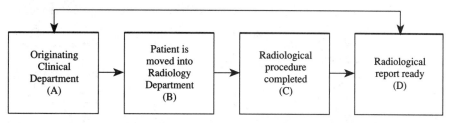

   The segment that was measured was the time it took to go through Steps (B) and (C). Mr. Pinckney was initiating steps to measure and report the total time delay—that is, for segments (A) through (D).

2. *Number of procedures performed* on a daily basis classified by *wards* which initiated the request as well as by *type of procedures*.

EXHIBIT 4

Patient's Waiting Time

April 14-20-73

Date	Minutes	Transport-Slips	Minutes (per slip)
April 14	624 minutes	15 slips	0:52 minutes/slip
15	585	14	0:42
16	2384	29	1:22
17	2828	37	1:16
18	5284	62	1:25
19	5791	47	1:31
20	923	19	:45
7 days total	18,419	223	1:23 average for week for <u>regular</u> cases

Specials

Date	Minutes	Transport-Slips	Minutes (per slip)
April 14	—	—	—
15	171 minutes	1 slip	2:51 minutes/slip
16	4680	29	2:41
17	3261	19	2:51
18	4270	40	1:47
19	3690	27	2:17
20	—	—	—
7 days total	16,072	116	2:18 average for week for <u>special</u> cases

Combined-Cases

	Minutes	Transport-Slips	Minutes
7 days total (April 14-20)	34,491	339	1:42 average wait for week for <u>all</u> cases

---

3. *A Technician Worksheet* (Exhibit 5), which shows the utilization of time of the technician. All log sheets which show a slack, like the one in Exhibit 5, are referred to Mr. Pinckney.
4. *Procedures per inpatient day* (Exhibit 6) as an index of the quality of service. The log sheet for the pediatrics department is shown in Exhibit 6.

EXHIBIT 5 Technician Worksheet

8am—4pm
4pm—12mid.
12mid.—8am

Signature *Cotton, M.R.T.*

Date *May 5, 1973*

Room No. *10*

Name	X-Ray No.	Examination	No. of Films	Time In	Time Out	Ward	Comments
1. BROWN, CHARLIE	1866	Rt. Ankle Chest	14'-8³	9:15	9:30	33	w/c
2. WASHINGTON, ANNA	1886	Lt. Hip L.S. Spine	10²-11²8	10:40	11:10	TR	w/c
3. WILDER, TYRONE	1890	Chest Lt. Ribs	14²	11:30	12:50	TR	str
4. McNEASE, NATHANIEL	1902	Rt. Forearm Skull	10⁴-11¹	1:05	1:30	TR	w.
5. FLOWERS, ANNIE	1912	Chest Skull, Cerv.	8³10⁴14²	2:00	2:35	10	str.
6. SMITH, JAMES	1927	Cer. Sp. Skull	8-10	3:40	4:00	TR	str

EXHIBIT 6 Procedures per Inpatient Day—Pediatrics

Mo.	Yr.	Inpatient Procedures	Days in Month	Average Procedures per Day	Average Daily Census	Procedures per Inpatient Day
Dec.	70	1012	31	33	281	.117
Jan.	71	1351	31	44	299	.147
Feb.		1291	28	46	296	.155
Mar.		1235	31	40	273	.147
Apr.		1198	30	40	239	.167
May		1174	31	38	227	.167
June		1096	30	37	296	.123
July		1004	31	32	313	.102
Aug.		1107	31	35	316	.113
Sept.		829	30	27	344	.078
Oct.		880	31	28	314	.089
Nov.		922	30	31	300	.109
Dec.		867	31	28	308	.091
Jan.	72	1030	31	33	312	.106
Feb.		1142	29	35	326	.107

EXHIBIT 7 Procedures per Employee—Total Diagnostic Department

Mo	Yr	Procedures	Days in Month	Average Daily Procedures	Payroll Employees	Procedures per Employee
Dec.		24372	31	786	140	4.11
Jan.	71	25937	31	836	140	5.97
Feb.		26037	28	992	135	7.34
Mar.		27297	31	880	140	6.29
Apr.		20700	30	693	144	4.81
May		19770	31	637	156	4.08
June		24014	30	827	168	4.76
July		32908	31	1061	177	5.94
Aug.		28519	31	933	207	4.50
Sept.		29566	30	985	227	4.03
Oct.		26267	31	847	222	3.06
Nov.		27559	30	918	224	4.05
Dec.		27934	31	901	221	4.07
Jan.	72	28699	31	732	227	3.22
Feb.		28589	29	986	221	4.46

5. *Procedures per employee* (Exhibit 7) as an index of productivity is measured on a monthly basis.

Mr. Pinckney relied heavily on the scheduling system for optimum utilization of his machines. This system worked as follows. The clerk in each clinic contacted the master scheduler at the radiology department and gave information on patients in his ward and the procedures called for. The master scheduler split the requests into routine, specials, and G.I.s (Gastro-intestinal) and passed it on to schedulers assigned to these groups. A log sheet was prepared by each group and, based on the loading chart, a transportation slip was prepared. Transportation personnel brought in patients to appropriate machine locations based on the transportation slips.

Mr. Pinckney reflected on the reports and the scheduling system and remarked:

We still do not have a comprehensive measure of activity. Our patient mix is changing, the nature of procedures are changing. So is the number of procedures per patient. We need to develop, in-house, a measure of activity which combines all these variations. This is the objective I have set for myself. In the meanwhile I will have to do with cruder measures of performance. I do not think financial measures and variance reports tell me what I want to know. I am confident that we can develop adequate systems. Some complain that we are slowly becoming a super-bureaucracy. Maybe. That doesn't bother me. What excites me here is that things are happening.

Questions

1. Evaluate the performance reporting system contained in Exhibits 4–7. What changes, if any, would you recommend?
2. What additional reports would you recommend be designed to meet Mr. Pinckney's needs? The needs of the Chief of Radiology?
3. How might these reports be modified for other departments in the hospital?

CASE 14–3   Union Medical Center*

Dr. Harriet Bingley, Manager of Clinical and Financial Systems, was discussing the theoretical underpinnings of the Diagnosis Related Group (DRG) system with one of her assistants and a representative of a western data analysis firm. The representative was at Union Medical Center (UMC) to present one of his classification systems and to explain its usefulness in comparison to other monitoring systems. Harriet was urging that the system wouldn't supply them with any information that they couldn't easily put together themselves. Already in her office stacked on shelves and up against walls were printouts of six different approaches to care monitoring and illness classification which she was in the process of evaluating.

Background

UMC was a 400-bed acute care teaching hospital located in an old downtown neighborhood undergoing considerable reconstruction. The physician staff was predominantly salaried under a contract with the hospital. Several years ago, the chief financial officer, Mr. Veller, joined UMC, bringing with him a strong interest in case mix, DRGs, and the belief that management of a hospital must revolve around its *products,* which are its cases. He intended to take an industrial model of management and apply it to the hospital.

Part of Mr. Veller's plan was to make those who manage the products responsible for resources used to produce them. This new structure thus required that a management team composed of a physician, nurse, and lay administrator be responsible for specific hospital products or case types. Another part of the plan was to merge clinical with financial data. This required changing the accounting system to track product costs in addition to departmental costs, the traditional focus of hospital cost accounting. To date, substantial progress had been made on the accounting system aspect of the plan.

---

* This case was prepared by Jill Piatek under the direction of Professor Nancy M. Kane, Harvard School of Public Health. Copyright © by the Massachusetts Health Data Consortium. Distributed by the Pew Curriculum Center, Harvard School of Public Health.

Harriet Bingley began working with Mr. Veller to implement these plans. Besides her M.D., she had an MBA from a prestigious local business school, which she felt gave her a better appreciation of the administrative aspects of clinical information. As Manager of Clinical and Financial Systems, her job entailed: (1) defining a care monitoring system; (2) refining the definitions of the hospital's products (case types); (3) development of standards of patient care by which future performance could be measured and goals set; (4) design of incentives for the departments and/or physicians to reach these goals; and (5) development of fixed prices for certain case types to bid for HMO business. Dr. Bingley reported to the vice-president of finance and to the assistant director and administrator of surgery.

Physician Relationships

As a first step toward implementation of the care monitoring system, Dr. Bingley launched an educational campaign for physicians. She began with the surgical department. With the backing of her superiors, she was given one physician from each surgical specialty with whom she discussed the care monitoring system development. The other departments would be undertaken in the future. Bingley planned four visits to each of the surgical specialty physicians. The first round, already completed, had been to introduce the physicians to the case concept, explain the types of information available about cases, and discuss the implications of the medicare prospective reimbursement system based on DRGs. The second visit, which Bingley was about to make, was to show them reports on their department and their own practice patterns, in terms of their Diagnosis Related Groups. In a future visit, Bingley expected to compare cases categorized by two other medically meaningful case classification systems which addressed severity of illness. In the last visit she hoped to sum up her analyses of the monitoring systems and methods used to estimate product costs.

Thus, the purposes of the physician interviews were to familiarize and educate physicians on product-based management information systems, to create a dialogue in which the physicians expressed their opinions on the utility of each system, and to lay the groundwork for their assuming accountability in the future for resources used for their patients. Bingley expected to employ their suggestions to modify the data in ways which would be most useful for the medical staff.

The Second Round

In November, Dr. Bingley began her second round of visits. She planned to begin the interviews by reiterating that DRGs are based on the principal diagnosis listed on the discharge summary, and that they are the basis by which medicare reimburses the hospital. She had prepared for each interview four (4) different sets of summary statistics (see Exhibits 1–4). Exhibit 1 showed a case summary for an

EXHIBIT 1   Clinical Case Summary

Unknown	
Department Surgery	
198 Total Cholecystectomy w/o C.D.E.	
Age < 70 w/o c.c.	
Patient Name	
Patient Number	
Admit-Date, Day, Time	05-27-87 Thursday 11 A.M.
Disch-Date, Day, Time	06-04-87 Friday 11 A.M.
Admission Source	Physician
Days Since Last Hospital Stay	No Previous Stay
Patient Age	61 years
Admit Weight	Unknown
Diagnosis	
Principal Diagnosis 57420	Cholelithiasis NOS
Admitting Diagnosis 57420	Cholelithiasis NOS
Total Secondary DXS	00
Infection/Complications	None
Operative Procedures	
Principal Proc (Hour 24)	Total Cholecystectomy
Associated Proc	Intraoper Cholangiogram
Associated Proc	Incidental Appendectomy
Associated Proc	Whole Blood Transfus NEC
Total Operative Episodes	01
Other Procedures	
Total Other Procedures	0
Physicians/Consultations	
Attend	Dr. Rair
Resident	Dr. Training
Surg Res	Dr. Intern
Total Consultations	Unknown
Discharge Disposition	
Deceased	
Nursing Home or Other Hospital	
Home, Home Care or Other	Home
Discharge Condition	
Afebrile	Unknown
Normal GI Function	Unknown
Ambulatory	Unknown
Physician Appointment	Unknown
Progress Satisfactory	Unknown
Instructions Understood	Unknown
Length of Stay	8 days
LOS excluding Deaths, etc.	
LOS vs. Region Median	Not Available
UR Uncertified Days	0 Days
Special Care Days	0 Days
Costs	
Routine Services	$2,152
Diagnostic Services	827
Therapeutic Services	2,134
Physician Services	0
Total Costs	$5,113
Medicare Reimbursement Rate	$4,300

EXHIBIT 2 Costs for the General Surgery Service (DRG 198, Total Cholecystectomy w/o C.D.E.; Age < 70 w/o c.c.)

Union Medical Center
Case Management System
Inpatient
Surgery, General

1	2	3	4	5	6	7	8	9	10	11	12
Base Period YTD					Current YTD		YTD Change		Change Due to		
No. of Pts.	Cost per Patient	Total Costs	Diagnostic Group	No. of Pts.	Cost per Patient	Total Costs	Costs	%	Volume/ Mix	Util.	Cost/ Unit
18	6,000	108,000	Cholecystec-tomy without common duct exploration age less than 70 without CC	20	5,940	118,800	(10,800)	10	(11,000)	8100	(7,900)

individual patient classified into Diagnosis Related Group (DRG) number 198, total cholecystectomy without common bile duct exploration, age under 70 years and/or without serious complications. The nature of information collected by the information system for each patient is shown.

Exhibit 2 described, for the same DRG, total costs incurred by the general surgery service in the base and current year, and the "variance" between years due to the changes in volume (number of patients), utilization (units, e.g., LOS per case) and cost per unit.

In Exhibit 3 each ancillary service used by the general surgery service in treating DRG 198 was broken out and the number of patients and units per patient were shown in the base and current years.

Finally, in Exhibit 4, the specific units used in one ancillary service, the clinical pathology lab, were broken down for the same DRG, for the general surgery department in the base and current years. Bingley used examples from the physicians' own departments, as well as their individual profiles.

The first physician visited was Dr. Farr in orthopedic surgery. Dr. Bingley pointed out the concern for efficiently managing cases under prospective reimbursement and suggested that cutting the quantity of lab tests might result in higher quality care. She also emphasized the excellent potential these data had as a research tool since all procedures, lab tests, and so on were documented for each case. Dr. Farr expressed interest in using the data to justify purchasing new equipment; he could see that it might be possible to cost out the possibility of trading off lower lengths of stay against higher ancillary costs. His final comment was: "That's interesting. It's nice that you can go into such detail to know what's going on."

EXHIBIT 3

Union Medical Center
Case Management System, Inpatient
Surgery, General—Cholecystectomy without C.D.E.
Age less than 70 without CC

1	2	3	4	5	6	7	8	9	10	11	12
Base Period YTD				Current YTD			YTD Change		Change Due to		
% of Pts.	Units/Pts. Receiving	Cost/Pt. in Dx Grp	Dept. Description	% of Pts.	Units/Pts. Receiving	Cost/Pt. in Dx Grp	Costs		Volume/Mix	Util.	Cost/Unit
100	20	250	Pharmacy	100	20	272	(940)		(500)	0	(440)
100	2	25	CSR	100	2	27	(90)		(50)	0	(40)
100	4	50	Pt. Care Eq.	100	4	54	(180)		(100)	0	(80)
100	1	15	SDS	100	1	16	(50)		(30)	0	(20)
100	1.5	20	SDS-P4	100	1.5	22	(80)		(40)	0	(40)
100	7	1750	P4 Room	100	7	1907	(6640)		(3500)	0	(3140)
100	2	40	Bacti Lab	100	1	24	240		(80)	400	(80)
100	17	160	Clin. Path	100	14	124	400		(320)	780	(60)
100	60	480	Chem. Lab	100	40	363	1380		(960)	3200	(860)
100	1	50	Path. Lab	100	1	54	(180)		(100)	0	(80)
100	2.5	250	Ad. Rad-Diag.	100	1.8	272	(940)		(500)	1400	(1840)
100	1	50	Rad-Nuclear Med.	10	1	42	(276)		260	0	16
100	1	75	Rad-UltraSnd	50	1	81	(135)		(75)	0	(60)
100	1	60	OR Monitoring	100	1	65	(220)		(120)	0	(100)
100	1	50	Ad. Card.	100	1	54	(180)		(100)	0	(80)
100	3	1700	Oper. Rm.	100	3	1653	(2460)		(3400)	0	940
100	14	200	OR Med. Sup.	100	14	218	(760)		(400)	0	(360)
100	1	65	OR Drgs	100	1	71	(250)		(130)	0	(120)
100	1	200	Rec. Rm.	100	1	218	(760)		(400)	0	(360)
100	55	350	IV Solutions	100	35	281	(682)		(700)	2544	(1162)
100	3	110	Blood Bank	80	2	87	588		220	586	(218)
100	5	50	Resp. Ther.	100	4	29	320		(100)	200	220
		6000	Total			5940	(10800)		(11000)	8100	(7900)

EXHIBIT 4

Union Medical Center
Case Management System
Inpatient
Surgery, General—Cholecystectomy without C.D.E.
Age less than 70 without CC

1	2	3	4	5	6	7	8	9	10	11	12
Base Period YTD					Current YTD		Total Variance		Variance Due to		
% of Pts.	Units per Pts. Receiving	Cost/ Pt. in Dx Grp	Service Unit Description	% of Pts.	Units per Pts. Receiving	Cost/ Pt. in Dx Grp	Costs		Volume/ Mix	Util.	Cost/ Unit
			Clinical Pathology Lab								
100	5	65	CBC	100	2	29	590		(130)	780	(60)
100	3	40	Differential	100	3	40	(80)		(80)	0	0
100	2	6	Routine urinalysis	100	2	6	(12)		(12)	0	0
100	1	13	PT	100	1	13	(26)		(26)	0	0
100	1	14	PTT	100	1	14	(28)		(28)	0	0
100	1	6	Platelet count	100	1	6	(12)		(12)	0	0
100	4	16	Stat test	100	4	16	(32)		(32)	0	0
	17	160	Total		14	124	400		(320)	780	(60)

Dr. Bingley's second interview was with Dr. Rair who was Chief of General Surgery. During the first interview with him, Rair had told her that he didn't need anyone to tell him about his patients, since he already knew everything about them. For the second interview he started with a similar position.

Dr. Rair felt that the DRG groupings were "terrible." He questioned several LOS measures and said that "he wouldn't point to those numbers and say anything since there was clearly something wrong with the system." He couldn't recognize some of the cases and attributed this to the residents and physician assistants who actually fill out the discharge summaries, which he usually only scans before signing. The number of people filling out the summaries and their carelessness were seen as compromising the accuracy of the database. Dr. Bingley commented that she had done a review of the primary diagnoses listed on the summaries and found an error rate of only 2–4% in coder interpretations of medical record data, but close to a 12% error rate in terms of the content expressed in the records.

Calming down a bit, Dr. Rair agreed that overuse of lab tests probably was a large problem. He didn't know if it could be stopped in a teaching hospital or if the administration would want to cut back since equipment like CAT scanners wouldn't pay for themselves. However, he primarily faulted the students: "Students are so into numbers, they can't practice medicine anymore. Residents, too. But if I told my residents to get a crit once a week and that's all, do you think that they're going to?"

Dr. Rair told Dr. Bingley that he applauded her efforts to combat these cost problems and wished her luck.

Bingley then visited Dr. Rand who was second in charge for all surgery at UMC. He was concerned with statistical meaningfulness of the data: he preferred the use of medians instead of means so that outliers wouldn't bias the data, and was concerned that the comparison of quarterly data should be to quarters having similar numbers of days. He also thought that a severity index would be more useful in terms of similarity of case costs. Bingley pointed out that severity indices weren't clinically meaningful, but he wasn't concerned about that, for his purposes. Rand said: "DRGs are worthwhile for year-to-year practice pattern changes but once the patterns are established, then severity is more important. You can't compare one of these, with one of these, with one of thats." Moreover, he felt that many of the DRG groupings in the department and physician profiles were "anecdotal" since they only contained one or a few cases.

Dr. Bingley also spoke with Dr. Bahr, a pediatric surgeon. It was apparent that the "pediatric" DRGs weren't very precise since actual pediatric cases were subsets of the categories. Bahr also was concerned about the lack of severity indices, especially for a tertiary referral hospital. Finally, he felt that the accuracy of the data was questionable since older physicians were less specific on the discharge summaries, writing "see old chart" or "multiple congenital anomalies" instead of listing each one.

Lab tests were discussed, and Bahr voiced a familiar opinion: "DRGs give us something to beat residents over the head with when they order too many electrolytes. Residents at UMC order 3–4 times too many tests, partly because it's a training institution. But even so, twice as many tests are ordered as a good training institution needs."

According to Bahr, pediatrics was different from the rest of the hospital in that it had fewer residents so there was more consistency in test ordering and lower numbers of "stats." But for less efficient departments and for people who didn't practice good medicine, DRGs were threatening. Bahr felt that there were two defects in the health care system: the second is that doctors control everything, and the first is that incentives are lacking for them to change.

Dr. Bingley had several more interviews before completing her second round. She wondered whether the third round, with the severity data, would be more popular with the doctors; she certainly hoped so. She also pondered Dr. Bahr's last comment about incentives; would severity information alone provide an incentive on the part of the doctors to change their behavior? Or should the administration develop additional incentives? What might those be? Before going on, Dr. Bingley decided to have another chat with Mr. Veller about these issues.

Questions

1. What are the physicians' concerns with respect to management uses of case mix information? How might management address those concerns?
2. What kinds of responsibility centers are there at UMC, and are they appropriate according to the criteria for the design of responsibility centers? Why or why not?
3. What is your assessment of the reports in use at UMC? In order to answer this question you will need to focus on the ways in which the reports relate to each other, and on the ways in which the chief of surgery (or any other chief) might use one or more of the reports.
4. What changes, if any, would you make to the management control system?

*Operations Analysis and
Program Evaluation*

In Chapters 11–14 we described the regular, recurring process of monitoring the current activities of an organization. In this chapter we describe two other processes that are used in analyzing and evaluating the performance of an organization and the effectiveness of its programs. One of these examines the operations of the organization as a whole, with the objective of assessing whether its efficiency and effectiveness can be improved. We call this *operations analysis*. The other focuses on individual programs, with the objective of recommending whether a program should be expanded, contracted, redirected, or discontinued. We call this *program evaluation*.

BASIC DISTINCTIONS

The operations analysis and program evaluation processes described in this chapter differ from the monitoring processes described in Chapters 13 and 14 in several respects. Specifically, an operations analysis or program evaluation usually: (1) is made at irregular, relatively long intervals, usually five years or so, rather than on a monthly or quarterly basis; (2) is much more thorough and time consuming than routine performance monitoring; (3) is conducted by an outside individual or team, or by a headquarters staff unit, rather than by an operating manager; and (4) uses different techniques than routine performance monitoring.

Differences between Operations Analysis and Program Evaluation

The essential difference between operations analysis and program evaluation is that the former is an evaluation of *process* and the latter an evaluation of *results*.[1] Because of this, operations analysis accepts the objectives of a responsibility center as given. Although there may be problems in finding out what these objectives are, once they have been identified, they are not challenged. Operations analysis assumes that a unit will continue its activities in achieving the overall goals of the organization (although occasionally the analysis may lead to the conclusion that an activity should be discontinued). The purpose of the analysis is to find more effective and efficient ways of carrying out these activities, whatever they are.

Program evaluation, by contrast, asks whether the objectives of a program are appropriate and whether the organization is attaining these objectives in the most effective and efficient way. The purpose of a program evaluation is to make a judgment about whether the program should be continued, redirected, or discontinued.

> *Example.* An operations analysis of a job training program would accept the fact that the responsibility center is supposed to train a certain target group for certain types of jobs and would examine ways of improving the efficiency and effectiveness of the training process. A program evaluation would attempt to determine whether the training in fact results in personnel who have acquired the desired skills, whether the benefits exceed the costs, and perhaps also whether society needs persons with these skills.

Essentially, then, the objective of operations analysis is reasonably clear-cut; it is to improve performance. The nature of a program evaluation is much more vague. The vagueness starts with the objectives of the program and continues through each step in the process. For this reason program evaluators usually prepare a careful plan and obtain the assent of the parties to this plan before undertaking the evaluation. Operations analysts can proceed with much less debate about what they are trying to do.

Skills Required.   The skills desirable in a program evaluation team differ considerably from those desirable for an operations analysis team. Operations analysis requires knowledge of the management process, principles of human behavior, efficient work methods, and other techniques. These principles and techniques are similar for most types of organizations. By contrast, a program evaluator must be knowledgeable about the specific type of program being evaluated. An expert in education, for example, is not likely to make a sound assessment of a health care

---

[1] The U.S. General Accounting Office uses the term *economy and efficiency audit* for what is labeled here *operations analysis* and the term *program results audit* for what is labeled *program evaluation*. (Comptroller General of the United States, *Standards for Audit of Governmental Organizations, Programs, Activities, and Functions*, rev. ed., 1981, p. 3).

program. Moreover, at least one member of the evaluation team must be an expert in sophisticated statistical and experimental methods if the evaluation method involves them, whereas operations analysis usually requires only rudimentary statistics.

OPERATIONS ANALYSIS

Although the techniques used in an operations analysis (which some people call a *management audit*) can be applied to any type of ongoing activity, they are especially applicable to service, support, and administration activities, to ongoing mission activities, such as police and fire protection, and to the regular activities of a hospital or educational institution. The need for continuing these activities in some form usually is not debatable. With respect to mission activities—where there may be questions about the appropriateness of the objectives or the continuation of the activity itself—an operations analysis is sometimes combined with a program evaluation.

Need for Operations Analysis

In many organization units, fat tends to accumulate with the passage of time. Senior management attempts to slow this accumulation by carefully examining budgets and monitoring current performance. However, adequate time for thorough analysis by these means often is not available. New technology and new production or service methods continually develop and tend to make current ways of doing things obsolete, but management, because of time limitations, often cannot consider the effect of these developments when reviewing the budget. Consequently, management usually relies on the current performance of the unit as a guide to what future performance should be.

To avoid the accumulation of fat, senior management in many organizations undertakes an occasional, basic review of activities. Such a review is often called a *zero-base review,* a term indicating that the analysis does not assume that any of the current ways of doing things are accepted as given; all are open to scrutiny. When people use the term *zero-base budgeting,* they usually mean zero-base review because there simply is not enough time in the annual budgeting process to conduct the thorough analysis that is implied by the term *zero base*.

Impetus for Operations Analysis

In some large organizations, operations analysis is conducted on a more-or-less regular cycle that covers all responsibility centers once every five to eight years. The results of this analysis are used to establish a new benchmark for the responsibility center. In subsequent budget reviews senior management attempts to maintain this benchmark, recognizing that it is likely to become gradually eroded over time until the next evaluation takes place.

In some organizations, an operations analysis is initiated because of a financial crisis. The citizens' revolt against increased property taxation in the late 1970s and 1980s led to operations analyses in many municipalities. A decrease in the inflow of financial resources, or, indeed, any situation in which expenses seem to be chronically in excess of revenues, is usually a signal that an operations analysis is warranted. Allegations, or even rumors, of fraud or gross inefficiency emanating from either inside or outside the organization also may touch off a crisis that calls for analysis. For example, spying scandals in the late 1980s led to the initiation of operations analyses in many U.S. embassies.

Who Conducts the Operations Analysis?

It is neither reasonable nor prudent to expect an operating manager to conduct an unbiased review of the activities of his or her own responsibility center or program. Presumably the manager is satisfied with the way these activities currently are carried out and will defend these practices in discussions with superiors. Occasionally, a cost-reduction program with adequate incentives can result in objective self-appraisals, but this is an exception to the rule. Most analyses must be conducted by a person or group not associated with the responsibility center being studied.

In organizations that have a systematic review process, operations analysis may be conducted by a staff unit whose full-time responsibility is to conduct such reviews. This unit may be designated as internal audit, industrial engineering, or, more recently, inspector general.

Outside consultants often are used for operations analysis. Although their hourly fees tend to be higher than the cost of internal personnel, they may be able to complete the analysis in fewer hours because of greater expertise and knowledge accumulated about how other organizations conduct the activities being reviewed.

Occasionally, a government agency may create a "blue ribbon commission" of qualified citizens to conduct an operations analysis. The largest such undertaking was the President's Private Sector Cost Survey, under the leadership of J. Peter Grace, in 1982–83. This survey covered most activities of the federal government. Its volunteer staff, recruited mostly from private business, numbered approximately 1,500.

Unless properly led, such evaluations by business executives can be unproductive, or even counterproductive. The group must understand the differences between the management of a government entity and the management of a for-profit business. As one city manager said: "All the Commission did was to describe the problems that we already knew about; they didn't help us find and implement solutions to them."

Colleges, universities, and hospitals have a type of operations analysis that is conducted by the agencies that accredit them. Typically, such reviews focus on the organization's effectiveness, especially on the quality of the services it provides.

The Operations Analysis Process

Depending on the size and complexity of the activity, an operations analysis may take anywhere from a few days to a year, or even longer. The U.S. General Accounting Office makes operations analyses of federal agencies on a regular basis, which it calls *economy and efficiency audits,* or, sometimes, *general management reviews*. As an indication of their magnitude, the following information is taken from a GAO internal planning document:

> The elapsed time, start to finish, should be estimated to be 12 months: 2 months for planning, scoping and assembling the team; 6 months for collecting information; 3 months for developing the report; and 1 month for briefing the agency.
>
> One review should involve approximately 2,200 staff days. The team should consist of not more than 10 persons, headed by an associate director.

There are seven principal steps in the operations analysis process. They are arranged in the order in which they usually are carried out:

- Obtain a mandate.
- Identify the organization's objectives.
- Identify fruitful areas of investigation.
- Decide how output is to be expressed.
- Conduct the analysis.
- Make recommendations and sell them.
- Follow up on implementation.

Obtaining a Mandate. Before work begins, the operations analysis team should obtain a clear mandate from senior management, the governing board, or whatever body has the power to ensure that recommendations are implemented. There must be a mutual understanding of the boundaries of the activities the analysis will encompass, freedom for the team to investigate within these boundaries, and assurance that the sponsoring body will provide support to the team conducting the analysis and be prepared to see that the recommendations are implemented. In some cases an analysis is instituted as a delaying action in response to public criticism, with the expectation that the furor—and the pressure for change—will eventually fade. Obviously, the analysis team is wasting time if it undertakes work sponsored for this purpose. Unfortunately, identifying such a motive may be difficult.

An operations analysis can be stressful to the operating managers of the unit being examined. As a minimum, the analysts' interviews take time that the manager could be using in day-to-day activities. More common is the manager's fear that the recommendations may lead to criticism or, in the extreme, dismissal. Consequently, the mandate from senior management or the outside body that sponsors the audit must be strong enough to assure full cooperation by operating managers. In fact, W. Edwards Deming, considered by many to be the founder of the total quality management (TQM) movement, emphasizes that *true cooperation*—and therefore a more successful analysis—can be gained only by establishing a trusting environment; that is, one where the unit managers are not threatened or (barring gross misconduct) punished. Not only does this environment foster cooperation, but it makes the whole analysis go faster.[2]

In organizations that must undergo an operations analysis to maintain accreditation, the accrediting body provides the mandate. Some government agencies are required by the legislature or a high-level body to have a periodic operations analysis; such requirements are not common, however. Many organizations do not have regularly scheduled operations analyses, and conduct them only when a crisis makes it necessary. Clearly, some crises could be averted if operations analyses were conducted at regular intervals. In many respects, this is the focus of the TQM efforts under way in some nonprofit organizations.

> *Example.* Hospitals in the United States report that a major move is planned toward greater use of process simplification. This practice analyzes a process and through steps, such as eliminating or minimizing nonvalue-adding activities, can greatly reduce costs and cycle time and improve the quality of outputs. Currently, only 6 percent of U.S. hospitals always or almost always apply process simplification practices. But in three years, that level is expected to rise dramatically to 40 percent.[3]

> *Example.* In a physician's office, a variety of questions can be asked that eventually will lead to an improvement in quality. When quality fails in your own work, why does it fail? Do you ever waste time waiting, when you should not have to? Do you ever redo your work because something failed the first time? Do the procedures you use waste steps, duplicate efforts, or frustrate you through their unpredictability? Is information you need ever lost? Does communication ever fail? If the answer to any of these is yes, then ask why. How can it be changed? What can be improved and how? Must you be a mere observer of problems, or can you lead toward their solution?[4]

Identifying Objectives. To improve operations, the analysis team begins by identifying the objectives of the organization; that is, what it is supposed to be doing. In many organizations, such as most health care or religious organizations, the objectives are fairly obvious. In other cases, such as certain charitable organizations, the objectives may be quite ambiguous. Furthermore, the work that the

---

[2] W. Edwards Deming, *Out of Crisis* (Cambridge, Mass.: MIT Press, 1986).

[3] Ernst & Young, *International Quality Study: Health Care Industry Report,* a joint project of Ernst & Young and the American Quality Foundation, Cleveland, Ohio, 1992, p. 36.

[4] Donald M. Berwick, "Continuous Improvement as an Ideal in Health Care," *New England Journal of Medicine* 320, no. 1 (January 5, 1989).

organization is actually doing may be different from what its sponsor, authorizing body, or governing board intended. For example, a charitable organization may undertake a campaign to achieve a political or social goal although this was not intended by its sponsors. Nevertheless, once the legitimate objectives are understood by the analysts, they are accepted. The purpose of the study is not to challenge the appropriateness of these objectives, but rather to analyze how well they are being achieved.

Identifying Fruitful Areas.   Operations analysis teams and consulting firms often have a checklist of possible topics that might be investigated, a list that includes every conceivable aspect of activities, organizational relationships, systems, personnel and other policies, communication devices, and the like. It is not worthwhile to analyze every topic on this list. Rather, the team uses it as a basis for identifying those areas where the opportunity for a significant payoff seems to exist.

> *Example.* A public accounting firm has developed a long checklist as a starting point in making an operations analysis of a hospital. It includes such questions as: Is the average age of physicians over 48 years? Is there difficulty in recruiting qualified specialist physicians? Is the amount of accounts receivable more than 75 days of revenues? Is there a backlog of incomplete medical record charts in excess of 14 days of discharges? Is the number of employees per occupied bed greater than 3.3? Is debt service more than 8 percent of revenue?

Experienced reviewers often can spot significant opportunities for improvement simply by visual inspection and by asking appropriate questions.

> *Example.* The following is the reminiscence of a member of the team that examined the operations of the Louisville, Kentucky, police court:
> "You remember one clerk, in particular, who was industriously banging away at a typewriter. You asked her what she was doing. She looked up briefly from her keyboard to explain that she was typing case dispositions. 'What happens to them when they're typed?' you asked. 'Why,' she answered, 'they go into the judge's order book.' 'What's the book used for?' you asked. She didn't know. So you went to her superior. 'Why is this done?' you asked. You learned why. It's done because a city ordinance says it must be done. But nobody ever uses the book. The same information is available in other records that are easier to use."

Deciding on Output Measures.   Many operations analyses involve comparisons of inputs and outputs, either explicitly or implicitly. As emphasized in earlier chapters, inputs are measured by costs. Although many organizations do not have good cost accounting systems, the nature of the information that is needed is fairly clear-cut. As we discussed in Chapter 12, the measurement of outputs is much more difficult. The team needs to decide on the most feasible way to measure what the organization is accomplishing. In many cases, no good quantitative measure exists, and judgment as to the quantity and quality of outputs is based strictly on the opinions of the analysis team.

Example. In 1971 the Standards Committee of the American Assembly of Collegiate Schools of Business voted to "look at the question of validation of current accreditation standards with special reference to performance and outcomes." In the late 1980s, after spending half a million dollars and "countless hours of volunteer and staff time," no measurements had been agreed on.[5]

Conducting the Analysis. Once it has a tentative list of areas to be investigated, the team discusses it with operating managers and senior management. After their concurrence, the team makes a detailed analysis of these areas. This may include an analysis of work flows, methods, and organizational relationships, using formal techniques developed for each area. Occasionally, it may involve sophisticated operations research techniques. Often the principal tools are an inquiring mind and common sense.

Example. Ishikawa's seven tools for quality control are relatively simple techniques that can be used to analyze numerical and categorical data. Ishikawa contends that the vast majority of quality problems can be solved with their use alone. The seven tools include such relatively common-sense techniques as cause-and-effect diagrams, check-sheets, histograms, graphs and control charts, and scatter diagrams.[6]

Cost Comparisons. An operations analysis frequently involves comparisons of unit costs for similar activities. These comparisons can be useful even though there are problems in achieving comparability and finding a "correct" relationship between cost and output. Such comparisons may identify costs that appear out of line, and thus lead to more thorough examination of certain activities. They often lead to the following interesting question: If other organizations get the job done for $X, why can't this one? Good cost data for such comparisons exist on a national basis for only a few types of nonprofit organizations, principally hospitals and certain municipal functions. Nevertheless, it may be possible to find data for activities within a state, or it may be feasible to compare units performing similar functions within a single organization, as in the case of local housing offices.

Example. A study of the costs of processing payroll in eight county governments showed results that ranged from one payroll employee for every 641 other employees down to one payroll employee for every 166 other employees, with an average of one per 424 other employees. If the two counties with the worst record improved to the average, they would need 38 fewer employees for their payroll functions.[7]

Example. In his 1988–89 President's Report, Derek Bok, then president of Harvard University, noted the difficulty with cost comparisons in universities: "It is [hard] to

---

[5] Quoted from a report of the Academy of Management.

[6] Masao Akiba, Shane J. Schvaneveldt, and Takao Enkawa, "Service Quality: Methodology and Japanese Perspectives," in G. Salvendy, *Handbook of Industrial Engineering,* 2nd ed. (New York: John Wiley & Sons, 1992). The authors cite K. Ishikawa, *Guide to Quality Control,* 2nd rev. ed. (Tokyo: Asian Productivity Organization, 1976).

[7] R. A. Smardon, "Cutting the Cost of Local Government," *Harvard Business Review*, March 1977, p. 25.

awaken a . . . zeal for finding ways to reduce administrative costs. After trying a number of conventional methods unsuccessfully, I eventually decided on a flat rule that the rate of increase in Central Administration expenses must be kept below that of the several faculties so that administrative costs would make up a gradually decreasing share of the University budget.''[8]

The comparisons in most cases are simple, such as the average cost per student in one school compared with the average cost per student in similar schools. In some circumstances, more sophisticated approaches are illuminating. For example, algorithms incorporating a number of interrelated variables have been developed for hospital costs.

Judging the Appropriate Level of Activity.   At some stage, possibly in the preliminary investigation, the analysis team should give some thought to the appropriate amount of service that the unit being evaluated should be furnishing. Although the overall objectives are accepted as given, the level of activity in attaining these objectives is a proper subject for analysis. In some situations, the services provided may be inadequate. More commonly, the question is: Is the unit doing more than really needs to be done for the overall good of the organization? The addition of functions of questionable value is often found in administrative units.

> *Example.*   Over a period of five years, the budget of a certain personnel department tripled, although the number of employees in the whole organization increased only slightly. The personnel department had instituted two in-house newsletters (one for professionals, the other for the entire staff); it had set up an elaborate computerized system of personnel records; it had started a clipping service which found and circulated published information about people in the organization; it conducted management training programs, clerical training programs, and interpersonal relations training programs; it had instituted psychological testing and counseling; its members went to and delivered papers at many professional meetings. There was general agreement that people in the personnel department worked diligently. The question was whether all this work was necessary.

Privatization.   As we discussed in Chapter 5, one possible approach to the improvement of efficiency in a nonprofit organization is to have certain activities performed by an outside organization, generally a for-profit one. The expectation is that the spur of competition that presumably exists in such organizations will result in lower costs. Possibilities for doing this are often explored in an operations analysis. Opportunities range from such specialized activities as building cleaning and maintenance to those that are usually thought of as belonging exclusively to the public sector, such as fire protection and other municipal services.

Managers of organization units whose functions might be taken over by an outside company naturally resist such threats to their continued existence. They frequently point out, quite correctly, that it should not be assumed that a for-profit

---

[8] Derek Bok, *The President's Report 1988–89* (Cambridge, Mass.: Harvard University).

company will perform a particular function more efficiently than their unit. The proper approach is, of course, to make a careful analysis of the cost of the alternative ways of performing the function. *Circular No. A-76* of the U.S. Office of Management and Budget, *Policies for Acquiring Commercial or Industrial Type Products and Services Needed by the Government,* provides excellent guidelines for making such comparisons. Even if such analyses lead to the conclusion that the function should continue to be performed by the organization itself, the fact that such comparisons are being made tends to keep managers on their toes.

Making and Selling Recommendations. In some cases, recommendations for improvements can be made, accepted, and implemented while the operations analysis is in process. To the extent that this can be done on a cooperative basis with the operating manager, the changes are likely to have longer lasting effects than those that are imposed by a higher authority. Thus, the team should forego public recognition of its own role in obtaining such changes and give credit to the operating manager.

The team cannot always count on a favorable reaction to its suggestions, however. Challenges to the established way of doing things are often not well received. Recommendations are subject to all the ploys used in the annual budget review, described in the appendix to Chapter 10, but the game is usually played with much more gusto because more is at stake. Managers under scrutiny can be expected to do their best to justify their current level of spending. Moreover, unless an atmosphere of trust is developed, they may attempt to undermine the entire effort. They consider the annual budget review as a necessary evil, but an operations analysis as something to be put off indefinitely in favor of "more pressing business." If all else fails, they may attempt to create enough doubts about the competence of the analysis team that the findings are inconclusive and the status quo prevails.[9]

A team that writes a report and then leaves is therefore not likely to accomplish much, if anything, of enduring value. In most cases, the team must devote a considerable amount of time to planning how its recommendations will be sold to those in a position to act, and to laying out a program of implementation and follow-up. If it turns out that the commitment to action obtained in the first stage of the process has, for some reason, disappeared, the team may decide to attempt a new approach to action, perhaps through publicity. This step is sometimes necessary with the blue-ribbon commission type of effort mentioned earlier.

Caution against Overselling. Having worked hard to develop good recommendations, there is a tendency for the analysts to attribute more validity to the results than is warranted. For example, the Grace Commission reported that the federal government would save $424 billion over three years if its recommenda-

---

[9] The General Accounting Office, although conducting operations analyses with statutory authority and with the full backing of the Congress, has difficulty in getting agencies to implement its recommendations, even those recommendations that the agency explicitly agreed were sound. See the GAO Report, *Disappointing Progress in Improving Systems for Resolving Billions in Audit Findings*, January 23, 1981.

tions were adopted, but an analysis of its report by the U.S. General Accounting Office concluded that the possible savings would be a small fraction of this amount. Such exaggeration casts doubt on the soundness of the whole effort. Indeed, a sound report should frankly reveal the limitations of the study.

Following up on Implementation.   The analysts' report presumably contains a list of recommended actions. Acceptance of the report by senior management by no means assures that these actions will be taken. The report itself should state who will be responsible for acting on each recommendation, specify how progress toward implementation will be measured, and, if feasible, establish a timetable. Senior management should be counseled to establish a mechanism for overseeing progress. This mechanism is a form of project control (discussed in Chapter 11).

PROGRAM EVALUATION

Programs tend to go on forever unless they are subject to periodic, hardheaded reexamination.[10] There is a need to look at operations in program terms to ascertain whether the benefits of each program continue to exceed their cost and whether there are ways to improve effectiveness. Although opportunities for improvement exist in every organization, there is a general feeling that these opportunities are especially significant in nonprofit organizations, primarily because the semiautomatic measure of efficiency provided by the bottom line on a business income statement does not exist in nonprofit organizations.

Evaluations of some type have been going on ever since there have been programs. It has been estimated that a moderately large metropolitan hospital is periodically evaluated by 100 or more agencies, ranging from fire inspection to the Joint Commission on Accreditation of Healthcare Organizations, without whose certificate the hospital cannot continue to operate. We are here concerned not with evaluation of specific aspects of a program, but rather with the broad evaluation of a program as a whole, particularly those programs whose continued existence is optional. If these programs are not effective, they should be discontinued or at least redirected.

Impetus for Program Evaluation

The legislative or other governing body that initially authorized and funded a program ordinarily wants to find out how well it is proceeding, as a basis for continuing, changing, or ending it. The public and the media become interested in certain programs, particularly those that they believe to be ineffective. Users or

---

[10] A Brookings study showed that of 175 federal government organizations that existed in 1923, 148 were in existence 50 years later; 246 more were created in the same period. Herbert Kaufman, *Are Government Organizations Immortal?* (Washington, D.C.: The Brookings Institution, 1976), p. 35.

potential users of the program, such as prospective students of a university or physicians considering the referral of patients to a hospital, want information about the program's quality. Donors or other fund providers to arts organizations, charities, museums, and the like, want to know how well the funds were spent.

The federal government carries out some 6,000 identifiable programs. Legislation requiring regular review of these programs was first enacted in the early 1970s when the federal government delegated to the states the task of providing many social services, and required, as a condition of funding these programs, that a formal means of evaluating them be established. At about the same time there was widespread interest in sunset legislation—laws that provided for the automatic discontinuance of a program unless it was evaluated every six to eight years and found to be effective. The majority of states now have such sunset laws. Usually, the evaluation is conducted under the direction of a committee of the legislature.

Program evaluation has become a growth industry. According to the General Accounting Office, in 1984 the nondefense departments and agencies of the federal government spent $139 million on program evaluations; their professional staffs of 1,179 persons conducted 2,291 evaluations.[11] Hundreds more are conducted annually at the state level. Professional journals, such as *Evaluation Quarterly, Evaluation and Program Planning,* and *Journal of Evaluation Research,* are now well established, along with a professional organization, the American Evaluation Association. Moreover, according to Eleanor Chelimsky, the assistant comptroller general for Program Evaluation and Methodology of the U.S. General Accounting Office:

> Today, program evaluations are a familiar adjunct of congressional policymaking; they now figure notably in program reauthorizations, legislative decisions and markups, oversight, and an informed public debate. One PEMD [Program Evaluation and Methodology Division] evaluation caused working mothers leaving AFDC to receive Medicaid health insurance for their children over longer periods; another set of studies held up production of the inadequately tested Bigeye bomb; another evaluation led to doubled funding for the high-quality Runaway and Homeless Youth program, whose appropriations the relevant executive agency had proposed halving; another (on employee stock ownership plans) was responsible for a reduction of nearly $2 billion in tax expenditures; still another—showing that an increase in the drinking age from 18 to 21 unambiguously reduces traffic fatalities—spurred legislation to this effect in 16 states, resulting in the estimated saving of 1,000 young lives in 1987 alone.[12]

Problems in Program Evaluation

A program evaluation seeks to answer broad, fundamental questions: Is the program being carried out according to the intent of those who authorized it? Why or why not? What would have happened if there had been no program? Answering

---

[11] U.S. General Accounting Office, *Federal Evaluation.* GAO/PEMD-87-9, January 1987, p. 22.

[12] Eleanor Chelimsky, "Expanding GAO's Capabilities in Program Evaluation," *The GAO Journal,* Winter/Spring 1990, p. 48.

these questions is an extraordinarily difficult task. Among the more important problems are:

- Objectives are often difficult to define.
- Output is often difficult to measure.
- The relationship between cause and effect is often obscure.
- The effort required to make a valid judgment may cost more than it is worth.
- Appropriate action may not be forthcoming.

These problems are discussed below.

Problems in Defining Objectives.   In general, those who initially approved a program had in mind one or more objectives that they hoped the program would accomplish. If the program is enacted by legislation, these objectives are supposed to be stated in the authorizing act. The fact is, however, that various supporters of a program may differ in their ideas about the program's objectives. Additionally, the stated objectives may be fuzzily worded to accommodate various points of view, and the objectives, either stated or unstated, may be numerous and possibly contradictory.

> *Example.* Some people viewed the purpose of the Comprehensive Employment and Training Act (CETA) as primarily to remove people from the unemployment rolls, others as a way of training unskilled persons so that they would qualify for better jobs, others as a device for channeling federal funds to reduce the tax burden of hard-pressed municipalities, others as a way of providing welfare payments, and still others as a device for reducing crime by taking youths off the street. Most advocates had more than one of these objectives in mind, but they differed as to the relative importance of each.

For other programs the objectives may be even more murky. Scholars have made many attempts to define the objectives of a liberal arts college in a way that permits evaluation, but with no success. A charitable organization may start out with a well-defined objective, such as providing a shelter for homeless people, but the objective may change over the years into providing other types of support. Sometimes this happens without an explicit decision by the governing body.

The evaluators must make every attempt to discern the real objectives and the relative importance of each. If they begin with the wrong objectives, the whole evaluation may be discredited on the grounds that it is based on a false premise.

Problems of Results Measures.   In Chapter 12 we discussed problems of measuring a program's output and the limitations of various output measures. For many programs there are no valid techniques for measuring what actually happened as a consequence of undertaking the program. In educational programs, for example, there are no reliable ways of measuring how much additional education a given program produces, except in the case of certain basic skills such as reading and arithmetic. Therefore, a comparison of some new educational effort, such as computer-assisted instruction, team teaching, or programmed learning, is unlikely to reveal any significant difference between those who learned in the new way and those who learned by conventional methods. (It is said, with considerable truth, that the best way to kill an educational experiment is to evaluate it. One can be almost certain in advance that the measurable results will not show a significant improvement.)

Example. The Manpower Development and Training Act of 1962 established an institutional program to provide training that would increase the future earnings of workers whose jobs had been eliminated for technological reasons, as well as those of other disadvantaged persons. It would appear that "earnings" is a quantity that could be measured fairly readily. Yet, 11 studies attempted to make such measurements, at a total cost of $180 million. Of the three studies that were considered to be well designed, none showed that the program had a significant effect on the earnings of participants. Of the other eight, six showed an improvement in earnings and two did not. However, these eight studies had such serious methodological weaknesses that no valid conclusion could be drawn from them.[13]

Problems of Cause-and-Effect Relationships. If the results of a program are favorable, there is a tendency to conclude that the program efforts caused this result, but this conclusion may be erroneous. In education, reference is often made to the *Coleman effect*, a term derived from a report by James S. Coleman and his colleagues,[14] which gave an impressive body of evidence to support the conclusion that no important quantifiable correlation exists between the cost of education and its quality, and specifically between pupil learning and class size, teachers' salary, teachers' experience, age of plant, or type of plant. The effects of these variables were swamped by the influence of the pupil's family environment. Although not everyone agrees with Coleman's conclusions, most people agree that it is extremely difficult to devise experiments that demonstrate quantitatively that one teaching tool or technique is more effective than another.

Even if the evaluation team does recognize that extraneous variables may have an effect, their importance in explaining program results may not be measurable.

Example. At the request of Senator John H. Chafee, the U.S. General Accounting Office compiled information on the effectiveness of government programs relating to teenage pregnancy. Senator Chafee asked for, among other things, evidence as to "What works and what doesn't work," as a basis for future legislation. The GAO located 1,170 references on this subject, and identified 37 evaluation reports of government-funded projects. In only 12 of these was the methodology sufficiently sound so that reliable inferences could be drawn. The GAO concluded: "[T]he lack of evidence from past programs means, unfortunately, that decisions about new programs and the expansion of old programs have to be based on common sense, logic, and plausible theory rather than on empirical data and knowledge."[15]

---

[13] Dave M. O'Neill, *The Federal Government and Manpower* (Washington, D.C.: American Enterprise Institute for Public Policy Research, 1973).

[14] James S. Coleman et al., *Equality of Educational Opportunity,* OE-38001 (Washington, D.C.: U.S. Department of HEW, 1966).

[15] U.S. General Accounting Office, *Teenage Pregnancy*, GAO/PEMD86-16BR, July 1986.

The use of any quantitative basis or comparison causes concern to some people. For example, Sol M. Linowitz, a highly respected business leader and university trustee, wrote:

> As to a numerical ratio of students per teacher, I am deeply disquieted—not because I am nurturing a romantic kind of Mark Hopkins hangover, but simply because I think this is the result of regarding a college as first a business operation and only secondarily as an educational institution trying to turn out the right kind of men and women.[16]

Although the faculty-student ratio can be misused, its proper use does not imply that a college is primarily a business operation and only secondarily an educational institution. A college is, in fact, both; neither aspect can be slighted.

An especially difficult problem is that of measuring the impact of a program, as contrasted with its output. For example, the Clean Air Act limits the amount of pollutants that industrial plants may release into the air, and the results of the Environmental Protection Agency's programs can be assessed by measuring the pollutants in the atmosphere. However, if the objective of these limitations is to reduce to tolerable limits the amount of acid rain that is damaging forests and water supplies, it is much more difficult to determine whether this objective has been achieved. In particular, the impact of such programs may not be measurable for many years after the presumed corrective action has occurred.

> ***Example.*** The Head Start Program, which was begun in the 1960s, was based on the assumption that a brief intervention in the early formative years could raise children's IQs. This was considered important, since IQ correlates with school achievement, persistence, motivation, social skills, and self-confidence. A 1969 report on Head Start performed by the Westinghouse Learning Corporation revealed that the IQ gains by children in preschool programs dissipated by the time they reached the third grade. Now, almost 25 years later, the Head Start Program still exists, not because it raises IQs, but because it enhances school readiness, improves health services for young children, educates parents about community services, and gets some parents involved in their children's education. In addition, it produces several important side effects, including employment for many low income people.[17]

Problems with the Scope of the Analysis. As is the case with any activity, the results of an evaluation should be worth more than the cost of obtaining them. Analyses range in complexity, cost, and time required; they vary from a simple observation to an elaborate experiment involving thousands of people and lasting several years. Before an evaluation is undertaken, the agency that authorizes it should give considerable thought to the likelihood of obtaining useful results within the available time and cost constraints.

---

[16] Sol M. Linowitz, "A Liberal Arts College Isn't a Railroad," *The Chronicle of Higher Education*, February 26, 1973, p. 12.

[17] Constance Holden, "Head Start Enters Adulthood," *Science* 247, no. 22 (March 23, 1990), pp. 1400–1402.

Problems in Obtaining Action.   Some groups who evaluate programs view the evaluation as a challenging research effort and lose interest when the research has been completed. They do not plan, or care about, how the results can be used as a basis for action. In other cases, the evaluation effort is undertaken by a program's manager to prove that the program is beneficial; if the evaluation comes to a contrary conclusion, it is buried. An unused program evaluation is just as wasteful as a useless program.

Furthermore, the conclusion that a program is worthwhile is a necessary but not sufficient reason for continuing it. In a world of finite resources, worthwhile programs must compete with other programs that may be even more worthwhile. The legislative body or other group that decides how best to use limited resources has a more complicated task than does the team that evaluates a single program; it must decide which of many worthwhile programs should continue to be supported and at what level.

Types of Program Evaluations

Before a full-scale evaluation is undertaken, the evaluators ordinarily make a preliminary analysis to settle on the evaluation type(s) to be used, and work out a plan for the evaluation effort. In this section, we list the principal types of evaluations and briefly describe the advantages and limitations of each. A more thorough description can be found in the references at the end of the chapter, particularly those of the U.S. General Accounting Office. The General Accounting Office is the largest and, in our opinion, the best evaluation organization in the United States. (Despite its name, the General Accounting Office is not primarily an accounting organization. Most of its more than 4,000 professionals are called *evaluators*; they include attorneys, actuaries, economists, engineers, computer specialists, management analysts, and personnel specialists, as well as accountants.)

Subjective Evaluations.   The majority of program evaluations are subjective; that is, they are judgments arrived at by personal observations of an individual or a small committee. The validity of such evaluations depends heavily on the expertise of those involved. Judgments also are influenced by the situations that the evaluators happen to observe; that is, they may be unduly impressed by what appear to be either excellent or poor results in particular cases.

Because support for the conclusions from such an evaluation is based on unsubstantiated evidence, decision makers may be unconvinced. For this reason, the evaluators may develop statistical or other data as a means for adding credence to their opinion.

In some situations the evaluation is subjective simply because a more elaborate approach is not warranted. If a team visits a vocational education school and observes that only half the students regularly attend class and that those who do attend are taught by incompetent teachers using ineffective methods, there is little need to collect data on the effectiveness of the school.

Peer Review Evaluation. As noted above, colleges, universities, and hospitals are regularly evaluated by accrediting organizations. The evaluation is conducted by a team of colleagues; that is, peers, who work at similar organizations. The team is guided in part by specified minimum standards (e.g., for a college, the number of books in the library, the proportion of faculty with advanced degrees) and, in part, by observation and discussion. This is a relatively inexpensive approach. A favorable conclusion means that the institution meets certain minimum requirements, but there is no attempt to rank the institution on a scale of excellence. In general, as we discussed above, these reviews are operations analyses rather than program evaluations. Sometimes they take on characteristics of a program evaluation, however. This happens when they question the appropriateness of the organization's goals, or when they suggest that certain programs' objectives do not fit well with the organization's goals.

Case Study Evaluations. In a case study, the evaluation team identifies a few situations that it believes to be typical and examines each in depth. Although statistically valid conclusions cannot be based on a small sample, the results may be informative. This approach is often used as a preliminary step in an evaluation; it gives the evaluators a feel for the situation. Based on what they uncover, the evaluators may decide not to proceed further; or, if they decide to proceed, the case studies help them select the appropriate research design.

> *Example.* In 1981 the Deputy Secretary of Defense directed the armed services to develop procedures for quantifying the effect of "technological risk" on the cost of weapons systems development projects. In 1983 the General Accounting Office was asked to evaluate this effort. It made a preliminary study of six weapons systems, two each from the Army, Navy, and Air Force. It did not find any case of quantified technological risk and therefore decided to describe what might be done, rather than to evaluate what had been done.[18]

Statistical Evaluation. An evaluation may be based at least in part on data about the program that have been collected routinely, or on data that have been collected for another purpose but can be recast to provide information relevant to the evaluation. There are four possible approaches, each of which has merit. The one or ones chosen will depend to a great extent upon the kinds of data that are available and the needs of the agency sponsoring the evaluation.

Compare Current Results with Performance Data Gathered Some Time Prior to the Initiation of the Program. This approach allows the sponsoring agency to determine if the program has had some impact over a baseline situation.

> *Example.* If the number of illiterate people in a community was 20 percent prior to a literacy training program and 15 percent after the program had been in operation for several years, there is some indication that the program is having an impact. Of course, as with most evaluations, the evaluators would need to look for other factors that could have had an impact on the community's literacy.

---

[18] U.S. General Accounting Office, *Designing Evaluations: A Workbook* February 1986, pp. 73–128.

Compare Current Results with Historical Trends. This approach allows the sponsoring agency to observe how well the program is performing over time.

Example. If a job training program placed 25 percent of its graduates during its first year, 30 percent during its second year, 40 percent during its third year, and 50 percent during its fourth year, there is some indication that the program is improving. Again, the evaluators would need to look for other factors, such as a change in the program's selection criteria.

Compare Current Results of the Program with the Results of Other, Presumably Similar, Programs. Using this approach assumes that a sufficiently similar program can be found, and that the available data will be comparable to those for the program being evaluated.

Example. A federally funded program to increase the quantity of low- or moderate income housing in one city can be compared with the same program in another city. If the two cities are reasonably similar in terms of the difficulty of constructing new housing, the comparative results should allow the sponsoring agency to determine which is the more successful.

Compare Current Results with the Results that Were Anticipated when the Program Was Initiated. The validity of this comparison obviously depends on the soundness of the original estimates of results.

Example. A program to provide literacy training projected that 3,000 people a year would become literate as a result of the training activities. This number can be compared with the actual number. If the actual is less than anticipated, the program's manager can be asked to explain why. The results can be used to set an objective either for the subsequent year or for similar programs in other locales.

Problems with Statistical Evaluations. Many problems are encountered in statistical evaluations. It may be difficult to:

1. Define the measures to be used.
2. Assure that data from different data bases are comparable.
3. Determine that the data are reliable.
4. Allow for extraneous factors.
5. Decide whether trends or comparisons are significant.

Evaluators need to determine in advance whether these problems are sufficiently manageable to make the results of the statistical analysis worth the considerable cost that may be involved in gathering and analyzing the data.

Sample Survey Evaluations. A survey of a sample of the target group (i.e., the individuals the program is intended to benefit) or of others who may be knowledgeable about the program may provide highly useful information. The survey may be either in the form of a written questionnaire or an interview. The latter technique is much more expensive, but permits more probing than is feasible with a questionnaire. Occasionally, some combination of the two may be feasible. To assure valid results, evaluators must word survey questions so that respondents' answers are unambiguous. They must also take care to select a sample so that the responses approximate those that would be given if the whole population were surveyed, and they must take steps to avoid any biases in administering the survey. Sampling theory is a complex topic; unless proper techniques are used, the results are likely to be questionable.

Field Experiments. In evaluating the efficacy of a new drug or a new medical or surgical procedure, medical researchers have a well-developed protocol. Two groups of subjects (animals or humans) are created: an experimental group and a control group. Individual subjects are assigned to one of these groups either randomly or in such a way that the factors that may affect the outcome of the experiment (e.g., age, sex, weight, health) are similar for each group. The experimental treatment is administered to the experimental group. (In a double-blind experiment, the experimenter does not know to which group an individual subject belongs nor whether the chemical administered is the test drug or a placebo.) Factors other than the experimental treatment that might affect the outcome are either insulated from the experiment or are observed and allowed for when results are analyzed. After results are measured, statistical tests are applied to determine if there is a significant difference (associated with the treatment) between the experimental group and the control group. If there is, the treatment is judged to be successful.

Much of the literature on program evaluation discusses ways of applying analogous experimental methods to social programs; such efforts frequently are called *social experiments*. Success has been minimal, however. In many cases, the analysis did not show a significant difference between the two groups. And in most cases with a statistically significant difference, critics maintain that the experiment did not satisfactorily answer the key question: Were the results caused by the treatment, or were they caused by something else?

> *Example.* One of the largest social experiments is that relating to proposals for income maintenance. It was designed to find out whether cash payments to low-income people (the negative income tax) are preferable to current welfare programs. The first effort was in New Jersey, begun in the late 1960s, and there have been experiments in six other states, with those in Denver and Seattle being the most comprehensive. These experiments involved 8,500 families at a cost of $112 million. Despite the wealth of data, there is no consensus on whether a negative income tax works better than a traditional welfare program.

Problems with Social Experiments. Social experiments carry special problems that do not exist for medical experiments. For one thing, most people do not like to be subjects. Guinea pigs can't object, and medical patients usually do not object because they see possible benefits to themselves. But subjects of social experiments often see no benefit in being treated like guinea pigs. In particular, control groups usually know from the beginning that they are not going to benefit, and dropout rates among these groups consequently are high. This upsets the statistical data base. Furthermore, to measure results, the experimenters usually must ask personal questions of the subjects, and despite pledges of confidentiality these are often regarded as an invasion of privacy. It therefore is difficult to determine whether the answers are honest. Even if they are honest, many answers depend on fallible memory.

Although field experiments have these limitations and although they are expensive, they can, if properly done, provide the best information on the results attributable to *the program*; that is, the relationship between cause and effect.

Steps in Making an Evaluation

There is no clear consensus among evaluators on the exact procedure an evaluation team should follow. Nevertheless, the following eight steps seem to take place in most evaluations.

1. Decide on the Purpose of the Evaluation.   Is it to appraise the success of the program as a basis for deciding its future? Is it to provide recommendations for improvement? Specifically, what questions is the evaluation intended to answer? Presumably, the body that requested the evaluation should state these questions. As a practical matter, however, the charge from that body may be vague, and the evaluation team may need to identify the most useful questions to address. These questions need to be carefully thought out and specifically stated; otherwise, the evaluation may proceed down the wrong road, with a waste of time and resources. The questions are subject to change, of course, if the team finds that the answers cannot feasibly be obtained, or if it uncovers better questions.

2. Examine the Available Information.   In some cases, information that is already available, either within the organization or from other researchers, may provide an adequate basis for evaluation. Alternatively, such information may provide a useful starting point.

3. Select a Tentative Strategy.   Which of the types of evaluations listed above is the most appropriate, considering the limitations of time, expertise, and money available for the study? What research design best suits the approach selected? In answering these questions, the evaluation team may assemble a panel of experts to provide guidance. The panel may use the *Delphi Technique;* that is, it may arrive at a conclusion by several iterations of proposed approaches. If the evaluation involves the use of quantitative data, a model showing how these data are to be analyzed needs to be constructed and examined for feasibility and for relevance to the evaluation questions. The team also should develop a project plan, showing personnel assigned to the project and a timetable.

The evaluation strategy should be presented to the body requesting the study, and that body should sign off on the strategy. If the resources initially available are inadequate, or if the completion time originally expected is too short, additional money or time should be negotiated with the requesting body. If additional money or time is not forthcoming, the scope of the project has to be narrowed or, in the extreme case, discontinued. All of these decisions need to be agreed to by the requesting body before the evaluation commences.

4. Test the Proposed Design.   Some sort of testing usually is feasible, and tests should be made before major resources are committed to the project. A pretest of questionnaires or interview questions, collection and tabulation of a sample of statistical data, or (if the evaluation is to be conducted at many sites) a complete test at one site may lead to a revision of the evaluation design—and significant cost savings.

5. Carry Out the Evaluation.   In carrying out the evaluation, the evaluation team should pay attention to both the agreed-upon timetable and the allowed budget. Exceeding either without prior approval, and usually without sound justification, can cost the team some of its credibility, even though the loss of credibility may have nothing to do with the quality of the evaluation itself. As Chelimsky notes:

> Evaluators working for the legislative branch much be extremely concerned about the timing of the final product and how it dovetails with congressional policy cycles and plans for use. We've learned that what is most important sometimes is not having the best design, but having an adequate design that will bring the findings in at the time they were promised.[19]

6. Draft a Tentative Report.   In doing so, the evaluation team should think about the best way of "selling" the results to those who are expected to act on them. Does the audience prefer a written report? An oral presentation? Both? Are there different audiences, with different desires? Initial response to the tentative report may, for example, lead the team to issue a formal report with wide circulation and an oral report of more sensitive findings.

7. Obtain Informal Feedback.   Within the organization conducting the evaluation, someone other than a member of the evaluation team should carefully examine the draft report. This quality control check should range from such details as arithmetic accuracy and proper grammar to the broad question of whether the conclusions are substantiated by the underlying data. In addition, the draft should be submitted for comment to the agency being evaluated. These comments may lead to changes in the report. Even if the evaluating team disagrees with the agency's comments, these comments should be noted in the report, together with the reasons for disagreement. It is much better to find out about errors or disagreements before the final report is submitted than to have it shot down after it has been formally submitted.

8. Sell the Findings.   By the time it has completed its final report, the evaluation team frequently has considerably more knowledge about the program than per-

---

[19] Eleanor Chelimsky, "What Have We Learned about the Politics of Program Evaluation?" *Evaluation Practice* 8, no. 1 (February 1987).

haps even the program's managers. When this is the case, there is a tendency to present too much information without appropriate summaries. The team must think about a reader with limited time, and present the information in such a way that it is both succinct and compelling. Key points should be highlighted in an executive summary, and most of the statistical computations should be relegated to appendices no matter how elegant the team thinks they are. As Chelimsky puts it:

> We have learned that telling all is tantamount to telling nothing. The important thing is to answer the policy question as clearly and simply as possible, to emphasize a few critical and striking numbers, and to do all that in such a way as to highlight those findings that give rise to policy action.[20]

In sum, the program evaluation process is as much political as it is scientific. The recommendations will not be implemented unless those who have the authority to do so are convinced that implementation is desirable.[21] The decision maker is often influenced by factors other than those set forth in the report, no matter how scientifically sound the analysis may be. The evaluation team should attempt to identify and deal with these political factors, even though they may be regarded as being illogical.

SUMMARY

In many respects, the process followed in an operations analysis parallels that in a program evaluation. In both activities, the team needs to: (1) obtain a mandate from a body that is prepared to act on its recommendations, (2) identify objectives, (3) determine a strategy for conducting the activity, (4) carry out the activity, and (5) make and sell recommendations.

Despite these similarities, there are some important differences. An operations analysis tends to be much more constrained than a program evaluation. Since the analysis team is focusing on *process* rather than *results,* it has a relatively easy time defining objectives, measuring output, and identifying areas where improvements might be made. Operations analysis is needed principally because fat tends to accumulate in any program, and a fat-trimming effort occasionally is necessary.

Program evaluation tends to be much more complicated than operations analysis. The objectives frequently are difficult to define, output frequently is tricky to measure, and cause-and-effect relationships can be elusive. Moreover, the choice of the most appropriate type of program evaluation frequently is highly debatable. Subjective, peer review, case study, statistical, sample survey, and field experiments are all candidates, and it frequently is not clear which will provide the best

---

[20] Ibid.

[21] For an expansion of this point, see Eleanor Chelimsky, "Politics of Evaluation," in D. S. Cordray, H. S. Bloom, and R. J. Light (eds.), *Evaluation Practices in Review: New Directions for Program Evaluation*, No. 34 (San Francisco, 1987).

information for assessing whether a program should continue as is, be modified, or be discontinued.

Despite these difficulties, governing bodies need to undertake program evaluations. In a world of scarce resources, they provide essential information for the difficult task of making trade-offs among a variety of possible programmatic endeavors. Indeed, without undertaking both operations analysis and program evaluation, a governing body cannot be certain that it is using resources in the most appropriate way to achieve the organization's goals.

SUGGESTED ADDITIONAL READINGS

Anderson, S., et al. *Statistical Methods for Comparative Studies*. New York: John Wiley & Sons, 1980.

Chelimsky, Eleanor, ed. *Program Evaluation: Patterns and Directions*. Washington, D.C.: American Society for Public Administration, 1985.

Deming, W. Edwards. *Out of Crisis*. Cambridge, Mass.: MIT Press, 1986.

Gronbach, L. J. *Designing Evaluations of Educational and Social Program*s. San Francisco: Jossey-Bass, 1982.

Ishikawa, K., ed. *Guide to Quality Control*. White Plains, N.Y.: Kraus International Publications, 1986.

James, B. C. *Quality Management for Health Care Delivery*. Chicago: The Hospital Research and Educational Trust of the American Hospital Association.

Judd, C. M., and D. A. Kenny. *Estimating the Effects of Social Interventions*. Cambridge, Eng.: Cambridge University Press, 1981.

Juran, J. M. *Juran on Planning for Quality*. New York: The Free Press, 1989.

Keppel, G. *Design and Analysis: A Researcher's Handbook*, 3rd ed. Englewood Cliffs, N.J.: Prentice Hall, 1991.

Kidder, L. H., and R. Judd. *Research Methods in Social Relations*, 4th ed. Fort Worth, Tex.: Holt, Rinehart & Winston, 1991.

Kruskal, W., and F. Mosteller. "Representative Sampling, I-IV." *International Statistical Review*, 1979 and 1980.

Light, Richard, and David Pillemer. *Summing up: The Science of Reviewing Research*. Cambridge, Mass.: Harvard University Press, 1984.

————, Judith Singer, and John Willett. *By Design*. Cambridge, Mass.: Harvard University Press, 1990.

Rossi, P. H., and H. E. Freeman. *Evaluation: A Systematic Approach*, 2nd ed. Beverly Hills, Calif.: Sage, 1989.

U.S. General Accounting Office, Program Evaluation and Methodology Division. Methodology Transfer Papers. Washington, D.C. (A series of papers on aspects of program evaluation. See especially, "Designing Evaluations," *Paper No. 4*, 1984; "Using Statistical Sampling," *Paper No. 6, 1986*; and *Designing Evaluations: A Workbook,* February 1986.

CASE 15–1   Bureau of Child Welfare*

Mr. Henry Brown, Special Assistant to the Director of the Bureau of Child Welfare, was evaluating the results of the Bureau's activities in its Adoption Program. Of concern to him was the fact that the number of adoptions had been declining over the past two years, and represented an increasingly smaller percentage of children in foster care (Exhibit 1). The Bureau had been emphasizing the importance of placing children in adoptive homes when the situation warranted such a move. Mr. Brown was uncertain as to why the private agencies, with which the Bureau contracted for the delivery of social services, were not making a greater effort to place children in adoptive homes.

Background

As indicated in Exhibit 1, the city's child welfare system provided care and delivered services to some 29,000 children at any given time. Approximately 8,000–10,000 children entered the child-care system during the course of a year and slightly fewer were discharged, so that the total population increased gradually from year to year.

Although the city was legally responsible for all children in its care, it had few programs and facilities of its own. Thus, the vast majority of children actually were under the direct supervision of some 80 private (or *voluntary*, as they were sometimes called) child-care agencies. The great majority of these children in placement resided with individual families in foster homes; the remaining children were distributed among facilities such as institutions, group homes, maternity shelters, and so forth.

The private agencies were funded by the city according to a reimbursement formula which was designed to cover approximately 85 to 90 percent of their reimbursable costs. The reimbursement for ongoing programs, such as foster care, was on a per diem basis; that is, the agency received a predetermined amount per day for each child in care. The amount of payment varied according to the type of program (foster home, group home, institution, and so on). A variety of costs either were not reimbursable or—as is the case with adoption—were reimbursed by means of a one-time fee. Payments made to agencies, regardless of whether they were per diem or a one-time fee, came from the Charitable Institutions Budget and totaled some $400 million per year.

Children entered the child-care system for a variety of reasons. In some instances the child's parents made a request to the city because they were unable to

---

* This case was prepared by Professor David W. Young. It is based on David W. Young and Brandt Allen, "Benefit Cost Analysis in the Social Services: The Example of Adoption Reimbursement." © 1983 by the University of Chicago. All rights reserved.

EXHIBIT 1 Number of Legal Adoptions, 1982–1986

	1982	1983	1984	1985	1986
Legal adoptions..........	1,000*	993	1,166	1,032	807
Children in foster care....	24,973	25,934	27,115	27,900	28,625
Percent adopted	4.0	3.8	4.3	3.7	2.8

* Estimate by Bureau of Child Welfare, all figures except percentages are from the same source.

provide adequate care in the home; in others the child entered by means of a court mandate for reasons such as neglect, abuse, delinquency, or potential delinquency. Although some children remained in care for only a few months, others remained in the system for several years, often until they reached the age of 21 and were no longer eligible for child welfare services.

A variety of changes had taken place over the past 5 to 10 years which affected not only the relationship between the city and the agencies, but the whole pattern of child care. One such change was in the characteristics of the children in care. Between 1980 and 1986 the mix of children in the child-care system shifted rather dramatically, such that there were now proportionately more older children and more children who were in care because of their own emotional and behavioral problems. As a result of this change, many agencies—and the city as well—had been left with inappropriate programs and service-delivery capabilities; consequently many children were residing in programs which were not appropriate to their needs.

Data

Mr. Brown realized that several complications existed which impinged on his evaluation. First, foster home care cost the city $24 a day, with payments made 365 days a year; this rate had remained unchanged for the full five years. The one-time adoption fee, by contrast, had risen from $800 in 1982 to $2,800 in 1986.

Second, over 40 percent of all adoptions in 1986 were "subsidized," that is, the adoptive parents received payments from the city of $2,880 per year. This percentage was up from only 1.1 percent in 1982 (see Exhibit 2).

EXHIBIT 2 Number of Subsidized Adoptions, 1982–1986

	1982	1983	1984	1985	1986
Subsidized adoptions	11	96	218	326	328
Percent of total adoptions ...	1.1	9.7	18.7	31.6	40.6

Source: All figures except percentages from the Bureau of Child Welfare.

Third, Mr. Brown had recently obtained some data on the cost to a voluntary agency of an adoptive effort. As he had learned, agencies incurred three types of costs in placing a child in an adoptive home. First, there were the rather standard direct costs for the adoption itself. These expenditures included legal fees, casework time, administrative time, testing, and the like. Second, there was a loss of per diem payments. That is, when a child was adopted, the agency's population level fell; since reimbursement was based on a per-child per-day payment, the agency lost this payment until a replacement child was admitted. The per diem payment was designed to cover both fixed and variable child-care costs, but when a child was adopted only the variable costs stopped—the fixed costs continued. Thus, until the agency could replace the adopted child it lost reimbursement for the fixed-cost portion of the per diem rate. Third, the child who replaced the one who was adopted was likely to have higher variable costs. Since children who were adopted usually required few special agency services, their variable costs were relatively low. On the other hand, new children entering the child-care system frequently had a need for one or more specialized services, so that when a replacement child was found he/she was likely to have higher variable costs, on the average, than the one who was adopted. As a result, the agency suffered a loss in the surplus of reimbursement over variable costs and consequently had fewer dollars available to cover its fixed costs.

As an example, if the fixed portion of the $24 per-child per-day reimbursement amount was $10.00, and if a month elapsed before a replacement child was admitted (which frequently was the case), the agency had lost approximately $300 ($10.00 per day × 30 days) of funds which it had previously planned to use for the payment of rent, salaries, and other expenses to which it had committed itself for the budget year. If the variable costs for the replacement child were $2.00 more per day than for the one who was adopted, the agency's annual fixed-cost reimbursement was depleted still further. Assuming children were adopted fairly consistently throughout the budget year, the $2.00 per day loss was in effect for an average of six months for each child adopted; the annual loss in reimbursement for fixed costs was thus about $360 ($2.00 per day × 180 days) per adopted child. Consequently, using the assumptions of a $10.00 fixed-cost portion, a one-month lapse before a replacement child was admitted, and $2.00 per day more in variable costs for the replacement child, an agency's direct adoption costs increased by some $660 per placement.

Of further significance was the fact that the direct cost of adoption itself frequently was understated. While the adoption fee might adequately account for the adoption-related costs of any *given* child, there were many children for whom adoption was attempted unsuccessfully. An agency incurred adoption-related costs for these children as well and yet received no reimbursement for them. The schematic diagram in Exhibit 3 illustrates the potential significance of unsuccessful attempts in the computation of adoption costs. In this example 100 children began the adoption process, but only 45 were successfully adopted. Exhibit 4 shows the costs of this process. When only successful attempts are used and when no home finding is necessary, the cost per adoption is $7,620. The inclusion of

EXHIBIT 3 Adoption Attempts for Children Considered Permanently Neglected (each symbol represents five children)

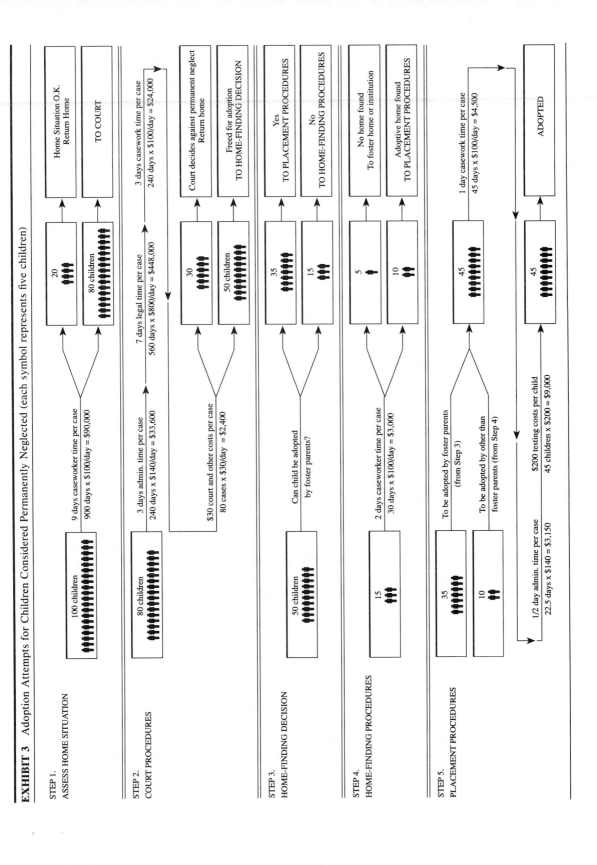

EXHIBIT 4 Adoption Costs for Permanently Neglected Children

		Using 100 Children	
Activity	*Cost for One Child*	*Number of Children Involved*	*Cost for Children Involved*
Caseworker assessment of home situation	$ 900	100	$ 90,000
Court procedures:			
Administrative time	420	80	33,600
Legal time	5,600	80	448,000
Casework time	300	80	24,000
Court and other costs	30	80	2,400
Caseworker time in home-finding procedures*	—	15	3,000
Placement procedures:			
Casework time	100	45	4,500
Administrative time	70	45	3,150
Testing costs	200	45	9,000
Total	$7,620	45	$617,650
Cost per adopted child	$7,620		$ 13,726

* Not necessary for the average child. Needed for only 15 children out of the 100. Cost is $200 per child when necessary. Therefore $3,000 is included in the cost for children involved.

unsuccessful attempts and home-finding efforts brings the cost to $13,726 per completed adoption; that is, the agency spent a total of $617,650 and completed only 45 adoptions.

Dr. Brown noted three points with respect to this example. First, the most significant cost was that of legal fees, which were quite high when there was a charge of permanent neglect because of both the relatively large number of days necessary per case and the fact that in this example the courts decided against the agency in 30 out of 80 cases. Second, not all adoptions followed this pattern. Different legal costs would be incurred, for example, in a case where the child had been surrendered, or where the agency went to court on an abandonment petition. Third, any projected savings would depend on the length of time a child *would have* remained in foster care if he/she were not adopted. He thought 10 years was a reasonable assumption.

In sum, he realized that agencies must consider a variety of costs when deciding whether to proceed toward adoption for a given child. In order to determine more specifically the level of these costs he analyzed 144 children who were adopted through one agency during the three years from 1984 to 1986.

Because this agency had deficit funding for its adoption program, it was able to undertake an adoption whenever it felt that adoption was in the best interests of the child, regardless of the financial consequences. Because it also accepted a relatively high proportion of children classified as "hard to place," it seemed feasible to conclude that the percentage of children adopted would not be biased

EXHIBIT 5   Adoption Analysis

| | Actual (1986) | | | | |
| | Agency | | City | | |
	Number	*Percent**	*Number*	*Percent**	*Cost per Adoption†*
Total children in care.........	596	—	28,625	—	—
Number of adoptions.........	43	7.22	807	2.82	—
Adoption breakdown:					
Surrendered................	27	4.53	—	—	$6,000
Abandoned.................	10	1.68	—	—	5,400
Permanently neglected......	6	1.01	—	—	9,200
Subsidized/unsubsidized breakdown:					
Subsidized	33	5.54	328	1.15	—
Unsubsidized..............	10	1.68	479	1.67	—

* Percent of total children in care.
† Includes "failures" and other associated costs.

by the children's characteristics. He classified these children into 36 categories based on legal status, age, and level of handicaps, and found that the average cost per successfully adopted child ranged from $5,400 in the lowest category to $9,200 in the highest.

In order to simplify his analysis, he decided to look only at 43 children whose adoptions were from this agency during 1986, and to collapse his 36 categories into 3, reflecting the most significant factor, legal status: surrendered, abandoned, or permanently neglected. Since this particular agency had had outside funding support for its adoption program, he thought that the results of its efforts might be indicative of what would happen citywide if further financial support for adoptions were made available to the agencies. The results of his analysis are contained in Exhibit 5.

With these data in hand, he began to reflect on the nature of the problem with adoptions, and what changes might be made in the Bureau's reimbursement policy in order to encourage agencies to move toward adoption when it was appropriate for the child.

Questions

1. What is your assessment of Dr. Brown's evaluation methodology? How might it have been improved?
2. Assuming the validity of the data he has gathered, what are the next steps he should take in the evaluation? What changes, if any, would you recommend the Bureau make in its reimbursement policies? In its other policies?

CASE 15–2   Comprehensive Employment and Training Act*

The Comprehensive Employment and Training Act (CETA) was scheduled to expire in 1983. As a basis for deciding whether programs of the type financed by CETA should be continued, the House Subcommittee on Employment Opportunities requested the U.S. General Accounting Office (GAO) to assess the effectiveness of various CETA services. The 139-page GAO report was issued June 14, 1982, with the title, "CETA Programs for Disadvantaged Adults—What Do We Know about Their Enrollees, Services, and Effectiveness?" This case focuses on one section of the GAO report, that relating to the effectiveness of CETA adult programs for classroom training, on-the-job training, work experience, and public service employment, as measured by annual earnings.

Nature of the Programs

In fiscal year 1979 about $9.4 billion was spent for programs delivered under CETA, out of about $14 billion spent for employment and training programs of all types. In 1976, about $1.7 billion was spent for classroom training, on-the-job training, and work experience programs, collectively called *comprehensive services programs,* and 1.7 million persons were enrolled in these programs. In 1976, 27 percent of these persons were in the classroom training program, 11 percent in on-the-job training, and 56 percent in work experience. (Five percent, although paid for with comprehensive services program money, were in the public services program.) In 1980, 48 percent were in classroom training, 13 percent in on-the-job training, and 39 percent in work experience.

Classroom training consisted of training in occupational skills (e.g., clerical and various types of crafts) and basic educational training. On average, participants received 21 weeks of training.

On-the-job training provided specific occupational skill training, primarily in operative and craft jobs, in actual job settings, usually in a private-sector company. CETA subsidized part of the wages paid to participants, and it was expected that they would continue working for the organization that trained them after the training period. On average, participants in this program received 20 weeks of training.

The work experience program provided subsidized employment that was intended to instill basic work habits and attitudes, rather than to teach specific job skills. The average participant was enrolled in this program for 20 weeks.

The public service employment program paid wages of persons employed in newly created public sector jobs. About $2.4 billion was spent for this program in 1976 and 600,000 persons were enrolled in it.

---

* This case was prepared by Professor Robert N. Anthony. Copyright © by Osceola Institute.

These programs were managed by state and local governments through mechanisms called *prime sponsors*. A prime sponsor had to represent at least 100,000 people; it could be a state, a county, a large city, or a group of smaller cities or counties. There were about 475 prime sponsors.

Criteria for Assessment

The GAO recognized that the effectiveness of the programs should be judged in terms of a number of criteria, including economic benefits to the participants, such as increased wages and skills; noneconomic benefits to the participants, such as improved family life and social status; economic benefits to society, such as increased skills in the labor force and reduced crime; and noneconomic benefits to society, such as better race relations and more equitable income distribution. Its report considered a number of these factors, but its monetary assessment of effectiveness focused on annual earnings.

The CETA program was administered by the Department of Labor. For some years, the department had engaged a private firm, Westat, Inc., to study the experience of a large sample of participants in the program. As of 1982, the most recent data were those for participants enrolled in 1976.[1] The lag was a function of the time required to collect data and interview participants one or two years after they left the program and to analyze these data. About 6,300 persons were in the CETA sample. Data about these persons were compared with data from a carefully matched sample of 5,200 persons whose earnings were reported in the Current Population Survey, a continuing sample survey sponsored by the Department of Labor.

Results of the Analysis

For the entire sample, 1977 annual earnings of CETA participants averaged $300 higher than those of the comparison group. For on-the-job training, the difference was $850; for classroom training, it was $350; for public service employment, $250, and for work experience it was a negative $150. The work experience amount was not statistically significant; the other numbers were statistically significant at the 0.05 level, or higher.

Annual earnings gains for men were not statistically significant for any program. Earnings gains for white females were $550 for classroom training, $550 for on-the-job training, and $950 for public service employment. Earnings gains for minority females were $500 for classroom training, $1,200 for on-the-job training,

---

[1] Westat, Inc., *Continuous Longitudinal Manpower Survey, Report No. 8* (Washington, D.C.: U.S. Department of Labor, March 1979), *Follow-Up Report No. 2* (March 1979), and *Follow-Up Report No. 3* (January 1981).

and $650 for public service employment. (Female earnings gains for work experience were not statistically significant.)

People with the lowest earnings before CETA gained the most from participation. When the sample was divided into three groups according to pre-CETA earnings, the group with the lowest pre-CETA earnings had $550 more annual earnings than the comparison group, while the middle and highest groups had no statistically significant change in earnings. For the lowest group, participants in classroom training had increased earnings (compared with the comparison group) of $600; on-the-job training, $1,300; and public service employment of $900 (work experience was not statistically significant).

Comparisons were also made by age groups, but the pattern was not clear.

The preceding numbers are averages for groups. The GAO report also reported frequency distributions. These showed that 36 percent of CETA participants had no gains or lower earnings in 1977 as compared with their pre-CETA earnings, whereas 24 percent had gains of $4,000 or more.

Conclusion

The summary section of the GAO report contained the following paragraphs under the heading, ''How effective were the services?'':

> The single effectiveness study available estimates that only $300–$400 of 1977 post-program earnings can be attributed directly to CETA participation in adult-oriented services during fiscal 1976. By service type, this study estimates gains of $850 for on-the-job training, $350 for classroom training, and $250–$750 for PSE and no significant gains for work experience.
>
> White and minority women had significant net gains of $500–$600, as did participants with the poorest earnings histories. Distributions of gross earnings changes over the period 1974–1977 suggest that even though the aggregate net gain was small, some women and poor earners had fairly substantial net gains from CETA.

Questions

1. Based on the earnings criterion, did some or all of the CETA programs probably have benefits that exceeded their costs?
2. In considering new legislation, what use could the House Committee reasonably make of the information in the GAO report?

CASE 15–3   Timilty Middle School*

Mary Grassa O'Neill, principal of the James P. Timilty Middle School, sat in her unadorned office. The walls were stripped and primed for a much-needed paint job. Ms. O'Neill brought 17 years of middle-school experience to this, her first principalship. Three years had passed since her appointment, and her decision to initiate the Project Promise Pilot Program. Now, after two complete years of the program, and a calm and orderly beginning of the third year, she had the luxury of some time to reflect on two important questions: What had Project Promise promised? and What had it delivered?

Background

The Timilty Middle School, located in historic John Eliot Square of the Fort Hill section of Boston, had a troubled history and had suffered for many years from a poor reputation. Founded in 1937 as a junior high school (Grades 7–9), and transformed to a middle school (Grades 6–8) in 1974, it had seen its racial and ethnic composition change dramatically—from 75 percent white and 25 percent black in 1942 to 52 percent black, 29 percent Hispanic, 7 percent Asian, and 9 percent white in 1988.

Following the assassinations of Dr. Martin Luther King and Robert Kennedy in the late sixties, the atmosphere at the school reflected the violence, racial tension, and turmoil of the surrounding community. In 1974, court-ordered desegregation resulted in turbulence and agitation in both the school and its community. In 1981, Proposition 2 ½[1] led to layoffs of 30 percent of the teachers, and a precipitous decline in both faculty and student morale. In December 1985, when Ms. O'Neill took over as principal, the school had more than its share of problems: low reading and math scores, low student and teacher attendance, high suspension and failure rates, and a general reputation as a low-achieving school. For many, including the press and the surrounding community, it was considered to be the "worst school in town."

The Timilty community included the black housing projects of Ruggles Street, several housing projects in all-white Charlestown, and most of Boston's South End, with its polyglot mix of Hispanic, Asian, white, and black. In the Boston Public School System (BPS), as in most other cities, students had no choice

---

* This case was prepared by Alexander D. Stankowicz under the direction of Professor David W. Young. Copyright © by David W. Young and Alexander D. Stankowicz.

[1] The result of a Massachusetts "taxpayer revolt," resulting in the limitation of property taxes to 2.50 percent of the assessed value of the property.

regarding their school assignment: all middle-school students living in specific neighborhoods were assigned to their geocoded school. As a result, the Timilty's student population consisted of racially mixed, urban poor, living in substandard housing, burdened with the struggles of poverty, drugs and alcohol, teenage pregnancy, family crises, and neighborhood violence. Indeed, according to an AFDC[2] report, and free-lunch statistics, the Timilty's students had the second lowest socioeconomic levels in the city.

The Program

Three days before the 1985 Christmas holiday, Ms. O'Neill found an application for the Project Promise Pilot Program in her morning mail. She discussed it with her staff, and decided to apply.

Project Promise, as introduced initially in Rochester, New York, was an intensive, academic remediation program designed to improve student performance in reading, mathematics, and writing. It was based on the theory that if underachieving students spent more time on the basics, their skills would improve.

Ms. O'Neill and her staff decided that the program at the Timilty would be for all students, not just those needing remediation. The Timilty's application was approved, and a Pilot Program was initiated in Spring, 1986. It had seven instructional components:

1. *Extended day.* Students attended school one and a half hours longer Monday through Thursday, from 7:40 A.M. until 3:10 P.M. Friday was a regular 7:40 to 1:40 school day. Teachers worked two hours longer, from 7:25 A.M. until 3:55 P.M., Monday to Friday. Overall, students were in school 37 percent longer; teachers worked 40 percent longer.

2. *Extended week.* Three hours of organized instruction were offered on Saturday mornings. Teachers used a variety of groupings and approaches to involve students in enrichment activities in reading, writing, and math.

3. *Interdisciplinary and team teaching.* Teachers worked together to use thematic teaching across the disciplines. The basic skills of reading and writing were taught across all subject areas. In order to determine effective ways of teaching across their specializations, teachers worked together in four separate clusters:[3] *(a)* Grade 6, *(b)* Grade 7, *(c)* Grade 8, and *(d)* multilevel, consisting of Grades 6, 7, and 8, with both monolingual and Spanish-speaking bilingual students (designed to assist in "mainstreaming" the Spanish-speaking stu-

---

[2] Aid to Families with Dependent Children, a program run by the State Department of Public Welfare.

[3] In the Timilty, students at each grade level received all their academic instruction from a small group of teachers; this was called the *cluster*. All nonacademic subjects (physical education, industrial arts, home economics, art) were taught by teachers outside the particular cluster.

dents). To facilitate interdisciplinary teaching, teachers also created opportunities to teach together.

4. *Smaller class size.*   This was achieved by adding academic staff—a teacher and a coordinator—to each cluster.

5. *Flexible schedule.*   The traditional day of 45-minute periods was replaced by a flexible schedule, determined by each team, allowing the scheduling of both longer and shorter classes in order to meet instructional needs.

6. *Planning time.*   Teachers had common planning time (approximately 4–6 hours per week) to develop interdisciplinary instruction in reading and writing and to discuss any issues relevant to their teaching.

7. *Parent outreach.*   To support these school-based innovations, two paid parent outreach workers undertook activities to inform and involve parents in their children's education.

The Pilot Program

The 8th grade had been targeted for the Pilot Program. Previously, the 8th grade consisted of five sections of about 30 children each. With the inception of the Pilot Program, the class structure changed. To the five academic teachers, two remediation specialists were added. Moreover, these seven teachers were a fairly autonomous group, with great scheduling latitude. They decided to structure the program around a seven-day cycle, not including Saturdays (which was to be different from the other school days). The teachers divided the students into groups, rearranged them according to their needs, and included the special needs students as much as possible.

Initially, the program was extremely challenging, especially in its attempt to dovetail the normal 6-hour day with a 7 ½-hour day, and to maintain consistency between Project Promise teachers and other teachers. As a result of this greater intensity, everyone involved had a totally new set of activities for the final 10 weeks of the school year. Teachers had smaller groups to work with—as few as 10 to 15 students for remediation, and approximately 20 to 25 for regular classes, rather than 30 students for both remediation and regular classes.

Although some of the teachers found the coordination demands challenging on occasion, in general, most would do things for the students that they would not have done in situations with larger class sizes. There was a new sense of mood in the building, due largely to the fact that there was now time to work things out. The common planning time that was built into the program allowed the faculty, students, and parents to bond together, and to dedicate themselves to a shared mission of education.

Laval Wilson, superintendent of the Boston Public Schools, had decided that Project Promise would not be a remedial program, targeted only for students with the lowest scores. Rather, the premise was that if the six academic components were good for students who needed remediation, then they were good for everyone. Jim Fewless, a 21-year veteran of the Timilty, and the 7th grade coordinator, explained the "promise" of Project Promise this way:

> If you are below average, we will work to see that you become an average student; if you are an average student, you can become an above average student; we want the above average student to excel; and if you are already an excellent student, there is always more to learn and more to do, and you will be given the time to do it.

The superintendent also had decided that the program would be initiated with only the 8th grade cluster, including one 7th grade homeroom that, for logistical reasons, was in that cluster. The 7th grade class made an interesting study group because, in the second year when the program was expanded to the entire school, this group already had had 10 solid weeks of Project Promise, and they were somewhat ahead of the other students in that cluster.

The 10-week period of the Pilot Program was considered an inadequate amount of time to accurately evaluate skill development. Nevertheless, the teachers felt they saw tremendous attitudinal changes at the school. As one observer commented:

> Teachers' Room conversations shifted from weekend activities, complaining about the kids, and counting how many days were left in the school year, to student-oriented topics like curriculum, sharing successful lessons, and brainstorming new ideas that might be tried in the classroom. There was a new excitement in the school, and both teachers and students seemed to be having fun.

Classroom observation and extensive interviews with teachers, students, and parents done in the summer of 1986 by Document Development, Inc., of Brookline, Massachusetts, an independent evaluation team, resulted in the conclusion that "The most significant effect of Project Promise was the increased interest and enthusiasm about the school exhibited by the students." Even before the evaluation had been received, however, Superintendent Wilson had decided that for the 1986–87 academic year the entire Timilty School would be a Project Promise program.

The 1986–87 Program

To implement the program, all academic and resource room position descriptions were rewritten and upgraded, and all former positions were abolished. Ms. O'Neill established a screening committee to fill the new positions, and before implementation of the first full year of Project Promise, 24 Timilty teachers had applied and 21 had been hired. This left 14 vacancies. Ms. O'Neill explained:

> There were three difficulties in attracting staff to the new positions: (1) many teachers simply didn't want to work in Project Promise, (2) the Boston Teachers' Union (BTU) lobbied against Project Promise because they maintained that teachers were being required to apply for their old jobs, and (3) there was a great deal of uncertainty associated

with the leap into an educational experiment of this magnitude, involving interdisciplinary teaching.

Although there were some grumblings about the recruitment process, most teachers felt that being chosen for the program bonded them together, and there was a strong belief that the program was going to work. The majority of teachers selected had worked in the school for over 15 years. Of the seven new people who were chosen to join the staff, only one was new to teaching. The remainder were experienced teachers, although some were from outside the BPS. According to one veteran, this was very good for the project:

> They had no old habits to break, and they were going to have to plunge in and learn all new habits. Also, they would be mentored by the more experienced teachers in the school. The new people who came in sometimes rose to be stars of the show. One teacher had a really rough time her first year in the school with 30 students in the classroom, unresponsive kids—your typical middle school experience. Now she's in her second year of teaching, this time as a Project Promise teacher. She is teaching what she wants, with a relatively small class size. She has suddenly become a shining star, with all of her talent and ability coming forth.

Administrative staff (consisting of a principal, an assistant principal, and a director of instruction) remained the same, and three additional instructional support teachers were included. According to Clem Pasquale, a veteran of 21 years' teaching at the school:

> What we have here now that we didn't have in the past is the support from the Instructional Coordinators, the Assistant Principal, and the Director of Instruction. There is now a framework of supports where you can go to work through and deal with problems that, in the past, would require you to take time away from your teaching. We now have the organization, a plan and a staff to do whatever has to be done to make the school work.

Jeff Cohen, a 19-year Timilty veteran, added:

> If there is something that happens that you can't handle yourself, you can send the student to someone who can deal with the problem. We are now spending most of the day teaching rather than doing paperwork or disciplining.

Cost

According to the BPS budget for the 1988–89 academic year, the Timilty Middle School cost $636,718 more than the average cost of other BPS middle schools. The average per pupil cost for FY88 for middle schools was $3,746, while the per pupil cost at the Timilty was $5,484, a difference of 46 percent. All of this was attributed to Project Promise. On the average, Project Promise teachers received $6,000–$7,000 more per year than other middle-school teachers, most of which was for overtime. The extra money bought several things: common planning time for teachers, smaller class sizes, remedial teachers, extended classroom time (90 minutes) for the students during the week, Saturday classes, and professional development (e.g., training) for the teachers.

Performance Measures

Several indicators of performance were available to Ms. O'Neill. One was student attendance. Prior to Project Promise, attendance at the Timilty ranged from 75 to 85 percent, about average for a middle school. Attendance for 1987–88, the first full year of Project Promise, was 90 percent; in the second full year, it rose to about 92 percent. Initially, on Saturdays, attendance was 45 percent, which rose to between 60 to 70 percent in the third year. One explanation given for this was that Timilty students now found school to be a place where they felt a strong sense of belonging, accomplishment, and in the process had some fun.

A second indicator was teacher attendance. Prior to Project Promise, teacher attendance, along with morale, at the Timilty was low. According to one veteran, ''The majority of staff members made sure that they took all their personal and sick days, usually right before or after a vacation, when we would have a quarter of the staff absent.'' In 1987–88, it was reported in the BPS School Profile that the Timilty's teacher attendance was the second highest in the city, even though teachers were required to put in two extra hours a day and three hours on Saturday. According to Mr. Fewless:

> Project Promise is a great deal of work for the staff. Because of the additional time, our weekends are shortened to a day and a half. Yet, besides the financial remuneration, the professional rewards of working together in a team gives us a sense that we are working together.

A third indicator was exam school[4] acceptances. Before Project Promise, the idea of Timilty's 8th graders applying for exam schools was almost unheard of. With the program, students were encouraged to apply, and the number admitted increased each year. Data on exam school acceptances are contained in Exhibit 1. Moreover, students who had graduated from Project Promise reported that they were not overloaded by the workload of high school, whereas in the past many students had reported being overwhelmed by the demands of regular high school.

A fourth indicator was suspensions. As Exhibit 1 indicates, the number of suspensions dropped dramatically by the second full year of Project Promise. In 1987–88, the Timilty's suspension rate was 8.7 per 1,000 students, the 10th lowest in the city. Rates at the Cleveland and Thompson Middle Schools, the two other Project Promise Schools, were 7.4 and 15.8, respectively.

---

[4] BPS had three high schools (Boston Latin, Boston Latin Academy, and Boston Technical High) that were called exam schools, because they required students to take SSAT (Secondary School Aptitude Test) in order to be accepted. These schools, known for their rigorous academic curriculum, prepared students for college.

EXHIBIT 1 Basic Information

Year	Average Number of Students in School*	Number of Exam School Acceptances	Suspensions	Suspensions per 1000 Students	Potential Nonpromote Percentage
1985–86	462	39	82	n.a.	n.a.
1986–87	510	52	83	n.a.	n.a.
1987–88	492	64	38	8.7	5.0

* Enrollment figures are determined three times each academic year: September, December, and June. This number is an average of the three.

Sources: Average number of students and exam school acceptances from Division of Implementation, Boston Public Schools. Other data from Michael Fung, ''1987–88 Middle School Statistics,'' Memorandum to William Abbott, Deputy Superintendent, Operations, May 22, 1989. (Most of Fung's data were obtained from *1987–88 School Profiles*, Research and Development Department, Boston Public Schools.)

A fifth indicator was potential nonpromotes. As Exhibit 1 also indicates, the Timilty's percentage of potential nonpromotes in 1987–88 was only 5 percent, the second lowest in the city. Rates at the Cleveland and Thompson Middle Schools were 13.1 and 9.0 percent, respectively.

A sixth indicator was parent involvement. With approximately 426 students in attendance, over 200 parents showed up for the annual open houses. According to Mr. Pasquale, ''In the old days there were usually twice as many teachers as parents at open house, and we would be lucky if 13 or 14 parents showed up.'' Indeed, following the initiation of Project Promise, over 100 parents frequently came on Saturdays to participate in school activities, such as the science fair, the international festival, and student and teacher appreciation days.

A final indicator was reading and math ability which can be measured by utilizing the MAT (Metropolitan Achievement Test) raw scores to summarize the overall picture for Grades 6, 7, and 8. Students at each grade level were given reading and math tests before they entered Project Promise and again after they had spent one year in the program. The scores of students who participated in Project Promise at the Timilty, as well as the Cleveland and Thompson Middle Schools, were compared to non-Project Promise students in the other BPS middle schools.

The results of these comparisons are shown in Exhibit 2. As this exhibit indicates, Project Promise students scored higher than non-Project Promise students at each grade level on the MAT reading test. In terms of percentile score, the largest difference was at the 7th grade level, where the median percentile was 7 points higher for Project Promise students than non-Project Promise ones. On the MAT math test, the largest difference was at the 8th grade level where Project Promise students had a median percentile 11 points higher than non-Project Promise ones.

Similar results could be seen from an analysis over a two-year period. In 1986, children who were to become Project Promise 6th grade students were 0.3 points

---

EXHIBIT 2 Average Percentile Scores for 1987–88 Project Promise versus Non-Project Promise Students

---

	Project Promise	*Non-Project Promise*
Reading:*		
Grade 6	63	57
Grade 7	50	43
Grade 8	45	41
Math:†		
Grade 6	72	64
Grade 7	51	46
Grade 8	54	43

* There were statistically significant differences favoring Project Promise in Grades 6 and 7.

† There were statistically significant differences favoring Project Promise in Grades 6, 7, and 8.

Note: Figures are based on students who were enrolled for the entire 1987–88 school year. For Project Promise, students had to be in the same Project Promise school for the entire year. Non-Project Promise does not include exam school students.

Source: Office of Research and Development, Boston Public Schools.

---

behind other 5th grade students. In 1987, after one year of the program, Project Promise students were 2.6 points ahead of students outside Project Promise. This meant that Project Promise students ended the 5th grade behind other students, went through the program, and at the end of the 6th grade had caught up with and surpassed their counterparts outside Project Promise.

Student performance on a school-by-school basis is shown in Exhibit 3, which shows the median percentile for students outside the program, and that of each Project Promise school in 1986, 1987, and 1988. For example, 6th grade students outside the program had a median reading score of 50 in 1986. The Cleveland School started quite behind, with a median score of 38, while Thompson and Timilty students started the 6th grade with scores of 53 and 48, respectively. In 1987, after the initiation of Project Promise, Cleveland 6th grade students improved somewhat (from 38 to 44), Thompson students stayed about the same, and Timilty students increased to a median score of 65. In 1988, Timilty students dropped slightly to 62, while Cleveland and Thompson students continued to improve.

After examining these reading and math scores, the BPS Office of Research and Development concluded:

Taken together, these data show a pattern of successful outcomes for Project Promise students. The Program seems to work for low-performing students who start out far behind their school counterparts, and also seems to accelerate the achievement of students who do not have a learning lag when they enter the Program.

EXHIBIT 3   Median Percentiles for Reading and Math by Grade, Year, and School

| | *School* | | | |
	All Non-Project Promise*	Cleveland	Thompson	Timilty
Grade 6:				
Reading:				
1986	50	38	53	48
1987	50	44	53	65
1988	n.a.	53	62	62
Math:				
1986	60	54	49	47
1987	57	65	71	71
1988	n.a.	63	65	74
Grade 7:				
Reading:				
1986	41	37	33	31
1987	38	41	45	50
1988	n.a.	46	38	50
Math:				
1986	47	46	28	30
1987	41	50	39	34
1988	n.a.	46	46	48
Grade 8:				
Reading:				
1986	35	35	29	30
1987	37	39	41	37
1988	n.a.	41	48	53
Math:				
1986	37	43	26	32
1987	38	38	34	34
1988	n.a.	41	56	54

* "Non-Project Promise" does not include students from the Latin Schools.

Source: Office of Research and Development, Boston Public Schools.

Long-Term Impact

One important question is whether the impact of Project Promise was cumulative or whether it would begin to wear off over time. Exhibit 4 shows the performance of students who had been in Project Promise for two full years, in comparison with other students for the same period. It suggests that, after participating in Project Promise for two years, current 7th graders had completely overcome the original gap in reading performance and were outperforming their non-Project Promise peers. For current 8th graders, the relative impact of Project Promise had decreased slightly, but this group was still scoring higher than their non-Project Promise peers.

As with reading, future Project Promise students were scoring lower on the MAT math test than other BPS students prior to the start of Project Promise. At

---

EXHIBIT 4   MAT Reading and Math: Progress over Time—Yearly Scaled Score Differences—
Project Promise minus Non-Project Promise*

	1985–86	1986–87	1987–88
Reading:			
7th Graders:			
Grade 5	−6		
Grade 6		−3	
Grade 7			+ 8
8th Graders:			
Grade 6	−8		
Grade 7		+8	
Grade 8			+7
Math:			
7th Graders:			
Grade 5	−11		
Grade 6		+2	
Grade 7			+6
8th Graders:			
Grade 6	−13		
Grade 7		−1	
Grade 8			+12

* Figures are based on students who were enrolled for the entire
1986–87 and 1987–88 school years. For Project Promise, students had
to be in the same Project Promise school for the entire year. Non-
Project Promise does not include exam school students.

Source: Office of Research and Development, Boston Public Schools.

the end of 1986–87 (i.e., after one year in the program), Project Promise 6th
graders had scored 2 points higher than non-Project Promise 6th graders. Project
Promise 7th graders performed similarly. After two years, 7th and 8th graders
continued to gain faster in math than other BPS students.

After two complete years of Project Promise, the Office of Research and Development concluded:

> The preliminary results strongly suggest that, as a whole, Project Promise students are
> improving at a relatively faster rate than their non-Project Promise peers. This is especially true in math. Future analyses will look at changes over time in more detail and
> include information from the CRTs [Criterion Reference Tests]. The final evaluation
> report will include information from teachers, students and parents regarding the impact
> of the project.

A Dissenting View

Although there were considerable data available to support the case that the
Project Promise Program at the Timilty School was a success, David Whall, the
budget director for the BPS, was skeptical. In his view:

While the Timilty reading and math scores improved, as they did at the Cleveland and Thompson, which were also Project Promise schools, there are nonetheless other schools that have shown equivalent improvement without the benefit of Project Promise (Exhibit 5). If you're looking at 1987 test scores, they are generally up from 1986 scores, which are down from 1985. And if you look at the middle school test scores as a whole and compare them from 1985 to 1988, there isn't any noticeable improvement.

The total expenditure of the BPS went from roughly $256 million in 1985 to $328 million in 1988, a 28 percent increase in aggregate expenditures (which is a 15 to 16 percent increase if you correct for inflation) for a student population that has not increased. From my budget perspective, there has been a very large increase in expenditures, but looking at the test scores, there has been no material improvement in academic performance.

Mr. Whall acknowledged that in many ways Project Promise was a desirable and successful program, but, in his view, it did not necessarily represent the optimal use of resources of the BPS.

Would the system be better off, on a whole, if the money were channeled into other resources? For example, as this analysis that I have prepared [Exhibit 6] shows, there are many ways the $1,265,326 for Project Promise for FY88 could have been spent. Since the students come into middle schools like the Timilty with basic academic deficiencies, it might be a more efficient allocation of resources to target an at-risk elementary population and provide an extended day program with academic remediation along with a social-cultural enrichment, including field trips, counseling and other social services.

In short, when evaluating Project Promise, you must look at what it costs the system as a whole, and then you have to ask yourself a couple of questions:

1. It would cost approximately $9 million to replicate Project Promise for the remaining 20 middle schools across the city. Is that the direction that the School Department wants to take?
2. Instead of continuing Project Promise, what else could be done with the money that would yield benefits equal to or greater than what was achieved at the Project Promise schools? Does the 46 percent differential in per pupil cost at the Timilty justify the increase in scores, or are there other alternatives? Does this represent the optimal use of financial resources?

Mr. Whall believed that in terms of cost-benefit analysis, the costs of Project Promise were

. . . perhaps, too high for the benefits derived, and the benefits for the system could have been attained for less money. Or, that equal benefits could have been distributed more widely across the system by doing something for other schools. Of course, that raises the question of scattering your resources across the four winds instead of channeling them into one site. But that gets back to the question: can we afford to replicate Project Promise over the system as a whole, especially during the present period of budgetary constraints?

He also commented about the leadership of Ms. O'Neill.

Part of Timilty's success has nothing to do with Project Promise, but is due to the leadership of Mary Grassa O'Neill. She is a very dynamic, very good administrator. In

EXHIBIT 5   MAT Reading and Mathematics: Rankings of Median Percentile Scores for Middle Schools Average Scale Score Change, 1987–88*

School	District	Average Scale Score Change
Reading:		
Lewenberg......	B	+16.33
M. Curley.......	A	+9.33
Dearborn	C	+9.00
McCormack.....	C	+8.67
Cleveland......	C	+7.00
Mackey........	E	+5.67
Timilty	D	+5.33
Barnes.........	D	+4.00
Thompson	B	+3.67
Tobin..........	A	+3.00
Edison.........	A	+2.67
Gavin	C	+2.00
Irving	B	+2.00
Wheatley	E	+1.33
Rogers.........	B	+1.00
Holmes.........	C	0.00
R. Shaw	B	0.00
Wilson.........	C	−0.67
Taft	A	−1.00
Edwards........	D	−1.67
Lewis	A	−7.67
King	E	−10.67
Mathematics:		
Lewenberg......	B	+12.67
Timilty	D	+12.00
Tobin..........	A	+12.00
Thompson	B	+7.33
Edison.........	A	+7.33
Barnes.........	D	+5.33
McCormack.....	C	+5.33
Gavin	C	+5.00
Irving	B	+2.67
Mackey........	E	+2.33
King	E	+1.67
Wilson.........	C	+1.00
Wheatley	E	+0.67
Cleveland......	C	−1.00
Taft	A	−1.67
Holmes.........	C	−2.33
R. Shaw	B	−3.00
Edwards........	D	−3.00
M. Curley.......	A	−5.00
Dearborn	C	−7.00
Rogers.........	B	−12.67
Lewis	A	−19.67

* Data for prior years are not available

Source: Department of Educational Testing, Boston Public Schools.

EXHIBIT 6 Budgetary Options*

School	Without Project Promise	School as Percent of Average	With Project Promise	School as Percent of Average	Project Promise Students	School as Percent of Average
Cleveland	$3,665	97.8%	$3,933	105.0%	$4,612	123.1%
Thompson	3,978	106.2	5,165	137.9	5,217	139.3
Timilty	4,165	111.2	5,466	145.9	5,484	146.4

* FY88 Middle School average cost per student: $3,746 (does not include overhead, transportation, etc.)

Note: Total city and externally funded budgets for Project Promise came to $1,265,326 in FY88. By comparison, this sum in FY88 could have done any of the following:

Purchase an additional 29 guidance counselors, including benefits.
Increase the instructional supply allocation by 26 percent for every student in the BPS.
Raise the BPS's library paraprofessional staff by 162 percent from 59 to 155 FTEs.
Provide another 35 elementary specialist teachers.
Nearly double the targeted reading work force, raising it from 37 to 69 teachers.
Give the middle schools another 33 instructional support teachers.
Expand outlays for middle school physical education and sports programs by 84%.
Double the size of Boston Prep and ACC.
Quadruple the size of our adult ed programs.
Pay for a nearly sixfold expansion of our summer programs.
Create another 35 extended day kdg classes, raising the total number by 71 percent from 49 to 84 FTE.
Push outlays for library and audiovisual materials up by over 1,500 percent.
Establish another 33 AWC classes versus the 55 in place in FY88.
Offer sabbaticals to 125 teachers.
Set up another four Barron Assessment Centers.
Double the number of bus monitors.
Or give every teacher a $285 raise.

Source: Budget Office, Boston Public Schools.

my assessment, she is capable of working minor miracles. She has the ability to instill enthusiasm, to communicate to her staff very clear-headed goals and how she wants them accomplished. So I think that leadership was very crucial to the success of the Timilty. Mary could have probably gotten the same results with less of an increase of money.

Ms. O'Neill's Response

Ms. O'Neill believed that Mr. Whall was making some incorrect interpretations of the available information. She also pointed out that Project Promise funds were not completely fungible:

First of all, you must bear in mind that David Whall is the budget director, not a statistician or researcher. This is important, because the statistics are complex in this field, and an expert is required to interpret them. David says there was no material improvement in academic performance at the Timilty. He definitely is wrong. Moreover, he doesn't mention that all the funding for Project Promise is in grants; that is, everything is outside the "formula" that is used to compute the distribution of the budget among BPS schools. He makes it sound as though we're taking money away from other things that could be funded through grants, which we're not. Also, the $1.2 million he mentions was for 3 schools. The Timilty never got $1.2 million; we got $636,000.

Also involved in the controversy was a statistician from the Office of Research and Development, of the Division of Planning and Resource Allocation, of the Boston Public Schools. The statistician pointed out that Mr. Whall was comparing apples and oranges, and that, if he were to make his case appropriately, he would need to find a school that was comparable to the Timilty. Unfortunately, no such school existed in the Boston school system.

Questions

1. What is your assessment of the data available for Project Promise? What additional information would you like to have? How might it be obtained?
2. What is your assessment of the issues and concerns raised by Mr. Whall?
3. What is your assessment of Ms. O'Neill's and the statistician's responses to Mr. Whall? How might Mr. Whall reply to them?
4. Has Project Promise been a success at the Timilty? Elsewhere? Should it be expanded to other schools in the BPS? In the country?

CASE 15–4   Massachusetts Housing Finance Agency*

In July 1985, Marvin Siflinger, Director of the Massachusetts Housing Finance Agency (MHFA), was evaluating the results of the State Housing Assistance for Rental Production (SHARP) program, one of several programs under the agency's auspices. SHARP, which had been in existence for only two years, had just completed its second "competitive round," and Mr. Siflinger felt that this was an opportune time to review the program's functioning. He was particularly interested in the system by which projects were selected for assistance, and questioned whether either the selection criteria that had been established and modified once, or the selection process itself, should be modified prior to the third competition.

Background

The Massachusetts Housing Finance Agency (MHFA) was created by a legislative mandate in 1966 for the purpose of increasing and improving the supply of standard housing for Massachusetts residents. It was intended to focus particular

---

* This case was prepared by Lynn B. Jenkins under the direction of Professor David W. Young. Copyright © by David W. Young. Distributed by the Accounting Curriculum Center, Boston University School of Management.

attention to the needs of low-income elderly, and other disadvantaged sectors of the population. The agency operated a variety of programs for homeowners and tenants, including mortgage assistance, loan arrangements, and interest subsidy payments for single- and multi-family housing.

Organizationally, the agency was a semi-autonomous arm of the state's Executive Office for Communities and Development (EOCD). The agency's Board of Directors was composed of nine community, housing, and financial representatives selected by the governor, plus two cabinet secretaries. The Board set overall policy and had veto power over virtually all agency activities and decisions. Because the MHFA was a semi-autonomous organization that functioned according to its own internal operating procedures, the state's role normally was limited to the involvement of its representatives on the Board of Directors, although on occasion it had exercised some discretionary authority over agency operations.

The MHFA staff consisted of approximately 200 people, many of whom had a background in banking, management, housing, architecture, and the real estate appraisal industry. An emphasis was placed on recruiting people with "real world experience" and technical expertise in the agency's line of business.

History of the SHARP Program

The MHFA traditionally had served as a channel for federal subsidies, including both the "236/Rent Supplement" and "Section 8" programs. These programs were subsidy programs that provided assistance to developers of rental housing, particularly for low-income and elderly residents. They were administered by the federal Department of Housing and Urban Development (HUD). Both programs were exceedingly generous, providing what have been termed "deep" subsidies, and existed in an environment where cost concerns did not significantly interfere with development goals.

As the political and financial support for these programs waned, MHFA was forced not only to develop alternative financing arrangements and to take responsibility for projects remaining in the Section 8 "pipeline," but also to cope with overspending and other programmatic inefficiencies that had developed. SHARP grew out of this need.

The impetus for the SHARP program also came from the realization that without federal (HUD) assistance, no new rental housing would be produced in Massachusetts. Indeed, in 1983–84 alone, there was a projected shortage of 200,000 rental units in the state.

In 1983, as part of the Comprehensive Housing Act, Governor Michael Dukakis signed the bill that created the SHARP program. The SHARP legislation itself was extremely brief and vaguely written. The specific program that emerged was formulated, for the most part, by Joseph Flatley, Assistant Secretary of the EOCD, and Eleanor White, Chief of Operations of the MHFA.

Central to the thinking of SHARP's designers was the desire to dispel the politicized reputation that the MHFA had developed, and to install a fair, consistent system of project appraisal. Drawing on the recommendation of a 1982 Housing Task Force, Flatley and White agreed that SHARP should meet some basic criteria. Specifically, it should *(a)* operate on the basis of competitive funding rounds, *(b)* require developers to put up more cash and assume greater financial risk than had been required of them under HUD assistance programs, *(c)* reserve at least 25 percent of the units for low-income tenants, and *(d)* incorporate incentives to use the lowest amount of SHARP funds necessary. The SHARP program was substantially more risky than its predecessors, since it depended largely upon the internal strengths of its chosen developers and their projects. Therefore, as underwriters, the agency needed to be concerned about the extent to which projects were economically successful, which depended in large part on their ability to meet the demands of the market.

Determination of Subsidies

The need for rental housing subsidies existed independently of the 25 percent low-income component that SHARP required of its developers. That is, because of a mismatch between construction costs, financing costs, and market rental rates, even if developers provided only market-rate units—and no low-income units—they generally were unable to build "affordable" rental housing. The result was an absence of rental construction in the early 1980s, leading to the previously cited shortage of units. Thus, the SHARP subsidy permitted not only the construction of low-income units but of rental units in general. As a result, since rent for low-income tenants was guaranteed by federal and state assistance programs, a developer's concern lay primarily with marketing the remaining 75 percent of the units.

To determine the maximum annual SHARP subsidy for a given year, the MHFA began with the estimated cost of producing a rental unit (of *X* number of bedrooms). It then calculated what it would cost the developer to finance construction at market interest rates, and recalculated it at a 5 percent rate. SHARP provided the difference between the two figures. In effect, then, SHARP was designed as a "shallow subsidy," to assist developments that could not be implemented by the private sector alone. For example, for a 2-bedroom unit that cost $60,000 to build, the Section 8 subsidy approached $8,000–$9,000 per year for certain developments; the SHARP subsidy, by contrast, might only provide $2,000–$2,200 per unit. Because it was a shallow subsidy program, SHARP required its developers to find supplemental means of ensuring their projects' viability.

In short, by reducing a developer's interest rate for project financing, SHARP lowered the effective cost of the mortgage loan and, in so doing, lowered the cost-based rent for *all* units to a level that local residents could afford to pay. State subsidies then further lowered the rent for the 25% low-income units that the MHFA required its developers to set aside.

Project Financing

In 1984, SHARP's first year of operations, the program received a $5 million appropriation from the state. This amount was increased to $13 million for 1985. In both years, the program supplemented its appropriation by raising funds through the sale of tax-exempt bonds to private investors. In addition to relying on the appeal of tax-exempt bonds, the MHFA used mortgage insurance, credit enhancement, and other "creative financing" strategies to make its bonds attractive to investors. The agency then translated the low interest rates it *paid* to its investors into below market interest rates it *charged* developers.

Projects selected for financing were awarded interest reduction subsidies for a maximum 15-year period, during which the subsidy was gradually diminished. Specific terms of both assistance and repayment were negotiated individually between the MHFA and each developer in accordance with the developer's projected cash flows. Importantly, though, the subsidy was not a grant, but a loan that was to be repaid once the project had been in operation for the 15 years (or less).

The Selection Process

SHARP selected its projects according to a set of firmly-established guidelines. Once each year there was a "competition" in which developers submitted projects, competing with one another for SHARP assistance. Out of approximately 60 submissions in the 1984 competition, 23 developments were chosen; there were 40 submissions in the 1985 competition, and 13 were chosen.

Projects submitted to the competition were scored and ranked according to a complex set of criteria. In designing these selection criteria, the EOCD and the MHFA asked the question, "What are the critical elements that make a project viable?" The resulting process brought together a variety of professional perspectives on these elements.

In developing the criteria, the MHFA and the EOCD initially disagreed about the balance between financial and social factors in determining the program's operations, although the two agencies agreed from the outset that both sets of criteria were necessary. They eventually agreed to set in place a scoring system prefaced by a group of threshold requirements that established the minimum viability of the project as a real estate venture. Both social and financial criteria were incorporated into the subsequent ranking system, and "gates" and cross-checks ensured that high priority conditions were adequately met. "All other things being equal," said one MHFA executive, "we would like to meet these important social goals, but our primary concerns have to be those of the lender."

In the threshold evaluation, projects were measured in terms of their acceptability as a credit risk and a real estate transaction. These terms included: (1) the quality of the project design, (2) the site, (3) the experience record of the development team, (4) the management company, and (5) the marketability of the project.

Applications that passed the threshold review were distributed within the MHFA for more intensive evaluations by each of the agency's functional subdivisions:

- Design and Technical Department—site specifications and architectural plans.
- Site Evaluation Department—site, market, and community needs.
- Mortgage Department—quality and history of development team, community impact, project's readiness to close, and amount of SHARP subsidy required.
- Equal Opportunity Department—affirmative action conditions.
- Management Department—qualifications of development team and management company.

Detailed evaluation criteria are contained in Exhibit 1.

At this second level of review, both social and financial criteria were given careful consideration. When the MHFA and EOCD designed the scoring system, they established cross-references for priority conditions, such as site, development quality, and zoning. These criteria were evaluated in both the set of initial threshold requirements and in subsequent scoring sections by different departments. This provided an opportunity for various professional viewpoints to be expressed on the merits of a particular aspect of the project. For example, the Design and Technical department and the Site Evaluation department might have evaluated different but equally important aspects of a project's site.

According to Ms. White, "the prime benefit of this strategy is that independent professional views are aired and the process remains open. Everyone on the staff knows what is going on, and the development teams understand the concept of the review process. The more eyes you have on a project, the more objective and defensible the review becomes."

After individual departments completed their reviews, the Mortgage department studied the resulting ranking order. "It's a bit like grading on a curve," noted Ms. White. "At this point, we could simply add up the scores, rank them, and fund from the top down . . . but we don't. Rather, the supervisory staff tries to flesh out discrepancies among the project scores, to make standards as uniform as possible. They ask: Did the scoring go properly? Did good projects fall out? Did bad ones rise?"

"For example, Mr. Jones may have four projects in one competitive round. If he has been given different scores by the Management and Development departments for certain criteria, the reasons for these differences need to be documented. It may be, for example, that he has experience in inner city rehabilitation but not in new construction, and the differences may therefore make sense. On the other hand, it may be that different individuals have done the scoring and may have judged him differently. Then, top management must be sure that there is consistency among the reviewers."

Following the departmental scoring, Mr. Siflinger, Ms. White, and selected Board members visited each of the proposed development sites to gain yet another angle on the project's desirability. Then, according to Ms. White, "we return to discuss the scoring with the Mortgage department and other departmen-

---

EXHIBIT 1 SHARP Project Selection Criteria

Projects that passed the set of initial threshold guidelines were competitively scored to determine how well they met certain policy objectives of the SHARP program. This review covered the following objectives:

A. Development Quality Goals: 10 points each, maximum of 50 points. Projects must score a minimum of 30 points and have an acceptable design score in order to remain in the competition.
   1. Design—the quality of the proposed design, including life-cycle costs and the treatment of special environmental conditions.
   2. Development Team—the record and capacity of the development team.
   3. Site—the suitability of the proposed site for housing. The presence of or plans for necessary utilities and amenities. Zoning and site control.
   4. Management—the prospective manageability of the development, the quality of the management plan, and the experience and capacity of the management agent.
   5. Marketability—the likely ability of the units to be marketed at the proposed rents.
B. Overall Impact Goals: 10 points each, maximum of 40 points.
   1. Community impacts—projects with demonstrable impacts upon the community, in support of local policies. Such projects include those which would rehabilitate a critical building in a business district, encourage additional nearby development, or promote investment in a locally targeted revitalization district. Evidence of local support would include contributions to the project from the community. Projects should not encourage displacement. Projects would ideally increase the supply of affordable housing in areas suffering displacement.
   2. Meet housing needs—projects which best meet the overall housing needs of communities in which they will be located (i.e., units of a certain size).
   3. Affirmative action—SHARP encourages developers to provide housing and job opportunities to minorities. Applications which provide vigorous affirmative action efforts, beyond the minimum requirements considered during the threshold review, will be given special preference.
   4. Readiness to move to construction—the readiness of proposals to move quickly to construction. Evidence of readiness would include proper zoning for the proposal, advanced design documents, building permits, etc.
C. Minimal SHARP Subsidy Goal: 10 points. Projects which require less than the maximum permitted amount of SHARP subsidy may earn up to 10 additional points. This criterion is consistent with a desire to generate the greatest level of housing production for the amount of SHARP funds authorized by the Legislature.

Maximum Total Points = 100

After the projects were scored and ranked, MHFA selected the highest ranked projects to receive subsidy awards, subject to consideration of two additional program objectives. Some of the selected projects should complement efforts to revitalize specific urban neighborhoods, and there should also be a reasonable distribution of selected projects throughout the State.

Following selection of a proposal for SHARP funding, the developer was invited to submit a full mortgage application for MHFA review. At this level of review, the technical feasibility of the accepted loan, and the value and marketability of the completed housing were evaluated.

---

tal staff. Evaluations are finely combed for inconsistencies. For example, in a given round, three inner city sites were proposed in one city. Two of them scored a '7' on a particular item, and the third scored a '5'. Yet the latter seemed to be better qualified. Why the discrepancy?''

"Ninety-nine percent of the time we (senior management, Board members, and the MHFA staff) come to a meeting of the minds on project scores, on problems such as this . . . through a good deal of negotiation, persuasion, discussion. In the 1 percent of the time we can't agree, Marvin and I can overrule the staff's evaluations, though we only do so when we have very compelling reasons to believe that their analysis is incorrect. The Board votes on the results and they, in turn, can overrule us.''

Developers were permitted to challenge the scores they received, beginning at the level of the Mortgage department and rising to the upper administrative levels of the agency, if necessary. As of 1985, however, not one developer had failed to agree with the staff's score after all challenges had taken place.

According to Ms. White, "Our atmosphere of open discussion and documentation of results is essential to maintaining the program's credibility and workability. The truth is that a group of individuals—developers, architects, planners, financial analysts—could probably sit around a table and come up with a list of projects that looks quite similar to the results of this elaborate scoring system. We know what kinds of qualities make a development successful . . . but we didn't want to make decisions behind closed doors. If you have a system that is open and fair, and if you show applicants the reasons for the weakness of their proposals and work with them to improve for the next round, they understand that you're not just being arbitrary.''

Political Issues

Political issues for SHARP assumed a variety of forms. One was that of community opposition to SHARP-assisted developments. In order to minimize such opposition, the MHFA advised developers to talk with local communities and their leaders before proceeding very far with their plans. As part of the site review process, the MHFA solicited the views of the mayor, chief executive, or selectmen of a project's locality. According to James Power of the MHFA Mortgage Department, in the second competitive round the MHFA had a 95 percent response rate from official community representatives, and letters from citizens and community groups (both favoring and opposing development) had increased many-fold over the first round when there was minimal community participation. "It is not so easy to bulldoze communities any more," said Mr. Power. "If a project doesn't have sufficient political support, it will have trouble all along the way.''

With this understanding, the MHFA encouraged developers to balance their interests with those of the businesses and residents in their prospective communities. Difficulties arose when, according to Mr. Power, "the business community wanted to see more multifamily housing, and the residents didn't want more growth in their neighborhoods." However, the MHFA—through its explicit procedures—was seemingly able to keep most political pressure at the level of "small-piece" politics. Said Mr. Power, "we try to help people to respect the system, and encourage cooperation with our goals."

When a project was politically and socially attractive, but financially weak, a second type of political issue arose. An example of this dilemma was a project in an economically depressed area, which had a minority development team and strong political support "from the local politicians all the way up to the EOCD and the legislature," but was deficient in terms of its architectural plans and its proposed rental scale.

According to Ms. White, "Everybody, including the MHFA, wanted this project to succeed, but it was simply not financially feasible. Marvin met with the EOCD, people from the governor's office, and the local elected officials—and told them very honestly that the project didn't meet the minimum standards; that it was not a prudent financial risk. They accepted the staff's recommendation, and most of the political pressure was diffused."

"The Board could have overruled us, but the last thing that it wants is a foreclosure. That's an embarrassment for everyone. So we worked with the project, and advised them of improvements. The developer reentered the competition this round, and his prospects are vastly improved."

The Future

Given SHARP's popularity in the legislature and the support it enjoyed from developers, there appeared to be no immediate possibility of major changes in the agency's operations. However, central to Mr. Siflinger's thinking as he reflected on the SHARP program's evaluation criteria and process, was the need to address the question of the kinds of changes that might be made to the project selection system to improve its functioning. He had approximately six months prior to the beginning of the third competition.

Questions

1. What are the key elements of SHARP's strategy?
2. What are the incentives for developers? Please be as specific as you can: If you were a developer, how would you make money on a SHARP project as compared to other potential projects?
3. What is your assessment of the project selection system? How does it help SHARP accomplish its goals?
4. What should Mr. Siflinger do?

Implementing a Management Control System

The value of understanding management control principles, and the concepts of structure and process that form the basis of management control systems, is in their application to real-world situations and problems. The ultimate goal is to develop management control systems that facilitate the improved operation of nonprofit organizations. The final section of the book discusses both the implementation of such systems and, by way of summary, the characteristics of a well-managed organization.

System Design and Installation

The structure of a management control system and the uses management can make of information flowing through such a system have been described in earlier chapters. This chapter focuses on problems involved in designing and installing a new or improved system. Technical aspects of systems design, such as the development of computer programs, coding schemes, forms, reports, and manuals are beyond the scope of this chapter. The emphasis here is primarily on behavioral considerations: the necessary preconditions for a successful installation, the problems that must be solved and ways of overcoming them, and the sequence of steps involved in developing and installing the system.

NECESSARY PRECONDITIONS

The introduction of a new management control system can be a traumatic experience for managers and others, particularly professionals, at all levels. A new system can change the way plans are made, alter the way performance is measured and judged, and establish new patterns of communication and discussion among managers. The information provided by the new system, while presumably better than before, frequently is quite different, and consequently takes some getting used to.

The problems involved in introducing a new system generally are more acute in a nonprofit organization than in a for-profit company. This is because a new system is likely to represent a greater degree of change from past practice in a nonprofit organization. In a for-profit company, many basic concepts are taken for granted: the use of accrual accounting, the relationship between results and personal responsibility, the importance of cost control, and so on. In this environment, a new system essentially is a refinement of existing concepts rather than the introduction of fundamentally new ones. By contrast, many nonprofit organizations have neither the rudiments of a satisfactory management control system nor the climate essential to the functioning of a good control system. Thus, the introduction of a new system often represents a substantial change in the established way of doing things.

These problems, incidentally, are much less severe in the installation of a task control system, as distinguished from a management control system. A new system for processing payroll or billing or tracking inventory, for example, may initially contain technical bugs that must be eliminated, but it is unlikely that such a system will cause serious organizational problems. If the system is technically well designed, organizational members are unlikely to resist its introduction; indeed, they will support it as soon as they recognize that it helps them do their jobs better.

Senior Management Support

The prime precondition for the successful installation of a new management control system is the active support and involvement of senior management. Ideally, senior management support should come from the chief executive officer (CEO). However, if the CEO is primarily involved in policymaking and relations with the outside world, then the necessary support can come from the principal deputy who in fact exercises most management authority. Without the support of one of these top people, the effort is unlikely to be successful.

Not everyone agrees with this precondition. There are those who believe that the impetus must come from operating managers, and that a new system cannot be installed successfully unless these managers request, welcome, or at least support it. In our view, however, the driving force for a new system must come from senior management. Moreover, in most organizations, operating managers are unlikely to embrace a new system voluntarily in advance of its installation, let alone be enthusiastic advocates of it. Although some people believe that a system development effort should not be initiated until a majority of operating managers are sold on the concept, we believe that if system designers (also referred to as systems designers) wait until that day arrives, they will be quite old.

Because of this need to encourage operating managers' involvement, senior management's support should include more than mere acquiescence. Although its time is precious, senior management nevertheless must be willing to allocate a significant amount of time and attention to the systems development effort. Senior management must understand the objectives and general concepts of the proposed system well enough to see its benefits, and must explain to operating managers how the system will help them as individuals, and help the organization as a whole. If roadblocks arise during the development and installation effort, senior management must be prepared to listen to the conflicting points of view and then make a decision that removes the roadblocks. In some situations, senior management must also do battle for the system with outside agencies that might otherwise prevent its adoption.

Example. According to George Turcott, then-associate director of the U.S. Bureau of Land Management, and the person responsible for the introduction of its highly regarded management by objectives (MBO) system, "The 'top dog' has got to get involved. Don't let the assistant director for administration do it. You have to get the line director or the associate to do it. It works. You've also got to have due process. You've got to have management reasonableness the whole way through and be a gentle tyrant."[1]

The systems designers should be convinced that this degree of senior management support will be forthcoming; otherwise, they should not begin a systems development effort for the organization as a whole. It is possible, however, that a management control system can be installed in some segment of the organization if it has the support of that segment's manager, and if there is reason to believe that senior management of the whole organization will at least acquiesce.

One way for senior management to convey its support for the new system is to allow operating managers time for involvement in the system's design. If such involvement inhibits operating managers' output, and hinders their ability to meet performance and evaluation measures, they will have no real incentive to participate. Thus, senior management must "invest" in the system design effort by allowing operating managers such time.

Support from Outside Agencies

A second precondition is that outside agencies who can influence the system either acquiesce in the development effort or are prevented by some higher authority from blocking it. Indeed, unless all influential agencies provide at least some support, the effort is unlikely to succeed.

> **Example.** In 1985, after many years of discussion, a new set of principles for accounting in the federal government was approved. The Department of the Treasury was assigned the task of implementation. The new principles were supported by the director of the Office of Management and Budget, representing the president, and by the Comptroller General of the United States. Unfortunately, the principles were not approved by the Appropriations Committee of the House of Representatives, which deals with budget requests. Since the Appropriations Committee had the "power of the purse," many federal agencies paid little attention to the proposed new system.

In many cases, outside agencies do not understand what a good management control system is. Furthermore, they cannot reasonably be expected to endorse the details of a new system until these details have been developed. The most that realistically can be hoped for in many situations, therefore, is that outside agencies will maintain an open mind and agree to support the system if it fulfills its promise.

To obtain this degree of acquiescence, all possible steps should be taken to minimize the impact of the system on outside agencies. This often requires a procedure called *crosswalking*, which we discuss later in the chapter.

---

[1] Paraphrased from an interview, reported in *GAO Review*, Fall 1981, pp. 23–27.

System Designers

A third prerequisite is an adequate staff to design and install the system. System designers should have not only the necessary competence and technical expertise, but they should also have a special set of relationships with the rest of the organization. System designers need ready access to senior management, either directly or through a single intermediary. If the system is to reflect the style of management that senior management wants, the system designers must discuss the proposed system personally with senior management.

System designers also must consult with operating managers, who are busy people, about their information needs. Few, if any, other staff specialists require a corresponding amount of an operating manager's time.

To do the job properly, the leader of the system design team ordinarily should work full time, or almost full time, on the project. Similarly, overall responsibility for the system project should be assigned to a single person. If it is divided, the pieces of the new system are unlikely to fit into a coordinated whole.

> *Example.* Since the mid-1970s, the U.S. Army has attempted to redesign its 60 separate accounting systems into a small family of standard systems. The project was expected to be completed in the 1990s at a cost of about $380 million. Originally, the project was the responsibility of a single manager, but in July 1986 the Comptroller of the Army reorganized the project and assigned responsibility to five separate managers. The U.S. General Accounting Office analyzed this situation and pointed out the likelihood that the necessary integration would be difficult to accomplish with such an arrangement. In response, the army again placed responsibility under a single manager.[2]

A systems design and installation effort requires a mix of skills not often found in a single person. It requires someone who can deal effectively with managers at all levels and who has broad understanding of the management control process; it also requires someone who pays careful attention to detail. A large fraction of the development work-hours are spent on tedious matters such as the exact definition of accounts, the design of forms, the preparation of flowcharts, and the writing of computer programs. Although most of this work can be delegated, the team leader must nevertheless have sufficient knowledge of the details to be able to detect mistakes that could affect the whole system.

Outside Consultants.　Since a small organization does not need a permanent full-time system designer, an outside consultant may provide the full-time attention in such an organization. Professional system design organizations have existed for several decades, and in the last 25 years all the large public accounting firms have created systems staffs. These firms employ many thousands of professionals.

There is a difference of opinion as to the circumstances under which an outside consultant should be employed. On the one hand, outside system designers can

---

[2] U.S. General Accounting Office, "Accounting Systems: Army's Efforts to Redesign Its Accounting Systems," GAO/AFMD-87-199, May 1987.

offer both general expertise and specific knowledge that may not exist within the organization. If an outside firm has done a good job of developing a system for one college, it is reasonable to expect that it can install a similar system in another college with little waste, even allowing for the inevitable differences between colleges. Furthermore, outsiders are often perceived by operating managers as unbiased: they are not associated with internal factions, they have no ax to grind, and they have a detached point of view. This objectivity, coupled with their expertise, means that outside consultants can add a degree of prestige and respectability to the effort.

On the other hand, outsiders are outsiders. The new system ultimately should be a vital part of the management process, and some people argue that consultants can never obtain the essential understanding of "how things really work" in an organization. Also, consultants may be expensive. Their daily cost is higher than that of insiders who might undertake the design and development task, although the higher daily cost may be offset by the fact that outsiders should require fewer workdays to develop the system.

In many situations, the organization has no choice. A mammoth systems effort, especially one undertaken to correct grave weaknesses in the current system, is likely to require more qualified people than are available within the organization, and more than can be recruited on short notice. Even under these circumstances, however, an outside firm should have only part of the responsibility for systems development and installation; in-house personnel must also be involved. Indeed, all good systems firms insist on such involvement. At some point in the system's development outsiders will depart; there then must be insiders who will regard the system as "theirs," and who will continue to work to ensure its success. This attitude can be generated only if in-house personnel are substantially involved in the system design effort.

A system designed by consultants, described in an impressive report, and then turned over to the organization for installation, is usually soon forgotten; competent systems firms are reluctant to accept an engagement if they believe this is likely to happen. Thus, although consultants do not want to do the whole job, neither do they want to walk away after completion of the design phase. They prefer to participate in the installation process also, departing gradually and only after the system is running smoothly.

Almost Enough Time

In a moderately large organization, at least two or three years usually will elapse between the time a decision is made to proceed with systems development and the date the new system becomes fully operational.[3] Even after this "cutover date,"

---

[3] The state of California Programming and Budgeting manual suggests that five years should be allowed for transition to a full PPB system.

much additional time is required to educate managers to obtain maximum use of the new information and to refine the system. A final precondition to a successful system, therefore, is that "almost enough time" be allowed between startup and the cutover date. The time allowed is never quite enough because there always is room for further refinements and additional training. But if enough time were allowed for all these worthy endeavors, the system never would go into operation.

PROBLEMS IN SYSTEM DESIGN AND IMPLEMENTATION

The system designer must address two sets of problems. First, there are technical problems associated with designing a management control system that best meets the needs of the organization, such as the choice of responsibility centers, the setting of transfer prices, and the design of budgetary and reporting processes that meet managers' needs. The relevant considerations for this set of problems were discussed in earlier chapters.

Second, there are problems that arise because the system designers are "change agents." That is, as a result of their efforts, managers will receive different information than before, and they quite likely will be expected to manage their responsibility centers differently. This latter set of problems includes: (1) the attitudes of managers toward the new system, (2) the information needs of operating managers, (3) the requirements of outside agencies, (4) the transition from the old to the new system, and (5) the need for education. We discuss each of these matters in this section.

Attitudes of Operating Managers

As discussed above, operating managers quite likely will resist efforts to introduce a new system, or at least they will be unenthusiastic about it. The reason is *not* that people resist all forms of change. A salary increase is a change, and no one resists a salary increase. Rather, people tend to resist a change when its effect on them is uncertain.

Even if operating managers perceive that the existing system is inadequate, it is nevertheless a system that they understand and are comfortable with. They have learned to interpret the information from the existing system, they know its virtues, and they also know and make allowances for its limitations. A new system means they must learn to interpret new information, and to recognize and allow for its limitations. Additionally, operating managers frequently are uncertain as to exactly how the new system will affect what they do. There is no way of removing this uncertainty completely because there is no way of communicating accurately to them what new sorts of demands will be made on them when the new system becomes operational. Although many operating managers are comfortable with computers and tend to want more rather than less technology, they are not necessarily comfortable with a new management control system.

Example. A management control system incorporating such conventional ideas as management participation in budgeting, variance analysis, and frequent review and revision of plans was described to 69 managers at naval field activities, and 85 percent stated that the system would be an improvement over that used currently. However, when they were asked to rate the acceptability of the proposed system on a scale of 1 (no) to 5 (excellent), the median rating was only 3.[4]

Concerns of Operating Managers. In addition to the effects of the new system itself, it is possible that studies made in developing the system may lead to changes in organizational relationships. A new system may raise questions such as the following: How will it change the way we conduct activities? Who benefits from it, and who is hurt by it? How will it affect relationships between superiors and subordinates? How will it affect the informal organization structure? Is it designed to help senior management at the expense of operating managers (or vice versa)? Will it provide information to politicians or other people outside the organization that can be used to hurt people inside the organization? Is it designed to help accountants or computer specialists, rather than operating managers?

A new system can change the style of management and the desired qualifications of managers. It may shift power from operating managers to senior management. Because it frequently requires understanding sophisticated techniques (such as variance analysis), it may require professionally educated managers rather than those qualified principally by experience. These tendencies, if perceived by the members of the organization, can easily lead to resistance. This is especially the case in a mature organization whose managers are interested primarily in job security.

Even if operating managers understand that the system will provide better information, their worries may not be allayed. Operating managers are part of an organizational hierarchy in which they have both subordinates and superiors. Operating managers may understand that the new system will provide them with more useful information about what their subordinates are doing, and therefore, improve control over their subordinates' efforts. This they welcome. By the same token, however, they may perceive that the new system provides better information to their superiors about what they are doing and, thus, gives their superiors an improved basis for controlling their efforts. They may not be so happy about this.

Managers who have previously collected information for their own use tend to resist a system in which information is collected, controlled, and furnished to them by an outside, impartial source. They may view their private data system as a source of power and prestige; other persons must come to them to obtain the information. Moreover, the value of information is that it reduces uncertainty. If a proposed system provides additional information that reduces the uncertainty of superiors about the performance of a subordinate's job, then the subordinate may

---

[4] W. J. Donnelly, *Budget Execution at Navy Shore Activities* (Monterey, Calif.: Naval Postgraduate School, 1980).

resist it. On the other hand, if the proposed system reduces the uncertainty about the tasks of others on the staff, the manager will support it. This leads to inevitable conflicts in proposing modifications to information systems, for the same proposal may be viewed as a threat by some people and as a valuable tool by others.

Educational efforts can reduce the force of these negative attitudes but probably cannot eliminate them. In general, negative attitudes will disappear only after the system has been in full operation for a substantial period of time. Nevertheless, system designers should not minimize the importance of this resistance; they must learn to live with it as best they can. They should be prepared for less than full cooperation in obtaining the information they need for systems design, and expect that some managers will attempt to delay the introduction of the system in the hope that, if delayed long enough, it may never materialize.

To overcome these delaying tactics, systems designers frequently must use the good offices of the senior manager who is sponsoring the system. They should understand, however, that in many respects, the installation of a new system is a political process. It involves pressure, persuasion, and compromise in proper proportions, as is the case with any important political action.

Aids to Changing Attitudes.   There are several ways to lessen hostility and resistance to a new system. First, to the extent that operating managers are convinced that the new system will benefit them, they usually will support it. Educational efforts should therefore stress the benefits, some of which are:

1. The system will help them do a better job, which will be perceived as such by their superiors.
2. The system will facilitate smoother coordination with other units.
3. The system will help them exercise better control over their subordinates.
4. The system will make life less hectic by providing an orderly, rapid flow of reliable information.
5. The system will permit improved resource allocation decisions (this is especially important in periods when budgets are tight).
6. The system will provide more equitable measurement of performance.

Second, the responsibility center concept should also be stressed. If too much emphasis is placed on programs and if the relationship of programs to personal responsibility is not made clear, operating managers are unlikely to perceive the new system as being helpful. They may instead regard it solely as a mechanism for reporting performance to top management; that is, as a "spy" system.

Third, designers should be aware of a natural bias that all aspects of the old system should be completely disregarded in the design of the new one. Operating managers will have much to learn about the new system, and to the extent that it incorporates familiar practices—particularly, familiar terms—it will seem less strange to them. System designers have their own preferred vocabulary; they should, however, be cautious about using these terms if those used in the old system are adequate.

One way of reducing hostility is to install the new system when operations are expanding. Operating managers will then associate it with increased budgets, whether or not such an association is warranted. If the system is installed in a period of contraction, it may be associated with the screw tightening characteristic of such periods, again without regard to whether such an association is warranted.

Identifying Information Needs

Notwithstanding the possible resistance described above, the system designer must work with operating managers to find out what information they need to do their job. At one time the recommended approach was for systems designers to ask managers what information they needed. In recent years, this approach has generally been abandoned because it was found that operating managers frequently do not know what information they need. In particular, they cannot visualize the nature of the new information that might be made available and therefore cannot comment on its usefulness.

Contributions from Operating Managers.   An alternative approach for the system designers is to find out by indirect methods what information the operating manager needs. In interviewing an operating manager, the systems designers focus primarily on the manager's job itself, the relationship of one responsibility center to another, the environmental influences that affect the work in the responsibility center, and so on. They also may, if for no other reason than courtesy, ask managers what information they need. The systems designers can then design a system that provides operating managers with the information they need. This, of course, is a difficult task since systems designers are not likely to be managers themselves, and sometimes will find it difficult to think of what an operating manager will need.

Operating managers can make important contributions to systems design. For one thing, they are the real experts on feasibility. When higher-level managers indicate a need for some information that cannot feasibly be collected, managers on the firing line can demonstrate the impracticability of collecting such information.

> *Example.* Senior management of a social service agency would like very much to have systematic, quantitative information on the results of an AIDS Awareness Program, but the social work supervisor may be able to demonstrate that reliable information on results cannot be obtained.

Discussions with operating managers are also necessary to test proposed reports, both those intended for the managers' use and those containing information that the managers generate. An operating manager can sometimes uncover mistaken assumptions about the availability of data or the exact nature of data.

Finally, discussions with operating managers are important—second only in importance to the support of senior management—to acceptance of the proposed system. To the extent that operating managers perceive that they are genuinely involved in the construction of the new system, their willingness to accept it is increased.

Using Existing Data. A study of what information gathering already goes on in the organization is also useful for uncovering operating information that can provide raw data for use in a management control system. It is much less expensive to develop management summaries from data prepared routinely for other purposes than to generate new data specifically for management control purposes. The system designer should be prepared to sacrifice some ideal type of management information if a slightly less desirable type of information can be obtained from existing sources. For example, if there are dozens of ways in which information on the status and flow of inventory can be summarized for management, the system designer is well advised to use a way that summarizes existing inventory records, rather than to insist on a change in the operating system for inventory control.

Line Needs versus Staff Needs. Information is needed both by operating managers for carrying out their line responsibilities and by staff people for planning and analyzing proposed programs and budgets. Unfortunately, there are inherent differences between the information needed by operating managers and the information needed by program planners. Program planners need approximate costs, full costs, and opportunity costs. Operating managers need more accurate cost information, direct costs, and historical costs. It may not be feasible to meet both sets of needs completely, so systems designers must help managers make compromises. As a general guide, the needs of operating managers should take precedence. If the system collects an inordinate amount of information that is useful only to planners, it tends to be regarded by operating managers as cumbersome and unnecessarily expensive.

Data Integrity. Data for the new system must be internally consistent and error free. Frequently, however, system designers fail to identify conditions that will lead to processing errors or inconsistencies. While generally not as severe as the somewhat apocryphal $1 million weekly paycheck, these conditions can easily cause problems with managers' confidence in a new system.

> *Example.* In an accounting system that was designed for a state government, the following situation was not completely allowed for by the system designers: A desk, ordered in April, was delivered in May; the voucher from the vendor was received in June, and the check sent in July. Since the voucher arrived in June, the expenditure report for May had already been produced. However, since the desk was delivered in May, it was not a June expenditure, and did not appear on that monthly report either. It was therefore thrown into the year-to-date column, with the result that managers were unable to track their spending in ways that were meaningful and familiar to them.[5]

---

[5] Paul R. Fisk, *Stalking the Wild Liability Date: New York's Safari to GAAP.* New York Case Studies in Public Management, The Nelson A. Rockefeller Institute of Government, State University of New York, and the Governor's Office of Employee Relations, no. 6, September 1984.

Requirements of Outside Agencies

As we noted above, influential outside agencies, especially those that have power of the purse, should at least acquiesce in the development of a new management control system. In an ideal world, this would not be a problem. Outside agencies should not need more information or different information than management needs; indeed, they should use the same type of information but in a summarized form. In the real world, however, an outside agency may not appreciate this fact. It may have become accustomed to receiving information in a certain format, and it may not view the new information as better. This is most likely when the new system is only a proposal on paper. Under these circumstances, the outside agency may specify that there is to be no change in the information it receives, and the systems designer usually must accommodate this demand.

It may be feasible to design an accounting system that meets both internal and external needs. If these needs are incompatible, however, two less desirable approaches are possible: crosswalking or operating a dual system.

Crosswalking. Crosswalking is a process used by federal organizations to translate management data into the format required by congressional appropriation committees. It is used by many state and municipal organizations for a similar purpose, and it is used by some organizations that are financed by grants to translate management information into the format prescribed by the grantor.

Crosswalking requires that information in the management accounts be reclassified in a manner prescribed by the outside agency. In some systems, this reclassification is exact; that is, detailed data exist in the accounts in a form that can be rearranged in the prescribed format. More commonly, the reclassification is only approximate; that is, some management accounts are subdivided and reclassified, more or less arbitrarily, to obtain the summaries required for outside agencies. Since the whole crosswalking operation is of no use to management, the organization devotes as little attention to it as possible.

Dual Systems. Some outside agencies insist that their preferred system of control also be used as the basis for control within the organization. Since their requirements may be fundamentally incompatible with the system that is best for management purposes, the consequence is often two systems that must be operated simultaneously. This can happen, for example, where an expense basis of accounting is obviously better for management purposes, but an outside agency insists on the obligation basis of accounting,[6] and prohibits the use of working capital accounts to reconcile the two bases. Some state legislative committees impose such requirements on state agencies.

When an organization is forced to operate a dual system, there is of course the problem of additional bookkeeping, but this is a relatively trivial matter. Much

---

[6] As we discussed in Chapter 11, the obligation basis of accounting focuses on contracts placed, and thus does not provide a record of expenses incurred classified by the responsibility centers that incur them.

more important is the problem of managerial behavior. Senior management wants operating managers to obtain their signals only from its management control system, but operating managers also receive signals from the system required by the outside agency. When these signals conflict, as can happen quite frequently, operating managers must decide which signal is more important. Since they know the outside system is associated with the agency that provides funds, they are quite likely to pay more attention to its signals than to those from the internal management control system.

> *Example.* Senior management in the Department of Labor wants operating managers to focus their attention on the information in the "Cost Center Detail Report." This report shows outputs, costs incurred in attaining them, and a comparison of actual and planned performance. The "Appropriation-Cost Center Report," which is specified by the Congress, requires that operating managers also think in terms of appropriations. The two approaches are not reconcilable, since the former report contains "unfunded" costs, that is, costs that have been incurred but are not included in the appropriation system.

Some people insist that a new system should not be pursued unless outside agencies are willing to accept information in the new format. They feel that the problems of operating a dual system are too formidable to make the attempt worthwhile. Such problems are indeed serious, especially if they include convincing operating managers to act in accordance with the signals given by the internal management control system. Others argue that attempting to build the prestige of a sound new system is preferable to the alternative of trying to manage solely with an unsatisfactory system prescribed by an outside agency. They hope that, as time goes on, the outside agency will appreciate the advantages of the new system and modify its requirements accordingly.

Transition from the Old to the New System

Except in rare circumstances, a new management control system usually replaces an existing system. (Even in a new organization, there is a tendency to install a system copied from another organization to get things going, even though this system may not be well suited to the new organization's needs.) The system designer has to decide how to make the transition from the old to the new system.

Some system designers advocate running a new system in parallel with the existing one until the bugs have been worked out. There are obvious advantages to doing this; in particular, it avoids the terrifying possibility of a new system bug that results in the permanent loss of vital data. On the other hand, there are situations where the time, cost, or complexity render a parallel run simply unfeasible.

> *Example.* In its attempt to convert from a cash to an accrual accounting system, New York state found that it did not have either the computer power or the staff to run two parallel accounting systems for the entire state. As a result, conversion to the new system entailed a complete switch in systems all at once.[7]

---

[7] Fisk, *Stalking the Wild Liability Date.*

Even if the systems run parallel, senior management should use information from the new system as soon as it becomes available and its accuracy is assured. Senior managers may be reluctant to do this because they do not feel comfortable with the new information. They should appreciate, however, that operating managers feel the same way, and that operating managers are unlikely to take the plunge until senior management breaks the ice.

Senior management's early use of the new system is especially important when a dual system is necessary. Senior management should use information from its management system exclusively; it should never use information from the system required by the outside agency, and it should insist that operating managers do the same. This is much more easily said than done, for it asks managers to give up something familiar for something strange.

If the old and new systems run parallel, the old system should be discarded as soon as the new system has been determined to be "bug free," even if managers are not completely comfortable with it. This does more than save bookkeeping costs. It prevents opponents of the new system from seeking ways to favor the old system over the new one. If the old system has disappeared completely, they have no choice but to use the new one.

Need for Education

All system designers are aware of the theoretical importance of a thorough educational program as a part of the system installation process. As a practical matter, however, they sometimes do not devote enough time to such a program. There are so many technical problems that must be solved by prescribed deadlines that often not enough time is left for adequate user education.

The preparation of manuals, explanations, sample reports, and other written material is a necessary part of the education process but is not the most important part. The most important part is to explain to managers how the new system can help them do a better job. System experts, who are the only ones with detailed familiarity with the new system, necessarily play a large role in these educational programs, but senior management also should be involved.

Above all else, operating managers must be convinced that the new system is in fact going to be used. System designers can say this, but they are, after all, only staff people. The only message that carries conviction comes from the words and deeds of senior management.

Within the limits of their knowledge about the new system, managers should teach each other about the system. That is, senior management should discuss the new system with immediate subordinates, who then convey the message to their subordinates, and so on. System designers can provide technical support at such meetings, of course, but it is preferable that the meetings be run by managers. Since teachers always also learn, this process aids in the education of those who are involved in it. Moreover, once the system goes into operation, even on a test basis, using the information that it generates is the best educational device available.

Danger of Overselling.   In their enthusiasm for the new system, system designers and the system's sponsors have a natural tendency to state its advantages more strongly than is warranted, and to minimize its limitations. A management control system aids management, but it does not lessen the need for management. Even with the best system, managers must analyze and interpret data. They must allow for its inadequacies, they must take into account much information not available in the system, they must use judgment in making decisions, and they must use behavioral skills in implementing these decisions. If a contrary impression is conveyed in the educational process, hardheaded managers who know the limitations of any system will be skeptical and regard the system effort as the work of impractical theorists.

STEPS IN SYSTEM DESIGN AND INSTALLATION

Details of the system design and installation process are set forth in many books. Assuming the preconditions listed earlier have been met, the eight main steps are as follows:

1. Diagnosis.   Analyze the objectives of the organization, the existing control system, and the existing organizational structure. This analysis may reveal defects in the existing system and the organizational structure, in part reflecting differences between senior management's objectives and the objectives as they are perceived by operating managers. Not much time should be spent defining objectives, however, for it is easy to get bogged down in semantics.

> *Example.* Although the objectives of a public school system are intuitively fairly obvious, the installation of a system in the Westport, Connecticut, school system was delayed for a year or more by attempts to elucidate objectives.[8]

2. Planning.   Develop a plan for system design and installation, including a timetable (preferably in the form of a PERT diagram or a similar scheduling device), an estimate of financial and other resources required, a statement of what units are to be responsible for each part of the development process, and a statement of the cooperation necessary from each part of the organization. Obtain senior management's approval of this plan.

3. Inventory of Current Information.   Examine the existing sources of information in detail. The use of information already collected for operating needs (e.g., payroll, inventory transactions) in the management control system involves little incremental cost.

---

[8] John Moore, "The Development of Long Range Plans in the Kirkwood School District (R-7)," Ph.D. dissertation, Harvard University.

4. Design. This involves the identification of responsibility centers, the development of a program structure, and decisions on the revenue, expense, and output elements that are to be incorporated in the system. These topics were discussed in earlier chapters. The most difficult problems are likely to be the development of a useful program structure and the choice of feasible output measures. In many cases, only crude output measures can be developed initially, and in some cases, no output measures at all are readily available. Nevertheless, the design effort should not be held up unduly because of these inadequacies. System design also requires determining where data will be collected, how it will be organized and stored, and how it will be presented on reports.

5. Test. Test the proposed structure and procedures, preferably in one part of the organization. Not only is this desirable for debugging, but it also provides a concrete example that is helpful in introducing the system and training people to use it.

6. Education. Develop and implement an education program for users of the system.

7. Implementation. If possible, initially run all or part of the new system concurrently with the existing system but, as soon as is feasible, eliminate obsolete parts of the existing system.

8. Documentation. Develop procedures and document all system flows and computer programs. Although sometimes slighted, documentation is extremely important because it makes the system independent of the designers, programmers, and operators.

Phased Installation

It is often desirable to install a system in stages, allowing enough time for managers to become accustomed to using the information available at one stage before proceeding to the next. There are three possible alternatives for such a phased effort: a pilot installation, a simple beginning that is later refined and expanded, and a stages approach.

Pilot Installation. The system can be installed initially in one part of the organization. Although information from the pilot study cannot be used to any great extent by senior management or headquarters staff for overall planning because it will not mesh with information provided by the system used in other parts of the organization, pilot information can be fully used by managers within the pilot segment. When this approach is used, senior management frequently "builds a fence" around the test site; that is, it exempts the test site from procedures and reports that are required of the remainder of the organization. To provide information about the organization as a whole, a unit may be created to "crosswalk" information from the new system to fit the requirements of the existing system. Such a unit should not be associated with the test site, however; all attention within the test site should be focused on the new system.

Once the system has been tested and debugged in the pilot installation, it can be installed in the rest of the organization. Depending on the nature and extent of the problems encountered in the test site, management may opt to install the system in a second test site, or it may move to an organizationwide installation.

Simple Beginning. A simple beginning contrasts with a pilot installation in that a scaled-down version of the final system is installed first, but it is installed throughout the organization. A simple beginning generally is used with a new system (i.e., one that does not replace an existing system). With a simple beginning, operating managers can assimilate the new information gradually. As such, a simple beginning avoids one of the principal causes of failure of a new system: excessive sophistication. When a system is too sophisticated, it can be time-consuming, contain many design errors, and pose difficulties in educating users.

Even though systems designers would like to demonstrate that they are familiar with the latest developments in their field, and even though they may feel open to criticism if they install a system that is less than the best, they should not bite off more than they or the organization can digest. If the basic elements of a system are installed first, refinements can be added as users become familiar with the essentials.

> *Example.* A state government installed a system for screening the validity of invoices submitted by physicians, pharmacists, and other health care providers under medicare and medicaid. Unfortunately, development of the computer programs for the system proved to be such a mammoth job that it required all the available programmers in the state, and the screening tests were so elaborate that, even with the largest computer, invoices could not be approved in time to permit payment of invoices by their due dates. Eventually, the system was scrapped.

Horror stories of overelaborate system installations are particularly common in developing countries. Designers have been known to develop systems as if they were to be operated and used by persons with technical and managerial skills typically found in American for-profit companies. With a simple beginning, both system designers and managers have the opportunity to learn and to grow with the system, and excessive costs for system development are often avoided.

Stages Approach. A simple beginning approach usually has only two phases: the simple one and the expanded one. By contrast, a system may be installed in several stages, permitting enough time for managers to become accustomed to using techniques available at one stage before proceeding to the next. This is called a *stages approach*. One feasible sequence is the following:

1. Prepare a budget by programs and responsibility centers, using out-of-pocket direct costs, with few service centers, and rough output measures. This usually does not require any changes to the accounting system.

2. Prepare a budget in the above terms, with perhaps improved output measures. This usually is possible since, once they have been using rough output measures for a while, managers have thought about improved ones.

3. Collect accounting information according to the new structure and educate managers in the use of this information. This usually requires changing the accounting system.

4. Continue development of better output measures.

5. Add sophistication by:

    a. Extending the service center concept and using transfer pricing.

    b. Collecting more detailed cost information, including cost allocations.

    c. Using a capital charge.

ROLE OF PERSONAL COMPUTERS

Widespread availability and use of personal computers (PCs) has done much to change the nature of system design and installation in both for-profit and nonprofit organizations. The ability to gather and process data within a single responsibility center, and to download data from a mainframe computer for analysis at the responsibility center level, has done much to assist managers in obtaining management control information in a more timely and action-oriented manner than had been possible previously. Personal computers offer several advantages to managers: lower cost information, quicker introduction of new applications, and more rapid processing turnaround (i.e., from data entry to report preparation).

At the same time that personal computers provide managers with potentially easier and less-expensive access to good management control information, they have also created their own set of system design and installation issues. These issues arise in the context of a set of information requirements that, for most organizations, can be classified into three categories: structured, semistructured, and unstructured. Each category can be further subdivided in terms of activities corresponding to strategic planning, management control, and task control discussed in Chapter 1. The resulting information requirements are shown in Exhibit 16–1.

As Exhibit 16–1 suggests, the kinds of computing power an organization needs will vary depending on how it sees its information requirements. Specifically, as one goes from the top left corner, where mainframes and minicomputers generally are most appropriate, both down and to the right, the value of a personal computer becomes higher and higher. That is, the more strategic the analyses that are undertaken, and the more unstructured the data, the greater value of a PC.

As their organizations grow in size and sophistication, senior managers in many nonprofit organizations need to engage in more management control and strategic planning activities using relatively unstructured information. As a result, they increasingly are relying on personal computers. Their flexibility and instant turn-around time allow managers to play with assumptions, tease them out, and ana-

---

EXHIBIT 16–1   Information Requirements by Type of Activity

Information Requirements	Type of Activity		
	Task Control	*Management Control*	*Strategic Planning*
Structured	Accounts receivable General ledger	Budget analysis (engineered) Short-term forecasting	Case mix forecasts ROI analysis
Semistructured	Client/patient scheduling and billing Cash management	Variance analysis Budget preparation (discretionary)	Merger and acquisition analysis Marketing analysis
Unstructured	Cost analysis	Client/case mix analyses	Product line planning

---

lyze the resulting implications. Generally, in the strategic and unstructured types of analyses, the greater flexibility and more rapid turnaround time of a personal computer outweigh the power advantage of a minicomputer or a mainframe.[9]

CONCLUDING COMMENT

We end this chapter with a comment by Aaron Wildavsky, one of the most perceptive observers of the nonprofit scene. The quote is taken from the concluding section of his review of Brewer's *Politicians, Bureaucrats, and the Consultant,* a description of tremendous failures in attempts to install new systems:

> Nothing anyone says will stop people from trying an available product; so a few rough rules may be offered to guide government officials contemplating the installation of information systems.
>
> First, the rule of skepticism: no one knows how to do it. As Brewer's account suggests, the people most deceived are not necessarily the clients but may well be the consultants. Their capacity for self-deception, for becoming convinced by listening to their own testimony, should never be underestimated. Thus it may be less important to discover whether they are telling the truth than whether the truth they think they are telling is true. Unless the idea is to subsidize employment of social scientists, the burden of proof should be on the proposer.
>
> Second, the rule of delay: if it works at all, it won't work soon. Be prepared to give it years.
>
> Third, the rule of complexity: nothing complicated works. When a new information system contains more variables than, shall we say, the average age of the officials who

---

[9] For a discussion of the use of a personal computer in strategic planning in a health care context, see Stephen D. Reiff, "Evaluating Strategic Change Using the Microcomputer," *Healthcare Financial Management*, June 1987.

are to use it, or more data bits than anyone can count in a year, the chances of failure are very high.

Fourth, the rule of thumb: if the data are thicker than your thumb (skeptics—see rule 1—may say "pinky") they are not likely to be comprehensible to anyone.

The fifth rule is to be like a child. Ask many questions; be literal in appraising answers. Unless you understand precisely who will use each data bit, how often, at what cost, relevant to which decisions they are empowered to make, don't proceed.

Sixth is the rule of length and width, or how to determine whether you will be all right in the end by visualizing the sequence of steps in the beginning and middle. Potential users of information should be able to envisage the length of the data flow over time, that is, who will pass what on to whom. If there are more than three or four links in the chain it is likely to become attenuated; data will be lost, diverted, or misinterpreted. The width of the chain is also important. If the data go to more than one level in the organization, the chances that they will be equally appropriate for all are exceedingly slim. The longer the sequence of steps, the wider the band of clientele, the less likely the information is to be of use.

Seventh, the rule of anticipated anguish (sometimes known as Murphy's Law): most of the things that can go wrong, will. Prepare for the worst. If you do not have substantial reserves of money, personnel, and time to help repair breakdowns, do not start.

Eighth, the rule of the known evil. People are used to working with and getting around what they have, they can estimate the "fudge factor" in it, they know whom to trust and what to ignore. They will have to re-estimate all these relationships under a new information system, without reasonable assurance they will know more at the end than they did at the beginning.

Ninth comes the most subtle rule of all, the rule of the mounting mirage. Everybody could use better information. No one is doing as well as he could do if only he knew better. The possible benefits of better information, therefore, are readily apparent in the present. The costs lie in the future. But because the costs arrive before the benefits, the mirage mounts, as it were, to encompass an even finer future that will compensate for the increasingly miserable present. Once this relationship is understood, however, it becomes possible to discount the difficulties by stating the tenth and final rule: Hypothetical benefits should outweigh estimated costs by at least ten to one before everyone concerned starts seeing things.[10]

Sadly, these rules have been violated countless times; nevertheless, they remain as valid today as they were in 1973, minicomputers and personal computers notwithstanding.

SUMMARY

The U.S. General Accounting Office, based on its experience in reviewing many system development projects, has described several factors that it considers critical for developing automated accounting and financial management systems (and, one would expect, most other management control systems as well). These provide a good summary of the thrust of this chapter.

---

[10] Aaron Wildavsky, *Science* 28 (December 1973), pp. 1335–38.

1. *Overall plan.*   There should be an overall system plan that establishes target deadlines, identifies the necessary resources, and designates who will be responsible for each part of the plan.
2. *Management commitment.*   Senior management must be willing to supply the skills of senior managerial and technical people, plus other resources as needed. Financial managers, system users, and others must be prepared to spend considerable time away from their normal duties to develop detailed operating requirements for the system. To assure senior management support, the GAO recommends the establishment of an Automated Data Processing (ADP) steering committee composed of senior managers who know the agency's information needs.
3. *Contracting process.*   When the system development and implementation task is contracted with a private consulting firm, the government agency must have skilled, competent people carry out the contracting function.
4. *Basic features.*   Although a number of basic features should be incorporated in the accounting and financial management system, the agency also should recognize that not everything will or should be computerized—some things will be done by people. A good systems project must deal with manual as well as automated processes.
5. *Systems methodology.*   This is a formal, structured approach to systems development that outlines and describes sequentially all phases, tasks, and requirements for a successful project. It ensures that each development phase is carefully planned, controlled, and approved; that it complies with standards; that it is adequately documented; and that it is staffed by competent people. When different segments of the system overlap, the steering committee must be sure that they are well integrated.
6. *Target dates.*   Target dates should be established for all phases, and regular written progress reports should be required. Everyone must recognize, however, that target dates occasionally must be changed. Nevertheless, as the project proceeds and greater understanding of its scope and complexity evolves, target dates should become more precise and reliable.
7. *Functional requirements.*   Functional requirements describe the accounting and financial management jobs that the system is to perform, the agency's information requirements, the operating environment, and a plan for developing the necessary computer programs. The study of functional requirements often is the most difficult part of a project because it asks specialists in three disciplines—management, accounting, and systems analysis—to communicate effectively with each other.
8. *Documentation.*   No matter how well and carefully a system is designed, it is of little value if inadequately documented. Documentation requirements include user manuals; operations manuals; system, subsystem, and program technical specifications; and program listings.
9. *Up-to-date technology.*   Projects should make optimal use of proven technology, not just in hardware but in software engineering and development. Although senior management and financial officials are not expected to be

technological experts, they should try to gain some awareness of recent innovations. However, they also should not be overly optimistic about present technology, which, despite some promises, rarely can assure that everything one would like to know is included in a single data base. Moreover, equipment should not be acquired before system requirements are clearly specified.

10. *Training.* Three primary groups need training: the system's information users, accountants, and operators. Moreover, some people's jobs will be changed, but since it is impossible to know in advance whose and to what extent, training may help mitigate some of the tension associated with the unknown.

11. *Independent testing.* The system—including documentation, equipment, and software—should be tested by a group independent of the developer, which, for complex systems, is a very formal process. Retesting should take place until all problems are satisfactorily resolved.

12. *System operation.* An agency should not try to place a new system in operation until all significant problems identified by testing have been corrected. To do otherwise is to risk losing the support of staff members who revert to manual processes. A parallel conversion, while appropriate in some instances, is not always necessary and can be quite costly and disruptive.

13. *Quality assurance review.* In long-term projects a fresh look by someone who has technical knowledge but is not close to the project can be helpful in spotting problem areas, omissions, or better ways of accomplishing the system's tasks. Typically, the reviewer should be equal to or higher in rank than the project manager, and must be able to exercise independent judgment similar to that of an inspector general.[11]

SUGGESTED ADDITIONAL READINGS

Austin, Charles J. *Information Systems for Hospital Administrators.* Ann Arbor, Mich.: Health Administration Press, 1991.

Boer, Germain. *Decision Support Systems for Management Accountants.* Montvale, N.J.: National Association of Accountants, 1987.

King, John L., and Edward L. Schrems. "Cost-Benefit Analysis in Information Systems Development and Operation," in Freemont J. Lyden and Ernest G. Miller, *Public Budgeting: Planning and Implementation,* 4th ed. (Englewood Cliffs, N.J.: Prentice Hall, 1982), Chap. 7, pp. 221–42.

McFarlan, F. Warren, ed. *The Information Systems Research Challenge Proceedings.* Boston: Harvard Business School Press, 1984.

Mowitz, Robert J. *The Design of Public Decision Systems.* Baltimore, Md.: University Park Press, 1980.

---

[11] U.S. General Accounting Office, *Critical Factors in Developing Automated Accounting and Financial Management Systems* (Gaithersburg, Md.: GAO, January 1987).

CASE 16–1   United Way*

In September 1986, Mark Mechanic, the director of a university computer center in upstate New York, was working at his desk when the phone rang. On the other end was Paul Powers, an executive in charge of evaluation at the local United Way. After some initial pleasantries, Paul began to describe a problem he was facing.

> Mark, I just came from a meeting with the directors of the various neighborhood agencies that we fund. They really unloaded on me. Paul Williams started complaining about the amount of paperwork he has to fill out. He says he has to do ours, then fill out still different forms for his other funding sources. Some of the agencies have money from the Federation of Settlements and Neighborhood Centers, and some even have private sources. Anyway, once he started it, the thing really began to snowball. Everyone in the place jumped on the bandwagon. The only way I could restore order was to promise them that I would look into a consolidated information system.
>
> At first the whole thing seemed like just another problem. But after thinking about it, I decided that they have given me a real opportunity. For years we have been trying to get good performance data. Here is a chance to do some real evaluation. The thought of comparing every center on the same set of objective measures turns me on. It would finally be possible to base funding on performance. We would have the capacity to compile longitudinal data and measure changes over time. Everyone wins: they cut out paperwork, and we get real control.
>
> I checked with some of the other funding agencies. They know it will be expensive, but they all are interested. The question is how to develop a system. We figured you are the best man we could contact for advice. You know some of their problems. What do you say? Can you help us out?

Mark Mechanic indicated that he was very interested. A week later he had his first meeting with the directors of eight neighborhood centers and executives from three funding agencies. The directors all had similar problems. Most of their agencies had evolved from local settlement houses to neighborhood centers that provided a number of services to local residents. Services varied widely but usually included housing, employment, recreation, food, clothing, child care, health services, and referrals and transportation to other agencies. Some centers had as few as 5 caseworkers; other centers had as many as 30. Each had its own unique variety of funding sources, and each was inundated with paperwork.

During the discussion of a potential information system, Mechanic explained what might be done to reduce the paperwork. He pointed out that the current narrative reports written by the caseworkers and the wide variety of forms could be reduced to several standardized forms. From the information on the standardized forms, the computer could produce summaries that would eliminate 80 per-

---

* This case was prepared by Professor Robert E. Quinn, Department of Public Administration, Graduate School of Public Affairs, State University of New York, Albany. Copyright © 1987 by Robert E. Quinn.

cent of the paperwork the directors were doing. The presentation generated considerable enthusiasm, and it was agreed that Mechanic's staff would begin to wade through the numerous forms used in each of the agencies.

After three months, the computer staff had conducted over 100 interviews with people from all levels of the eight agencies and had gathered 190 forms that were currently in use. For the next two months they sorted and analyzed the forms. By the end of five months the computer staff members felt that they had a rough understanding of information needs and were ready to begin designing a basic set of forms. In order to start that process they scheduled interviews with each of the eight directors. The purpose of the interviews was to present their initial conclusions and to determine the exact information needs of the directors. By the end of another month, the directors each had been interviewed at least twice. Shortly thereafter, Mechanic met with the members of his staff. At one point in the meeting the following discussion took place:

Mechanic: Up until now you have all been enthusiastic. All of a sudden you seem discouraged. What happened?

Bill Meadows (project director): Mark, the directors of the centers are idiots. They don't understand the first thing about information systems.

Mechanic: Idiots! What do you mean?

Meadows: We go in and ask them what information they need. They get a shocked look on their face, like they never thought of such a question. They hem and haw. We try a different tack and ask them what decisions they have to make. Again they are shocked. They can't even tell us what decisions they have to make. They have no vision of what an information system is or what it might do for them. No matter how many times we go back, they still cannot deal with the questions we need answered. Whenever we are around, the directors disappear.

Mechanic: If they disappear, what do you do?

Meadows: Well, it is sort of a tacit agreement. We don't bother them with questions and they don't bother us with objections. We show them the forms and they look at them and say O.K.

A Financial Break

Two months after Mechanic's discouraging conversation with Meadows, he received some great news. A local foundation had agreed to provide two years of funding for the project. Although the foundation's board had expressed concern about the amount of money that Mechanic requested, it had agreed to provide $150,000 a year for each of two years. It was anxious to see the project developed as a pilot that might later be transferred to cities all over the country. The arrangement not only covered costs but also took the burden of funding completely off the shoulders of local agencies. Paul Powers and other local officials were elated. Mechanic decided that the money and the new enthusiasm would provide the energy necessary to resolve all the problems that he had been encountering. Costs of transferring from a manual to a machine system, financial breakeven points, and numerous other money issues suddenly were eliminated. The new situation provided something for everyone. Mechanic, assured of a major success, was ready for anything.

A Fateful Memo

Several months later all the forms were completed and the system was ready for a trial run. Mechanic met with the directors to get their responses to the forms and to select several sites for the pretest. The meeting began with an explanation of six basic forms and how they would be used. When Mechanic finished his explanation he invited questions, but there were none. He knew that there had to be questions, so he pressed the group. Finally, one of the directors raised his hand and asked a question that was totally unrelated to the material that had been presented.

> You developed all these forms but what about confidentiality? How are the rights of the clients going to be protected? What if the police want the information that is on these forms?

The question ignited the group. For the next hour Mark Mechanic was peppered with questions about the system and what it would do. Finally he agreed to describe the system on paper. He would send them a memo and then meet with them again.

The next week he sent a memo (Exhibit 1) to the eight directors. Attached to the memo was an example of the sort of summary report Mr. Mechanic envisioned (Exhibit 2). This contrasted sharply with the narrative information most agencies now kept on their clients (Exhibit 3).

Trying Times

Several weeks passed with absolutely no response to the memo. Members of the computer staff began to complain that the directors of the centers were less cooperative than ever. Mechanic was baffled. He felt that the memo would clearly indicate the benefits that could be derived from the system, and thought that it would clear things up once and for all.

During the next six months, Mechanic spent his time in an endless series of meetings. Getting the pretest started turned into a monumental task. Three centers were initially involved in the pretest, but there was so much resistance from the other five that a decision was made to involve all the centers. However, even with every center involved, things kept getting worse. Finally at one meeting Mechanic reached his breaking point. Paul Williams, one of the directors, was complaining about confidentiality when Mechanic angrily interrupted.

> I am tired of hearing that nonsense! Every meeting for the last six months someone has stood up to complain about confidentiality and then the rest of you jump in to beat the same horse. Paul, I've been in your place a dozen times. Files on clients are lying all over the place. The file drawers are not locked at night and a kid could get through the front door of the center with a hairpin. Do you call that protecting confidentiality? Your

---

EXHIBIT 1   Memorandum from Mark Mechanic to Agency Directors

---

Subject: Nature and Purpose of the Information System

The purpose of this memo is to provide a summary statement of what the computer system will be like when it reaches completion. Provided here is an overview of the system, and a discussion of the output and how it might be used.

The purposes of the computer-based information system are (1) to provide relevant data which will permit an agency to conduct an internal audit of its overall performance and (2) to supply summarized data to an analytical system to monitor the community change process. This audit, made possible via data generated by the system, will provide to administrators the necessary insight to evaluate properly the agency's performance and to assist in making needed management decisions. The system's data can provide measurement information to show if objectives are being satisfactorily achieved. As a result of this matching of the system's data with objectives and goals, agency management can better determine if it is effectively serving its clients.

At its final state of evolution, the information system will revolve around the use of eight optical scanning forms. Each form, when properly completed, will touch on a particular aspect of a client's involvement with any given agency. This involvement will range from registration with the agency, to service rendered on an individual one-to-one basis, to services rendered on a group basis, to a change in status of the client in relation to the agency. Also recorded on the forms will be information which will indicate which worker completed the form, the time spent in providing a particular service, when the service was rendered, and other performance data on workers and the whole agency.

Early in the process of installing the system in a specific agency, employees will be taught how to use the basic forms properly. During this training, the importance of recording accurate data will be strongly emphasized and closely checked. Also in the early stages, representatives from the Computer Center will assist in the creation of a filing system (for every form turned in there will also be a carbon copy that is filed in the agency). They will also arrange for the proper pickup and delivery of forms for computer processing.

At regularly scheduled intervals the completed original copies of the forms will be sent to the computer center for recording. The information that is then generated will be stored on magnetic tapes. Computer printouts of the data will be made available to the participating agency. As a result of its confidential nature, the data will not be made available to any unauthorized persons. Use of the information retrieved from the systems will be controlled exclusively by the agency and its board. Agency printouts of overall agency operations will be available on a monthly, quarterly, and yearly basis along with a weekly printout of new client registration. These performance printouts include vital summaries of particular aspects of the operations which have priority to the agency's administrators.

Agency executives, the Community Action Commission, and the United Way will be able to assess the following items with the existing output:

1. The number of individuals and families registered by each agency.
2. The major needs of these families within the following categories: housing, employment, recreation, food, clothing, child care, health, legal, knowledge and learning, income, and counseling.
3. Basic information on all the individuals registered, such as whether they are employed, their age, education, place of birth, race, marital status, occupation, and income. These categories will be summarized by agency as well as by individual.
4. The number of referrals made by an agency to any other agency, the reason for referral, how long it took, the mode of referral, disposition of referral once a client gets to the intended agency, and the gross number of clients referred to any agency.
5. The number of clients directly served by an agency, the type of service given, and the length of contact.
6. The number of people receiving casework services. The data given basically will be the number of times served, the date, and the problems.
7. The number of groups and organizations and their general characteristics.
8. The number of meetings held by a group, the number present, the subject of the meeting, and several other characteristics.

The data produced by the system may be analyzed from three perspectives. First, individual workers can use it to get a quick profile of their clients. Second, the information can be used by heads of agencies for internal management decisions. Third, funding agencies can use the data for comparison of agencies or programs in making evaluations and decisions as to allocation of funds.

EXHIBIT 2 Example of Comparative Data Available to Funding Agencies

	Center 1	Center 2	Center 3	Center 4	Center 5	Center 6	Center 7
Total clients for the year to date	275	170	233	350	301	170	320
Total new clients	75	10	78	100	70	60	53
Total new households	59	8	61	83	65	51	42
Total direct services given	501	316	408	407	396	190	456
Total referrals made	78	61	98	105	129	70	62
Time consumed per unit of service	1.05	1.17	.55	1.01	1.30	1.25	1.09
Average units of service per staff member by day	8	3	6	8	7	3	7
Average cost per unit of service	4.59	8.60	5.37	5.05	4.68	7.43	5.00
Expenditure to date	$11,102	$14,350	$10,975	$9,996	$11,107	$12,801	$10,607

EXHIBIT 3 Typical Narrative Report Written by Caseworker

2/13

William Johnson came in today. I spent one hour of counseling time with him. We talked about family problems and jobs.

3/10

William Johnson—He still has no job. Family planning—referred.

3/17

William Johnson—Talked to his wife—She is the tall one from Seven Hills—They need food stamps.

4/4

William Johnson—He worked as a janitor this week but lost the job. He got his wife a job. I should tell Mary about that.

5/1

William Johnson—They are still not getting food stamps. I said I would call Gus. His wife is sick. I referred to Nancy. He is still not working.

people can't find files when they need them. Half the workers don't keep their narratives up to date. Most of you people can't get a single accurate statistic on what you are doing. The computerized system will be ten times safer than the information you have on clients now.

Mechanic's outburst was met with a long silence. A few minutes later the meeting ended, and people began to leave. Paul Powers stayed behind.

Powers: Mark, it seems pretty discouraging, doesn't it?

Mechanic: Paul, it is one of the most frustrating experiences I have ever had. These people are simply not rational. Their arguments about confidentiality simply do not make sense.

Powers: Do you think they're really worried about confidentiality?

Mechanic: That's all they ever talk about.

Powers: Mark, that's just a smoke screen. You have these people terrified. Most of them have no idea of what a computer can do. They have been totally uninvolved in developing those forms because they have no idea what their information needs are. Your people come in and talk in a language they can't begin to understand. Your people treat them as if they are idiots, and they resent it.

Mechanic: You mean they are scared because they don't want people to think they're dumb?

Powers: No. That's only a small part of the problem. The real problem emerged when you sent them that memo. When they realized what the computer system would produce, they were shocked. What terrifies them is evaluation. For years they have been able to get their funding by showing pictures of crippled kids in rags. Now you are actually going to assess what they are doing. Baby, those people are uptight.

Mechanic: I guess that would explain what's happened during the pretest. It's been a disaster.

Powers: What do you mean?

Mechanic: At most of the centers the caseworkers either have been ignoring the forms or complaining continually. Some insist on maintaining a narrative system and complain that the forms are a double burden. Some people wait until the reports are due and then simply fill out all the forms exactly the same way. Standardization is also a problem. Each center seems to have its own language. The same service gets coded completely differently at any two centers.

Powers: Are the directors giving you any support at all?

Mechanic: No. Most of them have completely withdrawn. We really were excited when we generated the computer printouts for the first reporting period. When we delivered them for the second period, our people were shocked. The envelopes from the first reports weren't even opened.

Powers: Like I said, it is pretty discouraging.

Mechanic: Discouraging! Paul, we have three years and $360,000 tied up in all this. What do I do next?

Questions

1. List the incentives of each of the key participants (or groups of participants). How, if at all, does this contribute to your understanding of the problems that developed?
2. What kinds of barriers arose to a successful implementation of the new system? Why did they arise?
3. What needs to happen now? Who should take the initiative?
4. If you were Mr. Mechanic, what would you do differently next time?

CASE 16–2   North Suffolk Mental Health Association*

Burt Lowe wondered what action he could take to address more effectively clinicians' dissatisfaction with the management information system (MIS) at North Suffolk Mental Health Association (NSMHA). Although many of the administration's objectives for the MIS had been met and some progress had been made in addressing clinicians' dissatisfaction, it was slow and time-consuming. Burt felt that the long-range success of the MIS depended upon its ability to meet the needs of clinical personnel, as well as those of central administration.

NSMHA was a mental health service delivery network serving 146,000 people in the Boston Harbor area. As Director of Planning and Evaluation, Burt Lowe was chiefly responsible for the development and implementation of the MIS at NSMHA. Since the inception of the MIS in 1977, he had worked with personnel at all levels of the organization in attempting to adapt it to their needs. The system had proven itself to be a useful tool for billing and government reporting purposes, but problems existed in its application to clinical work and program planning.

Some staff complained that the MIS was being used to demand unreasonable levels of productivity. Others protested that too little emphasis was placed on nonbillable activities affecting the quality of patient care. Still others objected to the use of the MIS on philosophical grounds, and questioned the reliability and usefulness of the information which it produced. Burt was aware of these complaints and wanted to remedy the problems related to clinical management and use of the MIS.

History and Operations of NSMHA

NSMHA evolved from the North Suffolk Child Guidance Clinic, which began operations in East Boston in 1959. It operated four outpatient counseling centers and other mental health agencies serving the East Boston/Winthrop, Revere, Chelsea, and Beacon Hill/West End of Boston areas. They served populations of 13,000 to 60,000 people with clinical staffs ranging from 16 to 28 full-time equivalents (FTEs) and administrative and support staffs ranging from 3 to 5 FTEs. The populations of two of these areas were predominantly Italian and of low socioeconomic level and had recently absorbed a large influx of transients. The population served by the third clinic was characterized by a high degree of unemployment, poverty, and social distress. Fifteen to 20 percent of its residents were Puerto Rican, and the center offered special programs to them. A larger number of young transients and deinstitutionalized chronic mental patients inhabited the

---

* This case was prepared by Stanley Alexander and Professor Martin P. Charns, Boston University School of Management. Copyright © 1981 by Stanley Alexander and Martin P. Charns. Used by permission. Distributed by The Accounting Curriculum Center, Boston University School of Management.

area served by the fourth clinic. Besides the four counseling centers, NSMHA also operated three day-treatment programs, an emergency services program, and several residential programs. Although the Massachusetts Department of Mental Health (MDMH) funded most of its clinical positions under a partnership agreement, NSMHA hired its own administrative and support staff. All staff were employed on a salaried basis, and no direct billing was done by clinical personnel at the centers. The Director of Clinical Services, Dr. Muriel Weckstein, supervised all clinical activities. The NSMHA central administrative office had final authority in all financial, operational, and personnel matters. In practice, however, most of this responsibility was delegated to administrative coordinators at the operating units. An organization chart is contained in Exhibit 1.

As a part of its contractual arrangements, NSMHA was obligated to report on its activities to MDMH personnel who oversaw the delivery of mental health services in the Greater Boston Area. NSMHA also was funded through federal grants and reimbursement mechanisms and had continuing reporting responsibility to federal authorities.

NSMHA could not refuse treatment to anyone requiring it. NSMHA programs, therefore, generally treated the sickest and neediest portions of the population, i.e., those rejected by private agencies because of an inability to pay or requiring too much case management to make their treatment cost-efficient. Burt Lowe felt that the organization had insufficient resources to serve all of its populations adequately, but attempted to spread its services as far as they would go.

Development and Implementation of the MIS

The need for some sort of information-gathering mechanism at NSMHA first was recognized by Eugene Thompson when he took over as business manager in 1976. At that time no budget or billing system existed. Thompson attempted to implement some rudimentary plans to organize these functions, as well as to gather statistical information regarding the delivery of services.

In 1977 Jim Cassetta had been installed as the Administrative Director for NSMHA, taking over direct responsibility for management of daily operations. Thompson had been promoted to Executive Director and his responsibilities had shifted to encompass longer-range planning and development efforts. He had explicitly incorporated responsibility for the development of a service data reporting and billing system into his role, however. His goal at that time was to develop a comprehensive system which would address all aspects of care provided by NSMHA in a useful and cost-effective manner. To this end he met with Burt Lowe, who at that time was a doctoral candidate in Clinical Psychology at Miami University of Ohio and was serving an internship in Massachusetts, split between clinical activity at a NSMHA clinic and the study of management information systems at the MDMH.

Implementation of the management information system was begun in the spring of 1977. The overall plan called for testing, debugging, and establishing the system by focusing on one unit and then successively implementing its use in other units

EXHIBIT 1   Organization Chart

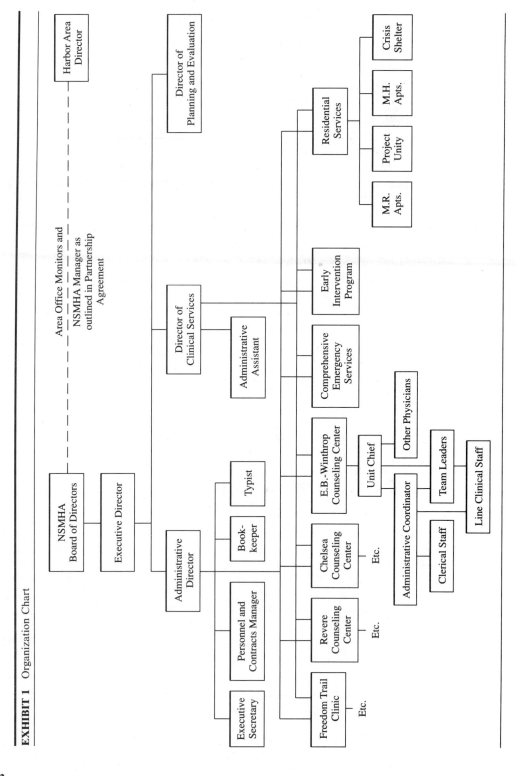

via the same process. According to Burt Lowe, adequate planning, phased implementation, and administrative support were key elements in the implementation process.

At the beginning of 1977, the existing service data collection system consisted of monthly service logs submitted by staff. These logs recorded face-to-face direct consultation services. There was about 40 percent compliance with the mandate to submit the logs, and of those logs received, the majority were two to six months late. Central administration also felt that much activity was going unreported, even by those staff who submitted logs. However, there was no way to determine this, since no quality control mechanisms existed.

Much of the impetus for more systematic data collection came from the need to maximize third-party reimbursements. It was estimated that up to 50 percent of potential reimbursement was not being recovered. The need for a functional MIS was also impelled by (1) data reporting requirements of the state and federal authorities, (2) grant proposal preparation needs, (3) monitoring affiliates and contracts, (4) managing existing programs, (5) inter-unit competition for resources, and (6) planning for growth and expansion.

Phased Implementation

Implementation of the MIS was phased, with gradual introduction in all of its dimensions, rather than beginning the entire system at once. Central administration conceptualized the system as having three dimensions: (1) location, or program; (2) data collected, or input; (3) reports produced, or output. Thus, implementation was initiated utilizing one form (the service ticket), collecting limited data (direct service only), in one clinic, and producing a single report (the Unit Summary). The MIS was restricted to these parameters for three months before expansion in any dimension was begun. The initial implementation was defined as a pilot project, and it was emphasized to administrative and clinical unit staff that their suggestions and criticisms were invited.

Training sessions in data preparation were given to both clinical and clerical staff. Burt Lowe was able to be on-site during the first two weeks of implementation, dealing with any problems on the spot and pitching in to work side by side with the staff as they coped with the new procedures. An additional half-time secretary/clerk, paid for by increased third-party reimbursement, was given to each unit as it started the MIS.

As more units were brought into the MIS, a bi-weekly meeting was organized of the senior clerical person (now titled administrative coordinator) of each of those units, plus the MIS staff. The meeting served to prepare the coordinators for new MIS requirements, facilitate their sharing of procedures and techniques, and general problem solving. In the opinion of central administration, the administrative coordinators were the key people in keeping the MIS functioning. The coordinators were viewed as the best resource for training the staff of new units about to join in the MIS.

Data from the MIS were presented and discussed regularly at the Steering Committee meeting, in which policy was formulated and area-wide decisions made. This meeting was attended by unit chiefs, selected board members, and key central administrative personnel. Burt Lowe reported that one of the results of this presentation was that unit chiefs, who were psychiatrists, began requesting to become part of the MIS, whereas their initial attitude had been the opposite.

Structure of the MIS

By spring 1981 Burt Lowe has assumed primary responsibility for the MIS. While Eugene Thompson continued to involve himself peripherally in the project, he awarded Lowe nearly complete authority for actual operation of the MIS. Lowe's qualifications for this responsibility stemmed from his involvement in the design and implementation of a number of community mental health management information systems. He was assisted in his efforts by Vic VanNeste, who performed data processing chores and aided in the continual revision and design of forms necessary to fully automate the system.

Through the implementation process various structural components were added to the system and other modifications made. Thus, the structure of the system evolved by early 1981 into that presented below.

Input Components

1. Client-tracing component: Records contact, registration, and evaluation information. Records treatment plans. Keeps track of client transfers to other Harbor Area programs, referrals to outside agencies, and terminations. (Four preprinted forms were used for this purpose.)
2. Service delivery component: Records type and amount of services rendered to clients and outside agencies. (See Exhibit 2.)
3. Staffing component: Records who is working and how much. Records which programs of treatment are delivered and how often. Keeps track of how much and what type of third-party reimbursable treatment is delivered and what degree of total service delivered is direct, i.e., billable.

Output Components

1. Billing component: Service ticket (Exhibit 2) produces a cash receipt and appointment slip for the client. Client monthly billing reports, unit billing summaries, and bills to third-party payors are produced.
2. Individual staff component: Monthly activities of each therapist are reported. Details include type and amount of service delivered, productivity in terms of

EXHIBIT 2 Service Ticket

SERVICE TICKET

CLIENT'S NAME

EAST BOSTON-WINTHROP
COUNSELING CENTER
10 GOVE STREET
EAST BOSTON, MA 02128

NO. E 0182

Cash Rec'd.

YOUR NEXT APPOINTMENT

Day _____
Date _____ Time _____
To see _____

PLEASE CALL US AT 727-7720
IF YOU ARE UNABLE TO KEEP
THIS APPOINTMENT. THANK YOU.

Cashier _____ Date _____

E 0182

MO	DAY	YR

PROGRAM	CLIENT ID	SUFFIX

SERVICE CODE

LOCATION
Center—Sched.
Center—Walkin
Other HA
Clients Home
Other Agency
Nursing Home
School
Court
Telephone
Other

TIME (MIN)

NUMBER CONTACTED
OR TREATED
Primary
Client
Family
Collateral
Other
Clients
Other
Professionals

CLINICIANS

SPECIAL DATA

DIRECT/SUPPORTIVE

REHABILITATION SERVICES
30–Counseling (vocational, etc.)
31–Education (sex, nutrition, etc.)
32–Occupational Therapy
38–Other Rehabilitation (individual)
39–Other Rehabilitation (group)

CLIENT-RELATED ACTIVITIES
40–Case Consultation
41–Case Conference
42–Supervision Provided
43–Supervision Received
44–Case Management
45–Court Appearance
46–Transportation of Client

OTHER ACTIVITIES
80–Intra-Unit Meeting
81–Inter-Unit Meeting
82–Travel
83–Administration
84–Inservice Training
97–No Show
99–Cancellation
99–Other Activity

SPECIALIZED PROGRAM
01–Authorized Code

EVALUATION SERVICES
0–Psychosocial Evaluation
1–Psychiatric/Medical Evaluation
2–Psychological Testing
3–CORE (Chap. 766) Evaluation
4–Evaluation Group
5–Occupational Therapy Evaluation
9–Other Evaluation

TREATMENT SERVICES
20–Individual Medication
21–Medication Group
22–Individual Therapy
23–Group Therapy
24–Family/Couple Therapy
25–Crisis Intervention
26–Combined Therapy and Medication
29–Other Treatment

Signature

CONSULTATION AND EDUCATION

FIRST CHARACTER
A—Client Centered
B—Staff Centered
C—Program Centered
D—Organization Centered
E—Community Planning
F—Outreach
G—Advocacy
H—Information & Education
J—Relationship Building
X—Other

SECOND CHARACTER
B—Planning, Preparing
C—Providing, Participating
D—Summarizing, Reporting
X—Other

direct service (as a percent of available hours), etc., as well as clients not seen for some time who might be terminated.

3. Unit and subunit (i.e., child, adult, and geriatric treatment teams) component: Various operating unit and subunit reports produced for unit chief, administrative coordinators, and team leaders. Included operating unit service summary, and summary of clinician hours. (An example is shown in Exhibit 3.)

4. Area-wide component: Reports summarizing all services in all operating units (Exhibit 4).

5. External reporting component: Produced information for state and federal reporting requirements, i.e., type and amount of services, etc.

6. Fiscal component: Reports on income, expenses, and variances from budget by cost center (operating unit). Reports not tied to service components.

EXHIBIT 3 Revere Community Counseling Center Service Summary (February 1 thru 29, 1980)

	Children 143	Adult 146	Geriatric 148	DDU 145	All Others	Totals
Type of direct service:						
10 Psychosocial evaluation . . .	17	28	5	4	0	54
11 Medication/medical evaluation	3	17	0	0	0	20
12 Psychological testing	1	0	0	0	0	1
14 Evaluation group	2	0	0	0	0	2
19 Other evaluation.	10	0	0	0	0	10
20 Individual medication	7	95	0	0	0	102
21 Medication group	0	3	0	0	0	3
22 Individual therapy	101	332	63	19	0	515
23 Group therapy	18	58	1	0	0	77
24 Family/couple therapy	17	32	14	8	0	71
25 Crisis intervention	12	12	9	2	0	35
26 Medication and therapy . . .	0	53	0	0	0	53
29 Other treatment	0	0	0	1	0	1
30 Counseling (voc., etc.)	0	21	0	0	0	21
38 Other rehab—individual . . .	0	2	0	0	0	2
40 Case consultation.	2	2	1	3	0	8
41 Case conference.	2	2	0	0	0	4
42 Supervision provided	8	0	1	0	0	9
43 Supervision received	0	1	0	0	0	1
44 Case management	9	3	2	0	0	14
46 Transportation of client . . .	1	0	0	0	0	1
80 Intra-unit meeting	3	0	0	0	0	3
81 Inter-unit meeting	3	0	0	0	0	3
82 Travel.	0	0	0	1	0	1
97 No show	18	72	8	0	0	98
98 Cancellation	39	86	10	0	0	135
99 Other activities	1	0	0	0	0	1

EXHIBIT 4   Harbor Area Service Summary (January 1 thru 31, 1980)

	Chelsea CCC	EB/WIN CC	Freedom Trail	Revere CCC	CES	DDU	AIPU	All Others	Total
Location of direct service:									
At unit—scheduled appointment....	777	1,111	767	901	0	197	0	0	3,753
At unit—walk-in..................	12	39	72	28	0	0	0	0	151
Other Harbor Area facility	1	99	6	14	0	1	0	0	121
Client's home	49	39	12	42	0	130	0	0	272
Other agency....................	5	86	41	2	0	0	0	0	134
Nursing home	0	18	1	2	0	0	0	0	21
School..........................	0	27	0	0	0	2	0	0	29
Court...........................	0	1	0	0	0	0	0	0	1
Other...........................	3	15	0	2	0	0	0	0	20
Length of direct service sessions:									
1–10 minutes....................	4	2	16	8	0	0	0	0	30
11–30 minutes...................	145	316	259	271	0	33	0	0	1,024
31–60 minutes...................	672	950	499	593	0	92	0	0	2,806
61–90 minutes...................	22	132	117	111	0	55	0	0	437
91 minutes	4	35	8	8	0	150	0	0	205
No. of staff in direct sessions:									
1 clinician......................	648	1,216	723	918	0	158	0	0	3,663
2 clinicians.....................	106	196	83	72	0	46	0	0	503
3 clinicians.....................	19	13	91	1	0	115	0	0	239
4 clinicians.....................	74	10	2	0	0	11	0	0	97
Direct service by program:									
Children's program...............	167	378	113	156	0	0	0	0	814
Adult program...................	608	850	776	710	0	0	0	0	2,944
Geriatric program................	60	131	10	98	0	0	0	0	299
Other..........................	12	17	0	27	0	0	0	0	56
Type of C and E service:									
Client-centered consultation........	17	25	7	7	0	0	0	1	57
Staff-centered consultation.........	7	5	6	2	0	0	0	0	20
Program-centered consultation	4	25	3	0	0	0	0	0	32
Outreach........................	0	1	3	0	0	0	0	0	4
Information and education	0	1	1	0	0	0	0	0	2
Other..........................	0	0	7	0	0	0	0	0	7
C and E by organization type:									
Educational systems	13	35	6	1	0	0	0	0	55
Health systems	3	23	0	8	0	0	0	0	34
Criminal justice system...........	2	0	0	0	0	0	0	0	2
Mental health...................	4	0	0	0	0	0	0	0	4
Social service—welfare............	6	0	21	0	0	0	0	0	27

Information Processing

Information processing varied slightly from unit to unit. There were two ways information originated: (1) from a schedule book (the service ticket was prepared in advance by clerical personnel and the therapist only filled in information regarding the type and duration of the service issued); (2) on a walk-in basis (either clerical personnel or the therapist filled in the service ticket). Service tickets were accumulated daily, and clerical staff entered the data at the operating unit terminal on the following day. Contact, registration, evaluation, transfer, termination, and staff information were entered in the same manner.

Between the second and the fifth day of each month all reports were generated and sent to the units. Central administration received reports which it utilized to review overall operating activities and fulfill funding and contract requirements. Special attention was paid to third-party billing in order to receive revenues as soon as possible.

The distribution policy on the MIS reports had both positive and negative effects. Formal policy adopted by the Board allowed information to go only one level higher in the organization than the level on which it was generated. This meant that individual information about a client only went to that client's therapist and supervisor—no higher. This policy successfully relieved clinical workers' fears regarding confidentiality. However, restrictive downward distribution policies had a detrimental effect. Workers complained that summary reports of unit activities were not available to line staff. Furthermore, clinicians generally did not know what the statistical data were used for, including their use for government reporting requirements.

Central Administration's Approach to Use of the System

By 1981 central administration felt that the impact of the MIS on billing and funding for services delivered by NSMHA had nearly been maximized. The objective of facilitating clinical management had not been met, however. Eugene Thompson felt that the system provided some valuable information to clinicians, but knew that Burt Lowe was bothered by persistent complaints from the clinicians. According to Lowe, however, the primary function of the MIS was to assist central administration to capture funding and revenue.

> Staff expect administration to take care of money and dealing with outside agencies, so that they are able to do clinical work. If administration can't bring in enough revenue from grants and third-party payors, it affects what line staff can do, the conditions under which they work and their morale . . . When we started the automated system, the amount of services reported per unit typically jumped about 250 percent. That wasn't due to more service being delivered. It was just that more of it was being captured.

Lowe considered one of the system's real benefits to be its effect on resource management. He emphasized the role of the MIS in centralizing control of the organization. In his opinion the MIS had sped up NSMHA's evolution from a fragmented network of independent clinics to a unified system with unified policies and operating procedures. He argued that much of the resistance around the MIS was due to the centers' loss of autonomy.

On the subject of staff resistance, Lowe first focused on the initial phase of the implementation of the system. He stated that a lot less resistance than was expected had occurred.

I think that we went overboard expecting a lot, planning for it . . . There's always resistance to change, but it was minimized here, since the system immediately replaced old forms (rather than adding new paperwork on top of old). So, it actually resulted in a reduction of paperwork . . . We were responsive. The system could be modified and was, frequently, in the early months, based on feedback from clinicians.

Some resistance around the MIS is irrational. That doesn't make it less important, but no logical approach can deal with it. People just have to find out that you're not going to misuse the information . . . There's still some resistance around some areas, mostly in terms of what standards are expected of clinicians and how that information will be used.

Lowe cited tension that arose from a fiscal crisis in 1980 as a more specific cause of resistance to the MIS. He related that some clinicians blamed those problems largely on central administration. Since some workers viewed the MIS as a tool of central administration, resentment toward the system lingered among clinical staff.

In spite of the resistance, Lowe estimated that approximately 98 percent of direct service was being accounted for by early 1981. He explained that clinicians were not asked to report on all hours of their available time. Central administration asked only for recording of billable service and consultation and education activities.

Clinician's Response to the MIS

Clinicians generally agreed that reports of their productivity in terms of direct, billable service were useful in assessing individual performances in this area. It was helpful for supervisors to see which employees were engaged in what amounts to face-to-face treatment with clients. This was the principal type of service for which the operating units and NSMHA received reimbursement from third-party payors, and both administrative and clinical supervisors at the centers stressed the importance of billable services to line staff. Reports were used to ferret out nonproductive individuals, so that supervisors might inquire about and urge them to correct their deficiencies. Such action had led to the dismissal of a number of staff who had failed to produce adequate levels of direct service despite repeated warnings.

The effectiveness of this system in getting all staff to share the load of billable service was recognized by most clinicians. However, there was opposition to the productivity levels proposed by central administration. Clinical workers felt that the emphasis placed on direct service created disincentives for other types of necessary, but nonbillable, services. Central administration was accused of fostering therapist "burn-out," i.e., workers overextending and exhausting themselves prematurely. Clinicians viewed central administration as being insensitive to the needs of line staff for supervision and consultation with other clinicians around difficult cases. They protested that case-management activities, such as advocacy appearances and interventions, assessment of client needs, development of treatment plans, and monitoring of client progress, were essential aspects of treatment.

For these reasons clinicians considered the need for increasing direct service to be a clinical rather than an administrative issue. It was felt that the service categories of the MIS excluded as nonbillable too many useful and necessary activities. Clinical staff were alarmed at what they perceived as an increasing tendency of central administration to focus on the numbers rather than on the nature of the services delivered. They feared the possibility of the numbers taking on too large a reality to the detriment of the quality of the treatment provided. This concern was shared by Vic VanNeste, who cited the "danger of the tail (the MIS) wagging the dog (clinical service)."

Broader concerns regarding the use of the MIS at NSMHA were voiced by East Boston unit personnel. One clinician stated, "Philosophically, the MIS doesn't pick up what it's like to work in East Boston with its population, as opposed to the other clinics." He noted the peculiarities of its population and the need for certain types of nonbillable services, e.g., outreach work. He felt that comparison of productivity levels across units was misleading due to difference in the populations served and the services demanded. Dr. Charles Carl, the unit chief at East Boston, felt that central administration needed to be educated regarding the relative importance of direct versus indirect services. He emphasized that his unit delivered "nonprofit, bottom-line service to the sickest people," and felt that direct service figures were not reflective of this. Dr. Carl suggested that service categories ought to be redesigned "to more accurately conceptualize activities which . . . are necessary for face-to-face service." He argued that an adequate level of understanding of clinical functioning might be hard to translate into MIS data and stated, "You can't define every minor nuance in terms of electronic data."

Dr. Carl also questioned whether the statistical data collected via the MIS was accurate enough to be used for actual planning purposes or whether it simply produced numbers in order to fulfill licensing and funding requirements. He stressed the importance of this, since taking the data seriously meant instituting change which people were not used to and often did not want.

Dr. Carl also argued that the cost of clinicians' time used in reporting to the MIS to get the most accurate data possible was an important consideration. This point was corroborated by other clinical personnel. One physician complained that the constant filling out of service tickets was a nuisance. A clinical team leader grumbled that use of the tickets was cumbersome, requiring constant interacting around the clerical staff and the data entry terminal. She also pointed out that the tickets were often inaccurate, so that supervisors had to go over every printed report carefully with each worker.

The MIS, however, received praise in other areas. Line staff remarked that, when accurately completed, the service tickets did keep track of appointment information for both clients and therapists. They also appreciated lists of clients who had not been seen for some time and might merit termination. It was also felt that the system had improved the allocation of resources to specific caseloads. One supervisor stated that the MIS had "clarified the process of supervision, since supervisors now have the information as to how clinicians spend their time and with whom.''

The most extreme sentiments expressed about use of the MIS, however, were that central administration attempted to compensate for its financial mistakes by suggesting arbitrarily high productivity levels. This radical view was the outgrowth of the 1980 fiscal crisis. Some acting-out against central administration via the MIS, i.e., clinicians failing to record services delivered, was noted at that time, but the level of this activity was minimal.

A host of other concerns existed around direct/support service categories and productivity data. Staff viewed some categories as too restrictive, i.e., not really descriptive of actual services. This led to a heavy use of ''other'' type categories in coding practice and ultimately to vague service delivery reports. Team leaders also reported that overestimates of direct service sometimes resulted from line staff coding indirect service as though it were billable. They attributed this behavior, when it was purposely deceptive, to laziness on the part of some staff but more often to frustration or disrespect for the MIS on the part of others.

Frustration arose from such incidents as no-shows (clients who do not cancel appointments beforehand but do not show up for them) not being counted into individual clinicians' direct service percentages. Clinicians considered this to be an unfair practice. They felt that no-shows should be counted into their productivity figures because workers had no control over whether or not clients showed up for scheduled appointments. If clients failed to appear under such circumstances, therapists were most often unable to schedule other direct services for the newly opened time slots on such short notice.

Central Administration's View on Productivity

Eugene Thompson intended to address the direct service issue at an upcoming meeting where the distribution of staff activities was to be discussed.

> We've been talking about ''productivity'' for a long time. We want to defuse that word, try to throw it out, and really talk about where staff resources are going.

He stated that, allowing for meetings, supervision, breaks, and other activities, only about 16 hours of an average 40 hour work week was available for direct service, consultation/education, case-management, and quality assurance activities. When looked at in this light, an average of 11 or 12 hours of direct service per week did not seem so bad. That meant only four or so hours per week was being spent on the phone, recording information, etc. Based on the flexibility evident in such an analysis, it appeared that clinicians were working very hard. But Thompson felt that NSMHA had to examine its assumptions regarding the amount of staff time allotted to staff meetings, supervision, and other nonbillable activities. While he remarked that the distribution of staff time seemed to work out pretty well, he noted that there were different costs and benefits to maintaining or changing the present system.

Thompson questioned whether pushing clinicians to increase their productivity from 28 percent to 40 percent would result in any fundamental change. Such action would create further disincentives for clinicians to allot time to case-management and treatment of difficult clients. But he pointed out that the alternative to increasing revenues might turn out to be cuts in staffing and services. This was due to the political climate existing in 1981 in which government sources of funding for mental health services were being cut back both on federal and state levels. As a result, central administration was deeply concerned about the financial strength of the organization. Thompson related that some veteran staff members understood the motivation behind central administration's emphasis on productivity. However, newer clinicians objected to what they perceived to be administrative tinkering with clinical activities.

Application of the MIS to Clinical Management

Broader issues surrounded the use of the MIS, though. One of these was the question of the appropriateness of the MIS as a clinical management tool. A number of clinicians had praised the income-producing capacities of the system, but they felt that, while it did a good job focusing on money matters, it was not very useful clinically. Thompson thought that this assessment was true in early 1981.

No external pressure had been exerted on NSMHA to produce treatment outcome information, but some clinicians had recently begun to press for such information. Thompson remarked that central administration had not pushed for this type of data in order to avoid creating further resistance to the MIS and short-circuiting those functions which it was performing well. Thompson said that central administration did consider this information to be useful though. Now that this mandate to produce clinically relevant information was coming from clinicians, it would hasten the process of gathering it. But he cited clinicians' reluctance to deal with paperwork, both of the input and output variety, as a real stumbling block in their utilizing the MIS effectively.

> The resistance, as it has presented itself to me, has just been generalized. A clinician will say, "I don't want to have to see any more paper of any kind. I don't care whether it has to do with billing or closing out records, or anything. I don't want to read another piece. Just let me see my clients and leave me alone."

Thompson claimed that such adamance about performing clinical work before all else was a traditional stance among clinicians.

> There's nothing that a management information system is going to do for a person who basically doesn't like paperwork . . . thinks that clinical work is an organic process and

it can't be managed . . . that it's mystical and it just has to flow . . . that if you have to be concerned about numbers and things that are going to be coming out on paper, it changes the clinical process.

MIS Effect on Decision Making

In early 1981, both Burt Lowe and Eugene Thompson agreed that implementation of the MIS at NSMHA had gone pretty much according to plan. But they also concurred that management decision-making processes, which were to have been transformed by the incorporation of data generated by the system, had remained little changed. The problem, as they saw it, had more to do with internal decision-making processes at NSMHA, than with the quality of the information which the MIS provided. Regarding this issue, Burt Lowe said:

> We still try to make most decisions by consensus, since the units are semi-autonomous. But decisions by consensus aren't necessarily rational or the best decisions. Therefore, the impact of the information which the MIS provides on those decisions is less than if they were made by a single person who could use that information. It clearly influences decisions, but I don't think it has the impact that it was originally envisioned that it would. That's not because the information isn't there. It's because internal decision-making processes don't allow that data to have the weight that I think it should.

Eugene Thompson echoed Lowe's sentiments:

> The thing we're still not great at is getting the management part of the information system into place. It does influence decisions, but not in a highly structured fashion . . . and they're clinicians. The managers are clinicians at heart and by training, and they aren't comfortable with management . . . so, we really haven't taken this management information system and used it to its maximum.

With these thoughts in mind, Burt wondered what steps to take. He hoped to come up with some solutions prior to the next monthly meeting with the unit chiefs. But, presently, he was at a loss for any answers.

Questions

1. What are the problems that Burt Lowe faces?
2. What steps should he take, and in what sequence should he take them?

CASE 16–3   Hennepin County*

As Bob Hanson, Director of the Hennepin County Information Services department (HCIS), strode through the Minneapolis skyway system back to his office, he paused for a moment to take in the view of the new modern office towers in downtown Minneapolis. He couldn't help wondering where all the change, especially the accelerating technological change and its associated hype, would lead in Hennepin County. With each technological change, end users in the county government demanded more information processing support from HCIS. Although he sympathized with users' concerns, Hanson knew his resources were limited and he could not satisfy all their wishes. It was becoming increasingly difficult to attract the necessary caliber of staff, and any expansion in staff would certainly require more money. Indeed, for the past five years the budget for HCIS had risen at a rate almost 60% faster than the growth in revenues.

Since 1980, pressure had been mounting from users who wanted to develop some of their own applications. The idea of delegating development tasks to users appealed to Hanson because it relieved some of the pressure on his department and increased its credibility with users. There were, however, risks. The key to success was to give the users only those tasks for which they were qualified and to leave the more complicated work to HCIS. Hanson was thankful that he and his managers had taken the time to develop the Application Approach Worksheet. While he knew the worksheet would not prevent every problem, it would help users develop realistic expectations about potential computer applications in county government.

Hennepin County

Hennepin County, Minnesota, covers 611 square miles, with over a third of its population of 940,080 located in Minneapolis, the county seat. In 1984, the county employed over 7,000 employees. Approximately three quarters of them worked in a beautiful, new 24-story government center complex, complete with ornamental pond and waterfall.

Hennepin was nationally recognized as one of the best managed counties in the United States. Its administrators were proud that the county was one of the few in the country with a triple-A bond rating. But, as with most state and local governments, the demand for services was rapidly outpacing the county's ability to provide them. This problem had been aggravated by federal government cutbacks and growing taxpayer resistance to tax increases. In the spring of 1984, Hennepin

---

* This case was prepared by Professor Leslie R. Porter, Harvard Business School. Copyright © by the President and Fellows of Harvard College. Harvard Business School case 9-185-005.

County completed Phase I of its new strategic planning process, and came to the following conclusions:

> The financing of county services promises to become increasingly problematic in the future due to a declining county tax base and a reduction in non-property tax revenues. At the same time, competition for funds to meet expanding and newly emerging service needs is growing. Resolution of this dilemma will require the county to develop new or expanded revenues, enlarge its tax base or reduce the costs of service provision. Without such strategies, the county will be forced to curtail needed services or confront untenable increases in property taxes.

The county was responsible for a wide range of services, from administering financial assistance programs to providing funds and administrative support to the justice system. To provide these services, the county's budget had grown by 56% since 1978 to almost $519 million in 1983.

The county government was comprised of semi-autonomous bureaus, boards, and miscellaneous offices. In 1967 the state legislature established the office of county administrator. In 1977 Dale Ackmann was appointed to that position and was responsible for the day-to-day operations of the government and reported directly to the Board of Commissioners.

Four bureaus reported directly to Ackmann. The largest of these was the Bureau of Social Services, which required 44% of the budget. Next in size was the Bureau of Health, which accounted for 20% of the budget, followed by the Bureau of Administration and Management at 8%, and the Bureau of Public Services at 7%.

Although the remaining county government offices reported on a line basis to either an elected official such as the county sheriff or to an appointed board such as the Library Board, they received their budget and most of their administrative support from the Bureau of Administration and Management. The Justice Department, largest of these groups, accounted for 12% of the county government budget. The remainder of the county budget went for capital improvements (7%) and for education and recreation (3%).

Hennepin County Information Services

The Bureau of Administration and Management provided support services for departments and divisions within the county government. Hennepin County Information Services (HCIS) was part of the Bureau of Administration and Management and provided information processing support for all branches of the county government.

In 1972, Information Services became the second public sector enterprise in the United States to embrace IBM's new planning methodology, Business Systems Planning (BSP). Hanson said they quickly realized that they could not build the "great data base in the sky" and so set about building a set of minimally redundant data bases that could be interfaced to meet the county's growing needs for information. Hanson proudly commented that "we stuck to the plan religiously and during this past winter we completed the last of the BSP systems." The county had 40 major on-line applications spread through the county offices. These applications accessed data in over 300 data bases using IBM's IMS data base systems software. Hanson's next objective was to develop index files which would connect all the related data.

Recognizing the growing importance of data processing, in 1978 the county formally established HCIS as a separate department whose director would report to the county deputy administrator. In the spring of 1984, Bob Hanson became the third director in two years.

HCIS employed over 200 people. Two assistant directors reported to Hanson: the assistant director for systems development and the assistant director for operations.

Systems Development.   Gary Kamp, the assistant director for systems development, was given a broad mandate that included developing and supporting application systems on the mainframe computer, as well as supporting end-user applications development using mainframe and personal computer tools. Three service groups reported to Kamp: quality support, development, and new technologies.

- *Quality Support.* The quality support group provided service to development groups. For instance, the group participated in quality reviews and provided technical writers for system documentation. In addition, this group trained users on HCIS-developed systems and provided training to help users develop their own systems. Quality support was also responsible for internal projects, such as improving the project management system and managing the use of the Spectrum software project development methodology. HCIS had adopted the latter to maintain and enhance the quality of the computer systems developed.
- *Development.* The development group, managed by Brandon Simpson, consisted of four project groups, each headed by a project manager. Twelve supervisors, 16 senior analysts, 26 programmer/analysts, and 42 programmers were each assigned to one of the four project groups. Each project group was assigned to a number of county departments. Each county department was allocated a fixed amount of resources. If a department made a request for service, it was routed through the department's MIS coordinator and/or MIS steering committee and assigned a priority rating, which determined if and when the service would be provided.

  For example, if a user required a new program or information from a data base, he or she completed a work request sheet (see Exhibit 1) and routed this sheet through the departmental MIS coordinator to the HCIS project manager assigned to that department. The HCIS project manager determined the appropriate course of action; this was then communicated back through the MIS coordinator to the user. Once the course of action was determined, the MIS coordinator, in consultation with the department manager and the HCIS project manager, determined the priority to assign to the request.

EXHIBIT 1   Hennepin County Data Processing—Work Request

User

Request Number 8 4 0 5 1   Requested by _____Victor Gage_____   Phone _____4242_____

Organization Name _____Coordinating Section_____   Organization Number _____2992_____

Sent to *(HCDP supervisor's name)* _____Chuck Krueger_____   Date _____1-20-84_____

Date Required 1-25-84   Explain _____
_____ See Attach. # _____

Urgency of Request   ____ Emergency   X Routine

Type of Request   ____ Investigation   ____ Change to Existing System _____
                         X New Development

Description of Request   *(problems, objectives, suggested solutions and organizational impact)*

Per request from Daniel F. Decowski, please provide an automatic
method for tracking Div. in process updates to owner, taxpayer,
address, & mtge. data. Per the discussion with you he
determines should be under Focus.
_____
_____
_____
_____
_____ See Attach. # _____

Reasons for Request   ____ Cost Avoidance   ____ Cost Reduction
                             ____ Legal Requirement   ____ Organizational Requirement
                             X Service Improvement   ____ Enhance Management Information
                             ____ Other
                             Explain Items Checked _____
                             _____ See Attach. # _____

User Management Approval   Signature   Phone   Date

System Coordinator   *Vic Gage*   4242   1-20-84

Organization Head

Project Sponsor

Data Processing

Received by _*Chuck Krueger*_   Date Received _1-23-84_

Classification   ____ Small Development   ____ Large Development
                        ____ Minor Maintenance   ____ Major Maintenance

Project Name *Dept. of Taxation I/c*   Project Number _2992_ 1593m

Action   ____ Prepare Project Plan   ____ Prepare Investigation Report
                ____ Begin Work   ____ Prepare Project Proposal
                ____ Other

Assigned to *Anjalee Khakar*   Phone *X-5149* Date 1-23-84
Expected Completion Date 1-25-84   Actual Completion Date 1-25-84

See reverse side for instructions.   HC 712 (8-80)

• *New Technologies.* Manager Jim Laurie came to the new technology group after working in several positions at HCIS, including project manager in the development group and data base administrator. He agreed to head up the New Technology area because he was excited about the potential impact it could have on the county government. His group had three areas of primary responsibility: (1) a large pilot office automation project which would use an IBM 36 in the Bureau of Social Services to support electronic mail, word processing, and calendaring; (2) managing the Personal Computer Center; (3) researching and evaluating new end-user tools.

Operations.   Since the assistant director's position in operations was not yet filled, two groups that normally would report to the assistant director reported to Hanson instead. The smaller group, Technical Support, maintained the data communications system, maintained and fine tuned the operating system for maximum performance, and planned systems growth. The larger group, Operations, was responsible for running Hennepin County's IBM 3081K with 32 megabytes of main memory. Operations scheduled jobs, distributed output, and provided data entry support.

In addition to Systems Development and Operations, three smaller departments reported to Hanson: data base administration, finance, and voice communications.

History of End-User Computing

From 1972 to 1980 almost all of HCIS's effort was directed toward getting the BSP systems up and operational. Many user requests (for specific applications) fell through the cracks. According to Hanson:

> As the users' sophistication increased, so did their demands on HCIS. Meanwhile, we continued to use only the traditional approach, regardless of the nature of the problem, because that is what we knew best. The inevitable consequence was that users became frustrated with the rigidity, expense, and delays associated with the traditional systems development approach. At the same time our development backlog of more than two years showed no signs of diminishing, so we began to look for new answers.

In the fall of 1980 HCIS management introduced an Information Center, which offered IBM's ADRS (a departmental reporting system) and several other "user friendly" packages. The use of these tools quickly caught on, and HCIS management realized that existing hardware resources could not support widespread use of ADRS. In the fall of 1981 ADRS was supplemented with FOCUS, a fourth generation applications development language. Four county departments were selected to serve as FOCUS pilots. HCIS staff trained users from these areas in the use of FOCUS and provided them with terminals, disk space, and machine time. Each user was charged the direct cost for the terminal, but was not charged directly for the disk space or machine time consumed.

Three concerns quickly arose. First, how could HCIS ensure that users developed appropriate applications? Second, the new organization required users to choose between the Information Center and the development group, which had supported them in the past. This confused users since they had only a rough idea of the differences between the two groups. Also, the publicity and excitement about the Information Center was beginning to hurt morale in the development groups. Brandon Simpson pointed out:

> By the following February, our development staff was beginning to feel left out. They felt that much of the savings that users were touting was arising because the users weren't adequately documenting what they were doing. The programmers felt that if they had "go fast" tools like FOCUS and the same lax documentation standards they could develop applications just as fast.

In November of 1982, Bruce Kurtz, weary of all the discussion over who should develop what and on which machine, suggested to HCIS management that they develop a method whereby users could determine for themselves where and by whom an application should be developed. Kurtz wanted to avoid a buzzword-laden document; he sought a simple, clear form, perhaps a matrix, that any employee could grasp. Application options would range from personal computers and word processors through minis and mainframes.

Hanson noted:

> We came up with more approaches than we could make recommendations for. We decided to concentrate on data automation and leave text processing out. This left the user three choices: the application could be developed on a personal computer, developed by the users with FOCUS, or developed by HCIS staff. Although minis were another viable alternative, we really lacked the experience to stand behind them so we felt we could not recommend them.

Starting with Kurtz's suggestion of a simple matrix, Hanson, Kamp, and Simpson arrived at the idea of the Application Approach Worksheet. The first draft of the worksheet contained 22 questions, several of which they quickly agreed were too technical. These questions were edited down to 18 (see Exhibit 2). In January of 1983 HCIS began testing the questionnaire internally with positive results.

Hanson commented on the concept behind the worksheet:

> When we began the criteria development process, we intended to create a tool that would promote more logical decision making than in the past. We hoped that by focusing on the real criteria for recommending different automation approaches, we could better manage user expectations.
>
> We also hoped that users would begin to identify applications that were suitable for personal computers. In short we wanted a vehicle to help us objectively identify the best application approach for a given automation effort.

EXHIBIT 2 Application Approach Worksheet

Note: The actual worksheet consisted of five pages on which the criteria were listed, with two or three categories under each criterion. There were three columns in which the points assigned to each of the three possible means of development were listed: (1) traditional, (2) user, and (3) personal computer. The criteria are listed below:

Criteria	Categories	Maximum Points
1. Number of concurrent users.....	1, 2–3, 4+	15
2. Number of locations............	1, 2–3, 4+	5
3. Number of workstations	1, 2–5, 6+	5
4. Output dynamics...............	Can schedule, moderate, cannot schedule	15
5. Processing dynamics...........	Structured, some "what if," unstructured	15
6. Data recovery	Automated recover to failed transaction, automated recovery to last backup, manual recovery to last backup	10
7. Application support	Require information services, user	10
8. Audit requirements............	Expected, moderate, minimum	10
9. Security requirement	Sensitive data, moderate, minimum	10
10. System transfer	Sectional, departmental, county wide	12
11. Data significance..............	Sectional, departmental, county wide	10
12. Processing access	Immediate/continuous, delayed/sporadic	10
13. Life expectancy...............	0–2 years, 2+ years	10
14. Data volume..................	0–320,000 characters, 320,000+ characters	10
15. Data source/currency..........	Existing permanent file/currency extract permanent file/previous day nonautomated data/currency required	10
16. Data retention	Legal retention required, not required	10
17. Employees that update.........	1, 2–4, 5+ concurrently	10
18. System complexity	Little, moderate, very	15

That March, HCIS began to require the worksheet as part of the regular work request process. While reaction to the new tool was generally favorable, many users found it a little confusing. To remedy this, Simpson included a session on completing the worksheet in her "Orientation to Information Services" class. In the first five months after the worksheet's introduction, 50 applications were evaluated. Of these, 17 were assigned to be developed by HCIS staff in the traditional manner, 9 were developed by users on the FOCUS system, and the remaining 24 were developed on personal computers.

To provide a central focus for users seeking automation support, the Information Center was closed down and responsibility for supporting personal computers was returned to the project development groups. Thus, when a department needed help to determine the best approach for an application or to develop an application, there was a single place to call. HCIS management felt this strengthened communications while still providing expertise in the new technologies.

In addition, the Information Center staff were assigned to a new Application

Support group that was part of the data base group. They were responsible for providing expert assistance and keeping current on emerging technologies.

In March of 1983, HCIS opened the Personal Computer (PC) Center where Hennepin County employees could learn about personal computers and try them out. The center had three full-time staff: one to provide assistance for those seeking help with personal computers, one to review and evaluate new technology, and one to assist user departments with word processing problems. Hennepin County standardized on the IBM PC; eight were available for users to try in the PC Center. The PC Center provided one-on-one tutoring and offered self-study videotaped training courses: one on Wordstar, a word processing package, and the other on Lotus 1-2-3, a popular spreadsheet package.

In order to purchase a personal computer, users first had to justify it to their own management. Then, through the use of the Application Approach Worksheet, they had to demonstrate to their department's HCIS project manager that the personal computer was the appropriate tool for the application. To complete the worksheet, the end user worked closely with the project manager, who helped resolve any ambiguities that might arise. Once the worksheet was reviewed and approved by the project manager, the PC Center would order the machine. Users who could not initially cost-justify the computer could borrow one from the PC Center for 45 days to develop the cost justification. In April of 1983, the county administrator published policies and guidelines for the acquisition and use of microcomputers (Exhibit 3).

Property Division Tracking Project

For almost two years, Dan Decowski, manager of the Property Identification and Election Division, had been seeking to computerize the tracking of property ownership undergoing divisions in the county but his department's management had not given it a high enough priority to warrant development. His problem seemed perfect for the computer. Each year about 1,200 to 1,400 tracts of land were subdivided within the county. One part of Decowski's group tracked the ownership of each parcel. Decowski described the process as follows:

> Let's assume there is a piece of property upon which the owners wish to build a condominium. Presently the property has a single tax record which includes who owns the property, a legal description of the property, the name and address of who pays the taxes, and the assessed value. When we are notified of this change, we set up a file for the property to be divided and insert a division sheet denoting each of the new parcel identities.
>
> Initially each sheet would be completed with the original owner's name and other pertinent information. Following this, new legal descriptions had to be added to the property records, and once this was done, a copy of the file would be sent to the assessor so the appropriate value could be assigned. Further, throughout the year each of the new pieces of property could be sold or any one of a variety of transactions could occur that

---

EXHIBIT 3   Application Analysis Guidelines for Acquisition of Microcomputers

---

What Is an "Application Analysis"?

In its simplest form, an application analysis is a study of the characteristics of a task or operation to be automated. The purpose of the study is to determine which automation approach is appropriate for those particular characteristics. These guidelines explain how the application analysis fits within the context of a potential microcomputer purchase.

The automation approaches used at Hennepin County range from major systems developed by the Information Services development staff using a large computer (e.g., Payroll) to small applications developed by individuals throughout the county using microcomputers (e.g., various VisiCalc applications). Between these two extremes is a range of approaches, most of which use the mainframe computer.

How Does the Process Work?

Phase I: Preliminary Analysis. The application analysis process always begins with an idea. The initiator of the idea then describes the idea in as much detail as possible to clarify his/her thinking. After the initiator of the idea has completed the written description, he/she works through an "Application Approach Worksheet" (available from Information Services project managers) to determine the most appropriate method of automation. If the initiator needs any help with this phase, Information Services project managers are available as consultants.

Once completed, the worksheet provides a general indication of the most appropriate automation approach.

If the preliminary analysis suggests either traditional or user development as the appropriate approach, the project manager will guide the initiator through the appropriate procedures. If the analysis suggests microcomputer development, Phases II through VI of this process should be completed.

Phase II: Introduction to Microcomputers. In this phase, the initiator contacts the Personal Computer Center to arrange a demonstration of the machine using the software that seems most appropriate for the application. If at this stage the software proves not to be appropriate, other software alternatives are identified and explored.

Phase III: Configuration Analysis. After exploring the software alternatives, the initiator will generally have a clearer picture of the work involved in developing the application. It is at this point that the initiator decides if the necessary staff are available to develop and maintain the application. If so, the initiator contacts the Information Services project manager responsible for his/her department. The initiator works with the project manager and the Personal Computer Center staff to identify the configuration of the hardware components. For example, if the application has a graphics component, a color terminal and a special printer may be needed. Or if a great deal of storage is needed, a hard disk drive may be necessary. In addition, the initiator estimates the amount of time the microcomputer will be needed per year.

Phase IV: Training and Testing. Then, the initiator takes the training necessary to use the software package chosen in Phase II. During and immediately after training, the initiator tries to use the software package on his/her application.

The testing can be done in a number of ways.

- If the testing is fairly simple and will require less than 20 hours to complete, the initiator may use one of the microcomputers in the Personal Computer Center.

EXHIBIT 3 *(concluded)*

- If the testing is complex, the initiator may apply for a computer loan. In this case, the initiator has 45 days to complete testing and decide whether or not to buy the loan unit.
- If testing is not required and the application is a short-term project that requires less than 20 hours per year, the initiator may use one of the microcomputers in the Personal Computer Center.

If the testing is not successful, the initiator and the project manager reevaluate the requirements of the application and change course as necessary.

Phase V: Purchase Justification. Once the initiator is satisfied that the microcomputer in conjunction with the software chosen in Phase IV can do the work needed, a purchase justification is prepared. For a complete description of purchase justification, see "Purchase Justification Guidelines."

Phase VI: Report Preparation. In this final phase of the application analysis, the results of each of the preceding phases are documented. Once the report has been completed, it is given to the head of the requesting department for approval.

---

would require recording, such as, mortgages are added or changed. The clerk responsible for tracking the division data had to manually file and process all changes.

Each year, usually in late January, HCIS would notify us that it had run the tax statements for the current year and that they were now ready to add the new division records to the tax data base. We would then scan each of the completed division sheets, highlighting changes for each of the properties and adding the supporting documentation. The completed division sheets would then be sent to the departmental data processing section for online keying. The last couple of weeks of February were usually very hectic as we got all the division information ready for the update to the tax data base. However, the rest of the year only required about a third to a half of a clerk's time.

The Department of Property Taxation, of which the Property Identification and Election Division was part, was one of the four pilot groups for FOCUS. Decowski asked Ken Felger, an analyst in his division, to learn FOCUS to increase his division's strength in its use. Felger decided that the divisions tracking project would be a good project for learning FOCUS. However, when Decowski asked Chuck Krueger, his HCIS project manager, for disk space to use FOCUS he was told that it was unavailable until he considered all approaches for developing this project. Krueger asked Decowski to complete an Application Approach Worksheet and a Work Request. After some initial help from Krueger, Decowski and Don Deutsch (the supervisor of the area responsible for division tracking), completed the worksheet, trying to be as objective as possible. As shown in Exhibit 1, the worksheet clearly indicated that FOCUS was an appropriate tool for developing this application. Delighted with their findings, Decowski and Deutsch wanted to proceed as quickly as possible.

On the review process, Krueger commented:

We don't go into the review just to initial the proposal. We review it. We explain what the criteria mean and talk about them. Occasionally we have to change a response. Data

Processing has to ensure that the requirements and the limits are well defined. Further, we make certain that the user has defined the data elements needed. These are the absolute bottom line tasks. Since we rely on our data base group to design the user data bases, we have to make certain that the user has put in enough thought so that the data base can be designed.

Upon receipt, Krueger reviewed the worksheet, work request, and agreed to provide the resources that they would need. However, to help prevent user systems development from returning to the chaotic days of the 1960s when systems were developed with no planning and no documentation, he created and required that his users use a specially modified version of the Spectrum life cycle development system methodology as a guideline. His hope was that the users would find these guidelines as beneficial as HCIS had found them in managing the larger systems development and maintenance projects. Krueger pointed out:

We want to see something documented such as screen designs and flow charts. Otherwise we will be back to the situation we had in the sixties with nothing documented. Something must be down on paper so we can survive and the user can survive. Not all managers require the users to use Spectrum, but I feel we must. This check list was created by Jim Laurie and myself. It's not perfect but it's a start and it will guarantee some level of success. The key is to do things right because no one ever has enough time nor energy to do things over.

With these guidelines in hand, Decowski and Deutsch plunged ahead.

The Future

Arriving at his office, Hanson looked down at the strategic planning document on his desk. He wondered which posed the greater threat to his ability to plan for the future: the pond and waterfall strategically located over his data center or the potential explosion in demand for computer resources for end-user systems. Last year the pond had seemed the greater threat, when the data center ceiling started leaking. Now they were prepared for any leaks with large sheets of plastic in the computer room. Was he as well prepared for end-user computing? Or would the swelling tide of demand overwhelm his group?

What would happen next year when users decided that they no longer wanted responsibility for running all these systems and wanted to turn them over to Operations? They now had a smooth system for handing over HCIS-developed systems to Operations, but this entailed strict enforcement of documentation standards. Would users adhere to these same documentation requirements? Was it appropriate to require those standards? What about data access? Users were always saying, "It's my data. What difference does it make if I store it in my filing cabinet or on the computer?" Hanson wondered what would happen when all the areas had their own data stored on the computer with different formats and different procedures for accessing it. Informal procedures for accessing the data from different departments might be impossible at that point. These were problems which he must address soon—before it was too late.

Questions

1. How can HCIS ensure that users develop appropriate applications? What should be the role of the development group and the HCIS project managers in this effort?
2. What is your assessment of the policies and guidelines for the acquisition and use of microcomputers? Is it appropriate for the organizational structure of Hennepin County? What modifications, if any, would you make?
3. What is your assessment of the criteria (and the weights given to them) on the Application Approach Worksheet? Is this a useful way of arriving at a decision on a proposed application? What modifications, if any, would you make?
4. How should Mr. Hanson address the problems raised in the last paragraph of the case?

Summary: The Well-Managed Nonprofit Organization

By way of summary, we describe in this chapter some management control practices that we believe are characteristic of well-managed nonprofit organizations. In this summary, we have in mind an organization of at least moderate size, say at least 100 employees and several million dollars of annual operating expenses. Smaller organizations can operate successfully with fewer formal management control techniques than those described here, although the basic concepts underlying these techniques are applicable even in small organizations.

THE BASIC PROBLEM

The principal characteristic that distinguishes the problem of management control in a nonprofit organization from that in a for-profit company is the absence of profit as: (1) an objective, (2) a criterion for appraising proposed alternative courses of action, and (3) a measure of performance. No comparable focus exists in a nonprofit organization, and consequently management control is more difficult.

In a well-managed nonprofit organization, this distinction is recognized, but does not lead to an attitude that management control is unimportant or inappropriate. Instead, it engenders a commitment to devise and implement the best possible management control system under the circumstances. Because profit is not an objective, management thinks carefully about the organization's objectives, even though they may be difficult to formulate. Because proposed courses of action cannot be judged in terms of how well they meet a profit objective, management develops other criteria for deciding on programs and budgets. Because there is no profit measure to provide a semiautomatic danger signal when performance is unsatisfactory, management develops substitute performance measures and other ways of evaluating the success of the organization.

ORGANIZATIONAL RELATIONSHIPS

The first requirement of good management control in a nonprofit organization is that senior management appreciate the importance of control, recognize its feasibility, understand how to use the management control system, and be willing to devote sufficient time to the management control process. Senior management appreciates that, although management control is not as glamorous as planning, and criticism is an unpleasant task, control is nevertheless essential. If, by contrast, senior management has the attitude that the effective and efficient use of resources is relatively unimportant in a nonprofit organization, or, even worse, that efforts to increase efficiency and effectiveness are beneath the dignity of the office, then management control will be ineffective no matter how well designed the system may be.

A well-managed organization has a strong governing body. Some members of this body spend considerable time examining program and budget proposals before they are submitted to the full board or legislative committee. Members of the governing body also analyze formal reports on performance and informal communications from clients and others on how well the organization is performing. Often they are assisted in this work by a staff.[1] In a private nonprofit organization, some members of the governing body are professional board members who devote substantial time to board activities, and may be members of several similar boards.

In performing these functions, the governing body is careful not to infringe on the prerogatives of management. The governing body ensures that the chief executive has full authority to execute policies, and that his or her decisions are supported by the board. The board also ensures that the CEO's compensation is appropriate.

Senior management is assisted by a professional staff, and it looks to this staff for innovative ideas and for the analysis of proposed programs. If the chief executive does not personally know where the levers of power exist and how to manipulate them, there is at least one staff member who has this knowledge about the organization and the skill to use it.

The controller is more than a chief accountant. The controller is responsible for the operation of all aspects of the management control system. Although the controller is management's principal adviser on management control matters, and the principal interpreter of information flowing from the system, he or she nevertheless is a staff person; line management makes the decisions.

Operating managers have the authority to use their judgment in running their responsibility centers and in accomplishing results. However, they are required to operate within somewhat closer budgetary and other constraints than is custom-

---

[1] In particular, legislative bodies in most states need larger staffs than they now have so that they can check on the performance of the executive branch.

ary in for-profit organizations. Operating managers reject the stereotype of civil servants as lazy, incompetent, rule-bound, self-serving, and immobile. They understand that, although job performance in any large organization is influenced by the inherent characteristics of bureaucracy, tolerance of laziness and incompetence is an indication of poor management, rather than an inherent characteristic of the system.

MANAGEMENT CONTROL PRINCIPLES

Account Classification

The control system contains two principal account classifications, one structured in terms of programs and the other in terms of organizational responsibility. At the lowest level are account building blocks, each of which relates both to a single program element and to a single responsibility center. Summaries are obtained by aggregating these building blocks by program elements and program categories in the program part of the structure, and by various levels of the organizational hierarchy in the responsibility part of the structure.

The system contains both historical data and data on estimated future costs and outputs. Historical data are defined and structured in the same way as estimated future data. An accounting system that collects historical data that are inconsistent with the program budget (e.g., estimated *future* costs and outputs) does not provide an adequate basis for control.

To facilitate control of operating expenses, the structure provides for a clean separation between capital costs and operating costs. The definition of capital costs is unambiguous, and is worded in such a way that items of minor importance are excluded even though they are long lived. If the organization makes grants, a third category of accounts is provided for this purpose.

External Financial Reporting

If required to do so by grantors or other external agencies, the organization prepares financial statements for external users according to principles set forth in AICPA *Accounting Guides*. If it is not constrained by these forces, it departs from those aspects of the *Accounting Guides* that inhibit the presentation of a clear picture of the results of operations. For example, it does not fragment the operating statement by setting up separate columns for various types of restricted funds.

The most important financial statement is the operating statement. Its central purpose is to show the extent to which management maintained the organization's operating capital. The organization maintains its operating capital—and hence is viable—if its revenues for a year equaled or exceeded expenses for that year.

The Accounting System

The accounting system is designed so that operating revenues are reported separately from capital contributions; that is, from gifts, grants, appropriations, or other resource inflows whose use is intended for the construction of plant, for endowment, or for other nonoperating purposes. The management control system also measures the expenses incurred during an accounting period.

Revenues arise from the sale of goods and services; from membership dues; from taxes, contributions, grants, and appropriations used for operating purposes (as contrasted with those intended for endowment or acquisition of plant and equipment); and from endowment earnings. The governing board establishes a firm policy regarding the types of contributions and grants that are to be treated as revenue and the types that are contributed capital. It also decides whether endowment revenues are to be measured by the spending-rate approach or by the traditional method of counting dividends, interest, rents, royalties, and similar inflows.

Expenses measure the resources used in operations during an accounting period, and decrease the organization's equity. The accounting system in a well-managed organization measures spending for programs and by responsibility centers in terms of expenses, rather than in terms of expenditures, because expenditures measure resources acquired, which do not necessarily correspond to resources used. Expenses include the total cost of the resources used, including, for example, the present value of the pension benefits that are associated with labor costs incurred during the period. The extent to which the expenses should include depreciation of long-lived assets (or debt service on these assets in lieu of depreciation) is controversial. There is considerable doubt about the desirability of measuring depreciation on "infrastructure" assets, such as roads, dams, and public buildings.

Even if required to keep accounts on an obligation or encumbrance basis, as is the case with government agencies, a well-managed organization measures expenses on an accrual basis and uses expense data as a basis for control. It reconciles these expenses with obligations or encumbrances in a separate calculation. Expenditures and corresponding liabilities are also recorded and controlled.

The accounting system also reports expenditures for long-lived assets. In many cases, however, it is not feasible to associate these with individual program elements.

Management Accounting

Most expenses recorded in management reports are measured according to the same principles that govern financial reporting, but in more detail. They are collected both by responsibility center and by program element. For responsibility center reporting, it may be desirable to measure only direct costs and to omit allocated costs, or to identify controllable expenses separately from noncontrollable expenses, but report both types. Some systems identify variable expenses separately from fixed expenses, although many organizations do not find such a separation useful.

Pricing Decisions

Except in unusual circumstances, such as those including public goods, a well-managed organization charges its clients for the services that they receive, sometimes through third-party payers, such as medicare. By charging for services, the organization generates a monetary measure of the quantity of its outputs and motivates managers to be concerned about the cost and quantity of services they provide.

The full cost of a service is its direct cost plus an equitable share of indirect or common costs. It includes depreciation if funds for the acquisition of new capital assets are provided from charges to clients, rather than from gifts or grants. To the extent that the organization's own resources are tied up in working capital or fixed assets, cost includes a charge for the use of capital. Cost also may include imputed costs, such as an amount in lieu of taxes, particularly when the price is used as a "yardstick" against which the prices of for-profit organizations are compared, as is the case with a publicly owned utility.

On average, the price charged for a service is set equal to the full cost of providing that service, including a capital charge. A higher price would take unfair advantage of what may be the organization's monopoly position and is in any event unnecessary. A lower price would provide services for less than they are worth and, hence, lead to misallocation of resources.

Although, on the average, prices of services are based on full cost, the organization may price some services below cost (a subsidy price) to encourage optimal use of resources, particularly the utilization of excess capacity in off-peak periods. In addition, an organization may use a subsidy price to encourage the use of certain socially needed services, or a penalty price to discourage the use of certain other services. Prices may also be somewhat higher than full costs to provide a cushion against unforeseen contingencies. On occasion, prices may include an amount that provides funds for expansion. As exceptions to the general rule, prices may be based on prevailing market prices when the nonprofit organization competes with for-profit companies, particularly in providing services that are not central to its mission.

The unit of pricing is made as specific as feasible because this provides a better measure of the quantity of services rendered and a better basis for decisions on the allocation of resources. The organization does not, by contrast, have a single overall rate, such as a blanket daily charge that takes no account of the types of services rendered. An exception to this principle occurs when the pricing of very small units would lead to unwise client decisions, as would happen, for example, if the price of each college course were based on its cost.

If feasible, prices are determined prospectively rather than retrospectively; that is, they are set before the fact on the basis of anticipated costs and volume, rather than after the fact on the basis of actual costs incurred. Retrospective pricing greatly diminishes the motivation to control costs.

THE MANAGEMENT CONTROL ENVIRONMENT

The management control system operates within both external and internal environments. These environments vary greatly from one organization to the next, and the management control system varies accordingly. The external environment includes legal and regulatory constraints, the degree of certainty of revenues, the nature of competition, and legislative and public pressures. The internal environment includes the organizational structure (both formal and informal), the program structure, the account structure, administrative factors, behavioral factors, and cultural factors.

Responsibility Structure

Part of the organizational structure is the network of responsibility centers. There are three principal types of responsibility centers: expense centers, profit centers, and investment centers. The selection of an appropriate type depends on senior management's assessment of the resources that a manager controls, and senior management attempts to hold managers responsible only for those resources over which they exert a reasonable amount of control. In general, a profit center is desirable, even when the unit "sells" its services internally; in this case, senior management makes sure that an appropriate set of transfer prices is developed to facilitate the control process.

Program Structure

Management has given much thought to designing a program structure that is useful in (1) making program decisions, (2) providing a basis for comparison of the costs and outputs of similar programs, and (3) providing a basis for setting prices for services that are sold. If the organization structure is such that each responsibility center is responsible for a single program, a separate program structure is not needed, and no effort is expended in creating "program" labels for the work done by these responsibility centers.

The program structure consists of about 10 main programs, plus as many program categories and program elements as are needed for the purposes mentioned above. One of the program categories is administration, so that administrative costs can be collected and analyzed separately from other costs. If fund-raising costs are significant, there is a separate program element for fund raising. Program elements and, if feasible, program categories are defined in such a way that quantitative output measures can be associated with each of them.

Account Structure

The responsibility account structure corresponds exactly to organization units. Some responsibility centers are expense centers; that is, their expenses are measured, but not their revenues. To the extent feasible, however, responsibility centers are designed as profit centers; that is, their managers are responsible for both expenses and revenues. The term *profit center* does not imply that the manager is necessarily expected to earn a profit. Rather, the objective is to achieve an agreed-upon relationship between revenues and expenses. Often, this is a breakeven relationship.

The program accounts and the responsibility accounts articulate with one another, as do the budgetary accounts (or amounts shown in the budget) and the historical accounts. Thus, the accounts collectively form a single system, in which each part can be related to the others.

THE CONTROL PROCESS

The control process in a well-managed organization consists of four phases—programming, budget preparation, operating and measuring, and reporting and evaluation. These phases occur at approximately the same time each year, and managers learn to adjust their schedules to them.

Programming

Unless the organization continues with the same activities, year after year, it has a procedure for generating ideas for new programs, analyzing these ideas, reaching decisions on them, and incorporating approved individual programs into an overall plan. This is the programming process.

Management creates an environment in which ideas for new programs are encouraged. When an idea is sufficiently attractive so that it gains the initial support of an influential advocate, it becomes a proposal. If the organization has many such proposals, it has a staff unit that analyzes and submits the analysis to senior management as a basis for decision. The analysis seeks to determine how well the proposal will help the organization achieve its goals.

To the extent feasible, the analysis includes an estimate in monetary terms of the benefits and costs of the proposal. A benefit/cost comparison is possible when the benefits can be measured in economic terms, such as savings in operating costs or increased output. Although many projects are of this character, most tend to be of relatively minor importance. A benefit/cost analysis also can be made by comparing two proposals, either of which will accomplish a desired objective satisfactorily; the proposal with the lower cost is preferred. If there is no plausible causal relationship between costs and benefits, however, the organization does not waste time in attempting a benefit/cost analysis.

If a program's benefits cannot be expressed in monetary terms, management attempts to estimate whether the benefits are at least as great as the costs. Management recognizes that a benefit/cost analysis does not by itself provide a basis for a decision because many relevant considerations cannot be measured. Nevertheless, the analysis reduces the area within which judgment must be applied.

In addition to an analysis of the merits of the proposal from an economic and social viewpoint, the decision maker considers its political implications, including such matters as its salability to those who must provide resources, and the effects it may have on the organization's constituencies. Usually, these political considerations are kept separate from the technical analysis.

Senior management recognizes that most proposals are advocacy proposals and that the accompanying analysis and justification is, at least to some extent, biased. Senior management attempts to offset this bias by having its own staff make a careful review of the proposal (recognizing that the staff itself may develop biases), or by setting up an adversary relationship in which natural opponents of the proposal are encouraged to criticize it.

Programming Systems.   If the organization is large, if it considers a sizable number of new programs, or if its activities change substantially over time, it has a formal programming system. This system provides a mechanism for incorporating the individual programs into an overall plan, often called a *long-range* or *strategic plan*, and testing this plan for balance and feasibility.

The programming system starts with the preparation and dissemination of guidelines that specify, among other things, the constraints within which program proposals are to be prepared. Working within these constraints, operating managers prepare program proposals that describe the activities they wish to undertake, the resources required for these activities, and the anticipated results. The proposals cover activities for a period of several future years, often five years. These proposals are first analyzed by a staff unit and then used as the basis for discussion between senior management and operating managers. The consensus that emerges from such a discussion constitutes approval in principle to proceed with the program, but the program's details are subject to refinement and modification in the budgeting process.

Operations Budgeting

Budgeting is a more important process in a nonprofit organization than in a for-profit one. In a for-profit organization, operating managers can be permitted to modify certain plans on their own initiative, provided the revised plan is likely to increase profits. By contrast, operating managers of nonprofit organizations, especially organizations whose annual revenue is essentially fixed, must adhere closely to plans as expressed in the budget.

The annual operating budget is derived from the approved programs. Essentially, it is a fine tuning of the next year's slice of each program. In the course of the budgeting process, more careful estimates of costs are made than those contained in the program proposal, and responsibility for execution of the program is assigned to individual responsibility centers. Budgeting is viewed as the most important part of the management control process because the budget specifies how activities are to be conducted in the coming year.

The budgeting process starts with a realistic estimate of revenues. Ordinarily, expenses are planned so that they are approximately equal to revenues. This matching of expenses and revenues differs from the approach used in for-profit organizations because in the latter, the amount budgeted for marketing expenses can influence the amount of revenues.

A nonprofit organization should plan to incur expenses that are almost equal to revenues. If budgeted expenses are below revenue by more than the amount needed to cover the organization's need for a surplus, the organization is not producing the quantity of services that those who provide the revenues have a right to expect. If budgeted expenses exceed revenues, the difference must be made up by the generally undesirable actions of drawing down endowment or other capital funds that are intended to provide services to future generations. If the first approximation of budgeted expenses exceeds estimated revenues, the prudent course of action usually is to reduce expenses rather than to anticipate that revenues can be increased.

The initial budget is a program budget; that is, one that focuses on the amounts to be spent on each program. Summary information on objects of expense (e.g., salaries, supplies, purchased services) may be included, but these are not the main focus. Programs are identified with the responsibility centers that are to execute them.

The first step in the budgeting process is the formulation of guidelines and their communication to operating managers. Operating managers prepare proposed budgets consistent with these guidelines and negotiate these proposals with their superiors. When agreement is reached, the budget becomes a commitment between the superior and the budgetee. The budgetee commits to accomplish the planned objectives within the spending limits specified in the budget, and the superior commits to agree that such accomplishment is satisfactory performance.

Although some people advocate that the analysis of a proposed budget start from a zero base, this is not feasible in the real world because of the limited amount of time available. Instead, senior management takes the current level of spending as a starting point, and reserves *zero-based review* for one or a few programs each year.

Control of Operations

The well-managed organization has a system to assure that actual spending is kept within limits specified in the approved budget, unless there are compelling reasons to depart from budgeted amounts. If budget limitations are stated as authority to encumber or obligate (i.e., to place contracts), as is the case in government and certain others, controls are correspondingly stated in obligation or encumbrance terms. The necessity for controlling encumbrances is not permitted to detract from a focus on expenses, however. Expenses measure the quantity of resources consumed and are therefore the best financial indication of the inputs that were used to accomplish whatever the organization did. To the extent feasible, the management control system insulates operating managers from the dysfunctional messages that are often signaled by obligation or encumbrance accounting.

The organization has a procedure for revising the budget when circumstances require it. Managers are required to follow this procedure, rather than to hide overruns by charging expenses to incorrect accounts.

Although conformance to the budget is emphasized, senior management is aware of the natural tendency to spend 100 percent of the amount authorized, whether needed or not, and attempts to counter this tendency by making appropriate rewards, including financial ones to those who reduce spending and still accomplish planned outputs.

In addition to financial controls, there are other rules and prescribed procedures. In promulgating these rules and procedures, management strikes an appropriate balance between the need to assure a reasonable degree of consistency in action taken by various managers and the need to avoid detailed rules that can stifle initiative and sound operating decisions.

Appropriate compliance audit and internal control techniques are used to minimize the possibility of loss by theft, fraud, or defalcation, to ensure that both financial and nonfinancial rules are adhered to, and to ensure that information flowing through the system is accurate.

The organization also engages in operational auditing. It recognizes, however, that this type of auditing requires different skills from compliance auditing and that, unless properly done, it can lead to friction and resentment that negate its possible benefits.

Measurement of Output

A nonprofit organization does not have a way of measuring output that is comparable to the measures of revenue, gross margin, or net income that are routinely prepared by a business enterprise, nor can it hope to develop a nonmonetary measure that is as good as these measures. Nevertheless, it needs the best possible substitutes that can be devised, because without some reasonable measure of output there is no way of assessing either the efficiency or the effectiveness of the organization's performance.

The well-managed organization therefore devotes considerable attention to developing satisfactory output measures. It recognizes that although many output measures are of limited validity, they are better than nothing. Since output should be related to an organization's goals and objectives, it is often worthwhile, as a first step, to try to state the more important objectives in quantitative terms, although this is not always feasible.

Output measures are in one of two categories: results measures, which indicate the organization's performance in accomplishing its objectives, and process measures, which indicate the quantity of work done. Reliable results measures are likely to be more difficult to devise than are process measures, but they generally are of more significance to higher level management. Process measures are relatively easy to identify and are more useful in the measurement of current, short-run performance. The management control system includes an appropriate mix of both types of measures. If industry associations have developed output measures, the members of the association use these data in analyzing outputs in their own organizations.

A third type of output measure, the social indicator, is of relatively little use in management control. It may be useful in strategic planning, however, provided users recognize its severe limitations; at best, it is a rough measure of performance.

The notion that the search for good output measures is fruitless because output cannot be measured perfectly is rejected. There is a never ending search for new, more valid measures. At the same time, the limitations of existing output measures are recognized. In particular, managers are not permitted to emphasize the attainment of a surrogate measure when this detracts from the attainment of the organization's actual objectives. The only output measures collected are those that are actually used. Management recognizes that many people, especially professionals, dislike the idea of accountability, which is associated with the measurement of outputs, but it proceeds with such measurements despite this resistance.

A measure of the quantity of output is more reliable and easier to develop than is a measure of the quality of output, but the well-managed organization does not permit this fact to lead to an overemphasis on quantity. Quality must be controlled, even though its measurement is subjective.

Reporting on Performance

Managers in the well-managed organization are provided with all the information they need (despite occasional attempts by some to inhibit the flow of information) but not with more than they can assimilate. An important type of information is a comparison of actual expenses and results with planned expenses and results in each responsibility center. Information on actual expenses is collected in a double-entry accounting system. This system uses accounts and rules for charging accounts that are entirely consistent with those in the budget. Reports containing this information are made available quickly. They are designed so as to highlight significant information. Where appropriate, variances between planned and actual spending are isolated by cause: volume, mix, price, and efficiency.

All levels of management, including senior management, are involved in the monitoring of current performance. Considerable attention is given to a review of output information in order to judge the organization's effectiveness. Quantitative measures of both the quantity and quality of outputs are used to the extent feasible, but the limitations of these measures are recognized. Peer reviews of quality are undertaken.

Evaluation

There are two general types of evaluation: operations evaluation and program evaluation. The well-managed organization engages in both.

Operations Evaluation. In many organizations, activities whose character and scope are relatively unchanged from one year to the next are not subject to much management attention. In a well-managed organization, a systematic examination of these operations is undertaken every five years or so. This process is called a *zero-base review*. Its purpose is to ascertain whether improvements in efficiency are feasible. The term is derived from the fact that such a review examines each function from scratch, rather than taking the existing level of spending as a starting point, which is usually done in the budgeting process. In making such a review, analysts carefully explore the possibility that certain functions could be performed more efficiently by a for-profit company.

A zero-base review is conducted by staff that is organized for this purpose, by outside consulting organizations, or occasionally by a "blue-ribbon commission" or task force of concerned citizens. The review can be conducted in various ways. One simple but effective approach is to ask naive questions about why operations are performed the way they are. Another is to compare costs of an activity with costs of similar activities in other organizations. Another is to apply work measurement techniques that have been developed by for-profit companies. Judgment is required in assessing the relationship between costs and outputs. The approach to the review is impersonal and factual.

Program Evaluation. In addition to an operations evaluation, the well-managed organization also undertakes a systematic evaluation of the effectiveness of its programs. Program evaluation requires persons with different skills than those of persons involved in evaluation of operations. In particular, it requires persons with expertise in the area of the program, whereas operations evaluation requires a knowledge of general management techniques.

Program evaluation involves, first, identification of the objectives of the program, and then a judgment as to the degree to which these objectives are being attained and whether the benefits exceed the costs. In the usual case, these judgments are based primarily on the intuition of the evaluators. The tendency to use sophisticated statistical or experimental techniques is resisted except in the relatively rare cases in which the data required for such techniques can be obtained.

Before undertaking either an operations evaluation or a program evaluation, those involved in it assure that they have adequate backing from senior management or other influential people. This increases the likelihood that recommendations will be implemented.

System Design and Installation

The preconditions for a successful system implementation effort are senior-management support, acquiescence from outside agencies, a competent system design team, and the allowance of *almost* enough time. Senior management is assumed to provide the first, and to devote time in discussions with outside agencies so as to assure the second. Senior management also assembles the necessary staff or hires outside system designers, and sets up a timetable covering one, two, or three years, depending on the complexity of the problem.

Senior management spends adequate time on the system development effort. It satisfies itself that the system is consistent with its own management style. It seeks to convince operating managers that the new system will in fact be used and that the former system will be discarded. It holds meetings with immediate subordinates to discuss how information can be used, and expects them to hold similar meetings with their subordinates. Once information from the new system becomes available and is reliable, senior management uses it exclusively. It discards the old system as soon as it is reasonably safe to do so.

In developing the system, the design staff relies primarily on an assessment of what information operating managers need, based on an analysis of their decision-making responsibilities. This analysis is carried out with operating managers but it goes beyond simply listening to what these managers say they need. Existing operating data are used to the maximum extent feasible. Crosswalks or other techniques are developed to permit information collected in the new system to meet the needs of outside agencies, and the staff spends a considerable fraction of the available time on education efforts.

If senior management decides that it is not feasible to install a complete new system all at once, it approaches the task in phases. Such an approach can consist of: (1) a pilot installation, (2) a simple beginning, or (3) a step-by-step installation. If the last method is followed, the first step is to have annual budgets prepared by programs and responsibility centers, but without an accounting backup.

MAIN LINES FOR IMPROVEMENT

In conclusion, and with considerable trepidation, we venture to list what seem to us to be the principal measures that will lead to improvement in the management control systems in nonprofit organizations. The items are listed roughly in the order of importance.

1. More active interest in the effective and efficient functioning of the organization by its governing board (including legislative committees in the case of government organizations). This is listed first because it can trigger all the other improvements.
2. More senior-management involvement in programming, in operations and program performance evaluation, and in systems improvement.

3. Extensive senior-management involvement in budgeting, with the delegation of much responsibility to operating managers as circumstances permit.
4. Better rewards for good management, including both better compensation for senior managers and refusal to tolerate poor management (including refusal to accept the cliché, that the Civil Service protects incompetents).
5. Use of expense accounting and a corresponding downgrading of obligation or expenditure accounting. Disregarding suggestions from auditors that financial statements should show detailed transactions by funds or, if this is not feasible, disregarding such reports in the management control process.
6. Structuring reports of actual performance so that they are entirely consistent with budgets.
7. Evaluation of operations on a regular basis, including the use of benchmark data from comparable organizations, and the support of industrywide efforts to improve such data. A search for opportunities to have functions performed by for-profit organizations.
8. Evaluation of program effectiveness on a regular basis, but not more sophisticated than is warranted by the nature of available data.
9. Use of a carefully designed program structure. This need is particularly significant in government organizations.
10. More use of benefit/cost analysis in appropriate circumstances, but with the recognition that in some circumstances, such analyses are of little value, and can even be misleading.
11. Creation of profit centers and a well-designed set of transfer prices.
12. More attention to setting appropriate prices of services, including the selection of units of pricing that are as specific as feasible. Recognition of the importance of basing prices on the full cost of services.
13. More emphasis on output measures, including more effort devoted to finding better measures, and the incorporation of output measures into both programs and budgets. The measurement of performance in terms of output as well as cost.

CONCLUDING REMARKS

The 1980s saw sizable cutbacks in federal funding for nonprofit organizations, coupled with the dual problem of reductions in spending by many states and increases in client demands for services in many sectors. The 1990s portend much of the same.

If needed services are to be provided in an era of scarcity, nonprofit organizations must take seriously the challenge of management control. This challenge exists for workers at all levels: governing boards, senior managers, operating managers, and professionals. Moreover, meeting the challenge is essential to both the well-being of an organization's clients and the viability of the organization itself.

CASE 17–1   The Johns Hopkins Hospital*

Early in May 1977, Robert M. Heyssel, M.D., executive vice president and director of The Johns Hopkins Hospital, was reviewing the hospital's annual operating plan for 1977–78. In 1972–73 a decentralized management structure had been initiated at Hopkins. The review of the 1977–78 operating plan provided an occasion to examine and assess the decentralization move.

Background

The Johns Hopkins Medical Institutions (JHMI) occupied a 44-acre site in the East Baltimore section of Baltimore, Maryland. A major American medical center, JHMI was made up of four components: the 1,037-bed Johns Hopkins Hospital and The Johns Hopkins University's professional health divisions—the School of Medicine; the School of Hygiene and Public Health; and the School of Health Services. The Johns Hopkins Medical Institutions described themselves as providing "a total environment in which the art of medicine and healing are carried out at a patient's bedside, in classrooms, clinics, and research laboratories, and in community outreach programs and innovative new prepaid medical plans such as those in East Baltimore and Columbia, Maryland." The John F. Kennedy Institute, located close to JHMI, was an independent institution affiliated with Hopkins; it had 40 long-term beds for mentally and physically handicapped children and was a center for training and research in mental retardation.

Johns Hopkins, in his will, provided $7 million to be divided between the university and the hospital; it was the largest single philanthropic bequest made in the United States up to that time. In an 1873 letter he stated "In all arrangements in relation to this hospital, you will bear constantly in mind that it is my wish and purpose that the institution shall ultimately form a part of the Medical School of that University . . ." The Johns Hopkins Hospital opened its doors in 1889.

The Johns Hopkins Hospital was a nonprofit corporation and was classified by the American Hospital Association in the 1970s as a "General Medical and Surgical" hospital. It treated all types of medical, surgical, and psychiatric patients in the acute stages of illness. As a teaching hospital, Johns Hopkins educated and trained over 400 residents and interns each year in multiple specialties. The JHMI also had contributed many advances in medicine: pioneering research in a host of diseases, development and improvement of surgical techniques, and the discovery of many drugs.

---

* This case was prepared by Srinivasan Umapathy, Research Assistant, under the direction of Eoin W. Trevelyan, Lecturer in Management, Harvard School of Public Health. Copyright © by the President and Fellows of Harvard College. Distributed by the Pew Curriculum Center, Harvard School of Public Health.

In 1965, the Johns Hopkins Medical Institutions considered moving to the suburbs. The 1976 Annual Report commented on the decision as follows:

> It was a watershed decision . . . to remain in Baltimore City . . . [and] bespoke a responsibility to improve the health care of our largely poor, medically underserved neighborhood and also to improve the area itself.

The Board of Trustees

The bylaws of The Johns Hopkins Hospital vested the Board of Trustees with "the control and management of the affairs, business, and properties of the Hospital." There were two board committees which helped coordinate the activities of the hospital with the rest of the Johns Hopkins Medical Institutions. The JHI Management Committee was the administrative policy-making body for the Johns Hopkins Medical Institutions; it met every Monday and focused its attention on issues which required coordination among the different divisions of JHMI. The JHMI Joint Administrative Committee met on the first and third Mondays of each month and dealt with policy and operational issues related to functions which were provided jointly to the institutions, such as library, student health services, and security.

The Board of Trustees appointed the Medical Board of the hospital. The Medical Board made recommendations to the board on matters relating to the welfare of the hospital and medical or surgical treatment of patients in the hospital. Formal appointments to the Medical Staff were made by the Board of Trustees of the hospital based on recommendations of the Medical Board, following nomination by the chief of each clinical service and review by a Quality Assurance Committee. Appointments, except for the chiefs of service, were for a period of not more than one year ending on the next June 30. The Medical Staff was divided into Active Staff, Courtesy Staff, Associate Staff, Resident Staff, and Honorary Staff categories. A chief of service was appointed by the Board of Trustees from among those recommended by the Medical Board, and served until a successor had been appointed. The chiefs of service were responsible not only for the care and treatment of patients in their respective departments, but also for the department's educational and research programs.

The Situation in 1972

The Johns Hopkins Hospital incurred annual operating losses of between $1.2 and $1.9 million throughout the period 1967–71. In the year ended June 30, 1972, the operating loss was reduced to $437,218; after the application of current gifts and endowment income, net income was $1,029,758—the first positive net income figure in four years.

The problems faced by the hospital in October 1972 were summarized in a 1976 note by Dr. Charles Buck, the director of planning, and covered personnel, organization, and finances. The number of hospital employees had increased by more than 40 percent in one decade, there was a perception that the hospital was overstaffed and inefficient, and an aggressive union had been organized to represent the hospital's service workers. Organizationally, there was a lack of a clear definition of responsibility and accountability for operations, the central service departments seemed to be operating more in their own self-interest than in meeting the needs of the operating departments, institutional goals and objectives were either unclear or unstated, and departmental goals were either undeveloped or unrelated to institutional goals. In the face of President Nixon's wage and price control program, and impending state-based regulation, the hospital's costs were rising at a rate of 11 to 14 percent per annum. Finally, allocation of limited capital resources on an annual basis was becoming increasingly difficult, and a high demand for renewal of facilities existed in the face of what was generally considered to be inefficient use of existing resources.

Developments during 1972–1973

Fiscal year 1972–73 saw an operating loss of $1.2 million. The hospital's Annual Report for that year observed:

> The Johns Hopkins Hospital has contributed more than $17 million in unreimbursed services to the community through its outpatient department.
>   The Hospital shoulders the loss by including a portion of it in its overall charges for care and by using a basic resource, the income earned by its endowment. It has not yet had to touch its endowment principal, but with hospital and medical care costs rising rapidly, an ominous threat to the lifeblood of Johns Hopkins has become very real.

Dr. Steven Muller, a specialist in comparative government and international relations, assumed office as the president of The Johns Hopkins University and president of The Johns Hopkins Hospital in 1972. He was the first person in this century to fill both the university and hospital presidencies.

In October 1972, Robert Heyssel, M.D., was appointed executive vice president and director of The Johns Hopkins Hospital. Dr. Heyssel had joined Johns Hopkins University School of Medicine in 1968 as associate dean, and at the same time was appointed director of Outpatient Services and director of the Office of Health Care Programs at The Johns Hopkins Hospital.

When Dr. Heyssel took charge, he found that there was "a strong hierarchy of central service departments; indicative of this is the fact that of the costs distributed to operating units, only 30 percent were direct costs and 70 percent were allocated or indirect costs. With control over only 30 percent of their costs, it was impossible to make any unit responsible or accountable for their total costs as related to budget or revenue." Dr. Heyssel also felt that the traditional organization structure of the hospital (Exhibit 1) was not suitable for Johns Hopkins. In addition, the budgeting process appeared to be taking place as a "top down" process with very little input from the patient care units. There were no agreed-

EXHIBIT 1 Organization Chart of The Johns Hopkins Hospital (1972)

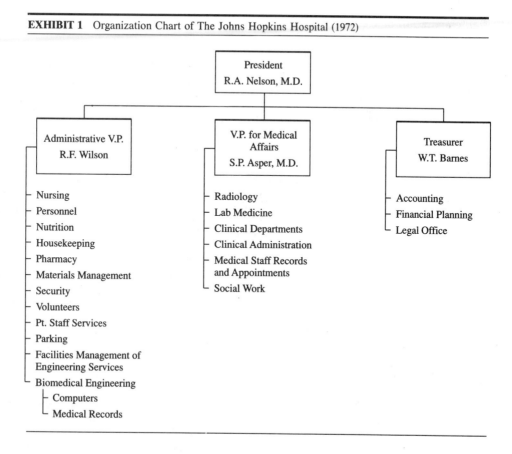

upon targets or goals which the units were expected to achieve with regard to occupancy of beds or other resources allocated to them, or to unit costs. For these reasons, it was decided to proceed with a process of decentralization.

In Dr. Heyssel's words:

> The chiefs of service [were] responsible for the overall operational planning, management, and results. The respective departmental administrative staff were to report directly to the chiefs. . . . Furthermore, the decision was made to decentralize the Department of Nursing for operational purposes with the departmental directors of nursing also responsible to the chiefs of service for operations but to a Central Nursing Staff for professional nursing standards. . . . Any service provided centrally which could logically be provided more effectively and at the same or lesser cost by the units would be provided by the unit itself. . . .

As the hospital's Annual Report noted:

> The objective of decentralization is to reduce operating costs by more efficient management, to improve and expedite the decision-making process, and to place budgetary responsibility at the level closest to the delivery of hospital services.

Implementation of Decentralization

The decision to "decentralize" was announced by Dr. Heyssel at the first meeting with the board of trustees after his appointment. This decision was made with the concurrence of the chairman of the board, Mr. William E. McGuirk, Jr. A graduate of the U.S. Naval Academy at Annapolis, Mr. McGuirk was chairman of the board of the Mercantile Safe Deposit and Trust Company (a bank holding company with headquarters in Baltimore) and a strong proponent of decentralization.

A Decentralization Committee was established and consulted with individuals throughout the institution on the implementation of decentralization. The committee, which consisted entirely of nonphysicians, recommended that the directors of functional units should be lay administrators. On this point, however, Dr. Heyssel differed and decided to give this responsibility to the chiefs of the clinical services.

In February 1973 Dr. Heyssel presented to the chiefs and senior administrative officers of the hospital a written report which described in broad terms the proposed plan for decentralization. The report stated in part:

> . . . responsibility for each functional management unit will be placed in the hands of the appropriate departmental chairman who will have a functional management unit administrator reporting to him . . . There will also be a director of nursing for each of the functional management units reporting to the chairman. Decision making with regard to allocation of resources to meet patient care needs and to attain objectives within stated fiscal goals will be the responsibility of the departmental chairman, who will confer with the administrator and the director of nursing service in his area . . .
>
> The departmental chairman will prepare one- and five-year budgets for his functional management unit. Upon review by hospital general management and approval by the board, such budgets became the operating plan of the hospital.
>
> Departmental chairmen will be expected both to achieve the occupancy rates necessary to attain the total budgeted revenues for their . . . units and to control expenses . . .

During the following months progress was made in anticipating and resolving problems and potential conflicts. As Dr. Heyssel noted in a status report in May 1973, one issue raised was the reason for pursuing decentralization:

> A valid question with regard to decentralization is "Why bother?" Won't there be additional costs? Why should the departments take on additional administrative workload? What are the real benefits? Why is decentralization necessary now if it wasn't necessary in the past?
>
> There are no easy answers to these questions. The fact is, however, that the hospital has grown considerably in size and complexity over the past few years. The advent of the state of Maryland hospital rate setting commission and utilization review impose new and critical demands on our operations. Most importantly, current trends of various critical measures of the hospital's own welfare, such as declining occupancy and rising per diem costs, must be reversed. This can only be accomplished by achieving a better alignment of responsibility and authority for patient care and fiscal matters, which is the primary objective of decentralization.

At this time, a schedule for decentralization had been developed. Yet, as Dr. Heyssel's report observed:

> Decentralization of management responsibility of the hospital is not going to take place overnight. The fiscal year beginning July 1, 1973, is regarded as a year of transition, but certain key changes will occur on or before July 1. Most of the organizational changes, new budgeting and reporting procedures, and new informational systems will become operational during that period . . . The objective, nonetheless, is to begin achieving the full benefits of decentralization during the next fiscal year starting July 1, 1974.

To evaluate and monitor performance under the new management plan, an outside consultant was retained early in 1973 to develop a rudimentary management information system and to advise concerning future information needs. The monthly management information report proposed by the consultant was designed to meet the informational needs of the executive vice president of the hospital. Functional units were also to receive complete copies of the report, although it was not designed to meet their information needs. Most of the raw data used in preparing the report were readily available. The report contained charts showing budgeted and actual amounts, and consisted of five sections: (1) summary reports, (2) inpatient statistics, (3) outpatient statistics, (4) patient care statistics, and (5) key operating ratios.

Other Developments, 1973–1977

Dr. Heyssel brought a number of persons into senior administrative posts in the hospital, including a new administrator of the outpatient clinics, an assistant director for planning and program development, a director of planning, a vice president for finance and management systems, a manager of employee relations, an administrator of cost improvement programs, and a vice president of nursing. Several of these persons had no prior hospital experience, but had had considerable experience in areas such as industrial engineering, commercial credit, computer operations, human resources planning, industrial relations, and manufacturing industry. The administrative organization structure created by Dr. Heyssel by 1977 is shown in Exhibits 2 and 3.

Operational planning and budgeting processes in the hospital were changed and now included the development of planning guidelines, planning meetings, and the creation of an annual operating plan. Charles Buck, director of planning, commented:

> We began to implement three years ago. Initially, it was viewed as a joint Medical School and Hospital effort and we initially focused on the clinical departments. During the first year the clinical departments were asked to prepare statements of their internal strengths and weaknesses and external threats and opportunities, along with their objectives for the forthcoming one or two years. This approach followed the corporate long-range planning model. In follow-up to these documents, the director of the hospital and

EXHIBIT 2   Organization Chart of The Johns Hopkins Hospital (April 1977)

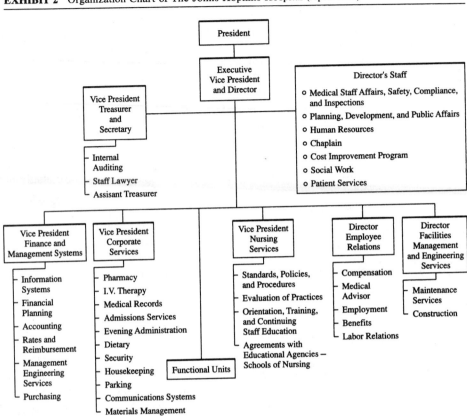

the dean of the medical school, along with the director of planning had a one- to two-hour discussion with each of the department chairmen centered on the issues raised in the documents. These discussions were "where are you headed?" types of issues and did not deal with money or budgets. In the next year we began to focus on action plans, or programs, desired in order to meet objectives. This approach turned out to generate a rather long "wish list" of desired programs which was unwieldy to work with and too expensive to fund. We also observed that the process has more applicability to the hospital than to the medical school. The major resource requests are related to the hospital. On the university side the dean supplies only a small portion of the total budget. We produced a list of approved projects from those originally submitted. This year, the process will take the form of reviewing new requests and updating that list. An important accomplishment is that the list has been made public; it will serve as a means for placing future requests in the context of our other outstanding needs. We will probably review this list and update it three times a year.

A budget reporting system also was developed to support the new decentralized structure. The new system related expenses to the output produced by the depart-

EXHIBIT 3   Organization Chart of The Johns Hopkins Hospital (April 1977)

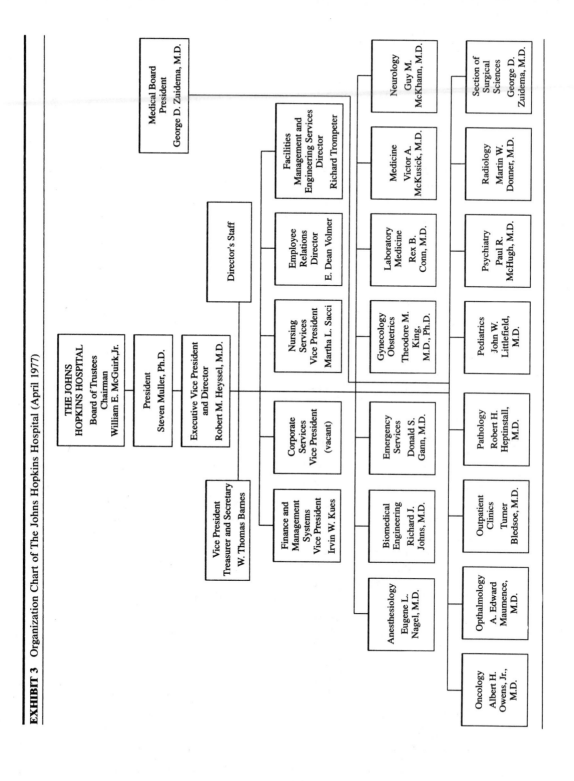

ment, both in terms of units of service and revenue (see Exhibits 4 and 5) and compared actuals with budgeted amounts for both the current month and the year to date. Supplementary reports provided detailed information on staffing patterns and salaries.

Several other changes and activities had also been initiated. For example:

In 1972 a revised University Faculty Incentive Plan for practice was introduced. Medical staff were encouraged to increase patient care income since this might be reflected in increased individual salaries or discretionary departmental surplus funds. This, and the addition of new members of the professional staff, were seen as means of increasing occupancy.

A Union Avoidance Program was initiated in 1976; a key element in this program was the establishment of nonbargaining unit grievance procedures which included an automatic review and approval mechanism by the executive vice president.

Late in 1976, a compensation study covering all employees of the hospital was initiated to ensure rationalization of pay scales.

A Performance Evaluation System was gradually developed. All salary increase requests considered in 1977 were to be decided only after considering information on the performance appraisal forms.

The Johns Hopkins Hospital Building Program

In 1976, on the occasion of their centennial, the Johns Hopkins Institutions launched the most ambitious fund raising effort in their history. The program sought endowment of 50 named professorships at $1 million each, bringing to 100 the number of such chairs, and $20 million to make possible a $100 million rebuilding program at the hospital.

The building program was designed in two phases. Phase I, completed in 1977, cost $49 million and was financed by a combination of federal and state funds ($10.7 million), Maryland Health and Higher Education Facilities Authority Loan ($24.7 million), university funds ($6.0 million), and hospital funds ($8.3 million). Phase II was to be completed in 1982 and was expected to involve expenditures of $40 to $60 million.

Results

A memorandum from Dr. Heyssel to all senior members of functional units and central staff dated April 22, 1977, stated some of the advantages and benefits of decentralization:

Our entire response to HSCRC [the state of Maryland's Health Services Cost Review Commission], as well as our ability to adopt to its methodology, was and is due to the

EXHIBIT 4 Statement of Direct Income and Expense

706 GENERAL OPERATING ROOMS
CURRENT PERIOD
FOR 5-31-77
YEAR TO DATE
ISSUED 6-18-77

	CURRENT PERIOD			YEAR TO DATE			
	ACTUAL	BUDGET	VARIANCE	ACTUAL	BUDGET	VARIANCE	PERCENT VARIANCE
TOTAL OPERATING PERFORMANCE							
GROSS REVENUE	673,907	407,778	266,129	5,284,600	4,284,328	1,000,272	23.00
DIRECT EXPENSES							
SALARIES	116,382	113,695	2,687-	1,201,922	1,213,453	11,531	.00
BENEFITS	18,621	18,850	229	203,076	203,539	463	.00
SUPPLIES	128,711	86,743	41,968-	1,296,889	954,107	342,782-	35.00-
JOINT AGREEMENT	10,066	10,066		105,967	110,718	4,751	4.00
REPAIRS	1,147	2,043	896	21,755	22,457	702	3.00
TRANSFERS	39,699	19,167	20,532-	317,902	210,833	107,069-	50.00-
TOTAL DIRECT EXPENSES	314,626	250,564	64,062-	3,147,511	2,715,107	432,404-	15.00-
TOTAL-(SEE FOOTNOTE)	359,281	157,214	202,067-	2,137,089	1,569,221	567,868-	36.00-
UNITS OF SERVICE	.00	1,930	1,930-	8,956	21,350	12,394-	58.00-
UNIT COST							
GROSS REVENUE	211.28	211.28	211.28-	590.06	200.67	389.39	194.00
DIRECT EXPENSES							
SALARIES	.00	58.90	58.90	134.20	56.83	77.36-	136.00-
BENEFITS	.00	9.76	9.76	22.67	9.53	13.14-	137.00-
SUPPLIES	.00	44.94	44.94	144.80	44.68	100.11-	224.00-
JOINT AGREEMENT	.00	5.21	5.21	11.83	5.18	6.64-	128.00-
PURCHASED SERVICES	.00	.00	.00	.00	.00	.00	999.99
REPAIRS	.00	1.05	1.05	2.42	1.05	1.37-	130.00-
TRANSFERS	.00	9.93	9.93	35.49	9.87	25.62-	259.00-
TOTAL DIRECT EXPENSES	.00	129.82	129.82	351.44	127.17	224.27-	176.00-
INCOME CONTRIBUTION	.00	81.45	81.45	238.62	73.49	165.12	224.00

```
****************************************************
* A NEGATIVE VARIANCE IS UNFAVORABLE, EXCEPT ON THE *
* "TOTAL" LINE. ON THE "TOTAL" LINE, A NEGATIVE VARIANCE IS *
* FAVORABLE IF THE COST CENTER HAS A "GROSS REVENUE" LINE. *
****************************************************
```

EXHIBIT 5 Departmental Expense with Budget

GENERAL FUND
706 GENERAL OPERATING ROOMS

For 5-31-77

| | CURRENT PERIOD | | | | YEAR TO DATE | | |
Account	ACTUAL	PLAN	VARIANCE	ACTUAL	PLAN	VARIANCE	PLAN BALANCE
140000 PROFESSIONAL & TECHNICAL	6,121	5,393	728-	61,308	57,870	3,438-	5,044
150000 NURSING	101,277	100,180	1,097-	1,046,725	1,069,292	22,567	93,490
160000 CLERICAL	5,196	4,809	387-	51,204	51,164	40-	4,504
170000 SERVICE	3,788	3,313	475-	42,685	35,127	7,558-	3,100
TOTAL SALARIES	116,382	113,695	2,687-	1,201,922	1,213,453	11,531	106,138
TOTAL FRINGE BENEFITS	0	0	0	0	0	0	0
302000 OFFICE SUPPLIES	228	175	53-	1,334	1,925	591	175
305000 MEDICAL & SURGICAL	16,302	15,084	1,218-	195,338	165,916	29,422-	15,084
307000 GLASSWARE	309	300	9-	3,884	3,300	584-	300
308000 BOOKS, PERIODICALS & SUBS	0	0	0	0	0	0	0
309000 FURNITURE, NON-CAPITAL	423	459	36	9,797	5,041	4,756-	459
310000 INSTRUMENTS	638	2,667	2,029	33,239	29,333	3,906-	2,667
310001 INSTRUMENTS-REPLACE LOSS	0	0	0	0	0	0	0
310002 INSTRUMENTS-REPLACE BREAK	68	0	68-	3,058	0	3,058-	0
311000 DIETARY	0	0	0	89	0	89-	0
315000 OTHER SUPPLIES & EQUIPMENT	0	0	0	0	0	0	0
319000 FILMS & SOLUTIONS	243	0	243-	2,172	0	2,172-	0
319001 SOLUTIONS-I V	3,136	1,834	1,302-	37,102	20,166	16,936-	1,834
319002 SOLUTIONS-IRRIGATING	2,447	1,584	863-	27,132	17,416	9,716-	1,584
320000 GASES	0	159	159	672	1,741	1,069	159
348000 REAGENT STRIPS & TABLETS	0	0	0	9	0	9-	0

Account	Description							
349000	SUTURES	2,921	2,921-	0	45,347	45,833	45,347-	0
349001	SUTURES—STANDARD	12,057	4,167	4,167	102,149	66,000	45,833-	4,167
349002	SUTURES—SPECIAL PURCHASES	15,732	6,057-	6,000	170,744	106,333	36,149-	6,000
352000	PUMP, OXYGENATOR	0	6,065-	9,667	2,645-	0	64,411-	9,667
354000	PACEMAKERS	5,362	1,112-	0	58,787	46,750	2,645-	0
373000	MATRONS	0	21	4,250	119	229	12,037-	4,250
376000	COPYING EXPENSE	3,889	305-	21	48,438	39,416	110-	21
377000	STOCK DRUGS	73	73-	3,584	7,384	0	9,022-	3,584
378000	STOCK DRUGS—CHG TO PATIENT	57,949	21,157-	0	510,607	404,708	7,384-	0
389000	DIRECT PURCHASES, SURG SPL	6,934	6,934-	36,792	42,133	0	105,899-	36,792
398000	MISCELLANEOUS						42,133-	
	TOTAL SUPPLIES	128,711	41,968-	86,743	1,296,889	954,107	342,782-	86,743
	TOTAL PURCHASED SERVICES	0	0	0	0	0	0-	0
520000	EQUIPMENT REPAIRS & MAINT	1,114	1,176	1,209	2,472	13,291	10,819-	1,209
540000	INSTRUMENT REPAIRS	1,147	280-	834	19,283	9,166	10,117-	834
	TOTAL REPAIRS & MAINTENANCE		896	2,043	21,755	22,457	702-	2,043
	TOTAL DEPRECIATION	0	0	0	0	0	0-	0
	TOTAL INTEREST	0	0	0	0	0	0-	0
704000	MAINTENANCE TRANSFER	2,367	2,292	2,292	21,587	25,208	3,421-	2,292
705000	CENTRAL SUPPLY TRANSFER	22,649	3,125	3,125	142,647	34,375	108,272-	3,125
707000	LAUNDRY LINEN TRANSFER	14,683	19,524-	13,750	153,668	151,250	2,418-	13,750
	TOTAL COST TRANSFER	39,699	20,532-	19,167	317,902	210,833	107,069-	19,167
832000	J/A—HOUSESTAFF	10,066	10,066	10,066	110,719	110,718	1-	10,066
899000	J/A—PRIOR YEAR SETTLEMENT	0	0		4,752-	0	4,752-	10,060
	TOTAL JOINT AGREEMENT	10,066		10,066	105,967	110,718	4,751-	
	TOTAL EXPENSES	296,005	64,291-	231,714	2,944,435	2,511,568	432,867-	224,157

EXHIBIT 6 Five-Year Trend in Operating Data* ($000)

	1973 Actual	1974 Actual	1975 Actual	1976 Actual	1977 Budget	1977 Est. Actual	1978 Budget	($000) Actual Growth Rate (Percent)
Gross revenue	$ 69,674	$ 72,742	$ 87,399	$101,718	$107,500	$109,000	$119,500	11.4%
Net operating revenue	59,946	64,822	75,136	88,538	96,842	96,023	107,601	12.4
Expenses:								
Salaries and benefits	37,218	39,681	44,144	51,656	56,011	55,950	61,200	10.6
Other expenses	23,975	26,589	31,864	36,626	40,081	39,964	45,201	13.6
Total expenses	61,193	66,270	76,008	88,282	96,092	95,914	106,401	11.7
Operating profit/(loss)	$ (1,247)	$ (1,448)	$ (872)	$ 256	$ 750	$ 109	$ 1,200	—
Visits	468,484	471,114	460,900	422,000	416,872	375,000	375,000	(4.5)%
Patients days	299,888	294,386	295,764	306,152	305,000	307,000	312,763	0.8
Cost per patient day	$ 155.20	$ 171.90	$ 194.70	$ 218.70	$ 238.90	$ 236.90	$ 258.24	10.7
Full-time equivalent personnel	3,963	3,921	4,043	4,080	4,230	4,090	4,200	1.2
Number of beds	1,063	1,077	1,100	1,058		1,037	1,077	1.4
Percent of revenue from Blue Cross, Medicare, and Medicaid	63%	62%	70%	70%	n.a.	n.a.	n.a.	

n.a. = not available.
* Data exclude Oncology Department, which was to be fully operational by July 1st.

generation of unit cost data for operating units under the decentralized mode of management.

The Statements of Financial Position of the Hospital provide hard evidence of the economic success of the process (Exhibit 6).

Since 1975 The Johns Hopkins Hospital had a progressive decline in its annual rate of unit cost increase (i.e., total expenses divided by total patient days). The rate of increase fell from a high of 14.6 percent (FY 1975 over FY 1974) to 12.2 percent (FY 1976 over FY 1975). The rate of cost increase for FY 1977 over FY 1976 was projected at slightly more than 10 percent (see Exhibit 7). Several factors were seen to have contributed to these results. As noted in the 1976 Annual Report:

> The one-year-old cost improvement program is showing commendable progress. Cost savings projects initiated in such areas as energy, preventive maintenance, and materials handling will achieve annualized savings of $650,000 . . . In the Employee Relations Department, a major program was launched to train and upgrade our supervisory personnel . . . Continuing to make more effective use of existing resources, we have increased bed occupancy from 76 percent in 1972 to 82 percent in 1976.

EXHIBIT 7   Summary of Functional Unit Performance Trends (unit cost increases*)

	Fiscal Year Increase (Percent)					
	74 over 73	*75 over 74*	*76 over 75*	*77E over 76*	*78 Budget over 77E*	*Average*
Hospital Average....................	10.3	14.6	12.2	10.0	8.9	11.4
Units						
Emergency medicine	25.5	28.2	16.5	12.9	6.7	17.7
OB-GYN..........................	15.2	14.5	25.2	7.2	12.6	14.7
Outpatient department—adult.........	13.6	7.4	11.5	20.2	16.6	13.8
Anesthesiology/adult ICUs...........	6.7	32.2	17.8	5.0	7.8	13.6
Pediatrics	25.5	10.0	17.5	7.4	7.4	13.4
Pharmacy	12.4	13.9	16.2	16.6	4.2	12.6
Radiology	24.3	11.0	11.0	6.8	6.3	11.7
Medicine..........................	13.5	18.7	8.1	8.4	7.0	11.1
Laboratory medicine	19.8	22.3	10.9	(2.6)	3.4	10.4
GOR..............................	20.0	6.6	6.9	1.0	12.0	9.1
Surgery	12.0	18.0	4.6	9.8	1.0	9.0
Psychiatry.........................	12.0	5.0	12.6	4.0	9.5	8.6
Pathology	6.8	16.9	2.4	7.2	6.2	7.8
Ophthalmology.....................	4.4	7.2	7.5	11.9	4.3	7.0
Rehabilitation medicine	1.1	5.5	9.0	7.2	11.9	6.9
Neurosciences	n.a.	n.a.	(8.3)	11.9	7.9	n.a.

n.a. = not available.
* Average without malpractice, utilities, and collection fees = 10.0 percent.

Comments of Senior Officials on Changes Made Since 1972

Edward Halle, administrator, Outpatient Clinics and Emergency Medical Services:

Decentralization has been an excellent motivator for all types of individuals. The absence of the profit motive has traditionally been a disincentive for efficiency and economy in the health care industry; the very fact that our managers are being measured serves as an incentive to do things better. The information system developed over the past five years has provided the means to manage as well as to communicate management information to the physicians.

In earlier days there was no pressure for conservation. The attitude was "if it's reimbursable (by third-party payers) it's okay to do it." Physicians were kept in the dark about financial matters. It was assumed they were interested only in medicine, but that has proved to be untrue. With a little education and some good information they were well able to assume some management responsibilities. For example, about six years ago we discovered that for the average outpatient visit the cost was $15; we were charging $10 and were actually collecting $7. Physician resistance to increased charges and to efforts to reduce costs and improve collections all but disappeared. Including physicians in the management process has resulted in a better operation with much less frustration.

Dr. Theodore King, chief of Gynecology and Obstetrics, had a favorable view of the decentralization process:

I am a great enthusiast of decentralization. It is a genuine attempt to bring responsibility to people. I am programmed to solve clinical problems not management problems. That is where business school is involved. Mr. Burch, the department administrator, is formally trained, while I have acquired some information on the job. The director of nursing, Mr. Burch, and I come together and determine the alternatives that are available. After decentralization, individuals within the departments are much more aware of the dollar costs.

Dr. Martin Donner, chief of Radiology, also held a positive view of decentralization:

I personally like decentralization. We do not have to get permission from the administration for minor internal expenditures, such as overtime, supplies, etc. As long as I am within my unit cost of service, such decisions are made by our managers. Of course, we must manage effectively and responsibly to stay within our unit cost of service. We are very happy with the reorganization. We can now respond more quickly to the requests from other departments. Supervision with flexibility is now possible. The concept of "units of production" used by us in analyzing and controlling costs, permits us to employ some of the principles used in manufacturing organizations, except that our "product" is superior health care at a reasonable cost.

Now we have the feeling of contributing to the overall management of the hospital. The physicians now spend less time with budgeting and other administrative details. My administrator's organization has permitted me and the other physicians to devote more time to teaching and research. This year as well as last year the award for the best teacher of the year, as voted by the senior class of medical students, was given to a member of this department. We have not lost any senior departmental faculty members or managers since the reorganization of the hospital and our department.

Dr. Charles Buck, director of planning, commented:

When Bob Heyssel came here he was uncomfortable with the organization as it was defined then. He felt that the physicians were major actors in the decisions to use hospital resources and that somehow this needed to be acknowledged in the organizational structure. We have been moving in this direction ever since under the banner of ''decentralization.'' Bob has a very good sense of timing as to how fast the organization can absorb new ways of doing things. None of this has caused much of an uproar.

As part of decentralization, we realized that better people were needed at the functional unit level. During his first 3 years, a number of managers were replaced. Now, if we look back, we see that a lot of people were replaced without any overt ''head chopping.'' Administrators in Medicine, Pediatrics, Psychiatry, Materials Management, Data Processing, Nursing, Employee Relations, and Medical Records were replaced.

We did not have good financial information systems. This, of course, was important if we were to move toward a decentralized form of management. The units needed the information to make better decisions, and central management needed the information to monitor the progress of the units.

As an early step toward initiating the concept of the chiefs of service being accountable for departmental operations, they were invited to the trustee meetings. Each of the chiefs, in turn, was asked to present an overview of his department's performance. While this certainly was not a vigorous review, it served the purpose of acknowledging that the chiefs, in fact, were now in charge.

An example of the ''decentralized'' approach is the method used to provide new administrative help in the clinical departments. Usually, a committee from central administration reviews candidates for clinical administrative jobs and presents a slate of acceptable candidates to the chiefs of service for final decision. They were grateful for this help and usually accepted our recommendations. Our clinical administrators are well paid. Some of them have been assistant directors of hospitals. This is important to the concept of decentralization.

Ms. Martha Sacci, vice president of Nursing, described her reactions:

I started here in February, 1977. Part of the lure was decentralization. Organizations are becoming more and more complex, and coordination between medicine, nursing, and administration is important. I think decentralization can help this process.

Currently I am working with head nurses from different clinics. Leadership development programs are needed. There is high turnover in some departments because of poor management.

The functional unit directors come to me if they are having trouble with their directors of Nursing. Otherwise, they don't. Selection of directors of Nursing is done jointly by me and the functional unit director. Regarding salaries for directors of Nursing, the manager for compensation calls me regularly, and some administrators have also called.

One of the administrators who had joined The Johns Hopkins Hospital about 10 years ago commented:

I feel that the job content of the administrator did not change after decentralization came in. After decentralization, doctors have become more involved, perhaps to their detriment. There has also been an infusion of administrators. Prior to decentralization there were only five or six administrators. Now there are 20 administrators, some of whom have not even had a college education. Everyone is calling himself an administrator.

The nurse-physician relationship has certainly improved, since the director of Nursing reports to the physician in her area of specialization, instead of reporting to an administrative nurse. There are no major problems in my functional unit since the director of Nursing reports to me for all administrative matters. The information system is okay, but it takes too long.

Annual Operating Plan, 1977–1978

During 1975–76 and 1976–77 the approach had been to develop plans at the hospital level and ask the functional units to respond with objectives that helped implement these plans. A major problem was trying to press an iterative process into a "top down" mold, with the result that there was some contradiction and/or overlapping in goal setting among the units.

For 1977–78 this planning process was superseded by one that dealt with goals and objectives by department at the JHMI level, that is, both the university and hospital sections of each clinical department. This comprehensive process was begun in November 1976 by sending out a request to the units to do a self assessment—their strengths, weaknesses, and their needs over the next two years.

The evaluation process was conducted through December 1976 and January 1977 by staff members (in conjunction with unit personnel) of both the university and the hospital and ended with a tentative JHMI program plan, including a total of 214 proposed new programs which were well defined and not overlapping or in conflict with each other.

This planning process was kept current by periodic updates and adjustments of priorities. The intent was to evolve it into a process of longer-range integrated planning, with financing and implementation to assure balanced growth among all departments.

The introduction to the Annual Operating Plan, 1977–78, stated:

As has been the case for the last few years, the functional unit has been the primary focal point for the planning process. However, several important changes were made this year. Instead of projecting the 1977–78 budget from the 1976–77 "actual" figures, the new budget was projected from the 1976–77 budget. This process adds a motivational factor to the decentralization concept in that functional units that underspent the current budget are rewarded . . . "unit costs" were separated into fixed and variable components to allow for volume change calculations. Each functional unit determined the fixed ratio for its "unit costs."

In addition to financial statements and evaluation of progress against fiscal 1977 unit objectives, the Annual Operating Plan presented budgets (by functional unit and by major expenditure category) for 1977–78 (Exhibits 8 and 9), capital equipment requests for fiscal 1978, full-time equivalent staffing levels analyzed by unit, and allocation and utilization of beds by unit. Exhibit 10 presents the availability and utilization of beds for 1976–1978. Exhibit 11 shows historical trends in staffing levels, by functional units.

EXHIBIT 8 Summary of Hospital 1977 Costs and 1978 Budgets ($000)

	77 Budget	Est. 77 Actual	78 Inflation $	78 Inflation %	78 Vol.	78 Tech. & Protocol	78 Budget w/o Onco.	Percent Increase over 77 Actual $	Percent Increase over 77 Actual Unit Cost	Oncology 77 Budget	Oncology 77 Est. Actual	Oncology Changes	Oncology 1978 Budget	Total Hospital
Direct patient care:														
Ophthalmology	$ 2,118.3	$ 2,152.2	$ 125.6	5.8	—	$ (33.9)	$ 2,243.9	4.3	4.3					$ 2,243.9
Psychiatry	2,126.9	2,080.5	144.4	6.9	—	18.0	2,242.9	7.8	7.8					2,242.9
Surgery	6,703.2	6,654.4	436.7	6.6	194.5	(26.8)	7,258.8	9.1	1.0					7,258.8
GOR	2,957.2	3,277.7	245.0	7.5	—	145.0	3,667.7	12.0	12.0					3,667.7
Neurosciences	1,105.9	1,089.0	77.3	7.1	1.7	16.9	1,184.9	8.9	7.9					1,184.9
OB-GYN	4,430.5	4,282.1	280.2	6.5	(74.0)	148.0	4,636.3	8.3	12.6					4,636.3
Anesthesiology	2,782.7	2,688.6	183.3	6.8	25.1	174.1	3,071.1	14.2	7.8					3,071.1
Adult ICU's	2,983.7	3,021.0	206.9	6.8	—	(77.8)	3,150.1	4.3	4.3					3,150.1
Medicine	6,135.4	6,106.5	429.8	7.0	—	—	6,536.3	7.0	7.0					6,536.3
Oncology	6,565.9	6,597.4	520.0	7.9	—	(31.5)	7,085.9	7.4	7.4	$5,176.1	$2,883.0	$3,260.4	$6,143.4	7,085.9
Pediatrics	1,421.8	1,379.4	76.9	5.6	—	16.0	1,472.3	6.7	6.7					1,472.3
Emergency medicine	1,722.6	1,636.9	112.8	6.9	(22.3)	50.0	1,777.4	8.6	14.4					1,777.4
Outpatient—adult gen'l	283.2	267.5	11.4	4.3	—	15.7	294.6	10.1	10.1					294.6
Outpatient—adult consult														
Subtotal	41,337.5	41,233.2	2,850.3	6.9	125.0	413.7	44,622.2	8.2	—	5,176.1	2,883.0	3,260.4	6,143.4	50,765.6
Patient care support:														
Pathology	1,528.3	1,526.4	91.9	6.0	—	1.9	1,620.2	6.2	6.2					1,620.2
Radiology	6,089.4	6,158.2	452.6	7.3	293.4	—	6,904.2	12.1	6.3					6,904.2
Laboratory medicine	6,450.2	6,444.5	358.0	5.6	130.0	—	6,932.5	7.6	3.4			348.3	348.3	7,280.8
Pharmacy	3,454.7	3,600.0	193.0	5.4	107.0	—	3,900.0	8.3	4.2	1,517.0	311.5	1,511.1	1,822.6	5,722.6
Social services	650.2	673.3	68.9	10.2	—	(23.1)	719.1	6.8	6.8					719.1
Rehabilitation medicine	546.8	516.3	30.9	6.0	—	30.5	577.7	11.9	11.9					577.7
IV therapy	953.9	1,060.7	60.0	5.7	18.7	(13.2)	1,126.2	2.1	2.1	75.0	30.0	70.0	100.0	1,226.2
Subtotal	19,673.5	19,979.4	1,255.3	6.3	549.1	(3.9)	21,779.9	9.0	—	1,592.0	341.5	1,929.4	2,270.9	24,050.8
Service:														
Finance	3,757.7	3,693.5	253.2	6.9	40.0	41.3	4,028.0	8.9	8.9					4,028.0
Systems, planning, M.R.	2,693.0	2,673.6	144.4	5.4	—	60.0	2,878.0	7.7	7.7					2,878.0
Materials management	1,655.2	1,698.1	85.0	5.0	—	—	1,783.1	5.0	5.0					1,783.1
Communications	1,042.1	1,085.2	51.2	4.7	—	71.0	1,207.4	11.3	11.3					1,207.4
FMLES	2,609.7	2,658.7	131.5	4.9	67.6	—	2,857.8	7.5	7.5	119.0	80.0	27.5	107.5	2,965.3
Patient services	1,142.5	1,116.7	79.3	7.1	11.7	—	1,207.7	8.1	8.1					1,207.7
General services	3,780.2	3,554.4	226.8	6.4	149.7	—	3,930.9	10.6	10.6	300.0	100.0	250.0	350.0	4,280.9
Nutrition	5,539.9	5,439.9	221.6	4.1	50.0	(45.4)	5,666.1	4.2	4.2	100.0	40.0	110.0	150.0	5,816.1
All other	4,831.0	4,802.1	384.2	8.0	0	40.0	5,226.3	8.8	8.8	14.0	14.0	50.0	64.0	5,290.3
Subtotal	27,051.3	26,722.2	1,577.2	5.9	319.0	166.9	28,785.3	7.7	—	533.0	234.0	437.5	671.5	29,456.8
Institutional:														
Malpractice insurance	1,543.0	1,480.0	—	0	—	(285.0)	1,195.0	(19.3)	—					1,195.0
Collection agency fees	471.0	455.0	—	0	39.0	—	494.0	8.6	—					494.0
Utilities	2,261.0	2,350.0	123.7	5.3	259.5	—	2,733.2	16.3	—	185.0	120.0	90.3	210.3	2,943.5
Blood fees	375.0	550.0	33.0	6.0	—	—	583.0	6.0	—					583.0
Depreciation (excl. P.P)	3,288.0	3,118.0	—	0	54.0	—	3,172.0	1.7	—	100.0	100.0	349.4	449.4	3,621.4
Interest	92.0	126.0	—	0	910.1	—	1,036.1	722.3	—	100.0	100.0	133.2	233.2	1,269.3
Subtotal	8,030.0	8,079.0	156.7	1.9	1,262.6	(285.0)	9,213.3	14.0	—	385.0	320.0	572.9	892.9	10,106.2
Total	$96,092.1	$96,013.8	$5,839.5	6.1	2,255.7	291.7	$104,400.7	6.7	6.7	$7,686.1	$3,778.5	$6,200.2	$9,978.7	$114,379.4
Program budget						2,100.0	2,100.0						—	2,100.0
Grand total							$106,500.7						$9,978.7	$116,479.4

897

EXHIBIT 9　Functional Unit Direct Revenue and Expense Statements, 1977 Budget ($000)

Units	Gross Revenue	Labor & Emp. Benefits	Sup. & Reps.	Pur. Ser.	Other	Joint Agreement	Total	Gross Margin
			Costs					
Direct patient care:								
Ophthalmology	$ 4,800	$ 1,517	$ 278	$ 28	$ 98	$ 323	$ 2,244	$ 2,556
Psychiatry	4,418	1,865	30	12	65	272	2,244	2,174
Surgery	13,637	5,830	273	19	719	418	7,259	6,378
GOR	7,800	1,741	1,525	4	256	142	3,668	4,132
Neurosciences	1,890	748	50	58	43	286	1,185	705
OB-GYN	7,600	3,529	357	11	408	331	4,636	2,964
Anesthesiology	5,000	942	408	17	51	1,653	3,071	1,929
Adult ICU's	4,950	2,146	252	50	465	237	3,150	1,800
Medicine	12,234	4,375	296	257	659	949	6,536	5,698
Pediatrics	12,500	5,041	433	46	663	903	7,086	5,414
Emergency medicine	2,933	1,086	146	8	(245)	477	1,472	1,461
Outpatient adult general	1,970	1,307	173	31	(66)	332	1,777	193
Outpatient adult consult.	—	231	30	—	21	13	295	(295)
Subtotal	79,732	30,358	4,251	541	3,137	6,336	44,623	35,109
Patient care support:								
Pathology	1,625	664	105	35	6	810	1,620	5
Radiology	11,350	2,775	1,521	244	155	2,209	6,904	4,446
Laboratory medicine	17,100	4,327	1,087	721	37	761	6,933	10,167
Pharmacy	6,420	1,284	2,363	90	163	—	3,900	2,520
Social services	—	678	15	24	2	—	719	(719)
Rehabilitation medicine	1,173	497	28	6	26	21	578	595
I.V. therapy	1,600	354	766	1	5	—	1,126	474
Subtotal	39,268	10,579	5,885	1,121	394	3,801	21,780	17,488
Service:								
Finance	—	2,181	160	473	1,214	—	4,028	
Systems, planning, & medical records	—	3,345	263	1,078	(1,857)	49	2,878	
Materials management	—	1,655	1,638	1,268	(2,781)	3	1,783	
Communications	—	413	30	758	6	—	1,207	
FM&ES	—	2,347	469	184	(165)	23	2,858	
Patient services	—	971	158	68	11	—	1,208	
General services	—	2,607	135	1,166	23	—	3,931	
Nutrition	—	2,691	6	2,916	53	—	5,666	
All other	—	3,040	291	—	357	1,538	5,226	
Subtotal	—	19,250	3,150	7,911	(3,139)	1,613	28,785	(28,785)
Institutional:								
Malpractice insurance	—	—	—	1,195	—	—	1,195	
Collection agency fees	—	—	—	494	—	—	494	
Utilities	—	—	2,601	132	—	—	2,733	
Blood fees	—	—	577	6	—	—	583	
Depreciation	—	—	—	—	3,172	—	3,172	
Interest	—	—	—	—	1,036	—	1,036	
Subtotal	—	—	3,178	1,827	4,208	—	9,213	(9,213)
Total hospital	$119,000	$60,187	$16,464	$11,400	$4,600	$11,750	$104,401	14,599
Adjustments:								
Other revenue								6,000
Bad debts & free work								(5,900)
Third-party discounts								(12,779)
Grand Total	$119,000							$ 1,920

EXHIBIT 10 Comparison of Census (1978 budget versus 1976 actual and 1977 estimate)

Units	1976 Beds Avail.	Days	Percent Occup.	1977 Estimate Beds Avail.	Days	Percent of Occupancy Plan	Actual	1978 Budget Beds Avail.	Days	Percent Occup.	Change Beds Avail.	Days	Percent Occup.
Wilmer*	78	23,471	82.4	78	23,900	82.5	83.9	78	23,500	82.5	—	(400)	(1.4)
Psychiatry	75	26,024	95.0	75	26,400	95.0	96.4	75	26,000	95.0	—	(400)	(1.4)
Surgery	292	87,021	88.4	263	84,100	87.5	87.6	290	91,586	86.5	27	7,486	(1.1)
Neurology	19	6,040	87.1	19	6,300	89.0	90.8	19	6,172	89.0	0	(128)	(1.8)
OB-GYN	100	29,017	80.1	100	29,100	81.4	79.7	96	27,927	79.7	(4)	(1,173)	0
Adult—ICU	35	9,140	71.5	35	9,800	71.9	76.7	36	9,528	72.5	1	(272)	(4.2)
Medicine	230	73,114	87.1	225	73,700	86.9	89.7	230	72,815	86.7	5	(885)	(3.0)
Pediatrics	207	52,325	69.2	197	53,700	74.4	74.7	197	55,235	76.8	—	1,535	2.1
Total	1,036	306,152	82.0	992	307,000	83.3	84.8	1,021	312,763	83.9	29	5,763	(.9)
Oncology	—	—	—	45	7,000	80.4	42.6	56	16,470	80.6	11	9,470	38.0
Grand total	1,036	306,152	82.0	1,037	314,000	82.6	83.0	1,077	329,233	83.8	40	15,233	.8

* Wilmer Ophthalmological Institute for the treatment of eye diseases; includes emergency room for eye injuries.

EXHIBIT 11 Full-Time-Equivalents Summary Comparison, 1973–1978B

	1973	1974	1975	1976	1977E	1978B	Percent Average Yearly Change
Ophthalmology	86	97	97	103	101	104	
Psychiatry	116	116	123	128	129	130	
Surgery	262	261	285	358*	368	378	
GOR	125	124	120	114	115	123	
Neurosciences	13	25	52	52	51	54	
OB-GYN	179	179	204	192	231	237	
Anesthesiology—ICU	189	203	199	178	182	195	
Medicine	301	321	328	250*	297	299	
Pediatrics	279	292	292	330	357	370	
Emergency medicine	67	70	74	69	67	70	
Outpatient—adult consult.	30	31	30	28	18	20	
Outpatient—adult general	110	116	117	115	72	77	
Subtotal	1,757	1,835	1,921	1,917	1,988	2,057	+3.2
Pathology	48	53	50	47	51	51	
Radiology	170	177	189	200	202	202	
Laboratory medicine	240	258	277	278	268	272	
Rehabilitation medicine	34	32	30	32	31	34	
Pharmacy	70	72	84	88	88	88	
Social services	28	23	41	41	42	43	
IV therapy	—	—	—	23	21	23	
Subtotal	590	615	671	709	703	713	+3.8
Service units	1,616	1,471	1,451	1,407	1,399	1,430	−2.5
Total	3,963	3,921	4,043	4,033	4,090	4,200	+1.2
Oncology: direct				29	180	293	—
service				—	19	35	—
Total w/ oncology				4,062	4,289	4,528	+2.7

* Administrative transfer of Marburg 3 and 4 from Medicine to Surgery. Earlier Marburg provided private rooms for both medical and surgical patients.

The Annual Operating Plan 1977–78 gave the following breakdown for the Capital Budget for Financial Year 1978:

Equipment:		
Under $20,000...........	$600,000	
Cost improvement	300,000	
Replacement	560,000	
Hospital equipment	646,000	
		$2,106,000
Less leasing...........		1,000,000
Subtotal		$1,106,000
Renovations:		
Hospital renovations		3,000,000
		$4,106,000

Referring to the above tabulation, the Annual Operating Plan noted:

In recent years capital investment to maintain and replace the hospital's plant and equipment has been restrained by annual operating deficits. Endowment and gift income has approximated annual losses, thus placing the capital burden upon depreciation, averaging less than $3.0 million a year.

Depreciation is not an adequate source of funding, causing necessary projects to be deferred. Further, with this limitation on capital, it is obvious that there is no provision for new high technology equipment, nor are there any funds provided for cost reduction capital investment, which ultimately is a self-supporting activity.

The financial plan for fiscal 1978 projects a profit for operations, which, if achieved, will provide more capital funds than have been available to this point.

Mr. Jack Murphy, Director of Operations, Planning, and Budgeting, explained the capital budgeting process:

The Financial Planning Department allocates, from the total funds available, the amount available for the capital budget. To handle requests over $20,000, a Capital Resource Allocation Committee has been set up. The committee meets three times a year and consists of Dr. Heyssel, Dr. Ross (Vice President for Medicine and Dean of the Medical Faculty at the Johns Hopkins University), the heads of service, and three or four faculty members.

Current Issues

In April 1977 Dr. Heyssel had established a Standing Committee for Policy Development Furthering Decentralization. This committee was expected to develop a policy framework to guide units and to address topics which had been raised by staff at different levels, such as:

Policies within which functional unit directors would have authority to adjust patient bills under a defined charity policy.

The degree to which functional units should have authority to let contracts to outside vendors.

The appropriate authority to grant to units to engage in capital equipment expenditures.

In discussing the decentralized management structure, Dr. Heyssel identified the major issues he faced in May 1977 as follows:

1. The division of program dollars and capital between functional units—and tying such decisions to unit plans and objectives.
2. Gaining a better understanding of the parameters within which functional units operate, development of units of measurement for assessing departments' performance, and clarification of the relationship between central staff and functional units.
3. Human development of management at the functional unit level.

Overall, Dr. Heyssel observed: "My life as director is a lot better now. I do not have to deal with trivial issues any longer. The next three to five years will be a testing period. But if we face a shortage of funds, we are now capable of taking quick action."

Questions

1. What are the most important changes that Dr. Heyssel has introduced into the organization?
2. What are the key characteristics of the new management control system? How do they relate to the changes that have taken place in the organization?
3. What changes, if any, should be made in the management control system?

CASE 17-2   Hoagland Hospital (B)*

Dr. Richard Wells, Chief of Surgery at Hoagland Hospital, recently had learned of the apparently smooth implementation of a new management control system at The Johns Hopkins Hospital (see Case 17–1). He wondered what lessons, if any, could be gleaned from this effort that might assist him in rethinking the approach he had taken in implementing his own management control system (see Case 1–1). He decided to contrast the process he had followed with that followed by Dr. Robert Heyssel at Johns Hopkins.

---

* This case was prepared by Professor David W. Young. Copyright © by David W. Young. Distributed by the Accounting Curriculum Center, Boston University School of Management.

Questions

1. Drawing on the material from Chapter 16, and information from other chapters as necessary, contrast the *process* followed in implementing the new management control system at The Johns Hopkins Hospital with that followed at Hoagland Hospital. What are the important differences?
2. What lessons, if any, can be learned from these two cases that would be useful in implementing a new management control system in another organization?

Author Index

Case Index

Subject Index